AMERICAN CONSTITUTIONAL LAW

CASES AND INTERPRETATION

Third Edition

AMERICAN CONSTITUTIONAL LAW

CASES AND INTERPRETATION

Third Edition

Ralph A. Rossum
Claremont McKenna College

G. Alan Tarr
Rutgers University, Camden

St. Martin's Press
New York

Senior editor: Don Reisman
Production supervisor: Alan Fischer
Cover design: Butler Udell Design
Cover photo: Louis M. Jawitz

Library of Congress Catalog Card Number: 89-63930

Manufactured in the United States of America.

5 4 3
f e d c b

For information, write:
St. Martin's Press, Inc.
175 Fifth Avenue
New York, NY 10010

ISBN: 0-312-03720-1

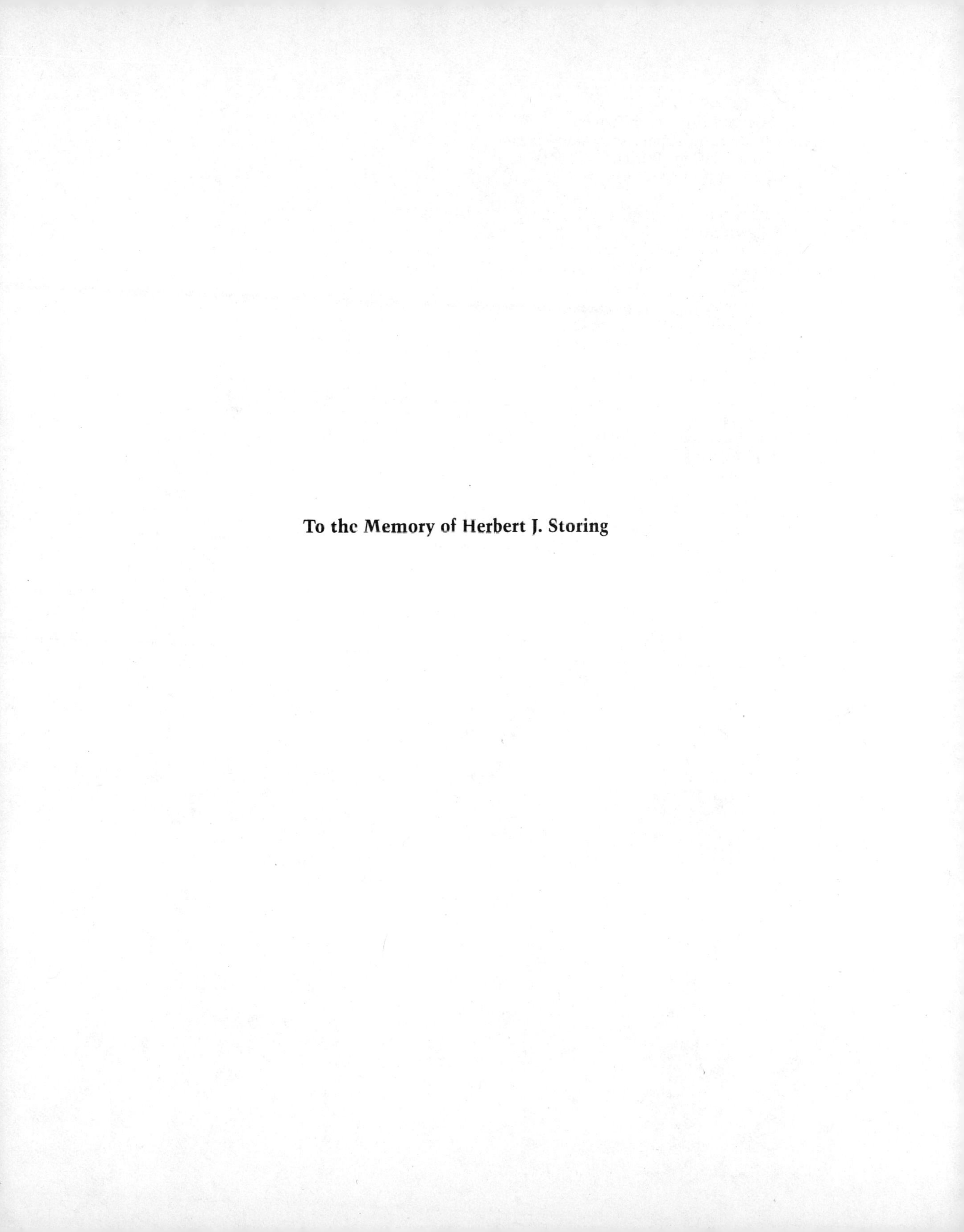

To the Memory of Herbert J. Storing

PREFACE

American Constitutional Law: Cases and Interpretation, third edition, is designed as a basic text for courses in constitutional law and civil liberties. Its approach to these subjects is based on three major premises.

First, the study of the Constitution and constitutional law is of fundamental importance to a full and coherent understanding of the principles, prospects, and problems of America's democratic republic. Cases should be examined not merely to foster an appreciation of what court majorities have thought of particular issues at certain points in time (although that is obviously important), but also to gain a deeper and fuller understanding of the principles that lie at the very heart of the American constitutional system. To that end, this text emphasizes precedent setting cases and presents comprehensive expositions of alternative constitutional positions. Substantial excerpts from cases and other constitutionally significant pronouncements have been included so that students can grapple with the arguments and justifications for these alternative positions. To ensure that the best arguments on all sides of a constitutional question are presented, extensive extracts of both concurring and dissenting opinions have been included.

Second, no interpretation of the Constitution can be evaluated properly without an appreciation of what those who initially drafted and ratified the Constitution sought to accomplish. The text incorporates documentary evidence in seeking to identify and explain the original purposes of the Constitution and the means provided for the achievement of those purposes. This inquiry into the Framers' understanding of the Constitution, in turn, furnishes one of the criteria for evaluating judicial decisions and constitutionally significant pronouncements from the executive and legislative branches.

Third, the study of the Constitution involves much more than an examination of its judicial interpretation. The Constitution is not merely what the Supreme Court says it is; its words are not so many empty vessels into which justices can pour meaning. Accordingly, this volume examines the interpretations of a variety of sources. The original understanding of the founding generation is one source. Another, equally indispensable source is, of course, the Supreme Court, whose decisions have influenced so profoundly our understanding of the Constitution and its principles. And because other governmental bodies have contributed significantly to the overall interpretation of the Constitution, this text includes decisions of the lower federal courts and state judiciaries and also extrajudicial materials of constitutional significance such as certain congressional acts and resolutions.

As we approach constitutional questions throughout this text, we begin by turning to the Framers. We do so, however, not so much for specific answers as for general guidance concerning what the Constitution was designed to accomplish. Obviously no interpretation can be expected to conform strictly to the expectations of the Framers. Other legitimate approaches may also contribute to an understanding of the Constitution, relying variously on analysis of the text itself, judicial precedent, constitutional doctrine, logical reasoning, and adaptation of constitutional provisions to changing circumstances. All these approaches are described in Chapter 1.

The structure of this book might be seen as a reflection of James Madison's observation in *The Federalist,* No. 51, that "in framing a government which is to be administered by men over men, the great difficulty lies in this: you must first enable the government to control the governed; and in the next place, oblige it to control itself." Chapter 1 explores in general how the Constitution was designed to resolve this difficulty, and Chapter 2 introduces the reader to the actual process of constitutional adjudication. The remainder of the book systematically examines how the Constitution and its amendments not only grant the national and state governments sufficient power to control the governed but also oblige these governments to control themselves. Chapters 3–6 consider the distribution of power in the national government. As a group, these chapters explore how the constitutional scheme of separation of powers and checks and balances both grants and controls power. Because of the importance of the distribution of power among the branches of the national government, we devote separate chapters to the Judiciary, the Congress, the Presidency, and war and foreign affairs. Chapters 7–10 consider the distribution of power between the national government and the states. These chapters focus on federalism, specifically how this institutional means carries out the ends of the Constitution. Finally, Chapters 11–17 examine the distribution of power between the government and the individual. The emphasis in these chapters is not so much on institutional contrivances that oblige the government to control itself as on the Bill of Rights and those subsequent amendments that guarantee specific rights and liberties, an emphasis that illuminates the way in which our most precious rights and liberties increasingly have become dependent for their vindication, not upon constitutional structure but upon what *The Federalist* called mere "parchment barriers."

With the exception of the first two chapters, each chapter opens with an introductory essay which is then followed by cases and, where appropriate, extrajudicial materials. Each essay includes extensive notes which provide valuable explanatory details and references to further materials, and ends with a list of suggested readings, including *Federalist* essays, additional cases, and scholarly books and articles. Each case also has its own introductory headnote, which provides historical perspective, indicates where the case stands in relation to current law, and gives the final court vote. Some cases have end notes that elaborate on the short- and long-term consequences of the decision. The text includes four appendices: the Constitution of the United States, a list of Supreme Court justices, a glossary of legal terms, and a table of cases.

The editorial staff at St. Martin's Press was cooperative, encouraging, and truly professional. We would particularly like to thank Don Reisman, Ed Cone, Carol Ewig, Emily Berleth, and Susanne Rosenberg. We are also grateful to several academic colleagues who reviewed drafts of the manuscripts and contributed valuable comments and suggestions to the three editions. We would also like to thank the following reviewers who supplied us with useful information to help guide our revisions for this third edition: Harry Balfe, Montclair State University; Robert C. Bradley, Illinois State University; Saul Brenner, University of North Carolina, Charlotte; Edgar Dyer, USC-Coastal Carolina College; Dr. Thomas E. Guild, Central State University; Robert P. Hunt, Kean College of New Jersey; Kent A. Kirwan, University of Nebraska, Omaha; Mark Landis, Hofstra University; Timothy O. Lenz, Florida Atlantic University; Earl Millen, Northeast Louisiana University; William S. Miller Jr., Marymount University; John M. Nickerson, University of Maine; R. Christopher Perry, Indiana State University; Dr. Jim L. Riley, Regis College; Willard Paul Tice, Oklahoma City University; Dr. John R. Vile, Middle Tennessee State University, who reviewed the third edition. Any errors of fact or interpretation, of course, are solely our responsibility. Finally, we wish to express our gratitude to our wives, Constance and Susan, and to our children, Kristin, Brent, and Pierce Rossum and Robert and Andrew Tarr, for their patience, understanding, and loving support throughout this project.

Ralph A. Rossum
G. Alan Tarr

CONTENTS

1. INTERPRETATION OF THE CONSTITUTION 1

APPROACHES TO CONSTITUTIONAL INTERPRETATION 3 • THE APPROACHES IN PERSPECTIVE 9 • THE ENDS OF THE CONSTITUTION 10 • THE MEANS TO THE ENDS 11 • NOTES 18 • SELECTED READINGS 20

2. CONSTITUTIONAL ADJUDICATION 22

HOW CASES GET TO THE SUPREME COURT 22 • HOW THE COURT DECIDES CASES 29 • THE IMPACT OF SUPREME COURT DECISIONS 32 • ANALYZING COURT DECISIONS 37 • SOURCES IN CONSTITUTIONAL LAW 40 • NOTES 42 • SELECTED READINGS 43

3. THE JUDICIAL POWER 45

THE POWER OF JUDICIAL REVIEW 46 • POLITICALLY IMPOSED RESTRAINTS ON JUDICIAL REVIEW 48 • COURT-IMPOSED RESTRAINTS ON JUDICIAL REVIEW 50 • THE EXPANDING ROLE OF THE COURTS 55 • THE COURTS, JUDICIAL REVIEW, AND THE PROBLEM OF LEGITIMACY 56 • NOTES 59 • SELECTED READINGS 62

CASES

***Marbury* v. *Madison* (1803)**	**64**
***Eakin* v. *Raub* (1825)**	**67**
***Ex Parte McCardle* (1869)**	**70**
***Frothingham* v. *Mellon* (1923)**	**71**
***Flast* v. *Cohen* (1968)**	**72**
***Allen* v. *Wright* (1984)**	**75**
***Luther* v. *Borden* (1849)**	**78**
***Baker* v. *Carr* (1962)**	**81**
***DeShaney* v. *Winnebago County Department of Social Services* (1989)**	**86**

4. THE LEGISLATIVE BRANCH **90**

THE SCOPE OF CONGRESSIONAL POWER **90** • POWERS THAT FACILITATE LEGISLATIVE ACTIVITY **92** • NONLEGISLATIVE POWERS **96** • SAFEGUARDING LEGISLATIVE POWER **99** • SOME CONCLUSIONS **101** • NOTES **102** • SELECTED READINGS **103**

CASES

***McCulloch* v. *Maryland* (1819)** **105**
***Gravel* v. *United States* (1972)** **109**
***McGrain* v. *Daugherty* (1927)** **112**
***Watkins* v. *United States* (1957)** **114**
***Schechter Poultry Corporation* v. *United States* (1935)** **117**
***Mistretta* v. *United States* (1989)** **119**
***Immigration and Naturalization Service* v. *Chadha* (1983)** **123**

5. THE EXECUTIVE BRANCH **129**

THE AIMS OF THE FRAMERS **130** • GRANTS OF POWER AND THEIR USE **131** • IMPLIED POWERS **132** • PREROGATIVE POWERS **136** • NOTES **138** • SELECTED READINGS **139**

CASES

***Youngstown Sheet & Tube Co.* v. *Sawyer* (1952)** **140**
***Myers* v. *United States* (1926)** **144**
***Morrison* v. *Olson* (1988)** **148**
***United States* v. *Nixon* (1974)** **152**
***In Re Neagle* (1890)** **154**

6. WAR AND FOREIGN AFFAIRS **157**

THE INTERBRANCH DISTRIBUTION OF POWER **158** • THE FOUNDATION AND EXTENT OF THE FOREIGN AFFAIRS POWER **163** • WAR AND INDIVIDUAL RIGHTS **165** • NOTES **167** • SELECTED READINGS **168**

CASES

***The Prize Cases* (1863)** **169**
The Gulf of Tonkin Resolution (1964) **170**
The War Powers Resolution (1973) **171**
***United States* v. *Curtiss-Wright Export Corp.* (1936)** **172**
***Missouri* v. *Holland* (1920)** **175**
***Ex Parte Milligan* (1866)** **176**
***Korematsu* v. *United States* (1944)** **179**

7. FEDERALISM **184**

FEDERALISM AND THE FOUNDING **184** • FEDERALISM AND THE MARSHALL COURT **188** • DUAL FEDERALISM **190** • FEDERALISM AND INTERPRETATION BASED ON STRUCTURE AND RELATIONSHIP **192** • THE POST-CIVIL WAR AMENDMENTS AND THE SHIFTING OF THE FEDERAL BALANCE **195** • NOTES **198** • SELECTED READINGS **199**

CASES

***Cohens* v. *Virginia* (1821)** **201**
***Younger* v. *Harris* (1971)** **205**
***Baldwin* v. *Montana Fish and Game Commission* (1978)** **207**
***Garcia* v. *San Antonio Metropolitan Transit Authority* (1985)** **210**
***The Civil Rights Cases* (1883)** **217**
***Jones* v. *Alfred H. Mayer Company* (1968)** **222**
***Patterson* v. *McLean Credit Union* (1989)** **225**

8. THE EXERCISE OF NATIONAL POWER **230**

THE COMMERCE POWER **231** • THE TAXING POWER **237** • THE SPENDING POWER **238** • LIMITATIONS ON NATIONAL POWER **239** • NOTES **240** • SELECTED READINGS **241**

CASES

***Gibbons* v. *Ogden* (1824)** **242**
***United States* v. *E.C. Knight Company* (1895)** **246**
***Hammer* v. *Dagenhart* (1918)** **248**
***NLRB* v. *Jones & Laughlin Steel Corp.* (1937)** **250**
***Wickard* v. *Filburn* (1942)** **252**
***Heart of Atlanta Motel* v. *United States* (1964)** **254**
***United States* v. *Butler* (1936)** **255**
***United States* v. *Kahriger* (1953)** **259**
***South Dakota* v. *Dole* (1987)** **260**

9. THE EXERCISE OF STATE POWER **263**

CONSTITUTIONAL PRINCIPLES **263** • PREEMPTION **264** • NEGATIVE IMPLICATIONS OF THE COMMERCE CLAUSE **265** • STATE REGULATION AND THE MODERN COURT **269** • THE ROLE OF THE COURT **270** • NOTES **271** • SELECTED READINGS **272**

CASES

***Pacific Gas & Electric Company* v. *State Energy Resources Conservation & Development Commission* (1983)** **273**

Cooley v. *Board of Wardens* (1852) 275
Dean Milk Company v. *City of Madison* (1951) 277
City of Philadelphia v. *New Jersey* (1978) 280
Southern Pacific Company v. *Arizona* (1945) 281

10. THE CONTRACT CLAUSE 285

MARSHALL'S EXPANSION OF THE CONTRACT CLAUSE 286 • THE DECLINE OF THE CONTRACT CLAUSE 287 • A CONTINUED RELEVANCE? 291 • NOTES 291 • SELECTED READINGS 292

CASES
Dartmouth College v. *Woodward* (1819) 293
Charles River Bridge Co. v. *Warren Bridge Co.* (1837) 296
Home Building and Loan Association v. *Blaisdell* (1934) 299
United States Trust Company v. *New Jersey* (1977) 303

11. ECONOMIC DUE PROCESS AND THE TAKINGS CLAUSE 307

THE FOURTEENTH AMENDMENT 308 • THE EMASCULATION OF THE PRIVILEGES OR IMMUNITIES CLAUSE 309 • ECONOMIC REGULATION AND THE RISE OF SUBSTANTIVE DUE PROCESS 310 • THE REPUDIATION OF SUBSTANTIVE DUE PROCESS 314 • THE TAKINGS CLAUSE 316 • NOTES 318 • SELECTED READINGS 318

CASES
The Slaughterhouse Cases (1873) 320
Munn v. *Illinois* (1877) 325
Lochner v. *New York* (1905) 327
West Coast Hotel Company v. *Parrish* (1937) 331
Williamson v. *Lee Optical Company* (1955) 333
United States v. *Carolene Products Company* (1938) 334
Hawaii Housing Authority v. *Midkiff* (1984) 334
Nollan v. *California Coastal Commission* (1987) 336

12. FREEDOM OF SPEECH, PRESS, AND ASSOCIATION 343

THE MEANING OF THE FIRST AMENDMENT 344 • FIRST AMENDMENT STANDARDS 346 • POLITICAL EXPRESSION

349 • THE REGULATION OF SPEECH 353 • RESTRAINTS ON THE PRESS 356 • LIBEL AND INVASION OF PRIVACY 358 • OBSCENITY 360 • SOME CONCLUSIONS 362 • NOTES 363 • SELECTED READINGS 364

CASES

Gitlow v. *New York* (1925) 366
Schenck v. *United States* (1919) 368
Dennis v. *United States* (1951) 369
Barenblatt v. *United States* (1959) 373
Brandenburg v. *Ohio* (1969) 377
Buckley v. *Valeo* (1976) 378
Texas v. *Johnson* (1989) 383
Village of Skokie v. *National Socialist Party* (1978) 386
Adderley v. *Florida* (1966) 387
Tinker v. *Des Moines* (1969) 389
Hazelwood School District v. *Kuhlmeier* (1988) 391
Near v. *Minnesota* (1931) 394
New York Times Co. v. *United States* (1971) 396
Branzburg v. *Hayes* (1972) 400
New York Times v. *Sullivan* (1964) 403
Miller v. *California* (1973) 405
Paris Adult Theater I v. *Slaton* (1973) 405
Indianapolis Anti-Pornography Ordinance (1984) 408

13. FREEDOM OF RELIGION 410

ESTABLISHMENT OF RELIGION 410 • FREE EXERCISE OF RELIGION 416 • RECONCILING THE RELIGION CLAUSES 418 • TRENDS AND PROSPECTS 420 • NOTES 420 • SELECTED READINGS 421

CASES

Everson v. *Board of Education* (1947) 422
School District of Abington v. *Schempp* (1963) 424
Lemon v. *Kurtzman* (1971) 427
Mueller v. *Allen* (1983) 430
Lynch v. *Donnelly* (1984) 433
Wallace v. *Jaffree* (1985) 436
Edwards v. *Aguillard* (1987) 440
West Virginia Board of Education v. *Barnette* (1943) 442
Sherbert v. *Verner* (1963) 445
Lyng v. *Northwest Indian Cemetery Protective Association* (1988) 447

14. DUE PROCESS AND CRIMINAL PROCEDURE **451**

DUE PROCESS AND THE BILL OF RIGHTS **452** • CRIMINAL PROCEDURE **458** • BASIC THEMES IN THE COURT'S CRIMINAL-PROCEDURE DECISIONS **475** • NOTES **476** • SELECTED READINGS **477**

CASES

***Palko* v. *Connecticut* (1937)** **479**
***Adamson* v. *California* (1947)** **481**
***Duncan* v. *Louisiana* (1968)** **483**
***New Jersey* v. *T.L.O.* (1985)** **487**
***National Treasury Employees Union* v. *Von Raab* (1989)** **490**
***Mapp* v. *Ohio* (1961)** **495**
***Olmstead* v. *United States* (1928)** **499**
***Katz* v. *United States* (1967)** **502**
***Powell* v. *Alabama* (1932)** **504**
***Gideon* v. *Wainwright* (1963)** **506**
***Miranda* v. *Arizona* (1966)** **507**
***Nix* v. *Williams* (1984)** **514**
***United States* v. *Leon* (1984)** **518**
***Caplin & Drysdale, Chartered* v. *United States* (1989)** **523**
Comprehensive Crime Control Act of 1984 **527**
***Gregg* v. *Georgia* (1976)** **529**
***Woodson* v. *North Carolina* (1976)** **534**
***Roberts* v. *Louisiana* (1976)** **536**
***Stanford* v. *Kentucky* (1989)** **537**
***Turner* v. *Safley* (1987)** **541**

15. THE EQUAL PROTECTION CLAUSE AND RACIAL DISCRIMINATION **545**

RACE AND THE FOUNDING **546** • RACIAL DESEGREGATION **550** • PRIVATE DISCRIMINATION AND THE CONCEPT OF STATE ACTION **559** • PROOF OF DISCRIMINATION: IMPACT VERSUS INTENT **562** • NOTES **564** • SELECTED READINGS **566**

CASES

***Dred Scott* v. *Sandford* (1857)** **568**
***Plessy* v. *Ferguson* (1896)** **573**
***Brown* v. *Board of Education* (1954)** **576**
***Bolling* v. *Sharpe* (1954)** **579**
***Brown* v. *Board of Education* (1955)** **580**
***Swann* v. *Charlotte-Mecklenburg Bd. of Ed.* (1971)** **581**
***Milliken* v. *Bradley* (1974)** **583**

Missouri v. *Jenkins* (1990) 590
Shelley v. *Kraemer* (1948) 595
Moose Lodge No. 107 v. *Irvis* (1972) 597
Palmore v. *Sidoti* (1984) 599
Wards Cove Packing Co. v. *Atonio* (1989) 601

16. SUBSTANTIVE EQUAL PROTECTION **605**

THE TWO-TIER APPROACH **606** • THE DEVELOPMENT OF AN INTERMEDIATE LEVEL OF REVIEW **607** • CLASSIFICATIONS WARRANTING HEIGHTENED SCRUTINY **610** • FUNDAMENTAL RIGHTS **621** • THE FUTURE OF EQUAL-PROTECTION ANALYSIS **624** • NOTES **626** • SELECTED READINGS **626**

CASES
Bakke v. *Regents of the University of California* (1976) 628
Regents of the Univeristy of California v. *Bakke* (1978) 632
Richmond v. *Croson Co.* (1989) 639
Foley v. *Connelie* (1978) 649
Trimble v. *Gordon* (1977) 652
Massachusetts Board of Retirement v. *Murgia* (1976) 655
Frontiero v. *Richardson* (1973) 659
Heckler v. *Mathews* (1984) 661
Rostker v. *Goldberg* (1981) 663
Shapiro v. *Thompson* (1969) 668
Reynolds v. *Sims* (1964) 671
Harper v. *Virginia State Board of Elections* (1966) 675
Dunn v. *Blumstein* (1972) 677
San Antonio School District v. *Rodriguez* (1973) 680

17. THE RIGHT TO PRIVACY **686**

THE CONSTITUTIONAL BASIS **687** • WHAT THE RIGHT TO PRIVACY PROTECTS **688** • QUALIFICATIONS ON THE RIGHT TO PRIVACY **694** • NOTES **696** • SELECTED READINGS **697**

CASES
Griswold v. *Connecticut* (1965) 698
Roe v. *Wade* (1973) 702
Webster v. *Reproductive Health Services* (1989) 707
Harris v. *McRae* (1980) 714
Bowers v. *Hardwick* (1986) 719
Paul v. *Davis* (1976) 723

THE CONSTITUTION OF THE UNITED STATES OF AMERICA 726

JUSTICES OF THE SUPREME COURT 737

GLOSSARY OF COMMON LEGAL TERMS 740

TABLE OF CASES 745

AMERICAN CONSTITUTIONAL LAW

CASES AND INTERPRETATION

Third Edition

1
INTERPRETATION OF THE CONSTITUTION

"We are under a Constitution, but the Constitution is what the Court says it is."[1] In the over half-century since Charles Evans Hughes, then governor of New York and later Chief Justice of the Supreme Court, uttered these now-famous words, they have been repeated so often and in so many contexts that they have assumed a prescriptive as well as a descriptive character. But exactly how valid is this prescription for understanding the Constitution?

Hughes's observation certainly contains a degree of truth. Many of the provisions of the Constitution are not self-defining and hence have been the objects of considerable judicial interpretation and construction. Various criminal procedural protections found in Amendments Four through Eight immediately spring to mind. What, after all, makes a particular search or seizure "unreasonable"? What is sufficient to establish "probable cause"? What constitutes "due process of law"? What is a "speedy" trial? What is an "excessive" fine or bail? What is "cruel and unusual punishment"? These constitutional provisions resemble empty vessels into which the United States Supreme Court has had to pour meaning.

Hughes's claim also portrays accurately the perspective taken by lower-court judges and practicing attorneys. However erroneous they may believe the Supreme Court's understanding of a particular constitutional provision to be, they generally shy away from breaking with the previous decisions of the High Bench and offering contrary interpretations. Rather, they usually attempt to accomplish their objectives within the framework of the prevailing Court view.

If valid to some extent, however, Hughes's assertion is also misleading in several ways. Above all, it fails to recognize that governmental bodies other than the Supreme Court also contribute to an overall interpretation of the Constitution. By passing the War Powers Resolution of 1973, for example, Congress undertook to define the constitutional limits of the president's powers to initiate and conduct undeclared war, an issue the Supreme Court refused to consider. In the Speedy Trial Act of 1974, to cite another example, Congress took upon itself constitutional interpretation in the sphere of criminal procedure, declaring that a defendant not brought to trial within one hundred days of arrest may move for a dismissal of the charges. By so doing, it gave meaning to a constitutional provision that the Supreme Court itself has acknowledged to be more vague than any other procedural right. Constitutionally significant pronouncements also have emanated from the executive branch (statements made by President Abraham Linclon during the Civil War, for example, have had more to do with defining the outer bounds of presidential prerogative than have any statements of the Court) and from the state and lower federal courts.

Another problem with Hughes's assertion is that it obscures the extent to which the meaning of the Constitution is agreed upon by all concerned parties. Most constitutional provisions are settled; what questions are raised about them pertain not to fundamental meaning, but rather to specific application. Relatively few constitutional provisions have sparked protracted debate and controversy: the Commerce Clause of Article I, Section 8, authorizing Congress to regulate commerce among the several states; the First Amendment guarantees of freedom of speech and of the press; the guarantees of the Fifth and Fourteenth Amendments that no person shall be deprived of life, liberty, or property without due process of law; the Fourteenth Amendment's guarantee that no person shall be denied the equal protection of the laws. Although these provisions are extremely important, the intense debate over them tends to obscure how ably the Constitution has governed our political actions for the past two centuries. By focusing exclusively on them and arguing, implicitly or explicitly, that they are fundamentally without meaning until construed by the Court, some jurists and legal scholars have reinforced the view that the Constitution is deficient in decisive respects and therefore unworthy of vital public support. As a result, the Constitution is deprived of what James Madison in *The Federalist,* No. 49, called "that veneration which time bestows on everything, and without which perhaps the wisest and freest governments would not possess the requisite stability." This is of no minor concern, for, as Madison continues, "the most rational government will not find it a superfluous advantage, to have the prejudices of the community on its side."[2]

The view that the Constitution is whatever the Court says it is further misleads by suggesting that the Constitution has no meaning in and of itself. If all meaning must be poured into it by the Court, we are unlikely to turn to it for basic instruction on the principles, problems, and prospects of the American regime. The proudest claim of those responsible for framing and ratifying the Constitution was that it provided "a Republican remedy for the diseases most incident to Republican Government."[3] If we strip the Constitution of all independent meaning, we are unlikely to remember the Founders' answers to the basic questions and dilemmas of democratic government—and what is even more regrettable, we are likely to forget the questions themselves.

Yet another negative by-product of presenting the Constitution as devoid of any independent meaning is the encouragement of uncritical public acceptance of Supreme Court decisions. If the Constitution has only that meaning which the Supreme Court gives it, on what basis, other than subjective preference, can anyone object to the Court's interpretations? To illustrate with concrete examples, if the Constitution has no meaning apart from its judicial gloss, on what constitutional basis can anyone object to the Supreme Court's decisions in *Dred Scott* (1857), declaring that blacks could not be citizens, and *Plessy* v. *Ferguson* (1896), upholding racial segregation? Students of the Court implicitly acknowledge this problem by routinely paying lip service to Hughes's assertion and then, as the scholarly journals attest, criticizing at length judicial interpretations that they find wanting in fidelity to the language of the Constitution, in scholarship, in craftsmanship, or in deference to the popularly elected branches.

Finally, Hughes's claim ignores the influence that political institutions may have on political behavior. The Court is seen as influencing the Constitution; rarely is the influence the Constitution may have on the Court, or on politics more generally, even considered.

APPROACHES TO CONSTITUTIONAL INTERPRETATION

To avoid the unpalatable ramifications of Hughes's aphorism, we will argue, along with Justice Felix Frankfurter, that the "ultimate touchstone of constitutionality is the Constitution itself and not what [the judges] have said about it."[4] But what, in fact, does the Constitution mean? How are we to understand its provisions and give them effect? In searching for satisfactory answers to these questions, students of the Constitution have come to employ several approaches to constitutional interpretation, each of which has its own strengths and weaknesses.

Textual Analysis

One approach to constitutional interpretation involves explicating the constitutional text simply on the basis of the words found there. The basic claim of this approach seems unarguable: If the Constitution is to control the outcome of a case, and its unadorned text is plain, then constitutional interpretation should stop right there. As Justice Noah Swayne observed in *United States* v. *Hartwell* (1868): "If the language be clear, it is conclusive. There cannot be construction where there is nothing to construe."

On the other hand, this approach often is difficult to apply. Although many provisions of the Constitution are perfectly clear, many require extensive construction. Moreover, even if the meanings of all relevant words are perfectly plain, problems of emphasis remain. In many cases, two or more constitutional provisions come into play, and the justices must decide which is to be given priority. To cite just one example of this problem: Does the First Amendment guarantee of freedom of speech and the press supersede the Sixth Amendment guarantee of a trial "by an impartial jury"? As this example indicates, the constitutional text in and of itself cannot resolve all the questions that the Constitution raises.

Precedent

When textual analysis alone is inadequate, many students of the Constitution turn to previously decided cases, searching for answers on the basis of precedent, or *stare decisis* ("to stand by decided matters"). Reliance on precedent, the primary method of legal reasoning in Anglo-American law, adds stability, continuity, and predictability to the entire legal enterprise.

For a variety of reasons, however, reliance on precedent has been applied only sporadically in constitutional law. Many jurists and scholars believe strongly that the Constitution itself, rather than previous decisions of the Court, should supply the standard for decision. Then, too, constitutional cases deal with momentous social and political issues that only temporarily take the form of litigation, and there is wide recognition that these issues cannot be resolved satisfactorily on the same basis as other legal problems. To the minds of some experts in the field, relying on precedent for constitutional interpretation is rather like driving an automobile down a busy street while looking only through the rear-view mirror: We get a good notion of where we have been, but not of where we should be going.[5] If this difficulty confronts the use of precedent in any legal matter, it seems especially troublesome and unnecessary in constitutional law. Most areas of law lack clearly defined ends or purposes and so must evolve via precedent. The common law, for example, is based mainly on longstanding usage or judicial precedent. Constitutional law, on the other hand, has before it (to borrow the language of Judge J. Skelly Wright) certain "directions, goals, and ideals" that are easily discernible in the Constitution. Once discerned, these guideposts make it possible for the Court to decide matters of political and social import not in terms of what previous Courts have held, but in light of what is most conducive to achieving the goals or purposes of the Constitution.[6]

Constitutional Doctrine

When neither the constitutional text nor precedent can provide an adequate account of the meaning of the Constitution, arguments from "constitutional doctrine" may be raised. Constitutional doctrines are formulas—sometimes nothing more than slogans—extracted from a combination of the constitutional text and a series of related cases. The Equal Protection Clause of the Fourteenth Amendment provides several examples of the development and use of constitutional doctrines. When considered as it applies to questions of race, this clause typically is understood to prohibit discrimination (although the word *discrimination* is nowhere to be found in the amendment); when considered as it applies to questions of legislative apportionment, it typically is understood to require "one person, one vote" (another phrase not found in the text). Similarly, the First Amendment's Establishment Clause, which charges Congress to "make no law respecting an establishment of religion," has been interpreted by many as erecting a "high wall of separatism" between church and state. In these illustrations, the constitutional doctrines enunciated serve as mediating principles that stand between specific controversies and the Constitution, giving meaning and content to ideals embodied in the text.

Over time, many of these doctrines have come to give the constitutional provision in question its only meaning as a guide for decision. This usurption of the original texts has profound and disturbing implications. As such doctrines become increasingly important, public debate tends to center on the meaning of the doctrines and not on the meaning of the Constitution itself. In reference to the Equal Protection Clause, for example, the contemporary debate over affirmative action/reverse discrimination has focused almost exclusively on such questions as whether this policy is discriminatory against whites and whether the majority should be free to discriminate against itself and on behalf of minority groups if it so wishes; the question of what "equal protection of the law" truly means has been all but forgotten. Equally disturbing is the fact that reducing constitutional provisions to doctrines or slogans often interferes with thoughtful consideration of the constitutional issues. The "one person, one vote" rule provides a case in point. On only the most elemental level does this rule have meaning; when examined outside a very narrow context, it becomes a simplistic and confusing slogan. After all, the question of permitting certain voters the opportunity to vote two, five, or ten times has never been raised by any of the legislative reapportionment cases. In *Baker* v. *Carr* (1962), for example, the central issue was how much the voter's one vote was to be worth—a question that moved Justice Frankfurter to ask:

> What is this question of legislative apportionment? Appellants invoke the right to vote and have their votes counted. But they are permitted to vote and their votes are counted. They go to the polls, they cast their ballots, they send their representatives to the state councils. Their complaint is simply that the representatives are not sufficiently numerous or powerful—in short, that Tennessee has adopted a basis of representation with which they are not satisfied. Talk of "debasement" or "dilution" is circular talk. One cannot speak of "debasement" or "dilution" of the value of a vote until there is first defined a standard of reference as to what a vote should be worth.

Emphasis on the slogan "one person, one vote" merely obscured these questions and added to doctrinal confusion. Because of this problem, Justice Abe Fortas broke from the Court majority in the legislative reapportionment cases, declaring that such "admittedly complex and subtle" matters must be governed by "substance, not shibboleth." Discussing simplistic formulas such as "one person, one vote," he complained that they "are not surgical instruments"; rather, "they have a tendency to hack deeply—to amputate."[7] Their bluntness often makes them brutally efficient, but such efficiency comes at the price of clarity in constitutional understanding. To a greater or lesser degree, the same criticism can be directed toward many other constitutional doctrines.

Logical Reasoning

Another approach to constitutional interpretation emphasizes the use of logical reasoning as exemplified in the syllogism, a formal argument consisting of a major premise, a minor premise, and a conclusion. The major premise sets forth a proposition, such as "A law repugnant to the Constitution is void." The minor premise contains an assertion related to the major premise: "This particular law is repugnant to the Constitution." From these premises the conclusion logically follows: "This particular law is void." The foregoing example represents the essence of Chief Justice John Marshall's reasoning in *Marbury* v. *Madison* (1803), which formally established the Court's power of judicial review (that is, the power to void legislative or executive acts that it finds unconstitutional.)

Marshall himself was well aware, however, that logical analysis is an insufficient method of interpreting the Constitution. Assuming the validity of the major premise, the soundness of the conclusion depends upon whether the minor premise is true. But logic cannot determine whether a particular law is repugnant to the Constitution. That question must be left to informed opinion and judgment—informed opinion about the purposes for which the Constitution was established, and judgment of whether the law in question is consistent with those ends or purposes. Logical analysis, therefore, must be supplemented with a clear understanding of what *The Federalist,* No. 10, calls the "great objects" of the Constitution. Even Marshall, the justice most commonly identified with the use of logical analysis, ultimately based his constitutional interpretations on his understanding of the ends the Constitution was intended to serve. Marshall believed that the Constitution points beyond itself to the purposes and policies that it serves, and that in the difficult (and most interesting) cases, constitutional interpretation must turn upon an understanding of the Constitution's proper ends. He confidently observed in *McCulloch* v. *Maryland* (1819) that the nature of the Constitution demands "that only its great outlines should be marked, its important objects designated." As for the "minor ingredients" that comprise these objects, he was convinced that they could be "deduced from the nature of the objects themselves."

The Living Constitution

Based upon changing conditions and the lessons of experience, the adaptive, or "living Constitution," approach treats the Constitution more as a political than as a legal document and holds that constitutional interpretation can and must be influenced by present-day values and the sum total of the American experience. Although they insist that each generation has the right to adapt the Constitution to its own needs, proponents of this approach acknowledge that these adaptations must be reconcilable with the language of the Constitution. They would concede, for example, that the provision that each state should have equal representation in the Senate cannot be interpreted to allow for proportional representation, no matter what the dictates of changing conditions. But, they argue, the meaning of the Commerce Clause or of the Eighth Amendment's prohibition of "cruel and unusual punishment" may legitimately change over a period of time.

Defenders of the adaptive approach often cite Marshall's observation in *McCulloch* that "We must never forget that it is a Constitution we are expounding," one that is "intended to endure for ages to come, and consequently, to be adapted to the various crises of human affairs,"[8] although, it should be noted, Marshall was not asserting that the Court should adapt the Constitution but was arguing instead that the powers of the Constitution should be understood as broad enough to provide Congress with latitude sufficient to confront various crises in the future. Also cited is the argument Justice Oliver Wendell Holmes put forward in *Missouri* v. *Holland* (1920):

> When we are dealing with words that also are a constituent act, like the Constitution of the United States, we must realize that they have called into life a being the development of which could not have been foreseen completely by the most gifted of its begetters. It was enough for them to realize or to hope that they had created an organism; it has taken a century and cost their successors much sweat and blood to prove that they created a nation. The case before us must be considered in the light of our whole experience and not merely in that of what was said a hundred years ago.

Like the other approaches to constitutional interpretation considered thus far, the adaptive approach has its problems. Most importantly, too much adaptation can render the Constitution and its various provisions so pliant that the original document is no longer able to provide guidance concerning what is to be done. Those who embrace the adaptive approach too often misuse Marshall's statements in *McCulloch* and seek not merely an adaptation *within* the Constitution but rather an adaptation *of* the Constitution; they want not only to devise new means to the ends of the Constitution, but also to adopt entirely new ends as well. Justice Brennan's objections to capital punishment are a case in point. He argues that the objective of the "cruel and unusual punishment" clause of the

Eighth Amendment is the promotion of "human dignity" and, by insisting that capital punishment is a denial of human dignity, concludes that capital punishment is unconstitutional,[9] despite the facts that the Constitution permits capital trials when preceded by a "presentment or indictment of a Grand Jury"; permits a person to be "put in jeopardy of life" provided it is not done twice "for the same offense"; and permits both the national government and the states to deprive persons of their lives provided it is not done "without due process of law." The consequences of such a course of action were recognized by James Madison: "If the sense in which the Constitution was accepted and ratified by the Nation . . . be not the guide in expounding it, there can be no security for a consistent and stable [government], more than for a faithful exercise of its powers."[10]

The Intent of the Framers

This approach is based on the premise that constitutional interpretation must proceed from an understanding of what those who initially drafted and ratified the Constitution intended for it to accomplish; as a consequence, it relies heavily on documentary evidence of the original understanding of the Constitution—especially on the notes taken by James Madison at the Federal Convention of 1787 and on *The Federalist*—in order to establish the ends of the American Constitution and the means for their achievement. Such reliance on the intent or aims of the Framers has often been subjected to harsh criticism. As critics have pointed out, the Framers' exact intentions are very difficult to determine in many cases. Of the fifty-five delegates present at one or more sessions of the 1787 Convention, for example, some took little or no part in the proceedings. Furthermore, what was said and the reasons given for votes cast are known largely through the remarkable yet necessarily incomplete notes of James Madison.[11] On only a few issues did a majority of the delegates speak, and on no issue did they all speak. Many decisions were compromises that completely satisfied no one, and others carried by the slimmest of majorities. And even if the intentions of the fifty-five delegates could somehow be divined, critics continue, how could we possibly know the intentions of the delegates to the states' ratifying conventions, whose votes put the Constitution into operation, or of the people who elected those delegates? As Justice Robert H. Jackson observed in *Youngstown Sheet and Tube Company* v. *Sawyer* (1952), "Just what our forefathers did envision, or would have envisioned had they foreseen modern conditions, must be divined from materials almost as enigmatic as the dreams Joseph was called to interpret for Pharoah."

Critics also raise a second and more fundamental objection—even if we could know the Framers' intention, why should we be bound by it? As Walton H. Hamilton has noted, "It is a little presumptuous for one generation, through a Constitution, to impose its will on posterity. Posterity has its own problems, and to deal with them adequately, it needs freedom of action, unhampered by the dead hand of the past."[12]

Although these criticisms seem forceful and cogent, they reflect a far too narrow understanding of the approach under discussion. To answer the most fundamental objection first, there should be no question of the founding generation "imposing its will on posterity." This approach seeks to understand the intentions of the Framers not because they were demigods whose judgments must be embraced unreservedly, but because they are and will remain the best possible guides to discovering the ends and purposes of the constitutional order under which we live. As long as that order remains in force, we need to know as much about the Constitution as possible, including the purposes it was designed to achieve and the evils it was intended to avert. When constitutional questions are raised, therefore, this approach turns to the Founders not for specific answers, but rather for general guidance as to what the Constitution was intended to accomplish and how constitutional questions can be resolved in a manner consistent with these overall intentions. In examining Congress's power under the Commerce Clause to legislate on a particular issue, for example, followers of this approach turn to the founding documents not to ascertain whether the Framers would have favored the specific legislation in question—in all probability, they would never have taken up this question; and even if they had, their specific answers are unlikely to have any contemporary bearing—but to identify the intentions of the Framers in order to determine whether the objectives of the legislation in question are consistent with the ends for which the Commerce Clause and the Constitution were created. The Framers' intentions are not always clear or definitive, of course. But protestations that it is very difficult to discover or verify these intentions miss the point. Any evidence pertaining to what the framers sought to accomplish can only enhance our appreciation of what the Constitution means and what purposes it was designed to achieve, and therefore ought to weigh heavily in our overall understanding of the Constitution.

THE APPROACHES IN PERSPECTIVE

Textual analysis, precedent, constitutional doctrine, logical analysis, adaptation, and identifying the intent of the Framers can all contribute to our understanding of the Constitution. We will be guided by all of them as appropriate, recognizing both the strengths and the weaknesses of each. In so doing, we will be following the prudent counsel given by Justice Joseph Story in his *Commentaries on the Constitution of the United States:*

> In construing the Constitution of the United States, we are, in the first instance, to consider, what are its nature and objects, its scope and design, as apparent from the structure of the instrument, viewed as a whole and also viewed in its component parts. Where its words are plain, clear and determinate, they require no interpretation. . . . Where the words admit of two senses, each of which is conformable to general usage, that sense is to be adopted, which without departing

> from the literal import of the words, best harmonizes with the nature and objects, the scope and design of the instrument. . . . In examining the Constitution, the antecedent situation of the country and its institutions, the existence and operations of the state governments, the powers and operations of the Confederation, in short all the circumstances, which had a tendency to produce, or to obstruct its formation and ratification, deserve careful attention.[13]

Taken together and employed with the "careful attention" that Justice Story urges, these approaches can contribute not only to our understanding of the Constitution but also to our ability to evaluate, in light of this understanding, the decisions of the federal and state judiciaries and the constitutional pronouncements of the executive and legislative branches. In order to take full advantage of all the approaches, we must first identify the Constitution's ends or purposes—what Justice Story calls its "nature and objects."

THE ENDS OF THE CONSTITUTION

Justice Jackson's sentiments notwithstanding, the documentary evidence is far from hopelessly "enigmatic" in spelling out the ends of the Constitution. The Founders set out to establish an efficient and powerful guarantor of rights and liberties based on the principle of qualitative majority rule, the principle that the majority not only should rule but should rule well. In *The Federalist,* No. 10, James Madison explicitly stated this goal:

> To secure the public good and private rights against the danger of [an overbearing majority], and at the same time to preserve the spirit and form of popular government is then the great object to which our inquiries are directed. Let me add that it is the desideratum by which alone this form of government can be rescued from the opprobrium under which it has so long labored and be recommended to the esteem and adoption of mankind.[14]

As Madison and his colleagues were well aware, the "great object" of their inquiries presented daunting difficulties. They were irrevocably committed to popular or republican government, but historically, popular governments led inevitably to majority tyranny. In such governments, measures were decided "not according to the rules of justice, and the rights of the minor party; but by the superior force of an interested and over-bearing majority." Minority rights were disregarded—as were the "permanent and aggregate interests of the community." Because popular governments too easily allowed for "unjust combinations of the majority as a whole," they typically had proved to be "incompatible with personal security, or the rights of property" and "as short in their lives, as they have been violent in their deaths."[15] Such, according to Madison, was the great "opprobrium" under which "this form of government" had "so long labored."

The most commonly prescribed palliative for the problems of majority tyranny was to render the government powerless. However eager a majority might be to "concert and carry into effect its schemes of oppression," if its governmental vehicle were sufficiently impotent, it would pose no real threat. As William Symmes commented in the Massachusetts State Constitutional Ratifying Convention, "Power was never given . . . but it was exercised, nor ever exercised but it was finally abused."[16] The implication was clear: To prevent abuses, power must be consciously and jealously withheld.

This prescription was not without its shortcomings, however. Carried to an extreme, it rendered government not only powerless but also altogether unworkable. To this view, the leading Framers justifiably and appropriately responded that although the spirit of jealousy was extremely valuable, when carried too far it impinged upon another equally important principle of government—that of "strength and stability in the organization of our government, and vigor in its operations."[17] They understood that a strong and stable government was necessary not only to cope with the problems that society faces, but also to render liberty fully secure. In order that popular government "be recommended to the esteem and adoption of mankind," they realized they would have to solve the twofold problem raised by majority rule: to establish a constitution capable of avoiding democratic tyranny on one hand and democratic ineptitude on the other. This problem had overwhelmed the government under the Articles of Confederation and led to the calling of the Federal Convention. Under the Articles, the member states were so powerful and their legislative assemblies so dominant and unchecked that the tyrannical impulses of the majority continually placed in jeopardy the life, liberty, and property of the citizenry; and the central federal government was so infirm and its responsibilities so few and limited that its situation often "bordered on anarchy." The Framers fully appreciated the challenge they faced. As Madison noted, "In framing a government which is to be administered by men over men, the great difficulty lies in this: You must first enable the government to controul the governed; and in the next place, oblige it to controul itself."[18] As we shall see, the Framers rose to this challenge by so arranging the various articles and provisions of the Constitution that they not only granted the federal and state governments sufficient power to control the governed but also obliged them to control themselves through such institutional arrangements and contrivances as the extended republic, separation of powers and checks and balances, and federalism.

THE MEANS TO THE ENDS

The Framers' solution to the problems of republican government was altogether consistent with republican principle. *The Federalist* is replete with references to this matter. Recognizing that "a dependence on the people is no doubt the primary controul on the government," the Framers also understood that experience had "taught mankind the necessity of auxiliary precautions."[19] This understanding was fundamentally shaped by their assessment of human nature. They believed mankind to be driven by self-interest and consumed by the desire for distinction. Men were seen as "ambitious, rapacious, and vindictive" creatures whose passions for "power and advantage" are so powerful and basic that it is folly to expect that they can be controlled adequately by traditional republican reliance on pure patriotism, respect for character, conscience, or religion, or even the not very lofty maxim that "honesty is the best policy." Inevitably, human avarice and lust for power divide men into parties, inflame them with mutual animosity, and render them much more disposed to oppress one another than to cooperate for the common good. Men are predictable in such matters. They will form factions, whether or not there are readily apparent reasons to do so. As their passions lead them in directions contrary to the "dictates of reason and justice," their reason is subverted into providing arguments for self-indulgence rather than incentives to virtue.[20]

Given these sentiments, it is hardly surprising that the Framers placed little faith in improving human nature through moral reformation or in the activities of "enlightened statesmen." The only hope for republican government, they concluded, was the establishment of institutions that would depend upon "the ordinary depravity of human nature."[21] Appreciating that human passion and pride were elemental forces that could never be stifled or contained by "parchment barriers,"[22] they sought to harness and direct these forces through the process of mutual checking. Consequently, they included in the Constitution checks and controls that might "make it the interest, even of bad men, to act for the public good."[23] Self-interest, the Framers contended, was one check that nothing could overcome, and the principal hope for security and stability in a republican government. The rather ignoble but always reliable inclination of people to follow their own "sober second thoughts of self-interest" would serve to minimize the likelihood of majority tyranny.[24] As the observant Alexis de Tocqueville would later describe it, the Framers relied on institutional mechanisms to check one personal interest with another and to direct the passions with the very same instruments that excite them.

But what kinds of institutional mechanisms—what constitutional means—could incorporate and redirect human self-interest in such a way as to enable the federal and state governments to control the governed and, at the same time, oblige those governments to control themselves? The answer to that question can be found in the three principal concepts underpinning the Constitution: the extended republic, separation of powers and checks and balances, and federalism.

The Extended Republic

The multiplicity of interests present in the extended commercial republic established by the Constitution represents one of the principal mechanisms by which the Framers sought to establish an energetic government based on the principle of qualitative majority rule. The advantages of an extended republic can be best seen by examining the defects of a small republic. As Madison noted in *The Federalist,* No. 10, the smaller the republic, "the fewer probably will be the distinct parties and interests composing it; the fewer the distinct parties and interests, the more frequently will a majority be found of the same party; and the smaller the compass within which they are placed, the more easily will they concert and execute their plans of oppression." Thus arises democratic tyranny, which can be prevented only by rendering the government impotent and thereby fostering democratic ineptitude. In contrast, the larger the republic, the greater the variety of interests, parties, and sects present within it and the more moderate and diffused the conflict. In the words of *The Federalist,* No. 10, "Extend the sphere, and you take in a greater variety of parties and interests; you make it less probable that a majority of the whole will have a common motive to invade the rights of other citizens; or if such a common motive exists, it will be more difficult for all who feel it to discover their own strength, and to act in unison with each other."[25]

Because of the "greater variety" of economic, geographic, religious, political, cultural, and ethnic interests that an extended republic takes in, rule by a majority is effectively replaced by rule by ever-changing coalitions of minorities that come together on one particular issue to act as a majority but break up on the next. The coalition of minorities that acts as a majority on the issue of import duties is not likely to remain intact on such issues as national defense or governmental aid to private schools. The very real possibility that allies in one coalition may be opponents in the next encourages a certain moderation in politics, in terms of both the political objectives sought and the political tactics employed. Political interests become reluctant to raise the political stakes too high: By scoring too decisive a political victory on one issue, an interest may find that it has only weakened itself, by devastating a potential ally and thus rendering itself vulnerable to similar treatment in the future. Accordingly, politics is moderated, not through idle appeals to conscience and beneficence but rather through the reliance on the inclination of individuals to look after their own self-interest. As Madison observed in *The Federalist,* No. 51, this diversity of interests assures that "a coalition of a majority of the whole society" will seldom take place "on any other principles than those of justice and the common good."[26] The extended republic thus helped to make it possible for the Framers to give the national government sufficient power to prevent democratic ineptitude without raising the spectre of democratic tyranny.

The Framers' recognition of and reliance on the moderating effects brought about by an extended republic is apparent in such constitutional provisions as the Contract Clause in Article I, Section 10, which prohibits any state from passing laws "impairing the obligation of contracts." Note that only the states are restrained, but the federal government is not—and for good reasons. It was thought that no state, however large, was or would be extensive enough to contain a variety of interests wide enough to prevent majorities from acting oppressively and using their legislative power to nullify contracts for their own advantage. Consequently they had to have their power to do so limited by the Constitution. The federal government, by contrast, was large enough and contained the multiplicity of interests necessary to prevent oppression of this sort, and so had no need of constitutional constraint. Thus could majority tyranny be avoided simply by relying on the popular principle to operate naturally in an extended republic. The elegant simplicity of this mechanism was pointed out by Madison: "In the extent and proper structure of the Union, therefore, we behold a Republican remedy for the disease most incident to Republican Government."[27]

Separation of Powers and Checks and Balances

For the Framers, the "great desideratum of politics" was the formation of a "government that will, at the same time, deserve the seemingly opposite epithets—efficient and free."[28] The extended republic was one means by which they sought to realize this objective; a "government of separated institutions sharing powers"[29] was another. They were aware that "the accumulation of all powers legislative, executive, and judiciary in the same hands, whether of one, a few, or many, and whether hereditary, self-appointed, or elective may justly be pronounced the very definition of tyranny," and therefore that "the preservation of liberty requires that the three great departments of power should be separate and distinct."[30] Thus, they sought to construct a government consisting of three coordinate and equal branches, with each performing a blend of functions, thereby balancing governmental powers. Their goal was to structure the government so that the three branches would "by their mutual relations, be the means of keeping each other in their proper places."[31] And this the Framers succeeded in doing. They began by giving most legislative power to the Congress, most executive power to the president, and most judicial power to the Supreme Court and to such inferior federal courts as Congress might establish. But they then set out to "divide and arrange" the remaining powers in such a manner that each branch could be "a check on the others." Principally, they introduced the principle of bicameralism, under which Congress was divided into the House of Representatives and the Senate, and arranged for the president to exercise certain important legislative powers by requiring yearly addresses on the State of the Union and by providing him with a conditional veto power. They also assumed that the Congress would be restrained by the Supreme Court's power of judicial review and sought to keep the president in check by requiring senatorial confirmation of executive appointees and judicial nominees, mandating that the Senate advise on and consent to treaties, and allowing for impeachment by the Congress. Finally, they supplied the means for keeping the Supreme Court in its "proper place" by giving the Congress budgetary control over the judiciary, the power of impeachment, and the power to regulate the Court's appellate jurisdiction. On top of these specific arrangements, they provided for staggered terms of office (two years for the House, six years for the Senate, four years for the President, and tenure "for good behavior" for the judiciary), to give each branch a further "constitutional check over the others."[32] Knowing that the various branches of the government, even though popularly elected, might from time to time be activated by "an official sentiment opposed to that of the General Government and perhaps to that of the people themselves,"[33] they felt that separation of powers was needed to ensure the fidelity of these popular agents. Separation of powers would provide for a "balance of the parts" that would consist "in the independent exercise of their separate powers and, when their powers are separately exercised, then in their mutual influence and operation on one another. Each part acts and is acted upon, supports and is supported, regulates and is regulated by the rest." This balance would assure that even if these separate parts were to become activated by separate interests, they would nonetheless move "in a line of direction somewhat different from that, which each acting by itself, would have taken; but, at the same time, in a line partaking of the natural direction of each, and formed out of the natural direction of the whole—the true line of publick liberty and happiness."[34]

Not only would such a separation and balancing of powers prevent any branch of government from tyrannizing the people, it would also thwart the majority from tyrannizing the minority. In creating an independent executive and judiciary, the Framers provided a means of temporarily blocking the will of tyrannical majorities as expressed through a compliant or demagogic legislature. Although separation of powers cannot permanently frustrate the wishes of the people, on those occasions when "the interests of the people are at variance with their inclinations" it so structures these institutions that they are able to "withstand the temporary delusions" of people, in order to give them "time and opportunity for more cool and sedate reflection."[35] The prospects for democratic tyranny are dimmed accordingly.

In addition to keeping society free, separation of powers was seen by the Framers as helping to render the government efficient—as minimizing the prospects for democratic ineptitude. Realizing that the democratic process of mutual deliberation and consent can paralyze the government when swift and decisive action is necessary, the Framers reasoned that government would be more efficient if its various functions were performed by separate and distinct agencies. According to James Wilson, a leading member of the Constitutional Convention,

> In planning, forming, and arranging laws, deliberation is always becoming, and always useful. But in the active scenes of government, there are emergencies, in which the man . . . who deliberates is lost. Secrecy may be equally necessary as dispatch. But can either secrecy or dispatch be expected, when, to every enterprise, mutual communication, mutual consultation, and mutual agreement among men, per-

> haps of discordant views, of discordant tempers, and discordant interests, are indispensably necessary? How much time will be consumed! and when it is consumed, how little business will be done! . . . If, on the other hand, the executive power of government is placed in the hands of one person, who is to direct all the subordinate officers of that department; is there not reason to expect, in his plans and conduct, promptitude, activity, firmness, consistency, and energy.[36]

For the Framers, then, separation of powers not only forestalled democratic tyranny, but also provided for an independent and energetic executive able to assure "that prompt and salutory execution of the laws, which enter into the very definition of good Government."[37]

Federalism

The American constitutional system rests on a federal arrangement in which power is shared by the national government and the states. The primary purpose of this arrangement was to provide for a strong central government; however, it has also had the effect of promoting qualitative majority rule. The federalism created by the Framers can best be understood when contrasted to the confederalism that existed under the Articles of Confederation. Confederalism was characterized by three principles:

(1) The central government exercised authority only over the individual governments (i.e., states) of which it was composed, never over the individual citizens of whom those governments were composed. Even this authority was limited, the resolutions of the federal authority amounting to little more than recommendations that the states could (and did) disregard.

(2) The central government had no authority over the internal affairs of the individual states; its rule was limited mainly to certain external tasks of mutual interest to the member states.

(3) Each individual state had an "exact equality of suffrage" derived from the equality of sovereignty shared by all states.[38]

The consequences of these three principles on the operation of the federal government were disastrous. They rendered the Articles of Confederation so weak that it was reduced, in Alexander Hamilton's words, "to the last stage of national humiliation."[39] There was obviously a need for a "more perfect union" and for new arrangements capable of rendering the political structure "adequate to the exigencies of Government and the preservation of the Union."[40]

The new federal structure erected by the Framers corrected each of the difficulties inherent in confederalism. To begin with, the power of the new federal government was enhanced considerably. Not only could it now operate directly on the individual citizen, just as the state governments could, but it could also deal with internal matters: for example, it now could regulate commerce among the several states, establish uniform rules of bankruptcy, coin money, establish a postal system, tax, and borrow money. Moreover, the federal government was made supreme over the states. As Article VI spelled out: "This Constitution, and the laws of the United States which shall be made in pursuance thereof . . . shall be the supreme law of the land."

If the federalism the Framers created strengthened the central government, it also contributed to qualitative majority rule, by preserving the presence of powerful states capable of checking and controlling not only the central government but each other as well. Federalism granted the new central government only those powers expressly or implicitly delegated to it in the Constitution and allowed the states to retain all powers not prohibited to them. The states were permitted to regulate intrastate commerce and the health, safety, and welfare of the citizenry (i.e., the police power) and even were authorized to exercise certain powers concurrently with the central government—for example the power of taxation and the power to regulate interstate commerce—so long as these powers were not exercised in a manner inconsistent with constitutional limitations or federal regulations. Finally, the Framers' federalism also contributed to qualitative majority rule by blending federal elements into the structure and procedures of the central government itself.[41] To take only the most obvious example, it mixed into the Senate the federal principle of equal representation of all states. When joined with bicameralism and separation of powers, this principle directly contributed to qualitative majority rule. For a measure to become law, it would have to pass the Senate, where because of the federal principle of equal representation of all states, the presence of a nationally distributed majority (with the moderating tendencies that provides) virtually would be guaranteed.

This division of power between the federal and state governments also provided another remedy for the ills of democratic ineptitude. As James Wilson emphasized, with two levels of government at their disposal, the people are in a position to assign their sovereign power to whichever level they believed to be more productive in promoting the common good. Moreover, efficiency is gained in still another way. The federal system permits the states to serve as, in the words of Justice John Marshall Harlan, "experimental social laboratories"[42] in which new policies and procedures can be implemented. If these experiments prove to be successful, they can be adopted elsewhere; if they fail, the damage is limited to the particular state in question. Since the risks are lessened, experimentation is encouraged, and the chances of positive reform and better governance are increased accordingly. In a wholly national or unitary system, on the other hand, experimentation can take place only on a national scale, and social inertia and a commitment to the status quo are encouraged.

The enhanced efficiency of the federal system, in turn, dims the prospect of democratic tyranny. As Madison observed in *The Federalist,* No.

20, "Tyranny has perhaps oftener grown out of the assumptions of power, called for, on pressing exigencies, by a defective constitution, than by the full exercise of the largest constitutional authorities."[43]

The Framers saw the multiplicity of interests present in an extended republic, separation of powers and checks and balances, and federalism as contributing to a government that is at once "efficient and free." These institutional mechanisms, operating in conjunction with each other, were designed to prevent the twin evils of democratic ineptitude and democratic tyranny. The Framers' intention was to institute an energetic and efficient government based on the principle of qualitative majority rule, and they systematically and consistently employed these means to achieve that end. This understanding is at the core of the approach to constitutional interpretation utilized in the discussion of the constitutional provisions that follows.

NOTES

1 For Chief Justice Hughes's subsequent qualification of these remarks, see *The Autobiographical Notes of Charles Evans Hughes,* eds. David J. Danielski and J. S. Tulshin (Cambridge, Mass.: Harvard University Press, 1973), p. 143.

2 Alexander Hamilton, James Madison, and John Jay, *The Federalist,* ed. Jacob E. Cooke (New York: World, 1961), p. 340. All subsequent references to *The Federalist* are to this edition.

3 Ibid., No. 10, p. 65.

4 *Graves* v. *O'Keefe* (1939). Justice Frankfurter concurring.

5 As Thomas Hobbes observed, "precedents prove only what was done, but not what was well done." See his *A Dialogue Between a Philosopher and a Student of the Common Laws of England,* ed. Joseph Cropsey (Chicago: University of Chicago Press, 1971), p. 129.

6 See J. Skelly Wright, "Professor Bickel, the Scholarly Tradition, and the Supreme Court," *Harvard Law Review* 84, no. 4 (February 1971):785.

7 *Avery* v. *Midland County* (1968). Mr. Justice Fortas dissenting.

8 See Christopher Wolfe, "A Theory of U.S. Constitutional History," *Journal of Politics* 43, no. 2 (May 1981):301.

9 William J. Brennan, "The Constitution of the United States: Contemporary Ratification," presentation at the Text and Teaching Symposium, Georgetown University, Washington, D.C., October 12, 1985.

10 James Madison, *The Writings of James Madison,* ed. Gaillard Hunt (New York: Putnam, 1900–1910), vol. 9, p. 191.

11 For a defense of Madison's notes, see his "Preface to the Debates in the Convention of 1787," in *The Records of the Federal Convention of 1787,* ed. Max Farrand (New Haven: Yale University Press, 1937), vol. 3, pp. 539–551.

12 Walton H. Hamilton, "The Constitution—Apropos of Crosskey," *University of Chicago Law Review* 21, no. 1 (Fall 1953): 82. For more contemporary critiques of original intent, see William J. Brennan, "The Constitution of the United States: Contemporary Ratification," Text and Teaching Symposium, Georgetown University, October 12, 1985; Arthur S. Miller, *Toward Increased Judicial Activism: The Political Role of the Supreme Court* (Westport, Conn.:

Greenwood Press, 1982); Leonard W. Levy, *Original Intent and the Framers' Constitution* (New York: Macmillan, 1988); and H. Jefferson Powell, "The Original Understanding of Original Intent," *Harvard Law Review* 98 (March 1985) 885–948. For responses to these critiques, see Raoul Berger, "Original Intent and Leonard Levy," *Rutgers Law Review* 42 (Fall 1989) 255–286; Raoul Berger, "The Founders' Views—According to Jefferson Powell," *Texas Law Review* 67 (April 1989): 1033–1096; James H. Hutson, "The Creation of the Constitution: The Integrity of the Documentary Record," *Texas Law Review* 65 (November 1986) 1–39; Charles A. Lofgren, "The Original Understanding of Original Intent?" *Constitutional Commentary* 5 (1988) 77–113; and Gary L. McDowell, *Curbing the Courts: The Constitution and the Limits of Judicial Power* (Baton Rouge: Louisiana State University Press, 1988).

13 Joseph Story, *Commentaries on the Constitution of the United States*, vol. 1 (Boston: Hilliard and Greay, 1833), pp. 387–388. See also pp. 322, 404, 412, and 417.

14 *The Federalist*, No. 10, p. 61.

15 *The Federalist*, No. 10, pp. 57–61; No. 51, p. 351.

16 Jonathan Elliot (ed.), *The Debates in the Several State Conventions on the Adoption of the Federal Constitution* 2d ed. (Philadelphia: Lippincott, 1863), vol. 2, p. 74.

17 Alexander Hamilton in the New York State Ratifying Convention: Elliot, *Debates*, vol. 2, p. 301.

18 *The Federalist*, No. 51, p. 349. See also No. 39, p. 233.

19 Ibid., No. 51, p. 349.

20 See *The Federalist*, No. 6, pp. 28–31; No. 10, pp. 59, 61; No. 15, pp. 96, 97; No. 30, p. 193; No. 42, p. 283; No. 48, p. 334; and No. 63, pp. 426–27. A qualification is necessary at this point According to *The Federalist:* "As there is a degree of depravity in mankind which requires a certain degree of circumspection and distrust; so there are other qualities in human nature which justify a certain portion of esteem and confidence. Republican government presupposes the existence of these qualities in a higher degree than any other form." *The Federalist*, No. 55, p. 378.

21 *The Federalist*, No. 10, p. 60; No. 78, p. 530.

22 *The Federalist*, No. 25, p. 163; No. 41, pp. 41, 270; No. 48, pp. 333, 338.

23 David Hume, *Political Essays*, ed. Charles W. Handel (Indianapolis: Bobbs-Merrill, 1953), p. 13.

24 The phrase is Frederick Douglass's. See his "The Destiny of Colored Americans," in *The North Star* of November 16, 1849.

25 *The Federalist*, No. 10, pp. 63–64.

26 Ibid., No. 51, p. 353.

27 Ibid., No. 10, p. 65.

28 *The Works of James Wilson*, ed. Robert Green McCloskey (Cambridge, Mass.: Belknap Press of Harvard University Press, 1967), p. 791.

29 Richard E. Neustadt, *Presidential Power* (New York: John Wiley, 1960), p. 33.

30 *The Federalist*, No. 47, p. 324.

31 *The Federalist*, No. 51, p. 348, 349.

32 Ibid., No. 48, p. 332.

33 James Wilson, in Farrand, *Records*, vol. 1, p. 359.

34 *The Works of James Wilson*, p. 300.

35 *The Federalist*, No. 71, pp. 482–83.

36 *The Works of James Wilson*, pp. 294, 296. See also *The Federalist*, No. 70.

37 *The Federalist,* No. 37, p. 233.
38 See Martin Diamond, "What the Framers Meant by Federalism," in *A Nation of States,* 2d ed., ed. Robert A. Goldwin (Chicago: Rand McNally, 1974), pp. 25–42.
39 See *The Federalist,* No. 9, p. 55; No. 15, p. 73; and No. 22, p. 138.
40 Resolution of the Congress calling for the Federal Convention of 1787, in Farrand, *Records,* vol. 3, p. 14.
41 See Martin Diamond, "*The Federalist* on Federalism: Neither a National Nor a Federal Constitution, But a Composition of Both," *Yale Law Journal* 86, no. 6 (May 1977), pp. 1273–85.
42 *Roth* v. *United States* (1957).
43 *The Federalist,* No. 20, p. 127.

SELECTED READINGS

The Federalist, Nos. 6, 9, 10, 15, 37, 39, 47–51, 63, 70–72, 78.

Agresto, John. *The Supreme Court and Constitutional Democracy* (Ithaca, New York: Cornell University Press, 1984).

Barber, Sotorios. *On What the Constitution Means* (Baltimore, Maryland: Johns Hopkins University Press, 1984).

Black, Charles L. *Decision According to Law* (New York: W. W. Norton, 1981).

Bork, Robert. *The Tempting of America: The Political Seduction of the Law* (New York: The Free Press, 1990).

Diamond, Martin. "Democracy and the Federalist: A Reconsideration of the Framers' Intent." *American Political Science Review* 53, no. 1 (March 1959): 52–68.

———. "The Ends of Federalism." *Publius* 3 (Fall 1973).

Douglas, William O. "Stare Decisis." *Columbia Law Review* 49 (1949).

Eidelberg, Paul. *The Philosophy of the American Constitution* (New York: Free Press, 1968).

Elliot, Jonathan, ed. *The Debates in the Several State Conventions on the Adoption of the Federal Constitution as Recommended by the General Convention in Philadelphia in 1787.* 5 vols (Philadelphia: Lippincott, 1863).

Ely, John Hart. *Democracy and Distrust: A Theory of Judicial Review* (Cambridge, Mass.: Harvard University Press, 1980).

Farrand, Max, ed. *The Records of the Federal Convention of 1787.* 4 vols. (New Haven: Yale University Press, 1937).

Faulkner, Robert K. *The Jurisprudence of John Marshall* (Princeton: Princeton University Press, 1937).

Hickok, Eugene W., ed. *The Bill of Rights: Original Meaning and Current Understanding* (Charlottesville: University Press of Virginia, 1991).

Kesler, Charles R., ed. *Saving the Revolution: The Federalist Papers and the American Founding* (New York: Free Press, 1987).

Kurland, Philip B., and Lerner, Ralph, eds. *The Founders' Constitution.* 5 vols. (Chicago: University of Chicago Press, 1987).

Levy, Leonard, and Mahoney, Dennis J., eds. *The Framing and Ratification of the Constitution* (New York: Macmillan Publishing Co., 1987).

Meese, Edwin. "Toward a Jurisprudence of Original Intention." *Benchmark* 2, no. 1 (1986): 1–10.

Perry, Michael J. *The Constitution, the Courts, and Human Rights* (New Haven: Yale University Press, 1982).

Rehnquist, William H. "The Notion of a Living Constitution." *Texas Law Review* 54 (May 1976): 693–707.

Rossum, Ralph A., and Gary L. McDowell, eds. *The American Founding: Politics, Statesmanship, and the Constitution* (Port Washington, N.Y.: Kennikat Press, 1981).

Storing, Herbert J., ed. *The Complete Anti-Federalist.* 7 vols. (Chicago: University of Chicago Press, 1981).

Wolfe, Christopher. *The Rise of Modern Judicial Review* (New York: Basic Books, 1986).

Wood, Gordon S. *The Creation of the American Republic.* (Chapel Hill, N.C.: University of North Carolina Press, 1969).

2
CONSTITUTIONAL ADJUDICATION

About 150 years ago, Alexis de Tocqueville observed that "there is hardly a political question in the United States which does not sooner or later turn into a judicial one."[1] Today, as then, Americans tend to transform policy disputes into constitutional issues and to seek resolutions in the courts in general, and in the Supreme Court in particular. The Supreme Court's political and legal roles are inextricably intertwined. By deciding cases that raise important issues concerning the extent, distribution, and uses of governmental power, the Court necessarily participates in governing.

The Court's dual role as an interpreter of the Constitution and an agency of government provides the focus for this chapter. Three basic questions will be considered: How are political questions transformed into legal issues and brought before the Court? How do the Justices go about deciding the cases involving those issues? What happens after the Court decides? The chapter's final section offers a framework for analyzing judicial decisions and supplies information about source materials in constitutional law.

HOW CASES GET TO THE SUPREME COURT

Each year over the past decade, the Court received about four thousand petitions for review and decided about 160 cases with full opinions. The cases the Court decides must fall within its jurisdiction: That is, it can only decide those cases it is empowered to hear by the Constitution or by statute. Once this requirement is fulfilled, the Court has broad discretion in determining what cases it will decide. The range of discretion available to the Court has increased over time, and with this expanded discretion have come significant shifts in its caseload.

Jurisdiction of the Court

The Supreme Court has both an original jurisdiction (over those cases in which the Court functions as a trial court) and an appellate jurisdiction (over those cases in which the Court may review the decisions of other courts). Article III, Section 2 of the Constitution defines the Court's original jurisdiction but confers its appellate jurisdiction subject to "such Exceptions, and under such Regulations, as Congress shall make."

Original Jurisdiction. The Supreme Court's original jurisdiction extends to cases involving foreign diplomatic personnel and to cases in which a state is a party. Altogether, the Court has decided fewer than two hundred cases under its original jurisdiction. Two developments have minimized the number of cases initiated in the Supreme Court. The Eleventh Amendment, adopted in 1798, withdrew part of the Court's original jurisdiction by prohibiting those who were not citizens of a state from suing it in federal court.[2] And more recently Congress has deflected many potential original-jurisdiction cases to the federal district courts by giving those courts concurrent jurisdiction.

As a result of legislation, the Supreme Court currently retains exclusive original jurisdiction only over legal disputes between two states, which commonly deal with boundaries or with water or mineral rights. Since hearing testimony in even these few cases could prove a major drain on the time and energies of the Court, it typically appoints a Special Master—usually a retired judge—to conduct hearings and report back to it. In deciding these cases, the justices often endorse the findings of the Master.

Appellate Jurisdiction. The Supreme Court hears the vast majority of its cases on appeal from either one of the fifty state court systems or from federal courts, in which instances it operates as the court of last resort. The Court's decisions are final because there is no court to which one can appeal to reverse them. Its interpretation of statutes can be reversed only by congressional legislation, and its constitutional rulings overturned only by constitutional amendment; in the absence of these remedies, all courts are obliged to follow the Supreme Court's direction in matters of federal law. The Court's decisions also are final in the sense that the Court generally decides cases only after the litigants have exhausted their available appeals to other courts (see Figure 2.1).

Cases initiated in state courts usually reach the U.S. Supreme Court on appeal from state supreme courts, although the Court occasionally hears a case on appeal from another state court when no further appeal is available in the state system. In *Thompson* v. *City of Louisville* (1960), for example, the justices accepted a case directly from the police court of Louisville, Kentucky, because under state law the defendant's fine was too low for appeal to any higher state court.[3] Cases initiated in federal district courts normally come to the Court following review by the appropriate court of appeals, but the Court can expedite consideration of cases. In *United States* v. *Nixon* (1974), which involved President Richard Nixon's refusal to surrender tapes of his conversations subpoenaed for use in a criminal prosecution, the importance of the dispute prompted the Court to hear the case immediately after the federal district court ruled.

Over the course of time, the Supreme Court has gained virtually total discretion in determining what cases it hears. Early in the twentieth century, cases on appeal (that is, cases in which the party appealing the case had a right to Supreme Court review) accounted for over 80 percent of the Court's appellate docket. Since many of these cases raised no significant legal issue, the justices actively lobbied for a reduction in the burden of obligatory review. Congress responded by passing the Judiciary Act of 1925, which drastically reduced the categories of cases in which parties had a right of appeal to the Court. In 1988, again at the urging of the justices, Congress eliminated almost all the Court's remaining mandatory jurisdiction, thereby according the Court nearly total control of its appellate docket.

Even prior to this legislation, the justices had exercised considerable control over the cases they decided. For one thing, over 90 percent of the

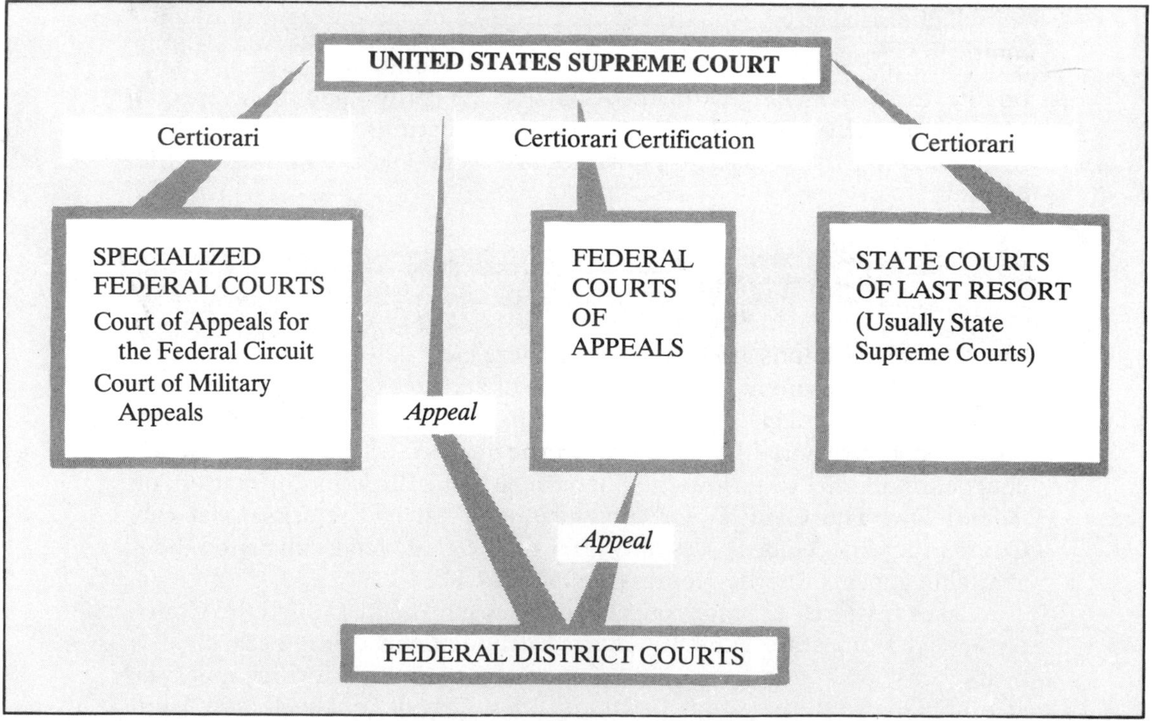

FIGURE 2.1 How Cases Reach the Supreme Court

BOX 2.1
The Justices—A Group Portrait

Selection. The president appoints the justices with the advice and consent of the Senate. On average, a vacancy on the Court occurs roughly every two years, so a president serving two full terms can expect to have a considerable impact on the membership of the Court. Ronald Reagan, for example, appointed three new members to the Court during his presidency. In recent decades the Senate has scrutinized nominees closely. From 1950 to 1990, it refused to confirm 4 of 24 nominees, either by a negative vote or by refusing to act on the nomination, and presidents withdrew other nominations in the face of opposition.

Backgrounds. Justices are usually appointed to the Court after long and active careers in public life. Among justices appointed up to 1990, 25 had served in Congress prior to appointment, and over 20 had held cabinet posts. Prior judicial experience is not a requirement—over one-third of the justices appointed since 1950 had none. In making appointments, presidents tend to consider prospective justices' political affiliation (almost 90 percent of appointees were members of the president's party), constitutional views, and demographic and geographic background. Thurgood Marshall (appointed 1967) was the first African-American elevated to the Supreme Court, and Sandra Day O'Connor (appointed 1981) the first woman.

Number. Although the Constitution establishes the Supreme Court, it does not specify the number of justices who shall serve on it. Therefore, Congress has the power to determine the size of the Court. Initially set at six, the number of justices fluctuated until 1869, when Congress established the number at nine. In 1937, President Franklin Roosevelt, frustrated by judicial decisions that had gutted major elements of his economic recovery program, proposed that the membership of the Court be expanded substantially. Congress, however, refused to enact this "court-packing" plan.

Tenure. The Constitution specifies that the justices, like other federal judges, shall hold office during "good behavior." Only one justice, Samuel Chase, has ever been impeached by the House of Representatives, and the Senate failed to convict him. Usually, appointment to the Court represents the culmination of a career, and justices tend to serve until death or retirement. Justice William Douglas, for example, served 36 years on the Court, and Justice Oliver Wendell Holmes did not retire until he was over 90. The average tenure for justices appointed during the twentieth century is over 14 years.

petitions for review came to the Court on writs of certiorari.[4] These petitions ranged from professionally drafted legal presentations in so-called paid cases to lay-drafted petitions submitted *in forma pauperis*.[5] In determining which certiorari petitions to accept, the Court has complete discretion. As the Supreme Court's Rule 17 states, "A review on writ of certiorari is not a matter of right, but of judicial discretion, and will be granted only when there are special and important reasons therefor."[6] In recent years the Court has granted certiorari in about 5 percent of the cases in which review was requested.

In addition, the Court had developed means to limit the burden posed by its mandatory appellate jurisdiction. Many cases on appeal had not warranted extended consideration by the Court; in such cases the Court summarily affirmed the decisions of federal courts without opinion or dismissed appeals from state courts "for want of a substantial federal question." In recent years, almost 80 percent of appeals were disposed of in this fashion. Thus the elimination of the Court's mandatory jurisdiction may not significantly affect the workload of the Court.

The Decision to Decide

The Supreme Court must be so selective in deciding what cases to hear because the number of cases in which review is sought far exceeds its capacities. Although congressional legislation has allowed the Court to choose for review only the most important cases, it has not alleviated the burden of screening petitions or established criteria for determining which cases warrant review.[7] It may be, as Chief Justice Earl Warren once suggested, that the standards which guide the justices' determinations "cannot be captured in any rule or guidelines that would be meaningful."[8] But this leaves unanswered the basic question of how the Court decides what to decide.

The Case Selection Process. The mechanics of case selection are relatively simple. Each justice has several law clerks (distinguished law school graduates selected annually by the justice after they have already served a year's clerkship), one of whose duties is to screen the petitions for review and prepare memos summarizing the materials. (Since 1972 the influx of cases has prompted several justices to pool their clerks for memo writing, so that the case memos each clerk prepares will be distributed to all participating justices.) Having evaluated the filings with the aid of his clerks' memos, the Chief Justice prepares a "discuss list" of the petitions he believes deserve collective consideration. Other justices can then add cases to the list. Unless a justice requests that a petition be discussed in conference, it is automatically denied. (More than 70 percent of all petitions are disposed of in this manner.)

Collective consideration of the petitions on the discuss list occurs during the three- or four-day conference prior to the beginning of the Court's term (in October) and at weekly conferences during the term. In the preterm conference, which is devoted exclusively to case selection, the justices dispose of the hundreds of petitions that have accumulated over the summer months. At the outset of its 1989 term, for example, the Court granted review in 24 cases, disposed of 3 more without opinion, and denied review in 988 cases.[9] No case is accepted for review, at either the preterm or the regular weekly conference, unless four justices vote to hear it (the so-called rule of four).

Criteria for Case Selection. Since the justices do not publish or explain their votes, it is difficult to determine what factors influenced decisions to grant or deny review in particular cases.[10] The considerations affecting case selection may vary from justice to justice and from case to case. We can identify, however, the general considerations that affect the Court's decisions on petitions for certiorari.

One such consideration is the Court's acknowledged responsibility to promote uniformity and consistency in federal law. Supreme Court Rule 17, "Considerations Governing Review on Certiorari," reflects this responsibility in listing the factors that might prompt the Court to grant certiorari: (1) important questions of Federal law on which the Court has not previously ruled; (2) conflicting interpretations of Federal law by lower courts; (3) lower-court decisions that conflict with previous Supreme Court decisions, and (4) lower-court departures 'from the accepted and usual course of judicial proceedings." This list is neither exhaustive nor binding: Reviews may be granted on the basis of other factors, or denied when one or more of the cited factors is present. At times the Court may deny review even when lower courts have reached conflicting decisions on an issue. In 1986, for example, the Court denied certiorari in a case challenging states' use of roadblocks to detect drunk drivers, even though several state courts had disagreed about whether the roadblocks violated the constitutional prohibition on unreasonable searches and seizures.[11]

In denying certiorari despite disagreement among lower courts, the justices often rely upon another case-selection criterion—the intrinsic importance of the issues raised in a case. Although occasionally the Court will reach out to correct gross miscarriages of justice, the justices recognize that they have important responsibilities in the governing of the nation, and they tend to be less concerned with correcting the errors of lower courts than with confronting "questions whose resolution will have immediate importance far beyond the particular facts and parties involved."[12] This criterion, of course, cannot be applied automatically. Some cases, because of the momentous political or legal issues they raise, clearly demand Supreme Court review. *United States* v. *Nixon,* which involved a confrontation over presidential claims of executive privilege, obviously fell into that category. Many other cases, including most *in forma pauperis* petitions, raise relatively minor issues that do not warrant the Court's attention. Whenever the choice is not so clear-cut, further considerations come into play.

Of paramount concern in some decisions whether or not to grant review is the effect the case might have on the long-run influence of the

Court. Historically, the Court has sought to maintain its influence by avoiding unproductive involvement in political disputes, as when it refused to hear cases challenging the constitutionality of the Vietnam War. The justices also attempt to select cases in which the issues are clear and well-defined enough to facilitate wise and persuasive constitutional decisions.

Finally, the Court usually seeks to avoid unnecessarily inflaming public opinion by limiting the number of controversial issues it addresses at one time and by considering public reaction in choosing cases in which to announce important rulings. Thus, for thirteen years after *Brown* v. *Board of Education* (1954), which outlawed state-mandated school segregation, it refused to consider constitutional challenges to state laws prohibiting interracial marriage.[13] And the Court chose *Gideon* v. *Wainwright* (1963) to announce that indigent defendants had a right to counsel at trial in part because it involved a relatively minor offense rather than a violent crime.[14]

Perhaps even more important than the maintenance of the Court's influence are the justices' constitutional views—their notions of what constitutional issues are most important and how those issues should be resolved. Specifically, justices may vote to hear a case when they believe that review would further their conception of desirable constitutional policy. In some cases, certain justices might favor review if they believe that a majority of the Court will support their constitutional position, particularly if they disagree with the lower court's decision. Alternatively, if they expect to be in a minority on the Court, they might oppose review rather than risk creation of an unfavorable precedent.

The Changing Agenda. Our discussion of case selection has focused thus far on the factors underlying the selection of particular cases for review. But the quotation from Tocqueville that opens the chapter suggests a broader perspective. If political questions tend to become judicial questions, then the cases from which the justices select presumably reflect the broad political issues confronting the nation. Put differently, if the Court seeks to decide cases of national concern, then the nation's political concerns necessarily furnish the Court's basic agenda.

The historical record confirms this point. Prior to the Civil War the paramount political issue was the distribution of political power between the national and state governments, and the constitutional cases considered by the Court characteristically required it to define the respective spheres of those governments. Following the Civil War the nation underwent rapid industrial development and the concurrent growth of large-scale economic enterprises, and governmental efforts to deal with these developments played a major role in the Court's constitutional decisions from the 1870s until the late 1930s. In the wake of the New Deal, an expansion in the scope of governmental concerns, facilitated by Court rulings permitting extensive regulation of economic activity, created new conflicts between government and the individual; accordingly, the contemporary Court's constitutional decisions have involved in large measure the delineation of individual rights.

HOW THE COURT DECIDES CASES

In deciding cases, the justices first of all inform themselves about the facts and legal issues in the case and about the more general consequences that can be expected from a ruling. After oral argument, they discuss the case in closed conference and reach a tentative decision. Finally, through the process of opinion writing and continuing discussion, the justices confirm (or in rare instances, reconsider) the decision reached in conference, clarify and develop the basis for the ruling, and attempt to reconcile intracourt differences.

As this summary suggests, the Court's decisions inevitably have a dual aspect. The litigants in a case usually are most concerned with winning or losing: To a convicted felon challenging the constitutionality of a police search that uncovered incriminating evidence, avoiding prison is the primary goal. In announcing decisions, however, the Court justifies its rulings on the basis of principles and standards whose ramifications extend far beyond the confines of the individual case. Indeed, the justices consciously use their discretion to review only cases of broad societal importance. An appreciation of this combination of the specific and the general, of immediate results and broader implications, is crucial to understanding the decision-making of the Supreme Court.

Informing and Persuading the Court

In weighing the merits of a particular case, the Court relies heavily on three sources of information: the briefs of the contending parties, *amicus curiae* (literally, "friend of the court") briefs, and oral argument. In all cases heard by the Court, the lawyers for both parties file legal briefs and then argue the case orally before the justices. In most cases other interested parties submit *amicus* briefs, which increase the range of information available to the justices. Since they resemble each other in basic purpose, the briefs of the parties and *amicus* briefs can be considered together.

Legal Briefs. A legal brief is first and foremost a partisan document—an attempt to persuade a court to rule in favor of one's client or position. Persuasion takes the form of marshalling and then interpreting favorably the legal materials (precedents, statutes, constitutional provisions) and the facts involved in the case. For *amicus* briefs as well as for those submitted by the parties, the ultimate goal is to gain a favorable ruling.

Amicus briefs do differ from the briefs filed by the litigants. They ordinarily are filed by parties who are interested primarily in the general constitutional issue the case raises, rather than in the fate of the particular litigants. Some organizations file *amicus* briefs out of concern for the effects the Court's decision might have on them or on their members. In

Regents of the University of California v. *Bakke* (1978), which involved an affirmative-action program for medical school admissions, several universities with similar programs filed *amicus* briefs, and so did the NAACP and several Jewish organizations. For other organizations, the principal concern is ideological: They wish to see the Constitution interpreted in a particular way. The American Civil Liberties Union (ACLU), for example, often files *amicus* briefs in First Amendment cases in an effort to gain or preserve a broad interpretation of the amendment's guarantees. But whatever the basis for their interest, those filing *amicus* briefs tend to be concerned largely with the constitutional standards that the Court announces and their implications.

Although legal briefs commonly focus on the interpretation of constitutional provisions, statutes, and precedents relevant to the case, they may also include nonlegal materials. In recent years lawyers have made extensive use of social science research to document conditions within the society, indicate the effects of governmental policies, or forecast the likely effects of a Court ruling. The prototype for such briefs was the famous "Brandeis brief" filed in *Muller* v. *Oregon* (1908). At issue in *Muller* was the constitutionality of an Oregon statute limiting female workers to a ten-hour work-day, which the plaintiff challenged as an arbitrary interference with economic liberty. In response, Louis Brandeis, then counsel for the state of Oregon and later a Supreme Court justice, claimed that the law served important public purposes—a claim backed up by over one hundred pages of social and economic data demonstrating that long working hours were dangerous to the health, safety, and morals of working women. Brandeis's success in *Muller* prompted counsel in later cases to adopt a similar approach. In *Brown* v. *Board of Education,* for example, legal arguments for outlawing racial segregation in public education were supplemented by the results of psychological tests showing the adverse effects of segregation on black children. More recently, contending parties in cases involving the constitutionality of the death penalty have included in their briefs extensive data on the deterrent or nondeterrent effect of capital punishment.

Oral Argument. In oral argument, the attorneys for each party have their last opportunity to influence the Court's decision. In the early nineteenth century, when the Court's docket was less crowded, the greatest lawyers in the country would spend several days arguing a case before the justices. Nowadays, oral presentations usually are limited to a half-hour for each party, although in particularly important cases more time may be allotted. In *Brown* v. *Board of Education* II (1955), which involved the question of how the Court's historic desegregation decision would be implemented, the Court permitted a total of fourteen hours of oral argument.

Despite severe time constraints, oral argument can provide an opportunity for influencing the justices, many of whom view it as vital for clarifying the written arguments presented in the briefs. Through their questions, the justices test the soundness of the opposing legal positions, and in this give-and-take, weaknesses in an argument or lack of preparation by attorneys soon becomes apparent. But the justices' questions can also indicate issues on which they are undecided, and effective response to their inquiries can substantially improve a client's chances. As Justice John Marshall Harlan has observed, oral argument "may in many cases make the difference between winning and losing, no matter how good the briefs are."[15]

The Decision-Making Process

On Wednesdays and Fridays during its annual term (October to late June), the Court meets in conference to consider the cases on which it has most recently heard oral argument. Since the confidentiality of these conferences is jealously guarded—only the justices themselves, without law clerks or other Court staff, attend them—our knowledge of them is necessarily fragmentary.

Deliberations begin only after the justices shake hands—a ritual instituted to symbolize that the inevitable disagreements are legal, not personal. The Chief Justice initiates discussion by indicating his views of the case at hand and his vote. The associate justices, in descending order of seniority, similarly present their views and votes. The discussion of the case, which in some instances is quite heated, and the tallying of votes produce a tentative decision. If the Chief Justice has voted with the majority, he determines who will write the opinion of the Court (majority opinion). He may assign the opinion to another member of the majority or retain it for himself. If the Chief Justice finds himself in the minority, the senior justice aligned with the majority assigns the opinion of the Court. The other justices are free to express their views in concurring or dissenting opinions.

How do the justices decide how they will vote? Experienced Court-watchers have suggested markedly different answers to this question, but some points are clear. Accounts of the justices' deliberations indicate that in conference they rely primarily on legal arguments to buttress their positions and persuade their colleagues.[16] The primacy of such arguments suggests that the justices acknowledge their duty to put aside personal preference and base their decisions on the Constitution. (Of course, whether they succeed in entirely banishing their personal policy views from their deliberations may well be another matter.) The requirement that decisions be legally justifiable rarely promotes consensus, however. Conscientious justices can and often do disagree about the difficult constitutional issues facing them. In recent terms, dissenting opinions were filed in about 70 percent of the cases the Court decided. Yet although interaction among the justices may have some effect on their votes and a substantial effect on their opinions, the decision-making process is more individual than collective in nature. As Justice Lewis Powell put it, "For the most part, perhaps as much as 90 percent of our total time, we function as nine small, independent law firms."[17] This high degree of individuality, which helps to account for the remarkable consistency of any given justice's voting patterns over time, reflects both the well-developed constitutional views the members of the Court bring to their cases and the limited resources available to them for changing the views of their colleagues.

The vote in conference comprises only the initial phase of decision making. Even after conference, discussion of cases continues, and during the extended period between the vote and announcement of the decision, the opinion of the Court and any concurring or dissenting opinions are prepared and circulated among the justices for their comments. Reviewing these opinions gives the justices an opportunity to reconsider their initial positions, and a particularly persuasive opinion may lead to a change of vote. On a closely divided Court, defection by a single justice can produce a new majority and, therefore, a different decision.

The likelihood of a postconference vote shift should not be exaggerated. A study of one ten-year period found that the justices' final votes differed from their votes in conference only about 9 percent of the time.[18] But even if no votes are changed, the period between the conference and the announcement of the Court's decision represents a crucial stage in the decisional process. During this time, the justices who comprise the majority carefully review the opinion of the Court; frequently, they require changes in its language or argument before they will endorse it. Justices Lewis Powell and William Brennan have acknowledged circulating as many as ten drafts of an opinion before one was accepted by the majority.[19] Even after prolonged discussions, deep-seated differences may prevent a Court majority from coalescing behind a single opinion. In *Furman* v. *Georgia* (1971), all five members of the Court majority wrote separate opinions that presented quite disparate grounds for invalidating Georgia's death penalty statute.

Such close scrutiny of the opinion of the Court reflects in part a concern for the soundness of the legal arguments it presents, since public and congressional acceptance of a decision may depend upon the persuasiveness of the arguments supporting it. The justices also realize that the justifications for their decision may play a large role in future decisions. The importance of this consideration was highlighted in the decision handed down in *United States* v. *Nixon,* in which the Court unanimously rejected the President's claim of executive privilege and voted to compel him to release the Watergate tapes. Before that decision was announced, several justices refused to join Chief Justice Warren Burger's opinion for the Court, because they felt that it provided too much support for future claims of executive power. Only after the Chief Justice agreed to extensive revisions of the original opinion did all the justices join it.

THE IMPACT OF SUPREME COURT DECISIONS

A Supreme Court decision not only resolves a dispute between particular litigants, but also may have serious and far-reaching consequences for the nation as a whole. In ruling on the constitutionality of a particular program or practice, the Court also indicates the likely validity of similar programs or practices. In interpreting a constitutional provision, the Court announces standards that may guide future decisions involving that provision. In elaborating constitutional principles, the Court may educate the public about what our basic principles of government require.

But Court decisions, like other governmental policies, do not always achieve their intended effects: Decisions may be misunderstood, misrepresented, or ignored; those responsible for carrying out the Court's mandates may seek to evade their responsibilities or may find ways to negate the effectiveness of the mandates; opposition to Court rulings may lead to attempts to overturn them or to limit their effects. Rather than resolving conflicts, then, Court decisions sometimes merely aggravate them. Only if we understand what happens *after* the Court rules can we fully appreciate the role that the Court plays in governing.

Legal Obligation

A Supreme Court decision invalidating a governmental program imposes legal obligations on three distinct sets of actors. Most immediately, the losing party in the case must either abandon the invalidated program or remedy its constitutional defects. In a case such as *Regents of the University of California* v. *Bakke*, in which it was held that the goal of the affirmative-action plan in question (increased minority-group representation in the medical profession) was within the law but the means employed to achieve this goal were unconstitutional, the university had merely to revise its program such that the goal could be achieved constitutionally. When, however, the aim of an invalidated program is itself unconstitutional, alternative programs designed to accomplish that goal cannot legally be instituted.

In addition, because of the Court's hierarchical position in the American judicial system, its decisions on matters of federal law constitute binding precedent for all other courts, both federal and state. This means that should a litigant challenge a program similar to one invalidated by the Court, lower-court judges are obliged to invalidate it. Moreover, in deciding other cases in which a federal law or constitutional provision comes into play, judges must treat the Court's interpretation as authoritative. As Judge Learned Hand of the Second Circuit Court of Appeals put it, "I have always felt that it was the duty of an inferior court to suppress its own opinions . . . and to try to prophesy what the appellate court would do. God knows, I have often been wrong in that too; but I have at least been obedient, which is as I conceive it a judge's prime duty."[20]

Finally, by striking down a program as unconstitutional, the Court may also oblige other governmental units to discontinue programs similar to the one invalidated. This consequence underlines the crucial importance of the opinion of the Court: The broader the basis for the ruling, the broader the range of affected programs. The progress of school-desegregation decisions clearly illustrates this point. In a series of decisions handed down from 1938 to 1954, the Court ruled that certain segregated school systems had violated the Equal Protection Clause of the Fourteenth Amendment by failing to provide equal educational facilities for black students; but since these rulings were tied to the conditions in specific districts, their effects were not felt outside those districts. Then, in 1954 the Court ruled in *Brown* v. *Board of Education* that separate school systems for blacks and whites were *inherently* unequal, and thereby obliged all states operating such systems to dismantle them. By choosing the broader basis for its decision in *Brown,* the Court assured that its ruling would have nationwide effects.

Yet there is considerable controversy over what obligations a Court ruling imposes on government officials. Although they may not legitimately defy the Court's decision in a specific case, they are not obliged in every instance to endorse the Court's interpretation of the Constitution. For such a requirement would imply that the Constitution is what the Court says it is or that the Court can never err in its reading of the Constitution. In the wake of the Court's infamous decision in *Dred Scott* v. *Sandford* (1857), for example, Abraham Lincoln, while professing respect for the Court and acknowledging the authority of its ruling in the case, denied that the Court had correctly interpreted the Constitution and indicated his intention to seek a reversal of the Court's position. More recently, critics of the Supreme Court's ruling in *Roe* v. *Wade* (1973) legalizing abortion adopted various restrictions on abortion that were susceptible to legal challenge, expecting that the resulting litigation would provide an opportunity for the Court to reconsider its position. Eventually this strategy succeeded.

Response to Court Mandates

In invalidating a program or practice, the Supreme Court imposes an obligation to cease the unconstitutional activity or take steps to remedy the constitutional violation. In most cases those affected by the Court's rulings comply with the legal requirements. The mere existence of legal obligations does not guarantee compliance, however, and the cases in which Court mandates have not been carried out have had an importance far greater than their numbers might suggest.

Communication of Court Mandates. If its decisions are to achieve their intended effects, the Court must identify clearly what actions are to be undertaken or what practices eliminated and communicate that mandate to the appropriate officials. Rulings that are unclear or that fail to reach their intended audience are unlikely to have much effect.

Confusion over the exact scope or meaning of Court mandates may stem from disagreement on the Court. Not once during the 1960s, for example, did a majority of the justices agree on standards defining what kinds of sexually explicit materials were protected by the First Amendment. As a result, the Court handed down decisions marked by a multiplicity of opinions, each offering a different standard for determining whether movies or publications were obscene. State and local officials who tried to respect constitutional limitations while enforcing obscenity legislation consequently received little guidance from the Court.

Even when the justices agree among themselves, ambiguities in the opinion of the Court can create uncertainty about the scope of the ruling, as happened in *Escobedo* v. *Illinois* (1964). In *Escobedo,* the Court for the first time recognized that suspects had a right to counsel during police interrogations; but because the opinion of the Court did not clearly define that right, lower courts developed widely divergent interpretations of the ruling. Only after the Court clarified its position in *Miranda* v. *Arizona* (1966) did lower courts consistently enforce the right to counsel.[21]

Finally, the clarity of a Court ruling may disappear as that ruling is transmitted to its intended audience. The transmission to police officers of the Supreme Court's landmark criminal-justice decisions illustrates how confusion can occur at this stage. In determining what the Court required, police officers typically relied for information on nonjudicial sources such as police training sessions, local officials, and the mass media. Often, the Court's message was simplified and distorted in the course of transmission. A study of the initial response to *Miranda* in four Wisconsin police departments, for example, found that despite the clarity of the Court's guidelines, more than half the officers in three departments incorrectly identified what the decision required.[22] However, this is likely to be a problem only in the short run.

Noncompliance. A more serious concern is noncompliance, the refusal to undertake or refrain from actions as required by Supreme Court rulings. State and federal courts at times have failed to follow or enforce Court decisions and state supreme courts, in particular, have displayed a penchant for ignoring Court precedents. More frequently, however, noncompliance crops up among state or local officials who resist Court directions to implement unpopular decisions or to observe new and potentially burdensome limitations on the exercise of their powers. Southern school boards, for instance, long sought to evade the Court's school desegregation requirements; and in more recent years, Northern school boards have done the same. School districts often ignored Court decisions requiring the elimination of prayer and Bible-reading from their schools. And when police officers believed that Court decisions hampered their efforts to control crime, they sought to evade limitations on their power to conduct searches and interrogate suspects.

That individuals evade, or seek to evade, their legal responsibilities is nothing new: the very existence of courts testifies to the need to enforce legal norms. Yet noncompliance—particularly if it is widespread—poses a grave threat to the Court's effectiveness, since its capacity to enforce its decisions is rather limited. As Alexander Hamilton noted in *The Federalist,* No. 78, the judiciary lacks control over "either the sword or the purse" and must "ultimately depend upon the aid of the executive arm even for the efficacy of its judgments." Should the executive prove reluctant to enforce its decisions vigorously, as happened initially after *Brown,* the Court can only depend on the willingness of litigants to initiate cases challenging instances of noncompliance. Even then, as earlier noted, it cannot always rely on the lower courts to enforce its rulings. In sum, the Court's effectiveness ultimately depends less on its ability to punish noncompliance than on its ability to persuade the targets of its decisions to comply voluntarily.

Political Impact

In addition to imposing legal obligations, Supreme Court decisions influence public opinion, political activity, and the development of public policies. By upholding a challenged governmental enactment, the justices authoritatively dispose of constitutional objections to its validity and thereby promote public acceptance of the law's legitimacy. The Court's decision in *Heart of Atlanta Motel* v. *United States* (1964), which upheld a controversial section of the Civil Rights Act of 1964, resolved constitutional questions about the national government's power to ban racial discrimination in public accommodations. Its decisions in *National Labor Relations Board* v. *Jones & Laughlin Steel Corporation* (1937) and in subsequent cases validated New Deal efforts to regulate the national economy. As these examples indicate, Supreme Court decisions have played a crucial role in legitimating the federal government's expanding exercise of power.[23] In addition, Court legitimation of one state's law may dispose other states to adopt similar measures. The full development of so-called Jim Crow laws, for example, did not occur until after the Court, in *Plessy* v. *Ferguson* (1896), upheld a Louisiana statute establishing racial segregation in public transportation.[24]

Decisions invalidating state or federal policies have produced varied effects. An adverse Court ruling frequently activates the political forces supporting a program to seek alternative means of accomplishing their objectives. Thus five constitutional amendments have been adopted, in whole or in part, to overturn Supreme Court decisions.[25] And during the past two decades, opponents of Court decisions have sought, unsuccessfully, to strip the Court of its power to hear cases involving school prayer, busing, and abortion.

The response to the Supreme Court's abortion decisions illustrates the potential political consequences of judicial rulings. The Supreme Court's decision in *Roe* v. *Wade* striking down state restrictions on abortion prompted the formation of the pro-life movement, which supported legislation discouraging abortions or making them more difficult to obtain and a constitutional amendment outlawing abortion. More recently, the Court's validation of state laws limiting abortion activated pro-choice forces, which sought to blunt the effect of the decision by supporting candidates sympathetic to their cause.

Yet controversial decisions often generate support as well as opposition. For example, *Brown* v. *Board of Education* produced not only intransigent resistance by segregationists but also efforts by civil rights groups to solidify and extend the gains they had made. Such decisions have the added effect of subtly changing the political context in which conflicts between such forces occur, by giving proponents of the Court's view the potent political advantage of being able to claim that the Constitution supports their position. Finally, the public support for the Court that promotes voluntary compliance also enables it to influence public opinion. According to public-opinion polls, public attitudes toward desegregation changed markedly after *Brown*.[26] This change may not have resulted solely from the Court's ruling, but it does suggest that the authority of the Court enables it to influence public opinion even on controversial matters.

In sum, Supreme Court decisions establish government policy, just as decisions made by the executive or legislative branches do, and thereby help shape American society. Indeed, if the Court is to fulfill its constitutional functions, it cannot avoid making policy. The important question to ask is whether its policies can be constitutionally justified.

ANALYZING COURT DECISIONS

Since judicial opinions provide justifications for constitutional positions, in reading cases you should bear in mind the modes of constitutional interpretation outlined in Chapter 1. Often it is helpful to "brief," or outline, a case in order to analyze its major elements (see Box 2.2 for an example). In general, you should look for the following elements that are common to all court cases.

Title and Citation. Case titles usually derive from the names of the parties to the controversy. The party listed first is seeking reversal of an unfavorable lower-court decision, whereas the party listed second typically wants that decision affirmed. If the case comes to the Court on appeal, the parties are referred to as the appellant and the appellee. If the case comes on a writ of certiorari, they are referred to as the petitioner and the respondent.

Facts of the Case. Because all Supreme Court cases arise as disputes between particular litigants, Court decisions represent attempts to apply constitutional principles to unique situations. Full understanding of a Court decision therefore requires an appreciation of the facts underlying the case, which have been established by testimony at trials. Supreme Court justices may differ in interpreting the facts, however; disagreement about the facts, as well as about the proper interpretation of the Constitution, may produce divisions on the Court. Frequently, the opinion of the Court, or majority opinion, summarizes the relevant facts before elaborating the Court's justification for its decision. In other cases, the facts must be pieced together from comments in several opinions. Preceding most cases presented in this volume are summaries of the facts, which indicate the factors you should look for in reading cases.

BOX 2.2
A Sample Case Brief

City of Philadelphia* v. *New Jersey
437 U.S. 617 (1978)

Facts of the Case. New Jersey passed a law banning the importation of most solid or liquid wastes into the state. This law, which was designed to protect the environment of the state and the health of its residents, was challenged by New Jersey landfill operators and by cities in neighboring states which used the landfills. The New Jersey Supreme Court upheld the law, and the Supreme Court granted certiorari.

The Law. The Commerce Clause (Article I, Section 8, Paragraph 3) of the U.S. Constitution.

Legal Questions.

1. Does the interstate transfer of solid and liquid wastes involve "commerce"? *Yes.*
2. Do state laws that discriminate against out-of-state commerce violate the Constitution? *Yes.*
3. Does the New Jersey law discriminate against out-of-state commerce? *Yes.*
4. Is New Jersey's discrimination against out-of-state commerce permissible because it is an environmental measure? *No.*
5. Is New Jersey's law similar to state quarantine measures which had previously been upheld by the Court? *No.*

Opinion of the Court (Stewart). Because all items of interstate trade, even noxious items, are protected by the Commerce Clause, the Court must consider whether New Jersey's ban on the importation of wastes violates that clause. Although New Jersey's law may not be protectionist in aim, it is protectionist in effect: It achieves its purpose by discriminating against articles of commerce coming from outside the state. Such protectionist measures violate the Commerce Clause, which was designed to promote a prosperous national economy and to end "economic isolation." The case differs from previous quarantine cases, in which discrimination against out-of-state articles was upheld, in that the wastes do not pose a danger during transportation into the state but only after their disposal at landfill sites, at which point they are indistinguishable from domestic wastes.

Concurring opinion. None.

Dissenting opinion (Rehnquist). The Court's distinction between its earlier quarantine cases and the present case is untenable, and the New

Jersey law should be upheld. In both the earlier cases and the present case, the aim was the same—to protect against dangers to the public health and safety—and the point at which these dangers arise is immaterial for Commerce Clause purposes. Moreover, the Court in earlier cases had sustained quarantines even though the states of necessity had to deal with domestic sources of danger as well. Hence the Commerce Clause does not require states to allow the importation of wastes merely because they must dispose of wastes produced within their borders.

Evaluation. The Court indicated that states could not use protectionist measures even to pursue valid non-economic objectives. By reaffirming that states cannot insulate themselves from common concerns, the decision probably promoted regional or national solutions to multi-state problems.

The Law. Supreme Court decisions usually involve the interpretation of three elements of law: constitutional provisions, statutes and/or administrative regulations, and Supreme Court precedents. Large bodies of law have sprung from most constitutional provisions, so it is important to note precisely which provision the Court is interpreting. For example, if a constitutional challenge is raised under the Fourteenth Amendment, the first thing to determine is whether the challenge is based on the Due Process Clause or the Equal Protection Clause.

The Legal Questions. A Court decision can be viewed as a response to a particular legal question or series of questions, a clear understanding of which is vital to any proper analysis of the opinions in a case and of the effects of the decision. One way of ensuring such clarity is to frame the questions involved in a yes-or-no format. (See Box 2.2 for an example.) Usually the Court's answers to the legal questions in a case can be determined from a close reading of the opinion of the Court. But in cases where five justices are unable to agree on a single opinion, one must search all opinions in the case for points of majority agreement.

The Opinion of the Court. This opinion announces the Court's decision and supplies the justifications for that ruling. Since the decision may serve as a precedent in future cases, close attention should be paid to the chain of reasoning supporting the decision and to its possible implications. Frequently, the best approach is to trace how the Court arrived at its answers to each of the legal questions previously identified.

Concurring Opinions. Members of the Court majority may write concurring opinions either because they agree with the Court's decision but disagree with its justification, in which instance the concurring opinion will offer an alternative justification, or because they agree with both the decision and its justification but wish either to clarify their own view of the case or to respond to arguments made in a dissenting opinion. Determining the basis for the concurrence should be the initial step in analyzing a concurring opinion.

Dissenting Opinions. Dissenting opinions attempt to demonstrate why the Court's decision is wrong. They may point to alleged errors in reasoning, misinterpretation of precedents or constitutional provisions, or misunderstanding of the facts in a case. Analysis of dissenting opinions should focus on the bases of disagreement with the opinion of the Court.

Evaluation. No analysis of a case is complete without an evaluation of the decision. Is the opinion of the Court convincing? Is the decision consistent with previous Court decisions? If not, does the Court provide persuasive reasons for departing from precedent? What are the likely effects of the Court's decision?

SOURCES IN CONSTITUTIONAL LAW

Court Decisions. The official edition of United States Supreme Court decisions, titled *United States Reports,* contains the text of all Supreme Court decisions handed down since 1790. For almost one hundred years, the volumes were issued under the names of individual court reporters. Thus, citations to cases in those volumes generally include the name of the particular reporter: *Marbury* v. *Madison,* 1 Cranch 137 (1803). After Volume 90 (1874), cases are cited only by the volume number of *U.S. Reports.* Thus *Adamson* v. *California,* 322 U.S. 46, can be found on page 46 of Volume 322.

Two other editions of the Supreme Court's decisions, published by private firms, contain supplementary material not found in the official edition. The *Supreme Court Reporter* prefaces the Court's decisions with summaries of the legal issues in the case. Citations are again by volume and page: for example, the citation for *Adamson* is 67 Sup. Ct. 1672. The *Lawyers' Edition of the United States Supreme Court Reports* includes legal analyses of the more important rulings and summarizes the oral arguments of counsel in each case. Citations are by volume and number: for *Adamson,* the citation is 91 L.Ed. 1903.

Prior to publication in bound volumes, copies of Supreme Court decisions are available in three forms. The Supreme Court itself issues pamphlets called "slip opinions," each of which contains the text of a single Court decision. *U.S. Law Week* publishes the full text of decisions in a loose-leaf format. Finally, all reporters of Supreme Court decisions issue "advance sheets"—booklets containing several decisions published prior to the accumulation of sufficient cases for a complete bound volume.

Decisions by lower federal courts and state courts may also be important in studying constitutional law. The *Federal Reporter* series publishes most decisions of the United States Courts of Appeals, and the *Federal Supplement* series publishes selected United States District Court decisions. Important state decisions are published in official versions by the various states. In addition, the privately published *National Reporter* series groups most decisions of state appellate courts in regional reporters. The *Southeastern Reporter,* for example, contains state appellate decisions from West Virginia, Virginia, North Carolina, South Carolina, and Georgia.

Statutes. Statutes (laws) comprise another important source material in constitutional law. The U.S. Government Printing Office initially publishes each Federal law separately as so-called slip laws, which are numbered chronologically: The Freedom of Information Act (1974) is cited as Pub. L 93-502, the *93* indicating the Congress and the *502* the numerical order in which the law appears. At the end of each session of Congress, the slip laws are collected and published in chronological order in *Statutes at Large.* Citations to *Statutes at Large* are by volume and page: The Freedom of Information Act is cited as 88 Stat. 1561, the *88* indicating the volume and the *1561* the initial page.

The single most useful official source for researching statutes is the *United States Code.* The *U.S. Code* arranges the law by subject into fifty titles, thus directing the researcher to all the Federal laws pertaining to a topic. Each of the fifty titles is subdivided further into chapters, sections, and subsections. Accordingly, the citation for the Freedom of Information Act is 5 U.S.C. § 552, the *5* indicating the title and the *552* the section of the code.

Executive-Branch Materials. Among the executive-branch materials that may be of interest in constitutional law are presidential documents, such as executive orders and presidential proclamations, and administrative agency rules and regulations. The most comprehensive source for presidential materials is the *Weekly Compilation of Presidential Documents,* published by the U.S. Government Printing Office. Orders and proclamations of general applicability and legal effect also can be found in the *Federal Register,* the daily official publication of executive branch actions.

The *Federal Register* also contains all rules, regulations, and orders issued by federal administrative agencies. Since the *Register* is published daily, it presents executive-branch materials chronologically. This mass of materials is organized topically in the *Code of Federal Regulations,* which divides the general and permanent rules published in the *Federal Register* into fifty titles representing broad areas subject to federal regulations. Each title is subdivided further into chapters, which usually bear the name of the issuing agency, and into parts, which pertain to specific regulatory areas. For example, the Department of Justice regulations pertaining to production or disclosure of information under the Freedom of Information Act are found at 28 CFR§ 16.

NOTES

1 Alexis de Tocqueville, *Democracy in America,* ed. J. P. Mayer (Garden City, N. Y.: Doubleday, 1969), p. 270.

2 Underlying the adoption of the Eleventh Amendment was widespread disenchantment with the Court's decision in *Chisholm* v. *Georgia* (1793), in which it was held that Chisholm, a citizen of South Carolina, could sue the state of Georgia in the federal courts.

3 "Shufflin' Sam" Thompson had been arrested for loitering while waiting in a bar for his bus and shuffling his feet in time to music from a jukebox. When he protested against his arrest, he was also charged with disorderly conduct. He was convicted on both charges and fined $10 for each. Since Kentucky law provided no opportunity to appeal fines of less than $20, Thompson petitioned for Supreme Court review. The Court accepted the case and ruled unanimously that the convictions were not supported by evidence and therefore amounted to a denial of due process of law.

4 Cases may also come to the Supreme Court by *certification.* Under this rarely used procedure, a lower federal court requests instruction from the Supreme Court on a point of law.

5 "Paid" cases are those in which the petitioners have paid the $200 filing fee and supplied the prescribed copies of briefs and other legal materials. An *in forma pauperis* case is one in which an impoverished petitioner requests review of a lower-court decision. These cases generally involve criminal appeals filed by prisoners who cannot afford expert legal assistance. In such cases the Court waives the filing fee and the other requirements it enforces in "paid" cases. For an excellent study of how one *in forma pauperis* petition led to a landmark Supreme Court decision guaranteeing indigent defendants a right to counsel at trial, see Anthony Lewis, *Gideon's Trumpet* (New York: Random House, 1964).

6 The Supreme Court established the procedural rules governing appeals to and the operations of the Court. These rules were revised most recently in 1980.

7 The increasing number of petitions for Supreme Court review has led to proposals for assisting the Court with this burden. The most controversial proposal came out of the "Freund study," the product of a committee appointed by Chief Justice Warren Burger, which recommended the creation of a new group to take over the Court's case selection function. See Federal Judicial Center, *Report of the Study Group on the Caseload of the Supreme Court* (Washington, D.C.: Administrative Office of the Courts, 1972).

8 "Retired Chief Justice Warren Attacks . . . Freund Study Group's Composition and Proposal," *American Bar Association Journal* 59 (July 1973): 728.

9 58 U.S. Law Week 3181 (October 3, 1989).

10 During his tenure on the Supreme Court (1947–58), Justice Harold Burton kept systematic records of the conference votes on whether to hear cases. Studies based on his paper include Doris Marie Provine, *Case Selection in the United States Supreme Court* (Chicago: University of Chicago Press, 1980); S. Sidney Ulmer, "The Decision to Grant Certiorari as an Indicator to Decision

'On the Merits,' " *Polity* 4 (1972); and Ulmer, "Selecting Cases for Supreme Court Review: An Underdog Model," *American Political Science Review* 72 (1978).

11 Lawrence Baum, *The Supreme Court,* 3d ed. (Washington, D.C.: Congressional Quarterly Press, 1989), p. 98.

12 Chief Justice Fred Vinson in "Work of the U.S. Supreme Court," *Texas Bar Journal* 12 (1949): 551.

13 It eventually struck down such laws in the aptly named *Loving* v. *Virginia,* 388 U.S. 1 (1967).

14 Baum, *The Supreme Court,* p. 103.

15 Harlan's statement is reported in Anthony Lewis, *Gideon's Trumpet,* p. 162, n. 23.

16 See, for example, Walter F. Murphy, *Elements of Judicial Strategy* (Chicago: University of Chicago Press, 1964); Alexander M. Bickel, *The Unpublished Opinions of Mr. Justice Brandeis: The Supreme Court at Work* (Cambridge, Mass.: Harvard University Press, 1957); and David O'Brien, *Storm Center; The Supreme Court in American Politics* (New York: W. W. Norton, 1986).

17 Lewis F. Powell, Jr., "What the Justices are Saying . . . ," *American Bar Association Journal* 62 (1976): 1454.

18 Saul Brenner, "Fluidity on the United States Supreme Court: A Reexamination," *American Journal of Political Science* 24 (1980).

19 Abraham, *The Judicial Process,* 5th ed. (New York: Oxford University Press, 1986), p. 223.

20 Hand's comment is contained in an intracourt memorandum quoted in Marvin Schick, *Learned Hand's Court* (Baltimore: Johns Hopkins Press, 1970), p. 167.

21 For a discussion of initial state-court responses to *Escobedo* v. *Illinois* and *Miranda* v. *Arizona,* see Neil T. Romans, "The Role of State Supreme Courts in Judicial Policy Making: *Escobedo, Miranda* and the Use of Impact Analysis," *Western Political Quarterly* 27 (1974).

22 Neil A. Milner, *The Court and Local Enforcement: The Impact of Miranda* (Beverly Hills, Cal.: Sage Publications, 1971), p. 225, Table 11-2.

23 For a discussion of the Court's legitimating role, see Charles L. Black, Jr., *The People and the Court* (New York: Macmillan, 1960).

24 See C. Vann Woodward, *The Strange Career of Jim Crow,* rev. ed. (New York: Oxford University Press, 1966).

25 The Eleventh Amendment overruled *Chisholm* v. *Georgia* (1793); the Fourteenth Amendment, *Dred Scott* v. *Sandford* (1857); the Sixteenth Amendment, *Pollock* v. *Farmers' Loan & Trust Co.* (1895); the Twenty-fourth Amendment, which overruled *Breedlove* v. *Suttles* (1937); and the Twenty-sixth Amendment, *Oregon* v. *Mitchell* (1970).

26 Data on changes in attitudes toward desegregation are summarized in Robert Weissberg, *Public Opinion and Popular Government* (Englewood Cliffs, N.J.: Prentice-Hall, 1976), pp. 110–121.

SELECTED READINGS

Abraham, Henry J. *The Judicial Process,* 5th ed. (New York: Oxford University Press, 1986).

Baum, Lawrence. *The Supreme Court,* 3d ed. (Washington, D.C.: Congressional Quarterly Press, 1989).

Fisher, Louis. *Constitutional Dialogues* (Princeton: Princeton University Press, 1988).

Frankfurter, Felix, and James Landis. *The Business of the Supreme Court: A Study of the Federal Judicial System* (New York: Macmillan, 1928).

Guide to the U.S. Supreme Court (Washington, D.C.: Congressional Quarterly Press, 1979).

Johnson, Charles A., and Bradley C. Canon. *Judicial Policies; Implementation and Impact* (Washington, D.C.: Congressional Quarterly Press, 1984).

O'Brien, David M. *Storm Center; The Supreme Court in American Politics* (New York: W. W. Norton, 1986).

Provine, Doris Marie. *Case Selection in the United States Supreme Court* (Chicago: University of Chicago Press, 1980).

Stern, Robert L., and Eugene Gressman. *Supreme Court Practice,* 5th ed. (Washington, D.C.: Bureau of National Affairs, 1978).

"Symposium on Supreme Court Advocacy." *Catholic University Law Review* 35 (1984): 525–632.

Tarr, G. Alan. *Judicial Impact and State Supreme Courts* (Lexington, Mass.: Lexington Books, 1977).

3
THE JUDICIAL POWER

Although Hamilton, in *The Federalist,* No. 78, described the federal judiciary as "beyond comparison the weakest of the three departments" of government, the courts are not entirely without power. Article III of the Constitution assigns to them the "judicial power" of the United States—a mandate never delineated clearly in the Constitution but usually understood to confer the power to decide conflicts between litigants and to issue writs and orders to carry them into effect. Also included under the umbrella of "judicial power" are the punishment of criminal contempts (to maintain the dignity of the court itself) and of civil contempts (to secure the rights of one party in a suit by forcing the other party to obey the court's ruling) and the issuance of writs of mandamus (ordering people or officials to do particular things), injunctions (ordering them to refrain from doing particular things), and habeas corpus (protecting citizens from illegal imprisonment).

Over and above these universally accepted powers, the federal courts have come to exercise the far more important power of judicial review: that is, the power to invalidate those actions of Congress, the executive, and the states that are, in the view of courts, contrary to the Constitution. Although this authority to determine the meaning and application of the Constitution is nowhere defined or even mentioned in the Constitution itself, the federal judiciary in general, and especially the Supreme Court, have come to wield it to such an extent as to have raised in the minds of some observers the specter of judicial supremacy or even of an emerging imperial judiciary. In this chapter, we examine the establishment and general justification of the power of judicial review and discuss the various restraints on its exercise imposed externally by the legislative and executive branches and internally by the courts themselves.

THE POWER OF JUDICIAL REVIEW

Since the power of judicial review is not explicitly spelled out in the Constitution, it cannot be defended by mere reference to the relevant constitutional text, and its defenders have had to engage in other forms of constitutional interpretation. Two of the earliest and most influential of these interpretations were made by Alexander Hamilton in *The Federalist,* No. 78, and Chief Justice John Marshall in *Marbury* v. *Madison* (1803).[1]

In *The Federalist,* Hamilton argued syllogistically that since "the interpretation of the law is the proper and peculiar province of the courts" and since the Constitution is a law (albeit a "fundamental" one), the courts must interpret the Constitution. Moreover, Hamilton continued, the power of the judiciary to interpret the Constitution, is justified not only by logical reasoning but also by the "natural feebleness of the judiciary." This feebleness arose from the judiciary's inherent incapacity, in comparison with the popularly elected branches, to injure the political rights of the Constitution:

> The executive not only dispenses the honors, but holds the sword of the community. The legislature not only commands the purse, but prescribes the rules by which the duties and rights of every citizen are to be regulated. The judiciary on the contrary has no influence over either the sword or the purse, no direction either of the strength or the wealth of the society, and can take no active resolution whatever. It may be truly be said to have neither Force nor Will, but merely judgment; and must ultimately depend upon the aid of the executive even for the efficacy of its judgments.

Hamilton trusted this very weakness to contribute greatly to "public justice and the public security." As he was well aware, one of the principal means to the ends of the Constitution was separation of powers—three separate and coequal branches sharing a balance of powers. Were either the legislative or the executive branch to exercise the power of constitutional review, the distribution of power in the government would become so lopsided that legislative or executive supremacy would inevitably arise. Conversely, no such drastic consequence would result from judicial exercise of this power. Even with judicial review, the judiciary would remain far too weak to become supreme; it would merely have sufficient strength to keep the legislative and executive branches within their assigned limits, thereby ensuring constitutional supremacy.

Chief Justice Marshall's defense of judicial review in *Marbury* draws heavily on Hamilton. In Marshall's own words, "It is emphatically the province and duty of the judicial department to say what the law is. Those who apply the rule to particular cases, must, of necessity, expound and interpret that rule." This argument leads him to the conclusion that "a law repugnant to the Constitution is void," and that "courts, as well as other departments, are bound by that instrument." Along with Hamilton, Marshall also argued that even though judicial review is not expressly mentioned in the Constitution, the principle of separation of powers requires that constitutional review be lodged in the judiciary, whose inherent weakness precludes the possibility of judicial supremacy.

But differences of opinion can and did arise over what "separation of powers" requires. In *Eakin* v. *Raub* (1825), Judge Gibson argued that

> it is the business of the judiciary, to interpret the laws, not scan the authority of the lawgiver; and without the latter, it cannot take cognizance of a collision between a law and the constitution. . . .
>
> But it has been said to be emphatically the business of the judiciary to ascertain and pronounce what the law is; and that this necessarily involves a consideration of the constitution. It does so: but how far? If the judiciary will inquire into anything beside the form of enactment, where shall it stop?

In its sharp opposition to the position of Hamilton and Marshall, Gibson's approach to judicial review indicates how differing understandings of "separation of powers" can shape contrasting views on the proper powers and responsibilities of the judiciary.[2]

Federalism, as well as separation of powers, played a role in the evolution of judicial review. In *Fletcher* v. *Peck* (1810), *Martin* v. *Hunter's Lessee* (1816), and *Cohens* v. *Virginia* (1821), the Marshall Court expanded its authority beyond that staked out in *Marbury* by asserting its powers to review the constitutionality of actions taken not only by the other branches of the national government, but also by the states. In *Fletcher*, it invalidated for the first time an act of a state legislature. Then, in *Martin* and *Cohens*, it defended the legitimacy of Supreme Court review of state court judgments in (respectively) civil and criminal cases that presented federal constitutional questions. These decisions rested primarily on the Marshall Court's interpretations of two constitutional provisions: Article III, Section 2, which provides that "the judicial Power shall extend to *all* Cases in Law and Equity, arising under this Constitution, the Laws of the United States, and Treaties made, or which shall be made, under their Authority"; and Article VI, Section 2, which declares that "this Constitution and the Laws of the United States which shall be made in Pursuance thereof; and all Treaties made, or which shall be made, under the Authority of the United States, shall be the supreme Law of the land; and the Judges in every State shall be bound thereby, any Thing in the Constitution or Laws of any State to the Contrary notwithstanding."

Justifying its exercise of judicial review on the grounds of separation of powers or of federalism, the Court through July of 1985 struck down a total of 135 different federal laws and voided over one thousand different state laws and municipal ordinances.[3] These statistics, however, do not reflect the most significant effect of the Court's power of judicial review. In giving the Court the power to strike down an unconstitutional legislative action, judicial review *ipso facto* empowers the Court to validate a legislative action as being within constitutionally granted powers and not violating constitutional limitations.[4] The significance of this legitimating function was pointed out by Chief Justice Hughes: "[F]ar more important to the development of the country than the decisions holding acts of Congress to be invalid, have been those in which the authority of Congress has been sustained and adequate national power to meet the necessities of a growing country has been found to exist within constitutional limitations."[5] Together, the validating function and the checking function of judicial review have contributed mightily to the power of the Court—and to its vulnerability.

POLITICALLY IMPOSED RESTRAINTS ON JUDICIAL REVIEW

The Court's power of judicial review has often brought it into conflict with those whose measures it has invalidated. Given the necessarily problematic nature of the Court's power to review the acts of the coequal branches of the national government, it should come as no surprise that most such controversies have involved Congress and the executive. Individually or together, these branches have imposed or threatened to impose on the Court such sanctions as impeachment, court packing, congressional review of judicial decisions, remedial constitutional amendments, the requirement of an extraordinary majority of the Court to invalidate legislation, and presidential refusal to enforce a decision.[6] (At the state level, nullification and even resort to force have greeted Court decisions.) Historically more important than any of those measures, however, have been sporadic congressional attempts to reduce the Court's appellate jurisdiction. Article III, Section 2 of the Constitution grants to the Supreme Court "appellate Jurisdiction, both as to Law and Fact, with such Exceptions, and under such Regulations, as the Congress shall make." In the post–Civil War period, for example, Congress invoked this constitutional authority in withdrawing from the Court's appellate jurisdiction a politically embarrassing case on which the justices had already heard argument. In *Ex Parte McCardle* (1869), the Court agreed unanimously that such drastic action lay within Congress's power and dismissed the case for want of jurisdiction.

The unanimous *McCardle* decision reflects the prevailing view that the Congress's power over the appellate jurisdiction of the Supreme Court is plenary, or absolute. Some scholars have argued, however, that Congress's power to make exceptions is constitutionally limited to such exceptions as will not interfere with the essential role of the Court.[7] According to Leonard Ratner, a leading proponent of this position, "Reasonably interpreted, the clause means 'with such exceptions and under such regulations as Congress may make, not inconsistent with the essential functions of the Supreme Court under this Constitution.' "

Ratner's argument is fraught with difficulties. To begin with, it is contrary to the clear words of the Constitution. There is absolutely nothing in the unqualified letter of the Exceptions Clause that either expressly or implicitly suggests that congressional authority under Article III, Section 2, is limited to making "inessential exceptions." And along with raising the problem of determining the Court's essential role, any circumscription of Congress's power makes the Court the final arbiter in any controversy over the extent of its own powers. In other words, despite the express grant of power to Congress given in the Constitution, Ratner and others of like mind maintain that no statute can constitutionally deprive the Court of its essential role *and* that that role is to be whatever the Court says it is. As Charles Rice points out in rebuttal, "It is hardly in keeping with the spirit of checks and balances to read such a virtually unlimited power into the Constitution. If the Framers intended so to permit the Supreme Court to define its own jurisdiction even against the will of Congress, it is fair to say that they would have made that intention explicit."[8] In fact, such an intention clearly contradicts the thinking of the Framers. Nothing in the records of the Federal Convention of 1787 or of the various state ratifying conventions contravenes the position set forth in *The Federalist,* No. 80, in which, in reviewing in detail the powers of the federal judiciary, Hamilton observed that "if some partial inconveniences should appear to be connected with the incorporation of any of them into the plan, it ought to be recollected that the national legislature will have ample authority to make such exceptions and to prescribe such regulations as will be calculated to obviate or remove these inconveniences."

Finally, the assertion that Congress's power under the Exceptions Clause is limited contradicts the firm, consistent, and unwavering understanding of the Supreme Court. No justice has ever denied Congress's broad power under Article III. As one scholar has observed, "the government body most ready to assert the power of Congress to deprive the Court of its appellate jurisdiction has been the Court itself."[9] In his dissent in *Glidden Co.* v. *Zdanok* (1962), Justice Douglas did declare that "[t]here is a serious question whether the *McCardle* case could command a majority today," and this passage is frequently cited to suggest that the contemporary Supreme Court would not accept congressional restrictions of its appellate jurisdiction equivalent to those upheld in *McCardle.* The context of Justice Douglas's dictum, however, suggests something quite different: namely, that if Congress were to attempt to deprive the Supreme Court of jurisdiction over a case that is already before the Court, it is questionable whether *McCardle* would be followed today. Douglas subsequently expressed his understanding of the broader question of Congress's power over the appellate jurisdiction of the Supreme Court in his concurrence in *Flast* v. *Cohen* (1968): "As respects our appellate jurisdiction, Congress may largely fashion it as Congress desires by reason of the express provisions of Section 2, Article III. See *Ex Parte McCardle*. . . ."

In the face of these formidable objections, those who would deny Congress's plenary power under the Exceptions Clause have failed to gain acceptance for their point of view.[10] Both the Warren and the Burger courts have been the targets of court-curbing initiatives. In 1957 the Jenner-Butler bill, prohibiting the Supreme Court from hearing on appeal cases that dealt with national security issues, failed by the narrowest of margins in the Senate.[11] Two decades later, Senator Jesse Helms's amendment to S. 210 (the bill creating the Department of Education), which would have forbade the Supreme Court to hear cases challenging state-sanctioned voluntary school prayers, passed the Senate but ultimately died in the House when the Ninety-sixth Congress adjourned. During the early 1980s, scores of bills were introduced in the Congress that would deprive the Supreme Court of appellate jurisdiction either to hear cases involving such issues as abortion rights and voluntary prayer in the public schools or to order school busing to achieve racial integration.[12]

COURT-IMPOSED RESTRAINTS ON JUDICIAL REVIEW

To minimize the likelihood of Congress or the executive seeking to impose restraints on its exercise of judicial review, the Court has developed a set of policies (Alexander Bickel calls them "passive virtues"[13]) restricting the general circumstances under which it and the lower courts will engage in constitutional adjudication. The part these restraints (at once both constitutionally based yet self-imposed) play in the exercise of judicial power is no less important than the part played by judicial review itself. As Professor John Roche observed,

> Judicial self-restraint and judicial power seem to be the opposite sides of the same coin: it has been by judicious application of the former that the latter has been maintained. A tradition beginning with Marshall's coup in *Marbury* v. *Madison* . . . suggests that the Court's power has been maintained by a wise refusal to employ it in unequal combat.[14]

The Court's self-declared limitations on its power of judicial review fall into the following categories.

Cases and Controversies

Article III, Section 2 declares that the judicial power of the federal courts shall extend to "Cases" and "Controversies": that is, to litigation involving a real conflict of interests or rights between contending parties. According to its interpretation of this mandate, the federal judiciary generally will not entertain hypothetical, feigned, or collusive suits or render advisory opinions.[15] In recent years, though, this self-imposed barrier to litigation has been lowered by the Supreme Court itself. Whereas in 1955

Justice Robert Jackson could call this restriction "perhaps the most significant . . . limitation upon judicial power," by 1976 Archibald Cox felt compelled to acknowledge that the Court has moved "away from the view that constitutional adjudication is only collateral to the essential judicial task of deciding lawsuits and towards the notion that the primary function of the Supreme Court of the United States is to ensure that other organs of government observe constitutional limitations."[16]

Standing to Sue

Closely related to the need for the presence of a case or controversy is the requirement that the party bringing suit must have standing to sue. To have standing, the party invoking judicial power must show "not only that the statute is invalid, but that he has sustained or is immediately in danger of sustaining some direct injury as the result of its enforcement, and not merely that he suffers in some indefinite way in common with people generally."[17] Standing is required because, as the Court noted in *Baker* v. *Carr,* "a personal stake in the outcome of the controversy . . . assure[s] that concrete adverseness which sharpens the presentation of issues upon which the court so largely depends for illumination of difficult constitutional questions."

One of the most interesting questions involving standing faced by the Court over the years has been whether or not the mere payment of taxes provides the taxpayer with sufficient standing to challenge governmental action involving the expenditure of funds. The Court's original answer to this question was given in *Frothingham* v. *Mellon* (1923), in which it rejected unequivocally the contention that taxpayers *qua* taxpayers have standing. In the unanimous opinion of the justices, a taxpayer's interest in the monies of the Treasury "is shared by millions of others; is comparatively minute and indeterminable; and the effect upon future taxation, of any payment out of the funds, so remote, fluctuating and uncertain, that no basis is afforded for an appeal to the preventive powers of a court of equity." Standing, the Court concluded, requires the demonstration of a personal interest that is sharp and distinct from the interests of taxpayers in general. In *Flast* v. *Cohen,* however, the Court qualified *Frothingham* by easing somewhat the requirements for standing. Under the revised guidelines, federal taxpayers would be allowed to challenge congressional spending if the legislation in question emanated from the Taxing and Spending Clause of Article I, Section 8, and if the taxpayers could show a nexus, or link, between their status as taxpayers and a specific constitutional limitation upon the exercise of the spending power.[18]

The relatively loose criteria for standing outlined in *Flast* made it easier for litigants to bring policy disputes before the judiciary, and they were soon tightened. In *United States* v. *Richardson* (1974) the Court held that a taxpayer as such has no standing to challenge the constitutionality of that provision of the Central Intelligence Agency Act which permits the CIA, unlike other federal agencies, to keep its budget secret. Five justices ruled that taxpayers are barred from using the courts as forums to air "general grievances" about governmental policies and procedures. Thus in *Richardson* (as well as in *Schlesinger* v. *Reservists' Committee to Stop the War*, announced the same day), the Court denied that *Flast* could be interpreted to allow a taxpayer's suit in the absence of a demonstrable and concrete injury suffered by the plaintiff.

An insistence that plaintiffs show something more than a generalized grievance in order to gain standing runs through the Court's rulings on the question of standing. In *Valley Forge Christian College* v. *Americans United for Separation of Church and State* (1982), the Court rejected the respondents' assertion that they had standing by virtue of an " 'injury in fact' to their shared individuated right to a government that 'shall make no law respecting an establishment of religion.' " As Justice Rehnquist observed for the Court majority, "although they claim that the Constitution has been violated, they claim nothing else. They fail to identify any personal injury suffered by the plaintiffs as a consequence of the alleged constitutional error, other than the psychological consequence presumably produced by observation of conduct with which one disagrees. That is not sufficient to confer standing under Article III, even though the disagreement is phrased in constitutional terms." Moreover, he continued, "Their claim that the government has violated the Establishment Clause does not provide a special license to roam the country in search of governmental wrongdoing and to reveal their discoveries in federal court. The federal courts were simply not constituted as ombudsmen of the general welfare." Finally, in *Allen* v. *Wright* (1984), the Court denied standing to black parents who sought to challenge the failure of the Internal Revenue Service to deny tax-exempt status to private schools that they alleged were practicing racial discrimination. The parents claimed that the tax exemptions harmed them directly and interfered with their children's opportunity to receive an education in desegregated public schools.

Mootness

Another barrier to judicial review is mootness, a doctrine closely related to the Court's insistence on standing and its refusal to render advisory opinions. When plaintiffs who clearly have standing to sue at the outset of litigation confront a change either in the facts or in the law that deprives them of a necessary stake in the outcome, the issue involved in the suit is rendered moot. The mootness doctrine requires that the case or controversy exist at all stages of review, not merely at the time the complaint was filed.

Although the Court in the main adheres to the mootness doctrine, fidelity to this technical barrier to adjudication is by no means absolute, as the contrasting holdings in *Roe* v. *Wade* (1973) and *DeFunis* v. *Odegaard* (1974) illustrate. In *Roe*, the plaintiff was an (initially) pregnant woman who challenged the constitutionality of abortion laws; her suit was initiated in 1970, but the Court's decision was not handed down until January of 1973. Even though the plaintiff was no longer pregnant, the Court refused to dismiss the case as moot. Justice Blackmun spoke for the Court: "Pregnancy provides a classic justification for a conclusion of nonmootness. It truly could be 'capable of repetition, yet evading review.' "

In *DeFunis,* on the other hand, the Court invoked the mootness doctrine to avoid ruling on the emotionally charged issue of affirmative action/reverse discrimination. Under a lower court order Marco DeFunis, Jr. was admitted to law school at the University of Washington, and by a Supreme Court stay he was able to remain in law school while he litigated his claim that the law school had practiced reverse discrimination and violated the Equal Protection Clause when it denied him admission while accepting minority applicants with less qualifications. He was in his final term when the Supreme Court handed down its decision, and the Court in its per curiam opinion found that fact sufficient to render the case moot: "Since he was now registered for his final term, it is evident that he will be given an opportunity to complete all academic and other requirements for graduation, and, if he does so, will receive his diploma regardless of any decision this Court might reach on the merits of this case."

The Court majority did not find persuasive Justice Brennan's objection that "any number of unexpected events—illness, economic necessity, even academic failure—might prevent his graduation at the end of the term. Were that misfortune to befall, and were petitioner required to register for yet another term, the prospect that he would again face the hurdle of the admissions policy is real, not fanciful."

Ripeness

Another technical barrier to adjudication of constitutional claims is the requirement that a suit not be brought to the courts prematurely, while the relationships between the parties are still developing or in flux. Unless a dispute is sufficiently real, well developed, and specific—in a word, *ripe*—any decision reached by the court necessarily will hinge on a series of predictions about the probable conduct of the parties, and those predictions will in turn depend upon contingencies and guesses about the future. Since no principled judgment is possible in such circumstances, the courts have developed the ripeness requirement to avoid having to speculate about contingencies and uncertainties.[19]

Nonjusticiable Political Questions

The presence of a case or controversy, standing to sue, the absence of mootness, and ripeness are characteristics that make a jurisdictional issue a justiciable one: that is, a case that the Supreme Court will decide. A different kind of restraint on judicial review comes into play when the Court considers a case to be nonjusticiable despite clear jurisdictional authority. The most common and controversial nonjusticiable cases are those in which the plaintiffs seek adjudication of questions that, in the view of the courts, can better be solved via the political process.

The first explicit application of the political-questions doctrine occured in *Luther* v. *Borden* (1849), in which the Court held that enforcement of Article IV, Section 4 of the Constitution, guaranteeing a republican form of government for all states, was the exclusive responsibility of the popularly elected branches. Until the Court's decision in *Baker* in 1962, questions involving legislative and congressional reapportionment were also deemed to be political. Specifically, in the crucial case of *Colegrove* v. *Green* (1946), Justice Frankfurter held for a plurality of the Court that districting was a political question beyond the reach of the Court, warning that "courts ought not to enter this political thicket." Sixteen years later, however, the justices did exactly that in *Baker* v. *Carr*, in which the Court directed a federal court in Tennessee to hear a case challenging legislative malapportionment as unconstitutional under the Equal Protection Clause. (The Court's principal decisions on reapportionment and a discussion of their significance can be found in Chapter 16.) Justice William Brennan's opinion for the Court in *Baker* is generally considered to be the authoritative statement by the Court on the political-questions doctrine.[20]

Avoiding the Constitutional Issue

In his concurrence in *Ashwander* v. *Tennessee Valley Authority* (1936), Justice Louis Brandeis spelled out yet another policy that the Court generally has followed to avoid antagonizing its coequal branches through too-frequent review of their actions:

> The Court will not pass on a constitutional question, although properly presented by the record, if there is also present some other ground on which the case may be disposed of. This rule has found some varied application. Thus, if a case can be decided on either of two grounds, one involving a constitutional question, the other a question of statutory construction or general law, the Court will decide only the latter. . . . Appeals from the highest court of a state challenging its decision of a question under the federal Constitution are frequently dismissed because the judgment can be sustained on an independent state ground.

Presumption of Constitutionality

In general, the Court presumes that a statute is constitutional unless the opposite is clearly demonstrated. Justice Bushrod Washington provided the rationale for this policy in his opinion for the Court in *Ogden* v. *Saunders* (1827): "It is but a decent respect due to the wisdom, integrity, and patriotism of the legislative body, by which any law is passed, to presume in favor of its validity. . . ." It must be emphasized, however, that today this presumption of constitutionality is confined almost exclusively to economic and social legislation. In the contemporary era, the Court usually has regarded as presumptively unconstitutional legislation that burdens "insular and discrete minorities" or that infringes upon First Amendment freedoms.[21]

THE EXPANDING ROLE OF THE COURTS

Although the set of policies described above is not exhaustive, it does indicate the range and variety of techniques and devices available to the judiciary when it wishes to avoid adjudicating constitutional claims. These techniques are not always employed. As Henry J. Abraham notes, they are little more than "maxims of judicial self-restraint." Different Courts and different justices have cleaved to them with varying degrees of fidelity.[22] Generally speaking, in recent decades, the Supreme Court has displayed less fidelity to these "passive virtues" than earlier Courts. Perceiving that its role includes representing those interests in society that failed to receive representation elsewhere in the government, it no longer embraces Justice Brandeis's observation that "The most important thing that we do is not doing."[23] Rather, it has felt compelled to lower the technical barriers to adjudication and, by reaching the constitutional merits of a case, to vindicate the rights of its clientele groups. Because the Burger and Rehnquist Courts have not raised these barriers appreciably, the federal judiciary as a whole has been faced with an expanded range of issues on which it must render final judgment.

Along with this lowering of barriers to constitutional adjudication, two other factors have contributed to an increased level of judicial activity in recent decades. The enormous expansion in the scope of government itself inevitably has raised the level of legal regulation, and thereby provided new opportunities for litigation. At the same time, special-interest groups have displayed an increasing willingness to use the courts to pursue political objectives. With the technical restrictions on constitutional adjudication eased, myriad organizations and lobbies—including civil rights groups, consumer groups, public interest groups, and environmental groups—have concluded that they may fare better in the courts than in the legislative and executive branches, and thus have sought to achieve their public policy objectives through litigation.[24]

Not only has the range of issues that the judiciary adjudicates expanded considerably, but the kind of response demanded from the courts by these new issues also is entirely different from past judicial responses. Previously, in the constitutional realm, the courts were called upon simply to protect the public from what the other branches of government may have wished to impose on it. Increasingly, however, they are now expected to participate more actively in the policy-making process and to expand what the popular branches must do, even when they do not wish, or know how, to act. Put another way, they are expected to be prescriptive as well as proscriptive and to address themselves not only to the government's "sins of commission" but also to its "sins of omission." This expectation that the judiciary engage in policy making has set off a lively debate between those who argue that the judiciary lacks the institutional capacity necessary to make effective policy (they stress that the very attributes of the adjudicative process that render courts so well-suited for specific grievance resolution also render them most ill-suited for general policy making) and those who insist that it is capable of dealing with policy issues and that, compared to the popularly elected branches and the bureaucracy, it does so quite well.[25] *DeShaney* v. *Winnebago County Department of Social Services* shows the Court debating an invitation to expand the Due Process Clause of the Fourteenth Amendment (and therewith its own power) in an emotionally laden case. Chief Justice Rehnquist for the majority relies on the actual words of the Constitution and on precedent to argue against further judicial control of the popular branches, while Justice Blackmun in his dissent invokes "Compassion" as his "only guide and comfort" to press for an expanded judicial role.

THE COURTS, JUDICIAL REVIEW, AND THE PROBLEM OF LEGITIMACY

Ever since *Marbury* v. *Madison,* the Supreme Court's first exercise of judicial review, the federal judiciary has had to grapple with the problem of legitimacy. How large a role should a nonmajoritarian institution play in shaping American public policy? How often and to what extent should federal judges substitute their judgment for that of the people's representatives? Judge Gibson's apprehensions in *Eakin* v. *Raub* have never been allayed completely, and debate over the appropriate role, function, or purpose of the federal judiciary has continued to this day among judges and students of public law. At the heart of this debate has been the question of judicial activism versus judicial self-restraint, with advocates for both positions finding support in *The Federalist,* No. 78.

Those who favor judicial activism stress that the judiciary "was designed to be an intermediate body between the people and the legislature, in order among other things to keep the latter within the limits assigned to their authority."[26] They see the judiciary as a "noble guard,"[27] protecting the people from the tyrannical excesses which might otherwise be visited upon them by their more immediate representatives and justify an activist judiciary on the grounds that it helps to promote qualitative, not simply quantitative, majority rule.

Those who favor judicial self-restraint or passivity also begin with *The Federalist,* No. 78. Reminding the judiciary that it is by far the weakest of the three branches of government, having neither the power of the purse nor the power of the sword but only that of judgment, they caution the Court to avoid placing itself in "continuous jeopardy of being overpowered, awed, or influenced by its coordinate branches." In the seminal words of James Bradley Thayer, the judiciary

> can only disregard [a legislative] act when those who have the right to make laws have not merely made a mistake, but have made a very clear one—so clear that it is not open to rational question. That is the standard of duty to which the Courts bring legislative acts; that is the test which they apply—not merely their own judgment as to constitutionality, but their conclusion as to what judgment is permissible to another

> department which the Constitution has charged with the duty of making it. This rule recognizes that, having regard to the great, complex, ever-unfolding exigencies of government, much which will seem unconstitutional to one man, or body of men, may reasonably not seem so to another; that the Constitution often admits of different interpretations; that the Constitution does not impose upon the legislature any one specific opinion, but leaves open this range of choice; and that whatever choice is rational is constitutional.[28]

Unless the federal judiciary employs this "reasonable doubt" test in exercising judicial review, the argument goes, the people will lose that "political experience and moral education and stimulus that comes from fighting the question out in the ordinary way and correcting their own errors."[29]

The federal judiciary periodically has swung between activism and self-restraint, alternately attracted to and repelled by the implications of these two basic positions.[30] But whatever its stand of the moment, it historically has sought to reassure the popularly elected branches by emphasizing its inherent weakness and by deliberately avoiding unnecessary conflicts with these branches, principally through the erection of technical barriers to adjudication. In recent years, however, the judiciary increasingly has embraced the arguments of judicial activism, eased restrictions on adjudication, and become an active participant in policy making.

The judiciary's embrace of judicial activism has been applauded and encouraged by many of the nation's most prominent legal scholars, who conceive the Supreme Court to be "the ultimate arbiter of social ethics in the nation," whose responsibility it is to "articulate the public good as . . . [the Justices] understand it."[31] In the name of "ethical norms" and "moral growth and evolution," they admonish the Court to "invent" new constitutional rights and to acknowledge openly "that the source of those rights is not the constitutional text but the enhanced seriousness of certain values in American society."[32] These scholars argue that the vast majority of those rights that the Court has come to protect are not constitutionally based (i.e., are not "applications of the value judgments constitutionalized by the Framers") but rather are wholly "extraconstitutional" (i.e., are newly invented rights that are the product of "our evolving, deepening moral understanding"[33]). They argue that "most political practices banned by the Supreme Court in human rights cases, including freedom of expression and equal protection cases, cannot plausibly be characterized as simply modern analogues of past, constitutionally-banned practices."[34] These practices are banned, not because they violate value judgments constitutionalized by the Framers but because they violate the value judgments of the judges, articulating, as they do, "the public good as they understand it."[35] Legal scholars who operate from this perspective argue that the Court must assume a "prophetic stance" and oppose itself to established conventions by submitting governmental actions to a moral critique and striking down such actions if they violate any human rights that the Court believes individuals ought to be deemed to have.[36] By institutionalizing prophecy in this manner, the Court provides the public with the occasion for "moral reevaluation and possible moral growth" in a way that the popular branches—guided by what these legal scholars consider to be "a stagnant or even repressive morality"—cannot.[37]

The Court, however, has been reluctant to admit candidly that it is performing this prophetic function and has displayed instead the "tendency to resort to bad legislative history and strained reading of constitutional language to support results that would be better justified by explication of contemporary moral and political ideals not drawn from the constitutional text." As Thomas Grey notes, this tendency undermines the Court's credibility for "if judges resort to bad interpretation in preference to honest exposition of deeply held but unwritten ideals, it must be because they perceive th[is] mode of decisionmaking to be . . . suspect."[38] Therefore, these legal scholars chide the Court for its lack of candor and admonish it to acknowledge openly that it is protecting human rights and dignity and fulfilling its prophetic mission. They urge the entire Court to follow the lead of Chief Justice Warren, who, in a peroration by Anthony Lewis, is described as "the closest thing the United States has had to a Platonic Guardian, dispensing law from a throne without any sensed limits of power except what was seen as the good of society."[39] As G. Edward White notes, "Most of Warren's energy on the Court was directed toward achieving the 'right' results. He did not often agonize, as did Frankfurter, over an outcome in a case, nor did he despair of finding an adequate constitutional basis for justifying his intuitions, nor did he worry about being overly activist. He spent his time on discerning results that seemed just and on marshalling support for those results by attempting to convince others of their inherent justice."[40] If the entire Court were to adopt this activist posture, these scholars insist, it would be more "effective" in its protection of human rights and better situated to foster "moral growth" among the citizenry;[41] it would lead the way to a "fuller realization of human dignity."[42]

The contention that constitutional rights can be identified and defended apart from the constitutional text is fraught with difficulties, the most serious of which is the way in which it undermines the legitimacy of the judiciary and its exercise of judicial review. Judicial activism has traditionally defended judicial review and voided acts of the popular branches in the name of the Constitution. It has drawn its strength from *The Federalist*, No. 78, and Hamilton's contention that judicial review does not suppose a superiority of the judiciary to the popular branches but "only supposes that the power of the people is superior to both; and that where the will of the legislature declared in its statutes, stands in opposition to that of the people declared in the constitution, the judges ought to be governed by the latter, rather than the former." However, the contention that the judiciary is justified in exercising judicial review in order to vindicate not the constitutional expression of the people's will but the "ethical premises" of the judges deprives the Courts of this defense and, therewith, of their fundamental legitimacy. As the federal judiciary expands both the reach, and vulnerability, of its judicial powers (and by so doing, reveals the limitations of their capacity to make policy), its legitimacy in the eyes of the public will depend as never before on the qualities of the judges themselves. As Tocqueville reminded us a century and a half ago, "They [the judges] are all-powerful so long as people respect the law; but they . . . [are] impotent against popular neglect or contempt of the law." Because of the intractability of public opinion, Tocqueville pointed out, judges must be more than "good citizens and men of the information and integrity which are indispensable to all magistrates"; they must also be "statesmen, wise to discern the signs of the time, not afraid to brave the obstacles that can be subdued, nor slow to turn away from the current when it threatens to sweep them off, and the supremacy of the Union and obedience due to the laws along with them."[43] Whether the judicial power will continue to serve as a means to the ends of the Constitution will in large measure depend upon the presence of these qualities in the members of the federal judiciary.

NOTES

1 See also P. Allan Dionisopoulos and Paul Peterson, "Rediscovering the American Origins of Judicial Review," *The John Marshall Law Review* 18 (1984): 49–76, who argue that the doctrine of judicial review "was first used by the federal courts in nullifying the two Invalid Acts of 1972 and 1793" in *Hayburn's Case* (1792) and *United States* v. *Yale Todd* (1794).

2 Whatever the understanding of separation of powers, it is significant to note that the Supreme Court did not wield the power of judicial review again until the *Dred Scott* decision in 1857. While several constitutional law scholars have recently begun to write of a second Marshall Court decision that held a provision of a congressional act unconstitutional—the obscure case of *Hodgson* v. *Bowerbank* (1809), this revisionist interpretation has been convincingly rebutted by Dennis J. Mahoney, "A Historical Note on *Hodgson* v. *Bowerbank*," *University of Chicago Law Review* 49 (1982): 725–740.

3 Henry J. Abraham, *The Judicial Process*, 5th ed. (New York: Oxford University Press, 1986), pp. 295–301.

4 Charles L. Black, Jr., *The People and the Court* (New York: Macmillan, 1960).

5 Charles Evans Hughes, *The Supreme Court of the United States* (New York: Columbia University Press, 1928), pp. 96–97.

6 Walter F. Murphy, *Congress and the Court* (Chicago: University of Chicago Press, 1962), p. 63.

7 See Henry M. Hart, Jr., "The Power of Congress to Limit the Jurisdiction of Federal Courts; An Exercise in Dialectic," *Harvard Law Review* 66 (June 1953): 1362; and Leonard G. Ratner, "Congressional Power Over the Appellate Jurisdiction of the Supreme Court," *University of Pennsylvania Law Review* 109 (December 1960): 157.

8 Charles Rice, "Limiting Federal Court Jurisdiction: The Constitutional Basis for the Proposals in Congress Today," *Judicature* 65, no. 4 (October 1981), p. 195. See also Ralph A. Rossum, "Congress, the Constitution, and the Appel-

late Jurisdiction of the Supreme Court: The Letter and Spirit of the Exceptions Clause," *William and Mary Law Review* 24 (April 1983): 385–428.

9 Comment, "Removal of Supreme Court Appellate Jurisdiction: A Weapon Against Obscenity?" 1969 *Duke Law Journal*:291, 297.

10 For citations to congressional attempts to limit the Supreme Court's appellate jurisdiction, see Gerald Gunther, "Congressional Power to Curtail Federal Court Jurisdiction: An Opinionated Guide to the Ongoing Debate," *Stanford Law Review* 36 (1984): 895–898.

11 See Murphy, *Congress and the Court.*

12 See Rossum, *Congressional Control of the Judiciary: The Article III Option.*

13 Alexander M. Bickel, *The Least Dangerous Branch: The Supreme Court at the Bar of Politics* (New York: Bobbs-Merrill, 1962), pp. 111–198.

14 John P. Roche, "Judicial Self-Restraint," *American Political Science Review* 49 (September 1955): 722.

15 See *Muskrat* v. *United States,* (1911). Although the federal courts do not render advisory opinions, they do render declaratory judgments. An advisory opinion is advice on a hypothetical question given by the judiciary to the executive or to the legislature. A declaratory judgment, by way of contrast, grows out of an adjudication of an actual controversy between adverse parties and differs from an ordinary judgment principally in that it involves no compulsory process.

16 Robert H. Jackson, *The Supreme Court in the American System of Government* (Cambridge, Mass.: Harvard University Press, 1955), p. 11; and Archibald Cox, *The Role of the Supreme Court in American Government* (New York: Oxford University Press, 1976), p. 101.

17 *Frothingham* v. *Mellon* (1923).

18 See *Valley Forge Christian College* v. *Americans United for Separation of Church and State* (1982), in which the Supreme Court refused to expand *Flast* and allow taxpayer suits challenging congressional action under the Property Clause of Article IV, section 3, clause 2.

19 See *United Public Workers* v. *Mitchell* (1947), and *Poe* v. *Ullman* (1961).

20 See also *Coleman* v. *Miller* (1939), in which the Court held that questions relating to the amending process of the United States Constitution are political.

21 See, for example, *United States* v. *Carolene Products Co.* (1938), fn. 4; and *New York Times* v. *United States* (1971).

22 Henry J. Abraham, *The Judicial Process,* p. 373. See also Wallace Mendelson, "Mr. Justice Douglas and Government by Judiciary," *Journal of Politics* 38, no. 4 (November 1976): 918–937.

23 Alexander M. Bickel, ed., *The Unpublished Opinions of Mr. Justice Brandeis: The Supreme Court at Work* (Cambridge, Mass.: Harvard University Press, 1957), p. 17.

24 Nathan Glazer, "Towards an Imperial Judiciary?" *The Public Interest,* no. 41 (Fall 1975): 119–121.

25. The critique is presented in Donald L. Horowitz, *The Courts and Social Policy* (Washington, D.C.: Brookings Institution Press, 1977), pp. 33–56. See also Horowitz's "The Judiciary: Umpire or Empire?" *Law and Human Behavior* 6 (1982): 129–143. For a contrasting point of view, see R. Cavanaugh and A. Sarat, "Thinking About Courts: Towards and Beyond a Jurisprudence of Judicial Competence," *Law and Society Review* 14, no. 2 (Winter 1980): 371–

420; and Stephen L. Wasby, "Arrogation of Power or Accountability: 'Judicial Imperialism' Revisited," *Judicature* 65, no. 4 (October 1981): 208–219.

26 *The Federalist*, No. 78, p. 525.

27 *The Works of James Wilson*, ed. by Robert Green McCloskey (Cambridge, Mass.: Harvard University Press, 1967), p. 330.

28 James Bradley Thayer, "The Origin and Scope of the American Doctrine of Constitutional Law," *Harvard Law Review* 7 (October 1893): 144. See also Philip Kurland, *Mr. Justice Frankfurter and the Supreme Court* (Chicago: University of Chicago Press, 1971), p. 5, who identifies six basic assumptions of the doctrine of self-restraint: "One is history and the obligation that constitutionalism imposes to adhere to the essential meaning put in the document by its framers. A second is the intrinsically undemocratic nature of the Supreme Court. A third is a corollary of the second, an abiding respect for the judgments of those branches of the government that are elected representatives of their constituents. A fourth is the recognition that judicial error at this level is more difficult of correction than other forms of judicial action. A fifth is respect for the judgments of earlier courts. But (sixth), the essential feature of judicial restraint that has gained most attention and aroused the greatest doubts—probably because few men are themselves big enough to abide by its command—is the notion of rejection of personal preference."

29 James Bradley Thayer, *John Marshall* (Boston: Houghton Mifflin, 1901), pp. 106–107. See also Sanford Gabin, *Judicial Review and the Reasonable Doubt Test* (New York: Kennikat Press, 1980), and Raoul Berger, *Government by Judiciary* (Cambridge, Mass.: Harvard University Press, 1977).

30 See Wallace Mendelson, "The Politics of Judicial Activism," *Emory Law Journal* 24 (1975): 43–66, who argues that periods of judicial activism coincide with periods of party decline: "judicial pretension appears to have thrived only in periods of unusual weakness in our political processes; at other times it has been effectively rebuffed. In short, 'government by judges' seems no more than flaws in the party system permit it to be." (p. 44)

31 See Arthur S. Miller, *Toward Increased Judicial Activism: The Political Role of the Supreme Court* (Westport, Conn.: Greenwood Press, 1982), pp. 28, 275.

32 G. Edward White, "Reflections on the Role of the Supreme Court: The Contemporary Debate and the 'Lessons' of History," *Judicature* 63, no. 4 (October 1979), p. 168.

33 Michael Perry, *The Constitution, the Courts, and Human Rights* (New Haven: Yale University Press, 1982), p. 41.

34 Ibid., p. 75.

35 Arthur S. Miller, *Toward Increased Judicial Activism*, p. 274.

36 Ibid., p. 20, and Michael Perry, *The Constitution, the Courts, and Human Rights*, pp. 97, 98, 101, 102, 112, 146, 162.

37 Michael Perry, *The Constitution, the Courts, and Human Rights*, pp. 100, 113.

38 Thomas C. Grey, "Do We Have an Unwritten Constitution?" *Stanford Law Review* 27 (1975): 706. For alternative justifications of judicial activism, see Ronald Dworkin, *Taking Rights Seriously* (Cambridge, Mass.: Harvard University Press, 1977), and Sotorios A. Barber, *On What the Constitution Means* (Baltimore: Johns Hopkins University Press, 1984).

39 Anthony Lewis, "Earl Warren," in L. Friedman and F. Israel, eds., *The Justices of the United States Supreme Court*, 4 vols. (New York: Chelsea, 1969), vol. 4, pp. 2726.

40 G. Edward White, *Earl Warren: A Public Life* (New York: Oxford University Press, 1982), p. 190. See also p. 359: "Warren . . . equated judicial lawmaking with neither the dictates of reason, as embodied in established precedent or doctrine, nor the demands imposed by an institutional theory of the judge's role, nor the alleged 'command' of the constitutional text, but rather with his own reconstruction of the ethical structure of the Constitution."

41 Michael Perry, *The Constitution, the Courts, and Human Rights*, pp. 141–143.

42 Arthur S. Miller, *Toward Increased Judicial Activism*, p. 317.

43 Alexis de Tocqueville, *Democracy in America*, vol. 1 (New York: Random House, 1945), p. 157.

SELECTED READINGS

The Federalist, Nos. 78, 80.

Ashwander v. *Tennessee Valley Authority*, 297 U.S. 288 (1936).
Colegrove v. *Green*, 328 U.S. 549 (1946).
Coleman v. *Miller*, 307 U.S. 433 (1939).
Laird v. *Tatum*, 408 U.S. 1 (1972).
Poe v. *Ullman*, 367 U.S. 497 (1961).
Powell v. *McCormack*, 395 U.S. 486 (1969).
United States v. *Nixon*, 418 U.S. 683 (1974).
Valley Forge Christian College v. *Americans United for Separation of Church and State*, 454 U.S. 464 (1982).

Agresto, John. *The Supreme Court and Constitutional Democracy* (Ithaca, New York: Cornell University Press, 1984).
Berger, Raoul. *Congress versus the Supreme Court* (Cambridge, Mass.: Harvard University Press, 1969).
Bickel, Alexander M. *The Least Dangerous Branch: The Supreme Court at the Bar of Politics* (New York: Bobbs-Merrill, 1962).
Chayes, Abram. "The Role of the Judge in Public Law Litigation," *Harvard Law Review* 89 (1976): 1281–1316.
Choper, Jesse H. *Judicial Review and the National Political Process* (Chicago: University of Chicago Press, 1980).
Cooper, Phillip J. *Hard Judicial Choices: Federal District Court Judges and State and Local Officials* (New York: Oxford University Press, 1988).
Currie, David P. "Misunderstanding Standing," 1981 *Supreme Court Review* 41–48.
Dworkin, Ronald. *Taking Rights Seriously* (Cambridge, Mass.: Harvard University Press, 1977).
Ely, John Hart. *Democracy and Distrust: A Theory of Judicial Review* (Cambridge, Mass.: Harvard University Press, 1980).
Horowitz, Donald L. *The Courts and Social Policy* (Washington, D.C.: Brookings Institution Press, 1977).
Jacobsohn, Gary L. *The Supreme Court and the Decline of Constitutional Aspiration* (Totawa, N.J.: Rowman & Littlefield, 1986).
Levinson, Sanford. *Constitutional Faith* (Princeton, N.J.: Princeton University Press, 1988).

Levy, Leonard, ed. *Judicial Review and the Supreme Court* (New York: Harper & Row, 1967).

McDowell, Gary L. *Curbing the Courts: The Constitution and the Limits of Judicial Power* (Baton Rouge: Louisiana State University Press, 1988).

McDowell, Gary L., ed. *Taking the Constitution Seriously: Essays on the Constitution and Constitutional Law* (Dubuque, Iowa: Kendall/Hunt, 1981).

Nagel, Robert F. *Constitutional Cultures: The Mentality and Consequences of Judicial Review* (Berkeley: University of California Press, 1989).

Perry, Michael J. *The Constitution, the Courts, and Human Rights* (New Haven: Yale University Press, 1982).

Perry, Michael J. *Morality, Politics, and the Law* (New York: Oxford University Press, 1988).

Rebell, Michael A. and Block, Arthur R. *Educational Policy Making and the Courts: An Empirical Study of Judicial Activism* (Chicago: University of Chicago Press, 1982).

Rossum, Ralph A. *Congressional Control of the Judiciary: The Article Three Option* (Washington, D.C.: Center for Judicial Studies, 1988).

Scalia, Antonin. "The Doctrine of Standing as an Essential Element of the Separation of Powers," *Suffolk University Law Review* 17 (1983): 881.

Scigliano, Robert. *The Supreme Court and the Presidency* (New York: Free Press, 1971).

Strumm, Philippa. *The Supreme Court and "Political Questions": A Study in Judicial Evasion* (University, Ala.: University of Alabama Press, 1974).

Thayer, James Bradley, "The Origin and Scope of the American Doctrine of Constitutional Law," *Harvard Law Review* 7 (1893): 129.

Van Alstyne, William W. "A Critical Guide to *Ex parte McCardle*," *Arizona Law Review* 15 (1973): 229.

Wolfe, Christopher. *The Rise of Modern Judicial Review: from Constitutional Interpretation to Judge-Made Law* (New York: Basic Books, 1986).

Marbury v. *Madison*

5 U.S. (1 Cranch) 137; 2 L. Ed. 60 (1803)

Before yielding control of the government to the Jeffersonians in 1801, the Federalist-controlled "lame duck" Congress created a number of new judicial posts. To fill the 42 justice-of-the-peace posts mandated for the District of Columbia, President John Adams nominated members of the Federalist Party, including one William Marbury. His commission, which had been confirmed by the Senate and signed by the president, was sealed by John Marshall, who, although appointed by President Adams as Chief Justice, was also serving as secretary of state. In the rush of the closing hours of the Adams administration, Marshall was unable to deliver Marbury's commission. When James Madison took over as Thomas Jefferson's secretary of state on March 4, he found Marbury's commission (and three others) and refused to deliver them. Marbury then brought suit in the Supreme Court to compel delivery of his commission, relying on Section 13 of the Judiciary Act of 1789, which, he claimed, gave the Supreme Court original jurisdiction in such a case. Despite his involvement in this matter, and with a bare quorum of four of the six justices participating, Chief Justice Marshall used this occasion to establish for the Court the power of judicial review. *Opinion of the Court: Marshall, Chase, Paterson, Washington. Not participating: Cushing, Moore.*

MR. JUSTICE MARSHALL delivered the opinion of the Court.

In the order in which the court has viewed this subject, the following questions have been considered and decided.

1. Has the applicant a right to the commission he demands?

2. If he has a right, and that right has been violated, do the laws of his country afford him a remedy?

3. If they do afford him a remedy, is it a *mandamus* issuing from this court?

. . . It is . . . the opinion of the court,

1. That, by signing the commission of Mr. Marbury, the President of the United States appointed him a justice of peace, for the county of Washington in the District of Columbia; and that the seal of the United States, affixed thereto by the Secretary of State, is conclusive testimony of the verity of the signature, and of the completion of the appointment; and that the appointment conferred on him a legal right to the office for the space of five years.

2. That, having this legal title to the office, he has a consequent right to the commission; a refusal to deliver which, is a plain violation of that right, for which the laws of this country afford him a remedy.

It remains to be enquired whether,

3. He is entitled to the remedy for which he applies. This depends on,

1. The nature of the writ applied for and
2. The power of this court.

. . . This, then, is a plain case for mandamus, either to deliver the commission, or a copy of it from the record; and it only remains to be enquired, whether it can issue from this court.

The act to establish the judicial courts of the United States authorizes the Supreme Court "to issue writs of mandamus in cases warranted by the principles and usages of law, to any courts appointed, or persons holding office, under the authority of the United States."

The Secretary of State, being a person holding an office under the authority of the United States,

Here and throughout the text, the authors of court opinions are underscored.

is precisely within the letter of the description, and if this court is not authorized to issue a writ of mandamus to such an officer, it must be because the law is unconstitutional, and therefore absolutely incapable of conferring the authority, and assigning the duties which its words purport to confer and assign.

The Constitution vests the whole judicial power of the United States in one supreme court, and such inferior courts as Congress shall, from time to time, ordain and establish. This power is expressly extended to all cases arising under the laws of the United States; and, consequently, in some form, may be exercised over the present case; because the right claimed is given by a law of the United States.

In the distribution of this power it is declared that "the Supreme Court shall have original jurisdiction in all cases affecting ambassadors, other public ministers and consuls, and those in which a state shall be a party. In all other cases, the Supreme Court shall have appellate jurisdiction."

It has been insisted at the bar, that, as the original grant of jurisdiction to the Supreme and inferior courts, is general, and the clause assigning original jurisdiction to the Supreme Court contains no negative or restrictive words, the power remains to the legislature to assign original jurisdiction to that court in other cases than those specified in the article which has been recited; provided those cases belong to the judicial power of the United States.

If it had been intended to leave it in the discretion of the legislature to apportion the judicial power between the Supreme and inferior courts according to the will of that body, it would certainly have been useless to have proceeded further than to have defined the judicial power, and the tribunals in which it should be vested. The subsequent part of the section is mere surplusage, is entirely without meaning. If Congress remains at liberty to give this court appellate jurisdiction, where the Constitution has declared their jurisdiction shall be original; and original jurisdiction where the Constitution has declared it shall be appellate, the distribution of jurisdiction made in the Constitution is form without substance.

Affirmative words are often, in their operation, negative of other objects than those affirmed; and in this case, a negative or exclusive sense must be given to them, or they have no operation at all.

It cannot be presumed that any clause in the Constitution is intended to be without effect; and, therefore, such a construction is inadmissible unless the words require it.

. . . To enable this court, then to issue a mandamus, it must be shown to be an exercise of appellate jurisdiction, or to be necessary to enable them to exercise appellate jurisdiction.

It has been stated at the bar that the appellate jurisdiction may be exercised in a variety of forms, and that, if it be the will of the legislature that a mandamus should be used for that purpose, that will must be obeyed. This is true, yet the jurisdiction must be appellate, not original.

It is the essential criterion of appellate jurisdiction that it revises and corrects the proceedings in a cause already instituted, and does not create that cause. Although, therefore, a mandamus may be directed to courts, yet to issue such a writ to an officer for the delivery of a paper is in effect the same as to sustain an original action for that paper, and, therefore, seems not to belong to appellate, but to original jurisdiction. Neither is it necessary, in such a case as this, to enable the court to exercise its appellate jurisdiction.

The authority, therefore, given to the Supreme Court by the act establishing the judicial courts of the United States, to issue writs of mandamus to public officers, appears not to be warranted by the Constitution; and it becomes necessary to inquire whether a jurisdiction so conferred can be exercised.

The question, whether an act repugnant to the Constitution can become the law of the land, is a question deeply interesting to the United States; but, happily, not of an intricacy proportioned to its interest. It seems only necessary to recognize certain principles, supposed to have been long and well established, to decide it.

That the people have an original right to establish, for their future government, such principles as, in their opinion, shall most conduce to their own happiness is the basis on which the whole American fabric had been erected. The exercise of this original right is a very great exertion; nor can it, nor ought it, to be frequently repeated. The principles, therefore, so established, are deemed fundamental. And as the authority from which they proceed is supreme, and can seldom act, they are designed to be permanent.

This original and supreme will organizes the

government, and assigns to different departments their respective powers. It may either stop here, or establish certain limits not to be transcended by those departments.

The government of the United States is of the latter description. The powers of the legislature are defined and limited; and that those limits may not be mistaken, or forgotten, the Constitution is written. To what purpose are powers limited, and to what purpose is that limitation committed to writing, if these limits may, at any time, be passed by those intended to be restrained? The distinction between a government with limited and unlimited powers is abolished if those limits do not confine the persons on whom they are imposed, and if acts prohibited and acts allowed are of equal obligation. It is a proposition too plain to be contested, that the Constitution controls any legislative act repugnant to it; or, that the legislature may alter the Constitution by an ordinary act.

Between these alternatives there is no middle ground. The Constitution is either a superior paramount law, unchangeable by ordinary means, or it is on a level with ordinary legislative acts, and, like other acts, is alterable when the legislature shall please to alter it.

If the former part of the alternative be true, then a legislative act contrary to the Constitution is not law: if the latter part be true, then written constitutions are absurd attempts on the part of the people to limit a power in its own nature illimitable.

Certainly all those who have framed written constitutions contemplate them as forming the fundamental and paramount law of the nation, and consequently, the theory of every such government must be, that an act of the legislature, repugnant to the constitution, is void.

This theory is essentially attached to a written constitution, and is, consequently, to be considered by this court as one of the fundamental principles of our society. It is not therefore to be lost sight of in the further consideration of this subject.

If an act of the legislature, repugnant to the Constitution, is void, does it, notwithstanding its invalidity, bind the courts, and oblige them to give it effect? Or, in other words, though it be not law, does it constitute a rule as operative as if it was a law? This would be to overthrow in fact what was established in theory; and would seem, at first view, an absurdity too gross to be insisted on. It shall, however, receive a more attentive consideration.

It is emphatically the province and duty of the judicial department to say what the law is. Those who apply the rule to particular cases must, of necessity, expound and interpret that rule. If two laws conflict with each other, the courts must decide on the operation of each.

So if a law be in opposition to the Constitution; if both the law and the Constitution apply to a particular case, so that the court must either decide that case conformably to the law, disregarding the Constitution; or conformably to the Constitution, disregarding the law; the court must determine which of these conflicting rules governs the case. This is of the very essence of judicial duty.

If, then, the courts are to regard the Constitution, and the Constitution is superior to any ordinary act of the legislature, the Constitution, and not such ordinary act, must govern the case to which they both apply.

Those, then, who controvert the principle that the Constitution is to be considered, in court, as a paramount law, are reduced to the necessity of maintaining that courts must close their eyes on the Constitution, and see only the law.

This doctrine would subvert the very foundation of all written constitutions. It would declare that an act which, according to the principles and theory of our government, is entirely void, is yet, in practice, completely obligatory. It would declare that if the legislature shall do what is expressly forbidden, such act, notwithstanding the express prohibition, is in reality effectual. It would be giving to the legislature a practical and real omnipotence, with the same breath which professes to restrict their powers within narrow limits. It is prescribing limits and declaring that those limits may be passed at pleasure.

That it thus reduces to nothing what we have deemed the greatest improvement on political institutions—a written constitution—would of itself be sufficient, in America, where written constitutions have been viewed with so much reverence, for rejecting the construction. But the peculiar expressions of the Constitution of the United States furnish additional arguments in favor of its rejection.

The judicial power of the United States is extended to all cases arising under the Constitution.

Could it be the intention of those who gave this power to say that, in using it, the Constitution should not be looked into? That a case arising under the Constitution should be decided without examining the instrument under which it rises?

This is too extravagant to be maintained.

In some cases then, the Constitution must be looked into by the judges. And if they can open it at all, what part of it are they forbidden to read or to obey?

There are many other parts of the Constitution which serve to illustrate this subject.

It is declared that "no tax or duty shall be laid on articles exported from any state." Suppose a duty on the export of cotton, of tobacco, or of flour; and a suit instituted to recover it. Ought judgment to be rendered in such a case? Ought the judges to close their eyes on the Constitution, and see only the law?

The Constitution declares that "no bill of attainder or ex post facto law shall be passed."

If, however, such a bill should be passed and a person should be prosecuted under it; must the court condemn to death those victims who the Constitution endeavours to preserve?

"No person," says the Constitution, "shall be convicted of treason unless on the testimony of two witnesses to the same overt act, or on confession in open court."

Here the language of the Constitution is addressed especially to the courts. It prescribes, directly for them, a rule of evidence not to be departed from. If the legislature should change that rule, and declare *one* witness, or a confession *out* of court, sufficient for conviction, must the constitutional principle yield to the legislative act?

From these, and many other selections which might be made, it is apparent that the framers of the Constitution contemplated that instrument as a rule for the government of *courts,* as well as of the legislature.

Why otherwise does it direct the judges to take an oath to support it? This oath certainly applies in an especial manner to their conduct in their official character. How immoral to impose it on them, if they were to be used as the instruments, and the knowing instruments, for violating what they swear to support?

The oath of office, too, imposed by the legislature, is completely demonstrative of the legislative opinion on this subject. It is in these words: "I do solemnly swear that I will administer justice without respect to persons, and do equal right to the poor and to the rich; and that I will faithfully and impartially discharge all the duties incumbent on me as—, according to the best of my abilities and understanding agreeably to the *Constitution* and laws of the United States."

Why does a judge swear to discharge his duties agreeably to the Constitution of the United States, if that Constitution forms no rule for his government? If it is closed upon him, and cannot be inspected by him?

If such be the real state of things, this is worse than solemn mockery. To prescribe, or take this oath, becomes equally a crime.

It is also not entirely unworthy of observation that, in declaring what shall be the *supreme* law of the land, the *Constitution* itself is first mentioned; and not the laws of the United States generally, but those only which shall be made in *pursuance* of the Constitution, have that rank.

Thus, the particular phraseology of the Constitution of the United States confirms and strengthens the principle, supposed to be essential to all written constitutions, that a law repugnant to the Constitution is void; and that *courts,* as well as other departments, are bound by that instrument.

The rule must be

Discharged.

Eakin v. *Raub*

12 Sergeant & Rawle (Pennsylvania Supreme Court) 330 (1825)

In this otherwise unimportant case, Judge Gibson of the Pennsylvania Supreme Court effectively presents, in a dissenting opinion, the opposite side of the argument made by Chief Justice Marshall in *Marbury* v. *Madi-*

son. Since the facts of the case and the opinion of the Court do not contribute to an understanding of Judge Gibson's argument, they have been omitted.

MR. JUSTICE GIBSON, dissenting. . . .

I am aware, that a right to declare all unconstitutional acts void . . . is generally held as a professional dogma; but I apprehend, rather as a matter of faith than of reason. I admit, that I once embraced the same doctrine, but without examination, and I shall, therefore, state the arguments that impelled me to abandon it, with great respect for those by whom it is still maintained. . . .

. . . The constitution is said to be a law of superior obligation; and consequently, that if it were to come into collision with an act of the legislature, the latter would have to give way; this is conceded. But it is a fallacy, to suppose, that they can come into collision *before the judiciary.* . . .

The constitution and the *right* of the legislature to pass the act, may be in collision; but is that a legitimate subject for judicial determination? If it be, the judiciary must be a peculiar organ, to revise the proceedings of the legislature, and to correct its mistakes; and in what part of the constitution are we to look for this proud preeminence? Viewing the matter in the opposite direction, what would be thought of an act of assembly in which it should be declared that the supreme court had, in a particular case, put a wrong construction on the constitution of the *United States,* and that the judgment should therefore be reversed? It would, doubtless, be thought a usurpation of judicial power. But it is by no means clear, that to declare a law void, which has been enacted according to the forms prescribed in the constitution, is not a usurpation of legislative power. . . . It is the business of the judiciary, to interpret the laws, not scan the authority of the lawgiver; and without the latter, it cannot take cognizance of a collision between a law and the constitution. So that to affirm that the judiciary has a right to judge of the existence of such collision, is to take for granted the very thing to be proved; and that a very cogent argument may be made in this way, I am not disposed to deny. . . . and pronounce what the law is; and that this necessarily involves a consideration of the constitution. It does so: but how far? If the judiciary will inquire into anything beside the form of enactment, where shall it stop? There must be some point of limitation to such an inquiry; for no one will pretend, that a judge would be justifiable in calling for the election returns, or scrutinizing the qualifications of those who composed the legislature. . . .

Every one knows how seldom men think exactly alike on ordinary subjects; and a government constructed on the principle of assent by all its parts, would be inadequate to the most simple operations. The notion of a complication of counter-checks has been carried to an extent in theory, of which the framers of the constitution never dreamt. When the entire sovereignty was separated into its elementary parts, and distributed to the appropriate branches, all things incident to the exercise of its powers were committed to each branch exclusively. The negative which each part of the legislature may exercise, in regard to the acts of the other, was thought sufficient to prevent material infractions of the restraints which were put on the power of the whole; for, had it been intended to interpose the judiciary as an additional barrier, the matter would surely not have been left in doubt. The judges would not have been left to stand on the insecure and ever-shifting ground of public opinion, as to constructive power; they would have been placed on the impregnable ground of an express grant; they would not have been compelled to resort to the debates in the convention, or the opinion that was generally entertained at the time. . . .

But the judges are sworn to support the constitution, and are they not bound by it as the law of the land? In some respects they are. In the very few cases in which the judiciary, and not the legislature, is the immediate organ to execute its provisions, they are bound by it, in preference to any act of assembly to the contrary; in such cases, the constitution is a rule to the courts. But what I have in view in this inquiry is, the supposed right of the judiciary, to interfere, in cases where the constitution is to be carried into effect through the instrumentality of the legislature, and where that organ must necessarily first decide on the constitutionality of its own act. The oath to support the constitution is not peculiar to the judges, but is taken indiscriminately by every officer of the government, and is designed rather as a test of the political principles of the man, than to bind the officer in the discharge of his duty: otherwise, it were difficult to determine, what operation it is to have in the case of a recorder of deeds, for instance, who, in the execution of his office, has nothing to do with the constitution. But granting it to relate to the official conduct of the judge, as well as every other officer, and not to his political principles, still, it must be understood in reference to supporting the constitution, *only as far as that may be involved in his official duty;* and consequently, if his official duty does not comprehend an inquiry into the authority of the legislature, neither does his oath. . . .

But do not the judges do a *positive* act in violation of the constitution, when they give effect to an unconstitutional law? Not if the law has been passed according to the forms established in the constitution. The fallacy of the question is, in supposing that the judiciary adopts the acts of the legislature as its own; whereas, the enactment of a law and the interpretation of it are not concurrent acts, and as the judiciary is not required to concur in the enactment, neither is it in the breach of the constitution which may be the consequence of the enactment; the fault is imputable to the legislature, and on it the responsibility exclusively rests. . . .

But it has been said, that this construction would deprive the citizen of the advantages which are peculiar to a written constitution, by at once declaring the power of the legislature, in practice, to be illimitable. . . . But there is no magic or inherent power in parchment and ink, to command respect, and protect principles from violation. In the business of government, a recurrence to first principles answers the end of an observation at sea, with a view to correct the dead-reckoning; and for this purpose, a written constitution is an instrument of inestimable value. It is of inestimable value also, in rendering its principles familiar to the mass of the people; for, after all, there is no effectual guard against legislative usurpation, but public opinion, the force of which, in this country, is inconceivably great. . . . Once let public opinion be so corrupt, as to sanction every misconstruction of the constitution, and abuse of power, which the temptation of the moment may dictate, and the party which may happen to be predominant, will laugh at the puny efforts of a dependent power to arrest it in its course.

For these reasons, I am of opinion that it rests with the people, in whom full and absolute sovereign power resides, to correct abuses in legislation, by instructing their representatives to repeal the obnoxious act. What is wanting to plenary power in the government, is reserved by the people, for their own immediate use; and to redress an infringement of their rights in this respect, would seem to be an accessory of the power thus reserved. It might, perhaps, have been better to vest the power in the judiciary; as it might be expected, that its habits of deliberation, and the aid derived from the arguments of counsel, would more frequently lead to accurate conclusions. On the other hand, the judiciary is not infallible; and an error by it would admit of no remedy but a more distinct expression of the public will, through the extraordinary medium of a convention; whereas, an error by the legislature admits of a remedy by an exertion of the same will, in the ordinary exercise of the right of suffrage—a mode better calculated to attain the end, without popular excitement. It may be said, the people would probably not notice an error of their representatives. But they would as probably do so, as notice an error of the judiciary; and beside, it is a *postulate* in the theory of our government, and the very basis of the superstructure, that the people are wise, virtuous, and competent to manage their own affairs: and if they are not so, in fact, still, every question of this sort must be determined according to the principles of the constitution, as it came from the hands of its framers, and the existence of a defect which was not foreseen, would not justify those who administer the government, in applying a corrective in practice, which can be provided only by a convention. . . .

Ex Parte McCardle

74 U.S. (7 Wallace) 506; 19 L. Ed. 264 (1869)

During the post–Civil War period, Radical Republicans in the Congress imposed upon the southern states a Reconstruction program. William McCardle, a Mississippi newspaper editor and opponent of Reconstruction, was held for trial before a military commission on charges that he had allowed to be published articles alleged to be "incendiary and libelous." As a civilian, McCardle asserted that he was being unlawfully restrained and sought a writ of habeas corpus before the Supreme Court under an 1867 statute. The Radical Republican leaders in the Congress feared that the Supreme Court—already hostile to Reconstruction—would use the occasion provided by *McCardle* to declare much of the Reconstruction program unconstitutional. Consequently, Congress, over President Andrew Johnson's veto, repealed the 1867 act on which McCardle's appeal was based. By this time, the Court had already heard full arguments in the case, but it had not yet announced its decision. *Opinion of the Court: Chase, Clifford, Davis, Field, Grier, Miller, Nelson, Swayne.*

MR. CHIEF JUSTICE CHASE delivered the opinion of the Court. . . .

The first question necessarily is that of jurisdiction; for, if the act of March, 1868, takes away the jurisdiction defined by the act of February, 1867, it is useless, if not improper, to enter into any discussion of other questions.

It is quite true, as was argued by the counsel for the petitioner, that the appellate jurisdiction of this court is not derived from acts of Congress. It is, strictly speaking, conferred by the Constitution. But it is conferred "with such exceptions and under such regulations as Congress shall make."

It is unnecessary to consider whether, if Congress had made no exceptions and no regulations, this court might not have exercised general appellate jurisdiction under rules prescribed by itself. For among the earliest acts of the first Congress, at its first session, was the act of September 24th, 1789, to establish the judicial courts of the United States. That act provided for the organization of this court, and prescribed regulations for the exercise of its jurisdiction.

The source of that jurisdiction, and the limitations of it by the Constitution and by statute, have been on several occasions subjects of consideration here. In the case of *Durousseau* v. *The United States* [1810] . . . particularly, the whole matter was carefully examined, and the court held, that while "the appellate powers of this court are not given by the judicial act, but are given by the Constitution," they are, nevertheless, "limited and regulated by that act, and by such other acts as have been passed on the subject." The court said, further, that the judicial act was an exercise of the power given by the Constitution to Congress "of making exceptions to the appellate jurisdiction of the Supreme Court." "They have described affirmatively," said the court, "its jurisdiction, and this affirmative description has been understood to imply a negation of the exercise of such appellate power as is not comprehended within it."

The principle that the affirmation of appellate jurisdication implies that negation of all such jurisdiction not affirmed having been thus established, it was an almost necessary consequence that acts of Congress, providing for the exercise of jurisdiction, should come to be spoken of as acts granting jurisdiction, and not as acts making exceptions to the constitutional grant of it.

The exception to appellate jurisdiction in the case before us, however, is not an inference from the affirmation of other appellate jurisdiction. It is made in terms. The provision of the act of 1867, affirming the appellate jurisdiction of this court in cases of *habeas corpus* is expressly repealed. It is hardly possible to imagine a plainer instance of positive exception.

We are not at liberty to inquire into the motives of the legislature. We can only examine into its power under the Constitution; and the power to make exceptions to the appellate jurisdiction of this court is given by express words.

What, then, is the effect of the repealing act upon the case before us? We cannot doubt as to this. Without jurisdiction the court cannot proceed at all in any cause. Jurisdiction is power to declare the law, and when it ceases to exist, the only function remaining to the court is that of announcing the fact and dismissing the cause. And this is not less clear upon authority than upon principle.

Several cases were cited by the counsel for the petitioner in support of the position that jurisdiction of this case is not affected by the repealing act. But none of them, in our judgment, afford any support to it. They are all cases of the exercise of judicial power by the legislature, or of legislative interference with courts in the exercising of continuing jurisdiction.

On the other hand, the general rule, supported by the best elementary writers, is, that "when an act of the legislature is repealed, it must be considered, except as to transactions past and closed, as if it never existed." . . .

It is quite clear, therefore, that this court cannot proceed to pronounce judgment in this case, for it has no longer jurisdiction of the appeal; and judicial duty is not less fitly performed by declining ungranted jurisdiction than in exercising firmly that which the Constitution and the laws confer.

Frothingham v. *Mellon*

262 U.S. 447; 43 S. Ct. 597; 67 L. Ed. 1078 (1923)

The Maternity Act of 1921 provided for grants from the United States Treasury to states that agreed to establish, under federal supervision, programs designed to reduce maternal and infant mortality and to protect the health of mothers and infants. Frothingham, a private citizen, brought suit as a taxpayer against Andrew Mellon, secretary of the treasury, alleging that this expenditure of federal funds violated the Due Process Clause of the Fifth Amendment. When the federal district court dismissed Frothingham's suit for want of jurisdiction and the court of appeals affirmed the lower court's decree, she appealed to the Supreme Court. *Opinion of the Court: Sutherland, Brandeis, Butler, Holmes, McKenna, McReynolds, Sanford, Taft, VanDevanter.*

MR. JUSTICE SUTHERLAND delivered the opinion of the Court. . . .

This . . . plaintiff alleges . . . that she is a taxpayer of the United States; and her contention, though not clear, seems to be that the effect of the appropriations complained of will be to increase the burden of future taxation and thereby take her property without due process of law. The right of a taxpayer to enjoin the execution of a federal appropriation act, on the ground that it is invalid and will result in taxation for illegal purposes, has never been passed upon by this Court. In cases where it was presented, the question has either been allowed to pass sub silentio or the determination of it expressly withheld. . . . The interest of a taxpayer of a municipality in the application of its moneys is direct and immediate and the remedy by injunction to prevent their misuse is not inappropriate. It is upheld by a large number of state cases and is the rule of this Court. . . . But the relation of a taxpayer of the United States to the Federal Government is very different. His interest in the moneys of the Treasury—partly realized from taxation and partly from other sources—is shared with millions of others; is comparatively minute and indeterminable; and the effect upon future taxation, of any payment out of the funds, so remote, fluctuating and uncertain, that no basis is afforded for an appeal to the preventive powers of a court of equity.

The administration of any statute, likely to produce additional taxation to be imposed upon a vast number of taxpayers, the extent of whose several liability is indefinite and constantly changing, is essentially a matter of public and not of individual concern. If one taxpayer may champion and litigate such a cause, then every other taxpayer may do the same, not only in respect of the statute here under review but also in respect of every other appropriation act and statute whose administration requires the outlay of public money, and whose validity may be questioned. The bare suggestion of such a result, with its attendant inconveniences, goes far to sustain the conclusion which we have reached, that a suit of this character cannot be maintained. It is of much significance that no precedent sustaining the right to maintain suits like this has been called to our attention, although, since the formation of the government, as an examination of the acts of Congress will disclose, a large number of statutes appropriating or involving the expenditure of moneys for non-federal purposes have been enacted and carried into effect.

The functions of government under our system are apportioned. To the legislative department has been committed the duty of making laws; to the executive the duty of executing them; and to the judiciary the duty of interpreting and applying them in cases properly brought before the courts. The general rule is that neither department may invade the province of the other and neither may control, direct or restrain the action of the other. We are not now speaking of the merely ministerial duties of officials. . . . We have no power per se to review and annul acts of Congress on the ground that they are unconstitutional. That question may be considered only when the justification for some direct injury suffered or threatened, presenting a justiciable issue, is made to rest upon such an act. Then the power exercised is that of ascertaining and declaring the law applicable to the controversy. It amounts to little more than the negative power to disregard an unconstitutional enactment, which otherwise would stand in the way of the enforcement of a legal right. The party who invokes the power must be able to show not only that the statute is invalid but that he has sustained or is immediately in danger of sustaining some direct injury as the result of its enforcement, and not merely that he suffers in some indefinite way in common with people generally. If a case for preventive relief be presented the court enjoins, in effect, not the execution of the statute, but the acts of the official, the statute notwithstanding. Here the . . . plaintiff [has] no such case. Looking through forms of words to the substance of [the] complaint, it is merely that officials of the executive department of the government are executing and will execute an act of Congress asserted to be unconstitutional; and this we are asked to prevent. To do so would be not to decide a judicial controversy, but to assume a position of authority over the governmental acts of another and coequal department, an authority which plainly we do not possess.

Flast v. *Cohen*

392 U.S. 83; 88 S. Ct. 1942; 20 L. Ed. 2d 947 (1968)

Florence Flast and other federal taxpayers filed suit in federal district court to enjoin Wilbur Cohen, secretary of health, education and welfare, from expending funds authorized by Congress under the Elementary and Secondary Education Act of 1965. The act provided funds to finance the instruction of and the purchase of textbooks in reading, arithmetic, and other subjects in religious schools. Flast and the other plaintiffs contended that these expenditures promoted religious programs in violation of the Establishment Clause of the First Amendment. The district court, on the authority of *Frothingham,* held that they lacked standing and dismissed the suit. They appealed to the Supreme Court. *Opinion of the Court: Warren, Black, Brennan, Marshall, White. Concurring opinions: Douglas; Fortas; Stewart. Dissenting opinion: Harlan.*

MR. CHIEF JUSTICE WARREN delivered the opinion of the Court. . . .

This Court first faced squarely the question whether a litigant asserting only his status as a taxpayer has standing to maintain a suit in a federal court in *Frothingham* v. *Mellon* . . . and that decision must be the starting point for analysis in this case. . . .

Although the barrier *Frothingham* erected against federal taxpayer suits has never been breached, the decision has been the source of some confusion and the object of considerable criticism. The confusion has developed as commentators have tried to determine whether *Frothingham* establishes a constitutional bar to taxpayer suits or whether the Court was simply imposing a rule of self-restraint which was not constitutionally compelled. The conflicting viewpoints are reflected in the arguments made to this Court by the parties in this case. The Government has pressed upon us the view that *Frothingham* announced a constitutional rule, compelled by the Article III limitations on federal court jurisdiction and grounded in considerations of the doctrine of separation of powers. Appellants, however, insist that *Frothingham* expressed no more than a policy of judicial self-restraint which can be disregarded when compelling reasons for assuming jurisdiction over a taxpayer's suit exist. The opinion delivered in *Frothingham* can be read to support either position. . . .

The jurisdiction of federal courts is defined and limited by Article III of the Constitution. In terms relevant to the question for decision in this case, the judicial power of federal courts is constitutionally restricted to "cases" and "controversies." As is so often the situation in constitutional adjudication, those two words have an iceberg quality, containing beneath their surface simplicity submerged complexities which go to the very heart of our constitutional form of government. Embodied in the words "cases" and "controversies" are two complementary but somewhat different limitations. In part those words limit the business of federal courts to questions presented in an adversary context and in a form historically viewed as capable of resolution through the judicial process. And in part those words define the role assigned to the judiciary in a tripartite allocation of power to assure that the federal courts will not intrude into areas committed to the other branches of government. Justiciability is the term of art employed to give expression to this dual limitation placed upon federal courts by the case-and-controversy doctrine.

. . . As we understand it, the Government's position is that the constitutional scheme of separation of powers, and the deference owed by the federal judiciary to the other two branches of government within that scheme, presents an absolute bar to taxpayer suits challenging the validity of federal spending programs. The Government views such suits as involving no more than the mere disagreement by the taxpayer "with the uses to which tax money is put." According to the Government, the resolution of such disagreements is committed to other branches of Federal Government and not to the judiciary. Consequently, the Government contends that, under no circumstances, should standing be conferred on federal taxpayers to challenge a federal taxing or spending program. An analysis of the function served by standing limitations compels a rejection of the Government's position.

Standing is an aspect of justiciability and as such, the problem of standing is surrounded by the same complexities and vagaries that inhere in justiciability. . . . The "gist of the question of standing" is whether the party seeking relief has "alleged such a personal stake in the outcome of the controversy as to assure that concrete adverseness which sharpens the presentation of issues upon which the court so largely depends for illumination of difficult constitutional questions." *Baker* v. *Carr* [1962]. . . . In other words, when standing is placed in issue in a case, the question is whether the person whose standing is challenged is a proper party to request an adjudication of a particular issue and not whether the issue itself is justiciable. . . .

. . . A taxpayer may or may not have the requisite personal stake in the outcome, depending upon the circumstances of the particular case. Therefore, we find no absolute bar in Article III to suits by federal taxpayers challenging allegedly unconstitutional federal taxing and spending programs. There remains, however, the problem of determining the circumstances under which a federal taxpayer will be deemed to have the personal stake and interest that imparts the necessary concrete adverseness to such litigation so that standing can be conferred on the taxpayer *qua* taxpayer consistent with the constitutional limitations of Article III. . . . Whether such individuals have standing to maintain that form of action turns on whether they can demonstrate the necessary stake as taxpayers in the outcome of the litigation to satisfy Article III requirements.

The nexus demanded of federal taxpayers has two aspects to it. First, the taxpayer must establish a logical link between that status and the type of legislative enactment attacked. Thus, a taxpayer will be a proper party to allege the unconstitutionality only of exercises of congressional power under the taxing and spending clause of Art. I, § 8, of the Constitution. It will not be sufficient to allege an incidental expenditure of tax funds in the administration of an essentially regulatory statute. Secondly the taxpayer must establish a nexus between that status and the precise nature of the constitutional infringement alleged. Under this requirement, the taxpayer must show that the challenged enactment exceeds specific constitutional limitations imposed upon the exercise of the congressional taxing and spending power and not simply that the enactment is generally beyond the powers delegated to Congress by Art. I, § 8. When both nexuses are established, the litigant will have shown a taxpayer's stake in the outcome of the controversy and will be a proper and appropriate party to invoke a federal court's jurisdiction. . . .

The taxpayer-appellants in this case have satisfied both nexuses to support their claim of standing under the test we announce today. Their constitutional challenge is made to an exercise by Congress of its power under Art. I, § 8, to spend for the general welfare, and the challenged program involves a substantial expenditure of federal tax funds. In addition, appellants have alleged that the challenged expenditures violate the Establishment and Free Exercise Clauses of the First Amendment. . . .

Reversed.

MR. JUSTICE HARLAN, dissenting.

The problems presented by this case are narrow and relatively abstract, but the principles by which they must be resolved involve nothing less than the proper functioning of the federal courts, and so run to the roots of our constitutional system. . . .

It is desirable first to restate the basic issues in this case. The lawsuits here and in *Frothingham.* They present the question whether federal taxpayers *qua* taxpayers may, in suits in which they do not contest the validity of their previous or existing tax obligations, challenge the constitutionality of the uses for which Congress has authorized the expenditure of public funds.

This Court has previously held that individual litigants have standing to represent the public interest, despite their lack of economic or other personal interests, if Congress has appropriately authorized such suits. . . . I would adhere to that principle. Any hazards to the proper allocation of authority among the three branches of the Government would be substantially diminished if public actions had been pertinently authorized by Congress and the President. I appreciate that this Court does not ordinarily await the mandate of other branches of the Government, but it seems to me that the extraordinary character of public actions, and of the mischievous, if not dangerous, consequences they involve for the proper functioning of our constitutional system, and in particular of the federal courts, makes such judicial forbearance the part of wisdom. It must be emphasized that the implications of these questions of judicial policy are of fundamental significance for the other branches of the Federal Government.

The question here is not, despite the Court's unarticulated premise, whether the religious clauses of the First Amendment are hereafter to be enforced by the federal courts; the issue is simply whether plaintiffs of an *additional* category, heretofore excluded from those courts, are to be permitted to maintain suits. The recent history of this Court is replete with illustrations, including even one announced today . . . that questions involving the religious clauses will not, if federal taxpayers are prevented from contesting federal expenditures, be left "unacknowledged, unresolved, and undecided."

Accordingly, for the reasons contained in this opinion, I would affirm the judgment of the District Court.

Allen v. *Wright*

468 U.S. 737, 104 S. Ct. 3315, 82 L. Ed. 2d 556 (1984)

The Internal Revenue Service (IRS) denies tax-exempt status under the Internal Revenue Code to racially discriminatory private schools and has established guidelines and procedures for determining whether a particular school is in fact racially discriminatory. A school denied tax-exempt status is also denied eligibility to receive charitable contributions deductible from income taxes under the Code. Inez Wright and other parents of black children who were attending public schools in seven states in school districts undergoing desegregation brought a nationwide class action in United States District Court for the District of Columbia against Treasury and IRS officials (W. Wayne Allen, the head of a private school identified in the complaint, intervened as a defendant), alleging that the IRS had not adopted sufficient standards and procedures to fulfill its obligation to deny tax-exempt status to racially discriminatory private schools and had thereby harmed the respondents directly and interfered with their children's opportunity to receive an education in desegregated public schools. They also alleged that many racially segregated private schools were created or expanded in their communities at the time the public schools were undergoing desegregation and had received tax exemptions despite the IRS policy and guidelines, and that these unlawful tax exemptions harmed them in that they constituted tangible financial aid for racially segregated educational institutions and encouraged the organization and expansion of institutions that provided segregated educational opportunities for white students avoiding attendance in the public schools. The respondents did not allege that their children had ever applied or would ever apply for admission to any private school. The District Court dismissed their complaint and request for declaratory and injunctive relief on the ground that the respondents lacked standing to bring the suit. The Court of Appeals for the District of Columbia reversed and remanded, and the Supreme Court granted certiorari. *Opinion of the Court: O'Connor, Burger, Powell, Rehnquist, White. Dissenting Opinions: Brennan; Stevens, Blackmun. Not participating: Marshall.*

JUSTICE O'CONNOR delivered the opinion of the Court.

Article III of the Constitution confines the federal courts to adjudicating actual "cases" and "controversies." As the Court explained in *Valley Forge Christian College* v. *Americans United for Separation of Church and State, Inc.* . . . the "case or controversy" requirement defines with respect to the Judicial Branch the idea of separation of powers on which the Federal Government is founded. The several doctrines that have grown up to elaborate that requirement are "founded in concern about the proper—and properly limited—role of the courts in a democratic society.". . .

The Art. III doctrine that requires a litigant to have "standing" to invoke the power of a federal court is perhaps the most important of these doctrines. . . . Standing doctrine embraces several judicially self-imposed limits on the exercise of federal jurisdiction, such as the general prohibition on a litigant's raising another person's legal rights, the rule barring adjudication of generalized grievances more appropriately addressed in the representative branches, and the requirement that a plaintiff's complaint fall within the zone of interests protected by the law invoked. . . . The requirement of standing, however, has a core component derived directly from the Constitution. A plaintiff must allege personal injury fairly traceable to the defendant's allegedly unlawful conduct and likely to be redressed by the requested relief. . . .

Like the prudential component, the constitutional component of standing doctrine incorporates concepts concededly not susceptible of precise definition. . . .

The absence of precise definitions, however, as this Court's extensive body of case law on standing illustrates, . . . hardly leaves courts at sea in applying the law of standing. Like most legal notions, the standing concepts have gained considerable definition from developing case law. In many cases the standing question can be answered chiefly by comparing the allegations of the particular complaint to those made in prior standing cases. . . . More important, the law of Art. III standing is built on a single basic idea—the idea of separation of powers. It is this fact which makes possible the gradual clarification of the law through judicial application. Of course, both federal and state courts have long experience in applying and elaborating in numerous contexts the pervasive and fundamental notion of separation of powers. . . .

Respondents allege two injuries in their complaint to support their standing to bring this lawsuit. First, they say that they are harmed directly by the mere fact of Government financial aid to discriminatory private schools. Second, they say that the federal tax exemptions to racially discriminatory private schools in their communities impair their ability to have their public schools desegregated.

. . . We conclude that neither suffices to support respondents' standing. The first fails under clear precedents of this Court because it does not constitute judicially cognizable injury. The second fails because the alleged injury is not fairly traceable to the assertedly unlawful conduct of the IRS.

Respondents' first claim of injury can be interpreted in two ways. It might be a claim simply to have the Government avoid the violation of law alleged in respondents' complaint. Alternatively, it might be a claim of stigmatic injury, or denigration, suffered by all members of a racial group when the Government discriminates on the basis of race. Under neither interpretation is this claim of injury judicially cognizable.

This Court has repeatedly held that an asserted right to have the Government act in accordance with law is not sufficient, standing alone, to confer jurisdiction on a federal court.

. . . Recently, in *Valley Forge,* we rejected a claim of standing to challenge a Government conveyance of property to a religious institution. Insofar as the plaintiffs relied simply on " 'their shared individuated right' " to a Government that made no law respecting an establishment of religion, we held that plaintiffs had not alleged a judicially cognizable injury. "[A]ssertion of a right to a particular kind of Government conduct, which the Government has violated by acting differently, cannot alone satisfy the requirements of Art. III without draining those requirements of meaning." Respondents here have no standing to complain simply that their Government is violating the law.

Neither do they have standing to litigate their claims based on the stigmatizing injury often caused by racial discrimination. There can be no doubt that this sort of noneconomic injury is one of the most serious consequences of discriminatory government action and is sufficient in some circumstances to support standing. . . . Our cases make clear, however, that such injury accords a basis for standing only to "those persons who are personally denied equal treatment" by the challenged discriminatory conduct.

If the abstract stigmatic injury were cognizable, standing would extend nationwide to all members of the particular racial groups against which the Government was alleged to be discriminating by its grant of a tax exemption to a racially discriminatory school, regardless of the location of that school. All such persons could claim the same sort of abstract stigmatic injury respondents assert in their first claim of injury. A black person in Hawaii could challenge the grant of a tax exemption to a racially discriminatory school in Maine. Recognition of standing in such circumstances would transform the federal courts into "no more than a vehicle for the vindication of the value interests of concerned bystanders." . . .Constitutional limits on the role of the federal courts preclude such a transformation.

It is in their complaint's second claim of injury that respondents allege harm to a concrete, personal interest that can support standing in some circumstances. The injury they identify—their children's diminished ability to receive an education in a racially integrated school—is, beyond any doubt, not only judicially cognizable but . . . one of the most serious injuries recognized in our legal system. Despite the constitutional importance of curing the injury alleged by respondents, however, the federal judiciary may not redress it unless standing requirements are met. In this case, respondents' second claim of injury cannot support standing because the injury alleged is not fairly traceable to the Government conduct respondents challenge as unlawful.

The diminished ability of respondents' children to receive a desegregated education would be fairly traceable to unlawful IRS grants of tax exemptions only if there were enough racially discriminatory private schools receiving tax exemptions in respondents' communities for withdrawal of those exemptions to make an appreciable difference in public-school integration. Respondents have made no such allegation. It is, first, uncertain how many racially discriminatory private schools are in fact receiving tax exemptions. Moreover, it is entirely speculative, as respondents themselves conceded in the Court of Appeals, . . . whether withdrawal of a tax exemption from any particular school would lead the school to change its policies. . . . It is just as speculative whether any given parent of a child attending such a private school would decide to transfer the child to public school as a result of any changes in educational or financial policy made by the private school once it was threatened with loss of tax-exempt status. It is also pure speculation whether, in a particular community, a large enough number of the numerous relevant school officials and parents would reach decisions that collectively would have a significant impact on the racial composition of the public schools.

The links in the chain of causation between the challenged Government conduct and the asserted injury are far too weak for the chain as a whole to sustain respondents' standing. . . .

The idea of separation of powers that underlies standing doctrine explains why our cases preclude the conclusion that respondents' alleged injury "fairly can be traced to the challenged action" of the IRS. . . . That conclusion would pave the way generally for suits challenging, not specifically identifiable Government violations of law, but the particular programs agencies establish to carry out their legal obligations. Such suits, even when premised on allegations of several instances of violations of law, are rarely if ever appropriate for federal-court adjudication.

"Carried to its logical end, [respondents'] approach would have the federal courts as virtually continuing monitors of the wisdom and soundness of Executive action; such a role is appropriate for the Congress acting through its committees and the 'power of the purse'; it is not the role of the judiciary, absent actual present or immediately threatened injury resulting from unlawful governmental action."

The Constitution, after all, assigns to the Executive Branch, and not to the Judicial Branch, the duty to "take Care that the Laws be faithfully executed." U.S. Const., Art. II, § 3. We could not recognize respondents' standing in this case without running afoul of that structural principle. . . .

JUSTICE BRENNAN, dissenting.

In these cases, the respondents have alleged at least one type of injury that satisfies the constitutional requirement of "distinct and palpable injury." In particular, they claim that the IRS' grant of tax-exempt status to racially discriminatory private schools directly injures their children's opportunity and ability to receive a desegregated education. . . .

Fully explicating the injury alleged helps to explain why it is fairly traceable to the governmental conduct challenged by the respondents. As the respondents specifically allege in their complaint:

"Defendants have fostered and encouraged the development, operation and expansion of many of these racially segregated private schools by recognizing them as "charitable" organizations described in Section 501(c)(3) of the Internal Revenue Code, and exempt from federal income taxation under Section 501(a) of the Code. Once the schools are classified as tax-exempt . . . , contributions made to them are deductible from gross income on individual and corporate income tax returns. . . . Moreover, [the] organizations . . . are also exempt from federal social security taxes. . . . and from federal unemployment taxes. . . . The resulting exemptions and deductions provide tangible financial aid and other benefits which support the operation of racially segregated private schools. In particular, the resulting deductions facilitate the raising of funds to organize new schools and expand existing schools in order to accommodate white students avoiding attendance in desegregating public school districts. Additionally, the existence of a federal tax exemption amounts to a federal stamp of approval which facilitates fund raising on behalf of racially segregated private schools. Finally, by supporting the development, operation and expansion of institutions providing racially segregated educational opportunities for white children avoiding attendance in desegregating public schools, defendants are thereby interfering with the efforts of courts, HEW and local school authorities to desegregate public school districts which have been operating racially dual school systems."

Viewed in light of the injuries they claim, the respondents have alleged a direct causal relationship between the government action they challenge and the injury they suffer: their inability to receive an education in a racially integrated school is directly and adversely affected by the tax-exempt status granted by the IRS to racially discriminatory schools in their respective school districts. Commonsense alone would recognize that the elimination of tax-exempt status for racially discriminatory private schools would serve to lessen the impact that those institutions have in defeating efforts to desegregate the public schools.

What is most disturbing about today's decision, therefore, is not the standing analysis applied, but the indifference evidenced by the Court to the detrimental effects that racially segregated schools, supported by tax-exempt status from the federal government, have on the respondents' attempt to obtain an education in a racially integrated school system. I cannot join such indifference, and would give the respondents a chance to prove their case on the merits.

Luther v. *Borden*

48 U.S. (7 Howard) 1; 12 L. Ed. 581 (1849)

In 1841, Rhode Island was still operating under a system of government established in 1663 under a colonial charter, granted by Charles II, that made no provision for amendment and strictly limited the right to vote. Dissident groups, protesting especially the limits on suffrage, combined that year to form a popular convention and draft a new constitution. In elections held in 1842, Thomas Dorr was elected governor. The old charter government continued to operate, however, and when it responded to the insurgent government by declaring martial law, the charter governor appealed to President John Tyler for military support. Although no federal troops were ever sent, the Dorr Rebellion was soon crushed, and the insurgent government collapsed.

On instructions from the charter government to gather up the dispersed and defeated insurgents, Luther Borden and other state militiamen set out to arrest Martin Luther, a Dorr supporter. In the process, they broke into and searched his home, whereupon Luther sued for illegal trespass, alleging that under Article IV, Section 4, which guarantees to each state a republican form of government, the charter government had been supplanted by the more representative insurgent government, and that as a consequence it was not the lawful government of the state. Because the charter government was not the lawful government, Luther continued, Borden and his men could not defend their actions by claiming to be agents of the state. Borden responded that the charter government was the lawful government and that his search was legitimate. Luther moved to Massachusetts in order to bring the case before the federal courts on the basis of diversity of citizenship. The federal courts were thus invited to determine which of the two governments was the lawful government of Rhode Island. After a federal circuit court ruled in Borden's favor, Luther brought the case to the Supreme Court on a writ of error. *Opinion of the Court: Taney, Grier, McLean, Nelson, Wayne. Dissenting opinion: Woodbury, Catron, Daniel. McKinley did not participate.*

Mr. Chief Justice Taney delivered the opinion of the Court. . . .

The fourth section of the fourth article of the Constitution of the United States provides that the United States shall guarantee to every State in the Union a republican form of government, and shall protect each of them against invasion; and on the application of the legislature or of the executive (when the legislature cannot be convened) against domestic violence.

Under this article of the Constitution it rests with Congress to decide what government is the established one in a State. For as the United States guarantee to each State a republican government, Congress must necessarily decide what government is established in the State before it can determine whether it is republican or not. And when the senators and representatives of a State are admitted into the councils of the Union, the authority of the government under which they are appointed, as well as its republican character, is recognized by the proper constitutional authority. And its decision is binding on every other department of the government, and could not be questioned in a judicial tribunal. It is true that the contest in this case did not last long enough to bring the matter to this issue; and as no senators or representatives were elected under the authority of the government of which Mr. Dorr was the head, Congress was not called upon to decide the controversy. Yet the right to decide is placed there, and not in the courts.

So, too, as relates to the clause in the above-mentioned article of the Constitution, providing for cases of domestic violence. It rested with Congress, too, to determine upon the means proper to be adopted to fulfill this guarantee. They might, if they had deemed it most advisable to do so, have placed it in the power of a court to decide when the contingency had happened which required the federal government to interfere. But Congress thought otherwise, and no doubt wisely; and by the act of February 28, 1795, provided, that "in case of an insurrection in any State against the government thereof, it shall be lawful for the President of the United States, on application of the legislature of such State or of the executive (when the legislature cannot be convened), to call forth such number of the militia of any other State or States, as may be applied for, as he may judge sufficient to suppress such insurrection."

By this act, the power of deciding whether the exigency had arisen upon which the government of the United States is bound to interfere, is given to the President. He is to act upon the application of the legislature or of the executive, and consequently he must determine what body of men constitute the legislature, and who is the governor, before he can act. The fact that both parties claim the right to the government cannot alter the case, for both cannot be entitled to it. If there is an armed conflict, like the one of which we are speaking, it is a case of domestic violence, and one of the parties must be in insurrection against the lawful government. And the President must, of necessity, decide which is the government, and which party is unlawfully arrayed against it, before he can perform the duty imposed upon him by the act of Congress.

After the President has acted and called out the militia, is a Circuit Court of the United States authorized to inquire whether his decision was right? Could the court, while the parties were actually contending in arms for the possession of the government, call witnesses before it and inquire which party represented a majority of the people? If it could, then it would become the duty of the court (provided it came to the conclusion that the President had decided incorrectly) to discharge those who were arrested or detained by the troops in the service of the United States or the government which the President was endeavoring to maintain. If the judicial power extends so far, the guarantee contained in the Constitution of the United States is a guarantee of anarchy, and not of order. Yet if this right does not reside in the courts when the conflict is raging, if the judicial power is at that time bound to follow the decision of the political, it must be equally bound when the contest is over. It cannot, when peace is restored, punish as offenses and crimes the acts which it before recognized, and was bound to recognize, as lawful.

It is true that in this case the militia were not called out by the President. But upon the application of the governor under the charter government, the President recognized him as the executive power of the State, and took measures to call out the militia to support his authority if it should be found necessary for the general government to interfere; and it is admitted in the argument, that it was the knowledge of this decision that put an end to the armed opposition to the charter government, and prevented any further efforts to establish by force the proposed constitution. The interference of the President, therefore, by announcing his determination, was as effectual as if the militia had been assembled under his orders. And it should be equally authoritative. For certainly no court of the United States, with a knowledge of this decision, would have been justified in recognizing the opposing party as the lawful government, or in treating as wrongdoers or insurgents the officers of the government which the President had recognized, and was prepared to support by an armed force. In the case of foreign nations, the government acknowledged by the President is always recognized by the courts of justice. And this principle has been applied by the act of Congress to the sovereign States of the Union.

It is said that this power in the President is dangerous to liberty, and may be abused. All power may be abused if placed in unworthy hands. But it would be difficult, we think, to point out any other hands in which this power would be more safe, and at the same time equally effectual. When citizens of the same State are in arms against each other, and the constituted authorities unable to execute the laws, the interposition of the United States must be prompt, or it is of little value. The ordinary course of proceedings in courts of justice would be utterly unfit for the crisis. And the elevated office of the President, chosen as he is by the people of the United States, and the high responsibility he could not fail to feel when acting in a case of so much moment, appear to furnish as strong safeguards against a wilful abuse of power as human prudence and foresight could well provide. At all events, it is conferred upon him by the Constitution and laws of the United States, and must therefore be respected and enforced in its judicial tribunals. . . .

Undoubtedly, if the President in exercising this power shall fall into error, or invade the rights of the people of the State, it would be in the power of Congress to apply the proper remedy. But the courts must administer the law as they find it. . . .

Much of the argument on the part of the plaintiff turned upon political rights and political questions, upon which the court has been urged to express an opinion. We decline doing so. The high power has been conferred on this court of passing judgment upon the acts of the State sovereignties, and of the legislative and executive branches of the federal government, and of determining whether they are beyond the limits of power marked out for them respectively by the Constitution of the United States. This tribunal, therefore, should be the last to overstep the boundaries which limit its own jurisdiction. And while it should always be ready to meet any question confided to it by the Constitution, it is equally its duty not to pass beyond its appropriate sphere of action, and to take care not to involve itself in discussions which properly belong to other forums. No one we believe, has ever doubted the proposition, that, according to the institutions of this country, the sovereignty in every State resides in the people of the State, and that they may alter and change their form of government at their own pleasure. But whether they have changed it or not by abolishing an old government, and establishing a new one in its place, is a question to be settled by the political power. And when that power has decided, the courts are bound to take notice of its decision, and to follow it.

The judgment of the circuit court must therefore be

Affirmed.

Baker v. *Carr*

369 U.S. 186; 82 S. Ct. 691; 7 L. Ed. 2d 663 (1962)

The Tennessee Constitution provides that representation in both houses of the state legislature shall be based on population and that legislators shall be apportioned every ten years on the basis of the federal census. Despite the constitutional requirement, the legislature had not reapportioned since 1901 when, in 1959, Charles Baker and other qualified voters in Tennessee brought suit in federal court against Joe Carr, Tennessee secretary of state, and other public officials, alleging deprivation of federal constitutional rights. The plaintiffs argued that the State's system of apportionment was "utterly arbitrary" and thereby deprived them of equal protection of the laws under the Fourteenth Amendment "by virtue of debasement of their votes." A three-member district court, relying on *Colegrove* v. *Green* (1946), dismissed their suit, whereupon the case went to the Supreme Court on appeal. *Opinion of the Court: Brennan, Black, Clark, Douglas, Stewart, Warren. Concurring opinions: Clark; Douglas; Stewart. Dissenting opinions: Frankfurter, Harlan; Harlan, Frankfurter. Not participating: Whittaker.*

MR. JUSTICE BRENNAN delivered the opinion of the Court. . . .

. . . We hold today only (a) that the [District Court] possessed jurisdiction of the subject matter; (b) that a justiciable cause of action is stated upon which appellants would be entitled to appropriate relief; and (c) because appellees raise the issue before this Court, that the appellants have standing to challenge the Tennessee apportionment statutes. Beyond noting that we have no cause at this stage to doubt the District Court will be able to fashion relief if violations of constitutional rights are found, it is improper now to consider what remedy would be most appropriate if appellants prevail at the trial.

Jurisdiction of the Subject Matter

The District Court was uncertain whether our cases withholding federal judicial relief rested upon a lack of federal jurisdiction or upon the inappropriateness of the subject matter for judicial consideration—what we have designated "nonjusticiability." The distinction between the two grounds is significant. In the instance of nonjusticiability, consideration of the cause is not wholly and immediately foreclosed; rather, the Court's inquiry necessarily proceeds to the point of deciding whether the duty asserted can be judicially identified and its breach judicially determined, and whether protection for the right asserted can be judicially molded. In the instance of lack of jurisdiction the cause either does not "arise under" the Federal Constitution, laws or treaties (or fall within one of the other enumerated categories of Art. III, § 2), or is not a "case or controversy" within the meaning of that section; or the cause is not one described by any jurisdictional statute. Our conclusion . . . that this cause presents no nonjusticiable "political question" settles the only possible doubt that it is a case or controversy. Under the present heading of "Jurisdiction of the Subject Matter" we hold only that the matter set forth in the complaint does arise under the Constitution. . . .

Standing

A federal court cannot "pronounce any statute, either of a state or of the United States, void, because irreconcilable with the constitution, except as it is called upon to adjudge the legal rights of litigants in actual controversies." *Liverpool, N.Y. & P. Steamship Co.* v. *Commissioners of Emigration*. . . . Have the appellants alleged such a personal stake in the outcome of the controversy as to assure that concrete adverseness which sharpens the presentation of issues upon which the court so largely depends for illumination of difficult constitutional questions? This is the gist of the question of standing. It is, of course, a question of federal law. . . .

We hold that the appellants do have standing to maintain this suit. Our decisions plainly support this conclusion. Many of the cases have assumed rather than articulated the premise in deciding the merits of similar claims. . . .

These appellants seek relief in order to protect or vindicate an interest of their own, and of those similarly situated. Their constitutional claim is, in substance, that the 1901 statute constitutes arbitrary and capricious state action, offensive to the Fourteenth Amendment in its irrational disregard of the standard of apportionment prescribed by the State's Constitution or of any standard, effecting a gross disproportion of representation to voting population. The injury which appellants assert is that this classification disfavors the voters in the counties in which they reside, placing them in a position of constitutionally unjustifiable inequality *vis-à-vis* voters in irrationally favored counties. . . .

It would not be necessary to decide whether appellants' allegations of impairment of their votes by the 1901 apportionment will, ultimately, entitle them to any relief, in order to hold that they have standing to seek it. If such impairment does produce a legally cognizable injury, they are among those who have sustained it. They are asserting "a plain, direct and adequate interest in maintaining the effectiveness of their votes," . . . not merely a claim of "the right possessed by every citizen 'to require that the government be administered according to law.' " . . .

Justiciability

In holding that the subject matter of this suit was not justiciable, the District Court relied on *Colegrove* v. *Green* [1946] . . . and subsequent *per curiam* cases. . . . We understand the District Court to have read the cited cases as compelling the conclusion that since the appellants sought to have a legislative apportionment held unconstitutional, their suit presented a "political question" and was therefore nonjusticiable. We hold that this challenge to an apportionment presents no nonjusticiable "political questions." The cited cases do not hold the contrary.

Of course the mere fact that the suit seeks protection of a political right does not mean it presents a political question. Such an objection "is little more than a play upon words." . . . Rather, it is argued that apportionment cases, whatever the actual wording of the complaint, can involve no federal constitutional right except one resting on the guaranty of a republican form of government, and that complaints based on that clause have been held to present political questions which are nonjusticiable.

We hold that the claim pleaded here neither rests upon nor implicates the Guaranty Clause and that its justiciability is therefore not foreclosed by our decisions of cases involving that clause. The District Court misinterpreted *Colegrove* v. *Green* and other decisions of this Court on which it relied. Appellants' claim that they are being denied equal protection is justiciable, and if "discrimination is sufficiently shown, the right to relief under the equal protection clause is not diminished by the fact that the discrimination relates to political rights." *Snowden* v. *Hughes [1944]*. . . . To show why we reject the argument based on the Guaranty Clause, we deem it necessary first to consider the contours of the "political question" doctrine.

Our discussion requires review of a number of political question cases, in order to expose the attributes of the doctrine. . . . That review reveals that in the Guaranty Clause cases and in the other "political question" cases, it is the relationship between the judiciary and the coordinate branches of the Federal Government, and not the federal judiciary's relationship to the States, which gives rise to the "political question." . . .

The nonjusticiability of a political question is primarily a function of the separation of powers. Much confusion results from the capacity of the "political question" label to obscure the need for case-by-case inquiry. Deciding whether a matter has in any measure been committed by the Constitution to another branch of government, or whether the action of that branch exceeds whatever authority has been committed, is itself a delicate exercise in constitutional interpretation, and is a responsibility of this Court as ultimate interpreter of the Constitution. . . .

. . . Prominent on the surface of any case held to involve a political question is found a textually demonstrable constitutional commitment of the issue to a coordinate political department; or a lack of judicially discoverable and manageable standards for resolving it; or the impossibility of deciding without an initial policy determination of a kind clearly for nonjudicial discretion; or the impossibility of a court's undertaking independent resolution without expressing lack of the respect due coordinate branches of government; or an unusual need for unquestioning adherence to a political decision already made; or the potentiality of embarrassment from multifarious pronouncements by various departments on one question.

Unless one of these formulations is inextricable from the case at bar, there should be no dismissal for nonjusticiability on the ground of a political question's presence. The doctrine of which we treat is one of "political questions," not one of "political cases." The courts cannot reject as "no law suit" a bona fide controversy as to whether some action denominated "political" exceeds constitutional authority. . . .

But it is argued that this case shares the characteristics of decisions that constitute a category not yet considered, cases concerning the Constitution's guaranty, in Art. IV, § 4, of a republican form of government. . . .

. . . A natural beginning is to note whether any of the common characteristics which we have been able to identify and label descriptively are present. We find none: The question here is the consistency of state action with the Federal Constitution. We have no question decided, or to be decided, by a political branch of government coequal with this Court. Nor do we risk embarrassment of our government abroad, or grave disturbance at home if we take issue with Tennessee as to the constitutionality of her action here challenged. Nor need the appellants, in order to succeed in this action, ask the Court to enter upon policy determinations for which judicially manageable standards are lacking. Judicial standards under the Equal Protection Clause are well developed and familiar, and it has been open to courts since the enactment of the Fourteenth Amendment to determine, if on the particular facts they must, that a discrimination reflects *no* policy, but simply arbitrary and capricious action.

This case does, in one sense, involve the allocation of political power within a State, and the appellants might conceivably have added a claim under the Guaranty Clause. Of course, as we have seen, any reliance on that clause would be futile. But because any reliance on the Guaranty Clause could not have succeeded it does not follow that appellants may not be heard on the equal protection claim which in fact they tender. True, it must be clear that the Fourteenth Amendment claim is not so enmeshed with those political question elements which render Guaranty Clause claims nonjusticiable as actually to present a political question itself. But we have found that not to be the case here. . . .

We conclude then that the nonjusticiability of claims resting on the Guaranty Clause which arises from their embodiment of questions that were thought "political," can have no bearing upon the justiciability of the equal protection claim presented in this case. Finally, we emphasize that it is the involvement in Guaranty Clause claims of the elements thought to define "political questions," and no other feature, which could render them nonjusticiable. Specifically, we have said that such claims are not held nonjusticiable because they touch matters of state governmental organization. . . .

We conclude that the complaint's allegations of a denial of equal protection present a justiciable constitutional cause of action upon which appellants are entitled to a trial and a decision. The right asserted is within the reach of judicial protection under the Fourteenth Amendment.

The judgment of the District Court is reversed and the cause is remanded for further proceedings consistent with this opinion.

Reversed and remanded.

MR. JUSTICE CLARK, concurring. . . .

Although I find the Tennessee apportionment statute offends the Equal Protection Clause, I would not consider intervention by this Court into so delicate a field if there were any other relief available to the people of Tennessee. But the majority of the people of Tennessee have no "practical opportunities for exerting their political weight at the polls" to correct the existing "invidious discrimination." Tennessee has no initiative and referendum. I have searched diligently for other "practical opportunities" present under the law. I find none other than through the federal courts. The majority of the voters have been caught up in a legislative strait jacket. Tennessee has an "informed, civically militant electorate" and "an aroused popular conscience," but it does not sear "the conscience of the people's representatives." This is because the legislative policy has riveted the present seats in the Assembly to their respective constituencies, and by the votes of their incumbents a reapportionment of any kind is prevented. The people have been rebuffed at the hands of the Assembly; they have tried the constitutional convention route, but since the call must originate in the Assembly it, too, has been fruitless. They have tried Tennessee courts with the same result and Governors have fought the tide only to flounder. It is said that there is recourse in Congress and perhaps that may be, but from a practical standpoint this is without substance. To date Congress has never undertaken such a task in any State. We therefore must conclude that the people of Tennessee are stymied and without judicial intervention will be saddled with the present discrimination in the affairs of their state government. . . .

MR. JUSTICE FRANKFURTER, whom MR. JUSTICE HARLAN joins, dissenting.

We were soothingly told at the bar of this Court that we need not worry about the kind of remedy a court could effectively fashion once the abstract constitutional right to have courts pass on a state-wide system of electoral districting is recognized as a matter of judicial rhetoric, because legislatures would heed the Court's admonition. This is not only an euphoric hope. It implies a sorry confession of judicial impotence in place of a frank acknowledgment that there is not under the Constitution a judicial remedy for every political mischief, for every undesirable exercise of legislative power. The Framers carefully and with deliberate forethought refused so to enthrone the judiciary. In this situation, as in others of like nature, appeal for relief does not belong here. Appeal must be to an informed, civically militant electorate. In a democratic society like ours, relief must come through an aroused popular conscience that sears the conscience of the people's representatives. In any event there is nothing judicially more unseemly nor more self-defeating than for this Court to make in terrorem pronouncements, to indulge in merely empty rhetoric, sounding a word of promise to the ear, sure to be disappointing to the hope. . . .

In sustaining appellants' claim, based on the Fourteenth Amendment, that the District Court may entertain this suit, this Court's uniform course of decision over the years is overruled or disregarded. Explicitly it begins with *Colegrove* v. *Green* . . . but its roots run deep in the Court's historic adjudicatory process. . . .

The *Colegrove* doctrine, in the form in which repeated decisions have settled it, was not an innovation. It represents long judicial thought and experience. From its earliest opinions this Court has consistently recognized a class of controversies which do not lend themselves to judicial standards and judicial remedies. . . .

The influence of . . . converging considerations—the caution not to undertake decision where standards meet for judicial judgment are lacking, the reluctance to interfere with matters of state government in the absence of an unquestionable and effectively enforceable mandate, the unwillingness to make courts arbiters of the broad issues of political organization historically committed to other institutions and for whose adjustment the judicial process is ill-adapted—has been decisive of the settled line of cases, reaching back more than a century, which holds that Article IV, Section 4, of the Constitution, guaranteeing to the States "a Republican Form of Government," is not enforceable through the courts. . . .

The present case involves all of the elements that have made the Guarantee Clause cases nonjusticiable. It is, in effect, a Guarantee Clause claim masquerading under a different label. But it cannot make the case more fit for judicial action that appellants invoke the Fourteenth Amendment rather then Article IV, Section 4, where, in fact, the gist of their complaint is the same—unless it can be found that the Fourteenth Amendment speaks with greater particularity to their situation. . . .

What, then, is this question of legislative apportionment? Appellants invoke the right to vote and to have their votes counted. But they are permitted to vote and their votes are counted. They go to the polls, they cast their ballots, they send their representatives to the state councils. Their complaint is simply that the representatives are not sufficiently numerous or powerful—in short, that Tennessee has adopted a basis of representation with which they are dissatisfied. Talk of "debasement" or "dilution" is circular talk. One cannot speak of "debasement" or "dilution" of the value of a vote until there is first defined a standard of reference as to what a vote should be worth. What is actually asked of the Court in this case is to choose among competing bases of representation—ultimately, really among competing theories of political philosophy—in order to establish an appropriate frame of government for the State of Tennessee and thereby for all the states of the Union.

What Tennessee illustrates is an old and still widespread method of representation—representation by local geographical division, only in part respective of population—in preference to others, others, forsooth, more appealing. Appellants contest this choice and seek to make this Court the arbiter of the disagreement. They would make the Equal Protection Clause the character of adjudication, asserting that the equality which it guarantees comports, if not the assurance of equal weight to every voter's vote, at least the basic conception that representation ought to be proportionate to the population, a standard by reference to which the reasonableness of apportionment plans may be judged.

To find such a political conception legally enforceable in the broad and unspecific guarantee of equal protection is to rewrite the Constitution. . . . Certainly, "equal protection" is no more secure a foundation for judicial judgment of the permissibility of varying forms of representative governments than is "Republican Form." Indeed since "equal protection of the laws" can only mean an equality of persons standing in the same relation to whatever governmental action is challenged, the determination whether treatment is equal presupposes a determination concerning the nature of the relationship. This, with respect to apportionment, means an inquiry into the theoretic base of representation in an acceptably republican state. For a court could not determine the equal-protection issue without in fact first determining the Republican-Form issue, simply because what is reasonable for equal protection purposes will depend upon what frame of government, basically, is allowed. To divorce "equal protection" from "Republican Form" is to talk about half a question.

The notion that representation proportioned to the geographic spread of population is so universally accepted as a necessary element of equality between man and man that it must be taken to be the standard of a political equality preserved by the Fourteenth Amendment—that it is, in appellants' words "the basic principle of representative government"—is, to put it bluntly, not true. However desirable and however desired by some among the great political thinkers and framers of our government, it has never been generally practiced, today or in the past. It was not the English system, it was not the colonial system, it was not the system chosen for the national government by the Constitution, it was not the system exclusively or even predominantly practiced by the States today. Unless judges, the judges of this Court, are to make their private views of political wisdom the measure of the Constitution—views which in all honesty cannot but give the appearance, if not reflect the reality, of involvement with the business of partisan politics so inescapably a part of apportionment controversies—the Fourteenth Amendment, "itself a historical product," . . . provides no guide for judicial oversight of the representation problem. . . .

Manifestly, the Equal Protection Clause supplies no clearer guide for judicial examination of apportionment methods than would the Guarantee Clause itself. Apportionment, by its character, is a subject of extraordinary complexity, involving—even after the fundamental theoretical issues concerning what is to be represented in a representative legislature have been fought out or compromised—considerations of geography, demography, electoral convenience, economic and social cohesions or divergencies among particular local groups, communications, the practical effects of political institutions like the lobby and the city machine, ancient traditions and ties of settled usage, respect for proven incumbents of long experience and senior status, mathematical mechanics, censuses compiling relevant data, and a host of others. Legislative responses throughout the country to the apportionment demands of the 1960 Census have glaringly confirmed that these are not factors that lend themselves to evaluations of a nature that are the staple of judicial determinations or for which judges are equipped to adjudicate by legal training or experience or native wit. And this is the more so true because in every strand of this complicated, intricate web of values meet the contending forces of partisan politics. The practical significance of apportionment is that the next election results may differ because of it. Apportionment battles are overwhelmingly party or intraparty contests. It will add a virulent source of friction and tension in federal-state relations to embroil the federal judiciary in them.

DeShaney v. *Winnebago County Department of Social Services*

109 S.Ct. 998 (1989)

The petitioner in this case, Joshua DeShaney, was subjected to a series of beatings by his father, Randy DeShaney, with whom he lived. The respondents, a county department of social services and several of its social workers, received complaints that Joshua was being abused by his father and took various steps to protect him; they did not, however, remove him from his father's custody. Joshua's father finally beat him so severely that he suffered massive and permanent brain damage and was rendered profoundly retarded. While Joshua's father was subsequently tried and convicted of child abuse, Joshua and his mother sued the respondents under 42 U.S.C. Section 1983, alleging that they had deprived Joshua of his "liberty interest in bodily integrity," in violation of his rights under the substantive component of the Fourteenth Amendment's Due Process Clause, by failing to intervene to protect him from his father's violence. The U.S. District Court for the Eastern District of Wisconsin granted summary judgment for the respondents; the Court of Appeals for the Seventh Circuit affirmed; and the Supreme Court granted certiorari. *Opinion of the Court: Rehnquist, Kennedy, O'Connor, Scalia, Stevens, White. Dissenting opinions: Brennan, Blackmun, Marshall; Blackmun.*

Chief Justice Rehnquist delivered the opinion of the Court. . . .

Petitioner is a boy who was beaten and permanently injured by his father, with whom he lived. The respondents are social workers and other local officials who received complaints that petitioner was being abused by his father and had reason to believe that this was the case, but nonetheless did not act to remove petitioner from his father's custody. Petitioner sued respondents claiming that their failure to act deprived him of his liberty in violation of the Due Process Clause of the Fourteenth Amendment to the United States Constitution. We hold that it did not. . . .

The Due Process Clause of the Fourteenth Amendment provides that "[n]o State shall . . . deprive any person of life, liberty, or property, without due process of law." Petitioners contend that the State deprived Joshua of his liberty interest in "free[dom] from . . . unjustified intrusions on personal security," . . . by failing to provide him with adequate protection against his father's violence. The claim is one invoking the substantive rather than procedural component of the Due Process Clause; petitioners do not claim that the State denied Joshua protection without according him appropriate procedural safeguards, . . . but that it was categorically obligated to protect him in these circumstances. . . .

But nothing in the language of the Due Process Clause itself requires the State to protect the life, liberty, and property of its citizens against invasion by private actors. The Clause is phrased as a limitation on the State's power to act, not as a guarantee of certain minimal levels of safety and security. It forbids the State itself to deprive individuals of life, liberty, or property without "due process of law," but its language cannot fairly be extended to impose an affirmative obligation on the State to ensure that those interests do not come to harm through other means. Nor does history support such an expansive reading of the constitutional text. Like its counterpart in the Fifth Amendment, the Due Process Clause of the Fourteenth Amendment was intended to prevent government "from abusing [its] power, or employing it as an instrument of oppression.". . . Its purpose was to protect the people from the State, not to ensure that the State protected them from each other. The Framers were content to leave the extent of governmental obligation in the latter area to the democratic political processes.

Consistent with these principles, our cases have recognized that the Due Process Clauses generally confer no affirmative right to governmental aid, even where such aid may be necessary to secure life, liberty, or property interests of which the government itself may not deprive the individual. . . . As we said in *Harris* v. *McRae* [1980], "[a]though the liberty protected by the Due Process Clause affords protection against unwarranted *government* interference . . . , it does not confer an entitlement to such [governmental aid] as may be necessary to realize all the advantages of that freedom." . . . If the Due Process Clause does not require the State to provide its citizens with particular protective services, it follows that the State cannot be held liable under the Clause for injuries that could have been averted had it chosen to provide them. As a general matter, then, we conclude that a State's failure to protect an individual against private violence simply does not constitute a violation of the Due Process Clause.

Petitioners contend, however, that even if the Due Process Clause imposes no affirmative obligation on the State to provide the general public with adequate protective services, such a duty may arise out of certain "special relationships" created or assumed by the State with respect to particular individuals. . . . Petitioners argue that such a "special relationship" existed here because the State knew that Joshua faced a special danger of abuse at his father's hands, and specifically proclaimed, by word and by deed, its intention to protect him against that danger. . . . Having actually undertaken to protect Joshua from this danger—which petitioners concede the State played no part in creating—the State acquired an affirmative "duty," enforceable through the Due Process Clause, to do so in a reasonably competent fashion. . . .

We reject this argument. It is true that in certain limited circumstances the Constitution imposes upon the State affirmative duties of care and protection with respect to particular individuals. In *Estelle* v. *Gamble* . . . [1976] we recognized that the Eighth Amendment's prohibition against cruel and unusual punishment . . . requires the State to provide adequate medical care to incarcerated prisoners. . . .

In *Youngberg* v. *Romeo* . . . [1982] we extended this analysis beyond the Eighth Amendment setting, holding that the substantive component of the Fourteenth Amendment's Due Process Clause requires the State to provide involuntarily committed mental patients with such services as are necessary to ensure their "reasonable safety" from themselves and others. . . .

But these cases afford petitioners no help. Taken together, they stand only for the proposition that when the State takes a person into its custody and holds him there against his will, the Constitution imposes upon it a corresponding duty to assume some responsibility for his safety and general well-being. . . . The rationale for this principle is simple enough: when the State by the affirmative exercise of its power so restrains an individual's liberty that it renders him unable to care for himself, and at the same time fails to provide for his basic human needs—*e.g.*, food, clothing, shelter, medical care, and reasonable safety—it transgresses the substantive limits on state action set by the Eighth Amendment and the Due Process Clause. . . . The affirmative duty to protect arises not from the State's knowledge of the individual's predicament or from its expressions of intent to help him, but from the limitation which it has imposed on his freedom to act on his own behalf. . . . In the substantive due process analysis, it is the State's affirmative act of restraining the individual's freedom to act on his own behalf—through incarceration, institutionalization, or other similar restraint of personal liberty—which is the "deprivation of liberty" triggering the protections of the Due Process Clause, not its failure to act to protect his liberty interests against harms inflicted by other means.

The *Estelle-Youngberg* analysis simply has no applicability in the present case. Petitioners concede that the harms Joshua suffered did not occur while he was in the State's custody, but while he was in the custody of his natural father, who was in no sense a state actor. While the State may have been aware of the dangers that Joshua faced in the free world, it played no part in their creation, nor did it do anything to render him any more vulnerable to them. That the State once took temporary custody of Joshua does not alter the analysis, for when it returned him to his father's custody, it placed him in no worse position than that in which he would have been had it not acted at all; the State does not become the permanent guarantor of an individual's safety by having once offered him shelter. Under these circumstances, the State had no constitutional duty to protect Joshua.

It may well be that, by voluntarily undertaking to protect Joshua against a danger it concededly played no part in creating, the State acquired a duty under state tort law to provide him with adequate protection against that danger. . . . But the claim here is based on the Due Process Clause of the Fourteenth Amendment, which, as we have said many times, does not transform every tort committed by a state actor into a constitutional violation. . . . Because . . . the State had no constitutional duty to protect Joshua against his father's violence, its failure to do so—though calamitous in hindsight—simply does not constitute a violation of the Due Process Clause.

Judges and lawyers, like other humans, are moved by natural sympathy in a case like this to find a way for Joshua and his mother to receive adequate compensation for the grievous harm inflicted upon them. But before yielding to that impulse, it is well to remember once again that the harm was inflicted not by the State of Wisconsin, but by Joshua's father. The most that can be said of the state functionaries in this case is that they stood by and did nothing when suspicious circumstances dictated a more active role for them. In defense of them it must also be said that had they moved too soon to take custody of the son away from the father, they would likely have been met with charges of improperly intruding into the parent-child relationship, charges based on the same Due Process Clause that forms the basis for the present charge of failure to provide adequate protection.

The people of Wisconsin may well prefer a system of liability which would place upon the State and its officials the responsibility for failure to act in situations such as the present one. They may create such a system, if they do not have it already, by changing the tort law of the State in accordance with the regular law-making process. But they should not have it thrust upon them by this Court's expansion of the Due Process Clause of the Fourteenth Amendment.

JUSTICE BRENNAN, with whom JUSTICE MARSHALL and JUSTICE BLACKMUN join, dissenting. . . .

To the Court, the only fact that seems to count as an "affirmative act of restraining the individual's freedom to act on his own behalf" is direct physical control. . . . I would not, however, give *Youngberg* and *Estelle* such a stingy scope. I would recognize, as the Court apparently cannot, that "the State's knowledge of [an] individual's predicament [and] its expressions of intent to help him" can amount to a "limitation of his freedom to act on his own behalf" or to obtain help from others. . . . Thus, I would read *Youngberg* and *Estelle* to stand for the much more generous proposition that, if a State cuts off private sources of aid and then refuses aid itself, it cannot wash its hands of the harm that results from its inaction.

Wisconsin has established a child-welfare system specifically designed to help children like Joshua. Wisconsin law places upon the local departments of social services such as respondent (DSS or Department) a duty to investigate reported instances of child abuse. . . . While other governmental bodies and private persons are largely responsible for the reporting of possible cases of child abuse, . . . Wisconsin law channels all such reports to the local departments of social services for evaluation and, if necessary, further action. . . . Even when it is the sheriff's office or police department that receives a report of suspected child abuse, that report is referred to local social services departments for action . . . the only exception to this occurs when the reporter fears for the child's *immediate* safety. . . . In this way, Wisconsin law invites—indeed, directs—citizens and other governmental entities to depend on local departments of social services such as respondent to protect children from abuse. . . .

In these circumstances, a private citizen, or even a person working in a government agency other than DSS, would doubtless feel that her job was done as soon as she had reported her suspicions of child abuse to DSS. Through its child-welfare program, in other words, the State of Wisconsin has relieved ordinary citizens and governmental bodies other than the Department of any sense of obligation to do anything more than report their suspicions of child abuse to DSS. If DSS ignores or dismisses these suspicions, no one will step in to fill the gap. Wisconsin's child-protection program thus effectively confined Joshua DeShaney within the walls of Randy DeShaney's violent home until such time as DSS took action to remove him. Conceivably, then, children like Joshua are made worse off by the existence of this program when the persons and entities charged with carrying it out fail to do their jobs. . . .

As the Court today reminds us, "the Due Process Clause of the Fourteenth Amendment was intended to prevent government 'from abusing [its] power, or employing it as an instrument of oppression.' " . . . My Disagreement with the Court arises from its failure to see that inaction can be every bit as abusive of power as action, that oppression can result when a State undertakes a vital duty and then ignores it. Today's opinion construes the Due Process Clause to permit a State to displace private sources of protection and then, at the critical moment, to shrug its shoulders and turn away from the harm that it has promised to try to prevent. Because I cannot agree that our Constitution is indifferent to such indifference, I respectfully dissent.

JUSTICE BLACKMUN, dissenting.

Today, the Court purports to be the dispassionate oracle of the law, unmoved by "natural sympathy." . . . But, in this pretense, the Court itself retreats into a sterile formalism which prevents it from recognizing either the facts of the case before it or the legal norms that should apply to those facts. As JUSTICE BRENNAN demonstrates, the facts here involve not mere passivity, but active state intervention in the life of Joshua DeShaney—intervention that triggered a fundamental duty to aid the boy once the State learned of the severe danger to which he was exposed. . . . The Court today claims that its decision, however harsh, is compelled by existing legal doctrine. On the contrary, the question presented by this case is an open one, and our Fourteenth Amendment precedents may be read more broadly or narrowly depending upon how one chooses to read them. Faced with the choice, I would adopt a "sympathetic" reading, one which comports with dictates of fundamental justice and recognizes that compassion need not be exiled from the province of judging. Cf. A. Stone, Law, Psychiatry, and Morality 262 (1984) ("We will make mistakes if we go forward, but doing nothing can be the worst mistake. What is required of us is moral ambition. Until our composite sketch becomes a true portrait of humanity we must live with our uncertainty; we will grope, we will struggle, and our compassion may be our only guide and comfort").

4
THE LEGISLATIVE BRANCH

Aware of the inadequacies of the Articles of Confederation, the Framers of the Constitution set out to create a national government powerful enough to rule a large and diverse nation. Broad powers were conferred on the legislative branch of government, which the Framers expected to be the most powerful of the three branches. Before examining in detail the important legislative powers vested in Congress, however, we must address four important preliminary questions:

1. What principles underlie the interpretation of the extent of the national legislative power?
2. What powers and privileges does the Constitution grant to Congress to facilitate its legislative activity?
3. What nonlegislative powers does the Constitution confer on Congress?
4. Given the growth of the Federal bureaucracy, what constitutional means are available for ensuring that Congress continues to make basic policy decisions?

THE SCOPE OF CONGRESSIONAL POWER

Article I of the Constitution grants Congress a broad range of legislative powers, including taxing and spending powers (which enable it to control the government's purse strings), the power to declare war, and the power to regulate commerce. Various constitutional amendments—in particular, the Thirteenth, Fourteenth, and Fifteenth—confer important additional powers. Finally, the Necessary and Proper Clause (Article I, Section

8) gives Congress the authority to "make all laws which shall be necessary and proper for carrying into Execution the foregoing Powers, and all other Powers vested by this Constitution in the Government of the United States, or in any Department or Officer thereof."

Yet although the Constitution vests broad powers in Congress, it also imposes various restrictions on congressional power. Some of these restrictions, such as the ban on *ex post facto* laws (those having a retroactive effect), were incorporated into the original Constitution. Others were added with the ratification of the Bill of Rights, the first ten amendments to the Constitution. Most important, Congress can exercise only the powers explicitly or implicitly conferred on it by the Constitution.

This mandate distinguishes Congress from the British Parliament, which (at least in theory) can pass any law it wishes. But it also means that Congress, unlike the legislature under the Articles of Confederation, is not limited to those powers expressly granted to it. How broad are Congress's implied powers? The answer to this question depends upon the interpretation of the Necessary and Proper Clause. By inserting such a clause, the Framers sought to give Congress the flexibility necessary for dealing with complex and changing conditions. Yet some political figures—most notably, Thomas Jefferson—charged that if Congress were allowed too much discretion in determining how it would achieve its objectives, this "sweeping clause" could transform a government of limited powers into one of unlimited powers. They therefore maintained that the phrase "necessary and proper" should be interpreted as limiting, rather than expanding, congressional power. According to this view, Congress could exercise implied powers only insofar as such powers were necessary for carrying out its enumerated powers. For example, if Congress's enumerated powers could be implemented without chartering a national bank, then the power to charter a bank was not necessary and hence not authorized.

This restrictive interpretation of congressional power was rejected in *McCulloch* v. *Maryland* (1819), in which the Supreme Court recognized Congress's power to charter the Bank of the United States and invalidated a Maryland tax on that bank. Speaking for a unanimous Court, Chief Justice John Marshall persuasively argued for a broad construction of congressional powers. Acknowledging that the Constitution did not specifically authorize Congress to charter a bank, Marshall reasoned that this omission was not in itself determinative. In establishing "a constitution intended to endure for ages to come," Marshall argued, the Framers deliberately avoided cluttering it with excessive detail, choosing instead merely to sketch the "great outlines" of congressional power. To determine whether Congress possessed a particular power, therefore, it was necessary to read the Constitution in light of the ends it was created to achieve.

Since the Constitution confers on Congress considerable responsibility for the economic prosperity of the nation, Marshall went on, it must be interpreted as furnishing Congress with sufficient power for securing that end; any other interpretation would be contradictory and self-defeating. And since effective congressional action is so essential, the Constitution must provide Congress with "that discretion, with respect to the means by which the powers it confers are to be carried into execution, which will enable that body to perform the high duties assigned to it, in the manner most beneficial to the people." To confine Congress to only those means necessary for carrying out its enumerated powers would be to jeopardize the ends for which the Constitution was established. Therefore, Marshall concluded, "Let the end be legitimate, let it be within the scope of the constitution, and all means which are appropriate, which are plainly adapted to that end, which are not prohibited, but consist with the letter and spirit of the constitution, are constitutional."

Marshall's opinion in *McCulloch* can serve as a model for interpreting the constitutional grants of power. By focusing on the ends the Framers sought to achieve, Marshall ensured that Congress neither overstepped its bounds nor was denied powers commensurate with its responsibilities. In allowing Congress to choose how best to achieve those ends, Marshall recognized (as did the Framers) that flexibility of response was essential for effective government. Although bitterly attacked at the time, his opinion was never successfully refuted and has remained the primary rationale for the broad exercise of congressional power.[1]

POWERS THAT FACILITATE LEGISLATIVE ACTIVITY

The broad scope of Marshall's interpretation of congressional power leads inescapably to the conclusion that, having vested Congress with important responsibilities, the Constitution provided the lawmakers with the powers and privileges necessary to fulfill those duties. To secure legislative independence, the Framers inserted into Article I the Speech and Debate Clause, which protects members of Congress from legal inquiry into their legislative activities, and other provisions guaranteeing Congress control over its proceedings.[2] Implicitly, they promoted well-informed deliberations through the Necessary and Proper Clause, under whose authority Congress has undertaken investigations, subpoenaed witnesses to testify, and punished refusals to supply pertinent information. But if the existence of these powers and privileges has long been recognized, their scope has remained the subject of controversy and litigation.

The Speech and Debate Clause

In Article I, Section 6 of the Constitution, members of Congress are guaranteed that "for any Speech or Debate in either House, they shall not be questioned in any other Place." This safeguard against executive harassment or intimidation of legislators, which originated during the British Parliament's struggle for legislative supremacy, excited little controversy for most of the nation's history. Since 1966, however, the Supreme Court has decided several cases involving the Speech and Debate Clause, and the deep divisions on the Court in these cases have revealed basic disagreements about the purposes the clause was designed to serve.

The justices have disagreed, first of all, over who is and who is not protected by the Speech and Debate Clause. Even though the clause expressly protects only senators and representatives, the Court has recognized that its protection cannot be so limited. Some congressional employees perform tasks so essential to the legislative process that denying them protection would defeat the basic purpose of the provision. Thus in *Gravel* v. *United States* (1972), which involved a grand jury investigation into how Senator Mike Gravel obtained and arranged to publish top-secret government documents, all the justices recognized that Gravel's legislative aide was entitled to the same immunity from legal inquiry as the senator. Most justices, however, have been unwilling to extend such protection to other congressional employees. In *Dombrowski* v. *Eastland* (1967), the Court decided that the counsel for a Senate committee could be sued for conspiring to violate the civil rights of various activists, even though the committee chairman could not. And in *Doe* v. *McMillan* (1973), it permitted parents to sue the Public Printer and Superintendent of Documents, who—with the authority of Congress—had publicly distributed a committee report that allegedly defamed and invaded the privacy of their children.

A more fundamental disagreement has developed over the range of activities protected by the Speech and Debate Clause. The Court recognized in *Kilbourn* v. *Thompson* (1881) that the clause covers not only debate within Congress but also all things "generally done in a session of the House by one of its members in relation to the business before it."[3] But the justices have disagreed sharply over what activities comprise "legislative acts" and are immune from inquiry or prosecution. In *Gravel* the Court held that the clause did not foreclose inquiry into how Gravel obtained and arranged for the publication of the Pentagon Papers. Noting that the Constitution specified "Speech or Debate," the *Gravel* majority argued that it protected only those activities directly related to such "internal" legislative functions as deliberation and voting. This distinction between internal and external functions also underlay the Court's rulings in *Doe* and in *Hutchinson* v. *Proxmire* (1979). The majority opinion in *Doe* argued that whereas the Speech and Debate Clause protected the committee hearings and the circulation of the committee's report to other members of Congress, it did not cover public dissemination of the committee report. Similarly, the justices held in *Hutchinson* that although the clause protected speeches on the Senate floor in which Senator William Proxmire attacked a government agency's funding of allegedly worthless research, he could be sued for libel for reproducing those speeches in a newsletter sent to his constituents. The dissenters in these cases rejected this interpretation of the legislative function as unduly narrow. According to these justices, legislators in a representative government have a responsibility to inform the electorate about governmental operations, and publication of material introduced in congressional hearings and of speeches dealing with the expenditure of public funds is a legitimate and appropriate means of fulfilling this responsibility. Such activity, they argued, thus came under the protection of the Speech and Debate Clause.

Bribery prosecutions of members of Congress have also raised Speech and Debate Clause issues. Because the clause protects both speeches delivered in Congress and the motivations for making them, the Court has held that such speeches and motivations could not be used in establishing criminal violations. But a prosecutor could introduce evidence at trial that a member of Congress had taken a bribe, since the clause "does not prohibit inquiry into activities that are casually or incidentally related to legislative affairs but not part of the process itself."[4] This position has facilitated prosecutions, and the three members of Congress who relied on the Speech and Debate Clause in conducting their defenses were all convicted after their cases were remanded to the lower courts.

Congressional Investigations

Since 1792, when the House of Representatives appointed a committee to inquire into General St. Clair's defeat by the Indians, congressional committees have conducted investigations to gather information for legislation, to oversee the implementation of laws, or to pursue various other ends. The House of Representatives and the Senate grant most of their committees the power to hold hearings, subpoena witnesses and materials, and cite for contempt witnesses who refuse to cooperate. The vast majority of these investigations proceed without fanfare or dispute, furnishing Congress with the information it needs to discharge its constitutional responsibilities. Some congressional investigations, such as the recent Iran-Contra hearings, however, have excited great controversy and prompted allegations of constitutional violations.

The most controversial and contentious of modern-day investigations were the inquiries into Communist subversion conducted by the House Un-American Activities Committee (HUAC) during the late 1940s and the 1950s. Empowered by the House to investigate subversive and un-American activities and propaganda, HUAC in this period called over three thousand witnesses, many for questioning about their own or their acquaintances' political beliefs and affiliations. Some witnesses, invoking the protection of the Fifth Amendment's privilege against self-incrimination, refused to testify. Others claimed that the committee's inquiries exceeded its legitimate authority and declined to appear before the committee or to answer its questions, and 144 of these uncooperative witnesses were cited by HUAC for contempt of Congress.[5]

In appealing subsequent contempt convictions, witnesses attacked the constitutionality of HUAC's proceedings on two grounds. They asserted, first of all, that the committee's inquiries were unconstitutional because they did not serve any valid legislative purpose. In making this claim, witnesses did not challenge Congress's power to investigate—the Supreme Court had recognized in *McGrain* v. *Daugherty* (1927) that the Necessary and Proper Clause authorized Congress to conduct investigations to secure the information it needed for wise legislation. They did insist, however, that the Court's position in *McGrain* implied a limitation on congressional committees: namely, that if the power to investigate derives from the power to legislate, then investigations that do not further the processes of legislation have no constitutional warrant. Such was the case, they charged, with HUAC's inquiries: because the committee sought to expose individuals' political beliefs rather than to obtain information for legislation, its investigations served no valid legislative purpose and were thus unconstitutional.

This argument enjoyed some initial success in *Watkins* v. *United States* (1957), in which the Court reversed the contempt conviction of a labor union official who refused to answer committee questions. Although the decision in *Watkins* rested on narrow grounds, Chief Justice Earl Warren expressly reaffirmed the *McGrain* limitation and pointedly noted that congressional committees had no power "to expose for the sake of exposure." Two years later, however, the Supreme Court in *Barenblatt* v. *United States* (1959) rejected the claim that HUAC's inquiries served no valid legislative purpose. The decisive consideration, the Court suggested, was not the motivation of individual committee members but the scope of Congress's legislative authority; and as long as the subject under investigation was one on which Congress could legislate, the Court would assume that the investigation was designed to secure information for possible legislation. This willingness to infer a valid legislative purpose from the subject under investigation virtually eliminated the *McGrain* requirement as a check on congressional investigations.[6]

Some witnesses also protested that the committee's inquiries into political beliefs and affiliations violated their First Amendment rights of freedom of speech and freedom of association. In *Barenblatt*, however, the Court noted that these rights were not absolute and must be balanced against the interest of the congressional committee in obtaining the information it needed to carry out its responsibilities. Applying this balancing test, the Court consistently upheld congressional inquiries against First Amendment challenge. But in *Gibson* v. *Florida Legislative Investigating Committee* (1963) the justices ruled that the First Amendment protected a witness who refused to divulge membership information to a state committee purportedly investigating Communist infiltration into the Miami NAACP.

Although the Court has rejected direct constitutional challenges to congressional investigations, it has developed various safeguards that protect witnesses against arbitrary committee actions. Among these are the requirements, enunciated in *McGrain*, that the scope of a committee's inquiry cannot exceed the authority granted to it by the House or Senate and that committee questions must be pertinent to the topic under investigation. Relying on these requirements of authorization and pertinency, the Supreme Court overturned contempt convictions in *Rumely* v. *United States* (1953) and in *Watkins*, noting in the latter case that neither HUAC's vague authorizing resolution nor the committee members' statements furnished any basis for determining whether the questions Watkins refused to answer were pertinent to the committee's legislative purpose.

In sum, the Court's decisions in cases involving congressional investigations manifest a combination of deference and intervention. On the one hand, the justices have avoided directly confronting Congress by curtailing the scope of its power to investigate. On the other hand, the rulings in *McGrain, Rumely, Watkins,* and other cases reflect an underlying concern for the rights of witnesses, and the Court has not been reluctant to police the activities of congressional committees.

NONLEGISLATIVE POWERS

Along with lawmaking responsibilities, the Constitution assigns to Congress the power of impeachment and important powers pertaining to the proposal and ratification of constitutional amendments.

Impeachment

Members of the executive and judicial branches can be removed from office upon impeachment by a majority vote in the House of Representatives and conviction by a two-thirds vote in the Senate. In assigning this power to Congress, the Framers generally followed English parliamentary practice, but departed from it in two important respects. Whereas under the Constitution impeachment and conviction carry purely political penalties—removal from office and ineligibility for future office—conviction by the House of Lords typically had led to the imposition of criminal penalties, including death. By eliminating such sanctions, the Framers sought to overcome legislative reluctance to use impeachment to punish official misconduct and to ensure impeached officials a trial by jury in subsequent prosecutions for any criminal offenses. The Constitution also departed from English practice in limiting impeachable offenses to "Treason, Bribery, or other high Crimes and Misdemeanors." Parliament had used impeachment as a political weapon in its struggles for power with the Crown, but the Framers did not intend that Congress should use the impeachment power to intimidate the executive. By specifying the grounds for impeachment and by defining treason in the Constitution (Article III, Section 3), they sought instead to create a check on executive misconduct that would not be subject to abuse.

Nevertheless, during both President Andrew Johnson's impeachment trial and President Richard Nixon's last year in office, considerable controversy arose over the constitutional grounds for impeachment, and in particular over the definition of "high Crimes and Misdemeanors." To some extent, purely partisan considerations dictated the positions taken—for example, Nixon's assertion that impeachment required a criminal violation. Yet these controversies reflected as well a genuine uncertainty about the Framers' intent. On the one hand, the Constitutional Convention's rejection of impeachment for "maladministration" bespeaks the Framers' determination to prevent impeachments motivated merely by political disagreements. On the other hand, the emphasis on "abuse or violation of some public trust" in *The Federalist,* No. 65, suggests that a criminal act is not necessary for impeachment. (This was the position taken by the House committee which recommended impeachment of President Nixon.) Most likely, no precise definition of "high Crimes or Misdemeanors" is possible. The Framers' concern about the proper forum for trying impeachments, as voiced both in the Constitutional Convention and *The Federalist,* suggests a recognition that ultimately these terms would be defined in the judgment of specific cases.

Constitutional Amendment

The Framers' experience with the Articles of Confederation on the one hand, and with the "mutability" of state laws on the other, convinced them of the dangers of making constitutional change either too difficult or too easy. The Constitution allows either Congress or specially elected representatives of the states to propose constitutional amendments (see Figure 4.1). For although the Framers expected that the national government would be more aware of defects in the constitutional system and thus more likely to propose remedies, they sought to ensure that it could not block popular demands for constitutional change.[7] The ratification process reflects the federal character of the American political system in requiring that amendments be supported not merely by a numerical majority but also by a geographically dispersed majority. As a final guarantee that any constitutional change would coincide with state public opinion, the Framers required ratification by state legislatures or specially elected conventions in each state.[8]

Thus far, all constitutional amendments have been adopted by the less-cumbersome national mode, under which Congress proposes amendments for adoption and determines the mode of ratification. In addition, because Article V leaves numerous procedural questions unresolved, Congress, acting under the Necessary and Proper Clause, has assumed a supervisory authority over the ratification process, recording state ratifications; determining when amendments have been adopted; and in this century, establishing time limits for ratification. In *Dillon* v. *Gloss* (1921) the Supreme Court upheld Congress's power to establish a "reasonable" timespan for ratification. Later, in *Coleman* v. *Miller* (1939), the justices refused to define the term *reasonable* in this context, asserting that the political-questions doctrine substantially limits judicial review of Congress's actions.

Nevertheless, congressional regulations governing the ratification process for the proposed Equal Rights Amendment (ERA) raised questions about constitutional limitations on this supervisory authority. As the initial deadline for ratification neared, Congress in 1978 extended it for thirty months and, noting that five state legislatures had voted to rescind their earlier ratifications, also prohibited such action.

Both these steps raised constitutional issues.[9] Proponents of the dead-

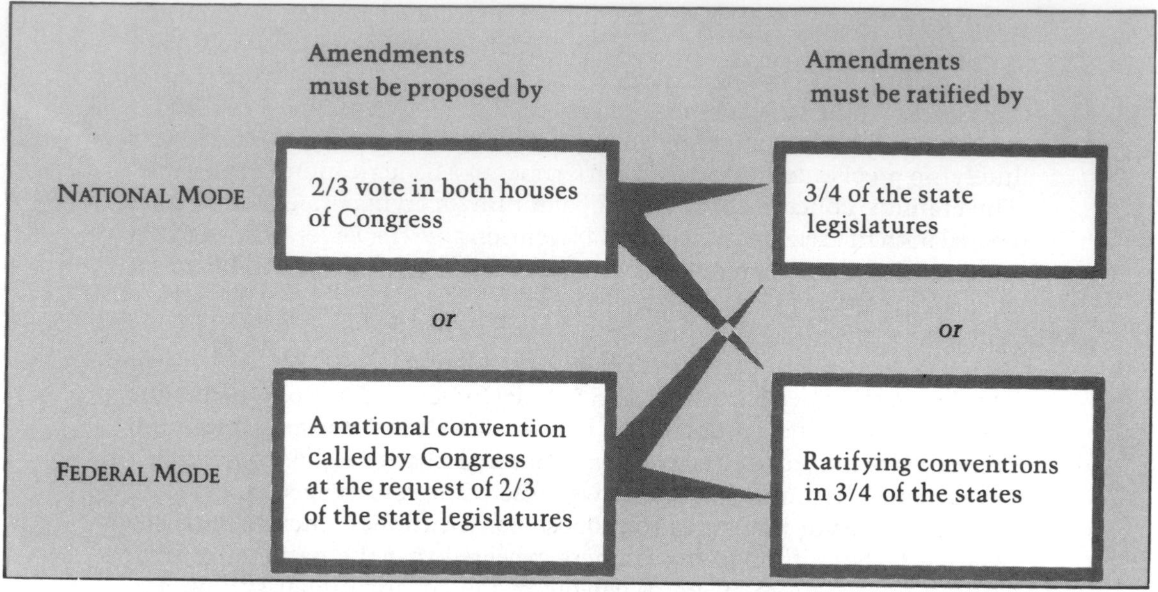

FIGURE 4.1 Methods of Amending the Constitution

line extension argued that since what constitutes a reasonable period for ratification might not be clear in advance, a later Congress should not be bound by an earlier determination. In the case of the ERA, they asserted, the unforeseen misrepresentations of the amendment's effects required an extension so that these distortions could be corrected. When opponents of the extension likened it to changing the rules in the middle of the game, proponents stressed that Congress's action served the Framers' aims by promoting informed consideration of a constitutional change.

But if the deadline was extended to permit a better-informed decision, why should the states not be able to reconsider their earlier ratifications of the amendment, as well as their earlier rejections? If the Framers wanted the ratification decision to reflect state public opinion, should not the more recent expression of that opinion be authoritative?

In countering these arguments, opponents of rescission emphasized the specific wording of Article V. Since the Constitution gives states the power to ratify amendments, they argued, failure to exercise that power on one occasion (i.e., rejection of a proposed amendment) cannot preclude its later exercise. And since Article V only mentions "ratification," the act of ratification exhausts state power in the amendment process, thus making rescission illegitimate. In addition, allowing rescission would create a disparity between the two modes of ratification, since rescission could not readily occur with ratification by state conventions. Finally, they maintained that making ratification irrevocable promotes a sense of political responsibility and ensures serious deliberation.

More recently, attention has focused on the federal mode of constitutional amendment, as proponents of a balanced budget amendment have campaigned for a constitutional convention to consider such an amendment. As of early 1990, 32 state legislatures—two short of the number required—had submitted petitions to Congress for a convention. If the movement succeeds, this would be the first convention under Article V.[10] But before the convention could meet, Congress, acting under the Necessary and Proper Clause, would have to resolve thorny questions about the apportionment of delegates among the states and the convention's mode of operation. Thus far Congress has failed to adopt legislation covering these matters, in part because opponents of a balanced budget amendment fear that this might encourage pro-convention forces.

SAFEGUARDING LEGISLATIVE POWER

Given the broad scope of national governmental concerns, it is not surprising that Congress increasingly has found it necessary to delegate power to the executive branch. In doing so, however, the legislators often have given executive officials broad discretion in defining policy aims and devising measures to achieve those aims—so broad, according to some commentators, that such delegations have produced a basic shift in the locus of national policy making.[11] Whatever the accuracy of this assessment, it is clear that extensive delegations of congressional power raise important questions about possible constitutional limits on Congress's power to delegate this authority and about the extent to which Congress can retain control over the direction of national policy.

Delegation of Power

Although particularly extensive during the twentieth century, congressional delegations of power have occurred throughout our history. As early as 1813 the Supreme Court, in *Brig Aurora* v. *United States,* upheld a statute authorizing the president to lift restrictions on trade with France and Great Britain if those nations ceased interfering with American shipping. Twelve years later, in *Wayman* v. *Southard* (1825), the justices upheld a provision of the Judiciary Act of 1789 that allowed the courts "to make and establish all necessary rules" for the transaction of judicial business.

In upholding these laws, however, the Court recognized that the Constitution imposes a limitation on congressional delegations: whatever powers are surrendered, the determination of basic policy must remain with Congress. The laws challenged in *Brig Aurora* and *Wayman* met this requirement by providing clear standards governing the use of the delegated powers. In *Brig Aurora* the justices emphasized that Congress had specified the conditions under which the president was to act and the acts to be performed; in *Wayman* they noted that the legislators had decided the most important matters and merely authorized those operating under the law to "fill up the details." In contrast, a congressional delegation without adequate standards—one that allowed executive officials to make basic policy—would constitute a transfer of legislative power to the executive branch and would thus be unconstitutional.

Despite continued judicial invocation, the requirement that Congress furnish standards has not impeded broad congressional delegations of power. Not until 1935 did the Court invalidate a congressional delegation. And although in *Panama Refining Company* v. *Ryan* (1935) and *Schecter Poultry Corporation* v. *United States* (1935) it did strike down provisions of the National Industrial Recovery Act, those cases marked both the zenith and the end of effective judicial supervision of congressional delegations. Since 1935 the Supreme Court has not invalidated a single delegation of congressional power.

Mistretta v. *United States* (1989), a constitutional challenge to the Sentencing Reform Act of 1984, exemplifies the Court's current approach in delegation cases. The Act authorized the United States Sentencing Commission, made up of three federal judges and four lay members, to establish mandatory sentencing guidelines for all persons convicted in federal courts. Despite this broad grant of power, the Court upheld the legislation, concluding that this complicated task was precisely the sort appropriate for delegation and that Congress had furnished adequate standards to guide the Commission in its work. In solitary dissent, Justice Antonin Scalia insisted that the Act involved a dangerous innovation. Previously, the realization that delegations aggrandized the executive branch, "its primary competitor for political power," had served as a check on Congress. By permitting Congress to delegate power outside the three branches of government, Scalia asserted, the Court in *Mistretta* removed the primary structural impediment to excessive congressional delegations.

The Legislative Veto

Rather than limiting administrative policy making by means of precisely drawn statutes, Congress in recent years typically has sought to safeguard its constitutional position by supervising the exercise of delegated power. One weapon Congress relied on for this purpose, particularly during the 1970s, was the legislative veto, under which it delegated power to the president or an administrative agency with the proviso that it could veto the exercise of that power. These conditional grants of power took various forms. The Budget and Impoundment Control Act of 1974 provided for a veto by congressional inaction: The president had to spend appropriated funds unless Congress affirmatively endorsed his failure to do so within forty-five days. The War Powers Resolution, in contrast, permitted Congress to terminate presidential commitments of troops by a concurrent resolution (one passed by both houses of Congress) not subject to presidential veto. Other statutes granted a single house of Congress—or even congressional committees—a veto over administrative regulations or actions of executive branch officials.

Such a one-house veto figured in *Immigration and Naturalization Service* v. *Chadha* (1983), the first Supreme Court ruling on the constitutionality of the legislative veto. Under the Immigration and Nationality Act, the Attorney General was authorized to allow deportable aliens to remain in the country, but a single house of Congress could invalidate the Attorney General's decision by majority vote. This procedure, the Court ruled in *Chadha,* violated the Constitution. Although Chief Justice Warren Burger acknowledged in the opinion of the Court that the legislative veto might at times promote efficiency, he insisted that it contravened "explicit and unambiguous provisions of the Constitution" defining the respective roles of Congress and the president in legislation. Whereas Article I directs that laws be enacted by majority vote in each house, the legislative veto in *Chadha* allowed action which was legislative in character and effect by majority vote in only one house, thus contravening the constitutional requirement of bicameralism. And whereas the Presentment Clause required that all legislation be submitted to the president before becoming law, the legislative veto enabled Congress to take legislative action without the threat of a presidential veto. Thus the legislative veto circumvented the procedures prescribed by the Constitution to ensure due deliberation, check ill-advised legislation, and maintain the separation of powers.

As Justice Byron White noted in his dissent, the Court's interpretation of the Presentment Clause doomed not only the one-house veto in *Chadha* but also "nearly 200 other statutory provisions in which Congress has reserved a 'legislative veto.' " Such a blanket condemnation, he insisted, was unwarranted. Because they made no new law but merely negatived actions of the executive branch, legislative vetoes did not violate the bicameralism requirement nor circumvent the Presentment Clause. In addition, all statutes incorporating legislative vetoes had been passed by both houses and presented to the president. More fundamentally, White faulted the Court majority for failing to recognize how the Federal Government had been transformed during the twentieth century. Since the 1930s the Federal Government had taken on a wide variety of new responsibilities. The number and complexity of these responsibilities necessitated broad delegations of power to executive and independent agencies, which then issued regulations having the force of law. The legislative veto was "an important if not indispensable political invention" for stemming the flow of law-making power to the executive branch, ensuring the accountability of executive and independent agencies, and vindicating Congress's role as the nation's lawmaker. Because it served important constitutional ends and was not prohibited by the document, White concluded that the legislative veto was a valid adaptation to a changing political reality.

SOME CONCLUSIONS

Several conclusions emerge from our review of the constitutional provisions defining Congress's powers and regulating their exercise. First, Congress's constitutional powers are exceedingly broad. Along with conferring on Congress important enumerated powers the Constitution, through the Necessary and Proper Clause, provides extensive additional powers that allow Congress necessary flexibility in fulfilling its constitutional responsibilities. And the Supreme Court, by foreclosing review through the "political-questions doctrine," has acknowledged Congress's broad discretion in the exercise of such nonlegislative powers as supervising the amendment process and hearing impeachments.

Second, the Constitution has provided Congress with important auxiliary powers and privileges that enable it to fulfill its constitutional responsibilities more effectively. Not only does the Constitution expressly confer on members of Congress various immunities that safeguard the independence of the legislative branch, but the Supreme Court also has recognized that the Constitution permits Congress to obtain necessary information for legislation by conducting investigations and punishing witnesses who refuse to supply pertinent information. Yet the Court's interpretation of these auxiliary powers and privileges offers considerable contrast. On the one hand, the justices have attempted to regulate congressional investigations without imposing requirements that would curtail the scope of congressional investigatory authority. On the other hand, in construing the Speech and Debate Clause, they have been much more willing to define the privilege narrowly and to rule against members of Congress.

Finally, the Constitution's generous grants of power have not ensured that Congress will play the decisive role in defining government policy. In recent decades the executive branch has increasingly dominated policy development. The Supreme Court's permissive interpretation of the nondelegation doctrine has facilitated the transfer of responsibility to the executive branch. During the 1970s and 1980s, Congress attempted to reclaim control, not by curtailing the scope of its delegations of power but by regulating the use of delegated power. With the Supreme Court's invalidation of the legislative veto in *Chadha,* however, Congress lost the prime weapon on which it had relied for overseeing the executive branch. What alternative means it will develop to reassert control over policy remains unclear.

NOTES

1 For the most forceful attacks on *McCulloch* and Marshall's responses, see Gerald Gunther, ed., *John Marshall's Defense of McCulloch* v. *Maryland* (Stanford: Stanford University Press, 1969).

2 Several constitutional provisions safeguard legislative independence. Each house of Congress can choose its own officers (Article I, Section 2, Paragraph 5, and Section 3, Paragraph 5) and determine the "Elections, Returns, and Qualifications of its own Members" (Article I, Section 5, Paragraph 1). Each house can also determine the rules of its proceedings and discipline or expel members (Article I, Section 5, Paragraph 2). Finally, members of Congress generally are immune from arrest during their attendance in Congress.

3 *Kilbourn* v. *Thompson,* 103 U.S. 168, 204 (1881).

4 *United States* v. *Brewster,* 408 U.S. 501, 528 (1972).

5 The figures in this paragraph are drawn from Carl Beck's *Contempt of Congress* (New Orleans: Hauser Press, 1959), Appendix B, pp. 217–241. For other accounts of HUAC's activities, see Alan Barth, *Government by Investigation* (New York: Viking, 1955); William F. Buckley, Jr., ed., *The Committee and Its Critics* (Chicago: Henry Regnery, 1962); and Walter Goodman, *The Committee: The Extraordinary Career of the House Committee on Un-American Activities* (New York: Farrar, Straus, & Giroux, 1968).

6 For a perceptive discussion of this point and a proposal for an alternative approach, see Martin Shapiro, *Law and Politics in the Supreme Court* (New York: The Free Press of Glencoe, 1964), Chapter 2.

7 Thus Alexander Hamilton emphasizes in *The Federalist,* No. 85, that when two-thirds of the states apply to Congress to call a convention for proposing amendments, Congress has no discretion and must do so.

8 The Twenty-First Amendment, which repealed Prohibition, was ratified by specially elected conventions. All other amendments have been ratified by the state legislatures.

9 A federal district court judge ruled in *Idaho* v. *Freeman,* 529 F. Supp. 1107 (1981), that the ERA deadline extension and prohibition on rescission were unconstitutional. However, the Supreme Court stayed the district court's ruling and granted certiorari, but the deadline for ratification passed before the Court ruled in the case, thereby rendering it moot.

10 However, there have been over 230 state constitutional conventions under state constitutions.

11 See, for example, Theodore J. Lowi, *The End of Liberalism,* 2d ed. (New York: W. W. Norton, 1979), especially Chapter 5.

SELECTED READINGS

The Federalist, Nos. 33, 44, 52–66, 85.

Barenblatt v. *United States,* Chapter 12.
Coleman v. *Miller,* 307 U.S. 433 (1939).
Doe v. *McMillan,* 412 U.S. 306 (1973).
Gibson v. *Florida Legislative Investigating Committee,* 372 U.S. 539 (1963).
Morrison v. *Olson,* Chapter 5.

Barber, Sotorios. *The Constitution and the Delegation of Congressional Power* (Chicago: University of Chicago Press, 1975).

Cella, Alexander J. "The Doctrine of Legislative Privilege of Speech or Debate: The New Interpretation as a Threat to Legislative Coequality." *Suffolk University Law Review* 8 (1974).

Craig, Barbara H. *Chadha: The Story of an Epic Constitutional Struggle* (New York: Oxford University Press, 1988).

Elliott, E. Donald. "INS v. Chadha: The Administrative Constitution, the Constitution, and the Legislative Veto." *The Supreme Court Review* (1983).

Fisher, Louis. *Constitutional Conflicts Between Congress and the President* (Princeton: Princeton University Press, 1985).

Hamilton, James. *The Power to Probe: A Study in Congressional Investigations* (New York: Random House, 1976).

Labovitz, John R. *Presidential Impeachment* (New York: Yale University Press, 1978).

"Note: the Equal Rights Amendment and Article V: A Framework for Analysis of the Extension and Recision Issues." *University of Pennsylvania Law Review* 127 (1978).

Shapiro, Martin. *Law and Politics in the Supreme Court* (New York: The Free Press of Glencoe, 1964) Chapter 2.

Weber, Paul J., and Barbara A. Perry. *Unfounded Fears; Myths and Realities of a Constitutional Convention* (New York: Praeger, 1989).

McCulloch v. *Maryland*

17 U.S. (Wheat.) 316; 4 L. Ed. 579 (1819)

In 1816, Congress chartered the Second Bank of the United States, one branch of which was established in Baltimore the next year. In 1818 the Maryland legislature passed a statute taxing "all banks or branches thereof" operating in Maryland but not chartered by the state. The act levied a tax of approximately 2 percent of the value of all notes issued or, alternatively, an annual fee of $15,000; it also provided for a $500 penalty for every violation. When James McCulloch, cashier of the Baltimore branch, issued notes and refused to pay the tax, suit was brought on behalf of the state of Maryland to recover the penalties. A judgment was rendered against McCulloch in lower court and affirmed by the Maryland court of appeals, the state's highest court. From there, the case was brought to the United States Supreme Court by a writ of error. *Opinion of the Court: Marshall, Washington, Johnson, Livingston, Todd, Duval, Story.*

Mr. Chief Justice Marshall delivered the opinion of the Court.

In the case now to be determined, the defendant, a sovereign State, denies the obligation of a law enacted by the legislature of the Union, and the plaintiff, on his part, contests the validity of an act which has been passed by the legislature of that State. The constitution of our country, in its most interesting and vital parts, is to be considered; the conflicting powers of the government of the Union and of its members, as marked in that constitution, are to be discussed; and an opinion given, which may essentially influence the great operations of the government. . . .

The first question made in the cause is, has Congress power to incorporate a bank? . . .

The government of the Union is acknowledged by all to be one of enumerated powers. . . . That principle is now universally admitted. But the question respecting the extent of the powers actually granted, is perpetually arising, and will probably continue to arise, as long as our system shall exist.

In discussing these questions, the conflicting powers of the general and State governments must be brought into view, and the supremacy of their respective laws, when they are in opposition, must be settled.

If any one proposition could command the universal assent of mankind, we might expect it would be this—that the government of the Union, though limited in its powers, is supreme within its sphere of action. This would seem to result necessarily from its nature. It is the government of all; its powers are delegated by all; it represents all, and acts for all. . . . The nation, on those subjects on which it can act, must necessarily bind its component parts. But this question is not left to mere reason: The people have, in express terms, decided it, by saying, "this constitution, and the laws of the United States, which shall be made in pursuance thereof," "shall be the supreme law of the land," and by requiring that the members of the State legislatures, and the officers of the executive and judicial departments of the States, shall take the oath of fidelity to it.

The government of the United States, then, though limited in its powers, is supreme; and its laws, when made in pursuance of the constitution, form the supreme law of the land, "any thing in the constitution or laws of any State to the contrary notwithstanding."

Among the enumerated powers, we do not find that of establishing a bank or creating a corporation. But there is no phrase in the instrument which, like the articles of confederation, excludes incidental or implied powers; and which requires that every thing granted shall be expressly and minutely described. Even the 10th amendment, which was framed for the purpose of quieting the excessive jealousies which had been excited, omits the word "expressly," and declares only that the powers "not delegated to the United States, nor prohibited to the States, are reserved to the States or to the people;" thus leaving the question, whether the particular power which may become the subject of contest has been delegated to the one government, or prohibited to the other, to depend on a fair construction of the whole instrument. The men who drew and adopted this amendment had experienced the embarrassments resulting from the insertion of this word in the articles of confederation, and probably omitted it to avoid those embarrassments. A constitution, to contain an accurate detail of all the subdivisions of which its great powers will admit, and of all the means by which they may be carried into execution, would partake of the prolixity of a legal code, and could scarcely be embraced by the human mind. It would probably never be understood by the public. Its nature, therefore, requires, that only its great outlines should be marked, its important objects designated, and the minor ingredients which compose those objects be deduced from the nature of the objects themselves. That this idea was entertained by the framers of the American constitution, is not only to be inferred from the nature of the instrument, but from the language. Why else were some of the limitations, found in the ninth section of the 1st article, introduced? It is also, in some degree, warranted by their having omitted to use any restrictive term which might prevent its receiving a fair and just interpretation. In considering this question, then, we must never forget, that it is *a constitution* we are expounding.

Although, among the enumerated powers of government, we do not find the word "bank" or "incorporation," we find the great powers to lay and collect taxes; to borrow money; to regulate commerce; to declare and conduct a war; and to raise and support armies and navies. The sword and the purse, all the external relations, and no inconsiderable portion of the industry of the nation, are entrusted to its government. It can never be pretended that these vast powers draw after them others of inferior importance, merely because they are inferiors. Such an idea can never be advanced. But it may with great reason be contended, that a government, entrusted with such ample powers, on the due execution of which the happiness and prosperity of the nation so vitally depends, must also be entrusted with ample means for their execution. The power being given, it is the interest of the nation to facilitate its execution. It can never be their interest, and cannot be presumed to have been their intention, to clog and embarrass its execution by withholding the most appropriate means. Throughout this vast republic . . . revenue is to be collected and expended, armies are to be marched and supported. The exigencies of the nation may require that the treasure raised in the north should be transported to the south, *that* raised in the east conveyed to the west, or that this order should be reversed. Is that construction of the constitution to be preferred which would render these operations difficult, hazardous, and expensive? Can we adopt that construction, (unless the words imperiously require it), which would impute to the framers of that instrument, when granting these powers for the public good, the intention of impeding their exercise by withholding a choice of means? If, indeed, such be the mandate of the constitution, we have only to obey; but that instrument does not profess to enumerate the means by which the powers it confers may be executed; nor does it prohibit the creation of a corporation, if the existence of such a being be essential to the beneficial exercise of those powers. It is, then, the subject of fair inquiry, how far such means may be employed.

It is not denied, that the powers given to the government imply the ordinary means of execution. That, for example, of raising revenue, and applying it to national purposes, is admitted to imply the power of conveying money from place to place, as the exigencies of the nation may require, and of employing the usual means of conveyance. But it is denied that the government has its choice of means; or, that it may employ the most convenient means, if, to employ them, it be necessary to erect a corporation.

But the constitution of the United States has not left the right of Congress to employ the necessary means, for the execution of the powers conferred on the government, to general reasoning. To its enumeration of powers is added that of making "all laws which shall be necessary and proper, for carrying into execution the foregoing powers, and all other powers vested by this constitution, in the government of the United States, or in any department thereof."

The counsel for the State of Maryland have urged various arguments, to prove that this clause, though in terms a grant of power, is not so in effect; but is really restrictive of the general right, which might otherwise be implied, of selecting means for executing the enumerated powers. . . .

The argument on which most reliance is placed, is drawn from the peculiar language of this clause. Congress is not empowered by it to make all laws, which may have relation to the powers conferred on the government, but such only as may be *"necessary and proper"* for carrying them into execution. The word *"necessary,"* is considered as controlling the whole sentence, and as limiting the right to pass laws for the execution of the granted powers, to such as are indispensable, and without which the power would be nugatory. That it excludes the choice of means, and leaves to Congress, in each case, that only which is most direct and simple.

Is it true, that this is the sense in which the word "necessary" is always used? Does it always import an absolute physical necessity, so strong, that one thing, to which another may be termed necessary, cannot exist without that other? We think it does not. . . . To employ the means necessary to an end, is generally understood as employing any means calculated to produce the end, and not as being confined to those single means, without which the end would be entirely unattainable. . . . Almost all compositions contain words, which, taken in their rigorous sense, would convey a meaning different from that which is obviously intended. It is essential to just construction, that many words which import something excessive, should be understood in a more mitigated sense—in that sense which common usage justifies. The word "necessary" is of this description. . . . It admits of all degrees of comparison; and is often connected with other words, which increase or diminish the impression the mind receives of the urgency it imports. A thing may be necessary, very necessary, absolutely or indispensably necessary. To no mind would the same idea by conveyed, by these several phrases. This comment on the word is well illustrated by the passage cited at the bar, from the 10th section of the 1st article of the constitution. It is, we think, impossible to compare the sentence which prohibits a State from laying "imposts, or duties on imports or exports, except what may be *absolutely* necessary for executing its inspection laws," with that which authorizes Congress "to make all laws which shall be necessary and proper for carrying into execution" the powers of the general government, without feeling a conviction that the convention understood itself to change materially the meaning of the word "necessary," by prefixing the word "absolutely." . . . This provision is made in a constitution intended to endure for ages to come, and, consequently, to be adapted to the various *crises* of human affairs. To have prescribed the means by which government should, in all future time; execute its powers, would have been to change, entirely, the character of the instrument, and give it the properties of a legal code. . . . To have declared that the best means shall not be used, but those alone without which the power given would be nugatory, would have been to deprive the legislature of the capacity to avail itself of experience, to exercise its reason, and to accommodate its legislation to circumstances. If we apply this principle of construction to any of the powers of the government, we shall find it so pernicious in its operation that we shall be compelled to discard it. . . .

Take, for example, the power "to establish post offices and post roads." This power is executed by the single act of making the establishment. But, from this has been inferred the power and duty of carrying the mail along the post road, from one post office to another. And, from this implied power, has again been inferred the right to punish those who steal letters from the post office, or rob the mail. It may be said, with some plausibility, that the right to carry the mail, and to punish those who rob it, is not indispensably necessary to the establishment of a post office and post road. This right is indeed essential to the beneficial exercise of the power, but not indispensably necessary to its existence. So, of the punishment of the crimes of stealing or falsifying a record or process of a Court of the United States, or of perjury in such Court. To punish these offences is certainly conducive to the due administration of justice. But courts may exist, and may decide the causes brought before them, though such crimes escape punishment. . . .

If this limited construction of the word "necessary" must be abandoned in order to punish, whence is derived the rule which would reinstate it, when the government would carry its powers into execution by means not vindictive in their nature? If the word "necessary" means "needful," "requisite," "essential," "conducive to," in order to let in the power of punishment for the infraction of law; why is it not equally comprehensive when required to authorize the use of means which facilitate the execution of the powers of government without the infliction of punishment?" . . .

But the argument which most conclusively demonstrates the error of the construction contended for by the counsel for the State of Maryland, is founded on the intention of the Convention, as manifested in the whole clause. . . . This clause, as construed by the State of Maryland, would abridge, and almost annihilate this useful and necessary right of the legislature to select its means. That this could not be intended, is, we should think, had it not been already controverted, too apparent for controversy. We think so for the following reasons.

1st. The clause is placed among the powers of Congress, not among the limitations on those powers.

2nd. Its terms purport to enlarge, not to diminish the powers vested in the government. It purports to be an additional power, not a restriction on those already granted. No reason has been, or can be assigned for thus concealing an intention to narrow the discretion of the national legislature under words which purport to enlarge it. The framers of the constitution wished its adoption, and well knew that it would be endangered by its strength, not by its weakness. Had they been capable of using language which would convey to the eye one idea, and, after deep reflection, impress on the mind another, they would rather have disguised the grant of power, than its limitation. If, then, their intention had been, by this clause, to restrain the free use of means which might otherwise have been implied, that intention would have been inserted in another place, and would have been expressed in terms resembling these. "In carrying into execution the foregoing powers, and all others," &c. "no laws shall be passed but such as are necessary and proper." Had the intention been to make this clause restrictive, it would unquestionably have been so in form as well as in effect. . . .

We admit, as all must admit, that the powers of the government are limited, and that its limits are not to be transcended. But we think the sound construction of the constitution must allow to the national legislature that discretion, with respect to the means by which the powers it confers are to be carried into execution, which will enable that body to perform the high duties assigned to it, in the manner most beneficial to the people. Let the end be legitimate, let it be within the scope of the constitution, and all means which are appropriate, which are plainly adapted to that end, which are not prohibited, but consist with the letter and spirit of the constitution, are constitutional. . . .

Should Congress, in the execution of its powers, adopt measures which are prohibited by the constitution; or should Congress, under the pretext of executing its powers, pass laws for the accomplishment of objects not entrusted to the government; it would become the painful duty of this tribunal, should a case requiring such a decision come before it, to say that such an act was not the law of the land. But where the law is not prohibited, and is really calculated to effect any of the objects entrusted to the government, to undertake here to inquire into the degree of its necessity, would be to pass the line which circumscribes the judicial department, and to tread on legislative ground. This court disclaims all pretensions to such a power. . . .

After the most deliberate consideration, it is the unanimous and decided opinion of this Court, that the act to incorporate the Bank of the United States is a law made in pursuance of the constitution and is a part of the supreme law of the land. . . .

It being the opinion of the Court, that the act incorporating the bank is constitutional . . . we proceed to inquire— . . . Whether the State of Maryland may, without violating the constitution, tax that branch?

The argument on the part of the State of Maryland, is, not that the States may directly resist a law of Congress, but that they may exercise their acknowledged powers upon it, and that the constitution leaves them this right in the confidence that they will not abuse it. . . .

That the power to tax involves the power to destroy; that the power to destroy may defeat and render useless the power to create; that there is a plain repugnance, in conferring on one government a power to control the constitutional measures of another, which other, with respect to those very measures, is declared to be supreme over that which exerts the control, are propositions not to be denied. But all inconsistencies are to be reconciled by the magic of the word CONFIDENCE. Taxation, it is said, does not necessarily and unavoidably destroy. To carry it to the excess of destruction would be an abuse, to presume which, would banish that confidence which is essential to all government.

But is this a case of confidence? Would the people of any one State trust those of another with a power to control the most insignificant operations of their State government? We know they would not. Why, then, should we suppose that the people of any one State should be willing to trust those of another with a power to control the operations of a government to which they have confided their most important and most valuable interests? In the legislature of the Union alone, are all represented. The legislature of the Union alone, therefore, can be trusted by the people with the power of controlling measures which concern all, in the confidence that it will not be abused. This, then, is not a case of confidence, and we must consider it as it really is.

If we apply the principle for which the State of Maryland contends, to the constitution generally, we shall find it capable of changing totally the character of that instrument. We shall find it capable of arresting all the measures of the government, and of prostrating it at the foot of the States. The American people have declared their constitution, and the laws made in pursuance thereof, to be supreme; but this principle would transfer the supremacy, in fact, to the States.

It has also been insisted, that, as the power of taxation in the general and State governments is acknowledged to be concurrent, every argument which would sustain the right of the general government to tax banks chartered by the States, will equally sustain the right of the States to tax banks chartered by the general government.

But the two cases are not on the same reason. The people of all the States have created the general government, and have conferred upon it the general power of taxation. The people of all the States, and the States themselves, are represented in Congress, and, by their representatives, exercise this power. When they tax the chartered institutions of the States, they tax their constituents; and these taxes must be uniform. But, when a State taxes the operations of the government of the United States, it acts upon institutions created, not by their own constituents, but by people over whom they claim no control. It acts upon the measures of a government created by others as well as themselves, for the benefit of others in common with themselves. The difference is that which always exists, and always must exist, between the action of the whole on a part, and the action of a part on the whole—between the laws of a government declared to be supreme, and those of a government which, when in opposition to those laws, is not supreme. . . .

The Court has bestowed on this subject its most deliberate consideration. The result is a conviction that the States have no power, by taxation or otherwise, to retard, impede, burden, or in any manner control, the operations of the constitutional laws enacted by Congress to carry into execution the powers vested in the general government. This is, we think, the unavoidable consequence of that supremacy which the constitution has declared.

We are unanimously of opinion, that the law passed by the legislature of Maryland, imposing a tax on the Bank of the United States, is unconstitutional and void. . . .

Gravel v. *United States*

408 U.S. 606, 92 S. Ct. 2614, 33 L. Ed. 2d 583 (1972)

In 1971 Senator Mike Gravel received from Daniel Ellsberg, a consultant to the Defense Department, a copy of the so-called Pentagon Papers, a classified Defense Department study on how the United States became involved in the Vietnam War. Gravel then convened a meeting of the Senate Subcommittee on Public Buildings and Grounds (of which he was chairman), read excerpts from the papers, and introduced all forty-seven volumes of the study into the record as an exhibit. Press reports indicated that the senator had also arranged with Beacon Press for private publication of the Pentagon Papers. A federal grand jury, impaneled to investigate possible violations of federal law in the release of the papers, subpoenaed Leonard Rodberg, a Gravel aide, to testify about his role in obtaining and arranging for publication of the Pentagon Papers. Senator Gravel intervened, contending that requiring Rodberg to testify about activities he undertook in Gravel's service would violate the Speech and Debate Clause. *Opinion of the Court: White, Burger, Blackmun, Powell, Rehnquist. Dissenting opinions: Stewart (in part); Douglas; Brennan, Douglas, Marshall.*

MR. JUSTICE WHITE delivered the opinion of the Court. . . .

Because the claim is that a Member's aide shares the Member's constitutional privilege, we consider first whether and to what extent Senator Gravel himself is exempt from process or inquiry by a grand jury investigating the commission of a crime. . . .

. . . His insistence is that the Speech or Debate Clause at the very least protects him from criminal or civil liability and from questioning elsewhere than in the Senate, with respect to the events occurring at the subcommittee hearing at which the Pentagon Papers were introduced into the public record. To us this claim is incontrovertible. The Speech or Debate Clause was designed to assure a co-equal branch of the government wide freedom of speech, debate, and deliberation without intimidation or threats from the Executive Branch. It thus protects Members against prosecutions that directly impinge upon or threaten the legislative process. . . .

Even so, the United States strongly urges that because the Speech or Debate Clause confers a privilege only upon "Senators and Representatives," Rodberg himself has no valid claim to constitutional immunity from grand jury inquiry. In our view both courts below correctly rejected this position. . . . It is literally impossible, in view of the complexities of the modern legislative process, with Congress almost constantly in session and matters of legislative concern constantly proliferating, for Members of Congress to perform their legislative tasks without the help of aides and assistants; the day-to-day work of such aides is so critical to the Members' performance that they must be treated as the latter's alter egos; and if they are not so recognized, the central role of the Speech or Debate Clause—to prevent intimidation of legislators by the Executive and accountability before a possibly hostile judiciary—will inevitably be diminished and frustrated. . . .

The United States fears the abuses that history reveals have occurred when legislators are invested with the power to relieve others from the operation of otherwise valid civil and criminal laws. But these abuses, it seems to us, are for the most part obviated if the privilege applicable to the aide is viewed, as it must be, as the privilege of the Senator, and invocable only by the Senator or by the aide on the Senator's behalf* and if in all events the privilege available to the aide is confined to those services that would be immune legislative conduct if performed by the Senator himself. This view places beyond the Speech and Debate Clause a variety of services characteristically performed by aides for Members of Congress, even though within the scope of their employment. . . . Thus our refusal to distinguish between Senator and aide in applying the Speech or Debate Clause does not mean that Rodberg is for all purposes exempt from grand jury questioning.

We are convinced also that the Court of Appeals correctly determined that Senator Gravel's alleged arrangement with Beacon Press to publish the Pentagon Papers was not protected speech or debate within the meaning of Art. I, § 6, cl. 1, of the Constitution.

Historically, the English legislative privilege was not viewed as protecting republication of an otherwise immune libel on the floor of the House. . . .

Prior cases have read the Speech or Debate Clause "broadly to effectuate its purposes," . . . and have included within its reach anything "generally done in a session of the House by one of its members in relation to the business before

*It follows that an aide's claim of privilege can be repudiated and thus waived by the Senator.

it." . . . But the Clause has not been extended beyond the legislative sphere. That Senators generally perform certain acts in their official capacity as Senators does not necessarily make all such acts legislative in nature. Members of Congress are constantly in touch with the Executive Branch of the Government and with administrative agencies—they may cajole, and exhort with respect to the administration of a federal statute—but such conduct, though generally done, is not protected legislative activity. . . . The heart of the Clause is speech or debate in either House. Insofar as the Clause is construed to reach other matters, they must be an integral part of the deliberative and communicative processes by which Members participate in committee and House proceedings with respect to the consideration and passage or rejection of propsed legislation or with respect to other matters which the Constitution places within the jurisdiction of either House . . .

Here, private publication by Senator Gravel through the cooperation of Beacon Press was in no way essential to the deliberations of the Senate; nor does questioning as to private publication threaten the integrity or independence of the Senate by impermissibly exposing its deliberation to executive influence. . . . We cannot but conclude that the Senator's arrangements with Beacon Press were not part and parcel of the legislative process. . . .

MR. JUSTICE BRENNAN, with whom MR. JUSTICE DOUGLAS and MR. JUSTICE MARSHALL join, dissenting. . . .

In holding that Senator Gravel's alleged arrangement with Beacon Press to publish the Pentagon Papers is not shielded from extrasenatorial inquiry by the Speech or Debate Clause, the Court adopts what for me is a far too narrow view of the legislative function. . . . The Court excludes from the sphere of protected legislative activity a function that I had supposed lay at the heart of our democratic system. I speak, of course, of the legislator's duty to inform the public about matters affecting the administration of government. . . .

The informing function has been cited by numerous students of American politics, both within and without the Government, as among the most important responsibilities of legislative office. . . . Though I fully share these . . . views on the educational values served by the informing function, there is yet another, and perhaps more fundamental, interest at stake. It requires no citation of authority to state that public concern over current issues—the war, race relations, governmental invasions of privacy—has transformed itself in recent years into what many believe is a crisis of confidence, in our system of government and its capacity to meet the needs and reflect the wants of the American people. Communication between Congress and the electorate tends to alleviate that doubt by exposing and clarifying the workings of the political system, the policies underlying new laws and the role of the Executive in their administration. To the extent that the informing function succeeds in fostering public faith in the responsiveness of Government, it is not only an "ordinary" task of the legislator but one that is essential to the continued vitality of our democratic institutions.

Unlike the Court, therefore, I think that the activities of Congressmen in communicating with the public are legislative acts protected by the Speech or Debate Clause. I agree with the Court that not every task performed by a legislator is privileged; intervention before Executive departments is one that is not. But the informing function carries a far more persuasive claim to the protections of the Clause. It has been recognized by this Court as something "generally done" by Congressmen, the Congress itself has established special concessions designed to lower the cost of such communication, and, most important, the function furthers several well-recognized goals of representative government. To say in the face of these facts that the informing function is not privileged merely because it is not necessary to the internal deliberations of Congress is to give the Speech or Debate Clause an artificial and narrow reading unsupported by reason. . . .

Whether the Speech or Debate Clause extends to the informing function is an issue whose importance goes beyond the fate of a single Senator or Congressman. What is at stake is the right of an elected representative to inform, and the public to be informed, about matters relating directly to the workings of our Government. The dialogue between Congress and people has been recognized, from the days of our founding, as one of the necessary elements of a representative system. We should not retreat from that view merely because, in the course of that dialogue, information may be revealed that is embarrassing to the other branches of government or violates their notions of necessary secrecy. A Member of Congress who exceeds the bounds of propriety in performing this official task may be called to answer by the other Members of his chamber. We do violence to the fundamental concepts of privilege, however, when we subject that same conduct to judicial scrutiny at the instance of the Executive. . . .

Equally troubling in today's decision is the Court's refusal to bar grand jury inquiry into the source of documents received by the Senator and placed by him in the hearing record. The receipt of materials for use in a congressional hearing is an integral part of the preparation for that legislative act. . . . It would accomplish little toward the goal of legislative freedom to exempt an official act from intimidating scrutiny, if other conduct leading up to the act and intimately related to it could be deterred by a similar threat. . . . I would hold that Senator Gravel's receipt of the Pentagon Papers, including the name of the person from whom he received them, may not be the subject of inquiry by the grand jury.

I would go further, however, and also exclude from grand jury inquiry any knowledge that the Senator or his aides might have concerning how the source himself first came to possess the Papers. This immunity, it seems to me, is essential to the performance of the informing function. Corrupt and deceitful officers of the government do not often post for public examination the evidence of their own misdeeds. That evidence must be ferreted out, and often is, by fellow employees and subordinates. Their willingness to reveal that information and spark congressional inquiry may well depend on assurances from their contact in Congress that their identities and means of obtaining the evidence will be held in strictest confidence. To permit the grand jury to frustrate that expectation through an inquiry of the Congressman and his aides can only dampen the flow of information to the Congress and thus to the American people. There is a similar risk, of course, when the Member's own House requires him to break the confidence. But the danger, it seems to me, is far less if the Member's colleagues, and not an "unfriendly executive" or "hostile judiciary," are charged with evaluating the propriety of his conduct. In any event, assuming that a Congressman can be required to reveal the sources of his information and the methods used to obtain that information, that power of inquiry, as required by the Clause, is that of the Congressman's House, and of that House only.

I respectfully dissent.

McGrain v. *Daugherty*

273 U.S. 135, 47 S. Ct. 319, 71 L. Ed. 580 (1927)

A Senate select committee investigating the Department of Justice's failure to prosecute key figures in the Teapot Dome scandal and other violators of federal statutes subpoenaed Mally Daugherty, a banker and the brother of the former attorney general, but Daugherty failed to appear. Acting on a warrant issued by the Senate, McGrain, the deputy sergeant at arms of the Senate, took Daugherty into custody so that the committee might question him. Daugherty successfully petitioned for a writ of habeas corpus from a federal district court, which ruled that the Senate had exceeded its constitutional powers in detaining him. The case was then appealed to the Supreme Court. *Opinion of the Court: Van Devanter, Taft, Holmes, McReynolds, Brandeis, Sutherland, Butler, Sanford. Not participating: Stone.*

Mr. Justice Van Devanter delivered the opinion of the Court. . . .

. . . The principal questions involved are . . . (a) whether the Senate—or the House of Representatives, both being on the same plane in this regard—has power, through its own process, to compel a private individual to appear before it or one of its committees and give testimony needed to enable it efficiently to exercise a legislative function belonging to it under the Constitution, and (b) whether it sufficiently appears that the process was being employed in this instance to obtain testimony for that purpose. . . .

. . . We are not now concerned with the right of the Senate to propound or the duty of the witness to answer specific questions, for as yet no questions have been propounded to him. He is asserting . . . that the Senate is without power to interrogate him, even if the questions propounded be pertinent and otherwise legitimate—which for present purposes must be assumed. . . .

. . . There is no provision expressly investing either house with power to make investigations and exact testimony to the end that it may exercise its legislative function advisedly and effectively. So the question arises whether this power is so far incidental to the legislative function as to be implied.

We are of the opinion that the power of inquiry—with process to enforce it—is an essential and appropriate auxiliary to the legislative function. It was so regarded and employed in American legislatures before the Constitution was framed and ratified. Both houses of Congress took this view of it early in their history . . . and both houses have employed the power accordingly up to the present time. . . . So, when their practice in the matter is appraised according to the circumstances in which it was begun and to those in which it has been continued, it falls nothing short of a practical construction, long continued, of the constitutional provisions respecting their powers, and therefore should be taken as fixing the meaning of those provisions, if otherwise doubtful.

We are further of opinion that the provisions are not of doubtful meaning, but . . . are intended to be effectively exercised, and therfore to carry with them such auxiliary powers as are necessary and appropriate to that end. . . . A legislative body cannot legislate wisely or effectively in the absence of information respecting the conditions which the legislation is intended to affect or change; and where the legislative body does not itself possess the requisite information—which not infrequently is true—recourse must be had to others who do possess it. Experience has taught that mere requests for such information often are unavailing, and also that information which is volunteered is not always accurate or complete; so some means of compulsion are essential to obtain what is needed. . . .

We come now to the question whether it sufficiently appears that the purpose for which the witness's testimony was sought was to obtain information in aid of the legislative function. . . .

It is quite true that the resolution directing the investigation does not in terms avow that it is intended to be in aid of legislation; but it does show that the subject to be investigated was the administration of the Department of Justice—whether its functions were being properly discharged or were being neglected or misdirected, and particularly whether the Attorney General and his assistants were performing or neglecting their duties in respect of the institution and prosecution of proceedings to punish crimes and enforce appropriate remedies against the wrongdoers—specific instances of alleged neglect being recited. Plainly the subject was one on which legislation could be had and would be materially aided by the information which the investigation was calculated to elicit. . . .

The only legitimate object the Senate could have in ordering the investigation was to aid it in legislating; and we think the subject-matter was such that the presumption should be indulged that this was the real object. . . .

We conclude that the investigation was ordered for a legitimate object; that the witness wrongfully refused to appear and testify before the committee and was lawfully attached; that the Senate is entitled to have him give testimony pertinent to the inquiry, either at its bar or before the committee; and that the district court erred in discharging him from custody under the attachment. . . .

Watkins v. *United States*

354 U.S. 178, 77 S. Ct. 1173, 1 L. Ed. 2d 1273 (1957)

As part of its investigation into communist influence in the labor movement, the House Un-American Activities Committee summoned John Watkins, an organizer for the United Auto Workers, to testify before it. Watkins willingly answered questions about his own personal involvement in Communist Party activities and about persons who he believed were still Communist Party members. He refused to respond, however, to questions about persons who had previously been active in the Communist Party but were no longer involved with it, maintaining that an inquiry into their activities was not pertinent to the committee's investigation. He was cited for contempt by the committee and subsequently convicted in federal district court. After the court of appeals upheld his conviction, the Supreme Court granted certiorari. *Opinion of the Court: Warren, Black, Douglas, Harlan, Brennan. Concurring opinion: Frankfurter. Dissenting opinion: Clark. Not participating: Burton, Whittaker.*

MR. CHIEF JUSTICE WARREN delivered the opinion of the Court.

We start with several basic premises on which there is general agreement. The power of the Congress to conduct investigations is inherent in the legislative process. That power is broad. It encompasses inquiries concerning the administration of existing laws as well as proposed or possibly needed statutes. It includes surveys of defects in our social, economic or political system for the purpose of enabling the Congress to remedy them. It comprehends probes into departments of the Federal Government to expose corruption, inefficiency or waste. But, broad as is this power of inquiry, it is not unlimited. There is no general authority to expose the private affairs of individuals without justification in terms of the functions of the Congress. . . . Nor is the Congress a law enforcement or trial agency. These are functions of the executive and judicial departments of government. No inquiry is an end in itself; it must be related to, and in furtherance of, a legitimate task of the Congress. Investigations conducted solely for the personal aggrandizement of the investigators or to "punish" those investigated are indefensible.

It is unquestionably the duty of all citizens to cooperate with Congress in its efforts to obtain the facts needed for intelligent legislative action. It is their unremitting obligation to respond to subpoenas, to respect the dignity of the Congress and its committees and to testify fully with respect to matters within the province of proper investigation. This, of course, assumes that the constitutional rights of witnesses will be respected by the Congress as they are in a court of justice. The Bill of Rights is applicable to investigations as to all forms of government action. . . .

Abuses of the investigative process may imperceptibly lead to abridgment of protected freedoms. The mere summoning of a witness and compelling him to testify, against his will, about his beliefs, expressions or associations is a measure of governmental interference. And when those forced revelations concern matters that are unorthodox, unpopular, or even hateful to the general public, the reaction in the life of the witness may be disastrous. This effect is even more harsh when it is past beliefs, expressions or associations that are disclosed and judged by current standards rather than those contemporary with the matters exposed. Nor does the witness alone suffer the consequences. Those who are identified by witnesses and thereby placed in the same glare of publicity are equally subject to public stigma, scorn and obloquy. Beyond that, there is the more subtle and immeasurable effect upon those who tend to adhere to the most orthodox and uncontroversial views and associations in order to avoid a similar fate at some future time. That this impact is partly the result of non-governmental activity by private persons cannot relieve the investigators of their responsibility for initiating the reaction. . . .

Petitioner has earnestly suggested that the difficult questions of protecting these rights from infringement by legislative inquiries can be surmounted in this case because there was no public purpose served in his interrogation. . . . The sole purpose of the inquiry, he contends, was to bring down upon himself and others the violence of public reaction because of their past beliefs, expressions and associations. In support of this argument, petitioner has marshalled an impressive array of evidence that some Congressmen have believed that such was their duty, or part of it.

We have no doubt that there is no congressional power to expose for the sake of exposure. . . . But a solution to our problem is not to be found in testing the motives of committee members for this purpose. Such is not our function. Their motives alone would not vitiate an investigation which had been instituted by a House of Congress if that assembly's legislative purpose is being served.

Petitioner's contentions do point to a situation of particular significance from the standpoint of the constitutional limitations upon congressional investigations. The theory of a committee inquiry is that the committee members are serving as the representatives of the parent assembly in collecting information for a legislative purpose. . . . An essential premise in this situation is that the House or Senate shall have instructed the committee members on what they are to do with the power delegated to them. It is the responsibility of the Congress, in the first instance, to insure that compulsory process is used only in furtherance of a legislative purpose. That requires that the instructions to an investigating committee spell out that group's jurisdiction and purpose with sufficient particularity. Those instructions are embodied in the authorizing resolution. That document is the committee's charter . . . The more vague the committee's charter is, the greater becomes the possibility that the committee's specific actions are not in conformity with the will of the parent House of Conress.

The authorizing resolution of the Un-American Activities Committee . . . defines the Committee's authority as follows:

"The Committee on Un-American Activities, as a whole or by subcommittee, is authorized to make from time to time investigations of (1) the extent, character, and objects of un-American propaganda activities in the United States, (2) the diffusion within the United States of subversive and un-American propaganda that is instigated from foreign countries or of a domestic origin and attacks the principle of the form of government as guaranteed by our Constitution, and (3) all other questions in relation thereto that would aid Congress in any necessary remedial legislation."

It would be difficult to imagine a less explicit authorization resolution. . . .

Combining the language of the resolution with the construction it has been given, it is evident that the preliminary control of the Committee exercised by the House of Representatives is slight or non-existent. No one could reasonably deduce from the charter the kind of investigation that the Committee was directed to make. . . .

In fulfillment of their obligation under [the statute for contempt of Congress], the courts must accord to the defendants every right which is guaranteed to defendants in all other criminal cases. Among these is the right to have available, through a sufficiently precise statute, information revealing the standard of criminality before the commission of the alleged offense. Applied to persons prosecuted under § 192, this raises a special problem in that the statute defines the crimes as a refusal to answer "any question pertinent to the question under inquiry." Part of the standard of criminality, therefore, is the pertinency of the questions propounded to the witness. . . .

It is obvious that a person . . . is entitled to have knowledge of the subject to which the interrogation is deemed pertinent. That knowledge must be available with the same degree of explicitness and clarity that the Due Process Clause requires in the expression of any element of a criminal offense. The "vice of vagueness" must be avoided here as in all other crimes. There are several sources that can outline the "question under inquiry" in such a way that the rules against vagueness are satisfied. The authorizing resolution, the remarks of the chairman or members of the committee, or even the nature of the proceedings themselves, might sometimes make the topic clear. . . .

The first possibility is that the authorizing resolution itself will so clearly declare the "question under inquiry" that a witness can understand the pertinency of questions asked him. The Government does not contend that the authorizing resolution of the Un-American Activities Committee could serve such a purpose. . . .

No aid is given as to the "question under inquiry" in the action of the full Committee that authorized the creation of the Subcommittee before which petitioner appeared. The Committee adopted a formal resolution giving the Chairman the power to appoint subcommittees ". . . for the purpose of performing any and all acts which the Committee as a whole is authorized to do." . . .

The Government believes that the topic of inquiry before the Subcommittee concerned Communist infiltration in labor. In his introductory remarks, the Chairman made reference to a bill, then pending before the Committee, which would have penalized labor unions controlled or dominated by persons who were, or had been, members of a "Communist-action" organization, as defined in the Internal Security Act of 1950. The Subcommittee, it is contended, might have been endeavoring to determine the extent of such a problem.

This view is corroborated somewhat by the witnesses who preceded and followed petitioner before the Subcommittee. Looking at the entire hearings, however, there is strong reason to doubt that the subject revolved about labor matters. The published transcript is entitled: Investigation of Community Activities in the Chicago Area, and six of the nine witnesses had no connection with labor at all.

The most serious doubts as to the Subcommittee's "question under inquiry," however, stem from the precise questions that petitioner has been charged with refusing to answer. Under the terms of the statute, after all, it is these which must be proved pertinent. Petitioner is charged with refusing to tell the Subcommittee whether or not he knew that certain named persons had been members of the Communist Party in the past. The Subcommittee's counsel read the list from the testimony of a previous witness who had identified them as Communists. Although this former witness was identified with labor, he had not stated that the persons he named were involved in union affairs. Of the thirty names propounded to petitioner, seven were completely unconnected with organized labor. . . .

The final source of evidence as to "the question under inquiry" is the Chairman's response when petitioner objected to the questions on the grounds of lack of pertinency. The Chairman then announced that the Subcommittee was investigating "subversion and subversive propaganda." This is a subject at least as broad and indefinite as the authorizing resolution of the Committee, if not more so.

Having exhausted the several possible indicia of the "question under inquiry," we remain unenlightened as to the subject to which the questions asked petitioner were pertinent. . . . Fundamental fairness demands that no witness be compelled to make such a determination with so little guidance. Unless the subject matter has been made to appear with undisputable clarity, it is the duty of the investigative body, upon objection of the witness on grounds of pertinency, to state for the record the subject under inquiry at that time and the manner in which the propounded questions are pertinent thereto. . . .

The statement of the Committee Chairman in this case, in response to petitioner's protest, was woefully inadequate to convey sufficient information as to the pertinency of the questions to the subject under inquiry. Petitioner was thus not accorded a fair opportunity to determine whether he was within his rights in refusing to answer, and his conviction is necessarily invalid under the Due Process Clause of the Fifth Amendment.

We are mindful of the complexities of modern government and the ample scope that must be left to the Congress as the sole constitutional depository of legislative power. Equally mindful are we of the indispensable function, in the exercise of that power, of congressional investigations. The conclusions we have reached in this case will not prevent the Congress, through its committees, from obtaining any information it needs for the proper fulfillment of its role in our scheme of government. The legislature is free to determine the kinds of data that should be collected. It is only those investigations that are conducted by use of compulsory process that give rise to a need to protect the rights of individuals against illegal encroachment. That protection can be readily achieved through procedures which prevent the separation of power from responsibility and which provide the constitutional requisites of fairness for witnesses. . . .

The Watkins decision provoked an immediate reaction in Congress. Senator Albert Jenner of Indiana introduced legislation withdrawing the Supreme Court's jurisdiction over "any function or practice of, or the jurisdiction of, any committee or sub-committee of the United States Congress or any action or proceedings against a witness charged with contempt of Congress." Although favorably reported by a Senate Committee, Jenner's bill was tabled by the Senate. Prior to its reintroduction, several of its supporters were defeated in the congressional elections of 1958, and the Supreme Court allayed congressional fears in Barenblatt v. United States. *As a result, the bill restricting the Court's jurisdiction was handily defeated in 1959.*

Schechter Poultry Corporation v. *United States*

295 U.S. 495, 55 S. Ct. 837, 79 L. Ed. 1570 (1935)

The National Industrial Recovery Act of 1933 was a major element in the Roosevelt administration's program to stimulate the economy and reduce unemployment. Under the act, trade associations were to propose industrywide codes of fair competition governing wages, hours, and modes of competition; these codes would take legal effect when the president endorsed them by executive order. The act specified that the trade associations should be truly representative, that the codes should not tend to produce monopolies, and that the codes should promote economic recovery.

The Schechter brothers were convicted for violating the Live Poultry Code by filing false sales and price reports and selling diseased chickens. They challenged their convictions, contending that the National Industrial Recovery Act constituted an unconstitutional delegation of legislative power and that their business activities were not part of interstate commerce and thus could not be regulated by the federal government. After a court of appeals generally sustained the district court, the Supreme Court granted certiorari. *Opinion of the Court: Hughes, Van Devanter, McReynolds, Brandeis, Sutherland, Butler, Roberts. Concurring opinion: Cardozo, Stone.*

MR. CHIEF JUSTICE HUGHES delivered the opinion of the Court. . . .

We are told that the provision of the statute authorizing the adoption of codes must be viewed in the light of the grave national crisis with which Congress was confronted. Undoubtedly, the conditions to which power is addressed are always to be considered when the exercise of power is challenged. Extraordinary conditions may call for extraordinary remedies. But the argument necessarily stops short of an attempt to justify action which lies outside the sphere of constitutional authority. Extraordinary conditions do not create or enlarge constitutional power. . . . Such assertions of extra-constitutional authority were anticipated and precluded by the explicit terms of the Tenth Amendment,—"The powers not delegated to the United States by the Constitution, nor prohibited by it to the States, are reserved to the States respectively, or to the people." . . .

. . . *The question of the delegation of legislative power.* . . . The Congress is not permitted to abdicate or to transfer to others the essential legislative functions with which it is thus vested. We have repeatedly recognized the necessity of adapting legislation to complex conditions involving a host of details with which the national legislature cannot deal directly. We pointed out in the *Panama Company* case [*Panama Refining Company* v. *Ryan* (1935)] that the Constitution has never been regarded as denying to Congress the necessary resources of flexibility and practicality, which will enable it to perform its function in laying down policies and establishing standards, while leaving to selected instrumentalities the making of subordinate rules within prescribed limits and the determination of facts to which the policy as declared by the legislature is to apply. But we said that the constant recognition of the necessity and validity of such provisions, and the wide range of administrative authority which has been developed by means of them, cannot be allowed to obscure the limitations of the authority to delegate, if our constitutional system is to be maintained. . . .

Accordingly, we look to the statute to see whether Congress has overstepped these limitations,—whether Congress in authorizing "codes of fair competition" has itself established the standards of legal obligation, thus performing its essential legislative function, or, by the failure to enact such standards, has attempted to transfer that function to others. . . .

What is meant by "fair competition" as the term is used in the Act? Does it refer to a category established in the law, and is the authority to make codes limited accordingly? Or is it used as a convenient designation for whatever set of laws the formulators of a code for a particular trade or industry may propose and the President may approve (subject to certain restrictions), or the President may himself prescribe, as being wise and beneficent provisions for the government of the trade or industry in order to accomplish the broad purposes of rehabilitation, correction and expansion which are stated in the first section of Title I?

The Government urges that the codes will "consist of rules of competition deemed fair for each industry by representative members of that industry—by the persons most vitally concerned and most familiar with its problems." Instances are cited in which Congress has availed itself of such assistance. . . . But would it be seriously contended that Congress could delgate its legislative authority to trade or industrial associations or groups so as to empower them to enact the laws they deem to be wise and beneficent for the rehabilitation and expansion of their trade or industries? . . . The answer is obvious. Such a delegation of legislative power is unknown to our law and is utterly inconsistent with the constitutional prerogatives and duties of Congress.

The question, then, turns upon the authority which § 3 of the Recovery Act vests in the President to approve or prescribe. If the codes have standing as penal statutes, this must be due to the effect of the executive action. But Congress cannot delegate legislative power to the President to exercise an unfettered discretion to make whatever laws he thinks may be needed or advisable for the rehabilitation and expansion of trade or industry. . . .

Section 3 of the Recovery Act is without precedent. It supplies no standards for any trade, industry or activity. It does not undertake to prescribe rules of conduct to be applied to particular states of fact determined by appropriate administrative procedure. Instead of prescribing rules of conduct, it authorizes the making of codes to prescribe them. For that legislative undertaking, § 3 sets up no standards, aside from the statement of the general aims of rehabilitation, correction and expansion described in section one. In view of the scope of that broad declaration, and of the nature of the few restrictions that are imposed, the discretion of the President in approving or prescribing codes, and thus enacting laws for the government of trade and industry throughout the country, is virtually unfettered. We think that the code-making authority thus conferred is an unconstitutional delegation of legislative power. . . .

On both the grounds we have discussed, the attempted delegation of legislative power, and the attempted regulation of intrastate transactions which affect interstate commerce only indirectly, we hold the code provisions here in question to be invalid and that the judgment of conviction must be reversed.

MR. JUSTICE CARDOZO, concurring.

The delegated power of legislation which has found expression in this code is not canalized within banks that keep it from overflowing. It is unconfined and vagrant. . . .

This court has held that delegation may be unlawful though the act to be performed is definite and single, if the necessity, time and occasion of performance have been left in the end to the discretion of the delgate. *Panama Refining Co.* v. *Ryan*, . . . I thought that ruling went too far. . . . Here, in the case before us, is an attempted delegation not confined to any single act nor to any class or group of acts identified or described by reference to a standard. Here in effect is a roving commission to inquire into evils and upon discovery correct them.

The code does not confine itself to the suppression of methods of competition that would be classified as unfair according to accepted business standards or accepted norms of ethics. It sets up a comprehensive body of rules to promote the welfare of the industry, if not the welfare of the nation, without reference to standards, ethical or commercial, that could be known or predicted in advance of its adoption. One of the new rules, the source of ten counts in the indictment, is aimed at an established practice, not unethical or oppressive, the practice of selective buying. Many others could be instanced as open to the same objection if the sections of the code were to be examined one by one. . . . Even if the statute itself has fixed the meaning of fair competition by way of contrast with practices that are oppressive or unfair, the code outruns the bounds of the authority conferred. What is excessive is not sporadic or superficial. It is deep-seated and pervasive.

. . . But there is another objection, far-reaching and incurable, aside from any defect of unlawful delegation.

If this code had been adopted by Congress itself, and not by the President on the advice of an industrial association, it would even then be void unless authority to adopt it is included in the grant of power "to regulate commerce with foreign nations and among the several states." . . .

I find no authority in that grant for the regulation of wages and hours of labor in the intrastate transactions that make up the defendants' business. As to this feature of the case little can be added to the opinion of the court. There is a view of causation that would obliterate the distinction between what is national and what is local in the activities of commerce. . . .

Mistretta v. *United States*

488 U.S. 109 S. Ct. 647, 102 L. Ed. 2d 714 (1989)

The Sentencing Act of 1984 was designed to eliminate the wide disparity in sentences which resulted from the broad sentencing discretion available to federal judges. In place of such discretion, the Act proposed a system of determinate sentencing, with mandatory sentencing guidelines to ensure similar sentences for comparable offenders and offenses. To devise this system, the Act created the U.S. Sentencing Commission, an independent commission within the judicial branch, with seven voting members (three of them federal judges) appointed by the president. The Commission was charged with developing sentencing guidelines, on the basis of criteria outlined in the Act, that would prescribe the range of sentences for various categories of offenses and offenders. If a federal judge departs from the guidelines in a particular case because of an aggravating or mitigating factor not considered by the Commission, the judge must give reasons for the deviation, and the sentence is subject to appellate review.

After the Commission announced its guidelines, their constitutionality was widely challenged in federal district courts—prior to the Supreme Court's decision in this case, over 150 district judges had declared the guidelines unconstitutional, while over 100 had upheld them. This case involved a challenge to the guidelines by John Mistretta, who was charged in connection with a sale of cocaine. After the District Court rejected

Mistretta's claim that the guidelines involved an excessive delegation of congressional power and violated the separation of powers, he pleaded guilty and was sentenced under the guidelines. When Mistretta filed a notice of appeal to the Court of Appeals, both he and the United States petitioned the Supreme Court for certiorari prior to judgment, and the Court granted the request. *Opinion of the Court: Blackmun, Rehnquist, Brennan (in part), White, Marshall, Stevens, O'Connor, Kennedy. Dissenting opinion: Scalia.*

Justice Blackmun delivered the opinion of the Court.

Delegation of Power

... Petitioner argues that in delegating the power to promulgate sentencing guidelines for every federal criminal offense to an independent Sentencing Commission, Congress has granted the Commission excessive legislative discretion in violation of the constitutionally based nondelegation doctrine. We do not agree.... The separation-of-powers principle, and the nondelegation doctrine in particular, do not prevent Congress from obtaining the assistance of its coordinate Branches. In a passage now enshrined in our jurisprudence, Chief Justice Taft, writing for the Court, explained our approach to such cooperative ventures: "In determining what [Congress] may do in seeking assistance from another branch, the extent and character of that assistance must be fixed according to common sense and the inherent necessities of the government co-ordination." *J. W. Hampton, Jr., & Co.* v. *United States* ... (1928). So long as Congress "shall lay down by legislative act an intelligible principle to which the person or body authorized to [exercise the delegated authority] is directed to conform, such legislative action is not a forbidden delegation of legislative power." *Id.*... The Act sets forth more than merely an "intelligible principle" or minimal standards. One court has aptly put it: "The statute outlines the policies which prompted establishment of the Commission, explains what the Commission should do and how it should do it, and sets out specific directives to govern particular situations." *United States* v. *Chambless* ... (1988).

Developing proportionate penalties for hundreds of different crimes by a virtually limitless array of offenders is precisely the sort of intricate, labor-intensive task for which delegation to an expert body is especially appropriate. Although Congress has delegated significant discretion to the Commission to draw judgments from its analysis of existing sentencing practice and alternative sentencing models, "Congress is not confined to that method of executing its policy which involves the least possible delegation of discretion to administrative officers." *Yakus* v. *United States* ... (1944).

Separation of Powers

Having determined that Congress has set forth sufficient standards for the exercise of the Commission's delegated authority, we turn to Mistretta's claim that the Act violates the constitutional principle of separation of powers.

This Court consistently has given voice to, and has reaffirmed, the central judgment of the Framers of the Constitution that, within our political scheme, the separation of governmental powers into three coordinate Branches is essential to the preservation of liberty.... Madison, in writing about the principle of separated powers, said: "No political truth is certainly of greater intrinsic value or is stamped with the authority of more enlightened patrons of liberty." The Federalist No. 47....

In applying the principle of separated powers in our jurisprudence, we have sought to give life to Madison's view of the appropriate relationship among the three coequal Branches. Accordingly, we have recognized, as Madison admonished at the founding, that while our Constitution mandates that "each of the three general departments of government [must remain] entirely free from the control of coercive influence, direct or indirect, of either of the others," *Humphrey's Executor* v. *United States* ... (1935), the Framers did not require—and indeed rejected—the notion that the three Branches must be entirely separate and distinct....

In adopting this flexible understanding of separation of powers, we simply have recognized Madison's teaching that the greatest security against tyranny—the accumulation of excessive authority in a single branch—lies not in a hermetic division between the Branches, but in a carefully crafted system of checked and balanced power within each Branch. . . .

Location of the Commission

The Sentencing Commission unquestionably is a peculiar institution within the framework of our Government. Although placed by the Act in the Judicial Branch, it is not a court and does not exercise judicial power. . . . Our constitutional principles of separated powers are not violated, however, by mere anomaly or innovation. . . . Congress' decision to create an independent rulemaking body to promulgate sentencing guidelines and to locate that body within the Judicial Branch is not unconstitutional unless Congress has vested in the Commission powers that are more appropriately performed by the other Branches or that undermine the integrity of the Judiciary. . . . Although the judicial power of the United States is limited by express provision of Article III to "Cases" and "Controversies," we have never held, and have clearly disavowed in practice, that the Constitution prohibits Congress from assigning to courts or auxiliary bodies within the Judicial Branch administrative or rulemaking duties that, in the words of Chief Justice Marshall, are "necessary and proper. . . for carrying into execution all the judgments which the judicial department has the power to pronounce." *Waymann* v. *Southard* (1825). . . .

Given the consistent responsibility of federal judges to pronounce sentence within the statutory range established by Congress, we find that the role of the Commission in promulgating guidelines for the exercise of that judicial function bears considerable similarity to the role of this Court in establishing rules of procedure under the various enabling acts. Such guidelines, like the Federal Rules of Criminal and Civil Procedure, are court rules—rules, to paraphrase Chief Justice Marshall's language in *Wayman,* for carrying into execution judgments that the judiciary has the power to pronounce. Just as the rules of procedure bind judges and courts in the proper management of the cases before them, so the Guidelines bind judges and courts in the exercise of their uncontested responsibility to pass sentence in criminal cases. In other words, the Commission's functions, like this Court's function in promulgating procedural rules, are clearly attendant to a central element of the historically acknowledged mission of the Judicial Branch. . . . Although the Guidelines are intended to have substantive effects on public behavior (as do the rules of procedure), they do not bind or regulate the primary conduct of the public or vest in the Judicial Branch the legislative responsibility for establishing minimum and maximum penalties for every crime. They do no more than fetter the discretion of sentencing judges to do what they have done for generations—impose sentences within the broad limits established by Congress. Given their limited reach, the special role of the Judicial Branch in the field of sentencing, and the fact that the Guidelines are promulgated by an independent agency and not a court, it follows that as a matter of "practical consequence" the location of the Sentencing Commission within the Judicial Branch simply leaves with the Judiciary what long has belonged to it. . . .

Composition of the Commission

. . . We now turn to petitioner's claim that Congress' decision to require at least three federal judges to serve on the Commission and to require those judges to share their authority with nonjudges undermines the integrity of the Judicial Branch. . . .

The text of the Constitution contains no prohibition against the service of active federal judges on independent commissions such as that established by the Act. The Constitution does include an Incompatibility Clause applicable to national legislators. . . . No comparable restriction applies to judges, and we find it at least inferentially meaningful that at the Constitutional Convention two prohibitions against plural officeholding by members of the judiciary were proposed, but did not reach the floor of the Convention for a vote.

. . . Our inferential reading that the Constitution does not prohibit Article III judges from undertaking extrajudicial duties finds support in the historical practice of the Founders after ratification. . . .

Subsequent history, moreover, reveals a frequent and continuing, albeit controversial, practice of extrajudicial service. . . .

. . . In light of the foregoing history and precedent, we conclude that the principle of separation of powers does not absolutely prohibit Article III judges from serving on commissions such as that created by the Act. The judges serve on the Sentencing Commission not pursuant to their status and authority as Article III judges, but solely because of their appointment by the President as the Act directs. Such power as these judges wield as Commissioners is not judicial power; it is administrative power derived from the enabling legislation. Just as the nonjudicial members of the Commission act as administrators, bringing their experience and wisdom to bear on the problems of sentencing disparity, so too the judges, uniquely qualified on the subject of sentencing, assume a wholly administrative role upon entering into the deliberations of the Commission. In other words, the Constitution, at least as a *per se* matter, does not forbid judges from wearing two hats; it merely forbids them from wearing both hats at the same time.

Presidential Control

The Act empowers the President to appoint all seven members of the Commission with the advice and consent of the Senate. The Act further provides that the President shall make his choice of judicial appointees to the Commission after considering a list of six judges recommended by the Judicial Conference of the United States. The Act also grants the President authority to remove members of the Commission, although "only for neglect of duty or malfeasance in office or for other good cause shown." . . .

Mistretta argues that this power of Presidential appointment and removal prevents the Judicial Branch from performing its constitutionally assigned functions. . . .

. . . Since the President has no power to affect the tenure or compensation of Article III judges, even if the Act authorized him to remove judges from the Commission at will, he would have no power to coerce the judges in the exercise of their judicial duties. In any case, Congress did not grant the President unfettered authority to remove Commission members. Instead, precisely to ensure that they would not be subject to coercion even in the exercise of their nonjudicial duties, Congress insulated the members from Presidential removal except for good cause. Under these circumstances, we see no risk that the President's limited removal power will compromise the impartiality of Article III judges serving on the Commission and, consequently, no risk that the Act's removal provision will prevent the Judicial Branch from performing its constitutionally assigned function of fairly adjudicating cases and controversies.

We conclude that in creating the Sentencing Commission—an unusual hybrid in structure and authority—Congress neither delegated excessive legislative power nor upset the constitutionally mandated balance of powers among the coordinate Branches. . . .

The judgment of United States District Court for the Western District of Missouri is affirmed.

It is so ordered.

Justice Scalia, dissenting.

While the products of the Sentencing Commission's labors have been given the modest name "Guidelines," . . . they have the force and effect of laws, prescribing the sentences criminal defendants are to receive. A judge who disregards them will be reversed. . . . I dissent from today's decision because I can find no place within our constitutional system for an agency created by Congress to exercise no governmental power other than the making of laws. . . .

Petitioner's most fundamental and far-reaching challenge to the Commission is that Congress' commitment of such broad policy responsibility to any institution is an unconstitutional delegation of legislative power. . . .

But while the doctrine of unconstitutional delegation is unquestionably a fundamental element of our constitutional system, it is not an element readily enforceable by the courts. Once it is conceded, as it must be, that no statute can be entirely precise, and that some judgments, even some judgments involving policy considerations, must be left to the officers executing the law and to the judges applying it, the debate over unconstitutional delegation becomes a debate not over a point of principle but over a question of degree. . . .

In short, I fully agree with the Court's rejection of petitioner's contention that the doctrine of unconstitutional delegation of legislative authority has been violated because of the lack of intelligible, congressionally prescribed standards to guide the Commission. . . .

Precisely because the scope of delegation is largely uncontrollable by the courts, we must be particularly rigorous in preserving the Constitution's structural restrictions that deter excessive delegation. The major one, it seems to me, is that the power to make law cannot be exercised by anyone other than Congress, except in conjunction with the lawful exercise of executive or judicial power.

The whole theory of *lawful* congressional "delegation" is not that Congress is sometimes too busy or too divided and can therefore assign its responsibility of making law to someone else; but rather that a certain degree of discretion, and thus of law-making, *inheres* in most executive or judicial action, and it is up to Congress, by the relative specificity or generality of its statutory commands, to determine—up to a point—how small or how large that degree shall be. . . . Strictly speaking, there is *no* acceptable delegation of legislative power. As John Locke put it almost three hundred years ago, "[t]he power of the *legislative* being derived from the people by a positive voluntary grant and institution, can be no other, than what the positive grant conveyed, which being only to make *laws*, and not to make *legislators*, the *legislative* can have no power to transfer their authority of making laws, and place it in other hands." . . . In the present case, however, a pure delegation of legislative power is precisely what we have before us. It is irrelevant whether the standards are adequate, because they are not standards related to the exercise of executive or judicial powers; they are, plainly and simply, standards for further legislation.

The lawmaking function of the Sentencing Commission is completely divorced from any responsibility for execution of the law or adjudication of private rights under the law. . . .

The delegation of lawmaking authority to the Commission is, in short, unsupported by any legitimating theory to explain why it is not a delegation of legislative power. To disregard structural legitimacy is wrong in itself—but since structure has purpose, the disregard also has adverse practical consequences. In this case, as suggested earlier, the consequence is to facilitate and encourage judicially uncontrollable delegation. Until our decision last Term in *Morrison* v. *Olson* . . . (1988), it could have been said that Congress could delegate lawmaking authority only at the expense of increasing the power of either the President or the courts. Most often, as a practical matter, it would be the President, since the judicial process is unable to conduct the investigations and make the political assessments essential for most policymaking. Thus, the need for delegation would have to be important enough to induce Congress to aggrandize its primary competitor for political power, and the recipient of the policymaking authority, while not Congress itself, would at least be politically accountable. . . .

By reason of today's decision, I anticipate that Congress will find delegation of its lawmaking powers much more attractive in the future. If rulemaking can be entirely unrelated to the exercise of judicial or executive powers, I foresee all manner of "expert" bodies, insulated from the political process, to which Congress will delegate various portions of its lawmaking responsibility. How tempting to create an expert Medical Commission (mostly MDs, with perhaps a few PhDs in moral philosophy) to dispose of such thorny, "no-win" political issues as the withholding of life-support systems in federally funded hospitals, or the use of fetal tissue for research. This is an undemocratic precedent that we set—not because of the scope of the delegated power, but because its recipient is not one of the three Branches of Government. The only governmental power the Commission possesses is the power to make law; and it is not the Congress.

Immigration and Naturalization Service v. *Chadha*

462 U.S. 919; 103 S. Ct. 2764; 77 L. Ed. 2d 317 (1983)

Jagdish Rai Chadha, an East Indian born in Kenya, was admitted to the United States in 1966 on a nonimmigrant student visa. When he remained in America after the visa expired in 1972, he became susceptible to deportation under the Immigration and Nationality Act. The Act authorized the Attorney General to suspend deportation if the alien had resided continuously in the United States for seven years, was of good moral character, and would suffer "extreme hardship" if deported. However, the Act reserved to each house of Congress the power to overrule the Attorney General's determinations. When Chadha's deportation was suspended and a report of the suspension was transmitted to Congress, the House of Representatives vetoed the action. Chadha challenged the House's authority to order his deportation, and when the Court of Appeals ruled the legislative veto in the Act unconstitutional, the case was appealed to the Supreme Court. *Opinion of the Court: Burger, Brennan, Marshall, Blackmun, Stevens, O'Connor. Concurring opinion: Powell. Dissenting opinions: White; Rehnquist, White.*

Chief Justice Burger delivered the opinion of the Court.

We turn . . . to the question whether action of one House of Congress under § 244(c)(2) violates strictures of the Constitution. We begin, of course, with the presumption that the challenged statute is valid. Its wisdom is not the concern of the courts; if a challenged action does not violate the Constitution, it must be sustained. . . .

By the same token, the fact that a given law or procedure is efficient, convenient, and useful in facilitating functions of government, standing alone, will not save it if it is contrary to the Constitution. Convenience and efficiency are not the primary objectives—or the hallmarks—of democratic government and our inquiry is sharpened rather than blunted by the fact that Congressional veto provisions are appearing with increasing frequency in statutes which delegate authority to executive and independent agencies. . . .

Explicit and unambiguous provisions of the Constitution prescribe and define the respective functions of the Congress and of the Executive in the legislative process. . . . The very structure of the articles delegating and separating powers under Arts I, II, and III exemplify the concept of separation of powers and we now turn to Art. I.

The Presentment Clauses

The records of the Constitutional Convention reveal that the requirement that all legislation be presented to the President before becoming law was uniformly accepted by the Framers. Presentment to the President and the Presidential veto were considered so imperative that the draftsmen took special pains to assure that these requirements could not be circumvented.

The decision to provide the President with a limited and qualified power to nullify proposed legislation by veto was based on the profound conviction of the Framers that the powers conferred on Congress were the powers to be most carefully circumscribed. . . .

The President's role in the lawmaking process also reflects the Framers' careful efforts to check whatever propensity a particular Congress might have to enact oppressive, improvident, or ill-considered measures. . . . The Court also has observed that the Presentment Clauses serve the important purpose of assuring that a "national" perspective is grafted on the legislative process.

Bicameralism

The bicameral requirement of Art I, §§ 1, 7 was of scarcely less concern to the Framers than was the Presidential veto and indeed the two concepts are interdependent. By providing that no law could take effect without the concurrence of the prescribed majority of the Members of both Houses, the Framers reemphasized their belief, already remarked upon in connection with the Presentment Clauses, that legislation should not be enacted unless it has been carefully and fully considered by the Nation's elected officials. . . .

. . . Apart from their fear that special interests could be favored at the expense of public needs, the Framers were also concerned, although not of one mind, over the apprehensions of the smaller states. Those states feared a commonality of interest among the larger states would work to their disadvantage; representatives of the larger states, on the other hand, were skeptical of a legislature that could pass laws favoring a minority of the people. It need hardly be repeated here that the Great Compromise, under which one House was viewed as representing the people and the other the states, allayed the fears of both the large and small states.

We see therefore that the Framers were acutely conscious that the bicameral requirement and the Presentment Clauses would serve essential constitutional functions. The President's participation in the legislative process was to protect the Executive Branch from Congress and to protect the whole people from improvident laws. The division of the Congress into two distinctive bodies assures that the legislative power would be exercised only after opportunity for full study and debate in separate settings. The President's unilateral veto power, in turn, was limited by the power of two thirds of both Houses of Congress to overrule a veto thereby precluding final arbitrary action of one person. It emerges clearly that the prescription for legislative action in Art I, §§ 1, 7 represents the Framers' decision that the legislative power of the Federal government be exercised in accord with a single, finely wrought and exhaustively considered, procedure.

The Constitution sought to divide the delegated powers of the new federal government into three defined categories, legislative, executive and judicial, to assure, as nearly as possible, that each Branch of government would confine itself to its assigned responsibility. The hydraulic pressure inherent within each of the separate Branches to exceed the outer limits of its power, even to accomplish desirable objectives, must be resisted.

Although not "hermetically" sealed from one another, the powers delegated to the three Branches are functionally identifiable. When any Branch acts, it is presumptively exercising the power the Constitution has delegated to it. When the Executive acts, it presumptively acts in an executive or administrative capacity as defined in Art II. And when, as here, one House of congress purports to act, it is presumptively acting within its assigned sphere.

Beginning with this presumption, we must nevertheless establish that the challenged action under § 244(c)(2) is of the kind to which the procedural requirements of Art I, § 7 apply. Not every action taken by either House is subject to the bicameralism and presentment requirements of Art I. Whether actions taken by either House are, in law and fact, an exercise of legislative power depends not on their form but upon "whether they contain matter which is properly to be regarded as legislative in its character and effect."

Examination of the action taken here by one House pursuant to § 244(c)(2) reveals that it was essentially legislative in purpose and effect. In purporting to exercise power defined in Art I, § 8, cl 4 to "establish an uniform Rule of Naturalization," the House took action that had the purpose and effect of altering the legal rights, duties and relations of persons, including the Attorney General, Executive Branch officials and Chadha, all outside the legislative branch. Section 244(c)(2) purports to authorize one House of Congress to require the Attorney General to deport an individual alien whose deportation otherwise would be cancelled under § 244. The one-House veto operated in this case to overrule the Attorney General and mandate Chadha's deportation; absent the House action, Chadha would remain in the United States. Congress has *acted* and its action has altered Chadha's status.

. . . Disagreement with the Attorney General's decision on Chadha's deportation—that is, Congress' decision to deport Chadha—no less than Congress' original choice to delegate to the Attorney General the authority to make that decision, involves determinations of policy that Congress can implement in only one way; bicameral passage followed by presentment to the President. Congress must abide by its delegation of authority until that delegation is legislatively altered or revoked.

Finally, we see that when the Framers intended to authorize either House of Congress to act alone and outside of its prescribed bicameral legislative role, they narrowly and precisely defined the procedure for such action. . . . These exceptions are narrow, explicit, and separately justified; none of them authorize the action challenged here. On the contrary, they provide further support for the conclusion that Congressional authority is not to be implied and for the conclusion that the veto provided for in § 244(c)(2) is not authorized by the constitutional design of the powers of the Legislative Branch.

The veto authorized by § 244(c)(2) doubtless has been in many respects a convenient shortcut; the "sharing" with the Executive by Congress of its authority over aliens in this manner is, on its face, an appealing compromise. In purely practical terms, it is obviously easier for action to be taken by one House without submission to the President; but it is crystal clear from the records of the Convention, contemporaneous writings, and debates, that the Framers ranked other values higher than efficiency. The records of the Convention and debates in the States preceding ratification underscore the common desire to define and limit the exercise of the newly created federal powers affecting the states and the people. There is unmistakable expression of a determination that legislation by the national Congress be a step-by-step, deliberate and deliberative process.

The choices we discern as having been made in the Constitutional Convention impose burdens on governmental processes that often seem clumsy, inefficient, even unworkable, but those hard choices were consciously made by men who had lived under a form of government that permitted arbitrary governmental acts to go unchecked. There is no support in the Constitution or decisions of this Court for the proposition that the cumbersomeness and delays often encountered in complying with explicity Constitutional standards may be avoided, either by the Congress or by the President. . . .

We hold that the Congressional veto provision in § 244(c)(2) is severable from the Act and that it is unconstitutional.

JUSTICE POWELL, concurring in the judgment.

The Court's decision, based on the Presentment Clauses, Art I, § 7, cl 2 and 3, apparently will invalidate every use of the legislative veto. The breadth of this holding gives one pause. Congress has included the veto in literally hundreds of statutes, dating back to the 1930s. Congress clearly views this procedure as essential to controlling the delegation of power to administrative agencies. One reasonably may disagree with Congress' assessment of the veto's utility, but the respect due its judgment as a coordinate branch of Government cautions that our holding should be no more extensive than necessary to decide this case. In my view, the case may be decided on a narrower ground. When Congress finds that a particular person does not satisfy the statutory criteria for permanent residence in this country it has assumed a judicial function in violation of the principle of separation of powers. Accordingly, I concur only in the judgment.

JUSTICE WHITE, dissenting.

Today the Court not only invalidates § 244(c)(2) of the Immigration and Nationality Act, but also sounds the death knell for nearly 200 other statutory provisions in which Congress has reserved a "legislative veto." . . .

The prominence of the legislative veto mechanism in our contemporary political system and its importance to Congress can hardly be overstated. It has become a central means by which Congress secures the accountability of executive and independent agencies. Without the legislative veto, Congress is faced with a Hobson's choice: either to refrain from delegating the necessary authority, leaving itself with a hopeless task of writing laws with the requisite specificity to cover endless special circumstances across the entire policy landscape, or in the alternative, to abdicate its lawmaking function to the executive branch and independent agencies. To choose the former leaves major national problems unresolved; to opt for the latter risks unaccountable policymaking by those not elected to fill that role. Accordingly, over the past five decades, the legislative veto has been placed in nearly 200 statutes.

[Justice White then reviewed at length the history of the legislative veto.]

Even this brief review suffices to demonstrate that the legislative veto is more than "efficient, convenient, and useful." It is an important if not indispensable political invention that allows the President and Congress to resolve major constitutional and policy differences, assures the accountability of independent regulatory agencies, and preserves Congress' control over lawmaking. Perhaps there are other means of accommodation and accountability, but the increasing reliance of Congress upon the legislative veto suggests that the alternatives to which Congress must now turn are not entirely satisfactory.

The history of the legislative veto also makes clear that it has not been a sword with which Congress has struck out to aggrandize itself at the expense of the other branches—the concerns of Madison and Hamilton. Rather, the veto has been a means of defense, a reservation of ultimate authority necessary if Congress is to fulfill its designated role under Article I as the nation's lawmaker. While the President has often objected to particular legislative vetoes, generally those left in the hands of congressional committees, the Executive has more often agreed to legislative review as the price for a broad delegation of authority. To be sure, the President may have preferred unrestricted power, but that could be precisely why Congress thought it essential to retain a check on the exercise of delegated authority.

. . . The constitutional question posed today is one of immense difficulty over which the executive and legislative branches—as well as scholars and judges—have understandably disagreed. That disagreement stems from the silence of the Constitution on the precise question: The Constitution does not directly authorize or prohibit the legislative veto. Thus, our task should be to determine whether the legislative veto is consistent with the purposes of Art I and the principles of Separation of Powers which are reflected in that Article and throughout the Constitution. We should not find the lack of a specific constitutional authorization for the legislative veto surprising, and I would not infer disapproval of the mechanism from its absence. From the summer of 1787 to the present the government of the United States has become an endeavor far beyond the contemplation of the Framers. Only within the last half century has the complexity and size of the Federal Government's responsibilities grown so greatly that the Congress must rely on the legislative veto as the most effective if not the only means to insure their role as the nation's lawmakers. But the wisdom of the Framers was to anticipate that the nation would grow and new problems of governance would require different solutions. Accordingly, our Federal Government was intentionally chartered with the flexibility to respond to contemporary needs without losing sight of fundamental democratic principles. . . .

This is the perspective from which we should approach the novel constitutional questions presented by the legislative veto. In my view, neither Article I of the Constitution nor the doctrine of separation of powers is violated by this mechanism by which our elected representatives preserve their voice in the governance of the nation. . . .

The terms of the Presentment Clauses suggest only that bills and their equivalent are subject to the requirements of bicameral passage and presentment to the President. . . . This reading is consistent with the historical background of the Presentation Clause itself which reveals only that the Framers were concerned with limiting the methods for enacting new legislation. The Framers were aware of the experience in Pennsylvania where the legislature had evaded the requirements attached to the passing of legislation by the use of "resolves," and the criticisms directed at this practice by the Council of Censors. There is no record that the Convention contemplated, let alone intended, that these Article I requirements would someday be invoked to restrain the scope of Congressional authority pursuant to duly-enacted law. . . .

When the Convention did turn its attention to the scope of Congress' lawmaking power, the Framers were expansive. The Necessary and Proper Clause, Art I, § 8, cl 18, vests Congress with the power "to make all laws which shall be necessary and proper for carrying into Execution the foregoing Powers [the enumerated powers of § 8], and all other Powers vested by this Constitution in the government of the United States, or in any Department or Officer thereof." It is long-settled that Congress may "exercise its best judgment in the selection of measures, to carry into execution the constitutional powers of the government," and "avail itself of experience, to exercise its reason, and to accommodate its legislation to circumstances." McCulloch v. Maryland.

The Court heeded this counsel in approving the modern administrative state. The Court's holding today that all legislative-type action must be enacted through the lawmaking process ignores that legislative authority is routinely delegated to the Executive branch, to the independent regulatory agencies, and to private individuals and groups. . . .

This Court's decisions sanctioning such delegations make clear that Article I does not require all action with the effect of legislation to be passed as a law. . . .

If Congress may delegate lawmaking power to independent and executive agencies, it is most difficult to understand Article I as forbidding Congress from also reserving a check on legislative power for itself. Absent the veto, the agencies receiving delegations of legislative or quasilegislative power may issue regulations having the force of law without bicameral approval and without the President's signature. It is thus not apparent why the reservation of a veto over the exercise of that legislative power must be subject to a more exacting test. In both cases, it is enough that the initial statutory authorizations comply with the Article I requirements.

. . . The Court concedes that certain administrative agency action, such as rulemaking, "may resemble lawmaking" and recognizes that" [t]his Court has referred to agency activity as being 'quasi-legislative' in character. . . . Under the Court's analysis, the Executive Branch and the independent agencies may make rules with the effect of law while Congress, in whom the Framers confided the legislative power, Art I, § 1, may not exercise a veto which precludes such rules from having operative force. If the effective functioning of a complex modern government requires the delegation of vast authority which, by virtue of its breadth, is legislative or "quasi-legislative" in character, I cannot accept that Article I—which is, after all, the source of the non-delegation doctrine—should forbid Congress from qualifying that grant with a legislative veto.

The central concern of the presentation and bicameralism requirements of Article I is that when a departure from the legal status quo is undertaken, it is done with the approval of the President and both Houses of Congress—or, in the event of a presidential veto, a two-thirds majority in both Houses. This interest is fully satisfied by the operation of § 244(c)(2). The President's approval is found in the Attorney General's action in recommending to Congress that the deportation order for a given alien be suspended. The House and the Senate indicate their approval of the Executive's action by not passing a resolution of disapproval within the statutory period. Thus, a change in the legal status quo—the deportability of the alien—is consummated only with the approval of each of the three relevant actors. The disagreement of any one of the three maintains the alien's pre-existing status: the Executive may choose not to recommend suspension; the House and Senate may each veto the recommendation. The effect on the rights and obligations of the affected individuals and upon the legislative system is precisely the same as if a private bill were introduced but failed to receive the necessary approval.

I do not suggest that all legislative vetoes are necessarily consistent with separation of powers principles. A legislative check on an inherently executive function, for example that of initiating prosecutions, poses an entirely different question. But the legislative veto device here—and in many other settings—is far from an instance of legislative tyranny over the Executive. It is a necessary check on the unavoidably expanding power of the agencies, both executive and independent, as they engage in exercising authority delegated by Congress.

5
THE EXECUTIVE BRANCH

In *The Federalist*, No. 51, James Madison suggested that "in republican government, the legislative authority necessarily predominates." Most contemporary observers of American government would disagree: certainly the development of American political institutions during the twentieth century has contributed to executive rather than legislative domination. The discrepancy between Madison's statement and current realities raises troubling constitutional questions. How has "an executive magistracy carefully limited . . . in the extent and duration of its power" become the most powerful branch of government?[1] And if American political development has not coincided with Madison's expectations, has the presidency exceeded its constitutional bounds? Can the modern presidency, in other words, be squared with the Constitution?

Constitutional scholars have long debated these questions. Some experts maintain that the constitutional system of checks and balances continues to operate. Others assert that those checks no longer effectively constrain the president and that the contemporary American government is largely presidential government. And whereas some scholars contend that the expansion of presidential power has occurred within the constitutional framework, others insist that "the history of the presidency is a history of aggrandizement."[2] This debate cannot be resolved conclusively in these pages. But careful analysis of the Framers' conception of the office, the powers constitutionally assigned to the president, and the means by which presidential power has expanded can provide the basis for an informed judgment on the legitimate scope of presidential power.

THE AIMS OF THE FRAMERS

The events leading to the American Revolution created a profound distrust of executive power that was reflected in the constitutions ratified following independence. The Articles of Confederation, which created a national government of very limited powers, did not establish a separate executive branch. Every state had a separate executive, but the state governors were rendered politically impotent by short terms of office, restrictions on reeligibility, election by the legislature, and/or the division of executive responsibilities among various officials.[3] The results, predictably, were disastrous. At the national level, the absence of a separate executive frustrated effective administration. At the state level, the lack of any effective check on the state legislatures led to the adoption of ill-considered and unjust laws. By the outset of the Constitutional Convention, most of the Framers were convinced of the need for a vigorous and independent executive. Alexander Hamilton reflected this view when he observed in *The Federalist,* No. 70, that "energy in the executive is a leading character in the definition of good government."

The delegates took several steps to ensure an energetic executive.[4] To begin with, they lodged the executive power in a single individual. Only a unified executive, they reasoned, could act with the necessary decisiveness and dispatch; moreover, such a concentration of power would promote accountability, since a single person would be responsible for the results of executive action. Second, they established a lengthy term of office and made the president eligible for reelection. An extended tenure, in their view, would not only promote continuity in administration but also give the president both the opportunity and the incentive to undertake long-range projects. The prospect of reelection, meanwhile, would encourage faithful performance of presidential duties and provide a basis for accountability. Third, they secured presidential independence by granting to the president powers (e.g., the veto) designed to safeguard his constitutional position and by creating a system of election (the electoral college) that rendered him independent of Congress. The electoral college had the additional advantage, according to *The Federalist,* No. 68, of ensuring that only figures of national stature would be elected, thereby affording "a moral certainty that the office of President will seldom fall to the lot of any man who is not in an eminent degree endowed with the requisite qualifications."

Most significantly, the Framers granted to the president extensive powers. Primary among these powers are those enumerated in Article II of the Constitution:

In the legislative sphere the president

- Must inform Congress as to the State of the Union (Section 3)
- Can recommend legislation to Congress (Section 3)
- Can call Congress into special session and, if the two houses disagree on the time of adjournment, adjourn it (Section 3)[5]
- Can veto legislation (Section 7, Paragraphs 2 and 3)

As chief executive the president

- Can appoint executive officers and fill vacancies in such offices (Section 2, Paragraphs 2 and 3)
- Can require the heads of executive departments to furnish advice, in writing, on subjects relating to the duties of their offices (Section 2, Paragraph 1)
- Must take care that the laws are faithfully executed (Section 3)

As chief law enforcer the president

- Can grant pardons and reprieves (Section 2, Paragraph 1)
- Must take care that the laws are faithfully executed (Section 3)

More generally, presidents have claimed broad powers to

- Exercise "the executive Power" vested in the President (Section 1, Paragraph 1)
- "Preserve, protect, and defend the Constitution," as required in the presidential oath of office (Section 1, Paragraph 8)

Presidential powers are not limited to those expressly listed in the Constitution, however. Much of the debate about the presidency has involved how far beyond those enumerated powers presidential power extends. What emerges from the Framers' discussions is a desire to give the president powers adequate to the responsibilities of the office.

GRANTS OF POWER AND THEIR USE

Surprisingly enough, presidential power has grown in large measure through the exercise of powers expressly granted in the Constitution. The executive branch has benefited greatly from historical developments that have increased the importance of particular governmental functions, and thereby the power of the branch assigned responsibility for those functions. For example, extensive American involvement in foreign affairs has augmented presidential power, because the Constitution assigns the president a major role in the conduct of foreign policy (see Chapter 6). In the domestic sphere, the vast expansion in the size of the federal government and the rise of administrative policy making have enhanced the significance of the president's power to make appointments and to supervise administration.

Presidential power also has been expanded through the more vigorous exercise of powers granted by the Constitution. Presidential activity in the legislative sphere provides the clearest instance of this expansion. From the Founding through the nineteenth century, presidents generally did not exploit the potentialities of the legislative functions assigned to the executive in the Constitution. Because the chief executives of this era neither recommended detailed legislative programs to Congress nor consistently used the veto to enforce their legislative priorities, Congress tended to dominate the legislative process. Then, in the twentieth century, presidents began to assume a more active role in legislation. Woodrow Wilson and the two Roosevelts established the idea that presidents should submit extensive legislative programs and work for their enactment, and they transformed the State of the Union address and other messages to Congress into vehicles for the announcement of presidential programs. Subsequent presidents, Republicans and Democrats, have continued this practice, to the point where in one year President Lyndon Johnson sought congressional action on 469 separate proposals. In a reversal of roles, Congress has come to depend upon presidential initiatives. As Representative Bob Eckhardt of Texas has described it, Congress is "a machine with a V-8 engine into which different forces come from different directions. The President is the ignition system."[6]

Presidential use of the veto presents a parallel case. During the first seventy-five years of the Republic, presidents were reluctant to veto legislation—no president before Andrew Johnson vetoed more than twelve bills—and even then the veto most frequently was used to prevent enactment of legislation the president believed unconstitutional. As presidents became more active participants in the legislative process, however, the veto emerged as a formidable weapon. It is extremely effective in preventing the enactment of legislation—only about 4 percent of all presidential vetoes have been overridden. Given its proven effectiveness, presidential willingness to use the veto inevitably increases the executive's influence on Congress. Just as the power to suggest legislation gives presidents considerable control over the issues Congress addresses, so the veto power ensures that their views will be taken into account in congressional deliberations, as members of Congress seek to avoid the threat of a veto.

Congressional legislation has also contributed to the growth of presidential power. By enacting broad legislation without clear standards for their exercise, Congress has allowed the executive branch to make important policy decisions and congressional requirements that the president submit programs or reports have created additional opportunities for presidential leadership in the legislative process. The Budget and Accounting Act of 1921 exemplifies how assignment of responsibilities to the president can enhance presidential power. The act requires that the president submit a budget to Congress each year, and thereby provide a basis for congressional action. Inevitably, however, the budget submitted represents not merely the aggregate requests of the various executive departments, but also the policy priorities of the president. Thus, simply by fulfilling their statutory responsibility, presidents necessarily set the agenda for public debate and congressional action. The success of President Ronald Reagan's budget initiatives in 1981–82 demonstrated the legislative leverage this process can give the executive.

IMPLIED POWERS

Presidential power has also increased through the recognition of the implied powers of the office. Chief Justice (and ex-President) William Howard Taft summarized the basis for claims of implied powers: "The true view of the Executive function is . . . that the President can exercise no power which cannot be fairly and reasonably traced to some specific grant of power or justly implied and included within such express grant as necessary and proper for its exercise."[7] In taking this position, Taft actually was arguing against a more expansive view of presidential power enunciated by Theodore Roosevelt.[8] Yet Taft's view also supports a broad exercise of executive power, for it suggests that the president is not restricted to the powers enumerated in Article II. Since those grants relate to particular governmental functions and since the Framers intended that the executive fulfill those functions, it follows that they must have provided the executive with the means necessary to carry them out. Thus, the character of the powers assigned to the president logically points to the existence of implied powers.

Taft's position has been endorsed in court decisions and incorporated into governmental practice. Yet acceptance of the principle of implied powers does not prevent disagreements about the scope of those powers. Examination of the president's powers as chief executive and the disputes over executive privilege and presidential immunity illustrates both the bases for claims of implied powers and possible limits on those powers.

The President as Chief Executive

Article II of the Constitution recognizes the president as head of the executive branch, assigning him "the Executive Power" and making him responsible for ensuring "that the laws be faithfully executed." To enable him to meet his responsibilities, it grants him the power to appoint major executive officers. This promotes presidential control over those who shall execute the laws—a necessary precondition for the effective supervision of administration. It also leads to accountability in the executive: a president who selects executive officials and has authority over them can be held responsible for their actions.

Yet the Constitution limits presidential control over the selection of executive-branch officials in several ways. To begin with, presidential nominees for most major offices must be confirmed by the Senate. Although usually they are—since 1789 only eight nominees for Cabinet posts have been rejected—on occasion presidents have been forced to withdraw nominations, and the necessity of securing senatorial confirmation also may affect presidential choices. In addition, Congress by statute defines the offices to be filled and can require Senate approval for appointment to them. Under legislation enacted in 1974, for example, the director of the Office of Management and the Budget must be confirmed by the Senate. Furthermore, Congress can establish qualifications for offices that restrict the president's range of choice in filling them.

Finally, the presidential appointment power extends only to principal officers. Article II authorizes Congress to vest the appointment of "inferior" officers in the president, the courts, or the heads of executive departments. Exactly what distinguishes principal from "inferior" officers is far from clear. In *Morrison* v. *Olson* (1988), for example, the Court ruled that an independent counsel with the power to investigate and prosecute violations of federal law largely free from executive-branch control was an inferior officer and upheld congressional legislation vesting her appointment in a federal court. Nevertheless, this congressional power is subject to an important separation-of-powers limitation: although Congress may designate who will appoint inferior officers, it cannot put the power in its own hands. When Congress attempted to vest in the president pro tem of the Senate and the speaker of the House the power to appoint a majority of the voting members of the Federal Election Commission, the Supreme Court in *Buckley* v. *Valeo* (1976) unanimously struck down the plan.

If the Constitution gives the president the power to appoint executive-branch officials to promote effective administration, does it also give him the power to remove them? This question is of vital concern, for the power to remove from office is in effect the power to control behavior in office. Aside from noting that "civil officers" are impeachable, however, the Constitution is silent on this point. Thus if the president has a constitutional power to remove officials, it must be an implied power.

The First Congress confronted this question in establishing a Department of Foreign Affairs. After prolonged debate, it concluded that the president acting alone could remove the secretary of state. Many members of Congress accepted the view, but presented by James Madison, that the removal power was implied in the grant of executive power to the president. Others insisted that Congress could determine who would exercise the removal power. The issue arose intermittently thereafter—most notably in the impeachment trial of President Andrew Johnson—but did not reach the Supreme Court until *Myers* v. *United States* [1926]. In *Myers* the Court upheld the president's removal of a postmaster in violation of legislation establishing a four-year term for postmasters and requiring senatorial consent for their removal. In support of this decision, Chief Justice Taft cited the actions of the First Congress, which he viewed as an authoritative recognition of an implied presidential power of removal. In addiiton, he noted, the president's responsibilities required that this implied power be recognized: "Made responsible under the Constitution for the effective enforcement of the law, the President needs as an indispensable aid to meet in the disciplinary influence upon those who act under him of a reserve power of removal."

The Court's ruling in *Myers* has not prevented disputes about the scope of the president's removal power. *Myers* seemed to imply that the president had the power to remove all those involved in the execution of the laws. If so, this raises questions about the constitutionality of independent regulatory commissions, such as the Federal Communications Commission, whose members can be removed by the president prior to the expiration of their terms only for dereliction of duty. However, the Court appears to have retreated from its position in *Myers*. It did recognize in *Bowsher* v. *Synar* (1986) that those exercising executive functions could not be under the control of Congress. But it has rejected presidential efforts to remove members of independent regulatory commissions prior to expiration of their terms of office, contending that the powers they exercised were only partly executive in character.[9] More recently, in *Morrison* v. *Olson*, it upheld restrictions on the removal of an independent counsel, who was involved in investigating and prosecuting official wrongdoing. The Court argued that the restrictions did not substantially impede the president's ability to perform his constitutional duty or unduly interface with the functioning of the executive branch. In dissent, Justice Antonin Scalia insisted that if prosecution of crimes is an executive function, then the president must have control over those exercising the function. Otherwise, the unity of the executive is compromised.

Executive Privilege and Presidential Immunity

More recent controversies over implied powers and privileges have involved presidential claims of executive privilege and immunity from suit. Executive privilege is the power of the president to refuse to provide information requested by the other branches of government. Since the Constitution does not explicitly grant this power to the executive, presidents generally have relied on three arguments to support claims of executive privilege. First, they have maintained that in order to fulfill their military, diplomatic, and national security responsibilities, they must at times withhold sensitive information from congressional and public scrutiny; otherwise, the argument runs, they could not successfully carry out the tasks assigned to the executive by the Framers. Another defense of executive privilege rests on the fact that presidents frequently depend on advice from associates and subordinates in implementing their policymaking responsibilities. Only by ensuring the confidentiality of these communications, they have argued, can they secure that candid interchange of views needed for wise decisions. Like the "national security" argument, this "candid interchange" argument suggests that the president's constitutional responsibilities by implication support claims of executive privilege. Some presidents have gone even further in claiming this privilege, asserting that the principle of separation of powers vests the president with control over the executive branch and, thereby, with the authority to control all communications emanating from that branch. This argument has been used to support the most extensive claims of executive privilege, since it implies that the provision of information to the other two branches is entirely a matter of presidential discretion.

Presidential invocation of executive privilege has become more frequent since World War II, in part because of increased American involvement in world affairs. Even so, conflicts between the president and Congress over the withholding of information were resolved by interbranch compromises, not by testing the legitimacy of executive privilege in the courts. This changed, however, when during the Watergate investigation President Richard Nixon relied on executive privilege to deny White House tapes and other records to congressional investigating committees, the Watergate special prosecutor, and the courts. When the president refused to turn over sixty-four tapes for use in the Watergate cover-up trial, the issue of executive privilege came to the Supreme Court, in *United States* v. *Nixon* (1974). Rejecting the broad separation-of-powers argument for executive privilege, the Court ordered the president to turn over the tapes. But the justices did not reject the notion of implied powers. They acknowledged that presidential claims of executive privilege had a basis in the Constitution and that such claims had particular force when information pertaining to war and foreign affairs was involved. To determine the scope of this implied power, therefore, it was necessary in each instance to balance the interest in confidentiality against the need for disclosure of the specific information.

The Supreme Court's resolution of this case suggests one possible limitation on the president's implied powers: although presidents legitimately can claim the powers necessary to fulfill their constitutional responsibilities, so too can Congress and the courts. When these claims conflict, the executive will not always prevail. In *United States* v. *Nixon*, for example, the Court ruled that the interest in securing evidence necessary for a fair trial outweighed the president's "generalized assertion of privilege."

When presidential claims of implied powers or privileges do not collide with the claims of a coequal branch of government, on the other hand, the Court has been receptive to them. In *Nixon* v. *Fitzgerald* (1982), for example, the Court narrowly held that the Constitution implicitly grants the president an absolute immunity from private suit for actions that fall "within the outer perimeter of his authority." The four dissenters in the case bitterly disputed this interpretation of presidential immunity, insisting that the scope of immunity should be defined by considering how the threat of private suit might impede the president's performance of the office's constitutional functions. All the justices, however, recognized that the Constitution provides the president with the powers and immunities necessary to carry out the responsibilities of the office. This agreement in principle among the justices is as noteworthy as their disagreement on outcome, in that they reaffirmed the existence of implied presidential powers.

PREROGATIVE POWERS

A third basis for the expansion of executive power has been presidential exercise of prerogative powers. The concept of prerogative powers derives from the writings of the English political philosopher John Locke, who defined *prerogative* as the power of the executive "to act according to discretion for the public good, without the prescription of law and sometimes even against it."[10] In the American context, prerogative justifies the use of powers beyond those granted or implied in Article II. According to this concept, presidential power varies with changes in circumstances, and under extraordinary conditions includes the power to go beyond or against the law. This absence of set limits on presidential power raises the question of whether prerogative is compatible with constitutional government.

There is some evidence that the Framers expected presidents to exercise prerogative powers. Whereas Article I restricts Congress to "all legislative powers herein granted," Article II vests the "executive power" in the president. The open-ended character of this provision suggests that the president can legitimately claim all powers, including prerogative powers, characteristically exercised by the executive in other governments. Certainly, the Framers were familiar with Locke's writings on the scope of executive power. And Hamilton's emphasis in *The Federalist* on "energy in the executive"—the ability of the president to respond swiftly and decisively to emergency situations—seems to presuppose the availability of prerogative powers.

Nevertheless, the status of prerogative under the Constitution has remained uncertain. Some assertions of prerogative powers have been accepted as justified responses to extraordinary conditions. At the outset of the Civil War, President Abraham Lincoln, acting on his own initiative while Congress was adjourned, ordered several measures of questionable legality (see Chapter 6). He later justified his actions on the grounds that they had been necessary to preserve the Union:

> I did understand, however, that my oath to preserve the constitution to the best of my ability, imposed upon me the duty of preserving, by every indispensable means, that government—that nation—of which that constitution was the organic law. Was it possible to lose the nation, and yet preserve the constitution? . . . I felt that measures, otherwise unconstitutional, might become lawful, by becoming indispensable to the preservation of the constitution, through the preservation of the nation.[11]

Once convened, Congress ratified Lincoln's actions, and the verdict of history has supported his forceful assertion of prerogative powers.

At times the Supreme Court has also lent support to the idea of prerogative powers. In *In Re Neagle* (1890), it ruled that the president did not need legislative authorization to assign a U.S. marshal to protect a Supreme Court justice. Although there was no statutory basis for such action, the justices held that the president's responsibility to "ensure that the laws be faithfully executed" extends beyond acts of Congress and includes "the rights, duties, and obligations growing out of the Constitution itself, our international relations, and all the protection implied by the nature of the government under the Constitution." Put differently, because the responsibility for preserving the peace of the nation—a requirement common to all societies—is lodged in the president, so is the power necessary to fulfill that responsibility.

Other assertions of prerogative powers have been viewed less sympathetically. In *Youngstown Sheet & Tube Company* v. *Sawyer* (1952) the Supreme Court invalidated President Harry Truman's order, given during the Korean War, that the nation's steel mills be seized to prevent a strike. The Court held that since Congress had designated steps to be followed in such emergencies, its determination bound the president and foreclosed consideration of alternative responses. And when President Richard Nixon attempted to justify actions taken during the Watergate scandal by invoking prerogative powers, the public reaction was overwhelmingly negative.

Yet the condemnation of presidential actions in these instances does not indicate a wholesale rejection of prerogative powers. Rather, it reflects a judgment that the situations involved did not warrant the exercise of such powers. The deeper issue remains: Are prerogative powers necessary in "a constitution intended to endure for ages to come, and consequently to be adapted to the various crises of human affairs"? And if they are, can they be entrusted to the executive without jeopardizing the system of republican government?

The problem raised by prerogative powers puts into clear focus the continuing problem of the presidency. When the proposed constitution was submitted for adoption, leading Anti-Federalists charged that, in the words of Patrick Henry, it "squints toward monarchy." The Framers sought to allay this concern by combining energy in the executive with "other ingredients which constitute safety in the republican sense." The debate over the modern presidency, with its greatly expanded powers, is largely a dispute over the success of their efforts.

NOTES

1 *The Federalist,* No. 48, p. 309.

2 The quotation is from Edward S. Corwin, *The President: Office and Powers,* 4th ed. (New York: New York University Press, 1957), pp. 29–30.

3 The sole exception, which served as a model to the delegates, was the governorship in New York.

4 The discussion here follows Hamilton's delineation in *The Federalist,* No. 70: "The ingredients which constitute energy in the executive are unity; duration; an adequate provision for its support; and competent powers."

5 With the advent of year-round congressional sessions, this power has ceased to be important.

6 Quoted in Arthur Maass, *Congress and the Common Good* (New York: Basic Books, 1983), p. 14.

7 William Howard Taft, *Our Chief Magistrate and His Powers* (New York: Columbia University Press, 1916), p. 139.

8 Roosevelt's view was spelled out in his autobiography: "My view was that every officer, and above all every executive officer in high position, was a steward of the people. . . . I declined to adopt the view that what was imperatively necessary for the Nation could not be done by the President unless he could find some specific authorization to do it. My belief was that it was not only his right but his duty to do anything that the needs of the Nation demanded unless such action was forbidden by the Constitution or the laws."

[Theodore Roosevelt, *An Autobiography* (New York: Charles Scribner's Sons, 1931), p. 388.]

9 See *Humphrey's Executor* v. *United States* (1935) and *Wiener* v. *United States* (1958).

10 Locke, *Second Treatise of Civil Government,* Chapter XIV, Section 160.

11 From the letter to A. G. Hodges, April 4, 1864, in *The Complete Works of Abraham Lincoln,* John Nicolay and John Hay, eds. (New York: Francis D. Tandy Co., 1894), vol. 10, pp. 65–68.

SELECTED READINGS

The Federalist, Nos. 67–77.

Bowsher v. *Synar,* 478 U.S. 714 (1986).
Buckley v. *Valeo,* Chapter 12.
Humphrey's Executor v. United States, 295 U.S. 602 (1935).
Mississippi v. *Johnson,* 4 Wall. 475 (1867).
Nixon v. *Administrator of General Services,* 433 U.S. 425 (1977).
Nixon v. *Fitzgerald,* 457 U.S. 731 (1982).

Berger, Raoul. *Executive Privilege: A Constitutional Myth* (Cambridge: Harvard University Press, 1974).

Bessette, Joseph, and Jeffrey Tulis. *The Presidency in the Constitutional Order* (Baton Rouge: Louisiana State University Press, 1981).

Corwin, Edward S. *The President: Office and Powers.* 4th rev. ed. (New York: New York University Press, 1957).

Fisher, Louis. *Constitutional Conflicts Between Congress and the President* (Princeton: Princeton University Press, 1985).

Pierce, Richard J. "Morrison v. Olson, Separation of Powers, and the Structure of Government," *The Supreme Court Review* (1988).

Pious, Richard M. *The American Presidency* (New York: Basic Books, 1970).

Scigliano, Robert. *The Supreme Court and the Presidency* (New York: Free Press, 1971).

Thach, Charles C., Jr. *The Creation of the Presidency, 1775–1789* (Baltimore: Johns Hopkins, 1922).

Westin, Alan F. *Anatomy of a Constitutional Law Case* (New York: Macmillan, 1958).

Youngstown Sheet & Tube Company v. Sawyer

343 U.S. 579, 72 S. Ct. 863, 96 L. Ed. 1153 (1952)

In order to avert an apparently imminent nationwide steel strike during the Korean War, President Harry Truman issued an executive order directing the secretary of commerce to seize and operate the nation's steel mills. By taking such a step, he implicitly rejected the remedy offered by the Taft-Hartley Act: the seeking of an injunction against the strike. Reporting his action to Congress, the president justified the seizure by citing his aggregate powers as chief executive and commander in chief. He also noted that Congress could reverse or endorse the seizure. Congress took no action prior to the Supreme Court's consideration of the case, however.

Shortly after the seizure, the steel companies obtained from a federal district court an injunction restraining the secretary of commerce from "continuing the seizure and possession of the plants"; but on the same day the court of appeals stayed the injunction. The Supreme Court granted certiorari and expedited consideration of the case, announcing its decision less than two months after the seizure. *Opinion of the Court: Black, Frankfurter, Burton, Jackson. Concurring opinions: Frankfurter; Burton; Jackson; Clark; Douglas. Dissenting opinion: Vinson, Reed, Minton.*

Mr. Justice Black delivered the opinion of the Court.

We are asked to decide whether the President was acting within his constitutional power when he issued an order directing the Secretary of Commerce to take possession of and operate most of the Nation's steel mills. . . .

The President's power, if any, to issue the order must stem either from an act of Congress or from the Constitution itself. There is no statute that expressly authorizes the President to take possession of property as he did here. Nor is there any act of Congress to which our attention has been directed from which such a power can fairly be implied. Indeed, we do not understand the Government to rely on statutory authorization for this seizure. . . .

It is clear that if the President had authority to issue the order he did, it must be found in some provision of the Constitution. And it is not claimed that express constitutional language grants this power to the President. The contention is that presidential power should be implied from the aggregate of his powers under the Constitution. Particular reliance is placed on provisions in Article II which say that "The executive Power shall be vested in a President . . ."; that "he shall take Care that the Laws be faithfully executed"; and that he "shall be Commander in Chief of the Army and Navy of the United States."

The order cannot properly be sustained as an exercise of the President's military power as Commander in Chief of the Armed Forces. The Government attempts to do so by citing a number of cases upholding broad powers in military commanders engaged in day-to-day fighting in a theater of war. Such cases need not concern us here. Even though "theater of war" be an expanding concept, we cannot with faithfulness to our constitutional system hold that the Commander in Chief of the Armed Forces has the ultimate power as such to take possession of private property in order to keep labor disputes from stopping production. This is a job for the Nation's lawmakers, not for its military authorities.

Nor can the seizure order be sustained because of the several constitutional provisions that grant executive power to the President. In the framework of our Constitution, the President's power to see that the laws are faithfully executed refutes the idea that he is to be a lawmaker. The Constitution limits his functions in the lawmaking process to the recommending of laws he thinks wise and the vetoing of laws he thinks bad. And the Constitution is neither silent nor equivocal about who shall make laws which the President is to execute. The first section of the first article says that "All legislative Powers herein granted shall be vested in a Congress of the United States. . . ." After granting many powers to the Congress, Article I goes on to provide that Congress may "make all Laws which shall be necessary and proper for carrying into Execution the foregoing Powers, and all other Powers vested by this Constitution in the Government of the United States, or in any Department or Officer thereof." . . .

The Founders of this Nation entrusted the lawmaking power to the Congress alone in both good and bad times. It would do no good to recall the historical events, the fears of power and the hopes for freedom that lay behind their choice. Such a review would but confirm our holding that this seizure order cannot stand.

The judgment of the District Court is

Affirmed.

MR. JUSTICE FRANKFURTER, concurring in the judgment and opinion of the Court.

Congress has frequently—at least 16 times since 1916—specifically provided for executive seizure of production, transportation, communications, or storage facilities. In every case it has qualified this grant of power with limitations and safeguards. . . .

Congress in 1947 was again called upon to consider whether governmental seizure should be used to avoid serious industrial shutdowns. . . . A proposal that the President be given powers to seize plants to avert a shutdown where the "health or safety" of the Nation was endangered, was thoroughly canvassed by Congress and rejected. No room for doubt remains that the proponents as well as the opponents of the bill which became the Labor Management Relations Act of 1947 clearly understood that as a result of that legislation the only recourse for preventing a shutdown in any basic industry, after failure of mediation, was Congress. . . . Perhaps as much so as is true of any piece of modern legislation, Congress acted with full consciousness of what it was doing and in the light of much recent history. . . .

It cannot be contended that the President would have had power to issue this order had Congress explicitly negated such authority in formal legislation. Congress has expressed its will to withhold this power from the President as though it had said so in so many words. The authoritatively expressed purpose of Congress to disallow such power to the President and to require him, when in his mind the occasion arose for such a seizure, to put the matter to Congress and ask for specific authority from it, could not be more decisive if it had been written into §§206–210 of the Labor Management Relations Act of 1947. . . .

MR. JUSTICE JACKSON, concurring in the judgment and opinion of the Court.

The actual art of governing under our Constitution does not and cannot conform to judicial definitions of the power of any of its branches based on isolated clauses or even single Articles torn from context. While the Constitution diffuses power the better to secure liberty, it also contemplates that practice will integrate the dispersed powers into a workable government. It enjoins upon its branches separateness but interdependence, autonomy but reciprocity. Presidential powers are not fixed but fluctuate, depending upon their disjunction or conjunction with those of Congress. We may well begin by a somewhat over-simplified grouping of practical situations in which a President may doubt, or others may challenge, his powers, and by distinguishing roughly the legal consequences of this factor of relativity.

1. When the President acts pursuant to an express or implied authorization of Congress, his authority is at its maximum, for it includes all that he possesses in his own right plus all that Congress can delegate. In these circumstances, and in these only, may he be said (for what it may be worth) to personify the federal sovereignty. If his act is held unconstitutional under these circumstances, it usually means that the Federal Government as an undivided whole lacks power. A seizure executed by the President pursuant to an Act of Congress would be supported by the strongest of presumptions and the widest latitude of judicial interpretation, and the burden of persuasion would rest heavily upon any who might attack it.

2. When the President acts in absence of ei-

ther a congressional grant or denial of authority, he can only rely upon his own independent powers, but there is a zone of twilight in which he and Congress may have concurrent authority, or in which its distribution is uncertain. Therefore, congressional inertia, indifference or quiescence may sometimes, at least as a practical matter, enable, if not invite, measures on independent presidential responsibility. In this area, any actual test of power is likely to depend on the imperatives of events and contemporary imponderables rather than on abstract theories of law.

3. When the President takes measures incompatible with the expressed or implied will of Congress, his power is at its lowest ebb, for then he can rely only upon his own constitutional powers minus any constitutional powers of Congress over the matter. Courts can sustain exclusive presidential control in such a case only by disabling the Congress from acting upon the subject. Presidential claim to a power at once so conclusive and preclusive must be scrutinized with caution, for what is at stake is the equilibrium established by our constitutional system.

Into which of these classifications does this executive seizure of the steel industry fit? It is eliminated from the first by admission, for it is conceded that no congressional authorization exists for this seizure. . . .

Can it then be defended under flexible tests available to the second category? It seems clearly eliminated from that class because Congress has not left seizure of private property an open field but has covered it by three statutory policies inconsistent with this seizure. . . . In choosing a different and inconsistent way of his own, the President cannot claim that it is necessitated or invited by failure of Congress to legislate upon the occasions, grounds and methods for seizure of industrial properties.

This leaves the current seizure to be justified only by the severe tests under the third grouping, where it can be supported only by any remainder of executive power after subtraction of such powers as Congress may have over the subject. In short, we can sustain the President only by holding that seizure of such strike-bound industries is within his domain and beyond control by Congress. Thus, this Court's first review of such seizures occurs under circumstances which leave presidential power most vulnerable to attack and in the least favorable of possible constitutional postures. . . .

That seems to be the logic of an argument tendered at our bar—that the President having, on his own responsibility, sent American troops abroad derives from that act "affirmative power" to seize the means of producing a supply of steel for them. . . .

I cannot foresee all that it might entail if the Court should indorse this argument. Nothing in our Constitution is plainer than that declaration of a war is entrusted only to Congress. Of course, a state of war may in fact exist without a formal declaration. But no doctrine that the Court could promulgate would seem to me more sinister and alarming than that a President whose conduct of foreign affairs is so largely uncontrolled, and often even is unknown, can vastly enlarge his mastery over the internal affairs of the country by his own commitment of the Nation's armed forces to some foreign venture. . . .

That military powers of the Commander in Chief were not to supersede representative government of internal affairs seems obvious from the Constitution and from elementary American history. . . .

We should not use this occasion to circumscribe, much less to contract, the lawful role of the President as Commander in Chief. I should indulge the widest latitude of interpretation to sustain his exclusive function to command the instruments of national force, at least when turned against the outside world for the security of our society. But, when it is turned inward, not because of rebellion but because of a lawful economic struggle between industry and labor, it should have no such indulgence. . . .

In view of the ease, expedition and safety with which Congress can grant and has granted large emergency powers, certainly ample to embrace this crisis, I am quite unimpressed with the argument that we should affirm possession of them without statute. Such power either has no beginning or it has no end. If it exists, it need submit to no legal restraint. I am not alarmed that it would plunge us straightway into dictatorship, but it is at least a step in that wrong direction. . . .

But I have no illusion that any decision by this Court can keep power in the hands of Congress if it is not wise and timely in meeting its problems. A crisis that challenges the President equally, or perhaps primarily, challenges Congress. If not good law, there was worldly wisdom in the maxim attributed to Napoleon that "The tools belong to the man who can use them." We may say that power to legislate for emergencies belongs in the hands of Congress, but only Congress itself can prevent power from slipping through its fingers.

The essence of our free Government is "leave to live by no man's leave, underneath the law"—to be governed by those impersonal forces which we call law. Our Government is fashioned to fulfill this concept so far as humanly possible. The Executive, except for recommendation and veto, has no legislative power. The executive action we have here originates in the individual will of the President and represents an exercise of authority without law. No one, perhaps not even the President, knows the limits of the power he may seek to exert in this instance and the parties affected cannot learn the limit of their rights. We do not know today what powers over labor or property would be claimed to flow from Government possession if we should legalize it, what rights to compensation would be claimed or recognized, or on what contingency it would end. With all its defects, delays and inconveniences, men have discovered no technique for long preserving free government except that the Executive be under the law, and that the law be made by parliamentary deliberations.

Such institutions may be destined to pass away. But it is the duty of the Court to be last, not first, to give them up.

MR. CHIEF JUSTICE VINSON, with whom MR. JUSTICE REED and MR. JUSTICE MINTON join, dissenting. . . .

In passing upon the question of Presidential powers in this case, we must first consider the context in which those powers were exercised. . . .

One is not here called upon even to consider the possibility of executive seizure of a farm, a corner grocery store or even a single industrial plant. Such considerations arise only when one ignores the central fact of this case—that the Nation's entire basic steel production would have shut down completely if there had been no Government seizure. Even ignoring for the moment whatever confidential information the President may possess as "the Nation's organ for foreign affairs," the uncontroverted affidavits in this record amply support the finding that "a work stoppage would immediately jeopardize and imperil our national defense."

Plaintiffs do not remotely suggest any basis for rejecting the President's finding that *any* stoppage of steel production would immediately place the Nation in peril. . . .

Focusing now on the situation confronting the President on the night of April 8, 1952, we cannot but conclude that the President was performing his duty under the Constitution to "take Care that the Laws be faithfully executed"—a duty described by President Benjamin Harrison as "the central idea of the office."

The President reported to Congress the morning after the seizure that he acted because a work stoppage in steel production would immediately imperil the safety of the Nation by preventing execution of the legislative programs for procurement of military equipment. And, while a shutdown could be averted by granting the price concessions requested by plaintiffs, granting such concessions would disrupt the price stabilization program also enacted by Congress. Rather than fail to execute either legislative program, the President acted to execute both.

Much of the argument in this case has been directed at straw men. We do not now have before us the case of a President acting solely on the basis of his own notions of the public welfare. Nor is there any question of unlimited executive power in this case. The President himself closed the door to any such claim when he sent his Message to Congress stating his purpose to abide by any action of Congress, whether approving or disapproving his seizure action. Here, the President immediately made sure that Congress was fully informed of the temporary action he had taken only to preserve the legislative programs from destruction until Congress could act.

The absence of a specific statute authorizing seizure of the steel mills as a mode of executing the laws—both the military procurement program and the anti-inflation program—has not until today been thought to prevent the President from executing the laws. Unlike an administrative commission confined to the enforcement of the statute under which it was created, or the head of a department when administering a particular statute, the President is a constitutional officer charged with taking care that a "mass of legislation" be executed. Flexibility as to mode of execution to meet critical situations is a matter of practical necessity. . . . Faced with the duty of executing the defense programs which Congress had enacted and the disastrous effects that any stoppage in steel production would have on those programs, the President acted to preserve those programs by seizing the steel mills. . . . The President immediately informed Congress of his action and clearly stated his intention to abide by the legislative will. No basis for claims of arbitrary action, unlimited powers or dictatorial usurpation of congressional power appears from the facts of this case. On the contrary, judicial, legislative and executive precedents throughout our history demonstrate that in this case the President acted in full conformity with his duties under the Constitution.

Myers v. *United States*

272 U.S. 52, 47 S. Ct. 21, 71 L. Ed. 160 (1926)

According to an act passed by Congress in 1876, "Postmasters of the first, second, and third classes shall be appointed and may be removed by the President by and with the advice and consent of the Senate, and shall hold their offices for four years unless sooner removed or suspended according to law." Myers was appointed to a first-class postmastership under this statute in 1917. The postmaster general, at the direction of President Woodrow Wilson, removed Myers from his post in 1920, prior to the expiration of Myers's term and without Senate approval. Myers protested his removal and sued to recover his lost salary in the U.S. Court of Claims. When the court of claims sustained the removal, the case was appealed to the Supreme Court. *Opinion of the Court: Taft, Sutherland, Butler, Sanford, Stone. Dissenting opinions: Holmes; Brandeis; McReynolds.*

MR. CHIEF JUSTICE TAFT delivered the opinion of the Court.

This case presents the question whether under the Constitution the President has the exclusive power of removing executive officers of the United States whom he has appointed by and with the advice and consent of the Senate. . . .

The question where the power of removal of executive officers appointed by the President by and with the advice and consent of the Senate was vested, was presented early in the first session of the First Congress. There is no express provision respecting removals in the Constitution, except as Section 4 of Article II, above quoted, provides for removal from office by impeachment. . . .

Mr. Madison and his associates in the discussion in the House dwelt at length upon the necessity there was for construing Article II to give the President the sole power of removal in his responsibility for the conduct of the executive branch, and enforced this by emphasizing his duty expressly declared in the third section of the Article to "take care that the laws be faithfully executed." . . .

The vesting of the executive power in the President was essentially a grant of the power to execute the laws. But the President alone and unaided could not execute the laws. He must execute them by the assistance of subordinates. This view has since been repeatedly affirmed by this Court. . . . As he is charged specifically to take care that they be faithfully executed, the reasonable implication, even in the absence of express words, was that as part of his executive power he should select those who were to act for him under his direction in the execution of the laws. The further implication must be, in the absence of any express limitation respecting removals, that as his selection of administrative officers is essential to the execution of the laws by him, so must be his power of removing those for whom he can not continue to be responsible. . . .

The power to prevent the removal of an officer who has served under the President is different from the authority to consent to or reject his appointment. When a nomination is made, it may be presumed that the Senate is, or may become, as well advised as to the fitness of the nominee as the President, but in the nature of things like defects in ability or intelligence or loyalty in the administration of the law of one who has served as an officer under the President, are facts as to which the President, or his trusted subordinates, must be better informed than the Senate, and the power to remove him may, therefore, be regarded as confined, for very sound and practical reasons, to the governmental authority which has administrative control. The power of removal is incident to the power of appointment, not to the power of advising and consenting to appointment, and when the grant of the executive power is enforced by the express mandate to take care that the laws be faithfully executed, it emphasizes the necessity for including within the executive power as conferred the exclusive power of removal. . . .

Made responsible under the Constitution for the effective enforcement of the law, the President needs as an indispensable aid to meet it the disciplinary influence upon those who act under him of a reserve power of removal. . . .

In all such cases, the discretion to be exercised is that of the President in determining the national public interest and in directing the action to be taken by his executive subordinates to protect it. In this field his cabinet officers must do his will. He must place in each member of his official family, and his chief executive subordinates, implicit faith. The moment that he loses confidence in the intelligence, ability, judgment or loyalty of any one of them, he must have the power to remove him without delay. To require him to file charges and submit them to the consideration of the Senate might make impossible that unity and co-ordination in executive administration essential to effective action.

The duties of the heads of departments and bureaus in which the discretion of the President is exercised and which we have described, are the most important in the whole field of executive action of the Government. There is nothing in the Constitution which permits a distinction between the removal of the head of a department or a bureau, when he discharges a political duty of the President or exercises his direction, and the removal of executive officers engaged in the discharge of their other normal duties. The imperative reasons requiring an unrestricted power to remove the most important of his subordinates in their most important duties must, therefore, control the interpretation of the Constitution as to all appointed by him.

But this is not to say that there are not strong reasons why the President should have a like power to remove his appointees charged with other duties than those above described. The ordinary duties of officers prescribed by statute come under the general administrative control of the President by virtue of the general grant to him of the executive power, and he may properly supervise and guide their construction of the statutes under which they act in order to secure that unitary and uniform execution of the laws which Article II of the Constitution evidently contemplated in vesting general executive power in the President alone. Laws are often passed with specific provision for the adoption of regulations by a department or bureau head to make the law workable and effective. The ability and judgment manifested by the official thus empowered, as well as his energy and stimulation of his subordinates, are subjects which the President must consider and supervise in his administrative control. Finding such officers to be negligent and inefficient, the President should have the power to remove them. Of course there may be duties so peculiarly and specifically committed to the discretion of a particular officer as to raise a question whether the President may overrule or revise the officer's interpretation of his statutory duty in a particular instance. Then there may be duties of a quasi-judicial character imposed on executive officers and members of executive tribunals whose decisions after hearing affect interests of individuals, the discharge of which the President can not in a particular case properly influence or control. But even in such a case he may consider the decision after its rendition as a reason for removing the officer, on the ground that the discretion regularly entrusted to that officer by statute has not been on the whole intelligently or wisely exercised. Otherwise he does not discharge his own constitutional duty of seeing that the laws be faithfully executed. . . .

We have devoted much space to this discussion and decision of the question of the Presidential power of removal in the First Congress, not because a Congressional conclusion on a constitutional issue is conclusive, but, first, because of our agreement with the reasons upon which it was avowedly based; second, because this was the decision of the First Congress, on a question of primary importance in the organization of the Government, made within two years after the Constitutional Convention and within a much shorter time after its ratification: and, third, because that Congress numbered among its leaders those who had been members of the Convention. It must necessarily constitute a precedent upon which many future laws supplying the machinery of the new Government would be based, and, if erroneous, it would be likely to evoke dissent and departure in future Congresses. It would come at once before the executive branch of the Government for compliance, and might well be brought before the judicial branch for a test of its validity. As we shall see, it was soon accepted as a final decision of the question by all branches of the Government.

An argument *ab inconvenienti* has been made against our conclusion in favor of the executive power of removal by the President, without the consent of the Senate—that it will open the door to a reintroduction of the spoils system. . . . Reform in the federal civil service was begun by the Civil Service Act of 1883. It has been developed from that time, so that the classified service now includes a vast majority of all the civil officers. It may still be enlarged by further legislation. The independent power of removal by the President alone, under present conditions, works no practical interference with the merit system. Political appointments of inferior officers are still maintained in one important class, that of the first, second and third class postmasters, collecters of internal revenue, marshals, collectors of customs and other officers of that kind, distributed through the country. They are appointed by the President with the consent of the Senate. It is the intervention of the Senate in their appointment, and not in their removal, which prevents their classification into the merit system. If such appointments were vested in the heads of departments to which they belong, they could be entirely removed from politics, and that is what a number of Presidents have recommended. . . .

For the reasons given, we must therefore hold that the provision of the law of 1876, by which the unrestricted power of removal of first class postmasters is denied to the President, is in violation of the Constitution, and invalid.

Judgment affirmed.

MR. JUSTICE HOLMES, dissenting. . . .

The arguments drawn from the executive power of the President, and from his duty to appoint officers of the United States (when Congress does not vest the appointment elsewhere), to take care that the laws be faithfully executed, and to commission all officers of the United States, seem to me spider's webs inadequate to control the dominant facts.

We have to deal with an office that owes its existence to Congress and that Congress may abolish tomorrow. Its duration and the pay attached to it while it lasts depend on Congress alone. Congress alone confers on the President the power to appoint to it and at any time may transfer the power to other hands. With such power over its own creation, I have no more trouble in believing that Congress has power to prescribe a term of life for it free from any interference than I have in accepting the undoubted power of Congress to decree its end. I have equally little trouble in accepting its power to prolong the tenure of an incumbent until Congress or the Senate shall have assented to his removal. The duty of the President to see that the laws be executed is a duty that does not go beyond the laws or require him to achieve more than Congress sees fit to leave within his power.

MR. JUSTICE BRANDEIS, dissenting. . . .

The ability to remove a subordinate executive officer, being an essential of effective government, will, in the absence of express constitutional provision to the contrary, be deemed to have been vested in some person or body. . . . But it is not a power inherent in a chief executive. The President's power of removal from statutory civil inferior offices, like the power of appointment to them, comes immediately from Congress. It is true that the exercise of the power of removal is said to be an executive act; and that when the Senate grants or withholds consent to a removal by the President, it participates in an executive act. But the Constitution has confessedly granted to Congress the legislative power to create offices, and to prescribe the tenure thereof; and it has not in terms denied to Congress the power to control removals. To prescribe the tenure involves prescribing the conditions under which incumbency shall cease. For the possibility of removal is a condition or qualification of the tenure. When Congress provides that the incumbent shall hold the office for four years unless sooner removed with the consent of the Senate, it prescribes the term of the tenure. . . .

To imply a grant to the President of the uncontrollable power of removal from statutory inferior executive offices involves an unnecessary and indefensible limitation upon the constitutional power of Congress to fix the tenure of inferior statutory offices. That such a limitation cannot be justified on the ground of necessity is demonstrated by the practice of our governments, state and national. . . .

The historical data submitted present a legislative practice, established by concurrent affirmative action of Congress and the President, to make consent of the Senate a condition of removal from statutory inferior, civil, executive offices to which the appointment is made for a fixed term by the President with such consent. They show that the practice has existed, without interruption, continuously for the last fifty-eight years; that, throughout this period, it has governed a great majority of all such offices; that the legislation applying the removal clause specifically to the office of postmaster was enacted more than half a century ago; and that recently the practice has, with the President's approval, been extended to several newly created offices. The data show further, that the insertion of the removal clause in acts creating inferior civil offices with fixed tenures is part of the broader legislative practice, which has prevailed since the formation of our Government, to restrict or regulate in many ways both removal from and nomination to such offices. A persistent legislative practice which involves a delimitation of the respective powers of Congress and the President, and which has been so established and maintained, should be deemed tantamount to judicial construction, in the absence of any decision by any court to the contrary. . . .

The persuasive effect of this legislative practice is strengthened by the fact that no instance has been found, even in the earlier period of our history, of concurrent affirmative action of Congress and the President which is inconsistent with the legislative practice of the last fifty-eight years to impose the removal clause. . . .

The separation of the powers of government did not make each branch completely autonomous. It left each, in some measure, dependent upon the others, as it left to each power to exercise, in some respects, functions in their nature executive, legislative and judicial. Obviously the President cannot secure full execution of the laws if Congress denies to him adequate means of doing so. . . . The President performs his full constitutional duty, if, with the means and instruments provided by Congress and within the limitations prescribed by it, he uses his best endeavors to secure the faithful execution of the laws enacted. . . .

The doctrine of the separation of powers was adopted by the Convention of 1787, not to promote efficiency but to preclude the exercise of arbitrary power. The purpose was, not to avoid friction, but, by means of the inevitable friction incident to the distribution of the governmental powers among three departments, to save the people from autocracy. . . . Nothing in support of the claim of uncontrollable power can be inferred from the silence of the Convention of 1787 on the subject of removal. For the outstanding fact remains that every specific proposal to confer such uncontrollable power upon the President was rejected. In America, as in England, the conviction prevailed then that the people must look to representative assemblies for the protection of their liberties. And protection of the individual, even if he be an official, from the arbitrary or capricious exercise of power was then believed to be an essential of free government.

Morrison v. *Olson*

487 U.S. 654, 108 S. Ct. 2597, 101 L. Ed. 2d 569 (1988)

The Ethics in Government Act of 1978 (Act) provides for the appointment of an independent counsel to investigate and prosecute violations of federal criminal laws by high-ranking officials of the executive branch. The executive branch's control over the independent counsel is quite limited: the counsel is appointed by a Special Division of the Court of Appeals (District of Columbia Circuit) and can be removed by the attorney general only for "good cause."

The constitutional challenge to the Act arose out of a congressional investigation of the Environmental Protection Agency (EPA). In 1982 two subcommittees of the House of Representatives issued subpoenas directing the EPA to produce documents relating to its implementation of the "Superfund Law." At that time Theodore Olson was assistant attorney general for the Office of Legal Counsel, Edward Schmults deputy attorney general, and Carol Dinkins assistant attorney general for the Land and Resources Division. President Reagan ordered the administrator of EPA to invoke executive privilege to withhold certain documents, but after the House voted to hold the administrator in contempt, a compromise was reached whereby the House obtained limited access to the documents. In 1984 the House Judiciary Committee began an investigation into the controversy over the withheld documents, at which Olson testified. Following the investigation, the committee issued a report which suggested that Olson had given false and misleading testimony and that Schmults and Dinkins had wrongfully withheld documents, thereby obstructing the investigation. The chairman of the Judiciary Committee sent the report to Attorney General Edwin Meese, requesting that he seek the appointment of an independent counsel to investigate the allegations.

Under the Act, the attorney general is obliged to request appointment of an independent counsel if there are "reasonable grounds" to believe further investigation or prosecution is warranted. When Meese did so, the Special Division designated Alexia Morrison as independent counsel. Morrison caused a grand jury to issue subpoenas to Olson, Schmults, and Dinkins, who moved to quash the subpoenas, claiming that the independent counsel provisions of the Act were unconstitutional and that Morrison therefore had no authority to proceed. The District Court rejected their motion, but the Court of Appeals reversed, ruling the Act unconstitutional, and Morrison appealed that decision to the Supreme Court. *Opinion of the Court: Rehnquist, Brennan, White, Marshall, Blackmun, Stevens O'Connor. Dissenting opinion: Scalia.*

Chief Justice Rehnquist delivered the opinion of the Court. . . .

This case presents us with a challenge to the independent counsel provisions of the Ethics in Government Act of 1978. . . . We hold today that these provisions of the Act do not violate the Appointments Clause of the Constitution, Art II, § 2, cl 2, or the limitations of Article III, nor do they impermissibly interfere with the President's authority under Article II in violation of the constitutional principle of separation of powers. . . .

The Appointments Clause of Article II reads as follows:

[The President] shall nominate, and by and with the Advice and Consent of the Senate, shall appoint Ambassadors, other public Ministers and Consuls, Judges of the supreme Court, and all other Officers of the United States, whose Appointments are not herein otherwise provided for, and which shall be established by Law: but the Congress may by Law vest the Appointment of such inferior Officers, as they think proper, in the President alone, in the Courts of Law, or in the Heads of Departments."

. . . The initial question is, accordingly, whether appellant is an "inferior" or a "principal" officer. . . .

The line between "inferior" and "principal" officers is one that is far from clear, and the Framers provided little guidance into where it should be drawn. . . . We need not attempt here to decide exactly where the line falls between the two types of officers, because in our view appellant clearly falls on the "inferior officer" side of that line. Several factors lead to this conclusion.

First, appellant is subject to removal by a higher Executive Branch official. Although appellant may not be "subordinate" to the Attorney General (and the President) insofar as she possesses a degree of independent discretion to exercise the powers delegated to her under the Act, the fact that she can be removed by the Attorney General indicates that she is to some degree "inferior" in rank and authority. Second, appellant is empowered by the Act to perform only certain, limited duties. An independent counsel's role is restricted primarily to investigation and, if appropriate, prosecution for certain federal crimes. Admittedly, the Act delegates to appellant "full power and independent authority to exercise all investigative and prosecutorial functions and powers of the Department of Justice," but this grant of authority does not include any authority to formulate policy for the Government or the Executive Branch, nor does it give appellant any administrative duties outside of those necessary to operate her office. The Act specifically provides that in policy matters appellant is to comply to the extent possible with the policies of the Department. . . .

Third, appellant's office is limited in jurisdiction. Not only is the Act itself restricted in applicability to certain federal officials suspected of certain serious federal crimes, but an independent counsel can only act within the scope of the jurisdiction that has been granted by the Special Division pursuant to a request by the Attorney General. Finally, appellant's office is limited in tenure. There is concededly no time limit on the appointment of a particular counsel. Nonetheless, the office of independent counsel is "temporary" in the sense that an independent counsel is appointed essentially to accomplish a single task, and when that task is over the office is terminated, either by the counsel herself or by action of the Special Division. Unlike other prosecutors, appellant has no ongoing responsibilities that extend beyond the accomplishment of the mission that she was appointed for and authorized by the Special Division to undertake. In our view, these factors relating to the "ideas of tenure, duration . . . and duties" of the independent counsel, . . . are sufficient to establish that appellant is an "inferior" officer in the constitutional sense. . . . Appellees argue that even if appellant is an "inferior" officer, the Clause does not empower Congress to place the power to appoint such an office outside the Executive Branch. They contend that the Clause does not contemplate congressional authorization of "interbranch appointments," in which an officer of one branch is appointed by officers of another branch. The relevant language of the Appointments Clause is worth repeating. It reads: ". . . but the Congress may by Law vest the Appointment of such inferior Officers, as they think proper, in the President alone, in the courts of Law, or in the Heads of Departments." On its face, the language of this "excepting clause" admits of no limitation on interbranch appointments. Indeed, the inclusion of "as they think proper" seems clearly to give Congress significant discretion to determine whether it is "proper" to vest the appointment of, for example, executive officials in the "courts of Law." . . .

We do not mean to say that Congress' power to provide for interbranch appointments of "inferior officers" is unlimited. In addition to separation of powers concerns, which would arise if such provisions for appointment had the potential to impair the constitutional functions assigned to one of the branches, [*Ex Parte*] Siebold [1880] itself suggested that Congress' decision to vest the appointment power in the courts would be improper if there was some "incongruity" between the functions normally performed by the courts and the performance of their duty to appoint. . . . In this case, however, we do not think it impermissible for Congress to vest the power to appoint independent counsels in a specially created federal court. . . . Congress of course was concerned when it created the office of independent counsel with the conflicts of interest that could arise in situations when the Executive Branch is called upon to investigate its own high-ranking officers. If it were to remove the appointing authority from the Executive Branch, the most logical place to put it was in the Judicial Branch. In the light of the Act's provision making the judges of the Special Division ineligible to participate in any matters relating to an independent counsel they have appointed . . . we do not think that appointment of the independent counsels by the court runs afoul of the constitutional limitation on "incongruous" interbranch appointments. . . .

We now turn to consider whether the Act is invalid under the constitutional principle of separation of powers. . . .

Two Terms ago we had occasion to consider whether it was consistent with the separation of powers for Congress to pass a statute that authorized a government official who is removable only by Congress to participate in what we found to be "executive powers." *Bowsher* v. *Synar*, . . . (1986). We held in *Bowsher* that "Congress cannot reserve for itself the power of removal of an officer charged with the execution of the laws except by impeachment." . . . A primary antecedent for this ruling was our 1926 decision in *Myers* v. *United States* . . . .

Unlike both *Bowsher* and *Myers*, this case does not involve an attempt by Congress itself to gain a role in the removal of executive officials other than its established powers of impeachment and conviction. The Act instead puts the removal power squarely in the hands of the Executive Branch; an independent counsel may be removed from office, "only by the personal action of the Attorney General, and only for good cause." . . . There is no requirement of congressional approval of the Attorney General's removal decision, though the decision is subject to judicial review. . . . In our view, the removal provisions of the Act make this case more analogous to *Humphrey's Executor* v. *United States* . . . (1935), and *Wiener* v. *United States* . . . (1958) [rulings denying presidential power to remove members of independent commissions before their terms expired], than to *Myers* or *Bowsher*. . . .

We undoubtedly did rely on the terms "quasi-legislative" and "quasi-judicial" to distinguish the officials involved in *Humphrey's Executor* and *Wiener* from those in *Myers*, but our present considered view is that the determination of whether the Constitution allows Congress to impose a "good cause"-type restriction on the President's power to remove an official cannot be made to turn on whether or not that official is classified as "purely executive." . . . But the real question is whether the removal restrictions are of such a nature that they impede the President's ability to perform his constitutional duty, and the functions of the officials in question must be analyzed in that light. . . . It is undeniable that the Act reduces the amount of control or supervision that the Attorney General and, through him, the President exercises over the investigation and prosecution of a certain class of alleged criminal activity. The Attorney General is not allowed to appoint the individual of his choice; he does not determine the counsel's jurisdiction; and his power to remove a counsel is limited. Nonetheless, the Act does give the Attorney General several means of supervising or controlling the prosecutorial powers that may be wielded by an independent counsel. Most importantly, the Attorney General retains the power to remove the counsel for "good cause," a power that we have already concluded provides the Executive with substantial ability to ensure that the laws are "faithfully executed" by an independent counsel. . . .

JUSTICE SCALIA, dissenting.

That is what this suit is about. Power. The allocation of power among Congress, the President and the courts in such fashion as to preserve the equilibrium the Constitution sought to establish—so that "a gradual concentration of the several powers in the same department," Federalist No. 51, p 321 (J. Madison), can effectively be resisted. Frequently an issue of this sort will come before the Court clad, so to speak, in sheep's clothing: the potential of the asserted principle to effect important change in the equilibrium of power is not immediately evident, and must be discerned by a careful and perceptive analysis. But this wolf comes as a wolf. . . .

. . . By the application of this statute in the present case, Congress has effectively compelled a criminal investigation of a high-level appointee of the President in connection with his actions arising out of a bitter power dispute between the President and the Legislative Branch. Mr. Olson may or may not be guilty of a crime; we do not know. But we do know that the investigation of him has been commenced, not necessarily because the President or his authorized subordinates believe it is the interest of the United States, in the sense that it warrants the diversion of resources from other efforts, and is worth the cost in money and in possible damage to other governmental interests; and not even, leaving aside those normally considered factors, because the President or his authorized subordinates necessarily believe that an investigation is likely to unearth a violation worth prosecuting; but only because the Attorney General cannot affirm, as Congress demands, that there are *no reasonable grounds to believe* that further investigation is warranted. The decisions regarding the scope of that further investigation, its duration, and, finally, whether or not prosecution should ensue, are likewise beyond the control of the President and his subordinates. . . .

If to describe this case is not to decide it, the concept of a government of separate and coordinate powers no longer has meaning. . . .

. . . Art III, § 1, cl 1 of the Constitution provides:

> The executive Power shall be vested in a President of the United States.

. . . This does not mean *some of* the executive power, but *all of* the executive power. It seems to me, therefore, that the decision of the Court of Appeals invalidating the present statute must be upheld on fundamental separation-of-powers principles if the following two questions are answered affirmatively: (1) Is the conduct of a criminal prosecution (and of an investigation to decide whether to prosecute) the exercise of purely executive power? (2) Does the statute deprive the President of the United States of exclusive control over the exercise of that power? Surprising to say, the Court appears to concede an affirmative answer to both questions, but seeks to avoid the inevitable conclusion that since the statute vests some purely executive power in a person who is not the President of the United States it is void. . . .

The utter incompatibility of the Court's approach with our constitutional traditions can be made more clear, perhaps, by applying it to the powers of the other two Branches. Is it conceivable that if Congress passed a statute depriving itself of less than full and entire control over some insignificant area of legislation, we would inquire whether the matter was "*so central* to the functioning of the Legislative Branch" as really to require complete control, or whether the statute gives Congress "*sufficient* control over the surrogate legislator to ensure that Congress is able to perform its constitutionally assigned duties"? Of course we would have none of that. Once we determined that a purely legislative power was at issue we would require it to be exercised, wholly and entirely, by Congress. Or to bring the point closer to home, consider a statute giving to non-Article III judges just a tiny bit of purely judicial power in a relatively insignificant field, with substantial control, though not total control, in the courts—perhaps "clear error" review, which would be a fair judicial equivalent of the Attorney General's "for cause" removal power here. Is there any doubt that we would not pause to inquire whether the matter was "*so central* to the functioning of the Judicial Branch" as really to require complete control, or whether we retained "*sufficient* control over the matters to be decided that we are able to perform our constitutionally assigned duties"? We would say that our "constitutionally assigned duties" include *complete* control over all exercises of the judicial power—or, as the plurality opinion said in *Northern Pipeline Construction Co.* v. *Marathon Pipe Line Co.* . . . (1982), that "[t]he inexorable command of [Article III] is clear and definite: The judicial power of the United States must be exercised by courts having the attributes prescribed in Art III." We should say here that the President's constitutionally assigned duties include *complete* control over investigation and prosecution of violations of the law, and that the inexorable command of Article II is clear and definite: the executive power must be vested in the President of the United States.

The Court has, nonetheless, replaced the clear constitutional prescription that the executive power belongs to the President with a "balancing test." What are the standards to determine how the balance is to be struck, that is, how much removal of presidential power is too much? Many countries of the world get along with an Executive that is much weaker than ours—in fact, entirely dependent upon the continued support of the legislature. Once we depart from the text of the Constitution, just where short of that do we stop? The most amazing feature of the Court's opinion is that it does not even purport to give an answer. It simply *announces,* with no analysis, that the ability to control the decision whether to investigate and prosecute the President's closest advisors, and indeed the President himself, is not "so central to the functioning of the Executive Branch" as to be constitutionally required to be within the President's control. . . . Evidently, the governing standard is to be what might be called the unfettered wisdom of a majority of this Court, revealed to an obedient people on a case-by-case basis. This is not only not the government of laws that the Constitution established; it is not a government of laws at all.

United States v. *Nixon*

418 U.S. 683, 94 S.Ct. 3090, 41 L. Ed. 2d 1039 (1974)

On March 1, 1974, a federal grand jury returned indictments against Attorney General John Mitchell, presidential assistants H. R. Haldeman and John Ehrlichman, and four other officials, charging them with conspiracy to defraud the government and obstruction of justice. The grand jury also named President Richard Nixon as an unindicted co-conspirator. Special Prosecutor Leon Jaworski obtained from the trial court a subpoena directing the president to produce as evidence certain tape recordings and memoranda of conversations held in the White House. Although he surrendered some of the subpoenaed materials, President Nixon refused to produce others, basing his right to refuse primarily on a claim of executive privilege. When the trial judge denied this claim, the president appealed the decision to the court of appeals. The special prosecutor petitioned the Supreme Court to expedite the matter by granting certiorari before the court of appeals reached a decision. The Supreme Court agreed to the prosecutor's request, heard oral argument in special session on July 8, and announced its decision on July 24. Six days later, the House Judiciary Committee voted articles of impeachment against the president. *Opinion of the Court: Burger, Douglas, Brennan, Stewart, White, Marshall, Blackmun, Powell. Not participating: Rehnquist.*

Mr. Chief Justice Burger delivered the opinion of the Court. . . .

Justiciability

In the District Court, the President's counsel argued that the court lacked jurisdiction to issue the subpoena because the matter was an intra-branch dispute between a subordinate and superior officer of the Executive Branch and hence not subject to judicial resolution. . . . Since the Executive Branch has exclusive authority and absolute discretion to decide whether to prosecute a case, it is contended that a President's decision is final in determining what evidence is to be used in a given criminal case. . . . The Special Prosecutor's demand for the items therefore presents, in the view of the President's counsel, a political question . . . since it involves a "textually demonstrable" grant of power under Art. II. The mere assertion of a claim of an "intra-branch dispute," without more, has never operated to defeat federal jurisdiction. . . .

Our starting point is the nature of the proceeding for which the evidence is sought—here a pending criminal prosecution. . . . Under the authority of Art. II. §2, Congress has vested in the Attorney General the power to conduct the criminal litigation of the United States Government. . . . It has also vested in him the power to appoint subordinate officers to assist him in the discharge of his duties. . . . Acting pursuant to those statutes, the Attorney General has delegated the authority to represent the United States in these particular matters to a Special Prosecutor with unique authority and tenure. The regulation gives the Special Prosecutor explicit power to contest the invocation of executive privilege in the process of seeking evidence deemed relevant to the performance of these specially delegated duties. . . . So long as this regulation is extant it has the force of law. Here at issue is the production or nonproduction of specified evidence deemed by the Special Prosecutor to be relevant and admissible in a pending criminal case. It is sought by one official of the Executive Branch within the scope of his express authority; it is resisted by the Chief Executive on the ground of his duty to preserve the confidentiality of the communications of the President. Whatever the correct answer on the merits, these issues are "of a type which are traditionally justiciable."

The Claim of Privilege

. . . we turn to the claim that the subpoena should be quashed because it demands "confidential conversations between a President and his close advisors that it would be inconsistent with the public interest to produce." . . . The first contention is a broad claim that the separation of powers doctrine precludes judicial review of a President's claim of privilege. The second contention is that if he does not prevail on the claim of absolute privilege, the court should hold as a matter of constitutional law that the privilege prevails over the subpoena *duces tecum*.

In the performance of assigned constitutional duties each branch of the Government must initially interpret the Constitution, and the interpretation of its powers by any branch is due great respect from the others. The President's counsel, as we have noted, reads the Constitution as providing an absolute privilege of confidentiality for all Presidential communications. Many decisions of this Court, however, have unequivocally reaffirmed the holding of *Marbury* v. *Madison* [1803] . . . that "it is emphatically the province and duty of the judicial department to say what the law is." . . .

In support of his claim of absolute privilege, the President's counsel urges two grounds, one of which is common to all governments and one of which is peculiar to our system of separation of powers. The first ground is the valid need for protection of communications between high Government officials and those who advise and assist them in the performance of their manifold duties; the importance of this confidentiality is too plain to require further discussion. Human experience teaches that those who expect public dissemination of their remarks may well temper candor with a concern for appearances and for their own interests to the detriment of the decisionmaking process. Whatever the nature of the privilege of confidentiality of Presidential communications in the exercise of Art. II powers, the privilege can be said to derive from the supremacy of each branch within its own assigned area of constitutional duties. Certain powers and privileges flow from the nature of enumerated powers; the protection of the confidentiality of Presidential communications has similar constitutional underpinnings. rests on the doctrine of separation of powers. Here it is argued that the independence of the Executive Branch within its own sphere . . . insulates a President from a judicial subpoena in an ongoing criminal prosecution, and thereby protects confidential Presidential communications.

However, neither the doctrine of separation of powers, nor the need for confidentiality of high-level communications, without more, can sustain an absolute, unqualified Presidential privilege of immunity from judicial process under all circumstances. The President's need for complete candor and objectivity from advisers calls for great deference from the courts. However, when the privilege depends solely on the broad, undifferentiated claim of public interest in the confidentiality of such conversations, a confrontation with other values arises. Absent a claim of need to protect military, diplomatic, or sensitive national security secrets, we find it difficult to accept the argument that even the very important interest in confidentiality of Presidential communications is significantly diminished by production of such material for *in camera* inspection with all the protection that a district court will be obliged to provide.

The impediment that an absolute, unqualified privilege would place in the way of the primary constitutional duty of the Judicial Branch to do justice in criminal prosecutions would plainly conflict with the function of the courts under Art. III. . . .

Since we conclude that the legitimate needs of the judicial process may outweigh Presidential privilege, it is necessary to resolve those competing interests in a manner that preserves the essential functions of each branch.

The expectation of a President to the confidentiality of his conversations and correspondence, like the claim of confidentiality of judicial deliberations, for example, has all the values to which we accord deference for the privacy of all citizens and, added to those values, is the necessity for protection of the public interest in candid, objective, and even blunt or harsh opinions in Presidential decisionmaking. . . .

But this presumptive privilege must be considered in light of our historic commitment to the rule of law. . . . The ends of criminal justice would be defeated if judgments were to be founded on a partial or speculative presentation of the facts. The very integrity of the judicial system and public confidence in the system depend on full disclosure of all the facts, within the framework of the rules of evidence. To ensure that justice is done, it is imperative to the function of courts that compulsory process be available for the production of evidence needed either by the prosecution or by the defense. . . . In this case the President challenges a subpoena served on him as a third party requiring the production of materials for use in a criminal prosecution; he does so on the claim that he has a privilege against disclosure of confidential communications. He does not place his claim of privilege on the ground they are military or diplomatic secrets. As to these areas of Art. II duties the courts have traditionally shown the utmost deference to Presidential responsibilities. . . No case of the Court, however, has extended this high degree of deference to a President's generalized interest in confidentiality. . . .

On the other hand, the allowance of the privilege to withhold evidence that is demonstrably relevant in a criminal trial would cut deeply into the guarantee of due process of law and gravely impair the basic function of the courts. . . . Without access to specific facts a criminal prosecution may be totally frustrated. . . .

We conclude that when the ground for asserting privilege as to subpoenaed materials sought for use in a criminal trial is based only on the generalized interest in confidentiality, it cannot prevail over the fundamental demands of due process of law in the fair administration of criminal justice. The generalized assertion of privilege must yield to the demonstrated, specific need for evidence in a pending criminal trial.

In Re Neagle

135 U.S. 1, 10 S. Ct. 658, 34 L. Ed. 55 (1890)

U.S. Marshal David Neagle was appointed by the attorney general to protect Supreme Court Justice Field while he rode circuit in California. When David Terry, a disappointed litigant with a grudge against Field, appeared about to attack the justice, Neagle shot and killed him. After California authorities arrested Neagle and charged him with murder, the United States sought to secure Neagle's release on habeas corpus. In the absence of any law specifically authorizing the president or the attorney general to assign marshals as bodyguards to the justices, the United States relied on a federal statute that made the writ available to those "in custody for an act done or omitted in pursuance of a law of the United States." *Opinion of the Court: Miller, Bradley, Harlan, Gray, Blatchford, Brewer. Dissenting opinion: Lamar, Fuller. Not participating: Field.*

Mr. Justice Miller delivered the opinion of the Court. . . .

. . . Without a more minute discussion of this testimony, it produces upon us the conviction of a settled purpose on the part of Terry and his wife, amounting to a conspiracy, to murder Justice Field. And we are quite sure that if Neagle had been merely a brother or a friend of Judge Field, travelling with him, and aware of all the previous relations of Terry to the Judge,—as he was,—of his bitter animosity, his declared purpose to have revenge even to the point of killing him, he would have been justified in what he did in defence of Mr. Justice Field's life, and possibly of his own.

But such a justification would be a proper subject for consideration on a trial of the case for murder in the courts of the State of California, and there exists no authority in the courts of the United States to discharge the prisoner while held in custody by the State authorities for this offence, unless there be found in aid of the defence of the prisoner some element of power and authority asserted under the government of the United States.

This element is said to be found in the facts that Mr. Justice Field, when attacked, was in the immediate discharge of his duty as judge of the Circuit Courts of the United States within California; that the assault upon him grew out of the animosity of Terry and wife, arising out of the previous discharge of his duty as circuit justice in the case for which they were committed for contempt of court; and that the deputy marshal of the United States, who killed Terry in defence of Field's life, was charged with a duty under the law of the United States to protect Field from the violence which Terry was inflicting, and which was intended to lead to Field's death. . . .

It is urged, however, that there exists no statute authorizing any such protection as that which Neagle was instructed to give Judge Field in the present case, and indeed no protection whatever against a vindictive or malicious assault growing out of the faithful discharge of his official duties; and that the language of section 753 of the Revised Statutes, that the party seeking the benefit of the writ of *habeas corpus* must in this connection show that he is "in custody for an act done or omitted in pursuance of a law of the United States," makes it necessary that upon this occasion it should be shown that the act for which Neagle is imprisoned was done by virtue of an act of Congress. It is not supposed that any special act of Congress exists which authorizes the marshals or deputy marshals of the United States in express terms to accompany the judges of the Supreme Court through their circuits, and act as a body-guard to them, to defend them against malicious assaults against their persons. But we are of opinion that this view of the statute is an unwarranted restriction of the meaning of a law designed to extend in a liberal manner the benefit of the writ of *habeas corpus* to persons imprisoned for the performance of their duty. And we are satisfied that if it was the duty of Neagle, under the circumstances, a duty which could only arise under the laws of the United States, to defend Mr. Justice Field from a murderous attack upon him, he brings himself within the meaning of the section we have recited. . . .

In the view we take of the Constitution of the United States, any obligation fairly and properly inferrible from that instrument, or any duty of the marshal to be derived from the general scope of his duties under the laws of the United States, is "a law" within the meaning of this phrase. It would be a great reproach to the system of government of the United States, declared to be within its sphere sovereign and supreme, if there is to be found within the domain of its powers no means of protecting the judges, in the conscientious and faithful discharge of their duties, from the malice and hatred of those upon whom their judgments may operate unfavorably. . . .

Where, then, are we to look for the protection which we have shown Judge Field was entitled to when engaged in the discharge of his official duties? . . . The Constitution, section 3, Article 2, declares that the President "shall take care that the laws be faithfully executed," and he is provided with the means of fulfilling this obligation by his authority to commission all the officers of the United States, and, by and with the advice and consent of the Senate, to appoint the most important of them and to fill vacancies. He is declared to be commander-in-chief of the army and navy of the United States. The duties which are thus imposed upon him he is further enabled to perform by the recognition in the Constitution, and the creation by acts of Congress, of executive departments, which have varied in number from four or five to seven or eight, the heads of which are familiarly called cabinet ministers. These aid him in the performance of the great duties of his office, and represent him in a thousand acts to which it can hardly be supposed his personal attention is called, and thus he is enabled to fulfil the duty of his great department, expressed in the phrase that "he shall take care that the laws be faithfully executed."

Is this duty limited to the enforcement of acts of Congress or of treaties of the United States according to their *express terms,* or does it include the rights, duties and obligations growing out of the Constitution itself, our international relations, and all the protection implied by the nature of the government under the Constitution? . . .

We cannot doubt the power of the President to take measures for the protection of a judge of one of the courts of the United States, who, while in the discharge of the duties of his office, is threatened with a personal attack which may probably result in his death. . . .

But there is positive law investing the marshals and their deputies with powers which not only justify what Marshal Neagle did in this matter, but which imposed it upon him as a duty. In chapter fourteen of the Revised Statutes of the United States, which is devoted to the appointment and duties of the district attorneys, marshals, and clerks of the courts of the United States, section 788 declares:

"The marshals and their deputies shall have, in each State, the same powers, in executing the laws of the United States, as the sheriffs and their deputies in such State may have, by law, in executing the laws thereof."

If, therefore, a sheriff of the State of California was authorized to do in regard to the laws of California what Neagle did, that is, if he was authorized to keep the peace, to protect a judge from assault and murder, then Neagle was authorized to do the same thing in reference to the laws of the United States.

That there is a peace of the United States; that a man assaulting a judge of the United States while in the discharge of his duties violates that peace; that in such case the marshal of the United States stands in the same relation to the peace of the United States which the sheriff of the county does to the peace of the State of California; are questions too clear to need argument to prove them. . . .

The result at which we have arrived upon this examination is, that in taking the life of Terry, under the circumstances, he was acting under the authority of the law of the United States, and was justified in so doing; and that he is not liable to answer in the courts of California on account of his part in that transaction.

We therefore affirm the judgment of the Circuit Court authorizing his discharge from the custody of the sheriff of San Joaquin County.

6
WAR AND FOREIGN AFFAIRS

Throughout the Vietnam War, congressional opponents of the conflict charged that it involved an executive usurpation of legislative war-making powers. More recently, President Ronald Reagan protested that Congress had undermined his ability to conduct foreign policy by imposing restrictions on aid to guerillas seeking to overthrow the Nicaraguan government. There is nothing novel in these conflicts. Within five years of the ratification of the Constitution, James Madison and Alexander Hamilton—the principal authors of *The Federalist*—disagreed about whether President George Washington had the authority to issue a proclamation of American neutrality in the war between France and Great Britain.[1] Since then, clashes over the constitutional distribution of power for the direction of foreign affairs and for the commitment of American troops have been a recurring feature of American politics. The constitutional separation of powers, in fact, virtually guarantees periodic interbranch conflict in these areas: as Edward Corwin has noted, the division of powers "is an invitation to struggle for the privilege of directing American foreign policy."[2]

The extent of the national power over war and foreign affairs also has raised constitutional questions. The Framers clearly intended to lodge power over these subjects in the national government. As Madison observed in *The Federalist*, No. 42, "If we are to be one nation in any respect, it clearly ought to be in respect to other nations." But this grant of power, in the view of some observers, may pose a threat to the general division of power between the national and state governments and to constitutional protections of individual rights. The difficulty of delineating the limits of the foreign affairs power, for instance, has fueled suspicions that the national government might use that power as a pretext to invade state prerogatives. Similar problems attend the protection of individual rights. Indisputably, the Framers sought to create a constitution "intended to endure for ages to come, and, consequently, to be adapted to the various crises of human affairs."[3] Less clear is whether this aim is compatible with the protection of individual rights, or whether a successful response to extreme crises of war or foreign affairs may not require a temporary sacrifice of those rights.

Conflicts over the constitutional distribution of power regarding foreign affairs and war characteristically involve the distribution of power (1) among the branches of the national government, (2) between the levels of the federal system, or (3) between government and the people. The material in this chapter is organized around these three basic conflicts.

THE INTERBRANCH DISTRIBUTION OF POWER

Table 6.1 summarizes the war and foreign affairs powers expressly granted in the Constitution to each department. Perhaps its most striking feature is the complete absence of the judiciary. Although the power of judicial review extends to the exercise of governmental power in war and foreign affairs, several interrelated factors have severely restricted the frequency and importance of judicial intervention in those areas.

Of prime importance is the nonjusticiability of most questions involving war and foreign affairs under the political questions doctrine (see Chapter 3). For example, although many people believed the Vietnam War to be unconstitutional, attempts to secure a judicial ruling consistently failed under the political questions doctrine or because the plaintiffs lacked standing.[4] More recently, the Supreme Court in *Goldwater* v. *Carter* (1979) invoked the political-questions doctrine to avoid a ruling on whether President Jimmy Carter could unilaterally terminate the nation's mutual defense treaty with Taiwan. An additional barrier has been the Court's understandable reluctance even to consider such delicate questions. On five separate occasions, for instance, the Court used its discretionary jurisdiction to refuse to hear challenges to the constitutionality of the Vietnam War. This unwillingness to rule on foreign policy issues tends to discourage potential litigants from pursuing their goals through the courts. Moreover, when the Court does intervene, it characteristically defers—because of its limited expertise and the lack of clear constitutional standards—to the judgment of other branches. The Court's decisions upholding President Carter's settlement of the Iran hostage crisis, the all-male draft registration system, and President Ronald Reagan's restrictions on travel to Cuba all reflect this deferential posture.[5] Overall, then, although the judiciary has on occasion considered the constitutional division of powers in war and foreign affairs, the most important sources of constitutional law in these spheres have been the executive and legislative branches.

TABLE 6.1 The Constitutional Distribution of Powers of War and Foreign Affairs

Presidential Powers	Congressional Powers	Senatorial Powers
	Foreign Relations Powers	
1. To make treaties (Senate consent required) 2. To appoint envoys (Senate consent required) 3. To receive envoys	1. To regulate foreign commerce 2. To lay duties 3. To define and punish piracies and felonies committed on the high seas and offenses against the law of nations	1. To advise on and consent to treaties 2. To advise on and consent to appointment of envoys
	Defense Powers	
1. Commander-in-Chief power 2. To repel sudden attacks on the United States or its armed forces (not mentioned in the constitutional text but indisputably granted)	1. To raise and support armies 2. To provide and maintain a navy 3. To make rules for the government and regulation of the land and naval forces 4. To provide for calling forth the militia to repel invasions 5. To suspend the writ of habeas corpus in cases of rebellion or invasion or when the public safety may require such action 6. To declare war	
	General Powers	
1. To inform the Congress about the state of the union and make recommendations 2. To convene both houses of Congress, or either one of them, on extraordinary occasions 3. To veto legislation 4. To execute the laws (which includes unmentioned, delegated rulemaking powers) 5. To appoint (Senate consent generally required)	1. To lay taxes, etc., and provide for the common defense and general welfare 2. To make all laws necessary and proper for carrying into execution congressional powers, and all other powers vested in the government, or in any department or officer thereof 3. To make appropriations 4. To impeach	1. To advise on and consent to appointments

Checks and Balances

Constitutional interpretations characteristically have emerged as a result of political interactions between the legislative and executive branches. Because both branches have long agreed that the president should serve as the "sole organ of the nation in its external relations," for example, this monopoly on communications with foreign governments has been recognized as constitutionally based.[6] On the other hand, dissatisfaction with the results of presidential control over commitment of troops led Congress to attempt to limit this control through the War Powers Resolution, which was passed over a presidential veto in 1973. Although these instances of interbranch cooperation and conflict mix policy and constitutional considerations, their outcomes do not represent merely "political" adjustments. For one thing, the participants in interbranch disputes generally have recognized the seriousness of constitutional questions and, rather than simply basing constitutional interpretations on their own policy positions, have sought correct solutions to them. More importantly, the Constitution itself regulates and in large measure determines the outcomes of such conflicts.

Under the system of checks and balances incorporated into the Constitution, powers are distributed to the various branches so that each branch can adequately defend its prerogatives and prevent domination of the government by any other single branch. These powers, in turn, represent political resources that can be brought to bear in interbranch conflicts. Should the dispute concern the regulation of foreign imports, both Congress and the president have constitutionally defined roles in the legislative process that prevent a single branch from acting alone. Should the president and the Senate conclude a treaty that the House of Representatives opposes, the House can refuse to pass legislation necessary to implement the treaty or to appropriate money for its implementation. The division of powers indicated in Table 6.1 suggests that these examples could be multiplied indefinitely. What is noteworthy is that the constitutional division of power provides each branch with the means to frustrate the achievement of foreign policy goals favored only by a single branch, and thereby places a premium on interbranch cooperation. Obviously no branch would cooperate if it believed that its constitutional powers were being usurped in the process.

The Constitution also influences the nature and outcomes of interbranch conflicts by imparting a particular character to each branch. The unity of the executive, Hamilton noted in *The Federalist,* No. 70, is conducive to "decision, activity, secrecy, and dispatch." These qualities enable the president to seize the initiative in foreign affairs—as President Carter did in the Middle East peace negotiations of the late 1970s—and to provide effective leadership during the nation's war efforts. In addition, the unity of the executive frequently allows the president to portray himself as the nation's representative in its dealings with other countries. In contrast, the two houses of Congress are deliberative bodies that more adequately reflect the varying viewpoints and interests in the nation.

These differences in composition have had two important ramifications. First, as relations with other countries increasingly have demanded swift and decisive reactions to events, the power of the executive naturally has increased. Second, the success over time of presidential initiatives—that is, whether they will lead to interbranch cooperation or conflict—depends upon the president's ability to convince the people and their representatives of the initiatives' wisdom. Woodrow Wilson's attempt to secure United States participation in the League of Nations, for example, foundered when the Senate refused to ratify the treaty leading to membership. President Harry Truman, on the other hand, gained congressional backing for the Marshall Plan by involving influential members in the negotiations setting up the plan. So although the character of the branches affects the roles they assume in foreign affairs, the constitutional structure again encourages interbranch cooperation.

War and Other Hostilities

The most severe test of the constitutional division of powers has been posed by the commitment of American troops in combat. As the Supreme Court ruled in *The Prize Cases* (1863), when the nation is attacked, the president may recognize that a state of war exists and, as commander-in-chief, respond accordingly. In all other circumstances the Constitution confers on Congress the choice between war and peace, by granting to the legislative branch the power to declare war. But does political practice reflect this constitutional assignment of power, or does the president in fact exercise decisive control?

Since World War II, American troops have been involved in hostilities ranging from short-term engagements for limited purposes (for example, rescuing the crew of the *Mayaguez* from their Cambodian captors in 1975[7]) to protracted conflicts in Korea and Vietnam. Many of these combat situations, like the invasion of Panama, have fallen somewhere in between these two extremes. On no occasion was the commitment of troops preceded by a declaration of war or other formal congressional authorization. Actually, this sort of presidential commitment of forces has not been confined to recent years—during the debates on the War Powers Resolution, one source listed 161 such instances of unilateral presidential action.[8] What is new is the willingness of some presidents to claim this power as a presidential preserve that is beyond congressional control. In support of this claim, presidents have asserted that the commander-in-chief power permits them to use the armed forces for various purposes short of war, such as protecting the lives and property of American citizens abroad, defending American troops from attack, and protecting American foreign policy interests.

Although the president can direct the movements of American troops, this power can lead—either inadvertently or by design—to the preemption of congressional decision-making. Once the forces committed are attacked, public opinion almost automatically supports retaliatory measures, and Congress is left with no choice but to endorse presidential requests for the continuation and expansion of hostilities. In the most blatant instance of presidential war-making, President James Polk in 1846 ordered troops to occupy disputed territory along the Rio Grande, thereby provoking a Mexican attack and in effect forcing Congress to declare war against Mexico.[9] Similarly, in 1964 President Lyndon Johnson used an alleged attack on American ships operating off North Vietnam to secure passage of the Gulf of Tonkin Resolution which provided the primary basis for the nation's involvement in Vietnam.

In an effort to clarify the limits of unilateral presidential action and reclaim lost powers, Congress in 1973 adopted the War Powers Resolution, which obliges the president to consult with Congress "in every possible instance" before committing troops "into hostilities or into situations where imminent involvement in hostilities is clearly indicated by the circumstances." If circumstances prevent prior consultation, the act requires the president to report his actions to Congress within forty-eight hours. Further, the president is required to terminate any use of military forces within sixty days after submitting such a report (with a possible extension of 30 days), unless Congress specifically authorizes their continued use. Finally, the act reserves to Congress a legislative veto over troop commitments: that is, the power to compel the withdrawal of troops by an unvetoable concurrent resolution.

How successful the War Powers Resolution has been in restoring the constitutional division of powers remains a matter of dispute. Some critics note that the law has neither prevented presidential commitment of troops nor promoted consultation beforehand—President Carter sent the rescue force to Iran without informing Congress, and President Reagan dispatched troops to Grenada on his own initiative.[10] Even when presidents have notified Congress or its leadership, as President George Bush did before dispatching troops to Panama, they have done so to announce a decision rather than to seek advice. And congressional control after the commitment of troops has been limited. When the Grenada incursion succeeded, Congress was hard-pressed to object to the unilateral presidential action; and when the Iran rescue failed, Congress was more concerned with the details of the failure than the lack of consultation. On the other hand, when a president seeks sustained American involvement in a conflict, the resolution's requirement that Congress specifically authorize prolonged troop commitments provides it with a weapon to ensure consultation.

Other critics have charged that the War Powers Resolution infringes on presidential authority and undermines the conduct of foreign policy.[11] Certainly presidents have been reluctant to comply with its provisions, and some have raised doubts about its constitutionality.[12] Most likely this dispute will be resolved through interbranch interaction rather than by a judicial decision.

THE FOUNDATION AND EXTENT OF THE FOREIGN AFFAIRS POWER

Although foreign relations is preeminently a national concern, the constitutional foundation for vesting this function exclusively in the national government is somewhat sketchy. For one thing, the Constitution's assignment of particular powers to various branches does not exhaust the range of powers necessary for the conduct of foreign affairs. The power to terminate treaties, the legal status of executive agreements, the circumstances under which the president may commit American troops to hostilities—none of these matters are dealt with expressly in the Constitution. Moreover, although the Constitution in no way limits national authority over foreign affairs, neither does it explicitly grant a comprehensive foreign affairs power.

This problem of the "missing powers" has generated two radically different approaches to providing a basis for national control. The so-called extrapolation approach suggests that the particular powers assigned to the various branches or denied to the states necessarily imply the missing powers required for the conduct of foreign affairs. Thus the power to make treaties implies the power to break them; the power to make war implies the power to make peace; the power to receive ambassadors (thereby granting diplomatic recognition) implies the power to refuse recognition by not receiving ambassadors; and so on. According to this view, a complete picture of the extent and distribution of the powers over foreign affairs can be derived from the express grants of power in the Constitution. A contrasting approach, suggested by Justice George Sutherland in *United States* v. *Curtiss-Wright Export Corporation* (1936), bases national control over foreign affairs on an extraconstitutional foundation. The Constitution, Sutherland maintained, distributed only the "internal powers" of government: that is, those powers pertaining to domestic affairs. In Sutherland's view the powers pertaining to foreign affairs—external powers—had already been lodged in the national government as an inheritance from the British Crown at the time that the United States became a sovereign nation, and thus did not rest on a delegation from the people or the states. What is assumed to be an incomplete grant of powers under the extrapolation approach, therefore, becomes for Sutherland merely the assignment of those powers that do not belong naturally to either the legislative or the executive branch.

Neither approach is altogether without difficulties. The extrapolation approach requires an extraordinarily broad reading of specific constitutional provisions that is not justified by anything within the document. Proponents of extrapolation argue, for example, that the power to appoint ambassadors includes the power to direct their activities and thus to define the ends, or policy objectives, to which those activities shall be directed. But this appointment power might as readily be interpreted as a narrow and specific grant of power that has nothing to do with the power to set foreign policy goals. In addition, this approach does not resolve conflicts about the distribution of powers: although the president may infer the power to set foreign policy objectives from the power to appoint ambassadors, Congress may conclude that its power to declare war carries with it a power to decide upon policies that might propel the nation into war. The Sutherland approach, on the other hand, relies upon a historical interpretation that is subject to challenge on two counts. Although Justice Sutherland contended that sovereignty—and therefore control over foreign affairs—passed directly from the Crown to a national government, the fact that several states during the post-Independence period acted independently in foreign affairs appears to belie Sutherland's assertion that a sense of nationhood was present. And although most people during the period were alarmed by the idea of a strong national government, there is no discussion of a preexisting foreign affairs power in the Constitution, in the records of the Constitutional Convention, or in other contemporary sources. It hardly seems credible that such a departure from the system of delegated powers would occur without discussion.

Whatever their differences, both approaches assign the foreign affairs power to the national government. The extent of this power remains a matter of controversy, however. In *Curtiss-Wright,* Justice Sutherland contended that national control over external affairs could be complete only if the line between external and internal affairs—and between external and internal powers—reflected changing world conditions. Sixteen years earlier, this argument had been advanced by Justice Oliver Wendell Holmes in *Missouri* v. *Holland* (1920), which upheld congressional legislation in pursuance of a treaty regulating the killing of migratory birds. To Holmes, neither the Framers' failure to anticipate treaties about migratory birds nor a lower court's invalidation of similar legislation prior to the treaty's ratification was decisive. As long as the treaty involved a matter of national concern that could be regulated through an international agreement, it constituted a valid exercise of the foreign affairs power. Holmes went on to point out that even if congressional legislation exceeded specific constitutional grants of power to Congress, it might nonetheless be valid if necessary and proper to implement a treaty or other exercise of the foreign affairs power.

Not surprisingly, the idea that the national government might expand its sphere of domestic control through the foreign affairs power has been disputed. Defenders of state prerogatives have argued that this interpretation threatens the division of power between nation and state, particularly because contemporary multilateral treaties (e.g., United Nations covenants on the elimination of racial discrimination) may involve matters of exclusively domestic concern. During the early 1950s, this concern led Senator John Bricker of Ohio to propose a constitutional amendment that would have required congressional legislation before any treaty became effective as internal law in the United States. Bricker's effort dramatized the concern that the states may lack constitutional protection against national foreign-policy decisions. However, the requirement that treaties be ratified by the Senate, in which the states are equally represented, probably affords the states adequate protection.

WAR AND INDIVIDUAL RIGHTS

The Framers of the Constitution sought to design a system of government that could respond successfully to crises of war and foreign affairs. In *The Federalist,* No. 23, Hamilton acknowledged that the achievement of this aim required a broad grant of power to the national government:

> The circumstances that endanger the safety of nations are infinite, and for this reason no constitutional shackles can wisely be imposed on the power to which the care of it is committed. This power ought to be coextensive with all the possible combinations of such circumstances; and ought to be under the direction of the same councils which are appointed to preside over the common defense.

Because war places a premium on swift and decisive action, Congress in wartime has characteristically concentrated this broad governmental power in the executive. During World War I, Congress delegated to President Woodrow Wilson virtually standardless regulatory power over major sectors of the economy, private communications with foreign countries, and numerous other concerns. Even prior to the United States' entry into World War II, the Lend-Lease Act empowered the president to transfer "defense articles" to the "government of any country whose defense [he] deems vital to the defense of the United States" under any terms that he deemed satisfactory. During the war, President Franklin Roosevelt was authorized to direct war production, to control the prices of goods, to introduce rationing, and generally to regulate the economic life of the country.

At times, presidents have relied upon their own authority rather than upon congressional delegations of power in responding to crisis situations. President Lincoln's actions during the ten weeks between the fall of Fort Sumter and the convening of Congress represent the prime example of unilateral executive action. During that period, Lincoln enlarged the army and navy, called up the state militias, spent unappropriated funds, and instituted a blockade of Southern ports. In defending his actions, he asserted that the "war power," a combination of the Commander-in-Chief Clause and of his responsibility to ensure that "the laws be faithfully executed," provided a sufficient constitutional justification. This extraordinary exercise of power was ratified by Congress shortly after it convened.

Several times in this century, presidents have claimed the power to act in crisis situations even without a declaration of war. During the undeclared war in Korea, President Harry Truman seized the steel mills to prevent a strike that would have stopped steel production; and during the

Vietnam conflict, President Richard Nixon attempted to halt publication of the Pentagon Papers, a classified study of how the United States became involved in the war. Although the Supreme Court in both instances rejected the claims of executive power, the justices implicitly recognized that the national government as a whole has sufficient power to deal with such crises.

Both governmental practice and judicial decisions, then, confirm that the national government possesses broad powers to deal with crises in external affairs, and that the exercise of these powers may justify the temporary overriding of the constitutional separation of powers. Does it also permit the temporary suspension of constitutionally protected rights? The question is not merely hypothetical. During the Civil War, President Lincoln suspended the writ of habeas corpus to all persons "guilty of any disloyal practice" and authorized trial and punishment of such persons by courts-martial and military tribunals. And early in World War II, President Franklin Roosevelt issued an executive order, later supported by congressional action, that led to the forced evacuation from the West Coast of 112,000 Japanese residents. Not surprisingly, those affected in both instances complained that the governmental actions taken had violated their constitutional rights. In *Ex Parte Milligan* (1866) and *Korematsu* v. *United States* (1944), the Supreme Court ruled directly upon these complaints.

Four alternative interpretations of the extent of governmental power during wartime have emerged from *Korematsu* and *Milligan.* According to the broadest interpretation of governmental power, which was espoused by the Court majority in *Korematsu* and by the four concurring justices in *Milligan,* the fundamental consideration is that the government's power to wage war is the power to wage war successfully. From this it follows that the national government possesses all powers necessary and proper to the successful prosecution of the war. When an area of the country is an actual or potential theater of military operations, accordingly, the government may engage in actions that would be unconstitutional during peacetime. As long as the actions taken are "reasonably expedient military precautions" relating to the public safety, they are constitutionally permissible under the Necessary and Proper Clause.

The Court majority in *Milligan* took a more restrictive view of governmental power, asserting that all constitutional limitations on governmental action apply with equal force during wartime. According to the *Milligan* majority, the decisive factor is the Framers' decision not to insert exceptions for wartime in the constitutional protections of rights. Their judgment that the government did not need the power to suspend constitutionally protected rights, based as it was on a personal familiarity with war during the Revolution, is authoritative for future generations. Therefore, any action that infringes upon rights during peacetime remains unconstitutional during wartime, because "the Constitution of the United States is a law for rulers and ruled, equally in war and in peace."

Justice Frank Murphy, dissenting in *Korematsu,* proposed a third constitutional standard. According to Murphy, military necessity can justify the deprivation of individual rights, but government assertions of necessity should not be accepted uncritically. When the government undertakes such a radical step, judges must scrutinize closely the bases for this action. Only when such deprivations can be "reasonably related to a public danger that is so immediate, imminent, and impending as not to admit of delay and not to permit the intervention of ordinary constitutional processes," Murphy concluded, should they be upheld.[19] The judiciary thus would play a major role in enforcing constitutional limitations.

In another dissent in *Korematsu*, Justice Robert Jackson offered a fourth interpretation of the extent of governmental power in wartime. Jackson maintained that what is expedient on military grounds may not be constitutionally permissible—a situation that obviously creates a dilemma for the Supreme Court. On the one hand, the judiciary cannot expect the national government to refrain from actions it deems essential to the public safety merely because of judicial disapproval. On the other hand, Court endorsement of unconstitutional actions on the basis of alleged military necessity would provide a precedent for similar abuses whenever "any authority . . . can bring forward a plausible claim of an urgent need." Because the Constitution does not provide sufficient power to deal with all the exigencies of war, necessity—self-preservation—and not constitutionality will inevitably (and properly) be the standard for governmental action during wartime. The Supreme Court, Jackson argued, should play no role in such situations.

NOTES

1 Hamilton defended the president's power to issue the Neutrality Proclamation in the "Pacificus" letters. See Alexander Hamilton, *The Works of Alexander Hamilton*, ed. Henry Cabot Lodge (New York: Federal Edition, 1904) 4:76. Madison challenged this view, at times quoting Hamilton's statements in *The Federalist* in the "Helvidius" letters. See James Madison, *The Writings of James Madison*, ed. Gaillard Hunt (New York: 1900–1910) 4:148.

2 Edward S. Corwin, *The President: Office and Powers*, 4th rev. ed. (New York: New York University Press, 1957), p. 171.

3 *McCulloch* v. *Maryland*, 4 Wheat. 316, 415 (1819).

4 Representative cases include *Katz* v. *Tyler*, (1967); and *Sarnoff* v. *Schultz*, (1972).

5 The relevant cases are *Dames & Moore* v. *Regan*, (1981); *Rostker* v. *Goldberg*, (1981), excerpted in Chapter 16; and *Regan* v. *Wald*, (1984).

6 John Marshall applied this label to the president during a debate in the House of Representatives in 1800.

7 In the *Mayaguez* incident, President Gerald Ford sent in naval and marine units to rescue the *Mayaguez*, a U.S. merchant ship, and its crew after Cambodia had seized them for intruding on its territorial waters.

8 American Enterprise Institute, *The War Powers Bill, Legislative Analysis No. 19*, (April 17, 1972), pp. 47–55.

9 The House of Representatives subsequently amended a resolution of thanks to

General Zachary Taylor to include a condemnation of President Polk for unconstitutionally involving the nation in war.

10 For discussions critical of the effectiveness of the War Powers Resolution, see Michael Glennon, "The War Powers Resolution: Sad Record, Dismal Promises," *Loyala of Los Angeles Law Review* 17 (1984): 657–670, and John Hart Ely, "Suppose Congress Wanted a War Powers Act That Worked," *Columbia Law* Review 88 (1988): 1379–1431.

11 See, for example, Robert F. Turner, "The War Powers Resolution: Unconstitutional, Unnecessary, and Unhelpful," *Loyola of Los Angeles Law Review* 17 (1984): 683–713.

12 In reporting his efforts to free the *Mayaguez,* President Gerald Ford stated that he did so "[i]n accordance with my desire that the Congress be informed on this matter and *taking note of sec. 4(a)(1)*" of the Resolution (emphasis added). Similarly, President Jimmy Carter's letter to Congress following the attempt to rescue the hostages in Iran stated that his report was "*consistent with*" the requirements of sec. 4(a)(1) (emphasis added). Thus in neither case did the president indicate that such a report was a legal responsibility.

SELECTED READINGS

The Federalist, Nos. 23–26, 64, 70, 75.

Dames & Moore v. *Regan,* 453 U.S. 654 (1981).
Ex Parte Endo, 323 U.S. 283 (1944).
United States v. *Pink,* 315 U.S. 203 (1942).

Casper, Gerhard. "Constitutional Constraints on the Conduct of Foreign and Defense Policy: A Nonjudicial Model," *University of Chicago Law Review* 43 (1976).

Corwin, Edward S. *The President: Office and Powers.* 4th rev. ed. (New York: New York University Press, 1957).

Henkin, Louis. *Constitutionalism, Democracy, and Foreign Affairs* (New York: Columbia University Press, 1990).

Irons, Peter H. *Justice at War* (New York: Oxford University Press, 1983).

Lofgren, Charles A. *"Government from Reflection and Choice;" Constitutional Essays on War, Foreign Relations, and Federalism* (New York: Oxford University Press, 1986).

May, Christopher N. *In the Name of War: Judicial Review and the War Powers Since 1918.* Cambridge: Harvard University Press, 1989.

Reveley, W. Taylor. *War Powers of the President and Congress* (Charlottesville: University of Virginia Press, 1981).

Scigliano, Robert. "The War Powers Resolution and the War Powers," in Joseph M. Bessette and Jeffrey Tulis, eds. *The Presidency in the Constitutional Order* (Baton Rouge: Louisiana State University Press, 1981).

"Symposium: The War Powers Resolution," *Loyola of Los Angeles Law Review* 17 (1984).

The Prize Cases

Black 635, 17 L. Ed. 459 (1863)

In April 1861, after the initial outbreak of Civil War hostilities but prior to the convening of a special session of Congress, President Abraham Lincoln proclaimed a blockade of Confederate ports. During the period between the issuance of the president's proclamation and the passage of congressional legislation endorsing the blockade, several ships were seized as blockade runners and their cargoes confiscated. The owners of the ships challenged the legality of the blockade, and questions arising from the litigation were certified to the Supreme Court. *Opinion of the Court: Grier, Wayne, Swayne, Miller, Davis. Dissenting opinion: Nelson, Taney, Catron, Clifford.*

MR. JUSTICE GRIER delivered the opinion of the Court.

Let us inquire whether, at the time this blockade was instituted, a state of war existed which would justify a resort to these means of subduing the hostile force. . . .

If a war be made by invasion of a foreign nation, the President is not only authorized but bound to resist force by force. He does not initiate the war, but is bound to accept the challenge without waiting for any special legislative authority. And whether the hostile "party be a foreign invader, or States organized in rebellion, it is nonetheless a war, although the declaration of it be *"unilateral."* . . .

Whether the President in fulfilling his duties, as Commander in-chief, in suppressing an insurrection, has met with such armed hostile resistance, and a civil war of such alarming proportions as will compel him to accord to them the character of belligerents, is a question to be decided *by him,* and this Court must be governed by the decisions and acts of the political department of the Government to which this power was entrusted. "He must determine what degree of force the crisis demands." The proclamation of blockade is itself official and conclusive evidence to the Court that a state of war existed which demanded and authorized a recourse to such a measure, under the circumstances peculiar to the case. . . .

If it were necessary to the technical existence of a war, that it should have a legislative sanction, we find it in almost every act passed at the extraordinary session of the Legislature of 1861, which was wholly employed in enacting laws to enable the Government to prosecute the war with vigor and efficiency. And finally, in 1861, we find Congress . . . passing an act "approving, legalizing, and making valid all the acts, proclamations, and orders of the President, &c., as if they had been *issued and done under the previous express authority* and direction of the Congress of the United States."

Without admitting that such an act was necessary under the circumstances, it is plain that if the President had in any manner assumed powers which it was necessary should have the authority or sanction of Congress, . . . this ratification has operated to perfectly cure the defect. . . .

. . . we are of the opinion that the President had a right, *jure belli,* to institute a blockade of ports in possession of the States in rebellion, which neutrals are bound to regard.

MR. JUSTICE NELSON, dissenting.

. . . The right of making war belongs exclusively to the supreme or sovereign power of the State. This power in all civilized nations is regulated by the fundamental laws or municipal constitution of the country. By our Constitution this power is lodged in Congress. . . .

An idea seemed to be entertained that all that was necessary to constitute a war was organized hostility in the district of country in a state of rebellion. . . .

Now, in one sense, no doubt this is war, and may be a war of the most extensive and threatening dimensions and effects, but it is a statement simply of its existence in a material sense, and has no relevancy or weight when the question is what constitutes war in a legal sense, in the sense of the law of nations, and of the Constitution of the United States? . . .

. . . Ample provision has been made under the Constitution and laws against any sudden and unexpected disturbance of the public peace from insurrection at home or invasion from abroad. The whole military and naval power of the country is put under the control of the President to meet the emergency. . . . But it is the exercise of a power under the municipal laws of the country and not under the law of nations. . . .

. . . I am compelled to the conclusion that no civil war existed between this Government and the States in insurrection till recognized by the Act of Congress 13th of July, 1861; that the President does not possess the power under the Constitution to declare war or recognize its existence within the meaning of the law of nations, which carries with it belligerent rights, and thus change the country and all its citizens from a state of peace to a state of war; that this power belongs exclusively to the Congress of the United States, and, consequently, that the President had no power to set on foot a blockade under the law of nations, and that the capture of the vessel and cargo in this case, and in all cases before us in which the capture occurred before the 13th of July, 1861 . . . are illegal and void, and that the decrees of condemnation should be reversed and the vessel and cargo restored.

The Gulf of Tonkin Resolution

On August 2, 1964, North Vietnamese torpedo boats allegedly attacked two U.S. destroyers in the Gulf of Tonkin. President Lyndon Johnson quickly called for a resolution from Congress to support his determination to repel attacks on American forces and to prevent further aggression. On August 7, the House and the Senate passed the requested resolution by margins of 416–0 and 88–2, respectively. Until its repeal by Congress in 1970, this so-called Gulf of Tonkin Resolution was relied upon to justify escalation and expansion of the Vietnam War.

Whereas naval units of the Communist regime in Vietnam, in violation of the principles of the Charter of the United Nations and of international law, have deliberately and repeatedly attacked United States naval vessels lawfully present in international waters, and have thereby created a serious threat to international peace: and

Whereas these attacks are part of a deliberate and systematic campaign of aggression that the Communist regime in North Vietnam has been waging against its neighbors and the nations joined with them in the collective defense of their freedom: and

Whereas the United States is assisting the people of southeast Asia to protect their freedom and has no territorial, military or political ambitions in that area, but desires only that these peoples should be left in peace to work out their own destinies in their own way: Now, therefore, be it

Resolved by the Senate, and House of Representatives of the United States of America in Congress assembled. That the Congress approves and supports the determination of the President, as Commander in Chief, to take all necessary measures to repel any armed attack against the forces of the United States and to prevent further aggression. . . .

Section 2. The United States regards as vital to its national interest and to world peace the maintenance of international peace and security in southeast Asia. Consonant with the Constitution of the United States and the Charter of the United Nations and in accordance with its obligations under the Southeast Asia Collective Defense Treaty, the United States is, therefore, prepared, as the President determines, to take all necessary steps, including the use of armed force, to assist any member or protocol state of the Southeast Asia Collective Defense Treaty requesting assistance in defense of its freedom.

Section 3. This resolution shall expire when the President shall determine that the peace and security of the area is reasonably assured by international conditions created by action of the United Nations or otherwise, except that it may be terminated earlier by concurrent resolution of the Congress.

The War Powers Resolution

87 Stat. 555, 50 U.S.C. 1541 (1973)

As criticism of the Vietnam War mounted during the early 1970s, members of Congress sought to reassert congressional control over the use of American troops. In 1972 the Senate passed a war powers bill that defined the circumstances under which the president could commit American troops to hostilities, but this bill was rejected by the House of Representatives. The following resolution, passed over President Richard Nixon's veto in 1973, does not specify when troops may be used, but it does require presidential consultation with Congress, when possible, and allows Congress to terminate American involvement in hostilities.

§1541 (a) It is the purpose of this joint resolution to fulfill the intent of the framers of the Constitution of the United States and insure that the collective judgment of both the Congress and the President will apply to the introduction of United States Armed Forces into hostilities, or into situations where imminent involvement in hostilities is clearly indicated by the circumstances, and to the continued use of such forces in hostilities or in such situations. . . .

(b) Under article I, section 8, of the Constitution, it is specifically provided that the Congress shall have the power to make all laws necessary and proper for carrying into execution, not only its own powers but also all other powers vested by the Constitution in the Government of the United States, or in any department or officer hereof.

(c) The constitutional powers of the President as Commander-in-Chief to introduce United States Armed Forces into hostilities, or into situations where imminent involvement in hostilities is clearly indicated by the circumstances, are exercised only pursuant to (1) a declaration of war (2) specific statutory authorization, or (3) a national emergency created by attack upon the United States, its territories or possessions, or its armed forces. . . .

§1542. . . . The President in every possible instance shall consult with Congress before introducing United States Armed Forces into hostilities or into situations where imminent involvement in hostilities is clearly indicated by the circumstances, and after every such introduction shall consult regularly with the Congress until United States Armed Forces are no longer engaged in hostilities or have been removed from such situations. . . .

§1543. . . .

(a) In the absence of a declaration of war, in any case in which United States Armed Forces are introduced—(1) into hostilities or into situations where imminent involvement in hostilities is clearly indicated by the circumstances; (2) into the territory, airspace or waters of a foreign nation, while equipped for combat, except for deployments which relate solely to supply, replacement, repair, or training of such forces; or (3) in numbers which substantially enlarge United States Armed Forces equipped for combat already located in a foreign nation; the President shall submit within 48 hours to the Speaker of the House of Representatives and to the President pro tempore of the Senate a report, in writing, setting forth—(A) the circumstances necessitating the introduction of the United States Armed Forces; (B) the constitutional and legislative authority under which such introduction took place; and (C) the estimated scope and duration of the hostilities or involvement.

(b) . . . The President shall provide such other information as the Congress may request in the fulfillment of its constitutional responsibilities with respect to committing the Nation to war and to the use of United States Armed Forces abroad. . . .

§1544. . . .

(b) . . . Within sixty calendar days after a report is submitted or is required to be submitted pursuant to section 1543(a)(1) of this title, whichever is earlier, the President shall terminate any use of United States Armed Forces with respect to which such report was submitted (or required to be submitted), unless the Congress (1) has declared war or has enacted a specific authorization for such use of United States Armed Forces, (2) has extended by law such sixty-day period, or (3) is physically unable to meet as a result of an armed attack upon the United States. Such sixty-day period shall be extended for not more than an additional thirty days if the President determines and certifies to the Congress in writing that unavoidable military necessity respecting the safety of United States Armed Forces requires the continued use of such armed forces in the course of bringing about a prompt removal of such forces.

(c) . . . Notwithstanding subsection (b) of this section, at any time that United States Armed Forces are engaged in hostilities outside the territory of the United States, its possessions and territories without a declaration of war or specific statutory authorization, such forces shall be removed by the President if the Congress so directs by concurrent resolution. . . .

§1547. . . . Authority to introduce United States Armed Forces into hostilities or into situations wherein involvement in hostilities is clearly indicated by the circumstances shall not be inferred—(1) from any provision of law (whether or not in effect before November 7, 1973), including any provision contained in any appropriation Act, unless such provision specifically authorizes the introduction of United States Armed Forces into hostilities or into such situations and states that it is intended to constitute specific statutory authorization within the meaning of this joint resolution; or (2) from any treaty heretofore or hereafter ratified unless such treaty is implemented by legislation specifically authorizing the introduction of United States Armed Forces into hostilities or into such situations and stating that it is intended to constitute specific statutory authorization within the meaning of this joint resolution.

(d) . . . Nothing in this joint resolution—(1) is intended to alter the constitutional authority of the Congress or of the President, or the provisions of existing treaties; or (2) shall be construed as granting any authority to the President with respect to the introduction of United States Armed Forces into hostilities or into situations wherein involvement in hostilities is clearly indicated by the circumstances which authority he would not have had in the absence of this joint resolution. . . .

United States v. *Curtiss-Wright Export Corporation*

299 U.S. 304; 57 S. Ct. 216; 81 L. Ed. 255 (1936)

On May 28, 1934, Congress passed a joint resolution authorizing the president to prohibit the sale of arms and munitions to the warring countries of Bolivia and Paraguay, should he determine that such a prohibition would "contribute to the reestablishment of peace between those countries." In pursuance of this authority, President Franklin D. Roosevelt immediately embargoed the sale of war materials to those countries. The defendants in this case, charged with conspiring to sell arms to Bolivia in violation of the embargo, contended that the presidential proclamation was invalid because Congress could not constitutionally delegate such broad power to the president. When a federal district court upheld this contention, the United States appealed directly to the Supreme Court. *Opinion of the Court: Sutherland, Hughes, Van Devanter, Brandeis, Butler, Roberts, Cardozo. Dissenting opinion: McReynolds. Not participating: Stone.*

MR. JUSTICE SUTHERLAND delivered the opinion of the Court. . . .

Whether, if the Joint Resolution had related solely to internal affairs it would be open to the challenge that it constituted an unlawful delegation of legislative power to the Executive, we find it unnecessary to determine. The whole aim of the resolution is to affect a situation entirely external to the United States, and falling within the category of foreign affairs. The determination which we are called to make, therefore, is whether the Joint Resolution, as applied to that situation, is vulnerable to attack under the rule that forbids a delegation of the law-making power. In other words, assuming (but not deciding) that the challenged delegation, if it were confirmed to internal affairs, would be invalid, may it nevertheless be sustained on the ground that its exclusive aim is to afford a remedy for a hurtful condition within foreign territory?

It will contribute to the elucidation of the question if we first consider the differences between the powers of the federal government in respect of foreign or external affairs and those in respect of domestic or internal affairs. That there are differences between them, and that these differences are fundamental, may not be doubted.

The two classes of powers are different, both in respect of their origin and their nature. The broad statement that the federal government can exercise no powers except those specifically enumerated in the Constitution, and such implied powers as are necessary and proper to carry into effect the enumerated powers, is categorically true only in respect of our internal affairs. In that field, the primary purpose of the Constitution was to carve from the general mass of legislative powers *then possessed by the states* such portions as it was thought desirable to vest in the federal government, leaving those not included in the enumeration still in the states. . . . Since the states severally never possessed international powers, such powers could not have been carved from the mass of state powers but obviously were transmitted to the United States from some other source. During the colonial period, those powers were possessed exclusively by and were entirely under the control of the Crown. By the Declaration of Independence, "the Representatives of the United States of America" declared the United [not the several] Colonies to be free and independent states, and as such to have "full Power to levy War, conclude Peace, contract Alliances, establish Commerce and to do all other Acts and Things which Independent States may of right do."

As a result of the separation from Great Britain by the colonies acting as a unit, the powers of external sovereignty passed from the Crown not to the colonies severally, but to the colonies in their collective and corporate capacity as the United States of America. Even before the Declaration, the colonies were a unit in foreign affairs, acting through a common agency—namely the Continental Congress, composed of delegates from the thirteen colonies. That agency exercised the powers of war and peace, raised an army, created a navy, and finally adopted the Declaration of Independence. Rulers come and go; governments end and forms of government change; but sovereignty survives. A political society cannot endure without a supreme will somewhere. Sovereignty is never held in suspense. When, therefore, the external sovereignty of Great Britain in respect of the colonies ceased, it immediately passed to the Union. . . .

The Union existed before the Constitution, which was ordained and established among other things to form "a more perfect Union." Prior to that event, it is clear that the Union, declared by the Articles of Confederation to be "perpetual," was the sole possessor of external sovereignty and in the Union it remained without change save in so far as the Constitution in express terms qualified its exercise. The Framers' Convention was called and exerted its powers upon the irrefutable postulate that though the states were several their people in respect of foreign affairs were one. . . .

It results that the investment of the federal government with the powers of external sovereignty did not depend upon the affirmative grants of the Constitution. The powers to declare and wage war, to conclude peace, to make treaties, to maintain diplomatic relations with other sovereignties, if they had never been mentioned in the Constitution, would have vested in the federal government as necessary concomitants of nationality. . . . As a member of the family of nations, the right and power of the United States in that field are equal to the right and power of the other members of the international family. Otherwise, the United States is not completely sovereign. . . .

Not only, as we have shown, is the federal power over external affairs in origin and essential character different from that over internal affairs, but participation in the exercise of the power is significantly limited. In this vast external realm, with its important, complicated, delicate and manifold problems, the President alone has the power to speak or listen as a representative of the nation. . . . As Marshall said in his great argument of March 7, 1800, in the House of Representatives, "The President is the sole organ of the nation in its external relations, and its sole representative with foreign nations." . . . It is important to bear in mind that we are here dealing not alone with an authority vested in the President by an exertion of legislative power, but with such an authority plus the very delicate, plenary and exclusive power of the President as the sole organ of the federal government in the field of international relations—a power which does not require as a basis for its exercise an act of Congress, but which, of course, like every other governmental power, must be exercised in subordination to the applicable provisions of the Constitution. It is quite apparent that if, in the maintenance of our international relations, embarrassment—perhaps serious embarrassment—is to be avoided and success for our aims achieved, congressional legislation which is to be made effective through negotiation and inquiry within the international field must often accord to the President a degree of discretion and freedom from statutory restriction which would not be admissible were domestic affairs alone involved. Moreover, he, not Congress, has the better opportunity of knowing the conditions which prevail in foreign countries, and especially is this true in time of war. He has his confidential sources of information. He has his agents in the form of diplomatic, consular and other officials. Secrecy in respect of information gathered by them may be highly necessary, and the premature disclosure of it productive of harmful results. Indeed, so clearly is this true that the first President refused to accede to a request to lay before the House of Representatives the instructions, correspondence and documents relating to the negotiation of the Jay Treaty—a refusal the wisdom of which was recognized by the House itself and has never since been doubted. . . .

The marked difference between foreign affairs and domestic affairs in this respect is recognized by both houses of Congress in the very form of their requisitions for information from the executive departments. In the case of every department except the Department of State, the resolution *directs* the official to furnish the information. In the case of the State Department, dealing with foreign affairs, the President is *requested* to furnish the information "if not incompatible with the public interest." A statement that to furnish the information is not compatible with the public interest rarely, if ever, is questioned.

When the President is to be authorized by legislation to act in respect of a matter intended to affect a situation in foreign territory, the legislator properly bears in mind the important consideration that the form of the President's action—or, indeed, whether he shall act at all—may well depend, among other things, upon the nature of the confidential information which he has or may thereafter receive, or upon the effect which his action may have upon our foreign relations. This consideration, in connection with what we have already said on the subject, discloses the unwisdom of requiring Congress in this field of governmental power to lay down narrowly definite standards by which the President is to be governed. As this court said in *Mackenzie* v. *Hare* [1915], "As a government, the United States is invested with all the attributes of sovereignty. As it has the character of nationality it has the powers of nationality, especially those which concern its relations and intercourse with other countries. *We should hesitate long before limiting or embarrassing such powers.*"

In the light of the foregoing observations, it is evident that this court should not be in haste to apply a general rule which will have the effect of condemning legislation like that under review as constituting an unlawful delegation of legislative power. The principles which justify such legislation find overwhelming support in the unbroken legislative practice which has prevailed almost from the inception of the national government to the present day. . . .

The result of holding that the joint resolution here under attack is void and unenforceable as constituting an unlawful delegation of legislative power would be to stamp this multitude of comparable acts and resolutions as likewise invalid. And while this court may not, and should not, hesitate to declare acts of Congress, however many times repeated, to be unconstitutional if beyond all rational doubt it finds them to be so, an impressive array of legislation such as we have just set forth, enacted by nearly every Congress from the beginning of our national existence to the present day, must be given unusual weight in the process of reaching a correct determination of the problem. A legislative practice such as we have here, evidenced not by only occasional instances, but marked by the movement of a steady stream for a century and a half of time, goes a long way in the direction of proving the presence of unassailable ground for the constitutionality of the practice, to be found in the origin and history of the power involved, or in its nature, or in both combined.

The judgment of the court below must be reversed and the cause remanded for further proceedings in accordance with the foregoing opinion.

Reversed.

Missouri v. *Holland*

252 U.S. 346; 91 S. Ct. 382; 64 L. Ed. 641 (1920)

In 1913, Congress passed legislation regulating the hunting of migratory birds. When two federal district courts ruled that the legislation was unconstitutional in that it lay beyond Congress's enumerated powers under the Constitution, the government accepted the decisions without appeal. In 1916, however, the United States entered into a treaty with Great Britain regulating the hunting of birds that migrated between the United States and Canada, and two years later, Congress passed the Migratory Bird Treaty Act in pursuance of that treaty. A lower federal court denied the state of Missouri's challenge to the legislation, and Missouri appealed. *Opinion of the Court: Holmes, McKenna, White, Day, McReynolds, Brandeis, Clarke. Dissenting (without opinion): VanDevanter, Pitney.*

MR. JUSTICE HOLMES delivered the opinion of the Court.

. . . The question raised is the general one whether the treaty and statute are void as an interference with the rights reserved to the States.

To answer this question it is not enough to refer to the Tenth Amendment, reserving the powers not delegated to the United States, because by Article II, § 2, the power to make treaties is delegated expressly, and by Article VI treaties made under the authority of the United States, along with the Constitution and laws of the United States made in pursuance thereof, are declared the supreme law of the land. If the treaty is valid there can be no dispute about the validity of the statute under Article I, § 8, as a necessary and proper means to execute the powers of the Government. The language of the Constitution as to the supremacy of treaties being general, the question before us is narrowed to an inquiry into the ground upon which the present supposed exception is placed.

It is said that a treaty cannot be valid if it infringes the Constitution, that there are limits, therefore, to the treaty-making power, and that one such limit is that what an act of Congress could not do unaided, in derogation of the powers reserved to the States, a treaty cannot do. An earlier act of Congress that attempted by itself and not in pursuance of a treaty to regulate the killing of migratory birds within the States had been held bad in the District Court. . . .

Whether the two cases were decided rightly or not they cannot be accepted as a test of the treaty power. Acts of Congress are the supreme law of the land only when made in pursuance of the Constitution, while treaties are declared to be so when made under the authority of the United States. It is open to question whether the authority of the United States means more than the formal acts prescribed to make the convention. We do not mean to imply that there are no qualifications to the treaty-making power; but they must be ascertained in a different way. It is obvious that there may be matters of the sharpest exigency for the national well being that an act of Congress could not deal with but that a treaty followed by such an act could, and it is not lightly to be assumed that, in matters requiring national action, "a power which must belong to and somewhere reside in every civilized government" is not to be found. . . . We are not yet discussing the particular case before us but only are considering the validity of the test proposed. With regard to that we may add that when we are dealing with words that also are a constituent act, like the Constitution of the United States, we must realize that they have called into life a being the development of which could not have been foreseen completely by the most gifted of its begetters. It was enough for them to realize or to hope that they had created an organism; it has taken a century and has cost their successors much sweat and blood to prove that they created a nation. The case before us must be considered in the light of our whole experience and not merely in that of what was said a hundred years ago. The treaty in question does not contravene any prohibitory words to be found in the Constitution. The only question is whether it is forbidden by some invisible radiation from the general terms of the Tenth Amendment. We must consider what this country has become in deciding what that Amendment has reserved.

The State as we have intimated founds its claim of exclusive authority upon an assertion of title to migratory birds, an assertion that is embodied in statute. . . . The whole foundation of the State's rights is the presence within their jurisdiction of birds that yesterday had not arrived, tomorrow may be in another State and in a week a thousand miles away. If we are to be accurate we cannot put the case of the State upon higher ground than that the treaty deals with creatures that for the moment are within the state borders, that it must be carried out by officers of the United States within the same territory, and that but for the treaty the State would be free to regulate this subject itself. . . .

Here a national interest of very nearly the first magnitude is involved. It can be protected only by national action in concert with that of another power. The subject-matter is only transitorily within the State and has no permanent habitat therein. But for the treaty and the statute there soon might be no birds for any powers to deal with. We see nothing in the Constitution that compels the Government to sit by while a food supply is cut off and the protectors of our forests and our crops are destroyed. It is not sufficient to rely upon the States. The reliance is vain, and were it otherwise, the question is whether the United States is forbidden to act. We are of opinion that the treaty and statute must be upheld. . . .

Decree affirmed.

Ex Parte Milligan

71 U.S. (4 Wall.) 2; 18 L. Ed. 281 (1866)

In 1862, President Abraham Lincoln ordered that all persons "guilty of any disloyal practice affording aid and comfort to rebels" should be subject to trial and punishment by "courts-martial or military commissions." Two years later, a military commission acting under this authority tried and convicted Lambdin P. Milligan, a notorious Confederate sympathizer in Indiana, on charges of disloyalty. Since the civil courts were functioning and Indiana was not a battle zone, Milligan charged that the commission lacked jurisdiction over him and sought a writ of habeas corpus in circuit court. He also contended that trial before the military commission violated his constitutional right to trial by jury. After failing to reach agreement on the issues Milligan raised, the circuit court certified the questions to the Supreme Court. *Opinion of the Court: Davis, Nelson, Grier, Clifford, Field. Concurring opinion: Chase, Wayne, Swayne, Miller.*

Mr. Justice Davis delivered the opinion of the Court.

. . . Milligan, not a resident of one of the rebellious states, or a prisoner of war, but a citizen of Indiana for twenty years past, and never in the military or naval service, is, while at his home, arrested by the military power of the United States, imprisoned and, on certain criminal charges preferred against him, tried, convicted, and sentenced to be hanged by a military commission, organized under the direction of the military commander of the military district of Indiana. Had this tribunal the legal power and authority to try and punish this man?

No graver question was ever considered by this court, nor one which more nearly concerns the rights of the whole people; for it is the birthright of every American citizen when charged with crime, to be tried and punished according to law. . . . The provisions of that instrument on the administration of criminal justice are too plain and direct to leave room for misconstruction or doubt of their true meaning. Those applicable to this case are found in that clause of the original Constitution which says "that the trial of all crimes, except in case of impeachment, shall be by jury;" and in the fourth, fifth, and sixth articles of the amendments. . . .

. . . Even these provisions, expressed in such plain English words, that it would seem the ingenuity of man could not evade them, are now, after the lapse of more than seventy years, sought to be avoided. . . . The Constitution of the United States is a law for rulers and people, equally in war and in peace, and covers with the shield of its protection all classes of men, at all times and under all circumstances. No doctrine, involving more pernicious consequences, was ever invented by the wit of man than that any of its provisions can be suspended during any of the great exigencies of government. Such a doctrine leads directly to anarchy or despotism, but the theory of necessity on which it is based is false; for the government, within the Constitution, has all the powers granted to it which are necessary to preserve its existence, as has been happily proved by the result of the great effort to throw off its just authority.

Have any of the rights guaranteed by the Constitution been violated in the case of Milligan? and if so, what are they?

Every trial involves the exercise of judicial power; and from what source did the Military Commission that tried him derive their authority? Certainly no part of the judicial power of the country was conferred on them: because the Constitution expressly vests it "in one Supreme Court and such inferior courts as the Congress may from time to time ordain and establish," and it is not pretended that the commission was a court ordained and established by Congress. They cannot justify on the mandate of the President: because he is controlled by law, and has his appropriate sphere of duty, which is to execute, not to make, the laws. . . .

But it is said that the jurisdiction is complete under the "laws and usages of war." found, and on whom they operate; they can never be applied to citizens in states which have upheld the authority of the government, and where the courts are open and their process unobstructed. This court has judicial knowledge that in Indiana the Federal authority was always unopposed, and its courts always open to hear criminal accusations and redress grievances; and no usage of war could sanction a military trial there for any offense whatever of a citizen in civil life, in nowise connected with the military service. Congress could grant no such power; and to the honor of our national legislature be it said, it has never been provoked by the state of the country even to attempt its exercise. One of the plainest constitutional provisions was, therefore, infringed when Milligan was tried by a court not ordained and established by Congress, and not composed of judges appointed during good behavior. . . .

Another guarantee of freedom was broken when Milligan was denied a trial by jury. . . . This privilege is a vital principle, underlying the whole administration of criminal justice; it is not held by sufferance, and cannot be frittered away on any plea of state or political necessity. When peace prevails, and the authority of the government is undisputed, there is no difficulty in preserving the safeguards of liberty; for the ordinary modes of trial are never neglected, and no one wishes it otherwise; but if society is disturbed by civil commotion—if the passions of men are aroused and the restraints of law weakened, if not disregarded—these safeguards need, and should receive, the watchful care of those intrusted with the guardianship of the Constitution and laws. . . .

It is claimed that martial law covers with its broad mantle the proceedings of this Military Commission. The proposition is this: That in a time of war the commander of an armed force (if in his opinion the exigencies of the country demand it, and of which he is to judge), has the power, within the lines of his military district, to suspend all civil rights and their remedies, and subject citizens as well as soldiers to the rule of his will; and in the exercise of his lawful authority cannot be restrained, except by his superior officer or the President of the United States. . . .

This nation, as experience has proved, cannot always remain at peace, and has no right to expect that it will always have wise and humane rulers, sincerely attached to the principles of the Constitution. Wicked men, ambitious of power, with hatred of liberty and contempt of law, may fill the place once occupied by Washington and Lincoln; and if this right is conceded, and the calamities of war again befall us, the dangers to human liberty are frightful to contemplate. . . .

. . . it is insisted that the safety of the country in time of war demands that this broad claim for martial law shall be sustained. If this were true, it could be well said that a country, preserved at the sacrifice of all the cardinal principles of liberty, is not worth the cost of preservation. Happily, it is not so. . . .

. . . Martial rule can never exist where the courts are open, and in the proper and unobstructed exercise of their jurisdiction. It is also confined to the locality of actual war. Because, during the late Rebellion it could have been enforced in Virginia, where the national authority was overturned and the courts driven out, it does not follow that it should obtain in Indiana, where that authority was never disputed, and justice was always administered.

MR. CHIEF JUSTICE CHASE delivered the following opinion.

. . . The opinion which has just been read . . . asserts not only that the Military Commission held in Indiana was not authorized by Congress, but that it was not in the power of Congress to authorize it.

We cannot agree to this. . . .

We think that Congress had power, though not exercised, to authorize the Military Commission which was held in Indiana. . . .

Congress has power to raise and support armies; to provide and maintain a navy; to make rules for the government and regulation of the land and naval forces; and to provide for governing such part of the militia as may be in the service of the United States.

It is not denied that the power to make rules for the government of the army and navy is a power to provide for trial and punishment by military courts without a jury. It has been so understood and exercised from the adoption of the Constitution to the present time.

Nor, in our judgment, does the fifth or any other amendment, abridge that power. . . .

. . . It is not necessary to attempt any precise definition of the boundaries of this power. But may it not be said that government includes protection and defense as well as the regulation of internal administration? And is it impossible to imagine cases in which citizens conspiring or attempting the destruction of great injury of the national forces may be subjected by Congress to military trial and punishment in the just exercise of this undoubted constitutional power? . . .

But we do not put our opinion, that Congress might authorize such a military commission as was held in Indiana, upon the power to provide for the government of the national forces.

Congress has the power not only to raise and support and govern armies, but to declare war. It has, therefore, the power to provide by law for carrying on war. This power necessarily extends to all legislation essential to the prosecution of war with vigor and success, except such as interferes with the command of the force and conduct of campaigns. That power and duty belong to the President as Commander-in-Chief. Both these powers are derived from the Constitution, but neither is defined by that instrument. Their extent must be determined: by their nature, and by the principles of our institutions. . . .

Where peace exists the laws of peace must prevail. What we do maintain is that when the nation is involved in war, and some portions of the country are invaded, and all are exposed to invasion, it is within the power of Congress to determine to what states or districts such great and imminent public danger exists as justifies the authorization of military tribunals for the trial of crimes and offenses against the discipline or security of the army or against the public safety.

In Indiana, for example, at the time of the arrest of Milligan and his co-conspirators, it is established by the papers in the record, that the state was a military district, was the theater of military operations, had been actually invaded, and was constantly threatened with invasion. It appears, also, that a powerful secret association, composed of citizens and others, existed within the state, under military organization, conspiring against the draft, and plotting insurrection, the liberation of the prisoners of war at various depots, the seizure of the state and national arsenals, armed co-operation with the enemy, and war against the national government.

We cannot doubt that, in such a time or public danger, Congress had power, under the Constitution, to provide for the organization of a military commission, and for trial by that commission of persons engaged in this conspiracy. The fact that the Federal courts were open was regarded by Congress as a sufficient reason for not exercising the power; but that fact could not deprive Congress of the right to exercise it. Those courts might be open and undisturbed in the execution of their functions, and yet wholly incompetent to avert threatened danger, or to punish, with adequate promptitude and certainty, the guilty conspirators.

In Indiana, the judges and officers of the courts were loyal to the government. But it might have been otherwise. In times of rebellion and civil war it may often happen, indeed, that judges and marshals will be in active sympathy with the rebels, and courts their most efficient allies. . . .

We think that the power of Congress, in such times and in such localities, to authorize trials for crimes against the security and safety of the national forces, may be derived from its constitutional authority to raise and support armies and to declare war, if not from its constitutional authority to provide for governing the national forces.

We have no apprehension that this power, under our American system of government, in which all official authority is derived from the people and exercised under direct responsibility to the people, is more likely to be abused than the power to regulate commerce or the power to borrow money. And we are unwilling to give our assent by silence to expressions of opinion which seem to us calculated, though not intended, to cripple the constitutional powers of the government, and to augment the public dangers in times of invasion and rebellion. . . .

Although Milligan *dealt with presidential actions, the opinion of the Court also stated that Congress could not have authorized the trial of civilians by military tribunals. After the Civil War, many members of Congress believed that the* Milligan *decision cast doubt on the constitutionality of the Reconstruction program in the Southern states. Its suspicions of the Court thus fueled, Congress responded in part by withdrawing the Court's jurisdiction to decide* Ex Parte McCardle *(see Chapter 3), which called into question a validity of the Reconstruction Acts.*

Korematsu v. *United States*

323 U.S. 214; 65 S. Ct. 193; 89 L. Ed. 194 (1944)

In February 1942, President Franklin D. Roosevelt issued Executive Order No. 9066, which authorized the creation of military areas from which individuals might be excluded to prevent espionage or sabotage. The order also permitted military commanders to regulate who might enter or remain in such areas. A month later, Congress passed legislation establishing criminal penalties for violations of these regulations. Acting pursuant to the authority delegated to him under the executive order, the commander of the Western Defense Command initially imposed a curfew on residents of Japanese ancestry and ultimately ordered that they be evacuated to inland detention centers. In *Hirabayashi* v. *United States* (1943), the Court upheld the curfew program in a narrow ruling that involved no consideration of the evacuation program. When Toyosaburo Korematsu, an American citizen of Japanese ancestry, refused to leave his home in California, he was convicted in federal district court of violating the exclusion order. After the conviction was upheld by the circuit court of appeals, the Supreme Court granted certiorari. *Opinion of the Court: Black, Stone, Reed, Frankfurter, Douglas, Rutledge. Concurring opinion: Frankfurter. Dissenting opinions: Roberts; Murphy; Jackson.*

MR. JUSTICE BLACK delivered the opinion of the Court.

... All legal restrictions which curtail the civil rights of a single racial group are immediately suspect. That is not to say that all such restrictions are unconstitutional. It is to say that courts must subject them to the most rigid scrutiny. Pressing public necessity may sometimes justify the existence of such restrictions; racial antagonism never can ...

In the light of the principles we announced in the *Hirabayashi* case [*Hirabayashi* v. *United States* (1943)], we are unable to conclude that it was beyond the war power of Congress and the Executive to exclude those of Japanese ancestry from the West Coast war area at the time they did.... Nothing short of apprehension by the proper military authorities of the gravest imminent danger to the public safety can constitutionally justify either. But exclusion from a threatened area ... has a definite and close relationship to the prevention of espionage and sabotage....

... It was because we could not reject the finding of the military authorities that it was impossible to bring about an immediate segregation of the disloyal from the loyal that we sustained the validity of the curfew order as applying to the whole group. In the instant case, temporary exclusion of the entire group was rested by the military on the same ground. The judgment that exclusion of the whole group was for the same reason a military imperative answers the contention that the exclusion was in the nature of group punishment based on antagonism to those of Japanese origin.

We uphold the exclusion order as of the time it was made and when the petitioner violated it.... In doing so, we are not unmindful of the hardships imposed by it upon a large group of American citizens.... But hardships are part of war, and war is an aggregation of hardships. All citizens alike, both in and out of uniform, feel the impact of war in greater or lesser measure. Citizenship has its responsibilities as well as its privileges, and in time of war the burden is always heavier. Compulsory exclusion of large groups of citizens from their homes, except under circumstances of direst emergency and peril, is inconsistent with our basic governmental institutions. But when under conditions of modern warfare our shores are threatened by hostile forces, the power to protect must be commensurate with the threatened danger....

It is said that we are dealing here with the case of imprisonment of a citizen in a concentration camp solely because of his ancestry, without evidence or inquiry concerning his loyalty and good disposition towards the United States. To cast this case into outlines of racial prejudice, without reference to the real military dangers which were presented, merely confuses the issue. Korematsu was not excluded from the Military Area because of hostility to him or his race. He *was* excluded because we are at war with the Japanese Empire, because the properly constituted military authorities feared an invasion of our West Coast and felt constrained to take proper security measures, because they decided that the military urgency of the situation demanded that all citizens of Japanese ancestry be segregated from the West Coast temporarily, and finally, because Congress, reposing its confidence in this time of war in our military leaders—as inevitably it must—determined that they should have the power to do just this. There was evidence of disloyalty on the part of some, the military authorities considered that the need for action was great, and time was short. We cannot—by availing ourselves of the calm perspective of hindsight—now say that at that time these actions were unjustified.

Affirmed.

MR. JUSTICE FRANKFURTER, concurring. . . .

The provisions of the Constitution which confer on the Congress and the President powers to enable this country to wage war are as much part of the Constitution as provisions looking to a nation at peace. And we have had recent occasion to quote approvingly the statement of former Chief Justice Hughes that the war power of the Government is "the power to wage war successfully." . . . Therefore, the validity of action under the war power must be judged wholly in the context of war. That action is not to be stigmatized as lawless because like action in times of peace would be lawless. To talk about a military order that expresses an allowable judgment of war needs by those entrusted with the duty of conducting war as "an unconstitutional order" is to suffuse a part of the Constitution with an atmosphere of unconstitutionality. . . . To recognize that military orders are "reasonably expedient military precautions" in time of war and yet to deny them constitutional legitimacy makes of the Constitution an instrument for dialectic subtleties not reasonably to be attributed to the hard-headed Framers, of whom a majority had had actual participation in war. If a military order such as that under review does not transcend the means appropriate for conducting war, such action by the military is as constitutional as would be any authorized action by the Interstate Commerce Commission within the limits of the constitutional power to regulate commerce. . . . To find that the Constitution does not forbid the military measures now complained of does not carry with it approval of that which Congress and the Executive did. That is their business, not ours.

MR. JUSTICE MURPHY, dissenting.

This exclusion of "all persons of Japanese ancestry, both alien and non-alien," from the Pacific Coast area on a plea of military necessity in the absence of martial law ought not to be approved. Such exclusion goes over "the very brink of constitutional power" and falls into the ugly abyss of racism.

In dealing with matters relating to the prosecution and progress of a war, we must accord great respect and consideration to the judgments of the military authorities who are on the scene and who have full knowledge of the military facts. The scope of their direction must, as a matter of necessity and common sense, be wide. And their judgments ought not to be overruled lightly by those whose training and duties ill-equip them to deal intelligently with matters so vital to the physical security of the nation.

At the same time, however, it is essential that there be definite limits to military discretion, especially where martial law has not been declared. Individuals must not be left impoverished of their constitutional rights on a plea of military necessity that has neither substance nor support.

The judicial test of whether the Government, on a plea of military necessity, can validly deprive an individual of any of his constitutional rights is whether the deprivation is reasonably related to a public danger that is so "immediate, imminent, and impending" as not to admit of delay and not to permit the intervention of ordinary constitutional processes to alleviate the danger. . . .

. . . In adjudging the military action taken in light of the then apparent dangers, we must not erect too high or too meticulous standards; it is necessary only that the action have some reasonable relation to the removal of the dangers of invasion, sabotage and espionage. But the exclusion, either temporarily or permanently, of all persons with Japanese blood in their veins has no such reasonable relation. And that relation is lacking because the exclusion order necessarily must rely for its reasonableness upon the assumption that *all* persons of Japanese ancestry may have a dangerous tendency to commit sabotage and espionage and to aid our Japanese enemy in other ways. . . . That this forced exclusion was the result in good measure of this erroneous assumption of racial guilt rather than bona fide military necessity is evidenced by the Commanding General's Final Report on the evacuation from the Pacific Coast area. In it he refers to all individuals of Japanese descent as "subversive," as belonging to "an enemy race" whose "racial strains are undiluted," and as constituting over 112,000 potential enemies . . . at large today" along the Pacific Coast.* In support of this blanket condemnation of all persons of Japanese descent, however, no reliable evidence is cited to show that such individuals were generally disloyal, or had generally so conducted themselves in this area as to constitute a special menace to defense installations or war industries, or had otherwise by their behavior furnished reasonable ground for their exclusion as a group.

Justification for the exclusion is sought, instead, mainly upon questionable racial and sociological grounds not ordinarily within the realm of expert military judgment, supplemented by certain semi-military conclusions drawn from an unwarranted use of circumstantial evidence.

No adequate reason is given for the failure to treat these Japanese Americans on an individual basis by holding investigations and hearings to separate the loyal from the disloyal, as was done in the case of persons of German and Italian ancestry. . . . It is asserted merely that the loyalties of this group "were unknown and time was of the essence." Yet nearly four months elapsed after Pearl Harbor before the first exclusion order was issued; nearly eight months went by until the last order was issued; and the last of these "subversive" persons was not actually removed until almost eleven months had elapsed. Leisure and deliberation seem to have been more of the essence than speed. And the fact that conditions were not such as to warrant a declaration of martial law adds strength to the belief that the factors of time and military necessity were not as urgent as they have been represented to be . . .

I dissent, therefore, from this legalization of racism. . . . All residents of this nation are kin in some way by blood or culture to a foreign land. Yet they are primarily and necessarily a part of the new and distinct civilization of the United States. They must accordingly be treated at all times as the heirs of the American experiment and as entitled to all the rights and freedoms guaranteed by the Constitution.

Mr. Justice Jackson, dissenting.

. . . It is said that if the military commander had reasonable military grounds for promulgating the orders, they are constitutional and become law, and the Court is required to enforce them. There are several reasons why I cannot subscribe to this doctrine.

It would be impracticable and dangerous idealism to expect or insist that each specific military command in an area of probable operations will conform to conventional tests of constitutionality. When an area is so beset that it must be put under military control at all, the paramount consideration is that its measures be successful, rather than legal. The armed services must protect a society, not merely its Constitution. The very essence of the military job is to marshal physical force, to remove every obstacle to its effectiveness, to give it every strategic advantage. Defense measures will not, and often should not, be held within the limits that bind civil authority in peace. No court can require such a commander in such circumstances to act as a reasonable man; he may be unreasonably cautious and exacting. Perhaps he should be. But a commander in temporarily focusing the life of a community on defense is carrying out a military program; he is not making law in the sense the courts know the term. He issues orders, and they may have a certain authority as military commands, although they may be very bad as constitutional law.

But if we cannot confine military expedients by the Constitution, neither would I distort the Constitution to approve all that the military may deem expedient. That is what the Court appears to be doing, whether consciously or not. I cannot say, from any evidence before me, that the orders of General DeWitt were not reasonably expedient military precautions, nor could I say that they were. But even if they were permissible military procedures, I deny that it follows that they are constitutional. If, as the Court holds, it does follow, then we may as well say that any military

*Further evidence of the Commanding General's attitude toward individuals of Japanese ancestry is revealed in his voluntary testimony . . .

"I don't want any of them [persons of Japanese ancestry] here. They are a dangerous element. There is no way to determine their loyalty. The west coast contains too many vital installations essential to the defense of the country to allow any Japanese on this coast. . . . The danger of the Japanese was, and is now—if they are permitted to come back—espionage and sabotage. It makes no difference whether he is an American citizen, he is still a Japanese. American citizenship does not necessarily determine loyalty. . . . But we must worry about the Japanese all the time until he is wiped off the map. Sabotage and espionage will make problems as long as he is allowed in this area . . ."

order will be constitutional and have done with it. . . .

In the very nature of things, military decisions are not susceptible of intelligent judicial appraisal. They do not pretend to rest on evidence, but are made on information that often would not be admissible and on assumptions that could not be proved. Information in support of an order could not be disclosed to courts without danger that it would reach the enemy. Neither can courts act on communications made in confidence. Hence courts can never have any real alternative to accepting the mere declaration of the authority that issued the order that it was reasonably necessary from a military viewpoint.

Much is said of the danger to liberty from the Army program for deporting and detaining these citizens of Japanese extraction. But a judicial construction of the due process clause that will sustain this order is a far more subtle blow to liberty than the promulgation of the order itself. A military order, however unconstitutional, is not apt to last longer than the military emergency. Even during that period a succeeding commander may revoke it all. But once a judicial opinion rationalizes such an order to show that it conforms to the Constitution, or rather rationalizes the Constitution to show that the Constitution sanctions such an order, the Court for all time has validated the principle of racial discrimination in criminal procedure and of transplanting American citizens. The principle then lies about like a loaded weapon ready for the hand of any authority that can bring forward a plausible claim of an urgent need. Every repetition imbeds that principle more deeply in our law and thinking and expands it to new purposes. . . .

I should hold that a civil court cannot be made to enforce an order which violates constitutional limitations even if it is a reasonable exercise of military authority. The courts can exercise only the judicial power, can apply only law, and must abide by the Constitution, or they cease to be civil courts and become instruments of military policy.

Of course the existence of a military power resting on force, so vagrant, so centralized, so necessarily heedless of the individual, is an inherent threat to liberty. But I would not lead people to rely on this Court for a review that seems to me wholly delusive. The military reasonableness of these orders can only be determined by military superiors. If the people ever let command of the war power fall into irresponsible and unscrupulous hands, the courts wield no power equal to its restraint. The chief restraint upon those who command the physical forces of the country, in the future as in the past, must be their responsibility to the political judgments of their contemporaries and to the moral judgments of history.

My duties as a justice as I see them do not require me to make a military judgment as to whether General DeWitt's evacuation and detention program was a reasonable military necessity. I do not suggest that the courts should have attempted to interfere with the Army in carrying out its task. But I do not think they may be asked to execute a military expedient that has no place in law under the Constitution. I would reverse the judgment and discharge the prisoner.

In 1948, following condemnation by a presidential commission of the forced evacuation of Japanese-Americans, Congress passed the Evacuation Claims Act, under which claimants received over $37 million. In 1984 another governmental commission concluded that internment resulted from "race prejudice, wartime hysteria, and a failure of political leadership" and recommended a national apology and further monetary compensation. That same year a Federal District Court vacated Korematsu's conviction based on newly discovered evidence that the government had deliberately withheld and falsified relevant evidence in the materials it presented in court. In 1988 Congress formally apologized for the internment and established a fund to pay reparations.

7
FEDERALISM

As a central feature of the American constitutional system, federalism is considered by many to be one of the most important contributions made by the Founders to the art of government and to represent the paradigm of what is called federal government. Most contemporary definitions of federalism amount to little more than generalized descriptions of the way governing power is divided in the United States between the states and the national government.[1] The Framers, however, did not consider the system they had designed to be federal. As their writings make clear, they thought that the Constitution was "in strictness, neither a national nor a federal Constitution, but a composition of both."[2] Further, James Madison argued, the "compound government" created by the Constitution must "be explained by itself, [and] not by similitudes or analogies."[3] In order to appreciate the difficulties facing the Supreme Court when it deals with questions of federalism and to evaluate its decisions in this area, we must attempt to comprehend the Framers' understanding of this "neither wholly federal, nor wholly national" political arrangement and how they thought that it contributed to the overall ends of the Constitution.

FEDERALISM AND THE FOUNDING

It is essential to understand that the Framers recognized only two fundamental modes, or elements, of political organization, the federal and the national,[4] which they thought they had combined into a compound system. Today, in contrast, it is commonplace to speak of three elemental forms: confederal, federal, and national or unitary. This modern typology treats the confederal and national forms as the extremes, with a confederation preserving the primacy and autonomy of the states and a nation giving unimpeded primacy to the government of the whole society. Federalism, in this view, stands between these two poles and combines the best characteristics of each. Specifically, federalism is thought to combine states, which confederally retain sovereignty within a certain sphere, with a central body that nationally possesses sovereignty within another sphere.

The Framers, however, saw no more difference between the confederal and the federal than we see, for example, between the words *inflammable* and *flammable:* nothing more was involved than the accidental presence or absence of a nonsignifying prefix. For them, the confederal or federal was opposed to the unitary or national, and they viewed the Constitution as a composition of both elemental modes. Today, we regard as a third fundamental mode or element what they regarded as a mere compound, bestowing the simple word *federal* on what the Framers considered to be a composition of both federal and national elements.

The founding generation's idea of confederal or federal arrangements, as represented in the Articles of Confederation, was characterized by three operative principles, each of which drastically limited the power of the federal authority and preserved the primacy of the member states.[5] First, the central federal authority did not govern individual citizens: it dealt only with the individual states that composed the federal system, and operated primarily by the voluntary consent of those states. Second, the central government had no authority to deal with the internal affairs of the member states; rather, its rule was narrowly confined to certain external tasks of mutual interest to all—for example, war and common defense. Third, each member state had an exact equality of sufferage—an equal vote derived from the equal sovereignty possessed by each state, regardless of size, strength, or wealth.

In the Founders' conception of a national government, in contrast, all power resided in the central authority and local units of government, if retained at all, were mere subdivisions that existed for administrative purposes only. Such powers as these localities possessed were delegated by the national government and could be overridden or withdrawn altogether at its will. The national authority, then, extended to all matters of internal administration and acted directly, through its own officials, not merely on the local governments but upon every citizen as well. Finally, since the national government was independent of the local units, it could continue in existence even if they were to disappear.

Given these two modes from which to choose, confederal or federal association traditionally had been preferred by those in favor of republican government, who regarded it as the only way in which the advantages of size could be combined with the blessings of republicanism. Proponents of this view argued that first of all, only small countries with homogeneous populations could possess republican government, for only small countries could secure the public's voluntary attachment to the government and voluntary obedience to the laws; and that secondly, when such small republics seek the advantages and safety of greater size, as inevitably they must, they can preserve their republican character only by uniting in a federal manner. Federalism would be, for them, the protective husk that preserved the kernels of free government.[6]

The leading Framers realized, however, that the traditional republican embrace of federalism, as incorporated in the Articles of Confederation, had reduced the people to "the last stage of national humiliation." As Alexander Hamilton complained, "There is scarcely anything that can wound the pride, or degrade the character of an independent nation, which we do not experience." The principles of federalism had rendered the Articles so weak that the situation "sometimes bordered on anarchy." Nor was the government's ineptitude limited to the realm of foreign affairs. Domestically, "the security of private rights" had been rendered precarious and the "steady dispensation of justice" interrupted by the practices of many states.[7] Convinced of the need for a more powerful government, many delegates to the Constitutional Convention supported the Virginia Plan. As amended, the plan declared that "a Union of the States merely federal will not accomplish the objects proposed by the Articles of Confederation, namely common defense, security of liberty, and general welfare" and proposed, therefore, that "a *national* Government ought to be established consisting of a *supreme* Legislative, Executive and Judiciary."[8]

At this juncture, a serious question arose: Could a national government be formed without jeopardizing republican liberty? Those who favored the establishment of such a government had to persuade their contemporaries that the proposed plan was also compatible with republican government—that federalism as it had been understood to that time was not indispensable to republicanism. To do so, they chose to undermine the prevailing notion that without federalism, only small countries could possess republican governments. Madison's arguments in this regard were decisive. Turning the small-republic view on its head, he contended that smallness, not largeness, was fatal to republican liberty. History demonstrated that small republics continuously were racked with faction and oppression; indeed, the Constitutional Convention itself had been instigated by the fear for liberty in the small American states. "Was it to be supposed that republican liberty could long exist under the abuses of it practiced in some of the States? . . . Were we not thence admonished to enlarge the sphere as far as the nature of the government would admit?" Because smallness had proven fatal to republicanism, "the only remedy is to enlarge the sphere, and thereby divide the community into so great a number of interests and parties, that in the first place a majority will not be likely at the same moment to have a common interest separate from that of the whole or of the minority; and in the second place, that in case they should have such an interest, they may not be apt to unite in the pursuit of it."[9] The multiplicity of interests present in a large republic thus was the true guardian of republican liberty—the republican remedy for the diseases most incident to republican government.[10]

Madison's arguments on behalf of a large extended republic effectively demolished the small-republic argument but failed to convince the convention to adopt a wholly national government. Most of the delegates, reluctant to abolish the states altogether, sought some means for preserving their existence and agency. Increasingly, they came to recognize that because, as William Johnson of Connecticut pointed out, the states were both distinct "political societies" and "districts of people composing one political society,"[11] neither a wholly federal nor a wholly national constitution was appropriate. Spurred on by, among others, George Mason of Virginia and James Wilson of Pennsylvania, they realized that it was possible for the people to create and assign power to more than "one set of immediate representatives."[12] The people could have their cake and eat it too: not only could they preserve the states while at the same time establishing a new national government, but they could also have a political structure in which both levels of government operated over the same geographic area. Power would be divided between these two levels according to a simple yet elegant formula: any object of government confined in operation and effect wholly within the bounds of a particular state would belong to the government of that state, and any object of government extended in its operation and effect beyond the bounds of the particular state would belong to the government of the United States.

Beyond this straightforward division of power between the central government and the states, federalism to the convention delegates also meant the presence of federal elements in the central government itself. They anticipated that the new constitution would "in some respects operate on the States, in others on the people."[13] Because the new central government would act upon both the states and the people, the delegates concluded that both ought to be represented in the new government. Accordingly, they mixed together varying proportions of federal and national elements to create a composition that was neither wholly federal nor wholly national. This blend of elements is apparent in such constitutional provisions as the mode by which the Constitution was to be ratified, the amending process, equal representation of the states in the Senate, and the electoral college.

When Alexis de Tocqueville examined the American Constitution, he described it as "neither exactly national nor exactly federal; but the new word which ought to express this novel thing does not yet exist."[14] While he was correct in declaring that a new word had not been devised, a familiar term from the beginning had been pressed into service to express this novel thing: the term *federal.* Well aware that federalism was generally thought to be essential for a republican government, the Framers seized the word for themselves and called their new compound arrangement federalism. This stratagem proved to be of considerable value during the ratification campaign, as it enabled them to present themselves as defenders of federalism and to refer to the adherents of true federalism as Anti-Federalists. But the Framers' identification of their compound government as federal, although an effective ploy at the time, has been the source of much subsequent confusion over exactly what federalism means and what mode of government the American Constitution establishes. Such confusion can be avoided by reference to the Constitution's Preamble. The Constitution was intended neither to provide for a perfect union (i.e., a wholly national government), nor to preserve the radically imperfect union of the Articles of Confederation; rather, it was ordained and established "in order to form a more perfect Union." The phrase "a more perfect Union" is no grammatical solecism; to the contrary, it is an accurate description of the compound government, made up of both federal and national elements, that the convention had devised.

It was, in part, through the means of this "more perfect Union" that the overall ends of the Constitution were to be served. As Madison had observed in *The Federalist,* No. 51, in framing the Constitution the convention's great object was "first [to] enable the government to control the governed; and in the next place, [to] oblige it to control itself." Madison and the other leading Framers recognized that the federal arrangements they had devised could contribute to the realization of both goals. The division of power between the states and the national government allowed them to entrust to the entire federal structure more power then they would have been willing to grant to either the states or the national government alone, and thereby to assure that the government would have sufficient power to control the governed and to avoid the near-anarchy that had existed under the Articles of Confederation. They also appreciated, on the other hand, that the federalism they had devised helped to oblige the government to control itself. By creating two levels of government and dividing power between them, the Framers made each level less threatening to liberty. And by interjecting federal elements into the national government itself, they checked the threat of tyranny from regionally concentrated factious majorities. In short, the Framers' federalism helped to provide energetic government organized around the principle of qualitative majority rule.

FEDERALISM AND THE MARSHALL COURT

As is true of many compounds, the government created by the Framers is potentially unstable. Under the pressure of events and with the proper catalytic agents present, it may break down into its elemental modes and become either wholly federal or wholly national. A principal responsibility of the Supreme Court, consistent with its claim in *Marbury* v. *Madison* (1803) that "it is emphatically the province and duty of the judicial department to say what the law is," has been to prevent such an occurrence and to preserve the "mixed nature" of the Constitution. In discharging this responsibility, the Court often has had to counteract whichever element is in danger of gaining ascendancy. For the most part, the justices have accomplished this task by the way in which they have drawn the line between the powers of the national government and those of the states. The line of demarcation cannot be fixed permanently or precisely. As Chief Justice John Marshall remarked in *McCulloch* v. *Maryland* (1819), "The question respecting the extent of the powers actually granted, is perpetually arising, and will probably continue to arise, as long as our system shall exist." The answers given by the Court to this "perpetually arising" question have helped to maintain a balance of power between the states and the national government, and thereby to preserve the compound nature of our constitutional system.[15]

Initially, under Marshall's leadership, the Court defined state and national powers in such a way as to benefit the national government. At that time, the people felt a "habitual attachment" to their state governments. As Hamilton pointed out in the Constitutional Convention, the state's "sovereignty is immediately before the eyes of the people: its protection is immediately enjoyed by them. From its hand distributive justice, and all those acts which familiarize and endear government to a people, are dispensed to them." Given that "the passions . . . of avarice, ambition, interest, which govern most individuals and all public bodies, fall into the current of the States and do not flow in the stream of the General Government," the states were likely to be "an overmatch for the General Government."[16] In the face of this imbalance in power, the compound government created by the Framers easily could be broken down into its elemental modes to such an extent that a simple confederation—with all its attendant evils, once again would emerge. To prevent such a calamity, Chief Justice Marshall systematically interpreted the Constitution so as to render secure the power and authority of the general government, as his opinions in *McCulloch* and in *Cohens* v. *Virginia* (1821) make clear.

In *McCulloch*, Marshall set forth three basic rules of constitutional interpretation that in general favored the national government and in particular supported his argument for upholding the constitutionality of the Bank of the United States and invalidating Maryland's tax on that bank. First, he argued that the enumerated powers of the national government ought to be seen as means to the accomplishment of certain ends. Because these powers helped designate the Constitution's "great outlines" and "important objects," Marshall contended, they should not be considered to be limitations on the national government. A broad and expansive construction of the powers of the national government was essential: "A constitution, to contain an accurate detail of all the subdivisions of which its great powers will admit, and of all the means by which they may be carried into execution, would partake of the prolixity of a legal code, and could scarcely be embraced by the human mind." The United States Constitution was not a statute, and it ought not to be read as one. Emphasizing that "we must never forget that it is *a constitution* we are expounding, . . . intended to endure for ages to come," Marshall advanced the following principle, which he felt would assure a "sound construction" of the Constitution: "Let the end be legitimate, let it be within the scope of the constitution, and all means which are appropriate, which are plainly adapted to that end, which are not prohibited, but consist with the letter and spirit of the constitution, are constitutional." To Marshall, this principle of constitutional construction was dictated not only by logic, but also by the presence of the Necessary and Proper Clause.

The second basic rule of constitutional interpretation advanced in *McCulloch* was related to the first: the Tenth Amendment, Marshall declared, constitutes no bar to a broad construction of even the incidental or implied powers of the national government. The Chief Justice drew attention to the fact that unlike the Articles of Confederation, which required "that everything granted shall be expressly and minutely described," the Tenth Amendment declares only that the powers "not delegated to the United States, nor prohibited to the States, are reserved to the States or to the people." Thus, the answer to the question of whether "the particular power which may become the subject of contest has been delegated to the one government or prohibited to the other, [is] to depend on a fair construction of the whole instrument."

Marshall's third and final rule arose out of his reading of the Supremacy Clause in Article VI. He contended that within its sphere the national government is supreme, and its policies must prevail, regardless of whatever state powers or functions it may touch: "It is of the very essence of supremacy to remove all obstacles to its action within its own sphere, and so to modify every power vested in subordinate governments, as to exempt its own operations from their own influence."

In *Cohens,* Marshall further sought to protect the compound nature of the American constitutional system from the excessive centrifugal forces generated by state loyalties, by establishing the authority of the Supreme Court to review state criminal court decisions. In countering the State of Virginia's argument that the state judiciaries were totally separate from and independent of the federal judiciary, the Chief Justice pointed out, first of all, that the states have "chosen to be, in many respects, and to many purposes, a nation; and for all these purposes, her government is complete; to all these objects, it is competent. The people have declared, that in the exercise of all powers given for these objects, it is supreme." From these facts, Marshall went on, it followed inevitably that in a government that is acknowledged to be supreme with respect to objects of vital interest to the nation, "the exercise of the appellate power over those judgments of the State tribunals which may contravene the Constitution or laws of the United States, is, we believe, essential to the attainment of those objects."[17]

DUAL FEDERALISM

Marshall's efforts to protect the national elements of the Constitution proved so successful that most subsequent concern for the preservation of the government's compound nature has been directed toward retaining its federal elements and ensuring the independent existence and agency of the states. From the appointment of Chief Justice Roger Brooke Taney as Marshall's successor in 1835 until President Franklin D. Roosevelt's clash with the Supreme Court during the New Deal era, this concern most often was manifested in what usually is called dual federalism. This doctrine was clearly defined by Justice Peter V. Daniel in the *License Cases* (1847): "Every power delegated to the federal government must be expounded in coincidence with a perfect right in the states to all that they have not delegated; in coincidence, too, with the possession of every power and right necessary for their existence and preservation." Dual federalism assumes that the two levels of government are coequal sovereignties and that each is supreme within its own sphere. Accordingly, the national government may not undertake any action, even in the exercise of its enumerated powers, that touches upon those functions that the Constitution has reserved to the states. The notorious decision handed down in *Dred Scott* v. *Sandford* (1857)—found in Chapter 15—in which the Court held unconstitutional the Missouri Compromise of 1820 and declared that Congress had no power to limit the spread of slavery in the territories, is based on these assumptions.

The proponents of dual federalism insist that the Constitution is a compact among the states, which have, on certain enumerated issues, ceded a portion of their sovereignty to the national government. All sovereignty not ceded, they argue, is retained. To prevent that retained sovereignty from slipping away, they interpret very narrowly the enumerated powers of the national government in general, and the Necessary and Proper Clause in particular. Also, they strongly emphasize the Tenth Amendment, which they consider to be an affirmative base of power from which the states may challenge the wide-ranging effects of national legislation.

All of these considerations are present in *Hammer* v. *Dagenhart* (1918), perhaps the Supreme Court's clearest statement of the theory of dual federalism. In *Hammer* the Court, by a 5–4 vote, invalidated a congressional statute that restricted the transportation in interstate commerce of goods produced by child labor. The majority held that despite the express delegation to the national government of the power "to regulate commerce among the several states," the national government was excluded from regulating any matter that was subject to state power. In the words of Justice William R. Day, author of the majority opinion, "The grant of authority over a purely federal [i.e., national] matter was not intended to destroy the local power always existing and carefully reserved to the States in the Tenth Amendment." He admonished all those who would interpret the Constitution to recall that "the powers not expressly delegated to the national government" are reserved to the states and to the people by the Tenth Amendment.

C. Herman Pritchett has pointed out that in the *Hammer* ruling, Justice Day misquoted the Tenth Amendment (the term *expressly* does not appear in the text), ignored judicial precedent (in *McCulloch* v. *Maryland,* Chief Justice Marshall had held that because the word *expressly* had been intentionally omitted from the amendment, the question of whether a particular power had been delegated to the national government could only be answered by a "fair construction of the whole instrument"), and denied the historical record (in considering the Tenth Amendment, the First Congress rejected a proposal to insert the word *expressly*).[18] These problems did not go unnoticed at the time. Speaking for the four dissenters, Justice Oliver Wendell Holmes declared, "I should have thought that the most conspicuous decisions of this Court had made it clear that the power to regulate commerce and other constitutional powers could not be cut down or qualified by the fact that it might interfere with the carrying out of the domestic policy of any State." Justice Day's argument in effect accorded such primacy to the purely federal elements in the constitutional system that it jeopardized the Constitution's mixed nature and gravely restricted the national government's ability to respond to nationwide problems.

In contending that Congress could not use its admitted powers if they interfered in any way with the states' exercise of their admitted powers, the advocates of dual federalism not only denied the compound nature of the Constitution but also ignored practical necessity. In the end, they did themselves a decided disservice: by the mid 1930s, not surprisingly, the doctrine had fallen into disgrace.[19] Dual federalism soon was replaced by what is often referred to as cooperative federalism—a pragmatic sharing of governmental functions by federal, state, and local authorities that takes little account of whether or not federal or national elements are present and governing.[20]

FEDERALISM AND INTERPRETATION BASED ON STRUCTURE AND RELATIONSHIP

By stubbornly insisting upon the virtual supremacy of federal elements, the defenders of dual federalism ultimately succeeded only in rendering the defense of those elements more difficult.[21] Such a defense is necessary, however. Even Chief Justice Marshall, who often favored the claims of the national government over those of the states, emphasized in *Cohens* that although the states are subordinate for some purposes, for other purposes they are sovereign. Marshall argued that the question of whether a state is to be considered as sovereign or subordinate must be answered through a "fair construction" of the entire Constitution. As Charles L. Black, Jr., has described it, his method was one of "inference from the structure and relationships created by the Constitution in all its parts," not one of elaborate interpretation or exegesis of a particular constitutional provision.[22]

After Marshall, Courts that attempted to preserve the federal elements in the Constitution without relying on dual federalism followed for the most part his example and reasoned from the total structure that the Constitution created. In *Coyle* v. *Smith* (1911), for example, the Court denied Congress the power to specify in Oklahoma's Enabling Act the location of the state's capital, arguing that congressional power was limited to admitting states into "a union of States, equal in power, dignity and authority, each competent to exert that residuum of sovereignty not delegated to the United States by the Constitution itself." To allow Congress selectively to impose conditions on some states would destroy the equality of status that the states enjoy as an inherent attribute of the federal union; more, it would mean that the powers of Congress, rather than being defined by the Constitution alone, in this instance could be enlarged or restricted by the conditions imposed upon new states by congressional legislation admitting them into the union. If such legislation were to be sanctioned, finally, new States might bargain away some of the powers reserved to them by the Constitution in an effort to gain admission into the Union.

The same emphasis on reasoning from the total structure of the Constitution is also apparent in *Younger* v. *Harris* (1971) and *Baldwin* v. *Montana Fish and Game Commission* (1978). In *Younger* the Court refused to enjoin a pending state criminal prosecution because of its commitment to what Justice Hugo Black called "Our Federalism." Stressing that the Court must be sensitive to the legitimate interests of both the states and the national government, Black declared that this sensitivity requires "a proper respect for state functions, a recognition of the fact that the entire country is made up of a Union of separate state governments, and a continuance of the belief that the National Government will fare best if the States and their institutions are left free to perform their separate functions in their separate ways." Later, the Court in *Baldwin* upheld a Montana law that mandated substantially higher hunting fees for nonresidents than for residents. Speaking for a six-member majority, Justice Harry Blackmun contended that this distinction between residents and nonresidents did not violate the Privileges and Immunities Clause of Article IV, Section 2:

> Some distinctions between residents and nonresidents merely reflect the fact that this is a Nation composed of individual States, and are permitted; other distinctions are prohibited because they hinder the formation, purpose, or development of a single Union of those States. Only with respect to those "privileges" and "immunities" bearing upon the vitality of the Nation as a single entity must the State treat all citizens, resident and nonresident, equally.

Blackmun rejected the contention of Justice William Brennan and other dissenters that the state must justify all distinctions, even those that neither trench upon the "basic rights" and "essential activities" of the citizenry nor "frustrate the purposes of the formation of the Union."[23]

Even when the entire court reasons from the structure and relationship created by the Constitution, there is no guarantee that all of the justices will reach the same conclusions, as *National League of Cities* v. *Usery* (1976) and *Garcia* v. *San Antonio Metropolitan Transit Authority* (1985) illustrate. In *National League of Cities,* the court invalidated a congressional attempt to apply minimum-wage and maximum-hours legislation to state governments and their political subdivisions because of the threat it posed to federalism. Justice Rehnquist argued for a five member majority that this congressional amendment to the Fair Labor Standards Act would "significantly alter or displace the States' abilities to structure employer-employee relationships in such areas as fire prevention, police protection, sanitation, public health, and parks and recreation." Yet those are the very functions and services that the state governments were created to provide, and "if Congress may withdraw from the States the authority to make those fundamental employment decisions upon which their systems for performance of these functions must rest, . . . there would be little left of the States' 'separate and independent existence.' " Rehnquist then noted that "the Constitution, in all its provisions, looks to an indestructible Union, composed of indestructible States." Reasoning from the total structure created by the Constitution, Justice Rehnquist concluded that Congress could no more use its commerce power to usurp the states' right to carry out their traditional functions than it could to deny the right to trial by jury contained in the Sixth Amendment or violate the Due Process Clause of the Fifth Amendment.

In his dissent, Justice William Brennan charged that Rehnquist in effect was embracing the discredited doctrine of dual federalism. He accused his fellow justice of finding in the Tenth Amendment an express limitation on the national government's delegated powers, and quoted approvingly from Justice Harlan Stone's opinion in *United States* v. *Darby Lumber* (1941): "The amendment states but a truism that all is retained which has not been surrendered. There is nothing in the history of its adoption to suggest that it was more than declaratory of the relationship between the national and state governments as it had been established by the Constitution before the amendment. . . ." Justice Brennan also insisted that since the "Congress is constituted of representatives in both Senate and House elected from the States, . . . decision upon the extent of federal intervention under the Commerce Clause into the affairs of the States are in that sense decisions of the States themselves."

In *Garcia,* in another 5-4 decision, the Supreme Court overruled *National League of Cities,* arguing that any attempt to draw the boundaries of state regulatory immunity in terms of "traditional governmental functions" is not only unworkable but is also inconsistent with the established principles of federalism on which *National League of Cities* purported to rest. Justice Blackmun declared for the Court majority that there is nothing in the overtime and minimum-wage requirements of the Fair Labor Standards Act that is destructive of state sovereignty or violative of any constitutional provision. In his dissent, Justice Powell excoriated the Court for its belief that "the role of the States in the federal system may depend upon the grace of elected federal officials, rather than on the Constitution as interpreted by this Court." Justice O'Connor also objected to the Court's refusal to fulfill its constitutional role of judicial review: "If federalism so conceived and so carefully cultivated by the Framers of our Constitution is to remain meaningful, this Court cannot abdicate its constitutional responsibility to oversee the Federal Government's compliance with its duty to respect the legitimate interests of the States."

THE POST-CIVIL WAR AMENDMENTS AND THE SHIFTING OF THE FEDERAL BALANCE

Thus far the discussion has been confined to the relationship between the national and state governments that originally was established by the Constitution, into which the Framers incorporated a balance of national and federal elements. Now we must consider the extent to which the mixed nature of the constitutional system has been altered by the Civil War amendments and the statutes flowing from them.

At a minimum, the Thirteenth, Fourteenth, and Fifteenth amendments were intended to safeguard the civil rights of the recently emancipated slaves. Although the protection of such civil rights previously had been among the broad mass of police powers reserved to the states, the last section of each of these amendments gave Congress the "power to enforce" them "by appropriate legislation." Pursuant to these grants of power, Congress passed the Civil Rights Acts of 1866 (which protected the right of blacks to make and enforce contracts and prohibited any person acting under color of state law from depriving any citizen of rights secured by the Constitution or federal law), 1870 (which protected voting rights), 1871 (which created a cause of civil action for deprivations, under color of state law, of secured rights), and 1875 (which secured for blacks the "full and equal enjoyment" of public accommodations). The pressures generated by the racial problems that these and subsequent civil rights acts were intended to address, together with the catalytic presence of the Civil War amendments themselves, have helped to break down the compound nature of the government and to give primacy to its national elements. However, the rate at which this process has taken place largely has been determined by Supreme Court decisions interpreting the 13th–15th amendments and the acts passed pursuant thereto.

Initially, the Court construed these constitutional and statutory provisions narrowly, in order to preserve the federal balance. In 1873, for example, it held in the *Slaughterhouse Cases*—found in Chapter 11—that the "privileges and immunities of citizens of the United States" protected from state abridgement by Section 1 of the Fourteenth Amendment were few in number and limited to such rights as access to the nation's seaports and the privilege of habeas corpus writs. That left the vast majority of legal rights and relations under the protection of the state governments. In reaching this decision, the Court majority pronounced itself reluctant to "fetter and degrade the State governments by subjecting them to the control of Congress, in the exercise of powers heretofore universally conceded to them of the most ordinary and fundamental character" and to change "the whole theory of the relations of the State and Federal governments to each other and of both these governments to the people . . . in the absence of language which expresses such a purpose too clearly to admit doubt." A similarly narrow view prevailed in the *Civil Rights Cases* (1883), in which the Court held that the public-accommodations provisions of the Civil Rights Act of 1875 were unconstitutional. Noting that the Fourteenth Amendment reads "no *state* shall . . .," it declared that the amendment prohibited only state actions of certain types, not "individual invasion of individual rights." Legislation that attempted to prohibit such purely private discrimination, therefore, was beyond the constitutional powers of Congress to enact.

The state-action doctrine promulgated in the *Civil Rights Cases* (see Chapter 15 for a detailed discussion), while providing an important means of preserving the federal balance, has not precluded the national government from intervening when the states themselves have violated constitutionally protected rights. To take perhaps the most famous example, the doctrine did not prevent the Supreme Court from declaring in *Brown* v. *Board of Education* (1954) that the defendant states were guilty of violating the Equal Protection Clause of the Fourteenth Amendment by requiring that schools be racially segregated. Nor has the theory of state action prevented federal prosecution of state officials and others who, while acting under color of state law, have deprived citizens of their constitutionally protected rights. Nonetheless, the state-action doctrine historically has sharply limited the ability of the national government to enter the domain of the states' police power and, to that extent, has helped to preserve the compound quality of the Constitution.

Increasingly, however, the doctrine is being effectively sidestepped by those who seek to expand the power of the national government to protect the civil rights of the citzenry. Of decisive importance in this respect is *Jones* v. *Alfred H. Mayer Company* (1968), in which the Court held that the national government has the power to regulate purely private property transactions where racial discrimination is present. In his majority opinion, Justice Potter Stewart exhumed the Civil Rights Act of 1866 and held that it "bars all racial discrimination, private as well as public, in the sale or rental of property, and that the statute, thus construed, is a valid exercise of the power of Congress to enforce the Thirteenth Amendment." Making many of the same arguments found in the first Justice Harlan's dissent in the *Civil Rights Cases,* Stewart insisted that the Thirteenth Amendment authorized Congress not only to dissolve the legal bonds by which slaves had been held to their masters, but also to determine rationally what the badges and the incidents of slavery are and to translate that determination into effective legislation.

Jones was followed by *Griffin* v. *Breckenridge* (1971) and *Runyon* v. *McCrary* (1976), in both of which the Court avoided the state-action doctrine and relied upon the Thirteenth Amendment to justify congressional bars to wholly private discrimination. In *Griffin* a unanimous Court, reversing its decision in *Collins* v. *Handyman* (1951), held that those sections of the Civil Rights Acts of 1866 and 1871 that granted civil remedies against racially motivated conspiracies to deprive individuals of their civil rights were applicable even to wholly private conspiracies. Speaking for the Court, Justice Stewart concluded that "Congress was wholly within its power under Section 2 of the Thirteenth Amendment in creating a statutory cause of action for Negro citizens who have been the victims of conspiratorial, racially discriminatory private action aimed at depriving them of the basic rights that the law secures to all free men." Employing the same arguments, Stewart held in *Runyon* that the section of the Civil Rights Act of 1866 that forbids discrimination in the making and enforcing of contracts prohibits private schools from excluding qualified students solely on the basis of race. In this particular case, blacks had been denied the opportunity to enter into a contract for the provision of educational services in return for the payment of tuition. This, in Justice Stewart's estimation, constituted a "class violation" of the law in question.[24]

In seeking to rectify glaring injustices, the decisions reached in these cases contributed to a shifting of the federal balance. The shift has been so pronounced that the Court seriously entertained overturning *Runyon* in its 1989 case of *Patterson* v. *McLean Credit Union*; it ultimately declined to do so and left the federal government free to continue to reach wholly private discriminatory conduct. *Patterson* and the Court's earlier decisions raise questions concerning the continued existence of our compound government—as do other Supreme Court decisions, including those incorporating the Bill of Rights into the Fourteenth Amendment (see Chapter 14) and those holding that national law preempts state law if considerations of national policy so warrant and if these considerations are consistent with either enumerated powers or broader national security interests.[25] Although undeniably beneficial in some respects, these decisions unfortunately have jeopardized the federal structure—one of the principal means by which the ends of the Constitution are to be achieved. Remarking on this cruel irony, Justice Harlan wrote, "We are accustomed to speak of the Bill of Rights and the Fourteenth Amendment as the principal guarantees of personal liberty. Yet it would surely be shallow not to recognize that the structure of our political system accounts no less for the free society we have." The Framers, in Justice Harlan's views "staked their faith that liberty would prosper in the new nation not primarily upon declaration of individual rights but upon the kind of government the Union was to have."[26] The problem that federalism has posed for the justices has been to ensure that the Court, itself a means to the ends of the Constitution, does not render decisions that jeopardize another means to those same ends.

NOTES

1 See Martin Diamond, "*The Federalist* on Federalism: 'Neither a National nor a Federal Constitution, But a Composition of Both,' " *Yale Law Journal* 86, no. 6 (May 1977): 1273–1285.
2 *The Federalist,* No. 39.
3 James Madison, "Outline," in *The Writings of James Madison,* ed. Gaillard Hunt, 9 vols. (New York: G. P. Putnam's Sons, 1910), 9:351.
4 The discussion that follows relies heavily on Martin Diamond, "What the Framers Meant by Federalism," in *A Nation of States,* 2d ed., Robert A. Goldwin, ed. (Chicago: Rand McNally, 1974), pp. 25–42.
5 See Martin Diamond, "The Ends of Federalism," *Publius,* 3, no. 2 (Fall 1973):131–132.
6 Herbert J. Storing, "Foreword," in Paul Eidelberg, *The Philosophy of the American Constitution* (New York: Free Press, 1968).
7 See *The Federalist,* Nos. 15, 16, and 22.
8 Max Farrand, ed., *The Records of the Federal Convention of 1787,* 4 vols. (New Haven, Conn.: Yale University Press, 1937), 1:33. Emphasis in the original.
9 *Ibid.,* 1:134–136.
10 *The Federalist,* No. 10.
11 Farrand, *Records,* 1:461.
12 See *Ibid,* 1:339, 405–406.
13 *Ibid,* 1:488.
14 Alexis de Tocqueville, *Democracy in America,* ed. Phillips Bradley, 2 vols. (New York: Random House, 1945), 1:165.
15 It should be noted that the Supreme Court's interest in federalism is limited almost exclusively to the balance between state power and the enumerated powers of the central government; the justices have not concerned themselves with the presence of federal elements in the design and the politics of the national government itself. This situation is understandable, as the former issue is far more amenable than the latter to legal disputation and judicial determination. Nevertheless, it should be recognized that the Court's treatment of federalism is not necessarily definitive or exhaustive, and that in this matter, as in others, the Constitution is not merely what the Supreme Court has said it is.
16 Farrand, *Records,* 1:284–285.
17 See also Justice Joseph Story's opinion in *Martin* v. *Hunter's Lessee* (1816), in which the Court had established federal judicial supremacy in strictly civil matters.
18 C. Herman Pritchett, *The American Constitution,* 3d ed. (New York: McGraw-Hill, 1977), pp. 50–51.
19 See *United States* v. *Darby Lumber Company* (1941).
20 See C. Herman Pritchett, *The American Constitutional System,* 4th ed. (New York: McGraw-Hill, 1976), pp. 25–27.
21 The defenders of economic due process suffered a similar fate. See Robert G. McCloskey, "Economic Due Process: An Exhumation and Reburial," 1962 *Supreme Court Review:* 42–43.
22 Charles L. Black, Jr., *Structure and Relationship in Constitutional Law* (Baton Rouge, La.: Louisiana State University Press, 1969), p. 7.
23 See *United Building and Construction Trades Council of Camden County* v.

Mayor and Council of the City of Camden (1984) where the Court employed *Baldwin* v. *Montana Fish and Game Commission* to hold that a city ordinance requiring that at least 40 percent of employees of contractors and subcontractors working on city construction projects be city residents was properly subject to the strictures of the privileges and immunities clause.

24 See also *Memphis* v. *Greene* (1981). In this case, black residents sued Memphis, Tennessee, because it had closed a street at the border between a white and a black neighborhood. The Supreme Court sustained the street closing, with Justice Stevens arguing for the majority that the City's interest in safety and tranquility was sufficient to "justify an adverse impact on motorists who are somewhat inconvenienced by the street closing. That inconvenience cannot be equated to an actual restraint on the liberty of black citizens that is in any sense comparable to the odious practice the Thirteenth Amendment was designed to eradicate."

25 See *Pennsylvania* v. *Nelson* (1956).

26 John M. Harlan, "The Bill of Rights and the Constitution," address at the dedication of the Bill of Rights Room, U.S. Subtreasury Building, New York City, Aug. 9, 1964.

SELECTED READINGS

The Federalist, Nos. 15, 16, 17, 18, 21, 22, 39.

Martin v. *Hunter's Lessee,* 1 Wheat. 304 (1816).
Moore v. *Sims,* 442 U.S. 415 (1979).
United States v. *Guest,* 383 U.S. 745 (1966).
Runyon v. *McCrary,* 427 U.S. 160 (1976).

Black, Charles L., Jr. *Structure and Relationship in Constitutional Law* (Baton Rouge: Louisiana State University Press, 1969).

Choper, Jesse H. "The Scope of National Power vis-à-vis the States: The Dispensability of Judicial Review." *Yale Law Journal* 86 (July 1977).

Cohen, William. "Congressional Power to Interpret Due Process and Equal Protection." *Stanford Law Review* 27 (February 1975).

Corwin, Edward S. "The Passing of Dual Federalism," *Virginia Law Review* 36 (February 1950).

Diamond, Martin. "The Ends of Federalism." *Publius* 3, no. 2 (Fall 1973).

________."*The Federalist* on Federalism." *Yale Law Journal* 86 (May 1977).

Goldwin, Robert A., ed. *A Nation of States.* 2d ed. (Chicago: Rand McNally, 1974).

Grodzins, Morton. *The American System: A New View of Government in the United States* (Chicago: Rand McNally, 1966).

McClellan, James. "Fiddling with the Constitution While *Rome* Burns: The Case Against the Voting Rights Act, 1965." *Louisiana Law Review* 42 (1981): 5–77.

Nagel, Robert F. "Federalism as a Fundamental Value: *National League of Cities* in Perspective." 1981 *Supreme Court Review.*

Riker, William H. "Federalism." *Handbook of Political Science.* Vol. 5. Edited by Fred I. Greenstein and Nelson Polsby (Reading, Mass.: Addison-Wesley, 1975).

Vile, M. J. C. *The Structure of American Federalism* (London: Oxford University Press, 1961).

Wechsler, Herbert. "The Political Safeguards of Federalism: The Role of the States in the Composition and Selection of the National Government." *Federalism: Mature and Emergent.* Edited by Arthur W. Macmahon (Garden City, N.Y.: Doubleday, 1955).

Zuckert, Michael P. "Federalism and the Founding: Toward a Reinterpretation of the Constitutional Convention," *The Review of Politics* 41 (Spring 1986): 166–210.

Cohens v. *Virginia*

19 U.S. (6 Wheaton) 264; 5 L. Ed. 257 (1821)

In 1802, Congress passed an act authorizing the District of Columbia to conduct lotteries to finance "any important improvements in the City, which the ordinary funds or revenue thereof will not accomplish." Pursuant to this act, the City of Washington passed an ordinance creating a lottery. The state of Virginia had a law that prohibited the sale of lottery tickets except for lotteries authorized by that state. P. J. and M. J. Cohen were arrested for selling the Washington lottery tickets at their office in Norfolk, Virginia. After the Cohens were found guilty in borough court and fined $100, the case went to the United States Supreme Court on a writ of error, and the justices unanimously upheld the Cohens' conviction on the grounds that Congress did not authorize the District of Columbia to "force the sale of these lottery tickets in States where such sales may be prohibited by law." *Cohens* v. *Virginia* is important not because of this holding, however, but because of Chief Justice John Marshall's powerful argument that the Supreme Court has the authority to review the judgments of state courts. The portion of the opinion that is presented below pertains solely to that argument. *Opinion of the Court: Marshall, Duvall, Johnson, Livingston, Story, Todd. Washington did not participate.*

MR. CHIEF JUSTICE MARSHALL delivered the opinion of the Court. . . .

The questions presented to the Court . . . are of great magnitude, and may be truly said vitally to affect the Union. They exclude the inquiry whether the constitution and laws of the United States have been violated by the judgment which the plaintiffs in error seek to review; and maintain that, admitting such violation, it is not in the power of the government to apply a corrective. They maintain that the nation does not possess a department capable of restraining peaceably, and by authority of law, any attempts which may be made, by a part, against the legitimate powers of the whole; and that the government is reduced to the alternative of submitting to such attempts, or of resisting them by force. They maintain that the constitution of the United States has provided no tribunal for the final construction of itself, or of the laws or treaties of the nation; but that this power may be exercised in the last resort by the Courts of every State in the Union. . . .

If such be the constitution, it is the duty of the Court to bow with respectful submission to its provisions. If such be not the constitution, it is equally the duty of this Court to say so; and to perform that task which the American people have assigned to the judicial department.

1st. The first question to be considered is, whether the jurisdiction of this Court is excluded by the character of the parties, one of them being a State, and the other a citizen of that State?

The second section of the third article of the constitution defines the extent of the judicial power of the United States. Jurisdiction is given to the Courts of the Union in two classes of cases. In the first, their jurisdiction depends on the character of the cause, whoever may be the parties. This class comprehends "all cases in law and equity arising under this constitution, the laws of the United States, and treaties made, or which shall be made, under their authority." This clause extends the jurisdiction of the Court to all the cases described, without making in its terms any exception whatever, and without any regard to the condition of the party. If there be any exception, it is to be implied against the express words of the article.

In the second class, the jurisdiction depends entirely on the character of the parties. In this are comprehended "controversies between two or more States, between a State and citizens of another State," "and between a State and foreign States, citizens or subjects." If these be the parties, it is entirely unimportant what may be the subject of controversy. Be it what it may, these parties have a constitutional right to come into the Court of the Union. . . .

The jurisdiction of the Court, then, being extended by the letter of the constitution to all cases arising under it, or under the laws of the United States, it follows that those who would withdraw any case of this description from that jurisdiction, must sustain the exemption they claim on the spirit and true meaning of the constitution, which spirit and true meaning must be so apparent as to overrule the words which its framers have employed.

The counsel for the defendant in error have undertaken to do this; and have laid down the general proposition, that a sovereign independent State is not suable, except by its own consent.

This general proposition will not be controverted. But its consent is not requisite in each particular case. It may be given in a general law. And if a State has surrendered any portion of its sovereignty, the question whether a liability to suit be a part of this portion, depends on the instrument by which the surrender is made. If, upon a just construction of that instrument, it shall appear that the State has submitted to be sued, then it has parted with this sovereign right of judging in every case on the justice of its own pretensions, and has entrusted that power to a tribunal in whose impartiality it confides.

The American States, as well as the American people, have believed a close and firm Union to be essential to their liberty and to their happiness. They have been taught by experience, that this Union cannot exist without a government for the whole; and they have been taught by the same experience that this government would be a mere shadow, that must disappoint all their hopes, unless invested with large portions of that sovereignty which belongs to independent States. Under the influence of this opinion, and thus instructed by experience, the American people, in the conventions of their respective States, adopted the present constitution.

If it could be doubted, whether from its nature, it were not supreme in all cases where it is empowered to act, that doubt would be removed by the declaration, that "this constitution, and the laws of the United States, which shall be made in pursuance thereof, and all treaties made, or which shall be made, under the authority of the United States, shall be the supreme law of the land; and the judges in every State shall be bound thereby; any thing in the constitution or laws of any State to the contrary notwithstanding."

This is the authoritative language of the American people; and, if gentlemen please, of the American States. It marks, with lines too strong to be mistaken, the characteristic distinction between the government of the Union, and those of the States. The general government, though limited as to its objects, is supreme with respect to those objects. This principle is a part of the constitution; and if there be any who deny its necessity, none can deny its authority.

To this supreme government ample powers are confided; and if it were possible to doubt the great purposes for which they were so confided, the people of the United States have declared, that they are given "in order to form a more perfect union, establish justice, ensure domestic tranquillity, provide for the common defence, promote the general welfare, and secure the blessings of liberty to themselves and their posterity."

With the ample powers confided to this supreme government, for these interesting purposes, are connected many express and important limitations on the sovereignty of the States, which are made for the same purposes. The powers of the Union, on the great subjects of war, peace, and commerce, and on many others, are in themselves limitations of the sovereignty of the States; but in addition to these, the sovereignty of the States is surrendered in many instances where the surrender can only operate to the benefit of the people and where, perhaps, no other power is conferred on Congress than a conservative power to maintain the principles established in the constitution. The maintenance of these principles in their purity, is certainly among the great duties of the government. One of the instruments by which this duty may be peaceably performed, is the judicial department. It is authorized to decide all cases of every description, arising under the constitution or laws of the United States. From this general grant of jurisdiction, no exception is made of those cases in which a State may be a party. When we consider the situation of the government of the Union and of a State, in relation to each other; the nature of our constitution; the subordination of the State governments to that constitution; the great purpose for which jurisdiction over all cases arising under the constitution and laws of the United States, is confided to the judicial department; are we at liberty to insert in this general grant, an exception of those cases in which a State may be a party? Will the spirit of the constitution justify this attempt to control its words? We think it will not. We think a case arising under the constitution or laws of the United States, is cognizable in the Courts of the Union, whoever may be the parties to that case. . . .

The mischievous consequences of the construction contended for on the part of Virginia, are also entitled to great consideration. It would prostrate, it has been said, the government and its laws at the feet of every State in the Union. And would not this be its effect? What power of the government could be executed by its own means, in any State disposed to resist its execution by a course of legislation? The laws must be executed by individuals acting within the several States. If these individuals may be exposed to penalties, and if the Courts of the Union cannot correct the judgments by which these penalties may be enforced, the course of the government may be, at any time, arrested by the will of one of its members. Each member will possess a *veto* on the will of the whole.

The answer which has been given to this argument, does not deny its truth, but insists that confidence is reposed, and may be safely reposed, in the State institutions; and that, if they shall ever become so insane or so wicked as to seek the destruction of the government, they many accomplish their object by refusing to perform the functions assigned to them.

. . . A constitution is framed for ages to come, and is designed to approach immortality as nearly as human institutions can approach it. Its course cannot always be tranquil. It is exposed to storms and tempests, and its framers must be unwise statesmen indeed, if they have not provided it, as far as its nature will permit, with the means of self-preservation from the perils it may be destined to encounter. No government ought to be so defective in its organization, as not to contain within itself the means of securing the execution of its own laws against other dangers than those which occur every day. Courts of justice are the means most usually employed; and it is reasonable to expect that a government should repose on its own Courts, rather than on others. There is certainly nothing in the circumstances under which our constitution was formed; nothing in the history of the times, which would justify the opinion that the confidence reposed in the States was so implicit as to leave in them and their tribunals the power of resisting or defeating in the form of law, the legitimate measures of the Union. . . .

It has been also urged, as an additional objection to the jurisdiction of the Court, that cases between a State and one of its own citizens, do not come within the general scope of the constitution; and were obviously never intended to be made cognizable in the federal Courts. . . .

If jurisdiction depended entirely on the character of the parties, and was not given where the parties have not an original right to come into Court, that part of the 2d section of the 3d article, which extends the judicial power to all cases arising under the constitution and laws of the United States, would be mere surplusage. It is to give jurisdiction where the character of the parties would not give it, that this very important part of the clause was inserted. It may be true, that the partiality of the State tribunals, in ordinary controversies between a State and its citizens, was not apprehended, and therefore the judicial power of the Union was not extended to such cases; but this was not the sole nor the greatest object for which this department was created. A more important, a much more interesting object, was the preservation of the constitution and laws of the United States, so far as they can be preserved by judicial authority; and therefore the jurisdiction of the Courts of the Union was expressly extended to all cases arising under that constitution and those laws. If the constitution or laws may be violated by proceedings instituted by a State against its own citizens, and if that violation may be such as essentially to affect the constitution and the laws, such as to arrest the progress of government in its constitutional course, why should these cases be excepted from that provision which expressly extends the judicial power of the Union to *all* cases arising under the constitution and laws? . . .

It is most true that this Court will not take jurisdiction if it should not: but it is equally true, that it must take jurisdiction if it should. The judiciary cannot, as the legislature may, avoid a measure because it approaches the confines of the constitution. We cannot pass it by because it is doubtful. With whatever doubts, with whatever difficulties, a case may be attended, we must decide it, if it be brought before us. We have no more right to decline the exercise of jurisdiction which is given, than to usurp that which is not given. The one or the other would be treason to the constitution. Questions may occur which we would gladly avoid; but we cannot avoid them. All we can do is, to exercise our best judgment, and conscientiously to perform our duty. In doing this, on the present occasion, we find this tribunal invested with appellate jurisdiction in *all* cases arising under the constitution and laws of the United States. We find no exception to this grant, and we cannot insert one. . . .

2d. The second objection to the jurisdiction of the Court is, that its appellate power cannot be exercised, in any case, over the judgment of a State Court.

This objection is sustained chiefly by arguments drawn from the supposed total separation of the judiciary of a state from that of the Union, and their entire independence of each other. The argument considers the federal judiciary as completely foreign to that of a State; and as being no more connected with it in any respect whatever, than the Court of a foreign State. If this hypothesis be just, the argument founded on it is equally so; but if the hypothesis be not supported by the constitution, the argument fails with it.

This hypothesis is not founded on any words in the constitution, which might seem to countenance it, but on the unreasonableness of giving a contrary construction to words which seem to require it; and on the incompatibility of the application of the appellate jurisdiction to the judgments of State Courts, with that constitutional relation which subsists between the government of the Union and the governments of those States which compose it.

Let this unreasonableness, this total incompatibility, be examined.

That the United States form, for many, and for most important purposes, a single nation, has not yet been denied. In war, we are one people. In making peace, we are one people. In all commercial regulations, we are one and the same people. In many other respects, the American people are one; and the government which is alone capable of controling and managing their interests in all these respects, is the government of the Union. It is their government, and in that character they have no other. America has chosen to be, in many respects, and to many purposes, a nation, and for all these purposes, her government is complete; to all these objects, it is competent. The people have declared, that in the exercise of all powers given for these objects, it is supreme. It can, then, in effecting these objects, legitimately control all individuals or governments within the American territory. The constitution and laws of a State, so far as they are repugnant to the constitution and laws of the United States, are absolutely void. These States are constituent parts of the United States. They are members of one great empire—for some purposes sovereign, for some purposes subordinate.

In a government so constituted, is it unreasonable that the judicial power should be competent to give efficacy to the constitutional laws of the legislature? That department can decide on the validity of the constitution or law of a State, if it be repugnant to the constitution or to a law of the United States. Is it unreasonable that it should also be empowered to decide on the judgment of a State tribunal enforcing such unconstitutional law? Is it so very unreasonable as to furnish a justification for controling the words of the constitution?

We think it is not. We think in a government acknowledgedly supreme, with respect to objects of vital interest to the nation, there is nothing inconsistent with sound reason, nothing incompatible with the nature of government, in making all its departments supreme, so far as respects those objects, and so far as is necessary to their attainment. The exercise of the appellate power over those judgments of the State tribunals which may contravene the constitution or laws of the United States, is, we believe, essential to the attainment of those objects.

The propriety of entrusting the construction of the constitution, and laws made in pursuance thereof, to the judiciary of the Union, has not, we believe, as yet, been drawn into question. It seems to be a corollary from this political axiom, that the federal Courts should either possess exclusive jurisdiction in such cases, or a power to revise the judgment rendered in them, by the State tribunals. If the federal and State Courts have concurrent jurisdiction in all cases arising under the constitution, laws, and treaties of the United States; and if a case of this description brought in a State Court cannot be removed before judgment, nor revised after judgment, then the construction of the constitution, laws, and treaties of the United States, is not confided particularly to their judicial department, but is confided equally to that department and to the State Courts, however they may be constituted. "Thirteen independent Courts," says a very celebrated statesman (and we have now more than twenty such Courts,) "of final jurisdiction over the same causes, arising upon the same laws, is a hydra in government, from which nothing but contradiction and confusion can proceed."

Dismissing the unpleasant suggestion, that any motives which may not be fairly avowed, or which ought not to exist, can ever influence a State or its Courts, the necessity of uniformity, as well as correctness in expounding the constitution and laws of the United States, would itself suggest the propriety of vesting in some single tribunal the power of deciding; in the last resort, all cases in which they are involved.

We are not restrained, then, by the political relations between the general and State governments, from construing the words of the constitution, defining the judicial power, in their true sense. We are not bound to construe them more restrictively than they naturally import.

They give to the Supreme Court appellate jurisdiction in all cases arising under the constitution, laws, and treaties of the United States. The words are broad enough to comprehend all cases of this description, in whatever Court they may be decided. In expounding them, we may be permitted to take into view those considerations to which Courts have always allowed great weight in the exposition of laws.

Younger v. *Harris*

401 U.S. 37; 91 S. Ct. 746; 27 L. Ed. 2d 669 (1971)

John Harris, a socialist, was indicted in California state court for violating California's Criminal Syndicalism Act, which prohibited "advocating, teaching or aiding and abetting the commission of crime, sabotage, . . . or unlawful acts of force and violence or unlawful methods of terrorism as a means of accomplishing a change in industrial ownership or control, or effecting any political change." After upholding the California statute in *Whitney* v. *California* (1927), the Supreme Court had subsequently overruled *Whitney* in *Brandenburg* v. *Ohio* (1969). Harris, alleging that the very existence of the statute had a "chilling effect" on his First Amendment rights, filed suit in federal district court seeking to enjoin Los Angeles County District Attorney Evelle Younger from prosecuting him under its provisions. A three-judge panel held the act void because of vagueness and overbreadth and enjoined Harris' prosecution. The state thereupon appealed to the Supreme Court. *Opinion of the Court: Black, Blackmun, Burger, Harlan, Stewart. Concurring opinion: Stewart, Harlan. Concurring in the result: Brennan, Marshall, White. Dissenting opinion: Douglas.*

MR. JUSTICE BLACK delivered the opinion of the Court. . . .

A federal lawsuit to stop a prosecution in a state court is a serious matter.

Since the beginning of this country's history Congress has, subject to few exceptions, manifested a desire to permit state courts to try state cases free from interference by federal courts. . . .

The precise reasons for this longstanding public policy against federal court interference with state court proceedings have never been specifically identified but the primary sources of the policy are plain. One is the basic doctrine of equity jurisprudence that courts of equity should not act, and particularly should not act to restrain a criminal prosecution, when the moving party has an adequate remedy at law and will not suffer irreparable injury if denied equitable relief. The doctrine . . . is . . . important under our Constitution, in order to prevent erosion of the role of the jury and avoid a duplication of legal proceedings and legal sanctions where a single suit would be adequate to protect the rights asserted. This underlying reason for restraining courts of equity from interfering with criminal prosecutions is reinforced by an even more vital consideration, the notion of "comity," that is, a proper respect for state functions, a recognition of the fact that the entire country is made up of a Union of separate state governments, and a continuance of the belief that the National Government will fare best if the States and their institutions are left free to perform their separate functions in their separate ways. This, perhaps for lack of a better and clearer way to describe it, is referred to by many as "Our Federalism," and one familiar with the profound debates that ushered our Federal Constitution into existence is bound to respect those who remain loyal to the ideals and dreams of "Our Federalism." The concept does not mean blind deference to "States' Rights" any more than it means centralization of control over every important issue in our National Government and its courts. The Framers rejected both these courses. What the concept does represent is a system in which there is sensitivity to the legitimate interests of both State and National Governments, and in which the National Government, anxious though it may be to vindicate and protect federal rights and federal interests, always endeavors to do so in ways that will not unduly interfere with the legitimate activities of the States. It should never be forgotten that this slogan, "Our Federalism," born in the early struggling days of our Union of States, occupies a highly important place in our Nation's history and its future. . . .

This is where the law stood when the Court decided *Dombrowski* v. *Pfister*. . . . (1965), and held that an injunction against the enforcement of certain state criminal statutes could properly issue under the circumstances presented in that case. In *Dombrowski*, unlike many of the earlier cases denying injunctions, the complaint made substantial allegations that: "the threats to enforce the statutes against appellants are not made with any expectation of securing valid convictions, but rather are part of a plan to employ arrests, seizures, and threats of prosecution under color of the statutes to harass appellants and discourage them and their supporters from asserting and attempting to vindicate the constitutional rights of Negro citizens of Louisiana." . . .

. . . These circumstances, as viewed by the Court sufficiently establish the kind of irreparable injury, above and beyond that associated with the defense of a single prosecution brought in good faith, that had always been considered sufficient to justify federal intervention.

The District Court, however, thought that the *Dombrowski* decision substantially broadened the availability of injunctions against state criminal prosecutions and that under that decision the federal courts may give equitable relief, without regard to any showing of bad faith or harassment, whenever a state statute is found "on its face" to be vague or overly broad, in violation of the First Amendment. We recognize that there are some statements in the *Dombrowski* opinion that would seem to support this argument. But, as we have already seen, such statements were unnecessary to the decision of that case, because the Court found that the plaintiffs had alleged a basis for equitable relief under the long-established standards. In addition, we do not regard the reasons adduced to support this position as sufficient to justify such a substantial departure from the established doctrines regarding the availability of injunctive relief. It is undoubtedly true, as the Court stated in *Dombrowski* that "[a] criminal prosecution under a statute regulating expression usually involves imponderables and contingencies that themselves may inhibit the full exercise of First Amendment Freedoms." But this sort of "chilling effect," as the Court called it, should not itself justify federal intervention. . . .

Beyond all this is another, more basic consideration. Procedures for testing the constitutionality of a statute "on its face" in the manner apparently contemplated by *Dombrowski*, and for then enjoining all action to enforce the statute until the State can obtain court approval for a modified version, are fundamentally at odds with the function of the federal courts in our constitutional plan. The power and duty of the judiciary to declare laws unconstitutional is in the final analysis derived from its responsibility for resolving concrete disputes brought before the courts for decision; a statute apparently governing a dispute cannot be applied by judges, consistently with their obligations under the Supremacy Clause, when such an application of the statute would conflict with the Constitution. . . . But this vital responsibility, broad as it is, does not amount to an unlimited power to survey the statute books and pass judgment on laws before the courts are called upon to enforce them. Ever since the Constitutional Convention rejected a proposal for having members of the Supreme Court render advice concerning pending legislation it has been clear that, even when suits of this kind involve a "case or controversy" sufficient to satisfy the requirements of Article III of the Constitution, the task of analyzing a proposed statute, pinpointing its deficiencies, and requiring correction of these deficiencies before the statute is put into effect, is rarely if ever an appropriate task for the judiciary. . . . In light of this fundamental conception of the Framers as to the proper place of the federal courts in the governmental processes of passing and enforcing laws, it can seldom be appropriate for these courts to exercise any such power of prior approval or veto over the legislative process.

For these reasons, fundamental not only to our federal system but also to the basic functions of the Judicial Branch of the National Government under our Constitution, we hold that the *Dombrowski* decision should not be regarded as having upset the settled doctrines that have always confined very narrowly the availability of injunctive relief against state criminal prosecutions. We do not think that opinion stands for the proposition that a federal court can properly enjoin enforcement of a statute solely on the basis of a showing that the statute "on its face" abridges First Amendment rights. . . .

The judgment of the District Court is reversed, and the case is remanded for further proceedings not inconsistent with this opinion.

Reversed.

Baldwin v. *Montana Fish and Game Commission*

436 U. S. 371; 98 S. Ct. 1852; 56 L. Ed. 2d 354 (1978)

Under Montana's elk-hunting license system, nonresidents were charged substantially higher fees than residents and were required to purchase a combination hunting and fishing license in order to be able to hunt elk. In 1976, for example, a Montana resident could purchase a license solely for elk for $9, whereas a nonresident had to pay $225 for a combination license. Lester Baldwin, a Montana hunting guide, and four nonresident elk-hunters brought suit in federal court seeking declaratory and injunctive relief and reimbursement of fees already paid. They contended that Montana's elk-hunting licensing scheme violated the Privileges and Immunities Clause of Article IV, Section 2. A divided three-judge district court denied all relief to the appellants, who appealed to the Supreme Court. *Opinion of the Court: Blackmun, Burger, Powell, Rehnquist, Stevens, Stewart. Concurring opinion: Burger. Dissenting opinion: Brennan, Marshall, White.*

MR. JUSTICE BLACKMUN delivered the opinion of the Court.

. . . Appellants strongly urge here that the Montana licensing scheme for the hunting of elk violates the Privileges and Immunities Clause of Art. IV, § 2, of our Constitution. That Clause is not one the contours of which have been precisely shaped by the process and wear of constant litigation and judicial interpretation over the years since 1789. . . . We are, nevertheless, not without some pronouncements by this Court as to the Clause's significance and reach. . . .

When the Privileges and Immunities Clause has been applied to specific cases, it has been interpreted to prevent a State from imposing unreasonable burdens on citizens of other States in their pursuit of common callings within the State, . . . in the ownership and disposition of privately held property within the State, . . . and in access to the courts of the State. . . .

It has not been suggested, however, that state citizenship or residency may never be used by a State to distinguish among persons. Suffrage, for example, always has been understood to be tied to an individual's identification with a particular State. . . . No one would suggest that the Privileges and Immunities Clause requires a State to open its polls to a person who declines to assert that the State is the only one where he claims a right to vote. The same is true as to qualification for an elective office of the State. . . . Nor must a State always apply all its laws or all its services equally to anyone, resident or nonresident, who may request it so to do. . . . Some distinctions between residents and nonresidents merely reflect the fact that this is a Nation composed of individual States, and are permitted; other distinctions are prohibited because they hinder the formation, the purpose, or the development of a single Union of those States. Only with respect to those "privileges" and "immunities" bearing upon the vitality of the Nation as a single entity must the State treat all citizens, resident and nonresident, equally. Here we must decide into which category falls a distinction with respect to access to recreational big-game hunting.

Many of the early cases embrace the concept that the States had complete ownership over wildlife within their boundaries, and, as well, the power to preserve this bounty for their citizens alone. It was enough to say "that in regulating the use of the common property of the citizens of [a] state, the legislature is [not] bound to extend to the citizens of all the other states the same advantages as are secured to their own citizens." *Corfield* v. *Coryell*, . . . (1825). It appears to have been generally accepted that although the States were obligated to treat all those within their territory equally in most respects, they were not obliged to share those things they held in trust for their own people. In *Corfield*, . . . Mr. Justice Washington, sitting as Circuit Justice, although recognizing that the States may not interfere with the "right of a citizen of one state to pass through, or to reside in any other state, for purposes of trade, agriculture, professional pursuits, or otherwise; to claim the benefit of the writ of habeas corpus; to institute and maintain actions of any kind in the courts of the state; to take, hold and dispose of property, either real or personal," . . . nonetheless concluded that access to oyster beds determined to be owned by New Jersey could be limited to New Jersey residents. This holding, and the conception of state sovereignty upon which it relied, formed the basis for similar decisions during later years of the 19th century. . . .

In more recent years, however, the Court has recognized that the States' interest in regulating and controlling those things they claim to "own," including wildlife, is by no means absolute. States may not compel the confinement of the benefits of their resources, even their wildlife, to their own people whenever such hoarding and confinement impedes interstate commerce. . . . And a State's interest in its wildlife and other resources must yield when, without reason, it interferes with a nonresident's right to pursue a livelihood in a State other than his own, a right that is protected by the Privileges and Immunities Clause. . . .

Appellants contend that the doctrine on which *Corfield*, . . . relied has no remaining vitality. We do not agree. . . . The fact that the State's control over wildlife is not exclusive and absolute in the face of federal regulation and certain federally protected interests does not compel the conclusion that it is meaningless in their absence. . . .

Appellants have demonstrated nothing to convince us that we should completely reject the Court's earlier decisions. In his opinion in *Coryell*, Mr. Justice Washington, although he seemingly relied on notions of "natural rights" when he considered the reach of the Privileges and Immunities Clause, included in his list of situations, in which he believed the States would be obligated to treat each other's residents equally, only those where a nonresident sought to engage in an essential activity or exercise a basic right. He himself used the term "fundamental," . . . in the modern as well as the "natural right" sense. . . . With respect to such basic and essential activities, interference with which would frustrate the purposes of the formation of the Union, the States must treat residents and nonresidents without unnecessary distinctions.

Does the distinction made by Montana between residents and nonresidents in establishing access to elk hunting threaten a basic right in a way that offends the Privileges and Immunities Clause? Merely to ask the question seems to provide the answer. . . . Elk hunting by nonresidents in Montana is a recreation and a sport. In itself—wholly apart from license fees—it is costly and obviously available only to the wealthy nonresident or to the one so taken with the sport that he sacrifices other values in order to indulge in it and to enjoy what it offers. It is not a means to the nonresident's livelihood. The mastery of the animal and the trophy are the ends that are sought; appellants are not totally excluded from these. The elk supply, which has been entrusted to the care of the State by the people of Montana, is finite and must be carefully tended in order to be preserved.

Appellants' interest in sharing this limited resource on more equal terms with Montana residents simply does not fall within the purview of the Privileges and Immunities Clause. Equality in access to Montana elk is not basic to the maintenance or well-being of the Union. . . . We do not decide the full range of activities that are sufficiently basic to the livelihood of the Nation that the States may not interfere with a nonresident's participation therein without similarly interfering with a resident's participation. Whatever rights or activities may be "fundamental" under the Privileges and Immunities Clause, we are persuaded, and hold, that elk hunting by nonresidents in Montana is not one of them. . . .

Mr. Justice Brennan, with whom Mr. Justice White and Mr. Justice Marshall join, dissenting.

Far more troublesome than the Court's narrow holding—elk hunting in Montana is not a privilege or immunity entitled to protection under Art. IV, § 2, cl. 1, of the Constitution—is the rationale of the holding that Montana's elk-hunting licensing scheme passes constitutional muster. The Court concludes that because elk hunting is not a "basic and essential activit[y], interference with which would frustrate the purposes of the formation of the Union," . . . the Privileges and Immunities Clause of Art. IV, § 2 . . . does not prevent Montana from irrationally, wantonly, and even invidiously discriminating against nonresidents seeking to enjoy natural treasures it alone among the 50 States possesses. I cannot agree that the Privileges and Immunities Clause is so impotent a guarantee that such discrimination remains wholly beyond the purview of that provision.

I think the time has come to confirm explicitly that which has been implicit in our modern privileges and immunities decisions, namely that an inquiry into whether a given right is "fundamental" has no place in our analysis of whether a State's discrimination against nonresidents—who "are not represented in the [discriminating] State's legislative halls," . . .—violates the Clause. Rather, our primary concern is the State's justification for its discrimination. . . . A State's discrimination against nonresidents is permissible where (1) the presence or activity of nonresidents is the source or cause of the problem or effect with which the State seeks to deal, and (2) the discrimination practiced against nonresidents bears a substantial relation to the problem they present. . . .

It is clear that under a proper privileges and immunities analysis Montana's discriminatory treatment of nonresident big-game hunters in this case must fall. . . . There are three possible justifications for charging nonresident elk hunters an amount at least 7.5 times the fee imposed on resident big game hunters.* The first is conservation. . . . There is nothing in the record to indicate that the influx of nonresident hunters created a special danger to Montana's elk or to any of its other wildlife species. . . . Moreover, . . . if Montana's discriminatorily high big-game license fee is an outgrowth of general conservation policy to discourage elk hunting, this too fails as a basis for the licensing scheme. Montana makes no effort similarly to inhibit its own residents. . . .

The second possible justification for the fee differential. . . . is a cost justification. . . . The licensing scheme, appellants contend, is simply an attempt by Montana to shift the costs of its

*This is the cost ratio of the 1976 nonresident combination license fee ($225) to the 1976 resident combination license fee ($30). Since a Montana resident wishing to hunt only elk could purchase an elk-hunting license for only $9, a nonresident who wanted to hunt only elk had to pay a fee 25 times as great as that charged a similarly situated resident of Montana.

conservation efforts, however commendable they may be, onto the shoulders of nonresidents who are powerless to help themselves at the ballot box. . . . The District Court agreed, finding that "[o]n a consideration of [the] evidence . . . and with due regard to the presumption of constitutionality . . . the ratio of 7.5 to 1 cannot be justified on any basis of cost allocation." . . . Montana's attempt to cost-justify its discriminatory licensing practices thus fails under the second prong of a correct privileges and immunities analysis—that which requires the discrimination a State visits upon nonresidents to bear a substantial relation to the problem or burden they pose.

The third possible justification for Montana's licensing scheme, . . . is actually no justification at all, but simply an assertion that a State "owns" the wildlife within its borders in trust for its citizens and may therefore do with it what it pleases.

In unjustifiably discriminating against nonresident elk hunters, Montana has not "exercised its police power in conformity with the . . . Constitution." The State's police power interest in its wildlife cannot override the appellants' constitutionally protected privileges and immunities right. I respectfully dissent and would reverse.

Garcia v. *San Antonio Metropolitan Transit Authority*

469 U.S. 528, 105 S. Ct. 1005, 83 L. Ed. 2d 1016 (1985)

San Antonio Metropolitan Transit Authority (SAMTA), a public mass-transit authority, is the major provider of public transportation in San Antonio, Texas. In 1979, the Wage and Hour Administration of the U.S. Department of Labor issued an opinion that SAMTA's operations were not immune from the minimum-wages and overtime provisions of the Fair Labor Standards Act (FLSA) under *National League of Cities* v. *Usery* (1976), in which it was held that the Commerce Clause does not empower Congress to enforce such requirements against the States in "areas of traditional governmental functions." SAMTA then brought action in the U.S. District Court for the Western District of Texas seeking declaratory judgment that municipal ownership and operation of a mass-transit system is a traditional governmental function and, under *National League of Cities,* exempt from the obligations imposed by the FLSA. The Department of Labor counterclaimed for enforcement of the overtime and record-keeping requirements of the FLSA, and Joe G. Garcia and several other SAMTA employees intervened, seeking overtime pay under the FLSA. The District Court granted SAMTA's motion for summary judgment, and the Department of Labor and the SAMTA employees appealed directly to the U.S. Supreme Court. *Opinion of the Court: Blackmun, Brennan, Marshall, Stevens, White. Dissenting Opinions: Powell, Burger, O'Connor, Rehnquist; O'Connor, Powell, Rehnquist; Rehnquist.*

JUSTICE BLACKMUN delivered the opinion of the Court.

We revisit in these cases an issue raised in *National League of Cities* v. *Usery* . . . (1976). In that litigation, this Court, by a sharply divided vote, ruled that the Commerce Clause does not empower Congress to enforce the minimum-wage and overtime provisions of the Fair Labor Standards Act (FLSA) against the States "in areas of traditional governmental functions." . . . Although *National League of Cities* supplied some examples of "traditional governmental functions," it did not offer a general explanation of how a "traditional" function is to be distinguished from a "nontraditional" one. Since then, federal and state courts have struggled with the task, thus imposed, of identifying a traditional function for purposes of state immunity under the Commerce Clause.

In the present cases, a Federal District Court concluded that municipal ownership and operation of a mass-transit system is a traditional governmental function and thus, under *National League of Cities,* is exempt from the obligations imposed by the FLSA. Faced with the identical question, three Federal Courts of Appeals and one state appellate court have reached the opposite conclusion.

Our examination of this "function" standard applied in these and other cases over the last eight years now persuades us that the attempt to draw the boundaries of state regulatory immunity in terms of "traditional governmental function" is not only unworkable but is inconsistent with established principles of federalism and, indeed, with those very federalism principles on which *National League of Cities* purported to rest. That case, accordingly, is overruled. . . .

The controversy in the present case has focused on the third . . . requirement—that the challenged federal statute trench on "traditional governmental functions." The District Court voiced a common concern: "Despite the abundance of adjectives, identifying which particular state functions are immune remains difficult." . . . . Just how troublesome the task has been is revealed by the results reached in other federal cases. Thus courts have held that regulating ambulance services, . . . licensing automobile drivers, . . . operating a municipal airport, . . . performing solid waste disposal, . . . and operating a highway authority . . . are functions *protected* under *National League of Cities.* At the same time, courts have held that issuance of industrial development bonds, . . . regulation of intrastate natural gas sales, . . . regulation of traffic on public roads, . . . regulation of air transportation, . . . operation of a telephone system, . . . leasing and sale of natural gas, . . . operation of a mental health facility, . . . and provision of in-house domestic services for the aged and handicapped . . . are *not* entitled to immunity. We find it difficult, if not impossible, to identify an organizing principle that places each of the cases in the first group on one side of a line and each of the cases in the second group on the other side. The constitutional distinction between licensing drivers and regulating traffic, for example, or between operating a highway authority and operating a mental health facility, is elusive at best. . . .

We believe, however, that there is a more fundamental problem at work here. The problem is that no distinction that purports to separate out important governmental functions can be faithful to the role of federalism in a democratic society. The essence of our federal system is that within the realm of authority left open to them under the Constitution, the States must be equally free to engage in any activity that their citizens choose for the common weal, no matter how unorthodox or unnecessary anyone else—including the judiciary—deems state involvement to be. Any rule of state immunity that looks to the "traditional," "integral," or "necessary" nature of governmental functions inevitably invites an unelected federal judiciary to make decisions about which state policies it favors and which ones it dislikes. . . .

The central theme of *National League of Cities* was that the States occupy a special position in our constitutional system and that the scope of Congress' authority under the Commerce Clause must reflect that position. . . .

What has proved problematic is not the perception that the Constitution's federal structure imposes limitations on the Commerce Clause, but rather the nature and content of those limitations. . . .

We doubt that courts ultimately can identify principled constitutional limitations on the scope of Congress' Commerce Clause powers over the States merely by relying on *a priori* definitions of state sovereignty. In part, this is because of the elusiveness of objective criteria for "fundamental" elements of state sovereignty, a problem we have witnessed in the search for "traditional governmental functions." There is, however, a more fundamental reason: the sovereignty of the States is limited by the Constitution itself. A variety of sovereign powers, for example, are withdrawn from the States by Article I, § 10. Section 8 of the same Article works an equally sharp contraction of state sovereignty by authorizing Congress to exercise a wide range of legislative powers and (in conjunction with the Supremacy Clause of Article

VI) to displace contrary state legislation. . . . By providing for final review of questions of federal law in this Court, Article III curtails the sovereign power of the States' judiciaries to make authoritative determinations of law. . . . Finally, the developed application, through the Fourteenth Amendment, of the greater part of the Bill of Rights to the States limits the sovereign authority that States otherwise would possess to legislate with respect to their citizens and to conduct their own affairs.

The States unquestionably do "retai[n] significant measure of sovereign authority." . . . They do so, however, only to the extent that the Constitution has not divested them of their original powers and transferred those powers to the Federal Government. In the words of James Madison to the Members of the First Congress: "Interference with the power of the States was no constitutional criterion of the power of Congress. If the power was not given, Congress could not exercise it; if given, they might exercise it, although it should interfere with the laws, or even the Constitution of the States."

As a result, to say that the Constitution assumes the continued role of the States is to say little about the nature of that role. . . . The fact that the States remain sovereign as to all powers not vested in Congress or denied them by the Constitution offers no guidance about where the frontier between state and federal power lies. In short, we have no license to employ freestanding conceptions of state sovereignty when measuring congressional authority under the Commerce Clause.

When we look for the States' "residuary and inviolable sovereignty," *The Federalist* No. 39, . . . in the shape of the constitutional scheme rather than in predetermined notions of sovereign power, a different measure of state sovereignty emerges. Apart from the limitation on federal authority inherent in the delegated nature of Congress' Article I powers, the principal means chosen by the Framers to ensure the role of the States in the federal system lies in the structure of the Federal Government itself. It is no novelty to observe that the composition of the Federal Government was designed in large part to protect the States from overreaching by Congress. The Framers thus gave the States a role in the selection both of the Executive and the Legislative Branches of the Federal Government. The States were vested with indirect influence over the House of Representatives and the Presidency by their control of electoral qualifications and their role in presidential elections. U.S. Const., Art. I, § 2, and Art. II, § 1. They were given more direct influence in the Senate, where each State received equal representation and each Senator was to be selected by the legislature of his State. Art. I, § 3. The significance attached to the States' equal representation in the Senate is underscored by the prohibition of any constitutional amendment divesting a State of equal representation without the State's consent. Art. V.

The extent to which the structure of the Federal Government itself was relied on to insulate the interests of the States is evident in the views of the Framers. James Madison explained that the Federal Government "will partake sufficiently of the spirit [of the States], to be disinclined to invade the rights of the individual States, or the prerogatives of their governments." *The Federalist* No. 46. . . . The Framers chose to rely on a federal system in which special restraints on federal power over the States inhered principally in the workings of the National Government itself, rather than in discrete limitations on the objects of federal authority. State sovereign interests, then, are more properly protected by procedural safeguards inherent in the structure of the federal system than by judicially created limitations on federal power. . . .

We realize that changes in the structure of the Federal Government have taken place since 1789, not the least of which has been the substitution of popular election of Senators by the adoption of the Seventeenth Amendment in 1913, and that these changes may work to alter the influence of the States in the federal political process. Nonetheless, against this background, we are convinced that the fundamental limitation that the constitutional scheme imposes on the Commerce Clause to protect the "States as States" is one of process rather than one of result. Any substantive restraint on the exercise of Commerce Clause powers must find its justification in the procedural nature of this basic limitation, and it must be tailored to compensate for possible failings in the national political process rather than to dictate a "sacred province of state autonomy." . . .

Insofar as the present cases are concerned, then, we need go no further than to state that we perceive nothing in the overtime and minimum-wage requirements of the FLSA, as applied to SAMTA, that is destructive of state sovereignty or violative of any constitutional provision. SAMTA faces nothing more than the same minimum-wage and overtime obligations that hundreds of thousands of other employers, public as well as private, have to meet.

In these cases, the status of public mass transit simply underscores the extent to which the structural protections of the Constitution insulate the States from federally imposed burdens. When Congress first subjected state mass-transit systems to FLSA obligations in 1966, and when it expanded those obligations in 1974, it simultaneously provided extensive funding for state and local mass transit. . . . In the two decades since it . . . has provided over $22 billion in mass transit aid to States and localities. . . . SAMTA and its immediate predecessor have received a substantial amount of . . . funding, including over $12 million during SAMTA's first two fiscal years alone. In short, Congress has not simply placed a financial burden on the shoulders of States and localities that operate mass-transit systems, but has provided substantial countervailing financial assistance as well, assistance that may leave individual mass transit systems better off than they would have been had Congress never intervened at all in the area. Congress' treatment of public mass transit reinforces our conviction that the national political process systematically protects States from the risk of having their functions in that area handicapped by Commerce Clause regulation.

This analysis makes clear that Congress' action in affording SAMTA employees the protections of the wage and hour provisions of the FLSA contravened no affirmative limit on Congress' power under the Commerce Clause. The judgment of the District Court therefore must be reversed.

Justice Powell, with whom The Chief Justice, Justice Rehnquist, and Justice O'Connor join, dissenting.

The Court today, in its 5–4 decision, overrules *National League of Cities* v. *Usery*, . . . (1976), a case in which we held that Congress lacked authority to impose the requirements of the Fair Labor Standards Act on state and local governments. Because I believe this decision substantially alters the federal system embodied in the Constitution, I dissent.

Whatever effect the Court's decision may have in weakening the application of *stare decisis*, it is likely to be less important than what the Court has done to the Constitution itself. A unique feature of the United States is the *federal* system of government guaranteed by the Constitution and implicit in the very name of our country. Despite some genuflecting in the Court's opinion to the concept of federalism, today's decision effectively reduces the Tenth Amendment to meaningless rhetoric when Congress acts pursuant to the Commerce Clause. . . .

To leave no doubt about its intention, the Court renounces its decision in *National League of Cities* because it "inevitably invites an unelected federal judiciary to make decisions about which state policies it favors and which ones it dislikes." . . . In other words, the extent to which the States may exercise their authority, when Congress purports to act under the Commerce Clause, henceforth is to be determined from time to time by political decisions made by members of the federal government, decisions the Court says will not be subject to judicial review. I note that it does not seem to have occurred to the Court that *it*—an unelected majority of five Justices—today rejects almost 200 years of the understanding of the constitutional status of federalism. In doing so, there is only a single passing reference to the Tenth Amendment. Nor is so much as a dictum of any court cited in support of the view that the role of the States in the federal system may depend upon the grace of elected federal officials, rather than on the Constitution as interpreted by this Court. . . .

Today's opinion does not explain how the States' role in the electoral process guarantees that particular exercises of the Commerce Clause power will not infringe on residual State sovereignty. Members of Congress are elected from the various States, but once in office they are members of the federal government. Although the States participate in the Electoral College, this is hardly a reason to view the President as a representative of the States' interest against federal encroachment. We noted recently "the hydraulic pressure inherent within each of the separate Branches to exceed the outer limits of its power. . . ." *Immigration and Naturalization Service* v. *Chadha*, . . . (1983). The Court offers no reason to think that this pressure will not operate when Congress seeks to invoke its powers under the Commerce Clause, notwithstanding the electoral role of the States.

The Court apparently thinks that the State's success at obtaining federal funds for various projects and exemptions from the obligations of some federal statutes is indicative of the "effectiveness of the federal political process in preserving the States' interests. . . ." . . . But such political success is not relevant to the question whether the political *processes* are the proper means of enforcing constitutional limitations. The fact that Congress generally does not transgress constitutional limits on its power to reach State activities does not make judicial review any less necessary to rectify the cases in which it does do so. The States' role in our system of government is a matter of constitutional law, not of legislative grace. "The powers not delegated to the United States by the Constitution, nor prohibited by it to the States, are reserved to the States, respectively, or to the people." U.S. Const., Amend. 10.

More troubling than the logical infirmities in the Court's reasoning is the result of its holding, i.e., that federal political officials, invoking the Commerce Clause, are the sole judges of the limits of their own power. This result is inconsistent with the fundamental principles of our constitutional system. . . . At least since *Marbury* v. *Madison* it has been the settled province of the federal judiciary "to say what the law is" with respect to the constitutionality of acts of Congress. . . . In rejecting the role of the judiciary in protecting the States from federal overreaching, the Court's opinion offers no explanation for ignoring the teaching of the most famous case in our history.

In our federal system, the States have a major role that cannot be preempted by the national government. As contemporaneous writings and the debates at the ratifying conventions make clear, the States' ratification of the Constitution was predicated on this understanding of federalism. Indeed, the Tenth Amendment was adopted specifically to ensure that the important role promised the States by the proponents of the Constitution was realized. . . .

The Framers had definite ideas about the nature of the Constitution's division of authority between the federal and state governments. . . .

The Framers believed that the separate sphere of sovereignty reserved to the States would ensure that the States would serve as an effective "counterpoise" to the power of the federal government. The States would serve this essential role because they would attract and retain the loyalty of their citizens. The roots of such loyalty, the Founders thought, were found in the objects peculiar to state government. For example, Hamilton argued that the States "regulat[e] all those personal interests and familiar concerns to which the sensibility of individuals is more immediately awake. . . ." *The Federalist* No. 17. . . . Thus, he maintained that the people would perceive the States as "the immediate and most visible guardian of life and property," a fact which "contributes more than any other circumstance to impressing upon the minds of the people affection, esteem and reverence towards the government." . . . Madison took the same position, explaining that "the people will be more familiarly and minutely conversant" with the business of state governments, and "with the members of these, will a greater proportion of the people have the ties of personal acquaintance and friendship, and of family and party attachments. . . ." *The Federalist* No. 46. . . . Like Hamilton, Madison saw the States' involvement in the everyday concerns of the people as the source of their citizens' loyalty. . . .

Thus, the harm to the States that results from federal overreaching under the Commerce Clause is not simply a matter of dollars and cents. . . . Nor is it a matter of the wisdom or folly of certain policy choices. . . . Rather, by usurping functions traditionally performed by the States, federal overreaching under the Commerce Clause undermines the constitutionally mandated balance of power between the States and the federal government, a balance designed to protect our fundamental liberties.

In *National League of Cities*, we spoke of fire prevention, police protection, sanitation, and public health as "typical of [the services] performed by state and local governments in discharging their dual functions of administering the public law and furnishing public services." . . . Not only are these activities remote from any normal concept of interstate commerce, they are also activities that epitomize the concerns of local, democratic self-government. . . . In emphasizing the need to protect traditional governmental functions, we identified the kinds of activities engaged in by state and local governments that affect the everyday lives of citizens. These are services that people are in a position to understand and evaluate, and in a democracy, have the right to oversee. We recognized that "it is functions such as these which governments are created to provide . . . " and that the states and local governments are better able than the national government to perform them. . . .

The Court maintains that the standard approved in *National League of Cities* "disserves principles of democratic self government." . . . In reaching this conclusion, the Court looks myopically only to persons elected to positions in the federal government. It disregards entirely the far more effective role of democratic self-government at the state and local levels. One must compare realistically the operation of the state and local governments with that of the federal government. Federal legislation is drafted primarily by the staffs of the congressional committees. In view of the hundreds of bills introduced at each session of Congress and the complexity of many of them, it is virtually impossible for even the most conscientious legislators to be truly familiar with many of the statutes enacted. Federal departments and agencies customarily are authorized to write regulations. Often these are more important than the text of the statutes. As is true of the original legislation, these are drafted largely by staff personnel. The administration and enforcement of federal laws and regulations necessarily are largely in the hands of staff and civil service employees. These employees may have little or no knowledge of the States and localities that will be affected by the statutes and regulations for which they are responsible. In any case, they hardly are as accessible and responsive as those who occupy analogous positions in State and local governments.

In drawing this contrast, I imply no criticism of these federal employees or the officials who are ultimately in charge. The great majority are conscientious and faithful to their duties. My point is simply that members of the immense federal bureaucracy are not elected, know less about the services traditionally rendered by States and localities, and are inevitably less responsive to recipients of such services, than are state legislatures, city councils, boards of supervisors, and state and local commissions, boards, and agencies. It is at these state and local levels—not in Washington as the Court so mistakenly thinks—that "democratic self-government" is best exemplified.

The Court emphasizes that municipal operation of an intracity mass transit system is relatively new in the life of our country. It nevertheless is a classic example of the type of service traditionally provided by local government. It is *local* by definition. State and local officials of course must be intimately familiar with these services and sensitive to their quality as well as cost. Such officials also know that their constituents and the press respond to the adequacy, fair distribution, and cost of these services. It is this kind of state and local control and accountability that the Framers understood would insure the vitality and preservation of the federal system that the Constitution explicitly requires. . . .

Justice O'Connor, with whom Justice Powell and Justice Rehnquist join, dissenting.

The Court today surveys the battle scene of federalism and sounds a retreat. Like Justice Powell, I would prefer to hold the field and, at the very least, render a little aid to the wounded. I join Justice Powell's opinion. I also write separately to note my fundamental disagreement with the majority's views of federalism and the duty of this Court. . . .

The true "essence" of federalism is that the States *as States* have legitimate interest which the National Government is bound to respect even though its laws are supreme. . . . If federalism so conceived and so carefully cultivated by the Framers of our Constitution is to remain meaningful, this Court cannot abdicate its constitutional responsibility to oversee the Federal Government's compliance with its duty to respect the legitimate interests of the States.

Due to the emergence of an integrated and industrialized national economy, this Court has been required to examine and review a breathtaking expansion of the powers of Congress. In doing so the Court correctly perceived that the Framers of our Constitution intended Congress to have sufficient power to address national problems.

But the Framers were not singleminded. The Constitution is animated by an array of intentions. . . . Just as surely as the Framers envisioned a National Government capable of solving national problems, they also envisioned a republic whose vitality was assured by the diffusion of power not only among the branches of the Federal Government, but also between the Federal Government and the States . . . . In the 18th century these intentions did not conflict because technology had not yet converted every local problem into a national one. A conflict has now emerged, and the Court today retreats rather than reconcile the Constitution's dual concerns for federalism and an effective commerce power.

. . . The Framers perceived the interstate commerce power to be important but limited, and expected that it would be used primarily if not exclusively to remove interstate tariffs and to regulate maritime affairs and large-scale mercantile enterprise. . . . This perception of a narrow commerce power is important not because it suggests that the commerce power should be as narrowly construed today. Rather, it explains why the Framers could believe the Constitution assured significant state authority even as it bestowed a range of powers, including the commerce power, on the Congress. In an era when interstate commerce represented a tiny fraction of economic activity and most goods and services were produced and consumed close to home, the interstate commerce power left a broad range of activities beyond the reach of Congress.

In the decades since ratification of the Constitution, interstate economic activity has steadily expanded. Industrialization, coupled with advances in transportation and communications, has created a national economy in which virtually every activity occurring within the borders of a State plays a part.

Incidental to this expansion of the commerce power, Congress has been given an ability it lacked prior to the emergence of an integrated national economy. Because virtually every *state* activity, like virtually every activity of a private individual, arguably "affects" interstate commerce, Congress can now supplant the States from the significant sphere of activities envisioned for them by the Framers. It is in this context that recent changes in the workings of Congress, such as the direct election of Senators and the expanded influence of national interest groups . . . become relevant. These changes may well have lessened the weight Congress gives to the legitimate interests of States as States. As a result, there is now a real risk that Congress will gradually erase the diffusion of power between state and nation on which the Framers based their faith in the efficiency and vitality of our Republic.

It is worth recalling the . . . passage in *McCulloch* v. *Maryland,* . . . that lies at the source of the recent expansion of the commerce power. "Let the end be legitimate, let it be within the scope of the constitution," Chief Justice Marshall said, "and all means which are appropriate, which are plainly adapted to that end, which are not prohibited, but consist with the letter *and spirit* of the constitution, are constitutional." (emphasis added). The *spirit* of the Tenth Amendment, of course, is that the States will retain their integrity in a system in which the laws of the United States are nevertheless supreme. . . .

It is not enough that the "end be legitimate"; the means to that end chosen by Congress must not contravene the spirit of the Constitution. Thus many of this Court's decisions acknowledge that the means by which national power is exercised must take into account concerns for state autonomy. . . .

. . . For example, Congress might rationally conclude that the location a State chooses for its capital may affect interstate commerce, but the Court has suggested that Congress would nevertheless be barred from dictating that location because such an exercise of a delegated power would undermine the state sovereignty inherent in the Tenth Amendment. *Coyle* v. *Oklahoma* . . . (1911).

The problems of federalism in an integrated national economy are capable of more responsible resolution than holding that the States as States retain no status apart from that which Congress chooses to let them retain. The proper resolution, I suggest, lies in weighing state autonomy as a factor in the balance when interpreting the means by which Congress can exercise its authority on the States as States. It is insufficient, in assessing the validity of congressional regulation of a State pursuant to the commerce power, to ask only whether the same regulation would be valid if enforced against a private party. That reasoning, embodied in the majority opinion, is inconsistent with the spirit of our Constitution. It remains relevant that a *State* is being regulated. . . . As far as the Constitution is concerned, a State should not be equated with any private litigant. . . . Instead, the autonomy of a State is an essential component of federalism. If state autonomy is ignored in assessing the means by which Congress regulates matters affecting commerce, then federalism becomes irrelevant simply because the set of activities remaining beyond the reach of such a commerce power "may well be negligible." . . .

It has been difficult for this Court to craft bright lines defining the scope of the state autonomy protected by *National League of Cities.* Such difficulty is to be expected whenever constitutional concerns as important as federalism and the effectiveness of the commerce power come into conflict. Regardless of the difficulty, it is and will remain the duty of this Court to reconcile these concerns in the final instance. That the Court shuns the task today by appealing to the "essence of federalism" can provide scant comfort to those who believe our federal system requires something more than a unitary, centralized government. I would not shirk the duty acknowledged by *National League of Cities* and it progeny.

I respectfully dissent.

With the decision in Garcia, *state and local governments across the United States were confronted with the prospect of having to pay up to $3 billion annually in overtime. Senator Pete Wilson of California predicted that his state, with over 89,000 state employees, would "be out some $300 million, with the city of Los Angeles accounting for perhaps $50 million." Worried about huge overtime bills and the likelihood of tax hikes to cover these costs, state and local governmental officials lobbied Congress for relief, and in November of 1985, President Reagan signed into law a bill that allowed state and local governments to continue offering compensatory time off in lieu of overtime pay.*

The Civil Rights Cases

109 U.S. 3; S. Ct. 18; 27 L. Ed. 835 (1883)

The Civil Rights Act of 1875 prohibited any person from denying a citizen "the full and equal enjoyment of the accommodations, advantages, facilities, and privileges of inns, public conveyences on land or water, theatres, and other places of public amusement." In the five cases that were heard together as the *Civil Rights Cases,* persons were indicted for violating the act by denying accommodations to blacks in a hotel, a theatre, an opera house, and a ladies' car on a train. Two of the five cases went to the Supreme Court on writs of error sued out by the plaintiffs in federal circuit courts. The other three were certified to the Supreme Court because the lower-court judges disagreed on the constitutionality of the act. *Opinion of the Court: Bradley, Blatchford, Field, Gray, Matthews, Miller, Waite, Woods. Dissenting opinion: Harlan.*

MR. JUSTICE BRADLEY delivered the opinion of the Court. . . .

It is obvious that the primary and important question in all the cases is the constitutionality of the law: for if the law is unconstitutional none of the prosecutions can stand. . . .

The essence of the law is, not to declare broadly that all persons shall be entitled to the full and equal enjoyment of the accommodations, advantages, facilities, and privileges of inns, public conveyances, and theatres; but that such enjoyment shall not be subject to any conditions applicable only to citizens of a particular race or color, or who had been in a previous condition of servitude. In other words, it is the purpose of the law to declare that, in the enjoyment of the accommodations and privileges of inns, public conveyances, theaters, and other places of public amusement, no distinction shall be made between citizens of different race or color, or between those who have, and those who have not, been slaves. . . .

Has Congress constitutional power to make such a law? Of course, no one will contend that the power to pass it was contained in the Constitution before the adoption of the last three amendments. The power is sought, first, in the Fourteenth Amendment, and the views and arguments of distinguished Senators, advanced whilst the law was under consideration, claiming authority to pass it by virtue of that amendment, are the principal arguments adduced in favor of the power. . . .

The first section of the Fourteenth Amendment (which is the one relied on), after declaring who shall be citizens of the United States, and of the several States, is prohibitory in its character, and prohibitory upon the States. It declares that:

"No State shall make or enforce any law which shall abridge the privileges or immunities of citizens of the United States; nor shall any State deprive any person of life, liberty, or property without due process of law; nor deny to any person within its jurisdiction the equal protection of the laws."

It is State action of a particular character that is prohibited. Individual invasion of individual rights is not the subject matter of the amendment. It has a deeper and broader scope. It nullifies and makes void all State legislation, and State action of every kind, which impairs the privileges and immunities of citizens of the United States, or which injures them in life, liberty or property without due process of law, or which denies to any of them the equal protection of the laws. It not only does this, but, in order that the national will, thus declared, may not be a mere *brutum fulmen*, the last section of the amendment invests Congress with power to enforce it by appropriate legislation. To enforce what? To enforce the prohibition. To adopt appropriate legislation for correcting the effects of such prohibited State laws and State acts, and thus to render them effectually null, void, and innocuous. This is the legislative power conferred upon Congress, and this is the whole of it. It does not invest Congress with power to legislate upon subjects which are within the domain of State legislation; but to provide modes of relief against State legislation, or State action, of the kind referred to. It does not authorize Congress to create a code of municipal law for the regulation of private rights; but to provide modes of redress against the operation of State laws, and the action of State officers executive or judicial, when these are subversive of the fundamental rights specified in the amendment. Positive rights and privileges are undoubtedly secured by the Fourteenth Amendment; but they are secured by way of prohibition against State laws and State proceedings affecting those rights and privileges, and by power given to Congress to legislate for the purpose of carrying such prohibition into effect. . . .

An inspection of the law shows that it makes no reference whatever to any supposed or apprehended violation of the Fourteenth Amendment on the part of the States. It is not predicated on any such view. It proceeds *ex directo* to declare that certain acts committed by individuals shall be deemed offences, and shall be prosecuted and punished by proceedings in the courts of the United States. It does not profess to be corrective of any constitutional wrong committed by the States; it does not make its operation to depend upon any such wrong committed. It applies equally to cases arising in States which have the justest laws respecting the personal rights of citizens, and whose authorities are ever ready to enforce such laws, as to those which arise in States that may have violated the prohibition of the amendment. In other words, it steps into the domain of local jurisprudence, and lays down rules for the conduct of individuals in society towards each other, and imposes sanctions for the enforcement of those rules, without referring in any manner to any supposed action of the State or its authorities.

If this legislation is appropriate for enforcing the prohibitions of the amendment, it is difficult to see where it is to stop. Why may not Congress with equal show of authority enact a code of laws for the enforcement and vindication of all rights of life, liberty, and property? If it is supposable that the States may deprive persons of life, liberty, and property without due process of law (and the amendment itself does suppose this), why should not Congress proceed at once to prescribe due process of law for the protection of every one of these fundamental rights, in every possible case, as well as to prescribe equal privileges in inns, public conveyances, and theatres? The truth is, that the implication of a power to legislate in this manner is based upon the assumption that if the States are forbidden to legislate or act in a particular way on a particular subject, and power is conferred upon Congress to enforce the prohibition, this gives Congress power to legislate generally upon that subject, and not merely power to provide modes of redress against such State legislation or action. The assumption is certainly unsound. It is repugnant to the Tenth Amendment of the Constitution, which declares that powers not delegated to the United States by the Constitution, nor prohibited by it to the States, are reserved to the States respectively or to the people. . . .

In this connection it is proper to state that civil rights, such as are guaranteed by the Constitution against State aggression, cannot be impaired by the wrongful acts of individuals, unsupported by State authority in the shape of laws, customs, or judicial or executive proceedings. The wrongful act of an individual, unsupported by any such authority, is simply a private wrong, or a crime of that individual; an invasion of the rights of the injured party, it is true, whether they affect his person, his property, or his reputation; but if not sanctioned in some way by the State, or not done under State authority, his rights remain in full force, and may presumably be vindicated by resort to the laws of the State for redress. An individual cannot deprive a man of his right to vote, to hold property, to buy and sell, to sue in the courts, or to be a witness or a juror; he may, by force or fraud, interfere with the enjoyment of the right in a particular case; he may commit an assault against the person, or commit murder, or use ruffian violence at the polls, or slander the good name of a fellow citizen; but, unless protected in these wrongful acts by some shield of State law or State authority, he cannot destroy or injure the right; he will only render himself amenable to satisfaction or punishment; and amenable therefore to the laws of the State where the wrongful acts are committed. Hence, in all those cases where the Constitution seeks to protect the rights of the citizen against discriminative and unjust laws of the State by prohibiting such laws, it is not individual offences, but abrogation and denial of rights, which it denounces, and for which it clothes the Congress with power to provide a remedy. This abrogation and denial of rights, for which the States alone were or could be responsible, was the great seminal and fundamental wrong which was intended to be remedied. And the remedy to be provided must necessarily be predicated upon that wrong. It must assume that in the cases provided for, the evil or wrong actually committed rests upon some State law or State authority for its excuse and perpetration.

Of course, these remarks do not apply to those cases in which Congress is clothed with direct and plenary powers of legislation over the whole subject, accompanied with an express or implied denial of such power to the States, as in the regulation of commerce with foreign nations, among the several States, and with the Indian tribes, the coining of money, the establishment of post offices and post roads, the declaring of war, etc. In these cases Congress has power to pass laws for regulating the subjects specified in every detail, and the conduct and transactions of individuals in respect thereof. But where a subject is not submitted to the general legislative power of Congress, but is only submitted thereto for the purpose of rendering effective some prohibition against particular State legislation or State action in reference to that subject, the power given is limited by its object, and any legislation by Congress in the matter must necessarily be corrective in its character, adapted to counteract and redress the operation of such prohibited State laws or proceedings of State officers. . . .

. . . The power of Congress to adopt direct and primary, as distinguished from corrective legislation, on the subject in hand, is sought . . . from the Thirteenth Amendment, which abolishes slavery. . . .

. . . It is assumed, that the power vested in Congress to enforce the article by appropriate legislation, clothes Congress with power to pass all laws necessary and proper for abolishing all badges and incidents of slavery in the United States: and upon this assumption it is claimed, that this is sufficient authority for declaring by law that all persons shall have equal accommodations and privileges in all inns, public conveyances, and places of amusement; the argument being, that the denial of such equal accommodations and privileges is, in itself, a subjection to a species of servitude within the meaning of the amendment. Conceding the major proposition to be true, that Congress has a right to enact all necessary and proper laws for the obliteration and prevention of slavery with all its badges and incidents, is the minor proposition also true, that the denial to any person of admission to the accommodations and privileges of an inn, a public conveyance, or a theatre, does subject that person to any form of servitude, or tend to fasten upon him any badge of slavery? If it does not, then power to pass the law is not found in the Thirteenth Amendment. . . .

It would be running the slavery argument into the ground to make it apply to every act of discrimination which a person may see fit to make as to the guests he will entertain, or as to the people he will take into his coach or cab or car, or admit to his concert or theatre, or deal with in other matters of intercourse or business. . . .

When a man has emerged from slavery, and by the aid of beneficent legislation has shaken off the inseparable concomitants of that state, there must be some stage in the progress of his elevation when he takes the rank of a mere citizen, and ceases to be the special favorite of the laws, and when his rights as a citizen, or a man, are to be protected in the ordinary modes by which other men's rights are protected. . . .

On the whole we are of opinion, that no countenance of authority for the passage of the law in question can be found in either the Thirteenth or Fourteenth Amendment of the Constitution; and no other ground of authority for its passage being suggested, it must necessarily be declared void at least so far as its operation in the several States is concerned. . . .

MR. JUSTICE HARLAN, dissenting.

The opinion in these cases proceeds, it seems to me, upon grounds entirely too narrow and artificial. I cannot resist the conclusion that the substance and spirit of the recent amendments of the Constitution have been sacrificed by a subtle and ingenious verbal criticism. . . .

There seems to be no substantial difference between my brethren and myself as to the purpose of Congress; for, they say that the essence of the law is, not to declare broadly that all persons shall be entitled to the full and equal enjoyment of the accommodations, advantages, facilities, and privileges of inns, public conveyances, and theatres; but that such enjoyment shall not be subject to conditions applicable only to citizens of a particular race or color, or who had been in a previous condition of servitude.

The court adjudges, I think erroneously, that Congress is without power, under either the Thirteenth or Fourteenth Amendment, to establish such regulations, and that the first and second sections of the statute are, in all their parts, unconstitutional and void. . . .

The Thirteenth Amendment, it is conceded, did something more than to prohibit slavery as an *institution*, resting upon distinctions of race, and upheld by positive law. My brethren admit that it established and decreed universal *civil freedom* throughout the United States. . . .

That there are burdens and disabilities which constitute badges of slavery and servitude, and that the power to enforce by appropriate legislation the Thirteenth Amendment may be exerted by legislation of a direct and primary character, for the eradication, not simply of the institution, but of its badges and incidents, are propositions which ought to be deemed indisputable. They lie at the foundation of the Civil Rights Act of 1866. Whether that act was authorized by the Thirteenth Amendment alone, without the support which it subsequently received from the Fourteenth Amendment, after the adoption of which it was re-enacted with some additions, my brethren do not consider it necessary to inquire. But I submit, with all respect to them, that its constitutionality is conclusively shown by their opinion. They admit, as I have said, that the Thirteenth Amendment established freedom; that there are burdens and disabilities, the necessary incidents of slavery, which constitute its substance and visible form; that Congress, by the act of 1866, passed in view of the Thirteenth Amendment, before the Fourteenth was adopted, undertook to remove certain burdens and disabilities, the necessary incidents of slavery, and to secure to all citizens of every race and color, and without regard to previous servitude, those fundamental rights which are the essence of civil freedom, namely, the same right to make and enforce contracts, to sue, be parties, give evidence, and to inherit, purchase, lease, sell, and convey, property as is enjoyed by white citizens; that under the Thirteenth Amendment, Congress has to do with slavery and its incidents; and that legislation, so far as necessary or proper to eradicate all forms and incidents of slavery and involuntary servitude, may be direct and primary, operating upon the acts of individuals, whether sanctioned by State legislation or not. These propositions being conceded, it is impossible, as it seems to me, to question the constitutional validity of the Civil Rights Act of 1866. I do not contend that the Thirteenth Amendment invests Congress with authority, by legislation, to define and regulate the entire body of the civil rights which citizens enjoy, or may enjoy, in the several States. But I hold that since slavery, . . . was the moving or principal cause of the adoption of that amendment, and since that institution rested wholly upon the inferiority, as a race, of those held in bondage, their freedom necessarily involved immunity from, and protection against, all discrimination against them, because of their race, in respect of such civil rights as belong to freemen of other races. Congress, therefore, under its express power to enforce that amendment, by appropriate legislation, may enact laws to protect that people against the deprivation, *because of their race*, of any civil rights granted to other freemen in the same State; and such legislation may be of a direct and primary character, operating upon States, their officers and agents, and, also, upon, at least, such individuals and corporations as exercise public functions and wield power and authority under the State. . . .

Congress has not, in these matters, entered the domain of State control and supervision. It does not, . . . assume to prescribe the general conditions and limitations under which inns, public conveyances, and places of public amusement, shall be conducted or managed. It simply declares, in effect, that since the nation has established universal freedom in this country, for all time, there shall be no discrimination, based merely upon race or color, in respect of the accommodations and advantages of public conveyances, inns, and places of public amusement.

I am of the opinion that such discrimination practised by corporations and individuals in the exercise of their public or quasi-public functions is a badge of servitude the imposition of which Congress may prevent under its power, by appropriate legislation, to enforce the Thirteenth Amendment; and, consequently, without reference to its enlarged power under the Fourteenth Amendment, the act of March 1, 1875, is not, in my judgment, repugnant to the Constitution.

It remains now to consider these cases with reference to the power Congress has possessed since the adoption of the Fourteenth Amendment. Much that has been said as to the power of Congress under the Thirteenth Amendment is applicable to this branch of the discussion, and will not be repeated. . . .

The assumption that [the Fourteenth] Amendment consists wholly of prohibitions upon State laws and State proceedings in hostility to its provisions, is unauthorized by its language. The first clause of the first section—"All persons born or naturalized in the United States, and subject to the jurisdiction thereof, are citizens of the United States, and of the State wherein they reside"—is of a distinctly affirmative character. In its application to the colored race, previously liberated, it created and granted, as well citizenship of the United States, as citizenship of the State in which they respectively resided. It introduced all of that race, whose ancestors had been imported and sold as slaves, at once, into the political community known as the "People of the United States." They became, instantly, citizens of the United States, *and* of their respective States.

The citizenship thus acquired, by that race, in virtue of an affirmative grant from the nation, may be protected, not alone by the judicial branch of the government, but by congressional legislation of a primary direct character; this, because the power of Congress is not restricted to the enforcement of prohibitions upon State laws or State action. It is, in terms distinct and positive, to enforce "the *provisions* of *this article*" of amendment; not simply those of a prohibitive character, but the provisions—*all* of the provisions—affirmative and prohibitive, of the amendment. It is, therefore, a grave misconception to suppose that the fifth section of the amendment has reference exclusively to express prohibitions upon State laws or State action. If any right was created by that amendment, the grant of power, through appropriate legislation, to enforce its provisions, authorizes Congress, by means of legislation, operating throughout the entire Union, to guard, secure, and protect that right. . . .

This construction does not in any degree intrench upon the just rights of the States in the control of their domestic affairs. It simply recognizes the enlarged powers conferred by the recent amendments upon the general government. In the view which I take of those amendments, the States possess the same authority which they have always had to define and regulate the civil rights which their own people, in virtue of State citizenship, may enjoy within their respective limits; except that its exercise is now subject to the expressly granted power of Congress, by legislation, to enforce the provisions of such amendments—a power which necessarily carries with it authority, by national legislation, to protect and secure the privileges and immunities which are created by or are derived from those amendments. That exemption of citizens from discrimination based on race or color, in respect to civil rights, is one of those privileges or immunities, can no longer be deemed an open question in this court. . . .

. . . Government has nothing to do with social, as distinguished from technically legal, rights of individuals. No government ever has brought, or ever can bring, its people into social intercourse against their wishes. Whether one person will permit or maintain social relations with another is a matter with which government has no concern. . . . The rights which Congress, by the act of 1875, endeavored to secure and protect are legal, not social rights. The right, for instance, of a colored citizen to use the accommodations of a public highway, upon the same terms as are permitted to white citizens, is no more a social right than his right, under the law, to use the public streets of a city or a town, or a turnpike road, or a public market, or a post office, or his right to sit.

My brethren say, that when a man has emerged from slavery, and by the aid of beneficent legislation has shaken off the inseparable concomitants of that state, there must be some state in the progress of his elevation when he takes the rank of a mere citizen, and ceases to be the special favorite of the laws, and when his rights as a citizen, or a man, are to be protected in the ordinary modes by which other men's rights are protected. It is, I submit, scarcely just to say that the colored race has been the special favorite of the laws. The statute of 1875, now adjudged to be unconstitutional, is for the benefit of citizens of every race and color. What the nation, through Congress, has sought to accomplish in reference to that race, is—what had already been done in every State of the Union for the white race—to secure and protect rights belonging to them as freemen and citizens; nothing more. . . . The supreme law of the land has decreed that no authority shall be exercised in this country upon the basis of discrimination, in respect of civil rights, against freemen and citizens because of their race, color, or previous condition of servitude. To that decree—for the due enforcement of which, by appropriate legislation, Congress has been invested with express power—every one must bow, whatever may have been, or whatever now are, his individual views as to the wisdom or policy, either of the recent changes in the fundamental law, or of the legislation which has been enacted to give them effect.

For the reasons stated I feel constrained to withhold my assent to the opinion of the court.

Jones v. *Alfred H. Mayer Company*

392 U. S. 409; 88 S. Ct. 2186; 20 L. Ed. 2d 1189 (1968)

Petitioners Joseph Lee Jones and his wife, alleging that the respondents had refused to sell them a home for the sole reason that he was black, filed a complaint in federal district court, seeking injunctive and other relief. They relied in part upon 42 U.S.C. § 1982, which provides that "all citizens of the United States shall have the same right, in every State and Territory, as is enjoyed by white citizens thereof to inherit, purchase, lease, sell, hold, and convey real and personal property." The district court dismissed the complaint, and the Court of Appeals for the Eighth Circuit affirmed, concluding that § 1982 applies only to state action and does not reach private refusals to sell. The Supreme Court granted certiorari. *Opinion of the Court: Stewart, Black, Brennan, Fortas, Marshall, Warren. Concurring opinion: Douglas. Dissenting opinion: Harlan, White.*

MR. JUSTICE STEWART delivered the opinion of the Court.

In this case we are called upon to determine the scope and the constitutionality of an Act of Congress, 42 U. S. C. § 1982 . . . .

For the reasons that follow, we reverse the judgment of the Court of Appeals. We hold that § 1982 bars *all* racial discrimination, private as well as public, in the sale or rental of property, and that the statute, thus construed, is a valid exercise of the power of Congress to enforce the Thirteenth Amendment. . . .

We begin with the language of the statute itself. In plain and unambiguous terms, § 1982 grants to *all* citizens, without regard to race or color, "the same right" to purchase and lease property "as is enjoyed by white citizens." As the Court of Appeals in this case evidently recognized, that right can be impaired as effectively by "those who place property on the market" as by the State itself. For, even if the State and its agents lend no support to those who wish to exclude persons from their communities on racial grounds, the fact remains that, whenever property "is placed on the market for whites only, whites have a right denied to Negroes." . . .

On its face, therefore, § 1982 appears to prohibit *all* discrimination against Negroes in the sale or rental of property—discrimination by private owners as well as discrimination by public authorities. Indeed, even the respondents seem to concede that, if § 1982 "means what it says"—to use the words of the respondents' brief—then it must encompass every racially motivated refusal to sell or rent and cannot be confined to officially sanctioned segregation in housing. Stressing what they consider to be the revolutionary implications of so literal a reading of § 1982, the respondents argue that Congress cannot possibly have intended any such result. Our examination of the relevant history, however, persuades us that Congress meant exactly what it said. . . .

In its original form, 42 U. S. C. § 1982 was part of § 1 of the Civil Rights Act of 1866. . . . The crucial language [of that section] was that which guaranteed all citizens "the same right, in every State and Territory in the United States, . . . to inherit, purchase, lease, sell, hold, and convey real and personal property . . . as is enjoyed by white citizens. . . ." To the Congress that passed the Civil Rights Act of 1866, it was clear that the right to do these things might be infringed not only by "State or local law" but also by "custom, or prejudice." Thus, when Congress provided in § 1 of the Civil Rights Act that the right to purchase and lease property was to be enjoyed equally throughout the United States by Negro and white citizens alike, it plainly meant to secure that right against interference from any source whatever, whether governmental or private. . . .

In attempting to demonstrate the contrary, the respondents rely heavily upon the fact that the Congress which approved the 1866 statute wished to eradicate the recently enacted Black Codes—laws which had saddled Negroes with "onerous disabilities and burdens, and curtailed their rights . . . to such an extent that their freedom was of little value . . . ." . . . The respondents suggest that the only evil Congress sought to eliminate was that of racially discriminatory laws in the former Confederate States. But the Civil Rights Act was drafted to apply throughout the country, and its language was far broader than would have been necessary to strike down discriminatory statutes.

That broad language, we are asked to believe, was a mere slip of the legislative pen. We disagree. For the same Congress that wanted to do away with the Black Codes *also* had before it an imposing body of evidence pointing to the mistreatment of Negroes by private individuals and unofficial groups, mistreatment unrelated to any hostile state legislation. . . .

Indeed, one of the most comprehensive studies then before Congress stressed the prevalence of private hostility toward Negroes and the need to protect them from the resulting persecution and discrimination. . . .

In this setting, it would have been strange indeed if Congress had viewed its task as encompassing merely the nullification of racist laws in the former rebel States. . . .

The remaining question is whether Congress has power under the Constitution to do what § 1982 purports to do: to prohibit all racial discrimination, private and public, in the sale and rental of property. Our starting point is the Thirteenth Amendment, for it was pursuant to that constitutional provision that Congress originally enacted what is now § 1982. . . .

. . . It has never been doubted . . . "that the power vested in Congress to enforce the article by appropriate legislation," . . . includes the power to enact laws "direct and primary, operating upon the acts of individuals, whether sanctioned by State legislation or not." . . .

. . . The constitutional question in this case, therefore, comes to this: Does the authority of Congress to enforce the Thirteenth Amendment "by appropriate legislation" include the power to eliminate all racial barriers to the acquisition of real and personal property? We think the answer to that question is plainly yes. . . .

. . . Surely Congress has the power under the Thirteenth Amendment rationally to determine what are the badges and the incidents of slavery, and the authority to translate that determination into effective legislation. Nor can we say that the determination Congress has made is an irrational one. For this Court recognized long ago that, whatever else they may have encompassed, the badges and incidents of slavery—its "burdens and disabilities"—included restraints upon "those fundamental rights which are that essence of civil freedom, namely, the same right . . . to inherit, purchase, lease, sell and convey property, as is enjoyed by white citizens." *Civil Rights Cases,* 109 U.S. 3, 22. Just as the Black Codes, enacted after the Civil War to restrict the free exercise of those rights, were substitutes for the slave system, so the exclusion of Negroes from white communities became a substitute for the Black Codes. And when racial discrimination herds men into ghettos and makes their ability to buy property turn on the color of their skin, then it too is a relic of slavery. . . . At the very least, the freedom that Congress is empowered to secure under the Thirteenth Amendment includes the freedom to buy whatever a white man can buy, the right to live wherever a white man can live. If Congress cannot say that being a free man means at least this much, then the Thirteenth Amendment made a promise the Nation cannot keep. . . .

MR. JUSTICE HARLAN, whom MR. JUSTICE WHITE joins, dissenting.

The decision in this case appears to me to be most ill-considered and ill-advised. . . .

The petitioners argue that the respondents' racially motivated refusal to sell them a house entitles them to judicial relief on two separate grounds. First, they claim that the respondents acted in violation of 42 U.S.C. § 1982; second, they assert that the respondents' conduct amounted in the circumstances to "state action" and was therefore forbidden by the Fourteenth Amendment even in the absence of any statute.

For reasons which follow, I believe that the Court's construction of § 1982 as applying to purely private action is almost surely wrong, and at the least is open to serious doubt. The issues of the constitutionality of § 1982, as construed by the Court, and of liability under the Fourteenth Amendment alone, also present formidable difficulties. Moreover, the political processes of our own era have, since the date of oral argument in this case, given birth to [the Civil Rights Act of 1968] embodying "fair housing" provisions which would at the end of this year make available . . . the type of relief which the petitioners now seek. It seems to me that this latter factor so diminishes the public importance of this case that by far the wisest course would be for this Court to refrain from decision and to dismiss the writ as improvidently granted. . . .

Like the Court, I begin analysis of § 1982 by examining its language. . . .

The Court finds it "plain and unambiguous," . . . that this language forbids purely private as well as state-authorized discrimination. With all respect, I do not find it so. For me, there is an inherent ambiguity in the term "right," as used in § 1982. The "right" referred to may either be a right to equal status under the law, in which case the statute operates only against state-sanctioned discrimination, or it may be an "absolute" right enforceable against private individuals. To me, the words of the statute, taken alone, suggest the former interpretation, not the latter. . . .

The Court rests its opinion chiefly upon the legislative history of the Civil Rights Act of 1866. . . . Those debates do not, as the Court would have it, overwhelmingly support the result reached by the Court, . . . in fact, a contrary conclusion may equally well be drawn.

[*Justice Harlan then engages in a lengthy review of the Act's legislative history.*]

The foregoing, I think, amply demonstrates that the Court has chosen to resolve this case by according to a loosely worded statute a meaning which is open to the strongest challenge in light of the statute's legislative history. In holding that the Thirteenth Amendment is sufficient constitutional authority for § 1982 as interpreted, the Court also decides a question of great importance. Even contemporary supporters of the aims of the 1866 Civil Rights Act doubted that those goals could constitutionally be achieved under the Thirteenth Amendment, and this Court has twice expressed similar doubts. . . . Thus, it is plain that the course of decision followed by the Court today entails the resolution of important and difficult issues. . . .

Patterson v. *McLean Credit Union*

109 S. Ct. 2363, 105 L. Ed. 2d 132 (1989)

Brenda Patterson, a black woman, was employed by the McLean Credit Union as a teller and file coordinator for 10 years until she was laid off in 1982. Thereafter, she brought suit in U.S. District Court under 42 U.S.C Section 1981, relying on *Runyon* v. *McCrary*, 427 U.S. 160 (1976) and alleging that the credit union had harassed her, failed to promote her to accounting clerk, and then discharged her, all because of her race. The District Court determined that a claim for racial harassment is not actionable under Section 1981 and declined to submit that part of the case to the jury. The court instructed the jury that in order to prevail in her promotion-discrimination claim Patterson had to prove that she was better qualified than the white employee who received the promotion. The jury found for the credit union on this claim, as well as on Patterson's discriminatory-discharge claim. The Court of Appeals for the Fourth Circuit affirmed the District Court's judgment, and the Supreme Court granted certiorari. *Opinion of the Court: Kennedy, O'Connor, Rehnquist, Scalia, White. Concurring in the judgment and dissenting in part: Brennan, Blackmun, Marshall, Stevens; Stevens.*

JUSTICE KENNEDY delivered the opinion of the Court.

In this case, we consider important issues respecting the meaning and coverage of one of our oldest civil rights statutes, 42 U. S. C. § 1981. . . .

We granted certiorari to decide whether petitioner's claim of racial harassment in her employment is actionable under § 1981, and whether the jury instruction given by the District Court on petitioner's § 1981 promotion claim was error. 484 U.S. 814 (1987). After oral argument on these issues, we requested the parties to brief and argue an additional question:

> Whether or not the interpretation of 42 U. S. C. § 1981 adopted by this Court in *Runyon* v. *McCrary* . . . (1976), should be reconsidered.

We now decline to overrule our decision in *Runyon* v. *McCrary*. . . . We hold . . . that racial harassment relating to the conditions of employment is not actionable under § 1981 because that provision does not apply to conduct which occurs after the formation of a contract and which does not interfere with the right to enforce established contract obligations. Finally, we hold that the District Court erred in instructing the jury regarding petitioner's burden in proving her discriminatory promotion claim. . . .

In *Runyon,* the Court considered whether § 1981 prohibits private schools from excluding children who are qualified for admission, solely on the basis of race. We held that § 1981 did prohibit such conduct, noting that it was already well established in prior decisions that § 1981 "prohibits racial discrimination in the making and enforcement of private contracts." . . . The arguments about whether *Runyon* was decided correctly in light of the language and history of the statute were examined and discussed with great care in our decision. It was recognized at the time that a strong case could be made for the view that the statute does not reach private conduct, . . . but that view did not prevail. Some Members of this Court believe that *Runyon* was decided incorrectly, and others consider it correct on its own footing, but the question before us is whether it ought now to be overturned. We conclude after reargument that *Runyon* should not be overruled, and we now reaffirm that § 1981 prohibits racial discrimination in the making and enforcement of private contracts. . . .

Our precedents are not sacrosanct, for we have overruled prior decisions where the necessity and propriety of doing so has been established. . . . Nonetheless, we have held that "any departure from the doctrine of *stare decisis* demands special justification." . . . We have said also that the burden borne by the party advocating the abandonment of an established precedent is greater where the Court is asked to overrule a point of statutory construction. Considerations of *stare decisis* have special force in the area of statutory interpretation, for here, unlike in the context of constitutional interpretation, the legislative power is implicated, and Congress remains free to alter what we have done. . . .

Our conclusion that we should adhere to our decision in *Runyon* that § 1981 applies to private conduct is not enough to decide this case. We must decide also whether the conduct of which petitioner complains falls within one of the enumerated rights protected by § 1981. . . .

Section 1981 reads as follows:

> All persons within the jurisdiction of the United States shall have the same right in every State and Territory to make and enforce contracts, to sue, be parties, give evidence, and to the full and equal benefit of all laws and proceedings for the security of persons and property as is enjoyed by white citizens, and shall be subject to like punishment, pains, penalties, taxes, licenses, and exactions of every kind, and to no other. Rev. Stat. § 1977.

The most obvious feature of the provision is the restriction of its scope to forbidding discrimination in the "mak[ing] and enforce[ment]" of contracts alone. Where an alleged act of discrimination does not involve the impairment of one of these specific rights, § 1981 provides no relief. Section 1981 cannot be construed as a general proscription of racial discrimination in all aspects of contract relations, for it expressly prohibits discrimination only in the making and enforcement of contracts. . . .

By its plain terms, the relevant provision in § 1981 protects two rights: "the same right . . . to make . . . contracts" and "the same right . . . to . . . enforce contracts." The first of these protections extends only to the formation of a contract, but not to problems that may arise later from the conditions of continuing employment. The statute prohibits, when based on race, the refusal to enter into a contract with someone, as well as the offer to make a contract only on discriminatory terms. But the right to make contracts does not extend, as a matter of either logic or semantics, to conduct by the employer after the contract relation has been established, including breach of the terms of the contract or imposition of discriminatory working conditions. Such postformation conduct does not involve the right to make a contract, but rather implicates the performance of established contract obligations and the conditions of continuing employment, matters more naturally governed by state contract law and Title VII. . . .

The second of these guarantees, "the same right . . . to . . . enforce contracts . . . as is enjoyed by white citizens," embraces protection of a legal process, and of a right of access to legal process, that will address and resolve contract-law claims without regard to race. In this respect, it prohibits discrimination that infects the legal process in ways that prevent one from enforcing contract rights, by reason of his or her race, and this is so whether this discrimination is attributed to a statute or simply to existing practices. It also covers wholly *private* efforts to impede access to the courts or obstruct nonjudicial methods of adjudicating disputes about the force of binding obligations, as well as discrimination by private entities, such as labor unions, in enforcing the terms of a contract. . . . The right to enforce contracts does not, however, extend beyond conduct by an employer which impairs an employee's ability to enforce through legal process his or her established contract rights. . . .

Applying these principles to the case before us, we agree with the Court of Appeals that petitioner's racial harassment claim is not actionable under § 1981. Petitioner has alleged that during her employment with respondent, she was subjected to various forms of racial harassment from her supervisor. As summarized by the Court of Appeals, petitioner testified that

> [her supervisor] periodically stared at her for several minutes at a time; that he gave her too many tasks, causing her to complain that she was under too much pressure; that among the tasks given her were sweeping and dusting, jobs not given to white employees. On one occasion, she testified, [her supervisor] told [her] that blacks are known to work slower than whites. According to [petitioner, her supervisor] also criticized her in staff meetings while not similarly criticizing white employees. . . .

Petitioner also alleges that she was passed over for promotion, not offered training for higher level jobs, and denied wage increases, all because of her race. . . .

This type of conduct, reprehensible though it be if true, is not actionable under § 1981, which covers only conduct at the initial formation of the contract and conduct which impairs the right to enforce contract obligations through legal process. Rather, such conduct is actionable under the more expansive reach of Title VII of the Civil Rights Act of 1964. The latter statute makes it unlawful for an employer to "discriminate against any individual with respect to his compensation, terms, conditions, or privileges of employment." . . . Racial harassment in the course of employment is actionable under Title VII's prohibition against discrimination in the "terms, conditions, or privileges of employment." . . .

Interpreting § 1981 to cover postformation conduct unrelated to an employee's right to enforce her contract, such as incidents relating to the conditions of employment, is not only inconsistent with that statute's limitation to the making and enforcement of contracts, but would also undermine the detailed and well-crafted procedures for conciliation and resolution of Title VII claims. In Title VII, Congress set up an elaborate administrative procedure, implemented through the EEOC [Equal Employment Opportunity Commission], that is designed to assist in the investigation of claims of racial discrimination in the workplace and to work towards the resolution of these claims through conciliation rather than litigation. . . . Only after these procedures have been exhausted, and the plaintiff has obtained a "right to sue" letter from the EEOC, may she bring a Title VII action in court. . . . Section 1981, by contrast, provides no administrative review or opportunity for conciliation.

Where conduct is covered by both § 1981 and Title VII, the detailed procedures of Title VII are rendered a dead letter, as the plaintiff is free to pursue a claim by bringing suit under § 1981 without resort to those statutory prerequisites. . . . We should be reluctant, however, to read an earlier statute broadly where the result is to circumvent the detailed remedial scheme constructed in a later statute. . . .

By reading § 1981 not as a general proscription of racial discrimination in all aspects of contract relations, but as limited to the enumerated rights within its express protection, specifically the right to make and enforce contracts, we may preserve the integrity of Title VII's procedures without sacrificing any significant coverage of the civil rights laws. . . .

Petitioner's claim that respondent violated § 1981 by failing to promote her, because of race, to a position as an intermediate accounting clerk is a different matter. As a preliminary point, we note that the Court of Appeals distinguished between petitioner's claims of racial harassment and discriminatory promotion, stating that although the former did not give rise to a discrete § 1981 claim, "[c]laims of racially discriminatory . . . promotion go to the very existence and nature of the employment contract and thus fall easily within § 1981's protection." . . . We think that somewhat overstates the case. Consistent with what we have said, . . . the question whether a promotion claim is actionable under § 1981 depends upon whether the nature of the change in position was such that it involved the opportunity to enter into a new contract with the employer. If so, then the employer's refusal to enter the new contract is actionable under § 1981. In making this determination, a lower court should give a fair and natural reading to the statutory phrase "the same right . . . to make . . . contracts," and should not strain in an undue manner the language of § 1981. Only where the promotion rises to the level of an opportunity for a new and distinct relation between the employee and the employer is such a claim actionable under § 1981. . . . Because respondent has not argued at any stage that petitioner's promotion claim is not cognizable under § 1981, we need not address the issue further here.

This brings us to the question of the District Court's jury instructions on petitioner's promotion claim. We think the District Court erred when it instructed the jury that petitioner had to prove that she was better qualified than the white employee who allegedly received the promotion. In order to prevail under § 1981, a plaintiff must prove purposeful discrimination. . . . Under our well-established framework, the plaintiff has the initial burden of proving, by the preponderance of the evidence, a prima facie case of discrimination. . . . The burden is not onerous. . . . Here, petitioner need only prove by a preponderance of the evidence that she applied for and was qualified for an available position, that she was rejected, and that after she was rejected respondent either continued to seek applicants for the position, or, as is alleged here, filled the position with a white employee.

Once the plaintiff establishes a prima facie case, an inference of discrimination arises. . . . In order to rebut this inference, the employer must present evidence that the plaintiff was rejected, or the other applicant was chosen, for a legitimate nondiscriminatory reason. . . . Here, respondent presented evidence that it gave the job to the white applicant because she was better qualified for the position, and therefore rebutted any presumption of discrimination that petitioner may have established. At this point, as our prior cases make clear, petitioner retains the final burden of persuading the jury of intentional discrimination.

Although petitioner retains the ultimate burden of persuasion, our cases make clear that she must also have the opportunity to demonstrate that respondent's proffered reasons for its decision were not its true reasons. . . . In doing so, petitioner is not limited to presenting evidence of a certain type. This is where the District Court erred. The evidence which petitioner can present in an attempt to establish that respondent's stated reasons are pretextual may take a variety of forms. . . . Indeed, she might seek to demonstrate that respondent's claim to have promoted a better-qualified applicant was pretextual by showing that she was in fact better qualified than the person chosen for the position. The District Court erred, however, in instructing the jury that in order to succeed petitioner was *required* to make such a showing. There are certainly other ways in which petitioner could seek to prove that respondent's reasons were pretextual. Thus, for example, petitioner could seek to persuade the jury that respondent had not offered the true reason for its promotion decision by presenting evidence of respondent's past treatment of petitioner, including the instances of the racial harassment which she alleges and respondent's failure to train her for an accounting position. . . . While we do not intend to say this evidence necessarily would be sufficient to carry the day, it cannot be denied that it is one of the various ways in which petitioner might seek to prove intentional discrimination on the part of respondent. She may not be forced to pursue any particular means of demonstrating that respondent's stated reasons are pretextual. It was, therefore, error for the District Court to instruct the jury that petitioner could carry her burden of persuasion only by showing that she was in fact better qualified than the white applicant who got the job. . . . The judgment of the Court of Appeals is therefore vacated insofar as it relates to petitioner's discriminatory promotion claim, and the case is remanded for further proceedings consistent with this opinion.

JUSTICE BRENNAN, with whom JUSTICE MARSHALL and JUSTICE BLACKMUN and JUSTICE STEVENS join, concuring in the judgment in part and dissenting in part.

What the Court declines to snatch away with one hand, it takes with the other. Though the Court today reaffirms § 1981's applicability to private conduct, it simultaneously gives this landmark civil rights statute a needlessly cramped interpretation. The Court has to strain hard to justify this choice to confine § 1981 within the narrowest possible scope, selecting the most pinched reading of the phrase "same right to make a contract," ignoring powerful historical evidence about the Reconstruction Congress' concerns, and bolstering its parsimonious rendering by reference to a statute enacted nearly a century after § 1981, and plainly not intended to affect its reach. When it comes to deciding whether a civil rights statute should be construed to further our Nation's commitment to the eradication of racial discrimination, the Court adopts a formalistic method of interpretation antithetical to Congress' vision of a society in which contractual opportunities are equal. I dissent from the Court's holding that § 1981 does not encompass Patterson's racial harassment claim. . . .

I turn now to the two issues on which certiorari was originally requested and granted in this case. The first of these is whether a plaintiff may state a cause of action under § 1981 based upon allegations that her employer harassed her because of her race. In my view, she may. . . .

The Court holds that § 1981, insofar as it gives an equal right to make a contract, "covers only conduct at the initial formation of the contract." . . . This narrow interpretation is not, as the Court would have us believe, . . . the inevitable result of the statutory grant of an equal right "to make contracts." On the contrary, the language of § 1981 is quite naturally read as extending to cover postformation conduct that demonstrates that the contract was not really made on equal terms at all.

. . . In my view, harassment is properly actionable under the language of § 1981 mandating that all persons "shall have the same right . . . to make . . . contracts . . . as is enjoyed by white citizens" if it demonstrates that the employer has in fact imposed discriminatory terms and hence has not allowed blacks to make a contract on an equal basis.

The question in a case in which an employee makes a § 1981 claim alleging racial harassment should be whether the acts constituting harassment were sufficiently severe or pervasive as effectively to belie any claim that the contract was entered into in a racially neutral manner. Where a black employee demonstrates that she has worked in conditions substantially different from those enjoyed by similarly situated white employees, and can show the necessary racial animus, a jury may infer that the black employee has not been afforded the same right to make an employment contract as white employees. . . .

Having reached its decision based upon a supposedly literal reading of § 1981, the Court goes on to suggest that its grudging interpretation of this civil rights statute has the benefit of not undermining Title VII. . . .

The Court's use of Title VII is . . . misleading. Section 1981 is a statute of general application, extending not just to employment contracts, but to *all* contracts. Thus we have held that it prohibits a private school from applying a racially discriminatory admissions policy . . . and a community recreational facility from denying membership based on race. . . . The Court, however, demonstrates no awareness at all that § 1981 is so much broader in scope than Title VII, instead focusing exclusively upon the claim that its cramped construction of § 1981 "preserve[s] the integrity of Title VII's procedures," . . . Rights as between an employer and employee simply are not involved in many § 1981 cases, and the Court's restrictive interpretation of § 1981, minimizing the overlap with Title VII, may also have the effect of restricting the availability of § 1981 as a remedy for discrimination in a host of contractual situations to which Title VII does not extend.

Applying the standards set forth above, I believe the evidence in this case brings petitioner's harassment claim firmly within the scope of § 1981.

8
THE EXERCISE OF NATIONAL POWER

The defects of the Articles of Confederation convinced the Framers that the United States needed a substantially stronger national government.[1] Under the Articles the national government could not regulate domestic commerce or levy taxes, and its powers were limited to those expressly enumerated. In the absence of a national commerce power, states taxed goods that were in transit for sale in other states and devised regulations to protect local producers from out-of-state competition, thereby impeding the flow of commerce and producing a stagnant national economy. The national government, meanwhile, was forced to rely on state contributions for its revenues—and because the states were notoriously unresponsive to requests for funds, forceful national action was impossible. Without implied powers, moreover, the national government lacked the flexibility necessary for effective responses to changing situations. To correct these problems, the Framers considerably augmented the powers of the national government. Article I, Section 8, of the new Constitution gives Congress the power "to regulate Commerce with foreign Nations, and among the several States, and with the Indian Tribes," the power to tax and to spend its revenues "to provide for the common Defense and the general Welfare of the United States," and all powers necessary and proper for carrying out its enumerated powers.

During the twentieth century, Congress has used these provisions to justify legislation affecting virtually every aspect of American life. On the basis of the commerce power, it has regulated interstate and intrastate economic activities of all sorts, to the extent that in 1970 it authorized the president to freeze all wages and prices throughout the United States.[2]

It has also relied on the commerce power in dealing with noneconomic concerns as diverse as civil rights, kidnapping, and pollution control. And relying on the spending power, Congress dispenses tax revenues through grant programs that account for about 20 percent of the expenditures of states and localities. As a result, according to one expert, "There is hardly an activity that does not involve the federal, state, and some local government in important responsibilities."[3] Is such an expansion of national concerns compatible with the constitutional division of powers between the national and state governments? Or does it threaten the federal system established by the Constitution? To answer these questions, we must trace the emergence of the contemporary interpretation of national power and analyze the constitutional arguments for and against the broad scope of that power.

THE COMMERCE POWER

Although Congress's power to regulate foreign trade has seldom been seriously challenged, its attempts to regulate commerce "among the several States" have aroused fierce resistance. The range of congressional control over commerce is crucial to American federalism because in large measure it determines the distribution of power between the national and state governments. Debate over the interpretation of the Commerce Clause generally has focused on three questions: (1) What activities constitute "commerce"? (2) If the power to regulate commercial activities is divided between the national and state governments, what portion of these activities can Congress regulate? (3) For what purposes may Congress regulate these activities? Different historical periods have supplied very different answers to these questions.

Marshall's Interpretation

Chief Justice John Marshall's opinion in *Gibbons* v. *Ogden* (1824) provides the starting point for all subsequent interpretations of the Commerce Clause. Although the case eventually was decided on the basis of an alleged conflict between federal and state law, Marshall used the occasion *Gibbons* provided to develop a broad interpretation of national power. First of all, Marshall observed, constitutional grants of power must be construed in terms of the ends for which they were conferred, for the Framers must have intended that those powers be sufficient to achieve their objectives. Since the Framers established a national commerce power to eliminate the economic chaos of the Confederation period, accordingly, the Commerce Clause at a minimum provides Congress with power adequate to accomplish this purpose. This premise supports an expansive definition of commerce. Because commerce "describes the commercial intercourse between nations, and parts of nations, in all its branches," the commerce power cannot be limited to the regulation of buying and selling but instead must encompass all aspects of economic activity. Elastic as well as broad, this power could be used to regulate new forms of commercial intercourse fostered by inventions and changes in business organization, including those unknown to the Framers. (In *Pensacola Telegraph Company* v. *Western Union Telegraph Company* (1878), for example, the Supreme Court recognized the authority of Congress to regulate telegraph companies.) With subsequent advances in transportation and communications, congressional authority has expanded accordingly.

In Marshall's view, the aims of the Commerce Clause also dictated a wide scope for congressional regulation. Since the commerce power was designed to promote the free flow of commerce among the states, he contended, Congress can deal with all obstacles to that flow, no matter how local they may be. Thus, congressional power necessarily extends to "that commerce which concerns more states than one"—a formulation that includes but is not limited to interstate commerce. Insofar as intrastate activities affect commerce "among the several states," they too are subject to congressional regulation. As the expansion of business enterprises has produced a more interdependent national economy, the range of economic activities subject to congressional regulation has increased accordingly.

Since the Marshall Court never confronted a congressional use of the Commerce Clause for noncommercial purposes, it never directly considered whether such a use was permissible. Marshall's opinion in *Gibbons* seems to suggest that Congress can regulate commerce for whatever purposes it wishes. The power to regulate, he noted, is the power "to prescribe the rules by which commerce is to be governed. This power, like all others vested in Congress, is complete in itself, may be exercised to its utmost extent, and acknowledges no limitations, other than are prescribed in the constitution. . . ." Yet in *McCulloch* v. *Maryland* and other cases, Marshall emphasized that the Constitution conveyed powers to the national government to achieve certain broad ends. The use of these powers for other ends may thus be constitutionally suspect.

Whatever the conclusion on this point, the *Gibbons* opinion did recognize that the Framers vested Congress with broad authority to regulate commerce. Within its sphere Congress was supreme, and that sphere included all economic transactions, of any nature, that affected more states than one. Although Congress did not immediately accept Marshall's implicit invitation to expand its use of the commerce power, his analysis supplied the justification that would be used in upholding vigorous congressional action during the twentieth century.

Contraction of the Commerce Power: 1888–1936

For almost a century after the Founding, the national commerce power was not a major issue, as Congress enacted little commercial legislation. The passage of the Interstate Commerce Act (1887), however, heralded a more active national role, and conflict over the scope of congressional power soon reached the Supreme Court. Starting from premises that differed from those that had guided Marshall's analysis, the Court in the late nineteenth and early twentieth centuries developed a more restrictive conception of the commerce power and invalidated important congressional legislation. Underlying the Court's interpretation of the Commerce Clause during this period was the doctrine of dual federalism (see Chapter 7), which suggests that in dividing governmental functions between the national and state governments, the Framers reserved important powers—including the police power—to the states.[4] In exercising their powers, therefore, neither the national nor the state governments may invade the other's sphere—and in particular, the national government may not use the pretext of its delegated powers to usurp the powers reserved to the states. The Court, accordingly, must interpret the Commerce Clause—along with other constitutional grants of power—so that the Framers' dual aims of adequate national power and a federal balance are both achieved. The restrictive interpretation of the Commerce Power required by this doctrine was justified in *United States* v. *E. C. Knight Company* (1895) by noting the dire effects that would presumably flow from a broad interpretation of that provision: "If the national power extends to all contracts and combinations in manufacture, agriculture, mining, and other productive industries, whose ultimate result may affect external commerce, comparatively little of business operations and affairs would be left for state control."

Under the influence of dual federalism, the Court attempted to safeguard state power by defining commerce narrowly, restricting the range of commercial activities under congressional control, and limiting the purposes for which the commerce power could be exercised. In *Knight,* which provided the authoritative interpretation of the Sherman Antitrust Act, the Court first announced its definition of commerce. At issue here were the activities of the American Sugar Refining Company, which controlled over 98 percent of the nations's sugar refining business. In holding that the antitrust act did not apply to the company's actions, the Court contended that congressional power extends only to commerce, and "commerce succeeds to manufacture, and is not a part of it." The implications of this distinction between commerce and production were enormous: at a stroke the justices had immunized from congressional regulation major elements of the national economy, including manufacturing, oil production, agriculture, and mining.

Even this artificial distinction between production and commerce might not have precluded congressional regulation if the Court had accepted Marshall's interpretation of the scope of congressional power: "that commerce which concerns more states than one." For production, even if not a part of commerce, unquestionably affects it and thus would fall within congressional control. The Court adopted a more exacting standard, however. Congress was permitted to regulate the flow of goods in interstate commerce, as well as those local transactions incidental to the transportation of goods in interstate commerce. In *Swift & Company.* v. *United States* (1905), for example, the justices ruled that the national government could prosecute stockyard firms that had conspired to monopolize the sale and distribution of fresh beef, because the purchase of cattle was merely an element in the "current of commerce" among the states. Congressional regulation of intrastate activities, on the other hand, was limited to cases in which such activities had a "direct effect," not merely an "indirect effect," on interstate commerce.

This distinction between "direct" and "indirect" effects, which in effect insulated some intrastate activities from congressional regulation, eventually proved unworkable. A vague criterion, it offered little guidance in the analysis of specific cases and contributed greatly to the inconsistency that marked the Court's decisions during this period. Judicial attempts to clarify the distinction between direct and indirect effects met with little success. When Justice George Sutherland undertook to do so in *Carter* v. *Carter Coal Company* (1936), which invalidated congressional regulation of labor relations throughout the mining industry, his explanation revealed the problems with this approach:

> The extent of the effect bears no logical relation to its character. The distinction between a direct and indirect effect turns, not upon the magnitude of either the cause or the effect, but entirely upon the manner in which the effect has been brought about. If the production by one man of a single ton of coal intended for interstate sale and shipment, and actually so sold and shipped, affects interstate commerce indirectly, the effect does not become direct by multiplying the tonnage, or increasing the number of men employed, or adding to the expense or complexities of the business, or by all combined.[5]

Following this line of logic, the Court in *Carter Coal* held that the distinction between direct and indirect effects turned on the proximity of the effect to interstate commerce, rather than on the extent of the effect. No matter how severe the effect on interstate commerce of intrastate activity, if the effect was indirect the remedy lay solely with the states. So Congress could not prevent such major interferences with the flow of commerce as nationwide strikes, because they affected commerce only "indirectly."

Even within Congress's recognized sphere of interstate commerce, the Court eventually discovered a further implicit limitation on legislative action, ruling that Congress could not use this power for noncommercial purposes. Initially, no such restriction was apparent to the Court. In *Champion* v. *Ames* (1903) the justices sustained legislation prohibiting the interstate transportation of lottery tickets, even though the law served police-power ends. Following *Champion*, Congress enacted extensive regulatory legislation—the Pure Food Act, the Narcotics Acts, and the White Slave Act, to name but a few—that also was upheld.[6] In *Hammer* v. *Dagenhart* (1918), however, the Court reversed its position in striking down a ban on interstate shipment of goods produced by child labor. Noting that the regulations in previous cases involved inherently harmful items, the majority in *Hammer* pointed out that items produced by child labor were indistinguishable from other goods except in terms of the workers involved, and that therefore the only congressional interest in banning their shipment was to prevent the employment of child labor. Because control over such matters was vested in the states, the justices concluded, Congress could not interfere in this matter. In reaching this decision, the Court followed the dictates of dual federalism, according to which grants of power to the national government were conditioned by the reserved powers of the states.

So long as Congress exercised the commerce power sparingly, collisions between Court and Congress were intermittent.[7] With the advent of the Great Depression, however, more active governmental intervention in the economy made confrontation almost inevitable. In 1935–1936 the Court struck down such important New Deal measures as the NIRA (National Industrial Recovery Act), the AAA (Agricultural Adjustment Act), and the Bituminous Coal Conservation Act,[8] and the bases for the Court's rulings presaged the invalidation of further New Deal recovery efforts. In 1937, following his landslide reelection, President Franklin Roosevelt proposed a plan to expand the membership of the Supreme Court.[9] Although defended as necessary to help the Court deal with its workload, the measure clearly was designed to secure a more favorable reception for New Deal legislation. With this "court-packing" legislation before Congress (where it ultimately died), the Court upheld the National Labor Relations Act and opened a new chapter in the interpretation of the Commerce Clause. Shortly thereafter, Justices Willis Van Devanter and George Sutherland retired, and Roosevelt's appointment of their successors solidified support for a broad view of the national commerce power.[10]

The Contemporary Era

In *National Labor Relations Board* v. *Jones & Laughlin Steel Corporation* (1937) the Court adopted Marshall's interpretation of the commerce power and applied it to contemporary economic conditions. Gone were the production/commerce dichotomy and the artificial distinction between direct and indirect effects. Asserting that judgments concerning interstate commerce must take into account "actual experience," the Court in *Jones & Laughlin* recognized that labor-management strife in nationwide industries threatens interstate commerce and so can be regulated by Congress. Other decisions indicated that the scope of congressional power turned on the *existence* of an effect on interstate commerce, not on the *extent* of the effect.[11] If Congress indicated that a class of activities had an effect on interstate commerce, then the Court would defer to that legislative judgment. The broad scope of this power was strikingly confirmed in *Wickard* v. *Filburn* (1942), in which the Court unanimously upheld congressional legislation governing the growing of wheat for domestic consumption.

Another series of decisions removed restrictions on the purposes for which Congress can employ the commerce power. In *United States* v. *Darby* (1941) the Court expressly overruled *Hammer,* holding that Congress could prohibit the interstate shipment of goods produced by workers receiving substandard wages. Justice Harlan Stone's opinion acknowledged that the *Darby* decision gave Congress wide leeway: "The motive and purpose of a regulation of interstate commerce are matters for the legislative judgment upon the exercise of which the Constitution places no restriction and over which the courts are given no control."[12]

In recent years Congress has relied on the commerce power in promoting such noncommercial ends as the protection of civil rights and the suppression of crime. Relying on the Commerce Clause, Congress in 1964 banned racial discrimination in public accommodations (restaurants, theatres, hotels, etc.) throughout the nation. The Court in *Heart of Atlanta Motel* v. *United States* (1964) upheld this ban as a valid exercise of the commerce power, and in later cases, citing *Wickard* v. *Fillburn,* sustained its application to small enterprises whose individual effect on interstate commerce was minimal.[13] In the matter of crime control, the justices ruled in *Perez* v. *United States* (1971) that the Commerce Clause provided Congress with broad authority to deal with crime. Previous Court decisions had endorsed congressional efforts to prevent misuse of the channels of interstate commerce, such as the transportation of stolen goods or kidnapped persons, and to protect the instrumentalities of interstate commerce against theft or destruction.[14] In *Perez,* however, the Court for the first time upheld congressional regulation of local criminal activity (loan sharking) that could supply funds for organized crime and thereby affect interstate commerce, even though the activities of the defendant in this particular case were purely intrastate, were unconnected to organized crime, and had no measurable effect on interstate commerce. Justice William Douglas, writing for the Court, noted that "where the *class of activities* is regulated and that *class* is within the reach of federal power, the courts have no power 'to excise as trivial, individual instances' of the class."[15] In solitary dissent Justice Potter Stewart complained that the Court's opinion offered no basis for distinguishing those crimes subject to congressional regulation from those traditionally dealt with by the states.[16]

The sole exception to the modern-day Court's expansive interpretation of the national commerce power occurred in *National League of Cities* v. *Usery* (1976), which struck down the extension of federal wages and hours requirements to state employees. Using language reminiscent of the dual-federalist Court, a five-member majority ruled in *Usery,* that Congress could not exercise its enumerated powers so as to interfere with the states' "integral governmental functions." In a series of subsequent cases, however, the Court has consistently rejected *Usery*-based challenges to federal regulations.[17] And in *Garcia* v. *San Antonio Metropolitan Transit Authority* (1985) the Court expressly overruled *Usery,* concluding that the "integral governmental functions" standard offered no clear direction for judicial decisions.

THE TAXING POWER

The Framers gave Congress the power to tax so that the national government could raise the revenues needed to finance the activities. The Constitution imposes only three express limitations on this power. Congress may not tax exports, must apportion direct taxes among the states in relation to their populations, and must impose taxes uniformly throughout the nation.[18] Only the limitation on "direct taxes"—a vague phrase neither discussed in the Constitutional Convention nor defined in the Constitution—has provoked much litigation. In *Hylton* v. *United States* (1796), the Supreme Court rejected a claim that a tax on carriages was a direct tax, noting that the term applied to head taxes and land taxes. And in *Springer* v. *United States* (1881) it concluded that the Civil War income tax was not a direct tax. But in *Pollock* v. *Farmer's Loan & Trust Company* (1895) it abandoned this position, holding that since taxes on real estate were direct taxes, so were taxes on the income from real estate. This decision, which in effect prevented the imposition of any type of federal income tax, was reversed by the ratification of the Sixteenth Amendment (1913).

A more serious constitutional issue stems from the uses Congress may make of its taxing power. All taxes, in addition to raising revenues, make goods more expensive, and thereby discourage their purchase. Obviously, this side effect of taxation can serve regulatory purposes. But does the mere fact that the Constitution places few restrictions on the goods and activities Congress can tax mean that the taxing power can be used for regulatory—as opposed to revenue-raising—purposes?

During the nineteenth century, debate over this question centered on protective tariffs, which both raise revenues and shield American industries from foreign competition. In pursuing the latter objective, Congress was using its taxing power for a regulatory purpose. Because the Constitution grants Congress regulatory authority over commerce with foreign nations, however, protective tariffs involve activities that Congress could regulate by other means, if it so chose. Thus the constitutionality of this use of the taxing power was generally recognized long before the Supreme Court upheld a protective tariff in *J. W. Hampton, Jr. & Company* v. *United States* (1928).

With the resolution of the controversy over protective tariffs, debate shifted to congressional use of the taxing power to reach activities it could not otherwise regulate. In *McCrary* v. *United States* (1904), the Court endorsed one such use of the taxing power, upholding a heavy excise tax on margarine that had been colored yellow to resemble butter. Although the tax clearly was designed to discourage purchase of the colored margarine, the Court insisted that it could not question the motives underlying the exercise of constitutionally granted powers. Yet it did exactly that in *Bailey* v. *Drexel Furniture Company* (1922), in which the justices struck down a law that imposed a 10 percent tax on the profits of all businesses employing children. Writing for the majority of the Court,

Chief Justice Howard Taft acknowledged that all taxes have regulatory effects but noted that "there comes a time in the extension of the penalizing features of the so-called tax when it loses its character as such and becomes a mere penalty, with the characteristics of regulation and punishment."[19] And if Congress cannot regulate an activity—and the Court in *Hammer* v. *Dagenhart* had ruled that it could not regulate child labor—then it cannot regulate indirectly through the subterfuge of a "so-called tax." Interestingly, although the Court was closely divided in *Hammer*, only one justice dissented in *Bailey*.

In *United States* v. *Butler* (1936) the Court employed the *Bailey* rationale in striking down the Agricultural Adjustment Act of 1933. Since 1937, however, the Court has refused to monitor the motives underlying congressional tax laws. An act virtually identical to the one struck down in *Butler* was upheld in *Mulford* v. *Smith* (1939), and in *United States* v. *Kahriger* (1953) an occupational tax on gamblers was upheld, even though the tax's primary aim was to suppress gambling. Although the Court eventually declared the tax unconstitutional on self-incrimination grounds in *Marchetti* v. *United States* (1968), in doing so it reasserted that only explicit constitutional prohibitions—not the reserved powers of the states—justify invalidation of congressional tax statutes. Thus the power to tax, like the power to regulate commerce, is plenary.

THE SPENDING POWER

Article I, Section 8 authorizes Congress "to pay the debts and provide for the common defense and general welfare of the United States." During the ratification debates, this broad grant of power worried critics of the Constitution, who asserted that it would transform the national government into a government of indefinite, rather than enumerated, powers. James Madison rejected this interpretation, maintaining in *The Federalist*, No. 41, that the enumeration of congressional powers that followed the general authorization served to "explain and qualify" it. To Madison, then, the spending power was subordinate to, rather than independent of, the Constitution's grants of legislative power. In his famous *Report on Manufactures*, however, Alexander Hamilton challenged Madison's view that the enumeration of powers served to limit the spending power and proposed a more expansive interpretation:

> The phrase is as comprehensive as any that could have been used, because it was not fit that the constitutional authority of the Union to appropriate its revenues should have been restricted within narrower limits than the "general welfare" and because this necessarily embraces a vast variety of particulars which are susceptible neither of specification nor of definition. It is therefore of necessity left to the discretion of the National Legislature to pronounce upon the objects

> which concern the general welfare, and for which, under the description, an appropriation of money is requisite and proper.[20]

Throughout most of the nation's history, Congressional practice has been guided by the Hamiltonian position, which the Supreme Court explicitly endorsed in *Butler.* Justice Owen Roberts did maintain in *Butler* that the spending power was limited by the reserved powers of the states, but the Court repudiated this position in *Steward Machine Company* v. *Davis* (1937) and *Helvering* v. *Davis* (1937).

Congress's power to spend is not completely unrestricted, however. All congressional expenditures must provide for the "common defense" or the "general welfare." In practice, this requirement is easily met: as the Court has recognized, Congress has primary responsibility for determining whether expenditures promote the general welfare, and courts may challenge only those determinations that are "clearly wrong, a display of arbitrary power, not an exercise of judgment."[21] Expenditures, like all other congressional actions, also are subject to express constitutional limitations such as the Bill of Rights. The requirement of standing (see Chapter 3), however, has limited judicial enforcement of these restrictions. In *Frothingham* v. *Mellon* (1923) the Court, rejecting a challenge to congressional appropriations in aid of expectant mothers, held that ordinary taxpayers generally lacked standing to contest Federal expenditures. This stricture was eased somewhat by the holding in *Flast* v. *Cohen* (1968) that taxpayers could sue when the "challenged enactment exceeds specific constitutional limitations imposed upon the exercise of the congressional taxing and spending power."[22] But later decisions—most notably *United States* v. *Richardson* (1974)—cast considerable doubt on the Court's willingness to entertain taxpayer challenges to appropriations.

LIMITATIONS ON NATIONAL POWER

Responding to the deficiencies of the Articles of Confederation, the Framers vested Congress with broad powers to tax, to spend, and to regulate commerce. In view of the modern Court's expansive interpretation of these powers, it seems fair to ask whether any limitations remain on the exercise of national power. *National League of Cities* v. *Usery* suggested that the preservation of state sovereignty furnished one such limitation, but it was overruled in *Garcia* v. *San Antonio Metropolitan Transit Authority.* Of greater importance are the limitations imposed by the Bill of Rights. It is no coincidence that as the scope of national activity has expanded, the Court has found increasing occasion to invalidate congressional legislation violating these protections.

Nevertheless, the primary limitation on the exercise of national power is political, not constitutional, in character. As Chief Justice Marshall observed in *Gibbons* v. *Ogden,* "The wisdom and the discretion of Congress, their identity with the people, and the influence which their constituents possess at election, are . . . the restraints on which the people must often rely solely, in all representative governments."

NOTES

1 Alexander Hamilton opens *The Federalist*, No. 1, by noting the "unequivocal experience of the inefficacy of the subsisting federal government," and many of the early papers are devoted to elaborating the defects of the Articles of Confederation.

2 The Economic Stabilization Act of 1970 was upheld against constitutional challenge in *Amalgamated Meat Cutters & Butcher Workmen* v. *Connally*, 337 F. Supp. 737 (D.D.C. 1971).

3 Morton Grodzins, *The American System; A New View of Government in the United States*, ed. Daniel J. Elazer (Chicago: Rand McNally, 1966), p. 4.

4 For a penetrating discussion of dual federalism, see Edward S. Corwin, "The Passing of Dual Federalism," in Robert G. McCloskey, ed., *Essays in Constitutional Law* (New York: Alfred A. Knopf, 1957).

5 *Carter* v. *Carter Coal Co.*, 298 U.S. 238, 308 (1936).

6 See *Hipolite Egg Co.* v. *United States* (1911) and *Hoke* v. *United States* (1913).

7 From 1888 to 1933 the Supreme Court struck down forty federal laws; from 1934 to 1936, it struck down thirteen. For a listing of these cases, see Henry J. Abraham, *The Judicial Process*, 5th ed. (New York: Oxford University Press, 1986), Table 9, pp. 295–298.

8 *Schecter Poultry Corp.* v. *United States* (1935), *United States* v. *Butler* (1936), and *Carter* v. *Carter Coal Co.* (1936).

9 This plan is discussed in Robert H. Jackson, *The Struggle for Judicial Supremacy* (New York: A. A. Knopf, 1941); and William E. Leuchtenburg, "The Origins of Franklin D. Roosevelt's 'Court-Packing' Plan," 1966 *Supreme Court Review.*

10 Justice Van Devanter retired in 1937 and was replaced by Justice Hugo Black. Justice Sutherland retired in 1938 and was replaced by Justice Stanley Reed.

11 This is illustrated in a series of cases, including *NLRB* v. *Friedman-Harry Marks Clothing Co.* (1937), *NLRB* v. *Fainblatt* (1939), and *Santa Cruz* v. *NLRB* (1938).

12 *United States* v. *Darby*, 312 U.S. 100, 115 (1941).

13 In *Katzenbach* v. *McClung* (1964) the Court upheld application of the Civil Rights Act of 1964 to Ollie's Barbecue, a family-owned restaurant that did not cater to interstate travelers; and in *Daniel* v. *Paul* (1969) the act was held to apply to a rural amusement park in Arkansas.

14 On interstate transportation of stolen automobiles, see *Brooks* v. *United States* (1925); on interstate transportation of kidnapped persons, see *Gooch* v. *United States* (1936).

15 *Perez* v. *United States*, 402 U.S. 146, 154 (1971).

16 The implications of *Perez* are surveyed in Robert L. Stern, "The Commerce Clause Revisited—the Federalization of Intrastate Crime," *Arizona Law Review* 15 (1973).

17 These cases include *Hodel* v. *Virginia Surface Mining & Reclamation Association*, 452 U.S. 264 (1981); *Hodel* v. *Indiana*, 452 U.S. 314 (1981); *Federal*

Energy Regulatory Commission v. *Mississippi*, 456 U.S. 742 (1982); and *Equal Employment Opportunities Commission* v. *Wyoming*, 460 U.S. 226 (1983).

18 These restrictions on the federal taxing power are found in Article I, Section 8, Paragraph 1, and Article I, Section 9, Paragraphs 4 and 5.

19 *Bailey* v. *Drexel Furniture Co.*, 259 U.S. 20, 38 (1922).

20 Alexander Hamilton, *The Works of Alexander Hamilton*, ed. Henry Cabot Lodge (New York: Federal Edition, 1904), 4:151.

21 *Helvering* v. *Davis*, 301 U.S. 619, 640 (1937).

22 *Flast* v. *Cohen*, 392 U.S. 83, 102–103 (1968).

SELECTED READINGS

The Federalist, Nos. 30–36, 41–42, 56.

Bailey v. *Drexel Furniture Company*, 259 U.S. 20 (1922).
Carter v. *Carter Coal Company*, 298 U.S. 238 (1936).
Garcia v. *San Antonio Metropolitan Transit Authority*, Chapter 7 (1985).
Perez v. *United States*, 402 U.S. 146 (1971).
United States v. *Darby*, 312 U.S. 100 (1941).

Barber, Sotorios A. *On What the Constitution Means* (Baltimore: Johns Hopkins University Press, 1984), Chapter 4.

Choper, Jesse H. *Judicial Review and the National Political Process; A Functional Reconsideration of the Role of the Supreme Court.* (Chicago: University of Chicago Press, 1980).

Corwin, Edward S. "The Passing of Dual Federalism." In Robert G. McCloskey, ed., *Essays in Constitutional Law.* (New York: Vintage, 1957).

Epstein, Richard A. "The Proper Scope of the Commerce Power," *Virginia Law Review* 73 (1987).

Frankfurter, Felix. *The Commerce Clause Under Marshall, Taney and Waite* (Chapel Hill: University of North Carolina Press, 1937).

McCoy, Thomas R., and Barry Friedman. "Conditional Spending: Federalism's Trojan Horse," *Supreme Court Review* (1988).

Swisher, Carl Brent. *The Growth of Constitutional Power in the United States.* 2d. ed. (Chicago: University of Chicago Press, 1963).

Gibbons v. *Ogden*

9 Wheat 1, 6 L. Ed. 23 (1824)

Robert Fulton and Robert Livingston, having obtained from the state of New York an exclusive right to operate steamboats in its waters, licensed Aaron Ogden to operate steamboats between New Jersey and New York. But Thomas Gibbons, armed with a federal license under the Coasting Act of 1793 (in which Congress provided for the licensing of "vessels employed in the coasting trade"), challenged the state-granted monopoly by running two steamboats between Elizabethtown, New Jersey, and New York City. When the New York Court of Chancery enjoined Gibbons from continuing to operate his boats, he appealed the decision to the United States Supreme Court. *Opinion of the Court: Marshall, Todd, Duval, Story, Thompson. Concurring opinion: Johnson.*

MR. CHIEF JUSTICE MARSHALL delivered the opinion of the Court.

As preliminary to the very able discussions of the constitution, which we have heard from the bar, and as having some influence on its construction, reference has been made to the political situation of these states, anterior to its formation. It has been said, that they were sovereign, were completely independent, and were connected with each other only by a league. This is true. But when these allied sovereigns converted their league into a government, when they converted their congress of ambassadors, deputed to deliberate on their common concerns, and to recommend measures of general utility into a legislature, empowered to enact laws on the most interesting subjects, the whole character in which the states appear, underwent a change, the extent of which must be determined by a fair consideration of the instrument by which that change was effected.

This instrument contains an enumeration of powers expressly granted by the people to their government. It has been said, that these powers ought to be construed strictly. But why ought they to be so construed? Is there one sentence in the constitution which gives countenance to this rule? In the last of the enumerated powers, that which grants, expressly, the means for carrying all others into execution, congress is authorized "to make all laws which shall be necessary and proper" for the purposes. But this limitation on the means which may be used, is not extended to the powers which are conferred; nor is there one sentence in the constitution which has been pointed out by the gentlemen of the bar, or which we have been able to discern, that prescribes this rule. We do not, therefore, think ourselves justified in adopting it. What do gentlemen mean, by a strict construction? If they contend only against that enlarged construction, which would extend words beyond their natural and obvious import, we might question the application of the term, but should not controvert the principle. If they contend for that narrow construction which, in support of some theory not to be found in the constitution, would deny to the government those powers which the words of the grant, as usually understood, import, and which are consistent with the general views and objects of the instrument—for that narrow construction, which would cripple the government, and render it unequal to the objects for which it is declared to be instituted, and to which the powers given, as fairly understood, render it competent—then we cannot perceive the propriety of this strict construction, nor adopt it as the rule by which the constitution is to be expounded. . . .

The words are, "congress shall have power to regulate commerce with foreign nations, and among the several states, and with the Indian tribes." The subject to be regulated is commerce; and our constitution being, as was aptly said at the bar, *one of enumeration, and not of definition,* to ascertain the extent of the power, it becomes necessary to settle the meaning of the word. The counsel for the appellee would limit it to traffic, to buying and selling, or the interchange of commodities, and do not admit that it comprehends navigation. This would restrict a general term, applicable to many objects, to one of its significations. Commerce, undoubtedly, is traffic, but it something more—it is intercourse. It describes the commercial intercourse between nations, and parts of nations, in all its branches, and is regulated by prescribing rules for carrying on that intercourse. The mind can scarcely conceive a system for regulating commerce between nations, which shall exclude all laws concerning navigation, which shall be silent on the admission of the vessels of the one nation into the parts of the other, and be confined to prescribing rules for the conduct of individuals, in the actual employment of buying and selling, or of barter. If commerce does not include navigation, the government of the Union has no direct power over that subject, and can make no law prescribing what shall constitute American vessels or requiring that they shall be navigated by American seamen. Yet this power has been exercised from the commencement of the government, has been exercised with the consent of all, and has been understood by all to be a commercial regulation. All America understands, and has uniformly understood, the word "commerce," to comprehend navigation. It was so understood, and must have been so understood, when the constitution was framed. The power over commerce, including navigation, was one of the primary objects for which the people of America adopted their government, and must have been contemplated in forming it. The convention must have used the word in that sense, because all have understood it in that sense; and the attempt to restrict it comes too late.

The word used in the constitution, then, comprehends, and has been always understood to comprehend, navigation within its meaning; and a power to regulate navigation, is as expressly granted, as if that term had been added to the word "commerce." To what commerce does this power extend? The constitution informs us, to commerce "with foreign nations, and among the several states, and with the Indian tribes." It has, we believe, been universally admitted, that these words comprehend every species of commercial intercourse between the United States and foreign nations. . . .

If this be the admitted meaning of the word, in its application to foreign nations, it must carry the same meaning throughout the sentence, and remain a unit, unless there be some plain intelligible cause which alters it. The subject to which the power is next applied, is to commerce, "among the several states." The word "among" means intermingled with. A thing which is among others, is intermingled with them. Commerce among the states, cannot stop at the external boundary line of each state, but may be introduced into the interior. It is not intended to say, that these words comprehend that commerce, which is completely internal, which is carried on between man and man in a state, or between different parts of the same state, and which does extend to or affect other states. Such a power would be inconvenient, and is certainly unnecessary. Comprehensive as the word "among" is, it may very properly be restricted to that commerce which concerns more states than one. . . . The genius and character of the whole government seem to be, that its action is to be applied to all the external concerns of the nation, and to those internal concerns which affect the states generally; but not to those which are completely within a particular state, which do not affect other states, and with which it is not necessary to interfere, for the purpose of executing some of the general powers of the government. The completely internal commerce of a state, then, may be considered as reserved for the state itself.

But in regulating commerce with foreign nations, the power of congress does not stop at the jurisdictional lines of the several states. . . . If congress has the power to regulate it, that power must be exercised whenever the subject exists. If it exists within the states, if a foreign voyage may commence or terminate at a port within a state, then the power of congress may be exercised within a state.

This principle is, if possible, still more clear, when applied to commerce "among the several states." They either join each other, in which case they are separated by a mathematical line, or they are remote from each other, in which case other states lie between them. What is commerce "among" them; and how is it to be conducted? Can a trading expedition between two adjoining states, commence and terminate outside of each? And if the trading intercourse be between two states remote from each other, must it not commence in one, terminate in the other, and probably pass through a third? . . . The power of congress, then, whatever it may be, must be exercised within the territorial jurisdiction of the several states. . . .

We are now arrived at the inquiry—what is the power? It is the power to regulate; that is, to prescribe the rule by which commerce is to be governed. This power, like all others vested in congress, is complete in itself, may be exercised to its utmost extent, and acknowledges no limitations, other than are prescribed in the constitution. If, as has always been understood, the sovereignty of congress, though limited to specified objects, is plenary as to those objects, the power over commerce with foreign nations, and among the several states, is vested in congress as absolutely as it would be in a single government, having in its constitution the same restrictions on the exercise of the power as are found in the constitution of the United States. The wisdom and the discretion of congress, their identity with the people, and the influence which their constituents possess at elections, are, in this, as in many other instances, as that, for example, of declaring war, the sole restraints on which they have relied, to secure them from its abuse. They are the restraints on which the people must often rely solely, in all representative governments.

But it has been urged, with great earnestness, that although the power of congress to regulate commerce with foreign nations, and among the several states, be co-extensive with the subject itself, and have no other limits than are prescribed in the constitution, yet the states may severally exercise the same power, within their respective jurisdictions.

The grant of the power to lay and collect taxes is, like the power to regulate commerce, made in general terms, and has never been understood to interfere with the exercise of the same power by the states; and hence has been drawn an argument which as been applied to the question under consideration. But the two grants are not, it is conceived, similar in their terms or their nature. Although many of the powers formerly exercised by the states, are transferred to the government of the Union, yet the state governments remain, and constitute a most important part of our system. The power of taxation is indispensable to their existence, and is a power which, in its own nature, is capable of residing in, and being exercised by, different authorities, at the same time. We are accustomed to see it placed, for different purposes, in different hands. Taxation is the simple operation of taking small portions from a perpetually accumulating mass, susceptible of almost infinite division; and a power in one to take what is necessary for certain purposes, is not, in its nature, incompatible with a power in another to take what is necessary for other purposes. Congress is authorized to lay and collect taxes, &c., to pay the debts, and provide for the common defense and general welfare of the United States. This does not interfere with the power of the states to tax for the support of their own governments; nor is the exercise of that power by the states, an exercise of any portion of the power that is granted to the United States. In imposing taxes for state purposes, they are not doing what congress is empowered to do. Congress is not empowered to tax for those purposes which are within the exclusive province of the states. When, then, each government exercises the power of taxation, neither is exercising the power of the other. But when a state proceeds to regulate commerce with foreign nations, or among the several states, it is exercising the very power that is granted to congress, and is doing the very thing which congress is authorized to do. There is no analogy, then, between the power of taxation and the power of regulating commerce.

In discussing the question, whether this power is still in the states, in the case under consideration, we may dismiss from it the inquiry, whether it is surrendered by the mere grant to congress, or is retained until congress shall exercise the power. We may dismiss that inquiry, because it has been exercised, and the regulations which congress deemed it proper to make, are now in full operation. The sole question is, can a state regulate commerce with foreign nations and among the states, while congress is regulating it?

. . . The inspection laws are said to be regulations of commerce and are certainly recognised in the constitution, as being passed in the exercise of a power remaining with the states. That inspection laws may have a remote and considerable influence on commerce, will not be denied: but that a power to regulate commerce is the source from which the right to pass them is derived cannot be admitted. The object of inspection laws, is to improve the quality of articles produced by the labor of a country: to do them for exportation; or, it may be, for domestic use. They act upon the subject, before it becomes an article of foreign commerce, or of commerce among the states, and prepare it for that purpose. They form a portion of that immense mass of legislation, which embraces everything within the territory of a state, not surrendered to the general government; all which can be most advantageously exercised by the states themselves. Inspection laws, quarantine laws, health laws of every description, as well as laws for regulating the internal commerce of a state, and those which respect turnpike-roads, ferries, &c., are component parts of this mass.

No direct general power over these objects is granted to congress; and, consequently, they remain subject to state legislation. If the legislative power of the Union can reach them, it must be for national purposes; it must be, where the power is expressly given for a special purpose, or is clearly incidental to some power which is expressly given. It is obvious, that the government of the Union, in the exercise of its express powers, that, for example, of regulating commerce with foreign nations and among the states, may use means that may also be employed by a state, in the exercise of its acknowledged powers; that, for example, of regulating commerce within the state. . . .

In our complex system, presenting the rare and difficult scheme of one general government, whose action extends over the whole, but which possesses only certain enumerated powers; and of numerous state governments, which retain and exercise all powers not delegated to the Union, contests respecting power must arise. Were it even otherwise, the measures taken by the respective governments to execute their acknowledged powers, would often be of the same description, and might, sometimes, interfere. This, however, does not prove that the one is exercising, or has a right to exercise, the powers of the other. . . .

Since, however, in exercising the power of regulating their own purely internal affairs, whether of trading or police, the states may sometimes enact laws, the validity of which depends on their interfering with, and being contrary to, an act of congress passed in pursuance of the constitution, the court will enter upon the inquiry, whether the laws of New York, as expounded by the highest tribunal of that state, have in their application to this case, come into collision with an act of congress and deprived a citizen of a right to which that act entitles him. Should this collision exist, it will be immaterial, whether those laws were passed in virtue of a concurrent power "to regulate commerce with foreign nations and among the several states" or in virtue of a power to regulate their domestic trade and police. In one case and the other, the acts of New York must yield to the law of congress; and the decision sustaining the privilege they confer, against a right given by a law of the Union, must be erroneous. This opinion has been frequently expressed in this court, and is founded, as well on the nature of the government, as on the words of the constitution. In argument, however, it has been contended, that if a law passed by a state, in the exercise of its acknowledged sovereignty, comes into conflict with a law passed by congress in pursuance of the constitution, they affect the subject, and each other, like equal opposing powers. But the framers of our constitution foresaw this state of things, and provided for it, by developing the supremacy not only of itself, but of the laws made in pursuance of it. The nullity of any act, inconsistent with the constitution is produced by the declaration, that the constitution is the supreme law. The appropriate application of that part of the clause which confers the same supremacy on laws and treaties, is to such acts of the state legislatures do not transcend their powers, by though enacted in the execution of acknowledged state powers, interfere with, or are contrary to the laws of congress, made in pursuance of the constitution, or some treaty made under the authority of the United States. In every such case the acts of congress, or the treaty, is supreme; and the law of the state, though enacted in the exercise of powers not controverted, must yield to it. . . .

But all inquiry into this subject seems to the court to be put completely at rest, by the act already mentioned, entitled, "an act for the enrolling and licensing of steamboats." This act authorizes a steam boat employed, or intended to be employed, only in a river or bay of the United States, owned wholly or in part by an alien, resident within the United States, to be enrolled and licensed as if the same belonged to a citizen of the United States. This act demonstrates the opinion of congress, that steamboats may be enrolled and licensed, in common with vessels using sails. They are, of course, entitled to the same privileges, and can no more be restrained from navigating waters, and entering ports which are free to such vessels, than if they were wafted on their voyage by the winds, instead of being propelled by the agency of fire. The one element may be as legitimately used as the other, for every commercial purpose authorized by the laws of the Union; and the act of a state inhibiting the use of either, to any vessel having a license under the act of congress, comes, we think, in direct collision with that act.

MR. JUSTICE JOHNSON, concurring.

The judgment entered by the court in this cause, has my entire approbation; but having adopted my conclusions on views of the subject materially different from those of my brethren, I feel it incumbent on me to exhibit those views....

In attempts to construe the constitution, I have never found much benefit resulting from the inquiry, whether the whole; or any part of it, is to be construed strictly or liberally. The simple, classical, precise, yet comprehensive language in which it is couched, leaves, at most, but very little latitude for construction; and when its intent and meaning are discovered, nothing remains but to execute the will of those who made it, in the best manner to effect the purposes intended. The great and paramount purpose was, to unite this mass of wealth and power, for the protection of the humblest individual; his rights, civil and political, his interests and prosperity, are the sole end; the rest are nothing but the means....

The history of the times will ... sustain the opinion, that the grant of power over commerce, if intended to be commensurate with the evils existing, and the purpose of remedying those evils, could be only commensurate with the power of the states over the subject....

... But what was that power? The states were, unquestionably, supreme; and each possessed that power over commerce, which is acknowledged to reside in every sovereign state.... The power of a sovereign state over commerce, therefore, amounts to nothing more than a power to limit and restrain it at pleasure. And since the power to prescribe the limits to its freedom, necessarily implies the power to determine what shall remain unrestrained, it follows, that the power must be exclusive: it can reside but in one potentate; and hence, the grant of this power carries with it the whole subject, leaving nothing for the state to act upon.

United States v. *E. C. Knight Company*

156 U.S. 1, 15 S. Ct. 249, 39 L. Ed. 325 (1895)

By purchasing the stock of four Philadelphia sugar refineries with shares of its own stock, the American Sugar Refining Company acquired control of over 98 percent of the nation's sugar refining business. The federal government charged that this action constituted a violation of the Sherman Antitrust Act, passed by Congress in 1890, which made it illegal to monopolize or restrain—or seek to monopolize or restrain—interstate or foreign commerce through any contact, combination, or conspiracy. The basic issue in this case was thus the interpretation of the statute: does the acquisition of control over the sugar refining business constitute a monopoly in interstate commerce? But in interpreting the statute, the Court sought to construe it so as to render it constitutional. Thus the Court's construction of the statute depended upon its understanding of the scope of national regulatory authority under the Commerce Clause. *Opinion of the Court: Fuller, Field, Gray, Brewer, Brown, Shiras, White, Peckham. Dissenting opinion: Harlan.*

Mr. Chief Justice Fuller . . . delivered the opinion of the Court.

The fundamental question is, whether conceding that the existence of a monopoly in manufacture is established by the evidence, that monopoly can be directly suppressed under the act of Congress in the mode attempted by this bill.

It cannot be denied that the power of a State to protect the lives, health, and property of its citizens, and to preserve good order and the public morals, "the power to govern men and things within the limits of its dominion," is a power originally and always belonging to the States, not surrendered by them to the general government, nor directly restrained by the Constitution of the United States, and essentially exclusive. . . . On the other hand, the power of Congress to regulate commerce among the several States is also exclusive. . . . That which belongs to commerce is within the jurisdiction of the United States, but that which does not belong to commerce is within the jurisdiction of the police power of the State. . . .

The argument is that the power to control the manufacture of refined sugar is a monopoly over a necessary of life, to the enjoyment of which by a large part of the population of the United States interstate commerce is indispensable, and that, therefore, the general government in the exercise of the power to regulate commerce may repress such monopoly directly and set aside the instruments which have created it. But this argument cannot be confined to necessaries of life merely, and must include all articles of general consumption. Doubtless the power to control the manufacture of a given thing involves in a certain sense the control of its disposition, but this is a secondary and not the primary sense; and although the exercise of that power may result in bringing the operation of commerce into play, it does not control it, and affects it only incidentally and indirectly. Commerce succeeds to manufacture, and is not a part of it. The power to regulate commerce is the power to prescribe the rule by which commerce shall be governed, and is a power independent of the power to suppress monopoly. But it may operate in repression of monopoly whenever that comes within the rules by which commerce is governed or whenever the transaction is itself a monopoly of commerce.

It is vital that the independence of the commercial power and of the police power, and the delimitation between them, however sometimes perplexing, should always be recognized and observed, for while the one furnishes the strongest bond of union, the other is essential to the preservation of the autonomy of the States as required by our dual form of government; and acknowledged evils, however grave and urgent they may appear to be, had better be borne, than the risk be run, in the effort to suppress them, of more serious consequences by resort to expedients of even doubtful constitutionality.

It will be perceived how far-reaching the proposition is that the power of dealing with a monopoly directly may be exercised by the general government whenever interstate or international commerce may be ultimately affected. The regulation of commerce applies to the subjects of commerce and not to matters of internal police. Contracts to buy, sell, or exchange goods to be transported among the several States, the transportation and its instrumentalities, and articles bought, sold, or exchanged for the purposes of such transit among the States, or put in the way of transit, may be regulated, but this is because they form part of interstate trade or commerce. The fact that an article is manufactured for export to another State does not of itself make it an article of interstate commerce, and the intent of the manufacturer does not determine the time when the article or product passes from the control of the State and belongs to commerce. . . .

Contracts, combinations, or conspiracies to control domestic enterprise in manufacture, agriculture, mining, production in all its forms, or to raise or lower prices or wages, might unquestionably tend to restrain external as well as domestic trade, but the restraint would be an indirect result, however inevitable and whatever its extent, and such result would not necessarily determine the object of the contract, combination, or conspiracy.

. . . Slight reflection will show that if the national power extends to all contracts and combinations in manufacture, agriculture, mining, and other productive industries, whose ultimate result may affect external commerce, comparatively little of business operations and affairs would be left for state control.

It was in the light of well-settled principles that the act of July 2, 1890, was framed. Congress did not attempt thereby to assert the power to deal with monopoly directly as such. . . . What the law struck at was combinations, contracts, and conspiracies to monopolize trade and commerce among the several States or with foreign nations; but the contracts and acts of the defendants related exclusively to the acquisition of the Philadelphia refineries and the business of sugar refining in Pennsylvania, and bore no direct relation to commerce between the States or with foreign nations. The object was manifestly private gain in the manufacture of the commodity, but not through the control of interstate or foreign commerce. It is true that the bill alleged that the products of these refineries were sold and distributed among the several States, and that all the companies were engaged in trade or commerce with the several States and with foreign nations; but this was no more than to say that trade and commerce served manufacture to fulfill its function. . . . It does not follow that an attempt to monopolize, or the actual monopoly of, the manufacture was an attempt, whether executory or consummated, to monopolize commerce, even though, in order to dispose of the product, the instrumentality of commerce was necessarily invoked. There was nothing in the proofs to indicate any intention to put a restraint upon trade or commerce, and the fact, was we have seen, that trade or commerce might be indirectly affected was not enough to entitle complainants to a decree. . . .

Decree affirmed.

Hammer v. *Dagenhart*

247 U.S. 251, 38 S. Ct. 529, 62 L. Ed. 1101 (1918)

The Federal Child Labor Act of 1916, which was designed to discourage the employment of child labor, prohibited the shipment in interstate commerce of goods produced in factories that employed children under the age of fourteen or permitted children under age sixteen to work either at night or for more than eight hours a day. Dagenhart, whose sons worked in his cotton mill, challenged the act in federal district court. When the district court invalidated the act, the case was appealed to the Supreme Court. *Opinion of the Court: Day, White, Van Devanter, Pitney, McReynolds. Dissenting opinion: Holmes, McKenna, Brandeis, Clarke.*

MR. JUSTICE DAY delivered the opinion of the Court. . . .

The controlling question for decision is: Is it within the authority of Congress in regulating commerce among the States to prohibit the transportation in interstate commerce of manufactured goods, the product of a factory in which, within thirty days prior to their removal therefrom, children under the age of fourteen have been employed or permitted to work, or children between the ages of fourteen and sixteen years have been employed or permitted to work more than eight hours in any day, or more than six days in any week, or after the hour of seven o'clock P.M. or before the hour of 6 o'clock A.M.? . . .

[*Mr. Justice Day then reviewed the Court's previous decisions regarding the use of the Commerce Clause for noncommercial purposes.*]

In each of these instances the use of interstate transportation was necessary to the accomplishment of harmful results. In other words, although the power over interstate transportation was to regulate, that could only be accomplished by prohibiting the use of facilities of interstate commerce to effect the evil intended.

This element is wanting in the present case. The thing intended to be accomplished by this statute is the denial of the facilities of interstate commerce to those manufacturers in the States who employ children within the prohibited ages. The act in its effect does not regulate transportation among the States, but aims to standardize the ages at which children may be employed in mining and manufacturing within the States. The goods shipped are of themselves harmless. The act permits them to be freely shipped after thirty days from the time of their removal from the factory. When offered for shipment, and before transportation begins, the labor of their production is over, and the mere fact that they were intended for interstate commerce transportation does not make their production subject to federal control under the commerce power. . . .

It is further contended that the authority of Congress may be exerted to control interstate commerce in the shipment of child-made goods because of the effects of the circulation of such goods in other States where the evil of this class of labor has been recognized by local legislation, and the right to thus employ child labor has been more rigorously restrained than in the State of production. In other words, that the unfair competition, thus engendered, may be controlled by closing the channels of interstate commerce to manufacturers in those States where the local laws do not meet what Congress deems to be the more just standard of other States.

There is no power vested in Congress to require the States to exercise their police power so as to prevent possible unfair competition. Many causes may cooperate to give one State, by reason of local laws or conditions, an economic advantage over others. The Commerce Clause was not intended to give to Congress a general authority to equalize such conditions. . . .

A statute must be judged by its natural and reasonable effect. The control by Congress over interstate commerce cannot authorize the exercise of authority not entrusted to it by the Constitution. . . . The maintenance of the authority of the States over matters purely local is as essential to the preservation of our institutions as is the conservation of the supremacy of the federal power in all matters entrusted to the Nation by the Federal Constitution. . . .

. . . To sustain this statute would not be in our judgment a recognition of the lawful exertion of congressional authority over interstate commerce, but would sanction an invasion by the federal power of the control of a matter purely local in its character, and over which no authority has been delegated to Congress in conferring the power to regulate commerce among the States.

In our view the necessary effect of this act is, by means of a prohibition against the movement in interstate commerce of ordinary commercial commodities, to regulate the hours of labor of children in factories and mines within the States, a purely state authority. Thus the act in a twofold sense is repugnant to the Constitution. It not only transcends the authority delegated to Congress over commerce but also exerts a power as to a purely local matter to which the federal authority does not extend. The far reaching result of upholding the act cannot be more plainly indicated than by pointing out that if Congress can thus regulate matters entrusted to local authority by prohibition of the movement of commodities in interstate commerce, all freedom of commerce will be at an end, and the power of the States over local matters may be eliminated, and thus our system of government be practically destroyed.

Affirmed.

MR. JUSTICE HOLMES, dissenting.

The first step in my argument is to make plain what no one is likely to dispute—that the statute in question is within the power expressly given to Congress if considered only as to its immediate effects and that if invalid it is so only upon some collateral ground. The statute confines itself to prohibiting the carriage of certain goods in interstate or foreign commerce. Congress is given power to regulate such commerce in unqualified terms. . . .

The question then is narrowed to whether the exercise of its otherwise constitutional power by Congress can be pronounced unconstitutional because of its possible reaction upon the conduct of the States in a matter upon which I have admitted that they are free from direct control. I should have thought that that matter had been disposed of so fully as to leave no room for doubt. I should have thought that the most conspicuous decisions of this Court had made it clear that the power to regulate commerce and other constitutional powers could not be cut down or qualified by the fact that it might interfere with the carrying out of the domestic policy of any State. . . .

The notion that prohibition is any less prohibition when applied to things now thought evil I do not understand. But if there is any matter upon which civilized countries have agreed—far more unanimously than they have with regard to intoxicants and some other matters over which this country is now emotionally aroused—it is the evil of premature and excessive child labor. I should have thought that if we were to introduce our own moral conceptions where in my opinion they do not belong, this was preeminently a case for upholding the exercise of all its powers by the United States.

But I had thought that the propriety of the exercise of a power admitted to exist in some cases was for the consideration of Congress alone and that this Court always had disavowed the right to intrude its judgment upon questions of policy or morals. . . .

The act does not meddle with anything belonging to the States. They may regulate their internal affairs and their domestic commerce as they like. But when they seek to send their products across the state line they are no longer within their rights. If there were no Constitution and no Congress their power to cross the line would depend upon their neighbors. Under the Constitution such commerce belongs not to the States but to Congress to regulate. It may carry out its views of public policy whatever indirect effect they may have upon the activities of the States. . . . The national welfare as understood by Congress may require a different attitude within its sphere from that of some self-seeking State. It seems to me entirely constitutional for Congress to enforce its understanding by all the means at its command.

National Labor Relations Board v. *Jones & Laughlin Steel Corporation*

301 U.S. 1; 57 S. Ct. 615; 81 L. Ed. 893 (1937)

The National Labor Relations Act (also called the Wagner Act) was designed to protect the rights of workers to form unions and to bargain collectively. The act prohibited a variety of unfair labor practices and authorized the National Labor Relations Board to issue cease-and-desist orders to employers who engaged in such practices. Jones & Laughlin, one of the nation's largest steel producers, violated the act by firing ten workers for engaging in union activities. The company then refused to comply with an NLRB order to reinstate the workers. After a court of appeals declined to enforce the board's order, the Supreme Court granted certiorari.

This decision—the so-called "switch in time that saved nine"—was announced amid intense controversy over the Supreme Court's rulings. Following his landslide reelection in 1936, President Franklin Roosevelt, frustrated by adverse Supreme Court rulings and sure that the nation supported his program of economic reform, sent to Congress a proposal to expand the number of Supreme Court justices. By upholding the Wagner Act, the Court largely defused the controversy and ensured the defeat of the so-called court-packing scheme. Shortly thereafter, President Roosevelt had the opportunity to name his first justice to the Court, and his appointment of eight justices by 1941 produced unanimous support for the conception of national power over the economy enunciated in this case. *Opinion of the Court: Hughes, Brandeis, Stone, Roberts, Cardozo. Dissenting opinion: McReynolds, Van Devanter, Sutherland, Butler.*

MR. CHIEF JUSTICE HUGHES delivered the opinion of the Court. . . .

First. The scope of the Act.—The Act is challenged in its entirety as an attempt to regulate all industry, thus invading the reserved powers of the States over their local concerns. It is asserted that the references in the Act to interstate and foreign commerce are colorable at best; that the Act is not a true regulation of such commerce or of matters which directly affect it but on the contrary has the fundamental object of placing under the compulsory supervision of the federal government all industrial labor relations within the nation. . . .

. . . The grant of authority to the Board does not purport to extend to the relationship between all industrial employees and employers. Its terms do not impose collective bargaining upon all industry regardless of effects upon interstate or foreign commerce. It purports to reach only what may be deemed to burden or obstruct that commerce and, thus qualified, it must be construed as contemplating the exercise of control within constitutional bounds. It is a familiar principle that acts which directly burden or obstruct interstate or foreign commerce, or its free flow, are within the reach of the congressional power. Acts having that effect are not rendered immune because they grow out of labor disputes. . . . It is the effect upon commerce, not the source of the injury, which is the criterion. . . . Whether or not particular action does affect commerce in such a close and intimate fashion as to be subject to federal control, and hence to lie within the authority conferred upon the Board, is left by the statute to be determined as individual cases arise. . . .

Second. The unfair practices in question. . . . In its present application, the statute goes no further than to safeguard the right of employees to self-organization and to select representatives of their own choosing for collective bargaining or other mutual protection without restraint or coercion by their employer.

That is a fundamental right. Employees have as clear a right to organize and select their representatives for lawful purposes as the respondent has to organize its business and select its own officers and agents. Discrimination and coercion to prevent the free exercise of the right of employees to self-organization and representation is a proper subject for condemnation by competent legislative authority. . . . Hence the prohibition by Congress of interference with the selection of representatives for the purpose of negotiation and conference between employers and employees, "instead of being an invasion of the constitutional right of either was based on the recognition of the rights of both." *Texas & N.O.R.C.* v. *Railway Clerks* [1930]. . . .

Third. The application of the Act to employees engaged in production.—The principle involved.—Respondent says that whatever may be said of employees engaged in interstate commerce, the industrial relations and activities in the manufacturing department of respondent's enterprise are not subject to federal regulation. The argument rests upon the proposition that manufacturing in itself is not commerce. . . .

. . . The congressional authority to protect interstate commerce from burdens and obstructions is not limited to transactions which can be deemed to be an essential part of a "flow" of interstate or foreign commerce. Although activities may be intrastate in character when separately considered if they have such a close and substantial relation to interstate commerce that their control is essential or appropriate to protect that commerce from burdens and obstructions, Congress cannot be denied the power to exercise that control. . . . Undoubtedly the scope of this power must be considered in the light of our dual system of government and may not be extended so as to embrace effects upon interstate commerce so indirect and remote that to embrace them, in view of our complex society, would effectually obliterate the distinction between what is national and what is local and create a completely centralized government. . . . The question is necessarily one of degree. . . .

It is thus apparent that the fact that the employees here concerned were engaged in production is not determinative. The question remains as to the effect upon interstate commerce of the labor practice involved. . . .

Fourth. Effects of the unfair labor practice in respondent's enterprise.—Giving full weight to respondent's contention with respect to a break in the complete continuity of the "stream of commerce" by reason of respondent's manufacturing operations, the fact remains that the stoppage of those operations by industrial strife would have a most serious effect upon interstate commerce. In view of respondent's far-flung activities, it is idle to say that the effect would be indirect or remote. It is obvious that it would be immediate and might be catastrophic. We are asked to shut our eyes to the plainest facts of our national life and to deal with the question of direct and indirect effects in an intellectual vacuum. Because there may be but indirect and remote effects upon interstate commerce in connection with a host of local enterprises throughout the country, it does not follow that other industrial activities do not have such a close and intimate relation to interstate commerce as to make the presence of industrial strife a matter of the most urgent national concern. When industries organize themselves on a national scale, making their relation to interstate commerce the dominant factor in their activities, how can it be maintained that their industrial labor relations constitute a forbidden field into which Congress may not enter when it is necessary to protect interstate commerce from the paralyzing consequences of industrial war? We have often said that interstate commerce itself is a practical conception. It is equally true that interferences with that commerce must be appraised by a judgment that does not ignore actual experience.

Experience has abundantly demonstrated that the recognition of the right of employees to self-organization and to have representatives of their own choosing for the purpose of collective bargaining is often an essential condition of industrial peace. Refusal to confer and negotiate has been one of the most prolific causes of strife. This is such an outstanding fact in the history of labor disturbances that it is a proper subject of judicial notice and requires no citation of instances. . . .

Our conclusion is that the order of the Board was within it competency and that the Act is valid as here applied. The judgment of the Circuit Court of Appeals is reversed and the cause is remanded for further proceedings in conformity with this opinion.

Reversed.

MR. JUSTICE MCREYNOLDS, dissenting.

The Court, as we think, departs from well-established principles followed in *Schechter Corp.* v. *United States* [1935] and *Carter* v. *Carter Coal Co* [1936]. Six district courts, on the authority of *Schechter's* and *Carter's* cases, have held that the Board has no authority to regulate relations between employers and employees engaged in local production. No decision or judicial opinion to the contrary has been cited, and we find none. Every consideration brought forward to uphold the Act before us was applicable to support the acts held unconstitutional in causes decided within two years. . . .

An effect on interstate commerce by the discharge of employees shown here, would be indirect and remote in the highest degree as consideration of the facts will show. [In *Jones & Laughlin*] ten men out of ten thousand were discharged: in the other cases only a few. The immediate effect in the factory may be to create discontent among all those employed and a strike may follow, which, in turn, may result in reducing production, which ultimately may reduce the volume of goods moving in interstate commerce. By this chain of indirect and progressively remote events we finally reach the evil with which it is said the legislation under consideration undertakes to deal. A more remote and indirect interference with interstate commerce or a more definite invasion of the powers reserved to the states is difficult, if not impossible, to imagine.

Wickard v. *Filburn*

317 U.S. 111, 63 S. Ct. 82, 87 L. Ed. 122 (1942)

The Agricultural Adjustment Act of 1938 imposed limitations on the acreage individual farmers could devote to wheat production. In setting such limits, Congress sought to control the volume of wheat moving in interstate and foreign commerce, in order to avoid surpluses and shortages and thereby prevent abnormally low or high wheat prices. Filburn, who owned a small farm in Ohio, exceeded his allotment of 11.1 acres for the 1941 wheat crop. He produced 23 acres of wheat, intending to keep the excess for use on his own farm. Penalized $117.11 for growing the excess wheat, he refused to pay and brought action to prevent collection. When the district court granted an injunction on nonconstitutional grounds, the government appealed. *Opinion of the Court: Jackson, Stone, Roberts, Black, Reed, Frankfurter, Douglas, Murphy, Byrnes.*

MR. JUSTICE JACKSON delivered the opinion of the Court.

It is urged that under the Commerce Clause of the Constitution, Article I, § 8, clause 3, Congress does not possess the power it has in this instance sought to exercise. The question would merit little consideration since our decision in *United States* v. *Darby* [1941] sustaining the federal power to regulate production of goods for commerce, except for the fact that this Act extends federal regulation to production not intended in any part for commerce but wholly for consumption on the farm. . . .

Appellee says that this is a regulation of production and consumption of wheat. Such activities are, he urges, beyond the reach of Congressional power under the Commerce Clause, since they are local in character, and their effects upon interstate commerce are at most "indirect." In answer the Government argues that the statute regulates neither production nor consumption, but only marketing, and, in the alternative, that if the Act does go beyond the regulation of marketing it is sustainable as a "necessary and proper" implementation of the power of Congress over interstate commerce. . . .

Whether the subject of the regulation in question was "production," "consumption," or "marketing" is . . . not material for purposes for deciding the question of federal power before us. That an activity is of local character may help in a doubtful case to determine whether Congress intended to reach it. . . . But even if appellee's activity be local and though it may not be regarded as commerce, it may still, whatever its nature, be reached by Congress if it exerts a substantial economic effect on interstate commerce, and this irrespective of whether such effect is what might at some earlier time have been defined as "direct" or "indirect."

The effect of consumption of home-grown wheat on interstate commerce is due to the fact that it constitutes the most variable factor in the disappearance of the wheat crop. Consumption on the farm where grown appears to vary in an amount greater than 20 percent of average production. The total amount of wheat consumed as food varies but relatively little, and use as seed is relatively constant.

The maintenance by government regulation of a price for wheat undoubtedly can be accomplished as effectively by sustaining or increasing the demand as by limiting the supply. The effect of the statute before us is to restrict the amount which may be produced for market and the extent as well to which one may forestall resort to the market by producing to meet his own needs. That appellee's own contribution to the demand for wheat may be trivial by itself is not enough to remove him from the scope of federal regulation where, as here, his contribution, taken together with that of many others similarly situated, is far from trivial. . . .

It is well established by decisions of this Court that the power to regulate commerce includes the power to regulate the prices at which commodities in that commerce are dealt in and practices affecting such prices. One of the primary purposes of the Act in question was to increase the market price of wheat, and to that end to limit the volume thereof that could affect the market. It can hardly be denied that a factor of such volume and variability as home-consumed wheat would have a substantial influence on price and market conditions. . . . This record leaves us in no doubt that Congress may properly have considered that wheat consumed on the farm where grown, if wholly outside the scheme of regulation, would have a substantial effect in defeating and obstructing its purpose to stimulate trade therein at increased prices.

It is said, however, that this Act, forcing some farmers into the market to buy what they could provide for themselves, is an unfair promotion of the markets and prices of specializing wheat growers. It is of the essence of regulation that it lays a restraining hand on the self-interest of the regulated and that advantages from the regulation commonly fall to others. The conflicts of economic interest between the regulated and those who advantage by it are wisely left under our system to resolution by the Congress under its more flexible and responsible legislative process. Such conflicts rarely lend themselves to judicial determination. And with the wisdom, workability, or fairness, of the plan of regulation we have nothing to do. . . .

Reversed.

Heart of Atlanta Motel v. *United States*

379 U.S. 241, 85 S. Ct. 348, 13 L. Ed. 2d 258 (1964)

The Heart of Atlanta Motel, located near major highways and interstates, sought patronage from outside Georgia through national advertising campaigns; and approximately 75 percent of its patrons were from out-of-state. Prior to passage of the Civil Rights Act of 1964, which outlawed discrimination in public accommodations, the motel refused to rent rooms to blacks. It indicated that it intended to continue this policy and sought a declaratory judgment attacking the validity of Title II (the public accommodations section). A three-judge district court sustained the challenged legislation, and the case was appealed to the Supreme Court. In a companion case argued at the same time—*Katzenbach* v. *McClung* (379 U.S. 294)—the Court upheld application of the act to a family-owned restaurant serving a primarily local clientele. *Opinion of the Court: Clark, Warren, Black, Douglas, Harlan, Brennan, Stewart, White, Goldberg. Concurring opinions: Black; Douglas.*

MR. JUSTICE CLARK delivered the opinion of the Court. . . .

It is admitted that the operation of the motel brings it within the provisions of § 201 (a) of the Act and that appellant refused to provide lodging for transient Negroes because of their race or color and that it intends to continue that policy unless restrained.

The sole question posed is, therefore, the constitutionality of the Civil Rights Act of 1964 as applied to these facts. The legislative history of the Act indicates that Congress based the Act on § 5 and the Equal Protection Clause of the Fourteenth Amendment as well as its power to regulate interstate commerce under Art. I. § 8, cl. 3, of the Constitution. . . .

While the act as adopted carried no congressional findings the records of its passage through each house is replete with evidence of the burdens that discrimination by race or color places upon interstate commerce. . . . This testimony included the fact that our people have become increasingly mobile with millions of people of all races traveling from State to State; that Negroes in particular have been the subject of discrimination in transient accommodations, having to travel great distances to secure the same; that often they have been unable to obtain accommodations and have had to call upon friends to put them up overnight. . . ; and that these conditions had become so acute as to require the listing of available lodging for Negroes in a special guidebook. . . . This testimony indicated a qualitative as well as quantitative effect on interstate travel by Negroes. The former was the obvious impairment of the Negro traveler's pleasure and convenience that resulted when he continually was uncertain of finding lodging. As for the latter, there was evidence that this uncertainty stemming from racial discrimination had the effect of discouraging travel on the part of a substantial portion of the Negro community. . . . The voluminous testimony presents overwhelming evidence that discrimination by hotels and motels impedes interstate travel.

[*Mr. Justice Clark then reviewed the Court's earlier decisions regarding the use of the Commerce Clause for noncommercial purposes.*]

That Congress was legislating against moral wrongs in many of these areas rendered its enactments no less valid. In framing Title II of this Act Congress was also dealing with what it considered a moral problem. But that fact does not detract from the overwhelming evidence of the disruptive effect that racial discrimination has had on commercial intercourse. It was this burden which empowered Congress to enact appropriate legislation and, given this basis for the exercise of its power, Congress was not restricted by the fact that the particular obstruction to interstate commerce with which it was dealing was also deemed a moral and social wrong.

It is said that the operation of the motel here is of a purely local character. But, assuming this to be true, "if it is interstate commerce that feels the pinch, it does not matter how local the operation which applies the squeeze." *United States* v. *Women's Sportswear Mfrs* [1949]. . . .

Thus the power of Congress to promote interstate commerce also includes the power to regulate the local incidents thereof, including local activities in both the States of origin and destination, which might have a substantial and harmful effect upon that commerce. One need only examine the evidence which we have discussed above to see that Congress may—as it has—prohibit racial discrimination by motels serving travelers, however "local" their operations may appear. . . .

Affirmed.

MR. JUSTICE DOUGLAS, concurring. . . .

Though I join the Court's opinion, I am somewhat reluctant here . . . to rest solely on the Commerce Clause. My reluctance is not due to any conviction that Congress lacks power to regulate commerce in the interests of human rights. It is rather my belief that the right of people to be free of state action that discriminates against them because of race, like the "right of persons to move freely from State to State" (*Edwards* v. *California* [1941]) "occupies a more protected position in our constitutional system than does the movement of cattle, fruit, steel and coal across state lines." *Ibid.* . . .

Hence I would prefer to rest on the assertation of legislative power contained in § 5 of the Fourteenth Amendment which states: "The Congress shall have power to enforce, by appropriate legislation, the provisions of this article"—a power which the Court concedes was exercised at least in part in this Act.

A decision based on the Fourteenth Amendment would have a more settling effect, making unnecessary litigation over whether a particular restaurant or inn is within the commerce definitions of the Act or whether a particular customer is an interstate traveler. Under my construction, the Act would apply to all customers in all the enumerated places of public accommodation. And that construction would put an end to all obstructionist strategies and finally close one door on a bitter chapter in American history.

United States v. *Butler*

297 U.S. 1; 56 S. Ct. 312; 80 L. Ed. 477 (1936)

The Agricultural Adjustment Act of 1933, in seeking to curtail excess farm production, provided that farmers who reduced their production be compensated. This compensation came from a tax, levied by the act, on the processing of agricultural commodities. Butler, the receiver for a cotton processing firm, refused to pay the tax. The district court ordered Butler to pay the tax, the court of appeals reversed, and the government appealed. *Opinion of the Court: Roberts, Hughes, Van Devanter, McReynolds, Sutherland, Butler. Dissenting opinion: Stone, Brandeis, Cardozo.*

MR. JUSTICE ROBERTS delivered the opinion of the Court.

. . . The Government asserts that even if the respondents may question the propriety of the appropriation embodied in the statute their attack must fail because Article I, § 8 of the Constitution authorizes the contemplated expenditure of the funds raised by the tax. This contention presents the great and the controlling question in the case. We approach its decision with a sense of our grave responsibility to render judgment in accordance with the principles established for the governance of all three branches of the Government.

There should be no misunderstanding as to the function of this court in such a case. It is sometimes said that the court assumes a power to overrule or control the action of the people's representatives. This is a misconception. The Constitution is the supreme law of the land ordained and established by the people. All legislation must conform to the principles it lays down.

When an act of Congress is appropriately challenged in the courts as not conforming to the constitutional mandate the judicial branch of the Government has only one duty—to lay the article of the Constitution which is invoked beside the statute which is challenged and to decide whether the latter squares with the former. All the court does, or can do, is to announce its considered judgment upon the question. The only power it has, if such it may be called, is the power of judgment. This court neither approves nor condemns any legislative policy. Its delicate and difficult office is to ascertain and declare whether the legislation is in accordance with, or in contravention of, the provisions of the Constitution; and, having done that, its duty ends.

The question is not what power the Federal Government ought to have but what powers in fact have been given by the people. It hardly seems necessary to reiterate that ours is a dual form of government; that in every state there are two governments,—the state and the United States. Each State has all governmental powers save such as the people, by their Constitution, have conferred upon the United States, denied to the States, or reserved to themselves. The federal union is a government of delegated powers. It has only such as are expressly conferred upon it and such as are reasonably to be implied from those granted. In this respect we differ radically from nations where all legislative power, without restriction or limitation, is vested in a parliament or other legislative body subject to no restrictions except the discretion of its members.

Article I, § 8, of the Constitution vests sundry powers in the Congress. But two of its clauses have any bearing upon the validity of the statute under review.

The clause thought to authorize the legislation,—the first,—confers upon the Congress power "to lay and collect Taxes, Duties, Imports and Excises, to pay the Debts and provide for the common Defence and general Welfare of the United States. . . ." It is not contended that this provision grants power to regulate agricultural production upon the theory that such legislation would promote the general welfare. The Government concedes that the phrase "to provide for the general welfare" qualifies the power "to lay and collect taxes." The view that the clause grants power to provide for the general welfare, independently of the taxing power, has never been authoritatively accepted. Mr. Justice Story points out that if it were adopted "it is obvious that under color of the generality of the words, to 'provide for the common defence and general welfare,' the government of the United States is, in reality, a government of general and unlimited powers, notwithstanding the subsequent enumeration of specific powers." The true construction undoubtedly is that the only thing granted is the power to tax for the purpose of providing funds for payment of the nation's debt and making provision for the general welfare.

Nevertheless the Government asserts that warrant is found in this clause for the adoption of the Agricultural Adjustment Act. The argument is that Congress may appropriate and authorize the spending of moneys for the "general welfare"; that the phrase should be liberally construed to cover anything conducive to national welfare; that decision as to what will promote such welfare rests with Congress alone, and the courts may not review its determination; and finally that the appropriation under attack was in fact for the general welfare of the United States.

The Congress is expressly empowered to lay taxes to provide for the general welfare. Funds in the Treasury as a result of taxation may be expended only through appropriation. (Art. I, § 9, cl. 7.) They can never accomplish the objects for which they were collected unless the power to appropriate is as broad as the power to tax. The necessary implication from the terms of the grant is that the public funds may be appropriated "to provide for the general welfare of the United States." These words cannot be meaningless, else they would not have been used. The conclusion must be that they were intended to limit and define the granted power to raise and to expend money. How shall they be construed to effectuate the intent of the instrument?

Since the foundation of the Nation sharp differences of opinion have persisted as to the true interpretation of the phrase. Madison asserted it amounted to no more than a reference to the other powers enumerated in the subsequent clauses of the same section; that, as the United States is a government of limited and enumerated powers, the grant of power to tax and spend for the general national welfare must be confined to the enumerated legislative fields committed to the Congress. In this view the phrase is mere tautology, for taxation and appropriation are or may be necessary incidents of the exercise of any of the enumerated legislative powers. Hamilton, on the other hand, maintained the clause confers a power separate and distinct from those later enumerated, is not restricted in meaning by the grant of them, and Congress consequently has a substantive power to tax and to appropriate, limited only by the requirement that it shall be exercised to provide for the general welfare of the United States. Each contention has had the support of those whose views are entitled to weight. This court has noticed the question, but has never found it necessary to decide which is the true construction. Mr. Justice Story, in his Commentaries, espouses the Hamiltonian position. We shall not review the writings of public men and commentators or discuss the legislative practice. Study of all these leads us to conclude that the reading advocated by Mr. Justice Story is the correct one. While, therefore, the power to tax is not unlimited, its confines are set in the clause which confers it, and not in those of § 8 which bestow and define the legislative powers of the Congress. It results that the power of Congress to authorize expenditure of public moneys for public purposes is not limited by the direct grants of legislative power found in the Constitution.

But the adoption of the broader construction leaves the power to spend subject to limitations. Story says that if the tax be not proposed for the common defence or general welfare, but for other objects wholly extraneous, it would be wholly indefensible upon constitutional principles. And he makes it clear that the powers of taxation and appropriation extend only to matters of national, as distinguished from local welfare.

We are not now required to ascertain the scope of the phrase "general welfare of the United States" or to determine whether an appropriation in aid of agriculture falls within it. Wholly apart from that question, another principle embedded in our Constitution prohibits the enforcement of the Agricultural Adjustment Act. The act invades the reserved rights of states. It is a statutory plan to regulate and control agricultural production, a matter beyond the powers delegated to the federal government. The tax, the appropriation of the funds raised, and the direction for their disbursement, are but parts of the plan. They are but means to an unconstitutional end.

From the accepted doctrine that the United States is a government of delegated powers, it follows that those not expressly granted, or reasonably to be implied from such as are conferred are reserved to the states or to the people. To forestall any suggestion to the contrary, the Tenth Amendment was adopted. The same proposition, otherwise stated, is that powers not granted are prohibited. None to regulate agricultural production is given, and therefore legislation by Congress for that purpose is forbidden.

It is an established principle that the attainment of a prohibited end may not be accomplished under the pretext of the exertion of powers which are granted. . . .

. . . If the taxing power may not be used as the instrument to enforce a regulation of matters of state concern with respect to which the Congress has no authority to interfere, may it, as in the present case, be employed to raise the money necessary to purchase a compliance which the Congress is powerless to command? The Government asserts that whatever might be said against the validity of the plan if compulsory, it is constitutionally sound because the end is accomplished by voluntary cooperation. The regulation is not in fact voluntary. The farmer, of course, may refuse to comply, but the price of such refusal is the loss of benefits. The amount offered is intended to be sufficient to exert pressure on him to agree to the proposed regulation. The power to confer or withhold unlimited benefits is the power to coerce or destroy.

But if the plan were one for purely voluntary co-operation it would stand no better so far as federal power is concerned. At best it is a scheme for purchasing with federal funds submission to federal regulation of a subject reserved to the states.

Congress has no power to enforce its commands on the farmer to the ends sought by the Agricultural Adjustment Act. It must follow that it may not indirectly accomplish those ends by taxing and spending to purchase compliance. The Constitution and the entire plan of our government negative any such use of the power to tax and to spend as the act undertakes to authorize. It does not help declare that local conditions throughout the nation have created a situation of national concern; for this is but to say that whenever there is a widespread similarity of local conditions, Congress may ignore constitutional limitations upon its own powers and usurp those reserved to the states. If, in lieu of compulsory regulation of subjects within the states' reserved jurisdiction, which is prohibited, the Congress could invoke the taxing and spending power as a means to accomplish the same end, clause 1 of § 8 of Article I would become the instrument for total subversion of the governmental powers reserved to the individual states.

If the act before us is a proper exercise of the federal taxing power, evidently the regulation of all industry throughout the United States may be accomplished by similar exercises of the same power. It would be possible to exact money from one branch of an industry and pay it to another branch in every field of activity which lies within the province of the states. The mere threat of such a procedure might well induce the surrender of rights and the compliance with federal regulation as the price of continuance in business. . . .

The judgment is

Affirmed.

Mr. Justice Stone, dissenting.

1. The power of courts to declare a statute unconstitutional is subject to two guiding principles of decision which ought never to be absent from judicial consciousness. One is that courts are concerned only with the power to enact statutes, not with their wisdom. The other is that while unconstitutional exercise of power by the executive and legislative branches of the government is subject to judicial restraint, the only check upon our own exercise of power is our own sense of self-restraint. For the removal of unwise laws from the statute books appeal lies not to the courts but to the ballot and to the processes of democratic government.

2. The constitutional power of Congress to levy an excise tax upon the processing of agricultural products is not questioned. The present levy is held invalid, not for any want of power in Congress to lay such a tax to defray public expenditures, including those for the general welfare, but because the use to which its proceeds are put is disapproved.

3. As the present depressed state of agriculture is nation wide in its extent and effects, there is no basis for saying that the expenditure of public money in aid of farmers is not within the specifically granted power of Congress to levy taxes to "provide for the . . . general welfare." The opinion of the Court does not declare otherwise. . . .

It is with these preliminary and hardly controverted matters in mind that we should direct our attention to the pivot on which the decision of the Court is made to turn. It is that a levy unquestionably within the taxing power of Congress may be treated as invalid because it is a step in a plan to regulate agricultural production and is thus a forbidden infringement of state power. The levy is not any the less an exercise of taxing power because it is intended to defray an expenditure for the general welfare rather than for some other support of government. Nor is the levy and collection of the tax pointed to as effecting the regulation. While all federal taxes inevitably have some influence on the internal economy of the states, it is not contended that the levy of a processing tax upon manufacturers using agricultural products as raw material has any perceptible regulatory effect upon either their production or manufacture. . . . Here regulation, if any there be, is accomplished not by the tax but by the method by which its proceeds are expended, and would equally be accomplished by any like use of public funds, regardless of their source. . . .

It is upon the contention that state power is infringed by purchased regulation of agricultural production that chief reliance is placed. It is insisted that, while the Constitution gives to Congress, in specific and unambiguous terms, the power to tax and spend, the power is subject to limitations which do not find their origin in any express provision of the Constitution and to which other expressly delegated powers are not subject.

Such a limitation is contradictory and destructive of the power to appropriate for the public welfare, and is incapable of practical application. The spending power of Congress is in addition to the legislative power and not subordinate to it. This independent grant of the power of the purse, and its very nature, involving in its exercise the duty to insure expenditure within the granted power, presuppose freedom of selection among divers ends and aims, and the capacity to impose such conditions as will render the choice effective. It is a contradiction in terms to say that there is power to spend for the national welfare while rejecting any power to impose conditions reasonably adapted to the attainment of the end which alone would justify the expenditure.

A tortured construction of the Constitution is not to be justified by recourse to extreme examples of reckless congressional spending which might occur if courts could not prevent—expenditures which even if they could be thought to effect any national purpose, would be possible only by action of a legislature lost to all sense of public responsibility. Such suppositions are addressed to the mind accustomed to belief that it is the business of courts to sit in judgment on the wisdom of legislative action. Courts are not the only agency of government that must be assumed to have capacity to govern. Congress and the courts both unhappily may falter or be mistaken in the performance of their constitutional duty. But interpretation of our great charter of government which proceeds on any assumption that the responsibility for the preservation of our institutions is the exclusive concern of any one of the three branches of government, or that it alone can save them from destruction is far more likely, in the long run, "to obliterate the constituent members" of "an indestructible union of indestructible states" than the frank recognition that language, even of a constitution, may mean what it says: that the power to tax and spend includes the power to relieve a nationwide economic maladjustment by conditional gifts of money.

United States v. *Kahriger*

345 U.S. 22, 73 S. Ct. 510; 97 L. Ed. 754 (1953)

Congress enacted a law levying an annual tax of $50 on persons in the business of taking bets. Persons paying the tax were required to register with the Federal Collector of Internal Revenue their names, addresses, and places of business. Kahriger was indicted for running a gambling business without paying the tax, but the district court dismissed the charge, ruling the law unconstitutional. The government then appealed the case to the Supreme Court. *Opinion of the Court: Reed, Warren, Jackson, Burton, Clark, Minton. Concurring opinion: Jackson. Dissenting opinions: Frankfurter, Douglas (in part); Black, Douglas.*

MR. JUSTICE REED delivered the opinion of the Court.

The issue raised by this appeal is the constitutionality of the occupational tax provisions of the Revenue Act of 1951, which levy a tax on persons engaged in the business of accepting wagers, and require such persons to register with the Collector of Internal Revenue. The unconstitutionality of the tax is asserted on two grounds. First, it is said that Congress, under the pretense of exercising its power to tax has attempted to penalize illegal intrastate gambling through the regulatory features of the Act. . . . and has thus infringed the police power which is reserved to the states. Secondly, it is urged that the registration provisions of the tax violate the privilege against self-incrimination and are arbitrary and vague, contrary to the guarantees of the Fifth Amendment. . . .

It is conceded that a federal excise tax does not cease to be valid merely because it discourages or deters the activities taxed. Nor is the tax invalid because the revenue obtained is negligible. Appellee, however, argues that the sole purpose of the statute is to penalize only illegal gambling in the states through the guise of a tax measure. . . . The instant tax has a regulatory effect. But regardless of its regulatory effect, the wagering tax produces revenue. As such it surpasses both the narcotics and firearms taxes which we have found valid.

. . . It is hard to understand why the power to tax should raise more doubts because of indirect effects than other federal powers. . . .

Appellee's second assertion is that the wagering tax is unconstitutional because it is a denial of the privilege against self-incrimination as guaranteed by the Fifth Amendment.

Since appellee failed to register for the wagering tax, it is difficult to see how he can now claim the privilege even assuming that the disclosure of violations of law is called for. . . .

Assuming that respondent can raise the self-incrimination issue, that privilege has relation only to past acts, not to future acts that may or may not be committed. . . . If respondent wishes to take wagers subject to excise taxes under § 3285, . . . he must pay an occupational tax and register. Under the registration provisions of the wagering tax, appellee is not compelled to confess to acts already committed, he is merely informed by the statute that in order to engage in the business of wagering in the future he must fulfill certain conditions.

MR. JUSTICE BLACK, with whom MR. JUSTICE DOUGLAS concurs, dissenting.

. . . The Act. . . creates a squeezing device contrived to put a man in federal prison if he refuses to confess himself into a state prison as a violator of state gambling laws. The coercion of confessions is a common but justly criticized practice of many countries that do not have or live up to a Bill of Rights. But we have a Bill of Rights that condemns coerced confessions, however refined or legalistic may be the technique of extortion. I would hold that this Act violates the Fifth Amendment. . . .

MR. JUSTICE FRANKFURTER, dissenting.

. . . Constitutional issues are likely to arise whenever Congress draws on the taxing power not to raise revenue but to regulate conduct. This is so, of course, because of the distribution of legislative power as between the Congress and the State Legislatures in the regulation of conduct. . . .

. . . When oblique use is made of the taxing power as to matters which substantively are not within the powers delegated to Congress, the Court cannot shut its eyes to what is obviously, because designedly, an attempt to control conduct which the Constitution left to the responsibility of the States, merely because Congress wrapped the legislation in the verbal cellophane of a revenue measure. . . .

. . . Congress, which cannot constitutionally grapple directly with gambling in the States, may [not] compel self-incriminating disclosures for the enforcement of State gambling laws, merely because it does so under the guise of a revenue measure obviously passed not for revenue purposes. The motive of congressional legislation is not for our scrutiny, provided only that the ulterior purpose is not expressed in ways which negative what the revenue words on their face express and which do not seek enforcement of the formal revenue purpose through means that offend those standards of decency in our civilization against which due process is a barrier.

I would affirm this judgment.

South Dakota v. *Dole*

483 U.S. 203, 107 S. Ct. 2793, 97 L. Ed. 2d 171 (1987)

In 1984 Congress enacted legislation directing the secretary of transportation to withhold 5 percent of federal highway funds from states that permitted purchase or public possession of alcoholic beverages by persons less than 21 years of age. South Dakota, which permitted persons 19 years of age or older to purchase 3.2 percent beer, sought a declaratory judgment that the law exceeded the constitutional limitations on the congressional spending power and violated the Twenty-First Amendment, which it viewed as granting the states exclusive authority to regulate the sale of alcohol within their borders. In support of this latter contention, South Dakota pointed to Section 2 of the amendment, which provides: "The transportation or importation into any State, Territory, or possession of the United States for delivery or use therein of intoxicating liquors, in violation of the laws thereof, is hereby prohibited." After its claims were rejected in federal district court and in the court of appeals, South Dakota appealed the case to the Supreme Court. *Opinion of the Court: Rehnquist, White, Marshall, Blackmun, Powell, Stevens, Scalia. Dissenting opinions: Brennan, O'Connor.*

CHIEF JUSTICE REHNQUIST delivered the opinion of the Court.

[W]e need not decide in this case whether [the Twenty-First] Amendment would prohibit an attempt by Congress to legislate directly a national minimum drinking age. Here, Congress has acted indirectly under its spending power to encourage uniformity in the States' drinking ages. As we explain below, we find this legislative effort within constitutional bounds even if Congress may not regulate drinking ages directly.

. . . The Constitution empowers Congress to "lay and collect Taxes, Duties, Imposts, and Excises, to pay the Debts and provide for the common Defence and general Welfare of the United States." Art. I, § 8, cl. 1. Incident to this power, Congress may attach conditions on the receipt of federal funds, and has repeatedly employed the power "to further broad policy objectives by conditioning receipt of federal moneys upon compliance by the recipient with federal statutory and administrative directives." *Fullilove* v. *Klutznick* . . . The breadth of this power was made clear in *United States* v. *Butler* . . . (1936), where the Court, resolving a longstanding debate over the scope of the Spending Clause, determined that "the power of Congress to authorize expenditure of public moneys for public purposes is not limited by the direct grants of legislative power found in the Constitution." Thus, objectives not thought to be within Article I's "enumerated legislative fields" . . . may nevertheless be attained through the use of the spending power and the conditional grant of federal funds. . . . We can readily conclude that the provision is designed to serve the general welfare, especially in light of the fact that "the concept of welfare or the opposite is shaped by Congress. . . ." *Helvering* v. *Davis* [1937] . . . Congress found that the differing drinking ages in the States created particular incentives for young persons to combine their desire to drink with their ability to drive, and that this interstate problem required a national solution. The means it chose to address this dangerous situation were reasonably calculated to advance the general welfare. The conditions upon which States receive the funds, moreover, could not be more clearly stated by Congress. . . . And the State itself, rather than challenging the germaneness of the condition to federal purposes, admits that it "has never contended that the congressional action was . . . unrelated to a national concern in the absence of the Twenty-first Amendment." . . . Indeed, the condition imposed by Congress is directly related to one of the main purposes for which highway funds are expended—safe interstate travel. . . .

The . . . basic point of disagreement between the parties—is whether the Twenty-first Amendment constitutes an "independent constitutional bar" to the conditional grant of federal funds. . . . Petitioner, relying on its view that the Twenty-first Amendment prohibits *direct* regulation of drinking ages by Congress, asserts that "Congress may not use the spending power to regulate that which it is prohibited from regulating directly under the Twenty-first Amendment." . . . But our cases show that this "independent constitutional bar" limitation on the spending power is not of the kind petitioner suggests. . . .

Our decisions have recognized that in some circumstances the financial inducement offered by Congress might be so coercive as to pass the point at which "pressure turns into compulsion." *Steward Machine Co.* v. *Davis* [1937]. . . .

Here Congress has offered relatively mild encouragement to the States to enact higher minimum drinking ages than they would otherwise choose. But the enactment of such laws remains the prerogative of the States not merely in theory but in fact. Even if Congress might lack the power to impose a national minimum drinking age directly, we conclude that encouragement to state action found in § 158 is a valid use of the spending power. Accordingly, the judgment of the Court of Appeals is

Affirmed.

JUSTICE O'CONNOR, dissenting.

My disagreement with the Court is relatively

narrow on the Spending Power issue: it is a disagreement about the application of a principle rather than a disagreement on the principle itself. I agree with the Court that Congress may attach conditions on the receipt of federal funds to further "the federal interest in particular national projects or programs." *Massachusetts* v. *United States,* . . . (1978). . . . In my view, establishment of a minimum drinking age of 21 is not sufficiently related to interstate highway construction to justify so conditioning funds appropriated for that purpose.

. . . The Court reasons that Congress wishes that the roads it builds may be used safely, that drunk drivers threaten highway safety, and that young people are more likely to drive while under the influence of alcohol under existing law than would be the case if there were a uniform national drinking age of 21. It hardly needs saying, however, that if the purpose of [this law] is to deter drunken driving, it is far too over- and under-inclusive. It is over-inclusive because it stops teenagers from drinking even when they are not about to drive on interstate highways. It is under-inclusive because teenagers pose only a small part of the drunken driving problem in this Nation. . . .

When Congress appropriates money to build a highway, it is entitled to insist that the highway be a safe one. But it is not entitled to insist as a condition of the use of highway funds that the State impose or change regulations in other areas of the State's social and economic life because of an attenuated or tangential relationship to highway use or safety. Indeed, if the rule were otherwise, the Congress could effectively regulate almost any area of a State's social, political, or economic life on the theory that use of the interstate transportation system is somehow enhanced. . . .

There is a clear place at which the Court can draw the line between permissible and impermissible conditions on federal grants. It is the line identified in the Brief for the National Conference of State Legislatures et al. as *Amici Curiae:*

> Congress has the power to *spend* for the general welfare, it has the power to *legislate* only for delegated purposes. . . . The appropriate inquiry, then, is whether the spending requirement or prohibition is a condition on a grant or whether it is regulation. The difference turns on whether the requirement specifies in some way how the money should be spent, so that Congress' intent in making the grant will be effectuated. Congress has no power under the Spending Clause to impose requirements on a grant that go beyond specifying how the money should be spent. A requirement that is not such a specification is not a condition, but a regulation, which is valid only if it falls within one of Congress' delegated regulatory powers.

This approach harks back to *United States* v. *Butler* . . . (1936), the last case in which this Court struck down an Act of Congress as beyond the authority granted by the Spending Clause. . . .

While *Butler*'s authority is questionable insofar as it assumes that Congress has no regulatory power over farm production, its discussion of the Spending Power and its description of both the power's breadth and its limitations remains sound. The Court's decision in *Butler* also properly recognizes the gravity of the task of appropriately limiting the Spending Power. If the Spending Power is to be limited only by Congress' notion of the general welfare, the reality, given the vast financial resources of the Federal Government, is that the Spending Clause gives "power to the Congress to tear down the barriers, to invade the states' jurisdiction, and to become a parliament of the whole people, subject to no restrictions save such as are self-imposed." *United States* v. *Butler.* . . . This, of course, as *Butler* held, was not the Framers' plan and it is not the meaning of the Spending Clause.

9
THE EXERCISE OF STATE POWER

The paramount development in American constitutional history has been the expansion of the power of the national government. This process has been aided by the Supreme Court's broad interpretation of the powers granted to Congress and by constitutional amendments—especially the 14th and 16th—that have conferred important additional powers on the legislative branch. So although the Tenth Amendment provides that the states retain those powers not delegated to the national government, the areas of exclusive state control have progressively narrowed. And as the national government has come to regulate areas traditionally dominated by the states, collisions between state and federal claims of authority have increased.

CONSTITUTIONAL PRINCIPLES

Alexander Hamilton observed in *The Federalist*, No. 32, that "the State governments would clearly retain all the rights of sovereignty which they before had, and which were not, by the ratification of the Constitution *exclusively* delegated to the United States." This statement suggests that the powers delegated to the national government can be divided into three categories: exclusive powers, which cannot be exercised by the states; concurrent powers, whose delegation to the national government do not restrict state power; and powers that are neither altogether exclusive nor altogether concurrent, whose delegation to the national government limit but do not completely preclude their exercise by the states.

The Constitution grants exclusive authority to the national government in various ways. Some exclusive powers, such as jurisdiction over the seat of government (Article I, Section 8), are granted expressly. Others are both granted to the national government and denied to the states: for example, the Constitution both authorizes the president to make treaties, with the advice and consent of the Senate (Article II, Section 2), and forbids the states to make them (Article I, Section 10). Finally, some powers granted to the national government, such as the power to declare war (Article I, Section 8), are by their very nature exclusive and thus cannot be exercised by the states.

In granting yet other powers to the national government, the Constitution neither expressly nor implicitly precludes state legislation. A prime example of these concurrent powers is the power to tax. Under the Supremacy Clause (Article VI), enactments made by the states under their concurrent powers may still be unconstitutional, if they conflict with Federal legislation. In this way, the vigorous exercise of national power can diminish state power. In the absence of conflicting federal legislation, however, the states remain free to exercise their concurrent powers.

Finally, some constitutional grants of power are neither wholly exclusive nor wholly concurrent. If the states exercised these powers to the fullest possible extent, the national government would be prevented from achieving the ends for which the powers were granted to it. Elimination of all state authority, on the other hand, would imperil legitimate state objectives. By far the most important of the powers that fall into this category is the commerce power. In the words of Thomas Reed Powell, "Congress may regulate interstate commerce. The states may also regulate interstate commerce, but not too much."[1] The responsibility for deciding what constitutes "too much" has fallen largely to the Supreme Court, which has heard hundreds of cases involving the validity of state regulations affecting interstate commerce.

PREEMPTION

Since 1937 the national government has entered a variety of policy areas—for example, pollution control, race relations, and consumer protection—that previously had been predominantly state concerns. This expansion of national power has not invariably produced conflict, because national and state policies often have been complementary. When national and state policies are incompatible, however, the Supremacy Clause mandates that national policy prevail. The process by which national policies supersede inconsistent state policies is referred to as preemption.

Congress may express its intention to exercise exclusive control over a field, thereby preempting all state regulation. More frequently, congressional legislation will contain no explicit reference to preemption. In such circumstances the Court may review congressional hearings and floor debates to determine Congress's intention. But if Congress did not consider the effect of its action on state laws, such a search is fruitless, and the Court then must consider "whether the state action stands as an obstacle to the accomplishment and execution of the full purposes and objectives of Congress."[2] In doing so the Court examines: (1) whether the state regulations conflict with federal requirements; (2) whether the pervasiveness of federal regulation signals an intention to "occupy the field" and exclude state regulation; and (3) whether the state regulations, although not directly in conflict with federal law, nevertheless may frustrate the purposes of that law.

Although these criteria may guide its decisions, the Court must analyze preemption claims on a case-by-case basis. From 1940, when it ruled in *Hines* v. *Davidowitz* that congressional legislation precluded state registration of aliens, through the late 1960s, the Court tended to assume the incompatibility of state law with federal initiatives. In recent years, however, the Court has been more reluctant to infer preemption in the absence of clear direction from Congress. In *Pacific Gas & Electric Company* v. *State Energy Resources and Development Commission* (1983), for example, the Court ruled that although the national government under the Federal Atomic Energy Act had occupied the field of nuclear safety, California's moratorium on the construction of new nuclear power plants could be upheld as an economic regulation. A year later in *Silkwood* v. *Kerr-McGee Corporation,* however, it also upheld a state-authorized award of punitive damages for conduct which created nuclear hazards, because Congress had not intended to preclude states from providing remedies for those suffering injuries from radiation in a nuclear plant.

The Court's current approach to preemption is designed to protect the legitimate concerns of both the state and national governments. Its refusal to infer preemption of state laws maximizes the exercise of state power. Yet national concerns remain protected, because Congress can override Court rulings by clarifying its preemptive intent. Thus Congress, rather than the Court, is accorded the primary responsibility for maintaining the federal balance.

NEGATIVE IMPLICATIONS OF THE COMMERCE CLAUSE

Where preemption is not an issue, state laws can violate the Constitution by invading the powers granted to the national government. In this respect, the Commerce Clause is particularly important. The Framers gave Congress the power to regulate commerce in order to promote enterprise throughout the nation, and, as Justice Robert Jackson observed in *H. P. Hood & Sons* v. *DuMond* (1949), accomplishment of this aim demands some exclusivity of regulation:

> Our system, fostered by the Commerce Clause, is that every farmer and every craftsman shall be encouraged by the certainty that he will have free access to every market in the Nation, that no home embargoes will withhold his exports, and no foreign state will by customs duties or regulations exclude them. Likewise, every consumer may look to the free competition from every producing area in the Nation to protect him from exploitation by any.[3]

On the other hand, the states traditionally have exercised considerable power over commerce, not only by regulating commerce for commercial purposes but also by taxing interstate commerce to raise revenue and by enacting "police power" regulations to protect the health, safety, welfare, and morals of the state population. If the Commerce Clause foreclosed all such regulation, the states would be deprived of much of their governing authority.

Not surprisingly, then, the Supreme Court in the first century of the Republic was called upon to render several important decisions relating to how the national commerce power affected state authority to regulate commerce, tax commercial activities, and enforce police-power regulations. Two questions were of particular concern: Was the grant of power to Congress an exclusive mandate that precluded all state regulation? And if not, what standards should govern the exercise of state power over commerce?

The Exclusivity Issue

The case for exclusivity is presented in the dormant-power theory, which suggests that by granting Congress the power to regulate commerce among the several states, the Constitution implicitly prohibited state regulation of that commerce. The scope of state power over commerce, accordingly, could be defined by subtraction: the states may regulate only those commercial transactions that Congress cannot regulate. With the expansion of national regulatory power during the twentieth century, this theory would virtually eliminate state power over commerce.

The most persuasive argument for this theory was offered by Justice William Johnson in his concurring opinion in *Gibbons* v. *Ogden* (1824). According to Johnson, economic warfare among the states during the Confederation period was one of the primary concerns of the Framers, who attempted to eliminate state barriers to the flow of commerce by vesting exclusive regulatory authority in Congress. If a state enactment conflicts with a congressional regulation, the congressional policy necessarily prevails. But even in failing to regulate, Johnson maintained, Congress makes a policy choice, for it indicates thereby that commerce should not be regulated. To allow state regulation when Congress fails to act, therefore, would frustrate national policy as surely as would permitting state regulations that are inconsistent with congressional action.

Chief Justice John Marshall acknowledged in *Gibbons* that "there is great force in the argument, and the Court is not satisfied that it has been refuted."[4] But adoption of the dormant-power theory, when joined with Marshall's expansive definition of the commerce power, would have stripped the states of much of their traditional regulatory authority. Perhaps for this reason, Marshall twice sidestepped the issue: in *Gibbons*, by concluding that the New York law involved was preempted by congressional legislation; and in *Willson* v. *Black Bird Creek Marsh Company* (1829), by asserting that the Delaware law authorizing a dam across a navigable stream was an exercise of the police power rather than a regulation of commerce. Some members of the Court majority in the *License Cases* (1847) did endorse the dormant-power theory, and the Court employed it in invalidating a state tax in the *Passenger Cases* (1849). In *Cooley* v. *Board of Wardens* (1852), however, the Court decisively rejected the dormant-power concept, and the position announced in that case has prevailed ever since.

The Court's rejection of the dormant-power theory left important questions unanswered. If the national commerce power does not foreclose all state regulation, does it foreclose any? And if it does, how does one determine the validity of state enactments? To understand how the Court answered these questions, we must return to *Gibbons.*

The Search for a Standard

In arguing for the validity of New York's regulation of ferry service in *Gibbons,* the counsel for Ogden maintained that national and state powers over commerce were altogether concurrent: that is, in conferring the commerce power on Congress, the Constitution did not thereby withdraw any field of endeavor from state regulation. In this respect the commerce power was analogous to the taxing power: just as the grant to Congress of the power to tax did not interfere with the states' taxing power, the power granted in the Commerce Clause did not limit the states' regulatory authority. Thus, state laws would be invalid only if they conflicted with congressional legislation.

Chief Justice Marshall persuasively disposed of the concurrent power theory in his opinion in *Gibbons.* The commerce power is not analogous to the taxing power, he noted, since it is not "in its own nature . . . capable of residing in, and being exercised by, different authorities at the same time." For in regulating commerce, a state "is exercising the very power that is granted to Congress, and is doing the very thing which Congress is authorized to do." Accordingly, Marshall concluded, the constitutional grant of power to Congress, by its own force and in the absence of congressional legislation, precludes some state regulations.

Another interpretation of state regulatory authority was provided by the mutual-exclusiveness theory, which was championed by Thomas Jefferson and other proponents of state power. According to this theory the Constitution, although conferring the commerce power on Congress, left the states free to exercise the police power—the power to protect the health, safety, welfare, and morals of their citizens. In doing so, it established separate spheres for state and federal activity, and neither government could trespass on the other's domain. These spheres were distinguished not by what was regulated—state and federal laws might touch the same activities—but by the ends served by regulation. Because the police power resided in the states, then, the validity of a state regulation affecting commerce depended upon whether or not the regulatory act served legitimate police-power ends. In his opinions in *Gibbons* and *Black Bird* Marshall neither endorsed nor rejected the mutual-exclusiveness theory. On the one hand, he recognized that the states had not surrendered all power to enact legislation that affected commerce. He acknowledged in *Gibbons* that the states could enact "[i]nspection laws, quarantine laws, health laws of every description, as well as laws for regulating the internal commerce of the state, and those which respect turnpike-roads, ferries, etc." And in *Black Bird* he ruled that a state law authorizing the damming of a navigable stream constituted a valid exercise of the police power rather than a regulation of commerce. On the other hand, Marshall also recognized that even state legislation which served valid state ends, might be "repugnant to the power to regulate commerce in its dormant state, or . . . in conflict with a law passed on the subject."[4] So although states in the exercise of their police power could enact laws that affected commerce, state laws could be struck down if they infringed on the field of regulation that the Commerce Clause reserved to the national government.

The search for an appropriate standard governing state regulation of commerce ended in the *Cooley* case, in which the Court adopted the selective-exclusiveness theory. Speaking for the Court, Justice Benjamin Curtis noted that since the Constitution does not expressly bar state regulation of commerce, such regulations are valid unless "the nature of the power, thus granted to Congress, requires a similar authority should not exist in the states." Whether or not such a requirement exists can only be determined by examining the nature of the subjects to be regulated. According to Curtis, previous theories upholding or denying state regulatory power had proved inadequate because no simple standard could take into account the diversity of the subjects that might be regulated. Having thus disposed of the dormant power and concurrent power theories, he proposed a different approach:

> Now the power to regulate commerce, embraces a vast field, containing not only many, but exceedingly various subjects, quite unlike in their nature; some imperatively demanding a single uniform rule, operating equally on the commerce of the United States in every port; and some like the subject now in question, as imperatively demanding that diversity which alone can meet the local necessities of navigation.

By directing attention to the particular factual situation in each case rather than to the nature of national and state power, the *Cooley* standard marked a major advance in Commerce Clause analysis. Exactly how the standard should be applied, however, is not always clear. For one thing, most subjects, rather than demanding national or state regulation, could "admit of" either. In addition, states might regulate a subject for either legitimate or illegitimate purposes. In *Dean Milk Company* v. *City of Madison* (1951), for example, the Court observed that a state could regulate milk sold in the state to protect the health of residents but not to protect its dairy industry from competition. In cases involving state regulations, therefore, the Court has undertaken to balance the national interest in uniformity against the interests served by state regulation.

STATE REGULATION AND THE MODERN COURT

The contemporary Court has adopted *Cooley*'s selective-exclusiveness standard for determining the validity of state regulations affecting interstate commerce. State regulations that serve no valid purpose or pose a major barrier to the flow of commerce have been struck down, whereas those that serve important state interests and impose a minimal burden on commerce have been upheld. In determining whether state regulations unduly impede interstate commerce the Court often has been required to strike a balance between state and national interests.

Discrimination against Interstate Commerce

The Supreme Court consistently has struck down state laws designed to shield local businesses from interstate competition. Such discrimination defeats the very purpose of the Commerce Clause—the creation of "a federal free trade unit"—and encourages retaliatory legislation reminiscent of the Confederation period. In *Foster-Fountain Packing Company* v. *Haydel* (1928), for example, the Court invalidated a Louisiana law forbidding the exportation of shrimp from which the heads and tails had not been removed— a measure designed to aid the state's processing and canning industries. In *Edwards* v. *California* (1941), it struck down a California law prohibiting any person from knowingly bringing nonresident indigents into the state, ruling that the measure had been designed in part to limit competition for jobs.[5] And, in *Crutcher* v. *Kentucky* (1891), it ruled that Kentucky could not require corporations to obtain permits in order to conduct interstate business within the state.

A more difficult problem is posed by state statutes that discriminate against interstate commerce but also (at least arguably) serve legitimate state interests. Examples have been plentiful: the New Jersey statute involved in *City of Philadelphia* v. *New Jersey* (1978) prohibited the importation of out-of-state wastes largely for environmental and health reasons; the New York law in *H. P. Hood & Sons* v. *DuMond* created a partial embargo on the export of New York milk to protect consumers from destructive competition; and the city ordinance in *Dean Milk Company* v. *City of Madison* purportedly safeguarded local health by prohibiting the sale of milk as pasteurized unless it was processed and bottled in an approved plant within five miles of the city's central square. In each of these cases, the Court struck down the challenged legislation, ruling that a legitimate state objective alone is not enough. When a state law blocks the flow of interstate commerce, the Court has indicated, it will be upheld only when it serves a particularly important state end that cannot be achieved by nondiscriminatory legislation. Few discriminatory regulations can survive such exacting scrutiny.

Burdens on Commerce

Even nondiscriminatory state regulations may impose diverse requirements that tend to make interstate commerce less convenient and more expensive. The Supreme Court nonetheless has upheld such regulations unless they unduly interfere with interstate commerce. Each case has required the Court to examine the operation of the state law and to balance the benefits it produces against the burden it imposes on interstate commerce.

The Court's case-by-case approach to this issue is reflected in several decisions involving interstate transportation. Whereas in *Missouri Pacific Company* v. *Norwood* (1931), the Court upheld state legislation requiring "full-crews" on trains, in *Southern Pacific Company* v. *Arizona* (1945) it struck down a law restricting the length of trains traveling through Arizona. These divergent rulings reflected the differing operation of the statutes. The train-length law produced negligible safety gains but posed a major obstacle to the flow of interstate train traffic. The "full-crew" laws, on the other hand, had demonstrable safety benefits and did not significantly interfere with interstate transportation.

Similar considerations have governed the Court's treatment of state laws dealing with highway safety. Although such laws burden interstate commerce, particularly when adjoining states impose different requirements, the Court has upheld state regulations that effectively promote highway safety and do not place interstate commerce at a competitive disadvantage. In *South Carolina Highway Department* v. *Barnwell Brothers, Inc.* (1938), for example, it upheld a South Carolina law that imposed weight and width limitations on trucks operating on state roads. When the safety benefits are negligible, however, the Court has struck down the state legislation. In *Raymond Motor Transportation, Inc.* v. *Rice* (1978), for example, it invalidated a Wisconsin law that imposed a fifty-five-foot length limitation on trucks and prohibited double-trailer trucks. The aim of the law was valid, the Court acknowledged, but it imposed a substantial burden on interstate commerce, and Wisconsin had offered no evidence supporting the safety benefits of the limitations. Similarly, in *Kassel* v. *Consolidated Freightways Corporation* (1981) the justices struck down an Iowa truck-length law, endorsing the trial court's conclusion that the state's safety evidence was unpersuasive.

THE ROLE OF THE COURT

The Supreme Court's delicate balancing of national and state interests in Commerce Clause cases has been questioned by several justices, among them Justice Hugo Black and, more recently, Chief Justice William Rehnquist and Justice Antonin Scalia.[6] These justices have argued that such balancing involves the Court in making policy judgments, which Congress and the state legislatures are more qualified to make. They therefore propose that the Court's role should be much narrower. As long as the states do not discriminate against interstate commerce, they should be allowed to determine how heavily commerce should be regulated and whether particular regulations effectively promote health and safety. If the regulations impose too heavy a burden on interstate commerce, Congress can always intervene to remedy the situation.[7]

Other justices—most eloquently, Justice Robert Jackson—have defended the Court's current approach. The question, they have insisted, is not one of competence but of responsibility. More specifically, the Court's responsibility to enforce the Constitution includes enforcement of the negative implications of the Commerce Clause. Furthermore, they point out, Congress lacks the time to oversee the multitude of state regulations that, although of limited importance individually, collectively can pose a serious barrier to interstate commerce and threaten the national common market the Framers sought to create. As Justice Oliver Wendell Holmes argued:

> I do not think the United States would come to an end if we lost our power to declare an Act of Congress void. I do think the Union would be imperiled if we could not make that declaration as to the laws of the several States. For one in my place sees how often a local policy prevails with those who are not trained to national views and how often action is taken that embodies what the Commerce Clause was meant to end.[8]

Although the Court has accepted this viewpoint, the more basic concern raised by Black and others remains valid. By dividing governing authority between nation and state, the Constitution created a potential for conflict between the levels of government. When state enactments are challenged as inconsistent with the Constitution or federal law, the Court must consider both the aims of union and the legitimate regulatory concerns of the states. The sensitivity of the Court in balancing these valid but competing claims can affect substantially the role that the states play in governing.

NOTES

1 Thomas Reed Powell, *Vagaries and Varieties in Constitutional Interpretation* (New York: Columbia University Press, 1956), p. ix.
2 *Hines* v. *Davidowitz*, 312 U. S. 52, 67.
3 336 U.S. 525, 539 (1949).
4 *Willson* v. *Black Bird Creek Marsh Co.*, 2 Pet. 245, 252 (1829).
5 Four justices would have struck down the law as a violation of the Privileges and Immunities Clause of the Fourteenth Amendment. More recently, the Court in *Hicklin* v. *Orbeck* (1978) struck down an "Alaska Hire" law on that basis.
6 Black presented this position in *Southern Pacific Co.* v. *Arizona* (1945) and in *Gwin, White & Prince, Inc.* v. *Henneford* (1939). For Rehnquist's views see *Kassel* v. *Consolidated Freightways Corp.* (1981); for Scalia's, see *Bendix Autolite Corp.* v. *Midwesco Enterprises, Inc.* (1988).
7 Even if the Court declares a state law unconstitutional, Congress can override

the Court's ruling and legitimize the regulation. This paradoxical situation is a natural consequence of the congressional power over commerce. Because Congress can prescribe the rules by which commerce is to be governed, it has the power to subject commerce to relevant state regulations. For an example of such congressional action, see *Prudential Insurance Co.* v. *Benjamin* (1946).

8 *Collected Legal Papers* (New York: Harcourt, Brace, 1921), pp. 295–296.

SELECTED READINGS

The Federalist, Nos. 31–34, 44–46.

Brown v. *Maryland,* 12 Wheat. 419 (1827).
CTS Corp. v. *Dynamics Corp.,* 481 U.S. 69 (1987).
Edwards v. *California,* 314 U.S. 160 (1941).
Gibbons v. *Ogden,* Chapter 8.
Hughes v. *Oklahoma,* 441 U.S. 322 (1979).
Hood v. *DuMond,* 336 U.S. 525 (1949).

In addition to the materials listed in Chapter 8, see:

Benson, Paul R. *The Supreme Court and the Commerce Power, 1937–1970* (New York: Dunellen, 1970).

Hellerstein, Walter. "Hughes v. Oklahoma: The Court, the Commerce Clause, and State Control of Natural Resources." *Supreme Court Review 1979:* 51–93.

Maltz, Earl M. "How Much Regulation Is Too Much—An Examination of Commerce Clause Jurisprudence." *George Washington Law Review* 50 (1981): 47–89.

Powell, Thomas Reed. *Vagaries and Varieties in Constitutional Interpretation* (New York: Columbia University Press, 1956).

"Pre-emption as a Preferential Ground: A New Canon of Constitutional Construction." *Stanford Law Review* 12 (1959): 208–225.

Tushnet, Mark. "Rethinking the Dormant Commerce Clause," 1979 *Wisconsin Law Review:* 125–165.

Pacific Gas & Electric Company v. *State Energy Resources Conservation & Development Commission*

461 U.S. 190, 103 S. Ct. 1713, 75 L. Ed. 2d 752 (1983)

The Federal Government has long regulated the development of nuclear energy under the Atomic Energy Act of 1954 and subsequent legislation. Growing opposition to nuclear power, however, has led some states to impose their own restrictions on its development. The present case involves a California law providing that before additional nuclear power plants could be built, the state energy commission had to determine on a case-by-case basis that there would be adequate capacity for storage of the plant's spent fuel rods. The statute also imposed a moratorium on the certification of new nuclear plants until the energy commission determined that an adequate technology had been developed for the disposal of high-level nuclear waste. Two electric utility companies challenged these provisions, claiming that they had been preempted by the Atomic Energy Act.

A federal district court ruled in favor of the utility companies. However, a federal court of appeals ruled that the moratorium on certification of new nuclear power plants was not preempted and that the provision dealing with capacity for storing spent fuel rods was not ripe for review. (For a discussion of ripeness, see Chapter 3.) The excerpts from the U.S. Supreme Court's decision presented below focus on whether federal legislation had preempted the state moratorium on certification of new plants.

Opinion of the Court: White, Burger, Brennan, Marshall, Powell, Rehnquist, O'Connor. Concurring opinion (in part): Blackmun, Stevens.

JUSTICE WHITE delivered the opinion of the Court.

It is well-established that within Constitutional limits Congress may preempt state authority by so stating in express terms. Absent explicit preemptive language, Congress' intent to supercede state law altogether may be found from a "scheme of federal regulation so pervasive as to make reasonable the inference that Congress left no room to supplement it," "because the Act of Congress may touch a field in which the federal interest is so dominant that the federal system will be assumed to preclude enforcement of state laws on the same subject," or because "the object sought to be obtained by the federal law and the character of obligations imposed by it may reveal the same purpose." Even where Congress has not entirely displaced state regulation in a specific area, state law is preempted to the extent that it actually conflicts with federal law. Such a conflict arises when "compliance with both federal and state regulations is a physical impossibility," or where state law "stands as an obstacle to the accomplishment and execution of the full purposes and objectives of Congress."

Petitioners, the United States, and supporting *amici*, present three major lines of argument as to why § 25524.2 is preempted. First, they submit that the statute—because it regulates construction of nuclear plants and because it is allegedly predicated on safety concerns—ignores the division between federal and state authority created by the Atomic Energy Act, and falls within the field that the federal government has preserved for its own exclusive control. Second, the statute, and the judgments that underlie it, conflict with decisions concerning the nuclear waste disposal issue made by Congress and the Nuclear Regulatory Commission. Third, the California statute frustrates the federal goal of developing nuclear technology as a source of energy. We consider each of these contentions in turn.

. . . From the passage of the Atomic Energy Act in 1954, through several revisions, and to the present day, Congress has preserved the dual regulation of nuclear-powered electricity generation: the federal government maintains complete control of the safety and "nuclear" aspects of energy generation; the states exercise their traditional authority over the need for additional generating capacity, the type of generating facilities to be licensed, land use, ratemaking, and the like.

The above is not particularly controversial. But deciding how § 25524.2 is to be construed and classified is a more difficult proposition. At the outset, we emphasize that the statute does not seek to regulate the construction or operation of a nuclear powerplant. It would clearly be impermissible for California to attempt to do so, for such regulation, even if enacted out of non-safety concerns, would nevertheless directly conflict with the NRC's exclusive authority over plant construction and operation. Respondents appear to concede as much. Respondents do broadly argue, however, that although safety regulation of nuclear plants by states is forbidden, a state may completely prohibit new construction until its safety concerns are satisfied by the federal government. We reject this line of reasoning. State safety regulation is not preempted only when it conflicts with federal law. Rather, the federal government has occupied the entire field of nuclear safety concerns, except the limited powers expressly ceded to the states. When the federal government completely occupies a given field or an identifiable portion of it, as it has done here, the test of preemption is whether "the matter on which the state asserts the right to act is in any way regulated by the federal government." A state moratorium on nuclear construction grounded in safety concerns falls squarely within the prohibited field. . . .

That being the case, it is necessary to determine whether there is a non-safety rationale for § 25524.2. . . .

Although [several] indicia of California's intent in enacting § 25524.2 are subject to varying interpretation, there are two reasons why we should not become embroiled in attempting to ascertain California's true motive. First, inquiry into legislative motive is often an unsatisfactory venture. What motivates one legislator to vote for a statute is not necessarily what motivates scores of others to enact it. Second, it would be particularly pointless for us to engage in such inquiry here when it is clear that the states have been allowed to retain authority over the need for electrical generating facilities easily sufficient to permit a state so inclined to halt the construction of new nuclear plants by refusing on economic grounds to issue certificates of public convenience in individual proceedings. In these circumstances, it should be up to Congress to determine whether a state has misused the authority left in its hands.

Therefore, we accept California's avowed economic purpose as the rationale for enacting § 25524.2. Accordingly, the statute lies outside the occupied field of nuclear safety regulation.

Petitioners' second major argument concerns federal regulation aimed at the nuclear waste disposal problem itself. It is contended that § 25524.2 conflicts with federal regulation of nuclear waste disposal, with the NRC's decision that it is permissible to continue to license reactors, notwithstanding uncertainty surrounding the waste disposal problem, and with Congress' recent passage of legislation directed at that problem. . . .

The NRC's imprimatur, however, indicates only that it is safe to proceed with such plants, not that it is economically wise to do so. Because the NRC order does not and could not compel a utility to develop a nuclear plant, compliance with both it and § 25524.2 are possible. Moreover, because the NRC's regulations are aimed at insuring that plants are safe, not necessarily that they are economical, § 25524.2 does not interfere with the objective of the federal regulation.

Nor has California sought through § 25524.2 to impose its own standards on nuclear waste disposal. The statute accepts that it is the federal responsibility to develop and license such technology. As there is no attempt on California's part to enter this field, one which is occupied by the federal government, we do not find § 25524.2 preempted any more by the NRC's obligations in the waste disposal field than by its licensing power over the plants themselves. . . .

Finally, it is strongly contended that § 25524.2 frustrates the Atomic Energy Act's purpose to develop the commercial use of nuclear power. . . .

There is little doubt that a primary purpose of the Atomic Energy Act was, and continues to be, the promotion of nuclear power. The Act itself states that it is a program "to encourage widespread participation in the development and utilization of atomic energy for peaceful purposes to the maximum extent consistent with the common defense and security and with the health and safety of the public." The House and Senate Reports confirmed that it was "a major policy goal of the United States" that the involvement of private industry would "speed the further development of the peaceful uses of atomic energy." The same purpose is manifest in the passage of the Price-Anderson Act, which limits private liability from a nuclear accident. The Act was passed "in order to protect the public and to encourage the development of the atomic energy industry. . . ."

The Court of Appeals' suggestion that legislation since 1974 has indicated a "change in congressional outlook" is unconvincing. . . . The Court of Appeals is right, however, that the promotion of nuclear power is not to be accomplished "at all costs." The elaborate licensing and safety provisions and the continued preservation of state regulation in traditional areas belie that. Moreover, Congress has allowed the States to determine—as a matter of economics—whether a nuclear plant vis-a-vis a fossil fuel plant should be built. The decision of California to exercise that authority does not, in itself, constitute a basis for preemption. Therefore, while the argument of petitioners and the United States has considerable force, the legal reality remains that Congress has left sufficient authority in the states to allow the development of nuclear power to be slowed or even stopped for economic reasons. Given this statutory scheme, it is for Congress to rethink the division of regulatory authority in light of its possible exercise by the states to undercut a federal objective. The courts should not assume the role which our system assigns to Congress.

The judgment of the Court of Appeals is

Affirmed.

JUSTICE BLACKMUN, with whom JUSTICE STEVENS joins, concurring in part and concurring in the judgment.

I join the Court's opinion, except to the extent it suggests that a State may not prohibit the construction of nuclear power plants if the State is motivated by concerns about the safety of such plants. . . .

Congress has not required States to "go nuclear," in whole or in part. The Atomic Energy Act's twin goals were to promote the development of a technology and to ensure the safety of that technology. Although that Act reserves to the NRC decisions about how to build and operate nuclear plants, the Court reads too much into the Act in suggesting that it also limits the States' traditional power to decide what types of electric power to utilize. Congress simply has made the nuclear option available, and a State may decline that option for any reason. Rather than rest on the elusive test of legislative motive, therefore, I would conclude that the decision whether to build nuclear plants remains with the States. In my view, a ban on construction of nuclear power plants would be valid even if its authors were motivated by fear of a core meltdown or other nuclear catastrophe.

Cooley v. *Board of Wardens*

53 U.S. (12 How.) 299, 13 L. Ed. 996 (1852)

In 1803, Pennsylvania passed a law requiring all ships entering or leaving the port of Philadelphia to engage a local pilot or to pay a fine amounting to half the pilotage fee for the "use of the society for the relief of distressed and decayed pilots" and their families. A 1789 Act of Congress had provided that "all pilots in the bays, inlets, rivers, harbors, and ports of the United States shall continue to be regulated in conformity with the existing laws of the states, respectively, wherein such pilots may be, or with such laws as the states may respectively hereafter enact for the purpose, until further legislative provision shall be made by Congress." After being fined for failure to engage a pilot, Aaron Cooley challenged the Pennsylvania law as an impermissible regulation of interstate commerce. *Opinion of the Court: Curtis, Taney, Catron, McKinley, Nelson, Grier. Concurring opinion: Daniel. Dissenting opinion: McLean, Wayne.*

MR. JUSTICE CURTIS delivered the opinion of the Court. . . .

That the power to regulate commerce includes the regulation of navigation, we consider settled. And when we look to the nature of the service performed by pilots, to the relations which that service and its compensations bear to navigation between the several states, and between the ports of the United States and foreign countries, we are brought to the conclusion, that the regulation of the qualifications of pilots, of the modes and times of offering and rendering their services, of the responsibilities which shall rest upon them, of the powers they shall possess, of the compensation they may demand, and of the penalties by which their rights and duties may be enforced, do constitute regulations of navigation, and consequently of commerce, within the just meaning of this clause of the Constitution. . . .

It becomes necessary, therefore, to consider whether this law of Pennsylvania, being a regulation of commerce, is valid. . . .

. . . We are brought directly and unavoidably to the consideration of the question, whether the grant of the commercial power to Congress, did *per se* deprive the states of all power to regulate pilots. This question has never been decided by this court, nor, in our judgment, has any case depending upon all the considerations which must govern this one, come before this court. The grant of commercial power to Congress does not contain any terms which expressly exclude the states from exercising an authority over its subject-matter. If they are excluded it must be because the nature of the power, thus granted to Congress, requires that a similar authority should not exist in the states. If it were conceded on the one side, that the nature of this power, like that to legislate for the District of Columbia, is absolutely and totally repugnant to the existence of similar power in the states, probably no one would deny that the grant of the power to Congress, as effectually and perfectly excludes the states from all future legislation on the subject, as if express words had been used to exclude them. And on the other hand, if it were admitted that the existence of this power in Congress, like the power of taxation, is compatible with the existence of a similar power in the states, then it would be in conformity with the contemporary exposition of the Constitution (Federalist, No. 32), and with the judicial construction, given from time to time by this court, after the most deliberate consideration, to hold that the mere grant of such a power to Congress, did not imply a prohibition on the states to exercise the same power; that it is not the mere existence of such a power, but its exercise by Congress, which may be incompatible with the exercise of the same power by the states, and that the states may legislate in the absence of congressional regulations. . . .

The diversities of opinion, therefore, which have existed on this subject, have arisen from the different views taken of the nature of this power. But when the nature of a power like this is spoken of, when it is said that the nature of the power requires that it should be exercised exclusively by Congress, it must be intended to refer to the subjects of that power, and to say they are of such a nature as to require exclusive legislation by Congress. Now the power to regulate commerce, embraces a vast field, containing not only many, but exceedingly various subjects, quite unlike in their nature; some imperatively demanding a single uniform rule, operating equally on the commerce of the United States in every port; and some, like the subject now in question, as imperatively demanding that diversity, which alone can meet the local necessities of navigation.

Either absolutely to affirm, or deny that the nature of this power requires exclusive legislation by Congress, is to lose sight of the nature of the subjects of this power, and to assert concerning all of them, what is really applicable but to a part. Whatever subjects of this power are in their nature national, or admit only of one uniform system, or plan of regulation, may justly be said to be of such a nature as to require exclusive legislation by Congress. That this cannot be affirmed of laws for the regulation of pilots and pilotage is plain. The act of 1789 contains a clear and authoritative declaration by the first Congress, that the nature of this subject is such, that until Congress should find it necessary to exert its power, it should be left to the legislation of the states; that it is local and not national; that it is likely to be the best provided for, not by one system, or plan of regulations, but by as many as the legislative discretion of the several states should deem applicable to the local peculiarities of the ports within their limits.

Viewed in this light, so much of this act of 1789 as declares that pilots shall continue to be regulated "by such laws as the states may respectively hereafter enact for that purpose," instead of being held to be inoperative, as an attempt to confer on the states a power to legislate, of which the Constitution had deprived them, is allowed an appropriate and important signification. It manifests the understanding of Congress, at the outset of the government, that the nature of this subject is not such as to require its exclusive legislation. The practice of the states, and of the national government, has been in conformity with this declaration, from the origin of the national government to this time; and the nature of the subject when examined, is such as to leave no doubt of the superior fitness and propriety, not to say the absolute necessity, of different systems of regulation, drawn from local knowledge and experience, and conformed to local wants. How then can we say that by the mere grant of power to regulate commerce, the states are deprived of all the power to legislate on this subject, because from the nature of the power the legislation of Congress must be exclusive. This would be to affirm that the nature of the power is in any case, something different from the nature of the subject to which, in such case, the power extends, and that the nature of the power necessarily demands, in all cases, exclusive legislation by Congress, while the nature of one of the subjects of that power, not only does not require such exclusive legislation, but may be best provided for by many different systems enacted by the states, in conformity with the circumstances of the ports within their limits. In construing an instrument designed for the formation of a government, and in determining the extent of one of its important grants of power to legislate, we can make no such distinction between the nature of the power and the nature of the subject on which that power was intended practically to operate, nor consider the grant more extensive by affirming of the power, what is not true of its subject now in question.

It is the opinion of a majority of the court that the mere grant to Congress of the power to regulate commerce, did not deprive the states of power to regulate pilots, and that although Congress has legislated on this subject, its legislation manifests an intention, with a single exception, not to regulate this subject, but to leave its regulation to the several states. . . .

We are of opinion that this state law was enacted by virtue of a power, residing in the state to legislate; that it is not in conflict with any law of Congress; that it does not interfere with any system which Congress has established by making regulations, or by intentionally leaving individuals to their own unrestricted action, that this law is therefore valid, and the judgment of the Supreme Court of Pennsylvania in each case must be affirmed.

Dean Milk Company v. *City of Madison*

340 U.S. 349; 71 S. Ct. 295; 95 L. Ed. 329 (1951)

A Madison, Wisconsin, ordinance prohibited the sale of milk in the city unless it came from a farm less than twenty-five miles from or was pasteurized and bottled at approved plants within five miles of the center of the city. Dean Milk was denied a license to sell milk because it pasteurized its milk at its plant in Illinois, beyond the five-mile limit. Both a county court and the Wisconsin Supreme Court upheld the ordinance, and the company appealed to the Supreme Court. *Opinion of the Court: Clark, Vinson, Reed, Frankfurter, Jackson, Burton. Dissenting opinion: Black, Douglas, Minton.*

Mr. Justice Clark delivered the opinion of the Court. . . .

. . . [W]e agree with appellant that the ordinance imposes an undue burden on interstate commerce.

This is not an instance in which an enactment falls because of federal legislation which, as a proper exercise of paramount national power over commerce, excludes measures which might otherwise be within the police power of the states. . . . There is no pertinent national regulation by the Congress, and statutes enacted for the District of Columbia indicate that Congress has recognized the appropriateness of local regulation of the sale of fluid milk. . . .

Nor can there be objection to the avowed purpose of this enactment. We assume that difficulties in sanitary regulation of milk and milk products originating in remote areas may present a situation in which "upon a consideration of all the relevant facts and circumstances it appears that the matter is one which may appropriately be regulated in the interest of the safety, health and well-being of local communities. . . ." . . . We also assume that since Congress has not spoken to the contrary, the subject matter of the ordinance lies within the sphere of state regulation even though interstate commerce may be affected. . . .

But this regulation . . . in practical effect excludes from distribution in Madison wholesome milk produced and pasteurized in Illinois. . . . In thus erecting an economic barrier protecting a major local industry against competition from without the State, Madison plainly discriminates against interstate commerce. This it cannot do, even in the exercise of its unquestioned power to protect the health and safety of its people, if reasonable nondiscriminatory alternatives, adequate to conserve legitimate local interests, are available. . . . A different view, that the ordinance is valid simply because it professes to be a health measure, would mean that the Commerce Clause of itself imposes no limitations on state action other than those laid down by the Due Process Clause, save for the rare instance where a state artlessly discloses an avowed purpose to discriminate against interstate goods. . . . Our issue then is whether the discrimination inherent in the Madison ordinance can be justified in view of the character of the local interests and the available methods of protecting them. . . .

It appears that reasonable and adequate alternatives are available. If the City of Madison prefers to rely upon its own officials for inspection of distant milk sources, such inspection is readily open to it without hardship for it could charge the actual and reasonable cost of such inspection to the importing producers and processors. . . . Moreover, appellee Health Commissioner of Madison testified that as proponent of the local milk ordinance he had submitted the provisions here in controversy and an alternative proposal based on § 11 of the Model Milk Ordinance recommended by the United States Public Health Service. The model provision imposes no geographical limitation on location of milk sources and processing plants but excludes from the municipality milk not produced and pasteurized conformably to standards as high as those enforced by the receiving city. In implementing such an ordinance, the importing city obtains milk ratings based on uniform standards and established by health authorities in the jurisdiction where production and processing occur. The receiving city may determine the extent of enforcement of sanitary standards in the exporting area by verifying the accuracy of safety ratings of specific plants or of the milkshed in the distant jurisdiction through the United States Public Health Service, which routinely and on request spot checks the local ratings. The Commissioner testified that Madison consumers "would be safeguarded adequately" under either proposal and that he had expressed no preference. . . .

To permit Madison to adopt a regulation not essential for the protection of local health interests and placing a discriminatory burden on interstate commerce would invite a multiplication of preferential trade areas destructive of the very purpose of the Commerce Clause. Under the circumstances here presented, the regulation must yield to the principle that "one state in its dealings with another may not place itself in a position of economic isolation." . . . *Baldwin* v. *G.A.F. Seelig, Inc.* [1935].

For these reasons we conclude that the judgment below sustaining the five-mile provision as to pasteurization must be reversed.

Mr. Justice Black, with whom Mr. Justice Douglas and Mr. Justice Minton concur, dissenting.

Today's holding invalidates § 7.21 of the Madison, Wisconsin, ordinance on the following reasoning: (1) the section excludes wholesome milk coming from Illinois; (2) this imposes a discriminatory burden on interstate commerce; (3) such a burden cannot be imposed where, as here, there are reasonable, nondiscriminatory and adequate alternatives available. I disagree with the Court's premises, reasoning, and judgment.

1. This ordinance does not exclude wholesome milk coming from Illinois or anywhere else. It does require that all milk sold in Madison must be pasteurized within five miles of the center of the city. But there was no finding in the state courts, nor evidence to justify a finding there or here, that appellant, Dean Milk Company, is unable to have its milk pasteurized within the defined geographical area. As a practical matter, so far as the record shows, Dean can easily comply with the ordinance whenever it wants to. Therefore, Dean's personal preference to pasteurize in Illinois, not the ordinance, keeps Dean's milk out of Madison.

2. Characterization of § 7.21 as a "discriminatory burden" on interstate commerce is merely a statement of the Court's result, which I think incorrect. The section does prohibit the sale of milk in Madison by interstate and intrastate producers who prefer to pasteurize over five miles distant from the city. But both state courts below found that § 7.21 represents a good-faith attempt to safeguard public health by making adequate sanitation inspections possible. While we are not bound by these findings, I do not understand the Court to overturn them. Therefore, the fact that § 7.21, like all health regulations, imposes some burden on trade, does not mean that it "discriminates" against interstate commerce.

3. This health regulation should not be invalidated merely because the Court believes that alternative milk-inspection methods might insure the cleanliness and healthfulness of Dean's Illinois milk. I find it difficult to explain why the Court uses the "reasonable alternative" concept to protect trade when today it refuses to apply the same principle to protect freedom of speech. . . .

If, however, the principle announced today is to be followed, the Court should not strike down local health regulations unless satisfied beyond a reasonable doubt that the substitutes it proposes would not lower health standards. I do not think that the Court can so satisfy itself on the basis of its judicial knowledge. And the evidence in the record leads me to the conclusion that the substitute health measures suggested by the Court do not insure milk as safe as the Madison ordinance requires.

One of the Court's proposals is that Madison require milk processors to pay reasonable inspection fees at the milk supply "sources." Experience shows, however, that the fee method gives rise to prolonged litigation over the calculation and collection of the charges. . . . To throw local milk regulation into such a quagmire of uncertainty jeopardizes the admirable milk-inspection systems in force in many municipalities. . . .

The Court's second proposal is that Madison adopt § 11 of the "Model Milk Ordinance." . . . The evidence indicates to me that enforcement of the Madison law would assure a more healthful quality of milk than that which is entitled to use the label of "Grade A" under the Model Ordinance. Indeed, the United States Board of Public Health, which drafted the Model Ordinance, suggests that the provisions are "minimum" standards only. The Model Ordinance does not provide for continuous investigation of all pasteurization plants as does § 7.21 of the Madison ordinance. Under § 11, moreover, Madison would be required to depend on the Chicago inspection system since Dean's plants, and the farms supplying them with raw milk, are located in the Chicago milkshed. But there is direct and positive evidence in the record that milk produced under Chicago standards did not meet the Madison requirements.

Furthermore, the Model Ordinance would force the Madison health authorities to rely on "spot checks" by the United States Public Health Service to determine whether Chicago enforced its milk regulations. The evidence shows that these "spot checks" are based on random inspection of farms and pasteurization plants: the United States Public Health Service rates the ten thousand or more dairy farms in the Chicago milkshed by a sampling of no more than two hundred farms. The same sampling technique is employed to inspect pasteurization plants. There was evidence that neither the farms supplying Dean with milk nor Dean's pasteurization plants were necessarily inspected in the last "spot check" of the Chicago milkshed made two years before the present case was tried.

From what this record shows, and from what it fails to show, I do not think that either of the alternatives suggested by the Court would assure the people of Madison as pure a supply of milk as they receive under their own ordinance. On this record I would uphold the Madison law. . . .

City of Philadelphia v. *New Jersey*

437 U.S. 617, 98 S. Ct. 2531, 57 L. Ed. 2d 475 (1978)

New Jersey's Waste Control Act made it illegal to import solid or liquid waste into the state. Landfill operators in New Jersey, along with several cities in adjoining states with which they had waste disposal agreements, challenged the statute as impermissibly burdening interstate commerce. In response, the state argued that the measure advanced vital health and environmental interests and had only a minimal effect on interstate commerce. The state trial court ruled the law unconstitutional, but the state supreme court reversed, and the case was appealed to the Supreme Court. *Opinion of the Court: Stewart, Brennan, White, Marshall, Blackmun, Powell, Stevens. Dissenting opinion: Rehnquist, Burger.*

MR. JUSTICE STEWART delivered the opinion of the Court. . . .

The New Jersey Supreme Court questioned whether the interstate movement of those wastes banned by ch. 363 is "commerce" at all within the meaning of the Commerce Clause. Any doubts on that score should be laid to rest at the outset. . . .

All objects of interstate trade merit Commerce Clause protection; none is excluded by definition at the outset. In *Bowman* v. *Chicago & Northwestern Ry.* (1888) and similar cases, the Court held simply that because the articles' worth in interstate commerce was far outweighed by the dangers inhering in their very movement, States could prohibit their transportation across state lines. Hence, we reject the state court's suggestion that the banning of "valueless" out-of-state wastes by ch. 363 implicates no constitutional protection. . . .

The opinions of the Court through the years have reflected an alertness to the evils of "economic isolation" and protectionism, while at the same time recognizing that incidental burdens on interstate commerce may be unavoidable when a State legislates to safeguard the health and safety of its people. Thus, where simple economic protectionism is effected by state legislation, a virtually *per se* rule of invalidity has been erected. . . .

The crucial inquiry, therefore, must be directed to determining whether ch. 363 is basically a protectionist measure, or whether it can fairly be viewed as a law directed to legitimate local concerns, with effects upon interstate commerce that are only incidental. . . .

The New Jersey law at issue in this case falls squarely within the area that the Commerce Clause puts off limits to state regulation. On its face, it imposes on out-of-state commercial interests the full burden of conserving the State's remaining landfill space. . . .

The appellees argue that not all laws which facially discriminate against out-of-state commerce are forbidden protectionist regulations. In particular, they point to quarantine laws, which this Court has repeatedly upheld even though they appear to single out interstate commerce for special treatment.

The New Jersey statute is not such a quarantine law. There has been no claim here that the very movement of waste into or through New Jersey endangers health, or that waste must be disposed of as soon and as close to its point of generation as possible. The harms caused by waste are said to arise after its disposal in landfill sites, and at that point, as New Jersey concedes, there is no basis to distinguish out-of-state waste from domestic waste. If one is inherently harmful, so is the other. Yet New Jersey has banned the former while leaving its landfill sites open to the latter. The New Jersey law blocks the importation of waste in an obvious effort to saddle those outside the State with the entire burden of slowing the flow of refuse into New Jersey's remaining landfill sites. That legislative effort is clearly impermissible under the Commerce Clause of the Constitution. . . .

The judgment is

Reversed.

MR. JUSTICE REHNQUIST, with whom THE CHIEF JUSTICE joins, dissenting. . . .

The question presented in this case is whether New Jersey must . . . continue to receive and dispose of solid waste from neighboring States even though these will inexorably increase . . . health problems. . . . The Court answers this question in the affirmative. New Jersey must either prohibit *all* landfill operations, leaving itself to cast about for a presently nonexistent solution to the serious problem of disposing of the waste generated within its own borders, or it must accept waste from every portion of the United States, thereby multiplying the health and safety problems which would result if it dealt only with such wastes generated within the State. Because past precedents establish that the Commerce Clause does not present appellees with such a Hobson's choice, I dissent. . . .

. . . [The Court's earlier quarantine cases] are dispositive of the present one. Under them, New Jersey may require germ-infected rags or diseased meat to be disposed of as best as possible within the State, but at the same time prohibit the *importation* of such items for disposal at the facilities that are set up within New Jersey for disposal of such material generated *within* the State. The physical fact of life that New Jersey must somehow dispose of its own noxious items does not mean that it must serve as a depository for those of every other State. Similarly, New Jersey should be free under our past precedents to prohibit the importation of solid waste because of the health and safety problems that such waste poses to its citizens. The fact that New Jersey continues to, and indeed must continue to, dispose of its own solid waste does not mean that New Jersey may not prohibit the importation of even more solid waste into the State. I simply see no way to distinguish solid waste, on the record of this case, from germ-infected rags, diseased meat, and other noxious items.

. . . According to the Court, the New Jersey law is distinguishable from these other laws, and invalid, because the concern of New Jersey is not with the *movement* of solid waste but of the present inability to safely *dispose* of it once it reaches its destination. . . .

Even if the Court is correct in its characterization of New Jersey's concerns, I do not see why a State may ban the importation of items whose movement risks contagion, but cannot ban the importation of items which, although they may be transported into the State without undue hazard, will then simply pile up in an ever increasing danger to the public's health and safety. The Commerce Clause was not drawn with a view to having the validity of state laws turn on such pointless distinctions.

. . . The Court implies that the challenged laws must be invalidated because New Jersey has left its landfills open to domestic waste. . . . New Jersey must out of sheer necessity treat and dispose of its solid waste in some fashion, just as it must treat New Jersey cattle suffering from hoof-and-mouth disease. It does not follow that New Jersey must, under the Commerce Clause, accept solid waste or diseased cattle from outside its borders and thereby exacerbate its problems.

The Supreme Court of New Jersey expressly found that ch. 363 was passed "to preserve the health of New Jersey residents by keeping their exposure to solid waste and landfill areas to a minimum.". . . The Court points to absolutely no evidence that would contradict this finding by the New Jersey Supreme Court. Because I find no basis for distinguishing the laws under challenge here from our past cases upholding state laws that prohibit the importation of items that could endanger the population of the State, I dissent.

Southern Pacific Company v. *Arizona*

325 U.S. 761, 65 S. Ct. 1515, 89 L. Ed. 1915 (1945)

The Arizona Train Limit Law prohibited passenger trains of more than fourteen cars and freight trains of more than seventy cars from operating in the state. When the Southern Pacific Railroad violated these safety restrictions by operating longer trains on interstate routes through the state, Arizona brought action in state court. The trial court ruled in favor of the company, the Arizona Supreme Court reversed, and Southern Pacific appealed to the Supreme Court. *Opinion of the Court: Stone, Reed, Frankfurter, Murphy, Jackson, Burton. Concurring in result: Rutledge. Dissenting opinions: Black, Douglas.*

MR. CHIEF JUSTICE STONE delivered the opinion of the Court. . . .

Although the commerce clause conferred on the national government power to regulate commerce, its possession of the power does not exclude all state power of regulation. . . . In the absence of conflicting legislation by Congress, there is a residuum of power in the state to make laws governing matters of local concern which nevertheless in some measure affect interstate commerce or even, to some extent, regulate it. . . . Thus the states may regulate matters which, because of their number and diversity, may never be adequately dealt with by Congress. . . . When the regulation of matters of local concern is local in character and effect, and its impact on the national commerce does not seriously interfere with its operation, and the consequent incentive to deal with them nationally is slight, such regulation has been generally held to be within state authority. . . .

But ever since *Gibbons* v. *Ogden* . . . the states have not been deemed to have authority to impede substantially the free flow of commerce from state to state, or to regulate those phases of the national commerce which, because of the need of national uniformity, demand that their regulation, if any, be prescribed by a single authority. . . .

In the application of these principles some enactments may be found to be plainly within and others plainly without state power. But between these extremes lies the infinite variety of cases, in which regulation of local matters may also operate as a regulation of commerce, in which reconciliation of the conflicting claims of state and national power is to be attained only by some appraisal and accommodation of the competing demands of the state and national interests involved. . . .

Hence the matters for ultimate determination here are the nature and extent of the burden which the state regulation of interstate trains, adopted as a safety measure, imposes on interstate commerce, and whether the relative weights of the state and national interests involved are such as to make inapplicable the rule, generally observed, that the free flow of interstate commerce and its freedom from local restraints in matters requiring uniformity of regulation are interests safeguarded by the commerce clause from state interference. . . .

The findings show that the operation of long trains, that is trains of more than fourteen passenger and more than seventy freight cars, is standard practice over the main lines of the railroads of the United States, and that, if the length of trains is to be regulated at all, national uniformity in the regulation adopted, such as only Congress can prescribe, is practically indispensable to the operation of an efficient and economical national railway system. On many railroads passenger trains of more than fourteen cars and freight trains of more than seventy cars are operated, and on some systems freight trains are run ranging from one hundred and twenty-five to one hundred and sixty cars in length. Outside of Arizona, where the length of trains is not restricted, appellant runs a substantial proportion of long trains. In 1939 on its comparable route for through traffic through Utah and Nevada from 66 to 85% of its freight trains were seventy cars in length and over 43% of its passenger trains included more than fourteen passenger cars.

In Arizona, approximately 93% of the freight traffic and 95% of the passenger traffic is interstate. Because of the Train Limit Law appellant is required to haul over 30% more trains in Arizona than would otherwise have been necessary. The record shows a definite relationship between operating costs and the length of trains, the increase in length resulting in a reduction of operating costs per car. The additional cost of operation of trains complying with the Train Limit Law in Arizona amounts for the two railroads traversing that state to about $1,000,000 a year. The reduction in train lengths also impedes efficient operation. More locomotives and more manpower are required; the necessary conversion and reconversion of train lengths at terminals and the delay caused by breaking up and remaking long trains upon entering and leaving the state in order to comply with the law, delays the traffic and diminishes its volume moved in a given time, especially when traffic is heavy. . . .

The unchallenged findings leave no doubt that the Arizona Train Limit Law imposes a serious burden on the interstate commerce conducted by appellant. . . . Compliance with a state statute limiting train lengths requires interstate trains of a length lawful in other states to be broken up and reconstituted as they enter each state according as it may impose varying limitations upon train lengths. The alternative is for the carrier to conform to the lowest train limit restriction of any of the states through which its trains pass, whose laws thus control the carriers' operations both within and without the regulating state. . . .

The trial court found that the Arizona law had no reasonable relation to safety, and made train operation more dangerous. . . .

The principal source of danger of accident from increased length of trains is the resulting increase of "slack action" of the train. . . . The length of the train increases the slack since the slack action of a train is the total of the free movement between its several cars. The amount of slack action has some effect on the severity of the shock of train movements, and on freight trains sometimes results in injuries to operatives, which most frequently occur to occupants of the caboose. The amount and severity of slack action, however, are not wholly dependent upon the length of train, as they may be affected by the mode and conditions of operation as to grades, speed, and load. . . .

On comparison of the number of slack action accidents in Arizona with those in Nevada, where the length of trains is now unregulated, the trial court found that with substantially the same amount of traffic in each state the number of accidents was relatively the same in long as in short train operations . . . reduction of the length of trains tends to increase the number of accidents because of the increase in the number of trains. . . . The accident rate in Arizona is much higher than on comparable lines elsewhere, where there is no regulation of length of trains. The record lends support to the trial court's conclusion that the train length limitation increased rather than diminished the number of accidents.

. . . [Arizona's] regulation of train lengths, admittedly obstructive to interstate train operation, and having a seriously adverse effect on transportation efficiency and economy, passes beyond what is plainly essential for safety since it does not appear that it will lessen rather than increase the danger of accident. . . . Examination of all the relevant factors makes it plain that the state interest is outweighed by the interest of the nation in an adequate, economical and efficient railway transportation service, which must prevail.

Reversed.

MR. JUSTICE BLACK, dissenting.

. . . I . . . think that the "findings" of the state court do not authorize today's decision. That court did not find that there is no unusual danger from slack movements in long trains. It did decide on disputed evidence that the long train "slack movement" dangers were more than offset by prospective dangers as a result of running a larger number of short trains, since many people might be hurt at grade crossing. There was undoubtedly some evidence before the state court from which it could have reached such a conclusion. There was undoubtedly as much evidence before it which would have justified a different conclusion.

Under those circumstances, the determination of whether it is in the interest of society for the length of trains to be governmentally regulated is a matter of public policy. Someone must fix that policy—either the Congress, or the state, or the courts. A century and a half of constitutional history and government admonishes this Court to leave that choice to the elected legislative representatives of the people themselves, where it properly belongs both on democratic principles and the requirements of efficient government. . . .

When we finally get down to the gist of what the Court today actually decides, it is this: Even though more railroad employees will be injured by "slack action" movements on long trains than on short trains, there must be no regulation of this danger in the absence of "uniform regulations" . . .

We are not left in doubt as to why, as against the potential peril of injuries to employees, the Court tips the scales on the side of "uniformity." For the evil it finds in a lack of uniformity is that it (1) delays interstate commerce, (2) increases its cost and (3) impairs its efficiency. All three of these boil down to the same thing, and that is that running shorter trains would increase the cost of railroad operations. . . .

. . . Thus the conclusion that a requirement for long trains will "burden interstate commerce" is a mere euphemism for the statement that a requirement for long trains will increase the cost of railroad operations. . . .

. . . I would affirm the judgment of the Supreme Court of Arizona.

10
THE CONTRACT CLAUSE

Article I, Section 10 of the Constitution declares that no state shall pass any "Law impairing the Obligations of Contracts." This language was included in order to protect "vested rights"—those so fundamental to an individual that they must remain beyond governmental control. Among the most important of these rights is the individual's right to security in the acquisition and possession of private property. The doctrine of vested rights thus precludes not only expropriation of an individual's property but also damaging interferences with future property interests, such as obligations embodied in contractual arrangements.[1]

As noted in Chapter One, a principal aim of the Constitution was to secure private rights (and especially property rights[2]) from the dangers of an overbearing majority while at the same time preserving the spirit and form of popular government. This goal was underscored in an exchange between Roger Sherman and James Madison early in the Constitutional Convention. Sherman suggested that the objects of the union include no more than defense against foreign danger and internal disputes and the establishment of a central authority to make treaties with foreign nations and to regulate foreign commerce. In rejoinder, Madison argued that another such object should be more effective provision "for the security of private rights, and the steady dispensation of justice." Interferences with these rights by state legislatures, Madison insisted, had been a principal force behind the calling of the convention.[3] And interferences there were. In Rhode Island, contemptuously referred to by many at the time as Rogues' Island, the legislature had passed a bill that allowed for the payment of debts with a worthless paper currency and that made it a criminal offense, punishable by death by hanging without benefit of clergy, for a creditor to refuse to accept such payment.[4] Such acts of oppression by the majority were not confined to the smaller, less important states: in Massachusetts, impoverished back-country farmers led by Daniel Shays had taken up arms against the government, demanding cheap paper money and a suspension of mortgage foreclosures.

The Framers adopted two principal defenses against the violation of property rights. At the national level, they relied upon the multiplicity of interests present in the extended republic they were creating. At the state level, where territorial and population restrictions precluded formation of a multiplicity of interests, the Framers trusted in the language of Article I, Section 10, whose prohibition of state laws that impair obligations of contracts helped to create a "constitutional bulwark in favor of personal security and private rights."

MARSHALL'S EXPANSION OF THE CONTRACT CLAUSE

In the hands of John Marshall, the Contract Clause became a powerful instrument for the protection of private property. The Marshall Court not only resisted any state encroachments on private contracts (i.e., contracts between individuals), but also expanded the scope of the term *contract* to include public contracts such as public grants and corporate charters.

Marshall's opinion for the Court in *Sturges* v. *Crowninshield* (1819) and his dissent in *Ogden* v. *Saunders* (1827) indicate how he sought to preserve private contractual relations against state interference. In *Sturges* the Court invalidated a New York bankruptcy act as it applied to a debt incurred before the law was passed. Although the Constitution had given Congress the power to establish uniform nationwide bankruptcy laws, Marshall recognized that until Congress exercised its power in such a way as to exclude state legislation on the subject, the states were free to regulate "such cases as the laws of the Union may not reach." But, he continued, New York's law violated the Contract Clause by relieving debtors of preexisting financial obligations. Marshall went even further in *Ogden,* insisting that the Contract Clause prevented legislative impairments not only of contracts already in force but also of contracts entered into after the passage of the legislation in question. A bankruptcy law already in force before a contract was made, he declared, should be unconstitutional. In this case, however, Marshall was unable to persuade a majority of the Court to accept his point of view, and for the only time in his thirty-four years as Chief Justice, he was forced to dissent on a constitutional issue.[5] The general position taken by the Court majority was that a statute in effect at the time a contract is formed is "the law of the contract," and "a part of the contract," and therefore cannot be held to impair its obligation. In the words of Justice William Johnson, the Contract Clause is "a general provision against arbitrary and tyrannical legislation over existing rights, whether personal or property." Bankruptcy legislation, accordingly, is no more constitutionally infirm than laws regulating usurious contracts or the collection of gaming debts. Since *Ogden*, this view of insolvency laws has been maintained consistently by the Court.

Of even greater importance for the protection of the vested rights of private property was Marshall's expansion of the constitutional definition of contract. In *Fletcher* v. *Peck* (1810), he extended the purview of the Contract Clause to public as well as private contracts, thereby making it applicable to transactions to which the state itself was a party. *Fletcher*, the first case in which a state statute was held void under the United States Constitution, originated in an action of the Georgia legislature, which in 1795 was induced by bribery to grant public lands, comprising much of what is now the states of Alabama and Mississippi, to four groups of purchasers known collectively as the Yazoo Land Companies.[6] Popular indignation forced the legislature in 1796 to rescind the grant, on the ground that it had been secured by fraud. By that time, however, some of the land had been purchased by innocent third parties in New England and other parts of the country. These buyers contested the validity of the rescinding act, contending that the original grant could not be repealed without violating the Contract Clause. Marshall, speaking for a unanimous Court, agreed: "Is a clause to be considered as inhibiting the State from impairing the obligation of contracts between two individuals, but as excluding from that inhibition contracts made with itself? The words themselves contain no such distinction. They are general, and are applicable to contracts of every description." Declaring that a public grant qualified as a contractual obligation and could not be abrogated without fair compensation, he therefore held that the rescinding act was an unconstitutional impairment of the obligations of contract.

Marshall further broadened the Contract Clause's coverage of public contracts in *Dartmouth College* v. *Woodward* (1819), in which a corporate charter was held to be a contract protected from infringement by state legislatures. Although this case concerned a college, it fostered the economic development of the nation by assuring business corporations that they would be protected from political interference. As Marshall's biographer, Albert J. Beveridge, has noted, *Dartmouth College* was announced at the very time that corporations were coming into their own, "springing up in response to the necessity for larger and more constant business units and because of the convenience and profit of such organizations. Marshall's opinion was a tremendous stimulant to this natural economic tendency. It reassured investors in corporate securities and gave confidence and steadiness to the business world."[7]

THE DECLINE OF THE CONTRACT CLAUSE

Marshall's efforts to transform the Contract Clause into a powerful guarantor of vested property rights profoundly affected constitutional law for the remainder of the nineteenth century. In a definitive study of the Contract Clause, Benjamin F. Wright noted that up to 1889, it figured in about 40 percent of all Supreme Court cases involving the validity of state legislation. During that time, moreover, it provided the constitutional justification for seventy-five invalidations of state legislation on constitutional grounds—on almost half of all cases in which such legislation was held invalid by the Court.[8]

Over time, however, the Contract Clause has come to lose much of the potency that Marshall gave it. One of the principal reasons for the decline in the importance of the Contract Clause was the increased use of reservation clauses. As Justice Joseph Story pointed out in his *Dartmouth College* concurrence, states could insert as a condition in a corporate charter the power to "amend, alter, and repeal" the charter. Because such a reservation would be a part of the charter, legislative interference would not constitute an impairment of obligations of contract. Several states, taking Story's argument one step further, passed general legislation incorporating the reservation in all subsequently granted charters. Reservation clauses soon became quite common, and by 1865, fourteen states had written general reservation clauses into their constitutions.[9]

The Contract Clause's ability to protect vested rights also was diminished by the Court's strict construction of public contracts or grants after Chief Justice Roger Taney's famous opinion in *Charles River Bridge Company* v. *Warren Bridge Company* (1837). Taney insisted that any ambiguity in the terms of a grant "must operate against the adventurers [i.e., grantees] and in favor of the public" and that the grantees can claim only what is clearly given to them. Nothing could pass to the grantees by implication. "While the rights of private property are sacredly guarded," Taney observed, "we must not forget that the community also have rights, and that the happiness and well being of every citizen depends on their faithful preservation."[10]

Yet a third contributor to the weakening of the Contract Clause was the rise of the doctrine of inalienable police power. Beginning with *Fertilizing Company* v. *Hyde Park* (1878), the Court has held that the states may not contract away certain police powers. At issue in *Fertilizing Company* was a municipal ordinance that rendered valueless a franchise to operate a fertilizer factory, by prohibiting the transportation of offal through the streets and forbidding the operation of such a factory within a certain distance of the town limits. In upholding the ordinance, Justice Noah Swayne emphasized the principle that all grants are to be construed in favor of the state and argued that because the franchise grant contained no expressed exemption from the power to abate a nuisance, it had been made subject to the police power of the state. Two years later, in *Stone* v. *Mississippi,* the Court held that the grant of a twenty-five-year charter to operate a lottery was subject to later application of the police power and did not bar a subsequent statute prohibiting lotteries. The statute in question had been passed to implement a recently ratified provision of Mississippi's new constitution. Insisting that the power of governing is a trust committed by the people to the government, no part of which can be granted away, the Court found in the charter an implied agreement that the privilege granted by the state was subject to the exercise of police power: "Anyone who accepts a lottery charter does so with the implied understanding that the people may resume it at any time when the public good shall require. . . . He has in legal effect nothing more than a license to enjoy the privilege on the terms named for the specified time, unless it be sooner abrogated by the sovereign power of the State."[11] Since these two decisions, the Court consistently has upheld the supremacy of the state's police power against claims deriving from previously existing business franchises and public grants.

The doctrine of inalienable police power, like strict construction of public contracts and the use of reservation clauses, was aimed at ensuring that governments would retain the ability to govern. In reaction, those business interests that traditionally had relied on the Contract Clause for protection turned increasingly to the Due Process Clause of the Fourteenth Amendment, which in time became an even more important vehicle for the protection of vested property rights. This trend confirmed the decline of the once-potent Contract Clause. According to Professor Wright, "The displacement of the contract clause by due process of law is but an incident in the continuous development of an idea. The former clause had become too circumscribed by judicially created or permitted limitations, and its place was gradually taken by another clause where the absence of restrictive precedent allowed freer play to judicial discretion."[12]

The demise of the Contract Clause is perhaps nowhere more apparent than in *Home Building and Loan Association* v. *Blaisdell* (1934). At issue here was a Depression-inspired Minnesota act providing for a moratorium on mortgage payments. In upholding the act, the Court declared that states have a reserved power to protect the interests of their citizens in times of emergency. Writing for the majority, Chief Justice Hughes argued that "state power exists to give temporary relief from the enforcement of contracts in the presence of disasters due to physical causes such as fire, flood or earthquake," and that the same power must exist "when the urgent public need demanding such relief is produced by other and economic causes." In the end, Hughes declared, "The question is no longer merely that of one party to a contract as against another, but of the use of reasonable means to safeguard the economic structure upon which the good of all depends. . . . The principle of this development is . . . that the reservation of the reasonable exercise of the protective power of the State is read into all contracts."

The majority opinion in *Blaisdell* seems directly to contradict the principle embodied in the contract clause, and in a lengthy dissent Justice George Sutherland severely criticized it on these grounds. After describing the economic conditions that prevailed when the Constitution was adopted, Sutherland pointed out that the Contract Clause was specifically intended to prevent the states from mitigating the effects of financial emergency. He charged that in asserting that the Depression legitimated remedial actions by the state, the *Blaisdell* majority violated the intentions of those who wrote the Constitution. "With due regard for the processes of logical thinking," he wrote, "it legitimately cannot be urged that conditions which produced the rule may now be invoked to destroy it."

Many defenders of *Blaisdell* accept Justice Sutherland's analysis of the intent of the Framers but contend that the Court must adapt the Constitution "to the various crises of human affairs."[13] Not every defender of *Blaisdell* accepts Sutherland's analysis, however. Professor Gary Jacobsohn, for example, argues that Chief Justice Hughes's majority opinion reveals a deeper and more profound appreciation for the Framers' enterprise than does Sutherland's dissent. Admitting that Sutherland was correct in asserting that the Contract Clause was intended to protect creditors from their debtors (even in times of emergencies), Jacobsohn insists that "beyond this, there was a deeper intent, which was to promote the conditions of economic stability."[14] The emergency conditions created by the Depression threatened the stability necessary for sound financial arrangements in a commercial economy. "An appropriate response to this problem required a recognition of the radical changes that had occurred in the nation's economy since the time of the founding fathers. Its new complexity, a consequence of modern industrialization, commerce, and technology, meant that the interests of the society were intimately intertwined with the interests of the parties joined in a private contract."[15] According to Jacobsohn, Hughes, unlike Sutherland, recognized that in some circumstances a temporary restraint of enforcement may be "consistent with the spirit and purpose of the constitutional provision and thus be found to be within the range of the reserved power of the State to protect the vital interests of the community." Hughes thus permitted the impairment of the obligations of a specific contract in order to preserve the principle embodied in the Contract Clause itself.

Although instructive, Jacobsohn's analysis of the "deeper intent" of the Framers raises a troubling question for defenders of *Blaisdell:* If the economic stability of the nation required the passage of a mortgage moratorium law, why was it appropriate that this law be passed by a particular state legislature rather than by the national legislature? Had Congress been persuaded that the economic stability of the nation required a mortgage moratorium law, it could have passed a law virtually identical to the Minnesota act, declaring therein that its provisions would go into effect in any state in which the mortgage foreclosure rate exceeded a predetermined level. A national problem then would have had a national solution, and no controversy would have arisen over the meaning of the Contract Clause, whose provisions are limited solely to the states.

Professor Wright has pointed out that Minnesota's mortgage moratorium law was a carefully drafted statute that attempted to protect the interests of the creditor and debtor alike.[16] Nonetheless, it could not possibly protect the interests of society as a whole as fully as could a national moratorium act. Only the multiplicity of interests present at the national level is sufficient to contribute to protection of "the public good and private rights." Specifically, not every creditor affected by Minnesota's law resided in that state; many were spread across the country and had no effective voice in the Minnesota legislature. To the extent that their interests were to be protected, they had to be protected at the national level. This point of view is in keeping with one of the principal means by which the ends of the Constitution are to be secured.

A CONTINUED RELEVANCE?

Many scholars of the Court believe that *Blaisdell* effectively ended the relevance of the Contract Clause.

United States Trust Company v. *New Jersey* (1977) indicated, however, that the contract clause has not become a dead letter—at least not in cases involving unilateral legislative impairment of government contracts. In *United States Trust,* the states were warned that they could not impair their obligations under contracts with private individuals in which the states receive direct, bargained-for benefits and are subject, in turn, to financial obligations that benefit the private parties to the contract. The reason is clear enough: in such instances, the states cannot be trusted to behave as referees, impartially acting in the best interests of the public. As Justice Blackmun noted for the Court majority in *United States Trust,* "Complete deference to a legislative assessment of reasonableness and necessity is not appropriate because the State's self-interest is at stake. A governmental entity can always find a use for extra money, especially when taxes do not have to be raised." Whatever the eventual significance of this revitalization of the Contract Clause, the standards enunciated in *United States Trust* reflect the fact that the clause remains a vital defense against self interested governments that attempt to impair their financial obligations.

NOTES

1 See Edward S. Corwin, "The Basic Doctrine of American Constitutional Law," *Michigan Law Review* 12 (February 1914): 255.

2 According to James Madison, This term in its particular application means "that dominion which one man claims and exercises over the external things of the world, in exclusion of every other individual." But in its larger and juster meaning, it embraces everything to which a man may attach a value and have a right; and which leaves to everyone else the like advantage. In the former sense, a man's land, or merchandise, or money is called his property. In the latter sense, a man has property in his opinions and a free communication of them. He has a property of peculiar value in his religious opinions, and in the profession and practice dictated by them. He has property very dear to him in the safety and liberty of his person. He has an equal property in the free use of his faculties and free choice of the objects on which to employ them. In a word, as a man is said to have a right to his property, he may be equally said to have a property in his rights. James Madison, "Essay on Property," in *The Writings of James Madison,* ed. Gaillard Hunt, 9 vols. (New York: G. P. Putnam's Sons, 1906), 6: 101. For a contemporary reaffirmation of this view, see Justice Stewart's opinion for the Court in *Lynch* v. *Household Finance Corporation* (1972).

3 Max Farrand, ed., *The Records of the Federal Convention of 1787,* 4 vols. (New Haven, Conn.: Yale University Press, 1937), 1: 133–134.
4 See Andrew C. McLaughlin, *The Confederation and the Constitution: 1787–1789* (New York: Collier, 1962), pp. 107–109.
5 Benjamin F. Wright, *The Contract Clause of the Constitution* (Cambridge, Mass.: Harvard University Press, 1938), p. 50.
6 For the details of this episode, see C. Peter Magrath, *Yazoo: Land and Politics in the New Republic* (Providence, R.I.: Brown University Press, 1966).
7 Albert J. Beveridge, *The Life of John Marshall,* 4 vols. (Boston: Houghton Mifflin, 1919), 4: 276.
8 Wright, *The Contract Clause,* p. 95.
9 See *Ibid.,* p. 84.
10 It must be emphasized that Chief Justice Taney's opinion in *Charles River Bridge Company* did not break with the Marshall tradition. Taney shared Marshall's view that "the rights of private property are sacredly guarded" and accepted without question Marshall's application of the Contract Clause to public as well as private contracts. See Wright, *The Contract Clause,* pp. 62–63, 245–246.
11 101 U. S. at 821. The police power prevails over private contracts with even greater force than over public contracts. As the Court observed in *Manigault* v. *Springs* (1905), "Parties by entering into contracts may not stop the legislature from enacting laws intended for the public good."
12 Wright, *The Contract Clause,* p. 258.
13 See Chapter 1 and its discussion of the adaptive approach to constitutional interpretation.
14 Gary J. Jacobsohn, *Pragmatism, Statesmanship, and the Supreme Court* (Ithaca, N.Y.: Cornell University Press, 1977), p. 188.
15 *Ibid.,* p. 192.
16 Wright, *The Contract Clause,* p. 110.

SELECTED READINGS

The Federalist, No. 44.

Fletcher v. *Peck,* 6 Cranch 87 (1810).
Sturges v. *Crowinshield,* 4 Wheaton 122 (1819).
Faitoute Iron & Steel Company v. *City of Asbury Park,* 316 U.S. 502 (1942).
El Paso v. *Simmons,* 379 U.S. 497 (1965).
Allied Structural Steel Company v. *Spannaus,* 438 U.S. 234 (1978).
Magrath, C. Peter. *Yazoo: Law and Politics in the New Republic: The Case of Fletcher* v. *Peck* (Providence, R.I.: Brown University Press, 1966).
"Revival of the Contract Clause." *Ohio State Law Journal* 39, no. 1 (1978): 195–213.
Story, Joseph. *Commentaries on the Constitution of the United States* (Boston: Hilliard, Gray, 1833), Vol. 3, pp. 240–269.
"The Constitutionality of the New York Municipal Wage Freeze and Debt Moratorium: Ressurrection of the Contract Clause." *University of Pennsylvania Law Review* 125, no. 1 (1976): 167–214.
Wright, Benjamin F. *The Contract Clause of the Constitution* (Cambridge, Mass.: Harvard University Press, 1938).

Dartmouth College v. *Woodward*

17 U.S. (4 Wheaton) 518; 4 L. Ed. 629 (1819)

In 1769 the British Crown granted a corporate charter to the trustees of Dartmouth College, conveying to them "forever" the right to govern the institution and to appoint their own successors. After remaining unchallenged through the revolutionary era, the charter was dramatically altered in 1816. The Republican governor and legislature of New Hampshire, having concluded that the old charter was based on principles more congenial to monarchy than to free government, sought to bring the college under public control by enacting three laws that took control of the college from the hands of the Federalist-dominated trustees and placed it under a board of overseers appointed by the governor. The trustees turned for relief to the state's judiciary. Contending that the 1816 laws impaired the obligation of contract contained in the original charter of 1769, they brought an action against William Woodward, the secretary and treasurer of the college, to recover the college's records, corporate seal, and other corporate property temporarily entrusted to him by one of the 1816 acts. The New Hampshire Supreme Court upheld the legislature's acts, chiefly on the grounds that the college was essentially a public corporation whose powers were exercised for public purposes and that it was therefore subject to public control. The trustees of the college then appealed the case upon a writ of error to the United States Supreme Court. *Opinion of the Court: Marshall, Johnson, Livingston, Story, Washington. Concurring opinions: Story, Livingston; Washington, Livingston. Dissent: Duvall.*

MR. CHIEF JUSTICE MARSHALL delivered the opinion of the Court. . . .

It can require no argument to prove, that the circumstances of this case constitute a contract. An application is made to the crown for a charter to incorporate a religious and literary institution. In the application, it is stated, that large contributions have been made for the object, which will be conferred on the corporation, as soon as it shall be created. The charter is granted, and on its faith the property is conveyed. Surely, in this transaction every ingredient of a complete and legitimate contract is to be found. The points for consideration are, 1. Is this contract protected by the constitution of the United States? 2. Is it impaired by the acts under which the defendant holds?

1. On the first point, it has been argued, that the word "contract," in its broadest sense, would comprehend the political relations between the government and its citizens, would extend to offices held within a state, for state purposes, and to many of those laws concerning civil institutions, which must change with circumstances, and be modified by ordinary legislation; which deeply concern the public, and which, to preserve good government, the public judgment must control. That even marriage is a contract, and its obligations are affected by the laws respecting divorces. That the clause in the constitution, if construed in its greatest latitude, would prohibit these laws. Taken in its broad, unlimited sense, the clause would be an unprofitable and vexatious interference with the internal concerns of a state, would unnecessarily and unwisely embarrass its legislation, and render immutable those civil institutions, which are established for purposes of internal government, and which, to subserve those purposes, ought to vary with varying circumstances. That as the framers of the constitution could never have intended to insert in that instrument, a provision so unnecessary, so mischievous, and so repugnant to its general spirit, the term "contract" must be understood in a more limited sense. That it must be understood as intended to guard against a power, of at least

doubtful utility, the abuse of which had been extensively felt; and to restrain the legislature in future from violating the right to property. That, anterior to the formation of the constitution, a course of legislation had prevailed in many, if not in all, of the states, which weakened the confidence of man in man, and embarrassed all transactions between individuals, by dispensing with a faithful performance of engagements. To correct this mischief, by restraining the power which produced it, the state legislatures were forbidden "to pass any law impairing the obligation of contracts," that is, of contracts respecting property, under which some individual could claim a right to something beneficial to himself; and that, since the clause in the constitution must in construction receive some limitation, it may be confined, and ought to be confined, to cases of this description; to cases within the mischief it was intended to remedy. . . .

The parties in this case differ less on general principles, less on the true construction of the constitution in the abstract, than on the application of those principles to this case, and on the true construction of the charter of 1769. This is the point on which the cause essentially depends. If the act of incorporation be a grant of political power, if it create a civil institution, to be employed in the administration of the government, or if the funds of the college be public property, or if the state of New Hampshire, as a government, be alone interested in its transactions, the subject is one in which the legislature of the state may act according to its own judgment, unrestrained by any limitation of its power imposed by the constitution of the United States.

But if this be a private eleemosynary institution, endowed with a capacity to take property, for objects unconnected with government, whose funds are bestowed by individuals, on the faith of the charter; if the donors have stipulated for the future disposition and management of those funds, in the manner prescribed by themselves; there may be more difficulty in the case. . . . It becomes then the duty of the court, most seriously to examine this charter, and to ascertain its true character. . . .

A corporation is an artificial being, invisible, intangible, and existing only in contemplation of law. Being the mere creature of law, it possesses only those properties which the charter of its creation confers upon it, either expressly, or as incidental to its very existence. These are such as are supposed best calculated to effect the object for which it was created. Among the most important are immortality, and, if the expression may be allowed, individuality; properties, by which a perpetual succession of many persons are considered as the same, and may act as a single individual. They enable a corporation to manage its own affairs, and to hold property, without the perplexing intricacies, the hazardous and endless necessity, of perpetual conveyances for the purpose of transmitting it from hand to hand. It is chiefly for the purpose of clothing bodies of men, in succession, with these qualities and capacities, that corporations were invented, and are in use. By these means, a perpetual succession of individuals are capable of acting for the promotion of the particular object, like one immortal being. But this being does not share in the civil government of the country, unless that be the purpose for which it was created. . . .

From the fact, then, that a charter of incorporation has been granted, nothing can be inferred, which changes the character of the institution, or transfers to the government any new power over it. The character of civil institutions does not grow out of their incorporation, but out of the manner in which they are formed, and the objects for which they are created. The right to change them is not founded on their being incorporated, but on their being the instruments of government, created for its purposes. The same institutions, created for the same objects, though not incorporated, would be public institutions, and, of course, be controllable by the legislature. The incorporating act neither gives nor prevents this control. Neither, in reason, can the incorporating act change the character of a private eleemosynary institution. . . .

. . . It appears, that Dartmouth College is an eleemosynary institution, incorporated for the purpose of perpetuating the application of the bounty of the donors, to the specified objects of that bounty; that its trustees or governors were originally named by the founder, and invested with the power of perpetuating themselves; that they are not public officers, nor is it a civil institution, participating in the administration of government; but a charity-school, or a seminary of education, incorporated for the preservation of its property, and the perpetual application of that property to the objects of its creation. . . .

This is plainly a contract to which the donors, the trustees and the crown (to whose rights and obligations New Hampshire succeeds) were the original parties. It is a contract made on a valuable consideration. It is a contract for the security and disposition of property. It is a contract, on the faith of which, real and personal estate has been conveyed to the corporation. It is, then, a contract within the letter of the constitution, and within its spirit also, unless the fact, that the property is invested by the donors in trustees, for the promotion of religion and education, for the benefit of persons who are perpetually changing, though the objects remain the same, shall create a particular exception, taking this case out of the prohibition created in the constitution.

It is more than possible, that the preservation of rights of this description was not particularly in the view of the framers of the constitution, when the clause under consideration was introduced into that instrument. It is probable, that interferences of more frequent occurrence, to which the temptation was stronger, and of which the mischief was more extensive, constituted the great motive for imposing this restriction on the state legislatures. But although a particular and a rare case may not, in itself, be of sufficient magnitude to induce a rule, yet it must be governed by the rule, when established, unless some plain and strong reason for excluding it can be given. It is not enough to say, that this particular case was not in the mind of the convention, when the article was framed, nor of the American people, when it was adopted. It is necessary to go further, and to say that, had this particular case been suggested, the language would have been so varied, as to exclude it, or it would have been made a special exception. The case being within the words of the rule, must be within its operation likewise, unless there be something in the literal construction, so obviously absurd or mischievous, or repugnant to the general spirit of the instrument, as to justify those who expound the constitution in making it an exception.

On what safe and intelligible ground, can this exception stand? There is no expression in the constitution, no sentiment delivered by its contemporaneous expounders, which would justify us in making it.

The opinion of the court, after mature deliberation, is, that this is a contract, the obligation of which cannot be impaired, without violating the constitution of the United States.

2. We next proceed to the inquiry, whether its obligation has been impaired by those acts of the legislature of New Hampshire, to which the special verdict refers?

From the review of this charter, which has been taken, it appears that the whole power of governing the college, of appointing and removing tutors, of fixing their salaries, of directing the course of study to be pursued by the students, and of filling up vacancies created in their own body, was vested in the trustees. On the part of the crown, it was expressly stipulated, that this corporation, thus constituted, should continue for ever. . . . By this contract, the crown was bound, and could have made no violent alteration in its essential terms, without impairing its obligation.

By the revolution, the duties, as well as the powers, of government devolved on the people of New Hampshire. It is admitted, that among the latter was comprehended the transcendent power of parliament, as well as that of the executive department. It is too clear, to require the support of argument, that all contracts and rights respecting property, remained unchanged by the revolution. The obligations, then, which were created by the charter to Dartmouth College, were the same in the new, that they had been in the old government. The power of the government was also the same. A repeal of this charter, at any time prior to the adoption of the present constitution of the United States, would have been an extraordinary and unprecedented act of power, but one which could have been contested only by the restrictions upon the legislature, to be found in the constitution of the state. But the constitution of the United States has imposed this additional limitation, that the legislature of a state shall pass no act "impairing the obligation of contracts." . . .

On the effect of this law . . . the whole power of governing the college is transferred from trustees, appointed according to the will of the founder, expressed in the charter, to the executive of New Hampshire. The management and application of the funds of this eleemosynary institution, which are placed by the donors in the hands of trustees named in the charter, and empowered to perpetuate themselves, are placed by this act under the control of the government of the state. The will of the state is substituted for the will of the donors, in every essential operation of the college. This may be for the advantage of this college in particular, and may be for the advantage of literature in general; but it is not according to the will of the donors, and is subversive of that contract, on the faith of which their property was given. . . .

It results from this opinion, that the acts of the legislature of New Hampshire, which are stated in the special verdict found in this cause, are repugnant to the constitution of the United States; and that the judgment on this special verdict ought to have been for the plaintiffs. The judgment of the state court must, therefore, be reversed.

Charles River Bridge Co. v. *Warren Bridge Co.*

36 U.S. (11 Peters) 420; 9 L. Ed. 773 (1837)

In 1785 the Massachusetts legislature granted a charter to the Charles River Bridge Company, authorizing it to construct a bridge between Charlestown and Boston and to collect tolls for forty years. (In 1792, the charter was extended to seventy years.) This franchise replaced an exclusive ferry right granted to Harvard College in 1650, and provision was made for compensating Harvard for the impairment of its ferry franchise. In 1828, however, the legislature incorporated the Warren Bridge Company and authorized it to construct another bridge, only 264 feet away from the Charles River Bridge on the Charlestown side and 825 feet away on the Boston side. No tolls were to be charged on the Warren Bridge after its construction costs were recovered or after a maximum period of six years. The Charles River Bridge Company entered state court and sought an injunction to prevent the erection of the Warren Bridge; then, after the bridge was constructed, they sought general relief, contending that the legislature, in authorizing the new bridge, had violated the contract clause. The Massachusetts Supreme Judicial Court dismissed the complaint, and the case went to the U.S. Supreme Court on a writ of error. *Opinion of the Court: Taney, Baldwin, Barbour, McLean, Wayne. Concurring opinion: McLean. Dissenting opinion: Story, Thompson.*

MR. CHIEF JUSTICE TANEY delivered the opinion of the Court. . . .

The plaintiffs in error insist that the acts of the legislature of Massachusetts of 1785, and 1792, by their true construction, necessarily implied that the legislature would not authorize another bridge, and especially a free one, by the side of this, and placed in the same line of travel, whereby the franchise granted to the "proprietors of the Charles River Bridge" should be rendered of no value; and the plaintiffs in error contend, that the grant of the charter to the proprietors of the bridge is a contract on the part of the state; and that the law authorizing the erection of the Warren Bridge in 1828, impairs the obligation of this contract. . . .

This brings us to the act of the legislature of Massachusetts, of 1785, by which the plaintiffs were incorporated by the name of "The Proprietors of the Charles River Bridge;" and it is here, and in the law of 1792, prolonging their charter, that we must look for the extent and nature of the franchise conferred upon the plaintiffs.

Much has been said in the argument of the principles of construction by which this law is to be expounded, and what undertakings, on the part of the state, may be implied. The Court think there can be no serious difficulty on that head. It is the grant of certain franchises by the public to a private corporation, and in a matter where the public interest is concerned. The rule of construction in such cases is well settled, both in England,

and by the decisions of our own tribunals. . . . The rule of construction in all such cases, is now fully established to be this; that any ambiguity in the terms of the contract, must operate against the adventurers, and in favour of the public, and the plaintiffs can claim nothing that is not clearly given them by the act." . . .

. . . The object and end of all government is to promote the happiness and prosperity of the community by which it is established; and it can never be assumed, that the government intended to diminish its power of accomplishing the end for which it was created. And in a country like ours, free, active, and enterprising, continually advancing in numbers and wealth; new channels of communication are daily found necessary, both for travel and trade; and are essential to the comfort, convenience, and prosperity of the people. A state ought never to be presumed to surrender this power, because, like the taxing power, the whole community have an interest in preserving it undiminished. And when a corporation alleges, that a state has surrendered for seventy years, its power of improvement and public accommodation, in a great and important line of travel, along which a vast number of its citizens must daily pass; the community have a right to insist . . . "that its abandonment ought not be presumed, in a case, in which the deliberate purpose of the state to abandon it does not appear." The continued existence of a government would be of no great value, if by implications and presumptions, it was disarmed of the powers necessary to accomplish the ends of its creation; and the functions it was designed to perform, transferred to the hands of privileged corporations. . . . No one will question that the interests of the great body of the people of the state, would, in this instance, be affected by the surrender of this great line of travel to a single corporation, with the right to exact toll, and exclude competition for seventy years. While the rights of private property are sacredly guarded, we must not forget that the community also have rights, and that the happiness and well being of every citizen depends on their faithful preservation.

Adopting the rule of construction above stated as the settled one, we proceed to apply it to the charter of 1785, to the proprietors of the Charles River Bridge. This act of incorporation is in the usual form, and the privileges such as are commonly given to corporations of that kind. It confers on them the ordinary faculties of a corporation, for the purpose of building the bridge; and establishes certain rates of toll, which the company are authorized to take. This is the whole grant. There is no exclusive privilege given to them over the waters of Charles river, above or below their bridge. No right to erect another bridge themselves, nor to prevent other persons from erecting one. No engagement from the state, that another shall not be erected; and no undertaking not to sanction competition, nor to make improvements that may diminish the amount of its income. Upon all these subjects the charter is silent; and nothing is said in it about a line of travel, so much insisted on in the argument, in which they are to have exclusive privileges. No words are used, from which an intention to grant any of these rights can be inferred. If the plaintiff is entitled to them, it must be implied, simply, from the nature of the grant; and cannot be inferred from the words by which the grant is made.

The relative position of the Warren Bridge has already been described. It does not interrupt the passage over the Charles River Bridge, nor make the way to it or from it less convenient. None of the faculties or franchises granted to that corporation, have been revoked by the legislature; and its right to take the tolls granted by the charter remains unaltered. In short, all the franchises and rights of property enumerated in the charter, and there mentioned to have been granted to it, remain unimpaired. But its income is destroyed by the Warren Bridge; which, being free, draws off the passengers and property which would have gone over it, and renders their franchise of no value. This is the gist of the complaint. For it is not pretended, that the erection of the Warren Bridge would have done them any injury, or in any degree affected their right of property; if it had not diminished the amount of their tolls. In order then to entitle themselves to relief, it is necessary to show, that the legislature contracted not to do the act of which they complain; and that they impaired, or in other words, violated the contract by the erection of the Warren Bridge.

The inquiry then is, does the charter contain such a contract on the part of the state? Is there any such stipulation to be found in that instrument? It must be admitted on all hands, that there is none—no words that even relate to another bridge, or to the diminution of their tolls, or to the line of travel. If a contract on that subject can be gathered from the charter, it must be by implication; and cannot be found in the words used. Can such an agreement be implied? The rule of construction before stated is an answer to the question. In charters of this description, no rights are taken from the public, or given to the corporation, beyond those which the words of the charter, by their natural and proper construction, purport to convey. There are no words which import such a contract as the plaintiffs in error contend for, and none can be implied. . . .

Indeed, the practice and usage of almost every state in the Union, old enough to have commenced the work of internal improvement, is opposed to the doctrine contended for on the part of the plaintiffs in error. Turnpike roads have been made in succession, on the same line of travel; the later ones interfering materially with the profits of the first. These corporations have, in some instances, been utterly ruined by the introduction of newer and better modes of transportation, and travelling. In some cases, rail roads have rendered the turnpike roads on the same line of travel so entirely useless, that the franchise of the turnpike corporation is not worth preserving. Yet in none of these cases have the corporations supposed that their privileges were invaded, or any contract violated on the part of the state. The absence of any such controversy, when there must have been so many occasions to give rise to it, proves that neither states, nor individuals, nor corporations, ever imagined that such a contract could be implied from such characters. It shows that the men who voted these laws, never imagined that they were forming such a contract; and if we maintain that they have made it, we must create it by a legal fiction, in opposition to the truth of the fact, and the obvious intention of the party. We cannot deal thus with the rights reserved to the states; and by legal intendments and mere technical reasoning, take away from them any portion of that power over their own internal police and improvement, which is so necessary to their well being and prosperity. . . .

The judgment of the supreme judicial court of the commonwealth of Massachusetts, dismissing the plaintiffs' bill, must, therefore, be affirmed, with costs.

Mr. Justice Story, dissenting. with it a necessary implication that the legislature shall do no act to destroy or essentially to impair the franchise; that (as one of the learned judges of the state court expressed it), there is an implied agreement of the state to grant the undisturbed use of the bridge and its tolls, so far as respects any acts of its own, or of any persons acting under its authority. In other words, the state, impliedly, contracts not to resume its grants, or to do any act to the prejudice or destruction of its grant. I maintain, that there is no authority or principle established in relation to the construction of crown grants, or legislative grants; which does not concede and justify this doctrine. Where the thing is given, the incidents, without which it cannot be enjoyed, are also given. . . . I maintain that a different doctrine is utterly repugnant to all the principles of the common law, applicable to all franchises of a like nature; and that we must overturn some of the best securities of the rights of property, before it can be established. . . . I maintain, that under the principles of the common law, there exists no more right in the legislature of Massachusetts, to erect the Warren bridge, to the ruin of the franchise of the Charles River bridge, than exists to transfer the latter to the former, or authorize the former to demolish the latter. If the legislature does not mean in its grant to give any exclusive rights, let it say so, expressly; directly; and in terms admitting of no misconstruction. . . .

My judgment is formed upon the terms of the grant, its nature and objects, its design and duties; and, in its interpretation, I seek for no new principles, but I apply such as are as old as the very rudiments of the common law. . . .

Upon the whole, my judgment is, that the act of the legislature of Massachusetts granting the charter of Warren bridge, is an act impairing the obligation of the prior contract and grant to the proprietors of Charles River bridge; and, by the constitution of the United States, it is therefore utterly void. I am for reversing the decree of the state court (dismissing the bill); and for remanding the cause to the state court for further proceedings, as to law and justice shall appertain.

Home Building and Loan Association v. *Blaisdell*

290 U.S. 398; 54 S. Ct. 231; 78 L. Ed. 413 (1934)

In 1933, at the depth of the Depression, Minnesota passed a mortgage moratorium act designed to prevent the loss of mortgaged property by individuals temporarily unable to meet their financial obligations. The act authorized the state courts, upon application of the mortgagor, to extend the period of redemption from foreclosure sales for such a period as the courts might deem equitable, but not beyond May 1, 1935. The act was to remain in effect "only during the continuance of the emergency and in no event beyond May 1, 1935." During the emergency period, the mortgagor was required to apply the income or reasonable rental value, as fixed by the courts, to the payment of taxes, interest, insurance, and the mortgage indebtedness. It was a carefully drafted statute that attempted to protect the interest of the creditor as well as those of the debtor. Despite the care that went into its drafting, the moratorium act did alter the arrangement of existing contracts and thus raised a question of whether or not the act was an unconstitutional impairment of the obligations of contract. This question ultimately was brought before the Supreme Court when John Blaisdell and his wife, owners of a lot that was mortgaged to the Home Building and Loan Association, applied to the District Court of Hennepin County for an extension of time so that they could retain ownership of their home. The District Court extended the redemption period, and the Supreme Court of Minnesota affirmed the judgment. The loan company appealed. *Opinion of the Court: Hughes, Brandeis, Cardozo, Roberts, Stone. Dissenting opinion: Sutherland, Butler, McReynolds, Van Devanter.*

Mr. Chief Justice Hughes delivered the opinion of the Court. . . .

The state court upheld the statute as an emergency measure. Although conceding that the obligations of the mortgage contract were impaired, the court decided that what it thus described as an impairment was, notwithstanding the contract clause of the Federal Constitution, within the police power of the State as that power was called into exercise by the public economic emergency which the legislature had found to exist. Attention is thus directed to the preamble and the first section of the statute, which described the existing emergency in terms that were deemed to justify the temporary relief which the statute affords. . . .

In determining whether the provision for this temporary and conditional relief exceeds the power of the State by reason of the clause in the Federal Constitution prohibiting impairment of the obligations of contracts, we must consider the relation of emergency to constitutional power, the historical setting of the contract clause, the development of the jurisprudence of this Court in the construction of that clause, and the principles of construction which we may consider to be established.

Emergency does not create power. Emergency does not increase granted power or remove or diminish the restrictions imposed upon power granted or reserved. The Constitution was adopted in a period of grave emergency. Its grants of power to the Federal Government and its limitations of the power of the States were determined in the light of emergency and they are not altered by emergency. What power was thus granted and what limitations were thus imposed are questions which have always been, and always will be, the subject of close examination under our constitutional system.

While emergency does not create power, emergency may furnish the occasion for the exercise of power. . . . The constitutional question presented in the light of an emergency is whether the power possessed embraces the particular exercise of it in response to particular conditions. Thus, the war power of the Federal Government is not created by the emergency of war, but it is a power given to meet that emergency. It is a power to wage war successfully, and thus it permits the harnessing of the entire energies of the people in a supreme cooperative effort to preserve the nation. But even the war power does not remove constitutional limitations safeguarding essential liberties. When the provisions of the Constitution, in grant or restriction are specific, so particularized as not to admit of construction, no question is presented. Thus, emergency would not permit a State to have more than two Senators in the Congress, or permit the election of President by a general popular vote without regard to the number of electors to which the States are respectively entitled, or permit the States to "coin money" or to "make anything but gold and silver coin a tender in payment of debts." But where constitutional grants and limitations of power are set forth in general clauses, which afford a broad outline, the process of construction is essential to fill in the details. That is true of the contract clause. . . .

In the construction of the contract clause, the debates in the Constitutional Covention are of little aid. But the reasons which led to the adoption of that clause, and of the other prohibitions of Section 10 of Article I, are not left in doubt and have frequently been described with eloquent emphasis. The widespread distress following the revolutionary period, and the plight of debtors, had called forth in the States an ignoble array of legislative schemes for the defeat of creditors and the invasion of contractual obligations. Legislative interferences had been so numerous and extreme that the confidence essential to prosperous trade had been undermined and the utter destruction of credit was threatened. . . .

But full recognition of the occasion and general purpose of the clause does not suffice to fix its precise scope. Nor does an examination of the details of prior legislation in the States yield criteria which can be considered controlling. To ascertain the scope of the constitutional prohibition we examine the course of judicial decisions in its application. These put it beyond question that the prohibition is not an absolute one and is not to be read with literal exactness like a mathematical formula. . . .

Not only is the constitutional provision qualified by the measure of control which the State retains over remedial processes, but the State also continues to possess authority to safeguard the vital interests of its people. It does not matter that legislation appropriate to that end "has the result of modifying or abrogating contracts already in effect." . . . Not only are existing laws read into contracts in order to fix obligations as between the parties, but the reservation of essential attributes of sovereign power is also read into contracts as a postulate of the legal order. The policy of protecting contracts against impairment presupposes the maintenance of a government by virtue of which contractual relations are worth while,—a government which retains adequate authority to secure the peace and good order of society. This principle of harmonizing the constitutional prohibition with the necessary residuum of state power has had progressive recognition in the decisions of this Court. . . .

The legislature cannot "bargain away the public health or public morals." Thus, the constitutional provision against the impairment of contracts was held not to be violated by an amendment of the state constitution which put an end to a lottery theretofore authorized by the legislature. *Stone* v. *Mississippi*, . . . (1880). . . . The lottery was a valid enterprise when established under express state authority, but the legislature in the public interest could put a stop to it. A similar rule has been applied to the control by the State of the sale of intoxicating liquors. . . . The States retain adequate power to protect the public health against the maintenance of nuisances despite insistence upon existing contracts. . . . Legislation to protect the public safety comes within the same category of reserved power. . . . This principle has had recent and noteworthy application to the regulation of the use of public highways by common carriers and "contract carriers," where the assertion of interference with existing contract rights has been without avail. . . .

The argument is pressed that in the cases we have cited the obligation of contracts was affected only incidentally. This argument proceeds upon a misconception. The question is not whether the legislative action affects contracts incidentally, or directly or indirectly, but whether the legislation is addressed to a legitimate end and the measures taken are reasonable and appropriate to that end. Another argument, which comes more closely to the point, is that the state power may be addressed directly to the prevention of the enforcement of contracts only when these are of a sort which the legislature in its discretion may denounce as being in themselves hostile to public morals, or public health, safety, or welfare, or where the prohibition is merely of injurious practices; that interference with the enforcement of other and valid contracts according to appropriate legal procedure, although the interference is temporary and for a public purpose, is not permissible. This is but to contend that in the latter case the end is not legitimate in the view that it cannot be reconciled with a fair interpretation of the constitutional provision.

Undoubtedly, whatever is reserved of state power must be consistent with the fair intent of the constitutional limitation of that power. The reserved power cannot be construed so as to destroy the limitation, nor is the limitation to be construed to destroy the reserved power in its essential aspects. They must be construed in harmony with each other. This principle precludes a construction which would permit the State to adopt as its policy the repudiation of debts or the destruction of contracts or the denial of means to enforce them. But it does not follow that conditions may not arise in which a temporary restraint of enforcement may be consistent with the spirit and purpose of the constitutional provision and thus be found to be within the range of the reserved power of the State to protect the vital interests of the community. It cannot be maintained that the constitutional prohibition should be so construed as to prevent limited and temporary interpositions with respect to the enforcement of contracts if made necessary by a great public calamity such as fire, flood, or earthquake. . . . The reservation of state power appropriate to such extraordinary conditions may be deemed to be as much a part of all contracts, as is the reservation of state power to protect the public interest in the other situations to which we have referred. And if state power exists to give temporary relief from the enforcement of contracts in the presence of disasters due to physical causes such as fire, flood or earthquake, that power cannot be said to be non-existent when the urgent public need demanding such relief is produced by other and economic causes. . . .

It is manifest from this review of our decisions that there has been a growing appreciation of public needs and of the necessity of finding ground for a rational compromise between individual rights and public welfare. The settlement and consequent contraction of the public domain, the pressure of a constantly increasing density of population, the interrelation of the activities of our people and the complexity of our economic interests, have inevitably led to an increased use of the organization of society in order to protect the very bases of individual opportunity. Where, in earlier days, it was thought that only the concerns of individuals or of classes were involved, and that those of the State itself were touched only remotely, it has later been found that the fundamental interests of the State are directly affected; and that the question is no longer merely that of one party to a contract as against another, but of the use of reasonable means to safeguard the economic structure upon which the good of all depends. . . .

Applying the criteria established by our decisions we conclude:

1. An emergency existed in Minnesota which furnished a proper occasion for the exercise of the reserved power of the State to protect the vital interests of the community. The declarations of the existence of this emergency by the legislature and by the Supreme Court of Minnesota cannot be regarded as a subterfuge or as lacking in adequate basis. . . . The finding of the legislature and state court has support in the facts of which we take judicial notice. . . .

2. The legislation was addressed to a legitimate end, that is, the legislation was not for the mere advantage of particular individuals but for the protection of a basic interest of society.

3. In view of the nature of the contracts in question—mortgages of unquestionable validity—the relief afforded and justified by the emergency, in order not to contravene the constitutional provision, could only be of a character appropriate to that emergency and could be granted only upon reasonable conditions.

4. The conditions upon which the period of redemption is extended do not appear to be

unreasonable. . . . The integrity of the mortgage indebtedness is not impaired; interest continues to run; the validity of the sale and the right of a mortgagee-purchaser to title or to obtain a deficiency judgment, if the mortgagor fails to redeem within the extended period, are maintained; and the conditions of redemption, if redemption there be, stand as they were under the prior law. . . . Also important is the fact that mortgagees, as is shown by official reports of which we may take notice, are predominantly corporations, such as insurance companies, banks, and investment and mortgage companies. These, and such individual mortgagees as are small investors, are not seeking homes or the opportunity to engage in farming. Their chief concern is the reasonable protection of their investment security. It does not matter that there are, or may be, individual cases of another aspect. The legislature was entitled to deal with the general or typical situation. The relief afforded by the statute has regard to the interest of mortgagees as well as to the interest of mortgagors. The legislation seeks to prevent the impending ruin of both by a considerate measure of relief.

5. The legislation is temporary in operation. It is limited to the exigency which called it forth. . . .

We are of the opinion that the Minnesota statute as here applied does not violate the contract clause of the Federal Constitution. Whether the legislation is wise or unwise as a matter of policy is a question with which we are not concerned.

MR. JUSTICE SUTHERLAND, dissenting.

Few questions of greater moment than that just decided have been submitted for judicial inquiry during this generation. He simply closes his eyes to the necessary implications of the decision who fails to see in it the potentiality of future gradual but ever-advancing encroachments upon the sanctity of private and public contracts. The effect of the Minnesota legislation, though serious enough in itself, is of trivial significance compared with the far more serious and dangerous inroads upon the limitations of the Constitution which are almost certain to ensue as a consequence naturally following any step beyond the boundaries fixed by that instrument. And those of us who are thus apprehensive of the effect of this decision would, in a matter so important, be neglectful of our duty should we fail to spread upon the permanent records of the court the reasons which move us to the opposite view.

A provision of the Constitution, it is hardly necessary to say, does not admit of two distinctly opposite interpretations. It does not mean one thing at one time and an entirely different thing at another time. If the contract impairment clause, when framed and adopted, meant that the terms of a contract for the payment of money could not be altered *in invitum* by a state statute enacted for the relief of hardly pressed debtors to the end and with the effect of postponing payment or enforcement during and because of an economic or financial emergency, it is but to state the obvious to say that it means the same now. This view, at once so rational in its application to the written word, and so necessary to the stability of constitutional principles, though from time to time challenged, has never, unless recently, been put within the realm of doubt by the decisions of this court. . . .

The whole aim of construction, as applied to a provision of the Constitution, is to discover the meaning, to ascertain and give effect to the intent, of its framers and the people who adopted it. . . . The necessities which gave rise to the provision, the controversies which preceded, as well as the conflicts of opinion which were settled by its adoption, are matters to be considered to enable us to arrive at a correct result. . . . The history of the times, the state of things existing when the provision was framed and adopted, should be looked to in order to ascertain the mischief and the remedy. . . . As nearly as possible we should place ourselves in the condition of those who framed and adopted it. . . . And if the meaning be at all doubtful, the doubt should be resolved, wherever reasonably possible to do so, in a way to forward the evident purpose with which the provision was adopted. . . .

An application of these principles to the question under review removes any doubt, if otherwise there would be any, that the contract impairment clause denies to the several states the power to mitigate hard consequences resulting to debtors from financial or economic exigencies by an impairment of the obligation of contracts of indebtedness. . . .

The lower court, and counsel for the appellees in their argument here, frankly admitted that the statute does constitute a material impairment of the contract, but contended that such legislation is brought within the state power by the present emergency. If I understand the opinion just delivered, this court is not wholly in accord with that view. The opinion concedes that emergency does not create power, or increase granted power, or remove or diminish restrictions upon power granted or reserved. It then proceeds to say, however, that while emergency does not create power, it may furnish the occasion for the exercise of power. I can only interpret what is said on that subject as meaning that while an emergency does not diminish a restriction upon power it furnishes an occasion for diminishing it; and this, as it seems to me, is merely to say the same thing by the use of another set of words, with the effect of affirming that which has just been denied.

It is quite true that an emergency may supply the occasion for the exercise of power, depending upon the nature of the power and the intent of the Constitution with respect thereto. But we are here dealing not with a power granted by the Federal Constitution, but with the state police power, which exists in its own right. Hence the question is not whether an emergency furnishes the occasion for the exercise of that state power, but whether an emergency furnishes an occasion for the relaxation of the restrictions upon the power imposed by the contract impairment clause; and the difficulty is that the contract impairment clause forbids state action under any circumstances, if it have the effect of impairing the obligation of contracts. That clause restricts every state power in the particular specified, no matter what may be the occasion. It does not contemplate that an emergency shall furnish an occasion for softening the restriction or making it any the less a restriction upon state action in that contingency than it is under strictly normal conditions.

The Minnesota statute either impairs the obligation of contracts or it does not. If it does not, the occasion to which it relates becomes immaterial, since then the passage of the statute is the exercise of a normal, unrestricted, state power and requires no special occasion to render it effective. If it does, the emergency no more furnishes a proper occasion for its exercise than if the emergency were non-existent. And so, while, in form, the suggested distinction seems to put us forward in a straight line, in reality it simply carries us back in a circle, like bewildered travelers lost in a wood, to the point where we parted company with the view of the state court. . . .

. . . The phrase, "obligation of a contract," in the constitutional sense imports a legal duty to perform the specified obligation of *that* contract, not to substitute and perform, against the will of one of the parties, a different, albeit equally valuable, obligation. And a state, under the contract impairment clause, has no more power to accomplish such a substitution than has one of the parties to the contract against the will of the other. It cannot do so either by acting directly upon the contract, or by bringing about the result under the guise of a statute in form acting only upon the remedy. If it could, the efficacy of the constitutional restriction would, in large measure, be made to disappear. . . .

I quite agree with the opinion of the court that whether the legislation under review is wise or unwise is a matter with which we have nothing to do. Whether it is likely to work well or work ill presents a question entirely irrelevant to the issue. The only legitimate inquiry we can make is whether it is constitutional. If it is not, its virtues, if it have any, cannot save it; if it is, its faults cannot be invoked to accomplish its destruction. If the provisions of the Constitution be not upheld when they pinch as well as when they comfort, they may as well be abandoned. Being unable to reach any other conclusion than that the Minnesota statute infringes the constitutional restriction under review, I have no choice but to say so.

United States Trust Company v. *New Jersey*

431 U.S. 1; 97 S. Ct. 1505; 52 L. Ed. 2d 92 (1977)

A 1962 interstate compact between New York and New Jersey limited the ability of the Port Authority of New York and New Jersey to subsidize mass transit from revenues and reserves pledged as security for consolidated bonds issued by the Authority. In 1974, in the face of an emerging national energy crisis, the New Jersey and New York legislatures, acting concurrently, retroactively repealed the 1962 covenant. United States Trust Company, a trustee and bondholder of the Port Authority, brought suit in a New Jersey Superior Court, attacking New Jersey's statutory repeal as a violation of the Contract Clause and seeking declaratory relief. The trial court dismissed the complaint on the grounds that the statute repealing the covenant was a reasonable exercise of New Jersey's police power. The New Jersey Supreme Court affirmed the decision, and the case was appealed to the Supreme Court. *Opinion of the Court: Blackmun, Burger, Rehnquist, Stevens. Concurring opinion: Burger. Dissenting opinion: Brennan, Marshall, White. Powell and Stewart did not participate.*

MR. JUSTICE BLACKMUN delivered the opinion of the Court. . . .

. . . Whether or not the protection of contract rights comports with current views of wise public policy, the Contract Clause remains a part of our written Constitution. We therefore must attempt to apply that constitutional provision to the instant case with due respect for its purpose and the prior decisions of this Court. . . .

Although the Contract Clause appears literally to proscribe "any" impairment, this Court observed in *Blaisdell* that "the prohibition is not an absolute one and is not to be read with literal exactness like a mathematical formula." . . . Thus, a finding that there has been a technical impairment is merely a preliminary step in resolving the more difficult question whether that impairment is permitted under the Constitution. In the instant case, as in *Blaisdell*, we must attempt to reconcile the strictures of the Contract Clause with the "essential attributes of sovereign power ". . . necessarily reserved by the States to safeguard the welfare of their citizens. . . .

The States must possess broad power to adopt general regulatory measures without being concerned that private contracts will be impaired, or even destroyed, as a result. Otherwise, one would be able to obtain immunity from state regulation by making private contractual arrangements. . . .

Yet private contracts are not subject to unlimited modification under the police power. . . . Legislation adjusting the rights and responsibilities of contracting parties must be upon reasonable conditions and of a character appropriate to the public purpose justifying its adoption. . . . As is customary in reviewing economic and social regulation, however, courts properly defer to legislative judgment as to the necessity and reasonableness of a particular measure. . . .

When a State impairs the obligation of its own contract, . . . complete deference to a legislative assessment of reasonableness and necessity is not appropriate because the State's self-interest is at stake. A governmental entity can always find a use for extra money, especially when taxes do not have to be raised. If a State could reduce its financial obligations whenever it wanted to spend the money for what it regarded as an important public purpose, the Contract Clause would provide no protection at all.

Mass transportation, energy conservation, and environmental protection are goals that are important and of legitimate public concern. Appellees contend that these goals are so important that any harm to bondholders from repeal of the 1962 covenant is greatly outweighed by the public benefit. We do not accept this invitation to engage in a utilitarian comparison of public benefit and private loss. . . . The Court has not "balanced away" the limitation on state action imposed by the Contract Clause. Thus a State cannot refuse to meet its legitimate financial obligations simply because it would prefer to spend the money to promote the public good rather than the private welfare of its creditors. We can only sustain the repeal of the 1962 covenant if that impairment was both reasonable and necessary to serve the admittedly important purposes claimed by the State.

The more specific justification offered for the repeal of the 1962 covenant was the States' plan for encouraging users of private automobiles to shift to public transportation. The States intended to discourage private automobile use by raising bridge and tunnel tolls and to use the extra revenue from those tolls to subsidize improved commuter railroad service. Appellees contend that repeal of the 1962 covenant was necessary to implement this plan because the new mass transit facilities could not possibly be self-supporting and the covenant's "permitted deficits" level had already been exceeded. We reject this justification because the repeal was neither necessary to achievement of the plan nor reasonable in light of the circumstances.

The determination of necessity can be considered on two levels. First, it cannot be said that total repeal of the covenant was essential; a less drastic modification would have permitted the contemplated plan without entirely removing the covenant's limitations on the use of Port Authority revenues and reserves to subsidize commuter railroads. Second, without modifying the covenant at all, the States could have adopted alternative means of achieving their twin goals of discouraging automobile use and improving mass transit. Appellees contend, however, that choosing among these alternatives is a matter for legislative discretion. But a State is not completely free to consider impairing the obligations of its own contracts on a par with other policy alternatives. Similarly, a State is not free to impose a drastic impairment when an evident and more moderate course would serve its purposes equally well. . . .

We also cannot conclude that repeal of the covenant was reasonable in light of the surrounding circumstances. . . .

. . . In the instant case the need for mass transportation in the New York metropolitan area was not a new development, and the likelihood that publicly owned commuter railroads would produce substantial deficits was well known. As early as 1922, over a half century ago, there were pressures to involve the Port Authority in mass transit. It was with full knowledge of these concerns that the 1962 covenant was adopted. Indeed, the covenant was specifically intended to protect the pledged revenues and reserves against the possibility that such concerns would lead the Port Authority into greater involvement in deficit mass transit. . . .

. . . We cannot conclude that the repeal was reasonable in the light of changed circumstances.

We therefore hold that the Contract Clause of the United States Constitution prohibits the retroactive repeal of the 1962 covenant. The judgment of the Supreme Court of New Jersey is reversed.

MR. JUSTICE BRENNAN, with whom MR. JUSTICE WHITE and MR. JUSTICE MARSHALL join, dissenting.

Decisions of this Court for at least a century have construed the Contract Clause largely to be powerless in binding a State to contracts limiting the authority of successor legislatures to enact laws in furtherance of the health, safety, and similar collective interests of the polity. In short, those decisions established the principle that lawful exercises of a State's police powers stand paramount to private rights held under contract. Today's decision, in invalidating the New Jersey Legislature's 1974 repeal of its predecessor's 1962 covenant, rejects this previous understanding and remolds the Contract Clause into a potent instrument for overseeing important policy determinations of the state legislature. At the same time, by creating a constitutional safe haven for property rights embodied in a contract, the decision substantially distorts modern constitutional jurisprudence governing regulation of private economic interests. I might understand, though I could not accept, this revival of the Contract Clause were it in accordance with some coherent and constructive view of public policy. But elevation of the Clause to the status of regulator of the municipal bond market at the heavy price of frustration of sound legislative policy-making is as demonstrably unwise as it is unnecessary. The justification for today's decision, therefore, remains a mystery to me, and I respectfully dissent. . . .

One of the fundamental premises of our popular democracy is that each generation of representatives can and will remain responsive to the needs and desires of those whom they represent. Crucial to this end is the assurance that new legislators will not automatically be bound by the policies and undertakings of earlier days. In accordance with this philosophy, the Framers of our Constitution conceived of the Contract Clause primarily as protection for economic transactions entered into by purely private parties, rather than obligations involving the State itself. . . . The Framers fully recognized that nothing would so jeopardize the legitimacy of a system of government that relies upon the ebbs and flows of politics to "clean out the rascals" than the possibility that those same rascals might perpetuate their policies simply by locking them into binding contracts.

I would not want to be read as suggesting that the States should blithely proceed down the path of repudiating their obligations, financial or otherwise. Their credibility in the credit market obviously is highly dependent on exercising their vast lawmaking powers with self-restraint and discipline, and I, for one, have little doubt that few, if any, jurisdictions would choose to use their authority "so foolish[ly] as to kill a goose that lays golden eggs for them," . . . But in the final analysis, there is no reason to doubt that appellant's financial welfare is being adequately policed by the political processes and the bond marketplace itself. The role to be played by the Constitution is at most a limited one. . . . For this Court should have learned long ago that the Constitution—be it through the Contract or Due Process Clause—can actively intrude into such economic and policy matters only if my Brethren are prepared to bear enormous institutional and social costs. Because I consider the potential dangers of such judicial interference to be intolerable, I dissent.

11
ECONOMIC DUE PROCESS AND THE TAKINGS CLAUSE

Prior to the Civil War, the only constitutional restrictions on the power of the states to regulate economic activity were those found in Article I, Section 10, which prohibits the states from emitting bills of credit, making anything but gold or silver a tender in payment of debts, and passing ex post facto laws or laws impairing obligations of contracts. With the adoption of the Fourteenth Amendment in 1868, this situation changed. As pointed out in Chapter 10, this amendment, especially through its Due Process Clause, supplied the Supreme Court with a potent weapon for invalidating state efforts at economic regulation and for protecting vested property rights. In the early part of the twentieth century, the Due Process Clause was wielded by the Court to strike down state laws that, in its estimation, arbitrarily, unreasonably, and capriciously interfered with the rights of life, liberty, and property.[1] During this period, various justices used the clause to justify substantive reviews of governmental actions, scrutinizing not only how the government acted but also what the government did.

As with the Contract Clause before it, substantive due process gradually lost its potency, until by the late 1930s it no longer represented a major obstacle to economic regulation by the states. Such obstacles as remain are found in the Takings Clause of the Fifth Amendment as incorporated to apply to the states, in the Court's expanding interpretations of congressional power to regulate commerce among the several states, or in the state constitutions themselves. It was wholly within the realm of civil liberties that substantive due process retained its potency and continued to serve as a constitutional limitation not only on legislative and executive procedure, but also on legislative and executive power to act at all. This chapter traces the rise and decline of substantive due process in the economic realm, as well as its subsequent revival as a strong check on the substance of legislation infringing upon civil liberties. It also explores the emerging significance of the Takings Clause as a check on state regulation of property rights.

THE FOURTEENTH AMENDMENT

The Fourteenth Amendment commands that "no state shall make or enforce any law which shall abridge the privileges or immunities of citizens of the United States; nor shall any State deprive any person of life, liberty, or property, without due process of law; nor deny to any person within its jurisdiction the equal protection of the laws." Out of an acrimonious debate over the specific intentions of the members of the Thirty-ninth Congress who framed this amendment[2] has emerged general agreement as to the overall ends that the amendment was intended to advance and as to how its three major provisions were to serve as means for the advancement of these ends. As a group, the Privileges or Immunities, Due Process, and Equal Protection clauses were intended to place economic and civil liberties on the safe and secure foundation of federal protection. To that end, the Privileges or Immunities Clause was to protect substantive rights (e.g., freedom of speech, religious freedom, the right to engage in lawful occupations, freedom from improper police violence) and the Equal Protection and Due Process clauses were to protect procedural rights, with the former barring legislative discrimination with respect to substantive rights and the latter guaranteeing procedural safeguards and judicial regularity in the enforcement of those rights.

The Fourteenth Amendment can be visualized as a platform erected above the surface of state action for the protection of economic and civil liberties. In this metaphor, the Privileges or Immunities, Due Process, and Equal Protection clauses represent the platform's three legs: each performs different functions, yet collectively they render the platform stable and secure. The amendment's framers believed that all three legs were essential, but that the Privileges or Immunities Clause would be the most important of the three, because it was designed to be the major load-bearing leg. This design is reflected clearly in Section 5 of the amendment, which provides that "Congress shall have power to enforce, by appropriate legislation, the provisions of this article." Looking at these provisions from the point of view of Congress, the Privileges or Immunities Clause provides the simplest framework for such enforcement legislation. Under that clause, Congress can set out, through a single act or a series of acts, a comprehensive list of the vast number of substantive rights that flow from United States citizenship and make it unlawful for any state, or its agents, to abridge such substantive rights.[3] In contrast, the Due Process and Equal Protection clauses, with their procedural emphases, represent far more elusive reference points for enforcement legislation, because of the formidable technical difficulties involved in avoiding unconstitutional vagueness while framing statutes that protect persons from state deprivation of their lives, liberty, or property "without due process of law" or that guarantee "equal protection of the laws" without interference with essential classificatory schemes.

Just five years after the Fourteenth Amendment was ratified, however, the Supreme Court in the *Slaughterhouse Cases* (1873) effectively kicked out the critical privileges-or-immunities leg and left the protective platform precariously supported by its two spindly procedural legs—due process and equal protection. To keep the platform of protections from collapsing altogether, subsequent Courts have found it imperative to increase substantially the size and strength of the procedural legs. Through judicial interpretation, the justices have added layer upon layer of meaning and coverage to these legs, in an effort to render secure those substantive economic and civil rights that originally were to have been protected by the Privileges or Immunities Clause.

THE EMASCULATION OF THE PRIVILEGES OR IMMUNITIES CLAUSE

In *Butcher's Benevolent Association* v. *Crescent City Livestock Landing and Slaughterhouse Company*, more commonly known as the *Slaughterhouse Cases*, the Court upheld an act of the Louisiana legislature that had conferred upon one firm what was in effect a monopoly of the slaughterhouse business in New Orleans. The plaintiffs had asserted, among other things, that the law in question was in violation of the Fourteenth Amendment. In a 5–4 decision, the Court rejected this claim, principally on the ground of an especially narrow construction of the Privileges or Immunities Clause. Speaking for the majority, Justice Samuel F. Miller drew a distinction between state citizenship and national citizenship and, hence, between those privileges or immunities that accrued to an individual by virtue of state citizenship and those that stemmed from national citizenship. Only the latter, he insisted, were protected by the Fourteenth Amendment.

In distinguishing the privileges or immunities of state citizenship from those of national citizenship, Justice Miller quoted earlier decisions in an effort to demonstrate that the whole body of commonly accepted civil and economic rights—including the right to pursue a lawful employment in a lawful manner, which lay at the heart of the *Slaughterhouse Cases*—fell within the privileges or immunities of state citizenship. Such rights included "protection by the government, with the right to acquire and possess property of every kind, and to pursue and obtain happiness and safety, subject, nevertheless, to such restraints as the [state] government may prescribe for the general good of the whole." Miller contended that the framers of the Fourteenth Amendment had not intended to transfer this whole body of rights to the protection of the federal government. To interpret the amendment otherwise, he argued, would be to accept consequences "so serious, so far-reaching and pervading" that they would alter radically "the whole theory of the relations of the state and Federal governments to each other." This the Court refused do, "in the absence of language which expresses such a purpose too clearly to admit of doubt."

Miller and the majority did not argue that national citizenship conferred no privileges or immunities. Although declining to define them precisely, they did suggest that such privileges or immunities included the right of a citizen "to come to the seat of the government to assert any claim he may have upon that government"; the "right of free access to its seaports"; and the right "to demand the care and protection of the Federal government over his life, liberty, and property when on the high seas, or within the jurisdiction of a foreign government." This list left the whole body of traditional economic and civil rights solely under the protection of the states. As far as the federal Constitution was concerned, therefore, the privileges or immunities of the citizens of the separate states remained exactly as they had been before the Fourteenth Amendment was adopted.

The *Slaughterhouse* decision knocked out the only substantive (and therefore, the most important) leg supporting the platform of economic and civil liberties erected by the Fourteenth Amendment. This leg has not been reassembled—with respect to the Privileges or Immunities Clause, the Court's decision in the *Slaughterhouse Cases* is still good law. The Court did announce in *Colgate* v. *Harvey* (1935) that the right of a U.S. citizen to do business and place a loan in a state other than that in which he resided was a privilege of national citizenship, but it expressly overruled that decision and returned to the old interpretation only five years later, holding in *Madden* v. *Kentucky* (1940) that "the right to carry out an incident to a trade, business or calling such as the deposit of money in banks is not a privilege of national citizenship." The *Slaughterhouse* interpretation also was affirmed in *Snowden* v. *Hughes* (1944), in which the Court held that the right to become a candidate for and be elected to a state office was an attribute of state citizenship, not a privilege of national citizenship. Those who had been denied this right, the Court declared, must look to their own state constitutions and laws for redress.[4]

ECONOMIC REGULATION AND THE RISE OF SUBSTANTIVE DUE PROCESS

The permanent emasculation of the Privileges or Immunities Clause left the substantive economic and civil liberties guaranteed by the Fourteenth Amendment wholly dependent for support upon the Due Process and Equal Protection clauses. The *Slaughterhouse* majority, however, also construed these clauses in a narrow, restrictive fashion.[5] In response to the plaintiffs' assertion that the Louisiana statute in question deprived them of their property without due process of law, the Court observed that "under no construction of that provision that we have ever seen, or that we deem admissible, can the restraint imposed by the State of Louisiana . . . be held to be a deprivation of property within the meaning of that provision."[6] And to a plea that the act deprived them of equal protection of the laws, the Court responded that the Equal Protection Clause had been aimed only at laws in the States where the newly emancipated negroes resided, "which discriminated with gross injustice and hardship against them as a class."

Over time, these narrow interpretations—these spindly legs—have been expanded and enlarged, until today the Due Process and Equal Protection clauses solidly support the protection of a vast array of substantive rights. This chapter and Chapters 12 through 14 explore the growth of the Due Process Clause, initially as a means of protecting economic rights and subsequently as a means of protecting civil liberties. Chapters 15 and 16 then explore the somewhat later growth of the Equal Protection Clause and the way that this procedural leg, too, has come to protect substantive civil liberties.

The narrow procedural interpretation given the Due Process Clause in the *Slaughterhouse Cases* gave way only gradually to a broader, more substantive understanding. In the significant case of *Munn* v. *Illinois* (1877), the Court reaffirmed the restrictive *Slaughterhouse* interpretation and refused to hold that Illinois legislation setting maximum rates for grain elevators denied the elevator operators use of their property without due process of law. Chief Justice Morrison Waite argued that since the days of the common law, grain elevators and warehouses had been recognized as businesses "clothed with a public interest," and as such were subject to public regulation by the legislature. Although he conceded that this regulatory power might be abused, the Chief Justice insisted that abuse "is no argument against [the law's] existence. For protection against abuses by legislatures the people must resort to the polls, not to the courts." In dissent, Justice Stephen J. Field argued that there was nothing in the character of the grain-elevator business that justified state regulation, and hence Illinois' legislation was "nothing less than a bold assertion of absolute power by the State to control at its discretion the property and business of the citizen, and fix the compensation he shall receive." To Field, this "unrestrained license" to regulate was incompatible with due process of law.

Field's broader conception of due process was articulated further by Justice Joseph Bradley in his concurring opinion in *Davidson* v. *New Orleans* (1878). Justice Miller, writing for the majority in *Davidson,* rejected a New Orleans landowner's claim that he had been deprived of his property without due process of law by being forced to pay a special assessment whose purpose (the draining of swamp lands) allegedly would not benefit him. After confessing that "the Constitutional meaning or value of the phrase 'due process of law' remains today without that satisfactory precision of definition which judicial decisions have given to nearly all the other guarantees of personal rights found in the constitutions of the several States and of the United States," Justice Miller went on to declare that the phrase's meaning, however unclear, must be understood in a procedural sense only:

> It is not possible to hold that a party has, without due process of law, been deprived of his property, when, as regards the issues affecting it, he has, by the laws of the State, a fair trial in a court of justice, according to the modes of proceedings applicable to such a case. . . . This proposition covers the present case. Before the assessment could be collected, or become effective, the statute required that the tableau of assessments should be filed in the proper District Court of the State; that personal service of notice, with reasonable time to object, should be served on all owners who were known and within reach of process, and due advertisement made as to those who were unknown, or could not be found. This was complied with; and the party complaining here appeared, and had a full and fair hearing in the court of first instance, and afterwards in the Supreme Court. If this be not due process of law, then the words can have no definite meaning as used in the Constitution.

Justice Bradley, although agreeing with the decision, insisted that the Due Process Clause had a substantive dimension as well. Making explicit what was implicit in Justice Field's dissent in *Munn,* he argued,

> I think . . . we are entitled under the fourteenth amendment, not only to see that there is some process of law, but "due process of law," provided by the State law when a citizen is deprived of his property; and that, in judging what is "due process of law," respect must be had to the cause and object of the taking, whether under the taxing power, the power of eminent domain, or the power of assessment for local improvements, or none of these: and if found to be suitable or admissible in the special case, it will be adjudged to be "due process of law;" but if found to be arbitrary, oppressive, and unjust, it may be declared to be not "due process of law."

According to this view, the Due Process Clause requires courts to review not only how, procedurally, the government acts (procedural due process)—but also what, substantively, the government does (substantive due process). If the Court discerns that a law is unreasonable—that is, "arbitrary, oppressive, and unjust"—then it is justified in declaring the law to be a denial of due process and, hence, constitutionally infirm.

These substantive due process arguments did not originate with Justices Field and Bradley. As far back as 1856, in *Wynehamer* v. *New York,* the New York Court of Appeals (the state's highest court) had invalidated a Prohibition law on the grounds that such an exercise of the police power infringed on the economic liberty of tavern proprietors to practice their livelihood and therefore denied them due process of law.[7] Justices Field and Bradley, however, were the first to give expression to these sentiments at the level of the United States Supreme Court, and the arguments that they introduced in *Munn* and *Davidson* were to gain ascendency in

Mugler v. *Kansas* (1887) and *Allgeyer* v. *Louisiana* (1897), and to receive their clearest constitutional expression in *Lochner* v. *New York* (1905).

In *Mugler* the Court upheld Kansas's Prohibition law but warned that it would begin examining the reasonableness of legislation. Justice John Marshall Harlan stressed that if "a statute purporting to have been enacted to protect the public health, the public morals, or the public safety has no real or substantial relation to those objects, or is a palpable invasion of rights secured by the fundamental law, it is the duty of the Courts to so adjudge." Then, in *Allgeyer,* the Court for the first time relied on substantive due process to invalidate state legislation. Louisiana had enacted legislation designed to regulate out-of-state insurance companies doing business in the state. Justice Rufus Peckham, writing for the majority, argued that the statute in question "is not due process of law, because it prohibits an act which under the federal constitution the defendant has a right to perform." The state's legitimate exercise of its police power, he contended, did not extend to "prohibiting a citizen from making contracts of the nature involved in this case outside of the limits of the jurisdiction of the state, and which are also to be performed outside of such jurisdiction." In the course of his opinion, Justice Peckham forthrightly announced the principle that the right to make contracts was a part of the liberty guaranteed by the Due Process Clause:

> The liberty mentioned in the [Fourteenth] Amendment means not only the right of the citizen to be free from the mere physical restraint of his person, as by incarceration, but the term is deemed to embrace the right of the citizen to be free in the enjoyment of all his faculties; to be free to use them in all lawful ways; to live and work where he will; to earn his livelihood by any lawful calling; to pursue any livelihood or avocation, and for that purpose to enter into all contracts which may be proper, necessary and essential to his carrying out to a successful conclusion the purposes above mentioned.

These substantive due process arguments received their clearest expression in *Lochner* v. *New York,* in which Justice Peckham declared that New York had unreasonably and arbitrarily interfered with the "freedom of master and employee to contract with each other in relation to their employment" by passing a law limiting the number of hours a baker could work in a bakery. Finding no valid health or safety reasons that could justify such a law, Peckham ruled that it amounted to an unreasonable deprivation of liberty (i.e., the liberty to contract) and violated the Due Process Clause.

By embracing the notion of substantive due process, the Court assumed the very role that Justice Miller had warned against in the *Slaughterhouse Cases:* it became a "perpetual censor," reviewing the reasonableness of state efforts at economic regulation. It continued to play this role at least through *Adkins* v. *Children's Hospital* (1923), in which the District of Columbia's minimum wage law for women and children was branded "the product of a naked arbitrary exercise of power" and thus a violation of the Fifth Amendment's Due Process Clause. Prior to *Adkins,* the Court had appeared to moderate its position toward economic legislation. In *Muller* v. *Oregon* (1908) and *Bunting* v. *Oregon* (1917), for example, the justices upheld the constitutionality of state legislation that, respectively, limited the workday for women to ten hours and extended that maximum-hours limitation to all mill and factory workers. Of decisive importance in both of these decisions, however, was the Court's belief that the regulations in question were a reasonable exercise of the state's police powers—not its subsequent conviction that any judicial inquiry into the substance or reasonableness of economic legislation was inappropriate.

THE REPUDIATION OF SUBSTANTIVE DUE PROCESS

As the Court's subsequent decision in *Adkins* makes apparent, *Muller* and *Bunting* did not represent a repudiation of substantive due process—in these cases the Court merely judged that the economic regulations in question were reasonable; it did not conclude that it was inappropriate for the Court to make such judgments in the first place. The disavowal of substantive due process began somewhat later in *Nebbia* v. *New York* (1934), in which the Court, by a 5–4 vote, upheld the validity of a Depression-era law regulating the price of milk. The New York legislature had sought to prevent ruinous price cutting by establishing a milk control board with power to fix minimum and maximum retail prices, and the appellant claimed that enforcement of the milk price regulations denied him due process of law by preventing him from selling his product at whatever price he desired. In rejecting this claim, Justice Owen Roberts, speaking for the majority, declared,

> So far as the requirement of due process is concerned, and in the absence of other constitutional restrictions, a state is free to adopt whatever economic policy may reasonably be deemed to promote public welfare, and to enforce that policy by legislation adapted to its purpose. The courts are without authority either to declare such policy, or, when it is declared by the legislature, to override it.

What was begun in *Nebbia* was completed in *West Coast Hotel Company* v. *Parrish* (1937). This case arose under a Washington state minimum-wage law that had been passed in 1913 and enforced continuously thereafter, quite irrespective of *Adkins.* In the midst of the intense political controversy generated by President Roosevelt's Court-packing plan, the Court upheld the law. Chief Justice Hughes insisted that the state legislature had the right to use its minimum-wage requirements to help implement its policy of protecting women from exploitive employers. He noted that "the adoption of similar requirements by many States evidences a deepseated conviction both as to the presence of the evil and as to the means adopted to check it. Legislative response to that conviction cannot be regarded as arbitrary or capricious, and that is all we have to decide." The Chief Justice then went even further: "Even if the wisdom of the policy is regarded as debatable and its effects uncertain, still the legislature is entitled to its judgment."

The Court's refusal in *Parrish* to contradict the judgment of the legislature on economic matters and its outright repudiation of substantive due process in the economic realm through the explicit overruling of *Adkins* remain controlling precedents. Subsequent decisions, in fact, suggest a reluctance to subject economic legislation to any constitutional test at all.[8] *Day-Brite Lighting* v. *Missouri* (1952) provides a clear example of this trend. In reviewing a state law that provided that employees could absent themselves from their jobs for four hours on election days and forbade employers from deducting wages for their absence, the Court admitted that the social policy embodied in the law was debatable but pointed out that "our recent decisions make plain that we do not sit as a superlegislature to weigh the wisdom of legislation nor to decide whether the policy it expresses offends the public welfare." This argument was repeated in *Williamson* v. *Lee Optical Company* (1955), which involved a statute that forbade any person but an ophthalmologist or an optometrist from fitting lenses to the face or duplicating or replacing lenses into frames, except on the prescription of an ophthalmologist or optometrist. After acknowledging that the law was "a needless, wasteful requirement in many cases," the Court went on to insist that "the day is gone" when it would strike down "state laws regulatory of business and industrial conditions, because they may be unwise, improvident, or out of harmony with a particular school of thought." Eight years later, in *Ferguson* v. *Skrupa* (1963), the Court applied the same reasoning in upholding a Kansas statute prohibiting anyone except lawyers from engaging in the business of debt adjustment, with Justice Black noting in his majority opinion that "it is up to legislatures, not Courts, to decide on the wisdom and utility of legislation." The *Ferguson* opinion elicited some judicial protests, however. Despite his abiding commitment to judicial self-restraint, Justice John Marshall Harlan felt compelled to protest against what he perceived to be judicial abdication. In his concurrence, he insisted that even economic legislation must bear "a rational relation to a constitutionally permissible objective"—a relationship that he found to exist in the instant case.

Justice Black's words in *Ferguson,* echoing as they do Chief Justice Waite's opinion in *Munn* v. *Illinois,* highlights the full circle traveled by the Court in its consideration of the Due Process Clause and economic rights. The spindly due-process leg in *Munn,* which by *Lochner* had grown enormously in size and strength, had lost its potency by *Parrish* and atrophied to the spindly reed it once again became by *Williamson.* At the very time that the Court was repudiating substantive due process in the economic realm, however, it was embracing that concept in the realm of civil liberties. In footnote four of the Court's opinion in *United States* v.

Carolene Products Company (1938), for example, Justice Harlan Fiske Stone outlined a justification for "more exacting judicial scrutiny" where infringements of civil liberties were involved. The Court's subsequent embrace of substantive due process in the realm of civil liberties will be an underlying concern in the chapters that follow.

THE TAKINGS CLAUSE

Just as the Due Process Clause supplanted the Contract Clause as a means of protecting property rights, so, too, the Takings Clause of the Fifth Amendment as incorporated to apply to the states by the Fourteenth Amendment appears to have supplanted due process. It states that private property shall not "be taken for public use, without just compensation," and is variously referred to as the Takings Clause, the Public Use Clause, or the Just Compensation Clause.

Both the federal and state governments have the power of eminent domain, the power to condemn or expropriate private property for public purposes upon just compensation of the owner. The decision to invoke the power of eminent domain is a legislative one, and the Court has been reluctant to question whether the compensation offered is "just" or whether the confiscated property has been taken for a "public use." In *Hawaii Housing Authority* v. *Midkiff* (1984), for example, the Supreme Court unanimously upheld Hawaii's use of its power of eminent domain to acquire property from large landowners and transfer it to lessees living on single-family residential lots on the land. The purpose of this land condemnation scheme was to reduce the concentration of land ownership, and Justice O'Connor declared that "our cases make clear that empirical debates over the wisdom of takings—no less than debates over the wisdom of other kinds of socioeconomic legislation—are not to be carried out in the federal courts."

While the Court has been hesitant to challenge legislative judgments concerning just compensation and public use, it has become increasingly assertive in concluding that various governmental regulations that restrict, diminish, or destroy the value of property can be as much a taking as eminent domain. In *First English Evangelical Lutheran Church* v. *Los Angeles County* (1987), the Court held in a 6–3 decision that a county decision to prohibit a church from constructing buildings on a campground it owned after there had been extensive damage from a flood constituted a taking for which the county must pay compensation. Moreover, the Court continued, once a taking has been determined, the government must compensate the owner for the period during which the taking was in effect. The mere fact that the taking was temporary—either because subsequently invalidated by the courts or repealed by a successor ordinance—does not eliminate the need for compensation. As Chief Justice Rehnquist noted: "[T]he Los Angeles County ordinances have denied appellant all use of its property for a considerable period of years, and we hold that invalidation of the ordinance without payment of fair value for the use of the property during this period of time would be a constitutionally insufficient remedy."

Nollan v. *California Coastal Commission* (1987) shows the Court's new assertiveness even more clearly. The coastal commission granted a permit to the Nollans to replace a small bungalow on their beachfront lot with a larger house. As a condition, however, the commission insisted that the Nollans grant an easement to the public across their land to the beach. The Nollans claimed that this requirement constituted a taking, and the Supreme Court, with Justice Scalia writing the majority opinion, agreed.

Among the justices on the Court, Justice Scalia appears the most willing to treat the Takings Clause as a successor to the Due Process Clause and use it to strike down governmental regulation of private property. In *Pennell* v. *City of San Jose* (1988), a case involving a rent control ordinance that allowed administrative reductions on rent in case of "tenant hardship," Justice Scalia dissented from Chief Justice Rehnquist's majority decision that the case was not ripe for judicial resolution, reached the merits on the hardship provision, and expanded on the themes he advanced in *Nollan*. He denied the landlords were the cause of the problem at which the hardship provision was aimed. Rather, he insisted that the provision was drafted "to meet a quite different social problem: the existence of some renters who are too poor to afford even reasonably priced housing. But that problem is no more caused or exploited by landlords than it is by the grocers who sell needy renters their food, or the department stores that sell them their clothes, or the employers who pay them their wages, or the citizens of San Jose holding the higher-paying jobs from which they are excluded." Moreover, Scalia continued, "even if the neediness of renters could be regarded as a problem distinctively attributable to landlords in general, it is not remotely attributable to the particular landlords that the ordinance singles out—namely, those who happen to have a 'hardship' tenant at the present time, or who may happen to rent to a 'hardship' tenant in the future, or whose current or future affluent tenants may happen to decline into the 'hardship' category." He then drove home his primary point: "The fact that government acts through the landlord-tenant relationship does not magically transform general public welfare, which must be supported by all the public, into mere 'economic regulation,' which can disproportionately burden particular individuals."

Justice Scalia's insistence that government (and hence taxpayers) pay for public welfare and not transfer these costs to particular discrete individuals takes on added significance today, with a public whose appetites for governmental services are greater than its willingness to pay for them. It also poses, as substantive due process before it, the question of the proper role of the Court. How much should the Court be a check on the wishes of the popular branches? How much should it protect the few from the wishes of the majority? How much should it protect the rights of property with the same dedication it displays for other rights?

NOTES

1 For an especially useful essay on this matter, see Edward S. Corwin, "The Supreme Court and the Fourteenth Amendment," *Michigan Law Review* 7 (June 1909): 643.

2 See Raoul Berger, *Government by Judiciary: The Transformation of the Fourteenth Amendment* (Cambridge, Mass.: Harvard University Press, 1977); Jacobus Tenbroek, *Equal under Law* (New York: Macmillan, 1965); Alexander M. Bickel, "The Original Understanding and the Segregation Decision," *Harvard Law Review* 69, no. 1. (November 1955); Charles Fairman, "Does the Fourteenth Amendment Incorporate the Bill of Rights?", *Stanford Law Review* 2, no. 1 (1949); and William W. Van Alstyne, "The Fourteenth Amendment, the 'Right to Vote,' and the Understanding of the Thirty-Ninth Congress," in *Supreme Court Review,* ed. Philip Kurland (Chicago: University of Chicago Press, 1966); and Alford H. Kelly, "Clio and the Court: An Illicit Love Affair," 1965 *Supreme Court Review.*

3 See Corwin, "The Supreme Court and the Fourteenth Amendment"; Tenbroek, *Equal under Law,* pp. 236–238; M. Glenn Abernathy, *Civil Liberties under the Constitution,* 3d ed. (New York: Harper and Row, 1977), pp. 32–33; and Berger, *Government by Judiciary,* pp. 18–19.

4 Unsuccessful attempts to broaden the scope of privileges and immunities include *Hague* v. *Committee for Industrial Organization* (1939); *Edwards* v. *California* (1941); and *Oyama* v. *California* (1948).

5 It could be said that with respect to the Due Process and Equal Protection clauses, the Court correctly identified the intentions of the Thirty-ninth Congress in drafting these clauses and acted accordingly. But given its concurrent construction of the Privileges or Immunities Clause, the Court's fidelity to the intentions of the Thirty-ninth Congress simply served to exacerbate matters and led directly to the development of substantive due process (discussed below).

6 The Court accepted without debate the procedural interpretation of due process. For differing views of what due process could have meant, however, see *Scott* v. *Sandford* (1857); *Hepburn* v. *Griswold* (1870); and Edward S. Corwin, "Due Process of Law before the Civil War," *Harvard Law Review* 24 (March 1911): 366ff. and (April 1911): 460*ff.*

7 As Justice Comstock put the question: "Do the prohibitions and penalties of the act for the prevention of intemperance, pauperism, and crime pass the utmost boundaries of mere regulation and police, and by their own force, assuming them to be valid and faithfully obeyed and executed, work the essential loss or destruction of the property at which they are aimed? . . . In my judgment, they do plainly work this result."

8 Guy Miller Struve, "The Less-Restrictive-Alternative Principle and Economic Due Process," *Harvard Law Review* 80 (1967): 1463–1488.

SELECTED READINGS

Adair v. *United States,* 208 U.S. 161 (1908).
Coppage v. *Kansas,* 236 U.S. 1 (1915).
Dean v. *Gadsden Times Publishing Company,* 412 U.S. 543 (1973).

Ferguson v. *Skrupa,* 372 U.S. 726 (1963).
First English Evangelical Lutheran Church of Glendale v. *Los Angeles County,* 482 U.S. 304 (1987).
Morehead v. *New York ex. rel. Tipaldo,* 298 U.S. 587 (1936).
New Orleans v. *Dukes,* 427 U.S. 297 (1976).
Pennell v. *City of San Jose,* 108 S. Ct. 849 (1988).

Berger, Raoul. *Government by Judiciary: The Transformation of the Fourteenth Amendment* (Cambridge, Mass.: Harvard University Press, 1977).

Dorn, James A., and Manne, Henry G., eds. *Economic Liberties and the Judiciary* (Fairfax, Va.: George Mason University Press, 1987).

Epstein, Richard A. *Takings: Property and the Power of Eminent Domain* (Cambridge, Mass.: Harvard University Press, 1985).

Galie, Peter J. "State Courts and Economic Rights," *Annals* 496 (1988): 76–87.

Kitch, Edmund W., and Clara Ann Bowler. "The Facts of *Munn* v. *Illinois*" *1978 Supreme Court Review* (Chicago: University of Chicago Press, 1978).

McCloskey, Robert. "Economic Due Process and the Supreme Court: An Exhumation and Reburial" *1962 Supreme Court Review* (Chicago: University of Chicago Press, 1962).

Nelson, William E. *The Fourteenth Amendment: From Political Principle to Judicial Doctrine* (Cambridge: Harvard University Press, 1988).

Porter, Mary Cornelia. "That Commerce Shall Be Free: A New Look at the Old Laissez-Faire Court" *1976 Supreme Court Review* (Chicago: University of Chicago Press, 1977).

Sallet, Jonathan D. "Regulatory 'Takings' and Just Compensation: The Supreme Court's Search for a Solution Continues," *Urban Lawyer* 18 (1986): 635.

Shapiro, Martin. "The Constitution and Economic Rights" In M. Judd Harmon, ed. *Essays on the Constitution of the United States* (Port Washington, N.Y.: Kennikat Press, 1978).

Siegan, Bernard H. *Economic Liberties and the Constitution* (Chicago: University of Chicago Press, 1981).

Struve, Guy Miller. "The Less-Restrictive-Alternative Principle and Economic Due Process" *Harvard Law Review* 80 (1967).

Tushnet, Mark. "The Newer Property: Suggestion for the Revival of Substantive Due Process" *1975 Supreme Court Review* (Chicago: University of Chicago Press, 1976).

The Slaughterhouse Cases

83 U.S. (16 Wallace) 36; 21 L. Ed. 394 (1873)

In 1869, the Louisiana legislature passed an act designed to "protect the health of the City of New Orleans" by granting to the Crescent City Livestock Landing and Slaughterhouse Co. a twenty-five-year monopoly on the sheltering and slaughtering of animals in the city and surrounding parishes. The law required that all other butchers in the New Orleans area come to that company and pay for the use of its abattoir. Although the law was in response to a cholera epidemic and represented an attempt to end contamination of the city's water supply caused by the dumping of refuse into the Mississippi River by small independent slaughterhouses, the state legislature at the time was dominated by carpetbag elements, and charges of corruption were rampant. The Butcher's Benevolent Association, a group of small independent slaughterers who had been deprived of their livelihood by the legislation, challenged the act on the grounds that it violated the Thirteenth Amendment and the Privileges and Immunities, Due Process, and Equal Protection clauses of the Fourteenth Amendment. A state district court and the Louisiana Supreme Court upheld the legislation, at which point this case, along with two others involving the same controversy, was brought to the United States Supreme Court on a writ of error. These three cases have come to be known simply as *The Slaughterhouse Cases. Opinion of the Court: Miller, Clifford, Davis, Hunt, Strong. Dissenting opinions: Bradley; Field, Bradley, Chase, Swayne; Swayne.*

MR. JUSTICE MILLER delivered the opinion of the Court. . . .

The plaintiffs in error . . . allege that the statute is a violation of the Constitution of the United States in these several particulars:

That it creates an involuntary servitude forbidden by the thirteenth article of amendment;

That it abridges the privileges and immunities of citizens of the United States;

That it denies to the plaintiffs the equal protection of the laws; and,

That it deprives them of their property without due process of law; contrary to the provisions of the first section of the fourteenth article of amendment.

This court is thus called upon for the first time to give construction to these articles.

. . . In the light of . . . recent . . . history, . . . and on the most casual examination of the language of these amendments, no one can fail to be impressed with the one pervading purpose found in them all, lying at the foundation of each, and without which none of them would have been even suggested; we mean the freedom of the slave race, the security and firm establishment of that freedom, and the protection of the newly-made freeman and citizen from the oppressions of those who had formerly exercised unlimited dominion over him. . . .

We do not say that no one else but the negro can share in this protection. . . . But what we do say, and what we wish to be understood is, that in any fair and just construction of any section or phrase of these amendments, it is necessary to look to the purpose which we have said was the pervading spirit of them all, the evil which they were designed to remedy, and the process of continued addition to the Constitution, until that purpose was supposed to be accomplished, as far as constitutional law can accomplish it.

The first section of the fourteenth article, to which our attention is more specially invited, opens with a definition of citizenship—not only citizenship of the United States, but citizenship of the States. . . .

"All persons born or naturalized in the United

States, and subject to the jurisdiction thereof, are citizens of the United States and of the State wherein they reside." . . .

It declares that persons may be citizens of the United States without regard to their citizenship of a particular State, and it overturns the Dred Scott decision by making *all persons* born within the United States and subject to its jurisdiction citizens of the United States. . . . Not only may a man be a citizen of the United States without being a citizen of a State, but an important element is necessary to convert the former into the latter. He must reside within the State to make him a citizen of it, but it is only necessary that he should be born or naturalized in the United States to be a citizen of the Union.

It is quite clear, then, that there is a citizenship of the United States, and a citizenship of a State, which are distinct from each other, and which depend upon different characteristics or circumstances in the individual.

We think this distinction and its explicit recognition in this amendment of great weight in this argument, because the next paragraph of this same section, which is the one mainly relied on by the plaintiffs in error, speaks only of privileges and immunities of citizens of the United States, and does not speak of those of citizens of the several States. The argument, however, in favor of the plaintiffs rests wholly on the assumption that the citizenship is the same, and the privileges and immunities guaranteed by the clause are the same.

The language is, "No State shall make or enforce any law which shall abridge the privileges or immunities of citizens of *the United States.*" It is a little remarkable, if this clause was intended as a protection to the citizen of a State against the legislative power of his own State, that the word citizen of the State should be left out when it is so carefully used, and used in contradistinction to citizens of the United States, in the very sentence which precedes it. It is too clear for argument that the change in phraseology was adopted understandingly and with a purpose.

Of the privileges and immunities of the citizen of the United States, and of the privileges and immunities of the citizen of the State, and what they respectively are, we will presently consider; but we wish to state here that it is only the former which are placed by this clause under the protection of the Federal Constitution, and that the latter, whatever they may be, are not intended to have any additional protection by this paragraph of the amendment.

If, then, there is a difference between the privileges and immunities belonging to a citizen of the United States as such, and those belonging to the citizen of the State as such, the latter must rest for their security and protection where they have heretofore rested; for they are not embraced by this paragraph of the amendment.

The first occurrence of the words "privileges and immunities" in our constitutional history, is to be found in the fourth of the articles of the old Confederation.

It declares "that . . . the free inhabitants of each of these States . . . shall be entitled to all the privileges and immunities of free citizens in the several States." . . .

In the Constitution of the United States, which superseded the Articles of Confederation, the corresponding provision is found in section two of the fourth article, in the following words: "The citizens of each State shall be entitled to all the privileges and immunities of citizens of the several States." . . .

That constitutional provision . . . did not create those rights, which it called privileges and immunities of citizens of the States. It threw around them in that clause no security for the citizen of the State in which they were claimed or exercised. Nor did it profess to control the power of the State governments over the rights of its own citizens.

Its sole purpose was to declare to the several States, that whatever those rights, as you grant or establish them to your own citizens, or as you limit or qualify, or impose restrictions on their exercise, the same, neither more nor less, shall be the measure of the rights of citizens of other States within your jurisdiction.

It would be the vainest show of learning to attempt to prove by citations of authority, that up to the adoption of the recent amendments, no claim or pretence was set up that those rights depended on the Federal government for their existence or protection, beyond the very few express limitations which the Federal Constitution imposed upon the States—such, for instance, as the prohibition against ex post facto laws, bills of attainder, and laws impairing the obligation of contracts. But with the exception of these and a few other restrictions, the entire domain of the privileges and immunities of citizens of the States, as above defined, lay within the constitutional and legislative power of the States, and without that of the Federal government. Was it the purpose of the fourteenth amendment, by the simple declaration that no State should make or enforce any law which shall abridge the privileges and immunities of *citizens of the United States*, to transfer the security and protection of all the civil rights which we have mentioned, from the States to the Federal government? And where it is declared that Congress shall have the power to enforce that article, was it intended to bring within the power of Congress the entire domain of civil rights heretofore belonging exclusively to the States?

All this and more must follow, if the proposition of the plaintiffs in error be sound. For not only are these rights subject to the control of Congress whenever in its discretion, any of them are supposed to be abridged by State legislation, but that body may also pass laws in advance, limiting and restricting the exercise of legislative power by the States, in their most ordinary and usual functions, as in its judgment it may think proper on all such subjects. And still further, such a construction followed by the reversal of the judgments of the Supreme Court of Louisiana in these cases, would constitute this court a perpetual censor upon all legislation of the States, on the civil rights of their own citizens, with authority to nullify such as it did not approve as consistent with those rights, as they existed at the time of the adoption of this amendment. The argument we admit is not always the most conclusive which is drawn from the consequences urged against the adoption of a particular construction of an instrument. But when, as in the case before us, these consequences are so serious, so far-reaching and pervading, so great a departure from the structure and spirit of our institutions; when the effect is to fetter and degrade the State governments by subjecting them to the control of Congress, in the exercise of powers heretofore universally conceded to them of the most ordinary and fundamental character; when in fact it radically changes the whole theory of the relations of the State and Federal governments to each other and of both these governments to the people; the argument has a force that is irresistible, in the absence of language which expresses such a purpose too clearly to admit of doubt.

We are convinced that no such results were intended by the Congress which proposed these amendments, nor by the legislatures of the States which ratified them.

Having shown that the privileges and immunities relied on in the argument are those which belong to citizens of the States as such, and that they are left to the State governments for security and protection, and not by this article placed under the special care of the Federal government, we may hold ourselves excused from defining the privileges and immunities of citizens of the United States which no State can abridge, until some case involving those privileges may make it necessary to do so.

But lest it should be said that no such privileges and immunities are to be found if those we have been considering are excluded, we venture to suggest some which owe their existence to the Federal government, its National character, its Constitution, or its laws.

One of these is well described in the case of *Crandall* v. *Nevada*. It is said to be the right of the citizen of this great country, protected by implied guarantees of its Constitution, "to come to the seat of government to assert any claim he may have upon that government, to transact any business he may have with it, to seek its protection, to share its offices, to engage in administering its functions. He has the right of free access to its seaports, through which all operations of foreign commerce are conducted, to the subtreasuries, land offices, and courts of justice in the several States." . . .

Another privilege of a citizen of the United States is to demand the care and protection of the Federal government over his life, liberty, and property when on the high seas or within the jurisdiction of a foreign government. Of this there can be no doubt, nor that the right depends upon his character as a citizen of the United States. The right to peaceably assemble and petition for redress of grievances, the privilege of the writ of *habeas corpus*, are rights of the citizen guaranteed by the Federal Constitution. The right to use the navigable waters of the United States, however they may penetrate the territory of the several States, all rights secured to our citizens by treaties with foreign nations, are dependent upon citizenship of the United States, and not citizenship of a State. One of these privileges is conferred by the very article under consideration. It is that a citizen of the United States can, of his own volition, become a citizen of any State of the Union by a *bonâ fide* residence therein, with the same rights as other citizens of that State. To these may be added the rights secured by the thirteenth and fifteenth articles of amendment, and by the other clause of the fourteenth, next to be considered.

But it is useless to pursue this branch of the inquiry, since we are of opinion that the rights claimed by these plaintiffs in error, if they have any existence, are not privileges and immunities of citizens of the United States within the meaning of the clause of the fourteenth amendment under consideration. . . .

The argument has not been much pressed in these cases that the defendant's charter deprives the plaintiffs of their property without due process of law. . . .

We are not without judicial interpretation, . . . both State and National, of the meaning of this clause. And it is sufficient to say that under no construction of that provision that we have ever seen, or any that we deem admissible, can the restraint imposed by the State of Louisiana upon the exercise of their trade by the butchers of New Orleans be held to be a deprivation of property within the meaning of that provision.

"Nor shall any State deny to any person within its jurisdiction the equal protection of the laws."

In the light of the history of these amendments, and the pervading purpose of them, which we have already discussed, it is not difficult to give a meaning to this clause. The existence of laws in the States where the newly emancipated negroes resided, which discriminated with gross injustice and hardship against them as a class, was the evil to be remedied by this clause, and by it such laws are forbidden. . . .

The judgments of the Supreme Court of Louisiana in these cases are

Affirmed.

Mr. Justice Field, dissenting. . . .

The question presented is . . . one of the gravest importance, not merely to the parties here, but to the whole country. It is nothing less than the question whether the recent amendments to the Federal Constitution protect the citizens of the United States against the deprivation of their common rights by State legislation. In my judgment the fourteenth amendment does afford such protection, and was so intended by the Congress which framed and the States which adopted it.

The counsel for the plaintiffs in error have contended, with great force, that the act in question is also inhibited by the thirteenth amendment.

. . . I have been so accustomed to regard it as intended to meet that form of slavery which had previously prevailed in this country, and to which the recent civil war owed its existence, that I was not prepared, nor am I yet, to give to it the extent and force ascribed by counsel. Still it is evident that the language of the amendment is not used in a restrictive sense. It is not confined to African slavery alone. It is general and universal in its application. . . .

It is not necessary, however, . . . to rest my objections to the act in question upon the terms and meaning of the thirteenth amendment. The provisions of the fourteenth amendment, which is properly a supplement to the thirteenth, cover, in my judgment, the case before us, and inhibit any legislation which confers special and exclusive privileges like these under consideration. . . . It first declares that "all persons born or naturalized in the United States, and subject to the jurisdiction thereof, are citizens of the United States and of the State wherein they reside." . . .

. . . It recognizes in express terms, if it does not create, citizens of the United States, and it makes their citizenship dependent upon the place of their birth, or the fact of their adoption, and not upon the constitution or laws of any State or the condition of their ancestry. A citizen of a State is now only a citizen of the United States residing in that State. The fundamental rights, privileges, and immunities which belong to him as a free man and a free citizen, now belong to him as a citizen of the United States, and are not dependent upon his citizenship of any State. . . .

The amendment does not attempt to confer any new privileges or immunities upon citizens, or to enumerate or define those already existing. It assumes that there are such privileges and immunities which belong of right to citizens as such, and ordains that they shall not be abridged by State legislation. If this inhibition has no reference to privileges and immunities of this character, but only refers, as held by the majority of the court in their opinion, to such privileges and immunities as were before its adoption specially designated in the Constitution or necessarily implied as belonging to citizens of the United States, it was a vain and idle enactment, which accomplished nothing, and most unnecessarily excited Congress and the people on its passage. With privileges and immunities thus designated or implied no State could ever have interfered by its laws, and no new constitutional provision was required to inhibit such interference. The supremacy of the Constitution and the laws of the United States always controlled any State legislation of that character. But if the amendment refers to the natural and inalienable rights which belong to all citizens, the inhibition has a profound significance and consequence.

What, then, are the privileges and immunities which are secured against abridgment by State legislation? . . .

The terms, privileges and immunities, are not new in the amendment; they were in the Constitution before the amendment was adopted. They are found in the second section of the fourth article, which declares that "the citizens of each State shall be entitled to all privileges and immunities of citizens in the several States," and they have been the subject of frequent consideration in judicial decisions. In *Corfield* v. *Coryell*, Mr. Justice Washington said he had "no hesitation in confining these expressions to those privileges and immunities which were, in their nature, fundamental; which belong of right to citizens of all free governments, and which have at all times been enjoyed by the citizens of the several States which compose the Union, from the time of their becoming free, independent, and sovereign;" and, in considering what those fundamental privileges were, he said that perhaps it would be more tedious than difficult to enumerate them, but that they might be "all comprehended under the following general heads: protection by the government; the enjoyment of life and liberty, with the right to acquire and possess property of every kind, and to pursue and obtain happiness and safety, subject, nevertheless, to such restraints as the government may justly prescribe for the general good of the whole." This appears to me to be a sound construction of the clause in question. The privileges and immunities designated are those *which of right belong to the citizens of all free governments*. Clearly among these must be placed the right to pursue a lawful employment in a lawful manner, without other restraint than such as equally affects all persons. . . .

What the clause in question did for the protection of the citizens of one State against hostile and discriminating legislation of other States, the fourteenth amendment does for the protection of every citizen of the United States against hostile and discriminating legislation against him in favor of others, whether they reside in the same or in different States. If under the fourth article of the Constitution equality of privileges and immunities is secured between citizens of different States, under the fourteenth amendment the same equality is secured between citizens of the United States. . . .

This equality of right, with exemption from all disparaging and partial enactments, in the lawful pursuits of life, throughout the whole country, is the distinguishing privilege of citizens of the United States. To them, everywhere, all pursuits, all professions, all avocations are open without other restrictions than such as are imposed equally upon all others of the same age, sex, and condition. The State may prescribe such regulations for every pursuit and calling of life as will promote the public health, secure the good order and advance the general prosperity of society, but when once prescribed, the pursuit or calling must be free to be followed by every citizen who is within the conditions designated, and will conform to the regulations. This is the fundamental idea upon which our institutions rest, and unless adhered to in the legislation of the country our government will be a republic only in name. The fourteenth amendment, in my judgment, makes it essential to the validity of the legislation of every State that this equality of right should be respected. . . .

MR. JUSTICE BRADLEY, dissenting. . . .

In my view, a law which prohibits a large class of citizens from adopting a lawful employment, or from following a lawful employment previously adopted, does deprive them of liberty as well as property, without due process of law. Their right of choice is a portion of their liberty;

their occupation is their property. Such a law also deprives those citizens of the equal protection of the laws, contrary to the last clause of the section.

It is futile to argue that none but persons of the African race are intended to be benefited by this amendment. They may have been the primary cause of the amendment, but its language is general, embracing all citizens, and I think it was purposely so expressed.

Munn v. *Illinois*

94 U.S. 113; 24 L. Ed. 77 (1877)

Pursuant to Article XIII of the Illinois Constitution of 1870, which empowered the state legislature to regulate the storage of grain, the Illinois General Assembly enacted a statute in 1871 that required grain warehouses and elevators to obtain operating licenses and that established the maximum rates they could charge for the handling and storage of grain. Ira Y. Munn was convicted in county court of operating a grain warehouse without a license and of charging higher rates than those allowed by the law, and was fined $100. The Illinois Supreme Court affirmed his conviction, and Munn brought the case to the United States Supreme Court on a writ of error. *Opinion of the Court: Waite, Bradley, Clifford, Davis, Hunt, Miller, Swayne. Dissenting opinion: Field, Strong.*

MR. CHIEF JUSTICE WAITE delivered the opinion of the Court.

The question to be determined in this case is whether the general assembly of Illinois can, under the limitations upon the legislative power of the States imposed by the Constitution of the United States, fix by law the maximum of charges for the storage of grain in warehouses at Chicago and other places in the State. . . .

It is claimed that such a law is repugnant— To that part of amendment 14 which ordains that no State shall "deprive any person of life, liberty, or property, without due process of law." . . .

The Constitution contains no definition of the word "deprive," as used in the Fourteenth Amendment. To determine its signification, therefore, it is necessary to ascertain the effect which usage has given it, when employed in the same or a like connection.

While this provision of the amendment is new in the Constitution of the United States, as a limitation upon the powers of the States, it is old as a principle of civilized government. It is found in Magna Charta, and, in substance if not in form, in nearly or quite all the constitutions that have been from time to time adopted by the several States of the Union. By the Fifth Amendment, it was introduced into the Constitution of the United States as a limitation upon the powers of the national government, and by the Fourteenth, as a guaranty against any encroachment upon an acknowledged right of citizenship by the legislatures of the States. . . .

When one becomes a member of society, he necessarily parts with some rights or privileges which, as an individual not affected by his relations to others, he might retain. . . . This does not confer power upon the whole people to control rights which are purely and exclusively private, . . . but it does authorize the establishment of laws requiring each citizen to so conduct himself, and so use his own property, as not unnecessarily to injure another. . . . From this source come the police powers. . . . Under these powers the government regulates the conduct of its citizens one towards another, and the manner in which each shall use his own property, when such regulation becomes necessary for the public good. In their exercise it has been customary in England from time immemorial, and in this country from its first colonization, to regulate ferries, common carriers, hackmen, bakers, millers, wharfingers, innkeepers, &c., and in so doing to fix a maximum of charge to be made for services rendered, accommodations furnished, and articles sold. To this day, statutes are to be found in many of the States upon some or all these subjects; and we think it has never yet been successfully contended that such legislation came within any of the constitutional prohibitions against interference with private property. . . .

This brings us to inquire as to the principles upon which this power of regulation rests, in order that we may determine what is within and what without its operative effect. Looking, then, to the common law, from whence came the right which the Constitution protects, we find that when private property is "affected with a public interest, it ceases to be *juris privati* only." This was said by Lord Chief Justice Hale more than two hundred years ago, in his treatise *De Portibus Maris*, . . . and has been accepted without objection as an essential element in the law of property ever since. Property does become clothed with a public interest when used in a manner to make it of public consequence, and affect the community at large. When, therefore, one devotes his property to a use in which the public has an interest, he, in effect, grants to the public an interest in that use, and must submit to be controlled by the public for the common good, to the extent of the interest he has thus created. He may withdraw his grant by discontinuing the use; but, so long as he maintains the use, he must submit to the control. . . .

. . . When private property is devoted to a public use, it is subject to public regulation. It remains only to ascertain whether the warehouses of these plaintiffs in error, and the business which is carried on there, come within the operation of this principle.

. . . It is difficult to see why, if the common carrier, or the miller, or the ferryman, or the innkeeper, or the wharfinger, or the baker, or the cartman, or the hackney-coachman, pursues a public employment and exercises "a sort of public office," these plaintiffs in error do not. They stand. . . in the very "gateway of commerce," and take toll from all who pass. Their business most certainly "tends to a common charge, and is become a thing of public interest and use." Every bushel of grain for its passage "pays a toll, which is a common charge," and, therefore, according to Lord Hale, every such warehouseman "ought to be under public regulation, viz., that he . . . take but reasonable toll." Certainly, if any business can be clothed "with a public interest, and cease to be *juris privati* only," this has been. . . .

. . . For our purposes we must assume that, if a state of facts could exist that would justify such legislation, it actually did exist when the statute now under consideration was passed. For us the question is one of power, not of expediency. If no state of circumstances could exist to justify such a statute, then we may declare this one void, because in excess of the legislative power of the State. But if it could, we must presume it did. Of the propriety of legislative interference within the scope of legislative power, the legislature is the exclusive judge. . . .

We know that this is a power which may be abused; but that is no argument against its existence. For protection against abuses by legislatures the people must resort to the polls, not to the courts. . . .

We conclude, therefore, that the statute in question is not repugnant to the Constitution of the United States, and that there is no error in the judgment. . . .

Judgment affirmed.

MR. JUSTICE FIELD, with whom MR. JUSTICE STRONG concurs, dissenting.

. . . I am compelled to dissent from the decision of the court in this case, and from the reasons upon which that decision is founded. The principle upon which the opinion of the majority proceeds is, in my judgment, subversive of the rights of private property, heretofore believed to be protected by constitutional guaranties against legislative interference. . . .

The question presented . . . is one of the greatest importance,—whether it is within the competency of a State to fix the compensation which an individual may receive for the use of his own property in his private business, and for his services in connection with it. . . .

. . . The court holds that property loses something of its private character when employed in such a way as to be generally useful. The doctrine declared is that property "becomes clothed with a public interest when used in a manner to make it of public consequence, and affect the community at large;" and from such clothing the right of the legislature is deduced to control the use of the property, and to determine the compensation which the owner may receive for it. When Sir Matthew Hale, and the sages of the law in his day, spoke of property as affected by a public interest, and ceasing from that cause to be *juris privati* solely, that is, ceasing to be held merely in private right, they referred to property dedicated by the owner to public uses, or to property the use of which was granted by the government, or in connection with which special privileges were conferred. Unless the property was thus dedicated, or some right bestowed by the government was held with the property, either by specific grant or by prescription of so long a time as to imply a grant originally, the property was not affected by any public interest so as to be taken out of the category of property held in private right. But it is not in any such sense that the terms "clothing property with a public interest" are used in this case. From the nature of the business under consideration—the storage of grain—which, in any sense in which the words can be used, is a private business, in which the public are interested only as they are interested in the storage of other products of the soil, or in articles of manufacture, it is clear that the court intended to declare that, whenever one devotes his property to a business which is useful to the public,—"affects the community at large,"—the legislature can regulate the compensation which the owner may receive for its use, and for his own services in connection with it.

If this be sound law, if there be no protection, either in the principles upon which our republican government is founded, or in the prohibitions of the Constitution against such invasion of private rights, all property and all business in the State are held at the mercy of a majority of its legislature. . . .

. . . It is only where some right or privilege is conferred by the government or municipality upon the owner, which he can use in connection with his property, or by means of which the use of his property is rendered more valuable to him, or he thereby enjoys an advantage over others, that the compensation to be received by him becomes a legitimate matter of regulation. Submission to the regulation of compensation in such cases is an implied condition of the grant, and the State, in exercising its power of prescribing the compensation, only determines the conditions upon which its concession shall be enjoyed. When the privilege ends, the power of regulation ceases.

There is nothing in the character of the business of the defendants as warehousemen which called for the interference complained of in this case. Their buildings are not nuisances; their occupation of receiving and storing grain infringes upon no rights of others, disturbs no neighborhood, infects not the air, and in no respect prevents others from using and enjoying their property as to them may seem best. The legislation in question is nothing less than a bold assertion of absolute power by the State to control at its discretion the property and business of the citizen, and fix the compensation he shall receive. The will of the legislature is made the condition upon which the owner shall receive the fruits of his property and the just reward of his labor, industry, and enterprise. . . . The decision of the court in this case gives unrestrained license to legislative will. . . .

I am of opinion that the judgment of the Supreme Court of Illinois should be reversed.

Lochner v. *New York*

198 U.S. 45; 25 S. Ct. 539; 49 L. Ed. 937 (1905)

Joseph Lochner, a Utica, New York, bakery proprietor, was found guilty and fined $50 for violating an 1897 New York law that limited the hours of employment in bakeries and confectionery establishments to ten hours a day and sixty hours a week. When his conviction was sustained by the New York appellate courts, Lochner brought the case to the Supreme Court on a writ of error. *Opinion of the Court: Peckham, Brewer, Brown, Fuller, McKenna. Dissenting opinions: Harlan, Day, White; Holmes.*

MR. JUSTICE PECKHAM delivered the opinion of the Court. . . .

The statute necessarily interferes with the right of contract between the employer and employés, concerning the number of hours in which the latter may labor in the bakery of the employer. The general right to make a contract in relation to his business is part of the liberty of the individual protected by the Fourteenth Amendment of the Federal Constitution. . . . Under that provision no State can deprive any person of life, liberty or property without due process of law. The right to purchase or to sell labor is part of the liberty protected by this amendment, unless there are circumstances which exclude the right. There are, however, certain powers, existing in the sovereignty of each State in the Union, somewhat vaguely termed police powers, the exact description and limitation of which have not been attempted by the courts. Those powers, broadly stated, . . . relate to the safety, health, morals and general welfare of the public. Both property and liberty are held on such reasonable conditions as may be imposed by the governing power of the State in the exercise of those powers, and with such conditions the Fourteenth Amendment was not designed to interfere. . . .

It must, of course, be conceded that there is a limit to the valid exercise of the police power by the State. There is no dispute concerning this general proposition. Otherwise the Fourteenth Amendment would have no efficacy and the legislatures of the States would have unbounded power, and it would be enough to say that any piece of legislation was enacted to conserve the morals, the health or the safety of the people; such legislation would be valid, no matter how absolutely without foundation the claim might be. The claim of the police power would be a mere pretext—become another and delusive name for the supreme sovereignty of the State to be exercised free from constitutional restraint. This is not contended for. In every case that comes before this court, therefore, where legislation of this character is concerned and where the protection of the Federal Constitution is sought, the question necessarily arises: Is this a fair, reasonable and appropriate exercise of the police power of the State, or is it an unreasonable, unnecessary and arbitrary interference with the right of the individual to his personal liberty or to enter into those contracts in relation to labor which may seem to him appropriate or necessary for the support of himself and his family? Of course the liberty of contract relating to labor includes both parties to it. The one has as much right to purchase as the other to sell labor.

This is not a question of substituting the judgment of the court for that of the legislature. If the act be within the power of the State it is valid, although the judgment of the court might be totally opposed to the enactment of such a law. But the question would still remain: Is it within the police power of the State? and that question must be answered by the court.

The question whether this act is valid as a labor law, pure and simple, may be dismissed in a few words. There is no reasonable ground for interfering with the liberty of person or the right of free contract, by determining the hours of labor, in the occupation of a baker. There is no contention that bakers as a class are not equal in intelligence and capacity to men in other trades or manual occupations, or that they are not able to assert their rights and care for themselves without the protecting arm of the State, interfering with their independence of judgment and of action. They are in no sense wards of the State. Viewed in the light of a purely labor law, with no reference whatever to the question of health, we think that a law like the one before us involves neither the safety, the morals nor the welfare of the public, and that the interest of the public is not in the slightest degree affected by such an act. The law must be upheld, if at all, as a law pertaining to the health of the individual engaged in the occupation of a baker. It does not affect any other portion of the public than those who are engaged in that occupation. Clean and wholesome bread does not depend upon whether the baker works but ten hours per day or only sixty hours a week. . . .

We think the limit of the police power has been reached and passed in this case. There is, in our judgment, no reasonable foundation for holding this to be necessary or appropriate as a health law to safeguard the public health or the health of the individuals who are following the trade of a baker. . . .

We think that there can be no fair doubt that the trade of a baker, in and of itself, is not an unhealthy one to that degree which would authorize the legislature to interfere with the right to labor, and with the right of free contract on the part of the individual, either as employer or employé. In looking through statistics regarding all trades and occupations, it may be true that the trade of a baker does not appear to be as healthy as some other trades, and is also vastly more healthy than still others. . . .

. . . The act is not, within any fair meaning of the term, a health law, but is an illegal interference with the rights of individuals, both employers and employés, to make contracts regarding labor upon such terms as they may think best, or which they may agree upon with the other parties to such contracts. Statutes of the nature of that under review, limiting the hours in which grown and intelligent men may labor to earn their living, are mere meddlesome interferences with the rights of the individual, and they are not saved from condemnation by the claim that they are passed in the exercise of the police power and upon the subject of the health of the individual whose rights are interfered with, unless there be some fair ground, reasonable in and of itself, to say that there is material danger to the public health or to the health of the employés, if the hours of labor are not curtailed. . . .

It was further urged on the argument that restricting the hours of labor in the case of bakers was valid because it tended to cleanliness on the part of the workers, as a man was more apt to be cleanly when not overworked, and if cleanly then his "output" was also more likely to be so. . . . The connection, if any exists, is too shadowy and thin to build any argument for the interference of the legislature. If the man works ten hours a day it is all right, but if ten and a half or eleven his health is in danger and his bread may be unhealthful, and, therefore, he shall not be permitted to do it. This, we think, is unreasonable and entirely arbitrary. . . .

It is manifest to us that the limitation of the hours of labor as provided for in this section of the statute . . . has no such direct relation to and no such substantial effect upon the health of the employé, as to justify us in regarding the section as really a health law. It seems to us that the real object and purpose were simply to regulate the hours of labor between the master and his employés . . . in a private business, not dangerous in any degree to morals or in any real and substantial degree, to the health of the employés. Under such circumstances the freedom of master and employé to contract with each other in relation to their employment, and in defining the same, cannot be prohibited or interfered with, without violating the Federal Constitution. . . .

Reversed.

MR. JUSTICE HARLAN, with whom MR. JUSTICE WHITE and MR. JUSTICE DAY concur, dissenting. . . .

I take it to be firmly established that what is called the liberty of contract may, within certain limits, be subjected to regulations designed and calculated to promote the general welfare or to guard the public health, the public morals or the public safety. . . .

Granting . . . that there is a liberty of contract which cannot be violated even under the sanction of direct legislative enactment, but assuming, as according to settled law we may assume, that such liberty of contract is subject to such regulations as the State may reasonably prescribe for the common good and the well-being of society, what are the conditions under which the judiciary may declare such regulations to be in excess of legislative authority and void? Upon this point there is no room for dispute; for, the rule is universal that a legislative enactment, Federal or state, is never to be disregarded or held invalid unless it be, beyond question, plainly and palpably in excess of legislative power. . . . If there be doubt as to the validity of the statute, that doubt must therefore be resolved in favor of its validity, and the courts must keep their hands off, leaving the legislature to meet the responsibility for unwise legislation. If the end which the legislature seeks to accomplish be one to which its power extends, and if the means employed to that end, although not the wisest or best, are yet not plainly and palpably unauthorized by law, then the court cannot interfere. In other words, when the validity of a statute is questioned, the burden of proof, so to speak, is upon those who assert it to be unconstitutional. . . .

Let these principles be applied to the present case. . . .

It is plain that this statute was enacted in order to protect the physical well-being of those who work in bakery and confectionery establishments. . . . I find it impossible, in view of common experience, to say that there is here no real or substantial relation between the means employed by the State and the end sought to be accomplished by its legislation. . . . Nor can I say that the statute has no appropriate or direct connection with that protection to health which each State owes to her citizens, . . . or that it is not promotive of the health of the employés in question, . . . or that the regulation prescribed by the State is utterly unreasonable and extravagant or wholly arbitrary. . . . Still less can I say that the statute is, beyond question, a plain, palpable invasion of rights secured by the fundamental law. . . . Therefore I submit that this court will transcend its functions if it assumes to annul the statute of New York. It must be remembered that this statute does not apply to all kinds of business. It applies only to work in bakery and confectionery establishments, in which, as all know, the air constantly breathed by workmen is not as pure and healthful as that to be found in some other establishments or out of doors. . . .

. . . There are many reasons of a weighty, substantial character, based upon the experience of mankind, in support of the theory that, all things considered, more than ten hours' steady work each day, from week to week, in a bakery or confectionery establishment, may endanger the health, and shorten the lives of the workmen, thereby diminishing their physical and mental capacity to serve the State, and to provide for those dependent upon them.

If such reasons exist that ought to be the end of this case, for the State is not amenable to the judiciary, in respect of its legislative enactments, unless such enactments are plainly, palpably, beyond all question, inconsistent with the Constitution of the United States. We are not to presume that the state of New York has acted in bad faith. Nor can we assume that its legislature acted without due deliberation, or that it did not determine this question upon the fullest attainable information, and for the common good. We cannot say that the State has acted without reason nor ought we to proceed upon the theory that its action is a mere sham. Our duty, I submit, is to sustain the statute as not being in conflict with the Federal Constitution, for the reason—and such is an all-sufficient reason—it is not shown to be plainly and palpably inconsistent with that instrument. . . .

I take leave to say that the New York statute, in the particulars here involved, cannot be held to be in conflict with the Fourteenth Amendment, without enlarging the scope of the Amendment far beyond its original purpose and without bringing under the supervision of this court matters which have been supposed to belong exclusively to the legislative departments of the several States when exerting their conceded power to guard the health and safety of their citizens by such regulations as they in their wisdom deem best. . . .

MR. JUSTICE HOLMES, dissenting. . . .

This case is decided upon an economic theory which a large part of the country does not entertain. If it were a question whether I agreed with that theory, I should desire to study it further and long before making up my mind. But I do not conceive that to be my duty, because I strongly believe that my agreement or disagreement has nothing to do with the right of a majority to embody their opinions in law. It is settled by various decisions of this court that state constitutions and state laws may regulate life in many ways which we as legislators might think as injudicious or if you like as tyrannical as this, and which equally with this interfere with the liberty to contract. Sunday laws and usury laws are ancient examples. A more modern one is the prohibition of lotteries. . . . The Fourteenth Amendment does not enact Mr. Herbert Spencer's Social Statics. . . . A constitution is not intended to embody a particular economic theory, whether of paternalism and the organic relation of the citizen to the State or of *laissez faire*. It is made for people of fundamentally differing views, and the accident of our finding certain opinions natural and familiar or novel and even shocking ought not to conclude our judgment upon the question whether statutes embodying them conflict with the Constitution of the United States.

. . . I think that the word liberty in the Fourteenth Amendment is perverted when it is held to prevent the natural outcome of a dominant opinion, unless it can be said that a rational and fair man necessarily would admit that the statute proposed would infringe fundamental principles as they have been understood by the traditions of our people and our law. It does not need research to show that no such sweeping condemnation can be passed upon the statute before us. A reasonable man might think it a proper measure on the score of health. Men whom I certainly could not pronounce unreasonable would uphold it as a first instalment of a general regulation of the hours of work. . . .

West Coast Hotel Company v. *Parrish*

300 U.S. 379; 57 S. Ct. 578; 81 L. Ed. 703 (1937)

In 1913 the state legislature of Washington enacted a minimum wage law covering women and minors. The law provided for the establishment of an Individual Welfare Commission, which was authorized "to establish such standards of wages and conditions of labor for women and minors employed within the State of Washington as shall be held hereunder to be reasonable and not detrimental to health and morals, and which shall be sufficient for the decent maintenance of women." Elsie Parrish, employed as a chambermaid by the West Coast Hotel Company, together with her husband brought suit to recover the difference between the wages paid her and the minimum wage fixed pursuant to the state law. The minimum wage for her job was $14.50 for a forty-eight hour week. The trial court decided against Parrish and declared the law to be repugnant to the Due Process Clause of the Fourteenth Amendment. The Washington Supreme Court reversed the trial court and sustained the statute. The hotel company brought the case to the U.S. Supreme Court on appeal. *Opinion of the Court: Hughes, Brandeis, Cardozo, Roberts, Stone. Dissenting opinion: Sutherland, Butler, McReynolds, Van Devanter.*

MR. CHIEF JUSTICE HUGHES delivered the opinion of the Court.

This case presents the question of the constitutional validity of the minimum wage law of the State of Washington. . . .

The appellant relies upon the decision of this Court in *Adkins* v. *Children's Hospital* . . . , which held invalid the District of Columbia Minimum Wage Act, which was attacked under the due process clause of the Fifth Amendment. . . . The state court has refused to regard the decision in the *Adkins* case as determinative and has pointed to our decisions both before and since that case as justifying its position. We are of the opinion that this ruling of the state court demands on our part a reëxamination of the *Adkins* case. The importance of the question, in which many States having similar laws are concerned, the close division by which the decision in the *Adkins* case was reached, and the economic conditions which have supervened, and in the light of which the reasonableness of the exercise of the protective power of the State must be considered, make it not only appropriate, but we think imperative, that in deciding the present case the subject should receive fresh consideration. . . .

. . . The violation alleged by those attacking minimum wage regulation for women is deprivation of freedom of contract. What is this freedom? The Constitution does not speak of freedom of contract. It speaks of liberty and prohibits the deprivation of liberty without due process of law. In prohibiting that deprivation the Constitution does not recognize an absolute and uncontrollable liberty. Liberty in each of its phases has its history and connotation. But the liberty safeguarded is liberty in a social organization which requires the protection of law against the evils which menace the health, safety, morals and welfare of the people. Liberty under the Constitution is thus necessarily subject to the restraints of due process, and regulation which is reasonable in relation to its subject and is adopted in the interests of the community is due process.

. . . What can be closer to the public interest than the health of women and their protection from unscrupulous and overreaching employers? And if the protection of women is a legitimate end of the exercise of state power, how can it be said that the requirement of the payment of a minimum wage fairly fixed in order to meet the very necessities of existence is not an admissible means to that end? The legislature of the State was clearly entitled to consider the situation of women in employment, the fact that they are in the class receiving the least pay, that their bargaining power is relatively weak, and that they are the ready victims of those who would take advantage of their necessitous circumstances. The legislature was entitled to adopt measures to reduce the evils of the "sweating system," the exploiting of workers at wages so low as to be insufficient to meet the bare cost of living, thus making their very helplessness the occasion of a most injurious competition. The legislature had the right to consider that its minimum wage requirements would be an important aid in carrying out its policy of protection. The adoption of similar requirements by many States evidences a deep-seated conviction both as to the presence of the evil and as to the means adapted to check it. Legislative response to that conviction cannot be regarded as arbitrary or capricious, and that is all we have to decide. Even if the wisdom of the policy be regarded as debatable and its effects uncertain, still the legislature is entitled to its judgment.

There is an additional and compelling consideration which recent economic experience has brought into a strong light. The exploitation of a class of workers who are in an unequal position with respect to bargaining power and are thus relatively defenceless against the denial of a living wage is not only detrimental to their health and well being but casts a direct burden for their support upon the community. What these workers lose in wages the taxpayers are called upon to pay. The bare cost of living must be met. . . . The community is not bound to provide what is in effect a subsidy for unconscionable employers. The community may direct its law-making power to correct the abuse which springs from their selfish disregard of the public interest. . . .

Our conclusion is that the case of *Adkins* v. *Children's Hospital* . . . should be, and it is, overruled. The judgment of the Supreme Court of the State of Washington is

Affirmed.

Mr. Justice Sutherland, dissenting.

It is urged that the question involved should now receive fresh consideration, among other reasons, because of "the economic conditions which have supervened"; but the meaning of the Constitution does not change with the ebb and flow of economic events. We frequently are told in more general words that the Constitution must be construed in the light of the present. If by that it is meant that the Constitution is made up of living words that apply to every new condition which they include, the statement is quite true. But to say, if that be intended, that the words of the Constitution mean today what they did not mean when written—that is, that they do not apply to a situation now to which they would have applied then—is to rob that instrument of the essential element which continues it in force as the people have made it until they, and not their official agents, have made it otherwise. . . .

The judicial function is that of interpretation; it does not include the power of amendment under the guise of intepretation. To miss the point of difference between the two is to miss all that the phrase "supreme law of the land" stands for and to convert what was intended as inescapable and enduring mandates into mere moral reflections. . . .

Coming, then, to a consideration of the Washington statute, it first is to be observed that it is in every substantial respect identical with the statute involved in the *Adkins* case. Such vices as existed in the latter are present in the former. And if the *Adkins* case was properly decided, as we who join in this opinion think it was, it necessarily follows that the Washington statute is invalid. . . .

Neither the statute involved in the *Adkins* case nor the Washington statute, so far as it is involved here, has the slightest relation to the capacity or earning power of the employee, to the number of hours which constitute the day's work, the character of the place where the work is to be done, or the circumstances or surroundings of the employment. The sole basis upon which the question of validity rests is the assumption that the employee is entitled to receive a sum of money sufficient to provide a living for her, keep her in health and preserve her morals. . . .

What we said further, in that case . . . is equally applicable here . . . : "A statute which prescribes payment without regard to any of these things and solely with relation to circumstances apart from the contract of employment, the business affected by it and the work done under it, is so clearly the product of a naked, arbitrary exercise of power that it cannot be allowed to stand under the Constitution of the United States." . . .

Williamson v. *Lee Optical Company*

348 U.S. 483; 75 S. Ct. 461; 99 L. Ed. 563 (1955)

In 1953 the Oklahoma legislature passed a law that made it unlawful for any person other than a licensed ophthalmologist or optometrist to fit lenses to the face or to duplicate or replace lenses, except upon written prescriptive authority of a licensed ophthalmologist or optometrist. Lee Optical challenged the constitutionality of this law before a federal district court of three judges, alleging in part that it violated the Due Process Clause of the Fourteenth Amendment. The district court agreed, holding portions of the act unconstitutional, and the state of Oklahoma appealed to the Supreme Court. *Opinion of the Court: Douglas, Black, Burton, Clark, Frankfurter, Minton, Reed, Warren. Harlan did not participate.*

MR. JUSTICE DOUGLAS delivered the opinion of the Court. . . .

An ophthalmologist is a duly licensed physician who specializes in the care of the eyes. An optometrist examines eyes for refractive error, recognizes (but does not treat) diseases of the eye, and fills prescriptions for eyeglasses. The optician is an artisan qualified to grind lenses, fill prescriptions, and fit frames.

The effect of § 2 is to forbid the optician from fitting or duplicating lenses without a prescription from an ophthalmologist or optometrist. In practical effect, it means that no optician can fit old glasses into new frames or supply a lens, whether it be a new lens or one to duplicate a lost or broken lens, without a prescription. The District Court . . . rebelled at the notion that a State could require a prescription from an optometrist or ophthalmologist "to take old lenses and place them in new frames and then fit the completed spectacles to the *face* of the eyeglass wearer." . . . It held that such a requirement was not "reasonably and rationally related to the health and welfare of the people." . . . It was, accordingly, the opinion of the court that this provision of the law violated the Due Process Clause by arbitrarily interfering with the optician's right to do business.

The Oklahoma law may exact a needless, wasteful requirement in many cases. But it is for the legislature, not the courts, to balance the advantages and disadvantages of the new requirement. It appears that in many cases the optician can easily supply the new frames or new lenses without reference to the old written prescription. It also appears that many written prescriptions contain no directive data in regard to fitting spectacles to the face. But in some cases the directions contained in the prescription are essential, if the glasses are to be fitted so as to correct the particular defects of vision or alleviate the eye condition. The legislature might have concluded that the frequency of occasions when a prescription is necessary was sufficient to justify this regulation of the fitting of eyeglasses. Likewise, when it is necessary to duplicate a lens, a written prescription may or may not be necessary. But the legislature might have concluded that one was needed often enough to require one in every case. Or the legislature may have concluded that eye examinations were so critical, not only for correction of vision but also for detection of latent ailments or diseases, that every change in frames and every duplication of a lens should be accompanied by a prescription from a medical expert. To be sure, the present law does not require a new examination of the eyes every time the frames are changed or the lenses duplicated. For if the old prescription is on file with the optician, he can go ahead and make the new fitting or duplicate the lenses. But the law need not be in every respect logically consistent with its aims to be constitutional. It is enough that there is an evil at hand for correction, and that it might be thought that the particular legislative measure was a rational way to correct it.

The day is gone when this Court uses the Due Process Clause of the Fourteenth Amendment to strike down state laws, regulatory of business and industrial conditions, because they may be unwise, improvident, or out of harmony with a particular school of thought. . . . We emphasize again what Chief Justice Waite said in *Munn* v. *Illinois,* . . . "For protection against abuses by legislatures the people must resort to the polls, not to the courts." . . .

United States v. *Carolene Products Company*

304 U.S. 144; 58 S. Ct. 778; 82 L. Ed. 1234 (1938)

In what has become a famous footnote in an otherwise unimportant case, Justice Stone developed the justification for "more exact judicial scrutiny" where infringements of civil liberties (as opposed to economic rights) are involved. *Opinion of the Court: Stone, Brandeis, Hughes, Roberts. Concurring opinions: Black; Butler. Dissenting opinion: McReynolds. Cardozo and Reed did not participate.*

Mr. Justice Stone delivered the opinion of the Court....

Regulatory legislation affecting ordinary commercial transactions is not to be pronounced unconstitutional unless in the light of the facts made known or generally assumed it is of such a character as to preclude the assumption that it rests upon some rational basis within the knowledge and experience of the legislators.*

*There may be narrower scope for operation of the presumption of constitutionality when legislation appears on its face to be within a specific prohibition of the Constitution, such as those of the first ten amendments, which are deemed equally specific when held to be embraced within the Fourteenth.

It is unnecessary to consider now whether legislation which restricts those political processes which can ordinarily be expected to bring about repeal of undesirable legislation, is to be subjected to more exacting judicial scrutiny under the general prohibitions of the Fourteenth Amendment than are most other types of legislation....

Nor need we enquire whether similar considerations enter into the review of statutes directed at particular religious . . . or national . . . or racial minorities . . . whether prejudice against discrete and insular minorities may be a special condition, which tends seriously to curtail the operation of those political processes ordinarily to be relied upon to protect minorities, and which may call for a correspondingly more searching judicial inquiry.

Hawaii Housing Authority v. *Midkiff*

467 U.S. 229, 104 S. Ct. 2321 81, L. Ed. 2d 186 (1984)

As a result of the feudal land tenure system of the early high chiefs of the Hawaiian Islands, land in Hawaii was concentrated in the hands of a few large landowners. In the mid-1960s, after extensive hearings, the Hawaii Legislature discovered that while the Federal and State Governments owned almost 49 percent of the State's land, another 47 percent was in the hands of only 72 private landowners. To reduce the perceived social and economic problems that resulted from this land concentration, the Hawaii Legislature enacted the Land Reform Act of 1967, which created a land condemnation scheme whereby title in real property could be taken from lessors and transferred to lessees. Under the Act, lessees living on single-family residential lots within tracts at least five acres in size can ask the Hawaii Housing Authority (HHA) to condemn the property on which they live. If the HHA determines that a "public purpose" will be served, it is authorized to designate some or all of the lots in the tract for acquisition. Once it has acquired the "right, title, and interest" in the land, at prices set by a condemnation trial or by negotiation between lessors and lessees, it can sell the land titles to the applicant lessees. After the HHA had held a public hearing on the proposed acquisition of Frank E. Midkiff's lands, he and other trustees of landholding estates filed suit in U.S. District Court for the District of Hawaii, asking that the Act be declared unconstitutional and that its enforcement be enjoined. The District Court held the Act constitutional under the Public Use Clause of the Fifth Amendment, made applicable to the State under the Fourteenth Amendment. The Court of Appeals for the Ninth Circuit reversed, holding that the Act violated the "public use" requirement of the Fifth Amendment, and the HHA appealed to the U.S. Supreme Court. *Unanimous Opinion of the Court: O'Connor, Burger, Blackmun, Brennan, Powell, Rehnquist, Steven, White. Marshall did not participate.*

JUSTICE O'CONNOR delivered the opinion of the Court.

The Fifth Amendment of the United States Constitution provides, in pertinent part, that "private property [shall not] be taken for public use, without just compensation." These cases present the question whether the Public Use Clause of that Amendment, made applicable to the States through the Fourteenth Amendment, prohibits the State of Hawaii from taking, with just compensation, title in real property from lessors and transferring it to lessees in order to reduce the concentration of ownership of fees simple in the State. We conclude that it does not. . . .

The starting point for our analysis of the Act's constitutionality is the Court's decision in *Berman* v. *Parker* . . . (1954). In *Berman,* the Court held constitutional the District of Columbia Redevelopment Act of 1945. That Act provided both for the comprehensive use of the eminent domain power to redevelop slum areas and for the possible sale or lease of the condemned lands to private interests. In discussing whether the takings authorized by that Act were for a "public use," . . . the Court stated:

"We deal, in other words, with what traditionally has been known as the police power. An attempt to define its reach or trace its outer limits is fruitless, for each case must turn on its own facts. The definition is essentially the product of legislative determinations addressed to the purposes of government, purposes neither abstractly nor historically capable of complete definition. Subject to specific constitutional limitations, when the legislature has spoken, the public interest has been declared in terms well-nigh conclusive. In such cases the legislature, not the judiciary, is the main guardian of the public needs to be served by social legislation, whether it be Congress legislating concerning the District of Columbia . . . or the States legislating concerning local affairs. . . . This principle admits of no exception merely because the power of eminent domain is involved. . . . " . . .

There is, of course, a role for courts to play in reviewing a legislature's judgment of what constitutes a public use, even when the eminent domain power is equated with the police power. But . . . the Court has made clear that it will not substitute its judgment for a legislature's judgment as to what constitutes a public use "unless the use be palpably without reasonable foundation." . . .

To be sure, the Court's cases have repeatedly stated that "one person's property may not be taken for the benefit of another private person without a justifying public purpose, even though compensation be paid." . . . But where the exercise of the eminent domain power is rationally related to a conceivable public purpose, the Court has never held a compensated taking to be proscribed by the Public Use Clause. . . .

On this basis, we have no trouble concluding that the Hawaii Act is constitutional. The people of Hawaii have attempted, much as the settlers of the original 13 Colonies did, to reduce the perceived social and economic evils of a land oligopoly traceable to their monarchs. The land oligopoly has, according to the Hawaii Legislature, created artificial deterrents to the normal functioning of the State's residential land market and forced thousands of individual homeowners to lease, rather than buy, the land underneath their homes. Regulating oligopoly and the evils associated with it is a classic exercise of a State's police powers. . . . We cannot disapprove of Hawaii's exercise of this power.

Nor can we condemn as irrational the Act's approach to correcting the land oligopoly problem. The Act presumes that when a sufficiently large number of persons declare that they are willing but unable to buy lots at fair prices the land market is malfunctioning. When such a malfunction is signalled, the Act authorizes HHA to condemn lots in the relevant tract. The Act limits the number of lots any one tenant can purchase and authorizes HHA to use public funds to ensure that the market dilution goals will be achieved. This is a comprehensive and rational approach to identifying and correcting market failure.

Of course, this Act, like any other, may not be successful in achieving its intended goals. But "whether *in fact* the provision will accomplish its objectives is not the question: the [constitutional requirement] is satisfied if . . . the . . . [state] Legislature *rationally could have believed* that the [Act] would promote its objective." . . . When the legislature's purpose is legitimate and its means are not irrational, our cases make clear that empirical debates over the wisdom of takings—no less than debates over the wisdom of other kinds of socioeconomic legislation—are not to be carried out in the federal courts. Redistribution of fees simple to correct deficiencies in the market determined by the state legislature to be attributable to land oligopoly is a rational exercise of the eminent domain power.

The mere fact that property taken outright by eminent domain is transferred in the first instance to private beneficiaries does not condemn that taking as having only a private purpose. The Court long ago rejected any literal requirement that condemned property be put into use for the general public. . . . As the unique way titles were held in Hawaii skewed the land market, exercise of the power of eminent domain was justified. The Act advances its purposes without the State taking actual possession of the land. In such cases, government does not itself have to use property to legitimate the taking; it is only the taking's purpose, and not its mechanics, that must pass scrutiny under the Public Use Clause.

Similarly, the fact that a state legislature, and not the Congress, made the public use determination does not mean that judicial deference is less appropriate. Judicial deference is required because, in our system of government, legislatures are better able to assess what public purposes should be advanced by an exercise of the taking power. State legislatures are as capable as Congress of making such determinations within their respective spheres of authority. . . . Thus, if a legislature, state or federal, determines there are substantial reasons for an exercise of the taking power, courts must defer to its determination that the taking will serve a public use.

The State of Hawaii has never denied that the Constitution forbids even a compensated taking of property when executed for no reason other than to confer a private benefit on a particular private party. A purely private taking could not withstand the scrutiny of the public use requirement; it would serve no legitimate purpose of government and would thus be void. But no purely private taking is involved in this case. The Hawaii Legislature enacted its Land Reform Act not to benefit a particular class of identifiable individuals but to attack certain perceived evils of concentrated property ownership in Hawaii—a legitimate public purpose. Use of the condemnation power to achieve this purpose is not irrational. Since we assume for purposes of this appeal that the weighty demand of just compensation has been met, the requirements of the Fifth and Fourteenth Amendments have been satisfied. Accordingly, we reverse the judgment of the Court of Appeals, and remand these cases for further proceedings in conformity with this opinion.

Nollan v. *California Coastal Commission*

483 U.S. 825, 107 S. Ct. 3141, 97 L. Ed. 2d 677 (1987)

The California Coastal Commission granted a permit to James and Marilyn Nollan to replace a small bungalow on their beachfront lot with a larger house upon the condition that they allow the public an easement to pass across their beach, which was located between two public beaches. The Nollans filed a petition for writ of administrative mandamus asking the Ventura County Superior Court to invalidate the access condition. They argued that the condition could not be imposed absent evidence that their proposed development would have a direct adverse impact on public access to the beach. The Court agreed and remanded the case to the Commission for a full evidentiary hearing on that issue. On remand, the Commission held a public hearing and made further factual findings; it reaffirmed its imposition of the condition, finding that the new house would increase blockage of the view of the ocean, thus contributing to the development of "a 'wall' of residential structures" that would prevent the public "psychologically . . . from realizing a stretch of coastline exists nearby that they have every right to visit." The Nollans filed a supplemental petition for a writ of administrative mandamus with the Superior Court, arguing that imposition of the access condition violated the Takings Clause of the Fifth Amendment, as incorporated against the states by the Fourteenth Amendment. The Superior Court avoided the constitutional question but ruled in their favor on statutory grounds. In its view, the administrative record did not provide an adequate factual basis for concluding that replacement of the bungalow with the house would create a direct or cumulative burden on public access to the sea. The Commission appealed to the California Court of Appeal, which reversed, holding that the access condition violated neither California statutes nor the Takings Clause of the U.S. Constitution. The Nollans appealed to the U.S. Supreme Court. *Opinion of the Court: Scalia, Rehnquist, O'Connor, Powell, White. Dissenting opinions: Brennan, Marshall; Blackmun; Stevens, Blackmun.*

JUSTICE SCALIA delivered the opinion of the Court. . . .

Had California simply required the Nollans to make an easement across their beachfront available to the public on a permanent basis in order to increase public access to the beach, rather than conditioning their permit to rebuild their house on their agreeing to do so, we have no doubt there would have been a taking. To say that the appropriation of a public easement across a landowner's premises does not constitute the taking of a property interest but rather (as JUSTICE BRENNAN contends) "a mere restriction on its use," is to use words in a manner that deprives them of all their ordinary meaning. Indeed, one of the principal uses of the eminent domain power is to assure that the government be able to require conveyance of just such interests, so long as it pays for them. . . . Perhaps because the point is so obvious, we have never been confronted with a controversy that required us to rule upon it, but our cases' analysis of the effect of other governmental action leads to the same conclusion. We have repeatedly held that, as to property reserved by its owner for private use, "the right to exclude [others is] 'one of the most essential sticks in the bundle of rights that are commonly characterized as property.' " . . .

JUSTICE BRENNAN argues that while this might ordinarily be the case, the California Constitution's prohibition on any individual's "exclu[ding] the right of way to [any navigable] water whenever it is required for any public purpose," Art X, § 4 produces a different result here. . . . There are a number of difficulties with that argument. Most obviously, the right of way sought here is not naturally described as one *to* navigable water (from the street to the sea) but *along* it; it is at least highly questionable whether the text of the California Constitution has any prima facie application to the situation before us. Even if it does, however, several California cases suggest that JUSTICE BRENNAN'S interpretation of the effect of the clause is erroneous, and that to obtain easements of access across private property the State must proceed through its eminent domain power. . . .

In light of these uncertainties, and given the fact that, as JUSTICE BLACKMUN notes, the Court of Appeal did not rest its decision on Art. X, § 4, we should assuredly not take it upon ourselves to resolve this question of California constitutional law in the first instance.

Given, then, that requiring uncompensated conveyance of the easement outright would violate the Fourteenth Amendment, the question becomes whether requiring it to be conveyed as a condition for issuing a land-use permit alters the outcome. We have long recognized that land-use regulation does not effect a taking if it "substantially advance[s] legitimate state interests" and does not "den[y] an owner economically viable use of his land," *Agins* v. *Tiburon,* 447 U. S. 255, 260 (1980). See also *Penn Central Transportation Co.* v. *New York City,* 438 U. S. 104, 127 (1978) ("[A] use restriction may constitute a 'taking' if not reasonably necessary to the effectuation of a substantial government purpose"). Our cases have not elaborated on the standards for determining what constitutes a "legitimate state interest" or what type of connection between the regulation and the state interest satisfies the requirement that the former "substantially advance" the latter. They have made clear, however, that a broad range of governmental purposes and regulations satisfies these requirements. . . . The Commission argues that among these permissible purposes are protecting the public's ability to see the beach, assisting the public in overcoming the "psychological barrier" to using the beach created by a developed shorefront, and preventing congestion on the public beaches. We assume, without deciding, that this is so—in which case the Commission unquestionably would be able to deny the Nollans their permit outright if their new house (alone, or by reason of the cumulative impact produced in conjunction with other construction,*) would substantially impede these purposes, unless the denial would interfere so drastically with the Nollans' use of their property as to constitute a taking. . . .

The Commission argues that a permit condition that serves the same legitimate police-power purpose as a refusal to issue the permit should not be found to be a taking if the refusal to issue the permit would not constitute a taking. We agree. Thus, if the Commission attached to the permit some condition that would have protected the public's ability to see the beach notwithstanding construction of the new house—for example, a height limitation, a width restriction, or a ban on fences—so long as the Commission could have exercised its police power (as we have assumed it could) to forbid construction of the house altogether, imposition of the condition would also be constitutional. Moreover (and here we come closer to the facts of the present case), the condition would be constitutional even if it consisted of the requirement that the Nollans provide a viewing spot on their property for passersby with whose sighting of the ocean their new house would interfere. Although such a requirement, constituting a permanent grant of continuous access to the property, would have to be considered a taking if it were not attached to a development permit, the Commission's assumed power to forbid construction of the house in order to protect the public's view of the beach must surely include the power to condition construction upon some concession by the owner, even a concession of property rights, that serves the same end. If a prohibition designed to accomplish that purpose would be a legitimate exercise of the police power rather than a taking, it would be strange to conclude that providing the owner an alternative to that prohibition which accomplishes the same purpose is not.

The evident constitutional propriety disappears, however, if the condition substituted for the prohibition utterly fails to further the end advanced as the justification for the prohibition. When that essential nexus is eliminated, the situation becomes the same as if California law forbade shouting fire in a crowded theater, but granted dispensations to those willing to contribute $100 to the state treasury. While a ban on shouting fire can be a core exercise of the State's police power to protect the public safety, and can thus meet even our stringent standards for regulation of speech, adding the unrelated condition

*If the Nollans were being singled out to bear the burden of California's attempt to remedy these problems, although they had not contributed to it more than other coastal landowners, the State's action, even if otherwise valid, might violate either the incorporated Takings Clause or the Equal Protection Clause. One of the principal purposes of the Takings Clause is "to bar Government from forcing some people alone to bear public burdens which, in all fairness and justice, should be borne by the public as a whole." *Armstrong* v. *United States,* 364 U. S. 40, 49 (1960); see also *San Diego Gas & Electric Co.* v. *San Diego,* 450 U. S. 621, 656 (1981) (BRENNAN, J., dissenting); *Penn Central Transportation Co.* v. *New York City,* 438 U. S. 104, 123 (1978). But that is not the basis of the Nollans' challenge here.

alters the purpose to one which, while it may be legitimate, is inadequate to sustain the ban. Therefore, even though, in a sense, requiring a $100 tax contribution in order to shout fire is a lesser restriction on speech than an outright ban, it would not pass constitutional muster. Similarly here, the lack of nexus between the condition and the original purpose of the building restriction converts that purpose to something other than what it was. The purpose then becomes, quite simply, the obtaining of an easement to serve some valid governmental purpose, but without payment of compensation. Whatever may be the outer limits of "legitimate state interests" in the takings and land-use context, this is not one of them. In short, unless the permit condition serves the same governmental purpose as the development ban, the building restriction is not a valid regulation of land use but "an out-and-out plan of extortion.". . .

The Commission claims that it concedes as much, and that we may sustain the condition at issue here by finding that it is reasonably related to the public need or burden that the Nollans' new house creates or to which it contributes. We can accept, for purposes of discussion, the Commission's proposed test as to how close a "fit" between the condition and the burden is required, because we find that this case does not meet even the most untailored standards. The Commission's principal contention to the contrary essentially turns on a play on the word "access." The Nollans' new house, the Commission found, will interfere with "visual access" to the beach. That in turn (along with other shorefront development) will interfere with the desire of people who drive past the Nollans' house to use the beach, thus creating a "psychological barrier" to "access." The Nollans' new house will also, by a process not altogether clear from the Commission's opinion but presumably potent enough to more than offset the effects of the psychological barrier, increase the use of the public beaches, thus creating the need for more "access." These burdens on "access" would be alleviated by a requirement that the Nollans provide "lateral access" to the beach.

Rewriting the argument to eliminate the play on words makes clear that there is nothing to it. It is quite impossible to understand how a requirement that people already on the public beaches be able to walk across the Nollans' property reduces any obstacles to viewing the beach created by the new house. It is also impossible to understand how it lowers any "psychological barrier" to using the public beaches, or how it helps to remedy any additional congestion on them caused by construction of the Nollans' new house. We therefore find that the Commission's imposition of the permit condition cannot be treated as an exercise of its land-use power for any of these purposes. Our conclusion on this point is consistent with the approach taken by every other court that has considered the question, with the exception of the California state courts.

JUSTICE BRENNAN argues that imposition of the access requirement is not irrational. In his version of the Commission's argument, the reason for the requirement is that in its absence, a person looking toward the beach from the road will see a street of residential structures including the Nollans' new home and conclude that there is no public beach nearby. If, however, that person sees people passing and repassing along the dry sand behind the Nollans' home, he will realize that there is a public beach somewhere in the vicinity. . . . The Commission's action, however, was based on the opposite factual finding that the wall of houses completely blocked the view of the beach and that a person looking from the road would not be able to see it at all.

Even if the Commission had made the finding that JUSTICE BRENNAN proposes, however, it is not certain that it would suffice. We do not share JUSTICE BRENNAN's confidence that the Commission "should have little difficulty in the future in utilizing its expertise to demonstrate a specific connection between provisions for access and burdens on access," . . . that will avoid the effect of today's decision. We view the Fifth Amendment's Property Clause to be more than a pleading requirement, and compliance with it to be more than an exercise in cleverness and imagination. As indicated earlier, our cases describe the condition for abridgment of property rights through the police power as a "*substantial* advanc[ing]" of a legitimate state interest. We are inclined to be particularly careful about the adjective where the actual conveyance of property is made a condition to the lifting of a land-use restriction, since in that context there is heightened risk that the purpose is avoidance of the compensation requirement, rather than the stated police power objective.

We are left, then, with the Commission's justification for the access requirement unrelated to land-use regulation:

> Finally, the Commission notes that there are several existing provisions of pass and repass lateral access benefits already given by past Faria Beach Tract applicants as a result of prior coastal permit decisions. The access required as a condition of this permit is part of a comprehensive program to provide continuous public access along Faria Beach as the lots undergo development or redevelopment. . . .

That is simply an expression of the Commission's belief that the public interest will be served by a continuous strip of publicly accessible beach along the coast. The Commission may well be right that it is a good idea, but that does not establish that the Nollans (and other coastal residents) alone can be compelled to contribute to its realization. Rather, California is free to advance its "comprehensive program," if it wishes, by using its power of eminent domain for this "public purpose," but if it wants an easement across the Nollans' property, it must pay for it.

Reserved.

JUSTICE BRENNAN, with whom JUSTICE MARSHALL joins, dissenting.

Appellants in this case sought to construct a new dwelling on their beach lot that would both diminish visual access to the beach and move private development closer to the public tidelands. The Commission reasonably concluded that such "buildout," both individually and cumulatively, threatens public access to the shore. It sought to offset this encroachment by obtaining assurance that the public may walk along the shoreline in order to gain access to the ocean. The Court finds this an illegitimate exercise of the police power, because it maintains that there is no reasonable relationship between the effect of the development and the condition imposed.

The first problem with this conclusion is that the Court imposes a standard of precision for the exercise of a State's police power that has been discredited for the better part of this century. Furthermore, even under the Court's cramped standard, the permit condition imposed in this case directly responds to the specific type of burden on access created by appellants' development. Finally, a review of those factors deemed most significant in takings analysis makes clear that the Commission's action implicates none of the concerns underlying the Takings Clause. The Court has thus struck down the Commission's reasonable effort to respond to intensified development along the California coast, on behalf of landowners who can make no claim that their reasonable expectations have been disrupted. The Court has, in short, given appellants a windfall at the expense of the public. . . .

The Commission is charged by both the State Constitution and legislature to preserve overall public access to the California coastline. . . . The Commission has sought to discharge its responsibilities in a flexible manner. It has sought to balance private and public interests and to accept tradeoffs: to permit development that reduces access in some ways as long as other means of access are enhanced. In this case, it has determined that the Nollans' burden on access would be offset by a deed restriction that formalizes the public's right to pass along the shore. In its informed judgment, such a tradeoff would preserve the net amount of public access to the coastline. The Court's insistence on a precise fit between the forms of burden and condition on each individual parcel along the California coast would penalize the Commission for its flexibility, hampering the ability to fulfill its public trust mandate.

The Court's demand for this precise fit is based on the assumption that private landowners in this case possess a reasonable expectation regarding the use of their land that the public has attempted to disrupt. In fact, the situation is precisely the reverse: it is private landowners who are the interlopers. The public's expectation of access considerably antedates any private development on the coast. Article X, § 4 of the California Constitution, adopted in 1879, declares:

> No individual, partnership, or corporation, claiming or possessing the frontage or tidal lands of a harbor, bay, inlet, estuary, or other navigable water in this State, shall be permitted to exclude the right of way to such water whenever it is required for any public pur-

> pose, nor to destroy or obstruct the free navigation of such water; and the Legislature shall enact such laws as will give the most liberal construction to this provision, so that access to the navigable waters of this State shall always be attainable for the people thereof.

It is therefore private landowners who threaten the disruption of settled public expectations. Where a private landowner has had a reasonable expectation that his or her property will be used for exclusively private purposes, the disruption of this expectation dictates that the government pay if it wishes the property to be used for a public purpose. In this case, however, the State has sought to protect *public* expectations of access from disruption by private land use. The State's exercise of its police power for this purpose deserves no less deference than any other measure designed to further the welfare of state citizens. . . .

Even if we accept the Court's unusual demand for a precise match between the condition imposed and the specific type of burden on access created by the appellants, the State's action easily satisfies this requirement. First, the lateral access condition serves to dissipate the impression that the beach that lies behind the wall of homes along the shore is for private use only. It requires no exceptional imaginative powers to find plausible the Commission's point that the average person passing along the road in front of a phalanx of imposing permanent residences, including the appellants' new home, is likely to conclude that this particular portion of the shore is not open to the public. If, however, that person can see that numerous people are passing and repassing along the dry sand, this conveys the message that the beach is in fact open for use by the public. Furthermore, those persons who go down to the public beach a quarter-mile away will be able to look down the coastline and see that persons have continuous access to the tidelands, and will observe signs that proclaim the public's right of access over the dry sand. The burden produced by the diminution in visual access—the impression that the beach is not open to the public—is thus directly alleviated by the provision for public access over the dry sand. The Court therefore has an unrealistically limited conception of what measures could reasonably be chosen to mitigate the burden produced by a diminution of visual access. . . .

The fact that the Commission's action is a legitimate exercise of the police power does not, of course, insulate it from a takings challenge, for when "regulation goes too far it will be recognized as a taking." *Pennsylvania Coal Co.* v. *Mahon.* Conventional takings analysis underscores the implausibility of the Court's holding, for it demonstrates that this exercise of California's police power implicates none of the concerns that underlie our takings jurisprudence. . . .

. . . The character of the regulation in this case is not unilateral government action, but a condition on approval of a development request submitted by appellants. The state has not sought to interfere with any pre-existing property interest, but has responded to appellants' proposal to intensify development on the coast. Appellants themselves chose to submit a new development application, and could claim no property interest in its approval. They were aware that approval of such development would be conditioned on preservation of adequate public access to the ocean. The State has initiated no action against appellants' property; had the Nollans' not proposed more intensive development in the coastal zone, they would never have been subject to the provision that they challenge.

Examination of the economic impact of the Commission's action reinforces the conclusion that no taking has occurred. Allowing appellants to intensify development along the coast in exchange for ensuring public access to the ocean is a classic instance of government action that produces a "reciprocity of advantage." . . . Appellants have been allowed to replace a one-story 521-square-foot beach home with a two-story 1,674-square foot residence and an attached two-car garage, resulting in development covering 2,464 square feet of the lot. Such development obviously significantly increases the value of appellants' property; appellants make no contention that this increase is offset by any diminution in value resulting from the deed restriction, much less that the restriction made the property less valuable than it would have been without the new construction. Furthermore, appellants gain an additional benefit from the Commission's permit condition program. They are able to walk along the beach beyond the confines of their own property only because the Commission has required deed restrictions as a condition of approving other new beach developments. Thus appellants benefit both as private landowners and as members of the public from the fact that new development permit requests are conditioned on preservation of public access. . . .

. . . The Court's insistence on a precise accounting system in this case is insensitive to the fact that increasing intensity of development in many areas calls for farsighted, comprehensive planning that takes into account both the interdependence of land uses and the cumulative impact of development. . . .

. . . State agencies therefore require considerable flexibility in responding to private desires for development in a way that guarantees the preservation of public access to the coast. They should be encouraged to regulate development in the context of the overall balance of competing uses of the shoreline. The Court today does precisely the opposite, overruling an eminently reasonable exercise of an expert state agency's judgment, substituting its own narrow view of how this balance should be struck. Its reasoning is hardly suited to the complex reality of natural resource protection in the 20th century. I can only hope that today's decision is an aberration, and that a broader vision ultimately prevails.

I dissent.

12
FREEDOM OF SPEECH, PRESS, AND ASSOCIATION

The First Amendment speaks in strikingly absolute terms: "Congress shall make no law . . . abridging the freedom of speech, or of the press." The Supreme Court's interpretation of these guarantees has been both broader and narrower than a literal reading of the amendment might suggest. The Court has ruled that the amendment protects channels of communication other than speech and press, including those (e.g., motion pictures and television) developed since the amendment's adoption. It has also extended some protection to actions undertaken with communicative intent (e.g., demonstrations, picketing, and symbolic acts), even if they do not entail speech. Acknowledging that "effective advocacy of both public and private points of view, particularly controversial ones, is undeniably enhanced by group association," the Court has recognized a First Amendment right to freedom of association.[1] Most importantly, in *Gitlow* v. *New York* (1925) the justices ruled that under the Due Process Clause of the Fourteenth Amendment, the First Amendment's restrictions likewise apply to state regulations of speech and press. Since *Gitlow,* the vast majority of the Court's free speech cases have involved challenges to state or local enactments.

On the other hand, the Court has never held that the First Amendment prohibits all regulation of speech and press.[2] It has upheld restrictions on the time, place, and manner of expression, such as the regulations governing the use of loudspeakers that were challenged in *Kovacs* v. *Cooper* (1949). Constitutional protection has been denied altogether to some categories of expression ("the lewd and the obscene, the profane, the libelous, and the insulting or 'fighting' words") and extended only in a limited way to others, such as commercial advertising.[3] Finally, it generally has held that the protection accorded expression depends upon the effects it is likely to produce. As Justice Oliver Wendell Holmes noted: "The most stringent protection of free speech would not protect a man in falsely shouting fire in a theater and causing a panic."[4]

General acceptance of these propositions notwithstanding, the Court has not achieved a consensus on First Amendment issues. The justices have disagreed sharply on the standards to be applied in evaluating First Amendment claims, on the application of these standards in individual cases, and on the level of deference to be accorded legislative judgments when they impinge upon speech and press. In exploring the bases of these differences, this chapter turns first to the debate over the aims of the First Amendment and shows how the differing interpretations of the ends of the First Amendment have found expression in the standards the Court has employed in press and speech cases.

THE MEANING OF THE FIRST AMENDMENT

Because the First Amendment prohibits all laws abridging the freedom of speech and of the press, the meaning of the amendment depends on the scope of those freedoms. In drawing up the Bill of Rights, the Framers were concerned more with protecting existing freedoms than with forging new liberties, and therefore the understanding of those freedoms which prevailed in English law is relevant to understanding the Framers' aims. William Blackstone, whose *Commentaries* clearly influenced the Framers, summarized the English law immediately prior to the American Revolution:

> The liberty of the press . . . consists in laying no previous restraints upon publications, and not in freedom from censure for criminal matter when published.
>
> . . . [T]o punish (as the law does at present) any dangerous or offensive writings, which when published, shall on a fair and impartial trial be adjudged of a pernicious tendency, is necessary for the preservation of peace and good order, a government and religion, the only solid foundations of civil liberty.[5]

Under English law, then, freedom of the press did not encompass the right to publish whatever one chose without fear of punishment, for that would jeopardize the peace and good order that government was charged with maintaining; it merely encompassed the right to be free from prior censorship. Under this system, the guarantee of a jury trial, which involved judgment by one's peers, presumably ensured that the power to punish press abuses could not be used to suppress legitimate publications.

Clearly, the Framers sought to provide protection as extensive as that existing in England. Many scholars and justices have concluded, however, that the Framers' aims were not so limited.[6] They have observed that because the First Amendment protects not only freedom of the press but also freedom of speech, which cannot be subjected to prior censorship, it must prohibit more than prior restraints on expression. In addition, they have noted that under English law, writers could be punished for seditious libel (criticism of the government)—a position which is inconsistent with the character of the government created by the Constitution. And indeed, when Congress outlawed seditious libel in the Sedition Act of 1798, opponents of the act contended that it violated the First Amendment, and it was repealed within three years.[7]

This focus on the character of the government established by the Constitution leads to a more expansive interpretation of the meaning of the First Amendment. As Justice Harlan Stone noted in his famous *Carolene Products* footnote (see Chapter 11), restrictions on political expression are constitutionally suspect because they cripple the political process and prevent the repeal of undesirable legislation. Only through the unfettered discussion of political alternatives, moreover, can the citizenry reach informed judgments about the policies government should pursue. Justice Louis Brandeis eloquently summarized the political importance of freedom of expression in *Whitney* v. *California* (1927):

> [The Framers] believed that freedom to think as you will and to speak as you think are means indispensable to the discovery of political truth; that without free speech and assembly, discussion would be futile; that with them, discussion affords ordinarily adequate protection against the dissemination of noxious doctrine; that the greatest menace to freedom is an inert people; that public discussion is a political duty; and that this should be a fundamental principle of the American government.[8]

Justice Brandeis' analysis left several important questions unanswered, however. First of all, if the First Amendment protects political speech because it is a prerequisite for self-government, does that protection extend only to speech advocating political alternatives consistent with a system of self-government? More specifically, does the First Amendment protect advocacy of unlawful actions or of the violent overthrow of the government? Then, too, Brandeis referred to free discussion as affording "ordinarily adequate protection against the dissemination of noxious doctrines," which implies that free discussion sometimes will not be adequate. Under what conditions, therefore, may other measures, including the suppression of speech, constitutionally be employed to combat the spread of dangerous views? Finally, in *Whitney* Brandeis dealt solely with political speech and its importance for self-government, thus leaving open the question of whether nonpolitical speech is entitled to First Amendment protection. On the one hand, some of the same arguments used to support political expression can be applied to nonpolitical expression: the suppression of unpopular moral or scientific ideas, like the suppression of political views, can enshrine error and thwart the search for truth. On the other hand, much nonpolitical speech is not concerned with the search for truth. Does the First Amendment extend protection to speech on all subjects? And if so, how broad is the protection it provides?

As these questions suggest, examination of the aims the Framers sought to achieve in adopting the First Amendment has not ended the debate about its meaning. Justices, as well as legal scholars, have arrived at quite different understandings of the ends the First Amendment was designed to serve, and these divergent views have been reflected in the various standards the Court has used in deciding First Amendment cases.

FIRST AMENDMENT STANDARDS

The Bad Tendency Test

The bad tendency test served as the Supreme Court's initial First Amendment standard. During the decade following World War I, in such cases as *Abrams* v. *United States* (1919), *Gitlow* v. *New York* (1925), and *Whitney* v. *California* (1927), the Court employed this standard in upholding the convictions of several political radicals. Underlying the bad tendency test is the assumption that the First Amendment, like other constitutional provisions, was designed to promote the public good. It follows that types of speech that have good effects are entitled to constitutional protection, whereas speech that threatens the security, order, or morals of the society may be regulated by the legislature. The decisive consideration, then, is whether the regulated speech is likely to produce bad effects—and this, the Court held, is primarily a legislative question. In defining its own role, the Court declared that "every presumption is to be indulged in favor of the validity of the statute."

In adopting this standard, the Court maintained that the First Amendment was never intended to protect all speech and publications; rather, this amendment, like other provisions of the Bill of Rights, merely embodied guarantees that had existed under English law. Because English law permitted prosecutions for abuses of freedom of the press, so did the First Amendment. And because legislators are popularly elected and are more familiar than judges with societal conditions, legislative judgments about the types of speech that are harmful generally should prevail. Under this standard, therefore, legislation affecting speech and press received no closer judicial scrutiny than did any other legislation.

The Clear-and-Present-Danger Test

Dissatisfaction with the suppression of speech and the press possible under the bad tendency test led to the development of the clear-and-present-danger test, which was first enunciated by Justice Oliver Wendell Holmes in *Schenck* v. *United States* (1919). In Holmes's words, "The question in every case is whether the words are used in such circumstances and are of such a nature as to create a clear and present danger that they will bring about the substantive evils that Congress has a right to prevent." This test resembles the bad tendency test in permitting the punishment of speech that produces harmful effects, but it imposes more exacting criteria for determining harm. The clear-and-present-danger test requires the government to demonstrate that the specific speech, in the context in which it occurred, created a danger to the achievement of permissible governmental objectives, and that the likelihood of harm was both substantial ("clear") and proximate ("present").

Throughout the decade following *Schenck,* Holmes and Justice Louis Brandeis sought to refine the test and clarify its constitutional foundations. Dissenting in *Abrams,* Holmes asserted that the "theory of our Constitution" was that the public interest was best served by fostering a "free trade in ideas." The First Amendment, he argued, reflected the Framers' conviction that "the best test of truth is the power of thought to get itself accepted in the competition of the market."[9] When government intervenes in this marketplace, suppressing harmful speech, it interferes with society's best mechanism for discovering truth. Such intervention, therefore, can be justified only when speech leads to substantial harm so immediately that there is no opportunity for further discussion to exert a corrective effect.

For over a decade the clear-and-present-danger test proved singularly ineffective in protecting speech and press. In no case was the test used to overturn a conviction; and only in *Schenck,* in which Justice Holmes upheld a conviction under the Espionage Act, did a majority of the justices endorse it. In *Herndon* v. *Lowry* (1937), however, the Court relied on it in reversing a conviction for distributing Communist Party literature. From that point until the early 1950s, the clear-and-present-danger test enjoyed broad support as a general standard for deciding First Amendment questions. Frequently alluding to the "preferred position" of First Amendment freedoms and its special responsibility to protect them, the Court applied the test in a wide range of cases to invalidate restrictions on speech and press.

Dennis v. *United States,* (1951) in which the Court upheld the convictions of Communist Party leaders for conspiring to advocate the overthrow of the government, marked a fundamental shift away from the clear-and-present-danger test. Speaking for four justices, Chief Justice Fred Vinson asserted that the situation in *Dennis* required a reformulation of Holmes's test: "In each case [courts] must ask whether the gravity of the evil, discounted by its improbability, justifies such invasion of free speech as is necessary to avoid the danger." In dissent, Justices Hugo Black and William Douglas observed that faithful application of Holmes's test meant reversal of the convictions. Yet this observation explains Vinson's modification of the test. Having determined that the clear-and-present-danger test offered too much protection—"the words cannot mean that before the Government may act, it must wait until the *putsch* is about to be executed, that plans have been laid and the signal is awaited"—Vinson sought to reconcile it with the community's need to deal with perceived threats to its safety. This perception that the clear-

and-present-danger test protected too much, together with the dissenters' belief that it protected too little, account for the Court's abandonment of the test. Since *Dennis*, it has rarely been invoked, as the justices have shied away from general standards for resolving First Amendment issues. On the other hand, the Court's opinions in cases such as *Brandenburg* v. *Ohio* (1969) have continued to reflect the concerns, if not always the language, of Holmes and Brandeis.

The Balancing Test

In *Kovacs* v. *Cooper* (1949), Justice Felix Frankfurter proposed the balancing test as an alternative to the clear-and-present-danger test and, in particular, to the Court's emphasis on a "preferred position" for First Amendment rights. The balancing test actually is less a standard than an approach. First Amendment cases typically involve conflicts between individual rights and the attainment of other governmental ends. Frankfurter contended that by automatically elevating individual rights to a "preferred position," the Court had oversimplified issues and predetermined outcomes. Such concentration on the single goal of protecting speech, he added, had no constitutional basis because the Constitution was designed to promote a variety of ends. What was necessary, rather, was an impartial balancing of competing claims on a case-by-case basis. Frankfurter urged that in undertaking this task, judges assign great weight to the balancing already undertaken by the legislative branch.

First endorsed by the Court in *American Communications Association* v. *Douds* (1950), balancing was employed during the 1950s and early 1960s in several cases involving legislative action against persons and groups viewed as subversive. More recently, however, the justices have tended to combine elements of balancing and of "preferred position." When government has sought to achieve legitimate ends by regulating the *mode* of expression, the Court typically has attempted to balance the competing claims of government and of those affected by the regulation, as in its decisions dealing with "symbolic speech" (actions designed to communicate ideas) and with time, place, and manner regulations. But when government has sought to achieve its ends by restricting the *content* or *extent* of expression, the Court usually has adopted a more stringent standard: "balancing of interests with an especially heavy weight given to the claims of speech."[10] Thus the Court in *Gibson* v. *Florida Legislative Investigating Committee* (1963) required that Florida demonstrate an "immediate, substantial and subordinating state interest" to justify a legislative inquiry that intruded on a witness's freedom of association. And in *Elrod* v. *Burns* (1976), it noted that "the interest advanced must be paramount, one of vital importance," in invalidating the patronage dismissal of government workers.[11] Although these requirements conceivably can be met—as *Buckley* v. *Valeo* (1976) demonstrates—the Court's "weighted" balancing affords substantially more protection for expression than did its earlier balancing approach.

Auxiliary Doctrines

The Court does not always decide First Amendment issues on the basis of broad constitutional standards; in some cases, various auxiliary doctrines have provided narrower grounds for the vindication of First Amendment rights. These doctrines focus not on the legitimacy of governmental regulation, but on the means the government has employed to achieve its ends.[12] Among the most important of these standards are the overbreadth and void-for-vagueness doctrines.

A statute is overbroad if it outlaws both unprotected and constitutionally protected speech. The basic defect of such statutes is their excessive deterrent effect. Speakers must guess whether their speech is constitutionally protected despite being proscribed by the statute and may refrain from speaking rather than risk possible punishment for violating it. As a result, the statute achieves its valid purpose only by infringing on First Amendment rights. *Coates* v. *City of Cincinnati* (1971) illustrates how the Court has employed the overbreadth doctrine. In invalidating a city ordinance that made it a criminal offense for "three or more persons to assemble . . . on any of the sidewalks . . . and then conduct themselves in a manner annoying to persons passing by," the Court did not concern itself with the details of Coates's conduct. Even if Coates's actions were not constitutionally protected, it ruled, the ordinance could not be upheld, because it established a standard for restricting the right of assembly that invaded First Amendment rights.

Closely related to the overbreadth standard is the void-for-vagueness doctrine. A statute is void for vagueness when it "either forbids or requires the doing of an act in terms so vague that men of common intelligence must necessarily guess at its meaning and differ as to its application."[13] By failing to provide adequate notice of what constitutes illegal behavior, vague statutes "chill" the exercise of First Amendment rights and delegate inordinate discretionary power to the officials charged with their enforcement.

POLITICAL EXPRESSION

Speaking for the Court in *New York Times* v. *Sullivan* (1964), Justice William Brennan observed that the nation was committed to the "principle that debate on public issues should be uninhibited, robust, and wide-open." Advocacy of radical political change through violence or other nondemocratic means, on the other hand, may threaten the very foundations of government. In addition, restrictions on political expression may be deemed necessary to prevent corruption of the political process or to serve other important societal purposes. This section details how the Court has dealt with governmental attempts to restrict political expression for national security or other purposes.

National Security

Governmental attempts to limit political expression have been most pronounced during periods of national crisis. The first major conflict over political expression occurred in the late 1790s, when the Sedition Act provoked a bitter controversy (see "Libel," below).

The next significant clash between the perceived requirements of national security and of political expression took place during and immediately after World War I. Following the assassination of President William McKinley by an anarchist in 1902, several states enacted legislation making it unlawful to advocate the violent overthrow of government; and by 1921, two thirds of the states had such laws. In 1917, Congress passed the Espionage Act, which, as amended in 1918, prohibited expression that interfered with the war effort.[14] During the war, almost two thousand prosecutions were brought under the Espionage Act, and many others under state law. Despite the development of the clear-and-present-danger test in *Schenck* v. *United States* (1919) and the incorporation of First Amendment guarantees in *Gitlow* v. *New York* (1925), the Court during this period consistently upheld convictions for political expression in national security cases.

Following World War II, the Cold War between the United States and the Soviet Union intensified concern about the activities of the Communist Party and so-called Communist-front groups. To deal with this perceived threat to national security, the government began to prosecute Communist Party officials under the Smith Act, which forbade advocating or organizing to advocate the overthrow of the government by force or violence. After *Dennis* v. *United States* (1951), in which the Supreme Court sustained the convictions of twelve Communist Party leaders for conspiring to violate the advocacy and organizing provisions of the Act, the government initiated additional prosecutions against Communist Party officials, which resulted in ninety-six convictions.

The Court's interpretation of the Smith Act in *Yates* v. *United States* (1957) and *Scales* v. *United States* (1961), however, severely restricted its usefulness. In *Yates* the Court ruled that the act only proscribed advocacy of participation in overthrowing the government: "Those to whom the advocacy is addressed must be urged to *do* something, now or in the future, rather than merely to *believe in* something."[15] Thus after *Yates*, convictions required proof of participation in a conspiracy to overthrow the government. In *Scales* the Court, although sustaining a conviction under the organizing provision of the act, indicated that mere membership in an organization advocating governmental overthrow was insufficient for conviction. Noting that members might disagree with positions taken by an organization, the Court ruled that the act applied only to "knowing" and "active" members who specifically intended to advance the organization's illegal aims. The importance of this distinction was underlined in *Noto* v. *United States* (1961), in which the justices set aside Noto's conviction because he belonged to an organization that merely engaged in discussions of Communist theory. In the aftermath of *Yates* and *Scales*, Smith Act prosecutions virtually ceased; and the Court's decision in *Brandenburg* v. *Ohio* (1969) has cast serious doubt on the continuing authority of *Dennis*.

During the Cold War era the national and state governments also either instituted or greatly expanded loyalty programs designed to deny public employment or positions of influence to those who might use them for subversive purposes. Initially, the Court endorsed most loyalty requirements. In *American Communications Association* v. *Douds* (1950), for example, it upheld a federal requirement that labor union officers file affidavits denying membership in the Communist Party or other organizations advocating overthrow of the government. Also, in *Adler* v. *Board of Education* (1952) the justices sustained a New York law that authorized the dismissal of teachers belonging to proscribed organizations, and in *Konigsberg* v. *State Bar of California* (1961) they ruled that persons who refused to answer questions about Communist Party membership could be denied admission to the bar. But gradually the Court imposed significant restrictions on governmental loyalty programs by extending procedural protections to public employees threatened with dismissal on loyalty grounds and by using the overbreadth and void-for-vagueness doctrines to limit the scope of loyalty inquiries. Thus in *United States* v. *Robel* (1967) it struck down as overbroad a federal statute prohibiting members of Communist organizations from working in defense facilities, and in *Keyishian* v. *Board of Regents* (1967) it overruled *Adler*, observing that the New York oath was unconstitutionally vague and penalized mere membership in the Communist Party. Finally, in *Law Students Civil Rights Research Council, Inc.* v. *Wadmond* (1971) the Court limited the *Konigsberg* ruling, restricting inquiries by bar-admission committees to whether prospective lawyers knowingly belonged to organizations committed to overthrowing the government.

Postwar legislative investigations into possible subversive activities also raised First Amendment issues. (See Chapter 4 for a discussion of the constitutional questions raised by congressional investigations.) During the 1950s, scores of witnesses were summoned before congressional and state legislative committees to testify about their past and present political associations, and witnesses who refused to testify were cited for contempt. In reviewing contempt convictions, the Supreme Court imposed procedural limitations on the conduct of investigations and announced that it would not tolerate "exposure for the sake of exposure." Not until *Barenblatt* v. *United States* (1959), however, did the Court consider the question of whether witnesses compelled to testify about political associations and beliefs were denied their First Amendment rights. The five-member majority in *Barenblatt* ruled that because the Communist Party was not "an ordinary political party" but an organization committed to the overthrow of the government, Congress's need for information about its activities overrode First Amendment objections.

Yet four years later the Court in *Gibson* v. *Florida Legislative Investi-*

gating Committee (1963) found that the head of the Miami chapter of the NAACP could not be compelled to furnish membership lists to a state committee investigating possible Communist infiltration.

Other Limitations on Political Expression

The Court has been reluctant to sustain restrictions on political expression that do not serve national security needs. Two decisions involving the freedom of association illustrate this. In *NAACP* v. *Alabama* (1958) the Court ruled that an Alabama law requiring out-of-state organizations to file their membership lists could not be enforced against the NAACP. Although it conceded that Alabama had a legitimate interest in the activities of organizations doing business in the state, the Court noted that disclosure of the NAACP's membership would subject members to reprisals and intimidation, and thereby abridge their right to associate in support of their beliefs. And in *Elrod* v. *Burns* (1976) the justices struck a major blow at the spoils system by invalidating the patronage dismissals of nonpolicymaking government employees. In the face of claims that patronage was necessary for strong political parties, the Court held that removals based on political affiliation violated government workers' rights of freedom of association and freedom of political belief.

In two areas, however, the Court has sustained limits on political expression. It has recognized, first of all, that the government's special interest in safeguarding the effectiveness and fairness of its operations may justify restrictions on political expression by governmental employees. This position is reflected in *U.S. Civil Service Commission* v. *National Association of Letter Carriers* (1973), in which the justices upheld restrictions on partisan political activity by federal civil servants. Yet public servants do not altogether forfeit their right to express opinions on political matters. In *Rankin* v. *McPherson* (1987), for example, the Court ruled that a clerical worker in a county constable's office could not be discharged for stating, after hearing of an attempt on the President's life, "If they go for him again, I hope they get him."

The Supreme Court has also recognized that government may act to protect the political process from corruption. Laws regulating lobbying and punishing election fraud, for example, present no First Amendment problem.

Recent regulations of the electoral process, such as the Federal Election Campaign Act Amendments of 1974, have raised constitutional questions. Enacted in response to the disclosures of Watergate and the spiraling costs of election campaigns, the act (1) restricted the size of individual and group contributions to political campaigns, (2) limited the amounts that candidates could spend in those campaigns, (3) required disclosure of campaign contributions and expenditures, (4) provided for public financing of presidential campaigns, and (5) established the Federal Election Commission to administer the act. A comprehensive challenge to this legislation was rejected in *Buckley* v. *Valeo* (1976). In this complicated case, the Court ruled that the limits on campaign contributions did not violate the First Amendment, because they served an important purpose (elimination of corruption) and impinged only minimally on speech interests. The justices did invalidate the limits on campaign expenditures, maintaining that such restrictions limited the communication of political views without contributing significantly to the control of corruption; but they also held that restrictions on expenditures could be imposed as a condition for public financing. Finally, they dismissed as hypothetical the claim that disclosure requirements invaded freedom of association by deterring support for unpopular minor parties.[16]

Perhaps the most important aspect of the *Buckley* decision was the Court's invalidation of the spending restrictions. The government had contended that these restrictions encouraged the dissemination of diverse viewpoints by equalizing candidates' opportunities to influence the electorate. The Court, however, emphasized that government could not achieve this legitimate end by limiting the dissemination of particular views. It reiterated this position in subsequent decisions—most notably in *Federal Election Commission* v. *National Conservative Political Action Committee* (1985), in which it struck down a Federal law prohibiting political action committees from making independent expenditures in support of presidential candidates who had accepted public financing. In so doing, it reasserted the traditional understanding of the First Amendment as creating a "marketplace of ideas" rather than permitting regulation in the public interest.

THE REGULATION OF SPEECH

In *Kunz* v. *United States* (1951) Justice Robert Jackson noted that "the vulnerability of various forms of communication to community control must be proportioned to their impact upon other community interests."[17] This observation explains why government may impose more stringent limitations on speech and expressive conduct than on publication. Because a speaker can address larger numbers of people simultaneously, speech is likely to have a more immediate impact than the press will have. And because expressive conduct ("symbolic speech") has an action component, it is more likely to interfere with the attainment of legitimate governmental ends unrelated to the suppression of speech. This section examines to what extent, and for what purposes, government can regulate speech and expressive conduct.

Symbolic Speech

Conduct, as well as speech, can promote the ends of the First Amendment. Demonstrations and picketing, by combining conduct with speech, often can be more effective than speech alone. Even conduct without speech—a refusal to salute a flag, for instance—can be an eloquent form of expression. Accordingly, the Court has long recognized that symbolic speech is entitled to some First Amendment protection. On the other hand, it has never ruled that the mere presence of a communicative element makes conduct immune from regulation. In each case the Court has had to balance the claims of free expression against the pursuit of other governmental objectives.

In *United States* v. *O'Brien* (1968) the Court upheld O'Brien's conviction for burning his draft card in protest against the Vietnam War. Speaking for the Court, Chief Justice Earl Warren proposed a four-part test for determining when a government interest permits the regulation of expressive conduct:

> [A] government regulation is sufficiently justified if it is within the constitutional power of the Government; if it furthers an important or substantial governmental interest; if the governmental interest is unrelated to the suppression of free expression; and if the incidental restriction of alleged First Amendment freedoms is no greater than is essential to the furtherance of that interest.[18]

When expression and conduct are intertwined, in other words, government can regulate the nonspeech element to achieve valid governmental ends. Thus in *O'Brien* the government's interest in the smooth operation of the Selective Service System justified the incidental burden imposed on free expression. More recently, in *Clark* v. *Community for Creative Non-Violence* (1984), the Court relied on the *O'Brien* test to uphold the National Park Service's ban on sleeping in national parks. Rejecting the challenge of a group that sought to conduct a "sleep-in" in parks near the nation's Capitol to dramatize the plight of the homeless, the Court observed that the prohibition was not designed to restrict expression and served the valid purpose of maintaining parks "in an attractive and intact condition."

For the governmental regulation to be valid, however, it must be content-neutral, that is, it must not regulate conduct as a means of restricting the expression of particular ideas. This requirement was decisive in the controversial case of *Texas* v. *Johnson* (1989), in which a sharply divided Court struck down the conviction of a political protestor who had violated Texas's flag-desecration statute by burning the American flag. According to the Court's five-member majority, the flaw in the Texas law was that it permitted the use of the flag to show support for the nation and its institutions but prevented its use to register dissent. Thus because the prohibition on flag desecration was not content-neutral, it violated the First Amendment.

Public Order

Government has a basic responsibility to maintain public order, and all states have statutes punishing actions such as disorderly conduct, breach of the peace, and incitement to riot. In *Chaplinsky* v. *New Hampshire* (1942) the Court noted that what it termed "fighting words" by their very nature posed an immediate threat to public order and thus were excluded from First Amendment protection. The Court has since defined "fighting words" narrowly. It is not enough that speech be offensive, or invite dispute, or provoke hostility among listeners: only face-to-face personal insults raise no First Amendment issues. Yet the difficulty of designing a statute confined to such insults has led the Court to overturn convictions on overbreadth or vagueness grounds even when the speech at issue clearly constituted "fighting words."

Other speech can be regulated if it poses a danger to public order. This problem usually arises when proponents of unpopular or controversial views use some form of public assembly—meetings, parades, demonstrations—to reach a broad audience. But that very fact complicates the issue: to penalize speakers merely because their views excite opposition would give unsympathetic listeners a "heckler's veto" over speech. The Supreme Court's decisions have not satisfactorily resolved this issue. In *Feiner* v. *New York* (1951) the Court upheld the conviction for disorderly conduct of a speaker who disobeyed police orders to end a speech that had produced some crowd hostility. In *Edwards* v. *South Carolina* (1963) and *Cox* v. *Louisiana* (1965), on the other hand, it overturned the breach-of-the-peace convictions of civil-rights activists whose demonstrations had also stirred crowd unrest. More recently, the Illinois Supreme Court in *Village of Skokie* v. *National Socialist Party* (1978) upheld the right of the American Nazi Party to demonstrate in Skokie, a predominantly Jewish suburb in which many Holocaust survivors resided. Although the intention of the demonstration's organizers clearly was provocative, the Illinois court concluded that the U.S. Supreme Court's decisions required it to overturn an injunction that would have prevented the demonstration and the displaying of the swastika.

Time, Place, and Manner Regulations

The Court has held that government can impose restrictions on the time, place, and manner of speech on public property in order to promote effective communication or accommodate other legitimate uses of that property, but that in imposing such restrictions it cannot discriminate on the basis of the content of expression. As the Court noted in *Police Department of Chicago* v. *Mosley* (1972), "Once a forum is opened up to assembly or speaking by some groups, government may not prohibit others from assembling or speaking on the basis of what they intend to say."[19] Thus the Court has struck down permit systems that distinguish on the basis of the content of speech, as in *Carey* v. *Brown* (1980), or that give excessive discretion, and thus the opportunity to discriminate, to local officials, as in *Lakewood* v. *Plain Dealer Publishing Co.* (1988).

Even nondiscriminatory regulations may be constitutionally suspect. Although government can regulate speech on public property in order to accommodate other interests, it may not deny all access to public property for expression. As Justice Owen Roberts emphasized in *Hague* v. *C.I.O.* (1939),

> Wherever the title of streets and parks may rest, they have immemorially been held in trust for the use of the public. . . . The privilege of a citizen of the United States to use the street and parks for communication of views on national questions may be regulated in the interest of all . . . but it must not, in the guise of regulation, be abridged or denied.[20]

On the question of what property must be made available for communicative purposes, the justices have divided. In *Adderley* v. *Florida* (1966), Justice Hugo Black, speaking for the Court, indicated that government could limit expression to that property which traditionally had been used as a public forum. However, in *Tinker* v. *Des Moines* (1969), a case involving the First Amendment rights of students, Justice Abraham Fortas, also speaking for the Court, insisted that the decisive consideration was whether the use of governmental property as a public forum significantly interfered with the purposes to which the property was dedicated. In *Hazelwood School District* v. *Kuhlmeier* (1988) the Court apparently retreated from that position, at least in dealing with the First Amendment rights of students.

RESTRAINTS ON THE PRESS

Prior Restraints

Prior restraints, which may involve either governmental licensing of publication or bans on publication of particular information, impose a particularly severe burden on communication. To require governmental approval prior to publication brings more materials under official scrutiny and, at minimum, delays even constitutionally protected expression. In addition, the decision to censor typically is reached without the adversarial proceedings and procedural safeguards which accompany criminal prosecutions. For these reasons, English law early on recognized that freedom from prior restraints was essential to freedom of the press. Because the Framers of the First Amendment clearly sought to secure as much press freedom as prevailed in England, the Supreme Court consistently has ruled that prior restraints are constitutionally suspect.

Near v. *Minnesota* (1931) established the Court's basic position on prior restraints. In *Near* the Court struck down a Minnesota law that permitted judges to enjoin publication of "malicious, scandalous and defamatory" newspapers. Speaking for the Court, Chief Justice Charles Evans Hughes recognized that the state had a legitimate interest in curbing such publications and could prosecute those who published them but argued that this interest did not justify prior restraints against publication, as such restraints could be tolerated only in "exceptional cases." To Hughes, prior restraints were impermissible unless the publication involved jeopardized the country's safety in wartime, threatened public decency (obscenity), incited violence or governmental overthrow, or invaded private rights.

Hughes's analysis in *Near* has governed subsequent decisions on prior restraints. In *Freedman* v. *Maryland* (1965), which upheld a state system of movie licensing, the Court indicated that as long as the government observed procedural requirements, it could employ prior restraints to protect public decency. The Court generally has refused to add to the exceptions Hughes listed, however. Thus in *Organization for a Better Austin* v. *Keefe* (1971), it struck down prior restraints on the distribution of nonobscene materials. In *Nebraska Press Association* v. *Stuart* (1976), it overturned a judicial "gag order" designed to prevent prejudicial publicity in a murder case. Finally, in *Hazelwood School District* v. *Kuhlmeier*, it emphasized that production of the student newspaper was part of the school curriculum in upholding censorship by school authorities.

The Court has also tended to construe Hughes's exceptions narrowly. In *New York Times* v. *United States* (1971) the justices lifted an injunction restraining publication of the Pentagon Papers, a top-secret account of the nation's involvement in the Vietnam War, despite objections that publication would threaten national security. In *Snepp* v. *United States* (1980), on the other hand, they upheld a contract requiring a former CIA agent to submit his writings for prepublication clearance by the agency.

Governmental Regulation of Newsgathering[21]

Some governmental regulations, even if adopted for legitimate purposes and applicable to all citizens, may restrict reporters' access to information or deter sources from confiding in them. By making newsgathering more difficult, these regulations may deprive the citizenry of information about matters of public concern. Since 1972 the Supreme Court has decided several cases involving regulations which impinge on the institutional press's access to information.

In *Richmond Newspapers Inc.* v. *Virginia* (1980) the Supreme Court recognized that, "absent a need to further a state interest of the highest order," the press cannot be prosecuted for publishing truthful information of public interest that is lawfully obtained. This does not mean that reporters have a right to obtain newsworthy information—as the Court noted in *Nixon* v. *Warner Communications* (1978), the First Amendment gives the media no right to information beyond that possessed by the general public. On that basis the justices in *Houchins* v. *KQED* (1978) upheld correctional authorities' refusal to grant reporters special access to prison facilities and to prisoners. Yet this does not mean that government can arbitrarily shield its proceedings from public scrutiny, particularly when those proceedings have historically been open to the public. Thus the Court recognized a right of public access to criminal trials in *Richmond Newspapers* and to certain preliminary hearings in criminal cases in *Press-Enterprise Co.* v. *Superior Court* (1986). Although reporters are accorded no special access, their status as members of the public serves to guarantee their admission.

The Court has also maintained that government may impose the same obligations on the press as on other citizens, even when those requirements may affect newsgathering. In *Branzburg* v. *Hayes* (1972), for example, the Court ruled that reporters must supply relevant information to grand juries, despite the alleged effects of such action on reporters' relationships with confidential sources. Similarly, in *Zurcher* v. *Stanford Daily* (1978) it upheld a warrant under which police searched a newsroom for evidence, despite claims that the search disrupted the newsroom and could lead to the disclosure of confidential sources and information.

In the face of the Court's refusal to provide special protection for the press, other branches have acted to facilitate newsgathering. Passage of the Freedom of Information Act (1966) by Congress and of "sunshine" legislation by state legislatures has expanded the availability of information about governmental activities to the press as well as to the general public. Although Congress has failed to approve legislation shielding reporters from grand jury questioning, fully half of the states currently provide some protection.[22] In the wake of *Zurcher,* finally, Congress enacted the Privacy Protection Act of 1980, which narrowly defined the circumstances under which federal, state, and local law-enforcement officers could conduct unannounced searches of newsrooms.

LIBEL AND INVASION OF PRIVACY

The Sedition Act of 1798, passed by the Federalist-dominated Congress in an effort to limit criticism of the Adams administration, provoked a serious First Amendment dispute by outlawing "seditious libel"; that is, defamation of government and its officials. The Jeffersonian Republicans challenged the act's constitutionality on the grounds (1) that with the ratification of the First Amendment, only the states had the authority to punish abuses of freedom of the press, and (2) that the crime of seditious libel was inconsistent with republican self-government. Although the Supreme Court never had occasion to rule on the act's constitutionality, President Thomas Jefferson did express his constitutional judgment by pardoning all persons who had been convicted under the act.

The political nature of the Sedition Act distinguishes it from most libel laws, which seek to protect private individuals from unfair damage to their reputations by authorizing either criminal penalties or civil suits for damages. In *Chaplinsky* v. *New Hampshire* (1942) the Court recognized that libel was one of the categories of expression not protected by the First Amendment. Because libel laws restrict the flow of information, however, the justices have attempted to reconcile the full discussion of public issues with adequate protection for individual reputations.

New York Times v. *Sullivan* (1964) marked the Court's first attempt to distinguish libel from protected expression. Sullivan, a police commissioner in Montgomery, Alabama, had been awarded $500,000 in damages stemming from a newspaper advertisement that contained partially erroneous statements criticizing police mistreatment of blacks. In unanimously overturning the libel judgment, the Court provided broad protection for criticism of public officials. The First Amendment, it asserted, abolished the crime of seditious libel and permits even "vehement, caustic, and unpleasantly sharp attacks on government and public officials." Because erroneous statements are unavoidable in the heat of public debate, "a rule compelling the critic of official conduct to guarantee the truth of all his factual assertions" would unjustifiably inhibit discussion of public affairs. Even false statements about official conduct, therefore, enjoy constitutional protection, unless they are made with "actual malice": that is, "with knowledge that [they were] false or with a reckless disregard of whether or not [they were] false."

Since the *New York Times* decision, the Court has focused on the questions of how "actual malice" can be proved and when this standard of proof is required. The justices declared in *Curtis Publishing Company* v. *Butts* (1967) that serious departures from standard journalistic practice could justify a finding of malice. Mere negligence or errors of judgment are not sufficient, although, as indicated in *Herbert* v. *Lando* (1979), the editorial practices of those responsible for publication may be explored in attempting to prove malice. In the *New York Times* case, this standard of proof was required for articles dealing with the official conduct of an elected official. In order to promote uninhibited discussion of public issues, however, the Court in subsequent cases extended the *New York Times* standard to statements made about candidates for public office, nonelected government employees with authority over the conduct of governmental affairs, and "public figures" in general—that is, individuals who "have thrust themselves to the forefront of particular public controversies in order to influence the resolution of the issues involved."[23] However, the Court has continued to distinguish between public figures and private individuals, rejecting the applicability of the *New York Times* standard to publications about private individuals involuntarily involved in events of public interest.

Two recent cases raise a related concern: does the First Amendment protect publications that violate the privacy of the individual or inflict emotional distress but do not contain malicious falsehoods? The first case, *Hustler Magazine* v. *Falwell* (1988), involved a parody of an advertisement depicting Jerry Falwell, a nationally prominent minister and founder of the Moral Majority, as having sexual relations with his mother. The Supreme Court unanimously ruled that Falwell, as a public figure, could not collect damages for infliction of emotional distress, because the parody did not pretend to be factual and hence did not involve "actual malice" as required by *New York Times* v. *Sullivan.* The second case, *Florida Star* v. *B.J.F.* (1989), involved a suit for invasion of privacy by a rape victim whose name was published in a newspaper, contrary to Florida law. In contrast to *Falwell,* the victim was not a public figure, but the publication contained information that was both accurate and legally obtained. A divided Court held that Florida could prohibit publication of such information only by a law narrowly tailored to achieve "a state interest of the highest order" and that the Florida law failed that demanding test.

OBSCENITY

Obscenity has historically been recognized as one of the categories of expression that does not receive First Amendment protection. But because not all expression dealing with sex is obscene, the Supreme Court has had to determine whether particular works enjoy First Amendment protection, and in developing and applying its standards for identifying obscenity, the justices have been badly divided. Between 1957, when the Court in *Roth* v. *United States* first announced its obscenity standards, and 1973, when it decided *Miller* v. *California,* in no case were five justices able to agree on standards for distinguishing obscene from non-obscene publications.

In *Roth* v. *United States* (1957), Justice William Brennan announced the Court's first test for identifying obscenity. Noting that obscenity is "utterly without redeeming social importance," Brennan held that material is obscene if "to the average person, applying contemporary community standards, the dominant theme of the material taken as a whole appeals to prurient interest." Later cases revealed that this test left crucial questions unanswered: If community standards are to be applied, what community should be consulted? In determining community standards, does one consider what the community proclaims to be its standards, or what the community is willing to tolerate? What is meant by "prurient interest"? (Brennan's opinion at various points appears to endorse two conflicting definitions: "arousing lustful thoughts and desires" and "arousing a morbid and shameful interest in sex.") What is the relationship between Brennan's emphasis on "utterly without redeeming social importance" and his definition of obscenity? And if a work fulfilling Brennan's definition has social importance, is it protected by the First Amendment?

During the 1960s the Court's answers to these questions in effect removed most restrictions on sexually explicit publications. In *Miller* v. *California* (1973), however, the Court reversed direction and renewed its efforts to define obscenity. Rejecting the dissenters' contention that regulation of obscenity inevitably encroaches on First Amendment values, Chief Justice Warren Burger, speaking for the Court, proposed a three-pronged test for identifying obscenity:

> (a) Whether "the average person, applying contemporary community standards" would find that the work, taken as a whole, appeals to the prurient interest, (b) whether the work depicts or describes, in a patently offensive way, sexual conduct specifically defined by the applicable state law, and (c) whether the work, taken as a whole, lacks serious literary, artistic, political, or scientific value.

The *Miller* decision introduced three changes in the Court's approach to obscenity. First, the Court no longer required application of a national community standard, maintaining that the diversity within the nation could properly be reflected in jury determinations of prurience and patent offensiveness. Second, it expressly defined the sorts of patently offensive materials that might constitutionally be banned. And third, it rejected the "utterly without redeeming social importance" standard in favor of consideration of the work as a whole.

Recent Supreme Court rulings have focused on three subsidiary issues. First, to what extent can localities regulate nonobscene adult entertainment? In *Erznoznick* v. *City of Jacksonville* (1975) the Court invalidated an ordinance forbidding drive-in theaters from showing films containing nudity when the screen was visible to the general public, and in *Schad* v. *Mount Ephraim* (1981) it struck down on overbreadth grounds a conviction for commercial displays of nude dancing in violation of a community ban on live entertainment. In *Renton* v. *Playtime Theaters* (1986), on the other hand, the justices upheld a zoning ordinance that prohibited adult motion picture theaters from locating within 1,000 feet of any residential zone, church, park, or school. These decisions, taken together, suggest that localities can regulate this type of protected expression, based on its content, as long as the regulation does not altogether suppress the expression and is closely related to a legitimate governmental objective.

Second, can states prohibit the dissemination of materials which show children engaged in sexual activity, regardless of whether the materials are obscene, in order to prevent sexual exploitation of children? A unanimous Court answered yes in *New York* v. *Ferber* (1982). However, the various opinions written in *Ferber* indicate that the justices remain divided about the adequacy of the *Miller* standards and the circumstances in which government may regulate sexually explicit materials.

Third, what penalties can states impose on those who violate obscenity laws? In *Fort Wayne Books* v. *Indiana* (1989) the Court upheld application of a "racketeering" law to those guilty of multiple obscenity offenses. Those convicted under the law not only receive stiff fines and jail sentences but conceivably could forfeit all their real and personal property used or acquired in the course of the offenses. The Court conceded that the heavy penalties might induce cautious booksellers to remove constitutionally protected materials from their shelves rather than risk prosecution. However, it concluded that deterrence of obscenity offenses was a valid state objective and that the risk of self-censorship was largely hypothetical.

Feminist opponents of pornography have recently proposed a different approach to its regulation. Pornography is objectionable, they claim, because it degrades and harms women by justifying their treatment as sexual objects. Because it differentially harms women, trafficking in pornography constitutes a form of sexual discrimination, and women should be able to sue those who engage in this type of discrimination. Thus whereas the traditional regulation of obscenity focused on the explicit portrayal of sexual activity, feminist critics are concerned with its implicit endorsement of sexual subordination, and whereas traditional regulation relied on criminal penalties, feminists have sought to control it through the threat of civil suits.

The feminist critique of pornography represents a fundamental challenge to First Amendment jurisprudence, because it asserts that some views are so clearly erroneous and harmful that they should be banished from the marketplace of ideas. In contrast, the Supreme Court has held that the First Amendment does not permit the outlawing of ideas, however loathsome. When the city council of Indianapolis enacted an ordinance incorporating the feminist approach to pornography regulation, lower federal courts quickly invalidated the law, and the Supreme Court affirmed.

SOME CONCLUSIONS

Although the number and variety of the Court's decisions preclude a summary evaluation, some general observations can be made about the Court's treatment of speech and press cases. To begin with, the Court has expanded substantially the range of expression that enjoys First Amendment protection. In large measure, this broadening of the amendment's coverage resulted from the incorporation of the speech and press guarantees in *Gitlow* v. *New York* (1925). The Court also has ruled, however, that some previously excluded categories of expression are entitled to First Amendment protection; decisions involving symbolic speech, commercial speech, and freedom of association have been particularly important in extending the scope of the First Amendment.

Second, the Court progressively has narrowed its definitions of the categories of speech—"the lewd and the obscene, the profane, the libelous, and the insulting or 'fighting' words"—that are not entitled to First Amendment protection. Despite the *Miller* ruling, the Court has continued to provide broad protection for sexually explicit materials. Its ruling in *New York Times* v. *Sullivan* (1964) and subsequent cases have rewritten the law of libel and provided broad protection for criticisms of governmental officials. In addition, its substantive rulings and its use of the void-for-vagueness and overbreadth doctrines virtually have eliminated prosecutions for "fighting words."

Finally, despite the movement, suggested by these developments, toward broader protection for expression, the Court has not developed a general standard for deciding First Amendment cases. Rather, the contemporary Court appears to be avoiding broad doctrine in favor of a case-by-case approach with standards limited to particular areas of First Amendment law (e.g., obscenity, libel). Whether this approach can ensure the principled development of First Amendment law remains to be seen.

NOTES

1 *NAACP* v. *Alabama*, 357 U.S. 449, 460 (1958). Since freedom of association is tied to expression, however, it does not require the invalidation of legislation which impinges on groups but has only a marginal effect on their expression. Thus in *Roberts* v. *United States Jaycees*, 468 U.S. 609 (1984), the Court upheld a state law which prohibited private associations from discriminating on the basis of sex.

2 Justice Hugo Black argued, albeit unsuccessfully, that the First Amendment imposed an absolute ban. His views are summarized in *Smith* v. *California* (1959) and in Edmund Cahn, "Mr. Justice Black and First Amendment Absolutes: A Public Interview," *New York University Law Review* 37 (1962). See also Justice William Douglas's opinion in *Brandenburg* v. *Ohio* (1969).

3 *Chaplinsky* v. *New Hampshire*, 315 U.S. 568, 572 (1942). For a discussion of the protection accorded commercial speech, see *Central Hudson Gas Company* v. *Public Service Commission* (1980).

4 *Schenck* v. *United States*, 249 U.S. 47, 52 (1919).

5 William Blackstone, *Commentaries on the Laws of England* (1765–1769), 2d rev. ed., ed. Thomas Cooley (Chicago: 1872), Book 4, pp. 151–152. For an analysis of the English and colonial background of the First Amendment, see Leonard Levy, *Legacy of Suppression: Freedom of Speech and Press in Early American History* (Cambridge, Mass.: Harvard University Press, 1960).

6 For contrasting views about the scope of First Amendment protection, see Thomas I. Emerson, *Toward a General Theory of the First Amendment* (New York: Random House, 1967); Alexander Meiklejohn, *Political Freedom: The Constitutional Powers of the People* (New York: Oxford University Press, 1960); and Robert Bork, "Neutral Principles and Some First Amendment Problems," *Indiana Law Journal* 47 (1971).

7 Those who opposed the Sedition Act on First Amendment grounds did not necessarily believe that prosecution for seditious libel was inconsistent with democratic government: the First Amendment imposed limitations only on Congress, and state legislatures remained free to punish the crime. See Walter Berns, *The First Amendment and the Future of American Democracy* (New York: Basic Books, 1977), Chapter 3.

8 *Whitney* v. *California*, 274 U.S. 357, 375 (1927).

9 *Abrams* v. *United States*, 250 U.S. 616, 630 (1919).

10 Martin Shapiro, *Freedom of Speech: The Supreme Court and Judicial Review* (Englewood Cliffs, N.J.: Prentice-Hall, 1966), p. 152.

11 *Gibson* v. *Florida Legislative Investigating Committee*, 372 U.S. 539, 551 (1963) and *Elrod* v. *Burns*, 427 U.S. 347, 362 (1976).

12 From this it follows that the government can replace a law invalidated as overbroad or void for vagueness with a more narrowly or precisely drawn statute that meets constitutional requirements.

13 *Connally* v. *General Construction Co.*, 269 U.S. 385, 391 (1926).

14 As Zechariah Chaffee observed, "It became criminal to advocate heavier taxation instead of bond issues, to state that conscription was unconstitutional though the Supreme Court had not yet held it valid, to say that the sinking of merchant ships was legal, to urge that a referendum should have preceded our declaration of war, to say that the war was contrary to the teachings of Christ. Men have been punished for criticizing the Red Cross and the Y.M.C.A., while under the Minnesota Espionage Act it has been held a crime to discourage

women from knitting by the remark, 'No soldier ever sees those socks.' " *Free Speech in the United States* (Cambridge, Mass.: Harvard University Press, 1941), pp. 51–52, note 12.

15 *Yates* v. *United States,* 354 U.S. 298, 325 (1957).

16 The Court in *Buckley* also upheld the constitutionality of the campaign finance program, which had been challenged as an invalid exercise of the spending power, and struck down congressional appointment of some members of the Federal Election Commission. After the latter ruling, Congress vested the appointment power in the president, as constitutionally required (see Chapter 5).

17 *Kunz* v. *United States,* 340 U.S. 290, 307–08 (1951).

18 *United States* v. *O'Brien,* 391 U.S. 367, 377 (1968).

19 *Police Department of Chicago* v. *Mosley,* 408 U.S. 92, 96 (1972).

20 *Hague* v. *C.I.O.,* 307 U.S. 496, 515–516 (1939).

21 Government may also restrict the flow of information to the public by classifying sensitive information over which it has control by restricting access to it. That government has a valid interest in maintaining the confidentiality of some information has long been recognized, and the inevitable complaints over excessive governmental secrecy have been dealt with largely through executive-branch actions and legislation such as the Freedom of Information Act.

22 See Maurice Van Gerpen, *Privileged Communication and the Press* (Westport, Conn.: Greenwood Press, 1979), Chapter 6.

23 This definition of a "public figure" is from *Gertz* v. *Robert Welch, Inc.,* 418 U.S. 323, 345 (1974).

SELECTED READINGS

American Booksellers Association v. *Hudnut,* 771 F.2d 323 (1985).

Central Hudson Gas Company v. *Public Service Commission,* 447 U.S. 557 (1980).

Hustler Magazine v. *Falwell,* 485 U.S. 46 (1988).

Red Lion Broadcasting Company v. *FCC,* 395 U.S. 367 (1969).

Richmond Newspapers Inc. v. *Virginia,* 448 U.S. 555 (1980).

United States Civil Service Commission v. *National Association of Letter Carriers,* 413 U.S. 548 (1973).

United States v. *O'Brien,* 391 U.S. 367 (1968).

West Virginia State Board of Education v. *Barnette* (Chapter 13).

Whitney v. *California,* 274 U.S. 357 (1927).

Baker, C. Edwin. *Human Liberty and Freedom of Speech* (New York: Oxford University Press, 1989).

Bollinger, Lee C. *The Tolerant Society* (New York: Oxford University Press, 1986).

Bork, Robert. "Neutral Principles and Some First Amendment Problems," *Indiana Law Journal* 47 (1971).

Clor, Harry. *Obscenity and Public Morality* (Chicago: University of Chicago Press, 1969).

Downs, Donald A. *Nazis in Skokie* (Notre Dame, Indiana: Notre Dame University Press, 1985).

Emerson, Thomas I. *The System of Freedom of Expression* (New York: Random House, 1970).

Haiman, Franklyn S. *Speech and Law in a Free Society* (Chicago: University of Chicago Press, 1981).

Levy, Leonard W. *Emergence of a Free Press* (New York: Oxford University Press, 1985).

Meiklejohn, Alexander. *Political Freedom: The Constitutional Powers of the People* (New York: Harper & Row, 1960).

O'Brien, David M. *The Public's Right to Know: The Supreme Court and the First Amendment* (New York: Praeger, 1981).

Van Alstyne, William. "The Hazards to the Press Claiming a 'Preferred Position.' " *Hastings Law Journal* 28 (January 1977).

Gitlow v. New York

268 U.S. 652, 45 S. Ct. 625, 69 L. Ed. 1138 (1925)

Benjamin Gitlow, a member of the Left Wing Section of the Socialist Party, was convicted of violating the New York criminal anarchy law by advocating the forceful overthrow of the government and circulating a paper advocating governmental overthrow. The specific basis for the indictment was Gitlow's publication of *The Left Wing Manifesto,* which proclaimed that the goal of so-called revolutionary socialism was to destroy the "bourgeois state" through "revolutionary mass action" and that depicted capitalism as "in the process of disintegration and collapse." No evidence of any effects following from circulation of Gitlow's publication was introduced at trial. When the New York Court of Appeals affirmed his conviction, Gitlow appealed his case to the Supreme Court. *Opinion of the Court: Sanford, Taft, Van Devanter, McReynolds, Sutherland, Butler, Stone. Dissenting opinion: Holmes, Brandeis.*

MR. JUSTICE SANFORD delivered the opinion of the Court. . . .

. . .The sole contention here is, essentially, that as there was no evidence of any concrete result flowing from the publication of the Manifesto or of circumstances showing the likelihood of such result, the statute as construed and applied by the trial court penalizes the mere utterance, as such, of "doctrine" having no quality of incitement, without regard either to the circumstances of its utterance or to the likelihood of unlawful sequences; and that, as the exercise of the right of free expression with relation to government is only punishable "in circumstances involving likelihood of substantive evil," the statute contravenes the due process clause of the Fourteenth Amendment. The argument in support of this contention rests primarily upon the following propositions: 1st, That the "liberty" protected by the Fourteenth Amendment includes the liberty of speech and of the press; and 2nd, That while liberty of expression "is not absolute," it may be restrained "only in circumstances where its exercise bears a causal relation with some substantive evil, consummated, attempted or likely," and as the statute "takes no account of circumstances," it unduly restrains this liberty and is therefore unconstitutional. . . .

The statute does not penalize the utterance or publication of abstract "doctrine" or academic discussion having no quality of incitement to any concrete action. It is not aimed against mere historical or philosophical essays. It does not restrain the advocacy of changes in the form of government by constitutional and lawful means. What it prohibits is language advocating, advising or teaching the overthrow of organized government by unlawful means. These words imply urging to action. . . .

The Manifesto, plainly, is neither the statement of abstract doctrine nor, as suggested by counsel, mere prediction that industrial disturbances and revolutionary mass strikes will result spontaneously in an inevitable process of evolution in the economic system. It advocates and urges in fervent language mass action which shall progressively foment industrial disturbances and through political mass strikes and revolutionary mass action overthrow and destroy organized parliamentary government. . . .

The means advocated for bringing about the destruction of organized parliamentary government, namely, mass industrial revolts usurping the functions of municipal government, political mass strikes directed against the parliamentary state, and revolutionary mass action for its final destruction, necessarily imply the use of force and violence, and in their essential nature are inherently unlawful in a constitutional government of law and order. That the jury were warranted in finding that the Manifesto advocated not merely the abstract doctrine of overthrowing organized government by force, violence and unlawful means, but action to that end, is clear.

For present purposes we may and do assume that freedom of speech and of the press—which are protected by the First Amendment from abridgment by Congress—are among the fundamental personal rights and "liberties" protected by the due process clause of the Fourteenth Amendment from impairment by the States. . . .

It is a fundamental principle, long established, that the freedom of speech and of the press which is secured by the Constitution, does not confer an absolute right to speak or publish, without responsibility, whatever one may choose, or an unrestricted and unbridled license that gives immunity for every possible use of language and prevents the punishment of those who abuse this freedom. . . .

That a State in the exercise of its police power may punish those who abuse this freedom by utterances inimical to the public welfare, tending to corrupt public morals, incite to crime, or disturb the public peace, is not open to question. . . .

By enacting the present statute the State has determined, through its legislative body, that utterances advocating the overthrow of organized government by force, violence and unlawful means, are so inimical to the general welfare and involve such danger of substantive evil that they may be penalized in the exercise of its police power. That determination must be given great weight. Every presumption is to be indulged in favor of the validity of the statute. . . . The State cannot reasonably be required to measure the danger from every such utterance in the nice balance of a jeweler's scale. A single revolutionary spark may kindle a fire that, smouldering for a time, may burst into a sweeping and destructive conflagration. It cannot be said that the State is acting arbitrarily or unreasonably when in the exercise of its judgment as to the measures necessary to protect the public peace and safety, it seeks to extinguish the spark without waiting until it has enkindled the flame or blazed into the conflagration. It cannot reasonably be required to defer the adoption of measures for its own peace and safety until the revolutionary utterances lead to actual disturbances of the public peace or imminent and immediate danger of its own destruction; but it may, in the exercise of its judgment, suppress the threatened danger in its incipiency. . . .

We cannot hold that the present statute is an arbitrary or unreasonable exercise of the police power of the State unwarrantably infringing the freedom of speech or press; and we must and do sustain its constitutionality.

This being so it may be applied to every utterance—not too trivial to be beneath the notice of the law—which is of such a character and used with such intent and purpose as to bring it within the prohibition of the statute. . . . In other words, when the legislative body has determined generally, in the constitutional exercise of its discretion, that utterances of a certain kind involve such danger of substantive evil that they may be punished, the question whether any specific utterance coming within the prohibited class is likely, in and of itself, to bring about the substantive evil, is not open to consideration. It is sufficient that the statute itself be constitutional and that the use of the language comes within its prohibition. . . .

MR. JUSTICE HOLMES, dissenting.

MR. JUSTICE BRANDEIS and I are of opinion that this judgment should be reversed. . . . If what I think the correct test is applied, it is manifest that there was no present danger of an attempt to overthrow the government by force on the part of the admittedly small minority who shared the defendant's views. It is said that this manifesto was more than a theory, that it was an incitement. Every idea is an incitement. It offers itself for belief and if believed it is acted on unless some other belief outweighs it or some failure of energy stifles the movement at its birth. The only difference between the expression of an opinion and an incitement in the narrower sense is the speaker's enthusiasm for the result. Eloquence may set fire to reason. But whatever may be thought of the redundant discourse before us it had no chance of starting a present conflagration. If in the long run the beliefs expressed in proletarian dictatorship are destined to be accepted by the dominant forces of the community, the only meaning of free speech is that they should be given their chance and have their way.

Schenck v. *United States*

249 U.S. 47, 39 S. Ct. 247, 63 L. Ed. 470 (1919)

Charles Schenck, general secretary of the Socialist Party, was convicted of violating the various provisions of the Espionage Act of 1917 by conspiring to obstruct military recruitment and cause insubordination in the armed forces. The charges stemmed from the fact that Schenck had mailed to fifteen thousand men who were eligible for military service leaflets that claimed that the draft was unconstitutional and urged the potential draftees to "assert your rights." *Opinion of the Court: Holmes, White, McKenna, Day, Van Devanter, Pitney, McReynolds, Brandeis, Clarke.*

MR. JUSTICE HOLMES delivered the opinion of the Court. . . .

The document in question upon its first printed side recited the first section of the Thirteenth Amendment, said that the idea embodied in it was violated by the Conscription Act and that a conscript is little better than a convict. In impassioned language it intimated that conscription was despotism in its worst form and a monstrous wrong against humanity in the interest of Wall Street's chosen few. It said "Do not submit to intimidation," but in form at least confined itself to peaceful measures such as a petition for the repeal of the act. The other and later printed side of the sheet was headed "Assert Your Rights." It stated reasons for alleging that any one violated the Constitution when he refused to recognize "your right to assert your opposition to the draft," and went on "If you do not assert and support your rights, you are helping to deny or disparage rights which it is the solemn duty of all citizens and residents of the United States to retain." It described the arguments on the other side as coming from cunning politicians and a mercenary capitalist press, and even silent consent to the conscription law as helping to support an infamous conspiracy. It denied the power to send our citizens away to foreign shores to shoot up the people of other lands, and added that words could not express the condemnation such cold-blooded ruthlessness deserves, &c., &c., winding up "You must do your share to maintain, support and uphold the rights of the people of this country." Of course the document would not have been sent unless it had been intended to have some effect, and we do not see what effect it could be expected to have upon persons subject to the draft except to influence them to obstruct the carrying of it out. The defendants do not deny that the jury might find against them on this point.

But it is said, suppose that that was the tendency of this circular, it is protected by the First Amendment to the Constitution. Two of the strongest expressions are said to be quoted respectively from well-known public men. It well may be that the prohibition of laws abridging the freedom of speech is not confined to previous restraints, although to prevent them may have been the main purpose. . . . We admit that in many places and in ordinary times the defendants in saying all that was said in the circular would have been within their constitutional rights. But the character of every act depends upon the circumstances in which it is done. . . . The most stringent protection of free speech would not protect a man in falsely shouting fire in a theatre and causing a panic. It does not even protect a man from an injunction against uttering words that may have all the effect of force. . . . The question in every case is whether the words used are used in such circumstances and are of such a nature as to create a clear and present danger that they will bring about the substantive evils that Congress has a right to prevent. It is a question of proximity and degree. When a nation is at war many things that might be said in time of peace are such a hindrance to its effort that their utterance will not be endured so long as men fight and that no Court could regard them as protected by any constitutional right. It seems to be admitted that if an actual obstruction of the recruiting service were proved, liability for words that produced that effect might be enforced. The statute of 1917 in § 4 punishes conspiracies to obstruct as well as actual obstruction. If the act, (speaking, or circulating a paper,) its tendency and the intent with which it is done are the same, we perceive no ground for saying that success alone warrants making the act a crime.

Judgments affirmed.

Dennis v. *United States*

341 U.S. 494, 71 S. Ct. 857 95 L. Ed. 1137 (1951)

In 1940, Congress passed the Smith Act, under which persons could be punished for advocating the overthrow of the government by force or violence or for organizing a group that advocated such action. In 1948, Eugene Dennis and ten other leaders of the Communist Party were indicted under the Smith Act for willfully and knowingly conspiring "(1) to organize as the Communist Party of the United States a society, group and assembly of persons who teach and advocate the overthrow and destruction of the Government of the United States by force and violence, and (2) knowingly and willfully to advocate and teach the duty and necessity of overthrowing and destroying the Government of the United States by force and violence." After a long and spectacular trial marked by conflict between the judge and the defense attorneys, all the defendants were convicted. When the convictions were upheld on appeal, the Supreme Court granted certiorari but limited its review to whether the relevant provisions of the Smith Act violated the First Amendment or were void for vagueness. *Plurality opinion: Vinson, Reed, Burton, Minton. Concurring opinions: Frankfurter; Jackson. Dissenting opinions: Black; Douglas. Not participating: Clark.*

MR. CHIEF JUSTICE VINSON announced the judgment of the Court and an opinion in which MR. JUSTICE REED, MR. JUSTICE BURTON and MR. JUSTICE MINTON join. . . .

The obvious purpose of the statute is to protect existing Government, not from change by peaceable, lawful and constitutional means, but from change by violence, revolution and terrorism. That it is within the *power* of the Congress to protect the Government of the United States from armed rebellion is a proposition which requires little discussion. The question with which we are concerned here is whether the *means* which it has employed conflict with the First and Fifth Amendments to the Constitution.

One of the bases for the contention that the means which Congress has employed are invalid takes the form of an attack on the face of the statute on the grounds that by its terms it prohibits academic discussion of the merits of Marxism-Leninism, that it stifles ideas and is contrary to all concepts of a free speech and a free press. . . .

The very language of the Smith Act negates the interpretation which petitioners would have us impose on that Act. It is directed at advocacy, not discussion. Thus, the trial judge properly charged the jury that they could not convict if they found that petitioners did "no more than pursue peaceful studies and discussions or teaching and advocacy in the realm of ideas." . . . Congress did not intend to eradicate the free discussion of political theories, to destroy the traditional rights of Americans to discuss and evaluate ideas without fear of governmental sanction.

. . . Speech is not an absolute, above and beyond control by the legislature when its judgment, subject to review here, is that certain kinds of speech are so undesirable as to warrant criminal sanction. Nothing is more certain in modern society than the principle that there are no absolutes, that a name, a phrase, a standard has meaning only when associated with the considerations which gave birth to the nomenclature. . . . To those who would paralyze our Government in the face of impending threat by encasing it in a semantic straitjacket we must reply that all concepts are relative.

In this case we are squarely presented with the application of the "clear and present danger" test, and must decide what that phrase imports. . . . Overthrow of the Government by force and violence is certainly a substantial enough interest for the Government to limit speech. Indeed, this is the ultimate value of any society, for if a society cannot protect its very structure from armed internal attack, it must follow that no subordinate value can be protected. If, then, this interest may be protected, the literal problem which is presented is what has been meant by the use of the phrase "clear and present danger" of the utterances bringing about the evil within the power of Congress to punish.

Obviously, the words cannot mean that before the Government may act, it must wait until the *putsch* is about to be executed, the plans have been laid and the signal is awaited. If Government is aware that a group aiming at its overthrow is attempting to indoctrinate its members and to commit them to a course whereby they will strike when the leaders feel the circumstances permit, action by the Government is required. The argument that there is no need for Government to concern itself, for Government is strong, it possesses ample powers to put down a rebellion, it may defeat the revolution with ease needs no answer. For that is not the question. Certainly an attempt to overthrow the Government by force, even though doomed from the outset because of inadequate numbers or power of the revolutionists, is a sufficient evil for Congress to prevent. The damage which such attempts create both physically and politically to a nation makes it impossible to measure the validity in terms of the probability of success, or the immediacy of a successful attempt. In the instant case the trial judge charged the jury that they could not convict unless they found that petitioners intended to overthrow the Government "as speedily as circumstances would permit." This does not mean, and could not properly mean, that they would not strike until there was certainty of success. What was meant was that the revolutionists would strike when they thought the time was ripe. We must therefore reject the contention that success or probability of success is the criterion. . . .

Chief Judge Learned Hand, writing for the majority below, interpreted the phrase as follows: "In each case [courts] must ask whether the gravity of the 'evil,' discounted by its improbability, justifies such invasion of free speech as is necessary to avoid the danger." . . . We adopt this statement of the rule. As articulated by Chief Judge Hand, it is as succinct and inclusive as any other we might devise at this time. It takes into consideration those factors which we deem relevant, and relates their significances. More we cannot expect from words.

Likewise, we are in accord with the court below, which affirmed the trial court's finding that the requisite danger existed. The mere fact that from the period 1945 to 1948 petitioners' activities did not result in an attempt to overthrow the Government by force and violence is of course no answer to the fact that there was a group that was ready to make the attempt. The formation by petitioners of such a highly organized conspiracy, with rigidly disciplined members subject to call when the leaders, these petitioners, felt that the time had come for action, coupled with the inflammable nature of world conditions, similar uprisings in other countries, and the touch-and-go nature of our relations with countries with whom petitioners were in the very least ideologically attuned, convince us that their convictions were justified on this score. And this analysis disposes of the contention that a conspiracy to advocate, as distinguished from the advocacy itself, cannot be constitutionally restrained, because it comprises only the preparation. It is the existence of the conspiracy which creates the danger. . . . If the ingredients of the reaction are present, we cannot bind the Government to wait until the catalyst is added. . . .

We hold that §§ 2 (a) (1), 2 (a) (3) and 3 of the Smith Act do not inherently, or as construed or applied in the instant case, violate the First Amendment and other provisions of the Bill of Rights, or the First and Fifth Amendments because of indefiniteness. Petitioners intended to overthrow the Government of the United States as speedily as the circumstances would permit. Their conspiracy to organize the Communist Party and to teach and advocate the overthrow of the Government of the United States by force and violence created a "clear and present danger" of an attempt to overthrow the Government by force and violence. They were properly and constitutionally convicted for violation of the Smith Act. The judgments of conviction are

Affirmed.

MR. JUSTICE FRANKFURTER, concurring in affirmance of the judgment.

Few questions of comparable import have come before this Court in recent years. The appellants maintain that they have a right to advocate a political theory, so long, at least, as their advocacy does not create an immediate danger of obvious magnitude to the very existence of our present scheme of society. On the other hand, the Government asserts the right to safeguard the security of the Nation by such a measure as the Smith Act. Our judgment is thus solicited on a conflict of interests of the utmost concern to the well-being of the country. This conflict of interests cannot be resolved by a dogmatic preference for one or the other, nor by a sonorous formula which is in fact only a euphemistic disguise for an unresolved conflict. If adjudication is to be a rational process, we cannot escape a candid examination of the conflicting claims with full recognition that both are supported by weighty title-deeds. . . .

But how are competing interests to be assessed? Since they are not subject to quantitative ascertainment, the issue necessarily resolves itself into asking, who is to make the adjustment?—who is to balance the relevant factors and ascertain which interest is in the circumstances to prevail? Full responsibility for the choice cannot be given to the courts. Courts are not representative bodies. They are not designed to be a good reflex of a democratic society. Their judgment is best informed, and therefore most dependable, within narrow limits. . . .

Primary responsibility for adjusting the interests which compete in the situation before us of necessity belongs to the Congress. . . . We are to set aside the judgment of those whose duty it is to legislate only if there is no reasonable basis for it. . . .

It is not for us to decide how we would adjust the clash of interests which this case presents were the primary responsibility for reconciling it ours. Congress has determined that the danger created by advocacy of overthrow justifies the ensuing restriction on freedom of speech. The determination was made after due deliberation, and the seriousness of the congressional purpose is attested by the volume of legislation passed to effectuate the same ends.

Can we then say that the judgment Congress exercised was denied it by the Constitution? Can we establish a constitutional doctrine which forbids the elected representatives of the people to make this choice? Can we hold that the First Amendment deprives Congress of what it deemed necessary for the Government's protection?

To make validity of legislation depend on judicial reading of events still in the womb of time—a forecast, that is, of the outcome of forces at best appreciated only with knowledge of the topmost secrets of nations—is to charge the judiciary with duties beyond its equipment. . . .

The wisdom of the assumptions underlying the legislation and prosecution is another matter. . . .

Civil liberties draw at best only limited strength from legal guaranties. Preoccupation by our people with the constitutionality, instead of with the wisdom, of legislation or of executive action is preoccupation with a false value. . . . Focusing attention on constitutionality tends to make constitutionality synonymous with wisdom. When legislation touches freedom of thought and freedom of speech, such a tendency is a formidable enemy of the free spirit. Much that should be rejected as illiberal, because repressive and envenoming, may well be not unconstitutional. The ultimate reliance for the deepest needs of civilization must be found outside their vindication in courts of law. . . .

MR. JUSTICE JACKSON, concurring. . . .

The "clear and present danger" test was an innovation by Mr. Justice Holmes in the *Schenck* [v. *United States (1919)*] case, reiterated and refined by him and Mr. Justice Brandeis in later cases, all arising before the era of World War II revealed the subtlety and efficacy of modernized revolutionary techniques used by totalitarian parties. In those cases, they were faced with convictions under so-called criminal syndicalism statutes aimed at anarchists but which, loosely construed, had been applied to punish socialism, pacifism, and left-wing ideologies, the charges often resting on farfetched inferences which, if true, would establish only technical or trivial violations. They proposed "clear and present danger" as a test for the sufficiency of evidence in particular cases.

I would save it, unmodified, for application as a "rule of reason" in the kind of case for which it was devised. . . . But its recent expansion has extended, in particular to Communists, unprecedented immunities. Unless we are to hold our Government captive in a judge-made verbal trap, we must approach the problem of a well-organized, nation-wide conspiracy, such as I have described, as realistically as our predecessors faced the trivialities that were being prosecuted until they were checked with a rule of reason.

I think reason is lacking for applying that test to this case.

MR. JUSTICE BLACK, dissenting. . . .

. . . The opinions for affirmance indicate that the chief reason for jettisoning the rule is the expressed fear that advocacy of Communist doctrine endangers the safety of the Republic. Undoubtedly, a governmental policy of unfettered communication of ideas does entail dangers. To the Founders of this Nation, however, the benefits derived from free expression were worth the risk. They embodied this philosophy in the First Amendment's command that "Congress shall make no law . . . abridging the freedom of speech, or of the press. . . ." I have always believed that the First Amendment is the keystone of our Government, that the freedoms it guarantees provide the best insurance against destruction of all freedom. At least as to speech in the realm of public matters, I believe that the "clear and present danger" test does not "mark the furthermost constitutional boundaries of protected expression" but does "no more than recognize a minimum compulsion of the Bill of Rights." *Bridges* v. *California*. . . .

So long as this Court exercises the power of judicial review of legislation, I cannot agree that the First Amendment permits us to sustain laws suppressing freedom of speech and press on the basis of Congress' or our own notions of mere "reasonableness." Such a doctrine waters down the First Amendment so that it amounts to little more than an admonition to Congress. The Amendment as so construed is not likely to protect any but those "safe" or orthodox views which rarely need its protection. . . .

Public opinion being what it now is, few will protest the conviction of these Communist petitioners. There is hope, however, that in calmer times, when present pressures, passions and fears subside, this or some later Court will restore the First Amendment liberties to the high preferred place where they belong in a free society.

MR. JUSTICE DOUGLAS, dissenting.

If this were a case where those who claimed protection under the First Amendment were teaching the techniques of sabotage, the assassination of the President, the filching of documents from public files, the planting of bombs, the art of street warfare, and the like, I would have no doubts. The freedom to speak is not absolute; the teaching of methods of terror and other seditious conduct should be beyond the pale along with obscenity and immorality. This case was argued as if those were the facts. The argument imported much seditious conduct into the record. That is easy and it has popular appeal, for the activities of Communists in plotting and scheming against the free world are common knowledge. But the fact is that no such evidence was introduced at the trial. There is a statute which makes a seditious conspiracy unlawful. Petitioners, however, were not charged with a "conspiracy to overthrow" the Government. They were charged with a conspiracy to form a party and groups and assemblies of people who teach and advocate the overthrow of our Government by force or violence and with a conspiracy to advocate and teach its overthrow by force and violence. It may well be that indoctrination in the techniques of terror to destroy the Government would be indictable under either statute. But the teaching which is condemned here is of a different character. . . .

There comes a time when even speech loses its constitutional immunity. . . . Yet free speech is the rule, not the exception. The restraint to be constitutional must be based on more than fear, on more than passionate opposition against the speech, on more than a revolted dislike for its contents. There must be some immediate injury to society that is likely if speech is allowed. . . .

The nature of Communism as a force on the world scene would, of course, be relevant to the issue of clear and present danger of petitioners' advocacy within the United States. But the primary consideration is the strength and tactical position of petitioners and their converts in this country. On that there is no evidence in the record. If we are to take judicial notice of the threat of Communists within the nation, it should not be difficult to conclude that *as a political party* they are of little consequence. . . . In America they are miserable merchants of unwanted ideas; their wares remain unsold. The fact that their ideas are abhorrent does not make them powerful.

The political impotence of the Communists in this country does not, of course, dispose of the problem. Their numbers; their positions in industry and government; the extent to which they have in fact infiltrated the police, the armed services, transportation, stevedoring, power plants, munitions works, and other critical places—these facts all bear on the likelihood that their advocacy of the Soviet theory of revolution will endanger the Republic. But the record is silent on these facts. If we are to proceed on the basis of judicial notice, it is impossible for me to say that the Communists in this country are so potent or so strategically deployed that they must be suppressed for their speech. . . .

. . . Free speech—the glory of our system of government—should not be sacrificed on anything less than plain and objective proof of danger that the evil advocated is imminent. On this record no one can say that petitioners and their converts are in such a strategic position as to have even the slightest chance of achieving their aims.

Barenblatt v. *United States*

360 U.S. 109, 79 S. Ct. 1081, 3 L. Ed. 2d 1115 (1959)

Lloyd Barenblatt, who had previously served as a psychology instructor at the University of Michigan and at Vassar College, was subpoenaed to testify by a subcommittee of the House Un-American Activities Committee, which was conducting hearings dealing with alleged Communist infiltration into the field of education. He refused to answer subcommittee questions pertaining to his past or present membership in the Communist Party and other groups, asserting that the First Amendment barred a legislative inquiry into his political beliefs and associations. After being convicted of contempt of Congress, he appealed the conviction primarily on First Amendment grounds. *Opinion of the Court: Harlan, Frankfurter, Clark, Whittaker, Stewart. Dissenting opinions: Black, Warren, Douglas; Brennan.*

MR. JUSTICE HARLAN delivered the opinion of the Court.

. . . The power of inquiry has been employed by Congress throughout our history, over the whole range of the national interests concerning which Congress might legislate or decide upon due investigation not to legislate; it has similarly been utilized in determining what to appropriate from the national purse, or whether to appropriate. The scope of the power of inquiry, in short, is as penetrating and far-reaching as the potential power to enact and appropriate under the Constitution.

Broad as it is, the power is not, however, without limitations. Since Congress may only investigate into those areas in which it may potentially legislate or appropriate, it cannot inquire into matters which are within the exclusive province of one of the other branches of the Government. . . . And the Congress, in common with all branches of the Government, must exercise its powers subject to the limitations placed by the Constitution on governmental action, more particularly in the context of this case the relevant limitations of the Bill of Rights. . . .

Petitioner's various contentions resolve themselves into three propositions: First, the compelling of testimony by the Subcommittee was neither legislatively authorized nor constitutionally permissible because of the vagueness of Rule XI of the House of Representatives, Eighty-third Congress, the charter of authority of the parent Committee. Second, petitioner was not adequately apprised of the pertinency of the Subcommittee's questions to the subject matter of the inquiry. Third, the questions petitioner refused to answer infringed rights protected by the First Amendment. . . .

. . . Rule XI authorized this Subcommittee to compel testimony within the framework of the investigative authority conferred on the Un-American Activities Committee. Petitioner contends that *Watkins* v. *United States* [1957] nevertheless held the grant of this power in all circumstances ineffective because of the vagueness of Rule XI in delineating the Committee jurisdiction to which its exercise was to be appurtenant. . . .

Petitioner also contends, independently of *Watkins,* that the vagueness of Rule XI deprived the Subcommittee of the right to compel testimony in this investigation into Communist activity. . . . Granting the vagueness of the Rule, we may not read it in isolation from its long history in the House of Representatives. Just as legislation is often given meaning by the gloss of legislative reports, administrative interpretation, and long usage, so the proper meaning of an authorization to a congressional committee is not to be derived alone from its abstract terms unrelated to the definite content furnished them by the course of congressional actions. The Rule comes to us with a "persuasive gloss of legislative history," . . . which shows beyond doubt that in pursuance of its legislative concerns in the domain of "national security" the House has clothed the Un-American Activities Committee with pervasive authority to investigate Communist activities in this country. . . .

. . . From the beginning, without interruption to the present time, and with the undoubted knowledge and approval of the House, the Committee has devoted a major part of its energies to the investigation of Communist activities. . . .

In the context of these unremitting pursuits, the House has steadily continued the life of the Committee at the commencement of each new Congress; it has never narrowed the powers of the Committee, whose authority has remained throughout identical with that contained in Rule XI; and it has continuingly supported the Committee's activities with substantial appropriations. Beyond this, the Committee was raised to the level of a standing committee of the House in 1945, it having been but a special committee prior to that time.

In light of this long and illuminating history it can hardly be seriously argued that the investigation of Communist activities generally, and the attendant use of compulsory process, was beyond the purview of the Committee's intended authority under Rule XI. . . .

Undeniably a conviction for contempt . . . cannot stand unless the questions asked are pertinent to the subject matter of the investigation. . . .

. . . What we deal with here is whether petitioner was sufficiently apprised of "the topic under inquiry" thus authorized "and the connective reasoning whereby the precise questions asked related to it." *Watkins*. . . . In light of his prepared memorandum of constitutional objections there can be no doubt that this petitioner was well aware of the Subcommittee's authority and purpose to question him as it did. . . . The subject matter of the inquiry had been identified at the commencement of the investigation as Communist infiltration into the field of education. . . . Further, petitioner had stood mute in the face of the Chairman's statement as to why he had been called as a witness by the Subcommittee. And, lastly, . . . petitioner refused to answer questions as to his own Communist Party affiliations, whose pertinency of course was clear beyond doubt. . . .

The precise constitutional issue confronting us is whether the Subcommittee's inquiry into petitioner's past or present membership in the Communist Party transgressed the provisions of the First Amendment, which of course reach and limit congressional investigations. . . .

. . . Undeniably, the First Amendment in some circumstances protects an individual from being compelled to disclose his associational relationships. However, the protections of the First Amendment, unlike a proper claim of the privilege against self-incrimination under the Fifth Amendment, do not afford a witness the right to resist inquiry in all circumstances. Where First Amendment rights are asserted to bar governmental interrogation resolution of the issue always involves a balancing by the courts of the competing private and public interests at stake in the particular circumstances shown. . . .

The first question is whether this investigation was related to a valid legislative purpose, for Congress may not constitutionally require an individual to disclose his political relationships or other private affairs except in relation to such a purpose. . . .

That Congress has wide power to legislate in the field of Communist activity in this Country, and to conduct appropriate investigations in aid thereof, is hardly debatable. The existence of such power has never been questioned by this Court, and it is sufficient to say, without particularization, that Congress has enacted or considered in this field a wide range of legislative measures, not a few of which have stemmed from recommendations of the very Committee whose actions have been drawn in question here. In the last analysis this power rests on the right of self-preservation, "the ultimate value of any society." *Dennis* v. *United States* [1951]. . . . Justification for its exercise in turn rests on the long and widely accepted view that the tenets of the Communist Party include the ultimate overthrow of the Government of the United States by force and violence, a view which has been given formal expression by the Congress.

. . . To suggest that because the Communist Party may also sponsor peaceable political reforms the constitutional issues before us should now be judged as if that Party were just an ordinary political party from the standpoint of national security, is to ask this Court to blind itself to world affairs which have determined the whole course of our national policy since the close of World War II. . . .

Nor can we accept the further contention that this investigation should not be deemed to have been in furtherance of a legislative purpose because the true objective of the Committee and of the Congress was purely "exposure." So long as Congress acts in pursuance of its constitutional power, the Judiciary lacks authority to intervene on the basis of the motives which spurred the exercise of that power. . . . Having scrutinized this record we cannot say that the unanimous panel of the Court of Appeals which first considered this case was wrong in concluding that "the primary purposes of the inquiry were in aid of legislative processes." . . .

We conclude that the balance between the individual and the governmental interests here at stake must be struck in favor of the latter, and that therefore the provisions of the First Amendment have not been offended.

We hold that petitioner's conviction for contempt of Congress discloses no infirmity, and that the judgment of the Court of Appeals must be

Affirmed.

MR. JUSTICE BLACK, with whom THE CHIEF JUSTICE and MR. JUSTICE DOUGLAS concur, dissenting. . . .

It goes without saying that a law to be valid must be clear enough to make its commands understandable. For obvious reasons, the standard of certainty required in criminal statutes is more exacting than in noncriminal statutes. This is simply because it would be unthinkable to convict a man for violating a law he could not understand. This Court has recognized that the stricter standard is as much required in criminal contempt cases as in all other criminal cases, and has emphasized that the "vice of vagueness" is especially pernicious where legislative power over an area involving speech, press, petition and assembly is involved. . . .

Measured by the foregoing standards, Rule XI cannot support any conviction for refusal to testify. . . .

. . . On the Court's own test, the issue is whether Barenblatt can know with sufficient certainty, at the time of his interrogation, that there is so compelling a need for his replies that infringement of his rights of free association is justified. The record does not disclose where Barenblatt can find what that need is. There is certainly no clear congressional statement of it in Rule XI. Perhaps if Barenblatt had had time to read all the reports of the Committee to the House, and in addition had examined the appropriations made to the Committee he, like the Court, could have discerned an intent by Congress to allow an investigation of communism in education. Even so he would be hard put to decide what the need for this investigation is since Congress expressed it neither when it enacted Rule XI nor when it acquiesced in the Committee's assertions of power. Yet it is knowledge of this need—what is wanted from him and why it is wanted—that a witness must have if he is to be in a position to comply with the Court's rule that he balance individual rights against the requirements of the State. I cannot see how that knowledge can exist under Rule XI. . . . I would hold that Rule XI is too broad to be meaningful and cannot support petitioner's conviction. . . .

The First Amendment says in no equivocal language that Congress shall pass no law abridging freedom of speech, press, assembly or petition. The activities of this Committee, authorized by Congress, do precisely that, through exposure, obloquy and public scorn. . . .

To apply the Court's balancing test under [present] circumstances is to read the First Amendment to say "Congress shall pass no law abridging freedom of speech, press, assembly and petition, unless Congress and the Supreme Court reach the joint conclusion that on balance the interest of the Government in stifling these freedoms is greater than the interest of the people in having them exercised." This is closely akin to the notion that neither the First Amendment nor any other provision of the Bill of Rights should be enforced unless the Court believes it is *reasonable* to do so. . . . This violates the genius of our *written* Constitution. . . .

But even assuming what I cannot assume, that some balancing is proper in this case, I feel that the Court after stating the test ignores it completely. At most it balances the right of the Government to preserve itself, against Barenblatt's right to refrain from revealing Communist affiliations. Such a balance, however, mistakes the factors to be weighed. In the first place, it completely leaves out the real interest in Barenblatt's silence, the interest of the people as a whole in being able to join organizations, advocate causes and make political "mistakes" without later being subjected to governmental penalties for having dared to think for themselves. It is this right, the right to err politically, which keeps us strong as a Nation. For no number of laws against communism can have as much effect as the personal conviction which comes from having heard its arguments and rejected them, or from having once accepted its tenets and later recognized their worthlessness. Instead, the obloquy which results from investigations such as this not only stifles "mistakes" but prevents all but the most courageous from hazarding any views which might at some later time become disfavored. This result, whose importance cannot be overestimated, is doubly crucial when it affects the universities, on which we must largely rely for the experimentation and development of new ideas essential to our country's welfare. It is these interests of society, rather than Barenblatt's own right to silence, which I think the Court should put on the balance against the demands of the Government, if any balancing process is to be tolerated. Instead they are not mentioned, while on the other side the demands of the Government are vastly overstated and called "self preservation." It is admitted that this Committee can only seek information for the purpose of suggesting laws, and that Congress' power to make laws in the realm of speech and association is quite limited, even on the Court's test. Its interest in making such laws in the field of education, primarily a state function, is clearly narrower still. Yet the Court styles this attenuated interest self-preservation and allows it to overcome the need our country has to let us all think, speak, and associate politically as we like and without fear of reprisal. Such a result reduces "balancing" to a mere play on words. . . .

Finally, I think Barenblatt's conviction violates the Constitution because the chief aim, purpose and practice of the House Un-American Activities Committee, as disclosed by its many reports, is to try witnesses and punish them because they are or have been Communists or because they refuse to admit or deny Communist affiliations. The punishment imposed is generally punishment by humiliation and public shame. . . .

The same intent to expose and punish is manifest in the Committee's investigation which led to Barenblatt's conviction. The declared purpose of the investigation was to identify to the people of Michigan the individuals responsible for the, alleged, Communist success there. . . . As a result of its Michigan investigation, the Committee called upon American labor unions to amend their constitutions, if necessary, in order to deny membership to any Communist Party member. This would, of course, prevent many workers from getting or holding the only kind of jobs their particular skills qualified them for. The Court, today, barely mentions these statements, which, especially when read in the context of past reports by the Committee, show unmistakably what the Committee was doing. . . .

I do not question the Committee's patriotism and sincerity in doing all this. I merely feel that it cannot be done by Congress under our Constitution. . . .

Brandenburg v. *Ohio*

395 U.S. 444, 89 S. Ct. 1827, 23 L. Ed. 2d 430 (1969)

Charles Brandenburg, a local Ku Klux Klan leader, was convicted under Ohio's Criminal Syndicalism Act, which prohibited "advocating . . . the duty, necessity, or propriety of crime, sabotage, violence, or unlawful methods of terrorism as a means of accomplishing industrial or political reform." The evidence in the case included two television films that showed Brandenburg addressing two Klan meetings. The most provocative element in his speeches was the statement that "if our President, our Congress, our Supreme Court, continues to suppress the white, Caucasian race, it's possible that there might have to be some revengence taken." *Opinion of the Court* per curiam: *Warren, Black, Douglas, Harlan, Brennan, Stewart, White, Fortas, Marshall. Concurring opinions: Black; Douglas, Black.*

PER CURIAM. . . .

The Ohio Criminal Syndicalism Statute was enacted in 1919. From 1917 to 1920, identical or quite similar laws were adopted by 20 States and two territories. . . . In 1927, this Court sustained the constitutionality of California's Criminal Syndicalism Act, the text of which is quite similar to that of the laws of Ohio. *Whitney* v. *California* [1927]. The Court upheld the statute on the ground that, without more, "advocating" violent means to effect political and economic change involves such danger to the security of the State that the State may outlaw it. . . . But *Whitney* has been thoroughly discredited by later decisions. . . . These later decisions have fashioned the principle that the constitutional guarantees of free speech and free press do not permit a State to forbid or proscribe advocacy of the use of force or of law violation except where such advocacy is directed to inciting or producing imminent lawless action and is likely to incite or produce such action. . . .

Measured by this test, Ohio's Criminal Syndicalism Act cannot be sustained. The Act punishes persons who "advocate or teach the duty, necessity, or propriety" of violence "as a means of accomplishing industrial or political reform"; or who publish or circulate or display any book or paper containing such advocacy; or who "justify" the commission of violent acts "with intent to exemplify, spread or advocate the propriety of the doctrines of criminal syndicalism"; or who "voluntarily assemble" with a group formed "to teach or advocate the doctrines of criminal syndicalism." Neither the indictment nor the trial judge's instructions to the jury in any way refined the statute's bald definition of the crime in terms of mere advocacy not distinguished from incitement to imminent lawless action.

Accordingly, we are here confronted with a statute which, by its own words and as applied, purports to punish mere advocacy and to forbid, on pain of criminal punishment, assembly with others merely to advocate the described type of action. Such a statute falls within the condemnation of the First and Fourteenth Amendments. The contrary teaching of *Whitney* v. *California* . . . cannot be supported, and that decision is therefore overruled.

Reversed.

MR. JUSTICE DOUGLAS, concurring.

While I join the opinion of the Court, I desire to enter a *caveat*. . . .

. . . I see no place in the regime of the First Amendment for any "clear and present danger" test, whether strict and tight as some would make it, or free-wheeling as the Court in *Dennis* rephrased it.

When one reads the opinions closely and sees when and how the "clear and present danger" test has been applied, great misgivings are aroused. First, the threats were often loud but always puny and made serious only by judges so wedded to the *status quo* that critical analysis made them nervous. Second, the test was so twisted and perverted in *Dennis* [v. *United States* (1951)] as to make the trial of those teachers of Marxism an all-out political trial which was part and parcel of the cold war that has eroded substantial parts of the First Amendment.

One's beliefs have long been thought to be sanctuaries which government could not invade. *Barenblatt* [v. *United States* (1959)] is one example of the ease with which that sanctuary can be violated. The lines drawn by the Court between the criminal act of being an "active" Communist and the innocent act of being a nominal or inactive Communist mark the difference only between deep and abiding belief and casual or uncertain belief. But I think that all matters of belief are beyond the reach of subpoenas or the probings of investigators. That is why the invasions of privacy made by investigating committees were notoriously unconstitutional. That is the deep-seated fault in the infamous loyalty-security hearings which, since 1947 when President Truman launched them, have processed 20,000,000 men and women. Those hearings were primarily concerned with one's thoughts, ideas, beliefs, and convictions. They were the most blatant violations of the First Amendment we have ever known.

The line between what is permissible and not subject to control and what may be made impermissible and subject to regulation is the line between ideas and overt acts.

The example usually given by those who would punish speech is the case of one who falsely shouts fire in a crowded theatre.

This is, however, a classic case where speech is brigaded with action. . . . They are indeed inseparable and a prosecution can be launched for the overt acts actually caused. Apart from rare instances of that kind, speech is, I think, immune from prosecution. Certainly there is no constitutional line between advocacy of abstract ideas as in *Yates* [v. *United States* (1957)] and advocacy of political action as in *Scales* [v. *United States* (1961)]. The quality of advocacy turns on the depth of the conviction; and government has no power to invade that sanctuary of belief and conscience.

Buckley v. *Valeo*

424 U.S. 1, 96 S. Ct. 612, 46 L. Ed. 2d 659 (1976)

Distressed by the campaign abuses documented during the Watergate investigations, Congress in 1974 amended the Federal Election Campaign Act of 1971, introducing a comprehensive set of electoral reforms. The Court of Appeals for the District of Columbia in large measure sustained the act, and the Supreme Court considered its constitutionality on appeal. The following excerpts deal primarily with the act's limits on contributions to candidates for federal office, its limits on expenditures in support of such candidates, and its provisions compelling disclosure of campaign contributions. In addition, the Court upheld the constitutionality of a system of federal financing of presidential campaigns and invalidated provisions for appointment of some members of the Federal Election Commission by the president *pro tem* of the Senate and the Speaker of the House. *Opinion of the Court* per curiam: *Burger, Brennan, Stewart, White, Marshall, Blackmun, Powell, Rehnquist. Concurring in part and dissenting in part: Burger; White; Marshall; Blackmun; Powell; Rehnquist. Not participating: Stevens.*

PER CURIAM.

. . . The statutes at issue summarized in broad terms, contain the following provisions: (a) individual political contributions are limited to $1,000 to any single candidate per election, with an overall annual limitation of $25,000 by any contributor; independent expenditures by individuals and groups "relative to a clearly identified candidate" are limited to $1,000 a year; campaign spending by candidates for various federal offices and spending for national conventions by political parties are subject to prescribed limits; (b) contributions and expenditures above certain threshold levels must be reported and publicly disclosed; (c) a system for public funding of Presidential campaign activities is established by Subtitle H of the Internal Revenue Code; and (d) a Federal Election Commission is established to administer and enforce the legislation.

I. CONTRIBUTION AND EXPENDITURE LIMITATIONS

A. General Principles

The Act's contribution and expenditure limitations operate in an area of the most fundamental First Amendment activities. Discussion of public issues and debate on the qualifications of candidates are integral to the operation of the system of government established by our Constitution. The First Amendment affords the broadest protection to such political expression. . . . Appellees contend that what the Act regulates is conduct, and that its effect on speech and association is incidental at most. Appellants respond that contributions and expenditures are at the very core of political speech, and that the Act's limitations thus constitute restraints on First Amendment liberty that are both gross and direct.

We cannot share the view that the present Act's contribution and expenditure limitations are comparable to the restrictions on conduct upheld in [*United States* v. *O'Brien* (1968)]. The expenditure of money simply cannot be equated with such conduct as destruction of a draft card. Some forms of communication made possible by the giving and spending of money involve speech alone, some involve conduct primarily, and some involve a combination of the two. Yet this Court has never suggested that the dependence of a communication on the expenditure of money operates itself to introduce a nonspeech element or to reduce the exacting scrutiny required by the First Amendment. . . .

Even if the categorization of the expenditure of money as conduct were accepted, the limitations challenged here would not meet the *O'Brien* test because the governmental interests advanced in support of the Act involve "suppressing communication." . . . Nor can the Act's contribution and expenditure limitations be sustained . . . by reference to the constitutional principles reflected in [the Court's time, place, and manner cases]. . . . The critical difference between this case and those . . . cases is that the present Act's contribution and expenditure limitations impose direct quantity restrictions on political communication and association by persons, groups, candidates, and political parties in addition to any reasonable time, place, and manner regulations otherwise imposed.

A restriction on the amount of money a person or group can spend on political communication during a campaign necessarily reduces the quantity of expression by restricting the number of issues discussed, the depth of their exploration, and the size of the audience reached. This is because virtually every means of communicating ideas in today's mass society requires the expenditure of money. . . .

The expenditure limitations contained in the Act represent substantial rather than merely theoretical restraints on the quantity and diversity of political speech. The $1,000 ceiling on spending "relative to a clearly identified candidate," . . . would appear to exclude all citizens and groups except candidates, political parties, and the institutional press from any significant use of the most effective modes of communication.

By contrast, . . . a limitation upon the amount that any one person or group may contribute to a candidate or political committee entails only a marginal restriction upon the contributor's ability to engage in free communication. A contribution serves as a general expression of support for the candidate and his views, but does not communicate the underlying basis for the support. . . . A limitation on the amount of money a person may give to a candidate or campaign organization thus involves little direct restraint on his political communication, for it permits the symbolic expression of support evidenced by a contribution but does not in any way infringe the contributor's freedom to discuss candidates and issues. While contributions may result in political expression if spent by a candidate or an association to present views to the voters, the transformation of contributions into political debate involves speech by someone other than the contributor.

. . . The overall effect of the Act's contribution ceilings is merely to require candidates and political committees to raise funds from a greater number of persons and to compel people who would otherwise contribute amounts greater than the statutory limits to expend such funds on direct political expression, rather than to reduce the total amount of money potentially available to promote political expression. . . .

B. Contribution Limitations

It is unnecessary to look beyond the Act's primary purpose—to limit the actuality and appearance of corruption resulting from large individual financial contributions—in order to find a constitutionally sufficient justification for the $1,000 contribution limitation. . . . To the extent that large contributions are given to secure a political *quid pro quo* from current and potential office holders, the integrity of our system of representative democracy is undermined. Although the scope of such pernicious practices can never be reliably ascertained, the deeply disturbing examples surfacing after the 1972 election demonstrate that the problem is not an illusory one.

Of almost equal concern . . . is the impact of the appearance of corruption stemming from public awareness of the opportunities for abuse inherent in a regime of large individual financial contributions. . . .

Appellants contend that the contribution limitations must be invalidated because bribery laws and narrowly drawn disclosure requirements constitute a less restrictive means of dealing with "proven and suspected *quid pro quo* arrangements." But . . . Congress was surely entitled to conclude that disclosure was only a partial measure, and that contribution ceilings were a necessary legislative concomitant. . . .

We find that, under the rigorous standard of review established by our prior decisions, the weighty interests served by restricting the size of financial contributions to political candidates are sufficient to justify the limited effect upon First Amendment freedoms caused by the $1,000 contribution ceiling. . . .

C. Expenditure Limitations . . .

We find that the governmental interest in preventing corruption and the appearance of corruption is inadequate to justify § 608 (e)(1)'s ceiling on independent expenditures. First, assuming, *arguendo,* that large independent expenditures pose the same dangers of actual or apparent *quid pro quo* arrangements as do large contributions, § 608 (e)(1) does not provide an answer that sufficiently relates to the elimination of those dangers. Unlike the contribution limitations' total ban on the giving of large amounts of money to candidates, § 608 (e)(1) prevents only some large expenditures. So long as persons and groups eschew expenditures that in express terms advocate the election or defeat of a clearly identified candidate, they are free to spend as much as they want to promote the candidate and his views. . . . It would naively underestimate the ingenuity and resourcefulness of persons and groups desiring to buy influence to believe that they would have much difficulty devising expenditures that skirted the restriction on express advocacy of election or defeat but nevertheless benefited the candidate's campaign. . . . Second, . . . the independent advocacy restricted by the provision does not presently appear to pose dangers of real or apparent corruption comparable to those identified with large campaign contributions. . . . Section 608 (b)'s contribution ceilings rather than § 608 (e)(1)'s independent expenditure limitation prevent attempts to circumvent the Act through prearranged or coordinated expenditures amounting to disguised contributions. . . .

It is argued, however, that the ancillary governmental interest in equalizing the relative ability of individuals and groups to influence the outcome of elections serves to justify the limitation on express advocacy of the election or defeat of candidates imposed by §608 (e)(1)'s expenditure ceiling. But the concept that government may restrict the speech of some elements of our society in order to enhance the relative voice of others is wholly foreign to the First Amendment. . . .

Limitation on Expenditures by Candidates from Personal or Family Resources.

The primary governmental interest served by the Act—the prevention of actual and apparent corruption of the political process—does not support the limitation on the candidate's expenditure of his own personal funds. . . . Indeed, the use of personal funds reduces the candidate's dependence on outside contributions and thereby counteracts the coercive pressures and attendant risks of abuse to which the Act's contribution limitations are directed.

The ancillary interest in equalizing the relative financial resources of candidates competing for elective office, therefore, provides the sole relevant rationale for §608 (a)'s expenditure ceiling. That interest is clearly not sufficient to justify the provision's infringement of fundamental First Amendment rights. . . .

Limitations on Campaign Expenditures.

The campaign expenditure ceilings appear to be designed primarily to serve the governmental interests in reducing the allegedly skyrocketing costs of political campaigns, . . . [But] the mere growth in the cost of federal election campaigns in and of itself provides no basis for governmental restrictions on the quantity of campaign spending and the resulting limitation on the scope of federal campaigns. The First Amendment denies government the power to determine that spending to promote one's political views is wasteful, excessive, or unwise. In the free society ordained by our Constitution it is not the government, but the people—individually as citizens and candidates and collectively as associations and political committees—who must retain control over the quantity and range of debate on public issues in a political campaign. . . .

II. REPORTING AND DISCLOSURE REQUIREMENTS

A. General Principles

. . . Unlike the overall limitations on contributions and expenditures, the disclosure requirements impose no ceiling on campaign-related activities. But we have repeatedly found that compelled disclosure, in itself, can seriously infringe on privacy of association and belief guaranteed by the First Amendment. . . . Since *NAACP* v. *Alabama* [1958] we have required that the subordinating interests of the State must survive exacting scrutiny. We also have insisted that there be a "relevant correlation" or "substantial relation" between the governmental interest and the information required to be disclosed. . . . But we have acknowledged that there are governmental interests sufficiently important to outweigh the possibility of infringement, particularly when the "free functioning of our national institutions" is involved. *Communist Party* v. *Subversive Activities Control Bd.* (1961). . . .

The governmental interests sought to be vindicated by the disclosure requirements are of this magnitude. They fall into three categories. First, disclosure provides the electorate with information "as to where political campaign money comes from and how it is spent by the candidate" in order to aid the voters in evaluating those who seek federal office. It allows voters to place each candidate in the political spectrum more precisely than is often possible solely on the basis of party labels and campaign speeches. The sources of a candidate's financial support also alert the voter to the interests to which a candidate is most likely to be responsive and thus facilitate predictions of future performance in office.

Second, disclosure requirements deter actual corruption and avoid the appearance of corruption by exposing large contributions and expenditures to the light of publicity. . . .

Third, and not least significant, recordkeeping, reporting, and disclosure requirements are an essential means of gathering the data necessary to detect violations of the contribution limitations described above.

B. Application to Minor Parties and Independents

Appellants contend that the Act's requirements are overbroad insofar as they apply to contributions to minor parties and independent candidates because the governmental interest in this information is minimal and the danger of significant infringement on First Amendment rights is greatly increased.

In *NAACP* v. *Alabama* the organization had "made an uncontroverted showing that on past occasions revelation of the identity of its rank-and-file members [had] exposed these members to economic reprisal, loss of employment, threat of physical coercion, and other manifestations of public hostility," . . . and the State was unable to show that the disclosure it sought had a "substantial bearing" on the issues it sought to clarify. . . . No record of harassment on a similar scale was found in this case. We agree with the Court of Appeals' conclusion that *NAACP* v. *Alabama* is inapposite where, as here, any serious infringement on First Amendment rights brought about by the compelled disclosure of contributors is highly speculative. . . .

MR. CHIEF JUSTICE BURGER, concurring in part and dissenting in part. . . .

. . . no legitimate public interest has been shown in forcing the disclosure of modest contributions that are the prime support of new, unpopular, or unfashionable political causes. There is no realistic possibility that such modest donations will have a corrupting influence especially on parties that enjoy only "minor" status. . . . In any event, the dangers to First Amendment rights here are too great. Flushing out the names of supporters of minority parties will plainly have a deterrent effect on potential contributors. . . .

I agree fully with that part of the Court's opinion that holds unconstitutional the limitations the Act puts on campaign expenditures which "place substantial and direct restrictions on the ability of candidates, citizens, and associations to engage in protected political expression, restrictions that the First Amendment cannot tolerate.". . . Yet when it approves similarly stringent limitations on contributions, the Court ignores the reasons it finds so persuasive in the context of expenditures. For me contributions and expenditures are two sides of the same First Amendment coin.

By limiting campaign contributions, the Act restricts the amount of money that will be spent on political activity—and does so directly.

The Court's attempt to distinguish the communication inherent in political *contributions* from the speech aspects of political *expenditures* simply "will not wash." We do little but engage in word games unless we recognize that people—candidates and contributors—spend money on political activity because they wish to communicate ideas, and their constitutional interest in doing so is precisely the same whether they or someone else utters the words.

The Court attempts to make the Act seem less restrictive by casting the problem as one that goes to freedom of association rather than freedom of speech. I have long thought freedom of association and freedom of expression were two peas from the same pod. The contribution limitations of the Act impose a restriction on certain forms of associational activity that are for the most part, as the Court recognizes, . . . harmless in fact. And the restrictions are hardly incidental in their effect upon particular campaigns. . . .

At any rate, the contribution limits are a far more severe restriction on First Amendment activity than the sort of "chilling" legislation for which the Court has shown such extraordinary concern in the past. . . .

MR. JUSTICE WHITE, concurring in part and dissenting in part.

. . . I dissent . . . from the Court's view that the expenditure limitations of 18 U.S.C. §§ 608 (c) and (e) . . . violate the First Amendment. . . .

Since the contribution and expenditure limitations are neutral as to the content of speech and are not motivated by fear of the consequences of the political speech of particular candidates or of political speech in general, this case depends on whether the nonspeech interests of the Federal Government in regulating the use of money in political campaigns are sufficiently urgent to justify the incidental effects that the limitations visit upon the First Amendment interests of candidates and their supporters.

. . . The Court . . . accepts the congressional judgment that the evils of unlimited contributions are sufficiently threatening to warrant restriction regardless of the impact of the limits on the contributor's opportunity for effective speech and in turn on the total volume of the candidate's political communications by reason of his inability to accept large sums from those willing to give.

. . . Congress was plainly of the view that these expenditures also have corruptive potential; but the Court strikes down the provision, strangely enough claiming more insight as to what may improperly influence candidates than is possessed by the majority of Congress that passed this bill and the President who signed it. Those supporting the bill undeniably included many seasoned professionals who have been deeply involved in elective processes and who have viewed them at close range over many years. . . .

Texas v. *Johnson*

491 U.S., 109 S. Ct. 2533, 105 L.Ed. 2d 342 (1989)

During the Republican National Convention in Dallas in 1984. Gregory Johnson participated in a demonstration, dubbed the "Republican War Chest Tour," to protest the policies of the Reagan administration and of certain Dallas-based corporations. The demonstrators marched through the Dallas streets, chanting slogans, and staged "die-ins" outside various corporate locations to dramatize the consequences of nuclear war. The demonstration ended in front of Dallas City Hall, where Johnson unfurled an American flag given to him by a fellow demonstrator (who had taken it from outside a building along the route), doused it with kerosene, and set it on fire. While the flag burned, the protestors chanted: "America, the red, white, and blue, we spit on you." Johnson was subsequently arrested and convicted of violating a Texas law prohibiting the "desecration of venerated objects," including the national flag. The law defined "desecrate" as "deface, damage, or otherwise physically mistreat in a way that the actor knows will seriously offend one or more persons likely to observe or discover his action."

The opinion of the Court applies the "*O'Brien* test," derived from *United States* v. *O'Brien* (1968), for determining the constitutionality of governmental regulations of expressive conduct. Under that test, "a governmental regulation is sufficiently justified if it is within the constitutional power of the government; if it furthers an important or substantial governmental interest; if the governmental interest is unrelated to the suppression of free expression; and if the incidental restriction of alleged First Amendment freedoms is no greater than is essential to the furtherance of that interest." *Opinion of the Court: Brennan, Marshall, Blackmun, Scalia, Kennedy. Concurring opinion: Kennedy. Dissenting opinions: Rehnquist, White, O'Connor: Stevens.*

JUSTICE BRENNAN delivered the opinion of the Court.

. . . After publicly burning an American flag as a means of political protest, Gregory Lee Johnson was convicted of desecrating a flag in violation of Texas law. This case presents the question whether his conviction is consistent with the First Amendment. We hold that it is not.

I

. . . Johnson was convicted of flag desecration for burning the flag rather than for uttering insulting words. This fact somewhat complicates our consideration of his conviction under the First Amendment. We must first determine whether Johnson's burning of the flag constituted expressive conduct, permitting him to invoke the First Amendment in challenging his conviction. . . . If his conduct was expressive, we next decide whether the State's regulation is related to the suppression of free expression. . . . If the State's regulation is not related to expression, then the less stringent standard we announced in *United States* v. *O'Brien* for regulations of noncommunicative conduct controls. . . . If it is, then we are outside of *O'Brien*'s test, and we must ask whether this interest justifies Johnson's conviction under a more demanding standard. . . .

In deciding whether particular conduct possesses sufficient communicative elements to bring the First Amendment into play, we have asked whether "[a]n intent to convey a particularized message was present, and [whether] the likelihood was great that the message would be understood by those who viewed it." . . .

. . . The State of Texas conceded for purposes

of its oral argument in this case that Johnson's conduct was expressive conduct, . . . Johnson burned an American flag as part—indeed, as the culmination—of a political demonstration that coincided with the convening of the Republican Party and its renomination of Ronald Reagan for President. The expressive, overtly political nature of this conduct was both intentional and overwhelmingly apparent. . . . In these circumstances, Johnson's burning of the flag was conduct "sufficiently imbued with elements of communication," . . . to implicate the First Amendment.

II

. . . In order to decide whether *O'Brien*'s test applies here, therefore, we must decide whether Texas has asserted an interest in support of Johnson's conviction that is unrelated to the suppression of expression. . . . The State offers two separate interests to justify this conviction: preventing breaches of the peace, and preserving the flag as a symbol of nationhood and national unity. We hold that the first interest is not implicated on this record and that the second is related to the suppression of expression.

A

. . . Texas claims that its interest in preventing breaches of the peace justifies Johnson's conviction for flag desecration. However, no disturbance of the peace actually occurred or threatened to occur because of Johnson's burning of the flag. . . . The only evidence offered by the State at trial to show the reaction to Johnson's actions was the testimony of several persons who had been seriously offended by the flag-burning. . . .

The State's position, therefore, amounts to a claim that an audience that takes serious offense at particular expression is necessarily likely to disturb the peace and that the expression may be prohibited on this basis. Our precedents do not countenance such a presumption. . . .

Thus, we have not permitted the Government to assume that every expression of a provocative idea will incite a riot, but have instead required careful consideration of the actual circumstances surrounding such expression, asking whether the expression "is directed to inciting or producing imminent lawless action and is likely to incite or produce such action." *Brandenburg* v. *Ohio*, . . . (1969). . . .

We . . . conclude that the State's interest in maintaining order is not implicated on these facts. . . .

B

The State also asserts an interest in preserving the flag as a symbol of nationhood and national unity. . . . The State, apparently, is concerned that such conduct will lead people to believe either that the flag does not stand for nationhood and national unity, but instead reflects other, less positive concepts, or that the concepts reflected in the flag do not in fact, exist, that is, we do not enjoy unity as a Nation. These concerns blossom only when a person's treatment of the flag communicates some message, and thus are related "to the suppression of free expression" within the meaning of *O'Brien.* We are thus outside of *O'Brien*'s test altogether.

III

It remains to consider whether the State's interest in preserving the flag as a symbol of nationhood and national unity justifies Johnson's conviction. . . . According to Texas, if one physically treats the flag in a way that would tend to cast doubt on either the idea that nationhood and national unity are the flag's referents or that national unity actually exists, the message conveyed thereby is a harmful one and therefore may be prohibited.

. . . If there is a bedrock principle underlying the First Amendment, it is that the Government may not prohibit the expression of an idea simply because society finds the idea itself offensive or disagreeable. . . .

We have not recognized an exception to this principle even where our flag has been involved. In *Street* v. *New York* . . . (1969), we held that a State may not criminally punish a person for uttering words critical of the flag. . . . Nor may the Government, we have held in *West Virginia State Board of Education* v. *Barnette* (1943), in which the Court invalidated a compulsory flag salute law], compel conduct that would evince respect for the flag. . . .

. . . In short, nothing in our precedents suggests that a State may foster its own view of the flag by prohibiting expressive conduct relating to it. . . . To conclude that the Government may permit designated symbols to be used to communicate only a limited set of messages would be to enter territory having no discernible or defensible boundaries. Could the Government, on this theory, prohibit the burning of state flags? Of copies of the Presidential seal? Of the Constitution? In evaluating these choices under the First Amendment, how would we decide which symbols were sufficiently special to warrant this unique status? To do so, we would be forced to consult our own political preferences, and impose them on the citizenry, in the very way that the First Amendment forbids us to do. . . .

. . . It is not the State's ends, but its means, to which we object. It cannot be gainsaid that there is a special place reserved for the flag in this Nation, and thus we do not doubt that the Government has a legitimate interest in making efforts to "preserv[e] the national flag as an unalloyed symbol of our country." . . . We reject the suggestion, urged at oral argument by counsel for Johnson, that the Government lacks "any state interest whatsoever" in regulating the manner in which the flag may be displayed. . . . Congress has, for example, enacted precatory regulations describing the proper treatment of the flag, . . . and we cast no doubt on the legitimacy of its interest in making such recommendations. To say that the Government has an interest in encouraging proper treatment of the flag, however, is not to say that it may criminally punish a person for burning a flag as a means of political protest. "National unity as an end which officials may foster by persuasion and example is not in question. The problem is whether under our Constitution compulsion as here employed is a permissible means for its achievement." Barnette. . . .

CHIEF JUSTICE REHNQUIST, with whom JUSTICE WHITE and JUSTICE O'CONNOR join, dissenting.

In holding this Texas statute unconstitutional, the Court ignores Justice Holmes' familiar aphorism that "a page of history is worth a volume of logic." *New York Trust Co.* v. *Eisner* . . . (1921). For more than 200 years, the American flag has occupied a unique position as the symbol of our Nation, a uniqueness that justifies a governmental prohibition against flag burning in the way respondent Johnson did here. . . .

The American flag . . . does not represent the views of any particular political party, and it does not represent any particular political philosophy. The flag is not simply another "idea" or "point of view" competing for recognition in the marketplace of ideas. Millions and millions of Americans regard it with an almost mystical reverence regardless of what sort of social, political, or philosophical beliefs they may have. I cannot agree that the First Amendment invalidates the Act of Congress, and the laws of 48 of the 50 States, which make criminal the public burning of the flag. . . .

. . . the Court insists that the Texas statute prohibiting the public burning of the American flag infringes on respondent Johnson's freedom of expression. . . . Johnson was free to make any verbal denunciation of the flag that he wished; indeed, he was free to burn the flag in private. He could publicly burn other symbols of the Government or effigies of political leaders. He did lead a march through the streets of Dallas, and conducted a rally in front of the Dallas City Hall. He engaged in a "die-in" to protest nuclear weapons. He shouted out various slogans during the march, including: "Reagan, Mondale which will it be? Either one means World War III"; "Ronald Reagan, killer of the hour, Perfect example of US power"; and "red, white and blue, we spit on you, you stand for plunder, you will go under." . . . For none of these acts was he arrested or prosecuted; it was only when he proceeded to burn publicly an American flag stolen from its rightful owner that he violated the Texas statute. . . . The Texas statute deprived Johnson of only one rather inarticulate symbolic form of protest—a form of protest that was profoundly offensive to many—and left him with a full panoply of other symbols and every conceivable form of verbal expression to express his deep disapproval of national policy. Thus, in no way can it be said that Texas is punishing him because his hearers—or any other group of people—were profoundly opposed to the message that he sought to convey. Such opposition is no proper basis for restricting speech or expression under the First Amendment. It was Johnson's use of this particular symbol, and not the idea that he sought to convey by it or by his many other expressions, for which he was punished. . . . But the Court today will have none of this. The uniquely deep awe and respect for our flag felt by virtually all of us are bundled off under the rubric of "designated symbols," . . . that the First Amendment prohibits the government from "establishing." But the government has not "established" this feeling; 200 years of history have done that. The government is simply recognizing as a fact the profound regard for the American flag created by that history when it enacts statutes prohibiting the disrespectful public burning of the flag.

Village of Skokie v. *National Socialist Party of America*

373 N.E. 2d 21, 69 Ill. 2d 605 (1978)

The National Socialist Party of America (the American Nazi Party) sought to conduct a demonstration in Skokie, Illinois, a predominantly Jewish suburb of Chicago in which over five thousand survivors of German concentration camps resided. Not surprisingly, the request generated a furor. After the Skokie Park District required the party to obtain a $350,000 bond before using a park for a public assembly, the party petitioned to conduct a half-hour demonstration protesting this action by marching in front of the village hall. Village officials denied the petition and obtained a court order enjoining party members from demonstrating in Skokie. After the Illinois courts refused to stay the court order, the United States Supreme Court reversed the decision and remanded the case. An Illinois appellate court then lifted the ban on the demonstration but prohibited the wearing or display of the swastika—a ruling the party appealed to the Illinois Supreme Court. *Opinion of the Court* per curiam: *Ward, Underwood, Goldenhersh, Ryan, Moran, Kluczynski. Dissenting without opinion: Clark.*

PER CURIAM. . . .

In defining the constitutional rights of the parties who come before this court, we are, of course, bound by the pronouncements of the United States Supreme Court in its interpretation of the United States Constitution. . . . The decisions of that court, particularly *Cohen* v. *California* (1971), . . . in our opinion compel us to permit the demonstration as proposed, including display of the swastika.

"It is firmly settled that under our Constitution the public expression of ideas may not be prohibited merely because the ideas are themselves offensive to some of their hearers" (*Bachellar* v. *Maryland* (1970) . . . and it is entirely clear that the wearing of distinctive clothing can be symbolic expression of a thought or philosophy. The symbolic expression of thought falls within the free speech clause of the first amendment, . . . and the plaintiff village has the heavy burden of justifying the imposition of a prior restraint upon defendants' right to freedom of speech. . . .

. . . The village of Skokie seeks to meet this burden by application of the "fighting words" doctrine first enunciated in *Chaplinsky* v. *New Hampshire* (1942). . . . That doctrine was designed to permit punishment of extremely hostile personal communication likely to cause immediate physical response, "no words being 'forbidden except such as have a direct tendency to cause acts of violence by the persons to whom, individually, the remark is addressed.' " . . . In *Cohen* the Supreme Court restated the description of fighting words as "those personally abusive epithets which, when addressed to the ordinary citizen, are, as a matter of common knowledge, inherently likely to provoke violent reaction." . . . Plaintiff urges, and the appellate court has held, that the exhibition of the Nazi symbol, the swastika, addresses to ordinary citizens a message which is tantamount to fighting words. Plaintiff further asks this court to extend *Chaplinsky,* which upheld a statute punishing the use of such words, and hold that the fighting-words doctrine permits a prior restraint on defendants' symbolic speech. . . .

. . . We do not doubt that the sight of this symbol is abhorrent to the Jewish citizens of

Skokie, and that the survivors of the Nazi persecutions, tormented by their recollections, may have strong feelings regarding its display. Yet it is entirely clear that this factor does not justify enjoining defendants' speech. The *Cohen* court spoke to this subject:

"Finally, in arguments before this Court much has been made of the claim that Cohen's distasteful mode of expression was thrust upon unwilling or unsuspecting viewers, and that the State might therefore legitimately act as it did in order to protect the sensitive from otherwise unavoidable exposure to appellant's crude form of protest. . . . While this Court has recognized that government may properly act in many situations to prohibit intrusion into the privacy of the home of unwelcome views and ideas which cannot be totally banned from the public dialogue. . . . we have at the same time consistently stressed that 'we are often "captives" outside the sanctuary of the home and subject to objectionable speech.' . . . The ability of government, consonant with the Constitution, to shut off discourse solely to protect others from hearing it is, in other words, dependent upon a showing that substantial privacy interests are being invaded in an essentially intolerable manner. Any broader view of this authority would effectively empower a majority to silence dissidents simply as a matter of personal predilections." . . .

. . . In summary, as we read the controlling Supreme Court opinions, use of the swastika is a symbolic form of free speech entitled to first amendment protections. Its display on uniforms or banners by those engaged in peaceful demonstrations cannot be totally precluded solely because that display may provoke a violent reaction by those who view it. Particularly is this true where, as here, there has been advance notice by the demonstrators of their plans so that they have become, as the complaint alleges, "common knowledge" and those to whom sight of the swastika banner or uniforms would be offensive are forewarned and need not view them. A speaker who gives prior notice of his message has not compelled a confrontation with those who voluntarily listen. . . .

We accordingly, albeit reluctantly, conclude that the display of the swastika cannot be enjoined under the fighting-words exception to free speech, nor can anticipation of a hostile audience justify the prior restraint. Furthermore, *Cohen* and *Erznoznik* [v. *City of Jacksonville* (1975)] direct the citizens of Skokie that it is their burden to avoid the offensive symbol if they can do so without unreasonable inconvenience. Accordingly, we are constrained to reverse that part of the appellate court judgment enjoining the display of the swastika. That judgment is in all other respects affirmed.

Adderley v. *Florida*

385 U.S. 39, 87 S. Ct. 242, 17L. Ed. 2d 149 (1966)

During the 1950s and 1960s the Court decided several cases involving demonstrations by civil rights groups. *Adderley* involved a group of students who demonstrated peacefully on the grounds of a county jail to protest the arrest of fellow demonstrators and local racial segregation. After ignoring a sheriff's warning to leave the premises, several demonstrators were arrested and convicted under a Florida trespass statute. The convictions were affirmed in the state courts, and the Supreme Court granted certiorari. *Opinion of the Court: Black, Clark, Harlan, Stewart, White. Dissenting opinion: Douglas, Brennan, Warren, Fortas.*

MR. JUSTICE BLACK delivered the opinion of the Court. . . .

Petitioners have insisted from the beginning of this case that it is controlled by and must be reversed because of our prior cases of *Edwards* v. *South Carolina* [1963] . . . and *Cox* v. *Louisiana* [1965]. . . . We cannot agree.

The *Edwards* case, like this one, did come up when a number of persons demonstrated on public property against their State's segregation policies.

They also sang hymns and danced, as did the demonstrators in this case. But here the analogies to this case end. In *Edwards,* the demonstrators went to the South Carolina State Capitol grounds to protest. In this case they went to the jail. Traditionally, state capitol grounds are open to the public. Jails, built for security purposes, are not. The demonstrators at the South Carolina Capitol went in through a public driveway and as they entered they were told by state officials there that they had a right as citizens to go through the State House grounds as long as they were peaceful. Here the demonstrators entered the jail grounds through a driveway used only for jail purposes and without warning to or permission from the sheriff. More importantly, South Carolina sought to prosecute its State Capitol demonstrators by charging them with the common-law crime of breach of the peace. This Court in *Edwards* took pains to point out at length the indefinite, loose, and broad nature of this charge. . . . South Carolina's power to prosecute, it was emphasized, . . . would have been different had the State proceeded under a "precise and narrowly drawn regulatory statute evincing a legislative judgment that certain specific conduct be limited or proscribed" such as, for example, "limiting the periods during which the State House grounds were open to the public. . . ." The South Carolina breach-of-the-peace statute was thus struck down as being so broad and all-embracing as to jeopardize speech, press, assembly and petition. . . . And it was on this same ground of vagueness that in *Cox* v. *Louisiana* . . . the Louisiana breach-of-the-peace law used to prosecute Cox was invalidated.

The Florida trespass statute under which these petitioners were charged cannot be challenged on this ground. It is aimed at conduct of one limited kind, that is, for one person or persons to trespass upon the property of another with a malicious and mischievous intent. There is no lack of notice in this law, nothing to entrap or fool the unwary. . . . Petitioners here contend that "Petitioners' convictions are based on a total lack of relevant evidence." If true, this would be a denial of due process. . . . [However,] petitioners' summary of facts, as well as that of the Circuit Court, shows an abundance of facts to support the jury's verdict of guilty in this case. . . .

[Justice Black then summarized the facts of the case.]

The sheriff, as jail custodian, had power . . . to direct that this large crowd of people get off the grounds. There is not a shred of evidence in this record that this power was exercised, or that its exercise was sanctioned by the lower courts, because the sheriff objected to what was being sung or said by the demonstrators or because he disagreed with the objectives of their protest. The record reveals that he objected only to their presence on that part of the jail grounds reserved for jail uses. There is no evidence at all that on any other occasion had similarly large groups of the public been permitted to gather on this portion of the jail grounds for any purpose. Nothing in the Constitution of the United States prevents Florida from even-handed enforcement of its general trespass statute against those refusing to obey the sheriff's order to remove themselves from what amounted to the curtilage of the jailhouse. The State, no less than a private owner of property, has power to preserve the property under its control for the use to which it is lawfully dedicated. For this reason there is no merit to the petitioners' argument that they had a constitutional right to stay on the property, over the jail custodian's objections, because this "area chosen for the peaceful civil rights demonstration was not only 'reasonable' but also particularly appropriate . . . ." Such an argument has as its major unarticulated premise the assumption that people who want to propagandize protests or views have a constitutional right to do so whenever and however and wherever they please. That concept of constitutional law was vigorously and forthrightly rejected [previously]. . . . We reject it again. The United States Constitution does not forbid a State to control the use of its own property for its own lawful nondiscriminatory purpose.

These judgments are

Affirmed.

MR. JUSTICE DOUGLAS, with whom THE CHIEF JUSTICE, MR. JUSTICE BRENNAN, and MR. JUSTICE FORTAS concur, dissenting.

The jailhouse, like an executive mansion, a legislative chamber, a courthouse, or the statehouse itself . . . is one of the seats of government, whether it be the Tower of London, the Bastille, or a small county jail. And when it houses political prisoners or those who many think are unjustly held, it is an obvious center for protest. The right to petition for the redress of grievances has an ancient history and is not limited to writing a letter or sending a telegram to a congressman; it is not confined to appearing before the local city council, or writing letters to the President or Governor or Mayor. . . . Conventional methods of petitioning may be, and often have been, shut off to large groups of our citizens. Legislators may turn deaf ears; formal complaints may be routed endlessly through a bureaucratic maze; courts may let the wheels of justice grind very slowly. Those who do not control television and radio, those who cannot afford to advertise in newspapers or circulate elaborate pamphlets may have only a more limited type of access to public officials. Their methods should not be condemned as tactics of obstruction and harassment as long as the assembly and petition are peaceable, as these were.

There is no question that petitioners had as their purpose a protest against the arrest of Florida A. & M. students for trying to integrate public theatres. . . . There was no violence; no threat of violence; no attempted jail break; no storming of a prison; no plan or plot to do anything but protest. The evidence is uncontradicted that the petitioners' conduct did not upset the jailhouse routine; things went on as they normally would. . . .

We do violence to the First Amendment when we permit this "petition for redress of grievances" to be turned into a trespass action. To say that a private owner could have done the same if the rally had taken place on private property is to speak of a different case, as an assembly and a petition for redress of grievances run to government, not to private proprietors. . . .

There may be some public places which are so clearly committed to other purposes that their use for the airing of grievances is anomalous. There may be some instances in which assemblies and petitions for redress of grievances are not consistent with other necessary purposes of public property. A noisy meeting may be out of keeping with the serenity of the statehouse or the quiet of the courthouse. No one, for example, would suggest that the Senate gallery is the proper place for a vociferous protest rally. And in other cases it may be necessary to adjust the right to petition for redress of grievances to the other interests inhering in the uses to which the public property is normally put. . . . But this is quite different from saying that all public places are off limits to people with grievances. . . . And it is farther yet from saying that the "custodian" of the public property in his discretion can decide when public places shall be used for the communication of ideas, especially the constitutional right to assemble and petition for redress of grievances. . . .

Tinker v. *Des Moines*

393 U.S. 503, 89 S. Ct. 733, 21 L. Ed. 2d 731 (1969)

The petitioners in this case—two high school students and a junior high student—were suspended from school for wearing black armbands to class as a protest against the Vietnam War and for failing to remove the armbands when requested to do so. They sought a Federal injunction against enforcement of the school regulation prohibiting students from wearing armbands to school, which had been adopted two days before, in anticipation of the protest. After the Court of Appeals divided evenly on the issue, the Supreme Court granted certiorari. *Opinion of the Court: Fortas, Warren, Douglas, Brennan, Stewart, White, Marshall. Concurring opinions: Stewart; White. Dissenting opinions: Black; Harlan.*

MR. JUSTICE FORTAS delivered the opinion of the Court. . . .

First Amendment rights, applied in light of the special characteristics of the school environment, are available to teachers and students. It can hardly be argued that either students or teachers shed their constitutional rights to freedom of speech or expression at the schoolhouse gate. This has been the unmistakable holding of this Court for almost 50 years. . . . On the other hand, the Court has repeatedly emphasized the need for affirming the comprehensive authority of the States and of school officials, consistent with fundamental constitutional safeguards, to prescribe and control conduct in the schools. . . . Our problem lies in the area where students in the exercise of First Amendment rights collide with the rules of the school authorities.

. . . Our problem involves direct, primary First Amendment rights akin to "pure speech." The school officials banned and sought to punish petitioners for a silent, passive expression of opinion, unaccompanied by any disorder or disturbance on the part of petitioners. There is here no evidence whatever of petitioners' interference, actual or nascent, with the schools' work or of collision with the rights of other students to be secure and to be let alone. Accordingly, this case does not concern speech or action that intrudes upon the work of the schools or the rights of other students. . . .

The District Court concluded that the action of the school authorities was reasonable because it was based upon their fear of a disturbance from the wearing of the armbands. But, in our system, undifferentiated fear or apprehension of disturbance is not enough to overcome the right to freedom of expression. . . .

In order for the State in the person of school officials to justify prohibition of a particular expression of opinion, it must be able to show that its action was caused by something more than a mere desire to avoid the discomfort and unpleasantness that always accompany an unpopular viewpoint. . . .

In the present case, the District Court made no such finding, and our independent examination of the record fails to yield evidence that the school authorities had reason to anticipate that the wearing of the armbands would substantially interfere with the work of the school or impinge upon the rights of other students. . . .

On the contrary, the action of the school authorities appears to have been based upon an urgent wish to avoid the controversy which might result from the expression, even by the silent symbol of armbands, of opposition to this Nation's part in the conflagration in Vietnam. . . .

It is also relevant that the school authorities did not purport to prohibit the wearing of all symbols of political or controversial significance. The record shows that students in some of the schools wore buttons relating to national political campaigns, and some even wore the Iron Cross, traditionally a symbol of Nazism. The order prohibiting the wearing of armbands did not extend to these. Instead, a particular symbol—black armbands worn to exhibit opposition to this Nation's involvement in Vietnam—was singled out for prohibition. Clearly, the prohibition of expression of one particular opinion, at least without evidence that it is necessary to avoid material and substantial interference with schoolwork or discipline, is not constitutionally permissible. . . .

The principle of these cases is not confined to the supervised and ordained discussion which takes place in the classroom. The principal use to which the schools are dedicated is to accommodate students during prescribed hours for the purpose of certain types of activities. Among those activities is personal intercommunication among the students. This is not only an inevitable part of the process of attending school; it is also an important part of the educational process. A student's rights, therefore, do not embrace merely the classroom hours. When he is in the cafeteria, or on the playing field, or on the campus during the authorized hours, he may express his opinions, even on controversial subjects like the conflict in Vietnam, if he does so without "materially and substantially interfer[ing] with the requirements of appropriate discipline in the operation of the school" and without colliding with the rights of others. . . . But conduct by the student, in class or out of it, which for any reason—whether it stems from time, place, or type of behavior—materially disrupts classwork or involves substantial disorder or invasion of the rights of others is, of course, not immunized by the constitutional guarantee of freedom of speech. . . .

Reversed and remanded.

MR. JUSTICE BLACK, dissenting.

Assuming that the Court is correct in holding that the conduct of wearing armbands for the purpose of conveying political ideas is protected by the First Amendment, . . . the crucial remaining questions are whether students and teachers may use the schools at their whim as a platform for the exercise of free speech "symbolic" or "pure"—and whether the courts will allocate to themselves the function of deciding how the pupils' school day will be spent. While I have always believed that under the First and Fourteenth Amendments neither the State nor the Federal Government has any authority to regulate or censor the content of speech, I have never believed that any person has a right to give speeches or engage in demonstrations where he pleases and when he pleases. . . .

While the record does not show that any of these armband students shouted, used profane language, or were violent in any manner, detailed testimony by some of them shows their armbands caused comments, warnings by other students, the poking of fun at them, and a warning by an older football player that other, nonprotesting students had better let them alone. There is also evidence that a teacher of mathematics had his lesson period practically "wrecked" chiefly by disputes with Mary Beth Tinker, who wore her armband for her "demonstration." Even a casual reading of the record shows that this armband did divert students' minds from their regular lessons, and that talk, comments, etc., made John Tinker "self-conscious" in attending school with his armband. While the absence of obscene remarks or boisterous and loud disorder perhaps justifies the Court's statement that the few armband students did not actually "disrupt" the classwork, I think the record overwhelmingly shows that the armbands did exactly what the elected school officials and principals foresaw they would, that is, took the students' minds off their classwork and diverted them to thoughts about the highly emotional subject of the Vietnam war. . . .

In my view, teachers in state-controlled public schools are hired to teach there. . . . Certainly a teacher is not paid to go into school and teach subjects the State does not hire him to teach as a part of its selected curriculum. Nor are public school students sent to the schools at public expense to broadcast political or any other views to educate and inform the public. The original idea of schools, which I do not believe is yet abandoned as worthless or out of date, was that children had not yet reached the point of experience and wisdom which enabled them to teach all of their elders. It may be that the Nation has outworn the old-fashioned slogan that "children are to be seen not heard," but one may, I hope, be permitted to harbor the thought that taxpayers send children to school on the premise that at their age they need to learn, not teach. . . .

Hazelwood School District v. *Kuhlmeier*

484 U.S. 260, 108 S. Ct. 562, 98 L. Ed. 2d 592 (1988)

As part of the Journalism II course at Hazelwood East High School, students edit and publish *Spectrum,* the school newspaper, which is distributed to students, school personnel, and members of the community. Prior to publication, the journalism teacher submitted page proofs of each issue to Principal Robert Reynolds. When proofs for the May 13, 1983, issue were submitted, Reynolds objected to two articles. One described three Hazelwood East students' experiences with pregnancy; the other discussed the impact of divorce on students at the school.

Reynolds maintained that although the first article used false names to mask the identity of the pregnant students, they might still be identifiable from the text. He also believed that the article's references to sexual activity and birth control might be inappropriate for younger students at the school. In the divorce story, he noted, a student identified by name complained that her father "was always out of town on business or out late playing cards with the guys" and "always argued about everything" with her mother. He contended that the parents should have had the opportunity to respond to these statements or to consent to their publication.

Because he believed that there was no time to make changes in the articles before the scheduled press run, he ordered that the two pages on which the articles appeared be deleted from the paper. When the paper appeared without those pages, three staff members of *Spectrum* sued, seeking a declaration that their First Amendment rights had been violated. The District Court rejected their claim, but the Court of Appeals reversed, and the Supreme Court granted certiorari. *Opinion of the Court: White, Rehnquist, Stevens, O'Connor, Scalia. Dissenting opinion: Brennan, Marshall, Blackmun.*

JUSTICE WHITE delivered the opinion of the Court.

. . . Students in the public schools do not "shed their constitutional rights to freedom of speech or expression at the schoolhouse gate." *Tinker,* [v. *Des Moines* (1969)]. . . .

. . . We have nonetheless recognized that the First Amendment rights of students in the public schools "are not automatically coextensive with the rights of adults in other settings," *Bethel School District No. 403* v. *Fraser* . . . (1986), and must be "applied in light of the special characteristics of the school environment." . . . A school need not tolerate student speech that is inconsistent with its "basic educational mission," . . . even though the government could not censor similar speech outside the school. . . .

A

. . . We deal first with the question whether *Spectrum* may appropriately be characterized as a forum for public expression. The public schools do not possess all of the attributes of streets, parks, and other traditional public forums that "time out of mind, have been used for purposes of assembly, communicating thoughts between citizens, and discussing public questions." *Hague* v. *CIO* . . . (1939). Hence, school facilities may be deemed to be public forums only if school authorities have "by policy or by practice" opened those facilities "for indiscriminate use by the general public," *Perry Education Assn.* v. *Perry Local Educators' Assn.* . . . (1983), or by some segment of the public, such as student organizations. . . . If the facilities have instead been reserved for other intended purposes, "communicative or otherwise," then no public forum has been created, and school officials may impose reasonable restrictions on the speech of students, teachers, and other members of the school community. . . . "The government does not create a public forum by inaction or by permitting limited discourse, but only by intentionally opening a nontraditional forum for public discourse." *Cornelius* v. *NAACP Legal Defense & Educational Fund, Inc.* . . . (1985).

The policy of school officials toward Spectrum was reflected in Hazelwood School Board Policy 348.51 and the Hazelwood East Curriculum Guide. Board Policy 348.51 provided that "[s]chool sponsored publications are developed within the adopted curriculum and its educational implications in regular classroom activities." . . .

School officials did not deviate in practice from their policy that production of Spectrum was to be part of the educational curriculum and a "regular classroom activit[y]." . . . Although the Statement of Policy published in the September 14, 1982, issue of *Spectrum* declared that "*Spectrum,* as a student-press publication, accepts all rights implied by the First Amendment," this statement, understood in the context of the paper's role in the school's curriculum, suggests at most that the administration will not interfere with the students' exercise of those First Amendment rights that attend the publication of a school-sponsored newspaper. It does not reflect an intent to expand those rights by converting a curricular newspaper into a public forum. . . . Accordingly, school officials were entitled to regulate the contents of *Spectrum* in any reasonable manner. . . .

B

The question whether the First Amendment requires a school to tolerate particular student speech—the question that we addressed in *Tinker* —is different from the question whether the First Amendment requires a school affirmatively to promote particular student speech. The former question addresses educators' ability to silence a student's personal expression that happens to occur on the school premises. The latter question concerns educators' authority over school-sponsored publications, theatrical productions, and other expressive activities that students, parents, and members of the public might reasonably perceive to bear the imprimatur of the school.

. . . Educators are entitled to exercise greater control over this second form of student expression to assure that participants learn whatever lessons the activity is designed to teach, that readers or listeners are not exposed to material that may be inappropriate for their level of maturity, and that the views of the individual speaker are not erroneously attributed to the school. . . .

Accordingly, we conclude that the standard articulated in *Tinker* for determining when a school may punish student expression need not also be the standard for determining when a school may refuse to lend its name and resources to the dissemination of student expression. Instead, we hold that educators do not offend the First Amendment by exercising editorial control over the style and content of student speech in school-sponsored expressive activities so long as their actions are reasonably related to legitimate pedagogical concerns.

This standard is consistent with our oft-expressed view that the education of the Nation's youth is primarily the responsibility of parents, teachers, and state and local school officials, and not of federal judges. . . . It is only when the decision to censor a school-sponsored publication, theatrical production, or other vehicle of student expression has no valid educational purpose that the First Amendment is so "directly and sharply implicate[d]," . . . as to require judicial intervention to protect students' constitutional rights. . . .

. . . We cannot reject as unreasonable Principal Reynolds' conclusion that neither the pregnancy article nor the divorce article was suitable for publication in Spectrum. Reynolds could reasonably have concluded that the students who had written and edited these articles had not sufficiently mastered those portions of the Journalism II curriculum that pertained to the treatment of controversial issues and personal attacks, the need to protect the privacy of individuals whose most intimate concerns are to be revealed in the newspaper, and "the legal, moral, and ethical restrictions imposed upon journalists within [a] school community" that includes adolescent subjects and readers. Finally, we conclude that the principal's decision to delete two pages of *Spectrum,* rather than to delete only the offending articles or to require that they be modified, was reasonable under the circumstances as he understood them. Accordingly, no violation of First Amendment rights occurred.

JUSTICE BRENNAN, with whom JUSTICE MARSHALL and JUSTICE BLACKMUN join, dissenting.

Even if we were writing on a clean slate, I would reject the Court's rationale for abandoning *Tinker* in this case. The Court offers no more than an obscure tangle of three excuses to afford educators "greater control" over school-sponsored speech than the *Tinker* test would permit: the public educator's prerogative to control curriculum; the pedagogical interest in shielding the high school audience from objectionable viewpoints and sensitive topics; and the school's need to dissociate itself from student expression. . . . None of the excuses, once disentangled, supports the distinction that the Court draws. *Tinker* fully addresses the first concern; the second is illegitimate; and the third is readily achievable through less oppressive means.

A

I fully agree with the Court that the First Amendment should afford an educator the prerogative not to sponsor the publication of a newspaper article that is "ungrammatical, poorly written, inadequately researched, biased or prejudiced," or that falls short of the "high standards for . . . student speech that is disseminated under [the school's] auspices. . . ." . . . But we need not abandon *Tinker* to reach that conclusion; we need only apply it. The enumerated criteria reflect the skills that the curricular newspaper "is designed to teach." The educator may, under *Tinker,* constitutionally "censor" poor grammar, writing, or research because to reward such expression would "materially disrup[t]" the newspaper's curricular purpose.

The same cannot be said of official censorship designed to shield the *audience* or dissociate the *sponsor* from the expression. Censorship so motivated . . . in no way furthers the curricular purposes of a student *newspaper,* unless one believes that the purpose of the school newspaper is to teach students that the press ought never report bad news, express unpopular views, or print a thought that might upset its sponsors. Unsurprisingly, Hazelwood East claims no such pedagogical purpose.

B

The Court's second excuse for deviating from precedent is the school's interest in shielding an impressionable high school audience from material whose substance is "unsuitable for immature audiences." . . .

Tinker teaches us that the state educator's undeniable, and undeniably vital, mandate to inculcate moral and political values is not a general warrant to act as "thought police" stifling discussion of all but state-approved topics and advocacy of all but the official position. . . .

The mere fact of school sponsorship does not, as the Court suggests, license such thought control in the high school, whether through school suppression of disfavored viewpoints or through official assessment of topic sensitivity. The former would constitute unabashed and unconstitutional viewpoint discrimination . . . as well as an impermissible infringement of the students' " 'right to receive information and ideas,' " . . .

Official censorship of student speech on the ground that it addresses "potentially sensitive topics" is, for related reasons, equally impermissible. I would not begrudge an educator the authority to limit the substantive scope of a school-sponsored publication to a certain, objectively definable topic, such as literary criticism, school sports, or an overview of the school year. Unlike those determinate limitations, "potential topic sensitivity" is a vaporous nonstandard . . . that invites manipulation to achieve ends that cannot permissibly be achieved through blatant viewpoint discrimination and chills student speech to which school officials might not object. In part because of those dangers, this Court has consistently condemned any scheme allowing a state official boundless discretion in licensing speech from a particular forum. . . .

C

The sole concomitant of school sponsorship that might conceivably justify the distinction that the Court draws between sponsored and nonsponsored student expression is the risk "that the views of the individual speaker [might be] erroneously attributed to the school." . . .

But " '[e]ven through the governmental purpose be legitimate and substantial, that purpose cannot be pursued by means that broadly stifle fundamental personal liberties when the end can be more narrowly achieved.' " *Keyishian* v. *Board of Regents* (1967) . . . Dissociative means short of censorship are available to the school. It could, for example, require the student activity to publish a disclaimer, such as the "Statement of Policy" that *Spectrum* published each school year announcing that "[a]ll . . . editorials appearing in this newspaper reflect the opinions of the *Spectrum* staff, which are not necessarily shared by the administrators or faculty of Hazelwood East," App. 26; or it could simply issue its own response clarifying the official position on the matter and explaining why the student position is wrong. Yet, without so much as acknowledging the less oppressive alternatives, the Court approves of brutal censorship.

Near v. *Minnesota*

283 U.S. 697, 51 S. Ct. 625, 75 L. Ed. 1357 (1931)

The Saturday Press published a series of articles charging that various Minneapolis public officials were dishonest and incompetent and that they were responsible for the racketeering and bootlegging in the city. The publication also called for a special grand jury to investigate the situation. Under a state law that authorized abatement of a "malicious, scandalous and defamatory newspaper," the state secured a court order that required *The Saturday Press* to cease publication. When the state supreme court affirmed the court order, the case was appealed to the United States Supreme Court. *Opinion of the Court: Hughes, Holmes, Brandeis, Stone, Roberts. Dissenting opinion: Butler, Van Devanter, McReynolds, Sutherland.*

MR. CHIEF JUSTICE HUGHES delivered the opinion of the Court. . . .

Without attempting to summarize the contents of the voluminous exhibits attached to the complaint, we deem it sufficient to say that the articles charged in substance that a Jewish gangster was in control of gambling, bootlegging and racketeering in Minneapolis, and that law enforcing officers and agencies were not energetically performing their duties. Most of the charges were directed against the Chief of Police; he was charged with gross neglect of duty, illicit relations with gangsters, and with participation in graft. The County Attorney was charged with knowing the existing conditions and with failure to take adequate measures to remedy them. The Mayor was accused of inefficiency and dereliction. One member of the grand jury was stated to be in sympathy with the gangsters. A special grand jury and a special prosecutor were demanded to deal with the situation in general, and, in particular, to investigate an attempt to assassinate one Guilford, one of the original defendants, who, it appears from the articles, was shot by gangsters after the first issue of the periodical had been published. There is no question but that the articles made serious accusations against the public officers named and others in connection with the prevalence of crimes and the failure to expose and punish them. . . .

This statute, for the suppression as a public nuisance of a newspaper or periodical, is unusual, if not unique, and raises questions of grave importance transcending the local interests involved in the particular action. It is no longer open to doubt that the liberty of the press, and of speech, is within the liberty safeguarded by the due process clause of the Fourteenth Amendment from invasion by state action. . . . In maintaining this guaranty, the authority of the State to enact laws to promote the health, safety, morals and general welfare of its people is necessarily admitted. The limits of this sovereign power must always be determined with appropriate regard to the particular subject of its exercise. . . . It is . . . important to note precisely the purpose and effect of the statute as the state court has construed it.

First. The statute is not aimed at the redress of individual or private wrongs. Remedies for libel remain available and unaffected. The statute, said the state court, "is not directed at threatened libel but at an existing business which, generally speaking, involves more than libel." It is aimed at the distribution of scandalous matter as "detrimental to public morals and to the general welfare," tending "to disturb the peace of the community" and "to provoke assaults and the commission of crime." . . .

Second. The statute is directed not simply at the circulation of scandalous and defamatory statements with regard to private citizens, but at the continued publication by newspapers and periodicals of charges against public officers of corruption, malfeasance in office, or serious neglect of duty. Such charges by their very nature create a public scandal. They are scandalous and defamatory within the meaning of the statute, which has its normal operation in relation to publications dealing prominently and chiefly with the alleged derelictions of public officers. . . .

Third. The object of the statute is not punishment, in the ordinary sense, but suppression of the offending newspaper or periodical. . . . Under this statute, a publisher of a newspaper or periodical, undertaking to conduct a campaign to expose and to censure official derelictions, and devoting his publication principally to that purpose, must face not simply the possibility of a verdict against him in a suit or prosecution for libel, but a determination that his newspaper or periodical is a public nuisance to be abated, and that this abatement and suppression will follow unless he is prepared with legal evidence to prove the truth of the charges and also to satisfy the court that, in addition to being true, the matter was published with good motives and for justifiable ends. This suppression is accomplished by enjoining publication and that restraint is the object and effect of the statute. . . .

Fourth. The statute not only operates to suppress the offending newspaper or periodical but to put the publisher under an effective censorship. When a newspaper or periodical is found to be "malicious, scandalous and defamatory," and is suppressed as such, resumption of publication is punishable as a contempt of court by fine or imprisonment. . . .

The question is whether a statute authorizing such proceedings in restraint of publication is consistent with the conception of the liberty of the press as historically conceived and guaranteed. In determining the extent of the constitutional protection, it has been generally, if not universally, considered that it is the chief purpose of the guaranty to prevent previous restraints upon publication. The struggle in England, directed against the legislative power of the licenser, resulted in renunciation of the censorship of the press. The liberty deemed to be established was thus described by Blackstone: "The liberty of the press is indeed essential to the nature of a free state; but this consists in laying no *previous* restraints upon publications, and not in freedom from censure for criminal matter when published. Every freeman has an undoubted right to lay what sentiments he pleases before the public; to forbid this, is to destroy the freedom of the press; but if he publishes what is improper, mischievous or illegal, he must take the consequence of his own temerity." . . .

The criticism upon Blackstone's statement has not been because immunity from previous restraint upon publication has not been regarded as deserving of special emphasis, but chiefly because that immunity cannot be deemed to exhaust the conception of the liberty guaranteed by state and federal constitutions. . . .

The objection has also been made that the principle as to immunity from previous restraint is stated too broadly, if every such restraint is deemed to be prohibited. That is undoubtedly true; the protection even as to previous restraint is not absolutely unlimited. But the limitation has been recognized only in exceptional cases. . . . No one would question but that a government might prevent actual obstruction to its recruiting service or the publication of the sailing dates of transports or the number and location of troops. On similar grounds, the primary requirements of decency may be enforced against obscene publications. The security of the community life may be protected against incitements to acts of violence and the overthrow by force of orderly government. The constitutional guaranty of free speech does not "protect a man from an injunction against uttering words that may have all the effect of force. . . . These limitations are not applicable here. Nor are we now concerned with questions as to the extent of authority to prevent publications in order to protect private rights according to the principles governing the exercise of the jurisdiction of courts of equity. . . .

The exceptional nature of its limitations places in a strong light the general conception that liberty of the press, historically considered and taken up by the Federal Constitution, has meant, principally although not exclusively, immunity from previous restraints or censorship. The conception of the liberty of the press in this country had broadened with the exigencies of the colonial period and with the efforts to secure freedom from oppressive administration. That liberty was especially cherished for the immunity it afforded from previous restraint of the publication of censure of public officers and charges of official misconduct. . . .

For these reasons we hold the statute, so far as it authorized the proceedings in this action under clause (b) of section one, to be an infringement of the liberty of the press guaranteed by the Fourteenth Amendment. . . .

Judgment reversed.

New York Times Co. v. *United States*

403 U.S. 713; 91 S. Ct. 2140; 29 L. Ed. 2d 822 (1971)

In late March 1971, *The New York Times* obtained from Daniel Ellsberg, who was associated with the Pentagon, a copy of the Pentagon Papers (a classified Defense Department study of United States involvement in Indochina). On June 12, 1971, after prolonged editorial consideration of the material, the *Times* began publication of excerpts from the multivolume study. When the *Times* ignored a Justice Department request to halt further publication, the attorney general obtained an injunction in federal district court—the first federal injunction ever sought against newspaper publication. From this point the case proceeded with extraordinary speed through the federal courts. By June 19, both the *Times* and the *Washington Post,* which had also begun publication of the materials, were under restraining orders imposed by federal courts of appeal. The Supreme Court agreed to hear the cases on June 25, heard oral argument a day later, and on June 29 announced its decision. (For a related case, see *Gravel* v. *United States,* in Chapter 4.) *Opinion of the Court* per curiam: *Black, Douglas, Brennan, Stewart, White, Marshall. Separate opinions: Black, Douglas; Douglas, Black; Brennan; Stewart, White; White, Stewart; Marshall. Dissenting opinions: Burger; Harlan, Burger, Blackmun; Blackmun.*

PER CURIAM. . . .

"Any system of prior restraints of expression comes to this Court bearing a heavy presumption against its constitutional validity." *Bantam Books, Inc.* v. *Sullivan* (1963). . . . The Government "thus carries a heavy burden of showing justification for the imposition of such a restraint." *Organization for a Better Austin* v. *Keefe* (1971). . . . The District Court for the Southern District of New York in the *New York Times* case and the District Court for the District of Columbia and the Court of Appeals for the District of Columbia Circuit in the *Washington Post* case held that the Government had not met that burden. We agree.

MR. JUSTICE BLACK, with whom MR. JUSTICE DOUGLAS joins, concurring.

I adhere to the view that the Government's case against the Washington Post should have been dismissed and that the injunction against the New York Times should have been vacated without oral argument when the cases were first presented to this Court. I believe that every moment's continuance of the injunctions against these newspapers amounts to a flagrant, indefensible, and continuing violation of the First Amendment. . . .

In the First Amendment the Founding Fathers gave the free press the protection it must have to fulfill its essential role in our democracy. The press was to serve the governed, not the governors. The Government's power to censor the press was abolished so that the press would remain forever free to censure the Government. The press was protected so that it could bare the secrets of government and inform the people. Only a free and unrestrained press can effectively expose deception in government. And paramount among the responsibilities of a free press is the duty to prevent any part of the government from deceiving the people and sending them off to distant lands to die of foreign fevers and foreign shot and shell. In my view, far from deserving condemnation for their courageous reporting, the New York Times, the Washington Post, and other newspapers should be commended for serving the purpose that the Founding Fathers saw so clearly. In revealing the workings of government that led to the Vietnam war, the newspapers nobly did precisely that which the Founders hoped and trusted they would do.

. . . We are asked to hold that despite the First Amendment's emphatic command, the Executive Branch, the Congress, and the Judiciary can make laws enjoining publication of current news and abridging freedom of the press in the name of "national security."

The word "security" is a broad, vague generality whose contours should not be invoked to abrogate the fundamental law embodied in the First Amendment. The guarding of military and diplomatic secrets at the expense of informed representative government provides no real security for our Republic. The Framers of the First Amendment, fully aware of both the need to defend a new nation and the abuses of the English and Colonial governments, sought to give this new society strength and security by providing that freedom of speech, press, religion, and assembly should not be abridged. . . .

MR. JUSTICE BRENNAN, concurring.

The error that has pervaded these cases from the outset was the granting of any injunctive relief whatsoever, interim or otherwise. The entire thrust of the Government's claim throughout these cases has been that publication of the material sought to be enjoined "could," or "might," or "may" prejudice the national interest in various ways. But the First Amendment tolerates absolutely no prior judicial restraints of the press predicated upon surmise or conjecture that untoward consequences may result. . . . Our cases have thus far indicated that such cases may arise only when the Nation "is at war," . . . during which times "[n]o one would question but that a government might prevent actual obstruction to its recruiting service or the publication of the sailing dates of transports or the number and location of troops." *Near* v. *Minnesota* [1931]. . . . Even if the present world situation were assumed to be tantamount to a time of war, or if the power of presently available armaments would justify even in peacetime the suppression of information that would set in motion a nuclear holocaust, in neither of these actions has the Government presented or even alleged that publication of items from or based upon the material at issue would cause the happening of an event of that nature. . . .

MR. JUSTICE STEWART, with whom MR. JUSTICE WHITE joins, concurring. . . .

In the absence of the governmental checks and balances present in other areas of our national life, the only effective restraint upon executive policy and power in the areas of national defense and international affairs may lie in an enlightened citizenry—in an informed and critical public opinion which alone can here protect the values of democratic government. For this reason, it is perhaps here that a press that is alert, aware, and free most vitally serves the basic purpose of the First Amendment. For without an informed and free press there cannot be an enlightened people.

Yet it is elementary that the successful conduct of international diplomacy and the maintenance of an effective national defense require both confidentiality and secrecy. Other nations can hardly deal with this Nation in an atmosphere of mutual trust unless they can be assured that their confidences will be kept. And within our own executive departments, the development of considered and intelligent international policies would be impossible if those charged with their formulation could not communicate with each other freely, frankly, and in confidence. In the area of basic national defense the frequent need for absolute secrecy is, of course, self-evident.

I think there can be but one answer to this dilemma, if dilemma it be. The responsibility must be where the power is. If the Constitution gives the Executive a large degree of unshared power in the conduct of foreign affairs and the maintenance of our national defense, then under the Constitution the Executive must have the largely unshared duty to determine and preserve the degree of internal security necessary to exercise that power successfully. It is an awesome responsibility, requiring judgment and wisdom of a high order. I should suppose that moral, political, and practical considerations would dictate that a very first principle of that wisdom would be an insistence upon avoiding secrecy for its own sake. . . . But be that as it may, it is clear to me that it is the constitutional duty of the Executive— as a matter of sovereign prerogative and not as a matter of law as the courts know law—through the promulgation and enforcement of executive regulations, to protect the confidentiality necessary to carry out its responsibilities in the fields of international relations and national defense.

This is not to say that Congress and the courts have no role to play. Undoubtedly Congress has the power to enact specific and appropriate criminal laws to protect government property and preserve government secrets. . . . And if a criminal prosecution is instituted, it will be the responsibility of the courts to decide the applicability of the criminal law under which the charge is brought. . . .

But in the cases before us we are asked neither to construe specific regulations nor to apply specific laws. We are asked, instead, to perform a function that the Constitution gave to the Executive, not the Judiciary. We are asked, quite simply, to prevent the publication by two newspapers of material that the Executive Branch insists should not, in the national interest, be published. I am convinced that the Executive is correct with respect to some of the documents involved. But I cannot say that disclosure of any of them will surely result in direct, immediate, and irreparable damage to our Nation or its people. That being so, there can under the First Amendment be but one judicial resolution of the issues before us. I join the judgments of the Court.

MR. JUSTICE WHITE, with whom MR. JUSTICE STEWART joins, concurring. . . .

The Government's position is simply stated: The responsibility of the Executive for the conduct of the foreign affairs and for the security of the Nation is so basic that the President is entitled to an injunction against publication of a newspaper story whenever he can convince a court that the information to be revealed threatens "grave and irreparable" injury to the public interest; and the injunction should issue whether or not the material to be published is classified, whether or not publication would be lawful under relevant criminal statutes enacted by Congress, and regardless of the circumstances by which the newspaper came into possession of the information.

At least in the absence of legislation by Congress, based on its own investigations and findings, I am quite unable to agree that the inherent powers of the Executive and the courts reach so far as to authorize remedies having such sweeping potential for inhibiting publications by the press. . . .

. . . Terminating the ban on publication of the relatively few sensitive documents the Government now seeks to suppress does not mean that the law either requires or invites newspapers or others to publish them or that they will be immune from criminal action if they do. . . .

. . . Congress has addressed itself to the problems of protecting the security of the country and the national defense from unauthorized disclosure of potentially damaging information. . . . It has not, however, authorized the injunctive remedy against threatened publication. It has apparently been satisfied to rely on criminal sanctions and their deterrent effect on the responsible as well as the irresponsible press.

MR. CHIEF JUSTICE BURGER, dissenting.

. . . In these cases, the imperative of a free and unfettered press comes into collision with another imperative, the effective functioning of a complex modern government and specifically the effective exercise of certain constitutional powers of the Executive. Only those who view the First Amendment as an absolute in all circumstances—a view I respect, but reject—can find such cases as these to be simple or easy. . . .

It is not disputed that the Times has had unauthorized possession of the documents for three to four months, during which it has had its expert analysts studying them, presumably digesting them and preparing the material for publication. . . . No doubt this was for a good reason; the analysis of 7,000 pages of complex material drawn from a vastly greater volume of material would inevitably take time and the writing of good news stories takes time. But why should the United States Government, from whom this information was illegally acquired by someone, along with all the counsel, trial judges, and appellate judges be placed under needless pressure? After these months of deferral, the alleged "right to know" has somehow and suddenly become a right that must be vindicated instanter.

. . . As I see it, we have been forced to deal with litigation concerning rights of great magnitude without an adequate record, and surely without time for adequate treatment either in the prior proceedings or in this Court. . . . I am not prepared to reach the merits [of the case].

I would affirm the Court of Appeals for the Second Circuit and allow the District Court to complete the trial aborted by our grant of certiorari, meanwhile preserving the status quo in the *Post* case.

MR. JUSTICE HARLAN, with whom THE CHIEF JUSTICE and MR. JUSTICE BLACKMUN join, dissenting.

. . . The scope of the judicial function in passing upon the activities of the Executive Branch of the Government in the field of foreign affairs is very narrowly restricted. This view is, I think, dictated by the concept of separation of powers upon which our constitutional system rests.

In a speech on the floor of the House of Representatives, Chief Justice John Marshall, then a member of that body, stated: "The President is the sole organ of the nation in its external relations, and its sole representative with foreign nations.". . . From that time, shortly after the founding of the Nation, to this, there has been no substantial challenge to this description of the scope of executive power. . . .

From this constitutional primacy in the field of foreign affairs, it seems to me that certain conclusions necessarily follow. Some of these were stated concisely by President Washington, declining the request of the House of Representatives for the papers leading up to the negotiation of the Jay Treaty:

"The nature of foreign negotiations requires caution, and their success must often depend on secrecy; and even when brought to a conclusion a full disclosure of all the measures, demands, or eventual concessions which may have been proposed or contemplated would be extremely impolitic; for this might have a pernicious influence on future negotiations, or produce immediate inconveniences, perhaps danger and mischief, in relation to other powers." . . .

The power to evaluate the "pernicious influence" of premature disclosure is not, however, lodged in the Executive alone. I agree that, in performance of its duty to protect the values of the First Amendment against political pressures, the judiciary must review the initial Executive determination to the point of satisfying itself that the subject matter of the dispute does lie within the proper compass of the President's foreign relations power. Constitutional considerations forbid "a complete abandonment of judicial control." Cf. *United States* v. *Reynolds*, [1953]. Moreover, the judiciary may properly insist that the determination that disclosure of the subject matter would irreparably impair the national security be made by the head of the Executive Department concerned—here the Secretary of State or the Secretary of Defense—after actual personal consideration by that officer. This safeguard is required in the analogous area of executive claims of privilege for secrets of state. . . .

But in my judgment the judiciary may not properly go beyond these two inquiries and redetermine for itself the probable impact of disclosure on the national security. . . .

Even if there is some room for the judiciary to override the executive determination, it is plain that the scope of review must be exceedingly narrow. I can see no indication in the opinions of either the District Court or the Court of Appeals in the *Post* litigation that the conclusions of the Executive were given even the deference owing to an administrative agency, much less that owing to a co-equal branch of the Government operating within the field of its constitutional prerogative.

Accordingly, I would vacate the judgment of the Court of Appeals for the District of Columbia Circuit on this ground and remand the case for further proceedings in the District Court. Before the commencement of such further proceedings, due opportunity should be afforded the Government for procuring from the Secretary of State or the Secretary of Defense or both an expression of their views on the issue of national security. The ensuing review by the District Court should be in accordance with the views expressed in this opinion. And for the reasons stated above I would affirm the judgment of the Court of Appeals for the Second Circuit.

Branzburg v. *Hayes*

408 U.S. 665, 92 S. Ct. 2646, 33 L. Ed. 2d 626 (1972)

In *Branzburg* the Court considered together three cases involving reporters' refusal to testify before grand juries. In one case, Paul Branzburg, a reporter for the Louisville *Courier-Journal*, refused to answer grand jury questions about the identity of persons he had observed processing hashish from marijuana. In the other two cases, Paul Pappas and Earl Caldwell refused to testify before grand juries investigating the activities of the Black Panthers, a radical group. *Opinion of the Court: White, Burger, Blackmun, Powell, Rehnquist. Concurring opinion: Powell. Dissenting opinions: Douglas; Stewart, Brennan, Marshall.*

MR. JUSTICE WHITE delivered the opinion of the Court. . . .

The issue in these cases is whether requiring newsmen to appear and testify before State or federal grand juries abridges the freedom of speech and press guaranteed by the First Amendment. We hold that it does not . . .

Petitioners Branzburg and Pappas and respondent Caldwell press First Amendment claims that may be simply put: that to gather news it is often necessary to agree either not to identify the source of information published or to publish only part of the facts revealed, or both; that if the reporter is nevertheless forced to reveal these confidences to a grand jury, the source so identified and other confidential sources of other reporters will be measurably deterred from furnishing publishable information, all to the detriment of the free flow of information protected by the First Amendment. . . . The heart of the claim is that the burden on news gathering resulting from compelling reporters to disclose confidential information outweighs any public interest in obtaining the information. . . .

It is clear that the First Amendment does not invalidate every incidental burdening of the press that may result from the enforcement of civil or criminal statutes of general applicability. . . . It has generally been held that the First Amendment does not guarantee the press a constitutional right of special access to information not available to the public generally. . . .

Despite the fact that news gathering may be hampered, the press is regularly excluded from grand jury proceedings, our own conferences, the meetings of other official bodies gathered in executive session, and the meetings of private organizations. Newsmen have no constitutional right of access to the scenes of crime or disaster when the general public is excluded, and they may be prohibited from attending or publishing information about trials if such restrictions are necessary to assure a defendant a fair trial before an impartial tribunal. . . .

It is thus not surprising that the great weight of authority is that newsmen are not exempt from the normal duty of appearing before a grand jury and answering questions relevant to a criminal investigation. . . .

A number of States have provided newsmen a statutory privilege of varying breadth, but the majority have not done so, and none has been provided by federal statute. Until now the only testimonial privilege for unofficial witnesses that is rooted in the Federal Constitution is the Fifth Amendment privilege against compelled self-incrimination. We are asked to create another by interpreting the First Amendment to grant newsmen a testimonial privilege that other citizens do not enjoy. This we decline to do. Fair and effective law enforcement aimed at providing security for the person and property of the individual is a fundamental function of government, and the grand jury plays an important, constitutionally mandated role in this process. On the records now before us, we perceive no basis for holding that the public interest in law enforcement and in ensuring effective grand jury proceedings is insufficient to override the consequential, but uncertain, burden on news gathering that is said to result from insisting that reporters, like other citizens, respond to relevant questions put to them in the course of a valid grand jury investigation or criminal trial.

. . . The administration of a constitutional newsman's privilege would present practical and conceptual difficulties of a high order. Sooner or later, it would be necessary to define those categories of newsmen who qualified for the privilege, a questionable procedure in light of the traditional doctrine that liberty of the press is the right of the lonely pamphleteer who uses carbon paper or a mimeograph just as much as of the large metropolitan publisher who utilizes the latest photocomposition methods. . . . Freedom of the press is a "fundamental personal right" which "is not confined to newspapers and periodicals. It necessarily embraces pamphlets and leaflets. . . . The press in its historic connotation comprehends every sort of publication which affords a vehicle of information and opinion." *Lovell* v. *Griffin* [1938]. . . . The informative function asserted by representatives of the organized press in the present cases in also performed by lecturers, political pollsters, novelists, academic researchers, and dramatists. Almost any author may quite accurately assert that he is contributing to the flow of information to the public, that he relies on confidential sources of information, and that these sources will be silenced if he is forced to make disclosures before a grand jury. . . .

Finally, . . . news gathering is not without its

First Amendment protections, and grand jury investigations if instituted or conducted other than in good faith, would pose wholly different issues for resolution under the First Amendment. Official harassment of the press undertaken not for purposes of law enforcement but to disrupt a reporter's relationship with his news sources would have no justification. Grand juries are subject to judicial control and subpoenas to motions to quash. We do not expect courts will forget that grand juries must operate within the limits of the First Amendment as well as the Fifth.

MR. JUSTICE STEWART, with whom MR. JUSTICE BRENNAN and MR. JUSTICE MARSHALL join, dissenting.

The Court's crabbed view of the First Amendment reflects a disturbing insensitivity to the critical role of an independent press in our society. . . . The Court in these cases holds that a newsman has no First Amendment right to protect his sources when called before a grand jury. The Court thus invites state and federal authorities to undermine the historic independence of the press by attempting to annex the journalistic profession as an investigative arm of government. Not only will this decision impair performance of the press' constitutionally protected functions, but it will, I am convinced, in the long run harm rather than help the administration of justice. . . .

The reporter's constitutional right to a confidential relationship with his source stems from the broad societal interest in a full and free flow of information to the public. It is this basic concern that underlies the Constitution's protection of a free press. . . .

Enlightened choice by an informed citizenry is the basic ideal upon which an open society is premised, and a free press is thus indispensable to a free society. Not only does the press enhance personal self-fulfillment by providing the people with the widest possible range of fact and opinion, but it also is an incontestable precondition of self-government. . . . As private and public aggregations of power burgeon in size and the pressures for conformity necessarily mount, there is obviously a continuing need for an independent press to disseminate a robust variety of information and opinion through reportage, investigation, and criticism, if we are to preserve our constitutional tradition of maximizing freedom of choice by encouraging diversity of expression. . . .

In keeping with this tradition, we have held that the right to publish is central to the First Amendment and basic to the existence of constitutional democracy. . . .

No less important to the news dissemination process is the gathering of information. News must not be unnecessarily cut off at its source, for without freedom to acquire information the right to publish would be impermissibly compromised. Accordingly, a right to gather news, of some dimensions, must exist. . . .

The right to gather news implies, in turn, a right to a confidential relationship between a reporter and his source. This proposition follows as a matter of simple logic once three factual predicates are recognized: (1) newsmen require informants to gather news; (2) confidentiality—the promise or understanding that names or certain aspects of communications will be kept off the record—is essential to the creation and maintenance of a news-gathering relationship with informants; and (3) an unbridled subpoena power—the absence of a constitutional right protecting, in *any* way, a confidential relationship from compulsory process—will either deter sources from divulging information or deter reporters from gathering and publishing information.

Posed against the First Amendment's protection of the newsman's confidential relationships in these cases is society's interest in the use of the grand jury to administer justice fairly and effectively. . . . Yet the longstanding rule making every person's evidence available to the grand jury is not absolute. The rule has been limited by the Fifth Amendment, the Fourth Amendment, and the evidentiary privileges of the common law. . . .

In striking the proper balance between the public interest in the efficient administration of justice and the First Amendment guarantee of the fullest flow of information, we must begin with the basic proposition that because of their "delicate and vulnerable" nature . . . and their transcendent importance for the just functioning of our society, First Amendment rights require special safeguards. . . .

Accordingly, when a reporter is asked to appear before a grand jury and reveal confidences, I would hold that the government must (1) show that there is probable cause to believe that the newsman has information which is clearly relevant to a specific probable violation of law; (2) demonstrate that the information sought cannot be obtained by alternative means less destructive of First Amendment rights; and (3) demonstrate a compelling and overriding interest in the information. . . .

New York Times v. *Sullivan*

376 U.S. 254, 84 S. Ct. 710, 11 L. Ed. 2d 686 (1964)

L. B. Sullivan, commissioner of public affairs in Montgomery, Alabama, brought suit charging that he had been libeled by an advertisement that a civil rights group published in *The New York Times.* The ad, which criticized the treatment of blacks by the Montgomery police, contained several minor factual errors. A jury in Alabama awarded Sullivan $500,000 in damages, and the state supreme court affirmed the trial judgment. Meanwhile, similar suits were filed by other plaintiffs in Alabama against the *Times* and the Columbia Broadcasting Company for combined damages of $7 million. *Opinion of the Court: Brennan, Warren, Clark, Harlan, Stewart, White. Concurring opinions: Black, Douglas; Goldberg, Douglas.*

MR. JUSTICE BRENNAN delivered the opinion of the Court.

We are required in this case to determine for the first time the extent to which the constitutional protections for speech and press limit a State's power to award damages in a libel action brought by a public official against critics of his official conduct. . . .

Under Alabama law as applied in this case, a publication is "libelous per se" if the words "tend to injure a person . . . in his reputation" or to "bring [him] into public contempt"; the trial court stated that the standard was met if the words are such as to "injure him in his public office, or impute misconduct to him in his office, or want of official integrity, or want of fidelity to a public trust. . . . "The jury must find that the words were published "of and concerning" the plaintiff, but where the plaintiff is a public official his place in the governmental hierarchy is sufficient evidence to support a finding that his reputation has been affected by statements that reflect upon the agency of which he is in charge. Once "libel per se" has been established, the defendant has no defense as to stated facts unless he can persuade the jury that they were true in all their particulars. . . . Unless he can discharge the burden of proving truth, general damages are presumed, and may be awarded without proof of pecuniary injury. . . .

The question before us is whether this rule of liability, as applied to an action brought by a public official against critics of his official conduct, abridges the freedom of speech and of the press that is guaranteed by the First and Fourteenth Amendments. . . .

. . . We consider this case against the background of a profound national commitment to the principle that debate on public issues should be uninhibited, robust, and wide-open, and that it may well include vehement, caustic, and sometimes unpleasantly sharp attacks on government and public officials. . . .

Authoritative interpretations of the First Amendment guarantees have consistently refused to recognize an exception for any test of truth—whether administered by judges, juries, or administrative officials—and especially one that puts the burden of proving truth on the speaker. . . . Erroneous statement is inevitable in free debate, and . . . it must be protected if the freedoms of expression are to have the "breathing space" that they "need . . . to survive," *N.A.A.C.P.* v. *Button,* [1963]. . . .

Injury to official reputation affords no more warrant for repressing speech that would otherwise be free than does factual error. . . . Criticism of . . . official conduct does not lose its constitutional protection merely because it is effective criticism and hence diminishes . . . official reputations.

If neither factual error nor defamatory content suffices to remove the constitutional shield from criticism of official conduct, the combination of the two elements is no less inadequate. This is the lesson to be drawn from the great controversy over the Sedition Act of 1798, . . . which first crystallized a national awareness of the central meaning of the First Amendment. . . .

Although the Sedition Act was never tested in this Court, the attack upon its validity has carried the day in the court of history. Fines levied in its prosecution were repaid by Act of Congress on the ground that it was unconstitutional. . . . [A broad consensus has developed] that the Act, because of the restraint it imposed upon criticism of government and public officials, was inconsistent with the First Amendment.

What a State may not constitutionally bring about by means of a criminal statute is likewise beyond the reach of its civil law of libel. The fear of damage awards under a rule such as that invoked by the Alabama courts here may be markedly more inhibiting than the fear of prosecution under a criminal statute. . . . The judgment awarded in this case—without the need for any proof of actual pecuniary loss—was one thousand times greater than the maximum fine provided by the Alabama criminal statute, and one hundred times greater than that provided by the Sedition Act. . . .

The state rule of law is not saved by its allowance of the defense of truth. . . . A rule compelling the critic of official conduct to guarantee the truth of all his factual assertions—and to do so on pain of libel judgments virtually unlimited in amount—leads to . . . "self-censorship." Allowance of the defense of truth, with the burden of proving it on the defendant, does not mean that only false speech will be deterred. . . . Under such a rule, would-be critics of official conduct may be deterred from voicing their criticism, even though it is believed to be true and even though it is in fact true, because of doubt whether it can be proved in court or fear of the expense of having to do so. They tend to make only statements which "steer far wider of the unlawful zone." *Speiser* v. *Randall* [1958]. . . . The rule thus dampens the vigor and limits the variety of public debate. It is inconsistent with the First and Fourteenth Amendments.

The constitutional guarantees require, we think, a federal rule that prohibits a public official from recovering damages for a defamatory falsehood relating to his official conduct unless he proves that the statement was made with "actual malice"—that is, with knowledge that it was false or with reckless disregard of whether it was false or not. . . .

Since respondent may seek a new trial, we deem that considerations of effective judicial administration require us to review the evidence in the present record to determine whether it could constitutionally support a judgment for respondent. . . .

Applying these standards, we consider that the proof presented to show actual malice lacks the convincing clarity which the constitutional standard demands, and hence that it would not constitutionally sustain the judgment for respondent under the proper rule of law. . . .

Reversed and remanded.

MR. JUSTICE BLACK, with whom MR. JUSTICE DOUGLAS joins, concurring.

I concur in reversing this half-million-dollar judgment against the New York Times Company and the four individual defendants. . . . I vote to reverse exclusively on the ground that the Times and the individual defendants had an absolute, unconditional constitutional right to publish in the Times advertisement their criticisms of the Montgomery agencies and officials. . . .

The half-million-dollar verdict . . . give[s] dramatic proof . . . that state libel laws threaten the very existence of an American press virile enough to publish unpopular views on public affairs and bold enough to criticize the conduct of public officials. . . .

In my opinion the Federal Constitution has dealt with this deadly danger to the press in the only way possible without leaving the free press open to destruction—by granting the press an absolute immunity for criticism of the way public officials do their public duty. . . . To punish the exercise of this right to discuss public affairs or to penalize it through libel judgments is to abridge or shut off discussion of the very kind most needed. This Nation, I suspect, can live in peace without libel suits based on public discussions of public affairs and public officials. But I doubt that a country can live in freedom where its people can be made to suffer physically or financially for criticizing their government, its actions, or its officials.

Miller v. *California*

413 U.S. 15, 93 S. Ct. 2607, 37 L. Ed. 2d 419 (1973)

Paris Adult Theater I v. *Slaton*

413 U.S. 49, 93 S. Ct. 2628, 37 L. Ed. 2d 446 (1973)

In these companion cases, the Burger Court sought to develop more adequate obscenity standards. In *Miller* the appellant had been convicted of violating a California law that prohibited the mailing of unsolicited obscene materials. The trial court in this case had instructed the jury to evaluate the materials' obscenity in light of the contemporary community standards in California. In *Slaton,* state officials had sued under Georgia civil law to enjoin the showing of two allegedly obscene films. The trial court ruled that the display of these films to consenting adults was constitutionally protected. The Georgia Supreme Court reversed, and the United States Supreme Court granted certiorari.

The Court divided identically on the two cases. Chief Justice Burger's opinion of the Court is taken from *Miller;* Justice Brennan's dissent, from *Slaton. Opinion of the Court: Burger, White, Powell, Blackmun, Rehnquist. Dissenting opinions: Douglas; Brennan, Stewart, Marshall.*

MR. CHIEF JUSTICE BURGER delivered the opinion of the Court. . . .

This much has been categorically settled by the Court, that obscene material is unprotected by the First Amendment. . . . We acknowledge, however, the inherent dangers of undertaking to regulate any form of expression. State statutes designed to regulate obscene materials must be carefully limited. . . .

The basic guidelines for the trier of fact must be: (*a*) whether "the average person, applying contemporary community standards" would find that the work, taken as a whole, appeals to the prurient interest . . . (*b*) whether the work depicts or describes, in a patently offensive way, sexual conduct specifically defined by the applicable state law; and (*c*) whether the work, taken as a whole, lacks serious literary, artistic, political, or scientific value. . . .

We emphasize that it is not our function to propose regulatory schemes for the States. That must await their concrete legislative efforts. It is possible, however, to give a few plain examples of what a state statute could define for regulation under the second part (*b*) of the standard announced in this opinion. . . .

(*a*) Patently offensive representations or descriptions of ultimate sexual acts, normal or perverted, actual or simulated.

(*b*) Patently offensive representations or descriptions of masturbation, excretory functions, and lewd exhibition of the genitals.

Sex and nudity may not be exploited without limit by films or pictures exhibited or sold in places of public accommodation any more than live sex and nudity can be exhibited or sold without limit in such public places. At a minimum, prurient, patently offensive depiction or description of sexual conduct must have serious literary, artistic, political, or scientific value to merit First Amendment protection. . . . For example, medical books for the education of physicians and related personnel necessarily use graphic illustrations and descriptions of human anatomy. In resolving the inevitably sensitive questions of fact and law, we must continue to rely on the jury system, accompanied by the safeguards that judges, rules of evidence, presumption of innocence and other protective features provide, as we do with rape, murder, and a host of other offenses against society and its individual members.

MR. JUSTICE BRENNAN, author of the opinions of the Court, or the plurality opinions in *Roth* v. *United States* [1957], *Jacobellis* v. *Ohio* [1964],

Ginzburg v. *United States* [1966], *Mishkin* v. *New York* [1966], and *Memoirs* v. *Massachusetts* [1966], has abandoned his former position and now maintains that no formulation of this Court, the Congress, or the States can adequately distinguish obscene material unprotected by the First Amendment from protected expression. . . . Paradoxically, Mr. Justice Brennan indicates that suppression of unprotected obscene material is permissible to avoid exposure to unconsenting adults, as in this case, and to juveniles, although he gives no indication of how the division between protected and nonprotected materials may be drawn with greater precision for these purposes than for regulation of commercial exposure to consenting adults only. . . . If the inability to define regulated materials with ultimate, god-like precision altogether removes the power of the States or the Congress to regulate, then "hard core" pornography may be exposed without limit to the juvenile, the passerby, and the consenting adult alike, as, indeed, Mr. Justice Douglas contends. . . .

It is certainly true that the absence, since *Roth* [v. *United States* (1957)], of a single majority view of this Court as to proper standards for testing obscenity has placed a strain on both state and federal courts. But today, for the first time since *Roth* was decided in 1957, a majority of this Court has agreed on concrete guidelines to isolate "hard core" pornography from expression protected by the First Amendment. . . . No amount of "fatigue" should lead us to adopt a convenient "institutional" rationale—an absolutist, "anything goes" view of the First Amendment—because it will lighten our burdens. . . .

Under a national Constitution, fundamental First Amendment limitations on the powers of the States do not vary from community to community, but this does not mean that there are, or should or can be, fixed, uniform national standards of precisely what appeals to the "prurient interest" or is "patently offensive." These are essentially questions of fact, and our nation is simply too big and too diverse for this Court to reasonably expect that such standards could be articulated for all 50 States in a single formulation, even assuming the prerequisite consensus exists. . . .

It is neither realistic nor constitutionally sound to read the First Amendment as requiring that the people of Maine or Mississippi accept public depiction of conduct found tolerable in Las Vegas, or New York City. . . . The primary concern with requiring a jury to apply the standard of "the average person, applying contemporary community standards" is to be certain that, so far as material is not aimed at a deviant group, it will be judged by its impact on an average person, rather than a particularly susceptible or sensitive person—or indeed a totally insensitive one. . . . We hold the requirement that the jury evaluate the materials with reference to "contemporary standards of the State of California" serves this protective purpose and is constitutionally adequate.

Vacated and remanded for further proceedings.

MR. JUSTICE BRENNAN, with whom MR. JUSTICE STEWART and MR. JUSTICE MARSHALL join, dissenting.

This case requires the Court to confront once again the vexing problem of reconciling state efforts to suppress sexually oriented expression with the protections of the First Amendment, as applied to the States through the Fourteenth Amendment. No other aspect of the First Amendment has, in recent years, demanded so substantial a commitment of our time, generated such disharmony of views, and remained so resistant to the formulation of stable and manageable standards. I am convinced that the approach initiated 15 years ago in *Roth* v. *United States* . . . and culminating in the Court's decision today, cannot bring stability to this area of the law without jeopardizing fundamental First Amendment values, and I have concluded that the time has come to make a significant departure from that approach. . . .

. . . We have failed to formulate a standard that sharply distinguishes protected from unprotected speech, and out of necessity, we have resorted to the *Redrup* [v. *New York* (1967)] approach, which resolves cases as between the parties, but offers only the most obscure guidance to legislation, adjudication by other courts, and primary conduct. . . .

Of course, the vagueness problem would be largely of our own creation if it stemmed primarily from our failure to reach a consensus on any one standard. But after 16 years of experimentation and debate I am reluctantly forced to the conclusion that none of the available formulas, including the one announced today, can reduce the vagueness to a tolerable level while at the same time striking an acceptable balance between the protections of the First and Fourteenth Amendments, on the one hand, and on the other the asserted state interest in regulating the dissemination of certain sexually oriented materials. Any effort to draw a constitutionally acceptable boundary on state power must resort to such indefinite concepts as "prurient interest," "patent offensiveness," "serious literary value," and the like. The meaning of these concepts necessarily varies with the experience outlook, and even idiosyncrasies of the person defining them. . . .

The vagueness of the standards in the obscenity area produces a number of separate problems, and any improvement must rest on an understanding that the problems are to some extent distinct. First, a vague statute fails to provide adequate notice to persons who are engaged in the type of conduct that the statute could be thought to proscribe. . . .

In addition to problems that arise when any criminal statute fails to afford fair notice of what it forbids, a vague statute in the areas of speech and press creates a second level of difficulty. We have indicated that "stricter standards of permissible statutory vagueness may be applied to a statute having a potentially inhibiting effect on speech; a man may the less be required to act at his peril here, because the free dissemination of ideas may be the loser." *Smith* v. *California* [1959]. . . . To implement this general principle, and recognizing the inherent vagueness of any definition of obscenity, we have held that the definition of obscenity must be drawn as narrowly as possible so as to minimize the interference with protected expression. . . . A vague statute in this area creates a third, although admittedly more subtle, set of problems. These problems concern the institutional stress that inevitably results where the line separating protected from unprotected speech is excessively vague. . . .

As a result of our failure to define standards with predictable application to any given piece of material, there is no probability of regularity in obscenity decisions by state and lower federal courts. That is not to say that these courts have performed badly in this area or paid insufficient attention to the principles we have established. The problem is, rather, that one cannot say with certainty that material is obscene until at least five members of this Court, applying inevitably obscure standards, have pronounced it so. The number of obscenity cases on our docket gives ample testimony to the burden that has been placed upon this Court.

But the sheer number of the cases does not define the full extent of the institutional problem. For, quite apart from the number of cases involved and the need to make a fresh constitutional determination in each case, we are tied to the "absurd business of perusing and viewing the miserable stuff that pours into the Court. . . . " *Interstate Circuit, Inc.* v. *Dallas*, [1959]. . . . In addition, the uncertainty of the standards creates a continuing source of tension between state and federal courts, since the need for an independent determination by this Court seems to render superfluous even the most conscientious analysis by state tribunals. And our inability to justify our decisions with a persuasive rationale—or indeed, any rationale at all—necessarily creates the impression that we are merely second-guessing state court judges.

. . . Given these inevitable side-effects of state efforts to suppress what is assumed to be *unprotected* speech, we must scrutinize with care the state interest that is asserted to justify the suppression. For in the absence of some very substantial interest in suppressing such speech, we can hardly condone the ill-effects that seem to flow inevitably from the effort. . . .

. . . While I cannot say that the interests of the State—apart from the question of juveniles and unconsenting adults—are trivial or nonexistent, I am compelled to conclude that these interests cannot justify the substantial damage to constitutional rights and to this Nation's judicial machinery that inevitably results from state efforts to bar the distribution even of unprotected material to consenting adults. . . . I would hold, therefore, that at least in the absence of distribution to juveniles or obtrusive exposure to unconsenting adults, the First and Fourteenth Amendments prohibit the state and federal governments from attempting wholly to suppress sexually oriented materials on the basis of their allegedly "obscene" contents. Nothing in this approach precludes those governments from taking action to serve what may be strong and legitimate interests through regulation of the manner of distribution of sexually oriented material. . . .

Indianapolis Anti-Pornography Ordinance (1984)

In 1984 the City-County Council of Indianapolis and Marion County, Indiana, pioneered a new approach to regulating pornography. The council concluded that pornography's implicit endorsement of the sexual subordination of women constitutes a form of sex discrimination which degrades and harms all women. It therefore authorized any woman to sue those trafficking in pornography for violating her civil rights.

The ordinance was struck down in *American Booksellers Association, Inc.* v. *Hudnut,* and the Supreme Court summarily affirmed that ruling.

Be it ordered by the City-County Council of the City of Indianapolis and of Marion County, Indiana:

(a) Findings. The City-County Council hereby makes the following findings: . . .

(2) Pornography is a discriminatory practice based on sex because its effect is to deny women equal opportunities in society. Pornography is central in creating and maintaining sex as a basis of discrimination. Pornography is a systematic practice of exploitation and subordination based on sex which differentially harms women. The bigotry and contempt it promotes, with the acts of aggression it fosters, harm women's opportunities for equality of rights in employment, education, access to and use of public accommodations, and acquisition of real property, and contribute significantly to restricting women in particular from full exercise of citizenship and participation in public life, including in neighborhoods.

(b) It is the purpose of this ordinance . . .

(8) To prevent and prohibit all discriminatory practices of sexual subordination or inequality through pornography.

(g) Discriminatory practice shall mean and include the following: . . .

(4) Trafficking in pornography: The production, sale, exhibition, or distribution of pornography.

(A) City, state and federally funded public libraries or private and public university and college libraries in which pornography is available for study, including on open shelves, shall not be construed to be trafficking in pornography, but special display presentations of pornography in said places is sex discrimination.

(B) The formation of private clubs or associations for purposes of trafficking in pornography is illegal and shall be considered a conspiracy to violate the civil rights of women.

(C) Any woman has a cause of action hereunder as a woman acting against the subordination of women. Any man, child or transsexual who alleges injury by pornography in the way women are injured by it shall also have a cause of action under this chapter.

(5) Coercion into pornographic performance. . . .

(6) Forcing pornography on a person: The forcing of pornography on any woman, man, child or transsexual in any place of employment, in education, in a home, or in any public place, except that a man, child or transsexual must allege and prove injury in the same way that a woman is injured in order to have a cause of action.

(7) Assault or physical attack due to pornography: The assault, physical attack, or injury of any woman, man, child, or transsexual in a way that is directly caused by specific pornography. The injured party shall have a claim for damages against the perpetrator(s), maker(s), distributor(s), seller(s), and exhibitor(s), and for an injunction against the specific pornography's further exhibition, distribution, or sale. . . .

(8) Defenses. Where the materials which are the subject matter of a cause of action under (4), (5), (6), or (7) of this section are pornography, it shall not be a defense that the defendant did not know or intend that the materials were pornography or sex discrimination. . . .

(v) Pornography shall mean the sexually explicit subordination of women, graphically depicted, whether in pictures or words, that includes one or more of the following:

(1) Women are presented as sexual objects who enjoy pain or humiliation; or

(2) Women are presented as sexual objects who experience sexual pleasure in being raped; or

(3) Woman are presented as sexual objects tied up or cut up or mutilated or bruised or physically hurt, or as dismembered or truncated or fragmented or severed into body parts; or

(4) Women are presented being penetrated by objects or animals; or

(5) Women are presented in scenarios of degradation, injury, abasement, torture, shown as filthy or inferior, bleeding, bruised, or hurt in a context that makes these conditions sexual. . . .

(bb) Sexually explicit shall mean actual or simulated:

(1) Sexual intercourse, including genital-genital, oral-genital, anal-genital or oral-anal, whether between persons of the same or opposite sex or between women and animals; or

(2) Uncovered exhibition of the genitals, pubic region, buttocks or anus of any person.

13
FREEDOM OF RELIGION

"Congress shall make no law respecting an establishment of religion, or prohibiting the free exercise thereof." The religion clauses of the First Amendment impose two restrictions: the Establishment Clause requires a degree of church-state separation, and the Free Exercise Clause recognizes a sphere of religious liberty that Congress cannot invade. For almost 150 years the Supreme Court had little occasion to construe these constitutional provisions. Since 1940, however, the Court has decided over seventy religion cases. This proliferation of cases has resulted in large part from the incorporation of the religion clauses in *Cantwell* v. *Connecticut* (1940) and *Everson* v. *Board of Education* (1947), which brought state and local accommodations of religion under constitutional scrutiny for the first time.[1] The expanding scope of governmental activity and an increasing religious diversity also have contributed to the rise in litigation. And along with the Court's greater involvement in disputes over religion has come intense controversy. This chapter describes how the Court has interpreted the Establishment and Free Exercise Clauses and analyzes the growing debate about the meaning of those provisions.

ESTABLISHMENT OF RELIGION

Everson and the Purposes of the Establishment Clause

In *Everson* v. *Board of Education* (1947) the Supreme Court outlined the interpretation of the Establishment Clause that guided its decisions through the early 1980s. Although the justices split, 5–4, in upholding

New Jersey's program of providing free bus transportation to both public and nonpublic school children, both the majority and dissenters in *Everson* agreed that the Establishment Clause was meant to erect a "wall of separation" between church and state. Justice Hugo Black summarized the Court's position:

> The "establishment of religion" clause of the First Amendment means at least this: Neither a state nor the Federal Government can set up a church. Neither can pass laws which aid one religion, aid all religions, or prefer one religion over another. Neither can force nor influence a person to go to or to remain away from church against his will or force him to profess a belief or disbelief in any religion. No person can be punished for entertaining or professing religious beliefs or disbeliefs, for church attendance or non-attendance. No tax in any amount, large or small, can be levied to support any religious activities or institutions, whatever they may be called, or whatever form they may adopt to teach or practice religion. Neither a state nor the Federal Government can, openly or secretly, participate in the affairs of any religious organizations or groups and vice versa.

Three aspects of the *Everson* decision, as reflected in Black's statement, deserve particular emphasis. First, the Court held that the Establishment Clause imposes restrictions on state activity as stringent as those imposed on the national government. Second, it ruled that the Establishment Clause prohibits any aid to religion and requires a strict neutrality not only among religions but also between religion and irreligion. Finally, as the divisions on the Court in *Everson* indicated, Black's standard did not lend itself to automatic application, and thus its endorsement by the Court did not foreclose disagreement in future Establishment Clause cases.

To support its interpretation of the Establishment Clause, the Court looked to the Framers' aims in adopting this provision. And in seeking those aims, the justices focused not on the debates in the First Congress, but on the struggle for religious liberty in Virginia, which had culminated in the disestablishment of the Episcopal Church. The history of this struggle, the Court maintained, supplied the key to a correct understanding of the Establishment Clause. To begin with, the long dispute in Virginia had engaged the attention of the other states, several of which were influenced by its outcome to eliminate their own religious establishments. Thus, the Court reasoned, the victory for religious liberty in Virginia created a national climate of opinion favorable to the separation of church and state. Even more important, the leaders of the anti-establishment forces in Virginia, James Madison and Thomas Jefferson, also played a major role in the development and adoption of the Bill of Rights. The Court therefore concluded that the views they expressed during the Virginia campaign in favor of a strict separation of church and state were incorporated into the First Amendment.

Although the Court subsequently devised various standards for detecting violations of the Establishment Clause, the decisions handed down until the 1980s for the most part reflected the view of the clause's purposes outlined in *Everson.* Thus the Court consistently ruled against government attempts to promote particular religious views. Examples include *School District of Abington Township* v. *Schempp* (1963), in which the Court invalidated requirements for Bible reading and the recitation of the Lord's Prayer in the public schools; and *Epperson* v. *Arkansas* (1968), in which it overturned an Arkansas law that prohibited teaching about evolution. It also has struck down enactments penalizing individuals for their religious beliefs or disbelief: in *Torasco* v. *Watkins* (1961), it unanimously invalidated a Maryland constitutional provision that established a religious test for public office; and in *McDaniel* v. *Paty* (1978), it struck down a Tennessee law that disqualified clergy from serving as state legislators. Finally, the justices have invalidated more even-handed efforts to aid religion on the ground that they violated governmental neutrality between religion and irreligion. New York's establishment of a nondenominational prayer for public school children, struck down in *Engel* v. *Vitale* (1962), fell into this category, as did a Champaign, Illinois, program of releasing students from classes for religious instruction on school premises, invalidated in *McCollum* v. *Board of Education* (1948).

The Challenge to *Everson*

Ever since *Everson,* some scholars have insisted that the justices, through excessive reliance on the Virginia struggle for religious liberty, had misinterpreted the religion clauses of the First Amendment.[2] Drawing upon this research in his dissent in *Wallace* v. *Jaffree* (1985), Justice William Rehnquist presented a substantially different understanding of the aims of the Establishment Clause. According to Rehnquist, the debate in the First Congress indicated that the Founders did not contemplate a "wall of separation" between church and state. Because most members of the founding generation believed that political liberty was more secure where religion flourished, they did not oppose using religious means, including nondiscriminatory aid to religion, to achieve valid governmental ends. Nor did they object to governmental support for religion and accommodation of the religious character of the American people. And both governmental practice and scholarly commentary for over a century after the ratification of the First Amendment reflected this view. As long as the national government neither established a national church nor gave preference to a particular religion, its actions supporting or accommodating religion were viewed as consistent with the Establishment Clause.

Acceptance of this interpretation of the Establishment Clause does not require repudiation of all the Court's decisions. If laws mandating prayer and Bible-reading in public schools entail governmental support for particular religious views, then their invalidation by the Court was correct. Equally unexceptionable were the Court's decisions in *McGowan* v. *Maryland* (1961), upholding Sunday closing laws, and in *Walz* v. *Tax*

Commission (1970), upholding tax exemptions for churches, in that the challenged programs served legitimate governmental purposes. And recent rulings which are difficult to square with *Everson*—such as *Lynch* v. *Donnelly* (1984), permitting inclusion of a creche in a Christmas display on public property, and *Marsh* v. *Chambers* (1985), upholding government payment of a chaplain to conduct prayers at the beginning of state legislative sessions—might be upheld as accommodations of the populace's religious beliefs.

On the other hand, some Court rulings cannot be reconciled with Justice Rehnquist's interpretation of the Establishment Clause. The Court's invalidation of Alabama's silent-prayer statute in *Jaffree* is a prime example, since government merely accommodated students' religious beliefs without favoring any particular creed. Even more important deviations are the Court's rulings on aid to nonpublic schools, to which we now turn.

Aid to Education

Perhaps the most difficult Establishment Clause question faced by the justices has been the validity of governmental aid to programs that benefit both sectarian and nonsectarian institutions. The aid program at issue in *Everson* v. *Board of Education* illustrates the difficulties posed by this question. On the one hand, state reimbursement for the cost of transporting children to sectarian schools clearly facilitates attendance at those schools and thus seems inconsistent with the no-aid requirement announced in *Everson*. On the other hand, for the state to deny transportation to students merely because they attend religious schools would appear to reflect governmental hostility to, rather than neutrality toward, religion. And as the expansion of governmental aid programs has made the consequences of exclusion from them more severe, conflicts over aid programs have increased in both intensity and frequency.

Initially, even while endorsing the view of the Establishment Clause announced in *Everson*, the Court concluded that some aid programs were constitutionally permissible. In *Everson* itself, the Court upheld New Jersey's transportation program, and in *Board of Education* v. *Allen* (1968) it rejected a challenge to a New York law requiring local school boards to lend textbooks to students in private and parochial schools. Even though these programs arguably facilitated attendance at sectarian schools, the Court noted that the aid served legitimate secular purposes, went to the students rather than to religious institutions, and did not directly assist those institutions in accomplishing their religious objectives. Dissenters in these cases, however, insisted that the programs violated the Establishment Clause's no-aid requirement and that the textbooks at issue in *Allen*, whatever their content, could be used to promote religious belief.[3] Apparently these arguments had some effect, for the Court in subsequent cases struck down various programs providing instructional materials and auxiliary services to parochial schools.

The Court first reviewed major aid programs to private (including sectarian) schools in *Lemon* v. *Kurtzman* (1971). At issue were two state programs: Pennsylvania's program directly reimbursed nonpublic elementary and secondary schools for the costs of teachers' salaries, textbooks, and instructional materials in specific secular subjects; and Rhode Island's provided a 15 percent salary supplement to teachers of secular subjects in nonpublic elementary and secondary schools. With only a single dissent, the Court invalidated both programs. Speaking for the Court, Chief Justice Warren Burger announced a three-pronged test, culled from previous Court decisions, for programs challenged under the Establishment Clause: "First, the statute must have a secular legislative purpose; second, its principal or primary effect must be one that neither advances nor inhibits religion; finally, the statute must not foster an excessive entanglement with religion." Applying this test to the programs in *Lemon*, Burger concluded that although both had secular legislative purposes, both involved excessive governmental entanglement with the sectarian schools. A prime purpose of sectarian elementary and secondary education, he noted, is to inculcate religious belief, not only through religious instruction but also by creating a pervasively religious atmosphere in the schools. And because all aspects of sectarian elementary and secondary education promote the schools' religious goals, aid to such schools unconstitutionally involves government in fostering religious belief. Moreover, Burger continued, even if a school sought to compartmentalize its religious and secular instruction, excessive governmental policing of the school's operations would be required to ensure that the aid served only secular purposes. Finally, the Chief Justice pointed out that such aid programs had the effect of promoting political divisions along religious lines, "one of the principal evils against which the First Amendment was intended to protect."

Nevertheless, in *Tilton* v. *Richardson* (1971) the Court sustained the constitutionality of the Higher Education Facilities Act of 1963, under which private colleges received federal grants and loans to construct buildings to be used solely for secular purposes.[4] Over the protests of three justices who had joined the *Lemon* majority, Chief Justice Burger distinguished the program in *Tilton* from those invalidated in *Lemon* on two bases: (1) the colleges receiving funds did not inject religious teaching into their secular courses nor view religious indoctrination as one of their primary functions; (2) that the character of the aid—one-time, single-purpose, and nonideological—precluded both political divisions along sectarian lines and excessive administrative entanglements.

In the numerous cases involving aid to nonpublic elementary and secondary education decided by the Court since 1971, the *Lemon* decision's emphasis on the educational mission of the schools receiving aid has played a crucial role. When states attempt to ensure that aid is not used to advance religion by policing its use, their programs run the risk of invalidation on entanglement grounds. However, state aid without policing may have a primary effect of advancing religion, since the Court has held that religious and secular education are inextricably mixed in sectarian elementary and secondary schools. Although this appears to suggest that any aid to sectarian schools violates the Constitution, the Court has not taken this position. Instead, it has attempted to distinguish between aid which advances the schools' religious mission and aid which does not.

The success of this endeavor is open to serious question. The justices have splintered badly in considering specific aid programs, and it has not been unusual for no opinion to command a majority on the Court. Moreover, as Box 13.1 indicates, the Court's rulings are difficult to reconcile, and insofar as they are reconcilable, they seem to rest on rather tenuous distinctions. As Justice Byron White put it, the Court's decisions have "sacrifice[d] clarity and predictability for flexibility."[5] This of course has created problems for states attempting to provide aid to students in sectarian schools without running afoul of constitutional limitations. Indeed, the number of school-aid questions coming to the Court testifies to the difficulties states have had in discerning the line between permissible and impermissible programs.

For Justice Rehnquist and other critics, however, the problems with the Court's approach go much deeper. It is not merely that the three-pronged test developed in *Lemon* is difficult to apply or that the requirement of monitoring aid without entanglement creates, in Rehnquist's view, an "insoluble paradox." Rather, because the test reflects the flawed historical understanding of the Establishment Clause announced in *Everson,* it improperly prevents government from pursuing legitimate secular ends, such as provision of education, through nondiscriminatory sectarian means. Put differently, adoption of Justice Rehnquist's position on the meaning of the Establishment Clause would require a fundamental reconsideration of the Court's rulings on aid to nonpublic schools.

BOX 13.1

Court Decisions on Aid to Nonpublic Elementary and Secondary Education

Tuition. Grants and tax benefits specifically geared to parents of children attending nonpublic schools were invalidated in *Committee for Public Education* v. *Nyquist* (1973), but tax credits made available to all parents for tuition and other educational expenses were upheld in *Mueller* v. *Allen* (1983).

Facility Maintenance. State funding for the upkeep of nonpublic-school facilities was invalidated in *Nyquist.*

Teacher Salaries. State payment of salaries, in whole or in part, for teachers of secular subjects in nonpublic schools was struck down in *Lemon* v. *Kurtzman* (1971).

Instructional Materials. Lending textbooks to pupils in nonpublic schools was upheld in *Board of Education* v. *Allen* (1968), *Meek* v. *Pittenger*

(1975), and *Wolman* v. *Walter* (1977). Lending other instructional materials (e.g., maps, films, laboratory equipment) was invalidated in *Meek* and *Wolman.* Reimbursement to nonpublic schools for textbooks and other instructional materials was struck down in *Lemon.*

Educational Services. State provision of counseling, testing, and psychological services for pupils in nonpublic schools was struck down when conducted by public-school personnel in nonpublic schools (*Meek*) but upheld when conducted off the nonpublic-school premises (*Wolman*). State provision of remedial and enrichment programs by public-school personnel in nonpublic schools was struck down in *School District of Grand Rapids* v. *Ball* (1985) and *Aguilar* v. *Felton* (1985).

Testing. Reimbursement for state-mandated testing was struck down when tests were prepared by nonpublic school personnel (*Levitt* v. *Committee for Public Education* [1973]) but upheld when the tests were prepared by the state (*Wolman* and *Committee for Public Education* v. *Regan* [1980]).

Transportation. State reimbursement to parents for public-transportation costs incurred by children attending nonpublic schools was upheld in *Everson* v. *Board of Education* (1947), but payment for field-trip transportation was struck down in *Wolman.*

FREE EXERCISE OF RELIGION

In a sense, the basic aims of the Free Exercise Clause have been achieved without judicial intervention. One reason the clause was inserted in the Constitution was to ensure that individuals could pursue their religious convictions without impediment, and the multiplicity of denominations in the United States today indicates that religious liberty is flourishing. Perhaps because no single denomination is predominant, overt governmental discrimination against religions seldom has posed a serious problem.[6] The free-exercise cases coming to the Court typically have involved a more delicate issue: how to resolve conflicts between governmental regulations serving secular ends and the demands of individuals' religious beliefs.

Governmental regulations can burden or conflict with the claims of conscience in a variety of ways. Some regulations may place an indirect burden on particular groups of believers. For example, by establishing a uniform day of rest, the Pennsylvania Sunday-closing law, which was upheld in *Braunfeld* v. *Brown* (1961), placed Orthodox Jews and other Sabbatarians at a competitive disadvantage by in effect requiring them to close their businesses two days a week. Other regulations may establish eligibility requirements for governmental benefits which force believers to choose between their religious convictions and those benefits. A prime example was South Carolina's denial of unemployment compensation to a Seventh-day Adventist who refused jobs that required her to work on

Saturday (her Sabbath)—an action the state based on an enactment requiring potential recipients to accept "available suitable work." (The Court in *Sherbert* v. *Verner* [1963] ruled that this denial of benefits violated the free exercise of religion.) Still other governmental regulations may oblige individuals to perform or refrain from actions in violation of their religious convictions. Among the cases raising such issues are *Jacobson* v. *Massachusetts* (1905), in which the Court upheld compulsory vaccination for smallpox despite resistance on religious grounds, and *Goldman* v. *Weinberger* (1986), in which the Court rejected the claim of an Orthodox Jewish psychologist that he be permitted to wear a yarmulke while on duty in uniform at a military hospital. Finally, as *Lyng* v. *Northwest Indian Cemetery Association* (1988) reveals, governmental actions may make it difficult for adherents of site-specific religions to practice their faith. In that case the Court refused to block development of portions of national forest, even though Native American groups viewed the land as sacred.

Braunfeld and *Sherbert* marked a major shift in the Court's interpretation of the Free Exercise Clause. Before 1960 the Court relied on the secular regulation rule in evaluating free-exercise claims. Under this rule, legislation was held to be invalid if it did not serve legitimate, nonreligious governmental ends or if it was directed against particular sects; if those requirements were met, however, the fact that the legislation involved conflicted with some persons' perceived religious obligations did not invalidate it or qualify them for exemptions. According to this interpretation, the Constitution does not require government to accord special recognition to religious beliefs or religiously motivated behavior. To hold that religious claims should prevail over the accomplishment of government's legitimate aims, the Court maintained, would be to admit their superior validity—a position that conflicts with the neutrality toward religion enjoined by the First Amendment. By granting religious exemptions from general legislation, moreover, government in effect would be providing an inducement for individuals to profess particular religious beliefs. Thus even when striking down enactments challenged on religious grounds, as in *West Virginia Board of Education* v. *Barnette* (1943), the Court emphasized that believers and nonbelievers alike were exempt from their requirements.

In *Braunfeld*, Chief Justice Earl Warren enunciated a more exacting standard for evaluating legislation challenged on free-exercise grounds. In upholding Pennsylvania's Sunday closing law, he noted that the state could not achieve its important secular goal of a uniform day of rest through any alternative means that was less burdensome on religious practice. Presumably, then, legislation that imposed a substantial burden on religious practices would be upheld only if (1) it served an important state aim and (2) that aim could not be advanced by a less restrictive means. The latter criterion provided the basis of the *Sherbert* ruling, in which Justice William Brennan, speaking for the Court, observed that even if South Carolina's aim of deterring fraudulent claims were a compelling one, it had not demonstrated that less restrictive means of preventing fraud were ineffective. In *Wisconsin* v. *Yoder* (1972) the Court emphasized the first aspect of Warren's test, ruling that requiring Amish children to attend school beyond the eighth grade did not serve an important state purpose.

This test, then, seeks to reduce conflicts between legal and religious obligations by extending greater protection to religiously motivated conduct. For under this more stringent free-exercise standard, the justices balance the claims of the government against those of the religious adherent. Adoption of this standard has had a beneficial influence on legislation, stimulating governmental efforts to accommodate religious interests in designing programs.[7] However, not all the results of the Court's new approach have been positive.

For one thing, the Court's current approach suffers from the difficulty common to all balancing tests: the outcome of the balancing often depends on who is doing it. Thus even those justices who have accepted this approach to free-exercise issues have disagreed sharply at times over how the balance should be struck in particular cases.

In addition, if religious beliefs qualify an individual for otherwise unavailable benefits or exemptions, then there is an inducement to profess such beliefs, and government must judge the validity of individual claims. This situation raises two problems. In the first place, officials must judge the sincerity of an individual's beliefs, since religious beliefs may be professed solely in order to escape obligations or prohibitions. And as the problems encountered in administering the conscientious objector exemption to military service reveal, such determinations can be exceedingly difficult. Secondly, even if an individual's beliefs clearly are sincere, officials must determine whether the beliefs are religious in nature: nonreligious beliefs, however strongly held, do not create an exemption from legal obligations. This judgment has been complicated by the broad definition of religion given by the Court in interpreting the conscientious objector exemption, under which nontheistic and purely personal beliefs may qualify as religious.[8] Paradoxically, then, the Court's aim of freeing religious belief from the burden of government regulation can be accomplished only by a much deeper governmental involvement in the religious realm: defining what constitutes a religion and judging the sincerity of individuals' beliefs. As early as 1948, the Supreme Court confronted this problem in *United States* v. *Ballard*, and since then the proliferation of cults and other religious movements has forced other courts to confront this perplexing issue.[9]

RECONCILING THE RELIGION CLAUSES

In interpreting the Establishment Clause, the Supreme Court has held that government may neither favor not disfavor religion. Yet in free-exercise cases, it has insisted that government must exempt believers from some general legal requirements, in effect using religion as a criterion for distributing benefits. Thus the aims of the religion clauses, at least under the Court's interpretation, seem inconsistent. How can one reconcile the Establishment Clause's mandate of neutrality between religion and irreligion with the Free Exercise Clause's demand for accommodation of religiously motivated actions?

Four answers to this question have been suggested. One is to admit that the Court's interpretations are inconsistent but to insist that this inconsistency is constitutionally warranted, since it reflects a natural antagonism between the two clauses. Thus in striking down aid to religion while requiring the accommodation of religious beliefs in the application of general legislation, the Court is merely fulfilling the somewhat opposed purposes of the two provisions. Although this view has prevailed on the Court, it is subject to two telling objections: it depreciates the Constitution by assuming that it incorporates an incoherent understanding of the proper relation between government and religion, and it offers no guidance for determining whether one should opt for neutrality or accommodation in resolving specific disputes.

The problems with this view have led some justices and constitutional scholars to locate the problem not in the Constitution but in the Court's interpretations. According to one view, the Court has interpreted the Establishment Clause in an overly rigid fashion that unduly restricts governmental efforts to promote the free exercise of religion. Justice Potter Stewart, dissenting in the school-prayer cases, voiced this criticism when he insisted that in providing opportunities for voluntary religious observances in the public schools, government merely accommodates the religious convictions of the populace. Justice Byron White has dissented from the Court's aid-to-education cases on similar grounds, asserting that governmental programs that make it possible for individuals to pursue a religious education constitute an accommodation consistent with—and indeed, appropriate to—the First Amendment's primary concern, the free exercise of religion.

Other observers have concluded that the Court has improperly interpreted the Free Exercise Clause. According to this view, best expressed in Justice John Marshall Harlan's dissent in *Sherbert,* a requirement that states accommodate religious convictions in their legislation violates that neutrality between religion and irreligion which was a prime purpose of the First Amendment. Only by reinstitution of the secular regulation rule, this argument goes, can the Court properly reconcile its establishment and free exercise positions.

Finally, Chief Justice Rehnquist has rejected the Court's interpretations of both the Establishment and Free Exercise Clauses. Agreeing with Justice Harlan that the secular regulation rule is the appropriate standard in free-exercise cases, he has insisted that states need not accommodate believers in designing legislation. Yet because his interpretation of the Establishment Clause does not require governmental neutrality between religion and irreligion, there is no constitutional bar to efforts to accommodate religion. His position thus allows government wide discretion in determining whether and when to grant exemptions from general statutory requirements.

TRENDS AND PROSPECTS

Although its rulings on school prayer and other publicly supported religious practices excited considerable controversy, for many years the Supreme Court continued to reaffirm its decisions and the understanding of the Establishment Clause underlying them. Thus as recently as 1981, the justices unanimously invalidated North Carolina's practice of publishing a "motorist's prayer" on its official highway map, and in 1980 they summarily struck down a Kentucky law directing that a copy of the Ten Commandments be posted in public school classrooms. Rulings since 1983, however, suggest that the Court is rethinking its separationist posture. In upholding Pawtucket's creche display in *Lynch* v. *Donnelly* and Nebraska's legislative prayer in *Marsh* v. *Chambers,* the Court indicated that the Establishment Clause did not bar some governmental efforts to recognize the nation's religious heritage. Even while invalidating Alabama's moment-of-silence law in *Wallace* v. *Jaffree,* several justices noted that more carefully drawn statutes would survive constitutional scrutiny.

A similar ferment is evident in the Court's recent aid-to-nonpublic-education cases. The narrow majorities supporting the Court's rulings indicate that fifteen years of dealing with the issue have not promoted a consensus among the justices. Indeed, several justices have openly expressed doubts about the course the Court has followed and the three-pronged test announced in *Lemon* v. *Kurtzman.* Whether the Court will abandon its current approach remains to be seen. But the divisions among the justices are likely to spur further litigation, thereby affording the opportunity for reconsideration of that approach.

NOTES

1 Some authorities assert that the Free Exercise Clause was incorporated in *Hamilton* v. *Board of Regents of the University of California (1934).*

2 Early works criticizing the Court's historical scholarship include James M. O'Neill, *Religion and Education Under the Constitution* (New York: Harper, 1949), and Mark DeWolfe Howe, *The Garden and the Wilderness* (Chicago: University of Chicago Press, 1965). More recent critical studies include Michael J. Malbin, *Religion and Politics* (Washington, D.C.: American Enterprise Institute, 1978), and Robert L. Cord, *Separation of Church and State: Historical Fact and Current Fiction* (New York: Lambeth Press, 1982).

3 It should be noted that Justice Hugo Black, who wrote the opinion of the Court in *Everson,* dissented in *Allen*—as did Justice William Douglas, the only other member of the *Everson* majority still on the Court at the time *Allen* was decided.

4 The Court did invalidate a provision of the law that permitted colleges to use the buildings for religious purposes twenty years after receiving the funds.

5 *Committee for Public Education* v. *Regan* (1980).

6 On the importance of religious diversity for religious liberty, see *The Federalist,* Nos. 10 and 51.

7 For parallel statutory developments, see Title VII of the Civil Rights Act of

1964, 42 U.S.C. secs. 200e *et seq.*, and the Equal Employment Opportunity Commission regulations on accommodating religious beliefs, 29 C.F.R. sec. 1605.1(a) (3).

8 See *United States* v. *Seeger* (1965) and *Welsh* v. *United States* (1970).

9 Recent cases involving "cults" demonstrate the difficulties of distinguishing religions and religious practices from secular groups and activities. Representative cases include *Katz* v. *Superior Court,* 73 Cal. App. 3d 952 (1977), which involved deprogramming of cult members, and *Holy Spirit Association for the Unification of World Christianity* v. *Tax Commission,* 435 N.E. 2d 662 (1982), which involved determinations of whether activities conducted by a religious group were religious in character.

SELECTED READINGS

Aguilar v. *Felton,* 473 U.S. 402 (1985).
Bob Jones University v. *United States,* 461 U.S. 574 (1983).
Cantwell v. *Connecticut,* 310 U.S. 296 (1940).
Reynolds v. *United States,* 98 U.S. 145 (1878).
United States v. *Ballard,* 322 U.S. 78 (1948).

Walter Berns, *The First Amendment and the Future of American Democracy* (New York: Basic Books, 1976).

Choper, Jesse H. "The Religion Clauses of the First Amendment: Reconciling the Conflict." *University of Pittsburgh Law Review* 41 (1980).

Cord, Robert L. *Separation of Church and State: Historical Fact and Current Fiction* (New York: Lambeth Press, 1982).

Curry, Thomas J. *The First Freedoms: Church and State in America to the Passage of the First Amendment.* New York: Oxford University Press, 1986.

"Developments in the Law—Religion and the State," *Harvard Law Review* 100 (1987).

Levy, Leonard W. *The Establishment Clause: Religion and the First Amendment.* New York: Macmillan, 1986.

Miller, William Lee. *The First Liberty: Religion and the American Republic.* New York: Knopf, 1985.

Sorauf, Frank J. *The Wall of Separation: The Constitutional Politics of Church and State.* Princeton: Princeton University Press, 1970.

Tarr, G. Alan. "Church and State in the States," *Washington Law Review* 64 (1989).

Everson v. *Board of Education*

330 U.S. 1, 67 S. Ct. 504, 91 L. Ed. 711 (1947)

A New Jersey statute authorized local school boards to make rules and contracts for the transportation of students to and from schools. Acting under this statute, the Ewing Township Board of Education authorized reimbursement to parents of money spent for transportation to Catholic parochial schools as well as to public schools. Arch Everson, a taxpayer in the school district, challenged the transportation program as a violation of the state constitution (a claim rejected by the state supreme court) and the Federal Constitution. *Opinion of the Court: Black, Vinson, Reed, Douglas, Murphy. Dissenting opinions: Jackson, Frankfurter; Rutledge, Frankfurter, Jackson, Burton.*

MR. JUSTICE BLACK delivered the opinion of the Court. . . .

This Court has previously recognized that the provisions of the First Amendment, in the drafting and adoption of which Madison and Jefferson played such leading roles, had the same objective and were intended to provide the same protection against governmental intrusion on religious liberty as the Virginia [Bill for Religious Liberty]. . . .

The "establishment of religion" clause of the First Amendment means at least this: Neither a state nor the Federal Government can set up a church. Neither can pass laws which aid one religion, aid all religions, or prefer one religion over another. Neither can force nor influence a person to go to or to remain away from church against his will or force him to profess a belief or disbelief in any religion. No person can be punished for entertaining or professing religious beliefs or disbeliefs, for church attendance or non-attendance. No tax in any amount, large or small, can be levied to support any religious activities or institutions, whatever they may be called, or whatever form they may adopt to teach or practice religion. Neither a state nor the Federal Government can, openly or secretly, participate in the affairs of any religious organizations or groups and *vice versa.* In the words of Jefferson, the clause against establishment of religion by law was intended to erect "a wall of separation between church and State." . . .

. . . New Jersey cannot consistently with the "establishment of religion" clause of the First Amendment contribute tax-raised funds to the support of an institution which teaches the tenets and faith of any church. On the other hand, other language of the amendment commands that New Jersey cannot hamper its citizens in the free exercise of their own religion. Consequently, it cannot exclude individual Catholics, Lutherans, Mohammedans, Baptists, Jews, Methodists, Non-believers, Presbyterians, or the members of any other faith, *because of their faith, or lack of it,* from receiving the benefits of public welfare legislation. While we do not mean to intimate that a state could not provide transportation only to children attending public schools, we must be careful, in protecting the citizens of New Jersey against state-established churches, to be sure that we do not inadvertently prohibit New Jersey from extending its general state law benefits to all its citizens without regard to their religious belief.

Measured by these standards, we cannot say that the First Amendment prohibits New Jersey from spending tax-raised funds to pay the bus fares of parochial school pupils as a part of a general program under which it pays the fares of pupils attending public and other schools. It is undoubtedly true that children are helped to get to church schools. There is even a possibility that some of the children might not be sent to the church schools if the parents were compelled to pay their children's bus fares out of their own pockets when transportation to a public school would have been paid for by the State. The same possibility exists where the state requires a local transit company to provide reduced fares to school children including those attending parochial schools, or where a municipally owned transportation system undertakes to carry all school children free of charge. Moreover, state-paid policemen, detailed to protect children going to and from church schools from the very real hazards of traffic, would serve much the same purpose and accomplish much the same result as state provisions intended to guarantee free transportation of a kind which the state deems to be best for the school children's welfare. And parents might refuse to risk their children to the serious danger of traffic accidents going to and from parochial schools, the approaches to which were not protected by policemen. Similarly, parents might be reluctant to permit their children to attend schools which the state had cut off from such general government services as ordinary police and fire protection, connections for sewage disposal, public highways and sidewalks. Of course, cutting off church schools from these services, so separate and so indisputably marked off from the religious function, would make it far more difficult for the schools to operate. But such is obviously not the purpose of the First Amendment. That Amendment requires the state to be a neutral in its relations with groups of religious believers and non-believers; it does not require the state to be their adversary. State power is no more to be used so as to handicap religions than it is to favor them. . . .

The First Amendment has erected a wall between church and state. That wall must be kept high and impregnable. We could not approve the slightest breach. New Jersey has not breached it here.

Affirmed.

MR. JUSTICE JACKSON, dissenting.

. . . The Court's opinion marshals every argument in favor of state aid and puts the case in its most favorable light, but much of its reasoning confirms my conclusions that there are no good grounds upon which to support the present legislation. In fact, the undertones of the opinion, advocating complete and uncompromising separation of Church from State, seem utterly discordant with its conclusion yielding support to their commingling in educational matters. The case which irresistibly comes to mind as the most fitting precedent is that of Julia who, according to Byron's reports, "whispering 'I will ne'er consent,'—consented." . . .

The Court sustains this legislation by assuming two deviations from the facts of this particular case. . . .

The Court concludes that this "legislation, as applied, does no more than provide a general program to help parents get their children, regardless of their religion, safely and expeditiously to and from accredited schools," and it draws a comparison between "state provisions intended to guarantee free transportation" for school children with services such as police and fire protection, and implies that we are here dealing with "laws authorizing new types of public services . . ." This hypothesis permeates the opinion. The facts will not bear that construction.

The Township of Ewing is not furnishing transportation to the children in any form; it is not operating school busses itself or contracting for their operation; and it is not performing any public service of any kind with this taxpayer's money. All school children are left to ride as ordinary paying passengers on the regular busses operated by the public transportation system. What the Township does, and what the taxpayer complains of, is at stated intervals to reimburse parents for the fares paid, provided the children attend either public schools or Catholic Church schools. This expenditure of tax funds has no possible effect on the child's safety or expedition in transit. As passengers on the public busses they travel as fast and no faster, and are as safe and no safer, since their parents are reimbursed as before.

In addition to thus assuming a type of service that does not exist, the Court also insists that we must close our eyes to a discrimination which does exist. The resolution which authorizes disbursement of this taxpayer's money limits reimbursement to those who attend public schools and Catholic schools. That is the way the Act is applied to this taxpayer.

The New Jersey Act in question makes the character of the school, not the needs of the children, determine the eligibility of parents to reimbursement. The Act permits payment for transportation to parochial schools or public schools but prohibits it to private schools operated in whole or in part for profit. . . .

MR. JUSTICE RUTLEDGE with whom MR. JUSTICE FRANKFURTER, MR. JUSTICE JACKSON and MR. JUSTICE BURTON agree, dissenting. . . .

The Amendment's purpose was not to strike merely at the official establishment of a single sect, creed or religion, outlawing only a formal relation such as had prevailed in England and some of the colonies. Necessarily it was to uproot all such relationships. But the object was broader than separating church and state in this narrow sense. It was to create a complete and permanent separation of the spheres of religious activity and civil authority by comprehensively forbidding every form of public aid or support for religion. . . .

No provision of the Constitution is more closely tied to or given content by its generating history than the religious clause of the First Amendment. It is at once the refined product and the terse summation of that history. The history includes not only Madison's authorship and the proceedings before the First Congress, but also the long and intensive struggle for religious freedom in America, more especially in Virginia, of which the Amendment was the direct culmination. . . .

All the great instruments of the Virginia struggle for religious liberty thus became warp and woof of our constitutional tradition, not simply by the course of history, but by the common unifying force of Madison's life, thought and sponsorship. He epitomized the whole of that tradition in the Amendment's compact, but nonetheless comprehensive, phrasing.

. . . Madison opposed every form and degree of official relation between religion and civil authority. For him religion was a wholly private matter beyond the scope of civil power either to restrain or to support. . . . In no phase was he more unrelentingly absolute than in opposing state support or aid by taxation. Not even "three pence" contribution was thus to be exacted from any citizen for such a purpose. . . .

In view of this history no further proof is needed that the Amendment forbids any appropriation, large or small, from public funds to aid or support any and all religious exercises. . . .

New Jersey's action . . . exactly fits the type of exaction and the kind of evil at which Madison and Jefferson struck. Under the test they framed it cannot be said that the cost of transportation is no part of the cost of education or of the religious instruction given. That it is a substantial and a necessary element is shown most plainly by the continuing and increasing demand for the state to assume it. Nor is there pretense that it relates only to the secular instruction given in religious schools or that any attempt is or could be made toward allocating proportional shares as between the secular and the religious instruction. It is precisely because the instruction is religious and relates to a particular faith, whether one or another, that parents send their children to religious schools. . . . And the very purpose of the state's contribution to defray the cost of conveying the pupil to the place where he will receive not simply secular, but also and primarily religious, teaching and guidance. . . .

. . . The matter is not one of quantity, to be measured by the amount of money expended. Now as in Madison's day it is one of principle, to keep separate the separate spheres as the First Amendment drew them; to prevent the first experiment upon our liberties; and to keep the question from becoming entangled in corrosive precedents. . . .

School District of Abington Township v. *Schempp*

374 U.S. 203, 83 S. Ct. 1560, 10 L. Ed. 2d 844 (1963)

One year after the Court in *Engel* v. *Vitale* invalidated the use of a government-composed prayer for voluntary recitation in New York public schools, it considered the more widespread practice of Bible reading in the public schools. A Pennsylvania law required daily Bible reading, and a Baltimore school board regulation required both Bible reading and daily recitation of the Lord's Prayer. Both programs permitted students to absent themselves from the religious exercises upon parental request.

Perhaps to allay the intense criticism that greeted the *Engel* decision, the opinion of the Court was assigned to Justice Clark, an elder in the Presbyterian Church, and concurring opinions were filed by Justice

Brennan, a Catholic, and Justice Goldberg, a Jew. *Opinion of the Court: Clark, Warren, Black, Douglas, Harlan, Brennan, White, Goldberg. Concurring opinions: Douglas; Brennan; Goldberg, Harlan. Dissenting opinion: Stewart.*

MR. JUSTICE CLARK delivered the opinion of the Court. . . .

The wholesome "neutrality" of which this Court's cases speak . . . stems from a recognition of the teachings of history that powerful sects or groups might bring about a fusion of governmental and religious functions or a concert or dependency of one upon the other to the end that official support of the State or Federal Government would be placed behind the tenets of one or of all orthodoxies. This the Establishment Clause prohibits. And a further reason for neutrality is found in the Free Exercise Clause, which recognizes the value of religious training, teaching and observance and, more particularly, the right of every person to freely choose his own course with reference thereto, free of any compulsion from the state. This the Free Exercise Clause guarantees. Thus, as we have seen, the two clauses may overlap. . . . the Establishment Clause has been directly considered by this Court eight times in the past score of years and, with only one Justice dissenting on the point, it has consistently held that the clause withdrew all legislative power respecting religious belief or the expression thereof. The test may be stated as follows: what are the purpose and the primary effect of the enactment? If either is the advancement or inhibition of religion then the enactment exceeds the scope of legislative power as circumscribed by the Constitution. That is to say that to withstand the strictures of the Establishment Clause there must be a secular legislative purpose and a primary effect that neither advances nor inhibits religion. . . . The distinction between the two clauses is apparent—a violation of the Free Exercise Clause is predicated on coercion while the Establishment Clause violation need not be so attended.

Applying the Establishment Clause principles to the cases at bar we find that the States are requiring the selection and reading at the opening of the school day of verses from the Holy Bible and the recitation of the Lord's Prayer by the students in unison. These exercises are prescribed as past of the curricular activities of students who are required by law to attend school. . . .

. . . Surely the place of the Bible as an instrument of religion cannot be gainsaid, and the State's recognition of the pervading religious character of the ceremony is evident from the rule's specific permission of the alternative use of the Catholic Douay version as well as the recent amendment permitting nonattendance at the exercises. None of these factors is consistent with the contention that the Bible is here used either as an instrument for nonreligious moral inspiration or as a reference for the teaching of secular subjects.

The conclusion follows that in both cases the laws require religious exercises and such exercises are being conducted in direct violation of the rights of the appellees and petitioners. . . .

It is insisted that unless these religious exercises are permitted a "religion of secularism" is established in the schools. We agree of course that the State may not establish a "religion of secularism" in the sense of affirmatively opposing or showing hostility to religion, thus "preferring those who believe in no religion over those who do believe" *Zorach* v. *Clauson* [1952]. We do not agree, however, that this decision in any sense has that effect. In addition, it might well be said that one's education is not complete without a study of comparative religion or the history of religion and its relationship to the advancement of civilization. It certainly may be said that the Bible is worthy of study for its literary and historic qualities. Nothing we have said here indicates that such study of the Bible or of religion, when presented objectively as part of a secular program of education, may not be effected consistently with the First Amendment. But the exercises here . . . are religious exercises, required by the States in violation of the command of the First Amendment that the Government maintain strict neutrality, neither aiding nor opposing religion.

Finally, we cannot accept that the concept of neutrality, which does not permit a State to require a religious exercise even with the consent of the majority of those affected, collides with the majority's right to free exercise of religion. While the Free Exercise Clause clearly prohibits the use of state action to deny the rights of free exercise to *anyone,* it has never meant that a majority could use the machinery of the State to practice its beliefs. . . .

MR. JUSTICE BRENNAN, concurring. . . .

. . . The specific question before us has aroused vigorous dispute whether the architects of the First Amendment—James Madison and Thomas Jefferson particularly—understood the prohibition against any "law respecting an establishment of religion" to reach devotional exercises in the public schools. . . . But I doubt that their view, even if perfectly clear one way or the other, would supply a dispositive answer to the question presented by these cases. A more fruitful inquiry, it seems to me, is whether the practices here challenged threaten those consequences which the Framers deeply feared; whether, in short, they tend to promote that type of interdependence between religion and state which the First Amendment was designed to prevent. . . .

A too literal quest for the advice of the Founding Fathers upon the issues of these cases seems to me futile and misdirected for several reasons: First, on our precise problem the historical record is at best ambiguous, and statements can readily be found to support either side of the proposition. The ambiguity of history is understandable if we recall the nature of the problems uppermost in the thinking of the statesmen who fashioned the religious guarantees; they were concerned with far more flagrant intrusions of government into the realm of religion than any that our century has witnessed. . . .

Second, the structure of American education has greatly changed since the First Amendment was adopted. In the context of our modern emphasis upon public education available to all citizens, any views of the eighteenth century as to whether the exercises at bar are an "establishment" offer little aid to decision. . . .

Third, our religious composition makes us a vastly more diverse people than were our forefathers. They knew differences chiefly among Protestant sects. Today the Nation is far more heterogeneous religiously, including as it does substantial minorities not only of Catholics and Jews but as well of those who worship according to no version of the Bible and those who worship no God at all. . . . In the face of such profound changes, practices which may have been objectionable to no one in the time of Jefferson and Madison may today be highly offensive to many persons, the deeply devout and the nonbelievers alike. . . .

Fourth, the American experiment in free public education available to all children has been guided in large measure by the dramatic evolution of the religious diversity among the population which our public schools serve. . . . It is implicit in the history and character of American public education that the public schools serve a uniquely *public* function: the training of American citizens in an atmosphere free of parochial, divisive, or separatist influences of any sort—an atmosphere in which children may assimilate a heritage common to all American groups and religions. . . . This is a heritage neither theistic nor atheistic, but simply civic and patriotic. . . .

MR. JUSTICE STEWART, dissenting.

I think the records in the two cases before us are so fundamentally deficient as to make impossible an informed or responsible determination of the constitutional issues presented. Specifically, I cannot agree that on these records we can say that the Establishment Clause has necessarily been violated. . . .

. . . While in many contexts the Establishment Clause and the Free Exercise Clause fully complement each other, there are areas in which a doctrinaire reading of the Establishment Clause leads to irreconcilable conflict with the Free Exercise Clause.

A single obvious example should suffice to make the point. Spending federal funds to employ chaplains for the armed forces might be said to violate the Establishment Clause. Yet a lonely soldier stationed at some faraway outpost could surely complain that a government which did *not* provide him the opportunity for pastoral guidance was affirmatively prohibiting the free exercise of his religion. And such examples could readily be multiplied. The short of the matter is simply that the two relevant clauses of the First Amendment cannot accurately be reflected in a sterile metaphor which by its very nature may distort rather than illumine the problems involved in a particular case. . . .

That the central value embodied in the First Amendment—and, more particularly, in the guarantee of "liberty" contained in the Fourteenth—is the safeguarding of an individual's right to free exercise of his religion has been consistently recognized. . . . It is this concept of constitutional protection . . . which makes the cases before us such difficult ones for me. For there is involved in these cases a substantial free exercise claim on the part of those who affirmatively desire to have their children's school day open with the reading of passages from the Bible. . . .

It might . . . be argued that parents who want their children exposed to religious influences can adequately fulfill that wish off school property and outside school time. With all its surface persuasiveness, however, this argument seriously misconceives the basic constitutional justification for permitting the exercises at issue in these cases. For a compulsory state educational system so structures a child's life that if religious exercises are held to be an impermissible activity in schools, religion is placed at an artificial and state-created disadvantage. Viewed in this light, permission of such exercises for those who want them is necessary if the schools are truly to be neutral in the matter of religion. And a refusal to permit religious exercises thus is seen, not as the realization of state neutrality, but rather as the establishment of a religion of secularism, or at the least, as government support of the beliefs of those who think that religious exercises should be conducted only in private. . . .

What our Constitution indispensibly protects is the freedom of each of us, be he Jew or Agnostic, Atheist, Buddhist or Freethinker, to believe or disbelieve, to worship or not worship, to pray or keep silent, according to his own conscience, uncoerced and unrestrained by government. It is conceivable that these school boards, or even all school boards, might eventually find it impossible to administer a system of religious exercises during school hours in such a way as to meet this constitutional standard—in such a way as completely to free from any kind of official coercion those who do not affirmatively want to participate. But I think we must not assume that school boards so lack the qualities of inventiveness and good will as to make impossible the achievement of that goal. . . .

The Court's decision in Schempp *provoked an angry reaction. A constitutional amendment was introduced in the House of Representatives to overturn the decision, but the measure remained bottled up in committee. At the local level, some school districts complied with the Court's decision; but many others, because of either disagreement or misunderstanding, continued their Bible reading programs. Although the issue of Bible reading in the public schools had become less salient over time, it attracted renewed attention when President Ronald Reagan endorsed a constitutional amendment which would overturn the Court's rulings and permit voluntary prayer in the schools.*

Lemon v. *Kurtzman*

403 U.S. 602, 91 S. Ct. 2105, 29 L. Ed. 745 (1971)

Lemon marked the Supreme Court's first consideration of the constitutionality of state programs providing aid to church-affiliated elementary and secondary schools. Under the Pennsylvania Nonpublic Elementary and Secondary Education Act, Pennsylvania purchased specified secular educational services from nonpublic schools by reimbursing them for the cost of teachers' salaries, textbooks, and instructional materials in various secular subjects. A three-judge federal district court dismissed the complaint regarding the program in *Lemon* v. *Kurtzman.* Under the Rhode Island Salary Supplement Act, Rhode Island paid teachers of secular subjects in nonpublic elementary schools a supplement of 15 percent of their annual salary. In *Early* v. *DiCenso* a three-judge federal district court struck down the act as a violation of the Establishment Clause. The Court consolidated these cases for argument with *Tilton* v. *Richardson. Opinion of the Court: Burger, Black, Douglas, Harlan, Stewart, Blackmun. Concurring opinions: Douglas, Black; Brennan. Dissenting opinion: White. Not participating: Marshall.*

MR. CHIEF JUSTICE BURGER delivered the opinion of the Court. . . .

Every analysis in this area must begin with consideration of the cumulative criteria developed by the Court over many years. Three such tests may be gleaned from our cases. First, the statute must have a secular legislative purpose; second, its principal or primary effect must be one that neither advances nor inhibits religion. . . ; finally, the statute must not foster "an excessive government entanglement with religion." . . .

Inquiry into the legislative purposes of the Pennsylvania and Rhode Island statutes affords no basis for a conclusion that the legislative intent was to advance religion. On the contrary, the statutes themselves clearly state that they are intended to enhance the quality of the secular education in all schools covered by the compulsory attendance laws. There is no reason to believe the legislatures meant anything else. A State always has a legitimate concern for maintaining minimum standards in all schools it allows to operate. . . .

The two legislatures, however, have . . . recognized that church-related elementary and secondary schools have a significant religious mission and that a substantial portion of their activities is religiously oriented. They have therefore sought to create statutory restrictions designed to guarantee the separation between secular and religious educational functions and to ensure that State financial aid supports only the former. . . . We need not decide whether these legislative precautions restrict the principal or primary effect of the programs to the point where they do not offend the Religion Clauses, for we conclude that the cumulative impact of the entire relationship arising under the statutes in each State involves excessive entanglement between government and religion. . . .

In order to determine whether the government entanglement with religion is excessive, we must examine the character and purposes of the institutions that are benefited, the nature of the aid that the State provides, and the resulting relationship between the government and the religious authority. . . .

Rhode Island Program

The District Court made extensive findings on the grave potential for excessive entanglement that inheres in the religious character and purpose of the Roman Catholic elementary schools of Rhode Island, to date the sole beneficiaries of the Rhode Island Salary Supplement Act.

The church schools involved in the program are located close to parish churches. This understandably permits convenient access for religious exercises since instruction in faith and morals is part of the total educational process. The school buildings contain identifying religious symbols such as crosses on the exterior and crucifixes, and religious paintings and statues either in the classrooms or hallways. Although only approximately 30 minutes a day are devoted to direct religious instruction, there are religiously oriented extracurricular activities. Approximately two-thirds of the teachers in these schools are nuns of various religious orders. Their dedicated efforts provide an atmosphere in which religious instruction and religious vocations are natural and proper parts of life in such schools.

On the basis of these findings the District Court concluded that the parochial schools constituted "an integral part of the religious mission of the Catholic Church."

The dangers and corresponding entanglements are enhanced by the particular form of aid that the Rhode Island Act provides. . . .

In [*Board of Education* v.] *Allen* [1968], the Court refused to make assumptions, on a meager record, about the religious content of the textbooks that the State would be asked to provide. We cannot, however, refuse here to recognize that teachers have a substantially different ideological character from books. In terms of potential for involving some aspect of faith or morals in secular subjects, a textbook's content is ascertainable, but a teacher's handling of a subject is not.

We need not and do not assume that teachers in parochial schools will be guilty of bad faith or any conscious design to evade the limitations imposed by the statute and the First Amendment. We simply recognize that a dedicated religious person, teaching in a school affiliated with his or her faith and operated to inculcate its tenets, will inevitably experience great difficulty in remaining religiously neutral. . . .

To ensure that no trespass occurs, the State has therefore carefully conditioned its aid with pervasive restrictions. An eligible recipient must teach only those courses that are offered in the public schools and use only those texts and materials that are found in the public schools. In addition the teacher must not engage in teaching any course in religion.

A comprehensive, discriminating, and continuing state surveillance will inevitably be required to ensure that these restrictions are obeyed and the First Amendment otherwise respected. Unlike a book, a teacher cannot be inspected once so as to determine the extent and intent of his or her personal beliefs and subjective acceptance of the limitations imposed by the First Amendment. These prophylactic contacts will involve excessive and enduring entanglement between state and church. . . .

There is another area of entanglement in the Rhode Island program that gives concern. The statute excludes teachers employed by nonpublic schools whose average per-pupil expenditures on secular education equal or exceed the comparable figures for public schools. In the event that the total expenditures of an otherwise eligible school exceed this norm, the program requires the government to examine the schools records in order to determine how much of the total expenditures is attributable to secular education and how much to religious activity. This kind of state inspection and evaluation of the religious content of a religious organization is fraught with the sort of entanglement that the Constitution forbids. It is a relationship pregnant with dangers of excessive government direction of church schools and hence of churches. . . .

Pennsylvania Program

. . . The very restrictions and surveillance necessary to ensure that teachers play a strictly nonideological role give rise to entanglements between church and state. The Pennsylvania statute, like that of Rhode Island, fosters this kind of relationship. . . .

The Pennsylvania statute, moreover, has the further defect of providing state financial aid directly to the church-related school. . . . The history of government grants of a continuing cash subsidy indicates that such programs have almost always been accompanied by varying measures of control and surveillance. The government cash grants before us now provide no basis for predicting that comprehensive measures of surveillance and controls will not follow. In particular the government's post-audit power to inspect and evaluate a church-related school's financial records and to determine which expenditures are religious and which are secular creates an intimate and continuing relationship between church and state. . . .

A broader base of entanglement of yet a different character is presented by the divisive political potential of these state programs. In a community where such a large number of pupils are served by church-related schools, it can be assumed that state assistance will entail considerable political activity. Partisans of parochial schools, understandably concerned with rising costs and sincerely dedicated to both the religious and secular educational mission of their schools, will inevitably champion this cause and promote political action to achieve their goals. Those who oppose state aid, whether for constitutional, religious, or fiscal reasons, will inevitably respond and employ all of the usual political campaign techniques to prevail. Candidates will be forced to declare and voters to choose. It would be unrealistic to ignore the fact that many people confronted with issues of this kind will find their votes aligned with their faith.

Ordinarily political debate and division, however vigorous or even partisan, are normal and healthy manifestations of our democratic system of government, but political division along religious lines was one of the principal evils against which the First Amendment was intended to protect. . . . The potential divisiveness of such conflict is a threat to the normal political process. . . .

The potential for political divisiveness related to religious belief and practice is aggravated in these two statutory programs by the need for continuing annual appropriations and the likelihood of larger and larger demands as costs and populations grow. . . .

MR. JUSTICE WHITE, dissenting.

Our prior cases have recognized the dual role of parochial schools in American society: they perform both religious and secular functions. It is enough for me that the States and the Federal Government are financing a separable secular function of overriding importance in order to sustain the legislation here challenged. That religion and private interests other than education may substantially benefit does not convert these laws into impermissible establishments of religion.

. . . Where a state program seeks to ensure the proper education of its young, in private as well as public schools, free exercise considerations at least counsel against refusing support for students attending parochial schools simply because in that setting they are also being instructed in the tenets of the faith they are constitutionally free to practice. . . .

The Court strikes down the Rhode Island statute on its face. No fault is found with the secular purpose of the program; there is no suggestion that the purpose of the program was aid to religion disguised in secular attire. Nor does the Court find that the primary effect of the program is to aid religion rather than to implement secular goals. The Court nevertheless finds that impermissible "entanglement" will result from administration of the program.

The Court thus creates an insoluble paradox for the State and the parochial schools. The State cannot finance secular instruction if it permits religion to be taught in the same classroom; but if it exacts a promise that religion not be so taught—a promise the school and its teachers are quite willing and on this record able to give—and enforces it, it is then entangled in the "no entanglement" aspect of the Court's Establishment Clause jurisprudence. . . .

With respect to Pennsylvania, the Court, accepting as true the factual allegations of the complaint, as it must for purpose of a motion to dismiss, would reverse the dismissal of the complaint and invalidate the legislation. The critical allegations, as paraphrased by the Court, are that "the church-related elementary and secondary schools are controlled by religious organizations, have the purpose of propagating and promoting a particular religious faith, and conduct their operations to fulfill that purpose." . . . From these allegations the Court concludes that forbidden entanglements would follow from enforcing compliance with the secular purpose for which the state money is being paid.

I disagree. There is no specific allegation in the complaint that sectarian teaching does or would invade secular classes supported by state funds. That the schools are operated to promote a particular religion is quite consistent with the view that secular teaching devoid of religious instruction can successfully be maintained. . . . I would no more here than in the Rhode Island case substitute presumption for proof that religion is or would be taught in state-financed secular courses or assume that enforcement measures would be so extensive as to border on a free exercise violation. . . .

I do agree, however, that the complaint should not have been dismissed for failure to state a cause of action. . . . Hence, I would reverse the judgment of the District Court and remand the case for trial, thereby holding the Pennsylvania legislation valid on its face but leaving open the question of its validity as applied to the particular facts of this case. . . .

Mueller v. *Allen*

463 U.S 388, 103 S. Ct. 3062, 77 L. Ed. 2d 721 (1983)

In computing their state income tax, Minnesota taxpayers were permitted a deduction from gross income for expenses for tuition, textbooks and supplies, and transportation of dependents attending elementary or secondary school. Although parents of all pupils benefited from the deduction for school materials, the major benefit accrued to parents of children attending private schools, who were able to deduct tuition costs. Over 95 percent of the children attending private schools were enrolled in sectarian schools. Several Minnesota taxpayers filed suit in federal district court, claiming that the deduction violated the Establishment Clause by providing financial assistance to sectarian schools. In doing so, they relied heavily on *Committee for Public Education* v. *Nyquist* (1973), in which the Supreme Court had struck down a program of tuition grants and tax credits which was restricted to parents of private-school pupils. The district court, however, upheld the Minnesota program, distinguishing it from the program invalidated in *Nyquist,* and after a court of appeals affirmed, the case was appealed to the Supreme Court. *Opinion of the Court: Rehnquist, Burger, White, Powell, O'Connor. Dissenting opinion: Marshall, Brennan, Blackmun, Stevens.*

JUSTICE REHNQUIST delivered the opinion of the Court.

Today's case is no exception to our oft-repeated statement that the Establishment Clause presents especially difficult questions of interpretation and application. . . .

One fixed principle in this field is our consistent rejection of the argument that "any program which in some manner aids an institution with a religious affiliation" violates the Establishment Clause. . . . For example, it is now well-established that a state may reimburse parents for expenses incurred in transporting their children to school, *Everson* v. *Board of Education,* and that it may loan secular textbooks to all schoolchildren within the state, *Board of Education* v. *Allen.*

Notwithstanding the repeated approval given programs such as those in *Allen* and *Everson,* our decisions also have struck down arrangements resembling, in many respects, these forms of assistance. In this case we are asked to decide whether Minnesota's tax deduction bears greater resemblance to those types of assistance to parochial schools we have approved, or to those we have struck down. Petitioners place particular reliance on our decision in *Committee for Public Education* v. *Nyquist,* where we held invalid a New York statute providing public funds for the maintenance and repair of the physical facilities of private schools and granting thinly disguised "tax benefits," actually amounting to tuition grants, to the parents of children attending private schools. As explained below, we conclude that § 290.09(22) bears less resemblance to the arrangement struck down in *Nyquist* than it does to assistance programs upheld in our prior decisions and those discussed with approval in *Nyquist.*

The general nature of our inquiry in this area has been guided, since the decision in *Lemon* v. *Kurtzman* by the "three-part" test laid down in that case: "First, the statute must have a secular legislative purpose; second, its principle or primary effect must be one that neither advances nor inhibits religion . . . ; finally, the statute must not foster 'an excessive government entanglement with religion.' " While this principle is well settled, our cases have also emphasized that it provides "no more than [a] helpful signpost" in dealing with Establishment Clause challenges. . . .

Little time need be spent on the question of whether the Minnesota tax deduction has a secular purpose. . . . A state's decision to defray the cost of educational expenses incurred by parents—regardless of the type of schools their children attend—evidences a purpose that is both secular and understandable. An educated populace is essential to the political and economic health of any community, and a state's efforts to assist parents in meeting the rising cost of educational expenses plainly serves this secular purpose of ensuring that the state's citizenry is well-educated. Similarly, Minnesota, like other states, could conclude that there is a strong public interest in assuring the continued financial health of private schools, both sectarian and non-sectarian. By educating a substantial number of students such schools relieve public schools of a correspondingly great burden—to the benefit of all taxpayers. In addition, private schools may serve as a benchmark for public schools. . . .

We turn therefore to the more difficult but related question whether the Minnesota statute has "the primary effect of advancing the sectarian aims of the nonpublic schools." In concluding that it does not, we find several features of the Minnesota tax deduction particularly significant. First, an essential feature of Minnesota's arrangement is the fact that § 290.09(22) is only one among many deductions—such as those for medical expenses and charitable contributions—available under the Minnesota tax laws. Our decisions consistently have recognized that traditionally "[l]egislatures have especially broad latitude in creating classifications and distinctions in tax statutes," in part because the "familiarity with local conditions" enjoyed by legislators especially enables them to "achieve an equitable distribution of the tax burden." Under our prior decisions, the Minnesota legislature's judgment that a deduction for educational expenses fairly equalizes the tax burden of its citizens and encourages desirable expenditures for educational purposes is entitled to substantial deference.

Other characteristics of § 290.09(22) argue equally strongly for the provision's constitutionality. Most importantly, the deduction is available for educational expenses incurred by *all* parents, including those whose children attend public schools and those whose children attend nonsectarian private schools or sectarian private schools. . . .

. . . [T]his case is vitally different from the scheme struck down in *Nyquist.* There, public assistance amounting to tuition grants, was provided only to parents of children in *nonpublic* schools. This fact had considerable bearing on our decision striking down the New York statute at issue. . . . Moreover, we intimated that "public assistance (e.g., scholarships) made available generally without regard to the sectarian-nonsectarian or public-nonpublic nature of the institution benefited" might not offend the Establishment Clause. We think the tax deduction adopted by Minnesota is more similar to this latter type of program than it is to the arrangement struck down in *Nyquist.* . . .

Petitioners argue that, notwithstanding the facial neutrality of § 290.09(22), in application the statute primarily benefits religious institutions. Petitioners rely . . . on a statistical analysis of the type of persons claiming the tax deduction. They contend that most parents of public school children incur no tuition expenses, and that other expenses deductible under § 290.09(22) are negligible in value; moreover, they claim that 96% of the children in private schools in 1978–1979 attended religiously-affiliated institutions. Because of all this, they reason, the bulk of deductions taken under § 290.09(22) will be claimed by parents of children in sectarian schools. . . .

We need not consider these contentions in detail. We would be loath to adopt a rule grounding the constitutionality of a facially neutral law on annual reports reciting the extent to which various classes of private citizens claimed benefits under the law. Such an approach would scarcely provide the certainty that this field stands in need of, nor can we perceive principled standards by which such statistical evidence might be evaluated. Moreover, the fact that private persons fail in a particular year to claim the tax relief to which they are entitled—under a facially neutral statute—should be of little importance in determining the constitutionality of the statute permitting such relief. . . .

Turning to the third part of the *Lemon* inquiry, we have no difficulty in concluding that the Minnesota statute does not "excessively entangle" the state in religion. The only plausible source of the "comprehensive, discriminating, and continuing state surveillance" necessary to run afoul of this standard would lie in the fact that state officials must determine whether particular textbooks qualify for a deduction. In making this decision, state officials must disallow deductions taken from "instructional books and materials used in the teaching of religious tenets, doctrines or worship, the purpose of which is to inculcate such tenets, doctrines or worship." Making decisions such as this does not differ substantially from making the types of decisions approved in earlier opinions of this Court. In *Board of Education* v. *Allen,* for example, the Court upheld the loan of secular textbooks to parents or children attending nonpublic schools; though state officials were required to determine whether particular books were or were not secular, the system was held not to violate the Establishment Clause.

JUSTICE MARSHALL, with whom JUSTICE BRENNAN, JUSTICE BLACKMUN and JUSTICE STEVENS join, dissenting.

The Establishment Clause of the First Amendment prohibits a State from subsidizing religious education, whether it does so directly or indirectly. In my view, this principle of neutrality forbids not only the tax benefits struck down in *Committee for Public Education* v. *Nyquist,* but any tax benefit, including the tax deduction at issue here, which subsidizes tuition payments to sectarian schools. I also believe that the Establishment Clause prohibits the tax deductions that Minnesota authorizes for the cost of books and other instructional materials used for sectarian purposes.

The majority attempts to distinguish *Nyquist* by pointing to two differences between the Minnesota tuition-assistance program and the program struck down in *Nyquist.* Neither of these distinctions can withstand scrutiny.

The majority first attempts to distinguish *Nyquist* on the ground that Minnesota makes all parents eligible to deduct up to $500 or $700 for each dependent, whereas the New York law allowed a deduction only for parents whose children attended nonpublic schools. Although Minnesota taxpayers who send their children to local public schools may not deduct tuition expenses because they incur none, they may deduct other expenses, such as the cost of gym clothes, pencils, and notebooks, which are shared by all parents of school-age children. This, in the majority's view, distinguishes the Minnesota scheme from the law at issue in *Nyquist.*

That the Minnesota statute makes some small benefit available to all parents cannot alter the fact that the most substantial benefit provided by the statute is available only to those parents who send their children to schools that charge tuition. It is simply undeniable that the single largest expense that may be deducted under the Minnesota statute is tuition. The statute is little more than a subsidy of general educational expenses. The other deductible expenses are *de minimis* in comparison to tuition expenses. . . .

That [the tuition] deduction has a primary effect of promoting religion can easily be determined without any resort to the type of "statistical evidence" that the majority fears would lead to constitutional uncertainty. The only factual inquiry necessary is . . . whether the deduction permitted for tuition expenses primarily benefits those who send their children to religious schools. . . .

In this case, it is undisputed that well over 90% of the children attending tuition-charging schools in Minnesota are enrolled in sectarian schools. History and experience likewise instruct us that any generally available financial assistance for elementary and secondary school tuition expenses mainly will further religious education because the majority of the schools which charge tuition are sectarian. . . .

. . . For the first time, the Court has upheld financial support for religious schools without any reason at all to assume that the support will be restricted to the secular functions of those schools and will not be used to support religious instruction. This result is flatly at odds with the fundamental principle that a State may provide no financial support whatsoever to promote religion. As the Court stated in *Everson* and has often repeated, "No tax in any amount, large or small, can be levied to support any religious activities or institutions, whatever they may be called, or whatever form they may adopt to teach or practice religion."

I dissent.

Lynch v. *Donnelly*

465 U.S. 668, 104 S. Ct. 1355, 79 L. Ed. 2d 664 (1984)

During the Christmas season each year, the city of Pawtucket, Rhode Island, erected a holiday display in a park owned by a nonprofit organization and located in the shopping district. The display included both secular figures and decorations associated with Christmas, such as reindeer pulling a sleigh and a Christmas tree, and a creche with figures of Jesus, Mary, Joseph, shepherds, angels, etc. The creche, originally purchased in

1973, cost the city $1365, and the city annually incurred nominal costs in erecting, lighting, and dismantling the creche. The respondents in the case challenged inclusion of the creche in the display as a violation of the Establishment Clause, arguing that it created both the appearance and reality of governmental endorsement of Christianity. They prevailed in both district court and the court of appeals, and the city appealed the case to the Supreme Court. *Opinion of the Court: Burger, White, Powell, Rehnquist, O'Connor. Concurring opinion: O'Connor. Dissenting opinion: Brennan, Marshall, Blackmun, Stevens.*

The CHIEF JUSTICE delivered the opinion of the Court.

In every Establishment Clause case, we must reconcile the inescapable tension between the objective of preventing unnecessary intrusion of either the church or the state upon the other, and the reality that, as the Court has so often noted, total separation of the two is not possible. . . .

Rather than mechanically invalidating all governmental conduct or statutes that confer benefits or give special recognition to religion in general or to one faith—as an absolutist approach would dictate—the Court has scrutinized challenged legislation or official conduct to determine whether, in reality, it establishes a religion or religious faith, or tends to do so.

In each case, the inquiry calls for line drawing; no fixed, *per se* rule can be framed. The Establishment Clause like the Due Process Clauses is not a precise, detailed provision in a legal code capable of ready application. . . .

In this case, the focus of our inquiry must be on the creche in the context of the Christmas season. . . .

The District Court inferred from the religious nature of the creche that the City has no secular purpose for the display. In so doing, it rejected the City's claim that its reasons for including the creche are essentially the same as it reasons for sponsoring the display as a whole. The District Court plainly erred by focusing almost exclusively on the creche. When viewed in the proper context of the Christmas Holiday season, it is apparent that, on this record, there is insufficient evidence to establish that the inclusion of the creche is a purposeful or surreptitious effort to express some kind of subtle governmental advocacy of a particular religious message. In a pluralistic society a variety of motives and purposes are implicated. The City, like the Congresses and Presidents, however, has principally taken note of a significant historical religious event long celebrated in the Western World. The creche in the display depicts the historical origins of this traditional event long recognized as a National Holiday. . . .

The District Court found that the primary effect of including the creche is to confer a substantial and impermissible benefit on religion in general and on the Christian faith in particular. . . .

We are unable to discern a greater aid to religion deriving from inclusion of the creche than from these benefits and endorsements previously held not violative of the Establishment Clause. What was said about the legislative prayers in *Marsh* [v. *Chambers*] and implied about the Sunday Closing Laws in *McGowan* is true of the City's inclusion of the creche: its "reason or effect merely happens to coincide or harmonize with the tenets of some . . . religions." . . .

The dissent asserts some observers may perceive that the City has aligned itself with the Christian faith by including a Christian symbol in its display and that this serves to advance religion. We can assume, *arguendo*, that the display advances religion in a sense; but our precedents plainly contemplate that on occasion some advancement of religion will result from governmental action. The Court has made it abundantly clear, however, that "not every law that confers an 'indirect,' 'remote,' or 'incidental' benefit upon [religion] is, for that reason alone, constitutionally invalid." Here, whatever benefit to one faith or religion or to all religions, is indirect, remote and incidental; display of the creche is no more an advancement or endorsement of religion than the Congressional and Executive recognition of the origins of the Holiday itself as "Christ's Mass," or the exhibition of literally hundreds of religious paintings in governmentally supported museums.

The District Court found that there had been no administrative entanglement between religion and state resulting from the City's ownership and use of the creche. But it went on to hold that some political divisiveness was engendered by this litigation. Coupled with its finding of an impermissible sectarian purpose and effect, this persuaded the court that there was "excessive entanglement." The Court of Appeals expressly declined to accept the District Court's finding that inclusion of the creche has caused political divisiveness along religious lines, and noted that this Court has never held that political divisiveness alone was sufficient to invalidate government conduct. . . .

The Court of Appeals correctly observed that this Court has not held that political divisiveness alone can serve to invalidate otherwise permissible conduct. And we decline to so hold today. This case does not involve a direct subsidy to church-sponsored schools or colleges, or other religious institutions, and hence no inquiry into potential political divisiveness is even called for. In any event, apart from this litigation there is no evidence of political friction or divisiveness over the creche in the 40-year history of Pawtucket's Christmas celebration. The District Court stated that the inclusion of the creche for the 40 years has been "marked by no apparent dissension" and that the display has had a "calm history." Curiously, it went on to hold that the political divisiveness engendered by this lawsuit was evidence of excessive entanglement. A litigant cannot, by the very act of commencing a lawsuit, however, create the appearance of divisiveness and then exploit it as evidence of entanglement. . . .

We hold that, notwithstanding the religious significance of the creche, the City of Pawtucket has not violated the Establishment Clause of the First Amendment. Accordingly, the judgment of the Court of Appeals is reversed.

Justice Brennan, with whom Justice Marshall, Justice Blackmun and Justice Stevens join, dissenting.

. . . After reviewing the Court's opinion, I am convinced that this case appears hard not because the principles of decision are obscure, but because the Christmas holiday seems so familiar and agreeable. Although the Court's reluctance to disturb a community's chosen method of celebrating such an agreeable holiday is understandable, that cannot justify the Court's departure from controlling precedent. In my view, Pawtucket's maintenance and display at public expense of a symbol as distinctively sectarian as a creche simply cannot be squared with our prior cases. And it is plainly contrary to the purposes and values of the Establishment Clause to pretend, as the Court does, that the otherwise secular setting of Pawtucket's nativity scene dilutes in some fashion the creche's singular religiosity, or that the City's annual display reflects nothing more than an "acknowledgment" of our shared national heritage. Neither the character of the Christmas holiday itself, nor our heritage of religious expression supports this result. . . .

The Court advances two principal arguments to support its conclusion that the Pawtucket creche satisfies the *Lemon* test. Neither is persuasive.

First, The Court, by focusing on the holiday "context" in which the nativity scene appeared, seeks to explain away the clear religious import of the creche and the findings of the District Court that most observers understood the creche as both a symbol of Christian beliefs and a symbol of the City's support for those beliefs. Thus, although the Court concedes that the City's inclusion of the nativity scene plainly serves "to depict the origins" of Christmas as a "significant historical religious event," and that the creche "is identified with one religious faith," we are nevertheless expected to believe that Pawtucket's use of the creche does not signal the City's support for the sectarian symbolism that the nativity scene evokes. The effect of the creche, of course, must be gauged not only by its inherent religious significance but also by the overall setting in which it appears. But it blinks reality to claim, as the Court does, that by including such a distinctively religious object as the creche in its Christmas display, Pawtucket has done no more than make use of a "traditional" symbol of the holiday, and has thereby purged the creche of its religious content and conferred only an "incidental and indirect" benefit on religion. . . .

Second. The Court also attempts to justify the creche by entertaining a beguilingly simple, yet faulty syllogism. The Court begins by noting that government may recognize Christmas day as a public holiday; the Court then asserts that the creche is nothing more than a traditional element of Christmas celebrations; and it concludes that the inclusion of a creche as part of a government's annual Christmas celebration is constitutionally permissible. The Court apparently believes that once it finds that the designation of Christmas as a public holiday is constitutionally acceptable, it is then free to conclude that virtually every form of governmental association with the celebration of the holiday is also constitutional. The vice of this dangerously superficial argument is that it overlooks the fact that the Christmas holiday in our national culture contains both secular and sectarian elements. To say that government may recognize the holiday's traditional, secular elements of giftgiving, public festivities and community spirit, does not mean that government may indiscriminately embrace the distinctively sectarian aspects of the holiday. . . .

When government decides to recognize Christmas day as a public holiday, it does no more than accommodate the calendar of public activities to the plain fact that many Americans will expect on that day to spend time visiting with their families, attending religious services, and perhaps enjoying some respite from pre-holiday activities. The Free Exercise Clause, of course, does not necessarily compel the government to provide this accommodation, but neither is the Establishment Clause offended by such a step. Because it is clear that the celebration of Christmas has both secular and sectarian elements, it may well be that by taking note of the holiday, the government is simply seeking to serve the same kinds of wholly secular goals—for instance, promoting goodwill and a common day of rest—that were found to justify Sunday Closing laws in *McGowan.* If public officials go further and participate in the *secular* celebration of Christmas—by, for example, decorating public places with such secular images as wreaths, garlands or Santa Claus figures—they move closer to the limits of their constitutional power but nevertheless remain within the boundaries set by the Establishment Clause. But when those officials participate in or appear to endorse the distinctively religious elements of this otherwise secular event, they encroach upon First Amendment freedoms. For it is at that point that the government brings to the forefront the theological content of the holiday, and places the prestige, power and financial support of a civil authority in the service of a particular faith. . . .

. . . The Court's approach suggests a fundamental misapprehension of the proper uses of history in constitutional interpretation. Certainly, our decisions reflect the fact that an awareness of historical practice often can provide a useful guide in interpreting the abstract language of the Establishment Clause. But historical acceptance of a particular practice alone is never sufficient to justify a challenged governmental action, since, as the Court has rightly observed, "no one acquires a vested or protected right in violation of the Constitution by long use, even when that span of time covers our entire national existence and indeed predates it." Attention to the details of history should not blind us to the cardinal purposes of the Establishment Clause, nor limit our central inquiry in these cases—whether the challenged practices "threaten those consequences which the Framers deeply feared."

. . . There is no evidence whatsoever that the Framers would have expressly approved a Federal celebration of the Christmas holiday including public displays of a nativity scene; accordingly, the Court's repeated invocation of the decision in *Marsh* is not only baffling, it is utterly irrelevant. Nor is there any suggestion that publicly financed and supported displays of Christmas creches are supported by a record of widespread, undeviating acceptance that extends throughout our history. Therefore, our prior decisions which relied upon concrete, specific historical evidence to support a particular practice simply have no bearing on the question presented in this case.

Wallace v. *Jaffree*

472 U.S. 38, 105 S. Ct. 2479, 86 L. Ed. 2d 29 (1985)

Beginning in the late 1970s, roughly half the states passed legislation authorizing a "moment of silence" at the outset of classes in public schools. This case provided the Supreme Court its first opportunity to consider constitutionality of such laws. At issue was a 1981 Alabama law, under which "a period of silence not to exceed one minute in duration shall be observed for meditation or voluntary prayer." (This law superseded a 1978 Alabama enactment which authorized a moment of silence but did not mention prayer.) Ishmael Jaffree, who had three children in Alabama public schools, challenged the 1981 law, claiming that it violated the First Amendment, made applicable to the states by the Fourteenth Amendment. The district court, in an unusual opinion, ruled against Jaffree, claiming that the Establishment Clause did not bar states from establishing a religion. The court of appeals reversed, ruling that the statute did not serve a secular purpose, and the state appealed to the Supreme Court. *Opinion of the Court: Stevens, Brennan, Marshall, Blackmun, Powell. Concurring opinions: Powell; O'Connor. Dissenting opinions: Burger; White; Rehnquist.*

JUSTICE STEVENS delivered the opinion of the Court.

When the Court has been called upon to construe the breadth of the Establishment Clause, it has examined the criteria developed over a period of many years. Thus, in *Lemon* v. *Kurtzman* (1971), we wrote:

"Every analysis in this area must begin with consideration of the cumulative criteria developed by the Court over many years. Three such tests may be gleaned from our cases. First, the statute must have a secular legislative purpose; second, its principal or primary effect must be one that neither advances nor inhibits religion; finally, the statute must not foster 'an excessive government entanglement with religion.' " It is the first of these three criteria that is most plainly implicated by this case. As the District Court correctly recognized, no consideration of the second or third criteria is necessary if a statute does not have a clearly secular purpose. . . .

In applying the purpose test, it is appropriate to ask "whether government's actual purpose is to endorse or disapprove of religion." In this case, the answer to that question is dispositive. For the record not only provides us with an unambiguous affirmative answer, but it also reveals that the enactment of § 16-1-20.1 was not motivated by any clearly secular purpose—indeed, the statute had *no* secular purpose.

The sponsor of the bill that became § 16-1-20.1, Senator Donald Holmes, inserted into the legislative record—apparently without dissent—a statement indicating that the legislation was an "effort to return voluntary prayer" to the public schools. Later Senator Holmes confirmed this purpose before the District Court. In response to the question whether he had any purpose for the legislation other than returning voluntary prayer to public schools, he stated, "No, I did not have no other purpose in mind." The State did not present evidence of *any* secular purpose. . . .

The legislative intent to return prayer to the public schools is, of course, quite different from merely protecting every student's right to engage in voluntary prayer during an appropriate moment of silence during the school day. The 1978 statute already protected that right, containing nothing that prevented any student from engaging in voluntary prayer during a silent minute of meditation. Appellants have not identified any secular purpose that was not fully served by § 16-1-20 before the enactment of § 16-1-20.1. Thus, only two conclusions are consistent with the text of § 16-1-20.1. (1) the statute was enacted to convey a message of State endorsement and promotion of prayer; or (2) the statute was enacted for no purpose. No one suggests that the statute was nothing but a meaningless or irrational act.

. . . The Legislature enacted § 16-1-20.1 despite the existence of § 16-1-20 for the sole purpose of expressing the State's endorsement of prayer activities for one minute at the beginning of each school day. The addition of "or voluntary prayer" indicates that the State intended to characterize prayer as a favored practice. Such an endorsement is not consistent with the established principle that the government must pursue a course of complete neutrality toward religion.

JUSTICE O'CONNOR, concurring in the judgment.

A state sponsored moment of silence in the public schools is different from state sponsored vocal prayer or Bible reading. First, a moment of silence is not inherently religious. Silence, unlike prayer or Bible reading, need not be associated with a religious exercise. Second, a pupil who participates in a moment of silence need not compromise his or her beliefs. During a moment of silence, a student who objects to prayer is left to his or her own thoughts, and is not compelled to listen to the prayers or thoughts of others. For these simple reasons, a moment of silence statute does not stand or fall under the Establishment Clause according to how the Court regards vocal prayer or Bible reading. . . .

The analysis above suggests that moment of silence laws in many States should pass Establishment Clause scrutiny because they do not favor the child who chooses to pray during a moment of silence over the child who chooses to meditate or reflect. Alabama Code § 16-1-20.1 does not stand on the same footing. However deferentially one examines its text and legislative history, however objectively one views the message attempted to be conveyed to the public, the conclusion is unavoidable that the purpose of the statute is to endorse prayer in public schools. I accordingly agree with the Court of Appeals that the Alabama statute has a purpose which is in violation of the Establishment Clause, and cannot be upheld.

JUSTICE REHNQUIST, dissenting.

Thirty-eight years ago this Court, in *Everson* v. *Board of Education* summarized its exegesis of Establishment Clause doctrine thus:

"In the words of Jefferson, the clause against establishment of religion by law was intended to erect 'a wall of separation between church and State.' "

It is impossible to build sound constitutional doctrine upon a mistaken understanding of constitutional history, but unfortunately the Establishment Clause has been expressly freighted with Jefferson's misleading metaphor for nearly forty years. When we turn to the record of the proceedings in the First Congress leading up to the adoption of the Establishment Clause of the Constitution, including Madison's significant contributions thereto, we see a far different picture of its purpose than the highly simplified "wall of separation between church and State." . . .

On the basis of record of these proceedings in the House of Representatives, James Madison was undoubtedly the most important architect among the members of the House of the amendments which became the Bill of Rights, but it was James Madison speaking as an advocate of sensible legislative compromise, not as an advocate of incorporating the Virginia Statute of Religious Liberty into the United States Constitution. . . . His original language "nor shall any national religion be established" obviously does not conform to the "wall of separation" between church and State idea which latter day commentators have ascribed to him. His explanation on the floor of the meaning of his language—"that Congress should not establish a religion, and enforce the legal observation of it by law" is of the same ilk. When he replied to Huntington in the debate over the proposal which came from the Select Committee of the House, he urged that the language "no religion shall be established by law" should be amended by inserting the word "national" in front of the word "religion."

It seems indisputable from these glimpses of Madison's thinking, as reflected by actions on the floor of the House in 1789, that he saw the amendment as designed to prohibit the establishment of a national religion, and perhaps to prevent discrimination among sects. He did not see it as requiring neutrality on the part of government between religion and irreligion. Thus the Court's opinion in *Everson*—while correct in bracketing Madison and Jefferson together in their exertions in their home state leading to the enactment of the Virginia Statute of Religious Liberty—is totally incorrect in suggesting that Madison carried these views onto the floor of the United States House of Representatives when he proposed the language which would ultimately become the Bill of Rights. . . .

None of the other Members of Congress who spoke during the August 15th debate expressed the slightest indication that they thought the language before them from the Select Committee, or the evil to be aimed at, would require that the Government be absolutely neutral as between religion and irreligion. The evil to be aimed at, so far as those who spoke were concerned, appears to have been the establishment of a national church, and perhaps the preference of one religious sect over another; but it was definitely not concern about whether the Government might aid all religions evenhandedly. . . .

The actions of the First Congress, which reenacted the Northwest Ordinance for the governance of the Northwest Territory in 1789, confirm the view that Congress did not mean that the Government should be neutral between religion and irreligion. . . . [This Ordinance] provided that "[r]eligion, morality, and knowledge, being necessary to good government and the happiness of mankind, schools and the means of education shall forever be encouraged." Land grants for schools in the Northwest Territory were not limited to public schools. It was not until 1845 that Congress limited land grants in the new States and Territories to nonsectarian schools. . . .

As the United States moved from the 18th into the 19th century, Congress appropriated time and again public moneys in support of sectarian Indian education carried on by religious organizations. Typical of these was Jefferson's treaty with the Kaskaskia Indians, which provided annual cash support for the Tribe's Roman Catholic priest and church. It was not until 1897, when aid to sectarian education for Indians had reached $500,000 annually, that Congress decided thereafter to cease appropriating money for education in sectarian schools. This history shows the fallacy of the notion found in *Everson* that "no tax in any amount" may be levied for religious activities in any form.

Joseph Story, a member of this Court from 1822 to 1845, and during much of that time a professor at the Harvard Law School, published by far the most comprehensive treatise on the United States Constitution that had then appeared. Volume 2 of Story's Commentaries on the Constitution of the United States discussed the meaning of the Establishment Clause of the First Amendment this way:

"Probably at the time of the adoption of the Constitution, and of the amendment to it now under consideration [First Amendment], the general if not the universal sentiment in America was, that Christianity ought to receive encouragement from the State so far as was not incompatible with the private rights of conscience and the freedom of religious worship. An attempt to level all religions, and to make it a matter of state policy to hold all in utter indifference, would have created universal disapprobation, if not universal indignation." . . .

It would seem from this evidence that the Establishment Clause of the First Amendment had acquired a well-accepted meaning: it forbade establishment of a national religion, and forbade preference among religious sects or denominations. . . . There is simply no historical foundation for the proposition that the Framers intended to build the "wall of separation" that was constitutionalized in *Everson*.

Notwithstanding the absence of an historical basis for this theory of rigid separation, the wall idea might well have served as a useful albeit misguided analytical concept, had it led this Court to unified and principled results in Establishment Clause cases. The opposite, unfortunately, has been true; in the 38 years since *Everson* our Establishment Clause cases have been neither principled nor unified. . . . Whether due to its lack of historical support or its practical unworkability, the *Everson* "wall" has proven all but useless as a guide to sound constitutional adjudication. . . . It should be frankly and explicitly abandoned. . . .

The Framers intended the Establishment Clause to prohibit the designation of any church as a "national" one. The Clause was also designed to stop the Federal Government from asserting a preference for one religious denomination or sect over others. Given the "incorporation" of the Establishment Clause as against the States via the Fourteenth Amendment in *Everson*, States are prohibited as well from establishing a religion or discriminating between sects. As its history abundantly shows, however, nothing in the Establishment Clause requires government to be strictly neutral between religion and irreligion, nor does that Clause prohibit Congress or the States from pursuing legitimate secular ends through nondiscriminatory sectarian means.

Edwards v. *Aguillard*

482 U.S. 578, 107 S. Ct. 2573, 96 L. Ed. 2d 510 (1987)

In 1982 the Louisiana legislature adopted the Balanced Treatment for Creation-Science and Evolution-Science in Public School Instruction Act. The act mandated that, in order to promote "academic freedom," the theory of evolution could not be taught in the state's public schools unless accompanied by instruction in the theory of creation science. A group including teachers, the parents of students, and religious leaders challenged the law as a violation of the Establishment Clause, and Louisiana agreed to delay implementation of the law pending the court test of its constitutionality. A federal district court struck down the act, concluding that its purpose was to endorse the views of fundamentalist Christians, a court of appeals affirmed that ruling, and the Supreme Court granted certiorari. *Opinion of the Court: Brennan, Marshall, Blackmun, Powell, Stevens, O'Connor (in part). Concurring opinions: Powell, O'Connor; White. Dissenting opinion: Scalia, Rehnquist.*

JUSTICE BRENNAN delivered the opinion of the Court.

The question for decision is whether Louisiana's "Balanced Treatment for Creation-Science and Evolution-Science in Public School Instruction" Act (Creationism Act) . . . is facially invalid as violative of the Establishment Clause of the First Amendment. . . .

The Establishment Clause forbids the enactment of any law "respecting an establishment of religion." The Court has applied a three-pronged test to determine whether legislation comports with the Establishment Clause. First, the legislature must have adopted the law with a secular purpose. Second, the statute's principal or primary effect must be one that neither advances nor inhibits religion. Third, the statute must not result in an excessive entanglement of government with religion. *Lemon* v. *Kurtzman* . . . (1971). State action violates the Establishment Clause if it fails to satisfy any of these prongs. . . .

Lemon's first prong focuses on the purpose that animated adoption of the Act. "The purpose prong of the *Lemon* test asks whether government's actual purpose is to endorse or disapprove of religion." *Lynch* v. *Donnelly* . . . (1984) (O'CONNOR, J., concurring). . . .

While the Court is normally deferential to a State's articulation of a secular purpose, it is required that the statement of such purpose be sincere and not a sham. . . .

It is clear from the legislative history that the purpose of the legislative sponsor, Senator Bill Keith, was to narrow the science curriculum. During the legislative hearings, Senator Keith stated: "My preference would be that neither [creationism nor evolution] be taught." . . . Such a ban on teaching does not promote—indeed, it undermines—the provision of a comprehensive scientific education.

It is equally clear that requiring schools to teach creation science with evolution does not advance academic freedom. The Act does not grant teachers a flexibility that they did not already possess to supplant the present science curriculum with the presentation of theories, besides evolution, about the origin of life. . . . The Act provides Louisiana schoolteachers with no new authority. Thus the stated purpose is not furthered by it. . . .

Furthermore, the goal of basic "fairness" is hardly furthered by the Act's discriminatory preference for the teaching of creation science and against the teaching of evolution. While requiring that curriculum guides be developed for creation science the Act says nothing of comparable guides for evolution. . . . Similarly, resource services are supplied for creation science but not for evolution. . . . Only "creation scientists" can serve on the panel that supplies the resource services. . . . The Act forbids school boards to discriminate against anyone who "chooses to be a creation-scientist" or to teach "creationism," but fails to protect those who choose to teach evolution or any other non-creation science theory, or who refuse to teach creation science. . . .

If the Louisiana Legislature's purpose was solely to maximize the comprehensiveness and effectiveness of science instruction, it would have encouraged the teaching of all scientific theories about the origins of humankind.* But under the Act's requirements, teachers who were once free to teach any and all facets of this subject are now unable to do so. Moreover, the Act fails even to ensure that creation science will be taught, but instead requires the teaching of this theory only when the theory of evolution is taught. Thus we agree with the Court of Appeals' conclusion that the Act does not serve to protect academic freedom, but has the distinctly different purpose of discrediting "evolution by counterbalancing its teaching at every turn with the teaching of creationism. . . ." . . .

. . . we need not be blind in this case to the legislature's preeminent religious purpose in enacting this statute. There is a historic and contemporaneous link between the teachers of certain religious denominations and the teaching of evolution. . . . Out of many possible science subjects taught in the public schools, the legislature chose to affect the teaching of the one scientific theory that historically has been opposed by certain religious sects. . . . The Establishment Clause, however, "forbids *alike* the preference of a religious doctrine *or* the prohibition of theory which is deemed antagonistic to a particular dogma." . . . Because the primary purpose of the Creationism Act is to advance a particular religious belief, the Act endorses religion in violation of the First Amendment.

JUSTICE SCALIA, with whom the CHIEF JUSTICE joins, dissenting.

*The dissent concludes that the Act's purpose was to protect the academic freedom of students, and not that of teachers. . . . Such a view is not at odds with our conclusion that if the Act's purpose was to provide comprehensive scientific education (a concern shared by students and teachers, as well as parents), that purpose was not advanced by the statute's provisions. . . .

Moreover, it is astonishing that the dissent, to prove its assertion, relies on a section of the legislation that was eventually deleted by the legislature. . . . The dissent contends that this deleted section—which was explicitly rejected by the Louisiana Legislature—reveals the legislature's "obviously intended meaning of the statutory terms 'academic freedom.' " . . .

. . . The Louisiana Legislature explicitly set forth its secular purpose ("protecting academic freedom") [by which it meant] . . . ". . . *students'* freedom from *indoctrination.* The legislature wanted to ensure that students would be free to decide for themselves how life began, based upon a fair and balanced presentation of the scientific evidence—that is, to protect "the right of each [student] voluntarily to determine what to believe (and what not to believe) free of any coercive pressures from the State." *Grand Rapids School District* v. *Ball* (1985). . . . Living up to its title of "*Balanced Treatment* for Creation-Science and Evolution-Science Act," . . . it treats the teaching of creation the same way. It does *not* mandate instruction in creation science . . .; *forbids* teachers to present creation science "as proven scientific fact," . . . and *bans* the teaching of creation science unless the theory is (to use the Court's terminology) "discredit[ed] '. . . at every turn' " with the teaching of evolution. . . . It surpasses understanding how the Court can see in this a purpose "to restructure the science curriculum to conform with a particular religious viewpoint," . . . "to provide a persuasive advantage to a particular religious doctrine," . . . "to promote the theory of creation science which embodies a particular religious tenet," . . . and "to endorse a particular religious doctrine." . . .

The Act's reference to "creation is not convincing evidence of religious purpose. The Act defines creation science as "*scientific evidenc[e],*" . . . and . . . [we] have no basis on the record to conclude that creation science need be anything other than a collection of scientific data supporting the theory that life abruptly appeared on earth. . . . The Louisiana legislators had been told repeatedly that creation scientists were scorned by most educators and scientists, who themselves had an almost religious faith in evolution. It is hardly surprising, then, that in seeking to achieve a balanced, "nonindoctrinating" curriculum, the legislators protected from discrimination only those teachers whom they thought were *suffering* from discrimination. . . . The two provisions respecting the development of curriculum guides are also consistent with "academic freedom" as the Louisiana Legislature understood the term. Witnesses had informed the legislators that, because of the hostility of most scientists and educators to creation science, the topic had been censored from or badly misrepresented in elementary and secondary school texts. In light of the unavailability of works on creation science suitable for classroom use (a fact appellees concede, see Brief for Appellees 27, 40) and the existence of ample materials on evolution, it was entirely reasonable for the legislature to conclude that science teachers attempting to implement the Act would need a curriculum guide on creation science, but not on evolution, and that those charged with developing the guide would need an easily accessible group of creation scientists. Thus, the provisions of the Act of so much concern to the Court *support* the conclusion that the legislature acted to advance "academic freedom." . . .

I have to this point assumed the validity of the *Lemon* "purpose" test. . . .

Given the many hazards involved in assessing the subjective intent of governmental decisionmakers, the first prong of *Lemon* is defensible, I think, only if the text of the Establishment Clause demands it. That is surely not the case. The Clause states that "Congress shall make no law respecting an establishment of religion." One could argue, I suppose, that any time Congress acts with the *intent* of advancing religion, it has enacted a "law respecting an establishment of religion"; but far from being an unavoidable reading, it is quite an unnatural one. . . .

In the past we have attempted to justify our embarrassing Establishment Clause jurisprudence on the ground that it "sacrifices clarity and predictability for flexibility." *Committee for Public Education & Religious Liberty* v. *Regan*. . . . One commentator has aptly characterized this as "a euphemism . . . for . . . the absence of any principled rationale." . . . I think it time that we sacrifice some "flexibility" for "clarity and predictability." Abandoning *Lemon*'s purpose test—a test which exacerbates the tension between the Free Exercise and Establishment Clauses, has no basis in the language or history of the Amendment, and, as today's decision shows, has wonderfully flexible consequences—would be a good place to start.

West Virginia Board of Education v. *Barnette*

319 U.S. 624; 63 S. Ct. 1178; 87 L. Ed. 1628 (1943)

In 1942 the West Virginia Board of Education adopted a regulation requiring the flag salute and Pledge of Allegiance as a part of regular public school activities. Students who refused to participate were deemed insubordinate and expelled, with readmission denied until compliance. During their expulsion, such students were considered "unlawfully absent," and both they and their parents were subject to prosecution. Walter Barnette, a Jehovah's Witness, brought suit to enjoin the compulsory flag salute, contending that it required his children to violate the religious commandment not to worship graven images.

The Supreme Court had considered the flag-salute issue only three years previously, in *Minersville School District* v. *Gobitis.* In that case Justice Felix Frankfurter, speaking for an eight–one majority, held that the compulsory flag salute did not violate the Free Exercise Clause of the First Amendment. Since *Gobitis,* however, Justices Robert Jackson and Wiley Rutledge had replaced two members of the Court majority. In addition, two other members of the *Gobitis* majority, Justices Hugo Black and William Douglas, had repudiated their *Gobitis* votes in *Jones* v. *Opelika* (1942). When a three-judge district court enjoined enforcement of the regulation, the Court agreed to hear the case on appeal. *Opinion of the Court: Jackson, Stone, Black, Douglas, Murphy, Rutledge. Concurring opinion: Black, Douglas. Dissenting opinions: Roberts, Reed; Frankfurter.*

MR. JUSTICE JACKSON delivered the opinion of the Court.

The freedom asserted by these appellees does not bring them into collision with rights asserted by any other individual. The sole conflict is between authority and rights of the individual. The State asserts power to condition access to public education on making a prescribed sign and profession and at the same time to coerce attendance by punishing both parent and child. The latter stand on a right of self-determination in matters that touch individual opinion and personal attitude.

As the present CHIEF JUSTICE said in dissent in the *Gobitis* case, the State may "require teaching by instruction and study of all in our history and in the structure and organization of our government, including the guaranties of civil liberty, which tend to inspire patriotism and love of country." . . . Here, however, we are dealing with a compulsion of students to declare a belief. They are not merely made acquainted with the flag salute so that they may be informed as to what it is or even what it means. The issue here is whether this slow and easily neglected route to aroused loyalties constitutionally may be short-cut by substituting a compulsory salute and slogan. . . .

There is no doubt that, in connection with the pledges, the flag salute is a form of utterance. Symbolism is a primitive but effective way of communicating ideas. The use of an emblem or flag to symbolize some system, idea, institution, or personality, is a short cut from mind to mind. . . .

It is also to be noted that the compulsory flag salute and pledge requires affirmation of a belief and an attitude of mind. It is not clear whether the regulation contemplates that pupils forego any contrary convictions of their own and become unwilling converts to the prescribed ceremony or whether it will be acceptable if they simulate assent by words without belief and by a gesture barren of meaning. It is now a commonplace that censorship or suppression of expression of opinion is tolerated by our Constitution only when the expression presents a clear and present danger of action of a kind the State is empowered to prevent and punish. It would seem that involuntary affirmation could be commanded only on even more immediate and urgent grounds than silence. But here the power of compulsion is invoked without any allegation that remaining passive during a flag salute ritual creates a clear and present danger that would justify an effort even to muffle expression. To sustain the compulsory flag salute we are required to say that a Bill of Rights which guards the individual's right to speak his own mind, left it open to public authorities to compel him to utter what is not in his mind. . . .

Nor does the issue as we see it turn on one's possession of particular religious views or the sincerity with which they are held. While religion supplies appellees' motive for enduring the discomforts of making the issue in this case, many citizens who do not share these religious views hold such a compulsory rite to infringe constitutional liberty of the individual. It is not necessary to inquire whether non-conformist beliefs will exempt from the duty to salute unless we first find power to make the salute a legal duty. . . .

. . . It was said that the flag-salute controversy confronted the Court with "the problem which Lincoln cast in memorable dilemma: 'Must a government of necessity be too *strong* for the liberties of its people, or too *weak* to maintain its own existence?' " and that the answer must be in favor of strength . . . . If validly applied to this problem, the utterance cited would resolve every issue of power in favor of those in authority and would require us to override every liberty thought to weaken or delay execution of their policies. . . . To enforce those rights today is not to choose weak government over strong government. It is only to adhere as a means of strength to individual freedom of mind in preference to officially disciplined uniformity for which history indicates a disappointing and disastrous end.

. . . It was also considered in the *Gobitis* case that functions of educational officers in States, counties and school districts were such that to interfere with their authority "would in effect make us the school board for the country." . . . The Fourteenth Amendment, as now applied to the States, protects the citizen against the State itself and all of its creatures—Boards of Education not excepted. These have, of course, important, delicate, and highly discretionary functions, but none that they may not perform within the limits of the Bill of Rights. . . .

Such Boards are numerous and their territorial jurisdiction often small. But small and local authority may feel less sense of responsibility to the Constitution, and agencies of publicity may be less vigilant in calling it to account. The action of Congress in making flag observance voluntary and respecting the conscience of the objector in a matter so vital as raising the Army contrasts sharply with these local regulations in matters relatively trivial to the welfare of the nation. . . .

. . . The *Gobitis* opinion reasoned that this is a field "where courts possess no marked and certainly no controlling competence," that it is committed to the legislatures as well as the courts to guard cherished liberties and that it is constitutionally appropriate to "fight out the wise use of legislative authority in the forum of public opinion and before legislative assemblies rather than to transfer such a contest to the judicial arena," since all the "effective means of inducing political changes are left free." . . .

The very purpose of a Bill of Rights was to withdraw certain subjects from the vicissitudes of political controversy, to place them beyond the reach of majorities and officials and to establish them as legal principles to be applied by the courts. One's right to life, liberty, and property, to free speech, a free press, freedom of worship and assembly, and other fundamental rights may not be submitted to vote; they depend on the outcome of no elections. . . . They are susceptible of restriction only to prevent grave and immediate danger to interests which the State may lawfully protect. . . .

. . . Lastly, and this is the very heart of the *Gobitis* opinion, it reasons that "National unity is the basis of national security," that the authorities have "the right to select appropriate means for its attainment," and hence reaches the conclusion that such compulsory measures toward "national unity" are constitutional. . . .

If there is any fixed star in our constitutional constellation, it is that no official, high or petty, can prescribe what shall be orthodox in politics, nationalism, religion, or other matters of opinion or force citizens to confess by word or act their faith therein. If there are any circumstances which permit an exception, they do not now occur to us. . . .

The decision of this Court in *Minersville School District* v. *Gobitis* . . . [is] overruled, and the judgment enjoining enforcement of the West Virginia regulation is

Affirmed.

MR. JUSTICE FRANKFURTER, dissenting.

One who belongs to the most vilified and persecuted minority in history is not likely to be insensible to the freedoms guaranteed by our Constitution. Were my purely personal attitude relevant I should wholeheartedly associate myself with the general libertarian views in the Court's opinion, representing as they do the thought and action of a lifetime. But as judges we are neither Jew nor Gentile, neither Catholic nor agnostic. We owe equal attachment to the Constitution and are equally bound by our judicial obligations whether we derive our citizenship from the earliest or the latest immigrants to these shores. As a member of this Court I am not justified in writing my private notions of policy into the Constitution, no matter how deeply I may cherish them or how mischievous I may deem their disregard. The duty of a judge who must decide which of two claims before the Court shall prevail, that of a State to enact and enforce laws within its general competence or that of an individual to refuse obedience because of the demands of his conscience, is not that of the ordinary person. It can never be emphasized too much that one's own opinion about the wisdom or evil of a law should be excluded altogether when one is doing one's duty on the bench. The only opinion of our own even looking in that direction that is material is our opinion whether legislators could in reason have enacted such a law. In the light of all the circumstances, including the history of this question in this Court, it would require more daring than I possess to deny that reasonable legislators could have taken the action which is before us for review. Most unwillingly, therefore, I must differ from my brethren with regard to legislation like this. I cannot bring my mind to believe that the "liberty" secured by the Due Process Clause gives this Court authority to deny to the State of West Virginia the attainment of that which we all recognize as a legitimate legislative end, namely, the promotion of good citizenship, by employment of the means here chosen. . . .

Under our constitutional system the legislature is charged solely with civil concerns of society. If the avowed or intrinsic legislative purpose is either to promote or to discourage some religious community or creed, it is clearly within the constitutional restrictions imposed on legislatures and cannot stand. But it by no means follows that legislative power is wanting whenever a general non-discriminatory civil regulation in fact touches conscientious scruples or religious beliefs of an individual or a group. . . . Were this so, instead of the separation of church and state, there would be the subordination of the state on any matter deemed within the sovereignty of the religious conscience. . . .

We are told that a flag salute is a doubtful substitute for adequate understanding of our institutions. The states that require such a school exercise do not have to justify it as the only means for promoting good citizenship in children, but merely as one of diverse means for accomplishing a worthy end. We may deem it a foolish measure, but the point is that this Court is not the organ of government to resolve doubts as to whether it will fulfill its purpose. Only if there be no doubt that any reasonable mind could entertain can we deny to the states the right to resolve doubts their way and not ours. . . .

Of course patriotism can not be enforced by the flag salute. But neither can the liberal spirit be enforced by judicial invalidation of illiberal legislation. Our constant preoccupation with the constitutionality of legislation rather than with its wisdom tends to preoccupation of the American mind with a false value. The tendency of focussing attention on constitutionality is to make constitutionality synonymous with wisdom, to regard a law as all right if it is constitutional. Such an attitude is a great enemy of liberalism. Particularly in legislation affecting freedom of thought and freedom of speech much which should offend a free-spirited society is constitutional. Reliance for the most precious interests of civilization, therefore, must be found outside of their vindication in courts of law. Only a persistent positive translation of the faith of a free society into the convictions and habits and actions of a community is the ultimate reliance against unabated temptations to fetter the human spirit.

Sherbert v. *Verner*

374 U.S. 398, 83 S. Ct. 1790, 10 L. Ed. 2d 965 (1963)

Under South Carolina's unemployment compensation act, a worker was considered ineligible for benefits if although able to work and available for work, he "failed, without good cause . . . to accept available suitable work when offered him by the employment office or the employer." Adell Sherbert, a Seventh-Day Adventist, was fired from her job and then refused other jobs because those jobs required her to work on Saturday, her Sabbath. Her application for unemployment compensation was denied because she had refused "available suitable work." She then sued the South Carolina Unemployment Security Commission, contending that the denial of benefits infringed upon the free exercise of her religion. *Opinion of the Court: Brennan, Warren, Black, Clark, Goldberg. Concurring opinions: Douglas; Stewart. Dissenting opinion: Harlan, White.*

MR. JUSTICE BRENNAN delivered the opinion of the Court.

We turn first to the question whether the disqualification for benefits imposes any burden on the free exercise of appellant's religion. We think it is clear that it does. . . . Here not only is it apparent that appellant's declared ineligibility for benefits derives solely from the practice of her religion, but the pressure upon her to forego that practice is unmistakable. The ruling forces her to choose between following the precepts of her religion and forfeiting benefits, on the one hand, and abandoning one of the precepts of her religion in order to accept work, on the other hand. Governmental imposition of such a choice puts the same kind of burden upon the free exercise of religion as would a fine imposed against appellant for her Saturday worship.

Nor may the South Carolina court's construction of the statute be saved from constitutional infirmity on the ground that unemployment compensation benefits are not appellant's "right" but merely a "privilege." It is too late in the day to doubt that the liberties of religion and expression may be infringed by the denial of or placing of conditions upon a benefit or privilege. . . . Conditions upon public benefits cannot be sustained if they so operate, whatever their purpose, as to inhibit or deter the exercise of First Amendment freedoms. . . .

We must next consider whether some compelling state interest enforced in the eligibility provisions of the South Carolina statute justifies the substantial infringement of appellant's First Amendment right. It is basic that no showing merely of a rational relationship to some colorable state interest would suffice; in this highly sensitive constitutional area."[o]nly the gravest abuses, endangering paramount interests, give occasion for permissible limitation," *Thomas* v. *Collins* [1945]. . . . No such abuse or danger has been advanced in the present case. The appellees suggest no more than a possibility that the filing of fraudulent claims by unscrupulous claimants feigning religious objections to Saturday work might not only dilute the unemployment compensation fund but also hinder the scheduling by employers of necessary Saturday work. . . . There is no proof whatever to warrant such fears of malingering or deceit as those which the respondents now advance . . . . It is highly doubtful whether such evidence would be sufficient to warrant a substantial infringement of religious liberties. For even if the possibility of spurious claims did threaten to dilute the fund and disrupt the scheduling of work, it would plainly be incumbent upon the appellees to demonstrate that no alternative forms of regulation would combat such abuses without infringing First Amendment rights. . . .

In holding as we do, plainly we are not fostering the "establishment" of the Seventh-day Adventist religion in South Carolina, for the extension of unemployment benefits to Sabbatarians in common with Sunday worshippers reflects nothing more than the governmental obligation of neutrality in the face of religious differences. . . . Our holding today is only that South Carolina may not constitutionally apply the eligibility provisions so as to constrain a worker to abandon his religious convictions respecting the day of rest. This holding but reaffirms a principle that we announced a decade and a half ago, namely that no State may "exclude individual Catholics, Lutherans, Mohammedans, Baptists, Jews, Methodists, Non-believers, Presbyterians, or the members of any other faith, *because of their faith, or lack of it,* from receiving the benefits of public welfare legislation." *Everson* v. *Board of Education* [1947]. . . .

The judgment of the South Carolina Supreme Court is reversed and the case is remanded for further proceeding not inconsistent with this opinion.

It is so ordered.

MR. JUSTICE STEWART, concurring in the result.

Although fully agreeing with the result which the Court reaches in this case, I cannot join the Court's opinion. This case presents a double-barreled dilemma, which in all candor I think the Court's opinion has not succeeded in papering over. The dilemma ought to be resolved. . . .

I am convinced that no liberty is more essential to the continued vitality of the free society which our Constitution guarantees than is the religious liberty protected by the Free Exercise Clause explicit in the First Amendment and imbedded in the Fourteenth. . . . There are many situations where legitimate claims under the Free Exercise Clause will run into head-on collision with the Court's insensitive and sterile construction of the Establishment Clause. The controversy now before us is clearly such a case. . . .

. . . If the appellant's refusal to work on Saturdays were based on indolence, or on a compulsive desire to watch the Saturday television programs, no one would say that South Carolina could not hold that she was not "available for work" within the meaning of its statute. That being so, the Establishment Clause as construed by this Court not only *permits* but affirmatively *requires* South Carolina equally to deny the appellant's claim for unemployment compensation when her refusal to work on Saturdays is based upon her religious creed. . . .

. . . This poses no problem for me, because I think the Court's mechanistic concept of the Establishment Clause is historically unsound and constitutionally wrong. . . . I think that the guarantee of religious liberty embodied in the Free Exercise Clause affirmatively requires government to create an atmosphere of hospitality and accommodation to individual belief or disbelief. In short, I think our Constitution commands the positive protection by government of religious freedom—not only for a minority, however small—not only for the majority, however large—but for each of us. . . .

MR. JUSTICE HARLAN, whom MR. JUSTICE WHITE joins, dissenting.

. . . What the Court is holding is that if the State chooses to condition unemployment compensation on the applicant's availability for work, it is constitutionally compelled to *carve out an exception*—and to provide benefits—for those whose unavailability is due to their religious convictions. Such a holding has particular significance in two respects.

First, despite the Court's protestations to the contrary the decision necessarily overrules *Braunfeld* v. *Brown*. . . . The secular purpose of the statute before us today is even clearer than that involved in *Braunfeld*. And just as in *Braunfeld*—where exceptions to the Sunday closing laws for Sabbatarians would have been inconsistent with the purpose to achieve a uniform day of rest and would have required case-by-case inquiry into religious beliefs—so here, an exception to the rules of eligibility based on religious convictions would necessitate judicial examination of those convictions and would be at odds with the limited purpose of the statute to smooth out the economy during periods of industrial instability. . . .

Second . . . The State . . . must *single out* for financial assistance those whose behavior is religiously motivated, even though it denies such assistance to others whose identical behavior (in this case, inability to work on Saturdays) is not religiously motivated. . . .

. . . I cannot subscribe to the conclusion that the State is constitutionally *compelled* to carve out an exception to its general rule of eligibility in the present case. Those situations in which the Constitution may require special treatment on account of religion are, in my view, few and far between. . . . Such compulsion in the present case is particularly inappropriate in light of the indirect, remote, and insubstantial effect of the decision below on the exercise of appellant's religion and in light of the direct financial assistance to religion that today's decision requires. . . .

Lyng v. *Northwest Indian Cemetery Protective Association*

485 U.S. 439, 108 S. Ct. 1319, 99 L. Ed. 2d 534 (1988)

In 1982 the United States Forest Service decided to build a six-mile paved road (the G-O road) through federal land, including the Chimney Rock area of the Six Rivers National Forest, to link two preexisting roads. In doing so, the Service rejected the recommendation of a study it had commissioned, which argued that the road not be built or that a route outside the Chimney Rock area be selected. Because this area had historically been used by certain Native Americans for religious rituals that depended upon privacy, silence, and an undisturbed natural setting, the study concluded that building the road would irreparably harm the religious areas.

Although the Forest Service rejected the study's recommendations, the route it selected avoided archeological sites and was removed as far as possible from the sites used for spiritual activities. At about the same time, the Service approved a management plan permitting limited timber harvesting in the area, with protective zones around all religious sites.

The respondents in this case filed suit in District Court, claiming that the road proposal and the decision to permit timber harvesting violated their rights under the Free Exercise Clause. The District Court issued a permanent injunction against the road construction and timber harvesting, and the Court of Appeals affirmed. *Opinion of the Court: O'Connor,*

Rehnquist, White, Stevens, Scalia. Dissenting opinion: Brennan, Marshall, Blackmun.

JUSTICE O'CONNOR delivered the opinion of the Court.

This case requires us to consider whether the First Amendment's Free Exercise Clause forbids the Government from permitting timber harvesting in, or constructing a road through, a portion of a National Forest that has traditionally been used for religious purposes by members of three American Indian tribes in northwestern California. We conclude that it does not. . . . It is undisputed that the Indian respondents' beliefs are sincere and that the Government's purposed actions will have severe adverse effects on the practice of their religion. Respondents contend that the burden on their religious practices is heavy enough to violate the Free Exercise Clause unless the Government can demonstrate a compelling need to complete the G–O road or to engage in timber harvesting in the Chimney Rock area. We disagree. . . .

In *Bowen* v. *Roy* . . . (1986), we considered a challenge to a federal statute that required the States to use Social Security numbers in administering certain welfare programs. Two applicants for benefits under these programs contended that their religious beliefs prevented them from acceding to the use of a Social Security number for their two-year-old daughter because the use of a numerical identifier would " 'rob the spirit' of [their] daughter and prevent her from attaining greater spiritual power." . . . The Court rejected this kind of challenge in *Roy:*

"The Free Exercise Clause simply cannot be understood to require the Government to conduct its own internal affairs in ways that comport with the religious beliefs of particular citizens. Just as the Government may not insist that [the Roys] engage in any set form of religious observance, so [they] may not demand that the Government join in their chosen religious practices by refraining from using a number to identify their daughter. . . .

". . . The Free Exercise Clause affords an individual protection from certain forms of governmental compulsion; it does not afford an individual a right to dictate the conduct of the Government's internal procedures." . . .

The building of a road or the harvesting of timber on publicly owned land cannot meaningfully be distinguished from the use of a Social Security number in *Roy.* In both cases, the challenged government action would interfere significantly with private persons' ability to pursue spiritual fulfillment according to their own religious beliefs. In neither case, however, would the affected individuals be coerced by the Government's action into violating their religious beliefs; nor would either governmental action penalize religious activity by denying any person an equal share of the rights, benefits, and privileges enjoyed by other citizens.

We are asked to distinguish this case from *Roy* on the ground that the infringement on religious liberty here is "significantly greater," or on the ground that the government practice in *Roy* was "purely mechanical" whereas this case involves "a case-by-case substantive determination as to how a particular unit of land will be managed." . . .

These efforts to distinguish *Roy* are unavailing. This Court cannot determine the truth of the underlying beliefs that led to the religious objections here or in *Roy,* . . . and accordingly cannot weigh the adverse effects on the Roys and compare them with the adverse effects on respondents. Without the ability to make such comparisons, we cannot say that the one form of incidental interference with an individual's spiritual activities should be subjected to a different constitutional analysis than the other. . . .

. . . Whatever may be the exact line between unconstitutional prohibitions on the free exercise of religion and the legitimate conduct by government of its own affairs, the location of the line cannot depend on measuring the effects of a governmental action on a religious objector's spiritual development. . . .

Even if we assume that we should accept the Ninth Circuit's prediction, according to which the G–O road will "virtually destroy the Indians ability to practice their religion," . . . the Constitution simply does not provide a principle that could justify upholding respondents' legal claims. However much we might wish that it were otherwise government simply could not operate if it were required to satisfy every citizen's religious needs and desires. A broad range of government activities—from social welfare programs to foreign aid to conservation projects—will always be considered essential to the spiritual well-being of some citizens, often on the basis of sincerely held religious beliefs. Others will find the very same activities deeply offensive, and perhaps incompatible with their own search for spiritual fulfillment and with the tenets of their religion. The First Amendment must apply to all citizens alike, and it can give to none of them a veto over public programs that do not prohibit the free exercise of religion. The Constitution does not, and courts cannot, offer to reconcile the various competing demands on government, many of them rooted in sincere religious belief, that inevitably arise in so diverse a society as ours. That task, to the extent that it is feasible, is for the legislatures and other institutions. Cf. The Federalist No. 10 (suggesting that the effects of religious factionalism are best restrained through competition among a multiplicity of religious sects). . . .

Perceiving a "stress point in the long-standing conflict between two disparate cultures," the dissent attacks us for declining to "balanc[e] these competing and potentially irreconcilable interests, choosing instead to turn this difficult task over to the federal legislature." . . . Seeing the Court as the arbiter, the dissent proposes a legal test under which it would decide which public lands are "central" or "indispensable" to which religions, and by implication which are "dispensable" or "peripheral," and would then decide which government programs are "compelling" enough to justify "infringement of those practices." . . . We would accordingly be required to weigh the value of every religious belief and practice that is said to be threatened by any government program. Unless a "showing of 'centrality,' " . . . is nothing but an assertion of centrality, . . . the dissent thus offers us the prospect of this Court holding that some sincerely held religious beliefs and practices are not "central" to certain religions, despite protestations to the contrary from the religious objectors who brought the lawsuit. In other words, the dissent's approach would require us to rule that some religious adherents misunderstand their own religious beliefs. We think such an approach cannot be squared with the Constitution or with our precedents, and that it would cast the judiciary in a role that we were never intended to play.

JUSTICE BRENNAN, with whom JUSTICE MARSHALL and JUSTICE BLACKMUN join, dissenting.

" '[T]he Free Exercise Clause,' " the Court explains today, " 'is written in terms of what the government cannot do to the individual, not in terms of what the individual can exact from the government.' " . . . Pledging fidelity to this unremarkable constitutional principle, the Court nevertheless concludes that even where the Government uses federal land in a manner that threatens the very existence of a Native American religion, the Government is simply not "*doing*" anything to the practitioners of that faith. Instead, the Court believes that Native Americans who request that the Government refrain from destroying their religion effectively seek to exact from the Government *de facto* beneficial ownership of federal property. These two astonishing conclusions follow naturally from the Court's determination that federal land-use decisions that render the practice of a given religion impossible do not burden that religion in a manner cognizable under the Free Exercise Clause, because such decisions neither coerce conduct inconsistent with religious belief nor penalize religious activity. The constitutional guarantee we interpret today, however, draws no such fine distinctions between types of restraints on religious exercise, but rather is directed against any form of governmental action that frustrates or inhibits religious practice. Because the Court today refuses even to acknowledge the constitutional injury respondents will suffer, and because this refusal essentially leaves Native Americans with absolutely no constitutional protection against perhaps the gravest threat to their religious practices, I dissent. . . .

The Court does not for a moment suggest that the interests served by the G–O road are in any way compelling, or that they outweigh the destructive effect construction of the road will have on respondents' religious practices. . . . Respondents here have demonstrated that construction of the G–O road will completely frustrate the practice of their religion, for as the lower courts found, the proposed logging and construction activities will virtually destroy respondents' religion, and will therefore necessarily force them into abandoning those practices altogether. Indeed, the Government's proposed activities will restrain religious practice to a far greater degree here than in any of the cases cited by the Court today. . . . The Court attempts to explain the line it draws by arguing that the protections of the Free Exercise Clause "cannot depend on measuring the effects of a governmental action on a religious objector's spiritual development," . . . for in a society as diverse as ours, the Government cannot help but offend the "religious needs and desires" of some citizens. . . . While I agree that governmental action that simply offends religious sensibilities may not be challenged under the Clause, we have recognized that laws that affect spiritual development by impeding the integration of children into the religious community or by increasing the expense of adherence to religious principles—in short, laws that frustrate or inhibit religious *practice*—trigger the protections of the constitutional guarantee. Both common sense and our prior cases teach us, therefore, that governmental action that makes the practice of a given faith more difficult necessarily penalizes that practice and thereby tends to prevent adherence to religious belief. The harm to the practitioners is the same regardless of the manner in which the Government restrains their religious expression, and the Court's fear that an "effects" test will permit religious adherents to challenge governmental actions they merely find "offensive" in no way justifies its refusal to recognize the constitutional injury citizens suffer when governmental action not only offends but actually restrains their religious practices. Here, respondents have demonstrated that the Government's proposed activities will completely prevent them from practicing their religion, and such a showing . . . entitles them to the protections of the Free Exercise Clause. . . .

I believe it appropriate, therefore, to require some showing of "centrality" before the Government can be required either to come forward with a compelling justification for its proposed use of federal land or to forego that use altogether. . . .

The Court today suggests that such an approach would place courts in the untenable position of deciding which practices and beliefs are "central" to a given faith and which are not, and invites the prospect of judges advising some religious adherents that they "misunderstand their own religious beliefs." In fact, however, courts need not undertake any such inquiries: like all other religious adherents, Native Americans would be the arbiters of which practices are central to their faith, subject only to the normal requirement that their claims be genuine and sincere. The question for the courts, then, is not whether the Native American claimants understand their own religion, but rather, whether they have discharged their burden of demonstrating, as the Amish did with respect to the compulsory school law in *Yoder,* that the land-use decision poses a substantial and realistic threat of undermining or frustrating their religious practices. Ironically, the Court's apparent solicitude for the integrity of religious belief and its desire to forestall the possibility that courts might second-guess the claims of religious adherents leads to far greater inequities than those the Court postulates: today's ruling sacrifices a religion at least as old as the Nation itself, along with the spiritual well-being of its approximately 5,000 adherents, so that the Forest Service can build a 6–mile segment of road that two lower courts found had only the most marginal and speculative utility, both to the Government itself and to the private lumber interests that might conceivably use it.

14
DUE PROCESS AND CRIMINAL PROCEDURE

The Constitution strongly emphasizes the protection of the rights of defendants in the criminal process. The original document contains no fewer than seven provisions specifically addressed to this matter—these are in keeping with the Founders' concern to protect minorities (in this case, unpopular criminal defendants) from the tyrannical excesses of an oppressive outraged majority. Article I, Section 9, restricts suspension of the privilege of the writ of habeas corpus "unless when in cases of rebellion or invasion the public safety may require it" and prohibits the passage of bills of attainder or ex post facto laws. Article II, Section 2, provides the president with the power to grant reprieves and pardons. Article III, Section 2, provides for trial by jury for "all crimes except in cases of impeachment" and further directs that the trial "shall be held in the state where the said crimes shall have been committed." Article III, Section 3, narrowly and precisely defines what constitutes treason against the United States. Finally, Article IV, Section 2, provides for extradition of criminal defendants.

The Bill of Rights places an even greater stress on criminal procedure. Of the twenty-three separate rights enumerated in the first eight amendments, thirteen relate to the treatment of criminal defendants. The Fourth Amendment guarantees the right of the people to be secure "in their persons, houses, papers, and effects" against unreasonable searches and seizures and prohibits the issuance of warrants without probable cause. The Fifth Amendment requires prosecution by grand-jury indictment for all "infamous crimes" (excepting certain military cases) and prohibits placing a person "twice in jeopardy of life or limb" for the same offense or compelling him to be "a witness against himself." The Sixth

Amendment lists several rights that the accused shall enjoy "in all criminal prosecutions": a speedy and public trial by an impartial jury of the state and district in which the crime has been committed, notice of the "nature and cause of the accusation," confrontation of hostile witnesses; compulsory process for obtaining favorable witnesses; and assistance of counsel. The Eighth Amendment adds prohibitions against the imposition of excessive bails and fines and the infliction of cruel and unusual punishments. And in addition to these specific guarantees, the Fifth Amendment adds a general prohibition against deprivation of life, liberty, or property without due process of law.

Those provisions spelled out in the original constitution obviously were understood to apply only to the federal government; and initially, so were the criminal procedural protections spelled out in the Bill of Rights. When the question of applying the Bill of Rights to the states first arose, Chief Justice John Marshall declared in *Barron* v. *Baltimore* (1833) that the first ten amendments were enacted as limitations upon the national government alone. Marshall observed that the opening sentence of the First Amendment begins with the phrase "Congress shall make no law . . ." and that nowhere in the subsequent provisions of the Bill of Rights can be found any limitations upon state action. Further, he reasoned,

> had the framers of these amendments intended them to be limitations on the powers of the state governments, they would have imitated the framers of the original Constitution, and have expressed that intention. Had Congress engaged in the extraordinary occupation of improving the constitutions of the several states by affording the people additional protection from the exercise of power by their own governments in matters which concerned themselves alone, they would have declared this purpose in plain and intelligible language.

With the adoption of the Fourteenth Amendment in 1868, however, the *Barron* ruling had to be reconsidered. Did the Fourteenth Amendment impose on the states the same restrictions that the Bill of Rights had imposed on the national government? Or, alternatively, did it impose either more lenient or more severe restrictions? These are critically important questions, because the vast majority of criminal prosecutions occur at the state level. From 1868 onward, the Supreme Court has had to grapple with the relationship between the limitations imposed on the states by the Fourteenth Amendment's Due Process Clause and the limitations imposed upon the federal government by the first eight amendments.

DUE PROCESS AND THE BILL OF RIGHTS

Three separate and distinct views of the appropriate relationship between the Due Process Clause and the Bill of Rights have been advanced: the "fundamental rights" interpretation, total incorporation, and selective incorporation.

"Fundamental Rights" Interpretation

Advocates of the "fundamental rights" interpretation find no necessary relationship between the Fourteenth Amendment and the guarantees of the Bill of Rights. Rather, they understand the Fourteenth Amendment as protecting "traditional notions" of due process, which were described variously by Justice Henry Brown in *Holden* v. *Hardy* (1898) as those "certain immutable principles of justice which inhere in the very idea of free government which no member of the Union may disregard" and by Justice Benjamin Cardozo in *Palko* v. *Connecticut* (1937) as those principles "implicit in the concept of ordered liberty." As applied to criminal procedure, this interpretation requires that a state grant the defendant "that fundamental fairness essential to the very concept of justice." The Bill of Rights is regarded as a likely, but not necessarily conclusive, indicator of "fundamental fairness." As Justice John Harlan observed in *Griswold* v. *Connecticut* (1965), "The Due Process Clause of the Fourteenth Amendment stands in my opinion on its own bottom." Just as this view of due process does not impose upon the states all the requirements of the Bill of Rights, neither does it restrict the reach of the Fourteenth Amendment to only those rights enumerated in the first eight amendments. Fundamental fairness, not mere compliance with the Bill of Rights, is its touchstone. Consequently, under the "fundamental rights" interpretation a state procedure may violate due process even though its operation is not contrary to any specific guarantee in the first eight amendments.

To its critics, the "fundamental rights" interpretation fosters subjective considerations based on some murky notion of natural justice, and thereby helps to promote an *ad hoc*, personal application of the Fourteenth Amendment. In reply, supporters of this interpretation contend that its application rests on a societal consensus that can be determined quite independently of the justice's personal views, and that various "objective" factors are available to the Court as it determines whether a particular procedural right traditionally has been recognized as an essential ingredient of fairness. Justice Benjamin Curtis cited two such factors in *Murray's Lessee* v. *Hoboken Land and Improvement Company* (1856): the significance attached to the right by the framers of the Constitution, and the importance of the right as recognized by "those settled usages and modes of proceedings existing in the common and statute law of England, before the immigration of our ancestors, and which are shown not to have been unsuited to their civil and political conditions by having been acted on by them after the settlement of this country." Other often-cited "objective" factors include the subsequent treatment of the right in state courts and legislatures and the significance attached to the right in countries with similar jurisprudential traditions. Although these factors do not provide "a mathematical calculus" for application of the Fourteenth Amendment, the argument continues, they go as far as is possible. After all, as Justice Felix Frankfurter observed,

> "Due Process", unlike some legal rules, is not a technical conception with a fixed content unrelated to time, place, and circumstances. Expressing as it does in its ultimate analysis respect enforced by law for the feeling of just treatment which has been evolved through centuries of Anglo-American constitutional history and civilization, "due process" cannot be imprisoned within the treacherous limits of any formula. Representing a profound attitude of fairness between man and man, and more particularly between the individual and the government, due process is compounded of history, reason, the past course of decisions, and stout confidence in the strength of the democratic faith which we profess. Due process is not a mechanical instrument. It is not a yardstick. It is a process.[1]

To Frankfurter and other proponents of the "fundamental rights" interpretation, judgment as to what due process requires must be made on a case-by-case basis. This interpretation, they continue, should prevail because it is the only interpretation of the Fourteenth Amendment that requires judges to engage in judgment—that activity that uniquely defines the behavior of a judge.

Total Incorporation

According to the "total incorporation" interpretation, the Fourteenth Amendment was intended simply and exclusively "to extend to all the people of the nation the complete protection of the Bill of Rights." Not only do the advocates of total incorporation believe that the legislative history and language of the amendment support total incorporation, but they also make the pragmatic argument that, by restricting judges to the specific language of the Bill of Rights, it avoids much of the subjectivity inherent in a "fundamental rights" approach.

Critics of total incorporation challenge these contentions. They argue that neither the legislative history nor the language of the amendment supports this view. Thus, they point out that the Due Process Clause of the Fourteenth Amendment merely restates a single provision of the Fifth Amendment of the Bill of Rights. Reflecting on this fact in *Hurtado* v. *California,* an 1884 decision in which the Court concluded that the Fourteenth Amendment's Due Process Clause did not require indictment by grand jury in state prosecutions, Justice Stanley Matthews observed:

> According to a recognized canon of interpretation, especially applicable to formal and solemn instruments of constitutional law, we are forbidden to assume, without clear reason to the contrary, that any part of . . . [the Fifth] Amendment is superfluous. The natural and obvious inference is, that in the sense of the Constitution, "due process of law" was not meant or intended to include . . . the institution and procedure of a grand jury in any case. The conclusion is equally

> irresistable, that when the same phrase was employed in the Fourteenth Amendment to restrain the action of the States, it was used in the same sense and with no greater extent; and that if in the adoption of that amendment it had been part of its purpose to perpetuate the institution of the grand jury in all the States, it would have embodied, as to the Fifth Amendment, express declaration to that effect.

Opponents of total incorporation also reject the notion that it avoids subjectivity. They criticize Justice Black—total incorporation's leading judicial exponent—for merely shifting the focus of judicial inquiry from the flexible concept of fundamental fairness to equally flexible terms in the specific amendments. Such terms as "probable cause," "speedy and public trial," and "cruel and unusual punishments," they observe are hardly self-defining and must be interpreted in light of the same contemporary notions of fairness considered in applying a "fundamental rights" standard. As Justice Harlan chided Justice Black in *Griswold,* " 'Specific' provisions of the Constitution, no less than 'due process' lend themselves readily to 'personal' interpretations by judges whose constitutional outlook is simply to keep the Constitution in supposed 'tune with the times.' " Finally, critics contend that total incorporation imposes an undue burden on the states and deprives them of any opportunity to act as social and legal laboratories—to experiment with reforms designed to enhance the protections and freedom of the people.

Selective Incorporation

Selective incorporation, the third view of the appropriate relationship between the Fourteenth Amendment and the Bill of Rights, combines aspects of both the "fundamental rights" and the total incorporation interpretations. Along with the "fundamental rights" interpretation, it holds that the Fourteenth Amendment encompasses all rights, substantive and procedural, that are "of the very essence of a scheme of ordered liberty." It recognizes that not all rights enumerated in the Bill of Rights are fundamental, and that some rights may be fundamental even if not specifically guaranteed in the Bill of Rights. But in determining whether an enumerated right is fundamental, this interpretation, like the total incorporation view, focuses on the *total* right guaranteed by the individual amendment, not merely on the element of that right before the Court or the application of that right in a particular case. In other words, by deciding that a particular guarantee within the first eight amendments is fundamental, the Supreme Court incorporates that guarantee into the Fourteenth Amendment "whole and intact" and enforces it against the states in every case, according to the same standards applied to the federal government. *Duncan* v. *Louisiana* (1968), which incorporated the right to a jury trial, expressed this understanding: "Because . . . trial by jury in criminal cases is fundamental to the American scheme of justice, we hold that the Fourteenth Amendment guarantees a right of jury trial in all criminal cases which—were they to be tried in a Federal court—would come within the Sixth Amendment's guarantee."

Proponents of selective incorporation maintain that it represents an improvement over both other interpretations. They argue that a fundamental right should not be denied merely because the "totality of circumstances" in a particular case does not disclose "a denial of fundamental fairness," pointing out that judicial evaluation of the factual circumstances surrounding any particular case often is extremely subjective and discretionary. On the other hand, they continue, selective incorporation avoids the rigidity and extremism of total incorporation, under which, for example, the Seventh Amendment right of trial by jury in all suits at common law in excess of twenty dollars logically should be incorporated.

In the view of its detractors, however, selective incorporation is an unacceptable compromise that is inconsistent with the logic and historical support of either of the doctrines it attempts to combine. Those who embrace total incorporation charge that it is merely another example of "natural law due process philosophy." Proponents of "fundamental rights," on the other hand, contend that selective incorporation fails to appreciate the special burdens it imposes on the administration of criminal justice at the state level. They fear that the imposition of a single standard regulating both state and federal practice would either place an unrealistic "constitutional straight-jacket" on the states or result in a relaxing of standards as applied to both state and federal officials, in order to meet the special problems of the states.

Despite these criticisms selective incorporation has replaced the "fundamental rights" interpretation as the dominant view on the Court. Justice William Brennan advanced the doctrine for the first time in his 1961 dissent in *Cohen* v. *Hurley,* and just two years later it had the support of at least four justices. It also was accepted by Justice Black, who, although remaining committed to total incorporation, accepted selective incorporation as a lesser evil than the "mysterious and uncertain law concepts" of the "fundamental rights" interpretation. With this majority support, selective incorporation was instrumental in making the following Bill of Rights guarantees applicable to the states: the right to have excluded from criminal trials any evidence obtained in violation of the Fourth Amendment, *Mapp* v. *Ohio* (1961); the privilege against compulsory self-incrimination, *Malloy* v. *Hogan* (1964); the guarantee against double jeopardy, *Benton* v. *Maryland* (1969); the right to assistance of counsel, *Gideon* v. *Wainwright* (1963) and *Argersinger* v. *Hamlin* (1972); the right to an impartial jury, *Parker* v. *Gladden* (1966); the right to a speedy trial, *Klopfer* v. *North Carolina* (1967); the right to a jury trial in nonpetty criminal cases, *Duncan* v. *Louisiana* (1968); the right to confront opposing witnesses, *Pointer* v. *Texas* (1965); the right to compulsory process for obtaining favorable witnesses, *Washington* v. *Texas* (1967); the protection against excessive bail, *Schilb* v. *Kuebel* (1971); and the protection against "cruel and unusual punishments," *Robinson* v. *California* (1962).

Before the selective-incorporation era, the Court had already incorporated the right to a public trial, *In Re Oliver* (1948), required states to provide defendants with notice of the nature and cause of the accusation against them, *Cole* v. *Arkansas* (1948), and extended to state court defendants the protection against unreasonable searches and seizures, *Wolf* v. *Colorado* (1949). The only Bill of Rights guarantees directly related to criminal procedure that have not been held to apply to the states are the Eighth Amendment prohibition against excessive fines and the Fifth Amendment requirement of prosecution by grand jury indictment. Remarkably, the Supreme Court has never been presented with an opportunity to rule on the prohibition against excessive fines, but it is generally assumed that this guarantee will be incorporated if the issue is squarely presented. The Fifth Amendment requirement of grand jury indictment, on the other hand, was specifically held not to be guaranteed by the Fourteenth Amendment in the *Hurtado* decision, which continues to be followed as valid precedent. (See Table 14.1.)

State Constitutional Guarantees

Although the extension of federal protection against states' violations of rights is a relatively recent phenomenon, this did not mean that previously defendants in state courts were altogether without rights. Rather, as propo-

TABLE 14.1 Incorporation of Criminal Procedure Rights to the States

Rights	Case and Year
Fourth Amendment	
Unreasonable Search and Seizure	*Wolf* v. *Colorado* (1949)
Exclusionary Rule	*Mapp* v. *Ohio* (1961)
Fifth Amendment	
Grand Jury Clause	Not Incorporated
Double Jeopardy Clause	*Benton* v. *Maryland* (1969)
Self-Incrimination Clause	*Malloy* v. *Hogan* (1964)
Sixth Amendment	
Speedy Trial Clause	*Klopfer* v. *North Carolina* (1967)
Public Trial Clause	*In Re Oliver* (1948)
Impartial Jury Clause	*Parker* v. *Gladden* (1966)
Jury Trial Clause	*Duncan* v. *Louisiana* (1968)
Notice Clause	*Cole* v. *Arkansas* (1948)
Confrontation Clause	*Pointer* v. *Texas* (1965)
Compulsory Process Clause	*Washington* v. *Texas* (1967)
Right to Counsel Clause	*Gideon* v. *Wainwright* (1963) / *Argersinger* v. *Hamlin* (1972)
Eighth Amendment	
Excessive Bail	*Schilb* v. *Kuebel* (1971)
Excessive Fines	Not Incorporated
Cruel and Unusual Punishment Clause	*Robinson* v. *California* (1962)

nents of the "fundamental rights" approach recognized, our federal system rested on the assumption of a rough division of labor in protecting rights. State laws and state constitutions were to serve as the primary guarantees against oppressive state governments, with the federal Constitution securing fundamental rights against state violation only when state judicial processes afforded no redress. Beginning in the mid-twentieth century, however, this balance began to shift. Defendants in state courts began looking primarily to the federal Constitution and federal judicial precedent for vindication of their rights, assuming that state constitutional guarantees either duplicated federal protections or were altogether irrelevant.

During the past decade and a half, however, lawyers and scholars have rediscovered state constitutions. Motivated both by rulings of the Burger Court and by its encouragement of reliance on state constitutional guarantees, they have begun to study state constitutions more closely and to fashion legal arguments based on the distinctive text and history of those state charters. Although it is unlikely that state constitutions will again become the primary guarantors of rights, this new attention to state constitutions represents a positive step toward reconciling federalism and the protection of rights.

CRIMINAL PROCEDURE

The following sections outline the development and current legal status of the major criminal procedural protections of Amendments Four through Eight.

Search and Seizure

Legal Parameters. The Fourth Amendment forbids "unreasonable searches and seizures"—not all searches and seizures, only those that are "unreasonable." In general, the Supreme Court has followed the rule that searches are reasonable if they are based on a warrant obtained from a magistrate, who may issue the warrant only if law enforcement officials have demonstrated, through introduction of evidence, that there is probable cause to believe that the search will uncover evidence of criminal activity. (In *Aguilar* v. *Texas* [1964] the Court ruled that probable-cause standards are the same for state and federal magistrates.)

Failure to obtain a warrant does not automatically render a search or seizure unreasonable. The Supreme Court has provided a number of exceptions to the requirement that a warrant be obtained, the most important of which is a search incident to a lawful arrest. The rationale for this exception is that an arresting officer needs to be free to search a defendant in order to remove weapons (to protect the officer's safety) and evidence (to prevent its destruction). Officers are not permitted, however, to search just anybody and then use the evidence thereby obtained to justify the original arrest. Generally speaking, officers cannot use the fruits of a search as justification for the arrest; grounds for arrest must exist for the search incident to the arrest to be valid. And as *Chimel* v. *California* (1968) made clear, neither do the officers have much latitude in searching premises under the control of validly arrested defendants. The officers in *Chimel* arrested the defendant in his house and, over his objections and without a search warrant, proceeded to search his entire three-bedroom house, including attic, garage, and workshop. Items obtained from this search subsequently were admitted in evidence against the defendant during his trial for burglary, and he was convicted. The Supreme Court, in a 7–2 decision, declared that such a widespread search was unreasonable and overturned his conviction. Justice Potter Stewart, speaking for the Court, noted that although there is solid justification for a search of the arrestee's person and of "the area 'within his immediate control'—construing that phrase to mean the area within which he might gain possession of a weapon or destructable evidence," there is no comparable justification for "routinely searching any room other than that in which an arrest occurs—or, for that matter, for searching through all the desk drawers or other closed or concealed areas in that room itself. Such searches, in the absence of well-organized exceptions, may be made only under the authority of a search warrant."[2]

A second exception to the warrant requirement is the "plain view" doctrine. As the Court held in *Harris* v. *United States* (1968), "It has long been settled that objects falling in the plain view of an officer who has a right to be in the position to have that view are subject to seizure and may be introduced in evidence." This doctrine covers observations made by officers standing on public property and peering into car windows or the windows of dwellings, as well as observations made by officers who are on a defendant's property in the pursuit of legitimate business.[3] *Chimel* did not qualify the "plain view" exception: incident to arrest, instrumentalities of crime can be seized if they are in plain view, even if they are not within the immediate control of the person arrested.[4]

Law officers also are permitted to search a vehicle on probable cause without a warrant. The Court first recognized this right during the Prohibition era, in *Carroll* v. *United States* (1925), citing as its justification the fact that a vehicle can be moved quickly out of the locality or jurisdiction in which the warrant must be sought. The so-called automobile exception has spawned considerable litigation, and the Court repeatedly has been obliged to clarify this area of the law and to determine whether particular warrantless searches have been justified. Unfortunately, its efforts at clarification often have been unsatisfactory, providing inadequate or even contradictory advice to police, prosecutors, and courts attempting to discharge their responsibilities in a manner consistent with the Fourth Amendment. Nowhere is this failure to provide specific guidance more apparent than in the cases of *Robbins* v. *California* (1981) and *New York* v. *Belton* (1981), both decided on the same day. In *Robbins* the justices held that a warrantless search of a package wrapped in opaque plastic and stored in the luggage area of a station wagon violated the Fourth Amendment; but in *Belton,* they ruled that a warrantless search of a zippered pocket of a jacket found in an automobile's passenger compartment did not violate the amendment. Following a public outcry over such vacillation, the Court addressed this matter again in *United States* v. *Ross* (1982). This time, a six-member majority set forth the ground rules for the "automobile exception." To begin with, the *Ross* majority announced, the exception applies to vehicle searches that are supported by probable cause to believe that the vehicle contains contraband or other evidence of criminality. In these cases, a search is reasonable if it is based on objective facts that would justify the issuance of a warrant by a magistrate. When police officers have probable cause to search an entire vehicle, the justices continued, they may conduct a warrantless search of every part of the vehicle and its contents, including all containers and packages, that may conceal the object of the search. In such cases, the scope of the search is not defined by the nature of the container in which the contraband or evidence of criminality is secreted, but rather by the object of the search and the places in which there is probable cause to believe that it may be found. As Justice Stevens noted for the majority, "Probable cause to believe that undocumented aliens are being transported in a van will not justify a warrentless search of a suitcase."[5]

Obtaining consent to search constitutes a fourth exception to the warrant requirement: Fourth Amendment rights, like other criminal-procedure rights, can be waived by the individual. (State courts generally have been more willing to assume consent than have the federal courts, which have gone on record as declaring that consent to search "is not lightly to be inferred."[6])

The Court's 1985 decision in *New Jersey* v. *T.L.O.* identified still another exception, permitting school officials to search students who are under their authority without a warrant. Justice White held for the Court majority that the legality of a search of a student should depend not on a showing of probable cause but simply on the reasonableness, under all the circumstances, of the search. Determining the reasonableness of any search involves a determination of whether the search was justified at its inception and whether, as conducted, it was reasonably related in scope to the circumstances that justified the school official's intervention in the first place.

Yet another exception, established in *Warden* v. *Hayden* (1967), allows the police to enter premises without an arrest or search warrant when in "hot pursuit" of a fleeing suspect, and having entered, to seize evidence uncovered in the search for the suspect.[7]

The seventh exception to the warrant requirement is the investigative technique known as stop and frisk, the long-established police practice of stopping suspicious persons on the street or in other public places for purposes of questioning them or conducting some other form of investigation and, incident to the stoppings, of searching ("frisking") the suspects for dangerous weapons. Because such searches commonly were employed when there were no grounds to arrest the suspect and to search him incident to arrest, their constitutionality was challenged in the courts. In *Terry* v. *Ohio* (1968), Chief Justice Earl Warren provided a clear answer to this question. Speaking for an eight-member majority (only Justice William Douglas dissented), he declared,

> When an officer is justified in believing that the individual whose suspicious behavior he is investigating at close range is armed and presently dangerous to the officer or to others, it would appear completely unreasonable to deny the officer the power to take necessary measures to determine whether the person is in fact carrying a weapon and to neutralize the threat of physical harm. . . . There must be a narrowly drawn authority to permit a reasonable search for weapons for the protection of the police officer, where he has reason to believe that he is dealing with an armed and dangerous individual, regardless of whether he has probable cause to arrest the individual for a crime. The officer need not be absolutely certain that the individual is armed; the issue is whether a reasonably prudent man in the circumstances would be warranted in the belief that his safety or that of others was in danger.

The 1973 decisions in *United States* v. *Robinson* and *Gustafson* v. *Florida* further modified the general rule that a warrantless search is valid only if it is incident to a lawful arrest. Both cases involved arrests for motor vehicle violations; and in both, subsequent searches of the offenders uncovered narcotics, and the evidence so obtained later was used to obtain convictions. In affirming both convictions, Justice William Rehnquist, writing for the majority in *Robinson* and a plurality in *Gustafson*, expanded the permissible limits of *Terry*'s stop-and-frisk doctrine. Under the circumstances of these cases, he held, a search incident to a valid arrest was not limited to a pat-down of the outer garments for weapons. These searches were not unreasonable, he continued, even though the arresting officers did not suspect either that the offenders were armed or that they might destroy evidence of the crime for which the arrests had been made. As Rehnquist declared in *Robinson*,

> As custodial arrest of a suspect based on probable cause is a reasonable intrusion under the Fourth Amendment, that intrusion being lawful, a search incident to the arrest requires no additional justification.

An eighth and final exception to the warrant requirement has recently been introduced by the Court: drug testing. In *Skinner* v. *Railway Labor Executives Association* (1989), the Court sustained drug testing of railroad employees involved in train accidents and held that, in certain circumstances, reasonableness does not require a warrant, probable cause, or even any measure of individualized suspicion. The Court concluded that the demonstrated frequency of drug and alcohol use by railroad employees and the demonstrated connection between such use and grave harm rendered the drug testing a reasonable means of protecting society. In *National Treasury Employees Union* v. *Von Raab,* decided the same day, the Court went even further and sustained the constitutionality of urine testing for those U.S. Customs Service employees involved directly in drug interdiction or whose positions required them to carry firearms. Justice Kennedy concluded for a five-member majority that the government had a "compelling interest" in "safeguarding our borders" and that public safety outweighs the privacy expectations of the Customs Service employees. Justice Scalia, who concurred in *Skinner,* filed a sharp dissent, describing the drug-testing rules of the Customs Service as "a kind of immolation of privacy and human dignity."

Electronic Surveillance. The Supreme Court first confronted the issue of electronic surveillance in *Olmstead* v. *United States* (1928), which involved the wiretapping of a gang of rumrunners. Here the justices concluded that the Fourth Amendment was not applicable, because there had been no trespass of a constitutionally protected area and no seizure of a physical object. The *Olmstead* doctrine was not repudiated until *Katz* v. *United States* (1967), in which the Court declared that the Fourth Amendment "protects people, not places" and held that electronic surveillance conducted outside the judicial process, whether or not it involves trespass, is *per se* unreasonable. In an attempt to limit *Katz* and to clarify exactly what was expected of law enforcement personnel, Congress included in the Omnibus Crime Control and Safe Streets Act of 1968 a title on the interception and disclosure of wire or oral communication, which provided for a system of judicially approved interceptions at the request of the attorney-general.

Remedies for Violations. Although the Fourth Amendment forbids unreasonable searches and seizures, it does not prescribe a remedy for those whose rights have been violated. Addressing this issue for the first time in *Weeks* v. *United States* (1914), the Supreme Court declared that the appropriate remedy was exclusion of the illegally obtained evidence. The justices did not hold that the Fourth Amendment of its own force barred from criminal prosecutions the use of illegally seized, or "tainted," items: that is, they did not consider the Fourth Amendment to constitute a rule of evidence. But without such an exclusionary rule, they argued, the Fourth Amendment would present no effective deterrent to improper searches and seizures. This holding meant that as a federal rule of evidence—which in its supervisory function the Court could impose on the entire federal judiciary—illegally obtained evidence could not be used in federal prosecutions.

The *Weeks* decision, however, dealt only with federal prosecutions. Because the Fourth Amendment had not yet been incorporated through the Fourteenth Amendment to apply to the states, most states continued to follow the old common-law rule that relevant evidence obtained under any circumstances was admissible. Not until *Wolf* v. *Colorado* (1949) did the

Supreme Court have occasion to rule on these state practices. In that decision the Court concluded, in an opinion written by Justice Frankfurter, that "the security of one's privacy against arbitrary intrusion by the police—which is at the core of the Fourth Amendment—is basic to a free society. It is therefore implicit in 'the concept of ordered liberty' and as such enforceable against the States through the Due Process Clause." Although holding that the Fourth Amendment guarantee against unreasonable searches and seizures was enforceable against the states through the Fourteenth Amendment, the *Wolf* majority did not consider the exclusionary rule announced in *Weeks* to be an "essential ingredient" of that guarantee. The Court denied that the exclusionary rule had any constitutional status, asserting instead that it was merely a pragmatic remedy developed under the Court's powers to supervise the federal judicial system. Not until *Mapp* v. *Ohio* (1961) did the Court finally abandon the *Wolf* doctrine and impose the exclusionary rule on state proceedings as well. In *Mapp,* it concluded that the exclusionary rule, by removing the incentive to disregard the Fourth Amendment, constituted "the only effectively available way . . . to compel respect for the constitutional guarantee."

Ever since *Mapp,* the exclusionary rule has been under heavy attack.[8] In his dissent in *Bivens* v. *Six Unknown Named Agents* (1971), Chief Justice Burger proposed its elimination and an end to what he called the "universal capital punishment we inflict on all evidence when police error is shown in its acquisition." He urged Congress to enact a statute that would waive sovereign immunity as to the illegal acts of law enforcement officials committed in the performance of assigned tasks; create a cause of action for damages sustained by any persons aggrieved by the conduct of governmental agents in violation of the Fourth Amendment or statutes regulating official conduct; create a quasijudicial tribunal, patterned after the U.S. Court of Claims, to adjudicate all claims under the statute; substitute this remedy for the exclusionary rule; and direct that no evidence, otherwise admissible, would be excluded from any criminal proceeding because of a violation of the Fourth Amendment. He believed this would provide a more "meaningful and effective remedy against unlawful conduct by governmental officials" and that it would afford "some remedy to completely innocent persons who are sometimes the victims of illegal police conduct."

While a majority of the Court has never accepted Chief Justice Burger's argument for the complete elimination of the exclusionary rule, it has come to recognize a "good faith" exception to it. In *United States* v. *Leon* (1984) and *Massachusetts* v. *Sheppard* (1984), the Court held that the exclusionary rule should not be applied so as to suppress the introduction of evidence at a criminal trial obtained in the reasonable belief that the search and seizure at issue was consistent with the Fourth Amendment.[9]

Self-Incrimination and Coerced Confessions

The Fifth Amendment provides that no person "shall be compelled in any criminal case to be a witness against himself." Along with other provisions of the Bill of Rights, this privilege originally was restricted to federal prosecutions. And in both *Twining* v. *New Jersey* (1908) and *Adamson* v. *California* (1947), the Supreme Court rejected the argument that the exception to compulsory self-incrimination was a "fundamental right" and hence necessary to a system of "ordered liberty." In the 1964 case of *Malloy* v. *Hogan,* however, it overruled those precedents and, through the Fourteenth Amendment, extended this protection to the states as well. As Justice William Brennan stated for the Court, "The Fourteenth Amendment secures against state invasion the same privilege that the Fifth Amendment guarantees against federal infringement—the right of a person to remain silent unless he chooses to speak in the unfettered exercise of his own will, and to suffer no penalty—for such silence."

Long before *Malloy,* the Court had placed limitations upon police interrogation techniques and the admissibility of confessions thereby obtained. In *Brown* v. *Mississippi* (1936) the Court overturned the conviction of three defendants whom police had physically tortured in order to extort confessions. Chief Justice Charles Evans Hughes made abundantly clear in *Brown* the Court's belief that the use of such confessions violated the Due Process Clause of the Fourteenth Amendment: "The freedom of the state in establishing its policy is the freedom of constitutional government and is limited by the requirement of due process of law. Because a state may dispense with a jury trial, it does not follow that it may substitute a trial by ordeal. The rack and torture chamber may not be substituted for the witness stand." *Brown* was extended in *Chambers* v. *Florida* (1940), in which the Court again overturned a state conviction—this time because the defendant had been arrested on suspicion, without a warrant; denied contact with friends or attorneys; and questioned for long periods of time by different squads of police officers.

Brown and *Chambers* were followed by a long line of cases in which the Court addressed admissibility-of-confessions questions on an *ad hoc* basis, employing the "totality of circumstances" rule: Under this guideline, the Court sought to determine whether the specific circumstances surrounding the obtaining of a particular confession (the nature of the charge; the age, maturity, and educational achievements of the defendant; the degree of pressure put upon him or her; the length of interrogation; etc.) constituted coercion and thereby rendered the confession inadmissible. This guideline suffered from one major drawback: it provided the police and the prosecution with little guidance as to what practices did or did not pass constitutional muster. As a consequence, the Court found itself confronted with a barrage of "coerced confessions" cases dealing with such police practices as attempts to gain the sympathy of the defendant through a childhood friend on the police force,[10] threats to bring a defendant's wife into custody for questioning,[11] threats to place the defendant's children in the custody of welfare officials,[12] and interrogations of wounded defendants under the influence of so-called truth serums.[13] To free itself from this perpetual stream of litigation, the Warren Court in *Miranda* v. *Arizona* (1966) broke completely with past cases and, rejecting the *ad hoc* "totality of circumstances" rule, announced specific procedures that the police would have to follow during interrogations, and declared that any statements elicited in violation of these procedures would be inadmissible.

The Burger and Rehnquist Courts have refused to overturn the *Miranda* decision,[14] but they have modified it in such decisions as *Harris* v. *New York* (1971), *Oregon* v. *Hass* (1975), *Nix* v. *Williams* (1984), *New York* v. *Quarles* (1984), and *Duckworth* v. *Eagan* (1989). The six-member majority in *Harris* held that although statements made to the police by defendants who have not been advised of their *Miranda* rights cannot be introduced as evidence for the prosecution's case-in-chief, they can be employed to impeach the credibility of defendants who testify in their own behalf and, in so doing, contradict earlier statements. In so ruling, the Court refused to construe the privilege against self-incrimination to include the right to commit perjury.[15] At issue in *Hass* were the rights of a suspect in police custody who, having received and accepted the full warnings prescribed by *Miranda,* later stated that he would like to telephone a lawyer; after being told he could not do so before reaching the station, he then provided inculpatory information. Such information, the Court ruled, was admissible in evidence at the suspect's trial solely for impeachment purposes after he had taken the stand and testified to the contrary, knowing that such information has been ruled inadmissible for the prosecution's case-in-chief.[16]

In *Williams,* the Court held in a 7–2 vote that evidence obtained in violation of the *Miranda* decision need not be suppressed if it would have been inevitably discovered by lawful means. And, in *Quarles,* the Court recognized a "public safety exception" to the requirement that *Miranda* warnings be given before a suspect's answers may be admitted into evidence. As Justice Rehnquist reasoned:

> The police, in this case, in the very act of apprehending a suspect, were confronted with the immediate necessity of ascertaining the whereabouts of a gun which they had every reason to believe the suspect had just removed from his empty holster and discarded in the supermarket. So long as the gun was concealed somewhere in the supermarket, with its actual whereabouts unknown, it obviously posed more than one danger to the public safety: an accomplice might make use of it, a customer or employee might later come upon it.

To insure that further danger to the public did not result from the concealment of the gun in a public area, the Court held that the police did not have to advise the suspect of his *Miranda* rights before questioning him about the whereabouts of the gun and that the suspect's response, in which he pointed out the gun's location, did not have to be excluded.

Finally, in *Duckworth,* the Court held that informing a suspect that an attorney would be appointed for him "if and when you go to court" does not render *Miranda* warnings inadequate. Chief Justice Rehnquist argued for a five-member majority that *Miranda* warnings need not be given in the exact form described in *Miranda* but simply must reasonably convey to suspects their rights.

It should be noted that not all self-incrimination cases are concerned with trial court procedures or pretrial police interrogation techniques. A recent case in point is *South Dakota* v. *Neville* (1983), in which Justice O'Connor held for a seven-member majority that admission into evidence of a defendant's refusal to submit to a blood-alcohol test does not offend his privilege against self-incrimination and that it is not fundamentally unfair in violation of due process to use a defendant's refusal to take the blood-alcohol test as evidence of guilt, even though the police failed to warn him that refusal could be used against him at trial. Another example is *Selective Service System* v. *Minnesota Public Interest Research Group* (1984), in which the Court held, 6–2, that a statute denying federal financial aid to male students who failed to register for the draft did not violate the privilege against self-incrimination of nonregistrants.

The Right to Counsel

The Sixth Amendment declares that "in all criminal prosecutions, the accused shall enjoy the right . . . to have Assistance of Counsel for his defense." Until well into the twentieth century, this language was construed to guarantee only that the accused could employ and bring to trial a lawyer of his own choosing. No provision was made for the indigent defendant who might want and even badly need assistance of counsel, but was unable to afford an attorney. The language was permissive only; it imposed no duty on the government to provide free counsel.

In 1932 the Court began to expand this interpretation, holding in *Powell* v. *Alabama* that in capital felony cases, right to counsel is secured by the Due Process Clause of the Fourteenth Amendment. Six years later, in *Johnson* v. *Zerbst*, the Court further broadened the right to counsel to include appointment of counsel for indigent defendants in all federal criminal proceedings, capital or noncapital: "The Sixth Amendment," the Court declared, "withholds from federal courts, in all criminal proceedings, the power and authority to deprive an accused of his life or liberty unless he has or waives the assistance of counsel."

Although the Court held that the Sixth Amendment required appointment of counsel for indigent criminal defendants in federal prosecutions, it was reluctant to interpret the Fourteenth Amendment's Due Process Clause in such a way as to impose the same requirements on the states. When presented with the opportunity to do so in *Betts* v. *Brady* (1942), Justice Owen Roberts examined the constitutional, judicial, and legislative history of the states from colonial days and concluded for a six-member majority that "this material demonstrates that, in the great majority of States, it has been the considered judgment of the people, their representatives and their courts that appointment of counsel is not a fundamental right essential to a fair trial. On the contrary, the matter has generally been deemed one of legislative policy. In the light of this evidence, we are unable to say that the concept of due process incorporated in the Fourteenth Amendment obligates the States, whatever may be their own views, to furnish counsel in every such case." In dissent, Justice Black stressed that "whether a man is innocent cannot be determined from a trial in which, as here, denial of counsel has made it impossible to conclude, with any satisfactory degree of certainty, that the defendant's case was adequately presented."

Justice Black's dissent eventually was vindicated in the celebrated case of *Gideon* v. *Wainwright* (1963), in which the Court overruled *Betts* and unanimously concluded that an indigent defendant's right to court-appointed counsel is fundamental and essential to a fair trial in state as well as federal felony prosecutions. Justice Black declared for the Court that precedent, reason, and reflection "require us to recognize that in our adversary system of criminal justice, any person hauled into court, who is too poor to hire a lawyer, cannot be assured a fair trial unless counsel is provided for him." Observing that the government hires lawyers to prosecute and defendants with money hire lawyers to defend, he concluded that "lawyers in criminal courts are necessities, not luxuries." The *Gideon* ruling did not extend the right to assistance of counsel to all criminal prosecutions, however. Misdemeanor offenses were excluded from coverage until *Argersinger* v. *Hamlin* (1972), in which the Court unanimously held that "absent a knowing and intelligent waiver, no person may be imprisoned for any offense, whether classified as petty, misdemeanor, or felony, unless he was represented by counsel at his trial."[17]

The Court has not only held that the right to assistance of counsel must be guaranteed in all trials where defendants can be sentenced to a term of imprisonment but has also held that this constitutional principle is not limited simply to the presence of counsel at trial. As it declared in *United States* v. *Wade* (1967),

> it is central to that principle that in addition to counsel's presence at trial, the accused is guaranteed that he need not stand alone against the state at any stage of the prosecution, formal or informal, in court or out, where counsel's absence might derogate from the accused's right to a fair trial.

On the basis of this principle, the Court has ruled that the accused has the right to counsel at such "critical stages" as in-custody police interrogation following arrest, *Escobedo* v. *Illinois* and *Miranda* v. *Arizona;* the police lineup held for eyewitness identification, *United States* v. *Wade* and *Gilbert* v. *California;* the preliminary hearing, *Coleman* v. *Alabama;* the arraignment, *Hamilton* v. *Alabama;* at his appeal, *Douglas* v. *California,* and even at a posttrial proceeding for the revocation of probation and parole, *Mempa* v. *Rhay.*

The Court's decisions from *Powell* to *Argersinger* raised a serious question: Does a defendant in a criminal trial have a constitutional right to proceed without counsel when he voluntarily and intelligently elects to do so? Stated another way, can a state constitutionally haul a person into its criminal courts and there force a lawyer upon him, even when he insists that he want to conduct his own defense? The Court gave a negative answer to this question in *Faretta* v. *California* (1975). Justice Stewart, speaking for a six-member majority, stressed that the language of the provision provides for "assistance" of counsel and that "an assistant, however expert, is still an assistant." Developing this argument further, he concluded that to thrust counsel upon an unwilling defendant would violate the logic of the amendment: "In such a case, counsel is not an assistant, but a master; and the right to make a defense is stripped of the personal character upon which the Amendment insists."

Justice Harry Blackmun challenged this conclusion in his dissent: "The Court seems to suggest that so long as the accused is willing to pay the consequences of his folly, there is no reason for not allowing a defendant the right to self-representation. . . . That view ignores the established principle that the interest of the State in a criminal prosecution 'is not that it shall win a case, but that justice shall be done.' "

Chaplin & Drysdale, Chartered v. *United States* (1989) posed for the Court an interesting right-to-counsel question arising out of the federal government's ongoing war against drugs: Can the federal government constitutionally enforce a statute authorizing forfeiture to the government of assets acquired as a result of drug law violations if the criminal defendant intends to use these assets to pay legal fees for his defense? In a 5–4 decision, Justice White concluded for the Court that the government can; he observed, among other things, that a defendant in a drug case has no more Sixth Amendment right to use funds obtained from an illegal drug enterprise to pay for his defense than a robbery suspect has "to use funds he has stolen from a bank."

The Right to a Speedy Trial

The Sixth Amendment assures the accused the right to a speedy trial. However, as Justice Powell remarked in *Barker* v. *Wingo* (1972), this right "is a more vague concept than other procedural rights. It is, for example, impossible to determine with precision when the right has been denied. We cannot definitely say how long is too long in a system where justice is supposed to be swift but deliberate." The vague quality of the right to a speedy trial led the Court in *Barker* to embrace a "balancing test" to determine whether the right had been violated. Four factors were to be weighed in the balance: length of delay, the reason for the delay, the defendant's assertion of his right, and prejudice to the defendant.

Conceding that this "difficult and sensitive balancing process" necessarily would compel the courts to approach speedy trial cases on an *ad hoc* basis, the Court insisted that this way of proceeding comported with the requirements of the judicial process. The Court was reluctant to go so far as to hold that the Constitution required a criminal defendant to be offered a trial within a specified time period. Against the undoubted clarity and definiteness of a time limit, the Court observed, must be weighed the fact that it would "require this Court to engage in legislative or rulemaking activity, rather than in the adjudicative process to which we should confine our efforts." It went on to note that although legislatures were free to prescribe reasonable periods of time, consistent with constitutional standards, within which criminal trials must begin, its own approach had to be less precise. Seeking such precision, Congress passed with the Speedy Trial Act of 1974, which ordered that criminal defendants be brought to trial within one hundred days.

Plea Bargaining

Plea bargaining, in which a defendant agrees to plead guilty in return for a reduced charge or sentence, has become such a central feature of the criminal justice system that it currently occurs in approximately 90 percent of all criminal cases in the United States. In *Brady* v. *United States* (1970) the Supreme Court gave its approval to most forms of plea bargaining. Speaking for the Court majority, Justice Byron White announced the Court's refusal to hold that "a guilty plea is compelled and invalid under the Fifth Amendment whenever motivated by the defendant's desire to accept the certainty or probability of a lesser penalty rather than face a wider range of possibilities extending from acquittal to conviction and a higher penalty authorized by law for the crime charged. . . . We cannot hold that it is unconstitutional for the State to extend a benefit to a defendant who in turn extends a substantial benefit to the State. . . ."

Since *Brady,* the Court has sought to formalize the procedures for plea bargaining. In *Santo Bello* v. *New York* (1971), for example, it held that if a defendant, relying upon a prosecutor's promise, enters a guilty plea, due process of law requires that the prosecutor's promise be kept or that the defendant be given some form of relief—typically, an opportunity to withdraw the guilty plea. Later, in its most comprehensive effort to define plea-bargaining procedures, the Court issued and sent to the Congress for approval a set of amendments to Rule 11 of the Federal Rules of Criminal Procedure. These amendments were approved, with several changes, by Congress and became effective in 1975.

Bail and Pretrial Detention

Bail and pretrial detention have perhaps raised fewer constitutional questions than any other practices in the criminal justice system. This is in part because the "excessive fines and bails" clause of the Eighth Amendment has never been incorporated to apply to the states and in part because the Supreme Court has never established an absolute right to bail. In determining whether bail will be granted, and the conditions under which it will be granted, courts have traditionally asked just one question: Will the accused abscond or appear as required at his trial? Increasingly, however, a second question is also being asked: Will the accused constitute a danger to the community and the safety of others by committing additional crimes while free on bail? Both the Supreme Court and the Congress have recently given their endorsement to the asking of this second question and to the use of preventive detention when the answer to this second question mandates it.

In *Schall* v. *Martin* (1984), the Supreme Court upheld by a vote of 7–2 the preventive detention provision of the New York Family Court Act that authorized pretrial detention of juveniles accused of acts of delinquency based on the finding that there was "serious risk" that the juvenile "may before the return date commit an act which if committed by an adult would constitute a crime." Justice Rehnquist held for the majority that preventive detention under the statute served the legitimate state objective of protecting both the juvenile and the society from the hazards of pretrial crime and that it was therefore "compatible with the 'fundamental fairness' demanded by the Due Process Clause." And, in the Comprehensive Crime Control Act of 1984, passed later that same year, Congress provided that, if, after a hearing pursuant to the provisions of that Act, a "judicial officer finds that no condition or combination of conditions will reasonably assure the appearance of the person as required and the safety of any other person and the community, he shall order the detention of the person prior to trial." Interestingly, given this chapter's previous discussion of the exclusionary rule, Congress specifically declared that "the rules concerning admissibility of evidence in criminal trials do not apply to the presentation and consideration of information" at the preventive detention hearing. These preventive detention provisions were upheld by the Supreme Court in *United States* v. *Salerno* (1987).

Cruel and Unusual Punishments

The Eighth Amendment protects against the infliction of "cruel and unusual punishments." This phraseology, derived from the English Bill of Rights of 1689, originally was understood to refer to such ancient practices as branding, drawing and quartering, burning alive, and crucifixion. But as Chief Justice Warren noted in *Trop* v. *Dulles* (1958), the Court must determine the meaning of the Eighth Amendment from the "evolving standards of decency that mark the progress of a maturing society." Put simply, whatever the amendment was originally intended to mean must be of less importance to the Court than what "evolving standards of decency" require. How the Court views these standards is of as much interest to the states as to federal government, because *Robinson* v. *California* (1962), which invalidated a California statute that made it a misdemeanor to be "addicted to the use of narcotics," made this particular provision applicable to the states through the Fourteenth Amendment.

Perhaps the most dramatic issue arising out of *Robinson* and its incorporation of the protection against cruel and unusual punishment has been that of capital punishment. In *Furman* v. *Georgia* (1972), a badly split Court rendered invalid every state death-penalty statute then in existence. In a brief *per curiam* order, the five members of the majority were able to agree that "the imposition and the carrying out of the death penalty in these cases constitute cruel and unusual punishment in violation of the Eighth and Fourteenth Amendments." They could agree on little more however—as attested by the fact that each member of the majority wrote a separate opinion.

Although *Furman* foreclosed executions under state statutes then in existence, it did not declare that capital punishment inevitably was unconstitutional. Encouraged by the fact that only Justices William Brennan and Thurgood Marshall regarded all death penalty statutes as *per se* unconstitutional, state legislatures were quick to adopt new capital-punishment statutes designed to meet the objections of the other members of the *Furman* majority. Ultimately, new death penalty schemes were adopted by at least 37 states. With the enactment of these new laws, the Court was forced once again to confront the question of the constitutionality of the death penalty. And in 1976, by a 7–2 vote in *Gregg* v. *Georgia,* it held the death penalty is a constitutionally permissible punishment, at least for carefully defined categories of murder.[18] The same plurality that spoke for the Court on this basic issue, however, went on to say that the Eighth Amendment requires that the sentencing authority be provided with carefully controlled discretion; a bifurcated trial was seen as the ideal procedure. Mandatory death penalty statutes were regarded as unconstitutional.

Since *Gregg* v. *Georgia,* a solid majority of the Supreme Court has refused to reconsider the general constitutionality of capital punishment. In fact, in *Barefoot* v. *Estelle* (1983), it upheld expedited procedures to review habeas corpus petitions filed by death row inmates, betraying an increasing impatience with the endless stays of execution that defense attorneys were securing in the lower courts. In *Pulley* v. *Harris* (1984), it rejected the contention that the Eighth Amendment requires that, before a state appellate court affirms a death sentence, it must engage in a comparative proportionality review, in which it compares the sentence in the case before it with the penalties imposed in similar cases to determine whether they are proportional. To inquire whether a penalty in a particular case is unacceptable because disproportionate to the punishment imposed on others convicted of the same crime would, Justice White wrote for a seven-member majority, depart from *Gregg* and the provisions for the exercise of controlled discretion approved there. In *McCleskey* v. *Kemp* (1987), the Court found no merit in the contention that Georgia's capital punishment process violated the Eighth and Fourteenth Amendments because a statistical study purported to show a disparity in Georgia's imposition of the death sentence based on the race of the murder victim. And in *Stanford* v. *Kentucky* (1989), it sustained the constitutionality of imposing capital punishment on individuals for crimes they had committed at 16 or 17 years of age.

In recent years the Court has reviewed other issues that also have raised questions concerning cruel and unusual punishment. In *Ingraham* v. *Wright* (1977), it held that the Cruel and Unusual Punishments Clause did not apply to "traditional disciplinary practices in public schools" such as paddling. And in *Solem* v. *Helm* (1983), it held that the Eighth Amendment prohibits sentences that are disproportionate to the crime committed and ruled that a sentence of life imprisonment without possibility of parole imposed under a South Dakota recidivist statute upon a defendant who was convicted of uttering a "no account" check for $100 and who had three prior convictions for third degree burglary, one prior conviction for obtaining money under false pretenses, one prior conviction for larceny, and one prior conviction of third-offense driving while intoxicated, was significantly disproportionate to his crime and prohibited by the Cruel and Unusual Punishments Clause.

Prisoners' Rights

Upon conviction and imprisonment, a profound change occurs in a person's legal status. Duly convicted prisoners lose entirely many freedoms enjoyed by free persons; however, they do not relinquish all rights. As the Supreme Court noted in *Wolf* v. *McDonald* (1974), "though his rights may be diminished by the needs and exigencies of the institutional environment, a prisoner is not wholly stripped of constitutional protections when he is imprisoned for crime. There is no iron curtain drawn between the Constitution and the prisons of this country."

There is no question that prisoners always retain the right to the minimal conditions necessary for human survival (i.e., the right to food, clothing, shelter, and medical care). The right of prisoners to a non-life-threatening environment goes beyond the provision of life's necessities; it includes their right to be protected from one another and from themselves. On this last point, lower courts have been more responsive to prisoners' claims than the Supreme Court and have found that prison crowding is unconstitutional. As a federal district court in Florida asserted in *Costello* v. *Wainwright* (1975), prison crowding "endangers the very lives of the inmates" and therefore violates the Eighth Amendment's guarantee against cruel and unusual punishments. The Supreme Court's reluctance to follow the lower courts is understandable, for empirical studies flatly contradict the assertion that crowding is life-threatening. Not only are the overall death rates, accidental death rates, and homicide and suicide rates of inmates two to three times lower than for comparable groups of parolees (controlling for age, race, and sex), but no statistically significant correlations exist between measures of crowding (density and occupancy) and inmate death rates.[19]

Beyond agreement that inmates have the minimal right to a non-life-threatening environment, legal debate rages. Some courts and legal scholars have taken their cues from the Sixth Circuit Court of Appeals in *Coffin* v. *Reichard* (1944) and have declared that prisoners retain all the rights of ordinary citizens except those expressly or by necessary implication taken by law. The Supreme Court's decision in *Procunier* v. *Martinez* (1974) followed this line of reasoning when it held that it would employ a strict scrutiny standard of review to evaluate claims that the rights of prisoners were being denied. It declared that it would sustain limitations of prisoners' rights only if they furthered an important or substantial governmental interest and if they were no greater than necessary to protect that interest.

Fundamentally opposed to *Coffin* and *Procunier* is the view, now dominant on the Supreme Court, that inmates are without rights except for those conferred by law or necessarily implied and that, as a consequence, courts should employ the reasonableness test to assess the legitimacy of restrictions on what prisoners assert to be their rights. In *Turner* v. *Safley* (1987), the Supreme Court articulated this position and rejected the use of strict scrutiny in prisoners' rights cases. Writing for a five-member majority, Justice O'Connor declared that "when a prison regulation impinges on inmates' constitutional rights, the regulation is valid if it is reasonably related to legitimate penological interests." O'Connor announced a four-prong test for measuring reasonableness: (1) Is there "a 'valid, rational connection' between the prison regulation and the legitimate government interest put forward to justify it"? (2) "Are alternative means of exercising the right . . . open to prison inmates"? (3) What is "the impact [that] accommodation of the asserted constitutional right will have on guards and other inmates, and on the allocation of prison resources generally"?, and (4) Is "the absence of ready alternatives . . . evidence of the reasonableness of the prison regulation"? Employing this four-prong test, Justice O'Connor rejected a First Amendment challenge to a Missouri ban on inmate-to-inmate correspondence because the prohibition on correspondence was "logically connected" to legitimate security concerns. In *O'Lone* v. *Shabazz* (1987), the Court applied the same reasonableness test to sustain New Jersey prison policies that resulted in Muslim inmates' inability to attend weekly congregational services.

Security concerns generally trump the claims of prisoners' rights; the Court is hesitant to recognize inmate claims that have the potential of putting at risk the prison itself, the guards, other inmates, or the petitioner. Justice Rehnquist in *Jones* v. *North Carolina Prisoners' Union* (1977) summarized well the Court's deferential approach to these issues: "It is enough to say that they [prison officials] have not been conclusively shown to be wrong in this view. The interest in preserving order and authority in prisons is self-evident."

Applying this reasoning, the Court has denied inmates' claims to a First Amendment right to organize as a prisoners' labor union; rejected the contention that an inmate's right to privacy protects against routine strip and body-cavity searches; and has refused to recognize any inmate legal rights in the ordinary classification process or interprison transfer. As the Court said in *Moody* v. *Daggett* (1976), no due process issues are implicated by "the discretionary transfer of state prisoners to a substantially less agreeable prison, even where the transfer visit[s] a 'grievious loss' upon the inmate. The same is true of prisoner classification and eligibility for rehabilitative programs."

Beyond assuring life's necessities for inmates, the Court has consistently recognized inmates' claims in only two areas: their due process right of access to the courts and their liberty interest in retaining "good time" and avoiding solitary confinement. Concerning the former, the Court has repeatedly insisted that inmates have the right to access to legal redress and that this right of access to the courts requires either an adequate law library or assistance from persons trained in the law (although not necessarily lawyers). Concerning the latter, the Court has held in *Wolf* v. *McDonnell* that inmates have a liberty interest in the good-time credit they have acquired and that they may not be stripped of these credits without a hearing before an impartial tribunal. The Court has not considered either of these rights to jeopardize prison security. Access to the courts poses no problems at all, and as the Court has made explicit in *Hewitt* v. *Helms* (1978) and *Superintendent* v. *Hill* (1985), prison disciplinary proceedings can follow (and need not precede) solitary confinement and can impose sanctions based on the lax evidentiary standard of "some evidence."

Retroactive Application of Criminal-Procedure Guarantees

In interpreting the provisions of the Bill of Rights in such a manner as to expand the procedural protections of criminal defendants and incorporating those provisions through the Fourteenth Amendment to apply to the states, the Court was forced to consider whether its interpretations and incorporations should be given retroactive effect: that is, whether they should be made available to criminal defendants whose cases had already been litigated under rules deemed constitutionally permissible at the time. Until 1965, this question was always answered in the affirmative, for reasons cited by Professor Herman Schwartz: "New constitutional doctrines are not conceptions but rather reflections of principles of 'ordered liberty' fundamental to our legal system. Such principles are equally applicable to past and present trials, for an ethical society cannot seek to retain the fruits of past defaults."[20]

Nevertheless, this commitment to unlimited retroactivity was abandoned in *Linkletter* v. *Walker* (1965), in which Justice Tom Clark concluded for a seven-member majority that the "Constitution neither prohibits nor requires retrospective effect." Instead, he argued, "We must . . . weigh the merits and demerits in each case by looking to the prior history of the rule in question, its purpose, effect, and whether retrospective operation will further or retard its operation."

Several factors contributed to the Court's shift in this matter. The most important, perhaps, was the essentially activist character of the Warren Court. Ineluctable retroactivity was an automatic check, an "inherent restraint," on judicial innovations, because it required that the new rule be applied to all relevant previous cases and that judicial hearings be granted to all those convicted under the old rule to determine whether their rights had been violated and whether, as a consequence, they were eligible for a new trial, outright release, return of all fines, or even damages. It compelled the Court to confront in a most direct manner the possible undesirable consequences of adopting a new rule.

A second factor for the Court's departure from unlimited retroactivity was its desire to forestall hostile public reaction to its more controversial decisions. A case in point was *Johnson* v. *New Jersey* (1966), which limited the retroactive effect of *Escobedo* v. *Illinois* and *Miranda* v. *Arizona* to those cases in which the trial actually had begun after the dates on which *Escobedo* and *Miranda* were decided. *Johnson* was an intensely practical decision by a Court attempting to minimize the hostility that *Escobedo* and *Miranda* had generated. A third, and closely related factor behind the Court's shift was the volatile and provocative problem of federalism. The need to sustain and, indeed, encourage viable and healthy federal-state relationships often intruded on the Court's considerations of retroactivity. Each time the Court incorporated another Bill of Rights guarantee to apply to the states, it imposed new responsibilities on the states in the realm of criminal procedure. The inevitable consequence was hostility to federal-court intervention. Aware of this exacerbating influence on already strained federal-state relations, the Court frequently sought to mitigate the tension by limiting the impact of its decisions through prospective application. Such Court awareness was apparent in *Linkletter* v. *Walker*, in which Justice Clark announced that retroactive application of *Mapp* would not "add harmony to the delicate state-federal relationship."

With virtually all the provisions of the Bill of Rights eventually incorporated to apply to the states, and with the advent of the more judicially restrained Burger and Rehnquist Courts, the problems posed by full retroactive application of criminal procedural guarantees largely disappeared. So, too, has the Court's adherence to *Linkletter*. In *Teague* v. *Lane* (1989), a majority of the Court rejected the *Linkletter* approach to retroactivity and agreed to apply the approach set forth by Justice Harlan in his opinions in *Desist* v. *United States* (1969) and *Mackey* v. *United States* (1971), pursuant to which new constitutional rules are to be applied to all cases on direct review that are not yet final but are not to be applied to previous final judgments attacked on collateral review, except in extraordinary cases in which "fundamental fairness" would be denied by not applying the new rule.

BASIC THEMES IN THE COURT'S CRIMINAL-PROCEDURE DECISIONS

Four basic themes emerge from our review of what the Supreme Court has done in the realm of criminal procedure. In the first place, the Court has been required to pour meaning into the many ambiguous provisions of the Bill of Rights—a task it has accomplished through its power of judgment.

A second theme is the emphasis the Court has placed on protecting minority interests from the potentially tyrannical tendencies of the majority. Recognizing the unequal impact that criminal procedure has had on the poor and on racial minorities the Court has undertaken to eliminate the official aspects of this inequality.

A third basic theme is the Court's growing insistence upon uniform constitutional standards applicable in both state and federal systems. In so insisting, the justices have all but repudiated the traditional view that states are to serve as laboratories, experimenting with novel social and legal schemes and thereby sparing the nation as a whole of the need to suffer the consequences of failure. Although the Court's approach has ensured a certain uniformity of criminal procedure throughout the land, it has also stifled creativity, checked innovation, and jeopardized federalism—an important means to the overall ends of the Constitution.

The final basic theme emerging from our review of the Court's decisions in criminal procedure is a movement toward broadly stated rulings. In recent years the Court has gone far beyond the proscription of particular unconstitutional practices to prescribe affirmative standards of conduct that it regards as essential to safeguard against such practices. In *Miranda,* for example, to avoid the potential violation of a defendant's privilege against self-incrimination during pretrial police interrogations, the Court required that the defendant be advised of his rights and given the right to consult with counsel before and during any interrogation. The use of such prescriptive rulings has certain obvious advantages. They reduce uncertainty and provide police, prosecutors, and lower-court personnel with specific instruction as to which procedures do or do not pass constitutional muster. And they spare the Court the need to pass individual judgment on each and every criminal prosecution, thereby enabling it to devote its time and attention to the further development and refinement of fundamental constitutional protections.

But the movement toward broadly stated rulings is not an unmixed blessing, for it represents a substantial departure from the "judicial" function. Instead of judging the merits of a particular "case or controversy," as charged by Article III of the Constitution, the Court increasingly has become involved in general lawmaking. The consequences of this shift are rather far-reaching. Lawmaking typically emphasizes the formulation and general administration of societywide policies; it is not concerned with the fates of particular individuals or the alleviation of specific instances of injustice. Traditionally, the latter concerns have been left to the judiciary, which understood its function to be the dispensation of justice and equity on an individual, case-by-case level. As the Court abandons this traditional role, there appears to be no other institution ready to step in and take its place.

NOTES

1 *Joint Anti-Fascist Refugee Committee* v. *McGrath* (1951).
2 See *New York* v. *Belton* (1981).
3 See *Oliver* v. *United States* (1984), in which the Supreme Court reaffirmed the "open fields" doctrine, which permits police officers to enter and search a field without a warrant.
4 See *Washington* v. *Chrisman* (1982).

5 Justices Brennan, White, and Marshall dissented in *Ross.* In his dissent, Justice Marshall declared that the majority opinion "not only repeals all realistic limits on warrantless automobile searches it repeals the Fourth Amendment warrant requirement itself."

6 See *Schneckloth* v. *Bustamonte* (1973).

7 See, however, *Steagald* v. *United States* (1981).

8 See Dallin H. Oaks, "Studying the Exclusionary Rule in Search and Seizure," *University of Chicago Law Review* 37 (1970): 665–753; John Kaplan, "The Limits of the Exclusionary Rule," *Stanford Law Review* 26 (1974): 1027–1055; and Steven Schlesinger, *Exclusionary Injustice* (New York: Marcel Dekker, 1977).

9 *Leon* and *Sheppard* were also preceded by *Illinois* v. *Gates* (1983), in which the Court had requested the parties to address specifically the question of the good-faith exception. In the course of its decision, however, the Court relaxed the standard for assessing probable cause and, employing that new standard, concluded that the police in the instant case had not violated the Fourth Amendment; consequently, it had no occasion to address the good-faith exception.

10 *Spano* v. *New York* (1959).

11 *Rodgers* v. *Richmond* (1961).

12 *Lynumn* v. *Illinois* (1963).

13 *Townsend* v. *Sain* (1963).

14 See *Brewer* v. *Williams* (1977).

15 *Harris* raises serious questions: Will not juries who hear statements, introduced as evidence, that the defendant is lying in the witness stand simply treat these statements as evidence of guilt? Will they be able to govern their thoughts by this subtle distinction?

16 See *Rhode Island* v. *Innis* (1980) and also *United States* v. *Havens* (1980).

17 Because the defendant in *Argersinger* had been convicted of carrying a concealed weapon and sentenced to ninety days in jail, the Court left unconsidered the question of whether counsel was required even in cases in which there was no prospect of imprisonment (i.e., in which only a fine was imposed). That issue was resolved in *Scott* v. *Illinois* (1979), in which the Court limited the *Argersinger* holding to instances in which the defendant is in fact sentenced to a term of imprisonment.

18 In *Coker* v. *Georgia* (1977) the Court held that the death penalty for rape constituted cruel and unusual punishment.

19 Ralph A. Rossum, "The Problem of Prison Crowding: On the Limits of Prison Capacity and Judicial Capacity," *Benchmark* I, no. 6: 22–30.

20 Herman Schwartz, "Retroactivity, Reliability, and Due Process," *University of Chicago Law Review* 33 (1966): 753.

SELECTED READINGS

Ake v. *Oklahoma,* 470 U.S. 68 (1985).
Argersinger v. *Hamlin,* 407 U.S. 25 (1972).
Brady v. *United States,* 397 U.S. 742 (1970).
Desist v. *United States,* 394 U.S. 244 (1969).
Furman v. *Georgia,* 408 U.S. 238 (1972).

Pulley v. *Harris*, 456 U.S. 37 (1984).
Stone v. *Powell*, 428 U.S. 465 (1976).
Twining v. *New Jersey*, 211 U.S. 78 (1908).
United States v. *United States District Court*, 407 U.S. 297 (1972).

Berger, Raoul. *The Fourteenth Amendment and the Bill of Rights* (Norman: University of Oklahoma Press, 1989).

Berkson, Larry. *The Concept of Cruel and Unusual Punishment* (Lexington, Mass.: Lexington Books, 1975).

Berns, Walter F. *For Capital Punishment: Crime and the Morality of the Death Penalty* (New York: Basic Books, 1979).

Black, Charles L. *Capital Punishment: The Inevitability of Caprice and Mistake* (New York: Norton, 1974).

Brennan, William J. "Constitutional Adjudication and the Death Penalty: A View from the Court," *Harvard Law Review* 100 (December 1986): 313–331.

Cohen, Fred. "The Law of Prisoners' Rights: An Overview," *Criminal Law Bulletin* 24 (1988): 321–349.

Fairman, Charles. "Does the Fourteenth Amendment Incorporate the Bill of Rights? The Original Understanding." *Stanford Law Review* 2 (1949).

Kamisar, Yale. "A Reply to Critics of the Exclusionary Rule." *Judicature* 62 (1978).

Lewis, Anthony. *Gideon's Trumpet* (New York: Vintage, 1964).

Oaks, Dallin H. "Studying the Exclusionary Rule in Search and Seizure." *University of Chicago Law Review* 37 (1970): 665–753.

Rossum, Ralph A. *The Politics of the Criminal Justice System: An Organizational Analysis* (New York: Marcel Dekker, 1978).

Schlesinger, Steven R. *Exclusionary Injustice* (New York: Marcel Dekker, 1977).

Sigler, Jay A. *Double Jeopardy: The Development of a Legal and Social Policy* (Ithaca, N.Y.: Cornell University Press, 1969).

Tarr, C. Alan and Porter, Mary Cornelia. *State Supreme Courts in State and Nation* (New Haven: Yale University Press, 1988).

Wilbanks, William. *The Myth of a Racist Criminal Justice System* (Monterey, Calif.: Brooks/Cole Publishing, 1987).

Wilson, James Q., ed. *Crime and Public Policy* (San Francisco: Institute for Contemporary Studies, 1983).

Palko v. *Connecticut*

302 U.S. 319; 58 S. Ct. 149; 82 L. Ed. 288 (1937)

Frank Palko was indicted for the crime of first-degree murder. A jury found him guilty of second-degree murder, and he was sentenced to life imprisonment. Thereafter, the state of Connecticut, with the permission of the trial judge, appealed to the Connecticut Supreme Court of Errors under a statute that permitted appeals from the rulings and decisions of the trial court "upon all questions of law arising on the trial of criminal cases . . . in the same manner and to the same effect as if made by the accused." The Supreme Court of Errors set aside the trial court's judgment and ordered a new trial, at which Palko was found guilty of first-degree murder and sentenced to death. The conviction was affirmed by the Supreme Court of Errors, and the case was appealed to the United States Supreme Court. Palko contended that the Connecticut statute was unconstitutional in that the Due Process Clause of the Fourteenth Amendment protected individuals from being tried twice for the same offense. *Opinion of the Court: Cardozo, Black, Brandeis, Hughes, McReynolds, Roberts, Stone, Sutherland. Dissent: Butler.*

MR. JUSTICE CARDOZO delivered the opinion of the Court. . . .

The argument for appellant is that whatever is forbidden by the Fifth Amendment is forbidden by the Fourteenth also. The Fifth Amendment, which is not directed to the states, but solely to the federal government, creates immunity from double jeopardy. No person shall be "subject for the same offense to be twice put in jeopardy of life or limb." The Fourteenth Amendment ordains, "nor shall any State deprive any person of life, liberty, or property, without due process of law." To retry a defendant, though under one indictment and only one, subjects him, it is said, to double jeopardy in violation of the Fifth Amendment, if the prosecution is one on behalf of the United States. From this the consequence is said to follow that there is a denial of life or liberty without due process of law, if the prosecution is one on behalf of the People of a State. . . .

We have said that in appellant's view the Fourteenth Amendment is to be taken as embodying the prohibitions of the Fifth. His thesis is even broader. Whatever would be a violation of the original bill of rights (Amendments I to VIII) if done by the federal government is now equally unlawful by force of the Fourteenth Amendment if done by a state. There is no such general rule.

The Fifth Amendment provides, among other things, that no person shall be held to answer for a capital or otherwise infamous crime unless on presentment or indictment of a grand jury. This court has held that, in prosecutions by a state, presentment or indictment by a grand jury may give way to informations at the instance of a public officer. . . . The Fifth Amendment provides also that no person shall be compelled in any criminal case to be a witness against himself. This court has said that, in prosecutions by a state, the exemption will fail if the state elects to end it. . . . The Sixth Amendment calls for a jury trial in criminal cases and the Seventh for a jury trial in civil cases at common law where the value in controversy shall exceed twenty dollars. This court has ruled that consistently with those amendments trial by jury may be modified by a state or abolished altogether. . . .

On the other hand, the due process clause of the Fourteenth Amendment may make it unlawful for a state to abridge by its statutes the freedom of speech which the First Amendment safeguards against encroachment by the Congress, . . . or the like freedom of the press, . . . or the free exercise of religion, . . . or the right of peaceable assembly without which speech would be unduly trammeled, . . . or the right of one accused of crime to the benefit of counsel. . . . In these and other situations immunities that are valid as against the federal government by force of the specific pledges of particular amendments have been found to be implicit in the concept of ordered liberty, and thus, through the Fourteenth Amendment, become valid as against the states.

The line of division may seem to be wavering and broken if there is a hasty catalogue of the cases on the one side and the other. Reflection and analysis will induce a different view. There emerges the perception of a rationalizing principle which gives to discrete instances a proper order and coherence. The right to trial by jury and the immunity from prosecution except as the result of an indictment may have value and importance. Even so, they are not of the very essence of a scheme of ordered liberty. To abolish them is not to violate a "principle of justice so rooted in the traditions and conscience of our people as to be ranked as fundamental." . . . Few would be so narrow or provincial as to maintain that a fair and enlightened system of justice would be impossible without them. What is true of jury trials and indictments is true also, as the cases show, of the immunity from compulsory self-incrimination . . . . This too might be lost, and justice still be done. Indeed, today as in the past there are students of our penal system who look upon the immunity as a mischief rather than a benefit, and who would limit its scope, or destroy it altogether. No doubt there would remain the need to give protection against torture, physical or mental. . . . Justice, however, would not perish if the accused were subject to a duty to respond to orderly inquiry. The exclusion of these immunities and privileges from the privileges and immunities protected against the action of the states has not been arbitrary or casual. It has been dictated by a study and appreciation of the meaning, the essential implications, of liberty itself.

We reach a different plane of social and moral values when we pass to the privileges and immunities that have been taken over from the earlier articles of the federal bill of rights and brought within the Fourteenth Amendment by a process of absorption. These in their origin were effective against the federal government alone. If the Fourteenth Amendment has absorbed them, the process of absorption has had its source in the belief that neither liberty nor justice would exist if they were sacrificed. . . . This is true, for illustration, of freedom of thought, and speech. Of that freedom one may say that it is the matrix, the indispensable condition, of nearly every other form of freedom. With rare aberrations a pervasive recognition of that truth can be traced in our history, political and legal. So it has come about that the domain of liberty, withdrawn by the Fourteenth Amendment from encroachment by the states, has been enlarged by latter-day judgments to include liberty of the mind as well as liberty of action. The extension became, indeed, a logical imperative when once it was recognized, as long ago it was, that liberty is something more than exemption from physical restraint, and that even in the field of substantive rights and duties the legislative judgment, if oppressive and arbitrary, may be overridden by the courts. . . . Fundamental too in the concept of due process, and so in that of liberty, is the thought that condemnation shall be rendered only after trial. . . . The hearing, moreover, must be a real one, not a sham or a pretense. . . . For that reason, ignorant defendants in a capital case were held to have been condemned unlawfully when in truth, though not in form, they were refused the aid of counsel. . . . The decision did not turn upon the fact that the benefit of counsel would have been guaranteed to the defendants by the provisions of the Sixth Amendment if they had been prosecuted in a federal court. The decision turned upon the fact that in the particular situation laid before us in the evidence the benefit of counsel was essential to the substance of a hearing.

. . . On which side of the line the case made out by the appellant has appropriate location must be the next inquiry and the final one. Is that kind of double jeopardy to which the statute has subjected him a hardship so acute and shocking that our polity will not endure it? Does it violate those "fundamental principles of liberty and justice which lie at the base of all our civil and political institutions"? . . . The answer surely must be "no." What the answer would have to be if the state were permitted after a trial free from error to try the accused over again or to bring another case against him, we have no occasion to consider. We deal with the statute before us and no other. The state is not attempting to wear the accused out by a multitude of cases with accumulated trials. It asks no more than this, that the case against him shall go on until there shall be a trial free from the corrosion of substantial legal error. . . . This is not cruelty at all, nor even vexation in any immoderate degree. If the trial had been infected with error adverse to the accused, there might have been review at his instance, and as often as necessary to purge the vicious taint. A reciprocal privilege, subject at all times to the discretion of the presiding judge, . . . has now been granted to the state. There is here no seismic innovation. The edifice of justice stands, its symmetry, to many, greater than before. . . .

Adamson v. California

332 U.S. 46; 67 S. Ct. 1672; 91 L. Ed. 1903 (1947)

The Constitution and penal code of California permitted the trial judge and prosecuting attorneys to comment adversely upon, and juries to consider as evidence of guilt, a defendant's failure to testify on his own behalf. Admiral Dewey Adamson had declined to testify at his trial for first-degree murder. In the presentation of the case to the jury, the prosecuting attorneys argued that Adamson's refusal to testify was an indication of his guilt. He was convicted and sentenced to death. His conviction was affirmed by the state supreme court and appealed to the United States Supreme Court. *Opinion of the Court: Reed, Burton, Frankfurter, Jackson, Vinson. Concurring opinion: Frankfurter. Dissenting opinions: Black, Douglas; Murphy, Rutledge.*

MR. JUSTICE REED delivered the opinion of the Court.

. . . Appellant urges that the provision of the Fifth Amendment that no person "shall be compelled in any criminal case to be a witness against himself" is a fundamental national privilege or immunity protected against state abridgment by the Fourteenth Amendment or a privilege or immunity secured, through the Fourteenth Amendment, against deprivation by state action because it is a personal right, enumerated in the federal Bill of Rights. . . .

It is settled law that the clause of the Fifth Amendment, protecting a person against being compelled to be a witness against himself, is not made effective by the Fourteenth Amendment as a protection against state action on the ground that freedom from testimonial compulsion is a right of national citizenship, or because it is a personal privilege or immunity secured by the Federal Constitution as one of the rights of man that are listed in the Bill of Rights.

The reasoning that leads to those conclusions starts with the unquestioned premise that the Bill of Rights, when adopted, was for the protection of the individual against the federal government and its provisions were inapplicable to similar actions done by the states. . . . With the adoption of the Fourteenth Amendment, it was suggested that the dual citizenship recognized by its first sentence secured for citizens federal protection for their elemental privileges and immunities of state citizenship. The *Slaughter-House Cases* decided, contrary to the suggestion, that these rights, as privileges and immunities of state citizenship, remained under the sole protection of the state governments. This Court, without the expression of a contrary view upon that phase of the issues before the Court, has approved this determination. . . . This leaves a state free to abridge, within the limits of the due process clause, the privileges and immunities flowing from state citizenship. This reading of the Federal Constitution has heretofore found favor with the majority of this Court as a natural and logical interpretation. It accords with the constitutional doctrine of federalism by leaving to the states the responsibility of dealing with the privileges and immunities of their citizens except those inherent in national citizenship. It is the construction placed upon the amendment by justices whose own experience had given them contemporaneous knowledge of the purposes that led to the adoption of the Fourteenth Amendment. This construction has become embedded in our federal system as a functioning element in preserving the balance between national and state power. We reaffirm the conclusion . . . that protection against self-incrimination is not a privilege or immunity of national citizenship. . . .

MR. JUSTICE FRANKFURTER, concurring. . . .

The short answer to the suggestion that the provision of the Fourteenth Amendment, which ordains "nor shall any State deprive any person of life, liberty, or property, without due process of law," was a way of saying that every State must thereafter initiate prosecutions through indictment by a grand jury, must have trial by such a jury of twelve in criminal cases, and must have trial by such a jury in common law suits where the amount in controversy exceeds twenty dollars, is that it is a strange way of saying it. It would be extraordinarily strange for a Constitution to convey such specific commands in such a roundabout and inexplicit way. . . . Those reading the English language with the meaning which it ordinarily conveys, those conversant with the political and legal history of the concept of due process, those sensitive to the relations of the States to the central government as well as the relation of some of the provisions of the Bill of Rights to the process of justice, would hardly recognize the Fourteenth Amendment as a cover for the various explicit provisions of the first eight Amendments. Some of these are enduring reflections of experience with human nature, while some express the restricted views of Eighteenth-Century England regarding the best methods for the ascertainment of facts. . . .

It may not be amiss to restate the pervasive function of the Fourteenth Amendment in exacting from the States observance of basic liberties. . . . The Amendment neither comprehends the specific provisions by which the founders deemed it appropriate to restrict the Federal Government nor is it confined to them. The Due Process Clause of the Fourteenth Amendment has an independent potency, precisely as does the Due Process Clause of the Fifth Amendment in relation to the Federal Government. It ought not to require argument to reject the notion that due process of law meant one thing in the Fifth Amendment and another in the Fourteenth. The Fifth Amendment specifically prohibits prosecution of an "infamous crime" except upon indictment; it forbids double jeopardy; it bars compelling a person to be a witness against himself in any criminal case; it precludes deprivation of "life, liberty, or property, without due process of law. . . ." Are Madison and his contemporaries in the framing of the Bill of Rights to be charged with writing into it a meaningless clause? To consider "due process of law" as merely a shorthand statement of other specific clauses in the same amendment is to attribute to the authors and proponents of this Amendment ignorance of, or indifference to, a historic conception which was one of the great instruments in the arsenal of constitutional freedom which the Bill of Rights was to protect and strengthen. . . .

. . . The relevant question is whether the criminal proceedings which resulted in conviction deprived the accused of the due process of law to which the United States Constitution entitled him. Judicial review of that guaranty of the Fourteenth Amendment inescapably imposes upon this Court an exercise of judgment upon the whole course of the proceedings in order to ascertain whether they offend those canons of decency and fairness which express the notions of justice of English-speaking peoples even toward those charged with the most heinous offenses. These standards of justice are not authoritatively formulated anywhere as though as they were prescriptions in a pharmacopoeia. But neither does the application of the Due Process Clause imply that judges are wholly at large. The judicial judgment in applying the Due Process Clause must move within the limits of accepted notions of justice and is not to be based upon the idiosyncrasies of a merely personal judgment. The fact that judges among themselves may differ whether in a particular case a trial offends accepted notions of justice is not disproof that general rather than idiosyncratic standards are applied. An important safeguard against such merely individual judgment is an alert deference to the judgment of the State court under review.

MR. JUSTICE BLACK, dissenting. . . .

This decision reasserts a constitutional theory spelled out in *Twining* v. *New Jersey* [1908], that this Court is endowed by the Constitution with boundless power under "natural law" periodically to expand and contract constitutional standards to conform to the Court's conception of what at a particular time constitutes "civilized decency" and "fundamental liberty and justice." Invoking this *Twining* rule, the Court concludes that although comment upon testimony in a federal court would violate the Fifth Amendment, identical comment in a state court does not violate today's fashion in civilized decency and fundamentals and is therefore not prohibited by the Federal Constitution as amended. . . .

. . . I would not reaffirm the *Twining* decision. I think that decision and the "natural law" theory of the Constitution upon which it relies degrade the constitutional safeguards of the Bill of Rights and simultaneously appropriate for this Court a broad power which we are not authorized by the Constitution to exercise. . . . My reasons for believing that the *Twining* decision should not be revitalized can best be understood by reference to the constitutional, judicial, and general history that preceded and followed the case. That reference must be abbreviated far more than is justified but for the necessary limitations of opinion-writing. . . .

My study of the historical events that culminated in the Fourteenth Amendment, and the expressions of those who sponsored and favored, as well as those who opposed its submission and passage, persuades me that one of the chief objects that the provisions of the Amendment's first section, separately, and as a whole, were intended to accomplish was to make the Bill of Rights, applicable to the states.

. . . I am attaching to this dissent an appendix which contains a résumé, by no means complete, of the Amendment's history. In my judgment that history conclusively demonstrates that the language of the first section of the Fourteenth Amendment, taken as a whole, was thought by those responsible for its submission to the people, and by those who opposed its submission, sufficiently explicit to guarantee that thereafter no state could deprive its citizens of the privileges and protections of the Bill of Rights. . . .

. . . I further contend that the "natural law" formula which the Court uses to reach its conclusion in this case should be abandoned as an incongruous excrescence on our Constitution. I believe that formula to be itself a violation of our Constitution, in that it subtly conveys to courts, at the expense of legislatures, ultimate power over public policies in fields where no specific provision of the Constitution limits legislative power. . . .

It is an illusory apprehension that literal application of some or of all the provisions of the Bill of Rights to the States would unwisely increase the sum total of the powers of this Court to invalidate state legislation. The Federal Government has not been harmfully burdened by the requirement that enforcement of federal laws affecting civil liberty conform literally to the Bill of Rights. Who would advocate its repeal? It must be conceded, of course, that the natural-law-due-process formula, which the Court today reaffirms, has been interpreted to limit substantially this Court's power to prevent state violations of the individual civil liberties guaranteed by the Bill of Rights. But this formula also has been used in the past, and can be used in the future, to license this Court, in considering regulatory legislation, to roam at large in the broad expanses of policy and morals and to trespass, all too freely, on the legislative domain of the states as well as the Federal Government. . . .

[Appendix to opinion of BLACK, J., omitted.]

MR. JUSTICE MURPHY, with whom MR. JUSTICE RUTLEDGE concurs, dissenting.

While in substantial agreement with the views of Mr. Justice Black, I have one reservation and one addition to make. . . .

I agree that the specific guarantees of the Bill of Rights should be carried over intact into the first section of the Fourteenth Amendment. But I am not prepared to say that the latter is entirely and necessarily limited by the Bill of Rights. Occasions may arise where a proceeding falls so far short of conforming to fundamental standards of procedure as to warrant constitutional condemnation in terms of a lack of due process despite the absence of a specific provision in the Bill of Rights. . . .

Duncan v. *Louisiana*

391 U.S. 145; 88 S. Ct. 1444; 20 L. Ed. 2d 491 (1968)

Gary Duncan, a black, was convicted in a Louisiana court of simple battery for slapping a white person on the elbow. Under state law, the maximum sentence for this misdemeanor was two years imprisonment and a $300 fine. During his court proceedings, Duncan requested a jury trial, but the judge denied his request, noting that the state constitution permitted jury trials only in instances in which hard labor or capital punishment might be imposed. Sentenced to sixty days in prison and a fine of $150, Duncan unsuccessfully petitioned the Louisiana Supreme Court for review, and then he appealed to the United States Supreme Court. He contended that the Sixth and Fourteenth amendments guaranteed the right to a jury trial in state prosecutions for crimes punishable by two years imprisonment or more. *Opinion of the Court: White, Black, Brennan, Douglas, Fortas, White, Marshall. Concurring opinions: Black, Douglas; Fortas. Dissenting opinion: Harlan, Stewart.*

MR. JUSTICE WHITE delivered the opinion of the Court. . . .

The test for determining whether a right extended by the Fifth and Sixth Amendments with respect to federal criminal proceedings is also protected against state action by the Fourteenth Amendment has been phrased in a variety of ways in the opinions of this Court. The question has been asked whether a right is among those " 'fundamental principles of liberty and justice which lie at the base of all our civil and political institutions,' " . . . whether it is "basic in our system of jurisprudence," . . . and whether it is "a fundamental right, essential to a fair trial." . . . The claim before us is that the right to trial by jury guaranteed by the Sixth Amendment meets these tests. The position of Louisiana, on the other hand, is that the Constitution imposes upon the States no duty to give a jury trial in any criminal case, regardless of the seriousness of the crime or the size of the punishment which may be imposed. Because we believe that trial by jury in criminal cases is fundamental to the American scheme of justice, we hold that the Fourteenth Amendment guarantees a right of jury trial in all criminal cases which—were they to be tried in a federal court—would come within the Sixth Amendment's guarantee. Since we consider the appeal before us to be such a case, we hold that the Constitution was violated when appellant's demand for jury trial was refused. . . .

The guarantees of jury trial in the Federal and State Constitutions reflect a profound judgment about the way in which law should be enforced and justice administered. A right to jury trial is granted to criminal defendants in order to prevent oppression by the Government. Those who wrote our constitutions knew from history and experience that it was necessary to protect against unfounded criminal charges brought to eliminate enemies and against judges too responsive to the voice of higher authority. The framers of the constitutions strove to create an independent judiciary but insisted upon further protection against arbitrary action. Providing an accused with the right to be tried by a jury of his peers gave him an inestimable safeguard against the corrupt or overzealous prosecutor and against the compliant, biased, or eccentric judge. If the defendant preferred the common-sense judgment of a jury to the more tutored but perhaps less sympathetic reaction of the single judge, he was to have it. Beyond this, the jury trial provisions in the Federal and State Constitutions reflect a fundamental decision about the exercise of official power—a reluctance to entrust plenary powers over the life and liberty of the citizen to one judge or to a group of judges. Fear of unchecked power, so typical of our State and Federal Governments in other respects, found expression in the criminal law in this insistence upon community participation in the determination of guilt or innocence. The deep commitment of the Nation to the right of jury trial in serious criminal cases as a defense against arbitrary law enforcement qualifies for protection under the Due Process Clause of the Fourteenth Amendment, and must therefore be respected by the States.

Louisiana's final contention is that even if it must grant jury trials in serious criminal cases, the conviction before us is valid and constitutional because here the petitioner was tried for simple battery and was sentenced to only 60 days in the parish prison. We are not persuaded. It is doubtless true that there is a category of petty crimes or offenses which is not subject to the

Sixth Amendment jury trial provision and should not be subject to the Fourteenth Amendment jury trial requirement here applied to the States. Crimes carrying possible penalties up to six months do not require a jury trial if they otherwise qualify as petty offenses. . . . But the penalty authorized for a particular crime is of major relevance in determining whether it is serious or not and may in itself, if severe enough, subject the trial to the mandates of the Sixth Amendment. . . . The penalty authorized by the law of the locality may be taken "as a gauge of its social and ethical judgments" . . . of the crime in question. . . . In the case before us the Legislature of Louisiana has made simple battery a criminal offense punishable by imprisonment for up to two years and a fine. The question, then, is whether a crime carrying such a penalty is an offense which Louisiana may insist on trying without a jury.

We think not. . . Of course the boundaries of the petty offense category have always been ill-defined, if not ambulatory. In the absence of an explicit constitutional provision, the definitional task necessarily falls on the courts, which must either pass upon the validity of legislative attempts to identify those petty offenses which are exempt from jury trial or, where the legislature has not addressed itself to the problem, themselves face the question in the first instance. In either case it is necessary to draw a line in the spectrum of crime, separating petty from serious infractions. This process, although essential, cannot be wholly satisfactory, for it requires attaching different consequences to events which, when they lie near the line, actually differ very little.

. . . In the federal system, petty offenses are defined as those punishable by no more than six months in prison and a $500 fine. In 49 of the 50 States crimes subject to trial without a jury, which occasionally include simple battery, are punishable by not more than one year in jail. Moreover, in the late 18th century in America crimes triable without a jury were for the most part punishable by no more than a six-month prison term, although there appear to have been exceptions to this rule. We need not, however, settle in this case the exact location of the line between petty offenses and serious crimes. It is sufficient for our purposes to hold that a crime punishable by two years in prison is, based on past and contemporary standards in this country, a serious crime and not a petty offense. Consequently, appellant was entitled to a jury trial and it was error to deny it.

MR. JUSTICE BLACK, with whom MR. JUSTICE DOUGLAS joins, concurring. . . .

In closing I want to emphasize that I believe as strongly as ever that the Fourteenth Amendment was intended to make the Bill of Rights applicable to the States. I have been willing to support the selective incorporation doctrine, however, as an alternative, although perhaps less historically supportable than complete incorporation. The selective incorporation process, if used properly, does limit the Supreme Court in the Fourteenth Amendment field to specific Bill of Rights' protections only and keeps judges from roaming at will in their own notions of what policies outside the Bill of Rights are desirable and what are not. And, most importantly for me, the selective incorporation process has the virtue of having already worked to make most of the Bill of Rights' protections applicable to the States.

MR. JUSTICE HARLAN, whom MR. JUSTICE STEWART joins, dissenting.

Every American jurisdiction provides for trial by jury in criminal cases. The question before us is not whether jury trial is an ancient institution, which it is; nor whether it plays a significant role in the administration of criminal justice, which it does; nor whether it will endure, which it shall. The question in this case is whether the State of Louisiana, which provides trial by jury for all felonies, is prohibited by the Constitution from trying charges of simple battery to the court alone. In my view, the answer to that question, mandated alike by our constitutional history and by the longer history of trial by jury, is clearly "no." . . .

The Court's approach to this case is an uneasy and illogical compromise among the views of various Justices on how the Due Process Clause should be interpreted. The Court does not say that those who framed the Fourteenth Amendment intended to make the Sixth Amendment applicable to the States. And the Court concedes that it finds nothing unfair about the procedure by which the present appellant was tried. Nevertheless, the Court reverses his conviction: it holds, for some reason not apparent to me, that the Due Process Clause incorporates the particular clause of the Sixth Amendment that requires trial by jury in federal criminal cases—including, as I read its opinion, the sometimes trivial accompanying baggage of judicial interpretation in federal contexts. . . .

A few members of the Court have taken the position that the intention of those who drafted the first section of the Fourteenth Amendment was simply, and exclusively, to make the provisions of the first eight Amendments applicable to state action. . . . Neither history, nor sense, supports using the Fourteenth Amendment to put the States in a constitutional straitjacket with respect to their own development in the administration of criminal or civil law.

Although I therefore fundamentally disagree with the total incorporation view of the Fourteenth Amendment, it seems to me that such a position does at least have the virtue, lacking in the Court's selective incorporation approach, of internal consistency: we look to the Bill of Rights, word for word, clause for clause, precedent for precedent because, it is said, the men who wrote the Amendment wanted it that way. . . .

Apart from the approach taken by the absolute incorporationists, I can see only one method of analysis that has any internal logic. That is to start with the words "liberty" and "due process of law" and attempt to define them in a way that accords with American traditions and our system of government. This approach, involving a much more discriminating process of adjudication than does "incorporation," is, albeit difficult, the one that was followed throughout the 19th and most of the present century. It entails a "gradual process of judicial inclusion and exclusion," seeking, with due recognition of constitutional tolerance for state experimentation and disparity, to ascertain those "immutable principles . . . of free government which no member of the Union may disregard." . . .

The relationship of the Bill of Rights to this "gradual process" seems to me to be twofold. In the first place it has long been clear that the Due Process Clause imposes some restrictions on state action that parallel Bill of Rights restrictions on federal action. Second, and more important than this accidental overlap, is the fact that the Bill of Rights is evidence, at various points, of the content Americans find in the term "liberty" and of American standards of fundamental fairness. . . .

Today's Court still remains unwilling to accept the total incorporationists' view of the history of the Fourteenth Amendment. This, if accepted, would afford a cogent reason for applying the Sixth Amendment to the States. The Court is also, apparently, unwilling to face the task of determining whether denial of trial by jury in the situation before us, or in other situations, is fundamentally unfair. Consequently, the Court has compromised on the case of the incorporationist position, without its internal logic. It has simply assumed that the question before us is whether the Jury Trial Clause of the Sixth Amendment should be incorporated into the Fourteenth, jot-for-jot and case-for-case, or ignored. Then the Court merely declares that the clause in question is "in" rather than "out." . . .

Since, as I see it, the Court has not even come to grips with the issues in this case, it is necessary to start from the beginning. When a criminal defendant contends that his state conviction lacked "due process of law," the question before this Court, in my view, is whether he was denied any element of fundamental procedural fairness. . . .

The argument that jury trial is not a requisite of due process is quite simple. The central proposition . . . is that "due process of law" requires only that criminal trials be fundamentally fair. As stated above, apart from the theory that it was historically intended as a mere shorthand for the Bill of Rights, I do not see what else "due process of law" can intelligibly be thought to mean. If due process of law requires only fundamental fairness, then the inquiry in each case must be whether a state trial process was a fair one. The Court has held, properly I think, that in an adversary process it is a requisite of fairness, for which there is no adequate substitute, that a criminal defendant be afforded a right to counsel and to cross-examine opposing witnesses. But it simply has not been demonstrated, nor, I think, can it be demonstrated, that trial by jury is the only fair means of resolving issues of fact. . . .

. . . There is a wide range of views on the desirability of trial by jury, and on the ways to make it most effective when it is used; there is also considerable variation from State to State in local conditions such as the size of the criminal caseload, the ease or difficulty of summoning jurors, and other trial conditions bearing on fairness. We have before us, therefore, an almost perfect example of a situation in which the celebrated dictum of Mr. Justice Brandeis should be invoked. It is, he said, "one of the happy incidents of the federal system that a single courageous State may, if its citizens choose, serve as a laboratory. . . ." [*New State Ice Co.* v. *Liebmann* . . . (dissenting opinion)]. This Court, other courts, and the political process are available to correct any experiments in criminal procedure that prove fundamentally unfair to defendants. That is not what is being done today: instead, and quite without reason, the Court has chosen to impose upon every State one means of trying criminal cases; it is a good means, but it is not the only fair means, and it is not demonstrably better than the alternatives States might devise.

New Jersey v. *T.L.O.*

469 U.S. 325, 105 S. Ct. 733; 83 L. Ed. 2d 720 (1985)

T.L.O., a fourteen-year-old freshman at Piscataway High School in Middlesex County, New Jersey, was discovered smoking cigarettes in a school lavatory and was brought to the Principal's Office. There, Assistant Vice Principal Theodore Choplick questioned her, and when she denied that she had been smoking, he demanded to see her purse. Upon opening the purse, he found a pack of cigarettes and also noticed cigarette rolling papers, commonly associated with the use of marijuana. He then proceeded to search the purse thoroughly and found some marijuana and drug paraphernalia, a substantial amount of money, a list of students who owed her money, and two letters implicating her in marijuana dealing. The State brought a delinquency petition against her, and the juvenile court, after denying her motion to suppress the evidence found in her purse, adjudged her to be delinquent. The Appellate Division of the New Jersey Superior Court affirmed that there had been no Fourth Amendment violation, but the New Jersey Supreme Court reversed and ordered the suppression of the evidence, holding that the search of her purse was unreasonable. The U.S. Supreme Court granted a writ of certiorari. *Opinion of the Court: White, Burger, O'Connor, Powell, Rehnquist. Concurring opinion: Powell, O'Connor. Concurring in the Judgment: Blackmun. Concurring in part and dissenting in part: Brennan, Marshall; Stevens, Brennan, Marshall.*

JUSTICE WHITE delivered the opinion of the Court.

In determining whether the search at issue in this case violated the Fourth Amendment, we are faced initially with the question whether that Amendment's prohibition on unreasonable searches and seizures applies to searches conducted by public school officials. We hold that it does.

To hold that the Fourth Amendment applies to searches conducted by school authorities is only to begin the inquiry into the standards governing such searches. Although the underlying command of the Fourth Amendment is always that searches and seizures be reasonable, what is reasonable depends on the context within which a search takes place. The determination of the standard of reasonableness governing any specific class of searches requires "balancing the need to search against the invasion which the search entails." . . . On one side of the balance are arrayed the individual's legitimate expectations of privacy and personal security; on the other, the government's need for effective methods to deal with breaches of public order.

How, then, should we strike the balance between the schoolchild's legitimate expectations of privacy and the school's equally legitimate need to maintain an environment in which learning can take place? It is evident that the school setting requires some easing of the restrictions to which searches by public authorities are ordinarily subject. The warrant requirement, in particular, is unsuited to the school environment: requiring a teacher to obtain a warrant before searching a child suspected of an infraction of school rules (or of the criminal law) would unduly interfere with the maintenance of the swift and informal disciplinary procedures needed in the schools. Just as we have in other cases dispensed with the warrant requirement when "the burden of obtaining a warrant is likely to frustrate the governmental purpose behind the search," . . . we hold today that school officials need not obtain a warrant before searching a student who is under their authority.

The school setting also requires some modification of the level of suspicion of illicit activity needed to justify a search. Ordinarily, a search—even one that may permissibly be carried out without a warrant—must be based upon "probable cause" to believe that a violation of the law has occurred. . . . However, "probable cause" is not an irreducible requirement of a valid search. The fundamental command of the Fourth Amendment is that searches and seizures be reasonable, and although "both the concept of probable cause and the requirement of a warrant bear on the reasonableness of a search, . . . in certain limited circumstances neither is required." . . . Thus, we have in a number of cases recognized the legality of searches and seizures based on suspicions that, although "reasonable," do not rise to the level of probable cause. . . . Where a careful balancing of governmental and private interests suggests that the public interest is best served by a Fourth Amendment standard of reasonableness that stops short of probable cause, we have not hesitated to adopt such a standard.

We join the majority of courts that have examined this issue in concluding that the accommodation of the privacy interests of schoolchildren with the substantial need of teachers and administrators for freedom to maintain order in the schools does not require strict adherence to the requirement that searches be based on probable cause to believe that the subject of the search has violated or is violating the law. Rather, the legality of a search of a student should depend simply on the reasonableness, under all the circumstances, of the search. Determining the reasonableness of any search involves a twofold inquiry: first, one must consider "whether the . . . action was justified at its inception," . . . second, one must determine whether the search as actually conducted "was reasonably related in scope to the circumstances which justified the interference in the first place." . . . Under ordinary circumstances, a search of a student by a teacher or other school official will be "justified at its inception" when there are reasonable grounds for suspecting that the search will turn up evidence that the student has violated or is violating either the law or the rules of the school. Such a search will be permissible in its scope when the measures adopted are reasonably related to the objectives of the search and not excessively intrusive in light of the age and sex of the student and the nature of the infraction.

This standard will, we trust, neither unduly burden the efforts of school authorities to maintain order in their schools nor authorize unrestrained intrusions upon the privacy of schoolchildren. By focusing attention on the question of reasonableness, the standard will spare teachers and school administrators the necessity of schooling themselves in the niceties of probable cause and permit them to regulate their conduct according to the dictates of reason and common sense. At the same time, the reasonableness standard should ensure that the interests of students will be invaded no more than is necessary to achieve the legitimate end of preserving order in the schools.

There remains the question of the legality of the search in this case. . . .

. . . Our review of the facts surrounding the search leads us to conclude that the search was in no sense unreasonable for Fourth Amendment purposes. The incident that gave rise to this case actually involved two separate searches, with the first—the search for cigarettes—providing the suspicion that gave rise to the second—the search for marihuana. Although it is the fruits of the second search that are at issue here, the validity of the search for marihuana must depend on the reasonableness of the initial search for cigarettes, as there would have been no reason to suspect that T.L.O. possessed marihuana had the first search not taken place. Accordingly, it is to the search for cigarettes that we first turn our attention.

. . . T.L.O. had been accused of smoking, and had denied the accusation in the strongest possible terms when she stated that she did not smoke at all. Surely it cannot be said that under these circumstances, T.L.O.'s possession of cigarettes would be irrelevant to the charges against her or to her response to those charges. T.L.O.'s possession of cigarettes, once it was discovered, would both corroborate the report that she had been smoking and undermine the credibility of her defense to the charge of smoking. To be sure, the discovery of the cigarettes would not prove that T.L.O. had been smoking in the lavatory; nor would it, strictly speaking, necessarily be inconsistent with her claim that she did not smoke at all. But it is universally recognized that evidence, to be relevant to an inquiry, need not conclusively prove the ultimate fact in issue, but only have "any tendency to make the existence of any fact that is of consequence to the determination of the action more probable or less probable than it would be without the evidence." . . . The relevance of T.L.O.'s possession of cigarettes to the question whether she had been smoking and to the credibility of her denial that she smoked supplied the necessary "nexus" between the item searched for and the infraction under investigation. . . .

Our conclusion that Mr. Choplick's decision to open T.L.O.'s purse was reasonable brings us to the question of the further search for marihuana once the pack of cigarettes was located. The suspicion upon which the search for marihuana was founded was provided when Mr. Choplick observed a package of rolling papers in the purse as he removed the pack of cigarettes. Although T.L.O. does not dispute the reasonableness of Mr. Choplick's belief that the rolling papers indicated the presence of marihuana, she does contend that the scope of the search Mr. Choplick conducted exceeded permissible bounds when he seized and read certain letters that implicated T.L.O. in drug dealing. This argument, too, is unpersuasive. The discovery of the rolling papers concededly gave rise to a reasonable suspicion that T.L.O. was carrying marihuana as well as cigarettes in her purse. This suspicion justified further exploration of T.L.O.'s purse, which turned up more evidence of drug-related activities: a pipe, a number of plastic bags of the type commonly used to store marihuana, a small quantity of marihuana, and a fairly substantial amount of money. Under these circumstances, it was not unreasonable to extend the search to a separate zippered compartment of the purse; and when a search of that compartment revealed an index card containing a list of "people who owe me money" as well as two letters, the inference that T.L.O. was involved in marihuana trafficking was substantial enough to justify Mr. Choplick in examining the letters to determine whether they contained any further evidence. In short, we cannot conclude that the search for marihuana was unreasonable in any respect.

Because the search resulting in the discovery of the evidence of marihuana dealing by T.L.O. was reasonable, the New Jersey Supreme Court's decision to exclude that evidence from T.L.O.'s juvenile delinquency proceedings on Fourth Amendment grounds was erroneous. Accordingly, the judgment of the Supreme Court of New Jersey is

Reversed.

JUSTICE BRENNAN, with whom JUSTICE MARSHALL joins, concurring in part and dissenting in part.

I fully agree [that] . . . teachers, like all government officials, must conform their conduct to the Fourth Amendment's protections of personal privacy and personal security, I do not, however, otherwise join the Court's opinion. . . .

I emphatically disagree with the Court's decision to cast aside the constitutional probable-cause standard when assessing the constitutional validity of a schoolhouse search. . . . This innovation finds support neither in precedent nor policy and portends a dangerous weakening of the purpose of the Fourth Amendment to protect the privacy and security of our citizens. Moreover, even if this Court's historic understanding of the Fourth Amendment were mistaken and a balancing test of some kind were appropriate, any such test that gave adequate weight to the privacy and security interests protected by the Fourth Amendment would not reach the preordained result the Court's conclusory analysis reaches today. Therefore, because I believe that the balancing test used by the Court today is flawed both in its inception and in its execution, I respectfully dissent.

Applying the constitutional probable-cause standard to the facts of this case, I would find that

Mr. Choplick's search violated T.L.O.'s Fourth Amendment rights. . . .

On my view of the case, we need not decide whether the initial search conducted by Mr. Choplick—the search for evidence of the smoking violation that was completed when Mr. Choplick found the pack of cigarettes—was valid. For Mr. Choplick at that point did not have probable cause to continue to rummage through T.L.O.'s purse. Mr. Choplick's suspicion of marihuana possession at this time was based *solely* on the presence of the package of cigarette papers. The mere presence without more of such a staple item of commerce is insufficient to warrant a person of reasonable caution in inferring both that T.L.O. had violated the law by possessing marihuana and that evidence of that violation would be found in her purse. Just as a police officer could not obtain a warrant to search a home based solely on his claim that he had seen a package of cigarette papers in that home, Mr. Choplick was not entitled to search possibly the most private possessions of T.L.O. based on the mere presence of a package of cigarette papers. Therefore, the fruits of this illegal search must be excluded and the judgment of the New Jersey Supreme Court affirmed.

National Treasury Employees Union v. *Von Raab*

109 S. Ct. 1384 (1989)

The United States Customs Service has as a primary enforcement mission the interdiction and seizure of illegal drugs smuggled into the country. It implemented a drug-screening program requiring urinalysis tests from Service employees seeking transfer or promotion to positions having a direct involvement in drug interdiction or whose positions required them to carry firearms or handle classified material. Among other things, the program required that applicants be notified that their selection depends upon successful completion of drug screening, sets forth procedures for collection and analysis of the requisite samples and procedures designed both to ensure against adulteration or substitution of specimens and to limit the intrusion on employee privacy, and provides that test results may not be turned over to any other agency, including criminal prosecutors, without the employees' written consent. The National Treasury Employees Union filed suit against the Commissioner of the U. S. Customs Service on behalf of Customs employees seeking covered positions, alleging that the drug-testing program violated the Fourth Amendment. The District Court for the Eastern District of Louisiana agreed and enjoined the program. The Court of Appeals for the Fifth Circuit vacated the injunction, holding that, while the program amounts to a search within the meaning of the Fourth Amendment, such searches are reasonable in light of their limited scope and the Customs Services's strong interest in detecting drug use among employees in covered positions. The Supreme Court granted certiorari.
Opinion of the Court: Kennedy, Blackmun, O'Connor, Rehnquist, White.
Dissenting opinions: Marshall, Brennan; Scalia, Stevens.

JUSTICE KENNEDY delivered the opinion of the Court.

We granted certiorari to decide whether it violates the Fourth Amendment for the United States Customs Service to require a urinalysis test from employees who seek transfer or promotion to certain positions. . . . We now affirm so much of the judgment of the court of appeals as upheld the testing of employees directly involved in drug interdiction or required to carry firearms.

We vacate the judgment to the extent it upheld the testing of applicants for positions requiring the incumbent to handle classified materials, and remand for further proceedings.

In *Skinner* v. *Railway Labor Executives Assn.*, . . . decided today, we hold that federal regulations requiring employees of private railroads to produce urine samples for chemical testing implicate the Fourth Amendment, as those tests invade reasonable expectations of privacy. . . . In view of our holding in *Railway Labor Executives* that urine tests are searches, it follows that the Customs Service's drug testing program must meet the reasonableness requirement of the Fourth Amendment.

While we have often emphasized, and reiterate today, that a search must be supported, as a general matter, by a warrant issued upon probable cause, . . . our decision in *Railway Labor Executives* reaffirms the longstanding principle that neither a warrant nor probable cause, nor, indeed, any measure of individualized suspicion, is an indispensable component of reasonableness in every circumstance. . . . *New Jersey* v. *T. L. O.* . . . As we note in *Railway Labor Executives,* our cases establish that where a Fourth Amendment intrusion serves special governmental needs, beyond the normal need for law enforcement, it is necessary to balance the individual's privacy expectations against the Government's interests to determine whether it is impractical to require a warrant or some level of individualized suspicion in the particular context. . . .

It is clear that the Customs Service's drug testing program is not designed to serve the ordinary needs of law enforcement. Test results may not be used in a criminal prosecution of the employee without the employee's consent. The purposes of the program are to deter drug use among those eligible for promotion to sensitive positions within the Service and to prevent the promotion of drug users to those positions. These substantial interests, no less than the Government's concern for safe rail transportation at issue in *Railway Labor Executives,* present a special need that may justify departure from the ordinary warrant and probable cause requirements. . . .

Petitioners do not contend that a warrant is required by the balance of privacy and governmental interests in this context, nor could any such contention withstand scrutiny. We have recognized before that requiring the Government to procure a warrant for every work-related intrusion "would conflict with 'the common-sense realization that government offices could not function if every employment decision became a constitutional matter.' " . . . The Customs Service has been entrusted with pressing responsibilities, and its mission would be compromised if it were required to seek search warrants in connection with routine, yet sensitive, employment decisions.

Furthermore, a warrant would provide little or nothing in the way of additional protection of personal privacy. A warrant serves primarily to advise the citizen that an intrusion is authorized by law and limited in its permissible scope and to interpose a neutral magistrate between the citizen and the law enforcement officer "engaged in the often competitive enterprise of ferreting out crime." . . . Under the Customs program, every employee who seeks a transfer to a covered position knows that he must take a drug test, and is likewise aware of the procedures the Service must follow in administering the test. A covered employee is simply not subject "to the discretion of the official in the field." . . . The process becomes automatic when the employee elects to apply for, and thereafter pursue, a covered position. Because the Service does not make a discretionary determination to search based on a judgment that certain conditions are present, there are simply "no special facts for a neutral magistrate to evaluate." . . .

Even where it is reasonable to dispense with the warrant requirement in the particular circumstances, a search ordinarily must be based on probable cause. . . . Our cases teach, however, that the probable-cause standard " 'is peculiarly related to criminal investigations.' " . . . In particular, the traditional probable-cause standard may be unhelpful in analyzing the reasonableness of routine administrative functions, . . . especially where the Government seeks to *prevent* the development of hazardous conditions or to detect violations that rarely generate articulable grounds for searching any particular place or person. . . . Our precedents have settled that, in certain limited circumstances, the Government's need to discover such latent or hidden conditions, or to prevent their development, is sufficiently compelling to justify the intrusion on privacy entailed by conducting such searches without any measure of individualized suspicion. . . . We think the Government's need to conduct the suspicionless searches required by the Customs program outweighs the privacy interests of employees engaged directly in drug interdiction, and of those who otherwise are required to carry firearms. . . . The Government has a compelling interest in ensuring that front-line interdiction personnel are physically fit, and have unimpeachable integrity and judgment. Indeed, the Government's interest here is at least as important as its interest in searching travelers entering the country. We have long held that travelers seeking to enter the country may be stopped and required to submit to a routine search without probable cause, or even founded suspicion, "because of national self protection reasonably requiring one entering the country to identify himself as entitled to come in, and his belongings as effects which may be lawfully brought in." . . . This national interest in self protection could be irreparably damaged if those charged with safeguarding it were, because of their own drug use, unsympathetic to their mission of interdicting narcotics. A drug user's indifference to the Service's basic mission or, even worse, his active complicity with the malefactors, can facilitate importation of sizable drug shipments or block apprehension of dangerous criminals. The public interest demands effective measures to bar drug users from positions directly involving the interdiction of illegal drugs.

The public interest likewise demands effective measures to prevent the promotion of drug users to positions that require the incumbent to carry a firearm, even if the incumbent is not engaged directly in the interdiction of drugs. Customs employees who may use deadly force plainly "discharge duties fraught with such risks of injury to others that even a monetary lapse of attention can have disastrous consequences." . . . We agree with the Government that the public should not bear the risk that employees who may suffer from impaired perception and judgment will be promoted to positions where they may need to employ deadly force. Indeed, ensuring against the creation of this dangerous risk will itself further Fourth Amendment values, as the use of deadly force may violate the Fourth Amendment in certain circumstances. . . .

Against these valid public interests we must weigh the interference with individual liberty that results from requiring these classes of employees to undergo a urine test. The interference with individual privacy that results from the collection of a urine sample for subsequent chemical analysis could be substantial in some circumstances. . . .

. . . It is plain that certain forms of public employment may diminish privacy expectations even with respect to such personal searches. Employees of the United States Mint, for example, should expect to be subject to certain routine personal searches when they leave the workplace every day. Similarly, those who join our military or intelligence services may not only be required to give what in other contexts might be viewed as extraordinary assurances of trustworthiness and probity, but also may expect intrusive inquiries into their physical fitness for those special positions. . . .

We think Customs employees who are directly involved in the interdiction of illegal drugs or who are required to carry firearms in the line of duty . . . have a diminished expectation of privacy in respect to the intrusions occasioned by a urine test. Unlike most private citizens or government employees in general, employees involved in drug interdiction reasonably should expect effective inquiry into their fitness and probity. Much the same is true of employees who are required to carry firearms. Because successful performance of their duties depends uniquely on their judgment and dexterity, these employees cannot reasonably expect to keep from the Service personal information that bears directly on their fitness. . . . While reasonable tests designed to elicit this information doubtless infringe some privacy expectations, we do not believe these expectations outweigh the Government's compelling interests in safety and in the integrity of our borders.

Without disparaging the importance of the governmental interests that support the suspicionless searches of these employees, petitioners nevertheless contend that the Service's drug testing program is unreasonable in two particulars. First, petitioners argue that the program is unjustified because it is not based on a belief that testing will reveal any drug use by covered employees. In pressing this argument, petitioners point out that the Service's testing scheme was not implemented in response to any perceived drug problem among Customs employees, and that the program actually has not led to the discovery of a significant number of drug users. . . . Counsel for petitioners informed us at oral argument that no more than 5 employees out of 3,600 have tested positive for drugs. . . . Second, petitioners contend that the Service's scheme is not a "sufficiently productive mechanism to justify [its] intrusion upon Fourth Amendment interests," . . . because illegal drug users can avoid detection with ease by temporary abstinence or by surreptitious adulteration of their urine specimens. . . . These contentions are unpersuasive.

Petitioners' first contention evinces an unduly narrow view of the context in which the Service's testing program was implemented. . . .

The mere circumstance that all but a few of the employees tested are entirely innocent of wrongdoing does not impugn the program's validity. . . . The Service's program is designed to prevent the promotion of drug users to sensitive positions as much as it is designed to detect these employees who use drugs. Where, as here, the possible harm against which the Government seeks to guard is substantial, the need to prevent its occurrence furnishes an ample justification for reasonable searches calculated to advance the Government's goal.

We think petitioners' second argument—that the Service's testing program is ineffective because employees may attempt to deceive the test by a brief abstention before the test date, or by adulterating their urine specimens—overstates the case. As the Court of Appeals noted, addicts may be unable to abstain even for a limited period of time, or may be unaware of the "fade-away effect" of certain drugs. . . . More importantly, the avoidance techniques suggested by petitioners are fraught with uncertainty and risks for those employees who venture to attempt them. A particular employee's pattern of elimination for a given drug cannot be predicted with perfect accuracy, and, in any event, this information is not likely to be known or available to the employee. . . . Thus, contrary to petitioners' suggestion, no employee reasonably can expect to deceive the test by the simple expedient of abstaining after the test date is assigned. Nor can he expect attempts at adulteration to succeed, in view of the precautions taken by the sample collector to ensure the integrity of the sample. . . .

In sum, we believe that Government has demonstrated that its compelling interests in safeguarding our borders and the public safety outweigh the privacy expectations of employees who seek to be promoted to positions that directly involve the interdiction of illegal drugs or that require the incumbent to carry a firearm. We hold that the testing of these employees is reasonable under the Fourth Amendment.

We are unable, on the present record, to assess the reasonableness of the Government's testing program insofar as it covers employees who are required "to handle classified material." . . .

It is not clear, however, whether the category defined by the Service's testing directive encompasses only those Customs employees likely to gain access to sensitive information. Employees who are tested under the Service's scheme include those holding such diverse positions as "Accountant," "Accounting Technician," "Animal Caretaker," "Attorney (All)," "Baggage Clerk," "Co-op Student (All)," "Electric Equipment Repairer," "Mail Clerk/Assistant," and "Messenger." . . . Yet it is not evident that those occupying these positions are likely to gain access to sensitive information, and this apparent discrepancy raises in our minds the question whether the Service has defined this category of employees more broadly than necessary to meet the purpose of the Commissioner's directive.

We cannot resolve this ambiguity on the basis of the record before us, and we think it is appropriate to remand the case to the court of appeals for such proceedings as may be necessary to clarify the scope of this category of employees subject to testing. . . .

The judgment of the Court of Appeals for the Fifth Circuit is affirmed in part and vacated in part, and the case is remanded for further proceedings consistent with this opinion.

Justice Marshall, with whom Justice Brennan joins, dissenting.

For the reasons stated in my dissenting opinion in *Skinner* v. *Railway Labor Executives Association*, . . . I also dissent from the Court's decision in this case. Here, as in *Skinner*, the Court's abandonment of the Fourth Amendment's express requirement that searches of the person rest on probable cause is unprincipled and unjustifiable. But even if I believed that balancing analysis was appropriate under the Fourth Amendment, I would still dissent from today's judgment, for the reasons stated by Justice Scalia in his dissenting opinion.

JUSTICE SCALIA, with whom JUSTICE STEVENS joins, dissenting. . . .

Until today this Court had upheld a bodily search separate from arrest and without individualized suspicion of wrongdoing only with respect to prison inmates, relying upon the uniquely dangerous nature of that environment. . . . Today, in *Skinner,* we allow a less intrusive bodily search of railroad employees involved in train accidents. I joined the Court's opinion there because the demonstrated frequency of drug and alcohol use by the targeted class of employees, and the demonstrated connection between such use and grave harm, rendered the search a reasonable means of protecting society. I decline to join the Court's opinion in the present case because neither frequency of use nor connection to harm is demonstrated or even likely. In my view the Customs Service rules are a kind of immolation of privacy and human dignity in symbolic opposition to drug use.

The Fourth Amendment protects the "right of the people to be secure in their persons, houses, papers, and effects, against unreasonable searches and seizures." While there are some absolutes in Fourth Amendment law, as soon as those have been left behind and the question comes down to whether a particular search has been "reasonable," the answer depends largely upon the social necessity that prompts the search. . . .

The Court's opinion in the present case, however, will be searched in vain for real evidence of a real problem that will be solved by urine testing of Customs Service employees. . . . It is not apparent to me that a Customs Service employee who uses drugs is significantly more likely to be bribed by a drug smuggler, any more than a Customs Service employee who wears diamonds is significantly more likely to be bribed by a diamond smuggler—unless, perhaps, the addiction to drugs is so severe, and requires so much money to maintain, that it would be detectable even without benefit of a urine test. Nor is it apparent to me that Customs officers who use drugs will be appreciably less "sympathetic" to their drug-interdiction mission, any more than police officers who exceed the speed limit in their private cars are appreciably less sympathetic to their mission of enforcing the traffic laws. (The only difference is that the Customs officer's individual efforts, if they are irreplaceable, can theoretically affect the availability of his own drug supply—a prospect so remote as to be an absurd basis of motivation.) Nor, finally, is it apparent to me that urine tests will be even marginally more effective in preventing gun-carrying agents from risking "impaired perception and judgment"than is their current knowledge that, if impaired, they may be shot dead in unequal combat with unimpaired smugglers—unless, again, their addiction is so severe that no urine test is needed for detection.

What is absent in the Government's justifications—notably absent, revealingly absent, and as far as I am concerned dispositively absent—is the recitation of *even a single instance* in which any of the speculated horribles actually occurred: an instance, that is, in which the cause of bribe-taking, or of poor aim, or of unsympathetic law enforcement, or of compromise of classified information, was drug use.

. . . In *Skinner,* . . . we pointed to a long history of alcohol abuse in the railroad industry, and noted that in an 8-year period 45 train accidents and incidents had occurred because of alcohol- and drug-impaired railroad employees, killing 34 people, injuring 66, and causing more than $28 million in property damage. . . . In the present case, by contrast, not only is the Customs Service thought to be "largely drug-free," but the connection between whatever drug use may exist and serious social harm is entirely speculative. . . .

Today's decision would be wrong, but at least of more limited effect, if its approval of drug testing were confined to that category of employees assigned specifically to drug interdiction duties. Relatively few public cmployees fit that description. But in extending approval of drug testing to that category consisting of employees who carry firearms, the Court exposes vast numbers of public employees to this needless indignity. . . .

There is only one apparent basis that sets the testing at issue here apart from all these other situations—but it is not a basis upon which the Court is willing to rely. I do not believe for a minute that the driving force behind these drug-testing rules was any of the feeble justifications put forward by counsel here and accepted by the

Court. The only plausible explanation, in my view, is what the Commissioner himself offered in the concluding sentence of his memorandum to Customs Service employees announcing the program: "Implementation of the drug screening program would set an important example in our country's struggle with this most serious threat to our national health and security." . . . Or as respondent's brief to this Court asserted: "if a law enforcement agency and its employees do not take the law seriously, neither will the public on which the agency's effectiveness depends." . . . What better way to show that the Government is serious about its "war on drugs" than to subject its employees on the front line of that war to this invasion of their privacy and affront to their dignity? To be sure, there is only a slight chance that it will prevent some serious public harm resulting from Service employee drug use, but it will show to the world that the Service is "clean," and—most important of all—will demonstrate the determination of the Government to eliminate this scourge of our society! I think it obvious that this justification is unacceptable; that the impairment of individual liberties cannot be the means of making a point; that symbolism, even symbolism for so worthy a cause as the abolition of unlawful drugs, cannot validate an otherwise unreasonable search.

Mapp v. *Ohio*

367 U.S. 643: 81 S. Ct. 1684; 6 L. Ed. 2d 1081 (1961)

On May 23, 1957, Cleveland police officers came to Dollree Mapp's residence, acting on information that a bombing-case suspect and betting equipment might be found there. They requested entrance, but Mapp refused to admit them without a search warrant. When she refused a second time, the police forced their way into her duplex apartment and subdued and handcuffed her when she grabbed and placed in her bosom a paper that they informed her was a valid search warrant. The officers subjected her entire residence and its contents to a thorough search and in a basement trunk found materials that provided the basis for her conviction of possessing obscene materials. The Ohio Supreme Court affirmed her conviction, and the United States Supreme Court granted certiorari. *Opinion of the Court: Clark, Black, Brennan, Douglas, Warren. Concurring opinions: Black; Douglas. Dissenting opinion: Harlan, Frankfurter, Whittaker. Separate memorandum: Stewart.*

MR. JUSTICE CLARK delivered the opinion of the Court.

Appellant stands convicted of knowingly having had in her possession and under her control certain lewd and lascivious books, pictures, and photographs in violation [of Ohio law]. . . . The Supreme Court of Ohio found that her conviction was valid though "based primarily upon the introduction in evidence of lewd and lascivious books and pictures unlawfully seized during an unlawful search of defendant's home." . . .

The State says that even if the search were made without authority, or otherwise unreasonably, it is not prevented from using the unconstitutionally seized evidence at trial, citing *Wolf* v. *Colorado*, . . . (1949), in which this Court did indeed hold "that in a prosecution in a State court for a State crime the Fourteenth Amendment does not forbid the admission of evidence obtained by an unreasonable search and seizure." . . .

. . . In the year 1914, in *Weeks* [v. *United States,*] this Court "for the first time" held that "in a federal prosecution the Fourth Amendment barred the use of evidence secured through an illegal search and seizure." . . . This Court has ever since required of federal law officers a strict adherence to that command which this Court has held to be a clear, specific, and constitutionally required—even if judicially implied—deterrent safeguard without insistence upon which the

Fourth Amendment would have been reduced to "a form of words." . . .

In 1949, 35 years after *Weeks* was announced, this Court, in *Wolf* v. *Colorado, supra,* again for the first time, discussed the effect of the Fourth Amendment upon the States through the operation of the Due Process Clause of the Fourteenth Amendment. Nevertheless, after declaring that the "security of one's privacy against arbitrary intrusion by the police" is "implicit in 'the concept of ordered liberty' and as such enforceable against the States through the Due Process Clause." . . . and announcing that it "stoutly adhere[d]" to the *Weeks* decision, the Court decided that the *Weeks* exclusionary rule would not then be imposed upon the States as "an essential ingredient of the right." . . .

Today we once again examine *Wolf's* constitutional documentation of the right to privacy free from unreasonable state intrusion, and after its dozen years on our books, are led by it to close the only courtroom door remaining open to evidence secured by official lawlessness in flagrant abuse of that basic right, reserved to all persons as a specific guarantee against that very same unlawful conduct. We hold that all evidence obtained by searches and seizures in violation of the Constitution is, by that same authority, inadmissible in a state court. . . .

Since the Fourth Amendment's right of privacy has been declared enforceable against the States through the Due Process Clause of the Fourteenth, it is enforceable against them by the same sanction of exclusion as is used against the Federal Government. Were it otherwise, then just as without the *Weeks* rule the assurance against unreasonable federal searches and seizures would be "a form of words," valueless and undeserving of mention in a perpetual charter of inestimable human liberties, so too, without that rule the freedom from state invasions of privacy would be so ephemeral and so neatly severed from its conceptual nexus with the freedom from all brutish means of coercing evidence as not to merit this Court's high regard as a freedom "implicit in the concept of ordered liberty."

. . . This Court has not hesitated to enforce as strictly against the States as it does against the Federal Government the rights of free speech and of a free press, the rights to notice and to a fair, public trial, including, as it does, the right not to be convicted by use of a coerced confession, however logically relevant it be, and without regard to its reliability. . . . Why should not the same rule apply to what is tantamount to coerced testimony by way of unconstitutional seizure of goods, papers, effects, documents, etc.? We find that as to the Federal Government, the Fourth and Fifth Amendments and, as to the States, the freedom from unconscionable invasions of privacy and the freedom from convictions based upon coerced confessions do enjoy an "intimate relation" in their perpetuation of "principles of humanity and civil liberty [secured] . . . only after years of struggle." . . . The very least that together they assure in either sphere is that no man is to be convicted on unconstitutional evidence. . . .

Moreover, our holding that the exclusionary rule is an essential part of both the Fourth and Fourteenth Amendments is not only the logical dictate of prior cases, but it also makes very good sense. There is no war between the Constitution and common sense. Presently, a federal prosecutor may make no use of evidence illegally seized, but a State's attorney across the street may, although he supposedly is operating under the enforceable prohibitions of the same Amendment. Thus the State, by admitting evidence unlawfully seized, serves to encourage disobedience to the Federal Constitution which it is bound to uphold. . . . In nonexclusionary States, federal officers, being human, were by it invited to and did, as our cases indicate, step across the street to the State's attorney with their unconstitutionally seized evidence. Prosecution on the basis of that evidence was then had in a state court in utter disregard of the enforceable Fourth Amendment. If the fruits of an unconstitutional search had been inadmissible in both state and federal courts, this inducement to evasion would have been sooner eliminated. . . .

There are those who say as did Justice (then Judge) Cardozo, that under our constitutional exclusionary doctrine "[t]he criminal is to go free because the constable has blundered." . . . In some cases this will undoubtedly be the result. But . . . "there is another consideration—the imperative of judicial integrity." . . . The criminal goes free, if he must, but it is the law that sets him free. Nothing can destroy a government more quickly than its failure to observe its own laws, or worse, its disregard of the charter of its own existence. . . .

The ignoble shortcut to conviction left open to the State tends to destroy the entire system of constitutional restraints on which the liberties of the people rest. Having once recognized that the right to privacy embodied in the Fourth Amendment is enforceable against the States, and that the right to be secure against rude invasions of privacy by state officers is, therefore, constitutional in origin, we can no longer permit that right to remain an empty promise. Because it is enforceable in the same manner and to like effect as other basic rights secured by the Due Process Clause, we can no longer permit it to be revocable at the whim of any police officer who, in the name of law enforcement itself, chooses to suspend its enjoyment. Our decision, founded on reason and truth, gives to the individual no more than that which the Constitution guarantees him, to the police officer no less than that to which honest law enforcement is entitled, and, to the courts, that judicial integrity so necessary in the true administration of justice. . . .

MR. JUSTICE BLACK, concurring . . .

I am still not persuaded that the Fourth Amendment, standing alone, would be enough to bar the introduction into evidence against an accused of papers and effects seized from him in violation of its commands. For the Fourth Amendment does not itself contain any provision expressly precluding the use of such evidence, and I am extremely doubtful that such a provision could properly be inferred from nothing more than the basic command against unreasonable searches and seizures. Reflection on the problem, however, in the light of cases coming before the Court since *Wolf,* has led me to conclude that when the Fourth Amendment's ban against unreasonable searches and seizures is considered together with the Fifth Amendment's ban against compelled self-incrimination, a constitutional basis emerges which not only justifies but actually requires the exclusionary rule. . . .

Memorandum of MR. JUSTICE STEWART. . . .

. . . I would . . . reverse the judgment in this case because I am persuaded that the provision of . . . the Ohio [obscenity law], upon which the petitioner's conviction was based, is, in the words of MR. JUSTICE HARLAN, not "consistent with the rights of free thought and expression assured against state action by the Fourteenth Amendment."

MR. JUSTICE HARLAN, whom MR. JUSTICE FRANKFURTER and MR. JUSTICE WHITTAKER join, dissenting.

In overruling the *Wolf* case the Court, in my opinion, has forgotten the sense of judicial restraint which, with due regard for *stare decisis,* is one element that should enter into deciding whether a past decision of this Court should be overruled. Apart from that I also believe that the *Wolf* rule represents sounder Constitutional doctrine than the new rule which now replaces it. . . .

From the Court's statement of the case one would gather that the central, if not controlling, issue on this appeal is whether illegally state-seized evidence is Constitutionally admissible in a state prosecution, an issue which would of course face us with the need for re-examining *Wolf.* However, such is not the situation. For, although that question was indeed raised here and below among appellant's subordinate points, the new and pivotal issue brought to the Court by this appeal is whether § 2905.34 of the Ohio Revised Code making criminal the *mere* knowing possession or control of obscene material, and under which appellant has been convicted, is consistent with the rights of free thought and expression assured against state action by the Fourteenth Amendment. That was the principal issue which was decided by the Ohio Supreme Court, which was tendered by appellant's Jurisdictional Statement, and which was briefed and argued in this Court.

In this posture of things, I think it fair to say that five members of this Court have simply "reached out" to overrule *Wolf.* With all respect for the views of the majority, and recognizing that *stare decisis* carries different weight in Constitutional adjudication than it does in nonconstitutional decision, I can perceive no justification for regarding this case as an appropriate occasion for re-examining *Wolf.* . . .

The occasion which the Court has taken here is in the context of a case where the question was briefed not at all and argued only extremely tangentially. The unwisdom of overruling *Wolf* without full-dress argument is aggravated by the circumstance that that decision is a comparatively recent one (1949) to which three members of the present majority have at one time or other expressly subscribed, one to be sure with explicit misgivings. I would think that our obligation to the States, on whom we impose this new rule, as well as the obligation of orderly adherence to our own processes would demand that we seek that aid which adequate briefing and argument lends to the determination of an important issue. It certainly has never been a postulate of judicial power that mere altered disposition, or subsequent membership on the Court, is sufficient warrant for overturning a deliberately decided rule of Constitutional law. . . .

I am bound to say that what has been done is not likely to promote respect either for the Court's adjudicatory process or for the stability of its decisions. Having been unable, however, to persuade any of the majority to a different procedural course, I now turn to the merits of the present decision. . . .

I would not impose upon the States this federal exclusionary remedy. The reasons given by the majority for now suddenly turning its back on *Wolf* seem to me notably unconvincing.

First, it is said that "the factual grounds upon which *Wolf* was based" have since changed, in that more States now follow the *Weeks* exclusionary rule than was so at the time *Wolf* was decided. While that is true, a recent survey indicates that at present one-half of the States still adhere to the common-law non-exclusionary rule . . . But in any case surely all this is beside the point, as the majority itself indeed seems to recognize. Our concern here, as it was in *Wolf,* is not with the desirability of that rule but only with the question whether the States are Constitutionally free to follow it or not as they may themselves determine, and the relevance of the disparity of views among the States on this point lies simply in the fact that the judgment involved is a debatable one. . . .

The preservation of a proper balance between state and federal responsibility in the administration of criminal justice demands patience on the part of those who might like to see things move faster among the States in this respect. Problems of criminal law enforcement vary widely from State to State. One State, in considering the totality of its legal picture, may conclude that the need for embracing the *Weeks* rule is pressing because other remedies are unavailable or inadequate to secure compliance with the substantive Constitutional principle involved. Another, though equally solicitous of Constitutional rights, may choose to pursue one purpose at a time, allowing all evidence relevant to guilt to be brought into a criminal trial, and dealing with Constitutional infractions by other means. Still another may consider the exclusionary rule too rough-and-ready a remedy, in that it reaches only unconstitutional intrusions which eventuate in criminal prosecution of the victims. Further, a State after experimenting with the *Weeks* rule for a time may, because of unsatisfactory experience with it, decide to revert to a non-exclusionary rule. And so on. From the standpoint of Constitutional permissibility in pointing a State in one direction or another, I do not see at all why "time has set its face against" the considerations which led Mr. Justice Cardozo, then chief judge of the New York Court of Appeals, to reject for New York in *People* v. *Defore,* . . . the *Weeks* exclusionary rule. For us the question remains, as it has always been, one of state power, not one of passing judgment on the wisdom of one state course or another. . . .

Further, we are told that imposition of the *Weeks* rule on the States makes "very good sense," in that it will promote recognition by state and federal officials of their "mutual obligation to respect the same fundamental criteria" in their approach to law enforcement, and will avoid " 'needless conflict between state and federal courts.' " . . .

An approach which regards the issue as one of achieving procedural symmetry or of serving administrative convenience surely disfigures the boundaries of this Court's functions in relation to the state and federal courts. Our role in promulgating the *Weeks* rule and its extensions . . . was quite a different one than it is here. There, in implementing the Fourth Amendment, we occupied the position of a tribunal having the ultimate responsibility for developing the standards and procedures of judicial administration within the judicial system over which it presides. Here we review state procedures whose measure is to be taken not against the specific substantive commands of the Fourth Amendment but under the flexible contours of the Due Process Clause. . . .

I regret that I find so unwise in principle and so

inexpedient in policy a decision motivated by the high purpose of increasing respect for Constitutional rights. But in the last analysis I think this Court can increase respect for the Constitution only if it rigidly respects the limitations which the Constitution places upon it, and respects as well the principles inherent in its own processes. In the present case I think we exceed both, and that our voice becomes only a voice of power, not of reason.

Olmstead v. *United States*

277 U.S. 438; 48 S. Ct. 564; 72 L. Ed. 944 (1928)

Roy Olmstead and several accomplices were convicted in federal district court of conspiring to violate the National Prohibition Act by unlawfully possessing, transporting, and importing intoxicating liquors. At trial, the government presented incriminating evidence obtained by federal agents who wiretapped telephone lines at points between the defendants' homes and their offices. The Court of Appeals for the Ninth Circuit affirmed the convictions over objections that this wiretap evidence was inadmissible under the Fourth Amendment protection from unreasonable searches and seizures and the Fifth Amendment guarantee against self-incrimination. The Supreme Court granted certiorari. *Opinion of the Court: Taft, McReynolds, Sanford, Sutherland, Van Devanter. Dissenting opinions: Brandeis; Butler; Holmes; Stone.*

MR. CHIEF JUSTICE TAFT delivered the opinion of the Court. . . .

There is no room in the present case for applying the Fifth Amendment unless the Fourth Amendment was first violated. There was no evidence of compulsion to induce the defendants to talk over their many telephones. They were continually and voluntarily transacting business without knowledge of the interception. Our consideration must be confined to the Fourth Amendment. . . .

The well known historical purpose of the Fourth Amendment, directed against general warrants and writs of assistance, was to prevent the use of governmental force to search a man's house, his person, his papers and his effects; and to prevent their seizure against his will. . . .

The Amendment itself shows that the search is to be of material things—the person, the house, his papers or his effects. The description of the warrant necessary to make the proceeding lawful, is that it must specify the place to be searched and the person or *things* to be seized. . . .

. . . The Amendment does not forbid what was done here. There was no searching. There was no seizure. The evidence was secured by the use of the sense of hearing and that only. There was no entry of the houses or offices of the defendants.

By the invention of the telephone, fifty years ago, and its application for the purpose of extending communications, one can talk with another at a far distant place. The language of the Amendment cannot be extended and expanded to include telephone wires reaching to the whole world from the defendant's house or office. The intervening wires are not part of his house or office any more than are the highways along which they are stretched. . . .

Congress may of course protect the secrecy of telephone messages by making them, when intercepted, inadmissible in evidence in federal criminal trials, by direct legislation, and thus depart from the common law of evidence. But the courts may not adopt such a policy by attributing an enlarged and unusual meaning to the Fourth Amendment. The reasonable view is that one who installs in his house a telephone instrument with connecting wires intends to project his voice to those quite outside, and that the wires beyond his house and messages while passing over them are not within protection of the Fourth Amendment. Here those who intercepted the projected voices were not in the house of either party to the conversation.

Neither the cases we have cited nor any of the many federal decisions brought to our attention hold the Fourth Amendment to have been violated as against a defendant unless there has been an official search and seizure of his person, or such a seizure of his papers or his tangible material effects, or an actual physical invasion of his house "or curtilage" for the purpose of making a seizure.

We think, therefore, that the wire tapping here disclosed did not amount to a search or seizure within the meaning of the Fourth Amendment.

What has been said disposes of the only question that comes within the terms of our order granting certiorari in these cases. But some of our number, departing from that order, have concluded that there is merit in the two-fold objection overruled in both courts below that evidence obtained through intercepting of telephone messages by government agents was inadmissible because the mode of obtaining it was unethical and a misdemeanor under the law of Washington. To avoid any misrepresentation of our views of that objection we shall deal with it in both of its phases.

While a Territory, the English common law prevailed in Washington and thus continued after her admission in 1889. The rules of evidence in criminal cases in courts of the United States sitting there, consequently are those of the common law. . . .

The common law rule is that the admissibility of evidence is not affected by the illegality of the means by which it was obtained. . . .

Nor can we, without the sanction of congressional enactment, subscribe to the suggestion that the courts have a discretion to exclude evidence, the admission of which is not unconstitutional, because unethically secured. This would be at variance with the common law doctrine generally supported by authority. There is no case that sustains, nor any recognized text book that gives color to such a view. Our general experience shows that much evidence has always been receivable although not obtained by conformity to the highest ethics. The history of criminal trials shows numerous cases of prosecutions of oath-bound conspiracies for murder, robbery, and other crimes, where officers of the law have disguised themselves and joined the organizations, taken the oaths and given themselves every appearance of active members engaged in the promotion of crime, for the purpose of securing evidence. Evidence secured by such means has always been received.

A standard which would forbid the reception of evidence if obtained by other than nice ethical conduct by government officials would make society suffer and give criminals greater immunity than has been known heretofore. In the absence of controlling legislation by Congress, those who realize the difficulties in bringing offenders to justice may well deem it wise that the exclusion of evidence should be confined to cases where rights under the Constitution would be violated by admitting it.

Mr. Justice Holmes, dissenting.

. . . It is desirable that criminals should be detected, and to that end that all available evidence should be used. It also is desirable that the Government should not itself foster and pay for other crimes, when they are the means by which the evidence is to be obtained. We have to choose, and for my part I think it a less evil that some criminals should escape than that the Government should play an ignoble part. . . .

Mr. Justice Brandeis, dissenting. . . .

The Government makes no attempt to defend the methods employed by its officers. Indeed, it concedes that if wire-tapping can be deemed a search and seizure within the Fourth Amendment, such wire-tapping as was practiced in the case at bar was an unreasonable search and seizure, and that the evidence thus obtained was inadmissible. But it relies on the language of the Amendment; and it claims that the protection given thereby cannot properly be held to include a telephone conversation.

"We must never forget," said Mr. Chief Justice Marshall in *McCulloch* v. *Maryland*, . . . "that it is a constitution we are expounding." Since then, this Court has repeatedly sustained the exercise of power by Congress, under various clauses of that instrument, over objects of which the Fathers could not have dreamed. . . . We have likewise held the general limitations on the powers of Government, like those embodied in the due process clauses of the Fifth and Fourteenth Amendments, do not forbid the United States or the States from meeting modern conditions by regulations which "a century ago, or even half a century ago, probably would have been rejected as arbitrary and oppressive." . . . Clauses guaranteeing to the individual protection against specific abuses of power, must have similar capacity of adaptation to a changing world.

When the Fourth and Fifth Amendments were adopted, "the form that evil had theretofore taken," had been necessarily simple. Force and violence were then the only means known to man by which a Government could directly effect self-incrimination. It could compel the individual to testify—a compulsion effected, if need be, by torture. It could secure possession of his papers and other articles incident to his private life—a seizure effected, if need be, by breaking and entry. Protection against such invasion of "the sanctities of a man's home and the privacies of life" was provided in the Fourth and Fifth Amendments by specific language. . . . But "time works changes, brings into existence new conditions and purposes." Subtler and more far-reaching means of invading privacy have become available to the Government. Discovery and invention have made it possible for the Government, by means far more effective than stretching upon the rack, to obtain disclosure in court of what is whispered in the closet.

Moreover, "in the application of a constitution, our contemplation cannot be only of what has been but of what may be." The progress of science in furnishing the Government with means of espionage is not likely to stop with wire tapping. Ways may some day be developed by which the Government, without removing papers from secret drawers, can reproduce them in court, and by which it will be enabled to expose to a jury the most intimate occurrences of the home. Advances in the psychic and related sciences may bring means of exploring unexpressed beliefs, thoughts and emotions. . . . Can it be that the Constitution affords no protection against such invasions of individual security?

. . . The makers of our Constitution undertook to secure conditions favorable to the pursuit of happiness. They recognized the significance of man's spiritual nature, of his feelings and of his intellect. They knew that only a part of the pain, pleasure and satisfactions of life are to be found in material things. They sought to protect Americans in their beliefs, their thoughts, their emotions and their sensations. They conferred, as against the Government, the right to be let alone—the most comprehensive of rights and the right most valued by civilized men. To protect that right, every unjustifiable intrusion by the Government upon the privacy of the individual, whatever the means employed, must be deemed a violation of the Fourth Amendment. And the use, as evidence in a criminal proceeding, of facts ascertained by such intrusion must be deemed a violation of the Fifth.

Applying to the Fourth and Fifth Amendments the established rule of construction, the defendants' objections to the evidence obtained by wire-tapping must, in my opinion, be sustained. It is, of course, immaterial where the physical connection with the telephone wires leading into the defendants' premises was made. And it is also immaterial that the intrusion was in aid of law enforcement. Experience should teach us to be most on our guard to protect liberty when the Government's purposes are beneficent. Men born to freedom are naturally alert to repel invasion of their liberty by evil-minded rulers. The greatest dangers to liberty lurk in insidious encroachment by men of zeal, well-meaning but without understanding.

Independently of the constitutional question, I am of opinion that the judgment should be reversed. By the laws of Washington, wire-tapping is a crime. . . . To prove its case, the Government was obliged to lay bare the crimes committed by its officers on its behalf. A federal court should not permit such a prosecution to continue. . . .

Decency, security and liberty alike demand that government officials shall be subjected to the same rules of conduct that are commands to the citizen. In a government of laws, existence of the government will be imperilled if it fails to observe the law scrupulously. Our Government is the potent, the omnipresent teacher. For good or for ill, it teaches the whole people by its example. Crime is contagious. If the Government becomes a lawbreaker, it breeds contempt for law; it invites every man to become a law unto himself; it invites anarchy. To declare that in the administration of the criminal law the end justifies the means—to declare that the Government may commit crimes in order to secure the conviction of a private criminal—would bring terrible retribution. Against that pernicious doctrine this Court should resolutely set its face.

Katz v. *United States*

389 U.S. 342; 88 S. Ct. 507; 19 L. Ed. 2d 576 (1967)

Charles Katz was convicted in federal district court of violating a federal statute by transmitting wagering information to Miami and Boston from a telephone booth in Los Angeles. At trial, the government introduced a recording of his phone conversations made by FBI agents using an electronic listening device attached to the outside of the booth. The court of appeals, in affirming Katz's conviction, rejected his contention that the recording had been obtained in violation of the Fourth Amendment, on the grounds that there was no physical entrance into the area occupied by the defendant. The Supreme Court granted certiorari. *Opinion of the Court: Stewart, Brennan, Douglas, Fortas, Harlan, Warren, White. Concurring opinions: Douglas, Brennan; Harlan; White. Dissenting opinion: Black. Marshall did not participate.*

MR. JUSTICE STEWART delivered the opinion of the Court.

. . . The petitioner has strenuously argued that the booth was a "constitutionally protected area." The Government has maintained with equal vigor that it was not. But this effort to decide whether or not a given "area," viewed in the abstract, is "constitutionally protected" deflects attention from the problem presented by this case. For the Fourth Amendment protects people, not places. What a person knowingly exposes to the public, even in his own home or office, is not a subject of Fourth Amendment protection. . . . But what he seeks to preserve as private, even in an area accessible to the public, may be constitutionally protected. . . .

The Government stresses the fact that the telephone booth from which the petitioner made his calls was constructed partly of glass, so that he was as visible after he entered it as he would have been if he had remained outside. But what he sought to exclude when he entered the booth was not the intruding eye—it was the uninvited ear. He did not shed his right to do so simply because he made his calls from a place where he might be seen. No less than an individual in a business office, in a friend's apartment, or in a taxicab, a person in a telephone booth may rely upon the protection of the Fourth Amendment. One who occupies it, shuts the door behind him, and pays the toll that permits him to place a call is surely entitled to assume that the words he utters into the mouthpiece will not be broadcast to the world. To read the Constitution more narrowly is to ignore the vital role that the public telephone has come to play in private communication.

The Government contends, however, that the activities of its agents in this case should not be tested by Fourth Amendment requirements, for the surveillance technique they employed involved no physical penetration of the telephone booth from which the petitioner placed his calls. It is true that the absence of such penetration was at one time thought to foreclose further Fourth Amendment inquiry, *Olmstead* v. *United States* . . .

. . . The underpinnings of *Olmstead* [v. *United States* (1928)] and *Goldman* have been so eroded by our subsequent decisions that the "trespass" doctrine there enunciated can no longer be regarded as controlling. The Government's activities in electronically listening to and recording the petitioner's words violated the privacy upon which he justifiably relied while using the telephone booth and thus constituted a "search and seizure" within the meaning of the Fourth Amendment. The fact that the electronic device employed to achieve that end did not happen to penetrate the wall of the booth can have no constitutional significance.

The question remaining for decision, then, is whether the search and seizure conducted in this case complied with constitutional standards. In that regard, the Government's position is that its agents acted in an entirely defensible manner: They did not begin their electronic surveillance until investigation of the petitioner's activities had established a strong probability that he was using the telephone in question to transmit gambling information to persons in other States, in violation of federal law. Moreover, the surveillance was limited, both in scope and in duration, to the specific purpose of establishing the contents of the petitioner's unlawful telephonic communications. The agents confined their surveillance to the brief periods during which he used the telephone booth, and they took great care to overhear only the conversations of the petitioner himself. . . .

The Government urges that, because its agents relied upon the decisions in *Olmstead* and *Goldman,* and because they did no more here than they might properly have done with prior judicial sanction, we should retroactively validate their conduct. That we cannot do. It is apparent that the agents in this case acted with restraint. Yet the inescapable fact is that this restraint was imposed by the agents themselves, not by a judicial officer. They were not required, before commencing the search, to present their estimate of probable cause for detached scrutiny by a neutral magistrate. They were not compelled, during the conduct of the search itself, to observe precise limits established in advance by a specific court order. Nor were they directed, after the search had been completed, to notify the authorizing magistrate in detail of all that had been seized. In the absence of such safeguards, this Court has never sustained a search upon the sole ground that officers reasonably expected to find evidence of a particular crime and voluntarily confined their activities to the least intrusive means consistent with that end. . . . "Over and again this Court has emphasized that the mandate of the [Fourth] Amendment requires adherence to judicial processes," . . . and that searches conducted outside the judicial process, without prior approval by judge or magistrate, are *per se* unreasonable under the Fourth Amendment—subject only to a few specifically established and well-delineated exceptions. . . .

MR. JUSTICE BLACK, dissenting. . . .

While I realize that an argument based on the meaning of words lacks the scope, and no doubt the appeal, of broad policy discussions and philosophical discourses on such nebulous subjects as privacy, for me the language of the Amendment is the crucial place to look in construing a written document such as our Constitution. The Fourth Amendment. . . . protects "persons, houses, papers, and effects, against unreasonable searches and seizures. . . ." These words connote the idea of tangible things with size, form, and weight, things capable of being searched, seized, or both. . . . The Amendment further establishes its Framers' purpose to limit its protection to tangible things by providing that no warrants shall issue but those "particularly describing the place to be searched, and the persons or things to be seized." A conversation overheard by eavesdroppings whether by plain snooping or wiretapping, is not tangible and, under the normally accepted meanings of the words, can neither be searched nor seized. In addition the language of the second clause indicates that the Amendment refers not only to something tangible so it can be seized but to something already in existence so it can be described. Yet the Court's interpretation would have the Amendment apply to overhearing future conversations which by their own nature are nonexistent until they take place. How can one "describe" a future conversation, and, if one cannot, how can a magistrate issue a warrant to eavesdrop one in the future? It is argued that information showing what is expected to be said is sufficient to limit the boundaries of what later can be admitted into evidence; but does such general information really meet the specific language of the Amendment which says "particularly describing"? Rather than using language in a completely artificial way, I must conclude that the Fourth Amendment simply does not apply to eavesdropping. . . .

Powell v. *Alabama*

287 U.S. 45; 53 S. Ct. 55; 77 L. Ed. 158 (1932)

In 1931, Ozie Powell and six other black defendants were convicted in Scottsboro, Alabama, for the rape of two white girls. Their trial lasted one day, and they were all sentenced to death. They had been arrested, tried, and sentenced in what Justice Sutherland was to call "an atmosphere of tense, hostile, and excited public sentiment." The defendants were too poor to retain counsel, and the trial judge vaguely appointed all members of the Alabama bar to represent them. The Alabama Supreme Court affirmed their conviction, with the chief justice writing a strong dissent on the grounds that the defendents had not been given a fair trial. The United States Supreme Court granted certiorari. The *Powell* case is the first of a series referred to as the Scottsboro cases, so termed because of the location of the trial. *Opinion of the Court: Sutherland, Brandeis, Cardozo, Hughes, Roberts, Stone, Van Devanter. Dissenting opinion: Butler, McReynolds.*

MR. JUSTICE SUTHERLAND delivered the opinion of the Court. . . .

The record shows that immediately upon the return of the indictment defendants were arraigned and pleaded not guilty. Apparently they were not asked whether they had, or were able to employ, counsel, or wished to have counsel appointed; or whether they had friends or relatives who might assist in that regard if communicated with. That it would not have been an idle ceremony to have given the defendants reasonable opportunity to communicate with their families and endeavor to obtain counsel is demonstrated by the fact that, very soon after conviction, able counsel appeared in their behalf. This was pointed out by Chief Justice Anderson in the course of his dissenting opinion. "They were nonresidents," he said, "and had little time or opportunity to get in touch with their families and friends who were scattered throughout two other states, and time has demonstrated that they could or would have been represented by able counsel had a better opportunity been given by a reasonable delay in the trial of the cases, judging from the number and activity of counsel that appeared immediately or shortly after their conviction." . . .

It is hardly necessary to say that, the right to counsel being conceded, a defendant should be afforded a fair opportunity to secure counsel of his own choice. Not only was that not done here, but such designation of counsel as was attempted was either so indefinite or so close upon the trial as to amount to a denial of effective and substantial aid in that regard.

. . . Until the very morning of the trial no lawyer had been named or definitely designated to represent the defendants. Prior to that time, the trial judge had "appointed all the members of the bar" for the limited "purpose of arraigning the defendants." Whether they would represent the defendants thereafter if no counsel appeared in their behalf, was a matter of speculation only, or, as the judge indicated, of mere anticipation on the part of the court. Such a designation, even if made for all purposes, would, in our opinion, have fallen short of meeting, in any proper sense, a requirement for the appointment of counsel. How many lawyers were members of the bar does not appear; but, in the very nature of things, whether many or few, they would not, thus collectively named, have been given that clear appreciation of responsibility or impressed with that individual sense of duty which should and naturally would accompany the appointment of a selected member of the bar, specifically named and assigned. . . .

. . . The Constitution of Alabama provides that in all criminal prosecutions the accused shall enjoy the right to have the assistance of counsel; and a state statute requires the court in a capital case, where the defendant is unable to employ counsel, to appoint counsel for him. The state supreme court held that these provisions had not been infringed, and with that holding we are powerless to interfere. The question, however, which it is our duty, and within our power, to decide, is whether the denial of the assistance of counsel contravenes the due process clause of the Fourteenth Amendment to the federal Constitution. . . .

One test which has been applied to determine whether due process of law has been accorded in given instances is to ascertain what were the settled usages and modes of proceeding under the common and statute law of England before the Declaration of Independence, subject, however, to the qualification that they be shown not to have been unsuited to the civil and political conditions of our ancestors by having been followed in this country after it became a nation. . . . Plainly, . . . this test, as thus qualified, has not been met in the present case. . . .

It never has been doubted by this court, or any other so far as we know, that notice and hearing are preliminary steps essential to the passing of an enforceable judgment, and that they, together with a legally competent tribunal having jurisdiction of the case, constitute basic elements of the constitutional requirement of due process of law. . . .

What, then, does a hearing include? Historically and in practice, in our country as least, it has always included the right to the aid of counsel when desired and provided by the party asserting the right. The right to be heard would be, in many cases, of little avail if it did not comprehend the right to be heard by counsel. Even the intelligent and educated layman has small and sometimes no skill in the science of law. If charged with crime, he is incapable, generally, of determining for himself whether the indictment is good or bad. He is unfamiliar with the rules of evidence. Left without the aid of counsel he may be put on trial without a proper charge, and convicted upon incompetent evidence, or evidence irrelevant to the issue or otherwise inadmissible. He lacks both the skill and knowledge adequately to prepare his defense, even though he have a perfect one. He requires the guiding hand of counsel at every step in the proceedings against him. Without it, though he be not guilty, he faces the danger of conviction because he does not know how to establish his innocence. If that be true of men of intelligence, how much more true is it of the ignorant and illiterate, or those of feeble intelligence. If in any case, civil or criminal, a state or federal court were arbitrarily to refuse to hear a party by counsel, employed by and appearing for him, it reasonably may not be doubted that such a refusal would be a denial of a hearing, and, therefore, of due process in the constitutional sense. . . .

In the light of the facts . . . —the ignorance and illiteracy of the defendants, their youth, the circumstances of public hostility, the imprisonment and the close surveillance of the defendants by the military forces, the fact that their friends and families were all in other states and communication with them necessarily difficult, and above all that they stood in deadly peril of their lives—we think the failure of the trial court to give them reasonable time and opportunity to secure counsel was a clear denial of due process.

But passing that, and assuming their inability, even if opportunity had been given, to employ counsel, as the trial court evidently did assume, we are of opinion that, under the circumstances just stated, the necessity of counsel was so vital and imperative that the failure of the trial court to make an effective appointment of counsel was likewise a denial of due process within the meaning of the Fourteenth Amendment. Whether this would be so in other criminal prosecutions, or under other circumstances, we need not determine. All that it is necessary now to decide, as we do decide, is that in a capital case, where the defendant is unable to employ counsel, and is incapable adequately of making his own defense because of ignorance, feeble mindedness, illiteracy, or the like, it is the duty of the court, whether requested or not, to assign counsel for him as a necessary requisite of due process of law; and that duty is not discharged by an assignment at such a time or under such circumstances as to preclude the giving of effective aid in the preparation and trial of the case. To hold otherwise would be to ignore the fundamental postulate, already adverted to, "that there are certain immutable principles of justice which inhere in the very idea of free government which no member of the Union may disregard." . . . In a case such as this, whatever may be the rule in other cases, the right to have counsel appointed, when necessary, is a logical corollary from the constitutional right to be heard by counsel. . . .

The judgments must be reversed and the causes remanded for further proceedings not inconsistent with this opinion.

Gideon v. *Wainwright*

372 U.S. 335; 83 S. Ct. 792; 9 L. Ed. 2d 799 (1963)

Clarence Gideon was charged in Florida state court with breaking into a pool hall with the intent to commit a misdemeanor—a felony under Florida law. Gideon appeared at his trial without a lawyer and without the funds necessary to retain one, and he requested the trial judge to appoint a lawyer for him. The trial judge refused, citing a Florida statute that permitted the appointment of counsel only in capital cases. Gideon then proceeded to conduct his own defense, and he was found guilty by the jury and sentenced to five years in prison by the judge. Once in prison, Gideon sought release by suing out a writ of habeas corpus against Wainwright, the state director of corrections. The Florida Supreme Court denied relief and Gideon presented an *in forma pauperis* petition to the United States Supreme Court, asserting that the trial judge's refusal to appoint counsel for him was a denial of rights guaranteed by the Sixth and Fourteenth Amendments. The Supreme Court granted certiorari and appointed Abe Fortas, later to serve as an associate justice of the Supreme Court, to represent him in this proceeding. *Opinion of the Court: Black, Brennan, Douglas, Goldberg, Stewart, Warren, White. Concurring opinion: Douglas, Concurring in result: Clark; Harlan.*

MR. JUSTICE BLACK delivered the opinion of the Court. . . .

. . . Since 1942, when *Betts* v. *Brady,* was decided by a divided Court, the problem of a defendant's federal constitutional right to counsel in a state court has been a continuing source of controversy and litigation in both state and federal courts. To give this problem another review here, we granted certiorari. . . . [We] requested both sides to discuss in their briefs and oral arguments the following: "Should this Court's holding in *Betts* v. *Brady* be reconsidered?" . . .

The Sixth Amendment provides, "In all criminal prosecutions, the accused shall enjoy the right . . . to have the Assistance of Counsel for his defence." We have construed this to mean that in federal courts counsel must be provided for defendants unable to employ counsel unless the right is competently and intelligently waived. Betts argued that this right is extended to indigent defendants in state courts by the Fourteenth Amendment. . . . The Court concluded that "appointment of counsel is not a fundamental right, essential to a fair trial.". . . It was for this reason the *Betts* Court refused to accept the contention that the Sixth Amendment's guarantee of counsel for indigent federal defendants was extended to or, in the words of that Court, "made obligatory upon the States by the Fourteenth Amendment.". . . .

We think the Court in *Betts* was wrong . . . in concluding that the Sixth Amendment's guarantee of counsel is not one of these fundamental rights. Ten years before *Betts* v. *Brady,* this Court, after full consideration of all the historical data examined in *Betts,* had unequivocally declared that "the right to the aid of counsel is of this fundamental character." *Powell* v. *Alabama* . . . (1932). While the Court at the close of its *Powell* opinion did by its language, as this Court frequently does, limit its holding to the particular facts and circumstances of that case, its conclusions about the fundamental nature of the right to counsel are unmistakable. Several years later, in 1936, the Court reemphasized what it had said about the fundamental nature of the right to counsel in this language:

"We concluded that certain fundamental rights, safeguarded by the first eight amendments against federal action, were also safeguarded against state action by the due process of law clause of the Fourteenth Amendment, and among them the fundamental right of the accused to the aid of counsel in a criminal prosecution." *Grosjean* v. *American Press Co.* (1936).

And again in 1938 this Court said:

"[The assistance of counsel] is one of the safeguards of the Sixth Amendment deemed necessary to insure fundamental human rights of life and liberty. . . . *Johnson* v. *Zerbst* . . . (1938). . . .

. . . In deciding as it did—that "appointment of counsel is not a fundamental right, essential to a fair trial"—the Court in *Betts* v. *Brady* made an abrupt break with its own well-considered precedents. In returning to these old precedents, sounder we believe than the new, we but restore constitutional principles established to achieve a fair system of justice. Not only these precedents but also reason and reflection require us to recognize that in our adversary system of criminal justice, any person haled into court, who is too poor to hire a lawyer, cannot be assured a fair trial unless counsel is provided for him. This seems to us to be an obvious truth. Governments, both state and federal, quite properly spend vast sums of money to establish machinery to try defendants accused of crime. Lawyers to prosecute are everywhere deemed essential to protect the public's interest in an orderly society. Similarly, there are few defendants charged with crime, few indeed, who fail to hire the best lawyers they can get to prepare and present their defenses. That government hires lawyers to prosecute and defendants who have the money hire lawyers to defend are the strongest indications of the widespread belief that lawyers in criminal courts are necessities, not luxuries. The right of one charged with crime to counsel may not be deemed fundamental and essential to fair trials in some countries, but it is in ours. From the very beginning, our state and national constitutions and laws have laid great emphasis on procedural and substantive safeguards designed to assure fair trials before impartial tribunals in which every defendant stands equal before the law. This noble ideal cannot be realized if the poor man charged with crime has to face his accusers without a lawyer to assist him. . . .

The judgment is reversed and the cause is remanded to the Supreme Court of Florida for further action not inconsistent with this opinion.

Miranda v. *Arizona*

384 U.S. 436; 86 S. Ct. 1602; L. Ed. 2d 694 (1966)

Miranda consolidates for decision four cases, all of which raised the issue of the admissibility into evidence of statements obtained from defendants during pretrial custodial police interrogation. In each of these cases, the defendants were convicted on the basis of confessions made after periods of police questioning during which they were not informed of their rights to counsel and to remain silent. The crimes for which they were convicted included murder, kidnapping, rape, and robbery. *Opinion of the Court: Warren, Black, Brennan, Douglas, Fortas. Dissenting opinions: Clark; Harlan, Stewart, White; White, Harlan, Stewart.*

MR. CHIEF JUSTICE WARREN delivered the opinion of the Court.

The cases before us raise questions which go to the roots of our concepts of American criminal jurisprudence: the restraints society must observe consistent with the Federal Constitution in prosecuting individuals for crime. More specifically, we deal with the admissibility of statements obtained from an individual who is subjected to custodial police interrogation and the necessity for procedures which assure that the individual is accorded his privilege under the Fifth Amendment to the Constitution not to be compelled to incriminate himself. . . .

Our holding will be spelled out with some specificity in the pages which follow but briefly stated it is this: the prosecution may not use statements, whether exculpatory or inculpatory, stemming from custodial interrogation of the defendant unless it demonstrates the use of procedural safeguards effective to secure the privilege against self-incrimination. By custodial interrogation, we mean questioning initiated by law enforcement officers after a person has been taken into custody or otherwise deprived of his freedom of action in any significant way. As for the procedural safeguards to be employed, unless other fully effective means are devised to inform accused persons of their right of silence and to assure a continuous opportunity to exercise it, the following measures are required. Prior to any questioning, the person must be warned that he has a right to remain silent, that any statement he does make may be used as evidence against him, and that he has a right to the presence of an attorney, either retained or appointed. The defendant may waive effectuation of these rights, provided the waiver is made voluntarily, knowingly and intelligently. If, however, he indicates in any manner and at any stage of the process that he wishes to consult with an attorney before speaking there can be no questioning. Likewise, if the individual is alone and indicates in any manner that he does not wish to be interrogated, the police may not question him. The mere fact that he may have answered some questions or volunteered some statements on his own does not deprive him of the right to refrain from answering any further inquiries until he has consulted with an attorney and thereafter consents to be questioned.

The constitutional issue we decide in each of these cases is the admissibility of statements obtained from a defendant questioned while in custody or otherwise deprived of his freedom of action in any significant way. In each, the defendant was questioned by police officers, detectives, or a prosecuting attorney in a room in which he was cut off from the outside world. In none of these cases was the defendant given a full and effective warning of his rights at the outset of the interrogation process. In all the cases, the questioning elicited oral admissions, and in three of them, signed statements as well which were admitted at their trials. They all thus share salient features—incommunicado interrogation of individuals in a police-dominated atmosphere, resulting in self-incriminating statements without full warnings of constitutional rights. . . .

An understanding of the nature and setting of this in-custody interrogation is essential to our decisions today. The difficulty in depicting what transpires at such interrogations stems from the fact that in this country they have largely taken place incommunicado. . . .

. . . Interrogation still takes place in privacy. Privacy results in secrecy and this in turn results in a gap in our knowledge as to what in fact goes on in the interrogation rooms. A valuable source of information about present police practices, however, may be found in various police manuals and texts, which document procedures employed with success in the past, and which recommend various other effective tactics. These texts are used by law enforcement agencies themselves as guides. It should be noted that these texts professedly present the most enlightened and effective means presently used to obtain statements through custodial interrogation. By considering these texts and other data, it is possible to describe procedures observed and noted around the country. . . .

From these representative samples of interrogation techniques, the setting prescribed by the manuals and observed in practice becomes clear. In essence, it is this: To be alone with the subject is essential to prevent distraction and to deprive him of any outside support. The aura of confidence in his guilt undermines his will to resist. He merely confirms the preconceived story the police seek to have him describe. Patience and persistence, at times relentless questioning, are employed. To obtain a confession, the interrogator must "patiently maneuver himself or his quarry into a position from which the desired objective may be attained." When normal procedures fail to produce the needed result, the police may resort to deceptive stratagems such as giving false legal advice. It is important to keep the subject off balance, for example, by trading on his insecurity about himself or his surroundings. The police then persuade, trick or cajole him out of exercising his constitutional rights. . . .

In the cases before us today, given this background, we concern ourselves primarily with this interrogation atmosphere and the evils it can bring. In No. 759, *Miranda* v. *Arizona,* the police arrested the defendant and took him to a special interrogation room where they secured a confession. In No. 760, *Vignera* v. *New York,* the defendant made oral admissions to the police after interrogation in the afternoon, and then signed an inculpatory statement upon being questioned by an assistant district attorney later the same evening. In No. 761, *Westover* v. *United States,* the defendant was handed over to the Federal Bureau of Investigation by local authorities after they had detained and interrogated him for a lengthy period, both at night and the following morning. After some two hours of questioning, the federal officers had obtained signed statements from the defendant. Lastly, in No. 584, *California* v. *Stewart,* the local police held the defendant five days in the station and interrogated him on nine separate occasions before they secured his inculpatory statement.

In these cases, we might not find the defendants' statements to have been involuntary in traditional terms. Our concern for adequate safeguards to protect precious Fifth Amendment rights is, of course, not lessened in the slightest. In each of the cases, the defendant was thrust into an unfamiliar atmosphere and run through menacing police interrogation procedures. The potentiality for compulsion is forcefully apparent, for example, in *Miranda,* where the indigent Mexican defendant was a seriously disturbed individual with pronounced sexual fantasies, and in *Stewart,* in which the defendant was an indigent Los Angeles Negro who had dropped out of school in the sixth grade. To be sure, the records do not evince overt physical coercion or patent psychological ploys. The fact remains that in none of these cases did the officers undertake to afford appropriate safeguards at the outset of the interrogation to insure that the statements were truly the product of free choice.

It is obvious that such an interrogation environment is created for no purpose other than to subjugate the individual to the will of his examiner. This atmosphere carries its own badge of intimidation. To be sure, this is not physical intimidation, but it is equally destructive of human dignity. The current practice of incommunicado interrogation is at odds with one of our Nation's most cherished principles—that the individual may not be compelled to incriminate himself. Unless adequate protective devices are employed to dispel the compulsion inherent in custodial surroundings, no statement obtained from the defendant can truly be the product of his free choice. . . .

From the foregoing, we can readily perceive an intimate connection between the privilege against self-incrimination and police custodial questioning. . . . We have recently noted that the privilege against self-incrimination—the essential mainstay of our adversary system—is founded on a complex of values. . . . All these policies point to one overriding thought: the constitutional foundation underlying the privilege is the respect a government—state or federal—must accord to the dignity and integrity of its citizens. To maintain a "fair state-individual balance," to require the government "to shoulder the entire load," . . . to respect the inviolability of human personality, our accusatory system of criminal justice demands that the government seeking to punish an individual produce the evidence against him by its own independent labors, rather than by the cruel, simple expedient of compelling it from his own mouth. . . . In sum, the privilege is fulfilled only when the person is guaranteed the right "to remain silent unless he chooses to speak in the unfettered exercise of his own will."

The question in these cases is whether the privilege is fully applicable during a period of custodial interrogation. In this Court, the privilege has consistently been accorded a liberal construction. . . . We are satisfied that all the principles embodied in the privilege apply to informal compulsion exerted by law-enforcement officers during in-custody questioning. An individual swept from familiar surroundings into police custody, surrounded by antagonistic forces, and subjected to the techniques of persuasion described above cannot be otherwise than under compulsion to speak. As a practical matter, the compulsion to speak in the isolated setting of the police station may well be greater than in courts or other official investigations, where there are often impartial observers to guard against intimidation or trickery. . . .

Today, then, there can be no doubt that the Fifth Amendment privilege is available outside of criminal court proceedings and serves to protect persons in all settings in which their freedom of action is curtailed in any significant way from being compelled to incriminate themselves. We have concluded that without proper safeguards the process of in-custody interrogation of persons suspected or accused of crime contains inherently compelling pressures which work to undermine the individual's will to resist and to compel him to speak where he would not otherwise do so freely. In order to combat these pressures and to permit a full opportunity to exercise the privilege against self-incrimination, the accused must be adequately and effectively apprised of his rights and the exercise of those rights must be fully honored.

It is impossible for us to foresee the potential alternatives for protecting the privilege which might be devised by Congress or the States in the exercise of their creative rule-making capacities. Therefore we cannot say that the Constitution necessarily requires adherence to any particular solution for the inherent compulsions of the interrogation process as it is presently conducted. Our decision in no way creates a constitutional straitjacket which will handicap sound efforts at reform, nor is it intended to have this effect. We encourage Congress and the States to continue their laudable search for increasingly effective ways of protecting the rights of the individual while promoting efficient enforcement of our criminal laws. However, unless we are shown other procedures which are at least as effective in apprising accused persons of their right of silence and in assuring a continuous opportunity to exercise it, the following safeguards must be observed.

At the outset, if a person in custody is to be subjected to interrogation, he must first be informed in clear and unequivocal terms that he has the right to remain silent. For those unaware of the privilege, the warning is needed simply to make them aware of it—the threshold requirement for an intelligent decision as to its exercise. More important, such a warning is an absolute prerequisite in overcoming the inherent pressures of the interrogation atmosphere. It is not just the subnormal or woefully ignorant who succumb to an interrogator's imprecations, whether implied or expressly stated, that the interrogation will continue until a confession is obtained or that silence in the face of accusation is itself damning and will bode ill when presented to a jury. Further, the warning will show the individual that his interrogators are prepared to recognize his privilege should he choose to exercise it.

The Fifth Amendment privilege is so fundamental to our system of constitutional rule and the expedient of giving an adequate warning as to the availability of the privilege so simple, we will not pause to inquire in individual cases whether the defendant was aware of his rights without a warning being given. Assessments of the knowledge the defendant possessed, based on information as to his age, education, intelligence, or prior contact with authorities, can never be more than speculation; a warning is a clearcut fact. More important, whatever the background of the person interrogated, a warning at the time of the interrogation is indispensable to overcome its pressures and to insure that the individual knows he is free to exercise the privilege at that point in time.

The warning of the right to remain silent must be accompanied by the explanation that anything said can and will be used against the individual in court. This warning is needed in order to make him aware not only of the privilege, but also of the consequences of forgoing it. It is only through an awareness of these consequences that there can be any assurance of real understanding and intelligent exercise of the privilege. Moreover, this warning may serve to make the individual more acutely aware that he is faced with a phase of the adversary system—that he is not in the presence of persons acting solely in his interest.

The circumstances surrounding in-custody interrogation can operate very quickly to overbear the will of one merely made aware of his privilege by his interrogators. Therefore, the right to have counsel present at the interrogation is indispensable to the protection of the Fifth Amendment privilege under the system we delineate today. Our aim is to assure that the individual's right to choose between silence and speech remains unfettered throughout the interrogation process. A once-stated warning, delivered by those who will conduct the interrogation, cannot itself suffice to that end among those who most require knowledge of their rights. A mere warning given by the interrogators is not alone sufficient to accomplish that end. . . . Thus, the need for counsel to protect the Fifth Amendment privilege comprehends not merely a right to consult with counsel prior to questioning, but also to have counsel present during any questioning if the defendant so desires. . . .

In order fully to apprise a person interrogated of the extent of his rights under this system then, it is necessary to warn him not only that he has the right to consult with an attorney, but also that if he is indigent a lawyer will be appointed to represent him. Without this additional warning, the admonition of the right to consult with counsel would often be understood as meaning only that he can consult with a lawyer if he has one or has the funds to obtain one. The warning of a right to counsel would be hollow if not couched in terms that would convey to the indigent—the person most often subjected to interrogation—the knowledge that he too has a right to have counsel present. As with the warnings of the right to remain silent and of the general right to counsel, only by effective and express explanation to the indigent of this right can there be assurance that he was truly in a position to exercise it. . . .

If the interrogation continues without the presence of an attorney and a statement is taken, a heavy burden rests on the government to demonstrate that the defendant knowingly and intelligently waived his privilege against self-incrimination and his right to retained or appointed counsel. This Court has always set high standards of proof for the waiver of constitutional rights, and we re-assert these standards as applied to in-custody interrogation. Since the State is responsible for establishing the isolated circumstances under which the interrogation takes place and has the only means of making available corroborated evidence of warnings given during incommunicado interrogation, the burden is rightly on its shoulders.

Whatever the testimony of the authorities as to waiver of rights by an accused, the fact of lengthy interrogation or incommunicado incarceration before a statement is made is strong evidence that the accused did not validly waive his rights. . . .

The warnings required and the waiver necessary in accordance with our opinion today are, in the absence of a fully effective equivalent, prerequisites to the admissibility of any statement made by a defendant. . . .

Our decision is not intended to hamper the traditional function of police officers in investigating crime. . . . When an individual is in custody on probable cause, the police may, of course, seek out evidence in the field to be used at trial against him. Such investigation may include inquiry of persons not under restraint. General on-the-scene questioning as to facts surrounding a crime or other general questioning of citizens in the fact-finding process is not affected by our holding. It is an act of responsible citizenship for individuals to give whatever information they may have to aid in law enforcement. In such situations the compelling atmosphere inherent in the process of in-custody interrogation is not necessarily present. . . .

Over the years the Federal Bureau of Investigation has compiled an exemplary record of effective law enforcement while advising any suspect or arrested person, at the outset of an interview, that he is not required to make a statement, that any statement may be used against him in court, that the individual may obtain the services of an attorney of his own choice and, more recently, that he has a right to free counsel if he is unable to pay. . . .

The practice of the FBI can readily be emulated by state and local enforcement agencies. The argument that the FBI deals with different crimes than are dealt with by state authorities does not mitigate the significance of the FBI experience.

The experience in some other countries also suggests that the danger to law enforcement in curbs on interrogation is overplayed. . . .

Because of the nature of the problem and because of its recurrent significance in numerous cases, we have to this point discussed the relationship of the Fifth Amendment privilege to police interrogation without specific concentration on the facts of the cases before us. We turn now to these facts to consider the application to these cases of the constitutional principles discussed above. In each instance, we have concluded that statements were obtained from the defendant under circumstances that did not meet constitutional standards for protection of privilege. . . .

MR. JUSTICE WHITE, with whom MR. JUSTICE HARLAN and MR. JUSTICE STEWART join, dissenting. . . .

. . . The Court's duty to assess the consequences of its action is not satisfied by the utterance of the truth that a value of our system of criminal justice is "to respect the inviolability of the human personality" and to require government to produce the evidence against the accused by its own independent labors. . . . More than the human dignity of the accused is involved; the human personality of others in the society must also be preserved. Thus the values reflected by the privilege are not the sole desideratum; society's interest in the general security is of equal weight.

The obvious underpinning of the Court's decision is a deep-seated distrust of all confessions. As the Court declares that the accused may not be interrogated without counsel present, absent a waiver of the right to counsel, and as the Court all but admonishes the lawyer to advise the accused to remain silent, the result adds up to a judicial judgment that evidence from the accused should not be used against him in any way, whether compelled or not. This is the not so subtle overtone of the opinion—that it is inherently wrong for the police to gather evidence from the accused himself. And this is precisely the nub of this dissent. I see nothing wrong or immoral, and certainly nothing unconstitutional, in the police's asking a suspect whom they have reasonable cause to arrest whether or not he killed his wife or in confronting him with the evidence on which the arrest was based, at least where he has been plainly advised that he may remain completely silent. . . . Until today, "the admissions or confessions of the prisoner, when voluntarily and freely made, have always ranked high in the scale of incriminating evidence." . . . Particularly when corroborated, as where the police have confirmed the accused's disclosure of the hiding place of implements or fruits of the crime, such confessions have the highest reliability and significantly contribute to the certitude with which we may believe the accused is guilty. Moreover, it is by no means certain that the process of confessing is injurious to the accused. To the contrary it may provide psychological relief and enhance the prospects for rehabilitation. . . .

The most basic function of any government is to provide for the security of the individual and of his property. . . . These ends of society are served by the criminal laws which for the most part are aimed at the prevention of crime. Without the reasonably effective performance of the task of preventing private violence and retaliation, it is idle to talk about human dignity and civilized values. . . . There is, in my view, every reason to believe that a good many criminal defendants who otherwise would have been convicted on what this Court has previously thought to be the most satisfactory kind of evidence will now, under this new version of the Fifth Amendment, either not be tried at all or will be acquitted if the State's evidence, minus the confession, is put to the test of litigation.

I have no desire whatsoever to share the responsibility for any such impact on the present criminal process.

In some unknown number of cases the Court's rule will return a killer, a rapist or other criminal to the streets and to the environment which produced him, to repeat his crime whenever it pleases him. As a consequence, there will not be a gain, but a loss, in human dignity. The real concern is not the unfortunate consequences of this new decision on the criminal law as an abstract, disembodied series of authoritative proscriptions, but the impact on those who rely on the public authority for protection and who without it can only engage in violent self-help with guns, knives and the help of their neighbors similarly inclined. There is, of course, a saving factor: the next victims are uncertain, unnamed and unrepresented in this case. . . .

Much of the trouble with the Court's new rule is that it will operate indiscriminately in all criminal cases, regardless of the severity of the crime or the circumstances involved. It applies to every defendant, whether the professional criminal or one committing a crime of momentary passion who is not part and parcel of organized crime. It will slow down the investigation and the apprehension of confederates in those cases where time is of the essence, such as kidnapping, . . . and some of those involving organized crime. In the latter context the lawyer who arrives may also be the lawyer for the defendant's colleagues and can be relied upon to insure that no breach of the organization's security takes place even though the accused may feel that the best thing he can do is to cooperate.

At the same time, the Court's *per se* approach may not be justified on the ground that it provides a "bright line" permitting the authorities to judge in advance whether interrogation may safely be pursued without jeopardizing the admissibility of any information obtained as a consequence. Nor can it be claimed that judicial time and effort, assuming that is a relevant consideration, will be conserved because of the ease of application of the new rule. Today's decision leaves open such questions as whether the accused was in custody, whether his statements were spontaneous or the product of interrogation, whether the accused has effectively waived his rights, and whether nontestimonial evidence introduced at trial is the fruit of statements made during a prohibited interrogation, all of which are certain to prove productive of uncertainty during investigation and litigation during prosecution. For all these reasons, if further restrictions on police interrogation are desirable at this time, a more flexible approach makes much more sense than the Court's constitutional straitjacket which forecloses more discriminating treatment by legislative or rule-making pronouncements.

MR. JUSTICE HARLAN with whom MR. JUSTICE STEWART and MR. JUSTICE WHITE join, dissenting.

I believe the decision of the Court represents poor constitutional law and entails harmful consequences for the country at large. How serious these consequences may prove to be only time can tell. But the basic flaws in the Court's justification seem to me readily apparent now once all sides of the problem are considered. . . .

While the fine points of this scheme are far less clear than the Court admits, the tenor is quite apparent. The new rules are not designed to guard against police brutality or other unmistakably banned forms of coercion. Those who use third-degree tactics and deny them in court are equally able and destined to lie as skillfully about warnings and waivers. Rather, the thrust of the new rules is to negate all pressures, to reinforce the nervous or ignorant suspect, and ultimately to discourage any confession at all. The aim in short is toward "voluntariness" in a utopian sense, or to view it from a different angle, voluntariness with a vengeance.

Without at all subscribing to the generally black picture of police conduct painted by the Court, I think it must be frankly recognized at the outset that police questioning allowable under due process precedents may inherently entail some pressure on the suspect and may seek advantage in his ignorance or weaknesses. The atmosphere and questioning techniques, proper and fair though they be, can in themselves exert a tug on the suspect to confess, and in this light "[t]o speak of any confessions of crime made after arrest as being 'voluntary' or 'uncoerced' is somewhat inaccurate, although traditional. A confession is wholly and incontestably voluntary only if a guilty person gives himself up to the law and becomes his own accuser." . . . Until today, the role of the Constitution has been only to sift out *undue* pressure, not to assure spontaneous confessions.

The Court's new rules aim to offset these minor pressures and disadvantages intrinsic to any kind of police interrogation. The rules do not serve due process interests in preventing blatant coercion since, as I noted earlier, they do nothing to contain the policeman who is prepared to lie from the start. The rules work for reliability in confessions almost only in the Pickwickian sense that they can prevent some from being given at all. . . .

How much harm this decision will inflict on law enforcement cannot fairly be predicted with accuracy. Evidence on the role of confessions is notoriously incomplete . . . and little is added by the Court's reference to the FBI experience and the resources believed wasted in interrogation. . . . We do know that some crimes cannot be solved without confessions, that ample expert testimony attests to their importance in crime control, and that the Court is taking a real risk with society's welfare in imposing its new regime on the country. The social costs of crime are too great to call the new rules anything but a hazardous experimentation. . . .

The Court in closing its general discussion invokes the practice in federal and foreign jurisdictions as lending weight to its new curbs on confessions for all the States. A brief résumé will suffice to show that none of these jurisdictions has struck so one-sided a balance as the Court does today. Heaviest reliance is placed on the FBI practice. Differing circumstances may make this comparison quite untrustworthy, but in any event the FBI falls sensibly short of the Court's formalistic rules. For example, there is no indication that FBI agents must obtain an affirmative "waiver" before they pursue their questioning. Nor is it clear that one invoking his right to silence may not be prevailed upon to change his mind. And the warning as to appointed counsel apparently indicates only that one will be assigned by the judge when the suspect appears before him; the thrust of the Court's rules is to induce the suspect to obtain appointed counsel before continuing the interview. . . .

In conclusion: Nothing in the letter or the spirit

of the Constitution or in the precedents squares with the heavy-handed and one-sided action that is so precipitously taken by the court in the name of fulfilling its constitutional responsibilities. . . .

Nix v. *Williams*

467 U.S. 431, 104 S. Ct. 2501, 81 L. Ed. 2d (1984)

The facts of this criminal case and its lengthy and intricate appellate history are summarized in the opinion below. *Opinion of the Court: Burger, Blackmun, O'Connor, Powell, Rehnquist, White. Concurring opinion: White. Concurring in the Judgment: Stevens. Dissenting opinion: Brennan, Marshall.*

CHIEF JUSTICE BURGER delivered the opinion of the Court.

We granted certiorari to consider whether, at respondent Williams' second murder trial in state court, evidence pertaining to the discovery and condition of the victim's body was properly admitted on the ground that it would ultimately or inevitably have been discovered even if no violation of any constitutional or statutory provision had taken place.

On December 24, 1968, 10-year-old Pamela Powers disappeared from a YMCA building in Des Moines, Iowa, where she had accompanied her parents to watch an athletic contest. Shortly after she disappeared, Williams was seen leaving the YMCA carrying a large bundle wrapped in a blanket; a 14-year-old boy who had helped Williams open his car door reported that he had seen "two legs in it and they were skinny and white."

Williams' car was found the next day 160 miles east of Des Moines in Davenport, Iowa. Later several items of clothing belonging to the child, some of Williams' clothing, and an army blanket like the one used to wrap the bundle that Williams carried out of the YMCA were found at a rest stop on Interstate 80 near Grinnell, between Des Moines and Davenport. A warrant was issued for Williams' arrest.

Police surmised that Williams had left Pamela Powers or her body somewhere between Des Moines and the Grinnell rest stop where some of the young girl's clothing had been found. On December 26, the Iowa Bureau of Criminal Investigation initiated a large-scale search. Two hundred volunteers divided into teams began the search 21 miles east of Grinnell, covering an area several miles to the north and south of Interstate 80. They moved westward from Poweshiek County, in which Grinnell was located, into Jasper County. Searchers were instructed to check all roads, abandoned farm buildings, ditches, culverts, and any other place in which the body of a small child could be hidden.

Meanwhile, Williams surrendered to local police in Davenport, where he was promptly arraigned. Williams contacted a Des Moines attorney who arranged for an attorney in Davenport to meet Williams at the Davenport police station. Des Moines police informed counsel they would pick Williams up in Davenport and return him to Des Moines without questioning him. Two Des Moines detectives then drove to Davenport, took Williams into custody, and proceeded to drive him back to Des Moines.

During the return trip, one of the policemen, Detective Leaming, began a conversation with Williams, saying:

"I want to give you something to think about while we're traveling down the road. . . . They are predicting several inches of snow for tonight, and I feel that you yourself are the only person that knows where this little girl's body is . . . and if you get a snow on top of it you yourself may be unable to find it. And since we will be going right past the area [where the body is] on the way into Des Moines, I feel that we could stop and locate the body, that the parents of this little girl should be entitled to a Christian burial for the little girl who was snatched away from them on Christmas [E]ve and murdered. . . . [A]fter a snow storm [we may not be] able to find it at all."

Leaming told Williams he knew the body was in the area of Mitchellville—a town they would be passing on the way to Des Moines. He concluded the conversation by saying, "I do not want you to answer me. . . . Just think about it. . . ."

Later, as the police car approached Grinnell, Williams asked Leaming whether the police had found the young girl's shoes. After Leaming replied that he was unsure, Williams directed the police to a point near a service station where he said he had left the shoes; they were not found. As they continued to drive to Des Moines, Williams asked whether the blanket had been found and then directed the officers to a rest area in Grinnell where he said he had disposed of the blanket; they did not find the blanket. At this point Leaming and his party were joined by the officers in charge of the search. As they approached Mitchellville, Williams, without any further conversation, agreed to direct the officers to the child's body.

The officers directing the search had called off the search at 3 P.M., when they left the Grinnell Police Department to join Leaming at the rest area. At that time, one search team near the Jasper County-Polk County line was only two and one-half miles from where Williams soon guided Leaming and his party to the body. The child's body was found next to a culvert in a ditch beside a gravel road in Polk County, about two miles south of Interstate 80, and essentially within the area to be searched.

First Trial

In February 1969 Williams was indicted for first-degree murder. Before trial in the Iowa court, his counsel moved to suppress evidence of the body and all related evidence including the condition of the body as shown by the autopsy. The ground for the motion was that such evidence was the "fruit" or product of Williams' statements made during the automobile ride from Davenport to Des Moines and prompted by Leaming's statements. The motion to suppress was denied.

The jury found Williams guilty of first-degree murder; the judgment of conviction was affirmed by the Iowa Supreme Court. . . . Williams then sought release on habeas corpus in the United States District Court for the Southern District of Iowa. That court concluded that the evidence in question had been wrongly admitted at Williams' trial; . . . a divided panel of the Court of Appeals for the Eighth Circuit agreed. . . .

We granted certiorari . . . and a divided Court affirmed, holding that Detective Leaming had obtained incriminating statements from Williams by what was viewed as interrogation in violation of his right to counsel. *Brewer* v. *Williams* . . . (1977). . . .

Second Trial

At Williams' second trial in 1977 in the Iowa court, the prosecution did not offer Williams' statements into evidence, nor did it seek to show that Williams had directed the police to the child's body. However, evidence of the condition of her body as it was found, articles and photographs of her clothing, and the results of post mortem medical and chemical tests on the body were admitted. The trial court concluded that the State had proved by a preponderance of the evidence that, if the search had not been suspended and Williams had not led the police to the victim, her body would have been discovered "*within a short time*" in essentially the same condition as it was actually found. The trial court also ruled that if the police had not located the body, "the search would clearly have been taken up again where it left off, given the extreme circumstances of this case and the body would [have] been found *in short order.*" . . .

In finding that the body would have been discovered in essentially the same condition as it was actually found, the court noted that freezing temperatures had prevailed and tissue deterioration would have been suspended. . . . The challenged evidence was admitted and the jury again found Williams guilty of first-degree murder; he was sentenced to life in prison.

On appeal, the Supreme Court of Iowa again affirmed. . . . That court held that there was in fact a "hypothetical independent source" exception to the Exclusionary Rule.

. . . The Iowa court then reviewed the evidence *de novo* and concluded that the State had shown by a preponderance of the evidence that, even if Williams had not guided police to the child's body, it would inevitably have been found by lawful activity of the search party before its condition had materially changed.

In 1980 Williams renewed his attack on the state-court conviction by seeking a writ of habeas corpus in the United States District Court for the Southern District of Iowa. The District Court conducted its own independent review of the evidence and concluded, as had the state courts, that the body would inevitably have been found by the searchers in essentially the same condition it was in when Williams led police to its discovery. The District Court denied Williams' petition. . . .

The Court of Appeals for the Eighth Circuit reversed. . . .

We granted the State's petition for certiorari, . . . and we reverse.

The Iowa Supreme Court correctly stated that the "vast majority" of all courts, both state and federal, recognize an inevitable discovery exception to the Exclusionary Rule. We are now urged to adopt and apply the so-called ultimate or inevitable discovery exception to the Exclusionary Rule.

. . . The Exclusionary Rule applies not only to the illegally obtained evidence itself, but also to other incriminating evidence derived from the primary evidence. . . .

The core rationale consistently advanced by this Court for extending the Exclusionary Rule to evidence that is the fruit of unlawful police conduct has been that this admittedly drastic and socially costly course is needed to deter police from violations of constitutional and statutory protections. This Court has accepted the argument that the way to ensure such protections is to exclude evidence seized as a result of such violations notwithstanding the high social cost of letting persons obviously guilty go unpunished for their crimes. On this rationale, the prosecution is not to be put in a better position than it would have been in if no illegality had transpired.

By contrast, the derivative evidence analysis ensures that the prosecution is not put in a *worse* position simply because of some earlier police error or misconduct. The independent source doctrine allows admission of evidence that has been discovered by means wholly independent of any constitutional violation. That doctrine, although closely related to the inevitable discovery doctrine, does not apply here; Williams' statements to Leaming indeed led police to the child's body, but that is not the whole story. The independent source doctrine teaches us that the interest of society in deterring unlawful police conduct and the public interest in having juries receive all probative evidence of a crime are properly balanced by putting the police in the same, not a *worse,* position than they would have been in if no police error or misconduct had occurred. . . . When the challenged evidence has an independent source, exclusion of such evidence would put the police in a worse position than they would have been in absent any error or violation. There is a functional similarity between these two doctrines in that exclusion of evidence that would inevitably have been discovered would also put the government in a worse position, because the police would have obtained that evidence if no misconduct had taken place. Thus, while the independent source exception would not justify admission of evidence in this case, its rationale is wholly consistent with and justifies our adoption of the ultimate or inevitable discovery exception to the Exclusionary Rule.

It is clear that the cases implementing the Exclusionary Rule "begin with the premise that the challenged evidence is *in some sense* the product of illegal governmental activity." . . . Of course, this does not end the inquiry. If the prosecution can establish by a preponderance of the evidence that the information ultimately or inevitably would have been discovered by lawful means—here the volunteers' search—then the deterrence rationale has so little basis that the evidence should be received. Anything less would reject logic, experience, and common sense.

Williams contends that because he did not waive his right to the assistance of counsel, the Court may not balance competing values in deciding whether the challenged evidence was properly admitted. He argues that, unlike the Exclusionary Rule in the Fourth Amendment context, the essential purpose of which is to deter police misconduct, the Sixth Amendment Exclusionary Rule is designed to protect the right to a fair trial and the integrity of the factfinding process. Williams contends that, when those interests are at stake, the societal costs of excluding evidence obtained from responses presumed involuntary are irrelevant in determining whether such evidence should be excluded. We disagree.

Exclusion of physical evidence that would inevitably have been discovered adds nothing to either the integrity or fairness of a criminal trial. The Sixth Amendment right to counsel protects against unfairness by preserving the adversary process in which the reliability of proffered evidence may be tested in cross-examination. . . . Here, however, Detective Leaming's conduct did nothing to impugn the reliability of the evidence in question—the body of the child and its condition as it was found, articles of clothing found on the body, and the autopsy. No one would seriously contend that the presence of counsel in the police car when Leaming appealed to Williams' decent human instincts would have had any bearing on the reliability of the body as evidence. Suppression, in these circumstances, would do nothing whatever to promote the integrity of the trial process, but would inflict a wholly unacceptable burden on the administration of criminal justice.

Nor would suppression ensure fairness on the theory that it tends to safeguard the adversary system of justice. To assure the fairness of trial proceedings, this Court has held that assistance of counsel must be available at pretrial confrontations where "the subsequent trial [cannot] cure a[n otherwise] one-sided confrontation between prosecuting authorities and the uncounseled defendant." . . . Fairness can be assured by placing the State and the accused in the same positions they would have been in had the impermissible conduct not taken place. However, if the government can prove that the evidence would have been obtained inevitably and, therefore, would have been admitted regardless of any overreaching by the police, there is no rational basis to keep that evidence from the jury in order to ensure the fairness of the trial proceedings. In that situation, the State has gained no advantage at trial and the defendant has suffered no prejudice. Indeed, suppression of the evidence would operate to undermine the adversary system by putting the State in a *worse* position than it would have occupied without any police misconduct. Williams' argument that inevitable discovery constitutes impermissible balancing of values is without merit.

. . . Three courts independently reviewing the evidence have found that the body of the child inevitably would have been found by the searchers. Williams challenges these findings, asserting that the record contains only the "*post hoc* rationalization" that the search efforts would have proceeded two and one-half miles into Polk County where Williams had led police to the body.

When that challenge was made at the suppression hearing preceding Williams' second trial, the prosecution offered the testimony of Agent Ruxlow of the Iowa Bureau of Criminal Investigation. Ruxlow had organized and directed some 200 volunteers who were searching for the child's body. . . . The searchers were instructed "to check all the roads, the ditches, any culverts. . . . If they came upon any abandoned farm buildings, they were instructed to go onto the property and search those abandoned farm buildings or any other places where a small child could be secreted." . . . Ruxlow testified that he marked off highway maps of Poweshiek and Jasper Counties in grid fashion, divided the volunteers into teams of four to six persons, and assigned each team to search specific grid areas. . . . Ruxlow also testified that, if the search had not been suspended because of Williams' promised cooperation, it would have continued into Polk County, using the same grid system. . . . Although he had previously marked off into grids only the highway maps of Poweshiek and Jasper Counties, Ruxlow had obtained a map of Polk County, which he said he would have marked off in the same manner had it been necessary for the search to continue. . . .

The search had commenced at approximately 10 A.M. and moved westward through Poweshiek County into Jasper County. At approximately 3 P.M., after Williams had volunteered to cooperate with the police, Officer Leaming, who was in the police car with Williams, sent word to Ruxlow and the other Special Agent directing the search to meet him at the Grinnell truck stop and the search was suspended at that time. . . . Ruxlow also stated that he was "under the impression that there was a possibility" that Williams would lead them to the child's body at that time. . . . The search was not resumed once it was learned that Williams had led the police to the body, . . . which was found two and one-half miles from where the search had stopped in what would have been the easternmost grid to be searched in Polk County. . . . There was testimony that it would have taken an additional three to five hours to discover the body if the search had been continued; . . . the body was found near a culvert, one of the kinds of places the teams had been specifically directed to search.

On this record it is clear that the search parties were approaching the actual location of the body and we are satisfied, along with three courts earlier, that the volunteer search teams would have resumed the search had Williams not earlier led the police to the body and the body inevitably would have been found. The evidence asserted by Williams as newly discovered, i.e., certain photographs of the body and deposition testimony of Agent Ruxlow made in connection with the federal habeas proceeding, does not demonstrate that the material facts were inadequately developed in the suppression hearing in state court or that Williams was denied a full, fair, and adequate opportunity to present all relevant facts at the suppression hearing.

The judgment of the Court of Appeals is reversed, and the case is remanded for further proceedings consistent with this opinion.

JUSTICE BRENNAN, with whom JUSTICE MARSHALL joins, dissenting.

... The Court concludes that unconstitutionally obtained evidence may be admitted at trial if it inevitably would have been discovered in the same condition by an independent line of investigation that was already being pursued when the constitutional violation occurred. As has every federal Court of Appeals previously addressing this issue, ... I agree that in these circumstances the "inevitable discovery" exception to the exclusionary rule is consistent with the requirements of the Constitution.

In its zealous efforts to emasculate the exclusionary rule, however, the Court loses sight of the crucial difference between the "inevitable discovery" doctrine and the "independent source" exception from which it is derived. When properly applied, the "independent source" exception allows the prosecution to use evidence only if it was, in fact, obtained by fully lawful means. It therefore does no violence to the constitutional protections that the exclusionary rule is meant to enforce. The "inevitable discovery" exception is likewise compatible with the Constitution, though it differs in one key respect from its next of kin: specifically, the evidence sought to be introduced at trial has not actually been obtained from an independent source, but rather would have been discovered as a matter of course if independent investigations were allowed to proceed.

In my view, this distinction should require that the government satisfy a heightened burden of proof before it is allowed to use such evidence. The inevitable discovery exception necessarily implicates a hypothetical finding that differs in kind from the factual finding that precedes application of the independent source rule. To ensure that this hypothetical finding is narrowly confined to circumstances that are functionally equivalent to an independent source, and to protect fully the fundamental rights served by the exclusionary rule, I would require clear and convincing evidence before concluding that the government had met its burden of proof on this issue. . . .

... Because the lower courts did not impose such a requirement, I would remand this case for application of this heightened burden of proof by the lower courts in the first instance. I am therefore unable to join either the Court's opinion or its judgment.

United States v. *Leon*

468 U.S. 897, 104 S. Ct. 3405, 82 L. Ed. 2d 677 (1984)

Acting on information supplied by a confidential informant, officers of the Burbank, California, police department initiated a drug-trafficking investigation involving the surveillance of Alberto Leon's activities. Based on an affidavit summarizing these officers' observations, the police prepared an application for a warrant to search the respondent's residences and automobiles for an extensive list of items. The application was reviewed by several deputy district attorneys, and a facially valid search warrant was issued by a state court judge. The ensuing searches produced large quantities of drugs and other evidence. Leon and his fellow defendants were indicted for federal drug offenses, and they filed motions to suppress the evidence seized pursuant to the warrant, contending that the affidavit was insufficient to establish probable cause. The U.S. District Court for the Central District of California granted the motions; it recognized that the police had acted in good faith, but rejected the federal government's suggestion that the exclusionary rule should not apply where evidence was seized on the basis of a reasonable, good-faith reliance on a search warrant. The Court of Appeals for the Ninth Circuit affirmed, also refusing to recognize a good-faith exception to the rule. The federal government petitioned for a writ of certiorari, presenting only the question of whether a good-faith exception to the exclusionary rule should be recognized. *Opinion of the Court: White, Burger, Blackmun, O'Connor, Powell, Rehnquist. Concurring opinion: Blackmun. Dissenting opinions: Brennan, Marshall; Stevens.*

JUSTICE WHITE delivered the opinion of the Court.

This case presents the question whether the Fourth Amendment exclusionary rule should be modified so as not to bar the use in the prosecution's case-in-chief of evidence obtained by officers acting in reasonable reliance on a search warrant issued by a detached and neutral magistrate but ultimately found to be unsupported by probable cause. To resolve this question, we must consider once again the tension between the sometimes competing goals of, on the one hand, deterring official misconduct and removing inducements to unreasonable invasions of privacy and, on the other, establishing procedures under which criminal defendants are "acquitted or convicted on the basis of all the evidence which exposes the truth." . . .

We have concluded that, in the Fourth Amendment context, the exclusionary rule can be modified somewhat without jeopardizing its ability to perform its intended functions. Accordingly, we reverse the judgment of the Court of Appeals.

Language in opinions of this Court and of individual Justices has sometimes implied that the exclusionary rule is a necessary corollary of the Fourth Amendment, . . . or that the rule is required by the conjunction of the Fourth and Fifth Amendments. . . . These implications need not detain us long. The Fifth Amendment theory has not withstood critical analysis or the test of time, . . . and the Fourth Amendment "has never been interpreted to proscribe the introduction of illegally seized evidence in all proceedings or against all persons." . . .

The Fourth Amendment contains no provision expressly precluding the use of evidence obtained in violation of its commands, and an examination of its origin and purposes makes clear that the use of fruits of a past unlawful search or seizure "work[s] no new Fourth Amendment wrong." . . . The wrong condemned by the Amendment is "fully accomplished" by the unlawful search or seizure itself, . . . and the exclusionary rule is neither intended nor able to "cure the invasion of the defendant's rights which he has already suffered." . . . The rule thus operates as "a judicially created remedy designed to safeguard Fourth Amendment rights generally through its deterrent effect, rather than a personal constitutional right of the person aggrieved." . . .

The substantial social costs exacted by the exclusionary rule for the vindication of Fourth Amendment rights have long been a source of concern. "Our cases have consistently recognized that unbending application of the exclusionary sanction to enforce ideals of governmental rectitude would impede unacceptably the truth-finding functions of judge and jury." . . . An objectionable collateral consequence of this interference with the criminal justice system's truth-finding function is that some guilty defendants may go free or receive reduced sentences as a result of favorable plea bargains. Particularly when law enforcement officers have acted in objective good faith or their transgressions have been minor, the magnitude of the benefit conferred on such guilty defendants offends basic concepts of the criminal justice system. . . . Indiscriminate application of the exclusionary rule, therefore, may well "generat[e] disrespect for the law and the administration of justice." . . . Accordingly, "[a]s with any remedial device; the application of the rule has been restricted to those areas where its remedial objectives are thought most efficaciously served.". . .

As yet, we have not recognized any form of

good-faith exception to the Fourth Amendment exclusionary rule. But the balancing approach that has evolved during the years of experience with the rule provides strong support for the modification currently urged upon us. As we discuss below, our evaluation of the costs and benefits of suppressing reliable physical evidence seized by officers reasonably relying on a warrant issued by a detached and neutral magistrate leads to the conclusion that such evidence should be admissible in the prosecution's case-in-chief.

Because a search warrant "provides the detached scrutiny of a neutral magistrate, which is a more reliable safeguard against improper searches than the hurried judgment of a law enforcement officer 'engaged in the often competitive enterprise of ferreting out crime,' " . . . we have expressed a strong preference for warrants and declared that "in a doubtful or marginal case a search under a warrant may be sustainable where without one it would fail." . . . Reasonable minds frequently may differ on the question whether a particular affidavit establishes probable cause, and we have thus concluded that the preference for warrants is most appropriately effectuated by according "great deference" to a magistrate's determination. . . .

Deference to the magistrate, however, is not boundless. It is clear, first, that the deference accorded to a magistrate's finding of probable cause does not preclude inquiry into the knowing or reckless falsity of the affidavit on which that determination was based. . . . Second, the courts must also insist that the magistrate purport to "perform his 'neutral and detached' function and not serve merely as a rubber stamp for the police." . . . A magistrate failing to "manifest that neutrality and detachment demanded of a judicial officer when presented with a warrant application" and who acts instead as "an adjunct law enforcement officer" cannot provide valid authorization for an otherwise unconstitutional search. . . .

. . . Third, reviewing courts will not defer to a warrant based on an affidavit that does not "provide the magistrate with a substantial basis for determining the existence of probable cause." . . . "Sufficient information must be presented to the magistrate to allow that official to determine probable cause; his action cannot be a mere ratification of the bare conclusions of others." . . . Even if the warrant application was supported by more than a "bare bones" affidavit, a reviewing court may properly conclude that, notwithstanding the deference that magistrates deserve, the warrant was invalid because the magistrate's probable-cause determination reflected an improper analysis of the totality of the circumstances, . . . or because the form of the warrant was improper in some respect.

Only in the first of these three situations, however, has the Court set forth a rationale for suppressing evidence obtained pursuant to a search warrant; in the other areas, it has simply excluded such evidence without considering whether Fourth Amendment interests will be advanced. To the extent that proponents of exclusion rely on its behavioral effects on judges and magistrates in these areas, their reliance is misplaced. First, the exclusionary rule is designed to deter police misconduct rather than to punish the errors of judges and magistrates. Second, there exists no evidence suggesting that judges and magistrates are inclined to ignore or subvert the Fourth Amendment or that lawlessness among these actors requires application of the extreme sanction of exclusion.

Third, and most important, we discern no basis, and are offered none, for believing that exclusion of evidence seized pursuant to a warrant will have a significant deterrent effect on the issuing judge or magistrate. Many of the factors that indicate that the exclusionary rule cannot provide an effective "special" or "general" deterrent for individual offending law enforcement officers apply as well to judges or magistrates. And, to the extent that the rule is thought to operate as a "systemic" deterrent on a wider audience, it clearly can have no such effect on individuals empowered to issue search warrants. Judges and magistrates are not adjuncts to the law enforcement team; as neutral judicial officers, they have no stake in the outcome of particular criminal prosecutions. The threat of exclusion thus cannot be expected significantly to deter them. Imposition of the exclusionary sanction is not necessary meaningfully to inform judicial officers of their errors, and we cannot conclude that admitting evidence obtained pursuant to a warrant while at the same time declaring that the warrant was somehow defective will in any way reduce judicial officers' professional incentives to comply with the Fourth Amendment, encourage them to repeat their mistakes, or lead to the granting of all colorable warrant requests.

If exclusion of evidence obtained pursuant to a subsequently invalidated warrant is to have any deterrent effect, therefore, it must alter the behavior of individual law enforcement officers or the policies of their departments.

We have frequently questioned whether the exclusionary rule can have any deterrent effect when the offending officers acted in the objectively reasonable belief that their conduct did not violate the Fourth Amendment. "No empirical researcher, proponent or opponent of the rule, has yet been able to establish with any assurance whether the rule has a deterrent effect. . . . " . . . But even assuming that the rule effectively deters some police misconduct and provides incentives for the law enforcement profession as a whole to conduct itself in accord with the Fourth Amendment, it cannot be expected, and should not be applied, to deter objectively reasonable law enforcement activity.

This is particularly true, we believe, when an officer acting with objective good faith has obtained a search warrant from a judge or magistrate and acted within its scope. In most such cases, there is no police illegality and thus nothing to deter. It is the magistrate's responsibility to determine whether the officer's allegations establish probable cause and, if so, to issue a warrant comporting in form with the requirements of the Fourth Amendment. In the ordinary case, an officer cannot be expected to question the magistrate's probable-cause determination or his judgment that the form of the warrant is technically sufficient. "[O]nce the warrant issues, there is literally nothing more the policeman can do in seeking to comply with the law." . . . Penalizing the officer for the magistrate's error, rather than his own, cannot logically contribute to the deterrence of Fourth Amendment violations.

We conclude that the marginal or nonexistent benefits produced by suppressing evidence obtained in objectively reasonable reliance on a subsequently invalidated search warrant cannot justify the substantial costs of exclusion. We do not suggest, however, that exclusion is always inappropriate in cases where an officer has obtained a warrant and abided by its terms. . . .

Suppression . . . remains an appropriate remedy if the magistrate or judge in issuing a warrant was misled by information in an affidavit that the affiant knew was false or would have known was false except for his reckless disregard of the truth. . . . Nor would an officer manifest objective good faith in relying on a warrant based on an affidavit "so lacking in indicia of probable cause as to render official belief in its existence entirely unreasonable." . . . Finally, depending on the circumstances of the particular case, a warrant may be so facially deficient—i.e., in failing to particularize the place to be searched or the things to be seized—that the executing officers cannot reasonably presume it to be valid. . . .

When the principles we have enunciated today are applied to the facts of this case, it is apparent that the judgment of the Court of Appeals cannot stand. . . . Accordingly, the judgment of the Court of Appeals is

Reversed.

Justice Brennan, with whom Justice Marshall joins, dissenting.

At bottom, the Court's decision turns on the proposition that the exclusionary rule is merely a " 'judicially created remedy designed to safeguard Fourth Amendment rights generally through its deterrent effect, rather than a personal constitutional right.' " . . . Although I had thought that such a narrow conception of the rule had been forever put to rest by our decision in *Mapp* v. *Ohio* . . . (1961), it has been revived by the present Court and reaches full flower with today's decision. The essence of this view is that the sole "purpose of the Fourth Amendment is to prevent unreasonable governmental intrusions into the privacy of one's person, house, papers, or effects. The wrong condemned is the unjustified governmental invasion of these areas of an individual's life. That wrong . . . is *fully accomplished* by the original search without probable cause." . . . This reading of the Amendment implies that its proscriptions are directed solely at those government agents who may actually invade an individual's constitutionally protected privacy. The courts are not subject to any direct constitutional duty to exclude illegally obtained evidence, because the question of the admissibility of such evidence is not addressed by the Amendment. This view of the scope of the Amendment relegates the judiciary to the periphery. Because the only constitutionally cognizable injury has already been "fully accomplished" by the police by the time a case comes before the courts, the Constitution is not itself violated if the judge decides to admit the tainted evidence. Indeed, the most the judge *can* do is wring his hands and hope that perhaps by excluding such evidence he can deter future transgressions by the police.

Such a reading appears plausible, because, as critics of the exclusionary rule never tire of repeating, the Fourth Amendment makes no express provision for the exclusion of evidence secured in violation of its commands. A short answer to this claim, of course, is that many of the Constitution's most vital imperatives are stated in general terms and the task of giving meaning to these precepts is therefore left to subsequent judicial decision-making in the context of concrete cases. . . .

A more direct answer may be supplied by recognizing that the Amendment, like other provisions of the Bill of Rights, restrains the power of the government as a whole; it does not specify only a particular agency and exempt all others. The judiciary is responsible, no less than the executive, for ensuring that constitutional rights are respected.

When that fact is kept in mind, the role of the courts and their possible involvement in the concerns of the Fourth Amendment comes into sharper focus. Because seizures are executed principally to secure evidence, and because such evidence generally has utility in our legal system only in the context of a trial supervised by a judge, it is apparent that the admission of illegally obtained evidence implicates the same constitutional concerns as the initial seizure of that evidence. Indeed, by admitting unlawfully seized evidence, the judiciary becomes a part of what is in fact a single governmental action prohibited by the terms of the Amendment. Once that connection between the evidence-gathering role of the police and the evidence-admitting function of the courts is acknowledged, the plausibility of the Court's interpretation becomes more suspect. Certainly nothing in the language or history of the Fourth Amendment suggests that a recognition of this evidentiary link between the police and the courts was meant to be foreclosed. It is difficult to give any meaning at all to the limitations imposed by the Amendment if they are read to proscribe only certain conduct by the police but to allow other agents of the same government to take advantage of evidence secured by the police in violation of its requirements. The Amendment therefore must be read to condemn not only the initial unconstitutional invasion of privacy—which is done, after all, for the purpose of securing evidence—but also the subsequent use of any evidence so obtained.

Even if I were to accept the Court's general approach to the exclusionary rule, I could not agree with today's result.

What the Court overlooks is that the deterrence rationale for the rule is not designed to be, nor should it be thought of as, a form of "punishment" of individual police officers for their failures to obey the restraints imposed by the Fourth Amendment. . . . Instead, the chief deterrent function of the rule is its tendency to promote institutional compliance with Fourth Amendment requirements on the part of law enforcement agencies generally. Thus, as the Court has previously recognized, "over the long term, [the] demonstration [provided by the exclusionary rule] that our society attaches serious consequences to violation of constitutional rights is thought to encourage those who formulate law enforcement policies, and the officers who implement them, to incorporate Fourth Amendment ideals into their value system." . . . It is only through such an institution-wide mechanism that information concerning Fourth Amendment standards can be effectively communicated to rank and file officers.

After today's decision, however, that institutional incentive will be lost. Indeed, the Court's "reasonable mistake" exception to the exclusionary rule will tend to put a premium on police ignorance of the law. Armed with the assurance provided by today's decision that evidence will always be admissible whenever an officer has "reasonably" relied upon a warrant, police departments will be encouraged to train officers that if a warrant has simply been signed, it is reasonable, without more, to rely on it. Since in close cases there will no longer be any incentive to err on the side of constitutional behavior, police would have every reason to adopt a "let's-wait-until-it's-decided" approach in situations in which there is a question about a warrant's validity or the basis for its issuance. . . .

Caplin & Drysdale, Chartered v. *United States*

109 S. Ct. 2646, 105 L. Ed. 2d 528 (1989)

Christopher Reckmeyer was indicted on charges of running a massive drug importation and distribution scheme that the government alleged was part of a continuing criminal enterprise (CCE) in violation of 21 U.S.C. Section 848. Relying on that portion of the CCE statute authorizing forfeiture to the federal government of property acquired as a result of drug law violations (Section 853), federal prosecutors sought forfeiture of specified assets in Reckmeyer's possession. After the District Court entered a restraining order forbidding Reckmeyer from transferring any of the potentially forfeitable assets, Reckmeyer moved to modify the order to allow him to use some of the restrained assets to pay legal fees to his attorneys, Caplin & Drysdale, Chartered, and to exempt such assets from postconviction forfeiture. Before the District Court could rule on his motion, Reckmeyer entered into a plea agreement in which he agreed, among other things, to forfeit all the specified assets. The Court then denied his motion and entered an order forfeiting virtually all his assets to the federal government. Caplin & Drysdale, deprived of its legal fees, filed a petition under the CCE statute seeking an adjudication of its third-party interest (a total of $195,000 for legal services) in the forfeited assets. It argued that assets used to pay an attorney are exempt from forfeiture under the statute, and, if they are not, the statute's failure to provide such an exemption renders it unconstitutional. The District Court granted the relief sought, but the Court of Appeals for the Fourth Circuit reversed, finding that the statute acknowledged no exception to its forfeiture requirement and that the statutory scheme was constitutional. The Supreme Court granted certiorari. *Opinion of the Court: White, Kennedy, O'Connor, Rehnquist, Scalia. Dissenting opinion: Blackmun, Brennan, Marshall, Stevens.*

JUSTICE WHITE delivered the opinion of the Court.

We are called on to determine whether the federal drug forfeiture statute includes an exemption for assets that a defendant wishes to use to pay an attorney who conducted his defense in the criminal case where forfeiture was sought. Because we determine that no such exemption exists, we must decide whether that statute, so interpreted, is consistent with the Fifth and Sixth Amendments. We hold that it is. . . . Petitioner contends that the statute infringes on criminal defendants' Sixth Amendment right to counsel of choice, and upsets the "balance of power" between the government and the accused in a manner contrary to the Due Process Clause of the Fifth Amendment. We consider these contentions in turn. . . .

Petitioner's first claim is that the forfeiture law makes impossible, or at least impermissibly burdens, a defendant's right "to select and be represented by one's preferred attorney," . . . Petitioner does not, nor could it defensibly do so, assert that impecunious defendants have a Sixth Amendment right to choose their counsel. The amendment guarantees defendants in criminal cases the right to adequate representation, but those who do not have the means to hire their own lawyers have no cognizable complaint so long as they are adequately represented by attorneys appointed by the courts. . . . Petitioner does not dispute these propositions. . . . Instead, petitioner urges that a violation of the Sixth Amendment arises here because of the forfeiture, at the instance of the Government, of assets that defendants intend to use to pay their attorneys.

Even in this sense, of course, the burden the forfeiture law imposes on a criminal defendant is limited. The forfeiture statute does not prevent a defendant who has nonforfeitable assets from retaining any attorney of his choosing. Nor is it necessarily the case that a defendant who possesses nothing but assets the Government seeks to have forfeited will be prevented from retaining counsel of choice. Defendants like Reckmeyer may be able to find lawyers willing to represent them, hoping that their fees will be paid in the event of acquittal, or via some other means that a defendant might come by in the future. The burden placed on defendants by the forfeiture law is therefore a limited one.

Nonetheless, there will be cases where a defendant will be unable to retain the attorney of his choice, when that defendant would have been able to hire that lawyer if he had access to forfeitable assets, and if there was no risk that fees paid by the defendant to his counsel would later be recouped under § 853(c). It is in these cases, petitioner argues, that the Sixth Amendment puts limits on the forfeiture statute.

This submission is untenable. Whatever the full extent of the Sixth Amendment's protection of one's right to retain counsel of his choosing, that protection does not go beyond "the individual's right to spend his own money to obtain the advice and assistance of . . . counsel." . . . A defendant has no Sixth Amendment right to spend another person's money for services rendered by an attorney, even if those funds are the only way that that defendant will be able to retain the attorney of his choice. A robbery suspect, for example, has no Sixth Amendment right to use funds he has stolen from a bank to retain an attorney to defend him if he is apprehended. The money, though in his possession, is not rightfully his; the government does not violate the Sixth Amendment if it seizes the robbery proceeds, and refuses to permit the defendant to use them to pay for his defense. . . .

Petitioner seeks to distinguish such cases for Sixth Amendment purposes by arguing that the bank's claim to robbery proceeds rests on "pre-existing property rights," while the Government's claim to forfeitable assets rests on a "penal statute" which embodies the "fictive property-law concept of . . . relation-back" and is merely "a mechanism for preventing fraudulent conveyances of the defendant's assets, not . . . a device for determining true title to property." . . . In light of this, petitioner contends, the burden placed on defendant's Sixth Amendment rights by the forfeiture statute outweighs the Government's interest in forfeiture. . . .

The premises of petitioner's constitutional analysis are unsound in several respects. First, the property rights given the Government by virtue of the forfeiture statute are more substantial than petitioner acknowledges. In § 853(c), the so-called "relation-back" provision, Congress dictated that "[a]ll right, title and interest in property" obtained by criminals via that illicit means described in the statute "vests in the United States upon the commission of the act giving rise to forfeiture." . . . § 853(c) reflects the application of the long-recognized and lawful practice of vesting title to any forfeitable assets, in the United States, at the time of the criminal act giving rise to forfeiture. . . . Petitioner's claim is that whatever part of the assets that is necessary to pay attorney's fees cannot be subjected to forfeiture. But given the Government's title to Reckmeyer's assets upon conviction, to hold that the Sixth Amendment creates some right in Reckmeyer to alienate such assets, or creates a right on petitioner's part to receive these assets, would be peculiar.

There is no constitutional principle that gives one person the right to give another's property to a third party, even where the person seeking to complete the exchange wishes to do so in order to exercise a constitutionally protected right. While petitioner and its supporting *amici* attempt to distinguish between the expenditure of forfeitable assets to exercise one's Sixth Amendment rights, and expenditures in the pursuit of other constitutionally protected freedoms, . . . there is no such distinction between, or hierarchy among, constitutional rights. If defendants have a right to spend forfeitable assets on attorney's fees, why not on exercises of the right to speak, practice one's religion, or travel? The full exercise of these rights, too, depends in part on one's financial wherewithal; and forfeiture, or even the threat of forfeiture, may similarly prevent a defendant from enjoying these rights as full as he might otherwise. Nonetheless, we are not about to recognize an antiforfeiture exception for the exercise of each such right; nor does one exist for the exercise of Sixth Amendment rights, either.

Petitioner's "balancing analysis" to the contrary rests substantially on the view that the Government has only a modest interest in forfeitable assets that may be used to retain an attorney. Petitioner takes the position that, in large part, once assets have been paid over from client to attorney, the principal ends of forfeiture have been achieved: dispossessing a drug dealer or racketeer of the proceeds of his wrongdoing. . . . We think that this view misses the mark for three reasons.

First, the Government has a pecuniary interest in forfeiture that goes beyond merely separating a criminal from his ill-gotten gains; that legitimate interest extends to recovering *all* forfeitable assets, for such assets are deposited in a Fund that supports law-enforcement efforts in a variety of important and useful ways. . . . The sums of money that can be raised for law-enforcement activities this way are substantial, and the Government's interest in using the profits of crime to fund these activities should not be discounted.

Second, the statute permits "rightful owners" of forfeited assets to make claims for forfeited assets before they are retained by the government. . . . The Government's interest in winning undiminished forfeiture thus includes the objective of returning property, in full, to those wrongfully deprived or defrauded of it. Where the Government pursues this restitutionary end, the government's interest in forfeiture is virtually indistinguishable from its interest in returning to a bank the proceeds of a bank robbery; and a forfeiture-defendant's claim of right to use such assets to hire an attorney, instead of having them returned to their rightful owners, is no more persuasive than a bank robber's similar claim

Finally, as we have recognized previously, a major purpose motivating congressional adoption and continued refinement of the RICO and CCE forfeiture provisions has been the desire to lessen the economic power of organized crime and drug enterprises. . . . This includes the use of such economic power to retain private counsel. As the Court of Appeals put it: "Congress has already underscored the compelling public interest in stripping criminals such as Reckmeyer of their undeserved economic power, and part of that undeserved power may be the ability to command high-priced legal talent." . . . The notion that the government has a legitimate interest in depriving criminals of economic power, even in so far as that power is used to retain counsel of choice, may be somewhat unsettling. . . . But when a defendant claims that he has suffered some substantial impairment of his Sixth Amendment rights by virtue of the seizure or forfeiture of assets in his possession, such a complaint is no more than the reflection of "the harsh reality that the quality of a criminal defendant's representation frequently may turn on his ability to retain the best counsel money can buy." . . . Again, the Court of Appeals put it aptly: "The modern day Jean Valjean must be satisfied with appointed counsel. Yet the drug merchant claims that his possession of huge sums of money . . . entitles him to something more. We reject this contention, and any notion of a constitutional right to use the proceeds of crime to finance an expensive defense."

It is our view that there is a strong governmental interest in obtaining full recovery of all forfeitable assets, an interest that overrides any Sixth Amendment interest in permitting criminals to use assets adjudged forfeitable to pay for their defense. Otherwise, there would be an interference with a defendant's Sixth Amendment rights whenever the government freezes or takes some property in a defendant's possession before, during or after a criminal trial. . . . Moreover, petitioner's claim to a share of the forfeited assets postconviction would suggest that the government could never impose a burden on assets within a defendant's control that could be used to pay a lawyer. Criminal defendants, however, are not exempted from federal, state, and local taxation simply because these financial levies may deprive them of resources that could be used to hire an attorney.

We therefore reject petitioner's claim of a Sixth Amendment right of criminal defendants to use assets that are the government's—assets adjudged forfeitable, as Reckmeyer's were—to pay attorneys' fees, merely because those assets are in their possession. . . .

JUSTICE BLACKMUN, with whom JUSTICE BRENNAN, JUSTICE MARSHALL, and JUSTICE STEVENS join, dissenting. . . .

Over 50 years ago, this Court observed: "It is hardly necessary to say that the right to counsel being conceded, a defendant should be afforded a fair opportunity to secure counsel of his own choice." *Powell* v. *Alabama*, . . . (1932). For years, that proposition was settled; the controversial question was whether the defendant's right to use his own funds to retain his chosen counsel was the outer limit of the right protected by the Sixth Amendment. . . . The Court's subsequent decisions have made clear that an indigent defendant has the right to appointed counsel . . . and that the Sixth Amendment guarantees at least minimally effective assistance of counsel. . . . But while court appointment of effective counsel plays a crucial role in safeguarding the fairness of criminal trials, it has never defined the outer limits of the Sixth Amendment's demands. The majority's decision in this case reveals that it has lost track of the distinct role of the right to counsel of choice in protecting the integrity of the judicial process, a role that makes "the right to be represented by privately retained counsel . . . the primary, preferred component of the basic right" protected by the Sixth Amendment. . . .

The right to retain private counsel serves to foster the trust between attorney and client that is necessary for the attorney to be a truly effective advocate. . . . Not only are decisions crucial to the defendant's liberty placed in counsel's hands, . . . but the defendant's perception of the fairness of the process, and his willingness to acquiesce in its results, depend upon his confidence in his counsel's dedication, loyalty, and ability. . . . When the Government insists upon the right to choose the defendant's counsel for him, that relationship of trust is undermined: counsel is too readily perceived as the Government's agent rather than his own.

The right to retain private counsel also serves to assure some modicum of equality between the Government and those it chooses to prosecute. The Government can be expected to "spend vast sums of money . . . to try defendants accused of crime," . . . and of course will devote greater resources to complex cases in which the punitive stakes are high. Precisely for this reason, "there are few defendants charged with crime, few indeed, who fail to hire the best lawyers they can get to prepare and present their defenses." . . . Where cases are complex, trials long, and stakes high, that problem is exacerbated.

In sum, our chosen system of criminal justice is built upon a truly equal and adversarial presentation of the case, and upon the trust that can exist only when counsel is independent of the Government. Without the right, reasonably exercised, to counsel of choice, the effectiveness of that system is imperilled. . . .

Had it been Congress' express aim to undermine the adversary system as we know it, it could hardly have found a better engine of destruction than attorney's-fee forfeiture. The main effect of forfeitures under the Act, of course, will be to deny the defendant the right to retain counsel, and therefore the right to have his defense designed and presented by an attorney he has chosen and trusts. If the Government restrains the defendant's assets before trial, private counsel will be unwilling to continue or to take on the defense. Even if no restraining order is entered, the possibility of forfeiture after conviction will itself substantially diminish the likelihood that private counsel will agree to take the case. The "message [to private counsel] is 'Do not represent this defendant or you will lose your fee.' That being the kind of message lawyers are likely to take seriously, the defendant will find it difficult or impossible to secure representation.' "

The resulting relationship between the defendant and his court-appointed counsel will likely begin in distrust, and be exacerbated to the extent that the defendant perceives his new-found "indigency" as a form of punishment imposed by the Government in order to weaken his defense. If the defendant had been represented by private counsel earlier in the proceedings, the defendant's sense that the Government has stripped him of his defenses will be sharpened by the concreteness of his loss. . . . Appointed counsel may be inexperienced and undercompensated and, for that reason, may not have adequate opportunity or resources to deal with the special problems presented by what is likely to be a complex trial. The already scarce resources of a public defender's office will be stretched to the limit. Facing a lengthy trial against a better-armed adversary, the temptation to recommend a guilty plea will be great. The result, if the defendant is convicted, will be a sense, often well grounded, that justice was not done.

Even if the defendant finds a private attorney who is "so foolish, ignorant, beholden or idealistic as to take the business," . . . the attorney-client relationship will be undermined by the forfeiture statute. . . .

Perhaps most troubling is the fact that forfeiture statutes place the Government in the position to exercise an intolerable degree of power over any private attorney who takes on the task of representing a defendant in a forfeiture case. The decision whether to seek a restraining order rests with the prosecution, as does the decision whether to waive forfeiture upon a plea of guilty or a conviction at trial. The Government will be ever tempted to use the forfeiture weapon against a defense attorney who is particularly talented or aggressive on the client's behalf—the attorney who is better than what, in the Government's view, the defendant deserves. The spectre of the Government's selectively excluding only the most talented defense counsel is a serious threat to the equality of forces necessary for the adversarial system to perform at its best. . . . An attorney whose fees are potentially subject to forfeiture will be forced to operate in an environment in which the Government is not only the defendant's adversary, but also his own. . . .

In short, attorney's-fee forfeiture substantially undermines every interest served by the Sixth Amendment right to chosen counsel, on the individual and institutional levels, over the short term and the long haul.

Comprehensive Crime Control Act of 1984

P.L. 98-473

Among the more controversial chapters of the Comprehensive Crime Control Act of 1984 was the Bail Reform Act of 1984, in which Congress, which had previously authorized preventive detention in the District of Columbia Court Reform and Criminal Procedures Act of 1970, increased its availability to the entire federal court system.

§3142. Release or Detention of a Defendant Pending Trial

(a) In General.—Upon the appearance before a judicial officer of a person charged with an offense, the judicial officer shall issue an order that, pending trial, the person be—

(1) released on his personal recognizance or upon execution of an unsecured appearance bond, pursuant to the provisions of subsection (b);

(2) released on a condition or combination of conditions pursuant to the provisions of subsection (c);

(3) temporarily detained to permit revocation of conditional release, deportation, or exclusion pursuant to the provisions of subsection (d); or

(4) detained pursuant to the provisions of subsection (e).

(e) Detention.—If, after a hearing pursuant to the provisions of subsection (f), the judicial officer finds that no condition or combination of conditions will reasonably assure the appearance of the person as required and the safety of any other person and the community, he shall order the detention of the person prior to trial. In a case described in (f)(1), a rebuttable presumption arises that no condition or combination of conditions will reasonably assure the safety of any other person and the community if the judge finds that—

(1) the person has been convicted of a Federal offense that is described in subsection (f)(1), or of a State or local offense that would have been an offense described in subsection (f)(1) if a circumstance giving rise to Federal jurisdiction had existed;

(2) the offense described in paragraph (1) was committed while the person was on release pending trial for a Federal, State, or local offense; and

(3) a period of not more than five years has elapsed since the date of conviction, or the release of the person from imprisonment, for the offense described in paragraph (1), whichever is later.

(f) Detention Hearing.—The judicial officer shall hold a hearing to determine whether any condition or combination of conditions set forth in subsection (c) will reasonably assure the appearance of the person as required and the safety of any other person and the community in a case—

(1) upon motion of the attorney for the Government, that involves—

(A) a crime of violence;

(B) an offense for which the maximum sentence is life imprisonment or death;

(C) an offense for which a maximum term of imprisonment of ten years or more is prescribed in the Controlled Substances Act . . ., the Controlled Substances Import and Export Act . . ., or section 1 of the Act of September 15, 1980 . . .; or

(D) any felony committed after the person had been convicted of two or more prior offenses described in sub-paragraphs (A) through (C), or two or more State or local offenses that would have been offenses described in sub-paragraphs (A) through (C) if a circumstance giving rise to Federal jurisdiction had existed; or

(2) upon motion of the attorney for the Government or upon the judicial officer's own motion, that involves—

(A) a serious risk that the person will flee;

(B) a serious risk that the person will obstruct or attempt to obstruct justice, or threaten, injure, or intimidate, or attempt to threaten, injure, or intimidate, a prospective witness or juror.

The hearing shall be held immediately upon the person's first appearance before the judicial officer unless that person, or the attorney for the Government, seeks a continuance. Except for good cause, a continuance on motion of the person may not exceed five days, and a continuance on motion of the attorney for the Government may not exceed three days. During a continuance, the person shall be detained, and the judicial officer, on motion of the attorney for the Government or on his own motion, may order that, while in custody, a person who appears to be a narcotics addict receive a medical examination to determine whether he is an addict. At the hearing, the person has the right to be represented by counsel, and, if he is financially unable to obtain adequate representation, to have counsel appointed for him. The person shall be afforded an opportunity to testify, to present witnesses on his own behalf, to cross-examine witnesses who appear at the hearing, and to present information by proffer or otherwise. The rules concerning admissibility of evidence in criminal trials do not apply to the presentation and consideration of information at the hearing. The facts the judicial officer uses to support a finding pursuant to subsection (e) that no condition or combination of conditions will reasonably assure the safety of any other person and the community shall be supported by clear and convincing evidence. The person may be detained pending completion of the hearing.

(g) Factors To Be Considered.—The judicial officer shall, in determining whether there are conditions of release that will reasonably assure the appearance of the person as required and the safety of any other person and the community, take into account the available information concerning—

(1) the nature and circumstances of the offense charged, including whether the offense is a crime of violence or involves a narcotic drug;

(2) the weight of the evidence against the person;

(3) the history and characteristics of the person, including—

(A) his character, physical and mental condition, family ties, employment, financial resources, length of residence in the community, community ties, past conduct, history relating to drug or alcohol abuse, criminal history, and record concerning appearance at court proceedings; and

(B) whether, at the time of the current offense or arrest, he was on probation, on parole, or on other release pending trial, sentencing, appeal, or completion of sentence for an offense under Federal, State, or local law; and

(4) the nature and seriousness of the danger to any person or the community that would be posed by the person's release. In considering the conditions of release . . . the judicial officer may upon his own motion, or shall upon the motion of the Government, conduct an inquiry into the source of the property to be designated for potential forfeiture or offered as collateral to secure a bond, and shall decline to accept the designation, or the use as collateral, of property that, because

of its source, will not reasonably assure the appearance of the person as required.

§3147. Penalty for an Offense Committed while on Release

A person convicted of an offense committed while released pursuant to this chapter shall be sentenced, in addition to the sentence prescribed for the offense to—

(1) a term of imprisonment of not less than two years and not more than ten years if the offense is a felony; or

(2) a term of imprisonment of not less than ninety days and not more than one year if the offense is a misdemeanor.

A term of imprisonment imposed pursuant to this section shall be consecutive to any other sentence of imprisonment.

Gregg v. *Georgia*

428 U.S. 153; 97 S. Ct. 2861; 49 L. Ed. 2d 859 (1976)

In *Furman* v. *Georgia* (1972), the Supreme Court in effect struck down all capital punishment laws as they then existed in the states. The reasons for the Court's action are summarized in the following opinion. In an effort to conform to what it understood to be the requirements of *Furman,* the Georgia legislature immediately revised its death penalty statute. Under the provisions of this revised statute, Troy Leon Gregg was charged with two counts of armed robbery and two counts of murder. At the trial stage of the bifurcated proceeding now required by the statute, the jury found Gregg guilty of all the charges against him. At the penalty stage, the judge instructed the jury that it could recommend either a sentence of death or a sentence of life in prison on each count; that it was free to consider mitigating or aggravating circumstances, if any, as presented by the parties; and that it would not be authorized to consider imposing the death sentence unless it first found beyond a reasonable doubt (1) that the murders were committed while Gregg was engaged in the commission of other capital felonies, *viz.,* the armed robberies of the victims; (2) that he committed the murders for the purpose of receiving the victims' money and automobile; or (3) that the murders were "outrageously and wantonly vile, horrible, and inhuman" in that they "involved the depravity of the mind of the defendant." The jury found the first and second of these aggravating circumstances and returned a sentence of death. Under Georgia's revised statute, the Georgia Supreme Court was required to review Gregg's conviction. After reviewing the trial transcript and record and considering the evidence and sentence in similar cases, the court upheld the death sentence for the murders, concluding that they had not resulted from prejudice or any other arbitrary factor and were not excessive or disproportionate to the penalty applied in similar cases. It vacated the armed robbery sentences, however, on the ground that the death penalty had rarely been imposed in Georgia for that offense. Gregg petitioned the Supreme Court for a writ of certiorari, charging that imposition of the death sentence under the Georgia statute was "cruel and unusual" punishment under the Eighth and Fourteenth amendments. *Judgment of the Court: Stewart, Powell, Stevens. Concurring in judgment: White, Burger, Rehnquist; Blackmun. Dissenting opinions: Brennan; Marshall.*

MR. JUSTICE STEWART, MR. JUSTICE POWELL, and MR. JUSTICE STEVENS announced the judgment of the Court and filed an opinion delivered by MR. JUSTICE STEWART. . . .

We address initially the basic contention that the punishment of death for the crime of murder is, under all circumstances, "cruel and unusual" in violation of the Eighth and Fourteenth Amendments of the Constitution. . . . Until *Furman* v. *Georgia* (1972), the Court never confronted squarely the fundamental claim that the punishment of death always, regardless of the enormity of the offense or the procedure followed in imposing the sentence, is cruel and unusual punishment in violation of the Constitution. Although this issue was presented and addressed in *Furman*, it was not resolved by the Court. Four Justices would have held that capital punishment is not unconstitutional *per se*;* two Justices would have reached the opposite conclusion;** and three Justices, while agreeing that the statutes then before the Court were invalid as applied, left open the question whether such punishment may ever be imposed.*** We now hold that the punishment of death does not invariably violate the Constitution.

. . . The Eighth Amendment has not been regarded as a static concept. As Chief Justice Warren said, in an oft-quoted phrase, "[t]he Amendment must draw its meaning from the evolving standards of decency that mark the progress of a maturing society." . . . Thus, an assessment of contemporary values concerning the infliction of a challenged sanction is relevant to the application of the Eighth Amendment. As we develop below more fully, . . . this assessment does not call for a subjective judgment. It requires, rather, that we look to objective indicia that reflect the public attitude toward a given sanction.

But our cases also make clear that public perceptions of standards of decency with respect to criminal sanctions are not conclusive. A penalty also must accord with "the dignity of man," which is the "basic concept underlying the Eighth Amendment." . . . This means, at least, that the punishment not be "excessive." When a form of punishment in the abstract (in this case, whether capital punishment may ever be imposed as a sanction for murder) rather than in the particular (the propriety of death as a penalty to be applied to a specific defendant for a specific crime) is under consideration, the inquiry into "excessiveness" has two aspects. First, the punishment must not involve the unnecessary and wanton infliction of pain. . . . Second, the punishment must not be grossly out of proportion to the severity of the crime. . . .

Of course, the requirements of the Eighth Amendment must be applied with an awareness of the limited role to be played by the courts. . . .

. . . In assessing a punishment selected by a democratically elected legislature against the constitutional measure, we presume its validity. We may not require the legislature to select the least severe penalty possible so long as the penalty selected is not cruelly inhumane or disproportionate to the crime involved. And a heavy burden rests on those who would attack the judgment of the representatives of the people.

. . . We now consider specifically whether the sentence of death for the crime of murder is a *per se* violation of the Eighth and Fourteenth Amendments to the Constitution. We note first that history and precedent strongly support a negative answer to this question. . . .

The imposition of the death penalty for the crime of murder has a long history of acceptance both in the United States and in England. The common-law rule imposed a mandatory death sentence on all convicted murderers. . . . And the penalty continued to be used into the 20th century by most American States, although the breadth of the common-law rule was diminished, initially by narrowing the class of murders to be punished by death and subsequently by widespread adoption of laws expressly granting juries the discretion to recommend mercy. . . .

It is apparent from the text of the Constitution itself that the existence of capital punishment was accepted by the Framers. At the time the Eighth Amendment was ratified, capital punishment was a common sanction in every State. Indeed, the First Congress of the United States enacted legislation providing death as the penalty for specified crimes. . . . The Fifth Amendment, adopted at the same time as the Eighth, contemplated the continued existence of the capital sanction by imposing certain limits on the prose-

*Blackmun, Burger, Powell, Rehnquist
**Brennan, Marshall
***Douglas, Stewart, White

cution of capital cases: "No person shall be held to answer for a capital, or otherwise infamous crime, unless on a presentment or indictment of a Grand Jury . . . ; nor shall any person be subject for the same offense to be twice put in jeopardy of life or limb; . . . nor be deprived of life, liberty, or property, without due process of law. . . ." And the Fourteenth Amendment, adopted over three-quarters of a century later, similarly contemplates the existence of the capital sanction in providing that no State shall deprive any person of "life, liberty, or property" without due process of law.

For nearly two centuries, this Court, repeatedly and often expressly, has recognized that capital punishment is not invalid *per se*. . . .

Four years ago, the petitioners in *Furman* and its companion cases predicated their argument primarily upon the asserted proposition that standards of decency had evolved to the point where capital punishment no longer could be tolerated. The petitioners in those cases said, in effect, that the evolutionary process had come to an end, and that standards of decency required that the Eighth Amendment be construed finally as prohibiting capital punishment for any crime regardless of its depravity and impact on society. This view was accepted by two Justices. Three other Justices were unwilling to go so far; focusing on the procedures by which convicted defendants were selected for the death penalty rather than on the actual punishment inflicted, they joined in the conclusion that the statutes before the Court were constitutionally invalid.

The petitioners in the capital cases before the Court today renew the "standards of decency" argument, but developments during the four years since *Furman* have undercut substantially the assumptions upon which their argument rested. Despite the continuing debate, dating back to the 19th century, over the morality and utility of capital punishment, it is now evident that a large proportion of American society continues to regard it as an appropriate and necessary criminal sanction.

The most marked indication of society's endorsement of the death penalty for murder is the legislative response to *Furman*. The legislatures of at least 35 States have enacted new statutes that provide for the death penalty for at least some crimes that result in the death of another person. And the Congress of the United States, in 1974, enacted a statute providing the death penalty for aircraft piracy that results in death. . . . All of the post-*Furman* statutes make clear that capital punishment itself has not been rejected by the elected representatives of the people.

The jury also is a significant and reliable objective index of contemporary values because it is so directly involved. . . . The action of juries in many States since *Furman* is fully compatible with the legislative judgments, reflected in the new statutes, as to the continued utility and necessity of capital punishment in appropriate cases. At the close of 1974 at least 254 persons had been sentenced to death since *Furman*, and by the end of March 1976, more than 460 persons were subject to death sentences.

As we have seen, however, the Eighth Amendment demands more than that a challenged punishment be acceptable to contemporary society. The Court also must ask whether it comports with the basic concept of human dignity at the core of the Amendment. . . . The sanction imposed cannot be so totally without penological justification that it results in the gratuitous infliction of suffering. . . .

The death penalty is said to serve two principal social purposes: retribution and deterrence of capital crimes by prospective offenders.

In part, capital punishment is an expression of society's moral outrage at particularly offensive conduct. This function may be unappealing to many, but it is essential in an ordered society that asks its citizens to rely on legal processes rather than self-help to vindicate their wrongs.

. . . "Retribution is no longer the dominant objective of the criminal law," . . . but neither is it a forbidden objective nor one inconsistent with our respect for the dignity of men. . . . Indeed, the decision that capital punishment may be the appropriate sanction in extreme cases is an expression of the community's belief that certain crimes are themselves so grievous an affront to humanity that the only adequate response may be the penalty of death.

Statistical attempts to evaluate the worth of the death penalty as a deterrent to crimes by potential offenders have occasioned a great deal of debate. The results simply have been inconclusive. . . .

Although some of the studies suggest that the

death penalty may not function as a significantly greater deterrent than lesser penalties, there is no convincing empirical evidence either supporting or refuting this view. We may nevertheless assume safely that there are murderers, such as those who act in passion, for whom the threat of death has little or no deterrent effect. But for many others, the death penalty undoubtedly is a significant deterrent. There are carefully contemplated murders, such as murder for hire, where the possible penalty of death may well enter into the cold calculus that precedes the decision to act. And there are some categories of murder, such as murder by a life prisoner, where other sanctions may not be adequate.

The value of capital punishment as a deterrent of crime is a complex factual issue the resolution of which properly rests with the legislatures, which can evaluate the results of statistical studies in terms of their own local conditions and with a flexibility of approach that is not available to the courts. . . . Indeed, many of the post-*Furman* statutes reflect just such a responsible effort to define those crimes and those criminals for which capital punishment is most probably an effective deterrent. . . . Considerations of federalism, as well as respect for the ability of a legislature to evaluate, in terms of its particular state, the moral consensus concerning the death penalty and its social utility as a sanction, require us to conclude, in the absence of more convincing evidence, that the infliction of death as a punishment for murder is not without justification and thus is not unconstitutionally severe.

Finally, we must consider whether the punishment of death is disproportionate in relation to the crime for which it is imposed. There is no question that death as a punishment is unique in its severity and irrevocability. . . . When a defendant's life is at stake, the Court has been particularly sensitive to insure that every safeguard is observed. . . . But we are concerned here only with the imposition of capital punishment for the crime of murder, and when a life has been taken deliberately by the offender, we cannot say that the punishment is invariably disproportionate to the crime. It is an extreme sanction, suitable to the most extreme of crimes.

We hold that the death penalty is not a form of punishment that may never be imposed, regardless of the circumstances of the offense, regardless of the character of the offender, and regardless of the procedure followed in reaching the decision to impose it. . . .

While *Furman* did not hold that the infliction of the death penalty *per se* violates the Constitution's ban on cruel and unusual punishments, it did recognize that the penalty of death is different in kind from any other punishment imposed under our system of criminal justice. Because of the uniqueness of the death penalty, *Furman* held that it could not be imposed under sentencing procedures that created a substantial risk that it would be inflicted in an arbitrary and capricious manner.

. . . The concerns expressed in *Furman* that the penalty of death not be imposed in an arbitrary or capricious manner can be met by a carefully drafted statute that ensures that the sentencing authority is given adequate information and guidance. As a general proposition these concerns are best met by a system that provides for a bifurcated proceeding at which the sentencing authority is apprised of the information relevant to the imposition of sentence and provided with standards to guide its use of the information.

. . . Georgia's new sentencing procedures require as a prerequisite to the imposition of the death penalty, specific jury findings as to the circumstances of the crime or the character of the defendant. Moreover to guard further against a situation comparable to that presented in *Furman*, the Supreme Court of Georgia compares each death sentence with the sentences imposed on similarly situated defendants to ensure that the sentence of death in a particular case is not disproportionate. On their face these procedures seem to satisfy the concerns of *Furman*. No longer should there be "no meaningful basis for distinguishing the few cases in which [the death penalty] is imposed from the many cases in which it is not." . . .

The basic concern of *Furman* centered on those defendants who were being condemned to death capriciously and arbitrarily. Under the procedures before the Court in that case, sentencing authorities were not directed to give attention to the nature or circumstances of crime committed or to the character or record of the defendant. Left unguided, juries imposed the death sentence in a way that could only be called freakish. The new Georgia sentencing procedures, by contrast, focus the jury's attention on the particularized nature of the crime and the particularized characteristics of the individual defendant. While the jury is permitted to consider any aggravating or mitigating circumstances, it must find and identify at least one statutory aggravating factor before it may impose a penalty of death. In this way the jury's discretion is channeled. No longer can a jury wantonly and freakishly impose the death sentence; it is always circumscribed by the legislative guidelines. In addition, the review function of the Supreme Court of Georgia affords additional assurance that the concerns that prompted our decision in *Furman* are not present to any significant degree in the Georgia procedure applied here.

For the reasons expressed in this opinion, we hold that the statutory system under which Gregg was sentenced to death does not violate the Constitution. Accordingly, the judgment of the Georgia Supreme Court is affirmed.

MR. JUSTICE BRENNAN, dissenting.

. . . Death for whatever crime and under all circumstances "is truly an awesome punishment. The calculated killing of a human being by the State involves, by its very nature, a denial of the executed person's humanity. . . . An executed person has indeed 'lost the right to have rights.' " Death is not only an unusually severe punishment, unusual in its pain, in its finality, and in its enormity, but it serves no penal purpose more effectively than a less severe punishment; therefore the principle inherent in the Clause that prohibits pointless infliction of excessive punishment when less severe punishment can adequately achieve the same purposes invalidates the punishment. . . .

The fatal constitutional infirmity in the punishment of death is that it treats "members of the human race as nonhumans, as objects to be toyed with and discarded. [It is] thus inconsistent with the fundamental premise of the Clause that even the vilest criminal remains a human being possessed of common human dignity." . . . As such it is a penalty that "subjects the individual to a fate forbidden by the principle of civilized treatment guaranteed by the [Clause]." I therefore would hold, on that ground alone, that death is today a cruel and unusual punishment prohibited by the Clause. "Justice of this kind is obviously no less shocking than the crime itself, and the new 'official' murder, far from offering redress for the offense committed against society, adds instead a second defilement to the first." . . .

MR. JUSTICE MARSHALL, dissenting. . . .

In *Furman* I concluded that the death penalty is constitutionally invalid for two reasons. First, the death penalty is excessive. . . . And second, the American people, fully informed as to the purposes of the death penalty and its liabilities would in my view reject it as morally unacceptable. . . .

Since the decision in *Furman*, the legislatures of 35 States have enacted new statutes authorizing the imposition of the death sentence for certain crimes, and Congress has enacted a law providing the death penalty for air piracy resulting in death. . . . I would be less than candid if I did not acknowledge that these developments have a significant bearing on a realistic assessment of the moral acceptability of the death penalty to the American people. But if the constitutionality of the death penalty turns, as I have urged, on the opinion of an *informed* citizenry, then even the enactment of new death statutes cannot be viewed as conclusive. In *Furman*, I observed that the American people are largely unaware of the information critical to a judgment on the morality of the death penalty, and concluded that if they were better informed they would consider it shocking, unjust, and unacceptable. . . . A recent study, conducted after the enactment of the post-*Furman* statutes, has confirmed that the American people know little about the death penalty, and that the opinions of an informed public would differ significantly from those of a public unaware of the consequences and effects of the death penalty.

Even assuming, however, that the post-*Furman* enactment of statutes authorizing the death penalty renders the prediction of the views of an informed citizenry an uncertain basis for a constitutional decision, the enactment of those statutes has no bearing whatsoever on the conclusion that the death penalty is unconstitutional because it is excessive. An excessive penalty is invalid under the Cruel and Unusual Punishments Clause "even though popular sentiment may favor" it. . . . The inquiry here, then, is simply whether the death penalty is necessary to accomplish the legitimate legislative purposes in punishment, or whether a less severe penalty—life imprisonment—would do as well. . . .

The two purposes that sustain the death penalty as nonexcessive in the Court's view are general deterrence and retribution. . . . The evidence I reviewed in *Furman* remains convincing, in my view, that "capital punishment is not necessary as a deterrent to crime in our society." The justification for the death penalty must be found elsewhere.

The other principal purpose said to be served by the death penalty is retribution. The notion that retribution can serve as a moral justification for the sanction of death finds credence in the opinion of my Brothers STEWART, POWELL, and STEVENS,. . . . It is this notion that I find to be the most disturbing aspect of today's unfortunate decision. . . . To be sustained under the Eighth Amendment, the death penalty must "[comport] with the basic concept of human dignity at the core of the Amendment". . . . The objective in imposing it must be "[consistent] with our respect for the dignity of other men." . . . Under these standards, the taking of life "because the wrong-doer deserves it" surely must fall, for such a punishment has as its very basis the total denial of the wrong-doer's dignity and worth. . . .

Woodson v. *North Carolina*

428 U.S. 280; 96 S. Ct. 2978; 49 L. Ed. 2d 944 (1976)

In *Gregg* v. *Georgia,* the Supreme Court rejected the argument that the imposition of the death penalty under any circumstances is cruel and unusual punishment in violation of the Eighth and Fourteenth Amendments and upheld the constitutionality of Georgia's capital punishment statute, in which the legislature channeled the jury's discretionary power to impose the death penalty through a bifurcated proceeding and mandatory appellate review. Not every state, however, responded in a like manner to the problem of unbridled jury discretion as raised by *Furman* v. *Georgia*. In North Carolina, for example, the legislature revised its capital punishment statute so as to make the death penalty mandatory for first-degree murder. In this companion case to *Gregg,* James Woodson was convicted of first-degree murder and, as required by the statute, was sentenced to death. The Supreme Court of North Carolina affirmed, and the United States Supreme Court granted certiorari. *Judgment of the Court: Stewart, Powell, Stevens. Concurring in the judgment: Brennan; Marshall. Dissenting opinions: Blackmun; Rehnquist; White, Burger, Rehnquist.*

MR. JUSTICE STEWART, MR. JUSTICE POWELL, and MR. JUSTICE STEVENS announced the judgment of the Court and filed an opinion delivered by MR. JUSTICE STEWART. . . .

. . . In ruling on the constitutionality of the sentences imposed on the petitioners under this North Carolina statute, the Court now addresses for the first time the question whether a death sentence returned pursuant to a law imposing a mandatory death penalty for a broad category of homicidal offenses constitutes cruel and unusual punishment within the meaning of the Eighth and Fourteenth Amendments. The issue, like that explored in *Furman,* involves the procedure employed by the State to select persons for the unique and irreversible penalty of death. . . .

. . . The history of mandatory death penalty statutes in the United States reveals that the practice of sentencing to death all persons convicted of a particular offense has been rejected as unduly harsh and unworkably rigid. The two crucial indicators of evolving standards of decency respecting the imposition of punishment in our society—jury determinations and legislative enactments—both point conclusively to the repudiation of automatic death sentences. At least since the Revolution, American jurors have, with some regularity, disregarded their oaths and refused to convict defendants where a death sentence was the automatic consequence of a guilty verdict. As we have seen, the initial movement to reduce the number of capital offenses and to separate murder into degrees was prompted in part by the reaction of jurors as well as by reformers who objected to the imposition of death as the penalty for any crime. Nineteenth century journalists, statesmen, and jurists repeatedly observed that jurors were often deterred from convicting palpably guilty men of first-degree murder under mandatory statutes. Thereafter, continuing evidence of jury reluctance to convict persons of capital offenses in mandatory death penalty jurisdictions resulted in legislative authorization of discretionary jury sentencing. . . . The consistent course charted by the state legislatures and by Congress since the middle of the past century demonstrates that the aversion of jurors to mandatory death penalty statutes is shared by society at large. . . .

It is now well established that the Eighth Amendment draws much of its meaning from "the evolving standards of decency that mark the progress of a maturing society." . . . As the above discussion makes clear, one of the most significant developments in our society's treatment of capital punishment has been the rejection of the common-law practice of inexorably imposing a death sentence upon every person convicted of a specified offense. North Carolina's mandatory death penalty statute for first-degree murder departs markedly from contemporary standards respecting the imposition of the punishment of death and thus cannot be applied consistently with the Eighth and Fourteenth Amendments' requirement that the State's power to punish "be exercised within the limits of civilized standards." . . .

A separate deficiency of North Carolina's mandatory death sentence statute is its failure to provide a constitutionally tolerable response to *Furman's* rejection of unbridled jury discretion in the imposition of capital sentences. Central to the limited holding in *Furman* was the conviction that the vesting of standardless sentencing power in the jury violated the Eighth and Fourteenth Amendments. . . . American juries have persistently refused to convict a significant portion of persons charged with first-degree murder of that offense under mandatory death penalty statutes. . . . In view of the historic record, it is only reasonable to assume that many juries under mandatory statutes will continue to consider the grave consequences of a conviction in reaching a verdict. North Carolina's mandatory death penalty statute provides no standards to guide the jury in its inevitable exercise of the power to determine which first-degree murderers shall live and which shall die. And there is no way under the North Carolina law for the judiciary to check arbitrary and capricious exercise of that power through a review of death sentences. . . .

A third constitutional shortcoming of the North Carolina statute is its failure to allow the particularized consideration of relevant aspects of the character and record of each convicted defendant before the imposition upon him of a sentence of death. . . . A process that accords no significance to relevant facets of the character and record of the individual offender or the circumstances of the particular offense excludes from consideration in fixing the ultimate punishment of death the possibility of compassionate or mitigating factors stemming from the diverse frailties of humankind. It treats all persons convicted of a designated offense not as uniquely individual human beings, but as members of a faceless, undifferentiated mass to be subject to the blind infliction of the penalty of death.

. . . Consideration of both the offender and the offense in order to arrive at a just and appropriate sentence has been viewed as a progressive and humanizing development. . . . While the prevailing practice of individualizing sentencing determinations generally reflects simply enlightened policy rather than a constitutional imperative, we believe that in capital cases the fundamental respect for humanity underlying the Eighth Amendment . . . requires consideration of the character and record of the individual offender and the circumstances of the particular offense as a constitutionally indispensable part of the process of inflicting the penalty of death. . . .

For the reasons stated, we conclude that the death sentences imposed upon the petitioners under North Carolina's mandatory death sentence statute violated the Eighth and Fourteenth Amendments and therefore must be set aside.

Roberts v. *Louisiana*

428 U.S. 325; 96 S. Ct. 3001; 49 L. Ed. 2d 974 (1976)

Stanislaus Roberts was found guilty of first-degree murder and was sentenced to death under Louisiana's capital punishment statute, which had been amended after *Furman* v. *Georgia* to make the death penalty mandatory for those convicted of first-degree murder. The Louisiana Supreme Court affirmed, and the United States Supreme Court granted certiorari. For the reasons stated in Justice Stewart's opinion in the companion case of *Woodson* v. *North Carolina*, Justice Stevens, speaking for himself and for Justices Stewart and Powell, announced the judgment of the court and invalidated Louisiana's mandatory death penalty statute. Justice White, dissenting, wrote an opinion that responds to the judgments of the Court in both *Roberts* and *Woodson*. *Judgment of the Court: Stewart, Powell, Stevens. Concurring in judgment: Brennan; Marshall. Dissenting opinions: Blackmun; Burger; White, Blackmun, Burger, Rehnquist.*

MR. JUSTICE WHITE, with whom THE CHIEF JUSTICE, MR. JUSTICE BLACKMUN, and MR. JUSTICE REHNQUIST join, dissenting. . . .

I cannot conclude that the current Louisiana first-degree murder statute is insufficiently different from the statutes invalidated in *Furman*'s wake to avoid invalidation under that case. . . .

The difference between a jury having and not having the lawful discretion to spare the life of the defendant is apparent and fundamental. It is undeniable that the unfettered discretion of the jury to save the defendant from death was a major contributing factor in the developments which led us to invalidate the death penalty in *Furman* v. *Georgia*. This factor Louisiana has now sought to eliminate by making the death penalty compulsory upon a verdict of guilty in first-degree murder cases. As I see it, we are now in no position to rule that the State's present law, having eliminated the overt discretionary power of juries, suffers from the same constitutional infirmities which led this Court to invalidate the Georgia death penalty statute in *Furman* v. *Georgia*. . . .

Nor am I convinced that the Louisiana death penalty for first-degree murder is . . . vulnerable because the prosecutor is vested with discretion as to the selection and filing of charges, by the practice of plea bargaining or by the power of executive clemency. . . . The Louisiana statutes . . . define the elements of first-degree murder, and I cannot accept the assertion that state prosecutors will systematically fail to file first-degree murder charges when the evidence warrants it or to seek convictions for first-degree murder on less than adequate evidence. Of course, someone *must* exercise discretion and judgment as to what charges are to be filed and against whom; but this essential process is nothing more than the rational enforcement of the State's criminal law and the sensible operation of the criminal justice system. The discretion with which Louisiana's prosecutors are invested and which appears to be no more than normal, furnishes no basis for inferring that capital crimes will be prosecuted so arbitrarily and frequently that the present death penalty statute is invalid under *Furman* v. *Georgia*. . . .

The plurality offers two additional reasons for invalidating the Louisiana statute. . . .

The plurality holds the Louisiana statute unconstitutional for want of a separate sentencing proceeding in which the sentencing authority may focus on the sentence and consider some or all of the aggravating and mitigating circumstances. Implicit in the plurality's holding that a separate proceeding might be held at which the sentencer may consider the character and record of the accused is the proposition that States are constitutionally prohibited from considering any crime no matter how defined so serious that every person who commits it should be put to death regardless of extraneous factors related to his character. . . . I cannot agree. It is axiomatic that the major justification for concluding that a given defendant deserves to be punished is that he committed a crime. Even if the character of the accused *must* be considered under the Eighth Amendment, surely a State is not constitutionally forbidden to provide that the commission of certain crimes conclusively establishes that the criminal's character is such that he deserves death. Moreover, quite apart from the character of a criminal, a State should constitutionally be able to conclude that the need to deter some crimes and that the likelihood that the death penalty will succeed in deterring these crimes is such that the death penalty may be made mandatory for all people who commit them. Nothing resembling a reasoned basis for the rejection of these propositions is to be found in the plurality opinion. The fact that juries at times refused to convict despite the evidence [does not] prove that the mandatory nature of the sentence was the burr under the jury's saddle rather than that one or more persons on those juries were opposed in principle to the death penalty under whatever system it might be authorized or imposed. Surely if every nullifying jury had been interrogated at the time and had it been proved to everyone's satisfaction that all or a large part of the nullifying verdicts occurred because certain members of these juries had been opposed to the death penalty in any form, rather than because the juries involved were reluctant to impose the death penalty on the particular defendants before them, it could not be concluded that either those juries or the country had condemned mandatory punishments as distinguished from the death penalty itself. The plurality nevertheless draws such an inference even though there is no more reason to infer that jury nullification occurred because of opposition to the death penalty in particular cases than because one or more of the 12 jurors on the critical juries were opposed to the death penalty in any form and stubbornly refused to participate in a guilty verdict. . . .

. . . The more fundamental objection than the plurality's muddled reasoning is that in *Gregg* v. *Georgia* . . . it lectures us at length about the role and place of the judiciary and then proceeds to ignore its own advice, the net effect being to suggest that observers of this institution should pay more attention to what we do than what we say. The plurality claims that it has not forgotten what the past has taught about the limits of judicial review; but I fear that it has again surrendered to the temptation to make policy for and to attempt to govern the country through a misuse of the powers given this Court under the Constitution.

Stanford v. *Kentucky*

109 S. Ct. 2969, 105 L. Ed. 2d 306 (1989)

The Supreme Court granted certiorari in two consolidated cases, *Stanford* v. *Kentucky* and *Wilkins* v. *Missouri,* to decide whether the Eighth Amendment precludes the death penalty for individuals who commit crimes at 16 or 17 years of age. The facts are presented in Justice Scalia's opinion below. *Opinion of the Court: Scalia, Kennedy, O'Connor, Rehnquist, White. Concurring opinion: O'Connor. Dissenting opinion: Brennan, Blackmun, Marshall, Stevens.*

Justice Scalia . . . delivered the opinion of the Court. . . .

These two consolidated cases require us to decide whether the imposition of capital punishment on an individual for a crime committed at 16 or 17 years of age constitutes cruel and unusual punishment under the Eighth Amendment.

The first case . . . involves the shooting death of 20-year-old Baerbel Poore in Jefferson County, Kentucky. Petitioner Kevin Stanford committed the murder on January 7, 1981, when he was approximately 17 years and 4 months of age. Stanford and his accomplice repeatedly raped and sodomized Poore during and after their commission of a robbery at a gas station where she worked as an attendant. They then drove her to a secluded area near the station, where Stanford shot her point-blank in the face and then in the back of her head. The proceeds from the robbery were roughly 300 cartons of cigarettes, two gallons of fuel and a small amount of cash. A corrections officer testified that petitioner explained the murder as follows: " '[H]e said, I had to shoot her, [she] lived next door to me and she would recognize me. . . . I guess we could have tied her up or something or beat [her up] . . . and tell her if she tells, we would kill her. . . . Then after he said that he started laughing.' " . . .

After Stanford's arrest, a Kentucky juvenile court conducted hearings to determine whether he should be transferred for trial as an adult under Ky. Rev. Stat. § 208.170. . . . The statute provided that juvenile court jurisdiction could be waived and an offender tried as an adult if he was either charged with a Class A felony or capital crime, or was over 16 years of age and charged with a felony. Stressing the seriousness of petitioner's offenses and the unsuccessful attempts of the juvenile system to treat him for numerous instances of past delinquency, the juvenile court found certification for trial as an adult to be in the best interest of petitioner and the community.

Stanford was convicted of murder, first-degree sodomy, first-degree robbery, and receiving stolen property, and was sentenced to death and 45 years in prison. The Kentucky Supreme Court affirmed the death sentence, rejecting Stanford's "deman[d] that he has a constitutional right to treatment" . . . Finding that the record clearly demonstrated that "there was no program or treatment appropriate for the appellant in the juvenile justice system," the court held that the juvenile court did not err in certifying petitioner for trial as an adult. The court also stated that petitioner's "age and the possibility that he might be rehabilitated were mitigating factors appropriately left to the consideration of the jury that tried him." . . .

The second case before us today . . . involves the stabbing death of Nancy Allen, a 26-year-old mother of two who was working behind the sales counter of the convenience store she and David Allen owned and operated in Avondale, Missouri. Petitioner Heath Wilkins committed the murder on July 27, 1985, when he was approximately 16 years and 6 months of age. The record reflects that Wilkins' plan was to rob the store and murder "whoever was behind the counter" because "a dead person can't talk." While Wilkins' accomplice, Patrick Stevens, held Allen, Wilkins stabbed her, causing her to fall to the floor. When Stevens had trouble operating the cash register, Allen spoke up to assist him, leading Wilkins to stab her three more times in her chest. Two of these wounds penetrated the victim's heart. When Allen began to beg for her life, Wilkins stabbed her four more times in the neck, opening her carotid artery. After helping themselves to liquor, cigarettes, rolling papers, and approximately $450 in cash and checks, Wilkins and Stevens left Allen to die on the floor.

Because he was roughly six months short of the age of majority for purposes of criminal prosecution, . . . Wilkins could not automatically be tried as an adult under Missouri law. Before that could happen, the juvenile court was required to terminate juvenile court jurisdiction and certify Wilkins for trial as an adult under § 211.071, which permits individuals between 14 and 17 years of age who have committed felonies to be tried as adults. Relying on the "viciousness, force and violence" of the alleged crime, petitioner's maturity, and the failure of the juvenile justice system to rehabilitate him after previous delinquent acts, the juvenile court made the necessary certification.

Wilkins was charged with first-degree murder, armed criminal action, and carrying a concealed weapon. After the court found him competent, petitioner entered guilty pleas to all charges. A punishment hearing was held, at which both the State and petitioner himself urged imposition of the death sentence. Evidence at the hearing revealed that petitioner had been in and out of juvenile facilities since the age of eight for various acts of burglary, theft, and arson, had attempted to kill his mother by putting insecticide into Tylenol capsules, and had killed several animals in his neighborhood. Although psychiatric testimony indicated that Wilkins had "personality disorders," the witnesses agreed that Wilkins was aware of his actions and could distinguish right from wrong. . . . On mandatory review of Wilkins' death sentence, the Supreme Court of Missouri affirmed, rejecting the argument that the punishment violated the Eighth Amendment. . . .

The thrust of both Wilkins' and Stanford's arguments is that imposition of the death penalty on those who were juveniles when they committed their crimes falls within the Eighth Amendment's prohibition against "cruel and unusual punishments." Wilkins would have us define juveniles as individuals 16 years of age and under; Stanford would draw the line at 17.

Neither petitioner asserts that his sentence constitutes one of "those modes or acts of punishment that had been considered cruel and unusual at the time that the Bill of Rights was adopted." . . . At that time, the common law set the rebuttable presumption of incapacity to commit any felony at the age of 14, and theoretically permitted capital punishment to be imposed on anyone over the age of 7. . . .

Thus petitioners are left to argue that their punishment is contrary to the "evolving standards of decency that mark the progress of a maturing society," *Trop* v. *Dulles*, . . . (1958). . . . They are correct in asserting that this Court has "not confined the prohibition embodied in the Eighth Amendment to 'barbarous' methods that were generally outlawed in the 18th century," but instead has interpreted the Amendment "in a flexible and dynamic manner." . . . In determining what standards have "evolved," however, we have looked not to our own conceptions of decency, but to those of modern American society as a whole. . . .

"[F]irst" among the "objective indicia that reflect the public attitude toward a given sanction' " are statutes passed by society's elected representatives. . . . Of the 37 States whose laws permit capital punishment, 15 decline to impose it upon 16-year-old offenders and 12 decline to impose it on 17-year-old offenders. This does not establish the degree of national consensus this Court has previously thought sufficient to label a particular punishment cruel and unusual. . . .

Petitioners make much of the recently enacted federal statute providing capital punishment for certain drug-related offenses, but limiting that punishment to offenders 18 and over. . . . That reliance is entirely misplaced. To begin with, the statute in question does not embody a judgment by the Federal Legislature that *no* murder is heinous enough to warrant the execution of such a youthful offender, but merely that the narrow class of offense it defines is not. The congressional judgment on the broader question, if apparent at all, is to be found in the law that permits 16- and 17-year-olds (after appropriate findings) to be tried and punished as adults for *all* federal offenses, including those bearing a capital penalty that is not limited to 18-year-olds. . . . Moreover, even if it were true that no federal statute permitted the execution of persons under 18, that would not remotely establish—in the face of a substantial number of state statutes to the contrary—a national consensus that such punishment is inhumane, any more than the absence of a federal lottery establishes a national consensus that lotteries are socially harmful. To be sure, the absence of a federal death penalty for 16- or 17-year-olds (if it existed) might be evidence that there is no national consensus *in favor* of such punishment. It is not the burden of Kentucky and Missouri, however, to establish a national consensus approving what their citizens have voted to do; rather, it is the "heavy burden" of petitioners . . . to establish a national consensus *against* it. . . .

Having failed to establish a consensus against capital punishment for 16- and 17-year-old offenders through state and federal statutes, . . . petitioners seek to demonstrate it through other indicia, including public opinion polls, the views of interest groups and the positions adopted by various professional associations. We decline the invitation to rest constitutional law upon such uncertain foundations. A revised national consensus so broad, so clear and so enduring as to justify a permanent prohibition upon all units of democratic government must appear in the operative acts (laws and the application of laws) that the people have approved.

We also reject petitioners' argument that we should invalidate capital punishment of 16- and 17-year-old offenders on the ground that it fails to serve the legitimate goals of penology. According to petitioners, it fails to deter because juveniles, possessing less developed cognitive skills than adults, are less likely to fear death; and it fails to exact just retribution because juveniles, being less mature and responsible, are also less morally blameworthy. In support of these claims, petitioners . . . marshall an array of socioscientific evidence concerning the psychological and emotional development of 16- and 17-year-olds.

If such evidence could conclusively establish the entire lack of deterrent effect and moral responsibility, resort to the Cruel and Unusual Punishments Clause would be unnecessary; the Equal Protection Clause of the Fourteenth Amendment would invalidate these laws for lack of rational basis. . . . But as the adjective "socioscientific" suggests (and insofar as evaluation of moral responsibility is concerned perhaps the adjective "ethicoscientific" would be more apt), it is not demonstrable that no 16-year-old is "adequately responsible" or significantly deterred. It is rational, even if mistaken, to think the contrary. The battle must be fought, then, on the field of the Eighth Amendment; and in that struggle socioscientific, ethicoscientific, or even purely scientific evidence is not an available weapon. The punishment is either "cruel *and* unusual" (*i.e.*, society has set its face against it) or it is not. The audience for these arguments, in other words, is not this Court but the citizenry of the United States. It is they, not we, who must be persuaded. For as we stated earlier, our job is to *identify* the "evolving standards of decency"; to determine, not what they *should* be, but what they *are.* We have no power under the Eighth Amendment to substitute our belief in the scientific evidence for the society's apparent skepticism. In short, we emphatically reject petitioner's suggestion that the issues in this case permit us to apply our "own informed judgment," . . . regarding the desirability of permitting the death penalty for crimes by 16- and 17-year-olds.

We reject the dissent's contention that our approach, by "largely return[ing] the task of defining the contours of Eighth Amendment protection to political majorities," leaves " '[c]onstitutional doctrine [to] be formulated by the acts of those institutions which the Constitution is supposed to limit' " . . . When this Court cast loose from the historical moorings consisting of the original application of the Eighth Amendment, it did not embark rudderless upon a wide-open sea. Rather, it limited the Amendment's extension to those practices contrary to the "evolving *standards* of decency that mark the progress of a maturing *society.*" . . . It has never been thought that this was a shorthand reference to the preferences of a majority of this Court. By reaching a decision supported neither by constitutional text nor by the demonstrable current standards of our citizens, the dissent displays a failure to appreciate that "those institutions which the Constitution is supposed to limit" include the Court itself. To say, as the dissent says, that "it is for *us* ultimately to judge whether the Eighth Amendment permits imposition of the death penalty," . . . —and to mean that as the dissent means it, *i.e.*, that it is for *us* to judge, not on the basis of what we perceive the Eighth Amendment originally prohibited, or on the basis of what we perceive the society through its democratic processes now overwhelmingly disapproves, but on the basis of what we think "proportionate" and "measurably contributory to acceptable goals of punishment"—to say and mean that, is to replace judges of the law with a committee of philosopher-kings. . . .

We discern neither a historical nor a modern societal consensus forbidding the imposition of capital punishment on any person who murders at 16 or 17 years of age. Accordingly, we conclude that such punishment does not offend the Eighth Amendment's prohibition against cruel and unusual punishment.

JUSTICE BRENNAN, with whom JUSTICE MARSHALL, JUSTICE BLACKMUN, and JUSTICE STEVENS join, dissenting.

I believe that to take the life of a person as punishment for a crime committed when below the age of 18 is cruel and unusual and hence is prohibited by the Eighth Amendment. . . . The rejection of the death penalty for juveniles by a majority of the States, the rarity of the sentence for juveniles, both as an absolute and a comparative matter, the decisions of respected organizations in relevant fields that this punishment is unacceptable, and its rejection generally throughout the world, provide to my mind a strong grounding for the view that it is not constitutionally tolerable that certain States persist in authorizing the execution of adolescent offenders. It is unnecessary, however, to rest a view that the Eighth Amendment prohibits the execution of minors solely upon a judgment as to the meaning to be attached to the evidence of contemporary values outlined above, for the execution of juveniles fails to satisfy two well-established and independent Eighth Amendment requirements—that a punishment not be disproportionate, and that it make a contribution to acceptable goals of punishment. . . .

JUSTICE SCALIA forthrightly states in his . . . opinion that Eighth Amendment analysis is at an end once legislation and jury verdicts relating to the punishment in question are analyzed as indicators of contemporary values. . . .

JUSTICE SCALIA's approach would largely return

the task of defining the contours of Eighth Amendment protection to political majorities. . . . The promise of the Bill of Rights goes unfulfilled when we leave "[c]onstitutional doctrine [to] be formulated by the acts of those institutions which the Constitution is supposed to limit," . . . as is the case under Justice Scalia's positivist approach to the definition of citizens' rights. This Court abandons its proven and proper role in our constitutional system when it hands back to the very majorities the Framers distrusted the power to define the precise scope of protection afforded by the Bill of Rights, rather than bringing its own judgment to bear on that question, after complete analysis. . . .

Proportionality analysis requires that we compare "the gravity of the offense," understood to include not only the injury caused, but also the defendant's culpability, with "the harshness of the penalty." . . . In my view, juveniles so generally lack the degree of responsibility for their crimes that is a predicate for the constitutional imposition of the death penalty that the Eighth Amendment forbids that they receive that punishment. . . .

Under a second strand of Eighth Amendment inquiry into whether a particular sentence is excessive and hence unconstitutional we ask whether the sentence makes a measurable contribution to acceptable goals of punishment. The two "principal social purposes" of capital punishment are said to be "retribution and the deterrence of capital crimes by prospective offenders." . . . Unless the death penalty applied to persons for offenses committed under 18 measurably contributes to one of these goals, the Eighth Amendment prohibits it. . . .

"[R]etribution as a justification for executing [offenders] very much depends on the degree of [their] culpability." . . . I have explained . . . why I believe juveniles lack the culpability that makes a crime so extreme that it may warrant, according to this Court's cases, the death penalty; and why we should treat juveniles as a class as exempt from the ultimate penalty. These same considerations persuade me that executing juveniles "does not measurably contribute to the retributive end of ensuring that the criminal gets his just deserts." . . . A punishment that fails the Eighth Amendment test of proportionality because disproportionate to the offender's blameworthiness by definition is not justly deserved.

Nor does the execution of juvenile offenders measurably contribute to the goal of deterrence. Excluding juveniles from the class of persons eligible to receive the death penalty will have little effect on any deterrent value capital punishment may have for potential offenders who are over 18: these adult offenders may of course remain eligible for a death sentence. The potential deterrent effect of juvenile executions on adolescent offenders is also insignificant. The deterrent value of capital punishment rests "on the assumption that we are rational beings who always think before we act, and then base our actions on a careful calculation of the gains and losses involved." . . . As noted, "[t]he likelihood that the teenage offender has made the kind of cost-benefit analysis that attaches any weight to the possibility of execution is so remote as to be virtually nonexistent." . . . Because imposition of the death penalty on persons for offenses committed under the age of 18 makes no measurable contribution to the goals of either retribution or deterrence, it is "nothing more than the purposeless and needless imposition of pain and suffering," . . . and is thus excessive and unconstitutional.

Turner v. *Safley*

482 U.S. 78, 107 S. Ct. 2254, 95 L. Ed. 2d 64 (1987)

Leonard Safley and other inmates brought a class action suit challenging two regulations of the Missouri Division of Corrections relating to inmate-to-inmate correspondence and inmate marriages. The U.S. District Court for the Western District of Missouri relied on *Procunier* v. *Martinez,* 416 U.S. 396 (1974), and, applying a strict scrutiny standard of review, found both regulations unconstitutional. The Court of Appeals for the Eighth Circuit affirmed, and the Supreme Court granted certiorari.

Opinion of the Court: O'Connor, Powell, Rehnquist, Scalia, White. Concurring in part and dissenting in part: Stevens, Blackmun, Brennan, Marshall.

JUSTICE O'CONNOR delivered the opinion of the Court.

This case requires us to determine the constitutionality of regulations promulgated by the Missouri Division of Corrections relating to inmate marriages and inmate-to-inmate correspondence. The Court of Appeals for the Eighth Circuit, applying a strict scrutiny analysis, concluded that the regulations violate respondents' constitutional rights. We hold that a lesser standard of scrutiny is appropriate in determining the constitutionality of the prison rules. Applying that standard, we uphold the validity of the correspondence regulation, but we conclude that the marriage restriction cannot be sustained. . . .

Two regulations are at issue here. The first of the challenged regulations relates to correspondence between inmates at different institutions. It permits such correspondence "with immediate family members who are inmates in other correctional institutions," and it permits correspondence between inmates "concerning legal matters." Other correspondence between inmates, however, is permitted only if "the classification/treatment team of each inmate deems it in the best interest of the parties involved." . . . The District Court found that the rule "as practiced is that inmates may not write non-family inmates." . . .

The challenged marriage regulation, . . . permits an inmate to marry only with the permission of the superintendent of the prison, and provides that such approval should be given only "when there are compelling reasons to do so." . . . The term "compelling" is not defined, but prison officials testified at trial that generally only a pregnancy or the birth of an illegitimate child would be considered a compelling reason. . . . The District Court issued a memorandum opinion and order finding both the correspondence and marriage regulations unconstitutional. The court, relying on *Procunier* v. *Martinez*, . . . applied a strict scrutiny standard. . . .

The Court of Appeals for the Eighth Circuit affirmed. . . . The Court of Appeals held that the District Court properly used strict scrutiny in evaluating the constitutionality of the Missouri correspondence and marriage regulations. Under *Procunier* v. *Martinez*, the correspondence regulation could be justified "only if it furthers an important or substantial governmental interest unrelated to the suppression of expression, and the limitation is no greater than necessary or essential to protect that interest." . . . The correspondence regulation did not satisfy this standard because it was not the least restrictive means of achieving the security goals of the regulation. In the Court of Appeals' view, prison officials could meet the problem of inmate conspiracies by exercising their authority to open and read all prisoner mail. . . . The Court of Appeals also concluded that the marriage rule was not the least restrictive means of achieving the asserted goals of rehabilitation and security. . . .

We begin, as did the courts below, with our decision in *Procunier* v. *Martinez*, . . . which described the principles that necessarily frame our analysis of prisoners' constitutional claims. The first of these principles is that federal courts must take cognizance of the valid constitutional claims of prison inmates. . . . Prison walls do not form a barrier separating prison inmates from the protections of the Constitution. Hence, for example, prisoners retain the constitutional right to petition the Government for the redress of grievances; . . . they are protected against invidious racial discrimination by the Equal Protection Clause of the Fourteenth Amendment; . . . and they enjoy the protections of due process. . . . Because prisoners retain these rights, "[w]hen a prison regulation or practice offends a fundamental constitutional guarantee, federal courts will discharge their duty to protect constitutional rights." . . .

. . . A second principle identified in *Martinez*, however, is the recognition that "courts are ill equipped to deal with the increasingly urgent problems of prison administration and reform." . . . As the *Martinez* Court acknowledged, "the problems of prisons in America are complex and intractable, and, more to the point, they are not readily susceptible of resolution by decree." . . . Running a prison is an inordinately difficult undertaking that requires expertise, planning, and the commitment of resources, all of which are peculiarly within the province of the Legislative and Executive Branches of Government. Prison administration is, moreover, a task that has been committed to the responsibility of those branches, and separation of powers concerns counsel a policy of judicial restraint. Where a state penal system is involved, federal courts have . . . additional reason to accord deference to the appropriate prison authorities. . . .

Our task, then, as we stated in *Martinez,* is to formulate a standard of review for prisoners' constitutional claims that is responsive both to the "policy of judicial restraint regarding prisoner complaints and [to] the need to protect constitutional rights." . . . As the Court of Appeals acknowledged, *Martinez* did not itself resolve the question that it framed. . . . We resolve it now: when a prison regulation impinges on inmates' constitutional rights, the regulation is valid if it is reasonably related to legitimate penological interests. In our view, such a standard is necessary if "prison administrators . . . , and not the courts, [are] to make the difficult judgments concerning institutional operations." . . . Subjecting the day-to-day judgments of prison officials to an inflexible strict scrutiny analysis would seriously hamper their ability to anticipate security problems and to adopt innovative solutions to the intractable problems of prison administration. The rule would also distort the decisionmaking process, for every administrative judgment would be subject to the possibility that some court somewhere would conclude that it had a less restrictive way of solving the problem at hand. Courts inevitably would become the primary arbiters of what constitutes the best solution to every administrative problem, thereby "unnecessarily perpetuat[ing] the involvement of the federal courts in affairs of prison administration." . . .

. . . Several factors are relevant in determining the reasonableness of the regulation at issue. First, there must be a "valid, rational connection" between the prison regulation and the legitimate governmental interest put forward to justify it. . . . Thus, a regulation cannot be sustained where the logical connection between the regulation and the asserted goal is so remote as to render the policy arbitrary or irrational. Moreover, the governmental objective must be a legitimate and neutral one. . . .

A second factor relevant in determining the reasonableness of a prison restriction, . . . is whether there are alternative means of exercising the right that remain open to prison inmates. Where "other avenues" remain available for the exercise of the asserted right, . . . courts should be particularly conscious of the "measure of judicial deference owed to corrections officials . . . in gauging the validity of the regulation."

A third consideration is the impact accommodation of the asserted constitutional right will have on guards and other inmates, and on the allocation of prison resources generally. . . .

. . . Finally, the absence of ready alternatives is evidence of the reasonableness of a prison regulation. . . . By the same token, the existence of obvious, easy alternatives may be evidence that the regulation is not reasonable, but is an "exaggerated response" to prison concerns. This is not a "least restrictive alternative" test: prison officials do not have to set up and then shoot down every conceivable alternative method of accommodating the claimant's constitutional complaint. . . . But if an inmate claimant can point to an alternative that fully accommodates the prisoner's rights at *de minimis* cost to valid penological interests, a court may consider that as evidence that the regulation does not satisfy the reasonable relationship standard. . . .

Applying our analysis to the Missouri rule barring inmate-to-inmate correspondence, we conclude that the record clearly demonstrates that the regulation was reasonably related to legitimate security interests. We find that the marriage restriction, however, does not satisfy the reasonable relationship standard, but rather constitutes an exaggerated response to petitioners' rehabilitation and security concerns. . . .

. . . According to the testimony at trial, the Missouri correspondence provision was promulgated primarily for security reasons. Prison officials testified that mail between institutions can be used to communicate escape plans and to arrange assaults and other violent acts. . . .

The prohibition on correspondence between institutions is logically connected to these legitimate security concerns. . . . Moreover, the correspondence regulation does not deprive prisoners of all means of expression. Rather, it bars communication only with a limited class of other people with whom prison officials have particular cause to be concerned—inmates at other institutions within the Missouri prison system.

. . . The Missouri marriage regulation prohibits inmates from marrying unless the prison superintendent has approved the marriage after finding that there are compelling reasons for doing so. . . . Generally only pregnancy or birth of a child is considered a "compelling reason" to approve a marriage. . . . Even under the reasonable relationship test, the marriage regulation does not withstand scrutiny. . . . No doubt legitimate security concerns may require placing reasonable restrictions upon an inmate's right to marry, and may justify requiring approval of the superintendent. The Missouri regulation, however, represents an exaggerated response to such security objectives. There are obvious, easy alternatives to the Missouri regulation that accommodate the right to marry while imposing a *de minimis* burden on the pursuit of security objectives. . . .

JUSTICE STEVENS, with whom JUSTICE BRENNAN, JUSTICE MARSHALL, and JUSTICE BLACKMUN join, concurring in part and dissenting in part. . . .

To the extent that this Court affirms the judgment of the Court of Appeals, I concur in its opinion. I respectfully dissent from the Court's partial reversal of that judgment on the basis of its own selective forays into the record. When all the language about deference and security is set to one side, the Court's erratic use of the record to affirm the Court of Appeals only partially may rest on an unarticulated assumption that the marital state is fundamentally different from the exchange of mail in the satisfaction, solace, and support it affords to a confined inmate. Even if such a difference is recognized in literature, history or anthropology, the text of the Constitution more clearly protects the right to communicate than the right to marry. In this case, both of these rights should receive constitutional recognition and protection.

15
THE EQUAL PROTECTION CLAUSE AND RACIAL DISCRIMINATION

The Fourteenth Amendment declares that "No state . . . shall deny any person within its jurisdiction the equal protection of the laws." As noted in Chapter 11, the meaning of this clause was first explored by the Supreme Court in the *Slaughterhouse Cases* (1873), in which case, Justice Samuel Miller construed its words narrowly and argued that it prohibited only racial discrimination. At that time, the Court refused to entertain the notion that the Equal Protection Clause could be used to protect the rights of other classes of citizens.

The exact words of the clause, however, guarantee equal protection to all "persons," not simply to ex-slaves or black persons, and over time, the narrow and spindly equal-protection leg of *Slaughterhouse* has grown into a substantial pillar upholding the protection of civil rights. Today, it is viewed as prohibiting all state action that invidiously discriminates against "suspect classifications" or that impinges upon "fundamental rights." As a result, the Court is now called upon to invoke its protections in cases in which discrimination against blacks is altogether absent, as in litigation challenging ameliorative racial preference (i.e., affirmative action/reverse discrimination), gender-based classifications, economic inequality, and restrictions on the exercise of the franchise. Chapter 16 takes up these "newer" equal-protection issues and reviews the various analytical frameworks the justices have employed in ruling on these controversial matters. In this chapter, we will concentrate exclusively on the race-discrimination issues raised by the Constitution and the Equal Protection Clause.

RACE AND THE FOUNDING

Although the post-Civil War amendments in general, and the Fourteenth Amendment in particular, have figured prominently in most analyses of race and the Constitution, the original Constitution also contains three provisions germane to this issue. The Founders have been subjected to considerable obloquy because of these provisions, which set forth the Three-fifths Compromise, allow for the importation of slaves for twenty years, and mandate the return of fugitive slaves to their masters. As Herbert Storing put it, the Founders' response to slavery and the problems of race usually is perceived to be "one to be lived down rather than lived up to."[1] The prominent black historian John Hope Franklin articulated a commonly held view when he charged the Founders with "betraying the ideals to which they gave lip service" by speaking "eloquently at one moment for the brotherhood of man" while denying it "in the next moment . . . to their black brothers." Particularly repugnant to Franklin and others was the Framers' apparent willingness to "degrade the human spirit by equating five black men [or more accurately, five black slaves] with three white men." Summarizing this moral legacy, Franklin declared: "Having created a tragically flawed revolutionary doctrine and a Constitution that did not bestow the blessings of liberty on its posterity, the Founding Fathers set the stage for every succeeding generation of Americans to apologize, compromise, and temporize on those principles of liberty that were supposed to be the very foundation of our system of government and way of life."[2] Citing as further evidence Chief Justice Roger Taney's pronouncement in *Dred Scott* v. *Sandford* (1857) that "the right of property in a slave is distinctly and expressly affirmed in the Constitution," advocates of this point of view assert confidently that the Founders first denied blacks the rights of man listed in the Declaration of Independence and then sanctioned slavery and black inferiority in the Constitution.

The historical record reads quite differently, however. To begin with, the Founders clearly understood that blacks, like all humans everywhere, were created equal and endowed with unalienable rights. As Professor Storing points out, "They did not say that all men were actually secured in the exercise of their rights or that they had the power to provide such security; but there was no doubt about the rights."[3] Powerful support for this point of view can be adduced from the nineteenth and final indictment against the British Crown included in Thomas Jefferson's initial draft of the Declaration of Independence:

> He [the King] has waged cruel war against human nature itself, violating its most sacred rights of life and liberty in the persons of a distant people who never offended him, captivating and carrying them into slavery in another hemisphere, or to incure miserable death in their transportation thither. This piratical warfare, the opprobrium of infidel powers, is the warfare of the Christian king of Great Britain.

> Determined to keep open a market where MEN should be bought and sold, he has prostituted his negative [used his veto power] for suppressing every legislative attempt to prohibit or to restrain this execrable commerce; and that this assemblage of horrors might want no fact of distinguished die, he is now exciting these very people to rise in arms among us, and to purchase that liberty of which he deprived them, by murdering the people upon whom he also obtruded them; thus paying off former crimes committed against the liberties of one people with crimes which he urges them to commit against the lives of another.[4]

This "vehement philippic against negro slavery," as John Adams termed it, eventually was dropped from the Declaration by the Continental Congress. First of all, it simply was not true that the British Crown was solely responsible for the evils of slavery: the colonists themselves were willing and active participants in the slave trade. Also, the Southern states would not have joined in a unanimous Declaration of Independence that contained language they deemed offensive to them and their "peculiar institution." Those outraged by slavery were willing to concede on this point, for they recognized that refusal to do so would not free a single slave and would in all likelihood destroy the possibility of political independence and union. Moreover, they comforted themselves in the knowledge that the Declaration's self-evident truth that all men are created equal had in no way been diluted and that the full force of its claims could be asserted and advanced under more propitious circumstances.

The Framers of the Constitution conceded no more to slavery than did the signers of the Declaration of Independence. No form of the word *slave* appears in the Constitution, and the text alone gives no clue that it concerns slavery at all. The Framers believed that some concessions to slavery were necessary in order to secure the Union, with its promise of a broad and long-lasting foundation of freedom. Their problem was to make the minimum concessions consistent with that end, to express those concessions in language that would not sanction slavery, and to avoid blotting the Constitution with the stain of slavery. How well they succeeded was revealed in the words of the former slave Frederick Douglass:

> I hold that the Federal Government was never, in its essence, anything but an anti-slavery government. Abolish slavery tomorrow, and not a sentence or syllable of the Constitution need be altered. It was purposely so framed as to give no claim, no sanction to the claim, of property in man. If in its origin slavery had relation to the government, it was only as the scaffolding to the magnificent structure, to be removed as soon as the building was completed.[5]

Douglass's reference to "scaffolding" is illuminating: the Framers' support of slavery was strong enough to allow the structure of the new Union to be built but unobtrusive enough to fade from view when the job was done. A detailed look at the three slave provisions reveals this point clearly.

Article 1, Section 2, provides that "Representatives and direct Taxes shall be apportioned among the several States . . . according to their respective Numbers, which shall be determined by adding to the whole Number of free Persons, including those bound to Service for a Term of Years, and excluding Indians not taxed, three fifths of all other Persons." The origins of the phrase "three fifths of all other Persons" (referring to slaves) lay in a dispute over whether legislative representation should be based on numbers of people or on wealth. During the Constitutional Convention, James Madison sought to sidestep that issue by suggesting that numbers were a good index, or proxy indicator, of wealth. The productivity of slaves, however, was generally understood to be lower than that of free men, and because wealth could claim inclusion in the basis for apportioning representation and was the sole basis for apportioning direct taxes, some discount for slaves seemed appropriate. In fact, the "three-fifths" figure had been used under the Articles of Confederation as a guide to apportioning population for purposes of laying requisitions on the states. So in actual fact, the Founders employed the Three-fifths Clause more as a guideline for measuring wealth than as a method of counting human beings represented in government.

The three-fifths rule was offensive to many of the Founders, as it suggested that slaves lacked full humanity. The antislavery Founders appreciated, however, that the South would not yield to a stronger national government unless its property interests were represented at least to the extent of the three-fifths standard. As Martin Diamond noted, "The Convention was faced with the same kind of problem that faced Lincoln later: Not striking the bargain would have freed not a single slave while it would have destroyed the possibility of union. And only a strong union, which would engender a national commercial economy, held out the hope that slavery would gradually be eliminated."[6] To most of the Founders, only the expectation that slavery would become unprofitable in a commercial republic and ultimately wither away rendered the three-fifths compromise palatable as a temporary expedient.

The second slave provision, found in Article 1, Section 9, reads: "The Migration or Importation of such Persons as any of the States now existing shall think proper to admit shall not be prohibited by the Congress prior to the year one thousand eight hundred and eight, but a tax or duty may be imposed on such Importation, not exceeding ten dollars for each Person." In *Dred Scott,* Chief Justice Taney relied on this provision to support his claim that the Constitution "distinctly and expressly" affirmed the right of property in a slave. And it was, in fact, a major concession to slavery: it protected not merely the existing slave population, but also the importation of new slaves, and thereby guaranteed a substantial increase in the slave population and an equally substantial augmentation of the slave problem. Yet this concession was carefully limited. To begin with, the provision did not guarantee a right, but, rather, postponed a power to prohibit. Further, it limited Congress's power to prohibit only to those states "now existing": in other words, the convention viewed slavery as a traditional or vested interest that was to be preserved for a time but that Congress did not have to allow to spread to new states. Fairly interpreted, then, the second slave provision gave only temporary respite to an illicit trade. The presumption was that after twenty years, Congress would forbid this trade—and in fact, Congress did so.

Article 4, Section 2, contains the third slave provision, which addresses the issue of fugitive slaves in the following terms: "No person held to Service or Labour in one State, under the Laws thereof, escaping into another, shall, in Consequence of any Law or Regulation thereof, be discharged from such Service or Labour, but shall be delivered up on Claim of the Party to whom such Service or Labour may be due." Another major concession to slavery, this provision amounted to a form of nationalization of slave property, in the sense that every resident of a free state was obliged to assist in the enforcement of the institution of slavery, at least insofar as fugitive slaves were involved. Like its model in the Northwest Ordinance, which outlawed slavery in the Northwest Territories, the fugitive-slave provision represented the price that had to be paid for a broader freedom. The Founders were willing to pay this price, although they were intent on defining it narrowly. An early version of this provision, agreed to by the convention, read: "If any person bound to service or labour in any of the U——— States shall escape into another State, he or she shall not be discharged from such service or labour, in consequence of any regulations subsisting in the State to which they escape, but shall be delivered up to the person justly claiming their service or labour." The Committee on Style subsequently revised it to read: "No person legally held to service or labour in one state, escaping into another, shall in consequence of regulations subsisting therein be discharged from such service or labour, but shall be delivered up on claim of the party to whom such service or labour may be due." The Committee on Style thus withdrew from the master the claim that he "justly claimed" the services of his slave and acknowledged only that the slave's labor "may be due" to the master. This was further revised so that a slave was no longer defined as one "legally held to service or labour," but rather as one "bound to service or labour." The Founders' motivation in these revisions is apparent. Knowing that a provision for the return of fugitive slaves had to be made to win ratification of the Constitution, they carefully chose language that would give as little sanction as possible to the idea that property in slaves had the same moral status as other kinds of property. Overall, the Founders' viewed slavery, in the words of Professor Storing, as "an evil to be tolerated, allowed to enter the Constitution only by the back door, grudgingly, unacknowledged, on the presumption that the house would be truly fit to live in only when it was gone, and that it would ultimately be gone."[7]

And ultimately, slavery was gone. It lasted longer than the Founders had anticipated, largely because the invention of the cotton gin made the growing of cotton profitable and the plantation slavery system that could grow cotton on a large scale economically viable. Only with the Civil War, the Emancipation Proclamation, and the ratification of the Thirteenth Amendment was slavery finally brought to an end. The former slaves then were made the political equals of their former masters via the Fourteenth Amendment's reversal of *Dred Scott* and its declaration that blacks are citizens of the United States and the states in which they reside, and the Fifteenth Amendment's conferral upon them of the franchise. Finally, the Privileges or Immunities, Due Process, and Equal Protection clauses of the Fourteenth Amendment provided the ex-slaves, and all others, with additional means to achieve the original ends of the Constitution and to check the tyrannical and discriminatory tendencies of the majority.

Of the three branches of government, the judiciary has been the most active and influential in interpreting and enforcing the momentous clauses of the Fourteenth Amendment. The Court's emasculation of the Privileges or Immunities Clause was discussed in Chapter 11, and its extensive and varied applications of the Due Process Clause were considered in Chapters 11 through 14. Here, we will examine the ways in which the Equal Protection Clause has been used as a means to protect against racial discriminations.

RACIAL DESEGREGATION

In interpreting the words of the Equal Protection Clause in the *Slaughter-house Cases* (1873), the Court declared that "the existence of laws in the States where the newly emancipated Negroes resided, which discriminated with gross injustice and hardship against them as a class, was the evil to be remedied by this clause, and by it such laws are forbidden." Thus, it argued that the Equal Protection Clause applied only to blacks. But, what protection did the clause provide them? As a result of the private and public discriminations perpetrated against the "newly emancipated Negroes," the Court was soon forced to define specifically what it understood the Equal Protection Clause to mean. Its response came in the *Civil Rights Cases* (1883) and in *Plessy* v. *Ferguson* (1896).

In the landmark *Civil Rights Cases* (see Chapter 7), the Court limited the protection of the Equal Protection Clause to "state action" only. It held that only discrimination by the states was prohibited and that Congress could not penalize private persons for discriminating against blacks. Absent state action (i.e., in the presence of private discrimination alone), the Court held, the Equal Protection Clause could not be invoked for protection. The concept of state action is in and of itself a complex issue that is discussed separately below. For the moment, the point to be stressed is that the *Civil Rights Cases* limited the concept of equal protection to a narrow class of cases and left entirely to the states the task of prohibiting private racial discriminations.

At this juncture came the *Plessy* decision, which limited the protections offered by the Equal Protection Clause even in cases in which state action was present. In upholding a Louisiana statute that ordered railroads to provide "equal but separate accommodations for the white and colored races," Justice Henry Brown, speaking for the *Plessy* majority, declared that the clause guaranteed to blacks political and civil equality but that it could not put them "on the same plane" socially with whites. Social equality could not be legislated, Brown argued, for it stemmed from "natural affinities, a mutual appreciation of each other's merits, and a voluntary consent of individuals." What the plaintiff Plessy sought, the Court believed, was social equality. To Plessy's contention that the enforced separation of the races stamped him with the badge of inferiority, the Court responded that nothing in the Louisiana statute pronounced him to be inferior, and if he and others of his race felt inferior, that was because they had chosen to put that construction upon the statute. At play here, the Court suggested, was a psychological problem, not a legal one:

> [Plessy's] argument necessarily assumes that if, as has been more than once the case, and is not unlikely to be so again, the colored race should become the dominant power in the state legislature, and should enact a law in precisely similar terms, it would thereby relegate the white race to an inferior position. We imagine that the white race, at least, would not acquiesce in this assumption.

Part of this psychological understanding of racial discrimination was subsequently "rejected" in *Brown* v. *Board of Education* (1954) in which the Court held that the "separate but equal" formula is inherently unequal because it generates feelings of inferiority in members of minority groups. It must be emphasized, however, that not all of the psychological understanding of discrimination present in *Plessy* has been repudiated. Justice Brown's belief that whites cannot be discriminated against because they will not feel stigmatized or inferior has never been overruled and, in fact, has been of decisive importance in sustaining the constitutional validity of, among other things, ameliorative racial preference. In *Regents of the University of California* v. *Bakke* (1978), for instance, Justice William Brennan offered the following observations in seeking to justify the use of racial quotas* by the medical school of the University of California at Davis:

> Nor was Bakke in any sense stamped as inferior by the Medical School's rejection of him. . . . [T]here is absolutely no basis for concluding that Bakke's rejection as a result of Davis's use of racial preference will affect him throughout his life in the same way as the segregation of the Negro school children in *Brown I* would have affected them. Unlike discrimination against racial minorities, the use of race

*This issue is dealt with at greater length in Chapter 16.

> preferences for remedial purposes does not inflict a pervasive injury upon individual whites in the sense that wherever they go or whatever they do there is a significant likelihood that they will be treated as second-class citizens because of their color.

Justice John Marshall Harlan, as the lone dissenter in *Plessy,* rebutted the majority's contention that if blacks felt that Louisiana's "equal but separate" statute branded them as inferior, it was simply because they had put that construction upon it: "Every one knows that the statute in question had its origin in the purpose, not so much to exclude white persons from railroad cars occupied by blacks, as to exclude colored people from coaches occupied by or assigned to white persons. . . . No one would be so wanting in candor to assert the contrary." More central to his dissent, however, was his eloquent and now-famous declaration that "our Constitution is color blind, and neither knows nor tolerates classes among citizens." It has become commonplace to assert that these words finally were vindicated by the Court's unanimous decision in *Brown.*[8] But here too, the Court's post-*Brown* decisions concerning ameliorative racial preference give pause. The principle that the Constitution is color blind is considered by many to be unduly simplistic and inappropriate for today's complexities; some observers have argued that although color blindness may be an appropriate long-term goal, "our society cannot be completely color blind in the short term if we are to have a color blind society in the long term."[9]

In sum, *Plessy* limited the protections of the Equal Protection Clause by legitimating the concept of "equal but separate" (or "separate but equal," as it soon came to be known). Once the principle of racial segregation was in place and constitutionally recognized, it proved difficult to remove. Despite decades of noble effort spearheaded in large part by the National Association for the Advancement of Colored People (NAACP),[10] not until the celebrated *Brown* decision, handed down fifty-eight years later, was "separate but equal" finally rooted out. Efforts to overturn *Plessy* largely were confined to, and ultimately prevailed in, the field of education. Although this focus on segregation in education unquestionably was a wise litigation strategy, as the fraudulent character of the protection afforded by "separate but equal" was nowhere more obvious, it did present a certain irony. In *Plessy,* Justice Brown relied heavily on the fact there was racial segregation in the schools of Boston and the District of Columbia to sustain racial segregation in railroad coaches in Louisiana: "The establishment of separate schools for white and colored children . . . has been held to be a valid exercise of the legislative power even by courts of States where the political rights of the colored race have been longest and most earnestly enforced."

The initial attempts to overturn *Plessy* and the "separate but equal" doctrine in education were inauspicious. In *Cumming* v. *Richmond County Board of Education* (1899), in fact, the plaintiffs found that the Court was willing to tolerate even "separate and unequal." This case arose out of a Georgia school board's decision to discontinue the existing black high school in order to use the building and facilities for black elementary education. Whereas no new black high school was established, the white high schools were continued, and black taxpayers and parents brought suit to restrain the school board from using money to support the white high school until equal facilities for black students had been provided. A unanimous Supreme Court sidestepped the question of segregation; denied that the discontinuance of the black school violated the Equal Protection Clause; and stressed that an injunction to close the white schools was not the proper legal remedy, as it would not help the black children.

The problems of reconciling *Cumming* and its progeny with the demands of equal protection finally prompted the Court in the 1930s to emphasize the need for equality in segregation. "Separate but equal" facilities were to be just that; "separate and unequal" treatment, at least in higher education, would no longer be tolerated. *Missouri Ex Rel Gaines* v. *Canada* (1938) is significant in this regard. Missouri had refused to admit blacks to the University of Missouri School of Law, providing instead state reimbursement of tuition fees for any of its black citizens who could gain admission to law schools in neighboring states in which segregation was not enforced. Missouri argued that this provision satisfied the "separate but equal" requirement, but the Supreme Court ruled that if facilities within the state were provided for the legal education of white students, equal facilities for black students also had to be made available in the state.

In subsequent cases the Court continued to insist on equal educational facilities for blacks pursuing postbaccalaureate studies. The most important of these was *Sweatt* v. *Painter* (1950), which held, in effect, that if educational facilities were segregated, they had to be equal not only quantitatively but also qualitatively. At issue was a law school for blacks that Texas had hastily established as a means of avoiding the desegregation of the University of Texas Law School. In the view of the Court, even if the black school were equal to the all-white law school "in terms of number of the faculty, variety of courses and opportunity for specialization, size of the student body, scope of the library, and availability of law review and other activities"—which it most assuredly was not—it clearly was unequal with respect to those "qualities which are incapable of objective measurement but which make for greatness in a law school. Such qualities, to name but a few, include reputation of the faculty, experience of the administration, position and influence of the alumni, standing in the community, traditions and prestige." The Court's message in *Sweatt* was plain and blunt: segregation *per se* was not yet unconstitutional, but the requirements of "separate but equal" henceforth would be all but impossible to meet.

The NAACP prudently had begun its assault on segregated education at the postgraduate and professional level, where the inequalities that black students suffered could be documented most easily. Because only a few blacks were seeking admission to these programs, moreover, the public's reaction to the Court's decisions would be uneventful. The *Missouri* and *Sweatt* decisions, however, paved the way for the NAACP's assault on segregation at all levels of public education, which bore fruit in *Brown.* In that landmark decision, handed down on May 17, 1954, by a unanimous Court, Chief Justice Earl Warren held that "in the field of public education the doctrine of 'separate but equal' has no place." Soon after the decision was rendered, *The New York Times* editorialized that "it is fifty-eight years since the Supreme Court, with Justice Harlan dissenting, established the doctrine of 'separate but equal' provision for the white and Negro races on interstate carriers. It is forty-three years since John Marshall Harlan passed from this earth. Now the words he used in his lonely dissent in an 8-to-1 decision in the case of *Plessy* v. *Ferguson* in 1896 have become a part of the law of the land." Although noting that *Brown* "dealt solely with segregation in the public schools," the *Times* insisted that "there was not one word in Chief Justice Warren's opinion that was inconsistent with the earlier views of Justice Harlan."[11]

The *Times*'s statement expresses the conventional wisdom that *Brown* realized Justice Harlan's famous dissenting dictum. A closer look at the *Brown* opinion, however, belies this claim. Chief Justice Warren did not invalidate "separate but equal" because it departed from the principle that the Constitution is color blind; he invalidated it because of the psychological damage it caused blacks. "Separate but equal" is inherently unequal, he insisted, because it "generates feelings of inferiority [in blacks] as to their status in the community that may affect their hearts and minds in a way unlikely ever to be undone"—a conclusion he supported by citations to the literature of social psychology. Accordingly, it can be argued that Chief Justice Warren's opinion had more in common with Justice Brown's majority opinion in *Plessy* than with Justice Harlan's dissent. Central to both Chief Justice Warren and Justice Brown was the question of the psychological damage caused by segregation; they differed only in the answers they gave, not in the questions they asked. Neither understood the Equal Protection Clause in the way that Justice Harlan did—as a flat prohibition against the use of race as the basis for classifying or categorizing individuals. Contrary to commonly held opinion, then, Justice Harlan's dissenting words have never been vindicated. This point must be understood if confusion is to be avoided, for the Supreme Court has continued to regard the Equal Protection Clause as a means for preventing or mitigating the psychological damage caused by racial discrimination, not as a barrier to race-conscious classifications.

In *Bolling* v. *Sharpe* (1954), a companion case to *Brown,* the Court also invalidated racial segregation in the public schools of the District of Columbia. Because the Equal Protection Clause of the Fourteenth Amendment applies only to the states, and not to the federal government, the justices based this decision on the Due Process Clause of the Fifth Amendment. In finding it "unthinkable" that the Constitution could impose a lesser duty on the federal government than on the states, they employed a substantive due-process argument to end this practice. Chief Justice Warren reasoned as follows: "Liberty . . . cannot be restricted except for a proper governmental objective. Segregation in public education is not reasonably related to any proper governmental objective, and thus imposes on Negro children of the District of Columbia a burden that constitutes an arbitrary deprivation of their liberty. . . ." The Court has relied on this same line of argument in subsequent cases to impose the standards of the Equal Protection Clause on national legislation—even though, to repeat, the Fourteenth Amendment is not directed toward the national government.

Brown and its companion cases established the fundamental principle that "racial discrimination in public education is unconstitutional"; they did not, however, address the question of how this fundamental principle was to be implemented. Instead, the Court postponed a decision on the application of *Brown*, restored the case to its docket for argument during the next term, and invited all interested parties to present their views on how its decision could be carried out. These hearings were held in April 1955, and on May 31 of that year the Court ruled in what is commonly called *Brown II* that the cases would be remanded to the courts in which they had originated, which were ordered to fashion decrees of enforcement on equitable principles and with regard to "varied local school problems."[12] The Supreme Court directed the lower courts to determine whether the actions or proposals of the various school authorities constituted "good faith implementation of the governing constitutional principles" and charged them with requiring a "prompt and reasonable start toward full compliance" with *Brown I* and with ensuring that the parties to these cases be admitted to public schools "on a racially non-discriminatory basis with all deliberate speed."[13]

Brown I and *Brown II* were met with stiff resistance throughout the South. The resisters redoubled their efforts after the Court, through a series of *per curiam* orders, extended the desegregation requirement, which originally had been confined to public education, to public recreational facilities, golf courses, bus transportation, public parks, athletic contests, airport restaurants, courtroom seating, public auditoriums, and jails.[14] Resistance took a number of forms, including threatened or actual violence. Major incidents involving violence occurred in Clinton, Tennessee, in 1956; in Little Rock, Arkansas, in 1957; in New Orleans in 1960; and at the University of Mississippi in 1962. On these occasions, the Court was quick to act and unequivocal in its condemnation. In the especially significant case of *Cooper* v. *Aaron* (1958), the Court unanimously held that the violent resistance to the desegregation plan of the schools of Little Rock was "directly traceable" to Arkansas's governor and legislature and warned that the constitutional prohibition of racial discrimination in school admissions "can neither be nullified openly and directly by state legislators or state executive or judicial officers, nor nullified indirectly by them through evasive schemes for segregation." Then, in extraordinary language, the Court explicitly asserted its supreme authority as constitutional expositor. Declaring that *Marbury* v. *Madison* established "the basic principle that the federal judiciary is supreme in the exposition of the law of the Constitution, and that [this] principle has ever since been respected by this Court and the Country as a permanent and indispensable feature of our Constitutional system," it held that "it follows that the interpretation of the Fourteenth Amendment enunciated by this Court in the *Brown* case is the Supreme Law of the Land, and Art. VI of the Constitution makes it of binding effect on the States."

More often, resistance took the form of delaying tactics by local school boards that, either on their own initiative or under the compulsion of a federal district court order, were charged with preparing desegregation plans. Even those boards willing to act usually preferred to await a court decision mandating such action, in order to justify their actions to those in the community opposed to *Brown* and to desegregation. When ordered to act, moreover, the boards often instituted measures that stopped short of actual desegregation. "Freedom of choice" plans, under which each pupil supposedly was free to choose the school to be attended but which in fact resulted in very few transfers out of black schools, represented one such measure. For some time, this foot-dragging proved successful—after all, the Supreme Court seemingly had sanctioned these measures in *Brown II,* as it had not required either the school authorities or the lower courts to take immediate steps to "admit pupils to public schools on a racially nondiscriminatory basis" but had only imposed on them the duty to realize this goal "with all deliberate speed." By 1968, however, the Court's patience had run out, and in *Green* v. *County School Board of New Kent County* it announced that school boards had a positive duty to eliminate, "root and branch," the historic and pervasive effects of racial discrimination. This required the formulation of plans that promised prompt conversion to a desegregated system. The goal, the Court underlined, was the achievement of a "unitary, nonracial system of public education." The following year, in *Alexander* v. *Holmes County Board of Education,* the Court more pointedly declared that the "continued operation of segregated schools under a standard of allowing 'all deliberate speed' for desegregation is no longer constitutionally permissible" and demanded that every district immediately end dual school systems and begin to operate unitary schools alone.

The question of exactly what the Court expected when it ordered the operation of unitary school systems has not yet been resolved definitively, but a review of its subsequent decisions yields some indications. In *Swann* v. *Charlotte-Mecklenburg Board of Eduation* (1971), it held that where *de jure* segregation existed in the past, school authorities must dismantle the dual school system by taking positive action to create an integrated school system. Among the measures deemed appropriate for eliminating "all vestiges of state-imposed segregation" were remedial altering of attendance zones, clustering, and busing. The Court acknowledged that these measures "may be administratively awkward, inconvenient, and even bizarre in some situations and may impose burdens on some," but it insisted that during this remedial period such inconveniences were necessary evils. In defending this extraordinary use of the judiciary's equity power, the Court emphasized that "absent a constitutional violation there would be no basis for judicially ordering assignment of students on a racial basis. All things being equal, with no history of discrimination, it might well be desirable to assign pupils to schools nearest their homes. But all things are not equal in a system that has been deliberately constructed and maintained to enforce racial segregation."

Soon thereafter, the Court in *Keyes* v. *School District No. 1, Denver, Colorado* (1973) brought school desegregation and busing to the northern states. Although *de facto* segregation—or, to use Nathan Glazer's phrase, racial concentration[15]—undeniably existed in the Denver schools, neither the city nor the state had ever required racial segregation by law. *Keyes* thus provided the Court with the opportunity to rule on whether such *de facto* segregation was unconstitutional, but the justices avoided this question. Noting that the Denver school authorities in drawing attendance boundaries, assigning teachers, and locating new schools, had acted and were continuing to support *de facto* segregation in a few of the district's schools, the Court argued that the school district had engaged in *de jure* segregation even in the absence of school segregation laws. In separate concurring opinions, however, Justices William Douglas and Lewis Powell argued that the *de jure/de facto* distinction should be abandoned and that segregation, for whatever reason, should be declared unconstitutional.

The Court continued to sidestep the question of whether *de facto* segregation is constitutionally proscribed in *Columbus Board of Education* v. *Penick* (1979) and *Dayton Board of Education* v. *Brinkman* (1979). In these companion cases, a badly split Supreme Court affirmed lower federal-court rulings ordering widescale busing to achieve racial balance in the public school systems of Columbus and Dayton, Ohio. However, the justices did not hold that *de facto* segregation resulting from housing patterns was unconstitutional; they merely accepted lower-court determinations that at the time that *Brown I* was decided, the public school systems of both cities were officially segregated on the basis of race, not by state law but as consequence of policies pursued by the cities' boards of education.

The breadth of what the Court majority in *Columbus* and *Dayton* was prepared to recognize as *de jure* segregation effectively obviated any need to clarify the constitutional status of *de facto* segregation. It also raised problems, however. As Justice Potter Stewart objected in his dissent, the Court appeared to reason that "if such an officially authorized segregated school system can be found to have existed in 1954, then any current racial separation in the schools will be presumed to have been caused by acts in violation of the Constitution." However, he continued,

> much has changed in 25 years, in the Nation at large and in Dayton and Columbus in particular. Minds have changed with respect to racial relationships. Perhaps more importantly, generations have

> changed. The prejudices of these School Boards of 1954 (and earlier) cannot realistically be assumed to haunt the school boards of today. Similarly . . . , school systems have changed. Dayton and Columbus are both examples of the dramatic growth and change in urban school districts. It is unrealistic to assume that the hand of 1954 plays any major part in shaping the current school systems in either city.

Continuing on this same theme, Justice William Rehnquist criticized the Court's finding of *de jure* segregation as running counter to the expectations "that the existence of violations of constitutional rights be carefully and clearly defined before a federal court invades the ambit of local control, and that the subsequent displacement of local authority be limited to that necessary to correct the identified violations." Given the majority's encompassing understanding of *de jure* segregation and the sweep of the remedies it was willing to sustain in the *Columbus* and *Dayton* cases, he speculated "that a school system's only hope of avoiding a judicial receivership [might] be a voluntary dismantling of its neighborhood school program."

In *Milliken* v. *Bradley* (1974) the Court addressed the question of whether increasingly black city school districts and largely white suburban school districts should be required, in the words of *Green* v. *New Kent County,* (1968), to consolidate into a "single unitary nonracial system of public education." In *Milliken,* however, a five-member majority rejected massive interdistrict busing as a remedy for the *de jure* segregation found in the Detroit school system. Chief Justice Warren Burger, speaking for the majority, ruled that the federal district court's decree bringing fifty-three suburban school districts into Detroit's desegregation plan was unjustified, because the Court had been shown no evidence of significant violations by these outlying school districts or any interdistrict violations. *Milliken* v. *Bradley* returned to the Supreme Court again in 1977, and at that time the Court upheld a district court order requiring remedial educational programs as part of its desegregation decrees. *Milliken II* marked the Court's first approval of desegregation remedies that not only involved assignment of students to schools on the basis of race but also pierced the core of educational programs; it involved the federal courts more than ever before in educational policymaking. How much more involved the courts have become since 1977 is apparent in *Missouri* v. *Jenkins* (1990). In *Jenkins,* Federal District Judge Russell Clark imposed a comprehensive and extraordinarily expensive desegregation remedy on the Kansas City, Missouri, School District that cost between $500,000,000 and $700,000,000 to implement. To pay for this remedy, he enjoined the operation of state tax limitation laws and ordered the doubling of the school district's property tax levy. While the Supreme Court unanimously concluded that Judge Clark had abused his discretion, a majority held that he abused it only by specifying the tax levy, not by demanding of the school district that it fully fund his remedy.

One final case must be mentioned in this review of the Court's efforts to clarify what *Alexander* v. *Holmes* requires: In *Pasadena City Board of Education* v. *Spangler* (1976), the Court held in a 6–2 decision that once the affirmative duty to desegregate has been accomplished (i.e., once a unitary school system has been achieved), school authorities are under no compulsion to readjust attendance zones each year to keep up with population shifts. Reaffirming what it had said in *Swann,* the Court declared that once dual school systems have been dismantled, subsequent changes in the racial composition of particular schools within these systems that are caused solely by shifts in population and in no way by segregatory actions by school officials, do not justify further district-court reassignment and busing orders.

PRIVATE DISCRIMINATION AND THE CONCEPT OF STATE ACTION

As noted above, the prohibitions of the Equal Protection Clause are limited to "state action" only. Since the *Civil Rights Cases* the Court consistently has held that private discriminations are not prohibited by the Fourteenth Amendment; only applicable state laws, it has ruled, can address this problem.[16] In hewing to this principle, the justices have had to address the question of what exactly constitutes "state action." The term obviously comprehends statutes enacted by national, state, or local legislative bodies and official actions of all governmental officers, but difficult problems arise when the conduct of private individuals or groups is challenged as racially discriminatory. In such cases the Court has had to determine whether these private actors are performing a government function or are sufficiently involved with or encouraged by the state so that they, too, should be held to the same constitutional obligations as the states themselves.

The "white primary" cases, which involved a series of ploys by the southern states to bar blacks from participating in primary elections, reflect how the Court has dealt with cases of governmental function. In *Newberry* v. *United States* (1921), the justices held that primary elections were "in no real sense part of the manner of holding elections" and thus were not subject to constitutional or congressional control. Many states in the "one-party South," aware that winning the Democratic primary was tantamount to winning the general election, thereupon openly set out to discriminate against black voters in primaries. For example, the Texas legislature in 1923 passed a law flatly prohibiting blacks from voting in that state's Democratic primaries. When the Supreme Court invalidated this statute in *Nixon* v. *Herndon* (1927), on the grounds that it was "a direct and obvious infringement" of the Equal Protection Clause, segregationist politicians sought to keep blacks from voting in ways that did not involve state action.[17] Again in Texas, the Democratic Party convention, on its own authority and without any state legislation on the subject, adopted a resolution confining party membership to white citizens. The Court unanimously concluded in *Grovey* v. *Townsend* (1935) that this action did not violate the Fourteenth Amendment, because it had been taken by the party and not by the state; the justices thus endorsed the view that political parties were private clubs, uncontrolled by constitutional limitations on official action, and that the primaries they held constitutionally were not part of the election process. This position was abandoned in *United States* v. *Classic* (1941), a Louisiana ballot-tampering case in which the Court held that the state's election laws made the primary an "integral part" of the process of electing congressmen and that the Democratic primary was actually "the only stage of the election procedure" in which a voter's choice was of any significance. *Classic* did not directly address the issue of the "white primary," but its implications were clear. After acknowledging that primaries performed a governmental function, the Court no longer could persist in the view that the parties conducting them were unaffected with public responsibilities. When the occasion to rule on "white primaries" presented itself in *Smith* v. *Allwright* (1944), the Court directly reversed the *Grovey* decision, announced that the Democratic Party was "an agency of the State," and declared that the party's use of the "white primary" constituted state action in violation of the Constitution.

State action can also result from state involvement in or encouragement of private discrimination. *Burton* v. *Wilmington Parking Authority* (1961) involved a parking facility owned and operated by an agency of the state of Delaware. To help finance the building, the agency leased some of its space to commercial operations, one of which was a segregated restaurant. A majority of the Court held that because of its location in and relationship to the parking facility, the restaurant had lost its "purely private" character. The relationship between the restaurant and parking facility was mutually beneficial—the former provided the latter with revenue and the latter provided the former with customers. By failing to require the restaurant to serve all customers, the state, in the words of the Court, had "made itself a party to the refusal of service" and had "elected to place its power, property and prestige behind the admitted discrimination."

The sit-in cases present even more dramatic evidence of how state encouragement of private discrimination can become state action. During the 1960s, civil-rights advocates frequently staged sit-ins at variety and drug stores that maintained segregated lunch counters. To protest such discrimination, blacks would take seats at lunch counters and, when refused service, continue to sit there until arrested, typically for breach of the peace or trespass. In a series of sit-in cases, the Court consistently reversed the convictions that resulted from these arrests, often on the ground that the policy of segregation that had led to the sit-ins was governmentally inspired and thus amounted to "state action" in violation of the Equal Protection Clause. In *Peterson* v. *Greenville* (1963), for example, a city ordinance actually required separation of the races in restaurants. *Lombard* v. *Louisiana* (1963) featured no such ordinance, but the Court ruled that city officials had coerced the restaurant manager to operate a segregated facility. In *Griffin* v. *Maryland* (1964) the Court held that an amusement park's exclusion of blacks constituted state action because, to enforce this private policy, the park had employed a deputy sheriff who, although off-duty, wore his badge and purported to exercise his official powers.

A more difficult state action question, which the Court has never answered fully, is whether state action is entirely a negative concept that prohibits states and their agents from practicing racial discrimination, or whether it is also a positive concept that imposes upon the states an affirmative obligation to prevent private racial discrimination. Initially, the Court was content to define equal protection negatively and to view the state action doctrine as simply prohibiting the states from acting in a discriminatory manner against blacks. Since *Shelley* v. *Kraemer* (1948), however, the Court increasingly has come to hold that the state must take positive steps to prevent racial discrimination by private parties or to overcome the effects of past discrimination.[18]

In *Shelley* the Court held that judicial enforcement of racially restrictive covenants (i.e., agreements entered into by property owners, binding them not to sell or lease their properties to blacks or other minorities) constituted governmental involvement in racial discrimination and thus amounted to state action. The Court reasoned as follows:

> We have no doubt that there has been state action in these cases in the full and complete sense of the phrase. The undisputed facts disclosed that petitioners were willing purchasers of properties upon which they desired to establish homes. The owners of the properties were willing sellers; and contracts of sale were accordingly consummated. It is clear that but for the active intervention of the state courts, supported by the full panoply of state power, petitioners would have been free to occupy the properties in question without restraint.

The Court thus reached the curious conclusion that a contract might be legally valid but unenforceable in court. It appeared to hold that courts would not enforce private property rights, however legal, that had been exercised in a discriminatory manner, on the ground that court enforcement would constitute discriminatory state action.[19] Because private rights count for little unless they can be legally enforced, the Court here came close to destroying the distinction between private action and state action. As a consequence, *Shelley* provoked the following line of inquiry: Could a police officer remove a black trespasser from the private residence of a white if the white concedes that the reason he wants the black removed is personal prejudice against blacks?

The Court continued to expand the concept of state action in *Reitman* v. *Mulkey* (1967). Voting 5–4, the Court, concluded in *Reitman* that California was guilty of violating the Equal Protection Clause because its citizens had ratified an amendment to the California state constitution that repealed a law prohibiting racial discrimination in the sale and rental of private dwellings. In his opinion for the Court, Justice Byron White acknowledged that California itself was not guilty of discrimination. He contended, however, that when the voters of California approved the amendment in question, which nullified existing open-housing laws and provided that property owners had "absolute discretion" to sell or rent to persons of their choice, "the right to discriminate, including the right to discriminate on racial grounds, was embodied in the state's basic charter, immune from legislative, executive or judicial regulation at any level of the state government. Those practicing racial discriminations need no longer rely on their personal choice. They could now evoke express constitutional authority."

According to the *Reitman* ruling, discriminatory private action becomes discriminatory state action if the state takes any action allowing such discrimination. Logically, the next step in this chain of reasoning would be the conclusion that discriminatory private action becomes discriminatory state action if the state fails to prohibit such discrimination. As *Moose Lodge No. 107* v. *Irvis* (1972) indicated, however, the Court was not willing to take such a step. In this 6–3 decision, the Court held that discrimination by a private club did not constitute state action simply because the club held a state liquor license. In so doing, the Court reaffirmed Justice Arthur Goldberg's statement in *Bell* v. *Maryland* (1964) that "rights pertaining to privacy and private association are themselves constitutionally protected liberties," and that included among those rights is the right of a person "to close his home or club to any person . . . on the basis of personal prejudices including race."

As *Palmore* v. *Sidoti* (1984) makes clear, however, this private racial prejudice cannot be invoked by any instrumentality of government to justify racial classifications. In unanimously holding that the reality of private biases and the possible injury they might inflict are not permissible considerations for removal of an infant child from the custody of its natural mother in racially mixed household custody cases, the Court offered one of its clearest statements on the constitutional test it employs in racial discrimination cases: Racial "classifications are subject to the most exacting scrutiny; to pass constitutional muster, they must be justified by a compelling governmental interest and must be 'necessary to the accomplishment of its legitimate purpose.' "

PROOF OF DISCRIMINATION: IMPACT VERSUS INTENT

By blurring the distinction between discriminatory private action and discriminatory state action, the Court expanded considerably the concept of state action. This approach to state action would have rendered the states much more vulnerable to charges of discrimination had the Court subsequently not sharpened the distinction between discriminatory impact and discriminatory intent or purpose. It did so by holding in *Washington* v. *Davis* (1976), *Village of Arlington Heights* v. *Metropolitan Housing Development Corporation* (1977), and *Mount Healthy City Board of Education* v. *Doyle* (1977) that the constitutionality of state action hinged not on a racially disproportionate impact, but only on the ground that the challenged action would not have been undertaken "but for" the presence of an invidious discriminatory purpose.

Washington and *Arlington Heights* represented substantial departures from the prevailing judicial belief, as stated by the Fifth Circuit Court of Appeals in *United States Ex Rel. Seals* v. *Wiman* (1962), that it should not be necessary for either the plaintiff or the judiciary "to go so far as to establish ill will, evil motive, or absence of good faith. . . . Objective results are largely to be relied on in the application of the Constitutional text." *Washington* upheld the recruiting procedures (including a written personnel test) of the District of Columbia police department, even though those procedures excluded a disproportionately large number of black applicants. The *Arlington Heights* case held that the Chicago suburb in question had not practiced racial discrimination by refusing to rezone a tract of land from single-family to multifamily usage so that a racially integrated low- and moderate-income housing project could be built. Together, these cases explicitly set forth the Court's position that in and of itself, the racially discriminatory effect of an official action is not sufficient to render that action unconstitutional. As the Court said in *Washington,* "Disproportionate impact is not irrelevant, but it is not the sole touchstone [of racial discrimination]." Henceforth, proof of racially discriminatory intent or purpose would be required to show a violation of the Equal Protection Clause. *Arlington Heights* not only reaffirmed this view but also offered the lower courts guidance on how to conduct a "proper and sensitive" inquiry into whether racially discriminatory intent exists. In addition to "the impact of the official action," which was viewed simply as one evidentiary source, Justice Powell's majority opinion directed a consideration of such other evidence as the historical background of the challenged action, the specific sequence of events leading up to the challenged action, departures from normal procedures, and contemporary statements of the decision-making body.

Mount Healthy and footnote 21 of *Arlington Heights* added the important "but for" qualification. In *Mount Healthy* the Court acknowledged that the petitioner school board's decision not to rehire a nontenured teacher had been motivated in part by conduct on the part of the teacher that was protected by the First Amendment. But that fact alone, the Court went on, did not necessarily amount to a constitutional violation justifying remedial action; rather, the trial court should have attempted to determine whether the school board had shown by a preponderance of the evidence that it would have dismissed the teacher even in the absence of the protected conduct. As a result of this decision, the courts will accept as constitutional an action that bears a rational relation to a legitimate state interest, even if an illegitimate purpose also motivated that action. Although *Mount Healthy* dealt only with freedom of speech, footnote 21 of *Arlington Heights* left no doubt that the principle it enunciated applied with no less force to cases involving racial discrimination. The footnote cited *Mount Healthy* and declared, "Proof that the decision by the Village was motivated in part by a racially discriminatory purpose would not necessarily have required invalidation of the challenged decision. Such proof would, however, have shifted to the Village the burden of establishing that the same decision would have resulted even had the impermissible purpose not been considered." This requirement that invidious discriminatory purpose be a "but for" cause of the challenged state action shows that what the Court may give with one hand (enhanced opportunity to bring discrimination suits based on an expanded concept of state action), it may take away with the other (increased difficulty in winning these suits because of the need to prove discriminatory intent or purpose). The Court's 1990 decision in *Wards Cove Packing Co.* v. *Atonio* is a case in point. While the Court was dealing with Title VII of the Civil Rights Act of 1964 and not the Equal Protection Clause, its language leaves no doubt that it implicitly overturned *Griggs* v. *Duke Power Co.* (1971) and that a majority of the Court does not consider the showing of disparate impact to be the same as the establishment of racial discrimination.

NOTES

1 Herbert J. Storing, "Slavery and the Moral Foundations of the American Republic," *The Moral Foundations of the American Republic,* ed. Robert H. Horwitz (Charlottesville, Va.: University Press of Virginia, 1977), p. 214. The discussion that follows relies heavily on this source.

2 John Hope Franklin, "The Moral Legacy of the Founding Fathers," *University of Chicago Magazine,* Summer 1975: 10–13.

3 Storing, "Slavery and the Moral Foundations of the American Republic," p. 214.

4 Quoted in Carl Becker, *The Declaration of Independence,* (New York: Vintage, 1942), p. 212.

5 Frederick Douglass, "Address for the Promotion of Colored Enlistments," July 6, 1863, in *The Life and Writings of Frederick Douglass,* ed. Philip S. Foner (New York: International Publishers, 1950), vol. 3, p. 365.

6 Martin Diamond, *The Founding of the Democratic Republic* (Itasca, Ill.: F. E. Peacock, 1981), p. 39.

7 Storing, "Slavery and the Moral Foundations of the American Republic," p. 225.

8 See, for examplc, Alfred H. Kelly and Winfred A. Harbison, *The American Constitution: Its Origins and Development,* 4th ed. (New York: W. W. Norton, 1970), p. 916.

9 *Associated General Contractors* v. *Altshuler* (First Cir., 1973).

10 On the critical role played by the NAACP throughout the entire desegregation process, see Daniel M. Berman, *It Is So Ordered: The Supreme Court Rules on School Segregation* (New York: W. W. Norton, 1966); Clement E. Vose, "Litigation as a Form of Pressure Group Activity," *Annals of the American Academy of Political and Social Science* 319 (September 1958); and Richard Kluger, *Simple Justice: The History of Brown v. Board of Education and Black America's Struggle for Equality* (New York: Knopf, 1976).

11 *New York Times,* May 23, 1954, p. 10E.

12 The primary responsibility for implementing *Brown* thus fell on the forty-eight federal district-court judges serving in the eleven southern states. Nearly all were southern and shared the views of the white southern establishment, and all were subject to the social pressures of their communities. In addition, many were personally unsympathetic to *Brown.* Not surprisingly, in many cases they moved very slowly in implementing school desegregation plans. The ten judges constituting the Federal Courts of Appeal for the Fourth and Fifth Circuits, who were responsible for reviewing the district judges' decisions, were somewhat further removed from the pressures of local situations and hence were able to take a more conscientious view of their obligations to enforce the Supreme Court's rulings. As a consequence, they overturned many district-court decisions. See Jack W. Peltason, *Fifty-eight Lonely Men* (New York: Harcourt, Brace & World, 1961).

13 The Court's implementation decision in *Brown II* has been subjected to harsh criticism. See Lino A. Graglia, *Disaster by Decree: The Supreme Court Decisions on Race and the Schools* (Ithaca, N.Y.: Cornell University Press, 1976), pp. 31–45. The Court's use of the phrase "all deliberate speed" has been particularly criticized. See Louis Lusky, "Racial Discrimination and the Federal Law," *Columbia Law Review* 63 (1963): 1172, n. 37: "Conceptually, the 'deliberate speed' formula is impossible to justify. . . . [J]udicial review has been founded in the judicial duty to give a litigant his rights under the Constitution. But the apparently successful plaintiff in the *Brown* case got no more than a promise that, some time in the indefinite future, other people would be given the rights which the Court said he had." In short, *Brown II* permitted the black plaintiffs in *Brown I* to be denied any relief from the legal wrongs that they were found to have suffered, provided that steps were taken to protect other blacks, at some later date, from similar wrongs.

14 *Mayor of Baltimore* v. *Dawson* (1955); *Holmes* v. *City of Atlanta* (1955); *Gayle* v. *Browder* (1956); *New Orleans City Park Improvement Association* v. *Detiege* (1958); *State Athletic Cmsn.* v. *Dorsey* (1959); *Turner* v. *Memphis* (1962); *Johnson* v. *Virginia* (1963); *Schiro* v. *Bynum* (1964); and *Lee* v. *Washington* (1968). These cases simply cited *Brown* as the controlling precedent. Because *Brown* addressed only segregation in public education, the Court opened itself up for a barrage of criticism—and not just from those who mourned the passing of segregation—when it failed to spell out constitutional principles and neglected to provide a reasoned argument against segregation in these other areas of public activity. See Herbert Wechsler, "Toward Neutral Principles of Constitutional Law," *Harvard Law Review* 73 (1959): 1, 22.

15 Nathan Glazer, *Affirmative Discrimination* (New York: Basic Books, 1975), p. 96.

16 However, recall the discussion in Chapter 7 concerning *Jones* v. *Alfred H. Mayer Company* (1968), *Runyon* v. *McCrary* (1976), *Patterson* v. *McLean Credit Union* (1989), and Congress's enforcement powers under Section 2 of Thirteenth Amendment.

17 See also *Nixon* v. *Condon* (1932).

18 This transformation of the concept of state action is akin to the transformation of the Sixth Amendment's right to counsel, discussed in Chapter 14. Originally, the Court had understood the guarantee of right to counsel in a negative sense (i.e., as prohibiting the federal government from denying to a defendant the right to employ counsel); only quite recently has the Court come to understand this right in a more positive or affirmative sense (i.e., as

imposing on the government the duty to provide counsel for those who cannot afford private representation).

19 As Professor Lino Graglia has noted: "*Shelley* has been rightly described as constitutional law's *Finnegan's Wake*: no one has ever claimed to understand the Court's reasoning or to think that it made sense. The Court purported to find unconstitutional state action in state court enforcement of a racially restrictive covenant between private parties, even though the Court would not find and has not found state action in state court enforcement of other private acts of discrimination. A state may, for example, enforce a will making a bequest contingent upon the beneficiary's marrying a person of a particular religious faith." Graglia, "Judicial Review on the Basis of 'Regime Principles': A Prescription for Government by Judiciary," *South Texas Law Journal* 26 (Fall 1985): 450.

SELECTED READINGS

The Federalist, Nos. 42, 54.

Barrows v. *Jackson,* 346 U.S. 249 (1953).
Cooper v. *Aaron,* 358 U.S. 1 (1958).
Dayton Board of Education v. *Brinkman,* 443 U.S. 526 (1979).
Griffin v. *County Board School Board of Prince Edward County,* 337 U.S. 218 (1964).
Mobile v. *Bolden,* 446 U.S. 55 (1980).
Reitman v. *Mulkey,* 387 U.S. 369 (1967).
Sweatt v. *Painter,* 339 U.S. 629 (1950).
Wright v. *Emporia City Council,* 407 U.S. 451 (1972).
Yick Wo v. *Hopkins,* 118 U.S. 356 (1886).

Berger, Raoul. *Government by Judiciary: The Transformation of the Fourteenth Amendment* (Cambridge, Mass.: Harvard University Press, 1977).
Bickel, Alexander M. "The Original Understanding and the Segregation Decision." *Harvard Law Review* 69 (1955): 1–65.
Glazer, Nathan. *Affirmative Discrimination: Ethnic Inequality and Public Policy* (New York: Basic Books, 1975).
Graglia, Lino A. *Disaster by Decree: The Supreme Court Decisions on Race and the Schools* (Ithaca, N.Y.: Cornell University Press, 1976).
Kluger, Richard. *Simple Justice* (New York: Knopf, 1976).
Lofgren, Charles A. *The Plessy Case: A Legal-Historical Interpretation* (New York: Oxford University Press, 1986).
McDowell, Gary L. *Equity and the Constitution: The Supreme Court, Equitable Relief, and Public Policy.* (Chicago: University of Chicago Press, 1982).
Peltason, Jack. *Fifty-eight Lonely Men: Southern Federal Judges and School Desegregation* (New York: HBJ, 1961).
Rist, Ray C., and Ronald J. Anson. *Education, Social Science, and the Judicial Process* (Totowah, N.J.: Teachers College Press, 1977).
Rossum, Ralph. "*Plessy, Brown,* and the Discrimination Cases: Consistency and Continuity in Judicial Approach." *American Behavioral Scientist* 28 (1985): 785–806.

TenBroek, Jacobus. *Equal under Law* (Berkeley: University of California Press, 1965).

Vose, Clement E. *Caucasians Only: The Supreme Court, the NAACP, and the Restrictive Covenant Cases* (Berkeley: University of California Press, 1959).

Wiecek, William M. "The Witch at the Christening: Slavery and the Constitution's Origins." *The Framing and Ratification of the Constitution.* Ed. by Leonard W. Levy and Dennis J. Mahoney (New York: Macmillan, 1987).

Wolf, Eleanor P. *Trial and Error: The Detroit School Segregation Case* (Detroit: Wayne State University Press, 1981).

Wolters, Raymond. *The Burden of Brown* (Knoxville: University of Tennessee Press, 1984).

Woodward, C. Vann. *The Strange Career of Jim Crow* (New York: Oxford University Press, 1966).

Dred Scott v. *Sandford*

60 U.S. (19 Howard) 393; 15 L. Ed. 691 (1857)

Dred Scott was a Negro slave belonging to Dr. Emerson, a U.S. Army surgeon stationed in Missouri. In 1834, Dr. Emerson was transferred to a military post in Rock Island, Illinois, a state in which slavery was forbidden, and he took Dred Scott with him. Two years later, Dr. Emerson again took Scott with him when he moved to Fort Snelling, in the territory of Louisiana (now Minnesota), an area in which slavery was prohibited by the terms of the Missouri Compromise of 1820. In 1838, Dr. Emerson returned with his slave to Missouri. In 1846, Dred Scott brought suit in a Missouri state court to obtain his freedom on the claim that his residence in a free territory conferred freedom upon him. Scott won, but the judgment was reversed by the Missouri Supreme Court. Seeking further judicial review of his case, abolitionists and other friends of Dred Scott arranged for a fictitious sale of Scott to John Sandford, a citizen of New York and a brother of the widow of the late Dr. Emerson, so that jurisdiction could be taken by the federal circuit court in Missouri. The federal court held against Scott, and he appealed his case to the Supreme Court on a writ of error. *Opinion of the Court: Taney, Campbell, Catron, Grier, Nelson, Wayne. Concurring opinions: Campbell; Cutron; Grier; Nelson; Wayne. Concurring in the result: Daniel. Dissenting opinions: Curtis; McLean.*

MR. CHIEF JUSTICE TANEY delivered the opinion of the Court.

. . . The question is simply this: can a negro whose ancestors were imported into this country and sold as slaves, become a member of the political community formed and brought into existence by the Constitution of the United States, and as such become entitled to all the rights, and privileges, and immunities, guaranteed by that instrument to the citizen. One of these rights is the privilege of suing in a court of the United States in the cases specified in the Constitution.

It will be observed, that the plea applies to that class of persons only whose ancestors were negroes of the African race, and imported into this country, and sold and held as slaves. The only matter in issue before the Court, therefore, is whether the descendants of such slaves, when they shall be emancipated, or who are born of parents who had become free before their birth, are citizens of a state, in the sense in which the word "citizen" is used in the Constitution of the United States. And this being the only matter in dispute on the pleadings, the Court must be understood as speaking in this opinion of that class only; that is, of those persons who are the descendants of Africans who were . . . imported into this country and sold as slaves.

The words "people of the United States" and "citizens" are synonymous terms, and mean the same thing. They both describe the political body, who according to our republican institutions, form the sovereignty, and who hold the power and conduct the government through their representatives. They are what we familiarly call the "sovereign people," and every citizen is one of this people, and a constituent member of this sovereignty. The question before us is, whether the class of persons described in the plea in abatement compose a portion of this people, and are constituent members of this sovereignty. We think they are not, and that they are not included and were not intended to be included, under the word "citizens" in the Constitution, and can, therefore, claim none of the rights and privileges which that instrument provided for and secures to citizens of the United States. On the contrary, they were at that time considered as a subordinate and inferior class of beings, who had been subjugated by the dominant race, and whether emancipated or not, yet remained subject to their authority, and had no rights or privileges but such as those who held the power and the government might choose to grant them. . . .

In discussing this question, we must not confound the rights of citizenship which a state may confer within its own limits, and the rights of citizenship as a member of the Union. It does not by any means follow, because he has all the rights and privileges of a citizen of a State, that he must be a citizen of the United States. He may have all the rights and privileges of a citizen of a State, and yet not be entitled to the rights and privileges of a citizen in any other State. For, previous to the adoption of the Constitution of the United States, every State had the undoubted right to confer on whomsoever it pleased the character of a citizen, and to endow him with all its rights. But this character, of course, was confined to the boundaries of the State, and gave him no rights or privileges in other States beyond those secured to him by the laws of nations and the comity of States. Nor have the several States surrendered the power of conferring these rights and privileges by adopting the Constitution of the United States. Each State may still confer them upon an alien, or any one it thinks proper, or upon any class or description of persons; yet he would not be a citizen in the sense in which that word is used in the Constitution of the United States, nor entitled to sue as such in one of its courts, nor to the privileges and immunities of a citizen in the other States. The rights which he would acquire would be restricted to the State which gave them. The Constitution has conferred on Congress the right to establish an uniform rule of naturalization, and this right is evidently exclusive, and has always been held by this Court to be so. Consequently, no State, since the adoption of the Constitution, can, by naturalizing an alien, invest him with the rights and privileges secured to a citizen of a State under the federal government, although, so far as the State alone was concerned, he would undoubtedly be entitled to the rights of a citizen, and clothed with all the rights and immunities which the Constitution and laws of the State attached to that character.

It is very clear, therefore, that no State can, by any Act or law of its own, passed, since the adoption of the Constitution, introduce a new member into the political community created by the Constitution of the United States. It cannot make him a member of this community by making him a member of its own. And for the same reason it cannot introduce any person, or description of persons, who were not intended to be embraced in this new political family, which the Constitution brought into existence, but were intended to be excluded from it. . . .

It is true, every person, and every class and description of persons, who were at the time of the adoption of the Constitution recognized as citizens in the several States, became also citizens of this new political body; but none other; it was formed by them, and for them and their posterity, but for no one else. And the personal rights and privileges guaranteed to citizens of this new sovereignty were intended to embrace those only who were then members of the several State communities, or who would afterwards by birthright or otherwise become members, according to the provisions of the Constitution and the principles on which it was founded. . . . And it gave to each citizen rights and privileges outside of his State which he did not before possess, and placed him in every other State upon a perfect equality with its own citizens as to rights of persons and rights of property; it made him a citizen of the United States.

It becomes necessary, therefore, to determine who were citizens of the several States when the Constitution was adopted. . . .

The legislation of the States . . . shows, in a manner not to be mistaken, the inferior and subject condition of . . . [the Negro] race at the time the Constitution was adopted, and long afterward, throughout the thirteen States by which that instrument was framed; and it is hardly consistent with the respect due to these States, to suppose that they regarded at that time as fellow-citizens and members of the sovereignty, a class of beings whom they had thus stigmatized; whom, as we are bound, out of respect to the State sovereignties, to assume they had deemed it just and necessary thus to stigmatize, and upon whom they had impressed such deep and enduring marks of inferiority and degradation; or, that when they met in convention to form the Constitution, they looked upon them as a portion of their constituents, or deigned to include them in the provisions so carefully inserted for the security and protection of the liberties and rights of their citizens. It cannot be supposed that they intended to secure to them rights, and privileges, and rank, in the new political body throughout the Union, which every one of them denied within the limits of its own dominion. More especially, it cannot be believed that the large slaveholding States regarded them as included in the word citizens, or would have consented to a Constitution which might compel them to receive them in that character from another State. For if they were so received, and entitled to the privileges and immunities of citizens, it would exempt them from the operation of the special laws and from the police regulations which they considered to be necessary for their own safety. It would give to persons of the Negro race, who were recognized as citizens in any one State of the Union, the right to enter every other State whenever they pleased, singly or in companies, whithout pass or passport, and without obstruction to sojourn there as long as they pleased, to go where they pleased at every hour of the day or night without molestation, unless they committed some violation of law for which a white man would be punished; and it would give them the full liberty of speech in public and in private upon all subjects upon which its own citizens might speak; to hold public meetings upon political affairs, and to keep and carry arms wherever they went. And all of this would be done in the face of the subject race of the same color, both free and slaves, and inevitably producing discontent and insubordination among them, and endangering the peace and safety of the State. . . .

Undoubtedly, a person may be a citizen, that is, a member of the community who form the sovereignty, although he exercises no share of the political power, and is incapacitated from holding particular offices. Women and minors, who form a part of the political family, cannot vote; and when a property qualification is required to vote or hold a particular office, those who have not the necessary qualification cannot vote or hold the office, yet they are citizens.

So, too, a person may be entitled to vote by the law of the State, who is not a citizen even of the State itself. And in some of the States of the Union foreigners not naturalized are allowed to vote. And the State may give the right to free negroes and mulattoes, but that does not make them citizens of the State, and still less of the United States. And the provisions in the Constitution giving privileges and immunities in other States does not apply to them.

Neither does it apply to a person who, being the citizen of a State, migrates to another State. For then he becomes subject to the laws of the State in which he lives, and he is no longer a citizen of the State from which he removed. And the State in which he resides may then, unquestionably, determine his status or condition, and place him among the class of persons who are not recognised as citizens, but belong to an inferior and subject race; and may deny him the privileges and immunities enjoyed by its citizens. . . .

No one, we presume, supposes that any change in public opinion or feeling, in relation to this unfortunate race, in the civilized nations of Europe or in this country, should induce the court to give to the words of the Constitution a more liberal construction in their favor than they were intended to bear when the instrument was framed and adopted. Such an argument would be altogether inadmissible in any tribunal called on to interpret it. If any of its provisions are deemed unjust, there is a mode prescribed in the instrument itself by which it may be amended; but while it remains unaltered, it must be construed now as it was understood at the time of its adoption. It is not only the same in words, but the same in meaning, and delegates the same powers to the Government, and reserves and secures the same rights and privileges to the citizen; and as long as it continues to exist in its present form, it speaks not only in the same words, but with the same meaning and intent with which it spoke when it came from the hands of its framers, and was voted on and adopted by the people of the United States. Any other rule of construction would abrogate the judicial character of this court, and make it the mere reflex of the popular opinion or passion of the day. This court was not created by the Constitution for such purposes. Higher and graver trusts have been confided to it, and it must not falter in the path of duty. . . .

. . . [T]he court is of opinion, that, . . . Dred Scott was not a citizen of Missouri within the meaning of the Constitution of the United States, and not entitled as such to sue in its courts: and, consequently, that the Circuit Court had no jurisdiction of the case. . . .

We proceed, therefore, to inquire whether the facts relied on by the plaintiff entitled him to his freedom. . . .

In considering this part of the controversy, two questions arise: (1.) Was he, together with his family, free in Missouri by reason of the stay in the territory of the United States . . . ? and (2.) If they were not, is Scott himself free by reason of his removal to Rock Island, in the State of Illinois. . . .

We proceed to examine the first question.

The act of Congress [Missouri Compromise] upon which the plaintiff relies, declares that slavery and involuntary servitude, except as a punishment for crime, shall be forever prohibited in all that part of the territory ceded by France, under the name of Louisiana, which lies north of 36°30′ north latitude, and not included within the limits of Missouri. And the difficulty which meets us at the threshold of this part of the inquiry is, whether Congress was authorized to pass this law under any of the powers granted to it by the Constitution; for if the authority is not given by that instrument, it is the duty of this court to declare it void and inoperative, and incapable of conferring freedom upon any one who is held as a slave under the laws of any one of the States.

The counsel for the plaintiff has laid much stress upon that article in the Constitution which confers on Congress the power "to dispose of and make all needful rules and regulations respecting the territory or other property belonging to the United States"; but, in the judgment of the court, that provision has no bearing on the present controversy, and the power there given, whatever it may be, is confined, and was intended to be confined, to the territory which at that time belonged to, or was claimed by, the United States, and was within their boundaries as settled by the treaty with Great Britain, and can have no influence upon a territory afterwards acquired from a foreign Government. It was a special provision for a known and particular territory, and to meet a persent emergency, and nothing more. . . .

This brings us to examine by what provision of the Constitution the present Federal Government, under its delegated and restricted powers, is authorized to acquire territory outside of the original limits of the United States, and what powers it may exercise therein over the person or property of a citizen of the United States, while it remains a Territory, and until it shall be admitted as one of the States of the Union.

There is certainly no power given by the Constitution to the Federal Government to establish or maintain colonies bordering on the United States or at a distance, to be ruled and governed at its own pleasure; nor to enlarge its territorial limits in any way, except by the admission of new States. That power is plainly given; and if a new State is admitted, it needs no further legislation by Congress, because the Constitution itself defines the relative rights and powers, and duties of the State, and the citizens of the State, and the Federal Government. But no power is given to acquire a Territory to be held and governed permanently in that character. . . .

. . . It may be safely assumed that citizens of the United States who migrate to a Territory belonging to the people of the United States, cannot be ruled as mere colonists, dependent upon the will of the General Government, and to be governed by any laws it may think proper to impose. The principle upon which our Governments rest, and upon which alone they continue to exist, is the union of States, sovereign and independent within their own limits in their internal and domestic concerns, and bound together as one people by a General Government possessing certain enumerated and restricted powers, delegated to it by the people of the several States, and exercising supreme authority within the scope of the powers granted to it, throughout the dominion of the United States. A power, therefore, in the General Government to obtain and hold colonies and dependent territories, over which they might legislate without restriction, would be inconsistent with its own existence in its present form. Whatever it acquires it acquires for the benefit of the people of the several States who created it. It is their trustee acting for them, and charged with the duty of promoting the interests of the whole people of the Union in the exercise of the powers specifically granted. . . .

. . . The Territory being a part of the United States, the Government and the citizen both enter it under the authority of the Constitution, with their respective rights defined and marked out; and the Federal Government can exercise no power over his person or property, beyond what that instrument confers, nor lawfully deny any right which it has reserved. . . .

Upon these considerations, it is the opinion of the court that the act of Congress which prohibited a citizen from holding and owning property of this kind in the territory of the United States north of the line therein mentioned, is not warranted by the Constitution, and is therefore void; and that neither Dred Scott himself, nor any of his family, were made free by being carried into this territory: even if they had been carried there by the owner, with the intention of becoming a permanent resident. . . .

But there is another point in the case which depends on State power and State law. And it is contended, on the part of the plaintiff, that he is made free by being taken to Rock Island, in the State of Illinois, independently of his residence in the territory of the United States; and being so made free, he was not again reduced to a state of slavery by being brought back to Missouri.

Our notice of this part of the case will be very brief; for the principle on which it depends was decided in this court, upon much consideration, in the case of *Strader et al.* v. *Graham*, reported in 19th Howard, 82, In that case, the slaves had been taken from Kentucky to Ohio, with the consent of the owner, and afterwards brought back to Kentucky. And this court held that their status or condition, as free or slave, depended upon the laws of Kentucky, when they were brought back into the State, and not of Ohio; and that this court had no jurisdiction to revise the judgment of a State court upon its own laws. . . .

So in this case. As Scott was a slave when taken into the State of Illinois by his owner, and was there held as such, and brought back in that character, his status, as free or slave, depended on the laws of Missouri, and not of Illinois. . . .

Upon the whole, therefore, it is the judgment of this court, that it appears by the record before us that the plaintiff in error is not a citizen of Missouri, in the sense in which that word is used in the Constitution; and that the Circuit Court of the United States, for that reason, had no jurisdiction in the case, and could give no judgment in it. Its judgment for the defendant must, consequently, be reversed, and a mandate issued, directing the suit to be dismissed for want of jurisdiction. . . .

MR. JUSTICE CURTIS, dissenting.

I dissent from the opinion pronounced by the Chief Justice, and from the judgment which the majority of the court think it proper to render in this case. . . .

To determine whether any free persons, descended from Africans held in slavery, were citizens of the United States under the Confederation, and consequently at the time of the adoption of the Constitution of the United States, it is only necessary to know whether any such persons were citizens of either of the States under the Confederation, at the time of the adoption of the Constitution.

Of this there can be no doubt. At the time of the ratification of the Articles of Confederation, all free native-born inhabitants of the States of New Hampshire, Massachusetts, New York, New Jersey, and North Carolina, though descended from African slaves, were not only citizens of those States, but such of them as had the other necessary qualifications possessed the franchise of electors, on equal terms with other citizens. . . .

Did the Constitution of the United States deprive them or their descendants of citizenship?

That Constitution was ordained and established by the people of the United States through the action, in each State, of those persons who were qualified by its laws to act thereon, in behalf of themselves and all other citizens of that State. In some of the States, as we have seen, colored persons were among those qualified by law to act on this subject. These colored persons were not only included in the body of "the people of the United States by whom the Constitution was ordained and established," but in at least five of the States they had the power to act, and doubtless did act, by their suffrages, upon the question of its adoption. It would be strange, if we were to find in that instrument anything which deprived of their citizenship any part of the people of the United States who were among those by whom it was established.

I can find nothing in the Constitution which deprives of their citizenship any class of persons who were citizens of the United States at the time of its adoption, or who should be native-born citizens of any State after its adoption; nor any power enabling Congress to disfranchise persons born on the soil of any State, and entitled to citizenship of such State by its constitution and laws. And my opinion is, that, under the Constitution of the United States, every free person born on the soil of a State, who is a citizen of that State by force of its Constitution or laws, is also a citizen of the United States. . . .

I dissent, therefore, from that part of the opinion of the majority of the court, in which it is held that a person of African descent cannot be a citizen of the United States; and I regret I must go further, and dissent both from what I deem their assumption of authority to examine the constitutionality of the act of Congress commonly called the Missouri Compromise act, and the grounds and conclusions announced in their opinion.

Having first decided that they were bound to consider the sufficiency of the plea to the jurisdiction of the Circuit Court, and having decided that this plea showed that the Circuit Court had not jurisdiction, and consequently that this is a case to which the judicial power of the United States does not extend, they have gone on to examine the merits of the case as they appeared on the trial before the court and jury, on the issues joined on the pleas in bar, and so have reached the question of the power of Congress to pass the act of 1820. On so grave a subject as this, I feel obliged to say that, in my opinion, such an exertion of judicial power transcends the limits of the authority of the court, as described by its repeated decisions and, as I understand, acknowledged in this opinion of the majority of the court. . . .

Plessy v. *Ferguson*

163 U.S. 537; 16 S. Ct. 1138; 41 L. Ed. 256 (1896)

An 1890 Louisiana statute required railroads to "provide equal but separate accommodations for the white and colored races." The law made it a criminal offense for any passenger to occupy a "coach or compartment to which by race he does not belong." Plessy, who was seven-eighths white and one-eighth black, refused to relinquish a seat assigned to white passengers. He was imprisoned in the parish jail in New Orleans and charged with violating the statute. During the course of his trial, Plessy petitioned the Louisiana Supreme Court to enjoin the trial judge, John Ferguson, from continuing the proceedings against him. After the court rejected his petition, Plessy brought the case to the United States Supreme Court on a writ of error. He claimed that Louisiana's statute violated the guarantees of the Thirteenth and Fourteenth amendments. *Majority opinion: Brown, Field, Fuller, Gray, Peckham, Shiras, White, Dissenting opinion: Harlan. Not participating: Brewer.*

MR. JUSTICE BROWN delivered the opinion of the Court. . . .

The constitutionality of this act is attacked upon the ground that it conflicts both with the Thirteenth Amendment of the Constitution, abolishing slavery, and the Fourteenth Amendment, which prohibits certain restrictive legislation on the part of the States.

1. That it does not conflict with the Thirteenth Amendment, which abolished slavery and involuntary servitude, except as a punishment for crime, is too clear for argument. Slavery implies involuntary servitude—a state of bondage; the ownership of mankind as a chattel, or at least the control of the labor and services of one man for the benefit of another, and the absence of a legal right to the disposal of his own person, property and services. . . .

A statute which implies merely a legal distinction between the white and colored races—a distinction which is founded in the color of the two races, and which must always exist so long as white men are distinguished from the other race by color—has no tendency to destroy the legal equality of the two races, or reestablish a state of involuntary servitude. Indeed, we do not understand that the Thirteenth Amendment is strenuously relied upon by the plaintiff in error in this connection.

2. By the Fourteenth Amendment, all persons born or naturalized in the United States, and subject to the jurisdiction thereof, are made citizens of the United States and of the State wherein they reside; and the States are forbidden from making or enforcing any law which shall abridge the privileges or immunities of citizens of the United States, or shall deprive any person of life, liberty or property without due process of law, or deny to any person within their jurisdiction the equal protection of the laws.

The proper construction of this amendment was first called to the attention of this court in the *Slaughterhouse Cases,* . . . which . . . said generally that its main purpose was to establish the citizenship of the negro; to give definitions of citizenship of the United States and of the States, and to protect from the hostile legislation of the States the privileges and immunities of citizens of the United States, as distinguished from those of citizens of the States.

The object of the amendment was undoubtedly to enforce the absolute equality of the two races before the law, but in the nature of things it could not have been intended to abolish distinctions based upon color, or to enforce social, as distinguished from political equality, or a commingling of the two races upon terms unsatisfactory to either. Laws permitting, and even requiring, their separation in places where they are liable to be brought into contact do not necessarily imply the inferiority of either race to the other, and have been generally, if not universally, recognized as within the competency of the state legislatures in the exercise of their police power. The most common instance of this is connected with the establishment of separate schools for white and colored children, which has been held to be a valid exercise of the legislative power even by courts of States where the political rights of the colored race have been longest and most earnestly enforced.

One of the earliest of these cases is that of *Roberts* v. *City of Boston* [1849], . . . in which the Supreme Judicial Court of Massachusetts held that the general schools committee of Boston had power to make provision for the instruction of colored children in separate schools established exclusively for them, and to prohibit their attendance upon the other schools. . . . Similar laws have been enacted by Congress under its general power of legislation over the District of Columbia, . . . as well as by the legislatures of many of the States, and have been generally, if not uniformly, sustained by the courts. . . .

So far, then, as a conflict with the Fourteenth Amendment is concerned, the case reduces itself to the question whether the statute of Louisiana is a reasonable regulation, and with respect to this there must necessarily be a large discretion on the part of the legislature. In determining the question of reasonableness it is at liberty to act with reference to the established usages, customs and traditions of the people, and with a view to the promotion of their comfort, and the preservation of the public peace and good order. Gauged by this standard, we cannot say that a law which authorizes or even requires the separation of the two races in public conveyances is unreasonable, or more obnoxious to the Fourteenth Amendment than the acts of Congress requiring separate schools for colored children in the District of Columbia, the constitutionality of which does not seem to have been questioned, or the corresponding acts of state legislatures.

We consider the underlying fallacy of the plaintiff's argument to consist in the assumption that the enforced separation of the two races stamps the colored race with a badge of inferiority. If this be so, it is not by reason of anything found in the act, but solely because the colored race chooses to put that construction upon it. The argument necessarily assumes that if, as has been more than once the case, and is not unlikely to be so again, the colored race should become the dominant power in the state legislature, and should enact a law in precisely similar terms, it would thereby relegate the white race to an inferior position. We imagine that the white race at least would not acquiesce in this assumption. The argument also assumes that social prejudices may be overcome by legislation, and that equal rights cannot be secured to the negro except by an enforced commingling of the two races. We cannot accept this proposition. If the two races are to meet upon terms of social equality, it must be the result of natural affinities, a mutual appreciation of each other's merits and a voluntary consent of individuals. . . . Legislation is powerless to eradicate racial instincts or to abolish distinctions based upon physical differences, and the attempt to do so can only result in accentuating the difficulties of the present situation. If the civil and political rights of both races be equal one cannot be inferior to the other civilly or politically. If one race be inferior to the other socially, the Constitution of the United States cannot put them upon the same plane. . . .

The judgment of the court below is, therefore,

Affirmed.

MR. JUSTICE HARLAN, dissenting.

The Thirteenth Amendment does not permit the withholding or the deprivation of any right necessarily inhering in freedom. It not only struck down the institution of slavery as previously existing in the United States, but it prevents the imposition of any burdens or disabilities that constitute badges of slavery or servitude. It decreed universal civil freedom in this country. The court has so adjudged. But that amendment having been found inadequate to the protection of the right of those who had been in slavery, it was followed by the Fourteenth Amendment, which added greatly to the dignity and glory of American citizenship and to the security of personal liberty. . . .

It was said in argument that the statute of Louisiana does not discriminate against either race, but prescribes a rule applicable alike to white and colored citizens. But this argument does not meet the difficulty. Every one knows that the statute in question had its origin in the purpose not so much to exclude white persons from railroad cars occupied by blacks, as to exclude colored people from coaches occupied by or assigned to white persons. Railroad corporations of Louisiana did not make discrimination among whites in the matter of accommodation for travellers. The thing to accomplish was, under the guise of giving equal accommodation for whites and blacks, to compel the latter to keep to themselves while travelling in railroad passenger coaches. No one would be so wanting in candor as to assert the contrary. The fundamental objection, therefore, to the statute is that it interferes with the personal freedom of citizens. "Personal liberty," it has been well said, "consists in the power of locomotion, of changing situation, or removing one's person to whatsoever places one's own inclination may direct, without imprisonment or restraint, unless by due course of law." . . . If a white man and a black man choose to occupy the same public conveyance on a public highway, it is their right to do so, and no government, proceeding alone on grounds of race, can prevent it without infringing the personal liberty of each. . . .

The white race deems itself to be the dominant race in this country. And so it is, in prestige, in achievements, in education, in wealth and in power. So, I doubt not, it will continue to be for all time, if it remains true to its great heritage and holds fast to the principles of constitutional liberty. But in view of the Constitution, in the eye of the law, there is in this country no superior dominant ruling class of citizens. There is no caste here. Our Constitution is color-blind, and neither knows nor tolerates classes among citizens. In respect of civil rights, all citizens are equal before the law. The humblest is the peer of the most powerful. The law regards man as man, and takes no account of his surroundings or of his color when his civil rights as guaranteed by the supreme law of the land are involved. It is, therefore, to be regretted that this high tribunal, the final expositor of the fundamental law of the land, has reached the conclusion that it is competent for a State to regulate the enjoyment by citizens of their civil rights solely upon the basis of race.

In my opinion, the judgment this day rendered will, in time, prove to be quite as pernicious as the decision made by this tribunal in the *Dred Scott* case. . . . The destinies of the two races, in this country, are indissolubly linked together, and the interests of both require that the common government of all shall not permit the seeds of race hate to be planted under the sanction of law. What can more certainly arouse race hate, what more certainly create and perpetuate a feeling of distrust between these races, than state enactments, which, in fact, proceed on the ground that colored citizens are so inferior and degraded that they cannot be allowed to sit in public coaches occupied by white citizens? That, as all will admit, is the real meaning of such legislation as was enacted in Louisiana. . . .

The arbitrary separation of citizens, on the basis of race, while they are on a public highway, is a badge of servitude wholly inconsistent with the civil freedom and the equality before the law established by the Constitution. It cannot be justified upon any legal grounds. . . .

Brown v. *Board of Education*

347 U.S. 483; 74 S. Ct. 693; 98 L. Ed. 591 (1954)

The facts in this landmark case are set out in the opinion. *Unanimous opinion: Warren, Black, Burton, Clark, Douglas, Frankfurter, Jackson, Minton, Reed.*

MR. CHIEF JUSTICE WARREN delivered the opinion of the Court.

These cases come to us from the States of Kansas, South Carolina, Virginia, and Delaware. They are premised on different facts and different local conditions, but a common legal question justifies their consideration together in this consolidated opinion.

In each of the cases, minors of the Negro race, through their legal representatives, seek the aid of the courts in obtaining admission to the public schools of their community on a nonsegregated basis. In each instance, they have been denied admission to schools attended by white children under laws requiring or permitting segregation according to race. This segregation was alleged to deprive the plaintiffs of the equal protection of the laws under the Fourteenth Amendment. In each of the cases other than the Delaware case, a three-judge federal district court denied relief to the plaintiffs on the so-called "separate but equal" doctrine announced by this Court in *Plessy* v. *Ferguson*. . . . Under that doctrine, equality of treatment is accorded when the races are provided substantially equal facilities, even though these facilities be separate. In the Delaware case, the Supreme Court of Delaware adhered to that doctrine, but ordered that the plaintiffs be admitted to the white schools because of their superiority to the Negro schools.

The plaintiffs contend that segregated public schools are not "equal" and cannot be made "equal," and that hence they are deprived of the equal protection of the laws. Because of the obvious importance of the question presented, the Court took jurisdiction. Argument was heard in the 1952 Term, and reargument was heard this Term on certain questions propounded by the Court.

Reargument was largely devoted to the circumstances surrounding the adoption of the Fourteenth Amendment in 1868. It covered exhaustively consideration of the Amendment in Congress, ratification by the states, then existing practices in racial segregation, and the views of proponents and opponents of the Amendment. This discussion and our own investigation convince us that, although these sources cast some light, it is not enough to resolve the problem with which we are faced. At best, they are inconclusive. The most avid proponents of the post-War Amendments undoubtedly intended them to remove all legal distinctions among "all persons born or naturalized in the United States." Their opponents, just as certainly, were antagonistic to both the letter and the spirit of the Amendments and wished them to have the most limited effect. What others in Congress and the state legislatures had in mind cannot be determined with any degree of certainty.

An additional reason for the inconclusive nature of the Amendment's history, with respect to segregated schools, is the status of public education at that time. In the South, the movement toward free common schools, supported by general taxation, had not yet taken hold. Education of white children was largely in the hands of private groups. Education of Negroes was almost nonexistent, and practically all of the race were illiterate. In fact, any education of Negroes was forbidden by law in some states. Today, in contrast, many Negroes have achieved outstanding success in the arts and sciences as well as in the business and professional world. It is true that public school education at the time of the Amendment had advanced further in the North, but the effect of the Amendment on Northern States was generally ignored in the congressional debates. Even in the North, the conditions of public education did not approximate those existing today. The curriculum was usually rudimentary; ungraded schools were common in rural areas; the school term was but three months a year in many states; and compulsory school attendance was virtually unknown. As a consequence, it is not surprising that there should be so little in the history of the Fourteenth Amendment relating to its intended effect on public education.

In the first cases in this Court construing the Fourteenth Amendment, decided shortly after its adoption, the Court interpreted it as proscribing all state-imposed discriminations against the Negro race.* The doctrine of "separate but equal" did not make its appearance in this Court until 1896 in the case of *Plessy* v. *Ferguson*, . . . involving not education but transportation. American courts have since labored with the doctrine for over half a century. In this Court, there have been six cases involving the "separate but equal" doctrine in the field of public education. In *Cumming* v. *Board of Education of Richmond County* [1899] . . . and *Gong Lum* v. *Rice* . . . , the validity of the doctrine itself was not challenged. In more recent cases, all on the graduate school level, inequality was found in that specific benefits enjoyed by white students were denied to Negro students of the same educational qualifications. . . . In none of these cases was it necessary to reexamine the doctrine to grant relief to the Negro plaintiff. And in *Sweatt* v. *Painter*, . . . the Court expressly reserved decision on the question whether *Plessy* v. *Ferguson* should be held inapplicable to public education.

In the instant cases, that question is directly presented. Here, unlike *Sweatt* v. *Painter*, there are findings below that the Negro and white schools involved have been equalized, or are being equalized, with respect to buildings, curricula, qualifications and salaries of teachers, and other "tangible" factors. Our decision, therefore, cannot turn on merely a comparison of these tangible factors in the Negro and white schools involved in each of the cases. We must look instead to the effect of segregation itself on public education.

In approaching this problem, we cannot turn the clock back to 1868 when the Amendment was adopted, or even to 1896 when *Plessy* v. *Ferguson* was written. We must consider public education in the light of its full development and its present place in American life throughout the Nation. Only in this way can it be determined if segregation in public schools deprives these plaintiffs of the equal protection of the laws.

Today, education is perhaps the most important function of state and local governments. Compulsory school attendance laws and the great expenditures for education both demonstrate our recognition of the importance of education to our democratic society. It is required in the performance of our most basic public responsibilities, even service in the armed forces. It is the very foundation of good citizenship. Today it is a principal instrument in awakening the child to cultural values, in preparing him for later professional training, and in helping him to adjust normally to his environment. In these days, it is doubtful that any child may reasonably be expected to succeed in life if he is denied the opportunity of an education. Such an opportunity, where the state has undertaken to provide it, is a right which must be made available to all on equal terms.

We come then to the question presented: Does segregation of children in public schools solely on the basis of race, even though the physical facilities and other "tangible" factors may be equal, deprive the children of the minority group of equal educational opportunities? We believe that it does.

In *Sweatt* v. *Painter* [1950], . . . , in finding that a segregated law school for Negroes could not provide them equal educational opportunities, this Court relied in large part on "those qualities which are incapable of objective measurement but which make for greatness in a law school." In *McLaurin* v. *Oklahoma State Regents* [1950], . . . the Court, in requiring that a Negro admitted to a white graduate school be treated like all other students, again resorted to intangible considerations: " . . . his ability to study, to engage in discussions and exchange views with other students, and, in general, to learn his profession." Such considerations apply with added force to children in grade and high schools. To separate them from others of similar age and qualifications solely because of their race generates a feeling of inferiority as to their status in the community that may affect their hearts and

*In Re *Slaughterhouse Cases*, 1873, . . . *Strauder* v. *West Virginia*, 1880. . . .

minds in a way unlikely ever to be undone. The effect of this separation on their educational opportunities was well stated by a finding in the Kansas case by a court which nevertheless felt compelled to rule against the Negro plaintiffs:

"Segregation of white and colored children in public schools has a detrimental effect upon the colored children. The impact is greater when it has the sanction of the law; for the policy of separating the races is usually interpreted as denoting the inferiority of the negro group. A sense of inferiority affects motivation of a child to learn. Segregation with the sanction of law, therefore, has a tendency to [retard] the education and mental development of negro children and to deprive them of some of the benefits they would receive in a racial[ly] integrated school system." Whatever may have been the extent of psychological knowledge at the time of *Plessy* v. *Ferguson*, this finding is amply supported by modern authority.** Any language in *Plessy* v. *Ferguson* contrary to this finding is rejected.

We conclude that in the field of public education the doctrine of "separate but equal" has no place. Separate educational facilities are inherently unequal. Therefore, we hold that the plaintiffs and others similarly situated for whom the actions have been brought are, by reason of the segregation complained of, deprived of the equal protection of the laws guaranteed by the Fourteenth Amendment. This disposition makes unnecessary any discussion whether such segregation also violates the Due Process Clause of the Fourteenth Amendment.

Because these are class actions, because of the wide applicability of this decision, and because of the great variety of local conditions, the formulation of decrees in these cases presents problems of considerable complexity. On reargument, the consideration of appropriate relief was necessarily subordinated to the primary question—the constitutionality of segregation in public education. We have now announced that such segregation is a denial of the equal protection of the laws. In order that we may have the full assistance of the parties in formulating decrees, the cases will be restored to the docket, and the parties are requested to present further argument on Questions 4 and 5 previously propounded by the Court for the reargument this Term.*** The Attorney General of the United States is invited to participate. The Attorneys General of the States requiring or permitting segregation in public education will also be permitted to appear as *amici curiae* upon request to do so by September 15, 1954, and submission of briefs by October 1, 1954. . . .

**K.B. Clark, Effect of Prejudice and Discrimination on Personality Development (Midcentury White House Conference on Children and Youth, 1950); Witmer and Kotinsky, Personality in the Making (1952), c. VI; Deutscher and Chein, The Psychological Effects of Enforced Segregation: A Survey of Social Science Opinion, 26 J. Psychol. 259 (1948); Chein, What are the Psychological Effects of Segregation Under Conditions of Equal Facilities?, 3 Int. J. Opinion and Attitude Res. 229(1949); Brameld, Educational Costs, in Discrimination and National Welfare (McIver, ed., 1949), 44–48; Frazier, The Negro in the United States (1949), 674–681. And see generally Myrdal, An American Dilemma (1944).

***4. Assuming it is decided that segregation in public schools violates the Fourteenth Amendment.

"(a) would a decree necessarily follow providing that, within the limits set by normal geographic school districting, Negro children should forthwith be admitted to schools of their choice, or

"(b) may this Court, in the exercise of its equity powers, permit an effective gradual adjustment to be brought about from existing segregated systems to a system not based on color distinctions?

"5. On the assumption on which questions 4(a) and (b) are based, and assuming further that this Court will exercise its equity powers to the end described in question 4(b),

"(a) should this Court formulate detailed decrees in these cases;

"(b) if so, what specific issues should decrees reach;

"(c) should this Court appoint a special master to hear evidence with a view to recommending specific terms for such decrees;

"(d) should this Court remand to the courts of first instance with directions to frame decrees in these cases, and if so, what general directions should the decrees of this Court include and what procedures should the courts of first instance follow in arriving at the specific terms of more detailed decrees?"

Bolling v. *Sharpe*

347 U.S. 497; 74 S. Ct. 686, 98 L. Ed. 583 (1954)

In this companion case to *Brown* v. *Board of Education,* the Supreme Court reviewed the validity of segregation in the public schools of the District of Columbia. *Unanimous opinion: Warren, Black, Burton, Clark, Douglas, Frankfurter, Jackson, Minton, Reed.*

MR. CHIEF JUSTICE WARREN delivered the opinion of the Court.

This case challenges the validity of segregation in the public schools of the District of Columbia. The petitioners, minors of the Negro race, allege that such segregation deprives them of due process of law under the Fifth Amendment. They were refused admission to a public school attended by white children solely because of their race. They sought the aid of the District Court for the District of Columbia in obtaining admission. That court dismissed their complaint. We granted a writ of certiorari before judgment in the Court of Appeals because of the importance of the constitutional question presented. . . .

We have this day held that the Equal Protection Clause of the Fourteenth Amendment prohibits the states from maintaining racially segregated public schools. The legal problem in the District of Columbia is somewhat different, however. The Fifth Amendment, which is applicable in the District of Columbia, does not contain an equal protection clause as does the Fourteenth Amendment, which applies only to the states. But the concepts of equal protection and due process, both stemming from our American ideal of fairness, are not mutually exclusive. The "equal protection of the laws" is a more implicit safeguard of prohibited unfairness than "due process of law," and, therefore, we do not imply that the two are always interchangeable phrases. But, as this Court has recognized, discrimination may be so unjustifiable as to be violative of due process.

Classifications based solely upon race must be scrutinized with particular care, since they are contrary to our traditions and hence constitutionally suspect. As long ago as 1896, this Court declared the principle "that the Constitution of the United States, in its present form, forbids, so far as civil and political rights are concerned, discrimination by the General Government, or by the States, against any citizen because of his race." And in *Buchanan* v. *Warley* [1917], . . . the Court held that a statute which limited the right of a property owner to convey his property to a person of another race was, as an unreasonable discrimination, a denial of due process of law.

Although the Court has not assumed to define "liberty" with any great precision, that term is not confined to mere freedom from bodily restraint. Liberty under law extends to the full range of conduct which the individual is free to pursue, and it cannot be restricted except for a proper governmental objective. Segregation in public education is not reasonably related to any proper governmental objective, and thus it imposes on Negro children of the District of Columbia a burden that constitutes an arbitrary deprivation of their liberty in violation of the Due Process Clause.

In view of our decision that the Constitution prohibits the states from maintaining racially segregated public schools, it would be unthinkable that the same constitution would impose a lesser duty on the Federal Government. We hold that racial segregation in the public schools of the District of Columbia is a denial of the due process of law guaranteed by the Fifth Amendment to the Constitution.

For the reasons set out in *Brown* v. *Board of Education,* this case will be restored to the docket for reargument on Questions 4 and 5 previously propounded by the Court. . . .

It is so ordered.

Brown v. Board of Education

349 U.S. 294; 75 S. Ct. 753; 99 L. Ed. 1083 (1955)

In this 1955 decision, often referred to as *Brown II,* the Supreme Court dealt with the question of how its decision in *Brown I* was to be implemented. *Unanimous opinion: Warren, Black, Burton, Clark, Douglas, Frankfurter, Harlan, Minton, Reed.*

MR. CHIEF JUSTICE WARREN delivered the opinion of the Court.

These cases were decided on May 17, 1954. The opinions of that date, declaring the fundamental principle that racial discrimination in public education is unconstitutional, are incorporated herein by reference. All provisions of federal, state, or local law requiring or permitting such discrimination must yield to this principle. There remains for consideration the manner in which relief is to be accorded. . . .

Full implementation of these constitutional principles may require solution of varied local school problems. School authorities have the primary responsibility for elucidating, assessing, and solving these problems; courts will have to consider whether the action of school authorities constitutes good faith implementation of the governing constitutional principles. Because of their proximity to local conditions and the possible need for further hearing, the courts which originally heard these cases can best perform this judicial appraisal. Accordingly, we believe it appropriate to remand the cases to those courts.

In fashioning and effectuating the decrees, the courts will be guided by equitable principles. Traditionally, equity has been characterized by a practical flexibility in shaping its remedies and by a facility for adjusting and reconciling public and private needs. These cases call for the exercise of these traditional attributes of equity power. At stake is the personal interest of the plaintiffs in admission to public schools as soon as practicable on a nondiscriminatory basis. To effectuate this interest may call for elimination of a variety of obstacles in making the transition to school systems operated in accordance with the constitutional principles set forth in our May 17, 1954, decision. Courts of equity may properly take into account the public interest in the elimination of such obstacles in a systematic and effective manner. But it should go without saying that the vitality of these constitutional principles cannot be allowed to yield simply because of disagreement with them.

While giving weight to these public and private considerations, the courts will require that the defendants make a prompt and reasonable start toward full compliance with our May 17, 1954, ruling. Once such a start has been made, the courts may find that additional time is necessary to carry out the ruling in an effective manner. The burden rests upon the defendants to establish that such time is necessary in the public interest and is consistent with good faith compliance at the earliest practicable data. To that end, the courts may consider problems related to administration, arising from the physical condition of the school plant, the school transportation system, personnel, revision of school districts and attendance areas into compact units to achieve a system of determining admission to the public schools on a nonracial basis, and revision of local laws and regulations which may be necessary in solving the foregoing problems. They will also consider the adequacy of any plans the defendants may propose to meet these problems and to effectuate a transition to a racially nondiscriminatory school system. During this period of transition, the courts will retain jurisdication of these cases. . . .

. . . The cases . . . are remanded to the district courts to take such proceedings and enter such orders and decrees consistent with this opinion as are necessary and proper to admit to public schools on a racially nondiscriminatory basis with all deliberate speed the parties to these cases.

It is so ordered.

Swann v. Charlotte-Mecklenburg Board of Education

402 U.S. 1; 91 S. Ct. 1267; 28 L. Ed. 2d 554 (1971)

Under a school desegregation plan approved by a federal district court in 1965 for the Charlotte-Mecklenburg County school system (the student population of which was 71 percent white and 29 percent black), nearly two-thirds of the system's black students attended schools that were at least 99 percent black. Following the Supreme Court's decision in *Green* v. *School District of New Kent County* (1968), which charged school districts with an "affirmative duty" to take whatever steps might be necessary to eliminate all vestiges of a dual school system and establish in its place "a unitary system in which racial discrimination would be eliminated root and branch," John Swann and other petitioners entered federal district court and sought further desegregation of the Charlotte-Mecklenburg system. As a result, the district court ordered the school board in 1969 to provide a plan for faculty and student desegregation. Finding the board's submission unsatisfactory, the court appointed a desegregation expert, Dr. John Finger, to submit a desegregation plan. In 1970 the court adopted a modified version of the board's plan for the faculty and for the junior and senior high schools, and the Finger plan for the elementary schools. The school board appealed to the Court of Appeals for the Fourth Circuit, where that part of the district court's orders relating to the faculty and secondary schools was affirmed but that part relating to the elementary schools was vacated. In the estimation of the Fourth Circuit, the Finger plan would have unreasonably burdened elementary school pupils and the board. After further court proceedings and consideration of additional desegregation plans, the district court again ordered that the Finger plan be put into effect. Both parties petitioned the Supreme Court for a writ of certiorari. *Unanimous opinion: Burger, Black, Blackmun, Brennan, Douglas, Harlan, Marshall, Stewart, White.*

MR. CHIEF JUSTICE BURGER delivered the opinion of the Court.

We granted certiorari in this case to review important issues as to the duties of school authorities and the scope of powers of federal courts under this Court's mandates to eliminate racially separate public schools established and maintained by state action. . . .

This case and those argued with it arose in states having a long history of maintaining two sets of schools in a single school system deliberately operated to carry out a governmental policy to separate pupils in schools solely on the basis of race. That was what *Brown* v. *Board of Education* was all about. These cases present us with the problem of defining in more precise terms than heretofore the scope of the duty of school authorities and district courts in implementing *Brown I* and the mandate to eliminate dual systems and establish unitary systems at once. . . .

The problems encountered by the district courts and courts of appeal make plain that we should now try to amplify guidelines, however incomplete and imperfect, for the assistance of school authorities and courts. . . .

The objective today remains to eliminate from the public schools all vestiges of state-imposed segregation. . . . If school authorities fail in their affirmative obligations under [our earlier] holdings, judicial authority may be invoked. Once a right and a violation have been shown, the scope of a district court's equitable powers to remedy past wrongs is broad, for breadth and flexibility are inherent in equitable remedies. . . . In seeking to define even in broad and general terms how far this remedial power extends it is important to remember that judicial powers may be exercised only on the basis of a constitutional violation. . . . Judicial authority enters only when local authority defaults.

The central issue in this case is that of student assignment, and there are essentially four problem areas. . . .

(1) Racial Balances or Racial Quotas

We do not reach in this case the question whether a showing that school segregation is a consequence of other types of state action, without any discriminatory action by the school authorities, is a constitutional violation requiring remedial action by a school desegregation decree. This case does not present that question and we therefore do not decide it. . . .

In this case it is urged that the District Court has imposed a racial balance requirement of 71–29% on individual schools. The fact that no such objective was actually achieved—and would appear to be impossible—tends to blunt that claim, yet in the opinion and order of the District Court . . . we find that court directing: "that efforts should be made to reach 71–29 ratio in the various schools so that there will be no basis for contending that one school is racially different from the others. . . . "

The District Judge went on to acknowledge that variation "from that norm may be unavoidable." This contains intimations that the "norm" is a fixed mathematical racial balance reflecting the pupil constituency of the system. If we were to read the holding of the District Court to require, as a matter of substantive constitutional right, any particular degree of racial balance or mixing, that approach would be disapproved and we would be obliged to reverse. The constitutional command to desegregate schools does not mean that every school in every community must always reflect the racial composition of the school system as a whole. . . .

Awareness of the racial composition of the whole school system is likely to be a useful starting point in shaping a remedy to correct past constitutional violations. In sum, the very limited use made of mathematical ratios was within the equitable remedial discretion of the District Court.

(2) One-Race Schools

The record in this case reveals that familiar phenomenon that in metropolitan areas minority groups are often found concentrated in one part of the city. . . . Schools all or predominately of one race in a district of mixed population will require close scrutiny to determine that school assignments are not part of state-enforced segregation.

In light of the above, it should be clear that the existence of some small number of one-race, or virtually one-race, schools within a district is not in and of itself the mark of a system which still practices segregation by law. . . .

The court should scrutinize such schools, and the burden upon the school authorities will be to satisfy the court that their racial composition is not the result of present or past discriminatory action on their part. . . .

(3) Remedial Altering of Attendance Zones

The maps submitted in these cases graphically demonstrate that one of the principal tools employed by school planners and by courts to break up the dual school system has been a frank—and sometimes drastic—gerrymandering of school districts and attendance zones. An additional step was pairing, "clustering," or "grouping" of schools with attendance assignments made deliberately to accomplish the transfer of Negro students out of formerly segregated Negro schools and transfer of white students to formerly all-Negro schools. More often than not, these zones are neither compact nor contiguous; indeed they may be on opposite ends of the city. As an interim corrective measure, this cannot be said to be beyond the broad remedial powers of a court.

Absent a constitutional violation there would be no basis for judicially ordering assignment of students on a racial basis. All things being equal, with no history of discrimination, it might well be desirable to assign pupils to schools nearest their homes. But all things are not equal in a system that has been deliberately constructed and maintained to enforce racial segregation. The remedy for such segregation may be administratively awkward, inconvenient and even bizarre in some situations and may impose burdens on some; but all awkwardness and inconvenience cannot be avoided in the interim period when remedial adjustments are being made to eliminate the dual school systems.

No fixed or even substantially fixed guidelines can be established as to how far a court can go, but it must be recognized that there are limits. The objective is to dismantle the dual school system. "Racially neutral" assignment plans proposed by school authorities to a district court may be inadequate; such plans may fail to counteract the continuing effects of past school segregation resulting from discriminatory location of school sites or distortion of school size in order to achieve or maintain an artificial racial separation. When school authorities present a district court with a "loaded game board," affirmative action in the form of remedial altering of attendance zones is proper to achieve truly nondiscriminatory assignments. . . . We hold that the pairing and grouping of noncontiguous school zones is a permissible tool and such action is to be considered in light of the objectives sought. . . .

(4) Transportation of Students

The scope of permissible transportation of students as an implement of a remedial decree has never been defined by this Court and by the very nature of the problem it cannot be defined with precision. No rigid guidelines as to student transportation can be given for application to the infinite variety of problems presented in thousands of situations. . . . The District Court's conclusion that assignment of children to the school nearest their home serving their grade would not produce an effective dismantling of the dual system is supported by the record.

Thus the remedial techniques used in the District Court's order were within that court's power to provide equitable relief; implementation of the decree is well within the capacity of the school authority.

The decree provided that the buses used to implement the plan would operate on direct routes. . . . The trips for elementary school pupils average about seven miles and the District Court found that they would take "not over 35 minutes at the most." This system compares favorably with the transportation plan previously operated in Charlotte under which each day 23,600 students on all grade levels were transported an average of 15 miles one way for an average trip requiring over an hour. In these circumstances, we find no basis for holding that the local school authorities may not be required to employ bus transportation as one tool of school desegregation. Desegregation plans cannot be limited to the walk-in school.

An objection to transportation of students may have validity when the time or distance of travel is so great as to risk either the health of the children or significantly impinge on the educational process. District courts must weigh the soundness of any transportation plan in light of what is said in subdivisions (1), (2), and (3) above. . . .

On the facts of this case, we are unable to conclude that the order of the District Court is not reasonable, feasible and workable. . . .

It does not follow that the communities served by such systems will remain demographically stable, for in a growing, mobile society, few will do so. Neither school authorities nor district courts are constitutionally required to make year-by-year adjustments of the racial composition of student bodies once the affirmative duty to desegregate has been accomplished and racial discrimination through official action is eliminated from the system. This does not mean that federal courts are without power to deal with future problems, but in the absence of a showing that either the school authorities or some other agency of the State has deliberately attempted to fix or alter demographic patterns to affect the racial composition of the schools, further intervention by a district court should not be necessary.

Milliken v. *Bradley*

418 U.S. 717; 94 S. Ct. 3112; 41 L. Ed. 2d 1069 (1974)

Ronald Bradley and other black students, together with the Detroit branch of the NAACP, brought a class action suit charging Michigan governor William Milliken, the state board of education, the state superintendent of public instruction, and the city school board and superintendent with racial segregation and seeking implementation of a plan to establish a unitary nonracial school system. The federal district court upheld the respondent's charges, found violations of constitutional rights by both city and state officials, and ordered the Detroit School Board to formulate a desegregation plan for the city; in addition, state officials were ordered to submit desegregation plans encompassing the three-county metropolitan area, despite the fact that the eighty-five school districts in these three counties were not parties to the action and there was no claim that they had committed constitutional violations. The district court subsequently permitted some of these surrounding school districts to appear and present arguments relevant to the formulation of a regional plan for racial balance in the schools, but prohibited them from asserting any claim or defense on issues previously adjudicated or from reopening any issue previously decided. Contending that "school districts are simply matters of political convenience and may not be used to deny constitutional rights," without citing any evidence that the suburban school districts had committed acts of *de jure* segregation, the district court appointed a panel to submit a desegregation plan encompassing a designated area consisting of 53 of the 85 suburban school districts plus Detroit. The court also ordered the Detroit school board to acquire at least 295 school buses for the purpose of transporting students to and from outlying districts. The Court of Appeals for the Sixth Circuit affirmed the substance of the district court's decision but remanded the case, in order to provide the affected suburban school districts with the opportunity to be heard as to the scope and implementation of such a remedy, and vacated the order as to the bus acquisitions, subject to its reimposition at an appropriate time. The governor and other state officials petitioned the Supreme Court for a writ of certiorari. *Majority opinion: Burger, Blackmun, Powell, Rehnquist, Stewart. Concurring opinion: Stewart. Dissenting opinions: Douglas; Marshall, Brennan, Douglas, White; White, Brennan, Douglas, Marshall.*

MR. CHIEF JUSTICE BURGER delivered the opinion of the Court.

We granted certiorari in these consolidated cases to determine whether a federal court may impose a multidistrict, areawide remedy to a single district *de jure* segregation problem absent any finding that the other included school districts have failed to operate unitary school systems within their districts, absent any claim or finding that the boundary lines of any affected school district were established with the purpose of fostering racial segregation in public schools, absent any finding that the included districts committed acts which effected segregation within the other districts, and absent a meaningful opportunity for the included neighboring school districts to present evidence or be heard on the propriety of a multidistrict remedy or on the question of constitutional violations by those neighboring districts. . . .

Viewing the record as a whole, it seems clear that the District Court and the Court of Appeals shifted the primary focus from a Detroit remedy to the metropolitan area only because of their conclusion that total desegregation of Detroit would not produce the racial balance which they perceived as desirable. Both courts proceeded on an assumption that the Detroit schools could not be truly desegregated—in their view of what constituted desegregation—unless the racial composition of the student body of each school substantially reflected the racial composition of the population of the metropolitan area as a whole. The metropolitan area was then defined as Detroit plus 53 of the outlying school districts. . . .

Here the District Court's approach to what constituted "actual desegregation" raises the fundamental question . . . as to the circumstances in which a federal court may order desegregation relief that embraces more than a single school district. The court's analytical starting point was its conclusion that school district lines are no more than arbitrary lines on a map "drawn for political convenience." Boundary lines may be bridged where there has been a constitutional violation calling for inter-district relief, but, the notion that school district lines may be casually ignored or treated as a mere administrative convenience is contrary to the history of public education in our country. No single tradition in public education is more deeply rooted than local control over the operation of schools; local autonomy has long been thought essential both to the maintenance of community concern and support for public schools and to quality of the educational process. . . .

The Michigan educational structure involved in this case, in common with most States, provides for a large measure of local control and a review of the scope and character of these local powers indicates the extent to which the inter-district remedy approved by the two courts could disrupt and alter the structure of public education in Michigan. The metropolitan remedy would require, in effect, consolidation of 54 independent school districts historically administered as separate units into a vast new super school district. . . . Entirely apart from the logistical and other serious problems attending large scale transportation of students, the consolidation would give rise to an array of other problems in financing and operating this new school system. Some of the more obvious questions would be: What would be the status and authority of the present popularly elected school boards? Would the children of Detroit be within the jurisdiction and operating control of a school board elected by the parents and residents of other districts? What board or boards would levy taxes for school operations in these 54 districts constituting the consolidated metropolitan area? What provisions could be made for assuring substantial equality in tax levies among the 54 districts, if this were deemed requisite? What provisions would be made for financing? Would the validity of long-term bonds be jeopardized unless approved by all of the component districts as well as the State? What body would determine that portion of the curricula now left to the discretion of local school boards? Who would establish attendance zones, purchase school equipment, locate and construct new schools, and indeed attend to all the myriad day-to-day decisions that are necessary to school operations affecting potentially more than three quarters of a million pupils? . . .

It may be suggested that all of these vital operational problems are yet to be resolved by the District Court, and that this is the purpose of the Court of Appeals' proposed remand. But it is obvious from the scope of the inter-district remedy itself that absent a complete restructuring of the laws of Michigan relating to school districts the District Court will become first, a *de facto* "legislative authority" to resolve these complex questions, and then the "school superintendent" for the entire area. This is a task which few, if any, judges are qualified to perform and one which would deprive the people of control of schools through their elected representatives.

Of course, no state law is above the Constitution. School district lines and the present laws with respect to local control, are not sacrosanct and if they conflict with the Fourteenth Amendment federal courts have a duty to prescribe appropriate remedies. . . . But our prior holdings have been confined to violations and remedies within a single school district. We therefore turn to address, for the first time, the validity of a remedy mandating cross-district or inter-district consolidation to remedy a condition of segregation found to exist in only one district.

The controlling principle consistently expounded in our holdings is that the scope of the remedy is determined by the nature and extent of the constitutional violation. . . . Before the boundaries of separate and autonomous school districts may be set aside by consolidating the separate units for remedial purposes or by imposing a cross-district remedy, it must first be shown that there has been a constitutional violation within one district that produces a significant segregative effect in another district. Specifically it must be shown that racially discriminatory acts of the state or local school districts, or of a single school district have been a substantial cause of inter-district segregation. Thus an inter-district remedy might be in order where the racially discriminatory acts of one or more school districts caused racial segregation in an adjacent district, or where district lines have been deliberately drawn on the basis of race. In such circumstances an inter-district remedy would be appropriate to eliminate the inter-district segregation directly caused by the constitutional violation. Conversely, without an inter-district violation and inter-district effect, there is no constitutional wrong calling for an inter-district remedy.

The record before us, voluminous as it is, contains evidence of *de jure* segregated conditions only in the Detroit schools; indeed, that was the theory on which the litigation was initially based and on which the District Court took evidence. . . . With no showing of significant violation by the 53 outlying school districts and no evidence of any inter-district violation or effect, the court went beyond the original theory of the case as framed by the pleadings and mandated a metropolitan area remedy. To approve the remedy ordered by the court would impose on the outlying districts, not shown to have committed any constitutional violation, a wholly impermissible remedy based on a standard not hinted at in *Brown I* and *II* or any holding of this Court.

In dissent MR. JUSTICE WHITE and MR. JUSTICE MARSHALL undertake to demonstrate that agencies having statewide authority participated in maintaining the dual school system found to exist in Detroit. They are apparently of the view that once such participation is shown, the District Court should have a relatively free hand to reconstruct school districts outside of Detroit in fashioning relief. . . . The difference between us arises instead from established doctrine laid down by our cases. . . . Terms such as "unitary" and "dual" systems, and "racially identifiable schools," have meaning, and the necessary federal authority to remedy the constitutional wrong is firmly established. But the remedy is necessarily designed, as all remedies are, to restore the victims of discriminatory conduct to the position they would have occupied in the absence of such conduct. Disparate treatment of White and Negro students occurred within the Detroit school system, and not elsewhere, and on this record the remedy must be limited to that system.

The constitutional right of the Negro respondents residing in Detroit is to attend a unitary school system in that district. Unless petitioners drew the district lines in a discriminatory fashion, or arranged for White students residing in the Detroit district to attend schools in Oakland and Macomb Counties, they were under no constitutional duty to make provisions for Negro students to do so. The view of the dissenters, that the existence of a dual system *in Detroit* can be made the basis for a decree requiring cross-district transportation of pupils cannot be supported on the grounds that it represents merely the devising of a suitable flexible remedy for the violation of rights already established by our prior decisions. It can be supported only by drastic expansion of the constitutional right itself, an expansion without any support in either constitutional principle or precedent.

Accepting, *arguendo,* the correctness of [the lower courts'] finding of State responsibility for the segregated conditions within the city of Detroit, it does not follow that an inter-district remedy is constitutionally justified or required. With a single exception, . . . there has been no showing that either the State or any of the 85 outlying districts engaged in activity that had a cross-district effect. The boundaries of the Detroit School District, which are coterminous with the boundaries of the city of Detroit, were established over a century ago by neutral legislation when the city was incorporated; there is no evidence in the record, nor is there any suggestion by the respondents, that either the original boundaries of the Detroit School District, or any other school district in Michigan, were established for the purpose of creating, maintaining or perpetuating segregation of races. There is no claim and there is no evidence hinting that petitioners and their predecessors, or the 40-odd other school districts in the tricounty area—but outside the District Court's "desegregation area"—have ever maintained or operated anything but unitary school systems. Unitary school systems have been required for more than a century by the Michigan Constitution as implemented by state law. Where the schools of only one district have been affected, there is no constitutional power in the courts to decree relief balancing the racial composition of that district's schools with those of the surrounding districts. . . .

We conclude that the relief ordered by the District Court and affirmed by the Court of Appeals was based upon an erroneous standard and was unsupported by record evidence that acts of the outlying districts affected the discrimination found to exist in the schools of Detroit. Accordingly, the judgment of the Court of Appeals is reversed and the case is remanded for further proceedings consistent with this opinion leading to prompt formulation of a decree directed to eliminating the segregation found to exist in Detroit city schools, a remedy which has been delayed since 1970.

Reversed and remanded.

MR. JUSTICE DOUGLAS, dissenting.

So far as equal protection is concerned we are now in a dramatic retreat from the 8-to-1 decision in 1896 that Blacks could be segregated in public facilities provided they received equal treatment. . . .

. . . There is so far as the school cases go no constitutional difference between *de facto* and *de jure* segregation. Each school board performs state action for Fourteenth Amendment purposes when it draws the lines that confine it to a given area, when it builds schools at particular sites, or when it allocates students. The creation of the school districts in Metropolitan Detroit either maintained existing segregation or caused additional segregation. Restrictive covenants maintained by state action or inaction build black ghettos. It is state action when public funds are dispensed by housing agencies to build racial ghettos. Where a community is racially mixed and school authorities segregate schools, or assign black teachers to black schools or close schools in fringe areas and build new schools in black areas and in more distant white areas, the State creates and nurtures a segregated school system, just as surely as did those States involved in *Brown* v. *Board of Education*, . . . when they maintained dual school systems.

. . . It is conceivable that ghettos develop on their own without any hint of state action. But since Michigan by one device or another has over the years created black school districts and white school districts, the task of equity is to provide a unitary system for the affected area where, as here, the State washes its hands of its own creations.

MR. JUSTICE WHITE, with whom MR. JUSTICE DOUGLAS, MR. JUSTICE BRENNAN, and MR. JUSTICE MARSHALL join, dissenting. . . .

Regretfully, and for several reasons, I can join neither the Court's judgment nor its opinion. The core of my disagreement is that deliberate acts of segregation and their consequences will go unremedied, not because a remedy would be infeasible or unreasonable in terms of the usual criteria governing school desegregation cases, but because an effective remedy would cause what the Court considers to be undue administrative inconvenience to the State. The result is that the State of Michigan, the entity at which the Fourteenth Amendment is directed, has successfully insulated itself from its duty to provide effective desegregation remedies by vesting sufficient power over its public schools in its local school districts. If this is the case in Michigan, it will be the case in most States. . . .

The Detroit school district is both large and heavily populated. It covers 139.6 square miles, encircles two entirely separate cities and school districts, and surrounds a third city on three sides. Also, whites and Negroes live in identifiable areas in the city. The 1970 public school enrollment in the city school district totalled 289,763 and was 63.6% Negro and 34.8% white. If "racial balance" were achieved in every school in the district, each school would be approximately 64% Negro. A remedy confined to the district could achieve no more desegregation. Furthermore, the proposed intracity remedies were beset with practical problems. None of the plans limited to the school district was satisfactory to the District Court. The most promising proposal, submitted by respondents, who were the plaintiffs in the District Court, would "leave many of its schools 75 to 90 per cent Black." . . . Transportation on a "vast scale" would be required; 900 buses would have to be purchased for the transportation of pupils who are not now bussed. . . . The District Court also found that the plan "would change a school system which is now Black and White to one that would be perceived as Black, thereby increasing the flight of Whites from the city and the system, thereby increasing the Black student population," . . . For the District Court,"[t]he conclusion, under the evidence in this case, is inescapable that relief of segregation in the public schools of the City of

Detroit cannot be accomplished within the corporate geographical limits of the city." . . .

Despite the fact that a metropolitan remedy, if the findings of the District Court accepted by the Court of Appeals are to be credited, would more effectively desegregate the Detroit schools, would prevent resegregation, and would be easier and more feasible from many standpoints, the Court fashions out of whole cloth an arbitrary rule that remedies for constitutional violations occurring in a single Michigan school district must stop at the school district line. . . .

I am surprised that the Court, sitting at this distance from the State of Michigan, claims better insight than the Court of Appeals and the District Court as to whether an interdistrict remedy for equal protection violations practiced by the State of Michigan would involve undue difficulties for the State in the management of its public schools.

I am even more mystified how the Court can ignore the legal reality that the constitutional violations, even if occurring locally, were committed by governmental entities for which the State is responsible and that it is the State that must respond to the command of the Fourteenth Amendment. An interdistrict remedy for the infringements that occurred in this case is well within the confines and powers of the State, which is the governmental entity ultimately responsible for desegregating its schools. . . . I cannot understand, nor does the majority satisfactorily explain, why a federal court may not order an appropriate interdistrict remedy, if this is necessary or more effective to accomplish this constitutionally mandated task. In this case, both the right and the States' Fourteenth Amendment violation have concededly been fully established, and there is no acceptable reason for permitting the party responsible for the constitutional violation to contain the remedial powers of the federal court within administrative boundaries over which the transgressor itself has plenary power. . . .

Until today, the permissible contours of the equitable authority of the district courts to remedy the unlawful establishment of a dual school system have been extensive, adaptable, and fully responsive to the ultimate goal of achieving "the greatest possible degree of actual desegregation." There are indeed limitations on the equity powers of the federal judiciary, but until now the Court had not accepted the proposition that effective enforcement of the Fourteenth Amendment could be limited by political or administrative boundary lines demarcated by the very State responsible for the constitutional violation and for the disestablishment of the dual system. . . .

Finally, I remain wholly unpersuaded by the Court's assertion that "the remedy is necessarily designed, as all remedies are, to restore the victims of discriminatory conduct to the position they would have occupied in the absence of such conduct." . . . In the first place, under this premise the Court's judgment is itself infirm; for had the Detroit school system not followed an official policy of segregation throughout the 1950's and 1960's, Negroes and whites would have been going to school together. There would have been no, or at least not as many, recognizable Negro schools and no, or at least not as many, white schools, but "just schools," and neither Negroes nor whites would have suffered from the effects of segregated education, with all its shortcomings. Surely the Court's remedy will not restore to the Negro community, stigmatized as it was by the dual school system, what it would have enjoyed over all or most of this period if the remedy is confined to present-day Detroit; for the maximum remedy available within that area will leave many of the schools almost totally black, and the system itself will be predominantly black and will become increasingly so. . . .

MR. JUSTICE MARSHALL, with whom MR. JUSTICE DOUGLAS, MR. JUSTICE BRENNAN, and MR. JUSTICE WHITE join, dissenting. . . .

I cannot subscribe to this emasculation of our constitutional guarantee of equal protection of the laws and must respectfully dissent. Our precedents, in my view, firmly establish that where, as here, state-imposed segregation has been demonstrated, it becomes the duty of the State to eliminate root and branch all vestiges of racial discrimination and to achieve the greatest possible degree of actual desegregation.

. . . The District Court's decision to expand its desegregation decree beyond the geographical limits of the city of Detroit rested in large part on its conclusions that the State of Michigan was ultimately responsible for curing the condition of segregation within the Detroit city schools, and that a Detroit-only remedy would not accomplish this task. In my view, both of these conclusions are well supported by the facts of this case and by this Court's precedents. . . .

We held in *Swann* that where *de jure* segregation is shown, school authorities must make "every effort to achieve the greatest possible degree of actual desegregation." . . . If these words have any meaning at all, surely it is that school authorities must, to the extent possible, take all practicable steps to ensure that Negro and white children in fact go to school together. This is, in the final analysis, what desegregation of the public schools is all about.

Because of the already high and rapidly increasing percentage of Negro students in the Detroit system, as well as the prospect of white flight, a Detroit-only plan simply has no hope of achieving actual desegregation. Under such a plan white and Negro students will not go to school together. Instead, Negro children will continue to attend all-Negro schools. The very event that *Brown I* was aimed at will not be cured, but will be perpetuated for the future. . . .

. . . The flaw of a Detroit-only decree is not that it does not reach some ideal degree of racial balance or mixing. It simply does not promise to achieve actual desegregation at all. It is one thing to have a system where a small number of students remain in racially identifiable schools. It is something else entirely to have a system where all students continue to attend such schools. . . .

Under a Detroit-only decree, Detroit schools will clearly remain racially identifiable in comparison with neighboring schools in the metropolitan community. Schools with 65% and more Negro students will stand in sharp and obvious contrast to schools in neighboring districts with less than 2% Negro enrollment. Negro students will continue to perceive their schools as segregated educational facilities and this perception will only be increased when whites react to a Detroit-only decree by fleeing to the suburbs to avoid integration. School district lines, however innocently drawn, will surely be perceived as fences to separate the races when, under a Detroit-only decree, white parents withdraw their children from the Detroit city schools and move to the suburbs in order to continue them in all-white schools. The message of this action will not escape the Negro children in the city of Detroit. . . . It will be of scant significance to Negro children who have for years been confined by *de jure* acts of segregation to a growing core of all-Negro schools surrounded by a ring of all-white schools that the new dividing line between the races is the school district boundary. . . .

The State must also bear part of the blame for the white flight to the suburbs which would be forthcoming from a Detroit-only decree and would render such a remedy ineffective. Having created a system where whites and Negroes were intentionally kept apart so that they could not become accustomed to learning together, the State is responsible for the fact that many whites will react to the dismantling of the segregated system by attempting to flee to the suburbs. Indeed, by limiting the District Court to a Detroit-only remedy and allowing that flight to the suburbs to succeed, the Court today allows the State to profit from its own wrong and to perpetuate for years to come the separation of the races it achieved in the past by purposeful state action. . . .

Desegregation is not and was never expected to be an easy task. Racial attitudes ingrained in our Nation's childhood and adolescence are not quickly thrown aside in its middle years. But just as the inconvenience of some cannot be allowed to stand in the way of the rights of others, so public opposition, no matter how strident, cannot be permitted to divert this Court from the enforcement of the constitutional principles at issue in this case. Today's holding, I fear, is more a reflection of a perceived public mood that we have gone far enough in enforcing the Constitution's guarantee of equal justice than it is the product of neutral principles of law. In the short run, it may seem to be the easier course to allow our great metropolitan areas to be divided up each into two cities—one white, the other black—but it is a course, I predict, our people will ultimately regret. I dissent.

Missouri v. *Jenkins*

110 S. Ct. 1651 (1990)

In a Section 1983 action, Judge Russell Clark of the District Court for the Western District of Missouri found that the Kansas City, Missouri, School District (KCMSD) and the State of Missouri were guilty of operating a segregated school system. Judge Clark ultimately issued an order detailing a desegregation remedy and the financing necessary to implement it. His remedy was comprehensive and extraordinarily expensive. Among other things, he mandated that every high school, every middle school, and half of the elementary schools in KCMSD become magnet schools; costs for implementing his remedial plan were placed between $500,000,000 and $700,000,000. To pay for this remedy, Judge Clark ordered the State of Missouri to cover 75 percent of the costs, with the KCMSD contributing the rest. When it became clear that state tax limitation laws prohibited the school district from raising property tax rates sufficiently to meet its 25 percent obligation, he enjoined the operation of these state laws and ordered the KCMSD property tax levy increased from $2.05 to $4.00 per $100 of assessed valuation. The Court of Appeals for the Eighth Circuit affirmed Judge Clark's order. However, concluding that federal/state principles of comity required the District Court to use minimally obtrusive methods to remedy constitutional violations, it held that in the future the lower court should not set the property tax rate itself but should authorize the KCMSD to submit a levy to state tax collection authorities and should enjoin the operating of state tax laws hindering KCMSD from adequately funding the remedy. The state and school district petitioned for a writ of certiorari, which the Supreme Court granted only with respect to the property tax increase. *Opinion of the Court: White, Blackmun, Brennan, Kennedy, Marshall, O'Connor, Rehnquist, Scalia, Stevens. Concurring in part and concurring in the judgment: Kennedy, O'Connor, Rehnquist, Scalia.*

JUSTICE WHITE delivered the opinion of the Court.

The United States District Court for the Western District of Missouri imposed an increase in the property taxes levied by the Kansas City, Missouri, School District (KCMSD) to ensure funding for the desegregation of KCMSD's public schools. We granted certiorari to consider the State of Missouri's argument that the District Court lacked the power to raise local property taxes. For the reasons given below, we hold that the District Court abused its discretion in imposing the tax increase. We also hold, however, that the modifications of the District Court's order made by the Court of Appeals do satisfy equitable and constitutional principles governing the District Court's power. . . .

We turn to the tax increase imposed by the District Court. The State urges us to hold that the tax increase violated Article III, the Tenth Amendment, and principles of federal/state comity. We find it unnecessary to reach the difficult constitutional issues, for we agree with the State that the tax increase contravened the principles of comity that must govern the exercise of the District Court's equitable discretion in this area.

It is accepted by all the parties, as it was by the courts below, that the imposition of a tax increase by a federal court was an extraordinary event. In assuming for itself the fundamental and delicate power of taxation the District Court not only intruded on local authority but circumvented it altogether. Before taking such a drastic step the District Court was obliged to assure itself that no permissible alternative would have accomplished the required task. We have emphasized that although the "remedial powers of an equity court must be adequate to the task, . . . they are not unlimited," . . . and one of the most important considerations governing the exercise of equitable power is a proper respect for the integrity and function of local government institutions. Especially is this true where, as here, those institutions are ready, willing, and—but for the operation of state law curtailing their powers—able to remedy the deprivation of constitutional rights themselves.

The District Court believed that it had no alternative to imposing a tax increase. But there was an alternative, the very one outlined by the Court of Appeals: it could have authorized or required KCMSD to levy property taxes at a rate adequate to fund the desegregation remedy and could have enjoined the operation of state laws that would have prevented KCMSD from exercising this power. . . . The difference between the two approaches is far more than a matter of form. Authorizing and directing local government institutions to devise and implement remedies not only protects the function of those institutions but, to the extent possible, also places the responsibility for solutions to the problems of segregation upon those who have themselves created the problems.

The District Court therefore abused its discretion in imposing the tax itself. The Court of Appeals should not have allowed the tax increase to stand and should have reversed the District Court in this respect. . . .

We stand on different ground when we review the modifications to the District Court's order made by the Court of Appeals. As explained supra, . . . the Court of Appeals held that the District Court in the future should authorize KCMSD to submit a levy to the state tax collection authorities adequate to fund its budget and should enjoin the operation of state laws that would limit or reduce the levy below that amount. . . .

The State argues that the funding ordered by the District Court violates principles of equity and comity because the remedial order itself was excessive. As the State puts it, [t]he only reason that the court below needed to consider an unprecedented tax increase was the equally unprecedented cost of its remedial programs. . . . We think this argument aims at the scope of the remedy rather than the manner in which the remedy is to be funded and thus falls outside our limited grant of certiorari in this case. . . .

We turn to the constitutional issues. The modifications ordered by the Court of Appeals cannot be assailed as invalid under the Tenth Amendment. The Tenth Amendment's reservation of nondelegated powers to the States is not implicated by a federal court judgment enforcing the express prohibitions of unlawful state conduct enacted by the Fourteenth Amendment. . . . "The Fourteenth Amendment . . . was avowedly directed against the power of the States," and so permits a federal court to disestablish local government institutions that interfere with its commands. . . .

Finally, the State argues that an order to increase taxes cannot be sustained under the judicial power of Article III. Whatever the merits of this argument when applied to the District Court's own order increasing taxes, . . . a court order directing a local government . . . body to levy its own taxes is plainly a judicial act within the power of a federal court . . .

The State maintains, however, . . . the federal judicial power can go no further than to require local governments to levy taxes AS AUTHORIZED UNDER STATE LAW. In other words, the State argues that federal courts cannot set aside state-imposed limitations on local taxing authority because to do so is to do more than to require the local government to exercise the power THAT IS THEIRS. We disagree.

. . . A local government with taxing authority may be ordered to levy taxes in excess of the limit set by state statute where there is reason based in the Constitution for not observing the statutory limitation . . . Here the KCMSD may be ordered to levy taxes despite the statutory limitations on its authority in order to compel the discharge of an obligation imposed on KCMSD by the Fourteenth Amendment. To hold otherwise would fail to take account of the obligations of local governments, under the . . . Supremacy Clause, to fulfill the requirements that the Constitution imposes on them. However wide the discretion of local authorities in fashioning desegregation remedies may be, "if a state-imposed limitation on a school authority's discretion operates to inhibit or obstruct the operation of a unitary school system or impede the disestablishing of a dual school system, it must fall; state policy must give way when it operates to hinder vindication of federal constitutional guarantees." . . . Even though a particular remedy may not be required in every case to vindicate constitutional guarantees, where (as here) it has been found that a particular remedy is required, the State cannot hinder the process by preventing a local government from implementing that remedy. . . . Accordingly, the judgment of the Court of Appeals is affirmed insofar as it required the District Court to modify its funding order and reversed insofar as it allowed the tax increase imposed by the District Court to stand. The case is remanded for further proceedings consistent with this opinion.

JUSTICE KENNEDY, with whom THE CHIEF JUSTICE, JUSTICE O'CONNOR, and JUSTICE SCALIA join, concurring in part and concurring in the judgment. . . .

I agree that the District Court exceeded its authority by attempting to impose a tax. The Court is unanimous in its holding, that the Court of Appeals' judgment affirming "the actions that the [district] court has taken to this point," . . . must be reversed. This is consistent with our precedents and the basic principles defining judicial power.

In my view, however, the Court transgresses these same principles when it goes further, much further, to embrace by broad dictum an expansion of power in the federal judiciary beyond all precedent. Today's casual embrace of taxation imposed by the unelected, life-tenured federal judiciary disregards fundamental precepts for the democratic control of public institutions. I cannot acquiesce in the majority's statements on this point, and should there arise an actual . . . dispute over the collection of taxes here contemplated in a case that is not, like this one, premature, we should not confirm the outcome of premises adopted with so little constitutional justification. The Court's statements, in my view, cannot be seen as necessary for its judgment, or as precedent for the future. . . .

Some essential litigation history is necessary for a full understanding of what is at stake here and what will be wrought if the implications of all the Court's statements are followed to the full extent. The District Court's remedial plan was proposed for the most part by the Kansas City, Missouri, School District (KCMSD) itself, which is in name a defendant in the suit. . . . The Court and the KCMSD decided to make a magnet of the district as a whole. The hope was to draw new nonminority students from outside the district. The KCMSD plan adopted by the Court provided that "every senior high school, every middle school, and approximately one-half of the elementary schools in the KCMSD will become magnet schools by the school year 1991–92." . . . The plan was intended to "improve the quality of education of all KCMSD students." . . . The District Court was candid to acknowledge that the "long-term goal of this Court's remedial order is to make available to ALL KCMSD students educational opportunities equal to or greater than those presently available in the average Kansas City, Missouri, metropolitan suburban school district." . . .

It comes as no surprise that the cost of this approach to the remedy far exceeded KCMSD's budget, or for that matter, its authority to tax. A few . . . examples are illustrative. Programs such as a "performing arts middle school," . . . a "technical magnet high school" that "will offer programs ranging from heating and air conditioning to cosmetology to robotics," . . . were approved. The plan also included a "25 acre farm and 25 acre wildland area" for science study. The Court rejected various proposals by the State to make "capital improvements necessary to eliminate health and safety hazards and to provide a good learning environment," because these proposals failed to "consider the criteria of suburban comparability." . . . The District Court stated: "This 'patch and repair' approach proposed by the State would not achieve suburban comparability or the visual attractiveness sought by the Court as it would result in floor coverings with unsightly sections of mismatched carpeting and tile, and individual walls possessing different shades of paint." . . . Finding that construction of new schools would result in more attractive facilities than renovation of existing ones, the District Court approved new construction at a cost ranging from $61.80 per square foot to $95.70 per square foot as distinct from renovation at $45 per square foot. . . . As the Eighth Circuit judges dissenting from denial of rehearing in banc put it: "The remedies ordered go far beyond anything previously seen in a school desegregation case. The sheer immensity of the programs encompassed by the district court's order—the large number of magnet schools and the quantity of capital renovations and new construction—are concededly without parallel in any other school district in the country. . . ."

The judicial taxation approved by the Eighth Circuit is also without parallel. Other Circuits that have faced funding problems arising from remedial decrees have concluded that, while courts have undoubted power to order that schools operate in compliance with the Constitution, the manner and methods of school financing are beyond federal judicial authority. . . . Whatever taxing power the KCMSD may exercise outside the boundaries of state law would derive from the federal court. The Court never confronts the judicial authority to issue an order for this purpose. Absent a change in state law, the tax is imposed by federal authority under a federal decree. The question is whether a district court possesses a power to tax under federal law, either directly or through delegation to the KCMSD.

Article III of the Constitution states that "[t]he judicial Power of the United States, shall be vested in one supreme Court, and in such inferior Courts as the Congress may from time to time ordain and establish." The description of the judicial power nowhere includes the word "tax" or anything that resembles it. This reflects the Framers' understanding that taxation was not a proper area for judicial involvement. "The judiciary . . . has no influence over either the sword or the purse, no direction either of the strength or of the wealth of the society, and can take no active resolution whatever." The Federalist No. 78. . . .

A judicial taxation order is but an attempt to exercise a power that always has been thought legislative in nature. The location of the federal taxing power sheds light on today's attempt to approve judicial taxation at the local level. Article I, s 1 states that "[A]LL legislative Powers herein granted shall be vested in a Congress of the United States, which shall consist of a Senate and House of Representatives" [emphasis added]. The list of legislative powers in Article I, s 8, cl. 1 begins with the statement that "[t]he Congress shall have Power to lay and collect Taxes. . . ." As we have said, "[t]axation is a legislative function, and Congress . . . is the sole organ for levying taxes." . . .

True, today's case is not an instance of one branch of the Federal Government invading the province of another. It is instead one that brings the weight of federal authority upon a local government and a State. This does not detract, however, from the fundamental point that the judiciary is not free to exercise all federal power; it may exercise only the judicial power. And the important effects of the taxation order discussed here raise additional federalism concerns that counsel against the Court's analysis. . . .

The confinement of taxation to the legislative branches, both in our Federal and State Governments, was not random. It reflected our ideal that the power of taxation must be under the control of those who are taxed. This truth animated all our colonial and revolutionary history. . . .

The power of taxation is one that the federal judiciary does not possess. In our system "the legislative department alone has access to the pockets of the people," The Federalist No. 48, . . . for it is the legislature that is accountable to them and represents their will. The authority that would levy the tax at issue here shares none of these qualities. Our federal judiciary, by design, is not representative or responsible to the people in a political sense; it is independent. Federal judges do not depend on the popular will for their office. They may not even share the burden of taxes they attempt to impose, for they may live outside the jurisdiction their orders affect. And federal judges have no fear that the competition for scarce public resources could result in a diminution of their salaries. It is not surprising that imposition of taxes by an authority so insulated from public communication or control can lead to deep feelings of frustration, powerlessness, and anger on the part of taxpaying citizens.

The operation of tax systems is among the most difficult aspects of public administration. It is not a function the judiciary as an institution is designed to exercise. Unlike legislative bodies, which may hold hearings on how best to raise revenues, all subject to the views of constituents to whom the legislature is accountable, the judiciary must grope ahead with only the assistance of the parties, or perhaps random amici curiae. Those hearings would be without principled direction, for there exists no body of juridical axioms by which to guide or review them. On this questionable basis, the Court today would give authority for decisions that affect the life plans of local citizens, the revenue available for competing public needs, and the health of the local economy.

Day-to-day administration of the tax must be accomplished by judicial trial and error, requisitioning the staff of the existing tax authority, or the hiring of a staff under the direction of the judge. . . .

The function of hiring and supervising a staff for what is essentially a political function has other complications. As part of its remedial order, for example, the District Court ordered the hiring of a "public information specialist," at a cost of $30,000. The purpose of the position was to "solicit community support and involvement" in the District Court's desegregation plan. . . . This type of order raises a substantial question whether a district court may extract taxes from citizens who have no right of representation and then use the funds for expression with which the citizens may disagree. . . .

Perhaps it is good educational policy to provide a school district with the items included in the KCMSD capital improvement plan, for example: high schools in which every classroom will have air conditioning, an alarm system, and 15 microcomputers; a 2,000-square-foot planetarium; greenhouses and vivariums; a 25-acre farm with an air-conditioned meeting room for 104 people; a Model United Nations wired for language translation; broadcast capable radio and television studios with an editing and animation lab; a temperature controlled art gallery; movie editing and screening rooms; a 3,500-square-foot dust-free diesel mechanics room; 1,875-square-foot elementary school animal rooms for use in a Zoo Project; swimming pools; and numerous other facilities. But these items are a part of legitimate political debate over educational policy and spending priorities, not the Constitution's command of racial equality. Indeed, it may be that a mere 12-acre petting farm, or other corresponding reductions in court-ordered spending, might satisfy constitutional requirements, while preserving scarce public funds for legislative allocation to other public needs, such as paving streets, feeding the poor, building prisons, or housing the homeless. Perhaps the KCMSD's Classical Greek theme schools emphasizing forensics and self-government will provide exemplary training in participatory democracy. But if today's dicta become law, such lessons will be of little use to students who grow up to become taxpayers in the KCMSD.

I am required in light of our limited grant of certiorari to assume that the remedy chosen by the District Court was a permissible exercise of its remedial discretion. But it is misleading to suggest that a failure to fund this particular remedy would leave constitutional rights without a remedy. In fact, the District Court acknowledged in its very first remedial order that the development of a remedy in this case would involve "a choice among a wide range of possibilities." . . .

The prudence we have required in other areas touching on federal court intrusion in local government . . . is missing here. Even on the assumption that a federal court might order taxation in an extreme case, the unique nature of the taxing power would demand that this remedy be used as a last resort. In my view, a taxation order should not even be considered, and this Court need never have addressed the question, unless there has been a finding that without the particular remedy at issue the constitutional violation will go unremedied. By this I do not mean that the remedy is, as we assume this one was, within the broad discretion of the district court. Rather, as a prerequisite to considering a taxation order, I would require a finding that any remedy less costly than the one at issue would so plainly leave the violation unremedied that its implementation would itself be an abuse of discretion. There is no showing in this record that, faced with the revenue shortfall, the District Court gave due consideration to the possibility that another remedy among the "wide range of possibilities" would have addressed the constitutional violations without giving rise to a funding crisis. . . .

This case is a stark illustration of the ever-present question whether ends justify means. Few ends are more important than enforcing the guarantee of equal educational opportunity for our Nation's children. But rules of taxation that override state political structures not themselves subject to any constitutional infirmity raise serious questions of federal authority, questions compounded by the odd posture of a case in which the Court assumes the validity of a novel conception of desegregation remedies we never before have approved. . . .

James Madison observed: "Justice is the end of government. It is the end of civil society. It ever has been, and ever will be pursued, until it be obtained, or until liberty be lost in the pursuit."

The Federalist, No. 51. . . . In pursuing the demand of justice for racial equality, I fear that the Court today loses sight of other basic political liberties guaranteed by our constitutional system, liberties that can coexist with a proper exercise of judicial remedial powers adequate to correct constitutional violations.

Shelley v. *Kraemer*

334 U.S. 1; 68 S. Ct. 836; 92 L. Ed. 1161 (1948)

J.D. Shelley, a black, purchased a house from Josephine Fitzgerald in a St. Louis neighborhood in which deeds held by three-fourths of the property owners contained a racially restrictive covenant—that is, an agreement by the property holders not to sell their property to "people of the Negro or Mongolian Race." The covenant had been in force since 1911, when the holders of the properties in question had entered into a fifty-year contract not to sell to "any person not of the Caucasian race." Neither Shelley nor Fitzgerald was aware of the restrictive covenant at the time of the sale. When Shelley refused to reconsider the purchase after learning of the racial exclusion, Louis Kraemer, a resident of the neighborhood whose deed contained a similar restriction, sued to enjoin Shelley from taking possession of the property. The Missouri Supreme Court ultimately granted Kraemer the relief he sought and directed the trial court to issue the injunction. Shelley appealed to the United States Supreme Court, where his case was heard in conjunction with a controversy from Michigan involving a similar restrictive covenant. *Majority opinion: Vinson, Black, Burton, Douglas, Frankfurter, Murphy. Not participating: Jackson, Reed, Rutledge.*

MR. CHIEF JUSTICE VINSON delivered the opinion of the Court.

These cases present for our consideration questions relating to the validity of court enforcement of private agreements, generally described as restrictive covenants, which have as their purpose the exclusion of persons of designated race or color from the ownership or occupancy of real property. Basic constitutional issues of obvious importance have been raised. . . .

It is well, at the outset, to scrutinize the terms of the restrictive agreements involved in these cases. In the Missouri case, the covenant declares that no part of the affected property shall be "occupied by any person not of the Caucasian race, it being intended hereby to restrict the use of said property . . . against the occupancy as owners or tenants of any portion of said property for resident or other purpose by people of the Negro or Mongolian Race." Not only does the restriction seek to proscribe use and occupancy of the affected properties by members of the excluded class, but as construed by the Missouri courts, the agreement requires that title of any person who uses his property in violation of the restriction shall be divested. The restriction of the covenant in the Michigan case seeks to bar occupancy by persons of the excluded class. It provides that "This property shall not be used or occupied by any person or persons except those of the Caucasian race." . . .

It cannot be doubted that among the civil rights intended to be protected from discriminatory state action by the Fourteenth Amendment are the rights to acquire, enjoy, own and dispose of property. Equality in the enjoyment of property rights was regarded by the framers of that Amendment as an essential pre-condition to the realization of other basic civil rights and liberties which the Amendment was intended to guarantee. . . .

It is likewise clear that restrictions on the right of occupancy of the sort sought to be created by the private agreements in these cases could not be squared with the requirements of the Fourteenth Amendment if imposed by state statute or local ordinance. We do not understand respondents to urge the contrary. . . .

But the present cases . . . do not involve action by state legislatures or city councils. Here the particular patterns of discrimination and the areas in which the restrictions are to operate, are determined, in the first instance, by the terms of agreements among private individuals. Participation of the State consists in the enforcement of the restrictions so defined. The crucial issue with which we are here confronted is whether this distinction removes these cases from the operation of the prohibitory provisions of the Fourteenth Amendment.

Since the decision of this Court in the *Civil Rights Cases*, . . . the principle has become firmly embedded in our constitutional law that the action inhibited by the first section of the Fourteenth Amendment is only such action as may fairly be said to be that of the States. That Amendment erects no shield against merely private conduct, however discriminatory or wrongful.

We conclude, therefore, that the restrictive agreements standing alone cannot be regarded as violative of any rights guaranteed to petitioners by the Fourteenth Amendment. So long as the purposes of those agreements are effectuated by voluntary adherence to their terms, it would appear clear that there has been no action by the State and the provisions of the Amendment have not been violated. . . .

But here there was more. These are cases in which the purposes of the agreements were secured only by judicial enforcement by state courts of the restrictive terms of the agreements.

We have no doubt that there has been state action in these cases in the full and complete sense of the phrase. The undisputed facts disclose that petitioners were willing purchasers of properties upon which they desired to establish homes. The owners of the properties were willing sellers; and contracts of sale were accordingly consummated. It is clear that but for the active intervention of the state courts, supported by the full panoply of state power, petitioners would have been free to occupy the properties in question without restraint.

These are not cases, as has been suggested, in which the States have merely abstained from action, leaving private individuals free to impose such discriminations as they see fit. Rather, these are cases in which the States have made available to such individuals the full coercive power of government to deny to petitioners, on the grounds of race or color, the enjoyment of property rights in premises which petitioners are willing and financially able to acquire and which the grantors are willing to sell. The difference between judicial enforcement and non-enforcement of the restrictive covenants is the difference to petitioners between being denied rights of property available to other members of the community and being accorded full enjoyment of those rights on an equal footing. . . .

. . . We have noted that previous decisions of this Court have established the proposition that judicial action is not immunized from the operation of the Fourteenth Amendment simply because it is taken pursuant to the state's common-law policy. Nor is the Amendment ineffective simply because the particular pattern of discrimination, which the State has enforced, was defined initially by the terms of a private agreement. State action, as that phrase is understood for the purposes of the Fourteenth Amendment, refers to exertions of state power in all forms. And when the effect of that action is to deny rights subject to the protection of the Fourteenth Amendment, it is the obligation of this Court to enforce the constitutional commands.

We hold that in granting judicial enforcement of the restrictive agreements in these cases, the States have denied petitioners the equal protection of the laws and that, therefore, the action of the state courts cannot stand. . . .

Respondents urge, however, that since the state courts stand ready to enforce restrictive covenants excluding white persons from the ownership or occupancy of property covered by such agreements, enforcement of covenants excluding colored persons may not be deemed a denial of equal protection of the laws to the colored persons who are thereby affected. This contention does not bear scrutiny. The parties have directed our attention to no case in which a court, state or federal, has been called upon to enforce a covenant excluding members of the white majority from ownership or occupancy of real property on grounds of race or color. But there are more fundamental considerations. The rights created by the first section of the Fourteenth Amendment are, by its terms, guaranteed to the individual. The rights established are personal rights. It is, therefore, no answer to these petitioners to say that the courts may also be induced to deny white persons rights of ownership and occupancy on grounds of race or color. Equal protection of the laws is not achieved through indiscriminate imposition of inequalities. . . .

The historical context in which the Fourteenth Amendment became a part of the Constitution should not be forgotten. Whatever else the framers sought to achieve, it is clear that the matter of primary concern was the establishment of equality in the enjoyment of basic civil and political rights and the preservation of those rights from discriminatory action on the part of the States based on considerations of race or color. Seventy-five years ago this Court announced that the provisions of the Amendment are to be construed with this fundamental purpose in mind. Upon full consideration, we have concluded that in these cases the States have acted to deny petitioners the equal protection of the laws guaranteed by the Fourteenth Amendment. . . .

For the reasons stated, the judgment of the Supreme Court of Missouri and the judgment of the Supreme Court of Michigan must be reversed.

Reversed.

Moose Lodge No. 107 v. *Irvis*

407 U.S. 163; 92 S. Ct. 1965; 32 L. Ed. 627 (1972)

Leroy Irvis, a black guest at the Moose Lodge in Harrisburg, Pennsylvania, was refused service at its dining room and bar solely because of his race. Irvis sued in federal district court for injunctive relief, charging that the discrimination was state action and thus in violation of the Equal Protection Clause of the Fourteenth Amendment, because the Pennsylvania liquor board had issued a liquor license to the Moose Lodge, a private club. The district court agreed with Irvis that state action was present and declared the Moose Lodge's liquor license invalid as long as it continued its discriminatory practices. The Moose Lodge appealed to the Supreme Court. *Majority opinion: Rehnquist, Blackmun, Burger, Powell, Stewart, White. Dissenting opinions: Brennan, Marshall; Douglas, Marshall.*

MR. JUSTICE REHNQUIST delivered the opinion of the Court. . . .

Moose Lodge is a private club in the ordinary meaning of that term. It is a local chapter of a national fraternal organization having well defined requirements for membership. It conducts all of its activities in a building that is owned by it. It is not publicly funded. Only members and guests are permitted in any lodge of the order; one may become a guest only by invitation of a member or upon invitation of the house committee.

Appellee, while conceding the right of private clubs to choose members upon a discriminatory basis, asserts that the licensing of Moose Lodge to serve liquor by the Pennsylvania Liquor Control Board amounts to such State involvement with the club's activities as to make its discriminatory practices forbidden by the Equal Protection Clause of the Fourteenth Amendment. The relief sought and obtained by appellee in the District Court was an injunction forbidding the licensing by the liquor authority of Moose Lodge until it ceased its discriminatory practices. We conclude that Moose Lodge's refusal to serve food and beverages to a guest by reason of the fact that he was a Negro does not, under the circumstances here presented, violate the Fourteenth Amendment.

In 1883, this Court in *The Civil Rights Cases* . . . set forth the essential dichotomy between discriminatory action by the State, which is prohibited by the Equal Protection Clause, and private conduct, "however discriminatory or wrongful," against which that clause "erects no shield," *Shelley* v. *Kraemer* . . . [1948]. . . .

While the principle is easily stated, the question of whether particular discriminatory conduct is private, on the one hand, or amounts to "State action," on the other hand, frequently admits of no easy answer. "Only by sifting facts and weighing circumstances can the nonobvious involvement of the State in private conduct be attributed its true significance." . . .

Our cases make clear that the impetus for the forbidden discrimination need not originate with the State if it is state action that enforces privately originated discrimination. . . . The Court held in *Burton* v. *Wilmington Parking Authority* [1962] . . . that a private restaurant owner who refused service because of a customer's race violated the Fourteenth Amendment, where the restaurant was located in a building owned by a state created parking authority and leased from the authority. The Court, after a comprehensive review of the relationship between the lessee and the parking authority concluded that the latter had "so far insinuated itself into a position of interdependence with Eagle [the restaurant owner] that it must be recognized as a joint participant in the challenged activity, which, on that account, cannot be considered to have been so 'purely private' as to fall without the scope of the Fourteenth Amendment." . . .

The Court has never held, of course, that discrimination by an otherwise private entity would be violative of the Equal Protection Clause if the private entity receives any sort of benefit or service at all from the State, or if it is subject to state regulation in any degree whatever. Since state-furnished services include such necessities of life as electricity, water, and police and fire protection, such a holding would utterly emasculate the distinction between private as distinguished from State conduct set forth in *The Civil Rights Cases* . . . and adhered to in subsequent decisions. Our holdings indicate that where the impetus for the discrimination is private, the State must have "significantly involved itself with invidious discriminations," . . . in order for the discriminatory action to fall within the ambit of the constitutional prohibition. . . .

Here there is nothing approaching the symbiotic relationship between lessor and lessee that was present in *Burton,* where the private lessee obtained the benefit of locating in a building owned by the State created parking authority, and the parking authority was enabled to carry out its primary public purpose of furnishing parking space by advantageously leasing portions of the building constructed for that purpose to commercial lessees such as the owner of the Eagle Restaurant. . . .

. . .The Pennsylvania Liquor Control Board plays absolutely no part in establishing or enforcing the membership or guest policies of the club which it licenses to serve liquor. There is no suggestion in this record that the Pennsylvania Act, either as written or as applied, discriminates against minority groups either in their right to apply for club licenses themselves or in their right to purchase and be served liquor in places of public accommodation. The only effect that the state licensing of Moose Lodge to serve liquor can be said to have on the right of any other Pennsylvanian to buy or be served liquor on premises other than those of Moose Lodge is that for some purposes club licenses are counted in the maximum number of licenses which may be issued in a given municipality. Basically each municipality has a quota of one retail license for each 1,500 inhabitants. Licenses issued to hotels, municipal golf courses and airport restaurants are not counted in this quota, nor are club licenses until the maximum number of retail licenses is reached. Beyond that point, neither additional retail licenses nor additional club licenses may be issued so long as the number of issued and outstanding retail licenses remains above the statutory maximum.

The District Court was at pains to point out in its opinion what it considered to be the "pervasive" nature of the regulation of private clubs by the Pennsylvania Liquor Control Board. As that court noted, an applicant for a club license must make such physical alterations in its premises as the board may require, must file a list of the names and addresses of its members and employees, and must keep extensive financial records. The board is granted the right to inspect the licensed premises at any time when patrons, guests or members are present.

However detailed this type of regulation may be in some particulars, it cannot be said to in any way foster or encourage racial discrimination. Nor can it be said to make the State in any realistic sense a partner or even a joint venturer in the club's enterprise. The limited effect of the prohibition against obtaining additional club licenses when the maximum number of retail licenses allotted to a municipality has been issued, when considered together with the availability of liquor from hotel, restaurant, and retail licensees falls far short of conferring upon club licensees a monopoly in the dispensing of liquor in any given municipality or in the State as a whole. We therefore hold that, with the exception hereafter noted, the operation of the regulatory scheme enforced by the Pennsylvania Liquor Control Board does not sufficiently implicate the State in the discriminatory guest policies of Moose Lodge so as to make the latter "State action" within the ambit of the Equal Protection Clause of the Fourteenth Amendment. . . .

MR. JUSTICE DOUGLAS, with whom MR. JUSTICE MARSHALL joins, dissenting. . . .

. . . Liquor licenses in Pennsylvania, unlike driver's licenses, or marriage licenses, are not freely available to those who meet racially neutral qualifications. There is a complex quota system, which the majority accurately describes. . . . What the majority neglects to say is that the Harrisburg quota, where Moose Lodge No. 107 is located, has been full for many years. No more club licenses may be issued in that city.

This state-enforced scarcity of licenses restricts the ability of blacks to obtain liquor, for liquor is commercially available *only* at private clubs for a significant portion of each week. Access by blacks to places that serve liquor is further limited by the fact that the state quota is filled. A group desiring to form a nondiscriminatory club which would serve blacks must purchase a license held by an existing club, which can exact a monopoly price for the transfer. The availability of such a license is speculative at best, however, for, as Moose Lodge itself concedes, without a liquor license a fraternal organization would be hard-pressed to survive.

Thus, the State of Pennsylvania is putting the weight of its liquor license, concededly a valued and important adjunct to a private club, behind racial discrimination.

MR. JUSTICE BRENNAN, with whom MR. JUSTICE MARSHALL joins, dissenting.

When Moose Lodge obtained its liquor license, the State of Pennsylvania became an active participant in the operation of the Lodge bar. Liquor licensing laws are only incidentally revenue measures; they are primarily pervasive regulatory schemes under which the State dictates and continually supervises virtually every detail of the operation of the licensee's business. Very few, if any, other licensed businesses experience such complete state involvement. . . .

Plainly, the State of Pennsylvania's liquor regulations intertwine the State with the operation of the Lodge bar in a "significant way [and] lend [the State's] authority to the sordid business of racial discrimination." . . .

Palmore v. *Sidoti*

446 U.S. 429, 104 S. Ct. 1879; 80 L. Ed. 2d 632 (1984)

When the Sidotis, both Caucasians, were divorced in Florida, Linda Sidoti was awarded custody of their three-year-old daughter. The following year, Anthony Sidoti sought custody of the child by filing a petition to modify the prior judgment because of changed conditions. The change was that Linda Sidoti was then cohabitating with Clarence Palmore, a Negro, whom she married later. The Florida trial court awarded custody to the father, concluding that the child's best interests would be served thereby. Acknowledging that there was no evidence that Linda Sidoti was unfit to continue the custody of her child, the court nevertheless shifted custody to the father in order to avoid the damaging impact on the child that would otherwise result from remaining in a racially mixed household. As it declared: "This Court feels that despite the strides that have been made in bettering relations between the races in this country, it is inevitable that . . . [the child] will, if allowed to remain in her present situation and attain school age and thus [be] more vulnerable to peer pressures, suffer from the social stigmatization that is sure to come." The Second District Court of Appeals affirmed without opinion, thereby denying the Florida Supreme Court jurisdiction to review the case. The U.S. Supreme Court granted certiorari. *Unanimous opinion of the Court: Burger, Blackmun, Brennan, Marshall, O'Connor, Powell, Rehnquist, Stevens, White.*

CHIEF JUSTICE BURGER delivered the opinion of the Court.

We granted certiorari to review a judgment of a state court divesting a natural mother of the custody of her infant child because of her remarriage to a person of a different race. . . .

The judgment of a state court determining or reviewing a child custody decision is not ordinarily a likely candidate for review by this Court. However, the court's opinion, after stating that the "father's evident resentment of the mother's choice of a black partner is not sufficient" to deprive her of custody, then turns to what it regarded as the damaging impact on the child from remaining in a racially-mixed household. . . . This raises important federal concerns arising from the Constitution's commitment to eradicating discrimination based on race.

The Florida court did not focus directly on the parental qualifications of the natural mother or her present husband, or indeed on the father's qualifications to have custody of the child. The court found that "there is no issue as to either party's devotion to the child, adequacy of housing facilities, or respect[a]bility of the new spouse of either parent." . . . This, taken with the absence of any negative finding as to the quality of the care provided by the mother, constitutes a rejection of any claim of petitioner's unfitness to continue the custody of her child.

The court correctly stated that the child's welfare was the controlling factor. But that court was entirely candid and made no effort to place its holding on any ground other than race. Taking the court's findings and rationale at face value, it is clear that the outcome would have been different had petitioner married a Caucasian male of similar respectability.

A core purpose of the Fourteenth Amendment was to do away with all governmentally-imposed discrimination based on race. . . . Classifying persons according to their race is more likely to reflect racial prejudice than legitimate public concerns; the race, not the person, dictates the category. . . . Such classifications are subject to the most exacting scrutiny; to pass constitutional muster, they must be justified by a compelling governmental interest and must be "necessary . . . to the accomplishment" of its legitimate purpose. . . .

The State, of course, has a duty of the highest order to protect the interests of minor children, particularly those of tender years. In common with most states, Florida law mandates that custody determinations be made in the best interests of the children involved. . . . The goal of granting custody based on the best interests of the child is indisputably a substantial governmental interest for purposes of the Equal Protection Clause.

It would ignore reality to suggest that racial and ethnic prejudices do not exist or that all manifestations of those prejudices have been eliminated. There is a risk that a child living with a step-parent of a different race may be subject to a variety of pressures and stresses not present if the child were living with parents of the same racial or ethnic origin.

The question, however, is whether the reality of private biases and the possible injury they might inflict are permissible considerations for removal of an infant child from the custody of its natural mother. We have little difficulty concluding that they are not. The Constitution cannot control such prejudices but neither can it tolerate them. Private biases may be outside the reach of the law, but the law cannot, directly or indirectly, give them effect. "Public officials sworn to uphold the Constitution may not avoid a constitutional duty by bowing to the hypothetical effects of private racial prejudice that they assume to be both widely and deeply held.". . . .

This is by no means the first time that acknowledged racial prejudice has been invoked to justify racial classifications. In *Buchanan* v. *Warley* . . . (1917), for example, this Court invalidated a Kentucky law forbidding Negroes from buying homes in white neighborhoods.

"It is urged that this proposed segregation will promote the public peace by preventing race conflicts. Desirable as this is, and important as is the preservation of the public peace, this aim cannot be accomplished by laws or ordinances which deny rights created or protected by the Federal Constitution."....

Whatever problems racially-mixed households may pose for children in 1984 can no more support a denial of constitutional rights than could the stresses that residential integration was thought to entail in 1917. The effects of racial prejudice, however real, cannot justify a racial classification removing an infant child from the custody of its natural mother found to be an appropriate person to have such custody.

The judgment of the District Court of Appeal is reversed.

Wards Cove Packing Co. v. *Atonio*

109 S. Ct. 2115, 104 L. Ed. 2d 733 (1989)

Jobs at the Alaskan canneries of Wards Cove Packing Co. were of two general types: unskilled "cannery" jobs on the cannery lines, filled predominantly by nonwhites, and higher-paying "noncannery" jobs, skilled posts filled predominantly by whites. Frank Atonio and other nonwhite cannery workers filed suit in U.S. District Court under Title VII of the Civil Rights Act of 1964, alleging that the petitioner's hiring and promotion practices were responsible for the racial stratification of the work force and denied them noncannery jobs on the basis of race. The District Court rejected the respondents' claims, but the U.S. Court of Appeals for the Ninth Court reversed, holding that the respondents had, on the basis of their statistics, made out a prima facie case of disparate impact in hiring for both skilled and unskilled jobs. The Supreme Court granted certiorari. *Opinion of the Court: White, Kennedy, O'Connor, Rehnquist, Scalia. Dissenting opinions: Blackmun, Brennan, Marshall; Stevens, Blackmun, Brennan, Marshall.*

JUSTICE WHITE delivered the opinion of the Court.

Title VII of the Civil Rights Act of 1964 . . . makes it an unfair employment practice for an employer to discriminate against any individual with respect to hiring or the terms and condition of employment because of such individual's race, color, religion, sex, or national origin; or to limit, segregate or classify his employees in ways that would adversely affect any employee because of the employee's race, color, religion, sex, or national origin. *Griggs* v. *Duke Power Co.* . . . (1971) construed Title VII to proscribe "not only overt discrimination but also practices that are fair in form but discriminatory in practice." Under this basis for liability, which is known as the "disparate impact" theory and which is involved in this case, a facially neutral employment practice may be deemed violative of Title VII without evidence of the employer's subjective intent to discriminate that is required in a "disparate treatment" case....

In holding that respondents had made out a prima facie case of disparate impact, the court of appeals relied solely on respondents' statistics showing a high percentage of nonwhite workers in the cannery jobs and a low percentage of such workers in the noncannery positions. Although statistical proof can alone make out a prima facie case, . . . the Court of Appeals' ruling here misapprehends our precedents and the purposes of Title VII, and we therefore reverse....

It is clear to us that the Court of Appeals' acceptance of the comparison between the racial composition of the cannery work force and that of the noncannery work force, as probative of a prima facie case of disparate impact in the selection of the latter group of workers, was flawed for several reasons. Most obviously, with respect to the skilled noncannery jobs at issue here, the cannery work force in no way reflected "the pool of *qualified* job applicants" or the "*qualified* population in the labor force." Measuring alleged discrimination in the selection of accountants, managers, boat captains, electricians, doctors, and engineers—and the long list of other "skilled" noncannery positions found to exist by the District Court . . .—by comparing the number of nonwhites occupying these jobs to the number of nonwhites filling cannery worker positions is nonsensical. If the absence of minorities holding such skilled positions is due to a dearth of qualified nonwhite applicants (for reasons that are not petitioners' fault), petitioners' selection methods or employment practices cannot be said to have had a "disparate impact" on nonwhites.

One example illustrates why this must be so. Respondents' own statistics concerning the noncannery work force at one of the canneries at issue here indicate that approximately 17% of the new hires for medical jobs, and 15% of the new hires for officer worker positions, were nonwhite. . . . If it were the case that less than 15–17% of the applicants for these jobs were nonwhite and that nonwhites made up a lower percentage of the relevant qualified labor market, it is hard to see how respondents . . . would have made out a prima facie case of disparate impact. Yet, under the Court of Appeals' theory, simply because nonwhites comprise 52% of the cannery workers at the cannery in question, . . . respondents would be successful in establishing a prima facie case of racial discrimination under Title VII.

Such a result cannot be squared with our cases or with the goals behind the statute. The Court of Appeals' theory, at the very least, would mean that any employer who had a segment of his work force that was—for some reason—racially imbalanced, could be haled into court and forced to engage in the expensive and time-consuming task of defending the "business necessity" of the methods used to select the other members of his work force. The only practicable option for many employers will be to adopt racial quotas, insuring that no portion of his work force deviates in racial composition from the other portions thereof; this is a result that Congress expressly rejected in drafting Title VII . . . The Court of Appeals' theory would "leave the employer little choice . . . but to engage in a subjective quota system of employment selection. This, of course, is far from the intent of Title VII."

The Court of Appeals also erred with respect to the unskilled noncannery positions. Racial imbalance in one segment of an employer's work force does not, without more, establish a prima facie case of disparate impact with respect to the selection of workers for the employer's other positions, even where workers for the different positions may have somewhat fungible skills (as is arguably the case for cannery and unskilled noncannery workers). As long as there are no barriers or practices deterring qualified nonwhites from applying for noncannery positions, if the percentage of selected applicants who are nonwhite is not significantly less than the percentage of qualified applicants who are nonwhite, the employer's selection mechanism probably does not operate with a disparate impact on minorities. Where this is the case, the percentage of nonwhite workers found in other positions in the employer's labor force is irrelevant to the question of a prima facie statistical case of disparate impact. As noted above, a contrary ruling on this point would almost inexorably lead to the use of numerical quotas in the workplace, a result that Congress and this Court have rejected repeatedly in the past.

Moreover, isolating the cannery workers as the potential "labor force" for unskilled noncannery positions is at once both too broad and too narrow in its focus. Too broad because the vast majority of these cannery workers did not seek jobs in unskilled noncannery positions; there is no showing that many of them would have done so even if none of the arguably "deterring" practices existed. Thus, the pool of cannery workers cannot be used as a surrogate for the class of qualified job applicants because it contains many persons who have not (and would not) be noncannery job applicants. Conversely, if respondents propose to use the cannery workers for comparison purposes because they represent the "qualified labor population" generally, the group is too narrow because there are obviously many qualified persons in the labor market for noncannery jobs who are not cannery workers. . . .

Consequently, we reverse the Court of Appeals' ruling that a comparison between the percentage of cannery workers who are nonwhite and the percentage of noncannery workers who are nonwhite makes out a prima facie case of disparate impact. Of course, this leaves unresolved whether the record made in the District Court will support a conclusion that a prima facie case of disparate impact has been established on some basis other than the racial disparity between cannery and noncannery workers. This is an issue that the Court of Appeals or the District Court should address in the first instance. . . . Because we remand for further proceedings, however, on whether a prima facie case of disparate impact has been made in defensible fashion in this case, we address two other challenges petitioners have made to the decision of the Court of Appeals. . . .

First is the question of causation in a disparate-impact case. . . .

Even if on remand respondents can show that nonwhites are underrepresented in the at-issue jobs . . . this alone will *not* suffice to make out a prima facie case of disparate impact. Respondents will also have to demonstrate that the disparity they complain of is the result of one or more of the employment practices that they are attacking here, specifically showing that each challenged practice has a significantly disparate impact on employment opportunities for whites and nonwhites. To hold otherwise would result in employers being potentially liable for "the myriad of innocent causes that may lead to statistical imbalances in the composition of their work forces." . . .

Some will complain that this specific causation requirement is unduly burdensome on Title VII plaintiffs. But liberal civil discovery rules give plaintiffs broad access to employers' records in an effort to document their claims. . . .

If, on remand, respondents meet the proof burdens outlined above, and establish a prima facie case of disparate impact with respect to any of petitioners' employment practices, the case will shift to any business justification petitioners offer for their use of these practices. . . .

In this phase, the employer carries the burden of producing evidence of a business justification for his employment practice. The burden of persuasion, however, remains with the disparate-impact plaintiff. . . . "[T]he ultimate burden of proving that discrimination against a protected group has been caused by a specific employment practice remains with the plaintiff *at all times*." . . . This rule conforms with the usual method for allocating persuasion and production burdens in the federal courts, . . . and more specifically, it conforms to the rule in disparate treatment cases that the plaintiff bears the burden of disproving an employer's assertion that the adverse employment action or practice was based solely on a legitimate neutral consideration. . . .

The persuasion burden here must remain with the plaintiff, for it is he who must prove that it was "because of such individual's race, color," etc., that he was denied a desired employment opportunity. . . .

For the reasons given above, the judgment of the Court of Appeals is reversed, and the case is remanded for further proceedings consistent with this opinion.

JUSTICE BLACKMUN, with whom JUSTICE BRENNAN and JUSTICE MARSHALL join, dissenting. . . .

This industry long has been characterized by a taste for discrimination of the old-fashioned sort: a preference for hiring nonwhites to fill its lowest-level positions, on the condition that they stay there. The majority's legal rulings essentially immunize these practices from attack under a Title VII disparate-impact analysis.

Sadly, this comes as no surprise. One wonders whether the majority still believes that race discrimination—or, more accurately, race discrimination against nonwhites—is a problem in our society, or even remembers that it ever was.

JUSTICE STEVENS, with whom JUSTICE BRENNAN, JUSTICE MARSHALL, and JUSTICE BLACKMUN join, dissenting

Fully 18 years ago, this Court unanimously held that Title VII of the Civil Rights Act of 1964 prohibits employment practices that have discriminatory effects as well as those that are intended to discriminate. *Griggs* v. *Duke Power Co.* . . . Federal courts and agencies consistently have enforced that interpretation, thus promoting our national goal of eliminating barriers that define economic opportunity not by aptitude and ability but by race, color, national origin, and other traits that are easily identified but utterly irrelevant to one's qualification for a particular job. Regrettably, the Court retreats from these efforts in its review of an interlocutory judgment respecting the "peculiar facts" of this lawsuit. Turning a blind eye to the meaning and purpose of Title VII, the majority's opinion perfunctorily rejects a longstanding rule of law and underestimates the probative value of evidence of a racially stratified work force. I cannot join this latest sojourn into judicial activism. . . .

The majority's opinion begins with recognition of the settled rule that that "a facially neutral employment practice may be deemed violative of Title VII without evidence of the employer's subjective intent to discriminate that is required in a 'disparate treatment' case." It then departs from the body of law engendered by this disparate impact theory, reformulating the order of proof and the weight of the parties' burdens. Why the Court undertakes these unwise changes in elementary and eminently fair rules is a mystery to me.

I respectfully dissent.

16
SUBSTANTIVE EQUAL PROTECTION

As Chapter 15 indicated, the Supreme Court initially viewed the Equal Protection Clause simply as a means for prohibiting racial discrimination. In keeping with this understanding, it customarily rejected invitations by counsel to employ the clause to strike down economic and social regulations that introduced distinctions among persons (i.e., that discriminated) on a nonracial basis. Even at the height of the *Lochner* era, when the justices were so willing to rely on the Due Process Clause to invalidate what were thought to be unduly restrictive (and hence, arbitrary and capricious) regulations, they flatly refused to consider using the Equal Protection Clause for matters unrelated to race. Clearly stating the Court's contempt for such equal-protection claims, Justice Oliver Wendell Holmes described them in *Buck v. Bell* (1927) as "the usual last resort of constitutional arguments."

However, the wording of the Equal Protection Clause guarantees equal protection of the laws to *all persons*, not merely to black persons or ex-slaves. In this respect, it advances ends identical to those advanced by the original Constitution: namely, the empowerment and employment of a powerful national government capable of protecting individual rights and liberties from the tyrannical tendencies of the majority while, in the words of *The Federalist*, "preserving the spirit and form of popular government."[1] On its face, then, the Equal Protection Clause mandates equality under the law for all persons, regardless of race, gender, socioeconomic condition, nationality, age, place or duration of residence, etc. Judicial acknowledgment of this fact came under the Warren Court (1953–1969), which for the first time systematically installed the clause as governing in cases involving types of unequal treatment wholly unrelated to traditional forms of racial discrimination. As a result of its seminal decisions, the judiciary has been called upon to determine whether the Equal Protection Clause has been violated by state laws and practices that, *inter alia*, discriminated in favor of (rather than against) blacks; imposed burdens on aliens and illegitimate children; treated the sexes differently; or impinged upon the rights to interstate travel, welfare assistance, educational opportunity, and exercise of the franchise.

This increased receptivity to a wide range of equal-protection challenges has posed new and difficult questions for the Court. So long as it understood the clause to prohibit only racial classifications, problems of interpretation remained manageable: the justices had only to look at the law or practice in question, determine whether it treated the races differently, and rule accordingly. Once the Court began employing the clause to evaluate other forms of unequal treatment, however, the problems grew in number and difficulty and became virtually identical to the problems the Court faced in the area of substantive due process. The primary question facing the Court then became, does equal protection of the laws prohibit all legal categories or classifications? In other words, must all people be treated identically with respect to all matters? Because virtually all laws and regulations create legal categories, the Court understandably refused to respond affirmatively to these questions; to do so would be to render government wholly inoperable. Instead, it sought to interpret the Equal Protection Clause in such a way as to permit what it considered to be legitimate classifications—which led, inevitably to the question of what constitutes a legitimate classification.

As the justices grappled with these and other problems, they found it necessary to develop standards or criteria for interpreting the Equal Protection Clause and for determining whether the laws and practices in question passed constitutional muster. This chapter spells out these standards, examines how and where they have been employed, and identifies the many criticisms that have been leveled against them.

THE TWO-TIER APPROACH

As an aid in determining whether particular classifications are legitimate and hence permissible under the Equal Protection Clause, the Court gradually developed what has been commonly called the two-tier approach. The tiers represent the level of scrutiny that the Court will give to the classification under review. The relatively lenient standard imposed on the lower tier usually is called the rational basis test. The upper tier imposes a much more stringent standard, referred to as the compelling-state-interest test or the strict scrutiny standard.

Most statutory categorizations or classifications have been reviewed under the rational basis test, which is governed by the operation of four general principles:

1. The Equal Protection Clause not only does not prohibit the state from creating legal categories but also allows a great deal of discre-

tion in this regard; such categories, therefore, should be invalidated only when they lack any reasonable basis and hence are purely arbitrary.

2. A classification having some reasonable basis does not offend against the Equal Protection Clause merely because it is not made with mathematical nicety or because in practice it results in some inequality.
3. When a classification in the law is called into question, it should not be set aside if any state of facts can be conceived to justify it, and the existence of that state of facts at the time the law was enacted must be assumed.
4. The party challenging the classification must carry the burden of showing that it does not rest upon any reasonable basis.

Some kinds of classifications have had to satisfy much more stringent standards. Under the two-tier system, the Court has subjected to strict scrutiny all laws that created "suspect classifications" or that impinged upon "fundamental rights" and has upheld them only if the state was able to show that they advanced a compelling governmental interest.

Whenever suspect classifications or fundamental rights have been involved, the Court has reversed the normal presumption of constitutionality, in that it has demanded that the state establish a compelling need for these statutory discriminations. And even if such a need is demonstrated, the state must show that no less-restrictive alternatives exist.[2] This is a stringent standard indeed, and it has been applied both to the ends that the state is seeking and the means it employs to achieve those ends. As Chief Justice Warren Burger noted in his dissent in *Dunn* v. *Blumstein* (1972), "To challenge [state policies] by the 'compelling state interest' standard is to condemn them all. So far as I am aware, no state law has ever satisfied this seemingly insurmountable standard and I doubt one ever will, for it demands nothing less than perfection." Scholarly commentators generally have concurred in this assessment. As Professor Gerald Gunther observed, use of this standard has been " 'strict' in theory and fatal in practice."[3]

THE DEVELOPMENT OF AN INTERMEDIATE LEVEL OF REVIEW

The two-tier approach has caused the Court a number of problems. To begin with, under this approach, the Court has experienced great difficulty in determining which classifications to label suspect. There has been complete agreement that blacks constitute a suspect class; the clear intention of the framers of the Fourteenth Amendment was to have blacks considered as such. Until recently, there also was general agreement that racial classifications of any kind should be considered formally suspect and hence should be subject to scrutiny under the compelling-state-interest test. That agreement, however, largely has broken up on the shoals of the controversy surrounding ameliorative racial preference.

Similar controversies have also raged over whether other classifications are suspect, and if so, why. The Court attempted to provide a framework for analyzing these questions when it declared in *Johnson* v. *Robinson* (1974) that a classification was suspect if based on "an immutable characteristic determined solely by the accident of birth, or a class saddled with such disabilities, or subjected to such a history of purposeful unequal treatment, or relegated to such political powerlessness as to command extraordinary protection from the majoritarian political process." These words, however, have failed to bind the Court together, and it has split badly when it has addressed equal-protection challenges to classifications based on alienage (the condition of being an alien), illegitimacy, age, gender, and indigency.

A second difficulty with the two-tier approach has been that it has provided the Court with very little guidance as to the definition of a fundamental right. Over time, the Court has come to recognize as fundamental the right to free speech, the right of freedom of religion, the right of freedom of association, the right of personal privacy, the right to vote, the right to procreate, the right to marry, and the right to travel from state to state. At the same time, it has refused to recognize as fundamental interests that many people would regard as equally important, including the rights to education, shelter, and food. The Court has defended its position by insisting that only those rights explicitly or implicitly guaranteed in the Constitution are fundamental, and that nothing in the Constitution guarantees that the government will provide individuals with an education, a house, or welfare benefits. But as Justice Thurgood Marshall mused in his dissent in *San Antonio* v. *Rodriguez,* "I would like to know where the Constitution guarantees the right to procreate, or the right to vote in state elections, or the right to appeal a criminal conviction. These are instances in which, due to the importance of the interests at stake, the Court has displayed a strong concern with the existence of discriminatory state treatment. But, the Court has never said or indicated that these are interests which independently enjoy full-blown constitutional protection." Marshall's critique could be underscored with other examples, but his point is well-taken. In fact the Court's method of determining fundamental rights appears to be of greater utility in providing the Court with an explanation for why it has refused to bestow fundamental status on a particular right than in assisting it in ascertaining what rights are fundamental. This approach, in Justice William Rehnquist's words in *Rostker* v. *Goldberg* (1981), "all too readily [lends itself to] facile abstractions used to justify a result."

Of the several major problems involved in the two-tier approach, perhaps the most serious has been its rigid, all-or-nothing character. The lenient rational-basis test almost never has resulted in the invalidation of legislation, whereas the stringent compelling-state-interest standard almost invariably has led to invalidation. Between these two widely varying levels of scrutiny, there is no room for rights and classes of intermediate importance. As Justice Thurgood Marshall complained in his dissent in *Massachusetts Board of Retirement* v. *Murgia* (1976), "All interests not fundamental and all classes not suspect are not the same; and it is time for the Court to drop the pretense that, for purposes of the Equal Protection Clause, they are." So long as the Court remained committed to the two-tier approach, however, that pretense could not be dropped, and the only critical decision facing the Court was, as Justice Marshall further remonstrated, "whether strict scrutiny should be invoked at all."

In place of this simplistic and rigid approach, Justice Marshall argued, in both *Murgia* and *San Antonio* v. *Rodriguez* (1973), for a "more sophisticated" approach in which "concentration is placed upon the character of the classification in question, the relative importance to the individuals in the class discriminated against of the governmental benefits they do not receive, and the asserted state interests in support of the classification." Other members of the Court, dissatisfied with the two-tier approach, have also come to employ an intermediate level of scrutiny when reviewing ameliorative racial preference and classifications based on illegitimacy and gender. Under this "middle-tier" approach, the classifications in question must "serve important governmental objectives" and be "substantially related to the achievement of those objectives." This standard is intermediate with respect both to ends and means. As Professor Gunther has observed: "Where ends must be 'compelling' to survive strict scrutiny and merely 'legitimate' under the 'old' mode, 'important' objectives are required here, and where means must be 'necessary' under the 'new' equal protection, and merely 'rationally related' under the 'old' equal protection, they must be 'substantially related' to survive the 'intermediate' level of review."[4]

The exact meaning of this new intermediate level of review, however, remains very much in doubt. This is in part because some justices have all but obliterated the distinctions between the lower and middle tiers. Justice Brennan's majority opinion in *Plyler* v. *Doe* (1982) is a case in point. In *Plyler*, the Court, in a 5–4 decision, invalidated on equal-protection grounds a Texas statute that withheld state funds from local school districts for the education of children who were illegal aliens and that further authorized the local school districts to deny enrollment to such children. Mixing language associated with different levels of review, Justice Brennan declared that a state law or practice "can hardly be considered rational unless it furthers some substantial goal of the State." The exact meaning of this new level of review is also in doubt because some of the justices who have employed it have been reluctant to admit a departure from the traditional two-tier approach; their comments concerning the intermediate standard have served more to confuse than to clarify. Justice Lewis Powell's comments in *Craig* v. *Boren* illustrate this point well. In that 1976 case, the Court employed an intermediate standard of review to invalidate a gender-based classification under which Oklahoma prohibited the sale of "nonintoxicating" 3.2 percent beer to males under the age of twenty-one and females under the age of eighteen. In his concurrence, Justice Powell admitted that "our decision today will be viewed by some as a 'middle-tier' approach." Attempting to qualify that view, he succeeded only in obscuring it further: "While I would not endorse that characterization and would not welcome a further subdividing of equal protection analysis, candor compels the recognition that the relatively deferential 'rational basis' standard normally applied takes on a sharper focus when we address a gender-based classification. So much is clear from our recent cases." This kind of language has prompted Professor Gunther to comment: "In form, the two-tier distinction between new, strict scrutiny and old, deferential review equal protection persists. In fact, the modern exercises of review in equal protection cases do not conform to that simple, bifurcated pattern."[5]

CLASSIFICATIONS WARRANTING HEIGHTENED SCRUTINY

Affirmative Action

Affirmative action raises two distinct and difficult questions that highlight the difficulties attending the Court's approach to equal-protection analysis: (1) Should racial classifications that burden whites be viewed as suspect? (2) Should classifications employed for the asserted purpose of aiding a minority (typically blacks) be subjected to the strict scrutiny to which invidious classifications have been subjected? The judiciary has split badly on both of these questions.

Some jurists have insisted that discriminations against whites should be subjected to the same stringent review under the Fourteenth Amendment used with discriminations against blacks. This position is consistent with the First Justice Harlan's famous dictum, given in his dissent in *Plessy* v. *Ferguson* (1896), that "the constitution is color-blind and neither knows nor tolerates classes among citizens." That position was taken by the California Supreme Court in *Bakke* v. *Regents of University of California* (1976), by Justice Powell in *Regents of the University of California* v. *Bakke* (1978), and most recently by a majority of the Supreme Court in *Richmond* v. *Croson* (1989). In *Croson,* the Court struck down Richmond's minority set-aside program requiring that 30% of the total dollar amount of all city contracts go to minority business enterprises. Justice Sandra Day O'Connor declared that "the standard of review under the Equal Protection Clause is not dependent on the race of those burdened or benefited by a particular classification." For the *Croson* majority, "racial classifications are suspect," regardless of the race of those discriminated against or the reason for the discrimination. In fact, Justice Scalia went so far in his concurrence as to brand all racial classifications impermissible except for those undertaken in response to "a social emergency rising to the level of imminent danger to life or limb—for example, a prison race riot, requiring temporary segregation of inmates." For Scalia, any lesser justification, including the need to ameliorate the effects of past discrimination, is insufficient, for "the difficulty of overcoming the effects of past discrimination is as nothing compared with the difficulty of eradicating from our society the source of those effects, which is the tendency—fatal to a nation such as ours—to classify and judge men and women on the basis of their country of origin or the color of their skin. A solution to the first problem that aggravates the second is no solution at all."

Other jurists, however, have argued that whites as a class have none of the "traditional indicia of suspectness." As a class, that is to say, whites have not been subjected to historical and pervasive discriminations and deprivations, have not been stigmatized and set apart, and have not been relegated to a position of political powerlessness. Relying on that portion of *Plessy* that *Brown* v. *Board of Education* (1954) did not repudiate, and on Chief Justice Warren's contention in *Brown* that the Equal Protection Clause merely proscribes classifications that "generate a feeling of inferiority" (i.e., that imply prejudice), advocates of this position have concluded that the clause offers whites no particular protections because discrimination in favor of blacks will not lead whites to assume that they are inferior. The most forceful defenders of this position have been Justice Thurgood Marshall in his dissent in *Croson* and Justice William Brennan in his opinions in *Bakke* and *Metro Broadcasting* v. *Federal Communications Commission* (1990). In *Metro Broadcasting,* Justice Brennan held in a 5–4 decision that benign race-conscious measures mandated by Congress, even though not remedial in the sense of being designed to compensate victims of past governmental or societal discrimination, are permissible under the equal protection component of the Fifth Amendment's Due Process Clause. He concluded, therefore, that the FCC's policy of giving preference to minority bids in competitive proceedings for new broadcast licenses and permitting limited categories of licenses to be transferred to minority-controlled firms in "distress sales" are mandated by Congress, serve an important government interest in promoting broadcasting diversity, are substantially related to the achievement of that objective, and do not violate the Fifth Amendment's equal protection component.

Intimately related to the dispute over whites as a suspect class has been the question of whether classifications employed for the asserted purpose of aiding minorities should be subjected to the same strict-scrutiny standard as invidious classifications. Those justices who have viewed whites as a suspect class invariably have invoked the strict-scrutiny standard; and because classifications intended to aid blacks almost inevitably come at the expense of whites, they typically have invalidated the offending classification as failing to advance a compelling state interest.[6] One exception to this generalization is Justice Powell. In his opinion in *Bakke,* he sustained the use of race in admissions decisions on the ground that it served the state's compelling interest in achieving a diverse student body; and in his concurrence in *Fullilove* v. *Klutznick* (1980) he defended Congress's enactment of a 10 percent set-aside requirement (the percentage of federal funds granted for local public-works projects that must be used by state and local grantees to procure services or supplies from businesses owned and controlled by minority-group members) as "designed to serve the compelling governmental interest in redressing racial discrimination." Justices who have not viewed whites as a suspect class, on the other hand, generally have refused to invoke the strict-scrutiny standard in reviewing ameliorative-racial-preference cases. Justice Brennan's opinion in *Bakke* reflected this point of view. The use of the compelling-state-interest test, he argued, would result in a denial of the aid that the classification was intended to provide. On the other hand, "because of the significant risk that racial classifications established for ostensibly benign purposes can be misused, causing effects not unlike that created by invidious classifications," he deemed it inappropriate to inquire only whether there was any conceivable basis on which to sustain such a classification. Instead, he argued, that such ameliorative racial preference be upheld if it could be shown that it served "an important and articulated purpose." Such a finding, he concluded, would require the same intermediate level of review appropriate in gender-based classifications—the classification in question "must serve important governmental objectives and be substantially related to the achievement of those objectives."

Alienage

The Court's responses to statutory classifications that deprive aliens of rights enjoyed by citizens have highlighted the problems confronting the justices in consistently applying strict-scrutiny standards to equal protection challenges. In *Graham* v. *Richardson* (1971) the Court held that aliens were a suspect class and that restrictions on aliens were to be treated by the Court with "heightened judicial solicitude." With *Graham* as precedent and employing the compelling-state-interest test, the justices subsequently voided a Connecticut law denying aliens the right to practice law, *In Re Griffiths* (1973); a New York statute barring aliens from holding positions in the competitive class of the state civil service, *Sugarman* v. *Dougall* (1973); a regulation of the Civil Service Commission limiting employment in the U.S. competitive civil service to citizens of the United States, *Hampton* v. *Wong* (1976); and a New York law denying resident aliens financial aid for higher education unless they applied for U.S. citizenship, *Nyquist* v. *Mauclet* (1977). In *Foley* v. *Connelie* (1978), however, the Court sustained a New York law barring aliens from the state police force. And in *Ambach* v. *Norwick* (1979) it upheld a New York statute forbidding certification as a public school teacher to any person who was not a citizen, unless that person had manifested an intention to apply for citizenship. In both cases, the Court insisted that not all limitations on aliens were suspect and employed the rational basis test to sustain the challenged classifications.

The Court argued in *Foley* and *Ambach* that some state functions, such as serving as a state trooper and teaching in the public schools, are so bound up with the operation of the state as a governmental entity as to permit the exclusion of all persons who have not become part of the process of self-government. "A discussion of the police function is essentially a description of one of the basic functions of government, especially in a complex modern society where police presence is pervasive," Chief Justice Burger wrote in *Foley*. Justice Powell in *Ambach* saw the teachers as performing an equally important and central function: "Public education, like the police function, 'fulfills a most fundamental obligation of government to its constituency.' The importance of public schools in the preparation of individuals for participation as citizens, and in the preservation of the values on which our society rests, long has been recognized by our decisions."

In recognizing this rule for governmental functions as an exception to the strict-scrutiny standard generally applicable to classifications based on alienage, the Court followed important principles inherent in the Constitution. The distinction between citizens and aliens, though ordinarily irrelevant to private activity, is fundamental to the definition and government of a state, and the constitutional references to such a distinction indicate that the status of citizenship was meant to have significance in the structure of our government. Because of this special significance, the Court ruled in *Foley* and *Ambach*, governmental entities, when exercising the functions of government, must have wide latitude in limiting the participation of aliens. The *Foley* and *Ambach* rulings, however, are difficult to reconcile with the Court's earlier holdings, especially *In Re Griffiths*. If a state may bar aliens from law enforcement or teaching because those tasks go to the heart of representative government, it is difficult to understand why a state may not also bar aliens from practicing law. Lawyers after all, serve as officers of the court and participate directly in the formulation, execution, and review of broad public policy. The Court, however, has neither overturned *In Re Griffiths* nor reconciled its apparently contradictory holdings on the exact status of alienage as a suspect classification.

Illegitimacy

The Court's course in reviewing classifications based on illegitimacy has been even more wavering than its course in reviewing classifications based on alienage. Although it has never labeled illegitimacy a suspect classification, the Court has exercised a degree of heightened scrutiny in most cases involving illegitimacy classifications, which have been struck down with some frequency. Nowhere in its rulings, however, has the Court explained what degree of heightened scrutiny is warranted, and why.

The Court's first encounter with illegitimacy classifications under the two-tier approach came in *Levy* v. *Louisiana* (1968), in which a law that denied unacknowledged illegitimate children the right to recover damages for the wrongful death of their mothers was found to violate the Equal Protection Clause. The exact reason for the law's unconstitutionality, however, was left in doubt, as Justice Douglas's majority opinion hinted at both the rational basis test and the compelling-state-interest standard. Three years later, in *Labine* v. *Vincent* (1971), the Court withdrew from the heightened scrutiny suggested in *Levy* and upheld an intestate succession provision that suboridinated the rights of acknowledged illegitimate children to those of the parent's other relatives. Employing the rational basis test, the *Labine* majority argued that absent an express constitutional guarantee, "it is for the legislature, not this Court, to select from among possible laws." Barely one year later, in *Weber* v. *Aetna Casualty and Surety Company* (1972), the Court abandoned what it had said in *Labine* and returned to its formulations in *Levy* by holding that the claims of dependent unacknowledged illegitimate children to death benefits under a workmen's compensation law could not be subordinated to the claims of legitimate children.

Such vacillation continued in *Mathews* v. *Lucas* (1976) and *Trimble* v. *Gordon* (1977). *Lucas* sustained death-benefits provisions of the Social Security Act that presumed legitimate children to have been dependent upon their fathers but required proof of dependency on the part of illegitimate children. In *Trimble,* on the other hand, the Court struck down a provision of the Illinois law governing intestate succession that barred illegitimate children from inheriting from their fathers.

Lucas and *Trimble* illustrate the Court's uneasy search for an articulable and consistently applicable standard of review for illegitimacy classifications. Both cases rejected the strict scrutiny standard while indicating that the rational basis test was only a minimum criterion and that sometimes the Court "requires more." Justice O'Connor's unanimous opinion in *Clark* v. *Jeter* (1988) identified that something more as the "intermediate" level of review, which the Court then used to conclude that Pennsylvania's six-year statute of limitations for support actions on behalf of illegitimate children "does not withstand heightened scrutiny."

Age

In reviewing classifications based on age, the Court consistently has adopted a deferential posture and employed the rational basis test. In *Massachusetts Board of Retirement* v. *Murgia* (1976) the Court upheld a state law mandating that state police officers retire at age fifty. Three years later, in *Vance* v. *Bradley* (1979), it rejected an equal-protection challenge to a federal law requiring Foreign Service personnel to retire at age sixty. The Court has refused to recognize the aged as a suspect class, noting in *Murgia* that old age is a universal condition and that "even if the statute could be said to impose a penalty upon a class defined as the aged, it would not impose a distinction sufficiently akin to those classifications that we have found suspect to call for strict judicial scrutiny." Both *Murgia* and *Vance* elicited strongly worded dissents from Justice Marshall, who urged the adoption of a more flexible approach in which the Court would review the importance of the governmental benefits denied, the character of the class, and the asserted state interests.

Mental Retardation

In *City of Cleburne, Texas* v. *Cleburne Living Center* (1985), the Supreme Court in a 6–3 decision refused to apply a "heightened" level of scrutiny to legislation affecting the mentally retarded. Cleburne Living Center had sought to lease a building for the operation of a group home for the mentally retarded; when it was denied a special use permit to do so by the city (which classified the group home under its zoning ordinance as a "hospital for the feebleminded"), it brought suit alleging that the zoning ordinance in question was unconstitutional, both on its face and as applied. The federal district court rejected its contentions, but the Court of Appeals for the Fifth Circuit reversed, holding that mental retardation was a "quasi-suspect" classification and that under a "heightened scrutiny equal protection test," the ordinance was unconstitutional, for it did not substantially further an important governmental purpose. Justice White spoke for the Court when he held that where individuals in a group affected by a statute or ordinance have distinguishing characteristics relevant to interests a state has the authority to implement, the Equal Protection Clause requires only that the classification drawn by the statute or ordinance be rationally related to a legitimate government interest. That requirement was met in the case; since mentally retarded persons have a reduced ability to cope with and function in the everyday world, they are in fact different from other persons, and the state's interest in dealing with and providing for them is legitimate. The Court, nonetheless, struck down Cleburne's zoning ordinance. Justice White found that requiring a permit in this case rested on "an irrational prejudice against the mentally retarded." Justice Marshall concurred in the Court's judgment but objected to its refusal to bring a heightened level of scrutiny to bear on legislation affecting the rights of the mentally retarded.

Gender-Based Classifications

The problems encountered by the Court in reviewing gender-based classifications have exposed clearly the deficiencies of the two-tier approach.

The Court's traditional stance toward sex discrimination claims was that exhibited in *Goesaert* v. *Cleary* (1948), in which it rejected an attack on a Michigan law that provided that no woman could obtain a bartender's license unless she was "the wife or daughter of the male owner" of a licensed liquor establishment. A radical break with that tradition occurred in 1971, when the Court in *Reed* v. *Reed* struck down a provision of Idaho's probate code that gave preference to men over women as administrators of estates. Employing the rational basis test, Chief Justice Burger declared for a unanimous Court in *Reed* that the question before it was "whether a difference in sex of competing applicants for letters of administration bears a rational relationship to a state objective that is sought to be advanced by the operation of [the Idaho law]." Finding no such relationship, he branded the mandatory preference given to men over women as "the very kind of arbitrary legislative choice" forbidden by the Equal Protection Clause.

This apparent consensus that classifications based on sex were to be reviewed under the rational basis test lasted a scant two years. In *Frontiero* v. *Richardson* (1973), four members of the Court argued that "classifications based upon sex, like classifications based upon race, alienage, and national origin, are inherently suspect." Justices Douglas, White, and Marshall joined Justice Brennan in applying the compelling-state-interest test to find unconstitutional a federal statute under which married servicemen automatically qualified for increased housing allowances and medical and dental benefits for their wives, whereas married servicewomen qualified for those fringe benefits only if their husbands were dependent upon them for at least one-half of their support. Four other justices concurred in Brennan's judgment that the statute was unconstitutional but rejected his claim that sex is a suspect classification in favor of *Reed*'s rational basis test. Justice Powell's concurrence in *Frontiero* was especially interesting in that one of his principal reasons for refusing to view sex as a suspect classification was that the Equal Rights Amendment (ERA) had been approved by the Congress and submitted to the states for ratification. If ratified, the amendment would have made sex-based classifications suspect, and Justice Powell saw no reason or need to "preempt by judicial action a major political decision" then in process of resolution.

Had a fifth member joined Justices Brennan, Douglas, White, and Marshall in either *Frontiero* or a subsequent case, a majority of the Court would have been on record as declaring that sex was a suspect classification. Ratification of the ERA would have had the same result. In the absence of either of these developments, sex-based classifications have failed to achieve suspect status, although some movement toward what Justice Brennan sought in *Frontiero* has occurred. In *Craig* v. *Boren* (1976), Brennan was able to prevail upon his judicial brethren to heighten somewhat the review given to sex-based classifications. Without formally acknowledging that the Court was about to embrace a new intermediate level of review, he announced that "classifications by gender must serve important governmental objectives and must be substantially related to achievement of those objectives." Using this middle-tier test, he invalidated sections of an Oklahoma statute that allowed females to purchase 3.2 percent beer at age eighteen but prohibited males from doing so until age twenty-one. He found unpersuasive the state's contention that such legislation was the proper way to deal with "the pervasiveness of youthful participation in motor vehicle accidents following the imbibing of alcohol." Then, in *Mississippi University for Women* v. *Hogan* (1982), Justice O'Connor applied an intermediate level of scrutiny to sustain an equal-protection challenge to Mississippi's policy of excluding men from MUW's School of Nursing. Interestingly, O'Connor never even mentioned *Craig* and, in fact, offered a different formulation of the middle tier: A governmental classification based on gender will be upheld, she insisted, only if the government meets the burden of showing a "legitimate" and "exceedingly persuasive justification" for the classification and demonstrating "the requisite direct, substantial relationship" between the governmental objective and the means it employs to achieve the objective.

Employing this intermediate level of review, the Court has also upheld a number of "benevolent" classifications that accord women preferential treatment. In every ruling of this type, the Court has based its decision on the argument that such treatment is a compensation for past economic discrimination. In *Kahn* v. *Shevin* (1974), for example, the Court sustained a Florida statute granting a $500 property tax exemption to widows but not to widowers. Justice Douglas wrote for the Court:

> There can be no dispute that the financial difficulties confronting the lone woman . . . exceed those facing the man. Whether from overt discrimination or from the socialization process of a male dominated culture, the job market is inhospitable to the woman seeking any but the lowest paid jobs. There are, of course, efforts under way to remedy this situation. . . . But firmly entrenched practices are resistant to such pressures. . . . We deal here with a state tax law reasonably designed to further the state policy of cushioning the financial impact of spousal loss upon the sex for whom that loss imposes a disproportionately heavy burden.

Similarly, in *Schlesinger* v. *Ballard* (1975) the Court sustained a sex classification in a congressional enactment providing for mandatory discharge of naval officers who, after designated periods of service, have failed to gain promotion. The service period was set at nine years for men and thirteen years for women. Ballard, a male officer who failed to receive promotion after nine years, challenged the statute. In sustaining it, the Court pointed out that female officers "because of restriction on their participation in combat . . . do not have equal opportunities for professional service equal to those of male line officers."[7]

Finally, in *Heckler* v. *Mathews* (1984), the Court upheld a temporary pension offset provision, applicable to nondependent men but not to similarly situated nondependent women, that required a reduction of spousal benefits by the amount of federal or state government pensions received by Social Security applicants. This provision temporarily revived a gender-based classification that the Court had invalidated earlier in *Califano* v. *Goldfarb* (1977), but, Justice Brennan insisted, it was "directly and substantially related to the important governmental interest of protecting individuals who planned their retirements in reasonable reliance on the law" invalidated in *Goldfarb*.

The Court has not upheld all "benevolent" classifications, however. Attempts to justify sex-based classifications as compensation for past discrimination against women have been rejected when the classifications involved have penalized women. Thus, in *Weinberger* v. *Wiesenfeld* (1975) the Court held void a provision of the Social Security Act that provided survivor's benefits for the widow of a deceased husband but not for the widower of a deceased wife. And in *Califano* v. *Goldfarb* (1977) it set aside a gender-based distinction in the Federal Old-Age, Survivors, and Disability Insurance Benefits program, under which a widow automatically received survivors' benefits based on the earnings of a deceased husband but a widower received benefits on the same basis only if he had been receiving at least one-half of his support from his deceased wife. In both cases, the Court rejected the government's claim that the provisions at issue were benevolent because they sought to compensate women beneficiaries as a group for the economic difficulties confronting women who sought to support themselves and their families. Instead, it found that the provisions discriminated against women in that their Social Security taxes produced less protection for their spouses than was produced by the taxes paid by men. The Court's 1979 decision in *Orr* v. *Orr* reinforced this approach to gender-based distinctions. Here the Court again employed the intermediate-scrutiny standard, this time to strike down an Alabama law authorizing the payment of alimony to wives but not to husbands. In his opinion for the Court, Justice Brennan stressed that "statutes purportedly designed to compensate for and ameliorate the effects of past discrimination must be carefully tailored," as benevolent gender classifications "carry the inherent risk of reinforcing stereotypes about the 'proper place' of women and their need for special protection." Brennan argued that the state's purposes could as well have been served "by a gender-neutral classification as by one that gender-classifies and therefore carries with it the baggage of sexual stereotypes."

It could be argued that *Wiesenfeld, Goldfarb,* and *Orr* also presented instances of discrimination against men. Although it was not made in those cases, this argument has been employed to challenge the constitutionality of various classifications, and the Court has responded inconsistently. In *Craig,* for example, it held that the Equal Protection Clause can be used to strike down statutory classifications that discriminate against men, at least where no claim of compensation on behalf of women is made to justify them. As Justice Brennan observed in a footnote, "*Kahn* v. *Shevin* and *Schlesinger* v. *Ballard,* upholding the use of gender-based classifications, rested upon the Court's perception of the laudatory purposes of those laws as remedying disadvantageous conditions suffered by women in economic and military life. Needless to say, in this case Oklahoma does not suggest that the age-sex differential was enacted to insure the availability of 3.2 percent beer for women as compensation for previous deprivations." In *Michael M.* v. *Sonoma County Superior Court* (1981), however, the Court upheld a California statutory rape statute that made it a criminal offense to have sexual intercourse with a female under the age of eighteen. It rejected the petitioner's gender-discrimination challenge that the law was unconstitutional because it did not make it illegal to have sexual intercourse with a male under the age of eighteen. In his opinion announcing the judgment of the Court, Justice Rehnquist declared that the operative standard for reviewing the law in question was "the principle that a legislature may not make overbroad generalizations based on sex which are entirely unrelated to any differences between men and women or which demean the ability or social status of the affected class." Employing this standard, he declared that the statute passed constitutional muster:

> Because virtually all of the significant harmful and inescapably identifiable consequences of teenage pregnancy fall on the young female, a legislature acts well within its authority when it elects to punish only the participant who, by nature, suffers few of the consequences of his conduct. It is hardly unreasonable for a legislature acting to protect minor females to exclude them from punishment. Moreover, risk of pregnancy itself constitutes a substantial deterrence to young females. No similar natural sanctions deter males. A criminal sanction imposed solely on males thus serves to roughly "equalize" the deterrents on the sexes.

Justice Brennan strenuously dissented, insisting that California had not shown that its statutory rape statute "is any more effective than a gender-neutral law would be in deterring minor females from engaging in sexual intercourse. It has, therefore, not met its burden of proving that the statutory classification is substantially related to the achievement of its asserted goal."

Adding to the Court's difficulties in this area has been the problem (given sex-specific traits) of determining what exactly constitutes discrimination, as illustrated in *Geduldig* v. *Aiello* (1974) and *Los Angeles Department of Water and Power* v. *Manhart* (1978). In *Geduldig* the Court upheld a California disability insurance program that exempted from coverage loss of wages resulting from normal pregnancy. Justice Stewart maintained that the program did not discriminate against women: "The program divides potential recipients into two groups—pregnant women and non-pregnant persons. While the first group is exclusively female, the second includes members of both sexes." That narrow understanding of discrimination was abandoned in *Manhart,* in which the Court distinguished *Geduldig* and held that a retirement plan that required women to make higher contributions than men discriminated against them and thereby violated Title VII of the 1964 Civil Rights Act, even though women's greater longevity meant that they probably would draw more benefits than men. Title VII, Justice John Paul Stevens argued for the Court, prohibits discrimination against any individual including those individual women who will "predecease the average woman." Justice Stevens acknowledged that "unless women as a class are assessed an extra charge, they will be subsidized, to some extent, by the class of male employees." Nonetheless, he continued, to treat women as a class would discriminate against those women who do not live as long as the average woman.

A final case involving gender-based classifications, *Rostker* v. *Goldberg* (1981), must be dealt with separately, because, as the Court majority noted, it arose "in the context of Congress' authority over national defense and military affairs, and perhaps in no other area has the Court accorded Congress greater deference." In this case the Court concluded that Congress did not violate the equal protection component of the Fifth Amendment when it authorized the registration of men only under the

Military Selective Service Act. In the majority opinion, Justice Rehnquist refused to clarify whether he was employing the rational relation test or some heightened level of scrutiny: "We do not think that the substantive guarantee of due process or certainty in the law will be advanced by any further 'refinement' in the applicable tests." Such refinement was unnecessary, as "this is not a case of Congress arbitrarily choosing to burden one of two similarly situated groups, such as would be the case with an all-black or all-white, or an all-Catholic or an all-Lutheran, or an all-Republican or an all-Democratic registration. Men and women, because of the combat restrictions on women, are simply not similarly situated for purposes of a draft or a registration for a draft." In his dissent, Justice Marshall accused the Court majority of focusing on the wrong question. What it should have asked, he maintained, was "whether the gender-based classification is itself substantially related to the achievement of the asserted governmental interest. Thus, the Government's task in this case is to demonstrate that excluding women from registration substantially furthers the goal of preparing a draft of combat troops. Or to put it another way, the government must show that drafting women would substantially impede its efforts to prepare for such a draft."

Indigency

In a variety of decisions, primarily in the realm of criminal justice, the Warren Court hinted that classifications based on indigency were suspect. In *Griffin* v. *Illinois* (1958), for example, it ruled that the state must provide indigent defendants with copies of trial transcripts necessary for filing a criminal appeal, and in *Douglas* v. *California* (1963) it declared that indigent defendants have a right of court-appointed counsel on appeal. The suspectness of indigency-based classifications seemed all the more clearly established when Justice Douglas declared for the Court in *Harper* v. *Virginia Board of Elections* (1966) that "lines drawn on the basis of wealth or property, like those of race, are traditionally disfavored," and when the Burger Court invalidated, in *Williams* v. *Illinois* (1970) and *Tate* v. *Short* (1971), the imprisonment of indigent defendants who lacked the means to avoid jail by paying fines.

These cases proved to be inconclusive, however. *Griffin* and *Douglas* came in a context involving the fundamental interest of access to the criminal process; *Williams* and *Tate* applied deferential review; and *Harper* involved the fundamental right of exercise of the franchise. In such subsequent decisions as *James* v. *Valtierra* (1971) and *San Antonio* v. *Rodriguez* (1973), moreover, the Court indicated that indigency-based classifications were far from being considered suspect. *Valtierra* involved an equal protection challenge to a California constitutional requirement that prohibited the state from developing low-rent housing projects "without prior approval in a local referendum." In upholding the requirement, Justice Black denied that lawmaking procedures which disadvantage the poor violate equal protection for that reason alone. Justice Powell argued along much the same lines in *Rodriguez,* holding that the Court had never held "that wealth discrimination alone provides an adequate basis for invoking strict scrutiny." Justice Marshall vigorously dissented in both cases. In his *Valtierra* opinion, in which Justices Brennan and Blackmun joined, he insisted that poverty-based classifications were suspect and thus demanded strict scrutiny. For him, "singling out the poor to bear a burden not placed on any other class of citizens tramples the values the Fourteenth Amendment was designed to protect." He resurrected this argument in *Rodriguez,* in which he contended that children living in impoverished school districts "constitute a sufficient class" to justify heightened review.

FUNDAMENTAL RIGHTS

The Court's efforts to identify and defend fundamental rights have sparked controversy but have not been characterized by the vacillation and indecision that have marked its endeavors to define suspect classifications and to determine the level of scrutiny with which those classifications should be reviewed. One of the first rights to be recognized as fundamental under the Warren Court's two-tier approach was the exercise of the franchise. Over time, this right came to embody three distinct principles: (1) each vote must count equally—i.e., the one-man, one-vote principle; (2) the franchise must be broadly available; and (3) for the vote to be meaningful, the ballot must reflect a sufficiently representative choice of parties and candidates.

Reynolds v. *Sims* (1964) illustrated the Warren Court's understanding of the one-man, one-vote principle. Chief Justice Warren argued in *Reynolds* that the right to exercise the franchise is "a fundamental matter in a free and democratic society" and the only way most citizens can enjoy their "inalienable right to full and effective participation in the political process" of their state governments. Accordingly, any "infringements" of that right must be "carefully and meticulously scrutinized." Employing this strict scrutiny standard, the Chief Justice ruled that both houses of a state legislature had to be apportioned strictly according to population.[8] The Court acknowledged in *Reynolds* that it would be almost impossible to arrange legislative districts so that each one had an identical number of "residents, or citizens, or voters" (terms it used interchangeably), and that "mathematical exactness or precision is hardly a workable constitutional requirement." This concession notwithstanding, the Warren Court later struck down a Missouri reapportionment plan that contained no more than a 5.97 percent disparity between the largest and smallest congressional district.[9] And the Burger Court, in the 1983 case of *Karcher* v. *Daggett* invalidated an apportionment plan for congressional districts in New Jersey in which each of the 14 districts differed from the "ideal" population figure by 0.1384 percent and in which the largest district had a population of 527,472, and the smallest district had a population of 523,798, with a difference between them being only 0.6984 percent of the average district. At the state legislative level, however, the Burger Court has expanded considerably the limits of constitutionality. In *Mahan* v. *Howell* (1973), it held a 16.4 percent deviation in the lower house of the Virginia legislature to be justified by "the State's policy of maintaining the integrity of political subdivision lines." And, in *Brown* v. *Thomson* (1983), it upheld an apportionment plan of Wyoming's House of Representatives which allowed an average deviation from population equality of 16 percent and a maximum deviation of 89 percent, noting that "Wyoming's constitutional policy—followed since statehood—of using counties as representative districts and ensuring that each county has one representative is supported by substantial and legitimate state concerns."

One consequence of the Court's one-person–one-vote decisions has been to free those who draw district lines from the need to respect geographic, historical, or political boundaries or to draw districts that are contiguous and compact. This has unleashed a political-gerrymandering revolution on the land. In California, for example, congressional district lines were drawn by the Democratically controlled state legislature after the 1980 census in such a way that Democratic candidates routinely win two-thirds of the seats from California in the U.S. House of Representatives even though they receive only one-half of the popular vote statewide. Partisan gerrymandering is, of course, a game that both parties play. In Indiana, the Republicans controlled reapportionment and drew lines to benefit themselves. The Indiana Democratic Party brought suit in federal court, alleging that the gerrymandered reapportionment in their state constituted an equal protection violation. A badly divided Supreme Court gave them some modest encouragement. Justice White spoke for a four-member plurality in *Davis* v. *Bandemer* (1986), when he held that an equal protection challenge to a gerrymander is not barred by the political questions doctrine. However, he rejected their specific equal protection claims, declaring that "the mere fact that a particular apportionment scheme makes it more difficult for a particular group in a particular district to elect the representatives of its choice does not render that scheme constitutionally infirm." Justice White insisted that "an individual or a group of individuals who votes for a losing candidate is usually deemed to be adequately represented by the winning candidate and to have as much opportunity to influence that candidate as other voters in the district. We cannot presume in such a situation, without actual proof to the contrary, that the candidate elected will entirely ignore the interests of those voters." He concluded that "a group's electoral power is not unconstitutionally diminished by the simple fact of an apportionment scheme that makes winning elections more difficult." White and the plurality departed from earlier cases that had categorically dismissed claims of gerrymandering by holding that "unconstitutional discrimination" could indeed occur if "the electoral system is arranged in a manner that will consistently degrade a voter's or a group of voters' influence on the political process as a whole." Such a finding of unconstitutionality would, however, have to "be supported by evidence of continued frustration of the will of a majority of the voters or effective denial to a minority of voters of a fair chance to influence the political process."

To advance its second principle of the right to vote, that the franchise be broadly available, the Warren Court undertook to strip away state-erected barriers to the ballot. In *Harper* v. *Virginia Board of Elections* (1966) it invalidated poll taxes as "having no relation to voting qualifications." The right to vote, it insisted, "is too precious, too fundamental, to be so burdened or conditioned." It also voided military status, in *Carrington* v. *Rush* (1965), and property ownership, in *Kramer* v. *Union Free School District* (1969), as conditions affecting the exercise of the franchise. The Burger Court, continuing this practice, in *Dunn* v. *Blumstein* (1972) invalidated durational residency as a condition of voting, on the ground that it could not be shown to further a compelling state interest. As Professor J. Harvie Wilkinson observed, the Court's decisions involving this principle implicitly rejected the view that the vote is a "privilege to be exercised only upon some demonstration of civic responsibility—whether of interest in public affairs by paying a poll tax, of a stake in political life stemming from ownership of property, or of a familiarity with and commitment to state politics resulting from living within the state's boundaries a respectable period."[10] That view was rejected, Justice Harlan complained in his dissent in *Harper*, because it was "not in accord with current egalitarian notions of how a modern democracy should be organized."

The third principle recognized by the Warren Court as implicit in the fundamental right to vote was that the exercise of the franchise be meaningful as well as available. Among "our most precious freedoms," the Court declared in *Williams* v. *Rhodes* (1968), is "the right of qualified voters, regardless of their political persuasion, to cast their votes effectively." In addition to greater ballot access for third-party and independent candidates such as George Wallace and John Anderson, this principle has required elimination of filing fees for indigent candidates. As the Burger Court held in *Lubin* v. *Panish* (1974), "It is to be expected that a voter hopes to find on the ballot a candidate who comes near to reflecting his policy preferences on competing issues."

Along with the franchise, the Warren Court also recognized as fundamental the right to travel from state to state. In *Shapiro* v. *Thompson* (1969), it found that this right of a citizen had been burdened for no compelling reason when Connecticut conditioned eligibility to receive public assistance upon having satisfied a one-year residency requirement. Justice Harlan, alarmed by this elevation of the right to travel to "fundamental" status, voiced his fear that the Court in *Shapiro* had understood the justification for strict scrutiny to stem entirely from the Equal Protection Clause itself, and not from any independent source elsewhere in the Constitution. The implications of such an understanding disturbed him greatly. Noting that almost all state statutes affect important rights, he charged that if the Court were "to pick out particular human activities, characterize them as 'fundamental,' and give them added protection under an unusually stringent equal protection test," it would soon become a "super-legislature."

Justice Harlan's fear were allayed, however, when the Burger Court refused to build on *Shapiro.* In *Dandridge* v. *Williams* (1970) it rejected the contention that the right to welfare was fundamental, and in *Lindsey* v. *Normet* (1972) it rebuffed efforts to establish "decent housing" and "possession of one's home" as fundamental rights. "It is not the province of this Court to create substantive constitutional rights in the name of guaranteeing equal protection of the laws," it declared in *San Antonio Independent School District* v. *Rodriguez* (1973), a case in which it denied that education is a fundamental right.[11] For a right to be fundamental, the Court insisted, it must be "expressly or implicitly guaranteed by the Constitution."

THE FUTURE OF EQUAL-PROTECTION ANALYSIS

As is apparent, the Court's approach to equal-protection issues is fraught with difficulties, which have prompted members of the Court to propose, and on occasion to employ, alternative analytical frameworks for resolving these issues. One such alternative is the "irrebuttable presumptions" doctrine. For a brief time in the mid-1970s, the Court flirted with and even embraced this approach, which asked whether the challenged classification simply presumes something to be the case while at the same time preventing an individual so classified from proving otherwise. In *Vlandis* v. *Kline* (1973), for example, the Court struck down Connecticut's residency requirements for favorable tuition status at state universities on the ground that the requirements did not allow students who had recently arrived in the state a chance to prove that they had in fact become bona fide residents.

The Court's embrace of the irrebuttable-assumptions approach was short-lived, however. In *Weinberger* v. *Salfi* (1975), it overturned a lower court decision that had invalidated, on irrebuttable-presumption grounds, a Social Security duration-of-relationship eligibility requirement for surviving wives and stepchildren of deceased wage earners. In like manner, it refused to acknowledge in *Murgia,* the presence in Massachusetts's mandatory retirement law of an irrebuttable presumption that policemen over the age of fifty are unfit for duty.

Another alternative to the Court's present approach would be the forthright acknowledgment and employment of the middle tier or intermediate level of scrutiny already discussed above. This middle-tier test would provide the Court with a flexibility (and, hence, an interventionist tool) not found in the Court's continued reliance on the rigid two-tier approach. However, that very flexibility can be a vice as well as a virtue. As Justice Rehnquist noted in his dissent in *Craig* v. *Boren,*

> I would think we have had enough difficulty with the two standards of review which our cases have recognized . . . so as to counsel weightily against the insertion of still another "standard" between those two. How is this Court to define what objectives are important? How is it to determine whether a particular law is "substantially" related to the achievement of such objectives, rather than related in some other way to its achievement? Both of the phrases used are so diaphanous and elastic as to invite subjective judicial preferences or prejudices relating to particular types of legislation, masquerading as judgments whether such legislation is directed at "important" objectives or whether the relationship to those objectives is "substantial" enough. . . . The introduction of the adverb "substantially" requires courts to make subjective judgments as to operational effects, for which neither their expertise nor their access to data fits them. And even if we manage to avoid both confusion and the mirroring of our own preferences in the development of this new doctrine, the thousands of judges in other courts who must interpret the Equal Protection Clause may not be so fortunate.

Justice Marshall's wish, expressed *San Antonio* v. *Rodriguez* (1973), to abandon the two-tier approach and to employ instead a "sliding scale" in which the level of scrutiny accorded individual classifications would depend upon the "constitutional and societal importance of the interest adversely affected and the recognized invidiousness of the basis upon which the particular classification is drawn" would not escape Rehnquist's strictures and has not been concurred in by his judicial brethren.

Still another approach to equal-protection analysis was suggested by Justice Rehnquist in his dissent in *Trimble* v. *Gordon.* The problems involved in reviewing equal protection claims, he argued, stemmed "not from the Equal Protection Clause but from the Court's insistence on reading so much into it." To his mind, anything more intensive than the most deferential kind of judicial scrutiny was indefensible, on both theoretical and practical grounds, "except in the area of the law in which the Framers obviously meant it to apply—classifications based on race or on national origin, the first cousin of race."

Rehnquist's proposal fell on the deaf ears of those who, with Justice Marshall in *James* v. *Valtierra* (1971), remained convinced that "it is far too late in the day to contend that the Fourteenth Amendment prohibits only racial discrimination." Thus, the Court has continued to search for a satisfactory and acceptable approach to the questions posed by substantive equal protection. The need for such an approach is great, for equal protection has gone from the "last resort of constitutional argument" to a prolific source of constitutional litigation. As Archibald Cox noted, "once loosed, the idea of Equality is not easily cabined."[12]

NOTES

1 *The Federalist,* No. 10, p. 61.
2 The need for strict scrutiny of classifications that are suspect or that burden fundamental rights may be found in Justice Harlan Stone's celebrated *Carolene Products* footnote (1938), which is reprinted in Chapter 11.
3 Gerald Gunther, "The Supreme Court, 1971 Term—Foreword: In Search of Evolving Doctrine on a Changing Court: A Model for a Newer Equal Protection" *Harvard Law Review* 86, (November 1972): 8.
4 Gerald Gunther, *Constitutional Law,* 11th ed. (Mineola, New York: Foundation Press, 1985), p. 591.
5 *Ibid.,* p. 589.
6 See also *Martin* v. *Wilks* (1989), in which the Supreme Court held in a 5–4 decision that white employees who allege that they have been the victims of racial discrimination because of the employment practices which their employer has undertaken pursuant to a consent decree, cannot be precluded from challenging those practices or consent decree.
7 Although both *Kahn* and *Ballard* were decided before *Craig* v. *Boren* and the de facto employment of the middle-tier test, *Califano* v. *Webster* left no doubt that the Court considered these earlier cases to be fully consistent with *Craig.*
8 The Warren Court ultimately came to apply this same one-man, one-vote principle not only to state legislatures but also to congressional districts, *Wesberry* v. *Sanders* (1964); local governments, *Avery* v. *Midland County* (1968); nominating petitions, *Moore* v. *Ogilvie* (1969); and elected junior-college trustees, *Hadley* v. *Junior College District of Metropolitan Kansas City* (1970). For a sustained criticism of these decisions, see Ralph A. Rossum, "Representation and Republican Government: Contemporary Court Variations on the Founders' Theme" *American Journal of Jurisprudence* 23 (1978).
9 *Kirkpatrick* v. *Preisler* (1969).
10 J. Harvie Wilkinson III, "The Supreme Court, the Equal Protection Clause, and the Three Faces of Constitutional Equality" *Virginia Law Review* 61 (June 1975): 958.
11 See, however, *Plyler* v. *Doe* (1982). Here Justice Brennan, although stating explicitly that education is not a fundamental right and that state denials of educational opportunity are not to be held to the compelling-state-interest test, appeared to argue that the right to education warrants some heightened level of review. The level of review he implicitly employed is the same middle-tier test that he used in *Boren* and *Bakke.*
12 Archibald Cox, "The Supreme Court, 1965 Term—Foreword: Constitutional Adjudication and the Promotion of Human Rights" *Harvard Law Review* 82 (November 1966): 91.

SELECTED READINGS

Ambach v. *Norwick,* 441 U.S. 68 (1979).
Brown v. *Thomson,* 462 U.S. 835 (1983).
Fullilove v. *Klutznick,* 448 U.S. 448 (1980).
James v. *Valtierra,* 402 U.S. 137 (1971).
Karcher v. *Daggett,* 462 U.S. 725 (1983).

Kramer v. *Union Free School District No. 15,* 395 U.S. 621 (1969).
Mississippi University for Women v. *Hogan,* 458 U.S. 718 (1982).
Morton v. *Mancari,* 417 U.S. 535 (1974).
Plyler v. *Doe,* 462 U.S. 725 (1983).
Sosna v. *Iowa,* 419 U.S. 393 (1975).
United Jewish Organizations of Williamsburgh v. *Carey,* 430 U.S. 144 (1977).
Weber v. *Aetna Casualty and Surety Company,* 406 U.S. 164 (1972).
Wengler v. *Druggists Mutual Insurance Company,* 446 U.S. 142 (1980).

Ackerman, Bruce L. "The Conclusive Presumption Shuffle." *University of Pennsylvania Law Review* 125 (April 1977): 761–810.

Baer, Judith A. *The Chains of Protection: The Judicial Response to Women's Labor Legislation* (Westport, Conn.: Greenwood Press, 1978).

———. *Equality Under the Constitution: Reclaiming the Fourteenth Amendment* (Ithaca, N.Y.: Cornell University Press 1983).

Eastland, Terry, and William J. Bennett. *Counting by Race: Equality from the Founding Fathers to Bakke and Weber* (New York: Basic Books, 1979).

Elliott, Ward E. Y. *The Rise of Guardian Democracy: The Supreme Court's Role in Voting Rights Disputes, 1845–1969* (Cambridge, Mass.: Harvard University Press, 1974).

Ely, John Hart. *Democracy and Distrust: A Theory of Judicial Review* (Cambridge, Mass.: Harvard University Press, 1980).

Gunther, Gerald. "The Supreme Court, 1971 Term—Foreword: In Search of Evolving Doctrine on a Changing Court: A Model for a Newer Equal Protection." *Harvard Law Review* 86 (November 1972): 1–48.

Jencks, Christopher. "Affirmative Action for Blacks." *American Behavioral Scientist* 28 (July/August 1985): 731–760.

Rossum, Ralph A. *Reverse Discrimination: The Constitutional Debate* (New York: Marcel Dekker, 1980).

Sindler, Allan P. *Bakke, DeFunis, and Minority Admissions: The Quest for Equal Opportunity* (New York: Longman, 1978).

Sowell, Thomas. *The Economics and Politics of Race* (New York: Morrow, 1983).

Wilkinson, Harvie J. "The Supreme Court, the Equal Protection Clause, and the Three Faces of Constitutional Equality." *Virginia Law Review* 61 (June 1975): 945–1018.

Bakke v. *Regents of the University of California*

553 P. 2d 1152 (1976)

Allan Bakke earned a baccalaureate degree in engineering from the University of Minnesota in 1962, graduating with a 3.51 grade-point average. He was employed as an engineer for a space-agency laboratory when he applied for admission to the 1973 entering class (and subsequently the 1974 entering class) of the Medical School of the University of California at Davis.

In an effort to increase the number of minority students attending the medical school, UC Davis had established a two-track system for applicants: Of the one hundred places available each year, sixteen were set aside for minority students and were filled under a special admissions program. Bakke's grade-point average and Medical College Admission Test (MCAT) scores were highly competitive with those of the regular admittees and much higher than those of the special admittees, as the following table indicates.

Class Entering in 1974

			MCAT (Percentiles)			
	Science GPA	Overall GPA	Verbal	Quantitative	Science	Gen. Infor.
Bakke	3.44	3.51	96	94	97	72
Average of Regular Admittees	3.36	3.29	69	67	82	72
Average of Special Admittees	2.42	2.62	34	30	37	18

Nonetheless, Bakke was denied admission both years. He thereupon filed suit in California Superior Court. The trial court judge held for Bakke, ruling, among other things, that Bakke was discriminated against because of his race in violation of the Equal Protection Clause of the Fourteenth Amendment. The judge also determined, however, that Bakke was *not* entitled to an order for admission to the university, because although he was qualified to be admitted both years in which he applied, he had not shown that he would have been selected even if there had been no special program for minorities. Both parties appealed to the California Supreme Court—Bakke from that portion of the judgment which denied him admission and the university from the determination that its special admissions program was unconstitutional. Because of the importance of the issues involved, the California Supreme Court took the case without intermediate appeal and ruled, six to one, for Bakke.

MR. JUSTICE MOSK delivered the opinion of the Court. . . .

We observe preliminarily that although it is clear that the special admission program classifies applicants by race, this fact alone does not render it unconstitutional. Classification by race has been upheld in a number of cases in which the purpose of the classification was to benefit rather than to disable minority groups.

Thus, such classifications have been approved to achieve integration in the public schools, to require a school system to provide instruction in

English to students of Chinese ancestry, and to uphold the right of certain non-English speaking persons to vote (*Katzenbach* v. *Morgan*). These cases differ from the special admission program in at least one critical respect, however. In none of them did the extension of a right or benefit to a minority have the effect of depriving persons who were not members of a minority group of benefits which they would otherwise have enjoyed.

The University suggests that this distinction is not apposite with respect to the school integration decisions because the effort to integrate schools discommodes nonminorities by requiring some to attend schools in neighborhoods other than their own. We cannot accept this as a valid analogy. Whatever the inconveniences and whatever the techniques employed to achieve integration, no child is totally deprived of an education because he cannot attend a neighborhood school, and all students, whether or not they are members of a minority race, are subject to equivalent burdens. As the Supreme Court has said numerous times since *Brown* v. *Board of Education* (1954), there is no right to a segregated education. The disadvantages suffered by a child who must attend school some distance from his home or is transferred to a school not of his qualitative choice cannot be equated with the absolute denial of a professional education, as occurred in the present case.

It is plain that the special admission program denies admission to some white applicants solely because of their race. Of the 100 admission opportunities available in each year's class, 16 are set aside for disadvantaged minorities, and the committee admits applicants who fall into this category until these 16 places are filled. Since the pool of applicants available in any year is limited, it is obvious that this procedure may result in acceptance of minority students whose qualifications for medical study, under the standards adopted by the University itself, are inferior to those of some white applicants who are rejected. . . .

The rating of some students admitted under the special program in 1973 and 1974 was as much as 30 points below that assigned to Bakke and other nonminority applicants denied admission. Furthermore, white applicants in the general admission program with grade point averages below 2.5 were, for that reason alone, summarily denied admission, whereas some minority students in the special program were admitted with grade point averages considerably below 2.5. In our view, the conclusion is inescapable that at least some applicants were denied admission to the medical school solely because they were not members of a minority race.

The issue to be determined thus narrows to whether a racial classification which is intended to assist minorities, but which also has the effect of depriving those who are not so classified of benefits they would enjoy but for their race, violates the constitutional rights of the majority.

Two distinct inquiries emerge at this point; first, what test is to be used in determining whether the program violates the equal protection clause; and second, does the program meet the requirements of the applicable test.

The general rule is that classifications made by government regulations are valid "if any state of facts reasonably may be conceived" in their justification. But in some circumstances a more stringent standard is imposed. Classification by race is subject to strict scrutiny, at least where the classification results in detriment to a person because of his race. In the case of such a racial classification, not only must the purpose of the classification serve a "compelling state interest," but it must be demonstrated by rigid scrutiny that there are no reasonable ways to achieve the state's goals by means which impose a lesser limitation on the rights of the group disadvantaged by the classification. The burden in both respects is upon the government. . . .

The University asserts that the appropriate standard to be applied in determining the validity of the special admission program is the more lenient "rational basis" test. It contends that the "compelling interest" measure is applicable only to a classification which discriminates against a minority, reasoning that racial classifications are suspect only if they result in invidious discrimination; and that invidious discrimination occurs only if the classification excludes, disadvantages, isolates, or stigmatizes a minority or is designed to segregate the races. The argument is that white applicants denied admission are not stigmatized in the sense of having cast about them an aura of inferiority; therefore, it is sufficient if the special admission program has a rational relation to the University's goals.

We cannot agree with the proposition that

deprivation based upon race is subject to a less demanding standard of review under the Fourteenth Amendment if the race discriminated against is the majority rather than a minority. We have found no case so holding, and we do not hesitate to reject the notion that racial discrimination may be more easily justified against one race than another, nor can we permit the validity of such discrimination to be determined by a mere census count of the races.

That whites suffer a grievous disadvantage by reason of their exclusion from the University on racial grounds is abundantly clear. The fact that they are not also invidiously discriminated against in the sense that a stigma is cast upon them because of their race, as is often the circumstance when the discriminatory conduct is directed against a minority, does not justify the conclusion that race is a suspect classification only if the consequences of the classification are detrimental to minorities.

Regardless of its historical origin, the equal protection clause by its literal terms applies to "any person," and its lofty purpose, to secure equality of treatment to all, is incompatible with the premise that some races may be afforded a higher degree of protection against unequal treatment than others.

We come, then, to the question whether the University has demonstrated that the special admission program is necessary to serve a compelling governmental interest and that the objectives of the program cannot reasonably be achieved by some means which would impose a lesser burden on the rights of the majority.

The University seeks to justify the program on the ground that the admission of minority students is necessary in order to integrate the medical school and the profession. The presence of a substantial number of minority students will not only provide diversity in the student body, it is said, but will influence the students and the remainder of the profession so that they will become aware of the medical needs of the minority community and be encouraged to assist in meeting those demands. Minority doctors will, moreover, provide role models for younger persons in the minority community, demonstrating to them that they can overcome the residual handicaps inherent from past discrimination.

Furthermore, the special admission program will assertedly increase the number of doctors willing to serve the minority community, which is desperately short of physicians. While the University concedes it cannot guarantee that all the applicants admitted under the special program will ultimately practice as doctors in disadvantaged communities, they have expressed an interest in serving those communities and there is a likelihood that many of them will thus fashion their careers.

Finally, it is urged, black physicians would have a greater rapport with patients of their own race and a greater interest in treating diseases which are especially prevalent among blacks, such as sickle cell anemia, hypertension, and certain skin ailments.

We reject the University's assertion that the special admission program may be justified as compelling on the ground that minorities would have more rapport with doctors of their own race and that black doctors would have a greater interest in treating diseases prevalent among blacks. The record contains no evidence to justify the parochialism implicit in the latter assertion; and as to the former, we cite as eloquent refutation to racial exclusivity the comment of Justice Douglas in his dissenting opinion in *DeFunis:* "The Equal Protection Clause commands the elimination of racial barriers, not their creation in order to satisfy our theory as to how society ought to be organized. The purpose of the University of Washington cannot be to produce black lawyers for blacks, Polish lawyers for Poles, Jewish lawyers for Jews, Irish lawyers for Irish. It should be to produce good lawyers for Americans. . . ." *DeFunis* v. *Odegaard* (1974).

We may assume *arguendo* that the remaining objectives which the University seeks to achieve by the special admission program meet the exacting standards required to uphold the validity of a racial classification insofar as they establish a compelling governmental interest. Nevertheless, we are not convinced that the University has met its burden of demonstrating that the basic goals of the program cannot be substantially achieved by means less detrimental to the rights of the majority.

The two major aims of the University are to integrate the student body and to improve medical care for minorities. In our view, the University has not established that a program which discriminates against white applicants because of their race is necessary to achieve either of these goals.

It is the University's claim that if special consideration is not afforded to disadvantaged minority applicants, almost none of them would gain admission because, no matter how large the pool of applicants, the grades and test scores of most minority applicants are lower than those of white applicants. . . .

While minority applicants may have lower grade point averages and test scores than others, we are aware of no rule of law which requires the University to afford determinative weight in admissions to these quantitative factors. In practice, colleges and universities generally consider matters other than strict numerical ranking in admission decisions. The University is entitled to consider, as it does with respect to applicants in the special program, that low grades and test scores may not accurately reflect the abilities of some disadvantaged students; and it may reasonably conclude that although their academic scores are lower, their potential for success in the school and the profession is equal to or greater than that of an applicant with higher grades who has not been similarly handicapped.

In addition, the University may properly as it in fact does, consider other factors in evaluating an applicant, such as the personal interview, recommendations, character, and matters relating to the needs of the profession and society, such as an applicant's professional goals. In short, the standards for admission employed by the University are not constitutionally infirm except to the extent that they are utilized in a racially discriminatory manner. Disadvantaged applicants of all races must be eligible for sympathetic consideration, and no applicant may be rejected because of his race, in favor of another who is less qualified, as measured by standards applied without regard to race. We reiterate, in view of the dissent's misinterpretation, that we do not compel the University to utilize only "the highest objective academic credentials" as the criterion for admission.

. . . The University has not shown that the second major objective of the program—the need for more doctors to serve the minority community—will be appreciably impaired. . . .

An applicant of whatever race who demonstrated his concern for disadvantaged minorities in the past and who declares that practice in such a community is his primary professional goal would be more likely to contribute to alleviation of the medical shortage than one who is chosen entirely on the basis of race and disadvantage. In short, there is no empirical data to demonstrate that any one race is more selflessly socially oriented or by contrast that another is more selfishly acquisitive.

Moreover, while it may be true that the influence exerted by minorities upon the student body and the profession will persuade some nonminority doctors to assist in meeting these community medical needs, it is at best a circuitous and uncertain means to accomplish the University's objective. It would appear that more directly effective methods can be devised, such as academic and clinical courses directed to the medical needs of minorities, and emphasis upon the training of general practitioners to serve the basic needs of the poor. . . .

While a program can be damned by semantics, it is difficult to avoid considering the University scheme as a form of an education quota system, benevolent in concept perhaps, but a revival of quotas nevertheless. No college admission policy in history has been so thoroughly discredited in contemporary times as the use of racial percentages. Originated as a means of exclusion of racial and religious minorities from higher education, a quota becomes no less offensive when it serves to exclude a racial majority. "No form of discrimination should be opposed more vigorously than the quota system."

To uphold the University would call for the sacrifice of principle for the sake of dubious expediency and would represent a retreat in the struggle to assure that each man and woman shall be judged on the basis of individual merit alone, a struggle which has only lately achieved success in removing legal barriers to racial equality. The safest course, the one most consistent with the fundamental interests of all races and with the design of the Constitution is to hold, as we do, that the special admission program is unconstitutional because it violates the rights guaranteed to the majority by the equal protection clause of the Fourteenth Amendment of the United States Constitution. . . .

Regents of the University of California v. *Bakke*

438 U.S. 265; 98 S. Ct. 2733; 57 L. Ed. 2d 750 (1978)

After the California Supreme Court held that the preferential admissions program of the Medical School of the University of California at Davis violated the Equal Protection Clause of the Fourteenth Amendment, the regents of the university successfully petitioned the United States Supreme Court for a writ of certiorari. *Judgment of the Court: Powell. Concurring in the judgment in part and dissenting: Brennan, Blackmun, Marshall, White. Concurring in the judgment in part and dissenting in part: Stevens, Burger, Rehnquist, Stewart.*

Mr. Justice Powell announced the judgment of the Court. . . .

The guarantees of the Fourteenth Amendment extend to persons. Its language is explicit: "No state shall . . . deny to any person within its jurisdiction the equal protection of the laws." It is settled beyond question that the "rights created by the first section of the Fourteenth Amendment are, by its terms, guaranteed to the individual. They are personal rights," *Shelley* v. *Kraemer*. . . . The guarantee of equal protection cannot mean one thing when applied to one individual and something else when applied to a person of another color. If both are not accorded the same protection, then it is not equal.

Nevertheless, petitioner argues that the court below erred in applying strict scrutiny to the special admissions programs because white males, such as respondent, are not a "discrete and insular minority" requiring extraordinary protection from the majoritarian political process. *Carolene Products Co.* . . . This rationale, however, has never been invoked in our decisions as a prerequisite to subjecting racial or ethnic distinctions to strict scrutiny. Nor has this Court held that discreteness and insularity constitute necessary preconditions to a holding that a particular classification is invidious. These characteristics may be relevant in deciding whether or not to add new types of classifications to the list of "suspect" categories or whether a particular classification survives close examination. . . . Racial and ethnic classifications, however, are inherently suspect and thus call for the most exacting judicial examination.

This perception of racial and ethnic distinctions is rooted in our Nation's constitutional and demographic history. The Court's initial view of the Fourteenth Amendment was that its "one pervading purpose" was "the freedom of the slave race, the security and firm establishment of that freedom, and the protection of the newly-made freeman and citizen from the oppressions of those who had formerly exercised dominion over him." *Slaughterhouse Cases* . . . (1873).

Although many of the Framers of the Fourteenth Amendment conceived of its primary function as bridging the vast distance between members of the Negro race and the white "majority," *Slaughterhouse Cases,* . . . the Amendment itself was framed in universal terms, without reference to color, ethnic origin, or condition of prior servitude. . . .

Petitioner urges us to adopt for the first time a more restrictive view of the Equal Protection Clause and hold that discrimination against members of the white "majority" cannot be suspect if its purpose can be characterized as "benign." The clock of our liberties, however, cannot be turned back to 1868. It is far too late to argue that the guarantee of equal protection to *all* persons permits the recognition of special wards entitled to a degree of protection greater than that accorded others. "The Fourteenth Amendment is not directed solely against discrimination due to a 'two-class theory'—that is, based upon differences between 'white' and Negro."

Once the artificial line of a "two-class theory" of the Fourteenth Amendment is put aside, the difficulties entailed in varying the level of judicial review according to a perceived "preferred" status of a particular racial or ethnic minority are intractable. The concepts of "majority" and "minority" necessarily reflect temporary arrangements and political judgments. As observed above, the white "majority" itself is composed of various minority groups, most of which can lay claim to a history of prior discrimination at the hands of the state and private individuals. Not all of these groups can receive preferential treatment and corresponding judicial tolerance of distinctions drawn in terms of race and nationality, for then the only "majority" left would be a new minority of White Anglo-Saxon Protestants. There is no principled basis for deciding which groups would merit "heightened judicial solicitude" and which would not. Courts would be asked to evaluate the extent of the prejudice and consequent harm suffered by various minority groups. Those whose societal injury is thought to exceed some arbitrary level of tolerability then would be entitled to preferential classifications at the expense of individuals belonging to other groups. Those classifications would be free from exacting judicial scrutiny. As these preferences began to have their desired effect, and the consequences of past discrimination were undone, new judicial rankings would be necessary. The kind of variable sociological and political analysis necessary to produce such rankings simply does not lie within the judicial competence—even if they otherwise were politically feasible and socially desirable.

Moreover, there are serious problems of justice connected with the idea of preference itself. First, it may not always be clear that a so-called preference is in fact benign. Courts may be asked to validate burdens imposed upon individual members of particular groups in order to advance the group's general interest. Nothing in the Constitution supports the notion that individuals may be asked to suffer otherwise impermissible burdens in order to enhance the societal standing of their ethnic groups. Second, preferential programs may only reinforce common stereotypes holding that certain groups are unable to achieve success without special protection based on a factor having no relationship to individual worth. Third, there is a measure of inequity in forcing innocent persons in respondent's position to bear the burdens of redressing grievances not of their making.

By hitching the meaning of the Equal Protection Clause to these transitory considerations, we would be holding, as a constitutional principle, that judicial scrutiny of classifications touching on racial and ethnic background may vary with the ebb and flow of political forces. Disparate constitutional tolerance of such classifications well may serve to exacerbate racial and ethnic antagonisms rather than alleviate them. Also, the mutability of a constitutional principle, based upon shifting political and social judgments, undermines the chances for consistent application of the Constitution from one generation to the next, a critical feature of its coherent interpretation. In expounding the Constitution, the Court's role is to discern "principles sufficiently absolute to give them roots throughout the community and continuity over significant periods of time and to lift them above the level of the pragmatic political judgments of a particular time and place." . . . The special admissions program purports to serve the purpose of obtaining the educational benefits that flow from an ethnically diverse student body. It is necessary to decide which, if any, of these purposes is substantial enough to support the use of a suspect classification.

The attainment of a diverse student body clearly is a constitutionally permissible goal for an institution of higher education. Academic freedom, though not a specifically enumerated constitutional right, long has been viewed as a special concern of the First Amendment. The freedom of a university to make its own judgments as to education includes the selection of its student body. Mr. Justice Frankfurter summarized the "four essential freedoms" that comprise academic freedom: "It is the business of a university to provide that atmosphere which is most conducive to speculation, experiment and creation. It is an atmosphere in which there prevail 'the four essential freedoms' of a university—to determine for itself on academic grounds who may teach, what may be taught, how it shall be taught, and who may be admitted to study" [*Sweezy* v. *New Hampshire* . . . (1957). . . .].

The atmosphere of "speculation, experiment and creation"—so essential to the quality of higher education—is widely believed to be promoted by a diverse student body. . . . It is not too much to say that the "nation's future depends upon leaders trained through wide exposure" to the ideas and mores of students as diverse as this Nation of many peoples.

Thus, in arguing that its universities must be accorded the right to select those students who will contribute the most to the "robust exchange of ideas," petitioner invokes a countervailing constitutional interest, that of the First Amendment. In this light, petitioner must be viewed as seeking to achieve a goal that is of paramount importance in the fulfillment of its mission.

Ethnic diversity, however, is only one element in a range of factors a university properly may consider in attaining the goal of a heterogeneous student body. Although a university must have wide discretion in making the sensitive judgments as to who should be admitted, constitutional limitations protecting individual rights may not be disregarded. Respondent urges—and the courts below have held—that petitioner's dual admissions program is a racial classification that impermissibly infringes his rights under the Fourteenth Amendment. As the interest of diversity is compelling in the context of a university's admissions program, the question remains whether the program's racial classification is necessary to promote this interest.

It may be assumed that the reservation of a specified number of seats in each class for individuals from the preferred ethnic groups would contribute to the attainment of considerable ethnic diversity in the student body. But petitioner's argument that this is the only effective means of serving the interest of diversity is seriously flawed. In a most fundamental sense the argument misconceives the nature of the state interest that would justify consideration of race or ethnic background. It is not an interest in simple ethnic diversity, in which a specified percentage of the student body is in effect guaranteed to be members of selected ethnic groups, with the remaining percentage an undifferentiated aggregation of students. The diversity that furthers a compelling state interest encompasses a far broader array of qualifications and characteristics of which racial or ethnic origin is but a single though important element. Petitioner's special admissions program, focused *solely* on ethnic diversity, would hinder rather than further attainment of genuine diversity.

The experience of other university admissions programs, which take race into account in achieving the educational diversity valued by the First Amendment, demonstrates that the assignment of a fixed number of places to a minority group is not a necessary means toward that end. An illuminating example is found in the Harvard College program.

In . . . [Harvard's] admissions program, race or ethnic background may be deemed a "plus" in a particular applicant's file, yet it does not insulate the individual from comparison with all other candidates for the available seats. The file of a particular black applicant may be examined for his potential contribution to diversity without the factor of race being decisive when compared, for example, with that of an applicant identified as an Italian-American if the latter is thought to exhibit qualities more likely to promote beneficial educational pluralism. Such qualities could include exceptional personal talents, unique work or service experience, leadership potential, maturity, demonstrated compassion, a history of overcoming disadvantage, ability to communicate with the poor, or other qualifications deemed important. In short, an admissions program operated in this way is flexible enough to consider all pertinent elements of diversity in light of the particular qualifications of each applicant, and to place them on the same footing for consideration, although not necessarily according them the same weight. Indeed, the weight attributed to a particular quality may vary from year to year depending upon the "mix" both of the student body and the applicants for the incoming class.

This kind of program treats each applicant as an individual in the admissions process. The applicant who loses out on the last available seat to another candidate receiving a "plus" on the basis of ethnic background will not have been foreclosed from all consideration for that seat simply because he was not the right color or had the wrong surname. It would mean only that his combined qualifications, which may have included similar nonobjective factors, did not outweigh those of the other applicant. His qualifications would have been weighed fairly and competitively, and he would have no basis to complain of unequal treatment under the Fourteenth Amendment.

It has been suggested that an admissions program which considers race only as one factor is simply a subtle and more sophisticated—but not less effective—means of according racial preference than the Davis program. A facial intent to discriminate, however, is evident in petitioner's preference program and not denied in this case. No such facial infirmity exists in an admissions program where race or ethnic background is simply one element—to be weighed fairly against other elements—in the selection process. "A boundary line," as Mr. Justice Frankfurter remarked in another connection, "is none the worse for being narrow." . . . And a Court would not assume that a university, professing to employ a facially nondiscriminatory admissions policy, would operate it as a cover for the functional equivalent of a quota system. In short, good faith would be presumed in the absence of a showing to the contrary in the manner permitted by our cases.

In summary, it is evident that the Davis special admission program involves the use of an explicit racial classification never before countenanced by this Court. It tells applicants who are not Negro, Asian, or "Chicano" that they are totally excluded from a specific percentage of the seats in an entering class. No matter how strong their qualifications, quantitative and extracurricular, including their own potential for contribution to educational diversity, they are never afforded the chance to compete with applicants from the preferred groups for the special admission seats. At the same time, the preferred applicants have the opportunity to compete for every seat in the class.

The fatal flaw in petitioner's preferential program is its disregard of individual rights as guaranteed by the Fourteenth Amendment. Such rights are not absolute. But when a State's distribution of benefits or imposition of burdens hinges on the color of a person's skin or ancestry, that individual is entitled to a demonstration that the challenged classification is necessary to promote a substantial state interest. Petitioner has failed to carry this burden. For this reason, that portion of the California court's judgment holding petitioner's special admissions program invalid under the Fourteenth Amendment must be affirmed.

In enjoining petitioner from ever considering the race of any applicant, however, the courts below failed to recognize that the State has a substantial interest that legitimately may be served by a properly devised admissions program involving the competitive consideration of race and ethnic origin. For this reason, so much of the California court's judgment as enjoins petitioner from any consideration of the race of any applicant must be reversed.

MR. JUSTICE BRENNAN, concurring in the judgment in part and dissenting.

Government may take race into account when it acts not to demean or insult any racial group, but to remedy disadvantages cast on minorities by past racial prejudice, at least when appropriate findings have been made by judicial, legislative, or administrative bodies with competence to act in this area. . . .

Against this background, claims that law must be "color-blind" or that the datum of race is no longer relevant to public policy must be seen as aspiration rather than as description of reality. This is not to denigrate aspiration; for reality rebukes us that race has too often been used by those who would stigmatize and oppress minorities. Yet we cannot—and as we shall demonstrate, need not under our Constitution or Title VI, which merely extends the constraints of the Fourteenth Amendment to private parties who receive federal funds—let color blindness become myopia which masks the reality that many "created equal" have been treated within our lifetimes as inferior both by the law and by their fellow citizens.

The assertion of human equality is closely associated with the proposition that differences in color or creed, birth or status, are neither significant nor relevant to the way in which persons should be treated. Nonetheless, the position that such factors must be "[c]onstitutionally an irrelevance," . . . summed up by the shorthand phrase "[o]ur Constitution is color-blind," . . . has never been adopted by this Court as the proper meaning of the Equal Protection Clause. Indeed, we have expressly rejected this proposition on a number of occasions.

Our cases have always implied that an "overriding statutory purpose" . . . could be found that would justify racial classifications. . . .

We conclude, therefore, that racial classifications are not *per se* invalid under the Fourteenth Amendment. Accordingly, we turn to the problem of articulating what our role should be in reviewing state action that expressly classifies by race. . . .

. . . We have held that a government practice or statute which restricts "fundamental rights" or which contains "suspect classifications" is to be subjected to "strict scrutiny" and can be justified only if it furthers a compelling government purpose and, even then, only if no less restrictive alternative is available. . . . But no fundamental right is involved here. Nor do whites as a class have any of the "traditional indicia of suspectness: the class is not saddled with such disabilities, or subjected to such a history of purposeful unequal treatment, or relegated to such a position of political powerlessness as to command extraordinary protection from the majoritarian political process."

On the other hand, the fact that this case does not fit neatly into our prior analytic framework for race cases does not mean that it should be analyzed by applying the very loose rational-basis standard of review that is the very least that is always applied in equal protection cases. "[T]he mere recitation of a benign, compensatory purpose is not an automatic shield which protects against any inquiry into the actual purposes underlying a statutory scheme." Instead, a number of considerations—developed in gender discrimination cases but which carry even more force when applied to racial classifications—lead us to conclude that racial classifications designed to further remedial purposes " 'must serve important governmental objectives and must be substantially related to achievement of those objectives.' "

First, race, like, "gender-based classifications too often [has] been inexcusably utilized to stereotype and stigmatize politically powerless segments of society." While a carefully tailored statute designed to remedy past discrimination could avoid these vices, we nonetheless have recognized that the line between honest and thoughtful appraisal of the effects of past discrimination and paternalistic stereotyping is not so clear and that a statute based on the latter is patently capable of stigmatizing all women with a badge of inferiority. State programs designed ostensibly to ameliorate the effects of past racial discrimination obviously create the same hazard of stigma, since they may promote racial separatism and reinforce the views of those who believe that members of racial minorities are inherently incapable of succeeding on their own.

Second, race, like gender and illegitimacy, is an immutable characteristic which its possessors are powerless to escape or set aside. While a classification is not *per se* invalid because it divides classes on the basis of an immutable characteristic, it is nevertheless true that such divisions are contrary to our deep belief that "legal burdens should bear some relationship to individual responsibility or wrongdoing," and that advancement sanctioned, sponsored, or approved by the State should ideally be based on individual merit or achievement, or at the least on factors within the control of an individual.

In sum, because of the significant risk that racial classifications established for ostensibly benign purposes can be misused, causing effects not unlike those created by invidious classifications, it is inappropriate to inquire only whether there is any conceivable basis that might sustain such a classification. Instead, to justify such a classification an important and articulated purpose for its use must be shown. In addition, any statute must be striken that stigmatizes any group or that singles out those least well represented in the political process to bear the brunt of a benign program.

Properly construed, therefore, our prior cases unequivocally show that a state government may adopt race-conscious programs if the purpose of such programs is to remove the disparate racial impact its actions might otherwise have and if there is reason to believe that the disparate impact is itself the product of past discrimination, whether its own or that of society at large. There is no question that Davis' program is valid under this test.

Certainly, on the basis of the undisputed factual submissions before this Court, Davis had a sound basis for believing that the problem of underrepresentation of minorities was substantial and chronic and that the problem was attributable to handicaps imposed on minority applicants by past and present racial discrimination. Until at least 1973, the practice of medicine in this country was, in fact, if not in law, largely the prerogative of whites. In 1950, for example, while Negroes comprised 10% of the total population, Negro physicians constituted only 2.2% of the total number of physicians. The overwhelming majority of these, moreover, were educated in two predominantly Negro medical schools, Howard and Meharry. By 1970, the gap between the proportion of Negroes in medicine and their proportion in the population had widened: The number of Negroes employed in medicine remained frozen at 2.2% while the Negro population had increased to 11.1%. The number of Negro admittees to predominantly white medical schools, moreover, had declined in absolute numbers during the years 1955 to 1964.

Moreover, Davis had very good reason to believe that the national pattern of underrepresentation of minorities in medicine would be perpetuated if it retained a single admissions standard. For example, the entering classes in 1968 and 1969, the years in which such a standard was used, included only one Chicano and two Negroes out of 100 admittees. Nor is there any relief from this pattern of underrepresentation in the statistics for the regular admissions program in later years.

Davis clearly could conclude that the serious and persistent underrepresentation of minorities in medicine depicted by these statistics is the result of handicaps under which minority applicants labor as a consequence of a background of deliberate, purposeful discrimination against minorities in education and in society generally, as well as in the medical profession.

The second prong of our test—whether the Davis program stigmatizes any discrete group or individual and whether race is reasonably used in light of the program's objectives—is clearly satisfied by the Davis program.

It is not even claimed that Davis' program in any way operates to stigmatize or single out any discrete and insular, or even any identifiable nonminority group. Nor will harm comparable to that imposed upon racial minorities by exclusion or separation on grounds of race be the likely result of the program. It does not, for example, establish an exclusive preserve for minority students apart from and exclusive of whites. Rather, its purpose is to overcome the effects of segregation by bringing the races together. True, whites are excluded from participation in the special admissions program, but this fact only operates to reduce the number of whites to be admitted in the regular admissions program in order to permit admission of a reasonable percentage—less than their proportion of the California population—of otherwise underrepresented qualified minority applicants.

Nor was Bakke in any sense stamped as inferior by the Medical School's rejection of him. Indeed, it is conceded by all that he satisfied those criteria regarded by the School as generally relevant to academic performance better than most of the minority members who were admitted. Moreover, there is absolutely no basis for concluding that Bakke's rejection as a result of Davis' use of racial preference will affect him throughout his life in the same way as the segregation of the Negro school children in *Brown I* would have affected them. Unlike discrimination against racial minorities, the use of racial preferences for remedial purposes does not inflict a pervasive injury upon individual whites in the sense that wherever they go or whatever they do there is a significant likelihood that they will be treated as second-class citizens because of their color. This distinction does not mean that the exclusion of a white resulting from preferential use of race is not sufficiently serious to require justification; but it does mean that the injury inflicted by such a policy is not distinguishable from disadvantages caused by a wide range of government actions, none of which has ever been thought impermissible for that reason alone.

In addition, there is simply no evidence that the Davis program discriminates intentionally or unintentionally against any minority group which it purports to benefit. The program does not establish a quota in the invidious sense of a ceiling on the number of minority applicants to be admitted. Nor can the program reasonably be regarded as stigmatizing the program's beneficiaries of their race as inferior. The Davis program does not simply advance less qualified applicants; rather it compensates applicants, whom . . . it is uncontested are fully qualified to study medicine, for educational disadvantage which it was reasonable to conclude was a product of state-fostered discrimination. Once admitted, these students must satisfy the same degree requirements as regularly admitted students; they are taught by the same faculty in the same classes, and their performance is evaluated by the same standards by which regularly admitted students are judged. Under these circumstances, their performance and degrees must be regarded equally with the regularly admitted students with whom they compete for standing. Since minority graduates cannot justifiably be regarded as less well qualified than nonminority graduates by virtue of the special admissions program, there is no reasonable basis to conclude that minority graduates at schools using such programs would be stigmatized as inferior by the existence of such programs.

We disagree with the lower courts' conclusion

that the Davis program's use of race was unreasonable in light of its objectives. First, as petitioner argues, there are no practical means by which it could achieve its ends in the foreseeable future without the use of race-conscious measures. With respect to any factor (such as poverty or family educational background) that may be used as a substitute for race as an indicator of past discrimination, whites greatly outnumber racial minorities simply because whites make up a far larger percentage of the total population and therefore far outnumber minorities in absolute terms at every socio-economic level. For example, of a class of recent medical school applicants from families with less than $10,000 income, at least 71% were white. Of all 1970 families headed by a person *not* a high school graduate which included related children under 18, 80% were white and 20% were racial minorities. Moreover, while race is positively correlated with differences in GPA and MCAT scores, economic disadvantage is not. Thus, it appears that economically disadvantaged whites do not score less well than economically advantaged whites, while economically advantaged blacks score less well than do disadvantaged whites. These statistics graphically illustrate that the University's purpose to integrate its classes by compensating for past discrimination could not be achieved by a general preferance for the economically disadvantaged or the children of parents of limited education unless such groups were to make up the entire class.

Second, the Davis admissions program does not simply equate minority status with disadvantage. Rather, Davis considers on an individual basis each applicant's personal history to determine whether he or she has likely been disadvantaged by racial discrimination. The record makes clear that only minority applicants likely to have been isolated from the mainstream of American life arc considered in the special program; other minority applicants are eligible only through the regular admissions program. True, the procedure by which disadvantage is detected is informal, but we have never insisted that educators conduct their affairs through adjudicatory proceedings, and such insistence here is misplaced. A case-by-case inquiry into the extent to which each individual applicant has been affected, either directly or indirectly, by racial discrimination, would seem to be, as a practical matter, virtually impossible, despite the fact that there are excellent reasons for concluding that such effects generally exist. When individual measurement is impossible or extremely impractical, there is nothing to prevent a State from using categorical means to achieve its ends, at least where the category is closely related to the goal. And it is clear from our cases that specific proof that a person has been victimized by discrimination is not a necessary predicate to offering him relief where the probability of victimization is great.

Finally, Davis' special admissions program cannot be said to violate the Constitution simply because it has set aside a predetermined number of places for qualified minority applicants rather than using minority status as a positive factor to be considered in evaluating the applications of disadvantaged minority applicants. For purposes of constitutional adjudication, there is no difference between the two approaches.

The "Harvard" program, as those employing it readily concede, openly and successfully employs a racial criterion for the purpose of ensuring that some of the scarce places in institutions of higher education are allocated to disadvantaged minority students. That the Harvard approach does not also make public the extent of the preference and the precise workings of the system while the Davis program employs a specific, openly stated number, does not condemn the latter plan for purposes of Fourteenth Amendment adjudication. It may be that the Harvard plan is more acceptable to the public than is the Davis "quota." But there is no basis for preferring a particular preference program simply because in achieving the same goals that the Davis Medical School is pursuing, it proceeds in a manner that is not immediately apparent to the public.

Richmond v. Croson Co.

109 S. Ct. 706 (1989)

The City of Richmond, Virginia, adopted a Minority Business Utilization Plan requiring prime contractors awarded city construction contracts to subcontract at least 30% of the total dollar amount of each contract to one or more Minority Business Enterprises (MBEs), which the city defined to include a business from anywhere in the country at least 51% of which is owned and controlled by black, Spanish-speaking, Oriental, Indian, Eskimo, or Aleut citizens. Although Richmond declared that the plan was "remedial" in nature, the city adopted it after a public hearing at which no direct evidence was presented that the city had discriminated on the basis of race in letting contracts or that its prime contractors had discriminated against minority subcontractors. What was introduced was a statistical study indicating that, while the city's population was 50% black, only .67% of its prime construction contracts had been awarded to minority subcontractors in recent years; figures showing that local contractors' associations had virtually no MBE members; the conclusion of the city's counsel that the plan was constitutional under *Fullilove* v. *Klutznick*, 448 U.S. 448 (1980); and statements of plan proponents indicating that there had been widespread racial discrimination in the local, state, and national construction industries.

Pursuant to this plan, the city adopted rules requiring individualized consideration of each bid or request for a waiver of the 30% set-aside, and providing that a waiver could be granted only upon proof that sufficient qualified MBEs were unavailable or unwilling to participate. After J.A. Croson Co., the sole bidder on a city contract, was denied a waiver and lost its contract, it brought suit in Federal District Court for the Eastern District of Virginia, alleging that the city's plan was unconstitutional under the Fourteenth Amendment's Equal Protection Clause. The District Court upheld the plan in all respects, and the Court of Appeals for the Fourth Circuit affirmed, applying a test derived from the Supreme Court's principal opinion in *Fullilove*, which accorded great deference to Congress's findings of past societal discrimination in holding that a 10% minority set-aside for certain federal construction grants did not violate the equal protection component of the Fifth Amendment. When Croson petitioned the Supreme Court for a writ of certiorari, the Court vacated the judgment from below and remanded the case for further consideration in light of its intervening decision in *Wygant* v. *Jackson Board of Education*, 476 U.S. 267 (1986), in which a plurality of the Supreme Court applied a strict scrutiny standard in holding that a race-based layoff program agreed to by a school district and the local teacher's union violated the Fourteenth Amendment's Equal Protection Clause. On remand, the Court of Appeals held that the city's plan violated both prongs of strict scrutiny in that it was not justified by a compelling governmental interest—the record revealed no prior discrimination by the city itself in awarding contracts—and the 30% set-aside was not narrowly tailored to accomplish a remedial purpose.

The City appealed. *Opinion of the Court: O'Connor, Kennedy, Rehnquist, Stevens, White. Concurring in part and concurring in the judgment: Kennedy; Stevens. Concurring in the judgment: Scalia. Dissenting opinion: Marshall, Brennan, Blackmun; Blackmun, Brennan.*

JUSTICE O'CONNOR . . . delivered the opinion of the Court. . . .

In this case, we confront once again the tension between the Fourteenth Amendment's guarantee of equal treatment to all citizens, and the use of race-based measures to ameliorate the effects of past discrimination on the opportunities enjoyed by members of minority groups in our society. In *Fullilove* v. *Klutznick* . . . (1980), we held that a congressional program requiring that 10% of certain federal construction grants be awarded to minority contractors did not violate the equal protection principles embodied in the Due Process Clause of the Fifth Amendment. Relying largely on our decision in *Fullilove,* some lower federal courts have applied a similar standard of review in assessing the constitutionality of state and local minority set-aside provisions under the Equal Protection Clause of the Fourteenth Amendment. . . . Since our decision two Terms ago in *Wygant* v. *Jackson Board of Education* . . . (1986), the lower federal courts have attempted to apply its standards in evaluating the constitutionality of state and local programs which allocate a portion of public contracting opportunities exclusively to minority-owned businesses. . . . We noted probable jurisdiction in this case to consider the applicability of our decision in *Wygant* to a minority set-aside program adopted by the city of Richmond, Virginia . . .

The parties and their supporting *amici* fight an initial battle over the scope of the city's power to adopt legislation designed to address the effects of past discrimination. Relying on our decision in *Wygant,* appellee argues that the city must limit any race-based remedial efforts to eradicating the effects of its own prior discrimination. This is essentially the position taken by the Court of Appeals below. Appellant argues that our decision in *Fullilove* is controlling, and that as a result the city of Richmond enjoys sweeping legislative power to define and attack the effects of prior discrimination in its local construction industry. We find that neither of these two rather stark alternatives can withstand analysis.

In *Fullilove,* we upheld the minority set-aside contained in § 103(f)(2) of the Public Works Employment Act of 1977, . . . against a challenge based on the equal protection component of the Due Process Clause . . .

The principal opinion in *Fullilove,* written by Chief Justice Burger, did not employ "strict scrutiny" or any other traditional standard of equal protection review. The Chief Justice noted at the outset that although racial classifications call for close examination, the Court was at the same time, "bound to approach [its] task with appropriate deference to the Congress, a co-equal branch charged by the Constitution with the power to 'provide for the . . . general Welfare of the United States' and 'to enforce by appropriate legislation,' the equal protection guarantees of the Fourteenth Amendment." . . . The principal opinion asked two questions: first, were the objectives of the legislation within the power of Congress? Second, was the limited use of racial and ethnic criteria a permissible means for Congress to carry out its objectives within the constraints of the Due Process Clause?

On the issue of congressional power, the Chief Justice found that Congress' commerce power was sufficiently broad to allow it to reach the practices of prime contractors on federally funded local construction projects. . . . Congress could mandate state and local government compliance with the set-aside program under its § 5 power to enforce the Fourteenth Amendment . . .

The Chief Justice next turned to the constraints on Congress' power to employ race-conscious remedial relief. His opinion stressed two factors in upholding the MBE set-aside. First was the unique remedial powers of Congress under § 5 of the Fourteenth Amendment:

"Here we deal . . . not with the limited remedial powers of a federal court, for example, but with the broad remedial powers of Congress. It is fundamental that *in no organ of government, state or federal, does there repose a more comprehensive remedial power than in the Congress,* expressly charged by the Constitution with competence and authority to enforce equal protection guarantees." . . .

Because of these unique powers, the Chief Justice concluded that "Congress not only may induce voluntary action to assure compliance with existing federal statutory or constitutional antidiscrimination provisions, but also, where Congress has authority to *declare certain conduct unlawful,* it may, as here, authorize and induce state action to avoid such conduct."

The second factor emphasized by the principal opinion in *Fullilove* was the flexible nature of the 10% set-aside. Two "congressional assumptions" underlay the MBE program: first, that the effects of past discrimination had impaired the competitive position of minority businesses, and second, that "adjustment for the effects of past discrimination" would assure that at least 10% of the funds from the federal grant program would flow to minority businesses. The Chief Justice noted that both of these "assumptions" could be "rebutted" by a grantee seeking a waiver of the 10% requirement. . . . Thus a waiver could be sought where minority businesses were not available to fill the 10% requirement or, more importantly, where an MBE attempted "to exploit the remedial aspects of the program by charging an unreasonable price, *i.e.,* a price not attributable to the present effects of prior discrimination." . . . The Chief Justice indicated that without this fine tuning to remedial purpose, the statute would not have "pass[ed] muster." . . .

Appellant and its supporting *amici* rely heavily on *Fullilove* for the proposition that a city council, like Congress, need not make specific findings of discrimination to engage in race-conscious relief. Thus, appellant argues "[i]t would be a perversion of federalism to hold that the federal government has a compelling interest in remedying the effects of racial discrimination in its own public works program, but a city government does not."

What appellant ignores is that Congress, unlike any State or political subdivision, has a specific constitutional mandate to enforce the dictates of the Fourteenth Amendment. The power to "enforce" may at times also include the power to define situations which *Congress* determines threaten principles of equality and to adopt prophylactic rules to deal with those situations. . . . The Civil War Amendments themselves worked a dramatic change in the balance between congressional and state power over matters of race. Speaking of the Thirteenth and Fourteenth Amendments in *Ex parte Virginia,* 100 U.S. 339, 345 (1880), the Court stated: "They were intended to be, what they really are, limitations of the powers of the States and enlargements of the power of Congress."

That Congress may identify and redress the effects of society-wide discrimination does not mean that, *a fortiori,* the States and their political subdivisions are free to decide that such remedies are appropriate. Section 1 of the Fourteenth Amendment is an explicit *constraint* on state power, and the States must undertake any remedial efforts in accordance with that provision. To hold otherwise would be to cede control over the content of the Equal Protection Clause to the 50 state legislatures and their myriad political subdivisions. The mere recitation of a benign or compensatory purpose for the use of a racial classification would essentially entitle the States to exercise the full power of Congress under § 5 of the Fourteenth Amendment and insulate any racial classification from judicial scrutiny under § 1. We believe that such a result would be contrary to the intentions of the Framers of the Fourteenth Amendment, who desired to place clear limits on the States' use of race as a criterion for legislative action, and to have the federal courts enforce those limitations. . . .

It would seem equally clear, however, that a state or local subdivision (if delegated the authority from the State) has the authority to eradicate the effects of private discrimination within its own legislative jurisdiction. This authority must, of course, be exercised within the constraints of § 1 of the Fourteenth Amendment. Our decision in *Wygant* is not to the contrary. *Wygant* addressed the constitutionality of the use of racial quotas by local school authorities pursuant to an agreement reached with the local teachers' union. It was in the context of addressing the school board's power to adopt a race-based layoff program affecting its own work force that the *Wygant* plurality indicated that the Equal Protection Clause required "some showing of prior discrimination by the governmental unit involved." . . . As a matter of state law, the city of Richmond has legislative authority over its procurement policies, and can use its spending powers to remedy private discrimination, if it identifies that discrimination with the particularity required by the Fourteenth Amendment. . . .

The Equal Protection Clause of the Fourteenth Amendment provides that "[N]o State shall . . . deny to *any person* within its jurisdiction the equal protection of the laws" (emphasis added). As this Court has noted in the past, the "rights created by the first section of the Fourteenth Amendment are, by its terms, guaranteed to the individual. The rights established are personal rights." *Shelly* v. *Kraemer*, . . . (1948). The Richmond Plan denies certain citizens the opportunity to compete for a fixed percentage of public contracts based solely upon their race. To whatever racial group these citizens belong, their "personal rights" to be treated with equal dignity and respect are implicated by a rigid rule erecting race as the sole criterion in an aspect of public decisionmaking.

Absent searching judicial inquiry into the justification for such race-based measures, there is simply no way of determining what classifications are "benign" or "remedial" and what classifications are in fact motivated by illegitimate notions of racial inferiority or simple racial politics. Indeed, the purpose of strict scrutiny is to "smoke out" illegitimate uses of race by assuring that the legislative body is pursuing a goal important enough to warrant use of a highly suspect tool. The test also ensures that the means chosen "fit" this compelling goal so closely that there is little or no possibility that the motive for the classification was illegitimate racial prejudice or stereotype.

Classifications based on race carry a danger of stigmatic harm. Unless they are strictly reserved for remedial settings, they may in fact promote notions of racial inferiority and lead to a politics of racial hostility. . . . We thus reaffirm the view expressed by the plurality in *Wygant* that the standard of review under the Equal Protection Clause is not dependent on the race of those burdened or benefited by a particular classification. . . .

Under the standard proposed by Justice Marshall's dissent, "[r]ace-conscious classifications designed to further remedial goals," . . . are forthwith subject to a relaxed standard of review. How the dissent arrives at the legal conclusion that a racial classification is "designed to further remedial goals," without first engaging in an examination of the factual basis for its enactment and the nexus between its scope and that factual basis we are not told. However, once the "remedial" conclusion is reached, the dissent's standard is singularly deferential, and bears little resemblance to the close examination of legislative purpose we have engaged in when reviewing classifications based either on race or gender. . . . The dissent's watered-down version of equal protection review effectively assures that race will always be relevant in American life, and that the "ultimate goal" of "eliminat[ing] entirely from governmental decisionmaking such irrelevant factors as a human being's race," . . . will never be achieved.

Even were we to accept a reading of the guarantee of equal protection under which the level of scrutiny varies according to the ability of different groups to defend their interests in the representative process, heightened scrutiny would still be appropriate in the circumstances of this case. One of the central arguments for applying a less exacting standard to "benign" racial classifications is that such measures essentially involve a choice made by dominant racial groups to disadvantage themselves. If one aspect of the judiciary's role under the Equal Protection Clause is to protect "discrete and insular minorities" from majoritarian prejudice or indifference, . . . some maintain that these concerns are not implicated when the "white majority" places burdens upon itself.

In this case, blacks comprise approximately 50% of the population of the city of Richmond. Five of the nine seats on the City Council are held by blacks. The concern that a political majority will more easily act to the disadvantage of a minority based on unwarranted assumptions or incomplete facts would seem to militate for, not against, the application of heightened judicial scrutiny in this case. . . .

Appellant argues that it is attempting to remedy various forms of past discrimination that are alleged to be responsible for the small number of minority businesses in the local contracting industry. Among these the city cites the exclusion of blacks from skilled construction trade unions and training programs. This past discrimination has prevented them "from following the traditional path from laborer to entrepreneur." The city also lists a host of nonracial factors which would seem to face a member of any racial group attempting to establish a new business enterprise, such as deficiencies in working capital, inability to meet bonding requirements, unfamiliarity with bidding procedures, and disability caused by an inadequate track record. . . .

While there is no doubt that the sorry history of both private and public discrimination in this country has contributed to a lack of opportunities for black entrepreneurs, this observation, standing alone, cannot justify a rigid racial quota in the awarding of public contracts in Richmond, Virginia. Like the claim that discrimination in primary and secondary schooling justifies a rigid racial preference in medical school admissions, an amorphous claim that there has been past discrimination in a particular industry cannot justify the use of an unyielding racial quota.

It is sheer speculation how many minority firms there would be in Richmond absent past societal discrimination, just as it was sheer speculation how many minority medical students would have been admitted to the medical school at Davis absent past discrimination in educational opportunities. Defining these sorts of injuries as "identified discrimination" would give local governments license to create a patchwork of racial preferences based on statistical generalizations about any particular field of endeavor.

These defects are readily apparent in this case. The 30% quota cannot in any realistic sense be tied to any injury suffered by anyone. The District Court relied upon five predicate "facts" in reaching its conclusion that there was an adequate basis for the 30% quota: (1) the ordinance declares itself to be remedial; (2) several proponents of the measure stated their views that there had been past discrimination in the construction industry; (3) minority businesses received .67% of prime contracts from the city while minorities constituted 50% of the city's population; (4) there were very few minority contractors in local and state contractors' associations; and (5) in 1977, Congress made a determination that the effects of past discrimination had stifled minority participation in the construction industry nationally. . . .

None of these "findings," singly or together, provide the city of Richmond with a "strong basis in evidence for its conclusion that remedial action was necessary." . . . There is nothing approaching a prima facie case of a constitutional or statutory violation by *anyone* in the Richmond construction industry. . . .

The District Court accorded great weight to the fact that the city council designated the Plan as "remedial." But the mere recitation of a "benign" or legitimate purpose for a racial classification, is entitled to little or no weight. . . . Racial classifications are suspect, and that means that simple legislative assurances of good intention cannot suffice.

The District Court also relied on the highly conclusionary statement of a proponent of the Plan that there was racial discrimination in the construction industry "in this area, and the State, and around the nation." . . . It also noted that the city manager had related his view that racial discrimination still plagued the construction industry in his home city of Pittsburg. . . . These statements are of little probative value in establishing identified discrimination in the Richmond construction industry. The factfinding process of legislative bodies is generally entitled to a presumption of regularity and deferential review by the judiciary. . . . But when a legislative body chooses to employ a suspect classification, it cannot rest upon a generalized assertion as to the classification's relevance to its goals. . . . A governmental actor cannot render race a legitimate proxy for a particular condition merely by declaring that the condition exists. . . . The history of racial classifications in this country suggests that blind judicial deference to legislative or executive pronouncements of necessity has no place in equal protection analysis. . . .

Reliance on the disparity between the number of prime contracts awarded to minority firms and the minority population of the city of Richmond is similarly misplaced. There is no doubt that "[w]here gross statistical disparities can be shown, they alone in a proper case may constitute prima facie proof of a pattern or practice of discrimination" under Title VII. . . . But it is equally clear that "[w]hen special qualifications are required to fill particular jobs, comparisons to the general population (rather than to the smaller group of individuals who possess the necessary qualifications) may have little probative value." . . .

In the employment context, we have recognized that for certain entry level positions or positions requiring minimal training, statistical comparisons of the racial composition of an employer's workforce to the racial composition of the relevant population may be probative of a pattern of discrimination. . . . But where special qualifications are necessary, the relevant statistical pool for purposes of demonstrating discriminatory exclusion must be the number of minorities qualified to undertake the particular task. . . .

In this case, the city does not even know how many MBEs in the relevant market are qualified to undertake prime or subcontracting work in public construction projects. . . . Nor does the city know what percentage of total city construction dollars minority firms now receive as subcontractors on prime contracts let by the city.

To a large extent, the set-aside of subcontracting dollars seems to rest on the unsupported assumption that white prime contractors simply will not hire minority firms. . . . Indeed, there is evidence in this record that overall minority participation in city contracts in Richmond is seven to eight percent, and that minority contractor participation in Community Block Development Grant *construction* projects is 17% to 22%. . . . Without any information on minority participation in subcontracting, it is quite simply impossible to evaluate overall minority representation in the city's construction expenditures.

The city and the District Court also relied on evidence that MBE membership in local contractors' associations was extremely low. Again, standing alone this evidence is not probative of any discrimination in the local construction industry. There are numerous explanations for this dearth of minority participation, including past societal discrimination in education and economic opportunities as well as both black and white career and entrepreneurial choices. Blacks may be disproportionately attracted to industries other than construction. . . . The mere fact that black membership in these trade organizations is low, standing alone, cannot establish a prima facie case of discrimination.

In sum, none of the evidence presented by the city points to any identified discrimination in the Richmond construction industry. We, therefore, hold that the city has failed to demonstrate a compelling interest in apportioning public contracting opportunities on the basis of race. To accept Richmond's claim that past societal discrimination alone can serve as the basis for rigid racial preferences would be to open the door to competing claims for "remedial relief" for every disadvantaged group. The dream of a Nation of equal citizens in a society where race is irrelevant to personal opportunity and achievement would be lost in a mosaic of shifting preferences based on inherently unmeasurable claims of past wrongs. . . .

The foregoing analysis applies only to the inclusion of blacks within the Richmond set-aside program. There is *absolutely no evidence* of past discrimination against Spanish-speaking, Oriental, Indian, Eskimo, or Aleut persons in any aspect of the Richmond construction industry. The District Court took judicial notice of the fact that the vast majority of "minority" persons in Richmond were black. . . . It may well be that Richmond has never had an Aleut or Eskimo citizen. The random inclusion of racial groups that, as a practical matter, may never have suffered from discrimination in the construction industry in Richmond, suggests that perhaps the city's purpose was not in fact to remedy past discrimination.

If a 30% set-aside was "narrowly tailored" to compensate black contractors for past discrimination, one may legitimately ask why they are forced to share this "remedial relief" with an Aleut citizen who moves to Richmond tomorrow? The gross overinclusiveness of Richmond's racial preference strongly impugns the city's claim of remedial motivation. . . .

As noted by the court below, it is almost impossible to assess whether the Richmond Plan is narrowly tailored to remedy prior discrimination since it is not linked to identified discrimination in any way. We limit ourselves to two observations in this regard.

First, there does not appear to have been any consideration of the use of race-neutral means to increase minority business participation in city contracting. . . .

Many of the barriers to minority participation in the construction industry relied upon by the city to justify a racial classification appear to be race neutral. If MBEs disproportionately lack capital or cannot meet bonding requirements, a race-neutral program of city financing for small firms would, *a fortiori,* lead to greater minority participation. . . . There is no evidence in this record that the Richmond City Council has considered any alternatives to a race-based quota.

Second, the 30% quota cannot be said to be narrowly tailored to any goal, except perhaps outright racial balancing. It rests upon the "completely unrealistic" assumption that minorities will choose a particular trade in lockstep proportion to their representation in the local population. . . .

Since the city must already consider bids and waivers on a case-by-case basis, it is difficult to see the need for a rigid numerical quota. As noted above, the congressional scheme upheld in *Fullilove* allowed for a waiver of the set-aside provision where an MBE's higher price was not attributable to the effect of past discrimination. Based upon proper findings, such programs are less problematic from an equal protection standpoint because they treat all candidates individually, rather than making the color of an applicant's skin the sole relevant consideration. Unlike the program upheld in *Fullilove*, the Richmond Plan's waiver system focuses solely on the availability of MBEs; there is no inquiry into whether or not the particular MBE seeking a racial preference has suffered from the effects of past discrimination by the city or prime contractors.

Given the existence of an individualized procedure, the city's only interest in maintaining a quota system rather than investigating the need for remedial action in particular cases would seem to be simple administrative convenience. But the interest in avoiding the bureaucratic effort necessary to tailor remedial relief to those who truly have suffered the effects of prior discrimination cannot justify a rigid line drawn on the basis of a suspect classification. . . . Under Richmond's scheme, a successful black, Hispanic, or Oriental entrepreneur from anywhere in the country enjoys an absolute preference over other citizens based solely on their race. We think it obvious that such a program is not narrowly tailored to remedy the effects of prior discrimination. . . .

Because the city of Richmond has failed to identify the need for remedial action in the awarding of its public construction contracts, its treatment of its citizens on a racial basis violates the dictates of the Equal Protection Clause. Accordingly, the judgment of the Court of Appeals for the Fourth Circuit is

Affirmed.

Justice Scalia, concurring in the judgment.

I agree with much of the Court's opinion, and, in particular, with its conclusion that strict scrutiny must be applied to all governmental classification by race, whether or not its asserted purpose is "remedial" or "benign." . . . I do not agree, however, with the Court's dicta suggesting that, despite the Fourteenth Amendment, state and local governments may in some circumstances discriminate on the basis of race in order (in a broad sense) "to ameliorate the effects of past discrimination."The difficulty of overcoming the effects of past discrimination is as nothing compared with the difficulty of eradicating from our society the source of those effects, which is the tendency—fatal to a nation such as ours—to classify and judge men and women on the basis of their country of origin or the color of their skin. A solution to the first problem that aggravates the second is no solution at all. I share the view expressed by Alexander Bickel that "[t]he lesson of the great decisions of the Supreme Court and the lesson of contemporary history have been the same for at least a generation: discrimination on the basis of race is illegal, immoral, unconstitutional, inherently wrong, and destructive of democratic society." A. Bickel, The Morality of Consent 133 (1975). At least where state or local action is at issue, only a social engineering rising to the level of imminent danger to life and limb—for example, a prison race riot, requiring temporary segregation of inmates. . . .—can justify an exception to the principle embodied in the Fourteenth Amendment that "[o]ur Constitution is color-blind, and neither knows nor tolerates classes among citizens," . . .

We have in some contexts approved the use of racial classifications by the Federal Government to remedy the effects of past discrimination. I do not believe that we must or should extend these holdings to the States. . . .

A sound distinction between federal and state (or local) action based on race rests not only upon the substance of the Civil War Amendments, but upon social reality and governmental theory. It is a simple fact that what Justice Stewart described in *Fullilove* as "the dispassionate objectivity [and] the flexibility that are needed to mold a race-conscious remedy around the single objective of eliminating the effects of past or present discrimination" . . . are substantially less likely to exist at the state or local level. The struggle for racial justice has historically been a struggle by the national society against oppression in the individual States. . . . What the record shows, in other words, is that racial discrimination against any group finds a more ready expression at the state and local than at the federal level. To the children of the Founding Fathers, this should come as no surprise. An acute awareness of the heightened danger of oppression from political factions in small, rather than large, political units dates to the very beginning of our national history. . . . As James Madison observed in support of the proposed Constitution's enhancement of national powers:

> "The smaller the society, the fewer probably will be the distinct parties and interests composing it; the fewer the distinct parties and interests, the more frequently will a majority be found of the same party; and the smaller the number of individuals composing a majority, and the smaller the compass within which they are placed, the more easily will they concert and execute their plan of oppression. Extend the sphere and you take in a greater variety of parties and interests; you make it less probable that a majority of the whole will have a common motive to invade the rights of other citizens; or if such a common motive exists, it will be more difficult for all who feel it to discover their own strength and to act in unison with each other." The Federalist No. 10. . . .

The prophesy of these words came to fruition in Richmond in the enactment of a set-aside clearly and directly beneficial to the dominant political group, which happens also to be the dominant racial group. The same thing has no doubt happened before in other cities (though the racial basis of the preference has rarely been made textually explicit)—and blacks have often been on the receiving end of the injustice. Where injustice is the game, however, turn-about is not fair play. . . .

In his final book, Professor Bickel wrote:

> "[A] racial quota derogates the human dignity and individuality of all to whom it is applied; it is invidious in principle as well as in practice. Moreover, it can easily be turned against those it purports to help. The history of the racial quota is a history of subjugation, not beneficence. Its evil lies not in its name, but in its effects: a quota is a divider of society, a creator of castes, and it is all the worse for its racial base, especially in a society desperately striving for an equality that will make race irrelevant." Bickel, The Morality of Consent, at 133.

Those statements are true and increasingly prophetic. Apart from their societal effects, however, which are "in the aggregate disastrous," . . . it is important not to lose sight of the fact that even "benign" racial quotas have individual victims, whose very real injustice we ignore whenever we deny them enforcement of their right not to be disadvantaged on the basis of race. . . . As Justice Douglas observed: "A DeFunis who is white is entitled to no advantage by virtue of that fact; nor is he subject to any disability, no matter what his race or color. Whatever his race, he had a constitutional right to have his application considered on its individual merits in a racially neutral manner." *DeFunis* v. *Odegaard* . . . (1974). When we depart from this American principle we play with fire, and much more than an occasional DeFunis . . . or Croson burns.

It is plainly true that in our society blacks have suffered discrimination immeasurably greater than any directed at other racial groups. But those who believe that racial preferences can help to "even the score" display, and reinforce, a manner of thinking by race that was the source of the injustice and that will, if it endures within our society, be the source of more injustice still. The relevant proposition is not that it was blacks, or Jews, or Irish who were discriminated against, but that it was individual men and women, "created equal," who were discriminated against. And the relevant resolve is that that should never happen again. Racial preferences appear to "even the score" (in some small degree) only if one embraces the proposition that our society is appropriately viewed as divided into races, making it right that an injustice rendered in the past to a black man should be compensated for by discriminating against a white. Nothing is worth that embrace. Since blacks have been disproportionately disadvantaged by racial discrimination, any race-neutral remedial program aimed at the disadvantaged *as such* will have a disproportionately beneficial impact on blacks. Only such a program, and not one that operates on the basis of race, is in accord with the letter and the spirit of our Constitution.

Since I believe that the appellee here had a constitutional right to have its bid succeed or fail under a decisionmaking process uninfected with racial bias, I concur in the judgment of the Court.

JUSTICE STEVENS, concurring in part and concurring in the judgment. . . .

The ordinance is . . . vulnerable because of its failure to identify the characteristics of the disadvantaged class of white contractors that justify the disparate treatment. . . . The composition of the disadvantaged class of white contractors presumably includes some who have been guilty of unlawful discrimination, some who practiced discrimination before it was forbidden by law, and some who have never discriminated against anyone on the basis of race. Imposing a common burden on such a disparate class merely because each member of the class is of the same race stems from reliance on a stereotype rather than fact or reason.

There is a special irony in the stereotypical thinking that prompts legislation of this kind. Although it stigmatizes the disadvantaged class with the unproven charge of past racial discrimination, it actually imposes a greater stigma on its supposed beneficiaries. For, as I explained in my *Fullilove* opinion:

> "[E]ven though it is not the actual predicate for this legislation, a statute of this kind inevitably is perceived by many as resting on an assumption that those who are granted this special preference are less qualified in some respect that is identified purely by their race." . . .
>
> "The risk that habitual attitudes toward classes of persons, rather than analysis of the relevant characteristics of the class, will serve as a basis for a legislative classification is present when benefits are distributed as well as when burdens are imposed. In the past, traditional attitudes too often provided the only explanation for discrimination against women, aliens, illegitimates, and black citizens. Today there is a danger that awareness of past injustice will lead to automatic acceptance of new classifications that are not in fact justified by attributes characteristic of the class as a whole.
>
> "When [government] creates a special preference, or a special disability, for a class of persons, it should identify the characteristic that justifies the special treatment. When the classification is defined in racial terms, I believe that such particular identification is imperative.
>
> "In this case, only two conceivable bases for differentiating the preferred classes from society as a whole have occurred to me: (1) that they were the victims of unfair treatment in the past and (2) that they are less able to compete in the future. Although the first of these factors would justify an appropriate remedy for past wrongs, for reasons that I have already stated, this statute is not such a remedial measure. The second factor is simply not true. Nothing in the record of this case, the legislative history of the Act, or experience that we may notice judicially provides any support for such a proposition."

JUSTICE MARSHALL, with whom JUSTICE BRENNAN and JUSTICE BLACKMUN join, dissenting

It is a welcome symbol of racial progress when the former capital of the Confederacy acts forthrightly to confront the effects of racial discrimination in its midst. In my view, nothing in the Constitution can be construed to prevent Richmond, Virginia, from allocating a portion of its contracting dollars for businesses owned or controlled by members of minority groups. Indeed, Richmond's set-aside program is indistinguishable in all meaningful respects from—and in fact was patterned upon—the federal set-aside plan which this Court upheld in *Fullilove* v. *Klutznick*. . . .

A majority of this Court holds today, however, that the Equal Protection Clause of the Fourteenth Amendment blocks Richmond's initiative. The essence of the majority's position is that Richmond has failed to catalogue adequate findings to prove that past discrimination has impeded minorities from joining or participating fully in Richmond's construction contracting industry. I find deep irony in second-guessing Richmond's judgment on this point. As much as any municipality in the United States, Richmond knows what racial discrimination is; a century of decisions by this and other federal courts has richly documented the city's disgraceful history of public and private racial discrimination. In any event, the Richmond City Council *has* supported its determination that minorities have been wrongly excluded from local construction contracting. Its proof includes statistics showing that minority-owned businesses have received virtually no city contracting dollars and rarely if ever belonged to area trade associations; testimony by municipal officials that discrimination has been widespread in the local construction industry; and the same exhaustive and widely publicized federal studies relied on in *Fullilove,* studies which showed that pervasive discrimination in the Nation's tight-knit construction industry had operated to exclude minorities from public contracting. These are precisely the types of statistical and testimonial evidence which, until today, this Court had credited in cases approving of race-conscious measures designed to remedy past discrimination.

More fundamentally, today's decision marks a deliberate and giant step backward in this Court's affirmative action jurisprudence. Cynical of one municipality's attempt to redress the effects of past racial discrimination in a particular industry, the majority launches a grapeshot attack on race-conscious remedies in general. The majority's unnecessary pronouncements will inevitably discourage or prevent governmental entities, particularly States and localities, from acting to rectify the scourge of past discrimination. This is the harsh reality of the majority's decision, but it is not the Constitution's command. . . . My view has long been that race-conscious classifications designed to further remedial goals "must serve important governmental objectives and must be substantially related to achievement of those objectives" in order to withstand constitutional scrutiny. . . . Analyzed in terms of this two-prong standard, Richmond's set-aside, like the federal program on which it was modeled, is "plainly constitutional." . . .

Turning first to the governmental interest inquiry, Richmond has two powerful interests in setting aside a portion of public contracting funds for minority-owned enterprises. The first is the city's interest in eradicating the effects of past racial discrimination. It is far too late in the day to doubt that remedying such discrimination is a compelling, let alone an important, interest. . . .

Richmond has a second compelling interest in setting aside, where possible, a portion of its contracting dollars. That interest is the prospective one of preventing the city's own spending decisions from reinforcing and perpetuating the exclusionary effects of past discrimination.

. . . When government channels all its contracting funds to a white-dominated community of established contractors whose racial homogeneity is the product of private discrimination, it does more than place its imprimatur on the practices which forged and which continue to define that community. It also provides a measurable boost to those economic entities that have thrived within it, while denying important economic benefits to those entities which, but for prior discrimination, might well be better qualified to receive valuable government contracts. In my view, the interest in ensuring that the government does not reflect and reinforce prior private discrimination in dispensing public contracts is every bit as strong as the interest in eliminating private discrimination—an interest which this Court has repeatedly deemed compelling. . . . The more government bestows its rewards on those persons or businesses that were positioned to thrive during a period of private racial discrimination, the tighter the deadhand grip of prior discrimination becomes on the present and future. Cities like Richmond may not be constitutionally required to adopt set-aside plans. . . . But there can be no doubt that when Richmond acted affirmatively to stem the perpetuation of patterns of discrimination through its own decisionmaking, it served an interest of the highest order. . . .

In my judgment, Richmond's set-aside plan also comports with the second prong of the equal protection inquiry, for it is substantially related to the interests it seeks to serve in remedying past discrimination and in ensuring that municipal contract procurement does not perpetuate that discrimination. The most striking aspect of the city's ordinance is the similarity it bears to the "appropriately limited" federal set-aside provision upheld in *Fullilove*. . . .

Today, for the first time, a majority of this Court has adopted strict scrutiny as its standard of Equal Protection Clause review of race-conscious remedial measures. . . . This is an unwelcome development. A profound difference separates governmental actions that themselves are racist, and governmental actions that seek to remedy the effects of prior racism or to prevent neutral governmental activity from perpetuating the effects of such racism. . . .

In concluding that remedial classifications warrant no different standard of review under the Constitution than the most brute and repugnant forms of state-sponsored racism, a majority of this Court signals that it regards racial discrimination as largely a phenomenon of the past, and that government bodies need no longer preoccupy themselves with rectifying racial injustice. . . .

I am also troubled by the majority's assertion that, even if it did not believe generally in strict scrutiny of race-based remedial measures, "the circumstances of this case" require this Court to look upon the Richmond City Council's measure with the strictest scrutiny. . . . The sole such circumstance which the majority cites, however, is the fact that blacks in Richmond are a "dominant racial grou[p]" in the city. . . . In support of this characterization of dominance, the majority observes that "blacks comprise approximately 50% of the population of the city of Richmond" and that "[f]ive of the nine seats on the City Council are held by blacks." . . .

While I agree that the numerical and political supremacy of a given racial group is a factor bearing upon the level of scrutiny to be applied, this Court has never held that numerical inferiority, standing alone, makes a racial group "suspect" and thus entitled to strict scrutiny review. . . .

In my view, the "circumstances of this case . . . underscore the importance of *not* subjecting to a strict scrutiny straitjacket the increasing number of cities which have recently come under minority leadership and are eager to rectify, or at least prevent the perpetuation of, past racial discrimination. In many cases, these cases will be the ones with the most in the way of prior discrimination to rectify. Richmond's leaders had just witnessed decades of publicly sanctioned racial discrimination in virtually all walks of life—discrimination amply documented in the decisions of the federal judiciary. . . . This history of "purposefully unequal treatment" forced upon minorities, not imposed by them, should raise an inference that minorities in Richmond had much to remedy—and that the 1983 set-aside was undertaken with sincere remedial goals in mind, not "simple racial politics." . . .

The majority today sounds a full-scale retreat from the Court's longstanding solicitude to race-conscious remedial efforts "directed toward deliverance of the century old promise of equality of economic opportunity." . . . The new and restrictive tests it applies scuttle one city's effort to surmount its discriminatory past, and imperil those of dozens more localities. I, however, profoundly disagree with the cramped vision of the Equal Protection Clause which the majority offers today and with its application of that vision to Richmond, Virginia's, laudable set-aside plan. The battle against pernicious racial discrimination or its effects is nowhere near won. I must dissent.

Foley v. *Connelie*

435 U.S. 291; 98 S. Ct. 1067; 55 L. Ed. 2d 287 (1978)

Edmund Foley, a lawfully admitted resident alien, applied for appointment as a New York state trooper, a position filled on the basis of competitive examinations. State authorities refused to allow Foley to take the examination, on the basis of a New York statute that provided that "no person shall be appointed to the New York state police force unless he shall be a citizen of the United States." Foley thereupon brought a class action suit in federal district court against the superintendent of the New York state police, seeking a declaratory judgment that the statute in question violated the Equal Protection Clause of the Fourteenth Amendment. A three-judge district court held the statute to be constitutional, and Foley appealed. *Opinion of the Court: Burger, Powell, Rehnquist, Stew-*

art, White. Concurring in result: Blackmun. Dissenting opinions: Marshall, Brennan, Stevens; Stevens, Brennan.

MR. CHIEF JUSTICE BURGER delivered the opinion of the Court. . . .

Appellant claims that the relevant New York statute violates his rights under the Equal Protection Clause.

The decisions of this Court with regard to the rights of aliens living in our society have reflected fine, and often difficult, questions of values. As a Nation we exhibit extraordinary hospitality to those who come to our country, which is not surprising for we have often been described as "a nation of immigrants." Indeed, aliens lawfully residing in this society have many rights which are accorded to noncitizens by few other countries. Our cases generally reflect a close scrutiny of restraints imposed by States on aliens. But we have never suggested that such legislation is inherently invalid, nor have we held that all limitations on aliens are suspect. . . . Rather, beginning with a case which involved the denial of welfare assistance essential to life itself, the Court has treated certain restrictions on aliens with "heightened judicial solicitude," *Graham* v. *Richardson* . . . (1971), a treatment deemed necessary since aliens—pending their eligibility for citizenship—have no direct voice in the political processes.

It would be inappropriate, however, to require every statutory exclusion of aliens to clear the high hurdle of "strict scrutiny," because to do so would "obliterate all the distinctions between citizens and aliens and thus depreciate the historic values of citizenship." . . . The act of becoming a citizen is more than a ritual with no content beyond the fanfare of ceremony. A new citizen has become a member of a Nation, part of a people distinct from others. . . . The individual, at that point, belongs to the polity and is entitled to participate in the processes of democratic decisionmaking. Accordingly, we have recognized "a State's historical power to exclude aliens from participation in its democratic political institutions" . . . as part of the sovereign's obligation " 'to preserve the basic conception of a political community.' " . . .

The practical consequence of this theory is that "our scrutiny will not be so demanding where we deal with matters firmly within a State's constitutional prerogatives." . . . The State need only justify its classification by a showing of some rational relationship between the interest sought to be protected and the limiting classification. This is not intended to denigrate the valuable contribution of aliens who benefit from our traditional hospitality. It is no more than recognition of the fact that a democratic society is ruled by its people. Thus, it is clear that a State may deny aliens the right to vote, or to run for elective office, for these lie at the heart of our political institutions. . . . Similar considerations support a legislative determination to exclude aliens from jury service. . . . Likewise, we have recognized that citizenship may be a relevant qualification for fulfilling those "important nonelective executive, legislative, and judicial positions," held by "officers who participate directly in the formulation, execution, or review of broad public policy." . . . This is not because our society seeks to reserve the better jobs to its members. Rather, it is because this country entrusts many of its most important policy responsibilities to these officers, the discretionary exercise of which can often more immediately affect the lives of citizens than even the ballot of a voter or the choice of a legislator. In sum, then, it represents the choice, and right, of the people to be governed by their citizen peers. To effectuate this result, we must necessarily examine each position in question to determine whether it involves discretionary decisionmaking, or execution of policy, which substantially affects members of the political community.

The essence of our holdings to date is that although we extend to aliens the right to education and public welfare, along with the ability to earn a livelihood and engage in licensed professions, the right to govern is reserved to citizens. . . .

A discussion of the police function is essentially a description of one of the basic functions of government, especially in a complex modern society where police presence is pervasive. The police function fulfills a most fundamental obligation of government to its constituency. Police officers in the ranks do not formulate policy, *per se,* but they are clothed with authority to exercise an almost infinite variety of discretionary powers. The execution of the broad powers vested in them affects members of the public significantly and often in the most sensitive areas of daily life. . . .

Clearly, the exercise of police authority calls for a very high degree of judgment and discretion, the abuse or misuse of which can have serious impact on individuals. . . . A policeman vested with the plenary discretionary powers we have described is not to be equated with a private person engaged in routine public employment or other "common occupations of the community" who exercises no broad power over people generally. Indeed, the rationale for the qualified immunity historically granted to the police rests on the difficult and delicate judgments these officers must often make. . . .

In short, it would be as anomalous to conclude that citizens may be subjected to the broad discretionary powers of noncitizen police officers as it would be to say that judicial officers and jurors with power to judge citizens can be aliens. It is not surprising, therefore, that most States expressly confine the employment of police officers to citizens, whom the State may reasonably presume to be more familiar with and sympathetic to American traditions. Police officers very clearly fall within the category of "important nonelective . . . officers who participate directly in the . . . *execution* . . . of broad public policy." . . . In the enforcement and execution of the laws the police function is one where citizenship bears a rational relationship to the special demands of the particular position. A State may, therefore, consonant with the Constitution, confine the performance of this important public responsibility to citizens of the United States.

Accordingly, the judgment of the District Court is

Affirmed.

MR. JUSTICE STEWART, concurring.

The dissenting opinions convincingly demonstrate that it is difficult if not impossible to reconcile the Court's judgment in this case with the full sweep of the reasoning and authority of some of our past decisions. It is only because I have become increasingly doubtful about the validity of those decisions (in at least some of which I concurred) that I join the opinion of the Court in this case.

MR. JUSTICE MARSHALL, with whom MR. JUSTICE BRENNAN and MR. JUSTICE STEVENS join, dissenting. . . .

Today the Court upholds a law excluding aliens from public employment as state troopers. It [argues] . . . that aliens may be barred from holding "state elective or important nonelective executive, legislative, and judicial positions," because persons in these positions "participate directly in the formulation, execution, or review of broad public policy." . . . I do not agree with the Court that state troopers perform functions placing them within this "narro[w] . . . exception" . . . to our usual rule that discrimination against aliens is presumptively unconstitutional. Accordingly I dissent. . . .

There is a vast difference between the formulation and execution of broad public policy and the application of that policy to specific factual settings. While the Court is correct that "the exercise of police authority calls for a very high degree of judgment and discretion," . . . the judgments required are factual in nature; the policy judgments that govern an officer's conduct are contained in the Federal and State Constitutions, statutes, and regulations. . . . It is . . . not a denigration of the important public role of the state trooper—who, as the Court notes, . . . operates "in the most sensitive areas of daily life"—to find that his law enforcement responsibilities do not "make him a formulator of governmental policy." . . . Since no other rational reason, let alone a compelling state interest, has been advanced in support of the statute here at issue, I would hold that the statute's exclusion of aliens from state trooper positions violates the Equal Protection Clause of the Fourteenth Amendment.

MR. JUSTICE STEVENS, with whom MR. JUSTICE BRENNAN joins, dissenting.

. . . What is the group characteristic that justifies the unfavorable treatment of an otherwise qualified individual simply because he is an alien?

No one suggests that aliens as a class lack the intelligence or the courage to serve the public as police officers. The disqualifying characteristic is apparently a foreign allegiance which raises a doubt concerning trustworthiness and loyalty so pervasive that a flat ban against the employment of any alien in any law enforcement position is thought to be justified. But if the integrity of all aliens is suspect, why may not a State deny aliens the right to practice law? Are untrustworthy or disloyal lawyers more tolerable than untrustworthy or disloyal policemen? Or is the legal profession better able to detect such characteristics on an individual basis than is the police department? Unless the Court repudiates its holding in *In re Griffiths* [1973], . . . it must reject any conclusive presumption that aliens, as a class, are disloyal or untrustworthy.

. . .The Court . . . should not uphold a statutory discrimination against aliens, as a class, without expressly identifying the group characteristic that justifies the discrimination. If the unarticulated characteristic is concern about possible disloyalty, it must equally disqualify aliens from the practice of law; yet the Court does not question the continuing vitality of its decision in *Griffiths.* Or if that characteristic is the fact that aliens do not participate in our democratic decisionmaking process, it is irrelevant to eligibility for this category of public service. If there is no group characteristic that explains the discrimination, one can only conclude that it is without any justification that has not already been rejected by the Court.

Trimble v. *Gordon*

430 U.S. 762; 97 S. Ct. 1459, 52 L. Ed. 2d 31 (1977)

According to Section 12 of the Illinois Probate Act, illegitimate children could inherit by intestate succession only from their mothers, whereas legitimate children could inherit by intestate succession from both their mothers and their fathers. When Sherman Gordon died intestate, an Illinois probate court, acting under the authority of Section 12, rejected the claim to heirship of Deta Trimble, Gordon's illegitimate daughter. After the Illinois Supreme Court dismissed her challenge to the constitutionality of Section 12, she appealed to the United States Supreme Court. *Opinion of the Court: Powell, Brennan, Marshall, Stevens, White. Dissenting opinions: Burger, Blackmun, Rehnquist, Stewart; Rehnquist.*

MR. JUSTICE POWELL delivered the opinion of the Court. . . .

. . . In weighing the constitutional sufficiency of these justifications, we are guided by our previous decisions involving equal protection challenges to laws discriminating on the basis of illegitimacy. "[T]his Court requires, at a minimum, that a statutory classification bear some rational relationship to a legitimate state purpose." *Weber* v. *Aetna Casualty & Surety Co.* . . . (1972). In this context, the standard just stated is a minimum; the Court sometimes requires more. "Though the latitude given state economic and social regulation is necessarily broad, when state statutory classifications approach sensitive and fundamental personal rights, this Court exercises a stricter scrutiny . . ." *Ibid.*

Appellants urge us to hold that classifications based on illegitimacy are "suspect," so that any justifications must survive "strict scrutiny." We considered and rejected a similar argument last Term in *Mathews* v. *Lucas* . . . (1976). As we recognized in *Lucas,* illegitimacy is analogous in many respects to the personal characteristics that have been held to be suspect when used as the basis of statutory differentiations. . . . We nevertheless concluded that the analogy was not sufficient to require "our most exacting scrutiny." . . . Despite the conclusion that classifications based on illegitimacy fall in a "realm of less than strictest scrutiny," *Lucas* also establishes that the scrutiny "is not a toothless one," . . . a proposition clearly demonstrated by our previous decisions in this area. . . .

The Illinois Supreme Court relied in part on the State's purported interest in "the promotion of [legitimate] family relationships." . . .

In a case like this, the Equal Protection Clause requires more than the mere incantation of a proper state purpose. No one disputes the appropriateness of Illinois' concern with the family unit, perhaps the most fundamental social institution of our society. The flaw in the analysis lies elsewhere. As we said in *Lucas,* the constitutionality of this law "depends upon the character of the discrimination and its relation to legitimate legislative aims." . . . We have expressly considered and [reject] the argument that a State may attempt to influence the actions of men and women by imposing sanctions on the children born of their illegitimate relationships. . . .

The Illinois Supreme Court also noted that the decedents whose estates were involved in the consolidated appeals could have left substantial parts of their estates to their illegitimate children by writing a will. . . .

By focusing on the steps that an intestate might have taken to assure some inheritance for his illegitimate children, the analysis loses sight of the essential question: the constitutionality of discrimination against illegitimates in a state intestate succession law. If the decedent had written a will devising property to his illegitimate child, the case no longer would involve intestate succession law at all. . . .

Finally, appellees urge us to affirm the decision below on the theory that the Illinois Probate Act, including § 12, mirrors the presumed intentions of the citizens of the State regarding the disposition of their property at death. Individualizing this theory, appellees argue that we must assume that Sherman Gordon knew the disposition of his estate under the Illinois Probate Act and that his failure to make a will shows his approval of that disposition. We need not resolve the question whether presumed intent alone can ever justify discrimination against illegitimates, for we do not think that § 12 was enacted for this purpose. . . . We find in § 12 a primary purpose to provide a system of intestate succession more just to illegitimate children than the prior law, a purpose tempered by a secondary interest in protecting against spurious claims of paternity. In the absence of a more convincing demonstration, we will not hypothesize an additional state purpose that has been ignored by the Illinois Supreme Court. . . .

For the reasons stated above, we conclude that § 12 of the Illinois Probate Act cannot be squared with the command of the Equal Protection Clause of the Fourteenth Amendment. Accordingly, we reverse the judgment of the Illinois Supreme Court and remand the case for further proceedings not inconsistent with this opinion. . . .

MR. JUSTICE REHNQUIST, dissenting.

The Fourteenth Amendment's prohibition against "any State . . . deny[ing] to any person . . . the equal protection of the laws" is undoubtedly one of the majestic generalities of the Constitution. If, during the period of more than a century since its adoption, this Court had developed a consistent body of doctrine which could reasonably be said to expound the intent of those who drafted and adopted the Clause of the Amendment, there would be no cause for judicial complaint, however unwise or incapable of effective administration one might find those intentions. If, on the other hand, recognizing that those who drafted and adopted this language had rather imprecise notions about what it meant, the Court had evolved a body of doctrine which both was consistent and served some arguable useful purpose, there would likewise be little cause for great dissatisfaction with the existing state of the law.

Unfortunately, more than a century of decisions under this Clause of the Fourteenth Amendment have produced neither of these results. They have instead produced a syndrome wherein this Court seems to regard the Equal Protection Clause as a cat-o'-nine-tails to be kept in the judicial closet as a threat to legislatures which may, in the view of the judiciary, get out of hand and pass "arbitrary," "illogical," or "unreasonable" laws. Except in the area of the law in which the Framers obviously meant it to apply—classifications based on race or on national origin, the first cousin of race—the Court's decisions can fairly be described as an endless tinkering with legislative judgments, a series of conclusions unsupported by any central guiding principle.

. . . In providing the Court with the duty of enforcing such generalities as the Equal Protection Clause, the Framers of the Civil War Amendments placed it in the position of Adam in the Garden of Eden. As members of a tripartite institution of government which is responsible to no constituency, and which is held back only by its own sense of self-restraint, . . . we are constantly subjected to the human temptation to hold that any law containing a number of imperfections denies equal protection simply because those who drafted it could have made it a fairer or a better law. The Court's opinion in the instant case is no better and no worse than the long series of cases in this line, a line which unfortunately proclaims that the Court has indeed succumbed to the temptation implicit in the Amendment.

The Equal Protection Clause is itself a classic paradox, and makes sense only in the context of a recently fought Civil War. It creates a requirement of equal treatment to be applied to the process of legislation—legislation whose very purpose is to draw lines in such a way that different people are treated differently. The problem presented is one of sorting the legislative distinctions which are acceptable from those which involve invidiously unequal treatment.

All constitutional provisions for protection of individuals involve difficult questions of line drawing. But most others have implicit within them an understandable value judgment that certain types of conduct have a favored place and are to be protected to a greater or lesser degree. Obvious examples are free speech, freedom from unreasonable search and seizure, and the right to a fair trial. The remaining judicial task in applying those guarantees is to determine whether, on given facts, the constitutional value judgment embodied in such a provision has been offended in a particular case.

In the case of equality and equal protection, the constitutional principle—the thing to be protected to a greater or lesser degree—is not even identifiable from within the four corners of the Constitution. For equal protection does not mean that all persons must be treated alike. Rather, its general principle is that persons similarly situated should be treated similarly. But that statement of the rule does little to determine whether or not a question of equality is even involved in a given case. For the crux of the problem is *whether persons are similarly situated* for the purposes of the state action in issue. Nothing in the words of the Fourteenth Amendment specifically addresses this question in any way.

The essential problem of the Equal Protection Clause is therefore the one of determining where the courts are to look for guidance in defining "equality" as that word is used in the Fourteenth Amendment. Since the Amendment grew out of the Civil War and the freeing of the slaves, the core prohibition was early held to be aimed at the protection of blacks. . . . If race was an invalid sorting tool where blacks were concerned, it followed logically that it should not be valid where other races were concerned either. . . . A logical, though not inexorable, next step, was the extension of the projection to prohibit classifications resting on national origin. . . .

The presumptive invalidity of all of these classifications has made decisions involving them, for the most part, relatively easy. But when the Court has been required to adjudicate equal protection claims not based on race or national origin, it has faced a much more difficult task. . . .

Illegitimacy, which is involved in this case, has never been held by the Court to be a "suspect classification." Nonetheless, in several opinions of the Court, statements are found which suggest that although illegitimates are not members of a "suspect class," laws which treat them differently from those born in wedlock will receive a more far-reaching scrutiny under the Equal Protection Clause than will other laws regulating economic and social conditions. . . . The Court's opinion today contains language to that effect. . . . In one sense this language is a source of consolation, since it suggests that parts of the Court's analysis used in this case will not be carried over to traditional "rational basis" or "minimum scrutiny" cases. At the same time, though, it is a source of confusion, since the unanswered question remains as to the precise sort of scrutiny to which classifications based on illegitimacy will be subject. . . .

The "difficulty" of the "judicial task" is, I suggest, a self-imposed one, stemming not from the Equal Protection Clause but from the Court's insistence on reading so much into it. I do not see how it can be doubted that the purpose (in the ordinary sense of that word) of the Illinois Legislature in enacting § 12 of the Illinois Probate Act was to make the language contained in that section a part of the Illinois law. I presume even the Court will concede that this purpose was accomplished. It was this particular language which the Illinois Legislature, by the required vote of both of its houses and the signature of the Governor, enacted into law. The use of the word "purpose" in today's opinion actually expands the normal meaning of the word into something more like motive. Indeed, the Court says that the law "must be considered in light of this motivating purpose." . . . The question of what "motivated" the various individual legislators to vote for this particular section of the Probate Act, and the Governor of Illinois to sign it, is an extremely complex and difficult one to answer even if it were relevant to the constitutional question. . . . This Court . . . takes it upon itself to inquire into whether the Act in question accomplished the "purpose" which the Court first determines the legislature had in mind. It should be apparent that litigants who wish to succeed in invalidating a law under the Equal Protection Clause must have a certain schizophrenia if they are to be successful in their advocacy: They must first convince this Court that the legislature had a particular purpose in mind in enacting the law, and then convince it that the law was not at all suited to the accomplishment of that purpose.

But a graver defect than this in the Court's analysis is that it also requires a conscious second-guessing of legislative judgment in an area where this Court has no special expertise whatever. Even assuming that a court has properly accomplished the difficult task of identifying the "purpose" which a statute seeks to serve, it then sits in judgment to consider the so-called "fit" between that "purpose" and the statutory means adopted to achieve it. In most cases, and all but invariably if the Court insists on singling out a unitary "purpose," the "fit" will involve a greater or lesser degree of imperfection. Then the Court asks itself: How much "imperfection" between means and ends is permissible? In making this judgment it must throw into the judicial hopper the whole range of factors which were first thrown into the legislative hopper. What alternatives were reasonably available? What reasons are there for the legislature to accomplish this "purpose" in the way it did? What obstacles stood in the way of other solutions?

The fundamental flaw, to me, in this approach is that there is absolutely nothing to be implied from the fact that we hold judicial commissions that would enable us to answer any one of these questions better than the legislators to whose initial decision they were committed. Without any antecedent constitutional mandate, we have created on the premises of the Equal Protection Clause a school for legislators, whereby opinions of this Court are written to instruct them in a better understanding of how to accomplish their ordinary legislative tasks.

Here the Illinois Legislature was dealing with a problem of intestate succession of illegitimates from their fathers, which as the Court concedes frequently presents difficult problems of proof. The provisions of Illinois Probate Act § 12, as most recently amended, alleviate some of the difficulties which previously stood in the way of such succession. The fact that the Act in question does not alleviate all of the difficulties, or that it might have gone further than it did, is to me wholly irrelevant under the Equal Protection Clause. The circumstances which justify the distinction between illegitimates and legitimates contained in § 12 are apparent with no great exercise of imagination; they are stated in the opinion of the Court, though they are there rejected as constitutionally insufficient. Since Illinois' distinction is not mindless and patently irrational, I would affirm the judgment of the Supreme Court of Illinois.

Massachusetts Board of Retirement v. *Murgia*

427 U.S. 307; 96 S. Ct. 2562; 49 L. Ed. 2d 520 (1976)

Robert Murgia, a uniformed officer in the Massachusetts State Police who was in excellent physical and mental health, was forced by state law to retire upon reaching his fiftieth birthday. He challenged the constitutionality of this law, arguing that such compulsory retirement discriminated on the basis of age in violation of the Equal Protection Clause. A three-judge federal district court agreed, holding that the statute lacked "a rational basis in furthering any substantial state interest." The Retirement Board appealed. *Per Curiam: Blackmun, Brennan, Burger, Powell,*

Rehnquist, Stewart, White. Dissenting opinion: Marshall. Not participating: Stevens.

PER CURIAM. . . .

. . . Uniformed state officers [must] pass a comprehensive physical examination biennially until age 40. After that, until mandatory retirement at age 50, uniformed officers must pass annually a more rigorous examination, including an electrocardiogram and tests for gastro-intestinal bleeding. Appellee Murgia had passed such an examination four months before he was retired, and there is no dispute that, when he retired, his excellent physical and mental health still rendered him capable of performing the duties of a uniformed officer.

The record includes the testimony of three physicians . . . that clearly established that the risk of physical failure, particularly in the cardiovascular system, increases with age, and that the number of individuals in a given age group incapable of performing stress functions increases with the age of the group. . . .

In assessing appellee's equal protection claim, the District Court found it unnecessary to apply a strict-scrutiny test, . . . for it determined that the age classification established by the Massachusetts statutory scheme could not in any event withstand a test of rationality. . . . Since there had been no showing that reaching age 50 forecasts even "imminent change" in an officer's physical condition, the District Court held that compulsory retirement at age 50 was irrational under a scheme that assessed the capabilities of officers individually by means of comprehensive annual physical examinations. We agree that rationality is the proper standard by which to test whether compulsory retirement at age 50 violates equal protection. We disagree, however, with the District Court's determination that the age 50 classification is not rationally related to furthering a legitimate state interest.

. . . Equal protection analysis requires strict scrutiny of a legislative classification only when the classification impermissibly interferes with the exercise of a fundamental right or operates to the peculiar disadvantage of a suspect class. Mandatory retirement at age 50 under the Massachusetts statute involves neither situation.

This Court's decisions give no support to the proposition that a right of governmental employment *per se* is fundamental. . . . Accordingly, we have expressly stated that a standard less than strict scrutiny "has consistently been applied to state legislation restricting the availability of employment opportunities."

Nor does the class of uniformed state police officers over 50 constitute a suspect class for purposes of equal protection analysis. . . . A suspect class is one "saddled with such disabilities, or subjected to such a history of purposeful unequal treatment, or relegated to such a position of political powerlessness as to command extraordinary protection from the majoritarian political process." While the treatment of the aged in this Nation has not been wholly free of discrimination, such persons, unlike, say, those who have been discriminated against on the basis of race or national origin, have not experienced a "history of purposeful unequal treatment" or been subjected to unique disabilities on the basis of stereotyped characteristics not truly indicative of their abilities. The class subject to the compulsory retirement feature of the Massachusetts statute consists of uniformed state police officers over the age of 50. It cannot be said to discriminate only against the elderly. Rather, it draws the line at a certain age in middle life. But even old age does not define a "discrete and insular" group . . . in need of "extraordinary protection from the majoritarian political process." Instead, it marks a stage that each of us will reach if we live out our normal span. Even if the statute could be said to impose a penalty upon a class defined as the aged, it would not impose a distinction sufficiently akin to those classifications that we have found suspect to call for strict judicial scrutiny.

Under the circumstances, it is unnecessary to subject the State's resolution of competing interests in this case to the degree of critical examination that our cases under the Equal Protection Clause recently have characterized as "strict judicial scrutiny." . . .

We turn then to examine this state classification under the rational-basis standard. This inquiry employs a relatively relaxed standard reflecting the Court's awareness that the drawing of lines that create distinctions is peculiarly a legislative task and an unavoidable one. Perfection in making the necessary classifications is neither possible nor necessary. . . . Such action by a legislature is presumed to be valid.

In this case, the Massachusetts statute clearly meets the requirements of the Equal Protection Clause, for the State's classification rationally furthers the purpose identified by the State: Through mandatory retirement at age 50, the legislature seeks to protect the public by assuring physical preparedness of its uniformed police. Since physical ability generally declines with age, mandatory retirement at 50 serves to remove from police service those whose fitness for uniformed work presumptively has diminished with age. This clearly is rationally related to the State's objective. There is no indication that [the statute] has the effect of excluding from service so few officers who are in fact unqualified as to render age 50 a criterion wholly unrelated to the objective of the statute.

That the State chooses not to determine fitness more precisely through individualized testing after age 50 is not to say that the objective of assuring physical fitness is not rationally furthered by a maximum-age limitation. It is only to say that with regard to the interest of all concerned, the State perhaps has not chosen the best means to accomplish this purpose. But where rationality is the test, a State "does not violate the Equal Protection Clause merely because the classifications made by its laws are imperfect." . . .

We do not make light of the substantial economic and psychological effects premature and compulsory retirement can have on an individual; nor do we denigrate the ability of elderly citizens to continue to contribute to society. The problems of retirement have been well documented and are beyond serious dispute. But "[w]e do not decide today that the [Massachusetts statute] is wise, that it best fulfills the relevant social and economic objectives that [Massachusetts] might ideally espouse, or that a more just and humane system could not be devised." . . . We decide only that the system enacted by the Massachusetts legislature does not deny appellee equal protection of the laws. . . .

MR. JUSTICE MARSHALL, dissenting. . . .

Although there are signs that its grasp on the law is weakening, the rigid two-tier model still holds sway as the Court's articulated description of the equal protection test. Again, I must object to its perpetuation. The model's two fixed modes of analysis, strict scrutiny and mere rationality, simply do not describe the inquiry the Court has undertaken—or should undertake—in equal protection cases. Rather, the inquiry has been much more sophisticated and the Court should admit as much. It has focused upon the character of the classification in question, the relative importance to individuals in the class discriminated against of the governmental benefits that they do not receive, and the state interests asserted in support of the classification. . . .

Although the Court outwardly adheres to the two-tier model, it has apparently lost interest in recognizing further "fundamental" rights and "suspect" classes. . . . In my view, this result is the natural consequence of the limitations of the Court's traditional equal protection analysis. If a statute invades a "fundamental" right or discriminates against a "suspect" class, it is subject to strict scrutiny. If a statute is subject to strict scrutiny, the statute always, or nearly always, . . . is struck down. Quite obviously, the only critical decision is whether strict scrutiny should be invoked at all. It should be no surprise, then, that the Court is hesitant to expand the number of categories of rights and classes subject to strict scrutiny, when each expansion involves the invalidation of virtually every classification bearing upon a newly covered category.

But however understandable the Court's hesitancy to invoke strict scrutiny, all remaining legislation should not drop into the bottom tier, and be measured by the mere rationality test. For that test, too, when applied as articulated, leaves little doubt about the outcome; the challenged legislation is always upheld. . . . It cannot be gainsaid that there remain rights, not now classified as "fundamental," that remain vital to the flourishing of a free society, and classes, not now classified as "suspect," that are unfairly burdened by invidious discrimination unrelated to the individual worth of their members. Whatever we call these rights and classes, we simply cannot forgo all judicial protection against discriminatory legislation bearing upon them, but for the rare instances when the legislative choice can be termed "wholly irrelevant" to the legislative goal. . . .

While the Court's traditional articulation of the rational-basis test does suggest just such an abdication, happily the Court's deeds have not matched its words. Time and again, met with cases touching upon the prized rights and burdened classes of our society, the Court has acted only after a reasonably probing look at the legislative goals and means, and at the significance of the personal rights and interests invaded. . . .

But there are problems with deciding cases based on factors not encompassed by the applicable standards. First, the approach is rudderless, affording no notice to interested parties of the standards governing particular cases and giving no firm guidance to judges who, as a consequence, must assess the constitutionality of legislation before them on an *ad hoc* basis. Second, and not unrelatedly, the approach is unpredictable and requires holding this Court to standards it has never publicly adopted. Thus, the approach presents the danger that, as I suggest has happened here, relevant factors will be misapplied or ignored. All interests not "fundamental" and all classes not "suspect" are not the same; and it is time for the Court to drop the pretense that, for purposes of the Equal Protection Clause, they are.

The danger of the Court's verbal adherence to the rigid two-tier test, despite its effective repudiation of that test in the cases, is demonstrated by its efforts here. There is simply no reason why a statute that tells able-bodied police officers, ready and willing to work, that they no longer have the right to earn a living in their chosen profession merely because they are 50 years old should be judged by the same minimal standards of rationality that we use to test economic legislation that discriminates against business interests. . . . Yet, the Court today not only invokes the minimal level of scrutiny, it wrongly adheres to it. Analysis of the three factors I have identified above—the importance of the governmental benefits denied, the character of the class, and the asserted state interests—demonstrates the Court's error.

Whether "fundamental" or not, " 'the right of the individual . . . to engage in any of the common occupations of life' " has been repeatedly recognized by this Court as falling within the concept of liberty guaranteed by the Fourteenth Amendment. . . .

While depriving any government employee of his job is a significant deprivation, it is particularly burdensome when the person deprived is an older citizen. Once terminated, the elderly cannot readily find alternative employment. The lack of work is not only economically damaging, but emotionally and physically draining. Deprived of his status in the community and of the opportunity for meaningful activity, fearful of becoming dependent on others for his support, and lonely in his new-found isolation, the involuntarily retired person is susceptible to physical and emotional ailments as a direct consequence of his enforced idleness. . . .

Not only are the elderly denied important benefits when they are terminated on the basis of age, but the classification of older workers is itself one that merits judicial attention. Whether older workers constitute a "suspect" class or not, it cannot be disputed that they constitute a class subject to repeated and arbitrary discrimination in employment. . . .

Of course, the Court is quite right in suggesting that distinctions exist between the elderly and traditional suspect classes such as Negroes, and between the elderly and "quasi-suspect" classes such as women or illegitimates. The elderly are protected not only by certain anti-discrimination legislation, but by legislation that provides them with positive benefits not enjoyed by the public at large. Moreover, the elderly are not isolated in society, and discrimination against them is not pervasive but is centered primarily in employment. The advantage of a flexible equal protection standard, however, is that it can readily accommodate such variables. The elderly are undoubtedly discriminated against, and when legislation denies them an important benefit—employment—I conclude that to sustain the legislation appellants must show a reasonably substantial interest and a scheme reasonably closely tailored to achieving that interest. . . .

. . . The Commonwealth's mandatory retirement law cannot stand when measured against the significant deprivation the Commonwealth's action works upon the terminated employees. I would affirm the judgment of the District Court.

Frontiero v. *Richardson*

411 U.S. 677; 93 S. Ct. 1764; 36 L. Ed. 2d 583 (1973)

Federal statutes provided that married servicemen would automatically qualify to receive increased quarters allowances and medical and dental benefits for their wives, but that female personnel in the armed services would not receive these fringe benefits unless their husbands were in fact dependent on them for over 50 percent of their support. Sharron Frontiero, a married Air Force officer, brought suit in federal district court against Secretary of Defense Elliott Richardson, challenging this sex-based differential treatment. She argued that it violated the equal protection component of the Due Process Clause of the Fifth Amendment, in that the statutes required a servicewoman to prove the actual dependency of her husband. A three-judge court denied relief, and she appealed. *Judgment of the Court: Brennan, Douglas, Marshall, White. Concurring in the judgment: Powell, Blackmun, Burger; Stewart. Dissenting opinion: Rehnquist.*

MR. JUSTICE BRENNAN announced the judgment of the Court. . . .

At the outset, appellants contend that classifications based upon sex, like classifications based upon race, alienage, and national origin, are inherently suspect and must therefore be subjected to close judicial scrutiny. We agree and, indeed, find at least implicit support for such an approach in our unanimous decision only last Term in *Reed* v. *Reed* . . . (1971). . . .

There can be no doubt that our Nation has had a long and unfortunate history of sex discrimination. Traditionally, such discrimination was rationalized by an attitude of "romantic paternalism" which, in practical effect, put women not on a pedestal, but in a cage. . . .

As a result . . . , our statute books gradually became laden with gross, stereotypical distinctions between the sexes and, indeed, throughout much of the 19th century the position of women in our society was, in many respects, comparable to that of blacks under the pre-Civil War slave codes. Neither slaves nor women could hold office, serve on juries, or bring suit in their own names, and married women traditionally were denied the legal capacity to hold or convey property or to serve as legal guardians of their own children. . . . And although blacks were guaranteed the right to vote in 1870, women were denied even that right—which is itself "preservative of other basic civil and political rights'—until adoption on the Nineteenth Amendment half a century later. It is true, of course, that the position of women in America has improved markedly in recent decades. Nevertheless, it can hardly be doubted that, in part because of the high visibility of the sex characteristic, women still face pervasive, although at times more subtle, discrimination in our educational institutions, on the job market and, perhaps most conspicuously, in the political arena. . . .

Moreover, since sex, like race and national origin, is an immutable characteristic determined solely by the accident of birth, the imposition of special disabilities upon the members of a particular sex because of their sex would seem to violate "the basic concept of our system that legal burdens should bear some relationship to individual responsibility. . . ." And what differentiates sex from such nonsuspect statutes as intelligence or physical disability, and aligns it with the recognized suspect criteria, is that the sex characteristic frequently bears no relation to ability to perform or contribute to society. As a result, statutory distinctions between the sexes often have the effect of invidiously relegating the entire class of females to inferior legal status without regard to the actual capabilities of its individual members. . . .

With these considerations in mind, we can only conclude that classifications based upon sex, like classifications based upon race, alienage, or national origin, are inherently suspect, and must therefore be subjected to strict judicial scrutiny.

Applying the analysis mandated by that statutory standard of review, it is clear that the statutory scheme now before us is constitutionally invalid.

The sole basis of the classification established in the challenged statutes is the sex of the individuals involved. . . .

Moreover, the Government concedes that the differential treatment accorded men and women under these statutes serves no purpose other than mere "administrative convenience." In essence, the Government maintains that, as an empirical matter, wives in our society frequently are dependent upon their husbands, while husbands rarely are dependent upon their wives. Thus, the Government argues that Congress might reasonably have concluded that it would be both cheaper and easier simply conclusively to presume that wives of male members are financially dependent upon their husbands, while burdening female members with the task of establishing dependency in fact.

The Government offers no concrete evidence, however, tending to support its views that such differential treatment in fact saves the Government any money. In order to satisfy the demands of strict judicial scrutiny, the Government must demonstrate, for example, that it is actually cheaper to grant increased benefits with respect to *all* male members, than it is to determine which male members are in fact entitled to such benefits and to grant increased benefits only to those members whose wives actually meet the dependency requirement. Here, however, there is substantial evidence that, if put to the test, many of the wives of male members would fail to qualify for benefits. And in light of the fact that the dependency determination with respect to the husbands of female members is presently made solely on the basis of affiddavits, rather than through the more costly hearing process, the Government's explanation of the statutory scheme is, to say the least, questionnable.

In any case, our prior decisions make clear that, although efficacious administration of governmental programs is not without some importance, "the Constitution recognizes higher values than speed and efficiency." . . . And when we enter the realm of "strict judicial scrutiny," there can be no doubt that "administrative convenience" is not a shibboleth, the mere recitation of which dictates constitutionality. . . . On the contrary, any statutory scheme which draws a sharp line between the sexes, *solely* for the purpose of achieving administrative convenience, necessarily commands "dissimilar treatment for men and women who are . . . similarly situated," and therefore involves the "very kind of arbitrary legislative choice forbidden by the [Constitution]." . . . We therefore conclude that, by according differential treatment to male and female members of the uniformed services for the sole purpose of achieving administrative convenience, the challenged statues violate the Due Process Clause of the Fifth Amendment insofar as they require a female member to prove the dependency of her husband.

Reversed.

MR. JUSTICE POWELL, with whom THE CHIEF JUSTICE and MR. JUSTICE BLACKMUN join, concurring.

I agree that the challenged statutes constitute an unconstitutional discrimination against service women in violation of the Due Process Clause of the Fifth Amendment, but I cannot join the opinion of MR. JUSTICE BRENNAN, which would hold that all classifications based upon sex, "like classifications based upon race, alienage, and national origin," are "inherently suspect and must therefore be subjected to close judicial scrutiny." . . . It is unnecessary for the Court in this case to characterize sex as a suspect classification, with all of the far-reaching implications of such a holding. *Reed* v. *Reed* . . . (1971), which abundantly supports our decision today, did not add sex to the narrowly limited group of classifications which are inherently suspect. In my view, we can and should decide this case on the authority of *Reed* and reserve for the future any expansion of its rationale.

There is another, and I find compelling, reason for deferring a general categorizing of sex classifications as invoking the strictest test of judicial scrutiny. The Equal Rights Amendment, which if adopted will resolve the substance of this precise question, has been approved by the Congress and submitted for ratification by the States. If this Amendment is duly adopted, it will represent the will of the people accomplished in the manner prescribed by the Constitution. By acting prematurely and unnecessarily, as I view it, the Court has assumed a decisional responsibility at the very time when state legislatures, functioning within the traditional democratic process, are debating the proposed Amendment. It seems to me that this reaching out to pre-empt by judicial action a major political decision which is currently in process of resolution does not reflect appropriate respect for duly prescribed legislature processes.

Heckler v. *Mathews*

465 U.S. 728, 104 S. Ct. 1387; 79 L. Ed. 2d 646 (1984)

Robert H. Mathews, a retired U.S. Postal Service employee, brought a class-action suit against Margaret Heckler, Secretary of the Department of Health and Human Services, alleging that 1977 amendments to the Social Security Act providing for a pension offset to him and other nondependent men but not to similarly situated nondependent women violated the equal protection component of the Due Process Clause of the Fifth Amendment. The United States District Court for the Northern District of Alabama held that the pension offset provision was unconstitutional, and the United States appealed directly to the Supreme Court. *Unanimous opinion of the Court: Brennan, Burger, Blackmun, Marshall, O'Connor, Powell, Rehnquist, Stevens, and White.*

JUSTICE BRENNAN delivered the opinion of the Court.

Califano v. *Goldfarb* . . . (1977) held that a gender-based classification in the spousal-benefit provisions of the Social Security Act violated the right to the equal protection of the laws guaranteed by the Due Process Clause of the Fifth Amendment. In this case, the United States District Court for the Northern District of Alabama held that amendments to the Act, adopted in 1977 partly in response to our decision, unjustifiably revive the gender-based classification that was invalidated in *Goldfarb* and therefore also violate the Fifth Amendment. . . . The Government appealed directly to this Court. We noted probable jurisdiction . . . and now reverse.

The Social Security Act (Act) provides spousal benefits for the wives, husbands, widows, and widowers of retired and disabled wage earners. . . . Prior to December 1977, benefits were payable only to those husbands or widowers who could demonstrate dependency on their wage-earning wives for one-half of their support. Wives and widows, on the other hand, were entitled to spousal benefits without any such showing of dependency on their husbands. . . . In March 1977, *Califano* v. *Goldfarb* affirmed the judgment of a three-judge District Court which held that the gender-based dependency requirement for widowers violated the equal protection component of the Due Process Clause of the Fifth Amendment. Subsequently, the Court summarily affirmed two District Court decisions invalidating the dependency requirement for husbands' benefits . . .

Following these decisions, as part of a general reform of the Social Security system, Congress repealed the dependency requirement for widowers and husbands. . . . It concluded, however, that elimination of the dependency test, by increasing the number of individuals entitled to spousal benefits, could create a serious fiscal problem for the Social Security trust fund. . . . This problem was particularly acute with respect to the large number of retired federal and state employees who would now become eligible for spousal benefits. Unlike most applicants, who must offset any dual Social Security benefits against each other, retired civil servants could, at the time of the 1977 Amendments, receive the full amount of both the spousal benefits and the government pensions to which they were entitled. Congress estimated that payment of unreduced spousal benefits to such individuals could cost the system an estimated $190 million in 1979. . . .

To avoid this fiscal drain, Congress included as part of the 1977 Amendments a "pension offset" provision that generally requires the reduction of spousal benefits by the amount of certain federal or state government pensions received by the Social Security applicant. . . . Congress estimated that 90 percent of the savings that would be achieved by the pension offset provision as proposed by the Senate would be attributable to a reduction in payments to nondependent husbands and widowers who had not been entitled to any spousal benefits prior to the decision in *Goldfarb*. . . . The remaining portion of the savings, however, would come from a reduction in benefits to individuals, mostly women but also dependent men, who had retired or were about to retire and who had planned their retirements in reliance on their entitlement, under pre-1977 law, to spousal benefits unreduced by government pension benefits. . . . In order to protect the reliance interests of this group, . . . Congress exempted from the pension offset requirement as ultimately enacted those spouses who were eligible to receive pension benefits prior to December 1982 and who would have qualified for unreduced spousal benefits under the Act "as it was in effect and being administered in January 1977." . . .

We recently reviewed the "firmly established principles" by which to evaluate a claim of gender discrimination like that made by appellee:

"Our decisions . . . establish that the party seeking to uphold a statute that classifies individuals on the basis of their gender must carry the burden of showing an 'exceedingly persuasive justification' for the classification. . . . The burden is met only by showing at least that the classification serves 'important governmental objectives and that the discriminatory means employed' are 'substantially related to the achievement of those objectives.' . . .

"Although the test for determining the validity of a gender-based classification is straightforward, it must be applied free of fixed notions concerning the roles and abilities of males and females. Care must be taken in ascertaining whether the statutory objective itself reflects archaic and stereotypic notions. Thus, if the statutory objective is to exclude or 'protect' members of one gender because they are presumed to suffer from an inherent handicap or to be innately inferior, the objective itself is illegitimate. . . .

"If the State's objective is legitimate and important, we next determine whether the requisite direct, substantial relationship between objective and means is present . . . *Mississippi University for Women* v. *Hogan*. . . ."

We therefore consider in turn whether the Secretary has carried her burden of (A) showing a legitimate and "exceedingly persuasive justification" for the gender-based classification of the pension offset provision and (B) demonstrating "the requisite direct, substantial relationship" between the classification and the important governmental objectives it purports to serve.

Although the offset exception temporarily revives the gender-based eligibility requirements invalidated in *Goldfarb*, Congress's purpose in adopting the exception bears no relationship to the concerns that animated the original enactment of those criteria. The Court concluded in *Goldfarb* that the original gender-based standards. . . which were premised on an assumption that females would normally be dependent on the earnings of their spouses but males would not.

The provision at issue here, in contrast, reflects no such illegitimate government purposes. As detailed above, . . . Congress adopted the offset exception in order to protect the expectations of persons, both men and women, who had planned their retirements based on pre-January 1977 law, under which they could receive spousal benefits unreduced by the amount of any government pensions to which they were also entitled.

Nor is that purpose rendered illegitimate by the fact that it is achieved through a temporary revival of an invalidated classification. We have recognized, in a number of contexts, the legitimacy of protecting reasonable reliance on prior law even when that requires allowing an unconstitutional statute to remain in effect for a limited period of time. . . . The protection of reasonable reliance interests is not only a legitimate governmental objective: it provides "an exceedingly persuasive justification" for the statute at issue here. . . .

In the years immediately preceding retirement, individuals make spending, savings, and investment decisions based on assumptions regarding the amount of income they expect to receive after they stop working. For such individuals reliance on the law in effect during those years may be critically important. In recognition of this fact, the offset exception, in the words of the Conference Report, protects "people who are already retired, or close to retirement, from public employment and who cannot be expected to readjust their retirement plans to take account of the 'offset' provision that will apply in the future." . . . That purpose, consistent with the principle that " '[g]reat nations, like great men, should keep their word,' " . . . provides an exceedingly persuasive justification for the gender-based classification incorporated in the offset exception.

Having identified the legitimate and important governmental purpose of the offset exception, we have little trouble concluding that the means employed by the statute is "substantially related to the achievement of [that] objectiv[e]." . . . By reviving for a five-year period the eligibility criteria in effect in January 1977, the exception is narrowly tailored to protect only those individuals who made retirement plans prior to the changes in the law that occurred after that date. Individuals who were eligible for spousal benefits before the law changed and who retire within five years of the statute's enactment may reasonably be assumed to have begun planning for their retirement prior to the adoption of the offset provision. . . . Such persons, men as well as women, may receive spousal benefits unreduced by their government pensions, while those persons, men as well as women, who first became eligible for benefits after January 1977 may not.

The exception to the pension offset requirement set out in . . . the 1977 Amendments to the Social Security Act, while temporarily reviving the gender-based classification invalidated in *Califano* v. *Goldfarb,* is directly and substantially related to the important governmental interest of protecting individuals who planned their retirements in reasonable reliance on the law in effect prior to that decision. Accordingly, the judgment of the District Court is

Reversed.

Rostker v. *Goldberg*

453 U.S. 57; 101 S. Ct. 2646; 69 L. Ed. 2d 478 (1981)

The Military Selective Service Act (MSSA) authorizes the president to require the registration for possible military service of males, but not females, the purpose of registration being to facilitate any eventual conscription under the act. Registration for the draft was discontinued by a presidential proclamation in 1975, but President Jimmy Carter decided in 1980 that it was necessary to reactivate the registration process and requested Congress to allocate funds for that purpose. He also recommended that Congress amend the MSSA to permit the registration and conscription of women. Although Congress agreed to reactivate the registration process, it declined to amend the MSSA to permit the registration of women and allocated funds only to register males. Thereafter, the president ordered the registration of specified groups of young men. A lawsuit was brought against Bernard Rostker, director of Selective Service, by several men, challenging the act's constitutionality. A three-judge district court held that the act's gender-based discrimination violated the Due Process Clause of the Fifth Amendment and enjoined registration under the Act, whereupon the United States government appealed to the Supreme Court. *Opinion of the Court: Rehnquist, Blackmun, Burger, Powell, Stevens, Stewart. Dissenting opinions: Marshall, Brennan; White, Brennan.*

Mr. Justice Rehnquist delivered the opinion of the Court.

The question presented is whether the Military Selective Service Act . . . violates the Fifth Amendment to the United States Constitution in authorizing the President to require the registration of males and not females. . . .

Congress is given the power under the Constitution "To raise and support Armies," "To provide and maintain a Navy," and "To make Rules for the Government and Regulation of the land and naval Forces." . . . Pursuant to this grant of authority Congress has enacted the Military Selective Service Act. . . . Section 3 of the Act . . .

empowers the President, by proclamation, to require the registration of "every male citizen" and male resident aliens between the ages of 18 and 26. . . . The MSSA registration provision serves no other purpose beyond providing a pool for subsequent induction.

Registration for the draft under § 3 was discontinued in 1975. . . . In early 1980, President Carter determined that it was necessary to reactivate the draft registration process. The immediate impetus for this decision was the Soviet armed invasion of Afghanistan. . . . The resulting crisis in Southwestern Asia convinced the President that the "time has come" "to use his present authority to require registration . . . as a necessary step to preserving or enhancing our national security interests." . . . The Selective Service System had been inactive, however, and funds were needed before reactivating registration. The President therefore recommended that funds be transferred from the Department of Defense to the separate Selective Service System. . . . He also recommended that Congress take action to amend the MSSA to permit the registration and conscription of women as well as men. . . .

Congress agreed that it was necessary to reactivate the registration process, and allocated funds for that purpose in a joint resolution which passed the House on April 22 and the Senate on June 12. . . . The resolution did not allocate all the funds originally requested by the President, but only those necessary to register males. . . . Although Congress considered the question at great length, . . . it declined to amend the MSSA to permit the registration of women.

On July 2, 1980, the President, by proclamation, ordered the registration of specified groups of young men pursuant to the authority conferred by § 3 of the Act. . . .

Whenever called upon to judge the constitutionality of an Act of Congress—"the gravest and most delicate duty that this Court is called upon to perform" . . . the Court accords "great weight to the decisions of Congress." . . . The Congress is a coequal branch of government whose members take the same oath we do to uphold the Constitution of the United States. . . . The customary deference accorded the judgments of Congress is certainly appropriate when, as here, Congress specifically considered the question of the Act's constitutionality. . . .

This is not, however, merely a case involving the customary deference accorded congressional decisions. The case arises in the context of Congress' authority over national defense and military affairs, and perhaps in no other area has the Court accorded Congress greater deference. In rejecting the registration of women, Congress explicitly relied upon its constitutional powers under Art. I, § 8, cls. 12–14. . . . This Court has consistently recognized Congress' "broad constitutional power" to raise and regulate armies and navies, *Schlesinger* v. *Ballard* . . . (1975).

Not only is the scope of Congress' constitutional power in this area broad, but the lack of competence on the part of the courts is marked. In *Gilligan* v. *Morgan* . . . (1973), the Court noted: "It is difficult to conceive of an area of governmental activity in which the courts have less competence. The complex, subtle, and professional decisions as to the composition, training, equipping, and control of a military force are essentially professional military judgments, subject always to civilian control of the Legislative and Executive branches." . . .

None of this is to say that Congress is free to disregard the Constitution when it acts in the area of military affairs. In that area as any other Congress remains subject to the limitations of the Due Process Clause, . . . but the tests and limitations to be applied may differ because of the military context. We of course do not abdicate our ultimate responsibility to decide the constitutional question, but simply recognize that the Constitution itself requires such deference to congressional choice. . . . In deciding the question before us we must be particularly careful not to substitute our judgment of what is desirable for that of Congress, or our own evaluation of evidence for a reasonable evaluation by the Legislative Branch.

The District Court purported to recognize the appropriateness of deference to Congress when that body was exercising its constitutionally delegated authority over military affairs, . . . but it stressed that "[w]e are not here concerned with military operations or day-to-day conduct of the military into which we have no desire to intrude." . . . Appellees also stress that this case involves civilians, not the military, and that "the impact of registration on the military is only indirect and attenuated." . . . We find these efforts to divorce registration from the military and national defense context, with all the deference called for in that context, singularly unpersuasive. . . . Registration is not an end in itself in the civilian world but rather the first step in the induction process into the military one, and Congress specifically linked its consideration of registration to induction. . . . Congressional judgments concerning registration and the draft are based on judgments concerning military operations and needs. . . . and the deference unquestionably due the latter judgments is necessarily required in assessing the former as well.

The Solicitor General argues . . . that this Court should scrutinize the MSSA only to determine if the distinction drawn between men and women bears a rational relation to some legitimate government purpose, . . . and should not examine the Act under the heightened scrutiny with which we have approached gender-based discrimination. . . . We do not think that the substantive guarantee of due process or certainty in the law will be advanced by any further "refinement" in the applicable tests as suggested by the Government. Announced degrees of "deference" to legislative judgments, just as levels of "scrutiny" which this Court announces that it applies to particular classifications made by a legislative body, may all too readily become facile abstractions used to justify a result. In this case the courts are called upon to decide whether Congress, acting under an explicit constitutional grant of authority, has by that action transgressed an explicit guarantee of individual rights which limits the authority so conferred. Simply labelling the legislative decision "military" on the one hand or "gender-based" on the other does not automatically guide a court to the correct constitutional result.

No one could deny that under the test of *Craig v. Boren* [1976] . . . the Government's interest in raising and supporting armies is an "important governmental interest." Congress and its committees carefully considered and debated two alternative means of furthering that interest: the first was to register only males for potential conscription, and the other was to register both sexes. Congress chose the former alternative. When that decision is challenged on equal protection grounds, the question a court must decide is not which alternative it would have chosen, had it been the primary decision-maker, but whether that chosen by Congress denies equal protection of the laws. . . .

This case is quite different from several of the gender-based discrimination cases we have considered in that, despite appellees' assertions, Congress did not act "unthinkingly" or "reflexively and not for any considered reason." . . . The question of registering women for the draft not only received considerable national attention and was the subject of wide-ranging public debate, but also was extensively considered by Congress in hearings, floor debate, and in committee. Hearings held by both Houses of Congress in response to the President's request for authorization to register women adduced extensive testimony and evidence concerning the issue. . . . These hearings built on other hearings held the previous year addressed to the same question.

The House declined to provide for the registration of women when it passed the Joint Resolution allocating funds for the Selective Service System. . . . When the Senate considered the Joint resolution, it defeated, after extensive debate, an amendment which in effect would have authorized the registration of women. . . .

While proposals to register women were being rejected in the course of transferring funds to register males, committees in both Houses which had conducted hearings on the issue were also rejecting the registration of women. The House Subcommittee on Military Personnel of the House Armed Services Committee tabled a bill which would have amended the MSSA to authorize registration of women. . . . The Senate Armed Services Committee rejected a proposal to register women, . . . as it had one year before. . . .

The foregoing clearly establishes that the decision to exempt women from registration was not the "accidental byproduct of a traditional way of thinking about women." . . . The issue was considered at great length and Congress clearly expressed its purpose and intent. . . .

The MSSA established a plan for maintaining "adequate armed strength . . . to ensure the security of [the] nation." . . . Registration is the first step "in a united and continuous process designed to raise an army speedily and efficiently," . . . and Congress provided for the reactivation of registration in order to "provide the means for the early delivery of inductees in an emergency." . . . Congress rather clearly linked the need for renewed registration with its views on the character of a subsequent draft. Any assessment of the congressional purpose and its chosen means must therefore consider the registration scheme as a prelude to a draft in a time of national emergency. Any other approach would not be testing the Act in light of the purposes Congress sought to achieve.

Congress determined that any future draft, which would be facilitated by the registration scheme, would be characterized by a need for combat troops. The Senate Report explained, in a specific finding later adopted by both Houses, that "if mobilization were to be ordered in a wartime scenario, the primary manpower need would be for combat replacements." . . .

Women as a group, however, unlike men as a group, are not eligible for combat. The restrictions on the participation of women in combat in the Navy and Air Force are statutory. . . . The Army and Marine Corps preclude the use of women in combat as a matter of established policy. . . . Congress specifically recognized and endorsed the exclusion of women from combat in exempting women from registration. In the words of the Senate Report: "The principle that women should not intentionally and routinely engage in combat is fundamental, and enjoys wide support among our people." . . .

The existence of the combat restrictions clearly indicates the basis for Congress' decision to exempt women from registration. The purpose of registration was to prepare for a draft of combat troops. Since women are excluded from combat, Congress concluded that they would not be needed in the event of a draft, and therefore decided not to register them. . . .

The District Court stressed that the military need for women was irrelevant to the issue of their registration. As that court put it: "Congress could not constitutionally require registration under MSSA of only black citizens or only white citizens, or single out any political or religious group simply because those groups contained sufficient persons to fill the needs of the Selective Service System." . . . This reasoning is beside the point. The reason women are exempt from registration is not because military needs can be met by drafting men. This is not a case of Congress arbitrarily choosing to burden one of two similarly situated groups, such as would be the case with an all-black or all-white, or an all-Catholic or all-Lutheran, or an all-Republican or all-Democratic registration. Men and women, because of the combat restrictions on women, are simply not similarly situated for purposes of a draft or registration for a draft.

Congress' decision to authorize the registration of only men, therefore, does not violate the Due Process Clause. The exemption of women from registration is not only sufficiently but closely related to Congress' purpose in authorizing registration. . . . The fact that Congress and the Executive have decided that women should not serve in combat fully justifies Congress in not authorizing their registration, since the purpose of registration is to develop a pool of potential combat troops. As was the case in *Schlesinger* v. *Ballard, supra,* "the gender classification is not invidious, but rather realistically reflects the fact that the sexes are not similarly situated" in this case. . . . The Constitution requires that Congress treat similarly situated persons similarly, not that it engage in gestures of superficial equality.

In holding the MSSA constitutionally invalid the District Court relied heavily on the President's decision to seek authority to register women and the testimony of members of the Executive Branch and the military in support of that decision. . . . As stated by the Administration's witnesses before Congress, however, the President's decision to ask for authority to register women is based on equity." . . . This was also the basis for the testimony by military officials. . . . The Senate Report, evaluating the testimony before the Committee, recognized that "the argument for registration and induction of women . . . is not based on military necessity, but on considerations of equity." . . . Congress was certainly entitled, in the exercise of its constitutional powers to raise and regulate armies and navies, to focus on the question of military need rather than "equity." . . .

In light of the foregoing, we conclude that Congress acted well within its constitutional authority when it authorized the registration of men, and not women, under the Military Selective Service Act. The decision of the District Court holding otherwise is accordingly

Reversed.

MR. JUSTICE MARSHALL, with whom MR. JUSTICE BRENNAN joins, dissenting.

The Court today places its imprimatur on one of the most potent remaining public expressions of "ancient canards about the proper role of women." ... It upholds a statute that requires males but not females to register for the draft, and which thereby categorically excludes women from a fundamental civic obligation. Because I believe the Court's decision is inconsistent with the Constitution's guarantee of equal protection of the laws, I dissent.

By now it should be clear that statutes like the MSSA, which discriminate on the basis of gender, must be examined under the "heightened" scrutiny mandated by *Craig* v. *Boren* . . . (1976). Under this test, a gender-based classification cannot withstand constitutional challenge unless the classification is substantially related to the achievement of an important governmental objective. . . . This test applies whether the classification discriminates against males or females. . . . The party defending the challenged classification carries the burden of demonstrating both the importance of the governmental objective it serves and the substantial relationship between the discriminatory means and the asserted end. . . . Consequently, before we can sustain the MSSA, the Government must demonstrate that the gender-based classification it employs bears "a close and substantial relationship to [the achievement of] important governmental objectives." . . .

. . . I agree with the majority, . . . that "none could deny that . . . the Government's interest in raising and supporting armies is an 'important governmental interest.' " Consequently, the first part of the *Craig* v. *Boren* test is satisfied. But the question remains whether the discriminatory means employed itself substantially serves the statutory end. . . . When, as here, a federal law that classifies on the basis of gender is challenged as violating this constitutional guarantee, it is ultimately for this Court, not Congress, to decide whether there exists the constitutionally required "close and substantial relationship" between the discriminatory means employed and the asserted governmental objective. . . . In my judgment, there simply is no basis for concluding in this case that excluding women from registration is substantially related to the achievement of a concededly important governmental interest in maintaining an effective defense. . . .

In the first place, although the Court purports to apply the *Craig* v. *Boren* test, the "similarly situated" analysis the Court employs is in fact significantly different from the *Craig* v. *Boren* approach. . . . The Court essentially reasons that the gender classification employed by the MSSA is constitutionally permissible because nondiscrimination is not necessary to achieve the purpose of registration to prepare for a draft of combat troops. In other words, the majority concludes that women may be excluded from registration because they will not be needed in the event of a draft.

This analysis, however, focuses on the wrong question. The relevant inquiry under the *Craig* v. *Boren* test is not whether a *gender-neutral* classification would substantially advance important governmental interests. Rather, the question is whether the gender-based classification is itself substantially related to the achievement of the asserted governmental interest. Thus, the Government's task in this case is to demonstrate that excluding women from registration substantially furthers the goal of preparing for a draft of combat troops. Or to put it another way, the Government must show that registering women would substantially impede its efforts to prepare for such a draft. Under our precedents, the Government cannot meet this burden without showing that a gender neutral statute would be a less effective means of attaining this end. . . . In this case, the Government makes no claim that preparing for a draft of combat troops cannot be accomplished just as effectively by *registering* both men and women but *drafting* only men if only men turn out to be needed. Nor can the Government argue that this alternative entails the additional cost and administrative inconvenience of registering women. This Court has repeatedly stated that the administrative convenience of employing a gender classification is not an adequate constitutional justification under the *Craig* v. *Boren* test. . . .

The fact that registering women in no way obstructs the governmental interest in preparing for a draft of combat troops points up a second flaw in the Court's analysis. The Court essentially reduces the question of the constitutionality of male-only *registration* to the validity of a hypothetical program for *conscripting* only men. The Court posits a draft in which *all* conscripts are either assigned to those specific combat posts presently closed to women or must be available for rotation into such positions. . . . If it could indeed be guaranteed in advance that conscription would be reimposed by Congress only in circumstances where, and in a form under which, all conscripts would have to be trained for and assigned to combat or combat rotation positions from which women are categorically excluded, then it could be argued that registration of women would be pointless.

But of course, no such guarantee is possible. Certainly, nothing about the MSSA limits Congress to reinstituting the draft only in such circumstances. . . .

. . . The discussion and findings in the Senate Report do not enable the Government to carry its burden of demonstrating that *completely* excluding women from the draft by excluding them from registration substantially furthers important governmental objectives. . . . Congressional enactments in the area of military affairs must, like all other laws, be *judged* by the standards of the Constitution. For the Constitution is the supreme law of the land and *all* legislation must conform to the principles it lay down. . . .

Furthermore, "[w]hen it appears that an Act of Congress conflicts with [a constitutional] provisio[n], we have no choice but to enforce the paramount commands of the Constitution. We are sworn to do no less. We cannot push back the limits of the Constitution merely to accommodate challenged legislation." . . . In some 106 instances since this court was established it has determined that congressional action exceeded the bounds of the Constitution. I believe the same is true of this statute. In an attempt to avoid its constitutional obligation, the Court today "pushes back the limits of the Constitution" to accommodate an Act of Congress.

I would affirm the judgment of the District Court.

Shapiro v. *Thompson*

394 U.S. 618; 89 S. Ct. 1322; 22 L. Ed. 2d 600 (1969)

Vivian Marie Thompson, a pregnant, nineteen-year-old unwed mother who already had one child, moved to Connecticut from Massachusetts in June 1966. Two months later, she applied for public assistance money under the Aid to Families with Dependent Children (AFDC) program. Her application was denied on the sole ground that she had not met the state's one-year residency requirement, which was a prerequisite for eligibility to receive aid. She thereupon brought suit against Bernard Shapiro, the Connecticut welfare commissioner, in federal district court. The three-judge court found the state residency requirement unconstitutional because of its "chilling effect on the right to travel." Shapiro appealed to the Supreme Court. The Court heard this case in conjunction with similar cases from Pennsylvania and the District of Columbia, both of which also involved the validity of one-year residency requirements. *Opinion of the Court: Brennan, Douglas, Fortas, Marshall, Stewart, White. Concurring opinion: Stewart. Dissenting opinions: Harlan; Warren, Black.*

Mr. Justice Brennan delivered the opinion of the Court. . . .

There is no dispute that the effect of the waiting-period requirement in each case is to create two classes of needy resident families indistinguishable from each other except that one is composed of residents who have resided a year or more, and the second of residents who have resided less than a year, in the jurisdiction. On the basis of this sole difference the first class is granted and the second class is denied welfare aid upon which may depend the ability of the families to obtain the very means to subsist—food, shelter, and other necessities of life. In each case, the District Court found that appellees met the test for residence in their jurisdictions, as well as all other eligibility requirements except the requirement of residence for a full year prior to their applications. On reargument, appellees' central contention is that the statutory prohibition of benefits to residents of less than a year creates a classification which constitutes an invidious discrimination denying them equal protection of the laws. We agree. The interests which appellants assert are promoted by the classification either may not constitutionally be promoted by government or are not compelling governmental interests.

Primarily, appellants justify the waiting-period requirement as a protective device to preserve the fiscal integrity of state public assistance programs. It is asserted that people who require welfare assistance during their first year of residence in a State are likely to become continuing burdens on state welfare programs. Therefore, the argument runs, if such people can be deterred from entering the jurisdiction by denying them welfare benefits during the first year, state programs to assist long-time residents will not be impaired by a substantial influx of indigent newcomers.

There is weighty evidence that exclusion from the jurisdiction of the poor who need or may need relief was the specific objective of these provisions. In the Congress, sponsors of federal legislation to eliminate all residence requirements have been consistently opposed by representatives of state and local welfare agencies who have stressed the fears of the States that elimination of the requirements would result in a heavy influx of individuals into States providing the most generous benefits. . . .

We do not doubt that the one-year waiting-period device is well suited to discourage the influx of poor families in need of assistance. An indigent who desires to migrate, resettle, find a new job, and start a new life will doubtless hesitate if he knows that he must risk making the move without the possibility of falling back on state welfare assistance during his first year of residence when his need may be most acute. But the purpose of inhibiting migration by needy persons into the State is constitutionally impermissible.

This Court long ago recognized that the nature of our Federal Union and our constitutional concepts of personal liberty unite to require that all citizens be free to travel throughout the length and breadth of our land uninhibited by statutes, rules, or regulations which unreasonably burden or restrict this movement. . . .

We have no occasion to ascribe the source of this right to travel interstate to a particular constitutional provision. It suffices that, as Mr. Justice Stewart said for the Court in *United States* v. *Guest* . . . (1966): "The constitutional right to travel from one State to another . . . occupies a position fundamental to the concept of our Federal Union. It is a right that has been firmly established and repeatedly recognized.

". . . [The] right finds no explicit mention in the Constitution. The reason, it has been suggested, is that a right so elementary was conceived from the beginning to be a necessary concomitant of the stronger Union the Constitution created. In any event, freedom to travel throughout the United States has long been recognized as a basic right under the Constitution." . . .

Alternatively, appellants argue that even if it is impermissible for a State to attempt to deter the entry of all indigents, the challenged classification may be justified as a permissible state attempt to discourage those indigents who would enter the State solely to obtain larger benefits. We observe first that none of the statutes before us is tailored to serve that objective. Rather, the class of barred newcomers is all-inclusive, lumping the great majority who come to the State for other purposes with those who come for the sole purpose of collecting higher benefits. In actual operation, therefore, the three statutes enact what in effect are nonrebuttable presumptions that every applicant for assistance in his first year of residence came to the jurisdiction solely to obtain higher benefits. Nothing whatever in any of these records supplies any basis in fact for such a presumption.

More fundamentally, a State may no more try to fence out those indigents who seek higher welfare benefits than it may try to fence out indigents generally. Implicit in any such distinction is the notion that indigents who enter a State with the hope of securing higher welfare benefits are somehow less deserving than indigents who do not take this consideration into account. But we do not perceive why a mother who is seeking to make a new life for herself and her children should be regarded as less deserving because she considers, among other factors, the level of a State's public assistance. Surely such a mother is no less deserving than a mother who moves into a particular State in order to take advantage of its better educational facilities. . . .

We recognize that a State has a valid interest in preserving the fiscal integrity of its programs. It may legitimately attempt to limit its expenditures, whether for public assistance, public education, or any other program. But a State may not accomplish such a purpose by invidious distinctions between classes of its citizens. It could not, for example, reduce expenditures for education by barring indigent children from its schools. Similarly, in the cases before us, appellants must do more than show that denying welfare benefits to new residents saves money. The saving of welfare costs cannot justify an otherwise invidious classification. . . .

Appellants next advance as justification certain administrative and related governmental objectives allegedly served by the waiting-period requirement. They argue that the requirement (1) facilitates the planning of the welfare budget; (2) provides an objective test of residency; (3) minimizes the opportunity for recipients fraudulently to receive payments from more than one jurisdiction; and (4) encourages early entry of new residents into the labor force.

. . . We reject appellants' argument that a mere showing of a rational relationship between the waiting period and these four admittedly permissible state objectives will suffice to justify the classification. . . . Any classification which serves to penalize the exercise of that right, unless shown to be necessary to promote a *compelling* governmental interest, is unconstitutional. . . .

MR. JUSTICE HARLAN, dissenting. . . .

In upholding the equal protection argument, the Court has applied an equal protection doctrine of relatively recent vintage: the rule that statutory classifications which either are based upon certain "suspect" criteria or affect "fundamental rights" will be held to deny equal protection unless justified by a "compelling" governmental interest.

I think that this branch of the "compelling interest" doctrine is sound when applied to racial classifications, for historically the Equal Protection Clause was largely a product of the desire to eradicate legal distinctions founded upon race. However, I believe that the more recent extensions have been unwise. . . .

The second branch of the "compelling interest" principle is even more troublesome. For it has been held that a statutory classification is subject to the "compelling interest" test if the result of the classification may be to affect a "fundamental right," . . . I think the "compelling interest" doctrine particularly unfortunate and unnecessary. It is unfortunate because it creates an exception which threatens to swallow the standard equal protection rule. Virtually every state statute affects important rights. This Court has repeatedly held, for example, that the traditional equal protection standard is applicable to statutory classifications affecting such fundamental matters as the right to pursue a particular occupation, the right to receive greater or smaller wages or to work more or less hours, and the right to inherit property. Rights such as these are in principle indistinguishable from those involved here, and to extend the "compelling interest" rule to all cases in which such rights are affected would go far toward making this Court a "super-legislature." But when a statute affects only matters not mentioned in the Federal Constitution and is not arbitrary or irrational, I must reiterate that I know of nothing which entitles this Court to pick out particular human activities, characterize them as "fundamental," and give them added protection under an unusually stringent equal protection test. . . .

I do not consider that the factors which have been urged . . . are sufficient to render unconstitutional these state and federal enactments. It is said, first, that this Court . . . has acknowledged that the right to travel interstate is a "fundamental" freedom. Second, it is contended that the governmental objectives mentioned above either are ephemeral or could be accomplished by means which do not impinge as heavily on the right to travel, and hence that the requirements are unconstitutional because they "sweep unnecessarily broadly and thereby invade the area of protected freedoms." . . .

Taking all of these competing considerations into account, I believe that the balance definitely favors constitutionality. In reaching that conclusion, I do not minimize the importance of the right to travel interstate. However, the impact of residence conditions upon that right is indirect and apparently quite insubstantial. On the other hand, the governmental purposes served by the requirements are legitimate and real, and the residence requirements are clearly suited to their accomplishment. To abolish residence requirements might well discourage highly worthwhile experimentation in the welfare field . . . Moreover, although the appellees assert that the same objectives could have been achieved by less restrictive means, this is an area in which the judiciary should be especially slow to fetter the judgment of Congress and of some 46 state legislatures in the choice of methods. Residence requirements have advantages, such as administrative simplicity and relative certainty, which are not shared by the alternative solutions proposed by the appellees. In these circumstances, I cannot find that the burden imposed by residence requirements upon ability to travel outweighs the governmental interests in their continued employment. Nor do I believe that the period of residence required in these cases—one year—is so excessively long as to justify a finding of unconstitutionality on that score.

I conclude with the following observations. Today's decision, it seems to me, reflects to an unusual degree the current notion that this Court possesses a peculiar wisdom all its own whose capacity to lead this Nation out of its present troubles is contained only by the limits of judicial ingenuity in contriving new constitutional principles to meet each problem as it arises. For anyone who, like myself, believes that it is an essential function of this Court to maintain the constitutional divisions between state and federal authority and among the three branches of the Federal Government, today's decision is a step in the wrong direction. This resurgence of the expansive view of "equal protection" carries the seeds of more judicial interference with the state and federal legislative process, much more indeed than does the judicial application of "due process" according to traditional concepts, . . . about which some members of this Court have expressed fears as to its potentialities for setting us judges "at large." I consider it particularly unfortunate that this judicial roadblock to the powers of Congress in this field should occur at the very threshold of the current discussions regarding the "federalizing" of these aspects of welfare relief.

Reynolds v. *Sims*

377 U.S. 533; 84 S. Ct. 1362; 12 L. Ed. 2d 506 (1964)

M.O. Sims and other Alabama residents brought suit against B.A. Reynolds and other state election officials, challenging the apportionment of the state legislature. The Alabama Constitution provided that the legislature be reapportioned dicennially on the basis of population, but with the qualification that each county be allocated one representative and that no county be apportioned more than one senator. Since no reapportionment had taken place since 1901, however, a substantial degree of malapportionment existed: some highly populous senatorial districts had over forty-one times as many people as others, and some legislative districts had populations sixteen times larger than others. It was possible, under the existing scheme of apportionment, for 25 percent of the population to elect a majority in the state senate and for approximately the same percentage to elect a majority of the state's representatives. A federal district court held that Alabama's scheme of apportionment violated the Equal Protection Clause of the Fourteenth Amendment. In response to this decision, the Alabama legislature adopted two alternative reapportionment plans, neither of which apportioned the legislature solely on the basis of population. When the district court also invalidated those plans, the defendants appealed to the Supreme Court. *Opinion of the Court:*

Warren, Black, Brennan, Douglas, Goldberg, White. Concurring in judgment: Clark; Stewart. Dissenting opinion: Harlan.

MR. CHIEF JUSTICE WARREN delivered the opinion of the Court. . . .

. . . Our problem is to ascertain . . . whether there are any constitutionally cognizable principles which would justify departures from the basic standard of equality among voters in the apportionment of seats in state legislatures.

A predominant consideration in determining whether a State's legislative apportionment scheme constitutes an invidious discrimination violative of rights asserted under the Equal Protection Clause is that the rights allegedly impaired are individual and personal in nature. . . . While the result of a court decision in a state legislative apportionment controversy may be to require the restructuring of the geographical distribution of seats in a state legislature, the judicial focus must be concentrated upon ascertaining whether there has been any discrimination against certain of the State's citizens which constitutes an impermissible impairment of their constitutionally protected right to vote. . . . Undoubtedly, the right of suffrage is a fundamental matter in a free and democratic society. Especially since the right to exercise the franchise in a free and unimpaired manner is preservative of other basic civil and political rights, any alleged infringement of the right of citizens to vote must be carefully and meticulously scrutinized.

Legislators represent people, not trees or acres. Legislators are elected by voters, not farms or cities or economic interests. As long as ours is a representative form of government, and our legislatures are those instruments of government elected directly by and directly representative of the people, the right to elect legislators in a free and unimpaired fashion is a bedrock of our political system. It could hardly be gainsaid that a constitutional claim had been asserted by an allegation that certain otherwise qualified voters had been entirely prohibited from voting for members of their state legislature. And, if a State should provide that the votes of citizens in one part of the State should be given two times, or five times, or 10 times the weight of votes of citizens in another part of the State, it could hardly be contended that the right to vote of those residing in the disfavored areas had not been effectively diluted. It would appear extraordinary to suggest that a State could be constitutionally permitted to enact a law providing that certain of the State's voters could vote two, five, or 10 times for their legislative representatives, while voters living elsewhere could vote only once. And it is inconceivable that a state law to the effect that, in counting votes for legislators, the votes of citizens in one part of the State would be multiplied by two, five, or 10, while the votes of persons in another area would be counted only at face value, could be constitutionally sustainable. Of course, the effect of state legislative districting schemes which give the same number of representatives to unequal numbers of constituents is identical. Overweighting and overvaluation of the votes of those living here has the certain effect of dilution and undervaluation of the votes of those living there. The resulting discrimination against those individual voters living in disfavored areas is easily demonstrable mathematically. Their right to vote is simply not the same right to vote as that of those living in a favored part of the State. Two, five, or 10 of them must vote before the effect of their voting is equivalent to that of their favored neighbor. Weighting the votes of citizens differently, by any method or means, merely because of where they happen to reside, hardly seems justifiable. One must be ever aware that the Constitution forbids "sophisticated as well as simple-minded modes of discrimination." . . .

. . . Representative government is in essence self-government through the medium of elected representatives of the people, and each and every citizen has an inalienable right to full and effective participation in the political processes of his State's legislative bodies. Most citizens can achieve this participation only as qualified voters through the election of legislators to represent them. Full and effective participation by all citizens in state government requires, therefore, that each citizen have an equally effective voice in the election of members of his state legislature. Modern and viable state government needs, and the Constitution demands, no less.

Logically, in a society ostensibly grounded on representative government, it would seem reasonable that a majority of the people of a State could elect a majority of that State's legislators. To conclude differently, and to sanction minority control of state legislative bodies, would appear to deny majority rights in a way that far surpasses any possible denial of minority rights that might otherwise be thought to result. Since legislatures are responsible for enacting laws by which all citizens are to be governed, they should be bodies which are collectively responsive to the popular will. And the concept of equal protection has been traditionally viewed as requiring the uniform treatment of persons standing in the same relation to the governmental action questioned or challenged. With respect to the allocation of legislative representation, all voters, as citizens of a State, stand in the same relation regardless of where they live. Any suggested criteria for the differentiation of citizens are insufficient to justify any discrimination, as to the weight of their votes, unless relevant to the permissible purposes of legislative apportionment. Since the achieving of fair and effective representation for all citizens is concededly the basic aim of legislative apportionment, we conclude that the Equal Protection Clause guarantees the opportunity for equal participation by all voters in the election of state legislators. Diluting the weight of votes because of place of residence impairs basic constitutional rights under the Fourteenth Amendment just as much as invidious discriminations based upon factors such as race . . . or economic status. . . . Our constitutional system amply provides for the protection of minorities by means other than giving them majority control of state legislatures. . . .

We are told that the matter of apportioning representation in a state legislature is a complex and many-faceted one. We are advised that States can rationally consider factors other than population in apportioning legislative representation. We are admonished not to restrict the power of the States to impose differing views as to political philosophy on their citizens. We are cautioned about the dangers of entering into political thickets and mathematical quagmires. Our answer is this: a denial of constitutionally protected rights demands judicial protection; our oath and our office require no less of us. . . . To the extent that a citizen's right to vote is debased, he is that much less a citizen. The fact that an individual lives here or there is not a legitimate reason for overweighting or diluting the efficacy of his vote. . . .

. . . Population is, of necessity, the starting point for consideration and the controlling criterion for judgment in legislative apportionment controversies.

We hold that, as a basic constitutional standard, the Equal Protection Clause requires that the seats in both houses of a bicameral state legislature must be apportioned on a population basis. Simply stated, an individual's right to vote for state legislators is unconstitutionally impaired when its weight is in a substantial fashion diluted when compared with votes of citizens living in other parts of the State. . . .

Since neither of the houses of the Alabama Legislature, under any of the three plans considered by the District Court, was apportioned on a population basis, we would be justified in proceeding no further. However, one of the proposed plans . . . at least superficially resembles the scheme of legislative representation followed in the Federal Congress. Under this plan, each of Alabama's 67 counties is allotted one senator, and no counties are given more than one Senate seat. Arguably, this is analogous to the allocation of two Senate seats, in the Federal Congress, to each of the 50 States, regardless of population. . . .

After considering the matter, the court below concluded that no conceivable analogy could be drawn between the federal scheme and the apportionment of seats in the Alabama Legislature under the proposed constitutional amendment. We agree with the District Court, and find the federal analogy inapposite and irrelevant to state legislative districting schemes. Attempted reliance on the federal analogy appears often to be little more than an after-the-fact rationalization offered in defense of maladjusted state apportionment arrangements.

The system of representation in the two Houses of the Federal Congress is one ingrained in our Constitution, as part of the law of the land. It is one conceived out of compromise and concession indispensable to the establishment of our federal republic. Arising from unique historical circumstances, it is based on the consideration that in establishing our type of federalism a group of formerly independent States bound themselves together under one national government. . . .

Political subdivisions of States—counties, cities, or whatever—never were and never have been considered as sovereign entities. Rather, they have been traditionally regarded as subordinate governmental instrumentalities created by the State to assist in the carrying out of state governmental functions. . . .

Since we find the so-called federal analogy inapposite to a consideration of the constitutional validity of state legislative apportionment schemes, we necessarily hold that the Equal Protection Clause requires both houses of a state legislature to be apportioned on a population basis. The right of a citizen to equal representation and to have his vote weighted equally with those of all other citizens in the election of members of one house of a bicameral state legislature would amount to little if States could effectively submerge the equal-population principle in the apportionment of seats in the other house. . . .

MR. JUSTICE HARLAN, dissenting.

The Court's constitutional discussion . . . is remarkable . . . for its failure to address itself at all to the Fourteenth Amendment as a whole. . . .

The Court relies exclusively on that portion of § 1 of the Fourteenth Amendment which provides that no State shall "deny to any person within its jurisdiction the equal protection of the laws," and disregards entirely the significance of § 2, which reads: "Representatives shall be apportioned among the several States according to their respective numbers, counting the whole number of persons in each State, excluding Indians not taxed. *But when the right to vote at any election for* the choice of electors for President and Vice President of the United States, Representatives in Congress, *the Executive and Judicial officers of a State, or the members of the Legislature thereof, is denied* to any of the male inhabitants of such State, being twenty-one years of age, and citizens of the United States, *or in any way abridged,* except for participation in rebellion, or other crime, the basis of representation therein shall be reduced in the proportion which the number of such male citizens shall bear to the whole number of male citizens twenty-one years of age in such State." (Emphasis added.)

The Amendment is a single text. It was introduced and discussed as such in the Reconstruction Committee, which reported it to the Congress. It was discussed as a unit in Congress and proposed as a unit to the States, which ratified it as a unit. A proposal to split up the Amendment and submit each section to the States as a separate amendment was rejected by the Senate. Whatever one might take to be the application to these cases of the Equal Protection Clause if it stood alone, I am unable to understand the Court's utter disregard of the second section which expressly recognizes the States' power to deny "or in any way" abridge the right of their inhabitants to vote for "the members of the [State] Legislature," and its express provision of a remedy for such denial or abridgment. The comprehensive scope of the second section and its particular reference to the state legislatures preclude the suggestion that the first section was intended to have the result reached by the Court today. If indeed the words of the Fourteenth Amendment speak for themselves, as the majority's disregard of history seems to imply, they speak as clearly as may be against the construction which the majority puts on them. . . .

. . . Note should be taken of the Fifteenth and Nineteenth Amendments. The former prohibited the States from denying or abridging the right to vote "on account of race, color, or previous condition of servitude." The latter, certified as part of the Constitution in 1920, added sex to the prohibited classifications. . . .

. . . Unless one takes the highly implausible view that the Fourteenth Amendment controls methods of apportionment but leaves the right to vote itself unprotected, the conclusion is inescapable that the Court has, for purposes of these cases, relegated the Fifteenth and Nineteenth Amendments to the same limbo of constitutional anachronisms to which the second section of the Fourteenth Amendment has been assigned. . . .

Although the Court—necessarily, as I believe—provides only generalities in elaboration of its main thesis, its opinion nevertheless fully demonstrates how far removed these problems are from fields of judicial competence. Recognizing that "indiscriminate districting" is an invitation to "partisan gerrymandering," . . . the Court nevertheless excludes virtually every basis for the formation of electoral districts other than "indiscriminate districting." . . . So far as presently appears, the *only* factor which a State may consider, apart from numbers, is political subdivisions. But even "a clearly rational state policy" recognizing this factor is unconstitutional if "population is submerged as the controlling consideration." . . .

. . . These decisions give support to a current mistaken view of the Constitution and the constitutional function of this Court. This view, in a nutshell, is that every major social ill in this country can find its cure in some constitutional "principle," and that this Court should "take the lead" in promoting reform when other branches of government fail to act. The Constitution is not a panacea for every blot upon the public welfare, nor should this Court, ordained as a judicial body, be thought of as a general haven for reform movements. The Constitution is an instrument of government, fundamental to which is the premise that in a diffusion of governmental authority lies the greatest promise that this Nation will realize liberty for all its citizens. This Court, limited in function in accordance with that premise, does not serve its high purpose when it exceeds its authority, even to satisfy justified impatience with the slow workings of the political process. For when, in the name of constitutional interpretation, the Court *adds* something to the Constitution that was deliberately excluded from it, the Court in reality substitutes its view of what should be so for the amending process.

Harper v. *Virginia State Board of Elections*

383 U.S. 663; 86 S. Ct. 1079; 16 L. Ed. 2d 169 (1966)

The state of Virginia imposed an annual poll tax of $1.50 on all residents over the age of twenty-one; payment of the tax was a precondition for voting in state elections. Proceeds from the tax were used to support local government activities, including education. A suit by Harper and others to have the poll tax declared unconstitutional was dismissed by a three-judge federal district court on the basis of *Breedlove* v. *Suttles (1937)*, in which the Court had unanimously rejected an equal-protection attack on Georgia's poll tax. Harper appealed to the United States Supreme Court.

Opinion of the Court: Douglas, Brennan, Clark, Fortas, Warren, White. Dissenting opinions: Black; Harlan, Stewart.

MR. JUSTICE DOUGLAS delivered the opinion of the Court. . . .

We conclude that a State violates the Equal Protection Clause of the Fourteenth Amendment whenever it makes the affluence of the voter or payment of any fee an electoral standard. Voter qualifications have no relation to wealth nor to paying or not paying this or any other tax. Our cases demonstrate that the Equal Protection Clause of the Fourteenth Amendment restrains the States from fixing voter qualifications which invidiously discriminate. . . .

Long ago in *Yick Wo* v. *Hopkins* [1886] . . . the Court referred to "the political franchise of voting" as a "fundamental political right, because preservative of all rights." Recently in *Reynolds* v. *Sims*, . . . we said, "Undoubtedly, the right of suffrage is a fundamental matter in a free and democratic society. Especially since the right to exercise the franchise in a free and unimpaired manner is preservative of other basic civil and political rights, any alleged infringement of the right of citizens to vote must be carefully and meticulously scrutinized." There we were considering charges that voters in one part of the State had greater representation per person in the State Legislature than voters in another part of the State. We concluded: "A citizen, a qualified voter, is no more nor no less so because he lives in the city or on the farm."

We say the same whether the citizen, otherwise qualified to vote, has $1.50 in his pocket or nothing at all, pays the fee or fails to pay it. The principle that denies the State the right to dilute a citizen's vote on account of his economic status or other such factors by analogy bars a system which excludes those unable to pay a fee to vote or who fail to pay.

It is argued that a State may exact fees from citizens for many different kind of licenses; that if it can demand from all an equal fee for a driver's license, it can demand from all an equal poll tax for voting. But we must remember that the interest of the State, when it comes to voting, is limited to the power to fix qualifications. Wealth, like race, creed, or color, is not germane to one's ability to participate intelligently in the electoral process. Lines drawn on the basis of wealth or property, like those of race . . . are traditionally disfavored. . . . To introduce wealth or payment of a fee as a measure of a voter's qualifications is to introduce a capricious or irrelevant factor. The degree of the discrimination is irrelevant. In this context—that is, as a condition of obtaining a ballot—the requirement of fee paying causes an "invidious" discrimination . . . that runs afoul of the Equal Protection Clause. Levy "by the poll," as stated in *Breedlove* v. *Suttles* . . . is an old familiar form of taxation; and we say nothing to impair its validity so long as it is not made a condition to the exercise of the franchise. *Breedlove* v. *Suttles* sanctioned its use as "a prerequisite of voting." . . . To that extent the *Breedlove* case is overruled. . . .

In a recent searching re-examination of the Equal Protection Clause, we held, as already noted, that "the opportunity for equal participation by all voters in the election of state legislators" is required. . . . We decline to qualify that principle by sustaining this poll tax. Our conclusion, like that in *Reynolds* v. *Sims*, is founded not on what we think governmental policy should be, but on what the Equal Protection Clause requires.

We have long been mindful that where fundamental rights and liberties are asserted under the Equal Protection Clause, classifications which might invade or restrain them must be closely scrutinized and carefully confined. . . .

Those principles apply here. For to repeat, wealth or fee paying has, in our view, no relation to voting qualifications; the right to vote is too precious, too fundamental to be so burdened or conditioned.

Reversed.

MR. JUSTICE BLACK, dissenting.

In *Breedlove* v. *Suttles* . . . decided December 6, 1937, a few weeks after I took my seat as a member of this Court, we unanimously upheld the right of the State of Georgia to make payment of its state poll tax a prerequisite to voting in state elections. We rejected at that time contentions that the state law violated the Equal Protection Clause of the Fourteenth Amendment because it put an unequal burden on different groups of people according to their age, sex, and ability to pay. . . . Later, May 28, 1951, I joined the Court's judgment in *Butler* v. *Thompson* . . . upholding, over the dissent of MR. JUSTICE DOUGLAS, the Virginia state poll tax law challenged here against the same equal protection challenges. Since the *Breedlove* and *Butler* cases were decided the Federal Constitution has not been amended in the only way it could constitutionally have been, that is, as provided in Article V of the Constitution. I would adhere to the holding of those cases. The Court, however, overrules *Breedlove* in part, but its opinion reveals that it does so not by using its limited power to interpret the original meaning of the Equal Protection Clause, but by giving that clause a new meaning which it believes represents a better governmental policy. From this action I dissent.

It should be pointed out at once that the Court's decision is to no extent based on a finding that the Virginia law as written or as applied is being used as a device or mechanism to deny Negro citizens of Virginia the right to vote on account of their color. . . .

. . . In view of the purpose of the terms to restrain the courts from a wholesale invalidation of state laws under the Equal Protection Clause it would be difficult to say that the poll tax requirement is "irrational" or "arbitrary" or works "invidious discriminations." State poll tax legislation can "reasonably," "rationally" and without an "invidious" or evil purpose to injure anyone be found to rest on a number of state policies including (1) the State's desire to collect its revenue, and (2) its belief that voters who pay a poll tax will be interested in furthering the State's welfare when they vote. . . .

The Court's failure to give any reasons to show that these purposes of the poll tax are "irrational," "unreasonable," "arbitrary," or "invidious" is a pretty clear indication to me that none exist. I can only conclude that the primary, controlling, predominant, if not the exclusive reason for declaring the Virginia law unconstitutional is the Court's deep-seated hostility and antagonism, which I share, to making payment of a tax a prerequisite to voting. . . .

. . . For us to undertake in the guise of constitutional interpretation to decide the constitutional policy question of this case amounts, in my judgment, to a plain exercise of power which the Constitution has denied us but has specifically granted to Congress. I cannot join in holding that the Virginia state poll tax law violates the Equal Protection Clause.

MR. JUSTICE HARLAN, whom MR. JUSTICE STEWART joins, dissenting. . . .

. . . Is there a rational basis for Virginia's poll tax as a voting qualification? I think the answer to that question is undoubtedly "yes."

. . . It is certainly a rational argument that payment of some minimal poll tax promotes civic responsibility, weeding out those who do not care enough about public affairs to pay $1.50 or thereabouts a year for the exercise of the franchise. It is also arguable, indeed it was probably accepted as sound political theory by a large percentage of Americans through most of our history, that people with some property have a deeper stake in community affairs, and are consequently more responsible, more educated, more knowledgeable, more worthy of confidence, than those without means, and that the community and Nation would be better managed if the franchise were restricted to such citizens. Nondiscriminatory and fairly applied literacy tests . . . find justification on very similar grounds.

These viewpoints, to be sure, ring hollow on most contemporary ears. Their lack of acceptance today is evidenced by the fact that nearly all of the States, left to their own devices, have eliminated property or poll-tax qualifications; by the cognate fact that Congress and three-quarters of the States quickly ratified the Twenty-Fourth Amendment; and by the fact that rules such as the "pauper exclusion" in Virginia law . . . have never been enforced.

Property and poll-tax qualifications, very simply, are not in accord with current egalitarian notions of how a modern democracy should be organized. It is of course entirely fitting that legislatures should modify the law to reflect such changes in popular attitudes. However, it is all wrong, in my view, for the Court to adopt the political doctrines popularly accepted at a particular moment of our history and to declare all others to be irrational and invidious, barring them from the range of choice by reasonably minded people acting through the political process. It was not too long ago that Mr. Justice Holmes felt impelled to remind the Court that the Due Process Clause of the Fourteenth Amendment does not enact the *laissez-faire* theory of society. . . . The times have changed, and perhaps it is appropriate to observe that neither does the Equal Protection Clause of that Amendment rigidly impose upon America an ideology of unrestrained egalitarianism.

Dunn v. Blumstein

405 U.S. 330; 92 S. Ct. 995; 31 L. Ed. 2d 274 (1972)

Tennessee law required a one-year residence in the state and a three-month residence in the county as a condition of voting. James Blumstein, a newly appointed faculty member at Vanderbilt University Law School, brought an action in federal district court against Governor Winfield Dunn and various other Tennessee public officials, challenging the constitutionality of this durational residency requirement. A three-judge court, in finding for Blumstein, concluded that the Tennessee law impermissibly interfered with the right to vote and created a "suspect" classification, penalizing some Tennessee residences because of recent interstate travel. Tennessee appealed to the U.S. Supreme Court. *Opinion of the Court: Marshall, Brennan, Douglas, Stewart, White. Concurring in judgment: Blackmun. Dissenting opinion: Burger. Not participating: Powell, Rehnquist.*

Mr. Justice Marshall delivered the opinion of the Court. . . .

Durational residence laws penalize those persons who have traveled from one place to another to establish a new residence during the qualifying period. Such laws divide residents into two classes, old residents and new residents, and discriminate against the latter to the extent of totally denying them the opportunity to vote. The constitutional question presented is whether the Equal Protection Clause of the Fourteenth Amendment permits a State to discriminate in this way among its citizens.

To decide whether a law violates the Equal Protection Clause, we look, in essence, to three things: the character of the classification in question; the individual interests affected by the classification; and the governmental interests asserted in support of the classification. . . . In considering laws challenged under the Equal Protection Clause, this Court has evolved more than one test, depending upon the interests affected and the classification involved. First, then, we must determine what standard of review is appropriate. In the present case, whether we look to the benefit withheld by the classification (the opportunity to vote) or the basis for the classifications (recent interstate travel) we conclude that the State must show a substantial and compelling reason for imposing durational residence requirements.

Durational residence requirements completely bar from voting all residents not meeting the fixed durational standards. By denying some citizens the right to vote, such laws deprive them of "a fundamental political right, . . . preservative of all rights." . . . If a challenged statute grants the right to vote to some citizens and denies the franchise to others, "the Court must determine whether the exclusions are *necessary* to promote a *compelling* state interest." . . . This is the test we apply here.

This exacting test is appropriate for another reason: . . . Tennessee's durational residence laws classify bona fide residents on the basis of recent travel, penalizing those persons, and only those persons, who have gone from one jurisdiction to another during the qualifying period. Thus, the durational residence requirement directly impinges on the exercise of a second fundamental personal right, the right to travel.

. . . Durational residence laws must be measured by a strict equal protection test: they are unconstitutional unless the State can demonstrate that such laws are "*necessary* to promote a *compelling* governmental interest." . . .

It is not sufficient for the State to show that durational residence requirements further a very substantial state interest. In pursuing that important interest, the State cannot choose means which unnecessarily burden or restrict constitutionally protected activity. Statutes affecting constitutional rights must be drawn with "precision" . . . , and must be "tailored" to serve their legitimate objectives. . . . And if there are other, reasonable ways to achieve those goals with a lesser burden on constitutionally protected activity, a State may not choose the way of greater interference. If it acts at all, it must choose "less drastic means." . . .

We turn, then, to the question of whether the State has shown that durational residence requirements are needed to further a sufficiently substantial state interest. We emphasize again the difference between bona fide residence requirements and durational residence requirements. We have in the past noted approvingly that the States have the power to require that voters be bona fide residents of the relevant political subdivision. . . . An appropriately defined and uniformly applied requirement of bona fide residence may be necessary to preserve the basic conception of a political community, and therefore could withstand close constitutional scrutiny. But *durational* residence requirements, representing a separate voting qualification imposed on bona fide residents, must be separately tested by the stringent standard. . . .

Tennessee tenders "two basic purposes" served by its durational residence requirements: "(1) INSURE PURITY OF BALLOT BOX—Protection against fraud through colonization and inability to identify persons offering to vote, and (2) KNOWLEDGEABLE VOTER—Afford some surety that the voter has, in fact, become a member of the community and that as such, he has a common interest in all matters pertaining to its government and is, therefore, more likely to exercise his right more intelligently" . . . .

Preservation of the "purity of the ballot box" is a formidable sounding state interest. The impurities feared, variously called "dual voting" and "colonization," all involve voting by nonresidents, either singly or in groups. The main concern is that nonresidents will temporarily invade the State or county, falsely swear that they are residents to become eligible to vote, and, by voting, allow a candidate to win by fraud. Surely the prevention of such fraud is a legitimate and compelling government goal. But it is impossible to view durational residence requirements as necessary to achieve that state interest.

Preventing fraud, the asserted evil which justifies state lawmaking, means keeping nonresidents from voting. But, by definition, a durational residence law bars *newly arrived* residents from the franchise along with nonresidents. . . .

Durational residence laws may once have been necessary to prevent a fraudulent evasion of state voter standards, but today in Tennessee, as in most other States, this purpose is served by a system of voter registration. . . .

Our conclusion that the waiting period is not the least restrictive means necessary for preventing fraud is bolstered by the recognition that Tennessee has at its disposal a variety of criminal laws which are more than adequate to detect and deter whatever fraud may be feared. . . .

The argument that durational residence requirements further the goal of having "knowledgeable voters" appears to involve three separate claims. The first is that such requirements "afford some surety that the voter has, in fact, become a member of the community." But here the State appears to confuse a bona fide residence requirement with a durational residence requirement. As already noted, a State does have an interest in limiting the franchise to bona fide members of the community. But this does not justify or explain the exclusion from the franchise of persons, not because their bona fide residence is questioned, but because they are recent rather than long-time residents.

The second branch of the "knowledgeable voters" justification is that durational residence requirements assure that the voter "has a common interest in all matters pertaining to [the community's] government. . . ." By this, presumably, the State means that it may require a period of residence sufficiently lengthy to impress upon its voters the local viewpoint. This is precisely the sort of argument this court has repeatedly rejected. . . .

. . . Tennessee's hopes for voters with a "common interest in all matters pertaining to [the community's] government" is impermissible. . . .

Finally, the State urges that a long-time resident is "more likely to exercise his right [to vote] more intelligently." To the extent that this is different from the previous argument, the State is apparently asserting an interest in limiting the franchise to voters who are minimally knowledgeable about the issues. In this case, Tennessee argues that people who have been in the State less than a year and the county less than three months are likely to be unaware of the issues involved in the congressional, state, and local elections, and therefore can be barred from the franchise. We note that the criterion of "intelligent" voting is an elusive one, and susceptible to abuse. But without deciding as a general matter the extent to which a State can bar less knowledgeable or intelligent citizens from the franchise, . . . we conclude that durational residence requirements cannot be justified on this basis.

The durational residence requirements in this case founder because of their crudeness as a device for achieving the articulated state goal of assuring the knowledgeable exercise of the franchise. The classifications created by durational residence requirements obviously permit any long-time resident to vote regardless of his knowledge of the issues—and obviously many long-time residents do not have any. On the other hand, the classifications bar from the franchise many other, admittedly new, residents who have become minimally, and often fully, informed about the issues. Indeed, recent migrants who take the time to register and vote shortly after moving are likely to be those citizens, such as appellee, who make it a point to be informed and knowledgeable about the issues. Given modern communications, and given the clear indication that campaign spending and voter education occur largely during the month before an election, the State cannot seriously maintain that it is "necessary" to reside for a year in the State and three months in the county in order to be minimally knowledgeable about congressional, state or even purely local elections. There is simply nothing in the record to support the conclusive presumption that residents who have lived in the State for less than a year and their county for less than three months are uninformed about elections. . . .

It is pertinent to note that Tennessee has never

made an attempt to further its alleged interest in an informed electorate in a universally applicable way. Knowledge or competence has never been a criterion for participation in Tennessee's electoral process for long-time residents. Indeed, the State specifically provides for voting by various types of absentee persons. These provisions permit many long-time residents who leave the county or State to participate in a constituency in which they have only the slightest political interest, and from whose political debates they are likely to be cut off. That the State specifically permits such voting is not consistent with its claimed compelling interest in intelligent, informed use of the ballot. If the State seeks to assure intelligent use of the ballot, it may not try to serve this interest only with respect to new arrivals. . . .

We are aware that classifications are always imprecise. By requiring classifications to be tailored to their purpose, we do not secretly require the impossible. Here, there is simply too attenuated a relationship between the state interest in an informed electorate and the fixed requirement that voters must have been residents in the State for a year and the county for three months. Given the exacting standard of precision we require of statutes affecting constitutional rights, we cannot say that durational residence requirements are necessary to further a compelling state interest. . . .

MR. CHIEF JUSTICE BURGER, dissenting.

. . . It is no more a denial of Equal Protection for a State to require newcomers to be exposed to state and local problems for a reasonable period such as one year before voting, than it is to require children to wait 18 years before voting. . . . In both cases some informed and responsible persons are denied the vote, while others less informed and less responsible are permitted to vote. Some lines must be drawn. To challenge such lines by the "compelling state interest" standard is to condemn them all. So far as I am aware, no state law has ever satisfied this seemingly insurmountable standard, and I doubt one ever will, for it demands nothing less than perfection. . . .

San Antonio Independent School District v. *Rodriguez*

411 U.S. 1; 93 S. Ct. 1278; 36 L. Ed. 2d 16 (1973)

The financing of public elementary and secondary education in Texas is a product of state and local participation. Almost half of the revenues are derived from a largely state-funded program designed to provide basic minimum education in every school. Each district then supplements this state aid through an *ad valorem* tax on property within its jurisdiction. Demetrio Rodriguez and others brought a class action on behalf of schoolchildren who were members of poor families that resided in school districts with low property-tax bases, claiming that the Texas system's reliance on local property taxation favored the more affluent and that it violated equal protection requirements because of the substantial interdistrict disparities in per-pupil expenditures that resulted primarily from differences in the value of assessable property among the districts. A three-judge federal district court, finding that wealth is a "suspect" classification and that education is a "fundamental right," concluded that the system could be upheld only upon a showing (which appellants failed to make) that there was a compelling state interest for the system. The court further concluded that appellants failed even to demonstrate a rational basis for Texas's system. The state appealed. *Opinion of the Court: Powell, Blackmun, Burger, Rehnquist, Stewart. Concurring opinion: Stewart. Dissenting opinions: Brennan; Marshall, Douglas; White, Brennan, Douglas.*

Mr. Justice Powell delivered the opinion of the Court. . . .

. . . We must decide, first, whether the Texas system of financing public education operates to the disadvantage of some suspect class or impinges upon a fundamental right explicitly or implicitly protected by the Constitution, thereby requiring strict judicial scrutiny. If so, the judgment of the District Court should be affirmed. If not, the Texas scheme must still be examined to determine whether it rationally furthers some legitimate, articulated state purpose and therefore does not constitute an invidious discrimination in violation of the Equal Protection Clause of the Fourteenth Amendment. . . .

We are unable to agree that this case, which in significant aspects is *sui generis*, may be so neatly fitted into the conventional mosaic of constitutional analysis under the Equal Protection Clause. Indeed, for the several reasons that follow, we find neither the suspect classification nor the fundamental interest analysis persuasive. . . .

The precedents of this Court provide the proper starting point. The individuals or groups of individuals who constituted the class discriminated against in our prior cases shared two distinguishing characteristics: because of their impecunity they were completely unable to pay for some desired benefit, and as a consequence, they sustained an absolute deprivation of a meaningful opportunity to enjoy that benefit. . . .

. . . Even a cursory examination, however, demonstrates that neither of the two distinguishing characteristics of wealth classifications can be found here. First, in support of their charge that the system discriminates against the "poor," appellees have made no effort to demonstrate that it operates to the peculiar disadvantage of any class fairly definable as indigent, or as composed of persons whose incomes are beneath any designated poverty level. Indeed, there is reason to believe that the poorest families are not necessarily clustered in the poorest property districts. A recent and exhaustive study of school districts in Connecticut concluded that "[i]t is clearly incorrect . . . to contend that the 'poor' live in 'poor' districts. . . . " Defining "poor" families as those below the Bureau of the Census "poverty level," the Connecticut study found, not surprisingly, that the poor were clustered around commercial and industrial areas—those same areas that provide the most attractive sources of property tax income for school districts. Whether a similar pattern would be discovered in Texas is not known, but there is no basis on the record in this case for assuming that the poorest people—defined by reference to any level of absolute impecunity—are concentrated in the poorest districts.

Second, neither appellees nor the District Court addressed the fact that, unlike each of the foregoing cases, lack of personal resources has not occasioned an absolute deprivation of the desired benefit. The argument here is not that the children in districts having relatively low assessable property values are receiving no public education; rather, it is that they are receiving a poorer quality education than that available to children in districts having more assessable wealth. Apart from the unsettled and disputed question whether the quality of education may be determined by the amount of money expended for it, a sufficient answer to appellees' argument is that at least where wealth is involved the Equal Protection Clause does not require absolute equality or precisely equal advantages. Nor, indeed, in view of the infinite variables affecting the educational process, can any system assure equal quality of education except in the most relative sense. . . .

For these two reasons—the absence of any evidence that the financing system discriminates against any definable category of "poor" people or that it results in the absolute deprivation of education—the disadvantaged class is not susceptible to identification in traditional terms. . . .

We thus conclude that the Texas system does not operate to the peculiar disadvantage of any suspect class. But in recognition of the fact that this Court has never heretofore held that wealth discrimination alone provides an adequate basis for invoking strict scrutiny, appellees have not relied solely on this contention. They also assert that the State's system impermissibly interferes with the exercise of a "fundamental" right and that accordingly the prior decisions of this Court require the application of the strict standard of judicial review. . . . It is this question—whether education is a fundamental right, in the sense that it is among the rights and liberties protected by the Constitution—which has so consumed the attention of courts and commentators in recent years.

In *Brown* v. *Board of Education* . . . (1954), a unanimous Court recognized that "education is perhaps the most important function of state and local governments." . . . What was said there in the context of racial discrimination has lost none of its vitality with the passage of time: "Compulsory school attendance laws and the great expenditures for education both demonstrate our recognition of the importance of education to our democratic society. It is required in the performance of our most basic responsibilities, even service in the armed forces. It is the very foundation of good citizenship. Today it is a principal instrument in awakening the child to cultural values, in preparing him for later professional training, and in helping him to adjust normally to his environment. In these days, it is doubtful that any child may reasonably be expected to succeed in life if he is denied the opportunity of an education. Such an opportunity, where the state has undertaken to provide it, is a right which must be made available to all on equal terms." . . . This theme, expressing an abiding respect for the vital role of education in a free society, may be found in numerous opinions of Justices of this Court writing both before and after *Brown* was decided. . . .

Nothing this court holds today in any way detracts from our historic dedication to public education. We are in complete agreement with the conclusion of the three-judge panel below that "the grave significance of education both to the individual and to our society" cannot be doubted. But the importance of a service performed by the State does not determine whether it must be regarded as fundamental for purposes of examination under the Equal Protection Clause.

. . . It is not the province of this Court to create substantive constitutional rights in the name of guaranteeing equal protection of the laws. Thus the key to discovering whether education is "fundamental" is not to be found in comparisons of the relative societal significance of education as opposed to subsistence or housing. Nor is it to be found by weighing whether education is as important as the right to travel. Rather, the answer lies in assessing whether there is a right to education explicitly or implicitly guaranteed by the Constitution. . . .

Education, of course, is not among the rights afforded explicit protection under our Federal Constitution. Nor do we find any basis for saying it is implicitly so protected. As we have said, the undisputed importance of education will not alone cause this Court to depart from the usual standard for reviewing a State's social and economic legislation. It is appellees' contention, however, that education is distinguishable from other services and benefits provided by the State because it bears a peculiarly close relationship to other rights and liberties accorded protection under the Constitution. Specifically, they insist that education is itself a fundamental personal right because it is essential to the effective exercise of First Amendment freedoms and to intelligent utilization of the right to vote. In asserting a nexus between speech and education, appellees urge that the right to speak is meaningless unless the speaker is capable of articulating his thoughts intelligently and persuasively. The "marketplace of ideas" is an empty forum for those lacking basic communicative tools. Likewise, they argue that the corollary right to receive information becomes little more than a hollow privilege when the recipient has not been taught to read, assimilate, and utilize available knowledge.

A similar line of reasoning is pursued with respect to the right to vote. Exercise of the franchise, it is contended, cannot be divorced from the educational foundation of the voter. The electoral process, if reality is to conform to the democratic ideal, depends on an informed electorate: a voter cannot cast his ballot intelligently unless his reading skills and thought processes have been adequately developed.

We need not dispute any of these propositions. The Court has long afforded zealous protection against unjustifiable governmental interference with the individual's rights to speak and to vote. Yet we have never presumed to possess either the ability or the authority to guarantee to the citizenry the most *effective* speech or the most *informed* electoral choice. That these may be desirable goals of a system of freedom of expression and of a representative form of government is not to be doubted. These are indeed goals to be pursued by a people whose thoughts and beliefs are freed from governmental interference. But they are not values to be implemented by judicial intrusion into otherwise legitimate state activities.

Even if it were conceded that some identifiable quantum of education is a constitutionally protected prerequisite to the meaningful exercise of either right, we have no indication that the present levels of educational expenditure in Texas provide an education that falls short. Whatever merit appellees' argument might have if a State's financing system occasioned an absolute denial of educational opportunities to any of its children, that argument provides no basis for finding an interference with fundamental rights where only relative differences in spending levels are involved and where—as is true in the present case—no charge fairly could be made that the system fails to provide each child with an opportunity to acquire the basic minimal skills necessary for the enjoyment of the rights of speech and of full participation in the political process. . . .

We have carefully considered each of the arguments supportive of the District Court's finding that education is a fundamental right or liberty and have found those arguments unpersuasive. In one further respect we find this a particularly inappropriate case in which to subject state action to strict judicial scrutiny. The present case, . . . involves the most persistent and difficult questions of educational policy, another area in which this Court's lack of specialized knowledge and experience counsels against premature interference with the informed judgments made at the state and local levels. . . . On even the most basic questions in this area the scholars and educational experts are divided. Indeed, one of the hottest sources of controversy concerns the extent to which there is a demonstrable correlation between educational expenditures and the quality of education—an assumed correlation underlying virtually every legal conclusion drawn by the District Court in this case. Related to the questioned relationship between cost and quality is the equally unsettled controversy as to the proper goals of a system of public education. And the question regarding the most effective relationship between state boards of education and local school boards, in terms of their respective responsibilities and degrees of control, is now undergoing searching re-examination. The ultimate wisdom as to these and related problems of education is not likely to be defined for all time even by the scholars who now so earnestly debate the issues. In such circumstances the judiciary is well advised to refrain from interposing on the States inflexible constitutional restraints that could circumscribe or handicap the continued research and experimentation so vital to finding even partial solutions to educational problems and to keeping abreast of ever changing conditions. . . .

The foregoing considerations buttress our conclusion that Texas' system of public school finance is an inappropriate candidate for strict judicial scrutiny. These same considerations are relevant to the determination whether that system, with its conceded imperfections, nevertheless bears some rational relationship to a legitimate state purpose. It is to this question that we next turn our attention. . . .

. . . The Texas plan is not the result of hurried, ill-conceived legislation. It certainly is not the product of purposeful discrimination against any group or class. On the contrary, it is rooted in decades of experience in Texas and elsewhere, and in major part is the product of responsible studies by qualified people. In giving substance to the presumption of validity to which the Texas system is entitled . . . it is important to remember that at every stage of its development it has constituted a "rough accommodation" of interests in an effort to arrive at practical and workable solutions. . . . One also must remember that the system here challenged is not peculiar to Texas or to any other State. In its essential characteristics the Texas plan for financing public education reflects what many educators for a half century have thought was an enlightened approach to a problem for which there is no perfect solution. We are unwilling to assume for ourselves a level of wisdom superior to that of legislators, scholars, and educational authorities in 49 States, especially where the alternatives proposed are only recently conceived and nowhere yet tested. The constitutional standard under the Equal Protection Clause is whether the challenged state action rationally furthers a legitimate state purpose or interest. . . . We hold that the Texas plan abundantly satisfies this standard.

MR. JUSTICE WHITE, with whom MR. JUSTICE DOUGLAS and MR. JUSTICE BRENNAN join, dissenting. . . .

The Equal Protection Clause permits discriminations between classes but requires that the classification bear some rational relationship to a permissible object sought to be attained by the statute. It is not enough that the Texas system before us seeks to achieve the valid, rational purpose of maximizing local initiative; the means chosen by the State must also be rationally related to the end sought to be achieved. . . .

Neither Texas nor the majority heeds this rule. If the State aims at maximizing local initiative and local choice, by permitting school districts to resort to the real property tax if they choose to do so, it utterly fails in achieving its purpose in districts with property tax bases so low that there is little if any opportunity for interested parents, rich or poor, to augment school district revenues. Requiring the State to establish only that unequal treatment is in furtherance of a permissible goal, without also requiring the State to show that the means chosen to effectuate that goal are rationally related to its achievement, makes equal protection analysis no more than an empty gesture. In my view, the parents and children in Edgewood, and in like districts, suffer from an invidious discrimination violative of the Equal Protection Clause. . . .

MR. JUSTICE MARSHALL, with whom MR. JUSTICE DOUGLAS concurs, dissenting. . . .

This Court has repeatedly held that state discrimination which either adversely affects a "fundamental interest" . . . or is based on a distinction of a suspect character . . . must be carefully scrutinized to ensure that the scheme is necessary to promote a substantial, legitimate state interest. . . . The majority today concludes, however, that the Texas scheme is not subject to such a strict standard of review under the Equal Protection Clause. Instead, in its view, the Texas scheme must be tested by nothing more than that lenient standard of rationality which we have traditionally applied to discriminatory state action in the context of economic and commercial matters. . . . By so doing, the Court avoids the telling task of searching for a substantial state interest which the Texas financing scheme, with its variations in taxable district property wealth, is necessary to further. I cannot accept such an emasculation of the Equal Protection Clause in the context of this case. . . .

To begin, I must once more voice my disagreement with the Court's rigidified approach to equal protection analysis. . . .

I therefore cannot accept the majority's labored efforts to demonstrate that fundamental interests, which call for strict scrutiny of the challenged classification, encompass only established rights which we are somehow bound to recognize from the text of the Constitution itself. To be sure, some interests which the Court has deemed to be fundamental for purposes of equal protection analysis are themselves constitutionally protected rights. . . . But it will not do to suggest that the "answer" to whether an interest is fundamental for purposes of equal protection analysis is *always* determined by whether that interest "is a right . . . explicitly or implicitly guaranteed by the Constitution." . . .

I would like to know where the Constitution guarantees the right to procreate, *Skinner* v. *Oklahoma ex rel. Williamson* . . . (1942), or the right to vote in state elections, *e.g., Reynolds* v. *Sims* . . . (1964), or the right to an appeal from a criminal conviction, *e.g., Griffin* v. *Illinois* . . . (1956). These are instances in which, due to the importance of the interests at stake, the Court has displayed a strong concern with the existence of discriminatory state treatment. But the Court has never said or indicated that these are interests which independently enjoy full-blown constitutional protection.

The majority is, of course, correct when it suggests that the process of determining which interests are fundamental is a difficult one. But I do not think the problem is insurmountable. And I certainly do not accept the view that the process need necessarily degenerate into an unprincipled, subjective "picking-and-choosing" between various interests or that it must involve this Court in creating "substantive constitutional rights in the name of guaranteeing equal protection of the laws." . . . Although not all fundamental interests are constitutionally guaranteed, the determination of which interests are fundamental should be firmly rooted in the text of the Constitution. The task in every case should be to determine the extent to which constitutionally guaranteed rights are dependent on interests not mentioned in the Constitution. As the nexus between the specific constitutional guarantee and the nonconstitutional interest draws closer, the nonconstitutional interest becomes more fundamental and the degree of judicial scrutiny applied when the interest is infringed on a discriminatory basis must be adjusted accordingly. Thus, it cannot be denied that interests such as procreation, the exercise of the state franchise, and access to criminal appellate processes are not fully guaranteed to the citizen by our Constitution. But these interests have nonetheless been afforded special judicial consideration in the face of discrimination because they are, to some extent, interrelated with constitutional guarantees. Procreation is now understood to be important because of its interaction with the established constitutional right of privacy. The exercise of the state franchise is closely tied to basic civil and political rights inherent in the First Amendment. And access to criminal appellate processes enhances the integrity of the range of rights implicit in the Fourteenth Amendment guarantee of due process of law. Only if we closely protect the related interests from state discrimination do we ultimately ensure the integrity of the constitutional guarantee itself. This is the real lesson that must be taken from our previous decisions involving interests deemed to be fundamental. . . .

A similar process of analysis with respect to the invidiousness of the basis on which a particular classification is drawn has also influenced the Court as to the appropriate degree of scrutiny to be accorded any particular case. The highly suspect character of classifications based on race, nationality, or alienage is well established. The reasons why such classifications call for close judicial scrutiny are manifold. Certain racial and ethnic groups have frequently been recognized as "discrete and insular minorities" who are relatively powerless to protect their interests in the political process. . . . Moreover, race, nationality, or alienage is " 'in most circumstances irrelevant' to any constitutionally acceptable legislative purpose. . . . Instead, lines drawn on such bases are frequently the reflection of historic prejudices rather than legislative rationality. It may be that all of these considerations, which make for particular judicial solicitude in the face of discrimination on the basis of race, nationality, or alienage, do not coalesce—or at least not to the same degree—in other forms of discrimination. Nevertheless, these considerations have undoubtedly influenced the care with which the Court has scrutinized other forms of discrimination. . . .

In summary, it seems to me inescapably clear that this Court has consistently adjusted the care with which it will review state discrimination in light of the constitutional significance of the interests affected and the invidiousness of the particular classification. In the context of economic interests, we find that discriminatory state action is almost always sustained for such interests are generally far removed from constitutional guarantees. Moreover, "[t]he extremes to which the Court has gone in dreaming up rational bases for state regulation in that area may in many instances be ascribed to a healthy revulsion from the Court's earlier excesses in using the Constitution to protect interests that have more than enough power to protect themselves in the legislative halls." . . . But the situation differs markedly when discrimination against important individual interests with constitutional implications and against particularly disadvantaged or powerless classes is involved. The majority suggests, however, that a variable standard of review would give this Court the appearance of a "superlegislature." . . . I cannot agree. Such an approach seems to me a part of the guarantees of our Constitution and of the historic experiences with oppression of and discrimination against discrete, powerless minorities which underlie that Document. In truth, the Court itself will be open to the criticism raised by the majority so long as it continues on its present course of effectively selecting in private which cases will be afforded special consideration without acknowledging the true basis of its action. . . . Such obfuscated action may be appropriate to a political body such as a legislature, but it is not appropriate to this Court. Open debate of the bases for the Court's action is essential to the rationality and consistency of our decisionmaking process. Only in this way can we avoid the label of legislature and ensure the integrity of the judicial process.

Nevertheless, the majority today attempts to force this case into the same category for purposes of equal protection analysis as decisions involving discrimination affecting commercial interests. By so doing, the majority singles this case out for analytic treatment at odds with what seems to me to be the clear trend of recent decisions in this Court, and thereby ignores the constitutional importance of the interest at stake and the invidiousness of the particular classification, factors that call for far more than the lenient scrutiny of the Texas financing scheme which the majority pursues. Yet if the discrimination inherent in the Texas scheme is scrutinized with the care demanded by the interest and classification present in this case, the unconstitutionality of that scheme is unmistakable.

17
THE RIGHT TO PRIVACY

Any consideration of the right to privacy must begin with Louis D. Brandeis. In a pioneering exposition, Brandeis, then a young legal scholar, asserted in the 1890 *Harvard Law Review* that the right to privacy means fundamentally "the right to be let alone."[1] The significance of this article, which he wrote with Samuel Warren, cannot be overstated; it generally is regarded as the most influential law review article ever published. Thirty-eight years later, as a justice of the Supreme Court, Brandeis expanded on the theme of the article in his dissent in *Olmstead* v. *United States* (1928): "The right to be let alone . . . [is] the most comprehensive of rights and the right most valued by civilized men. To protect that right, every unjustified intrusion of the government upon the privacy of the individual, whatever the means employed, must be deemed a [constitutional] violation." Another thirty-seven years would pass before Justice Brandeis's words were vindicated in *Griswold* v. *Connecticut* (1965), a landmark case in which the Court for the first time acknowledged the individual's constitutional right to privacy. Once vindicated, however, Brandeis's words, along with the right they declare, came to have a profound and troubling impact, for the right to privacy has figured prominently in some of the most controversial and divisive decisions the Court has ever rendered—those on abortion. This chapter explores three principal issues arising out of this right to privacy:

1. Is there a constitutional right to privacy, and if so, what is its constitutional basis?
2. What exactly does this right protect? Does the privacy to be protected inhere in places, relationships, or people?
3. What qualifications, if any, limit this right?

THE CONSTITUTIONAL BASIS

In his *Olmstead* dissent, Justice Brandeis considered the right to privacy to be "the most comprehensive of rights," and so it may well be. That same comprehensive nature, however, has made it exceedingly difficult for the Court to ascertain precisely what provision (or provisions) of the Constitution protect this right. Various justices have identified and relied upon different constitutional bases. Justice Brandeis in *Olmstead* (discussed in chapter 14) based the right to privacy on the Fourth Amendment's protections against unreasonable searches and seizures and on the Fifth Amendment's guarantee against self-incrimination. But Justice John Marshall Harlan, in his concurrence in *Griswold,* and Justice Harry Blackmun, in his opinion for the Court in *Roe* v. *Wade* (1973), declared that privacy claims were protected by the Due Process Clause of the Fourteenth Amendment; Justice William Brennan, in both his opinion for the Court in *Eisenstadt* v. *Baird* (1972) and his dissent in *Harris* v. *McRae* (1980), based the right to privacy on the Equal Protection Clause of the Fourteenth Amendment; Justice Arthur Goldberg, in his *Griswold* concurrence, relied on the Ninth Amendment; and Justice William Douglas, in his majority opinion in *Griswold,* unable to identify any single constitutional provision but taking comfort in the fact that "specific guarantees in the Bill of Rights have penumbras, formed by emanations from those guarantees that help give them life and substance," argued that a penumbral right of privacy emanates from particular guarantees found in the First, Third, Fourth, Fifth, and Ninth amendments.

These differences of opinion over the constitutional basis of the right to privacy apparently reflect a reluctance on the part of the Court to rely on the Due Process Clause. To many justices, grounding the right to privacy on the Due Process Clause and then employing that provision to bar legislative regulation of an entire area of conduct—as exemplified in *Griswold*—has raised the specter of substantive due process and provided too many parallels to the Court's pre-1937 espousal of "liberty of contract" as a defense against business regulation (see chapter 11). They have, therefore, pressed into service other constitutional provisions, including the Equal Protection Clause, the Ninth Amendment, and Justice Douglas's "penumbras." Reliance on these provisions has enabled the justices to provide the same level of protection for the right to privacy as would be provided by substantive due process. As Justice William Rehnquist has noted, these provisions—at least insofar as they have been employed by the Court in privacy cases—are "sisters under the skin" to substantive due process.[2] By invoking them, the justices apparently considered that they would escape the onus so often attached to substantive due process. Consider, for example, the following statement by Justice Douglas in *Griswold,* in which substantive due process is repudiated publicly but embraced *sub silentio.*

> We are met with a wide range of questions that implicate the Due Process Clause of the Fourteenth Amendment. Overtones of some

> arguments suggest that *Lochner* v. *State of New York* . . . should be our guide. But we decline that invitation. . . . We do not sit as a super-legislature to determine the wisdom, need, and propriety of laws that touch economic problems, business affairs, or social conditions.

That substantive due process is not without its merits was made clear by the Warren Court's embrace of it in *Bolling* v. *Sharpe* (1954). (See Chapter 15 for a full discussion of this issue.) The contemporary Court, however, is for the most part reluctant to employ substantive due process formally and defend it publicly, preferring instead to rely on its "sisters under the skin." As a result, the right to privacy has emerged as an issue in its own right, rather than as a dependency of due process, equal protection, or any other specific constitutional guarantee.

WHAT THE RIGHT TO PRIVACY PROTECTS

A second major issue arising out of the right to privacy centers on the question of what exactly does this right protect. In its initial decisions regarding privacy, the Court tended to view the right to privacy as place-oriented and property-based, and hence as narrow in the range of its protections. This tendency was understandable in view of the fact that these decisions invariably concerned questions of criminal procedure and the meaning and reach of the Fourth Amendment's protections against unreasonable searches and seizures. In the landmark *Olmstead* decision, for example, the Court majority upheld the courtroom use of wiretap evidence that had been obtained without a search warrant, arguing that because there had been no "actual physical invasion" or trespass of the defendants' homes or offices, there had been no search involved, and hence no violation of the Fourth Amendment and the privacy it guarantees. Justice Brandeis, in dissent, argued that privacy inheres in the individual (i.e., the person) and involves nothing less than the "right to be let alone." Despite this eloquent plea, the majority opinion in *Olmstead* remained in force well into the 1960s. A long line of cases, stretching from *Olmstead* through *Goldman* v. *United States* (1942) to *Silverman* v. *United States* (1961), consistently presented privacy as place-oriented and property-based (The frequent repetition by the courts of the aphorism "A man's home is his castle," underscored the judiciary's identification of privacy with property rights.). Anything less than physical trespass onto private premises, these cases held, fell outside the ambit of Fourth Amendment protection.

In the mid-1960s, however, this long-standing approach to privacy questions underwent drastic changes. In *Griswold*, the Court declared that privacy inheres in legally protected relationships (in this case, marriage). It went further in *Katz* v. *United States* (1967), declaring that the privacy component of the "Fourth Amendment protects people, not places"[3] and thus broadened considerably the scope of coverage of the right to privacy.

Griswold struck down a Connecticut statute that had made it a criminal offense either to use birth control devices or to give information or instruction on their use. In defending this decision, Justice Douglas observed that to enforce of the law, the police would have to search the bedrooms of married couples for evidence of contraceptive use—an idea that struck him as "repulsive to the notions of privacy surrounding the marriage relationship." Justice Douglas placed heavy emphasis on the "intimate relation of husband and wife": the privacy he sought to protect inhered in neither places nor persons, but in a relationship. He waxed poetic concerning this relationship: "Marriage is a coming together for better or for worse, hopefully enduring, and intimate to the degree of being sacred." Ironically, his efforts to protect the privacy of the conjugal bed by stressing the sacred intimacy of marriage soon were rendered superfluous by *Eisenstadt* v. *Baird* (1972), in which the Court invalidated a Massachusetts law that had made it a felony to give anyone other than a married person contraceptive medicines or devices. Justice Brennan, speaking for the Court, argued that the right to privacy inheres in the person and is not limited to certain relationships:

> If under *Griswold* the distribution of contraceptives to married persons cannot be prohibited, a ban on distribution to unmarried persons would be equally impermissible. It is true that in *Griswold* the right of privacy in question inhered in the marital relationship. Yet the marital couple is not an independent entity with a mind and heart of its own, but an association of two individuals each with a separate intellectual and emotional make-up. If the right of privacy means anything, it is the right of the individual, married or single, to be free from unwarranted governmental intrusion into matters so fundamentally affecting a person as the decision whether to bear or beget a child.

The ground for the Court's claim in *Eisenstadt* that the right to privacy inheres in the person and not necessarily in the relationship had been prepared in the *Katz* ruling that the privacy component of the Fourth Amendment "protects people, not places." Writing for the *Katz* majority, Justice Stewart had abandoned the line of cases from *Olmstead* through *Silverman* that had limited the reach of the Fourth Amendment to "constitutionally protected areas" and declared that "what a person knowingly exposes to the public, even in his own home or office, is not a subject of Fourth Amendment protection. . . . But what he seeks to preserve as private, even in an area accessible to the public, may be constitutionally protected." Because it emerged in a Fourth Amendment case, this new, person-oriented right to privacy initially was limited to cases involving unreasonable searches and seizures. In subsequent cases, however, the Court used this expanded conception of privacy not only to regulate particular practices in law enforcement and criminal procedure but also (and more importantly) to invalidate substantive governmental regulation of entire areas of conduct. Thus, it employed a broad conception of the right to privacy in banning legislative restrictions of birth control in *Eisenstadt* and in invalidating antiabortion statutes in the highly controversial case of *Roe* v. *Wade* (1973).

By declaring that "the personal right of privacy includes the abortion decision," *Roe,* together with the companion case of *Doe* v. *Bolton* (1973), generated a firestorm of controversy that has enveloped the Court ever since. To begin with, critics have charged that *Roe* and *Doe* gave an entirely new meaning to the term *privacy.* As Justice Rehnquist noted in his dissent, "A transaction resulting in an operation such as this is not 'private' in the ordinary usage of the word." Professor Louis Henkin elaborated:

> What the Court has been talking about is not at all what most people mean by privacy. . . . Ms. Roe sought her abortion openly, "publicly." In a word, the Court has been vindicating not a right to freedom from official intrusion, but to freedom from official regulation. . . . [T]hey are, I think, different notions conceptually, with different philosophical, political and social (and, one might have thought, legal) assumptions and consequences; they may look different also if viewed as aspects of the confrontation of private right with public good.[4]

This point leads to a second criticism. If what was at stake in *Roe* v. *Wade* was "freedom from official regulation," the Court was guilty of "*Lochnering*"; that is, of superimposing its own views of wise social policy on those of the legislature. The remarkable similarities between *Roe* and *Lochner* v. *New York* (1905) have led critics to ask why the right to be let alone should give a woman control over her body vis-à-vis an abortion but not, since the Court's repudiation of *Lochner,* control over her body vis-à-vis the sale of her labor (i.e., vis-à-vis the wages she shall receive and the hours she shall work). *Roe* and *Doe* also have been attacked on the ground that in them, the Court paid insufficient attention to protecting the interests of the fetus—that in protecting the woman's right to be let alone, it unnecessarily jeopardized the fetus's "right to be." Justice Harry Blackmun's majority opinion attempted with little success to parry this criticism. Blackmun admitted that if a fetus is a person, its right to life is guaranteed by the Fourteenth Amendment.[5] But he then skirted the question of whether a fetus is a person (i.e., the question of when the life of a person begins): "We need not resolve the difficult question of when life begins. When those trained in the respective disciplines of medicine, philosophy, and theology are unable to arrive at any consensus, the judiciary, at this point in the development of man's knowledge, is not in a position to speculate as to the answer."[6]

Despite these criticisms, the Court supported *Roe* in subsequent decisions. *Planned Parenthood of Central Missouri* v. *Danforth* (1976), an especially important case in this respect, involved a Missouri abortion statute passed in response to *Roe.* Although the Court upheld the statute's flexible definition of viability, affirmed the state's right to require the informed, voluntary, and written consent of the woman, and sustained the reporting and record-keeping provisions of the law, it emasculated the statute by declaring unconstitutional the following crucial elements:

1. The requirement that written consent must also be obtained from the spouse in nontherapeutic abortions.
2. The requirement that written consent must be obtained from the woman's parents if she is under 18 and unmarried, except in a life-saving situation.
3. The blanket prohibition on the use of saline amniocentesis as a technique for inducing abortion.
4. The imposition of a criminal penalty on the attending physicians for any failure on their part to exercise due care and skill to preserve the life and health of the fetus, insofar as that is possible.

Here, as in *Roe* v. *Wade,* the Court's decision hinged on the priority it placed on guaranteeing to the pregnant woman the right to be let alone. As for spousal consent, Justice Blackmun noted that the majority could not hold that the state "has the constitutional authority to give the spouse unilaterally the ability to prohibit the wife from terminating her pregnancy, when the State itself lacks that right." The spouse, then, was viewed as having no more of an interest in the abortion decision than the state had. And as to the parental consent requirement, Blackmun observed that "any independent interest the parent may have in the termination of the minor daughter's pregnancy is no more weighty than the right of privacy of the competent minor mature enough to have become pregnant." The Court thereby held, for the first time, that minors have constitutional rights as against their parents.[7]

In *Akron* v. *Akron Center for Reproductive Health* (1983), the Court dramatically reaffirmed *Roe* v. *Wade,* going so far as to announce that a woman has a "fundamental right" to have an abortion. The City of Akron had passed an ordinance that imposed a number of restrictions on the abortion process. Perhaps the most important was a requirement that any abortion performed after the first trimester of pregnancy had to be performed in a hospital. A six-member majority invalidated this requirement because it placed "a significant obstacle in the path of women seeking an abortion," a burden not justifiable as a reasonable health regulation. While hospitalization for abortions performed after the first trimester was recommended at the time of *Roe,* the safety of such abortions had "increased dramatically" since then because of improved technology and procedures, and there was no compelling reason why these abortions could not be performed on an outpatient basis in appropriate nonhospital settings. As Justice Powell declared for the majority: "[P]resent medical knowledge convincingly undercuts Akron's justification for requiring that all second-trimester abortions be performed in a hospital." Justice O'Connor dissented, observing that it was not until 1982, four years after Akron had passed its ordinance, that even the American College of Obstetricians and Gynecologists revised its standards and no longer recommended that all mid-trimester abortions be performed in a hospital. Her real objection, however, was with *Roe* itself. As she noted:

> The *Roe* framework . . . is clearly on a collision course with itself. As the medical risks of various abortion procedures decrease, the point at which the State may regulate for reasons of maternal health is moved further forward to actual childbirth. As medical science becomes better able to provide for the separate existence of the fetus, the point of viability is moved further back toward conception. Moreover, it is clear that the trimester approach violates the fundamental aspiration of judicial decision making through the application of neutral principles "sufficiently absolute to give them roots throughout the community and continuity over significant periods of time. . . ." The *Roe* framework is inherently tied to the state of medical technology that exists whenever particular litigation ensues. Although legislatures are better suited to make the necessary factual judgments in this area, the Court's framework forces legislatures, as a matter of constitutional law, to speculate about what constitutes "acceptable medical practice" at any given time. Without the necessary expertise or ability, courts must then pretend to act as science review boards and examine those legislative judgments.

Interestingly, when the opportunity for Justice O'Connor to help overturn *Roe* presented itself in *Webster* v. *Reproductive Health Services* (1989), she declined to do so on grounds of judicial self-restraint. The Missouri legislature had passed an abortion statute that, among other things, declared in its preamble that human life begins at conception and that "unborn children have protectable interests in life, health, and wellbeing." The law required medical tests to ascertain whether any fetus over 20 weeks old was viable and prohibited the use of public employees and facilities to perform abortions not necessary to save the life of the mother. Chief Justice Rehnquist wrote the judgment of the Court upholding all sections of the law. As O'Connor had done in *Akron,* he rejected the "rigid *Roe* framework" as "hardly consistent with the notion of a Constitution cast in general terms, as ours is, and usually speaking in general principles, as ours does. The key elements of the *Roe* framework—trimesters and viability—are not found in the text of the Constitution or in any place else one would expect to find a constitutional principle." Nonetheless, since he and his colleagues who joined in the Court's judgment believed that they could sustain the Missouri statute without overturning *Roe,* they, too, left it "undisturbed."

Justice Scalia was furious. Wishing the Court to overturn *Roe* completely and explicitly, he lamented that "the mansion of constitutionalized abortion-law, constructed overnight in *Roe* v. *Wade,* must be disassembled door-jamb by door-jamb, and never entirely brought down, no matter how wrong it may be." He expressed particular concern about the impact of *Webster* on the public's perception of the Court itself: "Alone sufficient to justify a broad holding is the fact that our retaining control, through *Roe,* of what I believe to be, and many of our citizens recognize to be, a political issue, continuously distorts the public perception of the role of this Court. We can now look forward to at least another Term with carts full of mail from the public, and streets full of demonstrators, urging us—their unelected and life-tenured judges who have been awarded those extraordinary, undemocratic characteristics precisely in order that we might follow the law despite the popular will—to follow the popular will."

While the Court's commitment to guaranteeing a woman's right to an abortion appears to be faltering—what it described as a "fundamental right" in *Akron* it called a "liberty interest" in *Webster*—its refusal to hold that the government is compelled to fund abortions for women in financial need is steadfast. In *Maher* v. *Roe* (1977), the Court held that Connecticut's decision not to pay for nontherapeutic abortions for indigent women, despite the fact that it did pay for childbirth, did not violate the Constitution. Justice Powell held for a six-member majority that the state's policy did not impinge upon *Roe's* recognition of a woman's fundamental right to protection "from unduly burdensome interference with her freedom to decide whether to terminate her pregnancy." That right, he declared, "implies no limitation on the authority of a State to make a value judgment favoring childbirth over abortion, and to implement that judgment by the allocation of public funds." He continued,

> The Connecticut regulation places no obstacles—absolute or otherwise—in the pregnant woman's path to an abortion. An indigent woman who desires an abortion suffers no disadvantage as a consequence of Connecticut's decision to fund childbirth; she continues as before to be dependent on private sources for the services she desires. The State may have made childbirth a more attractive alternative, thereby influencing the woman's decision, but it has imposed no restriction on access to abortions that was not already there. The indigency that may make it difficult—and in some cases, perhaps, impossible—for some women to have abortions is neither created nor in any way affected by the Connecticut regulation.

Justice Brennan, in dissent, accused the majority of a "distressing insensitivity to the plight of impoverished pregnant women." The Connecticut statute, he insisted, "unconstitutionally impinges upon the claim of privacy derived from the Due Process Clause," because of the "financial pressures on indigent women that force them to bear children they would not otherwise have."

In its 5–4 decision in *Harris* v. *McRae* (1980), the Court not only reaffirmed *Maher,* but also carried Justice Powell's argument one step further. Whereas *Maher* dealt only with nontherapeutic abortions, *Harris* sustained the constitutionality of the Hyde Amendment, which drastically limited federal funding for most medically necessary abortions as well. Justice Stewart's majority opinion relied heavily on the analysis in *Maher:*

> Although the liberty protected by the Due Process Clause affords protection against unwarranted governmental interference with freedom of choice in the context of certain personal decisions, it does not confer an entitlement to such funds as may be necessary to realize all the advantages of that freedom. To hold otherwise would make a drastic change in our understanding of the Constitution.

QUALIFICATIONS ON THE RIGHT TO PRIVACY

Professor Paul Freund observed that privacy is a "greedy legal concept."[8] In light of *Roe,* this observation seems especially apt. The Court has come to understand the "right to be let alone" to protect not only against official intrusion but also against official regulation. This expansion of what privacy is understood to secure could well render government itself problematic, were privacy to be regarded as an absolute right.

The Court has demonstrated, however, that it is aware of this problem. In *Roe,* the decision that more than any other has expanded the right to privacy, the Court stressed that "this right is not unqualified and must be considered against important state interests in regulation." Consistent with this understanding, it went on to argue that a pregnant woman's right to be let alone and to elect whether or not to have an abortion can be subordinated to the state's interest in "protecting fetal life after viability . . . except when it is necessary to preserve the life or health of the mother." The federal courts have also recognized the qualified nature of the right to privacy in such cases as *Bowers* v. *Hardwick* (1986). In *Bowers,* the Supreme Court overturned a decision of the Eleventh Circuit Court of Appeals that had invalidated a Georgia statute that made consensual homsexual sodomy a criminal offense. Justice White spoke for a five–member majority when he rejected the claim that the federal Constitution confers a "fundamental right upon homosexuals to engage in sodomy." He insisted that there should be "great resistance to expand the substantive reach" of the Due Process Clause, "particularly if it requires redefining the category of rights deemed to be fundamental. Otherwise, the Judiciary necessarily takes to itself further authority to govern the country without express constitutional authority. The claimed right pressed on us today falls far short of overcoming this resistance." In his dissent, Justice Blackmun charged that while the Court "claims that its decision today merely refuses to recognize a fundamental right to engage in homosexual sodomy, what the Court really has refused to recognize is the fundamental interest all individuals have in controlling the nature of their intimate associations with others."

While the judiciary has been reluctant to place the protections of the Constitution behind what most people would regard as unnatural sexual practices, and thereby to draw too heavily on its limited fund of public good will, it is nevertheless true that the Court's most expansive interpretations of the right to privacy have come in the area of sexual behavior. Claims to personal autonomy in other areas of life have met with a less favorable reception. *Kelley* v. *Johnson* and *Paul* v. *Davis,* both decided in 1976, are cases in point. In *Kelley,* decided 6–2, Justice Rehnquist held for the Court that a county regulation limiting the length of county policemen's hair did not violate any right guaranteed by the Fourteenth Amendment. In particular, he denied that the regulation impermissibly limited the right of privacy or the personal autonomy of the policemen, maintaining that the protections of this right were limited to "infringements on the individual's freedom of choice with respect to certain basic matters of procreation, marriage, and family life." Justice Marshall strenuously dissented: "To say that the liberty guarantee of the Fourteenth Amendment does not encompass matters of personal appearance would be fundamentally inconsistent with the values of privacy, self-identity, autonomy, and personal integrity that I have always assumed the Constitution was designed to protect." In *Paul,* Justice Rehnquist again spoke for the Court, this time to reject, among other things, a privacy claim made by a person who had been listed as an "active shoplifter" in a flyer made up by the Louisville police and distributed to city merchants. He had been arrested for shoplifting but never tried, and the charges against him ultimately had been dropped. Rehnquist held that because the police had not invaded any area traditionally regarded as private, such as "matters related to marriage, procreation, contraception, family relationships, and child rearing and education," there had been no constitutional violation of the right to privacy.

In *Whalen* v. *Roe* (1977), a related case, the Court unanimously sustained a New York statute requiring that the names of persons receiving dangerous prescription drugs be kept in a computer file. The statute had been challenged by an individual who claimed that such lists violated his right to privacy because of the risk that the information might become public. Justice Stevens noted for the Court that privacy cases involve, at minimum, two different types of interests: the individual interest in avoiding disclosure of a personal matter, of which the *Griswold* decision was representative; and the interest in securing independence in making certain kinds of important decisions, of which *Roe* v. *Wade* was illustrative. He concluded that "the New York program does not, on its face, pose a sufficiently grievous threat to either interest to establish a constitutional violation." With respect to a disclosure of personal matters, he emphasized the careful security provisions in the law and insisted that there was no justification for assuming that those provisions would be administered improperly. And with respect to an infringement of the interest in making important decisions independently, he dismissed the claim that patients would decline needed medication in order to keep their names out of the computerized file, insisting that the law did not significantly inhibit the patient-physician decision regarding needed medication.

NOTES

1 Samuel D. Warren and Louis D. Brandeis, "The Right to Privacy," *Harvard Law Review* 4, no. 5 (1890): 193.

2 William H. Rehnquist, "Is an Expanded Right to Privacy Consistent with Fair and Effective Law Enforcement? Or, Privacy, You've Come a Long Way, Baby" *Kansas Law Review* 23 (1974): 6.

3 It should be noted that these decisions, which conceptualized privacy as inhering in the relationship or in the person, supplemented but did not supplant the earlier view that privacy inheres in the place. In *Stanley* v. *Georgia* (1969), for example, the Court operated from the assumption that privacy inheres in the place when it declared that "[whereas] the States retain broad power to regulate obscenity, that power simply does not extend to mere possession by the individual in the privacy of his own home."

4 Louis Henkin, "Privacy and Autonomy" *Columbia Law Review* 74 (1974): 1410, 1424–1427.

5 Consider, however, Professor John Hart Ely's observations that a determination of whether a fetus is a "Fourteenth Amendment person" is irrelevant to the question of whether a fetus can be protected: "It has never been held or even asserted that the state interest needed to justify forcing a person to refrain from an activity, whether or not that activity is constitutionally protected, must implicate either the life or the constitutional rights of another person. Dogs are not "persons in the whole sense" nor have they constitutional rights, but that does not mean the state cannot prohibit killing them. It does not even mean the state cannot prohibit killing them in the exercise of the First Amendment right of political protest. Come to think of it, draft cards aren't persons either." John Hart Ely, "The Wages of Crying Wolf: A Comment on *Roe* v. *Wade*" *Yale Law Journal* 82 (1973): 929.

6 The Court's language here is of critical importance to the proponents of the Human Life Statute, which would declare that "the life of each human being begins at conception." They claim that the Court's refusal in *Roe* to treat the fetus as a person merely represented an admission that the judiciary was incapable of deciding the question of when human life begins. Further, they argue, under Section 5 of the Fourteenth Amendment, which empowers Congress to enforce by appropriate legislation the provisions of the amendment, Congress is the appropriate body to resolve that question and, if it finds life to begin at conception, to enforce the obligation of the states under the Fourteenth Amendment not to deprive persons (including unborn children) of life without due process of law. See Stephen H. Galebach, "A Human Life Statute" *The Human Life Review* 5 (1981).

7 See, however, *H.L.* v. *Matheson* (1981), in which the Court upheld, in a 6–3 decision, a Utah statute requiring the parents be notified by the attending physician that their unmarried minor daughter is seeking an abortion. Mere parental notice was not deemed by the Court to constitute an unwarranted interference with the minor daughter's right to be let alone.

8 Paul Freund, "Privacy: One Concept or Many" in *Privacy,* eds. J. Roland Pennock and John W. Chapman (New York: Atherton Press, 1971), p. 192.

SELECTED READINGS

Belloti v. *Baird,* 443 U.S. 622 (1979).
Carey v. *Population Services International,* 431 U.S. 678 (1977).
Eisenstadt v. *Baird,* 405 U.S. 438 (1972).
H. L. v. *Matheson,* 450 U.S. 398 (1981).
Lovisi v. *Slayton,* 363 F. Supp. 620 (1973).
Maher v. *Roe,* 432 U.S. 464 (1977).
Planned Parenthood of Central Missouri v. *Danforth,* 428 U.S. 52 (1976).
Time v. *Hill,* 385 U.S. 374 (1967).

Barnett, Randy, ed. *The Rights Retained by the People: The History and Meaning of the Ninth Amendment* (Fairfax, Va.: George Mason University Press, 1989).
Berger, Raoul. "The Ninth Amendment." *Cornell Law Review* 66 (1980): 1.
Dionisopoulos, P. Alan, and Craig R. Ducat. *The Right to Privacy: Essays and Cases* (St. Paul, Minn.: West. 1976).
Ely, John Hart. "The Wages of Crying Wolf: A Comment on *Roe* v. *Wade.*" *Yale Law Journal* 82 (1973): 920.
Galebach, Stephen H. "A Human Life Statute." *The Human Life Review* 5 (1981).
Hixson, Richard F. *Privacy in a Public Society: Human Rights in Conflict* (New York: Oxford University Press, 1987).
Miller, Arthur R. *The Assault on Privacy: Computers, Data Banks, and Dossiers* (Ann Arbor, Mich.: University of Michigan Press, 1971).
Pennock, J. Roland, and John W. Chapman, eds. *Privacy* (New York: Atherton Press, 1971).
Posner, Richard. "An Economic Theory of Privacy." *Regulation* 2, no. 3 (May–June 1978).
Rehnquist, William H. "Is an Expanded Right to Privacy Consistent with Fair and Effective Law Enforcement: Or, Privacy, You've Come a Long Way, Baby." *Kansas Law Review* 23 (1974): 1.
Rubin, Eva R. *Abortion, Politics, and the Courts: Roe v. Wade and Its Aftermath* (New York: Greenwood, 1987).
Warren, Samuel D., and Louis D. Brandeis. "The Right to Privacy." *Harvard Law Review* 4 (1890): 193.
Westin, Alan F. *Privacy and Freedom* (New York: Atheneum, 1967).

Griswold v. *Connecticut*

381 U.S. 479; 85 S. Ct. 1678; 14 L. Ed. 2d 510 (1965)

A Connecticut statute proscribed the use of birth control devices and made it a criminal offense for anyone to give information or instruction on their use. Estelle Griswold, executive director of the Planned Parenthood League of Connecticut, and Dr. Buxton, its medical director and a professor at the Yale Medical School, were convicted of dispensing such information to married persons in violation of the law and were fined $100. After a state appellate court and the Connecticut Supreme Court of Errors affirmed the convictions, the defendants appealed to the United States Supreme Court. It should be noted that the same statute had previously been unsuccessfully challenged in *Tileston* v. *Ullman* (1943) and *Poe* v. *Ullman* (1961). *Opinion of the Court: Douglas, Brennan, Clark, Goldberg, Warren. Concurring opinion: Goldberg, Brennan, Warren. Concurring in result: Harlan; White. Dissenting opinions: Black, Stewart; Stewart, Black.*

MR. JUSTICE DOUGLAS delivered the opinion of the Court. . . .

. . . We are met with a wide range of questions that implicate the Due Process Clause of the Fourteenth Amendment. Overtones of some arguments suggest that *Lochner* v. *State of New York* [1905] . . . should be our guide. But we decline that invitation as we did in *West Coast Hotel Co.* v. *Parrish* [1937] . . . We do not sit as a super-legislature to determine the wisdom, need, and propriety of laws that touch economic problems, business affairs, or social conditions. This law, however, operates directly on an intimate relation of husband and wife and their physician's role in one aspect of that relation.

The association of people is not mentioned in the Constitution nor in the Bill of Rights. The right to educate a child in a school of the parents' choice—whether public or private or parochial—is also not mentioned. Nor is the right to study any particular subject or any foreign language. Yet the First Amendment has been construed to include certain of those rights. . . .

[Previous] cases suggest that specific guarantees in the Bill of Rights have penumbras, formed by emanations from those guarantees that help give them life and substance. . . . Various guarantees create zones of privacy. The right of association contained in the penumbra of the First Amendment is one. . . . The Third Amendment in its prohibition against the quartering of soldiers "in any house" in time of peace without the consent of the owner is another facet of that privacy. The Fourth Amendment explicitly affirms the "right of the people to be secure in their persons, houses, papers, and effects, against unreasonable searches and seizures." The Fifth Amendment in its Self-Incrimination Clause enables the citizen to create a zone of privacy which government may not force him to surrender to his detriment. The Ninth Amendment provides: "The enumeration in the Constitution, of certain rights, shall not be construed to deny or disparage others retained by the people. . . .

The Fourth and Fifth Amendments were described in *Boyd* v. *United States* [1886] . . . as protection against all governmental invasions "of the sanctity of a man's home and the privacies of life." We recently referred in *Mapp* v. *Ohio* [1961] . . . to the Fourth Amendment as creating a "right to privacy, no less important than any other right carefully and particularly reserved to the people." . . .

We have had many controversies over these penumbral rights of "privacy and repose." . . . These cases bear witness that the right of privacy which presses for recognition here is a legitimate one.

The present case, then, concerns a relationship lying within the zone of privacy created by several fundamental constitutional guarantees. And it concerns a law which, in forbidding the *use* of contraceptives rather than regulating their manufacture or sale, seeks to achieve its goals by means having a maximum destructive impact upon that relationship. Such a law cannot stand in light of the familiar principle, so often applied by this Court, that a "governmental purpose to control or prevent activities constitutionally subject to state regulation may not be achieved by means which sweep unnecessarily broadly and thereby invade the area of protected freedoms." . . . Would we allow the police to search the sacred precincts of marital bedrooms for telltale signs of the use of contraceptives? The very idea is repulsive to the notions of privacy surrounding the marriage relationship.

We deal with a right of privacy older than the Bill of Rights—older than our political parties, older than our school system. Marriage is a coming together for better or worse, hopefully enduring, and initmate to the degree of being sacred. It is an association that promotes a way of life, not causes; a harmony in living, not political faiths; a bilateral loyalty, not commercial or social projects. Yet it is an association for as noble a purpose as any involved in our prior decisions.

Reversed.

MR. JUSTICE GOLDBERG, whom THE CHIEF JUSTICE and MR. JUSTICE BRENNAN join, concurring.

I agree with the Court that Connecticut's birth-control law unconstitutionally intrudes upon the right of marital privacy, and I join in its opinion and judgment. Although I have not accepted the view that "due process" as used in the Fourteenth Amendment includes all of the first eight Amendments, . . . I do agree that the concept of liberty protects those personal rights that are fundamental, and is not confined to the specific terms of the Bill of Rights. My conclusion that the concept of liberty is not so restricted and that it embraces the right of marital privacy though that right is not mentioned explicitly in the Constitution is supported both by numerous decisions of this Court, referred to in the Court's opinion, and by the language and history of the Ninth Amendment. In reaching the conclusion that the right of marital privacy is protected, as being within the protected penumbra of specific guarantees of the Bill of Rights, the Court refers to the Ninth Amendment. . . . I add these words to emphasize the relevance of that Amendment to the Court's holding.

The Court stated many years ago that the Due Process Clause protects those liberties that are "so rooted in the traditions and conscience of our people as to be ranked as fundamental." . . . This Court, in a series of decisions, has held that the Fourteenth Amendment absorbs and applies to the States those specifics of the first eight amendments which express fundamental personal rights. The language and history of the Ninth Amendment reveal that the Framers of the Constitution believed that there are additional fundamental rights, protected from governmental infringement, which exist alongside those fundamental rights specifically mentioned in the first eight constitutional amendments.

. . . It was proffered to quiet expressed fears that a bill of specifically enumerated rights could not be sufficiently broad to cover all essential rights and that the specific mention of certain rights would be interpreted as a denial that others were protected. . . .

A dissenting opinion suggests that my interpretation of the Ninth Amendment somehow "broaden[s] the powers of this Court." . . . I do not mean to imply that the Ninth Amendment is applied against the States by the Fourteenth. Nor do I mean to state that the Ninth Amendment constitutes an independent source of rights protected from infringement by either the States or the Federal Government. Rather, the Ninth Amendment shows a belief of the Constitution's authors that fundamental rights exist that are not expressly enumerated in the first eight amendments and an intent that the list of rights included there not be deemed exhaustive. As any student of this Court's opinions knows, this Court has held, often unanimously, that the Fifth and Fourteenth Amendments protect certain fundamental personal liberties from abridgment by the Federal Government or the States. . . . The Ninth Amendment simply shows the intent of the Constitution's authors that other fundamental personal rights should not be denied such protection or disparaged in any other way simply because they are not specifically listed in the first eight constitutional amendments. I do not see how this broadens the authority of the Court; rather it serves to support what this Court has been doing in protecting fundamental rights.

Nor am I turning somersaults with history in arguing that the Ninth Amendment is relevant in a case dealing with a *State's* infringement of a fundamental right. While the Ninth Amendment—and indeed the entire Bill of Rights—originally concerned restrictions upon *federal* power, the subsequently enacted Fourteenth Amendment prohibits the States as well from abridging fundamental personal liberties. And, the Ninth Amendment, in indicating that not all such liberties are specifically mentioned in the first eight amendments, is surely relevant in showing the existence of other fundamental personal rights, now protected from state, as well as federal, infringement. In sum, the Ninth Amendment simply lends strong support to the view that the "liberty" protected by the Fifth and Fourteenth Amendments from infringement by the Federal Government or the States is not restricted to rights specifically mentioned in the first eight amendments. . . .

The entire fabric of the Constitution and the purposes that clearly underlie its specific guarantees demonstrate that the rights to marital privacy and to marry and raise a family are of similar order and magnitude as the fundamental rights specifically protected.

Although the Constitution does not speak in so many words of the right of privacy in marriage, I cannot believe that it offers these fundamental rights no protection. The fact that no particular provision of the Constitution explicitly forbids the State from disrupting the traditional relation of the family—a relation as old and as fundamental as our entire civilization—surely does not show that the Government was meant to have the power to do so. Rather, as the Ninth Amendment expressly recognizes, there are fundamental personal rights such as this one, which are protected from abridgment by the Government though not specifically mentioned in the Constitution. . . .

The logic of the dissents would sanction federal or state legislation that seems to me even more plainly unconstitutional than the statute before us. Surely the Government, absent a showing of a compelling subordinating state interest, could not decree that all husbands and wives must be sterilized after two children have been born to them. Yet by their reasoning such an invasion of marital privacy would not be subject to constitutional challenge because, while it might be "silly," no provision of the Constitution specifically prevents the Government from curtailing the marital right to bear children and raise a family. While it may shock some of my Brethren that the Court today holds that the Constitution protects the right of marital privacy, in my view it is far more shocking to believe that the personal liberty guaranteed by the Constitution does not include protection against such totalitarian limitation of family size, which is at complete variance with our constitutional concepts. Yet, if upon a showing of a slender basis of rationality, a law outlawing voluntary birth control by married persons is valid, then, by the same reasoning, a law requiring compulsory birth control also would seem to be valid. In my view, however, both types of law would unjustifiably intrude upon rights of marital privacy which are constitutionally protected.

In sum, I believe that the right of privacy in the marital relation is fundamental and basic—a personal right "retained by the people" within the meaning of the Ninth Amendment. Connecticut cannot constitutionally abridge this fundamental right, which is protected by the Fourteenth Amendment from infringement by the States. I agree with the Court that petitioners' convictions must therefore be reversed.

MR. JUSTICE HARLAN, concurring.

I fully agree with the judgment of reversal, but find myself unable to join the Court's opinion. . . .

In my view, the proper constitutional inquiry in this case is whether this Connecticut statute infringes the Due Process Clause of the Fourteenth Amendment because the enactment violates basic values "implicit in the concept of ordered liberty," *Palko* v. *State of Connecticut.* [1937] . . . I believe that it does. While the relevant inquiry may be aided by resort to one or more of the provisions of the Bill of Rights, it is not dependent on them or any of their radiations. The Due Process Clause of the Fourteenth Amendment stands, in my opinion, on its own bottom. . . .

While I could not more heartily agree that judicial "self restraint" is an indispensable ingredient of sound constitutional adjudication, I do submit that the formula suggested for achieving it is more hollow than real. "Specific" provisions of the Constitution, no less than "due process," lend themselves as readily to "personal" interpretations by judges whose constitutional outlook is simply to keep the Constitution in supposed "tune with the times." . . .

Judicial self-restraint will not, I suggest, be brought about in the "due process" area by the historically unfounded incorporation formula long advanced by my Brother BLACK, and now in part espoused by my Brother STEWART. It will be achieved in this area, as in other constitutional areas, only by continual insistence upon respect for the teachings of history, solid recognition of the basic values that underlie our society, and wise appreciation of the great roles that the doctrines of federalism and separation of powers have played in establishing and preserving American freedoms. . . . Adherence to these principles will not, of course, obviate all constitutional differences of opinion among judges, nor should it. Their continued recognition will, however, go farther toward keeping most judges from roaming at large in the constitutional field than will the interpolation into the Constitution of an artificial and largely illusory restriction on the content of the Due Process Clause.

MR. JUSTICE BLACK, with whom MR. JUSTICE STEWART joins, dissenting.

I agree with my Brother STEWART's dissenting opinion. And like him I do not to any extent whatever base my view that this Connecticut law is constitutional on a belief that the law is wise or that its policy is a good one. In order that there may be no room at all to doubt why I vote as I do, I feel constrained to add that the law is every bit as [personally] offensive to me as it is my Brethren. . . .

. . . I get nowhere in this case by talk about a constitutional "right of privacy" as an emanation from one or more constitutional provisions. I like my privacy as well as the next one, but I am nevertheless compelled to admit that government has a right to invade it unless prohibited by some specific constitutional provision. For these reasons I cannot agree with the Court's judgment and the reasons it gives for holding this Connecticut law unconstitutional. . . .

I realize that many good and able men have eloquently spoken and written, sometimes in rhapsodical strains, about the duty of this Court to keep the Constitution in tune with the times. The idea is that the Constitution must be changed from time to time and that this Court is charged with a duty to make those changes. For myself, I must with all deference reject that philosophy. The Constitution makers knew the need for change and provided for it. Amendments suggested by the people's elected representatives can be submitted to the people or their selected agents for ratification. That method of change was good for our Fathers, and being somewhat old-fashioned I must add it is good enough for me. And so, I cannot rely on the Due Process Clause or the Ninth Amendment or any mysterious and uncertain natural law concept as a reason for striking down this state law. The Due Process Clause with an "arbitrary and capricious" or "shocking to the conscience" formula was liberally used by this Court to strike down economic legislation in the early decades of this century, threatening, many people thought, the tranquility and stability of the Nation. . . . That formula, based on subjective considerations of "natural justice," is no less dangerous when used to enforce this Court's views about personal rights than those about economic rights. I had thought that we had laid that formula, as a means for striking down state legislation to rest once and for all in cases like *West Coast Hotel Co.* v. *Parrish*. . . .

MR. JUSTICE STEWART, whom MR. JUSTICE BLACK joins, dissenting.

Since 1879 Connecticut has had on its books a law which forbids the use of contraceptives by anyone. I think this is an uncommonly silly law. As a practical matter, the law is obviously unenforceable, except in the oblique context of the present case. . . . But we are not asked in this case to say whether we think this law is unwise, or even asinine. We are asked to hold that it violates the United States Constitution. And that I cannot do.

In the course of its opinion the Court refers to no less than six Amendments to the Constitution: the First, the Third, the Fourth, the Fifth, the Ninth, and the Fourteenth. But the Court does not say which of these Amendments, if any, it thinks is infringed by this Connecticut law. . . .

The Court also quotes the Ninth Amendment, and my Brother GOLDBERG's concurring opinion relies heavily upon it. But to say that the Ninth Amendment has anything to do with this case is to turn somersaults with history. The Ninth

Amendment, like its companion the Tenth, which this Court held "states but a truism that all is retained which has not been surrendered," *United States* v. *Darby* [1941], . . . was framed by James Madison and adopted by the States simply to make clear that the adoption of the Bill of Rights did not alter the plan that the *Federal* Government was to be a government of express and limited powers, and that all rights and powers not delegated to it were retained by the people and the individual States. Until today no member of this Court has ever suggested that the Ninth Amendment meant anything else, and the idea that a federal court could ever use the Ninth Amendment to annul a law passed by the elected representatives of the people of the State of Connecticut would have caused James Madison no little wonder.

What provision of the Constitution, then, does make this state law invalid? The Court says it is the right of privacy "created by several fundamental constitutional guarantees." With all deference, I can find no such general right of privacy in the Bill of Rights, in any other part of the Constitution, or in any case ever before decided by this Court. . . .

Roe v. *Wade*

410 U.S. 113; 93 S. Ct. 705; 35 L. Ed. 2d 147 (1973)

A Texas abortion statute made it a felony for anyone to destroy a fetus except on "medical advice for the purpose of saving the life of the mother." This law was typical of abortion statutes in effect in most states for approximately a century. Jane Roe (the pseudonym for an unmarried pregnant woman) brought suit against District Attorney Wade of Dallas County for declaratory and injunctive relief. She challenged the statute on grounds that it denied equal protection (in that it forced women who did not have the money to have a baby when those who had money could go elsewhere and procure a safe, legal abortion), due process (because the statute was vague as to what "saving the life of the mother" actually meant), and the mother's right of privacy guaranteed under the First, Fourth, Fifth, Ninth, and Fourteenth Amendments. A three-judge federal district court found the statute unconstitutional, and Texas appealed to the Supreme Court. The Court heard *Roe* in conjunction with *Doe* v. *Bolton* (1973), in which a modern "reform" abortion statute from Georgia was also challenged. *Opinion of the Court: Blackmun, Brennan, Burger, Douglas, Marshall, Powell, Stewart. Concurring opinions: Burger, Douglas; Stewart. Dissenting opinions: White, Rehnquist; Rehnquist.*

MR. JUSTICE BLACKMUN delivered the opinion of the Court. . . .

We forthwith acknowledge our awareness of the sensitive and emotional nature of the abortion controversy, of the vigorous opposing views, even among physicians, and of the deep and seemingly absolute convictions that the subject inspires. One's philosophy, one's experiences, one's exposure to the raw edges of human existence, one's religious training, one's attitudes toward life and family and their values, and the moral standards one establishes and seeks to observe, are all likely to influence and to color one's thinking and conclusions about abortion.

In addition, population growth, pollution, poverty, and racial overtones tend to complicate and not to simplify the problem.

Our task, of course, is to resolve the issue by constitutional measurement, free of emotion and of predilection. We seek earnestly to do this, and, because we do, we have inquired into, and in this opinion place some emphasis upon, medical and medical-legal history and what that history reveals about man's attitudes toward the abortion procedure over the centuries. We bear in mind, too, Mr. Justice Holmes' admonition in his now-vindicated dissent in *Lochner* v. *New York* . . . (1905): "[The Constitution] is made for people of fundamentally differing views, and the accident of our finding certain opinions natural and familiar or novel and even shocking ought not to conclude our judgment upon the question whether statutes embodying them conflict with the Constitution of the United States." . . .

The principal thrust of appellant's attack on the Texas statutes is that they improperly invade a right, said to be possessed by the pregnant woman, to choose to terminate her pregnancy. Appellant would discover this right in the concept of personal "liberty" embodied in the Fourteenth Amendment's Due Process Clause; or in personal, marital, familial, and sexual privacy said to be protected by the Bill of Rights or its penumbras, . . . or among those rights reserved to the people by the Ninth Amendment. . . . Before addressing this claim, we feel it desirable briefly to survey, in several aspects, the history of abortion, for such insight as that history may afford us, and then to examine the state purposes and interests behind the criminal abortion laws. . . .

It perhaps is not generally appreciated that the restrictive criminal abortion laws in effect in a majority of States today are of relatively recent vintage. Those laws, generally proscribing abortion or its attempt at any time during pregnancy except when necessary to preserve the pregnant woman's life, are not of ancient or even of common-law origin. Instead, they derive from statutory changes effected, for the most part, in the latter half of the 19th century. . . .

Three reasons have been advanced to explain historically the enactment of criminal abortion laws in the 19th century and to justify their continued existence.

It has been argued occasionally that these laws were the product of a Victorian social concern to discourage illicit sexual conduct. Texas, however, does not advance this justification in the present case, and it appears that no court or commentator has taken the argument seriously. . . .

A second reason is concerned with abortion as a medical procedure. When most criminal abortion laws were first enacted, the procedure was a hazardous one for the woman. . . . Thus, it has been argued that a State's real concern in enacting a criminal abortion law was to protect the pregnant woman, that is, to restrain her from submitting to a procedure that placed her life in serious jeopardy.

Modern medical techniques have altered this situation. . . .

The third reason is the State's interest—some phrase it in terms of duty—in protecting prenatal life. Some of the argument for this justification rests on the theory that a new human life is present from the moment of conception. The State's interest and general obligation to protect life then extends, it is argued, to prenatal life. Only when the life of the pregnant mother herself is at stake, balanced against the life she carries within her, should the interest of the embryo or fetus not prevail. Logically, of course, a legitimate state interest in this area need not stand or fall on acceptance of the belief that life begins at conception or at some other point prior to live birth. In assessing the State's interest, recognition may be given to the less rigid claim that as long as at least *potential* life is involved, the State may assert interests beyond the protection of the pregnant woman alone. . . .

It is with these interests, and the weight to be attached to them, that this case is concerned. . . .

The Constitution does not explicitly mention any right of privacy. In a line of decisions, however, going back perhaps as far as . . . 1891, the Court has recognized that a right of personal privacy, or a guarantee of certain areas or zones of privacy, does exist under the Constitution. In varying contexts, the Court or individual Justices have, indeed, found at least the roots of that right in the First Amendment, . . . in the Fourth and Fifth Amendments, . . . in the penumbras of the Bill of Rights, . . . in the Ninth Amendment, . . . or in the concept of liberty guaranteed by the first section of the Fourteenth Amendment. . . . These decisions make it clear that only personal rights that can be deemed "fundamental" or "implicit in the concept of ordered liberty" . . . are included in this guarantee of personal privacy. They also make it clear that the right has some extension to activities relating to marriage, . . . procreation, . . . contraception, . . . family relationships, . . . and child rearing and education. . . .

This right of privacy, whether it be founded in the Fourteenth Amendment's concept of personal liberty and restrictions upon state action, as we feel it is, or, as the District Court determined, in the Ninth Amendment's reservation of rights to the people, is broad enough to encompass a woman's decision whether or not to terminate her pregnancy. The detriment that the State would impose upon the pregnant woman by denying this choice altogether is apparent. Specific and direct harm medically diagnosable even in early pregnancy may be involved. Maternity, or additional offspring, may force upon the woman a distressful life and future. Psychological harm may be imminent. Mental and physical health may be taxed by child care. There is also the distress, for all concerned, associated with the unwanted child, and there is the problem of bringing a child into a family already unable, psychologically and otherwise, to care for it. In other cases, as in this one, the additional difficulties and continuing stigma of unwed motherhood may be involved. All these are factors the woman and her responsible physician necessarily will consider in consultation.

On the basis of elements such as these, appellant and some *amici* argue that the woman's right is absolute and that she is entitled to terminate her pregnancy at whatever time, in whatever way, and for whatever reason she alone chooses. With this we do not agree. Appellant's arguments that Texas either has no valid interest at all in regulating the abortion decision, or no interest strong enough to support any limitation upon the woman's sole determination, is unpersuasive. The Court's decisions recognizing a right of privacy also acknowledge that some state regulation in areas protected by that right is appropriate. As noted above, a State may properly assert important interests in safeguarding health, in maintaining medical standards, and in protecting potential life. At some point in pregnancy, these respective interests become sufficiently compelling to sustain regulation of the factors that govern the abortion decision. The privacy right involved, therefore, cannot be said to be absolute. In fact, it is not clear to us that the claim asserted by some *amici* that one has an unlimited right to do with one's body as one pleases bears a close relationship to the right of privacy previously articulated in the Court's decisions. The Court has refused to recognize an unlimited right of this kind in the past. . . .

We, therefore, conclude that the right of personal privacy includes the abortion decision, but that this right is not unqualified and must be considered against important state interests in regulation. . . .

Where certain "fundamental rights" are involved, the Court has held that a regulation limiting these rights may be justified only by a "compelling state interest" . . . and that legislative enactments must be narrowly drawn to express only the legitimate state interests at stake. . . .

The District Court held that the appellee failed to meet his burden of demonstrating that the Texas statute's infringement upon Roe's rights was necessary to support a compelling state interest, and that, although the appellee presented "several compelling justifications for state presence in the area of abortions," the statutes outstripped these justifications and swept "far beyond any areas of compelling state interest." . . . Appellant and appellee both contest that holding. Appellant, as has been indicated, claims an absolute right that bars any state imposition of criminal penalties in the area. Appellee argues that the State's determination to recognize and protect prenatal life from and after conception constitutes a compelling state interest. . . . We do not agree fully with either formulation.

A. The appellee and certain *amici* argue that the fetus is a "person" within the language and meaning of the Fourteenth Amendment. In support of this, they outline at length and in detail the well-known facts of fetal development. If this suggestion of personhood is established, the appellant's case, of course, collapses, for the fetus' right to life is then guaranteed specifically by the Amendment. The appellant conceded as much on reargument. On the other hand, the appellee conceded on reargument that no case could be cited that holds that a fetus is a person within the meaning of the Fourteenth Amendment.

The Constitution does not define "persons" in so many words. . . . [I]n nearly all . . . instances [in which the word *person* is used], the use of the word is such that it has application only postnatally. None indicates, with any assurance, that it has any possible pre-natal application.

All this, together with our observation . . . that throughout the major portion of the 19th century prevailing legal abortion practices were far freer than they are today, persuades us that the word "person," as used in the Fourteenth Amendment, does not include the unborn. . . .

This conclusion, however, does not of itself fully answer the contentions raised by Texas, and we pass on to other considerations.

B. The pregnant woman cannot be isolated in her privacy. She carries an embryo and, later, a fetus, if one accepts the medical definitions of the developing young in the human uterus. . . . The situation therefore is inherently different from marital intimacy, or bedroom possession of obscene material, or marriage, or procreation, or education. . . . As we have intimated above, it is reasonable and appropriate for a State to decide that at some point in time another interest, that of health of the mother or that of potential human life, becomes significantly involved. The woman's privacy is no longer sole and any right of privacy she possesses must be measured accordingly.

Texas urges that, apart from the Fourteenth Amendment, life begins at conception and is present throughout pregnancy, and that, therefore, the State has a compelling interest in protecting that life from and after conception. We need not resolve the difficult question of when life begins. When those trained in the respective disciplines of medicine, philosophy, and theology are unable to arrive at any consensus, the judiciary, at this point in the development of man's knowledge, is not in a position to speculate as to the answer. . . .

In view of . . . this, we do not agree that, by adopting one theory of life, Texas may override the rights of the pregnant woman that are at stake. We repeat, however, that the State does have an important and legitimate interest in preserving and protecting the health of the pregnant woman, whether she be a resident of the State or a nonresident who seeks medical consultation and treatment there, and that it has still *another* important and legitimate interest in protecting the potentiality of human life. These interests are separate and distinct. Each grows in substantiality as the woman approaches term and, at a point during pregnancy, each becomes "compelling."

With respect to the State's important and legitimate interest in the health of the mother, the "compelling" point, in the light of present medical knowledge, is at approximately the end of the first trimester. This is so because of the now-established medical fact . . . that until the end of the first trimester mortality in abortion may be less than mortality in normal childbirth. It follows that, from and after this point, a State may regulate the abortion procedure to the extent that the regulation reasonably relates to the preservation and protection of maternal health. Examples of permissible state regulation in this area are requirements as to the qualifications of the person who is to perform the abortion; as to the licensure of that person; as to the facility in which the procedure is to be performed, that is, whether it must be a hospital or may be a clinic or some other place of less-than-hospital status; as to the licensing of the facility; and the like.

This means, on the other hand, that, for the period of pregnancy prior to this "compelling" point, the attending physician, in consultation with his patient, is free to determine, without regulation by the State, that, in his medical judgment, the patient's pregnancy should be terminated. If that decision is reached, the judgment may be effectuated by an abortion free of interference by the State. point is at viability. This is so because the fetus then presumably has the capability of meaningful life outside the mother's womb. State regulation protective of fetal life after viability thus has both logical and biological justifications. If the State is interested in protecting fetal life after viability, it may go so far as to proscribe abortion during that period, except when it is necessary to preserve the life or health of the mother.

Measured against these standards, Art. 1196 of the Texas Penal Code, in restricting legal abortions to those "procured or attempted by medical advice for the purpose of saving the life of the mother," sweeps too broadly. The statute makes no distinction between abortions performed early in pregnancy and those performed later, and it limits to a single reason, "saving" the mother's life, the legal justification for the procedure. The statute, therefore, cannot survive the constitutional attack made upon it here. . . .

To summarize and to repeat:

1. A state criminal abortion statute of the current Texas type, that excepts from criminality only a *lifesaving* procedure on behalf of the mother, without regard to pregnancy stage and without recognition of the other interests involved, is violative of the Due Process Clause of

the Fourteenth Amendment. (*a*) For the stage prior to approximately the end of the first trimester, the abortion decision and its effectuation must be left to the medical judgment of the pregnant woman's attending physician. (*b*) For the stage subsequent to approximately the end of the first trimester, the State, in promoting its interest in the health of the mother, may, if it chooses, regulate the abortion procedure in ways that are reasonably related to maternal health. (*c*) For the stage subsequent to viability, the State in promoting its interest in the potentiality of human life may, if it chooses, regulate, and even proscribe, abortion except where it is necessary, in appropriate medical judgment, for the preservation of the life or health of the mother. . . .

This holding, we feel, is consistent with the relative weights of the respective interests involved, with the lessons and examples of medical and legal history, with the lenity of the common law, and with the demands of the profound problems of the present day. . . .

MR. JUSTICE REHNQUIST, dissenting.

. . . I have difficulty in concluding, as the Court does, that the right of "privacy" is involved in this case. Texas, by the statute here challenged, bars the performance of a medical abortion by a licensed physician on a plaintiff such as Roe. A transaction resulting in an operation such as this is not "private" in the ordinary usage of that word. Nor is the "privacy" that the Court finds here even a distant relative of the freedom from searches and seizures protected by the Fourth Amendment to the Constitution, which the Court has referred to as embodying a right to privacy. . . .

If the Court means by the term "privacy" no more than that the claim of a person to be free from unwanted state regulation of consensual transactions may be a form of "liberty" protected by the Fourteenth Amendment, there is no doubt that similar claims have been upheld in our earlier decisions on the basis of that liberty. I agree with the statement of MR. JUSTICE STEWART in his concurring opinion that the "liberty," against deprivation of which without due process the Fourteenth Amendment protects, embraces more than the rights found in the Bill of Rights. But that liberty is not guaranteed absolutely against deprivation, only against deprivation without due process of law. The test traditionally applied in the area of social and economic legislation is whether or not a law such as that challenged has a rational relation to a valid state objective. . . . The Due Process Clause of the Fourteenth Amendment undoubtedly does place a limit, albeit a broad one, on legislative power to enact laws such as this. If the Texas statute were to prohibit an abortion even where the mother's life is in jeopardy, I have little doubt that such a statute would lack a rational relation to a valid state objective. . . . But the Court's sweeping invalidation of any restrictions on abortion during the first trimester is impossible to justify under that standard, and the conscious weighing of competing factors that the Court's opinion apparently substitutes for the established test is far more appropriate to a legislative judgment than to a judicial one.

The Court eschews the history of the Fourteenth Amendment in its reliance on the "compelling state interest" test. . . . But the Court adds a new wrinkle to this test by transposing it from the legal considerations associated with the Equal Protection Clause of the Fourteenth Amendment to this case arising under the Due Process Clause of the Fourteenth Amendment. Unless I misapprehend the consequences of this transplanting of the "compelling state interest test," the Court's opinion will accomplish the seemingly impossible feat of leaving this area of the law more confused than it found it.

While the Court's opinion quotes from the dissent of Mr. Justice Holmes in *Lochner* v. *New York*, . . . the result it reaches is more closely attuned to the majority opinion of Mr. Justice Peckham in that case. As in *Lochner* and similar cases applying substantive due process standards to economic and social welfare legislation, the adoption of the compelling state interest standard will inevitably require this Court to examine the legislative policies and pass on the wisdom of these policies in the very process of deciding whether a particular state interest put forward may or may not be "compelling." The decision here to break pregnancy into three distinct terms and to outline the permissible restrictions the State may impose in each one, for example, partakes more of judicial legislation than it does of a determination of the intent of the drafters of the Fourteenth Amendment.

Webster v. *Reproductive Health Services*

109 S. Ct. 3040, 106 L. Ed. 2d 410 (1989)

Reproductive Health Services, state-employed health professionals, and private nonprofit corporations providing abortion services brought suit against William L. Webster, Attorney General of Missouri, in the U.S. District Court for the Western District of Missouri. They sought declaratory and injunctive relief, challenging the constitutionality of a Missouri abortion statute. The statute set forth "findings" in its preamble that the "life of each human being begins at conception" and that "unborn children have protectable interests in life, health, and well-being." It specified that physicians, prior to performing an abortion on any woman whom they have reason to believe is 20 or more weeks pregnant, must ascertain whether the fetus is "viable" by performing "such medical examinations and tests as are necessary to make a finding of [the fetus's] gestational age, weight, and lung maturity." It also prohibited the use of public employees and facilities to perform or assist abortions not necessary to save the mother's life. The District Court struck down the statute and enjoined its enforcement. The Court of Appeals for the Eighth Circuit affirmed, ruling that the statute violated the Supreme Court decisions in *Roe* v. *Wade* and subsequent cases. *Judgment of the Court: Rehnquist, Kennedy, White. Concurring in part and concurring in the judgment: O'Connor; Scalia. Concurring in part and dissenting in part: Blackmun, Brennan, Marshall; Stevens.*

CHIEF JUSTICE REHNQUIST announced the judgment of the Court. . . .

Decision of this case requires us to address the preamble; . . . the prohibition on the use of public facilities or employees to perform abortions; . . . and . . . the requirement that physicians conduct viability tests prior to performing abortions. We address these *seriatim*. . . .

The Act's preamble, as noted, sets forth "findings" by the Missouri legislature that "[t]he life of each human being begins at conception," and that "[u]nborn children have protectable interests in life, health, and well-being." . . . The Act then mandates that state laws be interpreted to provide unborn children with "all the rights, privileges, and immunities available to other persons, citizens, and residents of this state," subject to the Constitution and this Court's precedents. . . . In invalidating the preamble, the Court of Appeals relied on this Court's dictum that " 'a State may not adopt one theory of when life begins to justify its regulation of abortions.' " . . . *Akron* v. *Akron Center for Reproductive Health, Inc.*, 462 U.S. 416, 444 . . . (1983). . . .

In our view, the Court of Appeals misconceived the meaning of the *Akron* dictum, which was only that a State could not "justify" an abortion regulation otherwise invalid under *Roe* v. *Wade* on the ground that it embodied the State's view about when life begins. Certainly the preamble does not by its terms regulate abortion or any other aspect of appellees' medical practice. The Court has emphasized that *Roe* v. *Wade* "implies no limitation on the authority of a State to make a value judgment favoring childbirth over abortion." . . . The preamble can be read simply to express that sort of value judgment. It will be time enough for federal courts to address the meaning of the preamble should it be applied to restrict the activities of appellees in some concrete way. Until then, this Court "is not empowered to decide . . . abstract propositions, or to declare, for the government of future cases, principles or rules of law which cannot affect the result as to the thing in issue in the case before it." . . .

Section 188.210 provides that "[i]t shall be unlawful for any public employee within the scope of his employment to perform or assist an abortion, not necessary to save the life of the mother," while § 188.215 makes it "unlawful for any public facility to be used for the purpose of performing or assisting an abortion not necessary to save the life of the mother." The Court of Appeals held that these provisions contravened this Court's abortion decisions. . . . We take the contrary view. . . .

In *Harris* v. *McRae*, . . . (1980), the Court upheld "the most restrictive version of the Hyde Amendment," . . . which withheld from States federal funds under the Medicaid program to reimburse the costs of abortions, " 'except where the life of the mother would be endangered if the fetus were carried to term.' " . . . Just as Congress' refusal to fund abortions in *McRae* left "an indigent woman with at least the same range of choice in deciding whether to obtain a medically necessary abortion as she would have had if Congress had chosen to subsidize no health care costs at all," . . . Missouri's refusal to allow public employees to perform abortions in public hospitals leaves a pregnant woman with the same choices as if the State had chosen not to operate any public hospitals at all. The challenged provisions only restrict a woman's ability to obtain an abortion to the extent that she chooses to use a physician affiliated with a public hospital. . . . Having held that the State's refusal to fund abortions does not violate *Roe* v. *Wade*, it strains logic to reach a contrary result for the use of public facilities and employees. If the State may "make a value judgment favoring childbirth over abortion and . . . implement that judgment by the allocation of public funds," . . . surely it may do so through the allocation of other public resources, such as hospitals and medical staff. . . .

Section 188.029 of the Missouri Act provides:

> "Before a physician performs an abortion on a woman he has reason to believe is carrying an unborn child of twenty or more weeks gestational age, the physician shall first determine if the unborn child is viable by using and exercising that degree of care, skill, and proficiency commonly exercised by the ordinarily skillful, careful, and prudent physician engaged in similar practice under the same or similar conditions. In making this determination of viability, the physician shall perform or cause to be performed such medical examinations and tests as are necessary to make a finding of the gestational age, weight, and lung maturity of the unborn child and shall enter such findings and determination of viability in the medical record of the mother."[12]

As with the preamble, the parties disagree over the meaning of this statutory provision. The State emphasizes the language of the first sentence, which speaks in terms of the physician's determination of viability being made by the standards of ordinary skill in the medical profession. Appellees stress the language of the second sentence, which prescribes such "tests as are necessary" to make a finding of gestational age, fetal weight, and lung maturity.

The viability-testing provision of the Missouri Act is concerned with promoting the State's interest in potential human life rather than in maternal health. Section 188.029 creates what is essentially a presumption of viability at 20 weeks, which the physician must rebut with tests indicating that the fetus is not viable prior to performing an abortion. It also directs the physician's determination as to viability by specifying consideration, if feasible, of gestational age, fetal weight, and lung capacity. The District Court found that "the medical evidence is uncontradicted that a 20-week fetus is *not* viable," and that "23½ to 24 weeks gestation is the earliest point in pregnancy where a reasonable possibility of viability exists." . . . But it also found that there may be a 4-week error in estimating gestational age, which supports testing at 20 weeks. . . .

We think that the doubt cast upon the Missouri statute . . . is not so much a flaw in the statute as it is a reflection of the fact that the rigid trimester analysis of the course of a pregnancy enunciated in *Roe* has resulted in . . . making constitutional law in this area a virtual Procrustean bed. . . .

Stare decisis is a cornerstone of our legal system, but it has less power in constitutional cases, where, save for constitutional amendments, this Court is the only body able to make needed changes. . . . We have not refrained from reconsideration of a prior construction of the Constitution that has proved "unsound in principle and unworkable in practice." . . . We think the *Roe* framework is hardly consistent with the notion of a Constitution cast in general terms, as ours is, and usually speaking in general principles, as ours does. The key elements of the *Roe* framework—trimesters and viability—are not found in the text of the Constitution or in any place else one would expect to find a constitutional principle. Since the bounds of the inquiry are essentially indeterminate, the result has been a web of legal rules that have become increasingly intricate, resembling a code of regulations rather than a body of constitutional doctrine. As Justice White has put it, the trimester framework has left this Court to serve as the country's "*ex officio* medical board with powers to approve or disapprove medical and operative practices and standards throughout the United States." . . .

In the second place, we do not see why the State's interest in protecting potential human life should come into existence only at the point of viability, and that there should therefore be a rigid line allowing state regulation after viability but prohibiting it before viability. . . .

The tests that § 188.029 requires the physician to perform are designed to determine viability. The State here has chosen viability as the point at which its interest in potential human life must be safeguarded. . . . It is true that the tests in question increase the expense of abortion, and regulate the discretion of the physician in determining the viability of the fetus. Since the tests will undoubtedly show in many cases that the fetus is not viable, the tests will have been performed for what were in fact second-trimester abortions. But we are satisfied that the requirement of these tests permissibly furthers the State's interest in protecting potential human life, and we therefore believe § 188.029 to be constitutional.

The dissent takes us to task for our failure to join in a "great issues" debate as to whether the Constitution includes an "unenumerated" general right to privacy as recognized in cases such as *Griswold* v. *Connecticut* . . . (1965), and *Roe*. . . . *Roe* v. *Wade* . . . sought to establish a constitutional framework for judging state regulation of abortion during the entire term of pregnancy. That framework sought to deal with areas of medical practice traditionally subject to state regulation, and it sought to balance once and for all by reference only to the calendar the claims of the State to protect the fetus as a form of human life against the claims of a woman to decide for herself whether or not to abort a fetus she was carrying. The experience of the Court in applying *Roe* v. *Wade* in later cases . . . suggests to us that there is wisdom in not unnecessarily attempting to elaborate the abstract differences between a "fundamental right" to abortion, . . . a "limited fundamental constitutional right," which Justice Blackmun's dissent today treats *Roe* as having established, . . . or a liberty interest protected by the Due Process Clause, which we believe it to be. The Missouri testing requirement here is reasonably designed to ensure that abortions are not performed where the fetus is viable—an end which all concede is legitimate—and that is sufficient to sustain its constitutionality.

. . . The dissent also accuses us, *inter alia*, of cowardice and illegitimacy in dealing with "the most politically divisive domestic legal issue of our time." . . .

But the goal of constitutional adjudication is surely not to remove inexorably "politically divisive" issues from the ambit of the legislative process, whereby the people through their elected representatives deal with matters of concern to them. The goal of constitutional adjudication is to hold true the balance between that which the Constitution puts beyond the reach of the democratic process and that which it does not. We think we have done that today. The dissent's suggestion . . . that legislative bodies, in a Nation where more than half of our population is women, will treat our decision today as an invitation to enact abortion regulation reminiscent of the dark ages not only misreads our views but does scant justice to those who serve in such bodies and the people who elect them.

Both appellants and the United States as *Amicus Curiae* have urged that we overrule our decision in *Roe* v. *Wade* . . . The facts of the present case, however, differ from those at issue in *Roe*. Here, Missouri has determined that viability is the point at which its interest in potential human life must be safeguarded. In *Roe*, on the other hand, the Texas statute criminalized the performance of *all* abortions, except when the mother's life was at stake. . . . This case therefore affords us no occasion to revisit the holding of *Roe*, which was that the Texas statute unconstitutionally infringed the right to an abortion derived from the Due Process Clause, . . . and we leave it undisturbed. To the extent indicated in our opinion, we would modify and narrow *Roe* and succeeding cases.

Because none of the challenged provisions of the Missouri Act properly before us conflict with the Constitution, the judgment of the Court of Appeals is

Reversed.

JUSTICE O'CONNOR, concurring in part and concurring in the judgment. . . .

In its interpretation of Missouri's "determination of viability" provision, . . . the plurality has proceeded in a manner unnecessary to deciding the question at hand. . . .

Unlike the plurality, I do not understand these viability testing requirements to conflict with any of the Court's past decisions concerning state regulation of abortion. Therefore, there is no necessity to accept the State's invitation to reexamine the constitutional validity of *Roe* v. *Wade*. . . . Where there is no need to decide a constitutional question, it is a venerable principle of this Court's adjudicatory processes not to do so for "[t]he Court will not 'anticipate a question of constitutional law in advance of the necessity of deciding it.' " *Ashwander* v. *TVA*, . . . (1936) (Brandeis, J., concurring). Neither will it generally "formulate a rule of constitutional law broader than is required by the precise facts to which it is to be applied." . . . Quite simply, "[i]t is not the habit of the court to decide questions of a constitutional nature unless absolutely necessary to a decision of the case." . . . The Court today has accepted the State's every interpretation of its abortion statute and has upheld, under our existing precedents, every provision of that statute which is properly before us. Precisely for this reason reconsideration of *Roe* falls not into any "good-cause exception" to this "fundamental rule of judicial restraint. . . ." . . . When the constitutional invalidity of a State's abortion statute actually turns on the constitutional validity of *Roe* v. *Wade*, there will be time enough to reexamine *Roe*. And to do so carefully. . . .

JUSTICE SCALIA, concurring in part and concurring in the judgment. . . .

The outcome of today's case will doubtless be heralded as a triumph of judicial statesmanship. It is not that, unless it is statesmanlike needlessly to prolong this Court's self-awarded sovereignty over a field where it has little proper business since the answers to most of the cruel questions posed are political and not juridical—a sovereignty which therefore quite properly, but to the great damage of the Court, makes it the object of the sort of organized public pressure that political institutions in a democracy ought to receive.

Justice O'Connor's assertion . . . that a "fundamental rule of judicial restraint" requires us to avoid reconsidering *Roe*, cannot be taken seriously. By finessing *Roe* we do not, as she suggests, . . . adhere to the strict and venerable rule that we should avoid "decid[ing] questions of a constitutional nature." We have not disposed of this case on some statutory or procedural ground, but have decided, and could not avoid deciding, whether the Missouri statute meets the requirements of the United States Constitution. The only choice available is whether, in deciding that constitutional question, we should use *Roe* v. *Wade* as the benchmark, or something else. What is involved, therefore, is not the rule of avoiding constitutional issues where possible, but the quite separate principle that we will not "formulate a rule of constitutional law broader than is required by the precise facts to which it is to be applied." . . . The latter is a sound general principle, but one often departed from when good reason exists. . . .

I have not identified with certainty the first instance of our deciding a case on broader constitutional grounds than absolutely necessary, but it is assuredly no later than *Marbury* v. *Madison*, . . . (1803), where we held that mandamus could constitutionally issue against the Secretary of State, although that was unnecessary given our holding that the law authorizing issuance of the mandamus by this Court was unconstitutional. . . .

The real question, then, is whether there are valid reasons to go beyond the most stingy possible holding today. It seems to me there are not only valid but compelling ones. Ordinarily, speaking no more broadly than is absolutely required avoids throwing settled law into confusion; doing so today preserves a chaos that is evident to anyone who can read and count. Alone sufficient to justify a broad holding is the fact that our retaining control, through *Roe*, of what I believe to be, and many of our citizens recognize to be, a political issue, continuously distorts the public perception of the role of this Court. We can now look forward to at least another Term with carts full of mail from the public, and streets full of demonstrators, urging us—their unelected and life-tenured judges who have been awarded those extraordinary, undemocratic characteristics precisely in order that we might follow the law despite the popular will—to follow the popular will. Indeed, I expect we can look forward to even more of that than before, given our indecisive decision today. And if these reasons for taking the unexceptional course of reaching a broader holding are not enough, then consider the nature of the constitutional question we avoid: In most cases, we do no harm by not speaking more broadly than the decision requires. Anyone affected by the conduct that the avoided holding would have prohibited will be able to challenge it himself, and have his day in court to make the argument. Not so with respect to the harm that many States believed, pre-*Roe,* and many may continue to believe, is caused by largely unrestricted abortion. That will continue to occur if the States have the constitutional power to prohibit it, and would do so, but we skillfully avoid telling them so. Perhaps those abortions cannot constitutionally be proscribed. That is surely an arguable question, the question that reconsideration of *Roe* v. *Wade* entails. But what is not at all arguable, it seems to me, is that we should decide now and not insist that we be run into a corner before we grudgingly yield up our judgment. The only sound reason for the latter course is to prevent a change in the law—but to think that desirable begs the question to be decided. . .

The result of our vote today is that we will not reconsider that prior opinion, even if most of the Justices think it is wrong, unless we have before us a statute that in fact contradicts it—and even then (under our newly discovered "no-broader-than-necessary" requirement) only minor problematical aspects of *Roe* will be reconsidered, unless one expects State legislatures to adopt provisions whose compliance with *Roe* cannot even be argued with a straight face. It thus appears that the mansion of constitutionalized abortion-law, constructed overnight in *Roe* v. *Wade,* must be disassembled door-jamb by door-jamb, and never entirely brought down, no matter how wrong it may be.

Of the four courses we might have chosen today—to reaffirm *Roe,* to overrule it explicitly, to overrule it *sub silentio,* or to avoid the question—the last is the least responsible. On the question of the constitutionality of § 188.029, I concur in the judgment of the Court and strongly dissent from the manner in which it has been reached.

Justice Blackmun, with whom Justice Brennan and Justice Marshall join, concurring in part and dissenting in part.

Today, *Roe* v. *Wade,* . . . (1973), and the fundamental constitutional right of women to decide whether to terminate a pregnancy, survive but are not secure. Although the Court extricates itself from this case without making a single, even incremental, change in the law of abortion, the plurality and Justice Scalia would overrule *Roe* (the first silently, the other explicitly) and would return to the States virtually unfettered authority to control the quintessentially intimate, personal, and life-directing decision whether to carry a fetus to term. Although today, no less than yesterday, the Constitution and the decisions of this Court prohibit a State from enacting laws that inhibit women from the meaningful exercise of that right, a plurality of this Court implicitly invites every state legislature to enact more and more restrictive abortion regulations in order to provoke more and more test cases, in the hope that sometime down the line the Court will return the law of procreative freedom to the severe limitations that generally prevailed in this country before January 22, 1973. Never in my memory has a plurality announced a judgment of this Court that so foments disregard for the law and for our standing decisions.

Nor in my memory has a plurality gone about its business in such a deceptive fashion. At every level of its review, from its effort to read the real meaning out of the Missouri statute, to its intended evisceration of precedents and its deafening silence about the constitutional protections that it would jettison, the plurality obscures the portent of its analysis. With feigned restraint, the plurality announces that its analysis leaves *Roe* "undisturbed," albeit "modif[ied] and narrow[ed]." . . . But this disclaimer is totally meaningless. The plurality opinion is filled with winks, and nods, and knowing glances to those who would do away with *Roe* explicitly, but turns a stone face to anyone in search of what the plurality conceives as the scope of a woman's right under the Due Process Clause to terminate a pregnancy free from the coercive and brooding influence of the State. The simple truth is that *Roe* would not survive the plurality's analysis, and that the plurality provides no substitute for *Roe's* protective umbrella.

I fear for the future. I fear for the liberty and equality of the millions of women who have lived and come of age in the 16 years since *Roe* was decided. I fear for the integrity of, and public esteem for, this Court.

I dissent.

. . .

. . . Tucked away at the end of its opinion, the plurality suggests a radical reversal of the law of abortion; and there, primarily, I direct my attention.

In the plurality's view, the viability-testing provision imposes a burden on second-trimester abortions as a way of furthering the State's interest in protecting the potential life of the fetus. Since under the *Roe* framework, the State may not fully regulate abortion in the interest of potential life (as opposed to maternal health) until the third trimester, the plurality finds it necessary, in order to save the Missouri testing provision, to throw out *Roe's* trimester framework. . . . In flat contradiction to *Roe*, the plurality concludes that the State's interest in potential life is compelling before viability, and upholds the testing provision because it "permissibly furthers" that state interest. . . .

The statute's plain language requires the physician to undertake whatever tests are necessary to determine gestational age, weight, and lung maturity, regardless of whether these tests are necessary to a finding of viability, and regardless of whether the tests subject the pregnant woman or the fetus to additional health risks or add substantially to the cost of an abortion.

Had the plurality read the statute as written, it would have had no cause to reconsider the *Roe* framework. As properly construed, the viability-testing provision does not pass constitutional muster under even a rational-basis standard, the least restrictive level of review applied by this Court. . . . By mandating tests to determine fetal weight and lung maturity for every fetus thought to be more than 20 weeks gestational age, the statute requires physicians to undertake procedures, such as amniocentesis, that, in the situation presented, have no medical justification, impose significant additional health risks on both the pregnant woman and the fetus, and bear no rational relation to the State's interest in protecting fetal life. As written, § 188.029 is an arbitrary imposition of discomfort, risk, and expense, furthering no discernible interest except to make the procurement of an abortion as arduous and difficult as possible. Thus, were it not for the plurality's tortured effort to avoid the plain import of § 188.029, it could have struck down the testing provision as patently irrational irrespective of the *Roe* framework. . . .

Having contrived an opportunity to reconsider the *Roe* framework, and then having discarded that framework, the plurality finds the testing provision unobjectionable because it "permissibly furthers the State's interest in protecting potential human life." . . . This newly minted standard is circular and totally meaningless. Whether a challenged abortion regulation "permissibly furthers" a legitimate state interest is the *question* that courts must answer in abortion cases, not the standard for courts to apply. In keeping with the rest of its opinion, the plurality makes no attempt to explain or to justify its new standard, either in the abstract or as applied in this case. Nor could it. The "permissibly furthers" standard has no independent meaning, and consists of nothing other than what a majority of this Court may believe at any given moment in any given case. The plurality's novel test appears to be nothing more than a dressed-up version of rational-basis review, this Court's most lenient level of scrutiny. One thing is clear, however: were the plurality's "permissibly furthers" standard adopted by the Court, for all practical purposes, *Roe* would be overruled.

The "permissibly furthers" standard completely disregards the irreducible minimum of *Roe:* the Court's recognition that a woman has a limited fundamental constitutional right to decide whether to terminate a pregnancy. That right receives no meaningful recognition in the plurality's written opinion. Since, in the plurality's view, the State's interest in potential life is compelling as of the moment of conception, and is therefore served only if abortion is abolished, every hindrance to a woman's ability to obtain an abortion must be "permissible." Indeed, the more severe the hindrance, the more effectively (and permissibly) the State's interest would be furthered. A tax on abortions or a criminal prohibition would both satisfy the plurality's standard. So, for that matter, would a requirement that a pregnant woman memorize and recite today's plurality opinion before seeking an abortion.

The plurality pretends that *Roe* survives. Explaining that the facts of this case differ from those in *Roe:* here, Missouri has chosen to assert its interest in potential life only at the point of viability, whereas, in *Roe,* Texas had asserted that interest from the point of conception, criminalizing all abortions, except where the life of the mother was at stake. . . . This, of course, is a distinction without a difference. The plurality repudiates every principle for which *Roe* stands; in good conscience, it cannot possibly believe that *Roe* lies "undisturbed" merely because this case does not call upon the Court to reconsider the Texas statute, or one like it. If the Constitution permits a State to enact any statute that reasonably furthers its interest in potential life, and if that interest arises as of conception, why would the Texas statute fail to pass muster? One suspects that the plurality opinion agrees. It is impossible to read the plurality opinion and especially its final paragraph, without recognizing its implicit invitation to every State to enact more and more restrictive abortion laws, and to assert their interest in potential life as of the moment of conception. All these laws will satisfy the plurality's non-scrutiny, until sometime, a new regime of old dissenters and new appointees will declare what the plurality intends: that *Roe* is no longer good law.

Thus, "not with a bang, but a whimper," the plurality discards a landmark case of the last generation, and casts into darkness the hopes and visions of every woman in this country who had come to believe that the Constitution guaranteed her the right to exercise some control over her unique ability to bear children. The plurality does so either oblivious or insensitive to the fact that millions of women, and their families, have ordered their lives around the right to reproductive choice, and that this right has become vital to the full participation of women in the economic and political walks of American life. The plurality would clear the way once again for government to force upon women the physical labor and specific and direct medical and psychological harms that may accompany carrying a fetus to term. The plurality would clear the way again for the State to conscript a woman's body and to force upon her a "distressful life and future." . . .

Of the aspirations and settled understandings of American women, of the inevitable and brutal consequences of what it is doing, the tough-approach plurality utters not a word. This silence is callous. It is also profoundly destructive of this Court as an institution. To overturn a constitutional decision is a rare and grave undertaking. To overturn a constitutional decision that secured a fundamental personal liberty to millions of persons would be unprecedented in our 200 years of constitutional history. . . .

For today, at least, the law of abortion stands undisturbed. For today, the women of this Nation still retain the liberty to control their destinies. But the signs are evident and very ominous, and a chill wind blows.

I dissent.

JUSTICE STEVENS, concurring in part and dissenting in part. . . .

The Missouri statute defines "conception" as "the fertilization of the ovum of a female by a sperm of a male," . . . even though standard medical texts equate "conception" with implantation in the uterus, occurring about six days after fertilization. Missouri's declaration therefore implies regulation not only of previability abortions, but also of common forms of contraception such as the IUD and the morning-after pill. Because the preamble, read in context, threatens serious encroachments upon the liberty of the pregnant woman and the health professional, I am persuaded that these plaintiffs, appellees before us, have standing to challenge its constitutionality.

To the extent that the Missouri statute interferes with contraceptive choices, I have no doubt that it is unconstitutional. . . .

Because I am not aware of any secular basis for differentiating between contraceptive procedures that are effective immediately before and those that are effective immediately after fertilization, I believe it inescapably follows that the preamble to the Missouri statue is invalid under *Griswold* and its progeny.

Indeed, I am persuaded that the absence of any secular purpose for the legislative declarations that life begins at conception and that conception occurs at fertilization makes the relevant portion of the preamble invalid under the Establishment Clause of the First Amendment to the Federal Constitution. . . .

Bolstering my conclusion that the preamble violates the First Amendment is the fact that the intensely divisive character of much of the national debate over the abortion issue reflects the deeply held religious convictions of many participants in the debate. The Missouri Legislature may not inject its endorsement of a particular religious tradition into this debate, for "[t]he Establishment Clause does not allow public bodies to foment such disagreement."

Harris v. *McRae*

448 U.S. 297; 100 S. Ct. 2671; 65 L. Ed. 2d 784 (1980)

In 1965, Congress created the Medicaid program, as Title XIX of the Social Security Act, to provide federal financial assistance to states that chose to reimburse certain costs of medical treatment for indigent persons. Beginning in 1976, Congress passed various versions of the so-called Hyde Amendment (named for its sponsor in the House) that severely restricted the use of any federal funds to reimburse the cost of abortions under the program. Specifically, the amendment barred the use of federal funds to perform abortions except "where the life of the mother would be endangered if the fetus were carried to term" or "for the victims of rape or incest when such rape or incest has been reported promptly to a law enforcement agency or public health service." Cora McRae, a pregnant Medicaid recipient, and other plaintiffs brought suit, attacking the Hyde Amendment as a violation of the right to privacy and on grounds that a participating state remained obligated, despite the restriction, to fund all medically necessary abortions. A federal district court rejected any such statutory obligation on the part of the states, but held the Hyde Amendment unconstitutional as an infringement of the plaintiffs' right to privacy. Patricia Harris, secretary of the Department of Health and Human Services (formerly HEW), thereupon appealed. *Opinion of the Court: Stewart, Burger, Powell, Rehnquist, White. Concurring opinion: White. Dissenting opinions: Brennan, Blackmun, Marshall; Blackmun; Marshall; Stevens.*

Mr. Justice Stewart delivered the opinion of the Court.

This case presents statutory and constitutional questions concerning the public funding of abortions under Title XIX of the Social Security Act, commonly known as the "Medicaid" Act, and recent annual appropriations acts containing the so-called "Hyde Amendment." The statutory question is whether Title XIX requires a State that participates in the Medicaid program to fund the cost of medically necessary abortions for which federal reimbursement is unavailable under the Hyde Amendment. The constitutional question, which arises only if Title XIX imposes no such requirement, is whether the Hyde Amendment, by denying public funding for certain medically necessary abortions, contravenes the liberty or equal protection guarantees of the Due Process Clause of the Fifth Amendment. . . .

It is well settled that if a case may be decided on either statutory or constitutional grounds, this Court, for sound jurisprudential reasons, will inquire first into the statutory question. This practice reflects the deeply rooted doctrine "that we ought not to pass on questions of constitutionality . . . unless such adjudication is unavoidable." . . . Accordingly, we turn first to the question whether Title XIX requires a State that participates in the Medicaid program to continue to fund those medically necessary abortions for which federal reimbursement is unavailable under the Hyde Amendment.

. . . The Medicaid program created by Title XIX is a cooperative endeavor in which the Federal Government provides financial assistance to participating States to aid them in furnishing health care to needy persons. Under this system of "cooperative federalism," . . . if a State agrees to establish a Medicaid plan that satisfies the requirements of Title XIX, which include several mandatory categories of health services, the Federal Government agrees to pay a specified percentage of "the total amount expended . . . as medical assistance under the State plan. . . ." 42 U.S.C. § 1396b (a)(1). The cornerstone of Medicaid is financial contribution by both the Federal Government and the participating State. Nothing in Title XIX as originally enacted, or in its legislative history, suggests that Congress intended to require a participating State to assume the full costs of providing any health services in its Medicaid plan. Quite the contrary, the purpose of Congress in enacting Title XIX was to provide federal financial assistance for all legitimate state expenditures under an approved Medicaid plan. . . .

Since the Congress that enacted Title XIX did not intend a participating State to assume a unilateral funding obligation for any health service in an approved Medicaid plan, it follows that Title XIX does not require a participating State to include in its plan any services for which a subsequent Congress has withheld federal funding. Title XIX was designed as a cooperative program of shared financial responsibility, not as a device for the Federal Government to compel a State to provide services that Congress itself is unwilling to fund. Thus, if Congress chooses to withdraw federal funding for a particular service, a State is not obliged to continue to pay for that service as a condition of continued federal financial support of other services. This is not to say that Congress may not now depart from the original design of Title XIX under which the Federal Government shares the financial responsibility for expenses incurred under an approved Medicaid plan. It is only to say that, absent an indication of contrary legislative intent by a subsequent Congress, Title XIX does not obligate a participating State to pay for those medical services for which federal reimbursement is unavailable. . . .

Having determined that Title XIX does not obligate a participating State to pay for those medically necessary abortions for which Congress has withheld federal funding, we must consider the constitutional validity of the Hyde Amendment. . . .

We address first the appellees' argument that the Hyde Amendment, by restricting the availability of certain medically necessary abortions under Medicaid, impinges on the "liberty" protected by the Due Process Clause as recognized in *Roe* v. *Wade* . . . and its progeny. . . .

In *Maher* v. *Roe* [1977] . . . the Court was presented with the question whether the scope of personal constitutional freedom recognized in *Roe* v. *Wade* included an entitlement to Medicaid payments for abortions that are not medically necessary. At issue in *Maher* was a Connecticut welfare regulation under which Medicaid recipients received payments for medical services incident to childbirth, but not for medical services incident to nontherapeutic abortions. . . .

. . . The constitutional freedom recognized in *Wade* and its progeny, the *Maher* Court explained, did not prevent Connecticut from making "a value judgment favoring childbirth over abortion, and . . . implement[ing] that judgment by the allocation of public funds." . . . As the Court elaborated: "The Connecticut regulation before us is different in kind from the laws invalidated in our previous abortions decisions The Connecticut regulation places no obstacles—absolute or otherwise—in the pregnant woman's path to an abortion. An indigent woman who desires an abortion suffers no disadvantage as a consequence of Connecticut's decision to fund childbirth; she continues as before to be dependent on private sources for the service she desires. The State may have made childbirth a more attractive alternative, thereby influencing the woman's decision, but it has imposed no restriction on access to abortions that was not already there. The indigency that may make it difficult—and in some cases, perhaps, impossible—for some women to have abortions is neither created nor in any way affected by the Connecticut regulation." . . .

. . . Thus, even though the Connecticut regulation favored childbirth over abortion by means of subsidization of one and not the other, the Court in *Maher* concluded that the regulation did not impinge on the constitutional freedom recognized in *Wade* because it imposed no governmental restriction on access to abortions.

The Hyde Amendment, like the Connecticut welfare regulation at issue in *Maher,* places no governmental obstacle in the path of a woman who chooses to terminate her pregnancy, but rather, by means of unequal subsidization of abortion and other medical services, encourages alternative activity deemed in the public interest. . . .

. . . Regardless of whether the freedom of a woman to choose to terminate her pregnancy for health reasons lies at the core or the periphery of the due process liberty recognized in *Wade*, it simply does not follow that a woman's freedom of choice carries with it a constitutional entitlement to the financial resources to avail herself of the full range of protected choices. The reason why was explained in *Maher:* although government may not place obstacles in the path of a woman's exercise of her freedom of choice, it need not remove those not of its own creation. Indigency falls in the latter category. The financial constraints that restrict an indigent woman's ability to enjoy the full range of constitutionally protected freedom of choice are the product not of governmental restrictions on access to abortions, but rather of her indigency. Although Congress has opted to subsidize medically necessary services generally, but not certain medically necessary abortions, the fact remains that the Hyde Amendment leaves an indigent woman with at least the same range of choice in deciding whether to obtain a medically necessary abortion as she would have had if Congress had chosen to subsidize no health care costs at all. We are thus not persuaded that the Hyde Amendment impinges on the constitutionally protected freedom of choice recognized in *Wade.**

Although the liberty protected by the Due Process Clause affords protection against unwarranted government interference with freedom of choice in the context of certain personal decisions, it does not confer an entitlement to such funds as may be necessary to realize all the advantages of that freedom. To hold otherwise would mark a drastic change in our understanding of the Constitution. It cannot be that because government may not prohibit the use of contraceptives . . . or prevent parents from sending their child to a private school, . . . government, therefore, has an affirmative constitutional obligation to ensure that all persons have the financial resources to obtain contraceptives or send their children to private schools. To translate the limitation on governmental power implicit in the Due Process Clause into an affirmative funding obligation would require Congress to subsidize the medically necessary abortion of an indigent woman even if Congress had not enacted a Medicaid program to subsidize other medically necessary services. Nothing in the Due Process Clause supports such an extraordinary result. Whether freedom of choice that is constitutionally protected warrants federal subsidization is a question for Congress to answer, not a matter of constitutional entitlement. Accordingly, we conclude that the Hyde Amendment does not impinge on the due process liberty recognized in *Wade*. . . .

The remaining question . . . is whether the Hyde Amendment is rationally related to a legiti-

*The appellees argue that the Hyde Amendment is unconstitutional because it "penalizes" the exercise of a woman's choice to terminate a pregnancy by abortion. . . . This argument falls short of the mark. In *Maher,* the Court found only a "semantic difference" between the argument that Connecticut's refusal to subsidize nontherapeutic abortions "unduly interfere[d]" with the exercise of the constitutional liberty recognized in *Wade* and the argument that it "penalized" the exercise of that liberty. . . . And, regardless of how the claim was characterized, the *Maher* Court rejected the argument that Connecticut's refusal to subsidize protected conduct, without more, impinged on the constitutional freedom of choice. This reasoning is equally applicable in the present case. A substantial constitutional question would arise if Congress had attempted to withhold all Medicaid benefits from an otherwise eligible candidate simply because that candidate had exercised her constitutionally protected freedom to terminate her pregnancy by abortion. This would be analogous to *Sherbert* v. *Verner* [1963] . . . where this Court held that a State may not, consistent with the First and Fourteenth Amendments, withhold *all* unemployment compensation benefits from a claimant who would otherwise be eligible for such benefits but for the fact that she is unwilling to work one day per week on her Sabbath. But the Hyde Amendment, unlike the statute at issue in *Sherbert,* does not provide for such a broad disqualification from receipt of public benefits. Rather, the Hyde Amendment, like the Connecticut welfare provision at issue in *Maher,* represents simply a refusal to subsidize certain protected conduct. A refusal to fund protected activity, without more, cannot be equated with the imposition of a "penalty" on that activity.

mate governmental objective. It is the Government's position that the Hyde Amendment bears a rational relationship to its legitimate interest in protecting the potential life of the fetus. We agree.

. . . By subsidizing the medical expenses of indigent women who carry their pregnancies to term while not subsidizing the comparable expenses of women who undergo abortions (except those whose lives are threatened), Congress has established incentives that make childbirth a more attractive alternative than abortion for persons eligible for Medicaid. These incentives bear a direct relationship to the legitimate congressional interest in protecting potential life. Nor is it irrational that Congress has authorized federal reimbursement for medically necessary services generally, but not for certain medically necessary abortions. Abortion is inherently different from other medical procedures, because no other procedure involves the purposeful termination of a potential life.

MR. JUSTICE BRENNAN, with whom MR. JUSTICE MARSHALL and MR. JUSTICE BLACKMUN join, dissenting. . . .

Roe v. *Wade* held that the constitutional right to personal privacy encompasses a woman's decision whether or not to terminate her pregnancy. *Roe* and its progeny established that the pregnant woman has a right to be free from state interference with her choice to have an abortion—a right which, at least prior to the end of the first trimester, absolutely prohibits any governmental regulation of that highly personal decision. The proposition for which these cases stand thus is not that the State is under an affirmative obligation to ensure access to abortions for all who may desire them; it is that the State must refrain from wielding its enormous power and influence in a manner that might burden the pregnant woman's freedom to choose whether to have an abortion. The Hyde Amendment's denial of public funds for medically necessary abortions plainly intrudes upon this constitutionally protected decision, for both by design and in effect it serves to coerce indigent pregnant women to bear children that they would otherwise elect not to have.

When viewed in the context of the Medicaid program to which it is appended, it is obvious that the Hyde Amendment is nothing less than an attempt by Congress to circumvent the dictates of the Constitution and achieve indirectly what *Roe* v. *Wade* said it could not do directly.

. . . The Hyde Amendment is a transparent attempt by the Legislative Branch to impose the political majority's judgment of the morally acceptable and socially desirable preference on a sensitive and intimate decision that the Constitution entrusts to the individual. Worse yet, the Hyde Amendment does not foist that majoritarian viewpoint with equal measure upon everyone in our Nation, rich and poor alike; rather, it imposes that viewpoint only upon that segment of our society which, because of its position of political powerlessness, is least able to defend its privacy rights from the encroachments of state-mandated morality. The instant legislation thus calls for more exacting judicial review than in most other cases. controversy, are simply two alternative medical methods of dealing with pregnancy. . . .' " *Beal* v. *Doe* . . . (BRENNAN, J., dissenting). . . . In every pregnancy, one of these two courses of treatment is medically necessary, and the poverty-stricken woman depends on the Medicaid Act to pay for the expenses associated with that procedure. But under the Hyde Amendment, the Government will fund only those procedures incidental to childbirth. By thus injecting coercive financial incentives favoring childbirth into a decision that is constitutionally guaranteed to be free from governmental intrusion, the Hyde Amendment deprives the indigent woman of her freedom to choose abortion over maternity, thereby impinging on the due process liberty right recognized in *Roe* v. *Wade*.

. . . What the Court fails to appreciate is that it is not simply the woman's indigency that interferes with her freedom of choice, but the combination of her own poverty and the government's unequal subsidization of abortion and childbirth.

. . . By funding all of the expenses associated with childbirth and none of the expenses incurred in terminating pregnancy, the government literally makes an offer that the indigent woman cannot afford to refuse. It matters not that in this instance the government has used the carrot rather than the stick. What is critical is the realization that as a practical matter, many poverty-stricken women will choose to carry their pregnancy to term simply because the government provides funds for the associated medical services, even though these same women would have chosen to have an abortion if the government had also paid for that option, or indeed if the government had stayed out of the picture altogether and had defrayed the costs of neither procedure. The fundamental flaw in the Court's due process analysis, then, is its failure to acknowledge that the discriminatory distribution of the benefits of governmental largesse can discourage the exercise of fundamental liberties just as effectively as can an outright denial of those rights through criminal and regulatory sanctions. . . .

MR. JUSTICE MARSHALL, dissenting. . . .

. . . Under the Hyde Amendment, federal funding is denied for abortions that are medically necessary and that are necessary to avert severe and permanent damage to the health of the mother. The Court's opinion studiously avoids recognizing the undeniable fact that for women eligible for Medicaid—poor women—denial of a Medicaid-funded abortion is equivalent to denial of legal abortion altogether. By definition, these women do not have the money to pay for an abortion themselves. If abortion is medically necessary and a funded abortion is unavailable, they must resort to back-alley butchers, attempt to induce an abortion themselves by crude and dangerous methods, or suffer the serious medical consequences of attempting to carry the fetus to term. Because legal abortion is not a realistic option for such women, the predictable result of the Hyde Amendment will be a significant increase in the number of poor women who will die or suffer significant health damage because of an inability to procure necessary medical services. . . .

This case is perhaps the most dramatic illustration to date of the deficiencies in the Court's obsolete "two-tiered" approach to the Equal Protection Clause. . . .

The Hyde Amendment . . . distinguishes between medically necessary abortions and other medically necessary expenses. As I explained in *Maher* v. *Roe*, . . . such classifications must be assessed by weighing " 'the importance of the governmental benefits denied, the character of the class, and the asserted state interests.' " . . . Under that approach, the Hyde Amendment is clearly invalid. As in *Maher*, the governmental benefits at issue here are "of absolutely vital importance in the lives of the recipients." . . .

The class burdened by the Hyde Amendment consists of indigent women, a substantial proportion of whom are members of minority races. As I observed in *Maher*, nonwhite women obtain abortions at nearly double the rate of whites. . . . In my view, the fact that the burden of the Hyde Amendment fall exclusively on financially destitute women suggests "a special condition, which tends seriously to curtail the operation of those political processes ordinarily to be relied upon to protect minorities, and which may call for a correspondingly more searching judicial inquiry." . . .

As I explained in *Maher*, the asserted state interest in protecting potential life is insufficient to "outweigh the deprivation or serious discouragement of a vital constitutional right of especial importance to poor and minority women." . . . In *Maher*, the Court found a permissible state interest in encouraging normal childbirth. . . . The governmental interest in the present case is substantially weaker than in *Maher*, for under the Hyde Amendment funding is refused even in cases in which normal childbirth will not result: one can scarcely speak of "normal childbirth" in cases where the fetus will die shortly after birth, or in which the mother's life will be shortened or her health otherwise gravely impaired by the birth. . . .

In this case, the Federal Government has taken upon itself the burden of financing practically all medically necessary expenditures. One category of medically necessary expenditure has been singled out for exclusion, and the sole basis for the exclusion is a premise repudiated for purposes of constitutional law in *Roe* v. *Wade*. The consequence is a devastating impact on the lives and health of poor women. I do not believe that a Constitution committed to the equal protection of the laws can tolerate this result. I dissent.

MR. JUSTICE STEVENS, dissenting. . . .

. . . The Court focuses exclusively on the "legitimate interest in protecting the potential life of the fetus." . . . It concludes that since the Hyde amendments further that interest, the exclusion they create is rational and therefore constitutional. But it is misleading to speak of the Government's legitimate interest in the fetus without reference to the context in which that interest was held to be legitimate. For *Roe* v. *Wade* squarely held that the States may not protect that interest when a conflict with the interest in a pregnant woman's health exists. It is thus perfectly clear that neither the Federal Government nor the States may exclude a woman from medical benefits to which she would otherwise be entitled solely to further an interest in potential life when a physician, "in appropriate medical judgment," certifies that an abortion is necessary "for the preservation of the life or health of the mother." *Roe* v. *Wade* . . . The Court totally fails to explain why this reasoning is not dispositive here. . . .

Having decided to alleviate some of the hardships of poverty by providing necessary medical care, the Government must use neutral criteria in distributing benefits. It may not deny benefits to a financially and medically needy person simply because he is a Republican, a Catholic, or an Oriental—or because he has spoken against a program the Government has a legitimate interest in furthering. In sum, it may not create exceptions for the sole purpose of furthering a governmental interest that is constitutionally subordinate to the individual interest that the entire program was designed to protect.

Bowers v. *Hardwick*

478 U.S. 186, 106 S. Ct. 2841, 926 L. Ed. 2d 140 (1986)

After being charged with violating Section 16-6-2 of the Georgia Code Annotated, which criminalized sodomy, by committing that act with another adult male in the bedroom of his home, Michael Hardwick brought suit in Federal District Court challenging the constitutionality of Section 16-6-2 insofar as it criminalized consensual sodomy. He asserted that he was a practicing homosexual, that the Georgia sodomy statute, as administered by Michael Bowers, Attorney General of Georgia, placed him in imminent danger of arrest, and that the statute for several reasons violated the federal Constitution. The District Court granted Bowers's motion to dismiss for failure to state a claim, relying on *Doe* v. *Commonwealth's Attorney for the City of Richmond,* 403 F. Supp. 1199 (ED Va. 1975). A divided panel of the Court of Appeals for the Eleventh Circuit reversed. Relying on the Supreme Court's decisions in *Griswold* v. *Connecticut* (1965), *Eisenstadt* v. *Baird* (1972), *Stanley* v. *Georgia* (1969), and *Roe* v. *Wade* (1973), it held that the Georgia statute violated Hardwick's fundamental rights because his homosexual activity is a private and intimate association that is beyond the reach of state regulation by reason of the Ninth Amendment and the Due Process Clause of the Fourteenth Amendment. Bowers petitioned the Supreme Court for a writ of certiorari. *Opinion of the Court: White, Burger, O'Connor, Powell, Rehnquist. Concurring opinions: Burger; Powell. Dissenting opinions: Blackmun, Brennan, Marshall, Stevens; Stevens, Brennan, Marshall.*

JUSTICE WHITE delivered the opinion of the Court.

This case does not require a judgment on whether laws against sodomy between consenting adults in general, or between homosexuals in particular, are wise or desirable. It raises no question about the right or propriety of state legislative decisions to repeal their laws that criminalize homosexual sodomy, or of state-court decisions invalidating those laws on state constitutional grounds. The issue presented is whether the Federal Constitution confers a fundamental right upon homosexuals to engage in sodomy and hence invalidates the laws of the many States that still make such conduct illegal and have done so for a very long time. The case also calls for some judgment about the limits of the Court's role in carrying out its constitutional mandate.

We first register our disagreement with the

Court of Appeals and with respondent that the Court's prior cases [*Griswold, Eisenstadt, Stanley,* and *Roe*] have construed the Constitution to confer a right of privacy that extends to homosexual sodomy and for all intents and purposes have decided this case. . . .

. . . , We think it evident that none of the right announced in those cases bears any resemblance to that claimed constitutional right of homosexuals to engage in acts of sodomy that is asserted in this case. No connection between family, marriage, or procreation on the one hand and homosexual activity on the other has been demonstrated, either by the Court of Appeals or by respondent. Moreover, any claim that these cases nevertheless stand for the proposition that any kind of private sexual conduct between consenting adults is constitutionally insulated from state proscription is unsupportable. . . .

Precedent aside, however, respondent would have us announce, as the Court of Appeals did, a fundamental right to engage in homosexual sodomy. This we are quite unwilling to do. It is true that despite the language of the Due Process Clauses of the Fifth and Fourteenth Amendments, which appears to focus only on the processes by which life, liberty, or property is taken, the cases are legion in which those Clauses have been interpreted to have substantive content, subsuming rights that to a great extent are immune from federal or state regulation or proscription. Among such cases are those recognizing rights that have little or no textual support in the constitutional language. *Meyer, Prince,* and *Pierce* fall in this category, as do the privacy cases from *Griswold* to *Carey.*

Striving to assure itself and the public that announcing rights not readily identifiable in the Constitution's text involves much more than the imposition of the Justices' own choice of values on the States and the Federal Government, the Court has sought to identify the nature of the rights qualifying for heightened judicial protection. In *Palko* v. *Connecticut* . . . (1937), it was said that this category includes those fundamental liberties that are "implicit in the concept of ordered liberty," such that "neither liberty nor justice would exist if [they] were sacrificed." A different description of fundamental liberties appeared in *Moore* v. *East Cleveland,* 431 U.S. 494, 503 (1977) (opinion of Powell, J.), where they are characterized as those liberties that are "deeply rooted in this Nation's history and tradition." . . .

It is obvious to us that neither of these formulations would extend a fundamental right to homosexuals to engage in acts of consensual sodomy. Proscriptions against that conduct have ancient roots. . . . Sodomy was a criminal offense at common law and was forbidden by the laws of the original 13 States when they ratified the Bill of Rights. In 1868, when the Fourteenth Amendment was ratified, all but 5 of the 37 States in the Union had criminal sodomy laws. In fact, until 1961, all 50 States outlawed sodomy, and today, 25 States and the District of Columbia continue to provide criminal penalties for sodomy performed in private and between consenting adults. . . . Against this background, to claim that a right to engage in such conduct is "deeply rooted in this Nation's history and tradition" or "implicit in the concept of ordered liberty" is, at best, facetious.

Nor are we inclined to take a more expansive view of our authority to discover new fundamental rights imbedded in the Due Process Clause. The Court is most vulnerable and comes nearest to illegitimacy when it deals with judge-made constitutional law having little or no cognizable roots in the language or design of the Constitution. That this is so was painfully demonstrated by the face-off between the Executive and the Court in the 1930's, which resulted in the repudiation of much of the substantive gloss that the Court had placed on the Due Process Clauses of the Fifth and Fourteenth Amendments. There should be, therefore, great resistance to expand the substantive reach of those Clauses, particularly if it requires redefining the category of rights deemed to be fundamental. Otherwise, the Judiciary necessarily takes to itself further authority to govern the country without express constitutional authority. The claimed right pressed on us today falls far short of overcoming this resistance.

Respondent, however, asserts that the result should be different where the homosexual conduct occurs in the privacy of the home. He relies on *Stanley* v. *Georgia,* 394 U.S. 557 (1969), where the Court held that the First Amendment prevents conviction for possessing and reading obscene material in the privacy of one's home: "If the First Amendment means anything, it means that a State has no business telling a man, sitting alone in his house, what books he may read or what films he may watch."

Stanley did protect conduct that would not have been protected outside the home, and it partially prevented the enforcement of state obscenity laws; but the decision was firmly grounded in the First Amendment. The right pressed upon us here has no similar support in the text of the Constitution, and it does not qualify for recognition under the prevailing principles for construing the Fourteenth Amendment. Its limits are also difficult to discern. Plainly enough, otherwise illegal conduct is not always immunized whenever it occurs in the home. Victimless crimes, such as the possession and use of illegal drugs, do not escape the law where they are committed at home. *Stanley* itself recognized that its holding offered no protection for the possession in the home of drugs, firearms, or stolen goods. . . . And if respondent's submission is limited to the voluntary sexual conduct between consenting adults, it would be difficult, except by fiat, to limit the claimed right to homosexual conduct while leaving exposed to prosecution adultery, incest, and other sexual crimes even though they are committed in the home. We are unwilling to start down that road.

Even if the conduct at issue here is not a fundamental right, respondent asserts that there must be a rational basis for the law and that there is none in this case other than the presumed belief of a majority of the electorate in Georgia that homosexual sodomy is immoral and unacceptable. This is said to be an inadequate rationale to support the law. The law, however, is constantly based on notions of morality, and if all laws representing essentially moral choices are to be invalidated under the Due Process Clause, the courts will be very busy indeed. Even respondent makes no such claim, but insists that majority sentiments about the morality of homosexuality should be declared inadequate. We do not agree, and are unpersuaded that the sodomy laws of some 25 States should be invalidated on this basis.

Accordingly, the judgment of the Court of Appeals is

Reversed.

JUSTICE POWELL, concurring.

I join the opinion of the Court. I agree with the Court that there is no fundamental right—*i.e.*, no substantive right under the Due Process Clause—such as that claimed by respondent Hardwick, and found to exist by the Court of Appeals. This is not to suggest, however, that respondent may not be protected by the Eighth Amendment of the Constitution. The Georgia statute at issue in this case, . . . authorizes a court to imprison a person for up to 20 years for a single private, consensual act of sodomy. In my view, a prison sentence for such conduct—certainly a sentence of long duration—would create a serious Eighth Amendment issue. . . .

JUSTICE BLACKMUN, with whom JUSTICE BRENNAN, JUSTICE MARSHALL, and JUSTICE STEVENS join, dissenting.

This case is no more about "a fundamental right to engage in homosexual sodomy," as the Court purports to declare, . . . than *Stanley* v. *Georgia*, 394 U.S. 557 (1969), was about a fundamental right to watch obscene movies, or *Katz* v. *United States*, 389 U.S. 347 (1967), was about a fundamental right to place interstate bets from a telephone booth. Rather, this case is about "the most comprehensive of rights and the right most valued by civilized men," namely, "the right to be let alone." *Olmstead* v. *United States*, 277 U.S. 438, 478 (1928) (Brandeis, J., dissenting).

The statute at issue . . . denies individuals the right to decide for themselves whether to engage in particular forms of private, consensual sexual activity. The Court concludes that § 16–6–2 is valid essentially because "the laws of . . . many States . . . still make such conduct illegal and have done so for a very long time." . . . But the fact that the moral judgments expressed by statutes like § 16–6–2 may be "natural and familiar . . . ought not to conclude our judgment upon the question whether statutes embodying them conflict with the Constitution of the United States." . . . Like Justice Holmes, I believe that "[i]t is revolting to have no better reason for a rule of law than that so it was laid down in the time of Henry IV. It is still more revolting if the grounds upon which it was laid down have vanished long since, and the rule simply persists from blind imitation of the past." Holmes, The Path of the Law, 10 Harv. L. Rev. 457, 469 (1897). I believe we must analyze respondent Hardwick's claim in the light of the values that underlie the constitutional right to privacy . . .

The Court concludes today that none of our prior cases dealing with various decisions that individuals are entitled to make free of governmental interference "bears any resemblance to the claimed constitutional right of homosexuals to engage in acts of sodomy that is asserted in this case." . . .

Only the most willful blindness could obscure the fact that sexual intimacy is "a sensitive, key relationship of human existence, central to family life, community welfare, and the development of human personality." . . . The fact that individuals define themselves in a significant way through their intimate sexual relationships with others suggests, in a Nation as diverse as ours, that there may be many "right" ways of conducting those relationships, and that much of the richness of a relationship will come from the freedom an individual has to *choose* the form and nature of these intensely personal bonds. . . .

. . . The Court claims that its decision today merely refuses to recognize a fundamental right to engage in homosexual sodomy; what the Court really has refused to recognize is the fundamental interest all individuals have in controlling the nature of their intimate associations with others. . . .

The behavior for which Hardwick faces prosecution occurred in his own home, a place to which the Fourth Amendment attaches special significance. The Court's treatment of this aspect of the case is symptomatic of its overall refusal to consider the broad principles that have informed our treatment of privacy in specific cases . . .

The Court's interpretation of the pivotal case of *Stanley* v. *Georgia* . . . is entirely unconvincing. *Stanley* held that Georgia's undoubted power to punish the public distribution of constitutionally unprotected, obscene material did not permit the State to punish the private possession of such material. According to the majority here, *Stanley* relied entirely on the First Amendment, and thus, it is claimed, sheds no light on cases not involving printed materials. . . . But that is not what *Stanley* said. Rather, the *Stanley* Court anchored its holding in the Fourth Amendment's special protection for the individual in his home. . . .

. . . I see no justification for the Court's attempt to equate the private, consensual sexual activity at issue here with the "possession in the home of drugs, firearms, or stolen goods," . . . to which *Stanley* refused to extend its protection. . . . None of the behavior so mentioned in *Stanley* can properly be viewed as "[v]ictimless": . . . drugs and weapons are inherently dangerous, . . . and for property to be "stolen," someone must have been wrongfully deprived of it. Nothing in the record before the Court provides any justification for finding the activity forbidden by § 16–6–2 to be physically dangerous, either to the persons engaged in it or to others. . . .

The assertion that "traditional Judeo-Christian values proscribe" the conduct involved, . . . cannot provide an adequate justification for § 16–6–2. That certain, but by no means all, religious groups condemn the behavior at issue gives the State no license to impose their judgments on the entire citizenry. The legitimacy of secular legislation depends instead on whether the State can advance some justification for its law beyond its conformity to religious doctrine . . .

JUSTICE STEVENS, with whom JUSTICE BRENNAN and JUSTICE MARSHALL join, dissenting.

Like the statute that is challenged in this case, the rationale of the Court's opinion applies equally to the prohibited conduct regardless of whether the parties who engage in it are married or unmarried, or are of the same or different sexes. Sodomy was condemned as an odious and sinful type of behavior during the formative period of the common law. That condemnation was equally damning for heterosexual and homosexual sodomy. Moreover, it provided no special exemption for married couples. The license to cohabit and to produce legitimate offspring simply did not include any permission to engage in sexual conduct that was considered a "crime against nature."

The history of the Georgia statute before us clearly reveals this traditional prohibition of heterosexual, as well as homosexual, sodomy. . . .

Because the Georgia statute expresses the traditional view that sodomy is an immoral kind of conduct regardless of the identity of the persons who engage in it, I believe that a proper analysis of its constitutionality requires consideration of two questions: First, may a State totally prohibit the described conduct by means of a neutral law applying without exception to all persons subject to its jurisdiction? If not, may the State save the statute by announcing that it will only enforce the law against homosexuals? The two questions merit separate discussion. . . .

Our prior cases make two propositions abundantly clear. First, the fact that the governing majority in a State has traditionally viewed a particular practice as immoral is not a sufficient reason for upholding a law prohibiting the practice; neither history nor tradition could save a law prohibiting miscegenation from constitutional attack. Second, individual decisions by married persons, concerning the intimacies of their physical relationship, even when not intended to produce offspring, are a form of "liberty" protected by the Due Process Clause of the Fourteenth Amendment. *Griswold* v. *Connecticut,* 381 U.S. 479 (1965). Moreover, this protection extends to intimate choices by unmarried as well as married persons. *Carey* v. *Population Services International,* 431 U.S. 678 (1977); *Eisenstadt* v. *Baird,* 405 U.S. 438 (1972). . . .

Paradoxical as it may seem, our prior cases thus establish that a State may not prohibit sodomy within "the sacred precincts of marital bedrooms," . . . or, indeed, between unmarried heterosexual adults . . . In all events, it is perfectly clear that the State of Georgia may not totally prohibit the conduct proscribed by § 16–6–2 of the Georgia Criminal Code. . . .

If the Georgia statute cannot be enforced as it is written—if the conduct it seeks to prohibit is a protected from of liberty for the vast majority of Georgia's citizens—the State must assume the burden of justifying a selective application of its law. Either the persons to whom Georgia seeks to apply its statute do not have the same interest in "liberty" that others have, or there must be a reason why the State may be permitted to apply a generally applicable law to certain persons that it does not apply to others.

The first possibility is plainly unacceptable. Although the meaning of the principle that "all men are created equal" is not always clear, it surely must mean that every free citizen has the same interest in "liberty" that the members of the majority share. From the standpoint of the individual, the homosexual and the heterosexual have the same interest in deciding how he will live his own life, and, more narrowly, how he will conduct himself in his personal and voluntary associations with his companions. State intrusion into the private conduct of either is equally burdensome.

The second possibility is similarly unacceptable. A policy of selective application must be supported by a neutral and legitimate interest—something more substantial than a habitual dislike for, or ignorance about, the disfavored group. Neither the State nor the Court has identified any such interest in this case. The Court has posited as a justification for the Georgia statute "the presumed belief of a majority of the electorate in Georgia that homosexual sodomy is immoral and unacceptable." . . . But the Georgia electorate has expressed no such belief—instead, its representatives enacted a law that presumably reflects the belief that *all sodomy* is immoral and unacceptable. Unless the Court is prepared to conclude that such a law is constitutional, it may not rely on the work product of the Georgia Legislature to support its holding. For the Georgia statute does not single out homosexuals as a separate class meriting special disfavored treatment. . . .

I respectfully dissent.

Paul v. *Davis*

424 U.S. 693; 96 S. Ct. 455; 47 L. Ed. 2d 405 (1976)

A photograph of Edward C. Davis III bearing his name was included in a flyer of "active shoplifters" after he was arrested on a shoplifting charge in Louisville, Kentucky. When the charge subsequently was dismissed, Davis brought an action under 42 U.S.C. § 1983 against Edgar Paul, chief of police of Louisville, and other petitioners who had distributed the flyer to area merchants, alleging that their action under color of law had deprived him of his constitutional rights. Specifically, he alleged that distribution of the flyer had deprived him of his constitutional right to privacy and of liberty and property rights secured by the Due Process Clause of the Fourteenth Amendment. The district court granted petitioners' motion to dismiss. The court of appeals reversed on due process grounds, and the Supreme Court granted certiorari. Presented here is that portion of the Supreme Court's decision pertaining to the question of Davis's claim of a violation of the right to privacy. *Opinion of the Court: Rehnquist, Blackmun, Burger, Powell, Stewart. Dissenting opinion: Brennan, Marshall, White. Stevens did not participate.*

MR. JUSTICE REHNQUIST delivered the opinion of the Court. . . .

Respondent's complaint also alleged a violation of a "right to privacy guaranteed by the First, Fourth, Fifth, Ninth, and Fourteenth Amendments." The Court of Appeals did not pass upon this claim since it found the allegations of a due process violation sufficient to require reversal of the District Court's order. As we have agreed with the District Court on the due process issue, we find it necessary to pass upon respondent's other theory in order to determine whether there is any support for the litigation he seeks to pursue.

While there is no "right of privacy" found in any specific guarantee of the Constitution, the Court has recognized that "zones of privacy" may be created by more specific constitutional guarantees and thereby impose limits upon government power. . . . Respondent's case, however, comes within none of these areas. He does not seek to suppress evidence seized in the course of an unreasonable search. . . . And our other "right of privacy" cases, while defying categorical description, deal generally with substantive aspects of the Fourteenth Amendment. In *Roe* [v. *Wade* (1973)] the Court pointed out that the personal rights found in this guarantee of personal privacy must be limited to those which are "fundamental" or "implicit in the concept of ordered liberty" as described in *Palko* v. *Connecticut* . . . (1937). The activities detailed as being within this definition were ones very different from that for which respondent claims constitutional protection—matters relating to marriage, procreation, contraception, family relationships, and child rearing and education. In these areas it has been held that there are limitations on the States' power to substantively regulate conduct.

Respondent's claim is far afield from this line of decisions. He claims constitutional protection against the disclosure of the fact of his arrest on a shoplifting charge. His claim is based not upon any challenge to the State's ability to restrict his freedom of action in a sphere contended to be "private," but instead on a claim that the State may not publicize a record of an official act such as an arrest. None of our substantive privacy decisions hold this or anything like this, and we decline to enlarge them in this manner.

MR. JUSTICE BRENNAN, with whom MR. JUSTICE MARSHALL concurs and MR. JUSTICE WHITE concurs in part, dissenting. . . .

I had always thought that one of this Court's most important roles is to provide a formidable bulwark against governmental violation of the constitutional safeguards securing in our free society the legitimate expectations of every person to innate human dignity and sense of worth. It is a regrettable abdication of that role and a saddening denigration of our majestic Bill of Rights when the Court tolerates arbitrary and capricious official conduct branding an individual as a criminal without compliance with constitutional procedures designed to ensure the fair and impartial ascertainment of criminal culpability. Today's decision must surely be a short-lived aberration.* . . .

*In light of my conviction that the State may not condemn an individual as a criminal without following the mandates of the trial process, I need not address the question whether there is an independent right of privacy which would yield the same result. Indeed, privacy notions appear to be inextricably interwoven with the considerations which require that a State not single an individual out for punishment outside the judicial process. Essentially, the core concept would be that a State cannot broadcast even such factual events as the occurrence of an arrest that does not culminate in a conviction when there are no legitimate law enforcement justifications for doing so, since the State is chargeable with the knowledge that many employers will treat an arrest the same as a conviction and deny the individual employment or other opportunities on the basis of a fact that has no probative value with respect to actual criminal culpability. . . . A host of state and federal courts, relying on both privacy notions and the presumption of innocence, have begun to develop a line of cases holding that there are substantive limits on the power of the government to disseminate unresolved arrest records outside the law enforcement system. . . . I fear that after today's decision, these nascent doctrines will never have the opportunity for full growth and analysis. Since the Court of Appeals did not address respondent's privacy claims, and since there has not been substantial briefing or oral argument on that point, the Court's pronouncements are certainly unnecessary. Of course, States that are more sensitive than is this Court to the privacy and other interests of individuals erroneously caught up in the criminal justice system are certainly free to adopt or adhere to higher standards under state law. . . . Mr. Justice White does not concur in this footnote.

THE CONSTITUTION OF THE UNITED STATES OF AMERICA

We the People of the United States, in Order to form a more perfect Union, establish Justice, insure domestic Tranquility, provide for the common defence, promote the general Welfare, and secure the Blessings of Liberty to ourselves and our Posterity, do ordain and establish this CONSTITUTION for the United States of America.

ARTICLE I

SECTION 1. All legislative Powers herein granted shall be vested in a Congress of the United States, which shall consist of a Senate and House of Representatives.

SECTION 2. [1] The House of Representatives shall be composed of Mcmbers chosen every second Year by the People of the several States, and the Electors in each State shall have the Qualifications requisite for Electors of the most numerous Branch of the State Legislature.

[2] No person shall be a Representative who shall not have attained to the Age of twenty-five Years, and been seven Years a Citizen of the United States, and who shall not, when elected, be an Inhabitant of that State in which he shall be chosen.

[3] Representatives and direct Taxes shall be apportioned among the several States which may be included within this Union, according to their respective Numbers, which shall be determined by adding to the whole Number of free Persons, including those bound to Service for a Term of Years, and excluding Indians not taxed, three fifths of all other Persons. The actual Enumeration shall be made within three Years after the first Meeting of the Congress of the United States, and within every subsequent Term of ten Years, in such Manner as they shall by Law direct. The Number of Representatives shall not exceed one for every thirty Thousand, but each State shall have at Least one Representative; and until such enumeration shall be made, the State of New Hampshire shall be entitled to chuse three, Massachusetts eight, Rhode-Island and Providence Plantations one, Connecticut five, New York six, New Jersey four, Pennsylvania eight,

Delaware one, Maryland six, Virginia ten, North Carolina five, South Carolina five, and Georgia three.

[4] When vacancies happen in the Representation from any State, the Executive Authority thereof shall issue Writs of Election to fill such Vacancies.

[5] The House of Representatives shall chuse their Speaker and other Officers; and shall have the sole Power of Impeachment.

SECTION 3. [1] The Senate of the United States shall be composed of two Senators from each State, chosen by the Legislature thereof, for six Years; and each Senator shall have one Vote.

[2] Immediately after they shall be assembled in Consequence of the first Election, they shall be divided as equally as may be into three Classes. The Seats of the Senators of the first Class shall be vacated at the Expiration of the Second Year, of the second Class at the Expiration of the fourth Year, and of the third Class at the Expiration of the sixth Year, so that one-third may be chosen every second Year; and if Vacancies happen by Resignation, or otherwise, during the Recess of the Legislature of any State, the Executive thereof may make temporary Appointments until the next Meeting of the Legislature, which shall then fill such Vacancies.

[3] No person shall be a Senator who shall not have attained to the Age of thirty Years, and been nine Years a Citizen of the United States, and who shall not, when elected, be an Inhabitant of that State for which he shall be chosen.

[4] The Vice President of the United States shall be President of the Senate, but shall have no Vote, unless they be equally divided.

[5] The Senate shall chuse their Officers, and also a President pro tempore, in the absence of the Vice President, or when he shall exercise the Office of the President of the United States.

[6] The Senate shall have the sole Power to try all Impeachments. When sitting for that Purpose, they shall be on Oath or Affirmation. When the President of the United States is tried, the Chief Justice shall preside: And no Person shall be convicted without the Concurrence of two-thirds of the Members present.

[7] Judgment in Cases of Impeachment shall not extend further than to removal from Office, and disqualification to hold and enjoy any Office of honor, Trust, or Profit under the United States: but the Party convicted shall nevertheless be liable and subject to Indictment, Trial, Judgment, and Punishment, according to Law.

SECTION 4. [1] The Times, Places and Manner of holding Elections for Senators and Representatives, shall be prescribed in each State by the Legislature thereof; but the Congress may at any time by Law make or alter such Regulations, except as to the Places of chusing Senators.

[2] The Congress shall assemble at least one in every Year, and such Meeting shall be on the first Monday in December, unless they shall by Law appoint a different Day.

SECTION 5. [1] Each House shall be the Judge of the Elections, Returns, and Qualifications of its own Members, and a Majority of each shall constitute a Quorum to do Business, but a smaller Number may adjourn for day to day, and may be authorized to compel the Attendance of absent Members, in such Manner, and under such Penalties as each House may provide.

[2] Each House may determine the Rules of its Proceedings, punish its Members for disorderly Behavior, and with the Concurrence of two thirds, expel a Member.

[3] Each House shall keep a Journal of its Proceedings, and from time to time publish the same, excepting such Parts as may in their Judgment require Secrecy; and the Yeas and Nays of the Members of either House on any question shall, at the Desire of one fifth of those Present, be entered on the Journal.

[4] Neither House, during the Session of Congress, shall, without the Consent of the other, adjourn for more than three days, nor to any other Place than that in which the two Houses shall be sitting.

SECTION 6. [1] The Senators and Representatives shall receive a Compensation for their Services, to be ascertained by Law, and paid out of the Treasury of the United States. They shall in all Cases, except Treason, Felony and Breach of the Peace, be privileged from Arrest during their Attendance at the Session of their respective Houses, and in going to and returning from the same; and for any Speech or Debate in either House, they shall not be questioned in any other Place.

[2] No Senator or Representative shall, during the Time for which he was elected, be appointed to any civil Office under the Authority of the United States, which shall have been created, or the Emoluments whereof shall have been encreased during such time; and no Person holding any Office under the United States, shall be a Member of either House during his Continuance in Office.

SECTION 7. [1] All Bills for raising Revenue shall originate in the House of Representatives; but the Senate may propose or concur with Amendments as on other Bills.

[2] Every Bill shall have passed the House of Representatives and the Senate, shall, before it become a Law, be presented to the President of the United States; if he approve he shall sign it, but if not he shall return it, with his Objections to that House in which it shall have originated, who shall enter the Objections at large on their Journal, and proceed to reconsider it. If after such Reconsideration two thirds of that House shall agree to pass the Bill, it shall be sent, together with the Objections, to the other House, by which it shall likewise be reconsidered, and if approved by two thirds of that House, it shall become a Law. But in all such Cases, the Votes of both Houses shall be determined by Yeas and Nays, and the Names of the Persons voting for and against the Bill shall be entered on the Journal of each House respectively. If any Bill shall not be returned by the President within ten Days (Sundays excepted) after it shall have been presented to him, the Same shall be a Law, in like Manner as if he had signed it, unless the Congress by their Adjournment prevent its Return, in which Case it shall not be a Law.

[3] Every Order, Resolution, or Vote to which the Concurrence of the Senate and House of Representatives may be necessary (except on a question of Adjournment) shall be presented to the President of the United States; and before the Same shall take Effect, shall be approved by him, or being disapproved by him, shall be repassed by two thirds of the Senate and House of Representatives, according to the Rules and Limitations prescribed in the Case of a Bill.

SECTION 8. The Congress shall have Power

[1] To lay and collect Taxes, Duties, Imposts and Excises, to pay the Debts and provide for the common Defence and general Welfare of the United States, but all Duties, Imposts and Excises shall be uniform throughout the United States;

[2] To borrow money on the credit of the United States;

[3] To regulate Commerce with foreign Nations, and among the several States, and with the Indian Tribes;

[4] To establish an uniform Rule of Naturalization, and uniform Laws on the subject of Bankruptcies throughout the United States;

[5] To coin Money, regulate the Value thereof, and of foreign Coin, and fix the Standard of Weights and Measures;

[6] To provide for the Punishment of counterfeiting the Securities and current Coin of the United States;

[7] To Establish Post Offices and post Roads;

[8] To promote the Progress of Science and useful Arts, by securing for limited Times to Authors and Inventors the exclusive Right to their respective Writings and Discoveries;

[9] To constitute Tribunals inferior to the Supreme Court;

[10] To define and punish Piracies and Felonies committed on the high Seas, and Offenses against the Law of Nations;

[11] To declare War, grant Letters of Marque and Reprisal, and make Rules concerning Captures on Land and Water;

[12] To raise and support Armies, but no Appropriation of Money to that Use shall be for a longer Term than two Years;

[13] To provide and maintain a Navy;

[14] To make Rules for the Government and Regulation of the land and naval Forces;

[15] To provide for calling forth the Militia to execute the Laws of the Union, suppress Insurrections and repel Invasions;

[16] To provide for organizing, arming, and disciplining the Militia, and for governing such Part of them as may be employed in the Service of the United States, reserving to the States respectively, the Appointment of the Officers, and the Authority of training the Militia according to the discipline prescribed by Congress;

[17] To exercise exclusive Legislation in all Cases whatsoever, over such District (not exceeding ten Miles square) as may, by Cession of particular States, and the acceptance of Congress, become the Seat of the Government of the United States, and to exercise like Authority over all

Places purchased by the Consent of the Legislature of the State in which the Same shall be, for the Erection of Forts, Magazines, Arsenals, dock-Yards, and other needful Buildings;—And

[18] To make all Laws which shall be necessary and proper for carrying into Execution the foregoing Powers, and all other Powers vested by this Constitution in the Government of the United States, or in any Department or Officer thereof.

SECTION 9. [1] The Migration or Importation of Such Persons as any of the States now existing shall think proper to admit, shall not be prohibited by the Congress prior to the Year one thousand eight hundred and eight, but a tax or duty may be imposed on such Importation, not exceeding ten dollars for each Person.

[2] The privilege of the Writ of Habeas Corpus shall not be suspended, unless when in Cases of Rebellion or Invasion the public Safety may require it.

[3] No Bill of Attainder or ex post facto Law shall be passed.

[4] No capitation, or other direct, Tax shall be laid, unless in Proportion to the Census or Enumeration herein before directed to be taken.

[5] No Tax or Duty shall be laid on Articles exported from any State.

[6] No preference shall be given by any Regulation of Commerce or Revenue to the Ports of one State over those of another; nor shall Vessels bound to, or from, one State be obliged to enter, clear, or pay Duties in another.

[7] No money shall be drawn from the Treasury, but in Consequence of Appropriations made by Law; and a regular Statement and Account of the Receipts and Expenditures of all public Money shall be published from time to time.

[8] No Title of Nobility shall be granted by the United States: And no Person holding any Office of Profit or Trust under them, shall, without the Consent of the Congress, accept of any present, Emolument, Office, or Title, of any kind whatever, from any King, Prince, or foreign State.

SECTION 10. [1] No State shall enter into any Treaty, Alliance, or Confederation; grant Letters of Marque and Reprisal; coin Money; emit Bills of Credit; make any Thing but gold and silver Coin a Tender in Payment of Debts; pass any Bill of Attainder, ex post facto Law, or Law impairing the Obligation of Contracts, or grant any Title of Nobility.

[2] No State shall, without the Consent of the Congress, lay any Imposts or Duties on Imports or Exports, except what may be absolutely necessary for executing its inspection Laws: and the net Produce of all Duties and Imposts, laid by any State on Imports or Exports, shall be for the Use of the Treasury of the United States; and all such Laws shall be subject to the Revision and Control of the Congress.

[3] No State shall, without the Consent of Congress, lay any duty of Tonnage, keep Troops, or Ships of War in time of Peace, enter into any Agreement or Compact with another State, or with a foreign Power, or engage in War, unless actually invaded, or in such imminent Danger as will not admit of delay.

ARTICLE II

SECTION 1. [1] The executive Power shall be vested in a President of the United States of America. He shall hold his Office during the Term of four Years, and together with the Vice President, chosen for the same Term, be elected, as follows:

[2] Each State shall appoint, in such Manner as the Legislature thereof may direct, a Number of Senators and Representatives to which the State may be entitled in the Congress: but no Senator or Representative, or Person holding an Office of Trust or Profit under the United States, shall be appointed an Elector.

[3] The Electors shall meet in their respective States, and vote by Ballot for two persons, of whom one at least shall not be an Inhabitant of the same State with themselves. And they shall make a List of all the Persons voted for, and of the Number of Votes for each; which List they shall sign and certify, and transmit sealed to the Seat of the Government of the United States, directed to the President of the Senate. The President of the Senate shall, in the Presence of the Senate and House of Representatives, open all the Certificates, and the Votes shall then be counted. The Person having the greatest Number of Votes shall be the President, if such Number be a Majority of the whole Number of Electors appointed; and if there be more than one who have such Majority, and have an equal Number of Votes, then the

House of Representatives shall immediately chuse by Ballot one of them for President; and if no Person have a Majority, then from the five highest on the List the said House shall in like Manner chuse the President. But in chusing the President, the Votes shall be taken by States, the Representation from each State having one Vote; A quorum for this Purpose shall consist of a Member or Members from two-thirds of the States, and a Majority of all the States shall be necessary to a Choice. In every Case, after the Choice of the President, the Person having the greatest Number of Votes of the Electors shall be the Vice President. But if there shall remain two or more who have equal Votes, the Senate shall chuse from them by Ballot the Vice President.

[4] The Congress may determine the Time of chusing the Electors, and the Day on which they shall give their Votes; which Day shall be the same throughout the United States.

[5] No person except a natural born Citizen, or a Citizen of the United States, at the time of the Adoption of this Constitution, shall be eligible to the Office of President; neither shall any Person be eligible to that Office who shall not have attained to the Age of thirty-five Years, and been fourteen Years a Resident within the United States.

[6] In case of the removal of the President from Office, or of his Death, Resignation, or Inability to discharge the Powers and Duties of the said Office, the same shall devolve on the Vice President, and the Congress may by Law provide for the Case of Removal, Death, Resignation or Inability, both of the President and Vice President, declaring what Officer shall then act as President, and such Officer shall act accordingly, until the Disability be removed, or a President shall be elected.

[7] The President shall, at stated Times, receive for his Services, a Compensation, which shall neither be encreased nor diminished during the Period for which he shall have been elected, and he shall not receive within that Period any other Emolument from the United States, or any of them.

[8] Before he enter on the Execution of his Office, he shall take the following Oath or Affirmation:—"I do solemnly swear (or affirm) that I will faithfully execute the Office of President of the United States, and will to the best of my Ability, preserve, protect and defend the Constitution of the United States."

SECTION 2. [1] The President shall be Commander in Chief of the Army and Navy of the United States, and of the Militia of the several States, when called into the actual Service of the United States; he may require the Opinion, in writing, of the Principal Officer in each of the executive Departments, upon any subject relating to the Duties of their respective Offices, and he shall have Power to grant Reprieves and pardons for Offenses against the United States, except in Cases of Impeachment.

[2] He shall have Power, by and with the Advice and Consent of the Senate, to make Treaties, provided two-thirds of the Senators present concur; and he shall nominate, and by and with the Advice and Consent of the Senate, shall appoint Ambassadors, other public Ministers and Consuls, Judges of the Supreme Court, and all other Officers of the United States, whose Appointments are not herein otherwise provided for, and shall be established by Law, but the Congress may by Law vest the Appointment of such inferior Officers, as they think proper, in the President alone, in the Courts of Law, or in the Heads of Departments.

[3] The President shall have Power to fill up all Vacancies that may happen during the Recess of the Senate, by granting Commissions which shall expire at the End of their next Session.

SECTION 3. He shall from time to time give to the Congress Information of the State of the Union, and recommend to their Consideration such Measures as he shall judge necessary and expedient; he may, on extraordinary Occasions, convene both Houses, or either of them, and in Case of Disagreement between them, with Respect to the Time of Adjournment, he may adjourn them to such Time as he shall think proper; he shall receive Ambassadors and other public Ministers; he shall take Care that the Laws be faithfully executed, and shall Commission all the Officers of the United States.

SECTION 4. The President, Vice President and all civil Officers of the United States, shall be removed from Office on Impeachment for, and Conviction of, Treason, Bribery, or other high Crimes and Misdemeanors.

ARTICLE III

SECTION 1. The judicial Power of the United States, shall be vested in one supreme Court, and in such inferior Courts as the Congress may from time to time ordain and establish. The Judges, both of the supreme and inferior Courts, shall hold their Offices during good Behaviour, and shall, at stated Times, receive for their Services a Compensation which shall not be diminished during their Continuance in Office.

SECTION 2. [1] The judicial Power shall extend to all Cases, in Law and Equity, arising under this Constitution, the Laws of the United States, and Treaties made, or which shall be made under their Authority;—to all Cases affecting Ambassadors, other public Ministers and Consuls;—to all Cases of admiralty and maritime Jurisdiction;—to Controversies to which the United States shall be a Party;—to Controversies between two or more States;—between a State and Citizens of another State;—between Citizens of different States;—between Citizens of the same State claiming Lands under Grants of different States, and between a State, or the Citizens thereof, and foreign States, Citizens or Subjects.

[2] In all Cases affecting Ambassadors, other public Ministers and Consuls, and those in which a State shall be Party, the supreme Court shall have original Jurisdiction. In all the other Cases before mentioned, the supreme Court shall have appellate Jurisdiction, both as to Law and Fact, with such Exceptions, and under such Regulations as the Congress shall make.

[3] The trial of all Crimes, except in Case of Impeachment, shall be by Jury; and such Trial shall be held in the State where the said Crimes shall have been committed, but when not committed within any State, the Trial shall be at such Place or Places as the Congress may by Law have directed.

SECTION 3. [1] Treason against the United States, shall consist only in levying War against them, or, in adhering to their Enemies, giving them Aid and Comfort. No Person shall be convicted of Treason unless on the Testimony of two Witnesses to the same overt Act, or on Confession in open Court.

[2] The Congress shall have power to declare the Punishment of Treason, but no Attainder of Treason shall work Corruption of Blood, or Forfeiture except during the Life of the Person attainted.

ARTICLE IV

SECTION 1. Full Faith and Credit shall be given in each State to the public Acts, Records, and judicial Proceedings of every other State. And the Congress may by general Laws prescribe the Manner in which such Acts, Records and Proceedings shall be proved, and the Effect thereof.

SECTION 2. [1] The Citizens of each State shall be entitled to all Privileges and Immunities of Citizens in the several States.

[2] A Person charged in any State with Treason, Felony, or other Crime, who shall flee from Justice, and be found in another State, shall on demand of the executive Authority of the State from which he fled, be delivered up, to be removed to the State having Jurisdiction of the Crime.

[3] No Person held to Service or Labour in one State, under the Laws thereof, escaping into another, shall, in Consequence of any Law or Regulation therein, be discharged from such Service or Labour, but shall be delivered up on Claim of the Party to whom such Service or Labour may be due.

SECTION 3. [1] New States may be admitted by the Congress into this Union; but no new State shall be formed or erected within the Jurisdiction of any other State; nor any State be formed by the Junction of two or more States, or parts of States, without the Consent of the Legislature of the States concerned as well as of the Congress.

[2] The Congress shall have Power to dispose of and make all needful Rules and Regulations respecting the Territory or other Property belonging to the United States; and nothing in this Constitution shall be so construed as to Prejudice any Claims of the United States, or of any particular State.

SECTION 4. The United States shall guarantee to every State in this Union a Republican Form of Government, and shall protect each of them against Invasion; and on Application of the Legislature, or of the Executive (when the Legislature cannot be convened) against domestic Violence.

ARTICLE V

The Congress, whenever two-thirds of both Houses shall deem it necessary, shall propose Amendments to this Constitution, or, on the Application of the Legislatures of two-thirds of the several States, shall call a Convention for proposing Amendments, which, in either Case, shall be valid to all Intents and Purposes, as part of this Constitution, when ratified by the Legislatures of three-fourths of the several States, or by Conventions in three-fourths thereof, as the one or the other Mode of Ratification may be proposed by the Congress; Provided that no Amendment which may be made prior to the Year One thousand eight hundred and eight shall in any Manner affect the first and fourth Clauses in the Ninth Section of the first Article; and that no State, without its Consent, shall be deprived of its equal Suffrage in the Senate.

ARTICLE VI

[1] All Debts contracted and Engagements entered into, before the Adoption of this Constitution shall be valid against the United States under this Constitution, as under the Confederation.

[2] This Constitution, and the Laws of the United States which shall be made in Pursuance thereof; and all Treaties made, or which shall be made, under the Authority of the United States, shall be the supreme Law of the Land; and the Judges in every State shall be bound thereby, any Thing in the Constitution or Laws of any State to the Contrary notwithstanding.

[3] The Senators and Representatives before mentioned, and the Members of the several State Legislatures, and all executive and judicial Officers, both of the United States and of the several States, shall be bound by Oath or Affirmation, to support this Constitution; but no religious Test shall ever be required as a Qualification to any Office or public Trust under the United States.

ARTICLE VII

The Ratification of the Conventions of nine States shall be sufficient for the Establishment of this Constitution between the States so ratifying the Same.

ARTICLES IN ADDITION TO, AND AMENDMENT OF, THE CONSTITUTION OF THE UNITED STATES OF AMERICA, PROPOSED BY CONGRESS, AND RATIFIED BY THE LEGISLATURES OF THE SEVERAL STATES, PURSUANT TO THE FIFTH ARTICLE OF THE ORIGINAL CONSTITUTION

AMENDMENT I [1791]

Congress shall make no law respecting an establishment of religion, or prohibiting the free exercise thereof; or abridging the freedom of speech, or of the press; or the right of the people peaceably to assemble and to petition the Government for a redress of grievances.

AMENDMENT II [1791]

A well regulated Militia, being necessary to the security of a free State, the right of the people to keep and bear Arms, shall not be infringed.

AMENDMENT III [1791]

No Soldier shall, in time of peace be quartered in any house, without the consent of the Owner, nor in time of war, but in a manner to be prescribed by Law.

AMENDMENT IV [1791]

The right of the people to be secure in their persons, houses, papers, and effects, against unreasonable searches and seizures, shall not be violated, and no Warrants shall issue, but upon probable cause, supported by Oath or affirmation, and particularly describing the place to be searched, and the persons or things to be seized.

AMENDMENT V [1791]

No person shall be held to answer for a capital, or otherwise infamous crime, unless on a presentment or indictment of a Grand Jury, except in cases arising in the land or naval forces, or in the Militia, when in acutal service in time of War or public danger; nor shall any person be subject for the same offence to be twice put in jeopardy of life or limb; nor shall be compelled in any criminal case to be a witness against himself, nor be deprived of life, liberty, or property, without due process of law; nor shall private property be taken for public use, without just compensation.

AMENDMENT VI [1791]

In all criminal prosecutions, the accused shall enjoy the right to a speedy and public trial, by an impartial jury of the State and district wherein the crime shall have been committed, which district shall have been previously ascertained by law, and to be informed of the nature and cause of the accusation; to be confronted with the witnesses against him; to have compulsory process for obtaining witnesses in his favor, and to have the Assistance of Counsel for his defence.

AMENDMENT VII [1791]

In suits at common law, where the value in controversy shall exceed twenty dollars, the right of trial by jury shall be preserved, and no fact tried by jury, shall be otherwise reexamined in any Court of the United States, than according to the rules of the common law.

AMENDMENT VIII [1791]

Excessive bail shall not be required, nor excessive fines imposed, nor cruel and unusual punishments inflicted.

AMENDMENT IX [1791]

The enumeration in the Constitution, of certain rights, shall not be construed to deny or disparage others retained by the people.

AMENDMENT X [1791]

The powers not delegated to the United States by the Constitution, nor prohibited by it to the States, are reserved to the States respectively, or to the people.

AMENDMENT XI [1798]

The Judicial power of the United States shall not be construed to extend to any suit in law or equity, commenced or prosecuted against one of the United States by Citizens of another State, or by Citizens or Subjects of any Foreign State.

AMENDMENT XII [1804]

The electors shall meet in their respective states and vote by ballot for President and Vice-President, one of whom, at least, shall not be an inhabitant of the same state with themselves; they shall name in their ballots the person voted for as President, and in distinct ballots the person voted for as Vice-President, and they shall make distinct lists of all persons voted for as President, and of all persons voted for as Vice-President, and of the number of votes for each, which lists they shall sign and certify, and transmit sealed to the seat of the government of the United States, directed to the President of the Senate;—The President of the Senate shall, in presence of the Senate and House of Representatives, open all the certificates and the votes shall then be counted;—The person having the greatest number of votes for President, shall be the President, if such number be a majority of the whole number of Electors appointed; and if no person have such majority, then from the persons having the highest numbers not exceeding three on the list of those voted for as President, the House of Representatives shall choose immediately, by ballot, the President. But in choosing the President, the votes shall be taken by states, the representation from each state have one vote; a quorum for this purpose shall consist of a member or members from two-thirds of the states, and a majority of all the states shall be necessary to a choice. And if the House of Representatives shall not choose a President whenever the right of choice shall devolve upon them, before the fourth day of March next following, then the Vice-President shall act as President, as in the case of the death or other constitutional disability of the President.—The person having the greatest number of votes as Vice-President, shall be the Vice-President, if such number be a majority of the whole number of Electors appointed, and if no person have a majority, then from the two highest numbers on the list, the Senate shall choose the Vice-President; a quorum for the purpose shall consist of two-thirds of the whole number of Senators, and a majority of the whole number shall be necessary to a choice. But no person constitutionally ineligible to the office of President shall be eligible to that of Vice-President of the United States.

AMENDMENT XIII [1865]

SECTION 1. Neither slavery nor involuntary servitude, except as a punishment for crime whereof the party shall have been duly convicted, shall exist within the United States, or any place subject to their jurisdiction.

SECTION 2. Congress shall have power to enforce this article by appropriate legislation.

AMENDMENT XIV [1868]

SECTION 1. All persons born or naturalized in the United States, and subject to the jurisdiction thereof, are citizens of the United States and of the State wherein they reside. No State shall make or enforce any law which shall abridge the privileges or immunities of citizens of the United States; nor shall any State deprive any person of life, liberty, or property, without due process of law; nor deny to any person within its jurisdiction the equal protection of the laws.

SECTION 2. Representatives shall be apportioned among the several States according to their respective numbers, counting the whole number of persons in each State, excluding Indians not taxed. But when the right to vote at any election for the choice of electors for President and Vice-President of the United States, Representatives in Congress, the Executive and Judicial officers of a State, or the members of the Legislature thereof, is denied to any of the male inhabitants of such State, being twenty-one years of age, and citizens of the United States, or in any way abridged, except for participation in rebellion, or other crime, the basis of representation therein shall be reduced in the proportions which the number of such male citizens shall bear to the whole number of male citizens twenty-one years of age in such State.

SECTION 3. No person shall be a Senator or Representative in Congress, or elector of President and Vice-President, or hold any office, civil or military, under the United States, or under any State, who, having previously taken an oath, as a member of Congress, or as an officer of the United States, or as a member of any State legislature, or as an executive or judicial officer of any State, to support the Constitution of the United States, shall have engaged in insurrection or rebellion against the same, or given aid or comfort to the enemies thereof. But Congress may by a vote of two-thirds of each House, remove such disability.

SECTION 4. The validity of the public debt of the United States, authorized by law, including debts incurred for payment of pensions and bounties for services in suppressing insurrection or rebellion, shall not be questioned. But neither the United States nor any State shall assume or pay any debt or obligation incurred in aid of insurrection or rebellion against the United States, or any claim for the loss or emancipation of any slave; but all such debts, obligations and claims shall be held illegal and void.

SECTION 5. The Congress shall have power to enforce, by appropriate legislation, the provisions of this article.

AMENDMENT XV [1870]

SECTION 1. The right of citizens of the United States to vote shall not be denied or abridged by the United States or by any State on account of race, color, or previous condition of servitude.

SECTION 2. The Congress shall have power to enforce this article by appropriate legislation.

AMENDMENT XVI [1913]

The Congress shall have power to lay and collect taxes on incomes, from whatever source derived, without apportionment among the several States, and without regard to any census or enumeration.

AMENDMENT XVII [1913]

The Senate of the United States shall be composed of two Senators from each State, elected by the people thereof, for six years, and each Senator shall have one vote. The electors in each State shall have the qualifications requisite for electors of the most numerous branch of the State legislatures.

When vacancies happen in the representation of any State in the Senate, the executive authority of such State shall issue writs of election to fill such vacancies: *Provided,* That the legislature of any State may empower the executive thereof to make temporary appointments until the people fill the vacancies by election as the legislature may direct.

This amendment shall not be so construed as to affect the election or term of any Senator chosen before it becomes valid as part of the Constitution.

AMENDMENT XVIII [1919]

SECTION 1. After one year from the ratification of this article the manufacture, sale, or transportation of intoxicating liquors within, the importation thereof into, or the exportation thereof from the United States and all territory subject to the jurisdiction thereof for beverage purposes is hereby prohibited.

SECTION 2. The Congress and the several States shall have concurrent power to enforce this article by appropriate legislation.

SECTION 3. This article shall be inoperative unless it shall have been ratified as an amendment to the Constitution by the legislatures of the several States, as provided in the Constitution, within seven years from the date of the submission hereof to the States by the Congress.

AMENDMENT XIX [1920]

The right of citizens of the United States to vote shall not be denied or abridged by the United States or by any State on account of sex.

Congress shall have the power to enforce this article by appropriate legislation.

AMENDMENT XX [1933]

SECTION 1. The terms of the President and Vice President shall end at noon on the 20th day of January, and the terms of Senators and Representatives at noon on the 3d day of January, of the years in which such terms would have ended if this article had not been ratified; and the terms of their successors shall then begin.

SECTION 2. The Congress shall assemble at least once in every year, and such meeting shall begin at noon on the 3rd day of January, unless they shall by law appoint a different day.

SECTION 3. If, at the time fixed for the beginning of the term of the President, the President elect shall have died, the Vice President elect shall become President. If a President shall not have been chosen before the time fixed for the beginning of his term, or if the President elect shall have failed to qualify, then the Vice President elect shall act as President until a President shall have qualified; and the Congress may by law provide for the case wherein neither a President elect nor a Vice President elect shall have qualified, declaring who shall then act as President, or the manner in which one who is to act shall be selected, and such person shall act accordingly until a President or Vice President shall have qualified.

SECTION 4. The Congress may by law provide for the case of the death of any of the persons from whom the House of Representatives may choose a President whenever the right of choice shall have devolved upon them, and for the case of the death of any of the persons from whom the Senate may choose a Vice President whenever the right of choice shall have devolved upon them.

SECTION 5. Sections 1 and 2 shall take effect on the 15th day of October following the ratification of this article.

SECTION 6. This article shall be inoperative unless it shall have been ratified as an amendment to the Constitution by the legislatures of three-fourths of the several States within seven years from the date of its submission.

AMENDMENT XXI [1933]

SECTION 1. The eighteenth article of amendment to the Constitution of the United States is hereby repealed.

SECTION 2. The transportation or importation into any State, Territory, or possession of the United States for delivery of use therein of intoxicating liquors, in violation of the laws thereof, is hereby prohibited.

SECTION 3. This article shall be inoperative unless it shall have been ratified as an amendment to the Constitution by conventions in the several States, as provided in the Constitution, within seven years from the date of the submission hereof to the States by the Congress.

AMENDMENT XXII [1951]

SECTION 1. No person shall be elected to the office of the President more than twice, and no person who has held the office of President, or acted as President, for more than two years of a term to which some other person was elected President shall be elected to the office of the President more than once. But this Article shall not apply to any person holding the office of President when this Article was proposed by the Congress, and shall not prevent any person who may be holding the office of President, or acting as President, during the tem within which the Article becomes operative from holding the office of President or acting as President during the remainder of such term.

SECTION 2. This article shall be inoperative unless it shall have been ratified as an amendment to the Constitution by the legislatures of three-fourths of the several States within seven years from the date of its submission to the States by the Congress.

AMENDMENT XXIII [1961]

SECTION 1. The District constituting the seat of Government of the United States shall appoint in such manner as the Congress may direct:

A number of electors of President and Vice President equal to the whole number of Senators and Representatives in Congress to which the District would be entitled if it were a State, but in no event more than the least populous State; they shall be in addition to those appointed by the States, but they shall be considered, for the purposes of the election of President and Vice President, to be electors appointed by a State; and they shall meet in the District and perform such duties as provided by the twelfth article of amendment.

SECTION 2. The Congress shall have power to enforce this article by appropriate legislation.

AMENDMENT XXIV [1964]

SECTION 1. The right of citizens of the United States to vote in any primary or other election for President or Vice President, for electors for President or Vice President, or for Senator or Representative in Congress, shall not be denied or abridged by the United States or any State by reason of failure to pay any poll tax or other tax.

SECTION 2. The Congress shall have power to enforce this article by appropriate legislation.

AMENDMENT XXV [1967]

SECTION 1. In case of the removal of the President from office or his death or resignation, the Vice President shall become President.

SECTION 2. Whenever there is a vacancy in the office of the Vice President, the President shall nominate a Vice President who shall take the Office upon confirmation by a majority vote of both houses of Congress.

SECTION 3. Whenever the President transmits to the President pro tempore of the Senate and the Speaker of the House of Representatives his written declaration that he is unable to discharge the powers and duties of his office, and until he transmits to them a written declaration to the contrary, such powers and duties shall be discharged by the Vice President as Acting President.

SECTION 4. Whenever the Vice President and a majority of either the principal officers of the executive departments, or of such other body as Congress may by law provide, transmit to the President pro tempore of the Senate and the Speaker of the House of Representatives their written declaration that the President is unable to discharge the powers and duties of his office, the Vice President shall immediately assume the powers and duties of the office as Acting President.

Thereafter, when the President transmits to the President pro tempore of the Senate and the Speaker of the House of Representatives his written declaration that no inability exists, he shall resume the powers and duties of his office unless the Vice President and a majority of either the principal officers of the executive department, or of such other body as Congress may by law provide, transmit within four days to the President pro tempore of the Senate and the Speaker of the House of Representatives their written declaration that the President is unable to discharge the powers and duties of his office. Thereupon Congress shall decide the issue, assembling within 48 hours for that purpose if not in session. If the Congress, within 21 days after receipt of the latter written declaration, or, if Congress is not in session, within 21 days after Congress is required to assemble, determines by two-thirds vote of both houses that the President is unable to discharge the powers and duties of his office, the Vice President shall continue to discharge the same as Acting President; otherwise, the President shall resume the powers and duties of his office.

AMENDMENT XXVI [1971]

SECTION 1. The right of citizens of the United States, who are eighteen years of age, or older, to vote shall not be denied or abridged by the United States or by any state on account of age.

SECTION 2. The Congress shall have the power to enforce this article by appropriate legislation.

JUSTICES OF THE SUPREME COURT

	Term	*Appointed by*	*Replaced*
*John Jay**	1789–1795	Washington	
John Rutledge	1789–1791	Washington	
William Cushing	1789–1810	Washington	
James Wilson	1789–1798	Washington	
John Blair	1789–1796	Washington	
James Iredell	1790–1799	Washington	
Thomas Johnson	1791–1793	Washington	Rutledge
William Paterson	1793–1806	Washington	Johnson
John Rutledge	1795	Washington	Jay
Samuel Chase	1796–1811	Washington	Blair
Oliver Ellsworth	1796–1800	Washington	Rutledge
Bushrod Washington	1798–1829	J. Adams	Wilson
Alfred Moore	1799–1804	J. Adams	Iredell
John Marshall	1801–1835	J. Adams	Ellsworth
William Johnson	1804–1834	Jefferson	Moore
Brockholst Livingston	1806–1823	Jefferson	Paterson
Thomas Todd	1807–1826	Jefferson	(new seat)
Gabriel Duval	1811–1835	Madison	Chase
Joseph Story	1811–1845	Madison	Cushing
Smith Thompson	1823–1843	Monroe	Livingston
Robert Trimble	1826–1828	J.Q. Adams	Todd
John McLean	1829–1861	Jackson	Trimble
Henry Baldwin	1830–1844	Jackson	Washington
James Wayne	1835–1867	Jackson	Johnson

*The names of the Chief Justices are italicized.

Roger Taney	1836–1864	Jackson	Marshall
Philip Barbour	1836–1841	Jackson	Duval
John Catron	1837–1865	Van Buren	(new seat)
John McKinley	1837–1852	Van Buren	(new seat)
Peter Daniel	1841–1860	Van Buren	Barbour
Samuel Nelson	1845–1872	Tyler	Thompson
Levi Woodbury	1845–1851	Polk	Story
Robert Grier	1846–1870	Polk	Baldwin
Benjamin Curtis	1851–1857	Fillmore	Woodbury
John Campbell	1853–1861	Pierce	McKinley
Nathan Clifford	1858–1881	Buchanan	Curtis
Noah Swayne	1862–1881	Lincoln	McLean
Samuel Miller	1862–1890	Lincoln	Daniel
David Davis	1862–1877	Lincoln	Campbell
Stephen Field	1863–1897	Lincoln	(new seat)
Salmon Chase	1864–1873	Lincoln	Taney
William Strong	1870–1880	Grant	Grier
Joseph Bradley	1870–1892	Grant	Wayne
Ward Hunt	1872–1882	Grant	Nelson
Morrison Waite	1874–1888	Grant	Chase
John Marshall Harlan	1877–1911	Hayes	Davis
William Woods	1880–1887	Hayes	Strong
Stanley Matthews	1881–1889	Garfield	Swayne
Horace Gray	1881–1902	Arthur	Clifford
Samuel Blatchford	1882–1893	Arthur	Hunt
Lucius Lamar	1888–1893	Cleveland	Woods
Melville Fuller	1888–1910	Cleveland	Waite
David Brewer	1889–1910	Harrison	Matthews
Henry Brown	1890–1906	Harrison	Miller
George Shiras	1892–1903	Harrison	Bradley
Howell Jackson	1893–1895	Harrison	Lamar
Edward White	1894–1910	Cleveland	Blatchford
Rufus Peckham	1895–1909	Cleveland	Jackson
Joseph McKenna	1898–1925	McKinley	Field
Oliver Wendell Holmes	1902–1932	T. Roosevelt	Gray
William Day	1903–1922	T. Roosevelt	Shiras
William Moody	1906–1910	T. Roosevelt	Brown
Horace Lurton	1909–1914	Taft	Peckham
Charles Evans Hughes	1910–1916	Taft	Brewer
Edward White	1910–1921	Taft	Fuller
Willis Van Devanter	1910–1937	Taft	White
Joseph Lamar	1910–1916	Taft	Moody
Mahlon Pitney	1912–1922	Taft	Harlan
James McReynolds	1914–1941	Wilson	Lurton
Louis Brandeis	1916–1939	Wilson	Lamar
John Clarke	1916–1922	Wilson	Hughes
William Taft	1921–1930	Harding	White
George Sutherland	1922–1938	Harding	Clarke
Pierce Butler	1922–1939	Harding	Day
Edward Sanford	1923–1930	Harding	Pitney
Harlan Stone	1925–1941	Coolidge	McKenna

Charles Evans Hughes	1930–1941	Hoover	Taft
Owen Roberts	1932–1945	Hoover	Sanford
Benjamin Cardozo	1932–1938	Hoover	Holmes
Hugo Black	1937–1971	F. Roosevelt	Van Devanter
Stanley Reed	1938–1957	F. Roosevelt	Sutherland
Felix Frankfurter	1939–1962	F. Roosevelt	Cardozo
William Douglas	1939–1975	F. Roosevelt	Brandeis
Frank Murphy	1940–1949	F. Roosevelt	Butler
James Byrnes	1941–1942	F. Roosevelt	McReynolds
Harlan Stone	1941–1946	F. Roosevelt	Hughes
Robert Jackson	1941–1954	F. Roosevelt	Stone
Wiley Rutledge	1943–1949	F. Roosevelt	Byrnes
Harold Burton	1945–1958	Truman	Roberts
Fred Vinson	1946–1953	Truman	Stone
Tom Clark	1949–1967	Truman	Murphy
Sherman Minton	1949–1956	Truman	Rutledge
Earl Warren	1953–1969	Eisenhower	Vinson
John Harlan	1955–1971	Eisenhower	Jackson
William Brennan	1956–1990	Eisenhower	Minton
Charles Whittaker	1957–1962	Eisenhower	Reed
Potter Stewart	1958–1981	Eisenhower	Burton
Arthur Goldberg	1962–1965	Kennedy	Frankfurter
Byron White	1962–	Kennedy	Whittaker
Abe Fortas	1965–1969	Johnson	Goldberg
Thurgood Marshall	1967–	Johnson	Clark
Warren Burger	1969–1986	Nixon	Warren
Harry Blackmun	1970–	Nixon	Fortas
Lewis Powell	1972–1987	Nixon	Black
William Rehnquist	1972–1986	Nixon	Harlan
John Stevens	1975–	Ford	Douglas
Sandra Day O'Connor	1981–	Reagan	Stewart
William Rehnquist	1986–	Reagan	Burger
Antonin Scalia	1986–	Reagan	Rehnquist
Anthony Kennedy	1988–	Reagan	Powell
David Souter	1990–	Bush	Brennan

GLOSSARY OF COMMON LEGAL TERMS

Abstention The doctrine under which the U.S. Supreme Court and other federal courts choose not to rule on state cases, even when empowered to do so, so as to allow the issue to be decided on the basis of state law.

Advisory Opinion A legal opinion rendered at the request of the government or another party indicating how the court would rule if the issue arose in an adversary context.

Amicus Curiae "Friend of the court." A person or group not directly involved in a particular case that volunteers or is requested by the court to supply its views on the case (usually through the submission of a brief).

Appeal The procedure whereby a case is brought from an inferior to a superior court. In the Supreme Court, certain cases are designated as appeals under federal law and must be heard formally by the court.

Appellant The party who appeals a decision from a lower to a higher court.

Appellate Jurisdiction The authority of a court to hear, determine, and render judgment in an action on appeal from an inferior court.

Appellee The party against whom an appeal to a superior court is taken and who has an interest in upholding the lower court's decision.

Arraignment The formal process of charging a person with a crime, reading the charge, and asking for and entering his plea.

Bail The security (cash or a bail bond) given as a guarantee that a released prisoner will appear at trial.

Bill of Attainder A legislative act declaring a person guilty of a crime and passing sentence without benefit of trial.

Brief A document prepared by counsel as the basis for an argument in court. It sets forth the facts of the case and the legal arguments in support of the party's position.

Case Law The law as defined by previously decided cases.

Certification A method of appeal whereby a lower court requests a higher court to rule on certain legal questions so that the lower court can make the correct decision in light of the answer given.

Certiorari, Writ of An order from a superior court to an inferior court to forward the entire record of a case to the superior court for review. The U.S. Supreme Court may issue such writs at its discretion.

Civil Action A lawsuit, usually brought by a private party, seeking redress for a noncriminal act (e.g., a suit in negligence, contract, or defamation).

Class Action A lawsuit brought by one person or by a group on behalf of all persons similarly situated.

Comity Courtesy and respect. In the legal sense, the respect federal courts give to the decisions of state courts.

Common Law Principles and rules of action, particularly from unwritten English law, whose authority stems from long-standing usage and custom or from judicial recognition and enforcement of those customs.

Concurrent Powers Powers which may be exercised by both the national government and state governments.

Concurring Opinion An opinion submitted by a member of a court who agrees with the result by the court in a case but either disagrees with the court's reasons for the decision or wishes to address matters not touched in the opinion of the court.

Declaratory Judgment A judicial pronouncement declaring the legal rights of the parties involved in an actual case or controversy but not ordering a specific action.

De Facto "In fact." The existence of something in fact or reality, as opposed to *de jure* (by right).

Defendant The person against whom a civil or criminal charge is brought.

De Jure "By right." Lawful, rightful, legitimate; as a result of official action.

Dissenting Opinion An opinion submitted by a member of a court who disagrees with the result reached by the court.

Distinguish To point out why a previous decision is not applicable.

Diversity Jurisdiction The authority of federal courts to hear cases involving citizens of different states.

Dual Federalism The view that national powers should be interpreted so as not to invade traditional spheres of state activity.

Equity The administration of justice based upon principles of fairness rather than upon strictly applied rules found in the law.

Error, Writ of A writ issued by a superior court directing a lower court to send it the record of a case in which the lower court has entered a final judgment, for the purpose of reviewing alleged errors made by the lower court.

Exclusionary Rule The rule that evidence obtained by illegal means, such as unreasonable searches and seizures, cannot be introduced by the prosecution in a criminal trial.

Ex parte "From (or on) one side." A hearing in the presence of only one of the parties to a case, such as a hearing to review a petition for a writ of habeas corpus.

Ex Post Facto "After the fact." A law which makes an action for a crime after it has already been committed.

Ex Rel "By (or on) the information of." The designation of suit instituted by a state but at the instigation of a private individual interested in the matter.

Federal Question A case that contains a major issue involving the U.S. Constitution, or U.S. laws or treaties. (The jurisdiction of the federal courts is limited to federal questions and diversity suits.)

Habeas Corpus "You have the body." A writ inquiring of an official who has custody of a person whether that person is imprisoned or detained lawfully.

In Camera "In chambers." The hearing of a case or part of a case in private (without spectators).

Incorporation The process by which provisions of the Bill of Rights were applied as limitations on state governments through the Due Process Clause of the Fourteenth Amendment.

In Forma Pauperis "In the manner of a pauper." Permission for indigents to bring legal action without payment of the required fees.

Injunction A writ prohibiting the person to whom it is directed from performing some specified act.

In Re "In the matter of; concerning." The designation of judicial proceedings in which there are no adversaries.

Judgment of the Court The ruling of the court (independent of the reasons for the court's ruling).

Judicial Review The power of a court to review legislation or other governmental action in order to determine its validity with respect to the U.S. constitution or state constitutions.

Juris Belli "Under the law of war." That part of the law of nations which defines the rights of belligerent and neutral nations during wartime.

Jurisdiction The authority of a court to hear, determine, and render final judgment in an action, and to enforce its judgments by legal process.

Justiciability The question of whether a matter is appropriate for judicial decision. A justiciable issue is one that appropriately can be decided by a court.

Litigant An active participant in a lawsuit.

Mandamus "We command." A court order directing an individual or organization to perform a particular act.

Moot Unsettled, undecided. A moot question is one in which either the result sought by the lawsuit has occurred or the conditions have so changed as to render it impossible for the court to grant the relief sought.

Obiter Dicta (Also called *dictum* or *dicta.*) That part of the reasoning in a judicial opinion which is not necessary to resolve the case. Dicta are not necessarily binding in future cases.

Opinion of the Court The opinion which announces the court's decision and is adhered to by a majority of the participating judges.

Original Jurisdiction The authority of a court to hear, determine, and render judgment in an action as a trial court.

Per Curiam "By the court." An unsigned opinion by the court, or a collectively authored opinion.

Petitioner The party who files a petition with a court seeking action.

Plaintiff The party who brings a civil action or sues to obtain a remedy for an injury to his or her rights.

Plea Bargain Negotiations between the prosecution and defense aimed at exchanging a plea of guilty for concessions by the prosecution.

Police Power The power of the states to protect the health, safety, welfare, and morals of their citizens.

Political Question An issue that the court believes should be decided by a nonjudicial unit of government.

Precedent A prior case relied upon in deciding a present dispute.

Preemption The doctrine under which issues previously subject to state control are brought, through congressional action, within the primary or exclusive jurisdiction of the national government.

Prima Facie "At first sight." Evidence that, unless contradicted, is sufficient to establish a claim without investigation or evaluation.

Pro Bono "For the good." Legal services rendered without charge.

Ratio Decidendi "Reason for the decision." The principle of the case.

Remand To send back. In remanding a decision, a higher court sends it, for further action, back to the court from which it came.

Respondent The party against whom a legal action is taken.

Special Master A person designated by a court to hear evidence and submit findings and recommendations based on that evidence. The Supreme Court typically uses special masters in original jurisdiction cases.

Standing The qualifications needed to bring or participate in a case. To have standing to sue, plaintiffs must demonstrate the existence of a controversy in which they personally have suffered or are about to suffer an injury or infringement of a legally protected right.

Stare Decisis "Let the decision stand." The doctrine that a point settled in a previous case is a precedent that should be followed in subsequent cases with similar facts.

State Action Action by the state or by a private entity closely associated with it ("under color of state law"). The basis for redress under the Due Process and Equal Protection Clauses of the Fourteenth Amendments.

Stay To halt or suspend further judicial proceedings.

Subpoena An order to present oneself and to testify before a court, grand jury, or legislative hearing.

Subpoena Duces Tecum An order by a court or other authorized body that specified documents or papers be produced.

Tort Willful or negligent injury to the person, property, or reputation of another.

Ultra Vires "Beyond power." An action beyond the legal authority of the person or body performing it.

Vacate To make void, annul, or rescind.

Venue The jurisdiction in which a case is to be heard.

Vested Rights Long established rights which government should recognize and protect and which a person cannot be deprived of without injustice.

Writ A written court order commanding the recipient to perform or refrain from performing acts specified in the order.

TABLE OF CASES

Case titles in capital letters are reprinted in this volume; the underscored page number indicates where the case is reprinted here.

Abrams v. *United States*, 250 U.S. 616 (1919) **346, 347, 363n**
Adair v. *United States*, 208 U.S. 161 (1908) **318**
ADAMSON v. *CALIFORNIA*, 332 U.S. 46 (1947) **40, 464, 481**
ADDERLEY v. *FLORIDA*, 385 U.S. 39 (1966) **356, 387**
Adkins v. *Children's Hospital*, 261 U.S. 525 (1923) **313–314**
Adler v. *Board of Education*, 342 U.S. 485 (1952) **351**
Aguilar v. *Felton*, 473 U.S. 401 (1985) **416, 421**
Aguilar v. *Texas*, 378 U.S. 108 (1964) **458**
Ake v. *Oklahoma*, 105 S. Ct. 1087 (1985) **477**
Akron v. *Akron Center for Reproductive Health* (1983) **691–692, 693**
Alexander v. *Holmes County Board of Education*, 396 U.S. 19 (1969) **556, 559**
ALLEN v. *WRIGHT*, 468 U.S. 737 (1984) **52, 75**
Allgeyer v. *Louisiana*, 156 U.S. 578 (1897) **313**
Allied Structural Steel Company v. *Spannaus*, 438 U.S. 234 (1978) **292**
Amalgamated Meat Cutters & Butcher Workmen v. *Connally*, 337 F. Supp. 737 (D.D.C. 1971) **240n**
Ambach v. *Norwick*, 441 U.S. 68 (1979) **612–613, 626**
American Booksellers Association v. *Hudnut*, 771 F. 2d 323 (1985) **364**
American Communications Association v. *Douds*, 339 U.S. 382 (1950) **348, 351**
Argersinger v. *Hamlin*, 407 U.S. 25 (1972) **456, 457, 467, 477n**
Arlington Heights, Village of v. *Metropolitan Housing Development Corporation*, 429 U.S. 252 (1977) **562–563**
Ashwander v. *Tennessee Valley Authority*, 297 U.S. 288 (1936) **54, 62**
Associated General Contractors v. *Altshuler* (First Cir., 1973) **564n**
Autolite Corp. v. *Midwesco Enterprises, Inc.* (1988) **271n**
Avery v. *Midland County*, 390 U.S. 474 (1968) **18n, 626n**

Bailey v. *Drexel Furniture Company,* 259 U.S. 20 (1922) **237–238, 241n**

BAKER v. *CARR,* 369 U.S. 186 (1962) **5, 51, 54, 81**

BAKKE v. *REGENTS OF THE UNIVERSITY OF CALIFORNIA,* 553 P. 2d 1152 (1976) **610, 628**

BALDWIN v. *MONTANA FISH AND GAME COMMISSION,* 436 U.S. 371 (1978) **193, 199n, 207**

Barefoot v. *Estelle* (1983) **471**

BARENBLATT v. *UNITED STATES,* 360 U.S. 109 (1959) **95, 103, 351, 373**

Barker v. *Wingo,* 407 U.S. 514 (1972) **468**

Barron v. *Baltimore,* 7 Pet. 243 (1833) **452**

Barrows v. *Jackson,* 346 U.S. 249 (1953) **566**

Bell v. *Maryland,* 378 U.S. 226 (1964) **562**

Belloti v. *Baird,* 443 U.S. 622 (1979) **697**

Benton v. *Maryland,* 395 U.S. 784 (1969) **456, 457**

Betts v. *Brady,* 316 U.S. 455 (1942) **466, 467**

Bivens v. *Six Unknown Named Agents,* 403 U.S. 388 (1971) **463**

Board of Education v. *Allen,* 392 U.S. 236 (1968) **413, 415, 420n**

Bob Jones University v. *United States,* 461 U.S. 574 (1983) **421**

BOLLING v. *SHARPE,* 347 U.S. 497 (1954) **554–555, 579, 688**

Bowers v. *Hardwick,* 478 U.S. 186 (1986) **694, 719**

BOWSHER v. *SYNAR,* 478 U.S. 714 (1986) **134, 139**

Brady v. *United States,* 397 U.S. 742 (1970) **469, 477**

BRANDENBURG v. *OHIO,* 395 U.S. 444 (1969) **348, 351, 363n, 377**

BRANZBURG v. *HAYES,* 408 U.S. 665 (1972) **358, 400**

Braunfeld v. *Brown,* 366 U.S. 599 (1961) **416, 417**

Breedlove v. *Suttles,* 302 U.S. 277 (1937) **43n**

Brewer v. *Williams,* 430 U.S. 387 (1977) **477n**

Brig Aurora v. *United States,* 7 Cr. 382 (1813) **99**

Brooks v. *United States* (1925) **240n**

BROWN v. *BOARD OF EDUCATION,* 347 U.S. 483 (1954) **28, 30, 34, 36–37, 196, 551, 552, 554, 555, 556, 557, 565n, 576, 611**

BROWN v. *BOARD OF EDUCATION II,* 349 U.S. 294 (1955) **30, 555, 556, 565n, 580**

Brown v. *Maryland,* 12 Wheat. 419 (1827) **272**

Brown v. *Mississippi,* 197 U.S. 278 (1936) **464**

Brown v. *Thomson,* 462 U.S. 835 (1983) **622, 626**

Buck v. *Bell,* 274 U.S. 200 (1927) **605**

BUCKLEY v. *VALEO,* 424 U.S. 1 (1976) **134, 139, 348, 352–353, 364n, 378**

Bunting v. *Oregon,* 243 U.S. 426 (1917) **314**

Burton v. *Wilmington Parking Authority,* 365 U.S. 715 (1961) **560**

Butcher's Benevolent Association v. *Crescent City Livestock Landing and Slaughterhouse Company.* See *The Slaughterhouse Cases*

Califano v. *Goldfarb,* 430 U.S. 199 (1977) **617–618**

Califano v. *Webster,* 430 U.S. 313 (1977) **626n**

Cantwell v. *Connecticut*, 310 U.S. 296 (1940) **410, 421**
CAPLIN & DRYSDALE, CHARTERED v. *UNITED STATES*, 109 S. Ct. 2646 (1989) **468, 523**
Carey v. *Brown*, 447 U.S. 455 (1980) **355**
Carey v. *Population Services International*, 431 U.S. 678 (1977) **697**
Carrington v. *Rush*, 380 U.S. 89 (1965) **623**
Carroll v. *United States*, 267 U.S. 132 (1925) **459**
Carter v. *Carter Coal Company*, 298 U.S. 238 (1936) **234, 240n, 241**
Central Hudson Gas Company v. *Public Service Commission*, 447 U.S. 557 (1980) **363n, 364**
Chambers v. *Florida*, 309 U.S. 227 (1940) **464**
Champion v. *Ames*, 188 U.S. 321 (1903) **234**
Chaplinsky v. *New Hampshire*, 315 U.S. 568 (1942) **354–355, 358, 363n**
CHARLES RIVER BRIDGE COMPANY v. *WARREN BRIDGE COMPANY*, 36 U.S. (11 Peters) 420 (1837) **288, 292n, 296**
Chimel v. *California*, 395 U.S. 752 (1968) **459**
Chisholm v. *Georgia*, 2 U.S. 419 (1793) **42n, 43n**
City of Cleburne, Texas v. *Cleburne Living Center*. See *Cleburne, Texas, City of* v. *Cleburne Living Center*
City of Philadelphia v. *New Jersey*. See *Philadelphia, City of* v. *New Jersey*
THE CIVIL RIGHTS CASES, 109 U.S. 3 (1883) **196, 217, 550, 559**
Clark v. *Community for Creative Non-Violence* (1984) **354**
Clark v. *Jeter* (1988) **614**
Cleburne, Texas, City of v. *Cleburne Living Center* (1985) **614–615**
Coates v. *City of Cincinnati*, 402 U.S. 611 (1971) **349**
Coffin v. *Reichard* (1944) **472–473**
Cohen v. *Hurley*, 366 U.S. 117 (1961) **456**
COHENS v. *VIRGINIA*, 19 U.S. (6 Wheaton) 264 (1821) **47, 189, 190, 192, 201**
Coker v. *Georgia*, 433 U.S. 584 (1977) **477n**
Cole v. *Arkansas*, 333 U.S. 196 (1948) **457**
Colegrove v. *Green*, 328 U.S. 549 (1946) **54, 62**
Coleman v. *Alabama*, 399 U.S. 1 (1970) **467**
Coleman v. *Miller*, 307 U.S. 433 (1939) **60n, 62, 97, 103**
Colgate v. *Harvey*, 296 U.S. 404 (1935) **310**
Collins v. *Handyman*, 341 U.S. 651 (1951) **197**
Columbus Board of Education v. *Penick*, 443 U.S. 499 (1979) **557, 558**
Committee for Public Education v. *Nyquist*, 413 U.S. 758 (1973) **415**
Committee for Public Education v. *Regan*, 444 U.S. 648 (1980) **416, 420n**
Connally v. *General Construction Co.*, 269 U.S. 385 (1926) **363n**
COOLEY v. *BOARD OF WARDENS*, 53 U.S. (12 How.) 299 (1852) **267, 268, 269, 275**
Cooper v. *Aaron*, 358 U.S. 1 (1958) **555, 566**
Coppage v. *Kansas*, 236 U.S. 1 (1915) **318**

Costello v. *Wainwright* (1975) **472**
Cox v. *Louisiana*, 379 U.S. 536 (1965) **355**
Coyle v. *Smith*, 221 U.S. 559 (1911) **193**
Craig v. *Boren*, 429 U.S. 190 (1976) **609–610, 616, 618, 624–625, 626n**
CTS Corp. v. *Dynamics Corp.*, 481 U.S. 69 (1987) **272**
Cumming v. *Richmond County Board of Education*, 175 U.S. 528 (1899) **552–553**
Curtis Publishing Company v. *Butts*, 388 U.S. 130 (1967) **359**

Dames & Moore v. *Regan*, 453 U.S. 654 (1981) **167n, 168**
Dandridge v. *Williams*, 397 U.S. 471 (1970) **624**
Daniel v. *Paul*, 395 U.S. 298 (1969) **240n**
DARTMOUTH COLLEGE v. *WOODWARD*, 17 U.S. (4 Wheaton) 518 (1819) **287, 288, 293**
Davidson v. *New Orleans*, 96 U.S. 97 (1878) **311–312**
Davis v. *Bandemer* (1986) **622**
Day-Brite Lighting v. *Missouri*, 342 U.S. 421 (1952) **315**
Dayton Board of Education v. *Brinkman*, 443 U.S. 526 (1979) **557, 558, 566**
Dean v. *Gadsden Times Publishing Company*, 412 U.S. 543 (1973) **318**
DEAN MILK COMPANY v. *CITY OF MADISON*, 340 U.S. 349 (1951) **268, 269, 277**
DENNIS v. *UNITED STATES*, 341 U.S. 494 (1951) **347–348, 350, 351, 369**
DeFunis v. *Odegaard*, 416 U.S. 312 (1974) **52–53**
DeSHANEY v. *WINNEBAGO COUNTY DEPARTMENT OF SOCIAL SERVICES*, 109 S. Ct. 998 (1989) **56, 86**
Desist v. *United States*, 394 U.S. 244 (1969) **475, 477**
Dillon v. *Gloss* (1921) **97**
Doe v. *Bolton*, 410 U.S. 479 (1973) **690**
Doe v. *McMillan*, 412 U.S. 306 (1973) **93, 103**
Dombrowski v. *Eastland*, 387 U.S. 82 (1967) **93**
Douglas v. *California*, 372 U.S. 353 (1963) **467, 620**
DRED SCOTT v. *SANDFORD*, 60 U.S. (19 Howard) 393 (1857) **3, 34, 43n, 59n, 191, 546, 548, 550, 568**
Duckworth v. *Eagan* (1989) **465**
DUNCAN v. *LOUISIANA*, 391 U.S. 145 (1968) **455, 456, 457, 483**
DUNN v. *BLUMSTEIN*, 405 U.S. 330 (1972) **607, 623, 677**

EAKIN v. *RAUB*, 12 Sergeant & Rawle 330 (1825) **47, 56, 67**
EDWARDS v. *AGUILLARD*, 482 U.S. 578 (1987) **440**
Edwards v. *California*, 314 U.S. 160 (1941) **269, 272, 318n**
Edwards v. *South Carolina*, 372 U.S. 229 (1963) **355**
Eisenstadt v. *Baird*, 405 U.S. 438 (1972) **687, 689, 690, 697**
El Paso v. *Simmons*, 379 U.S. 497 (1965) **292**
Elrod v. *Burns*, 427 U.S. 347 (1976) **348, 352, 363n**
Endo, Ex Parte, 323 U.S. 283 (1944) **168**

Engel v. *Vitale*, 370 U.S. 421 (1962) **412**
Epperson v. *Arkansas*, 393 U.S. 97 (1968) **412**
Equal Employment Opportunities Commission v. *Wyoming*, 460 U.S. 226 (1983) **240n**
Erznoznick v. *City of Jacksonville*, 442 U.S. 205 (1975) **361**
Escobedo v. *Illinois*, 387 U.S. 478 (1964) **35, 43n, 467, 475**
EVERSON v. *BOARD OF EDUCATION*, 330 U.S. 1 (1947) **410–411, 412, 413, 415, 416, 420n, 422**
Ex Parte Endo. See *Endo, Ex Parte*
Ex Parte McCardle. See *McCardle, Ex Parte*
Ex Parte Milligan. See *Milligan, Ex Parte*

Faitoute Iron & Steel Company v. *City of Asbury Park*, 316 U.S. 502 (1942) **292**
Faretta v. *California* (1975) **468**
Federal Election Commission v. *National Conservative Political Action Committee* (1985) **353**
Federal Energy Regulatory Commission v. *Mississippi*, 456 U.S. 742 (1982) **240n–241n**
Feiner v. *New York*, 340 U.S. 315 (1951) **355**
Ferguson v. *Skrupa*, 372 U.S. 726 (1963) **315, 319**
Fertilizing Company v. *Hyde Park*, 97 U.S. 659 (1878) **288**
First English Evangelical Lutheran Church of Glendale v. *Los Angeles County*, 482 U.S. 304 (1987) **316–317, 319**
FLAST v. *COHEN*, 392 U.S. 83 (1968) **49–50, 51, 52, 72, 239, 241n**
Fletcher v. *Peck*, 6 Cranch 87 (1810) **47, 287, 292**
Florida Star v. *B.J.F.* (1989) **359–360**
FOLEY v. *CONNELIE*, 435 U.S. 291 (1978) **612–613, 649**
Fort Wayne Books v. *Indiana* (1989) **361**
Foster-Fountain Packing Company v. *Haydel* (1928) **269**
Freedman v. *Maryland*, 380 U.S. 51 (1965) **357**
FRONTIERO v. *RICHARDSON*, 411 U.S. 677 (1973) **615–616, 659**
FROTHINGHAM v. *MELLON*, 262 U.S. 447 (1923) **51, 60n, 71, 239**
FULLILOVE v. *KLUTZNICK*, 448 U.S. 448 (1980) **611, 626**
Furman v. *Georgia*, 408 U.S. 238 (1972) **32, 470–471, 477**

GARCIA v. *SAN ANTONIO METROPOLITAN TRANSIT AUTHORITY*, 469 U.S. 528 (1985) **194–195, 210, 236, 239, 241**
Gayle v. *Browder*, 352 U.S. 903 (1956) **565n**
Geduldig v. *Aiello*, 417 U.S. 484 (1974) **619**
Gertz v. *Robert Welch, Inc.*, 418 U.S. 323 (1974) **364n**
GIBBONS v. *OGDEN*, 9 Wheat. 1 (1824) **231, 232, 239–240, 242, 266, 267–268, 272**
Gibson v. *Florida Legislative Investigating Committee*, 372 U.S. 539 (1963) **95, 103, 348, 351–352, 363n**
GIDEON v. *WAINWRIGHT*, 372 U.S. 335 (1963) **28, 456, 457, 467, 506**
Gilbert v. *California* **467**

GITLOW v. *NEW YORK*, 268 U.S. 652 (1925) **343, 346, 350, 362, 366**
Glidden Company v. *Zdanok*, 370 U.S. 530 (1962) **49**
Goesaert v. *Cleary*, 335 U.S. 464 (1948) **615**
Goldman v. *United States*, 316 U.S. 129 (1942) **688**
Goldman v. *Weinberger* (1986) **417**
Goldwater v. *Carter*, 444 U.S. 996 (1979) **158**
Gooch v. *United States* (1936) **240n**
Graham v. *Richardson*, 403 U.S. 365 (1971) **612**
GRAVEL v. *UNITED STATES*, 408 U.S. 606 (1972) **93, 109**
Graves v. *O'Keefe*, 306 U.S. 466 (1939) **18n**
Green v. *County School Board of New Kent County*, 391 U.S. 430 (1968) **556, 558**
GREGG v. *GEORGIA*, 428 U.S. 153 (1976) **471, 529**
Griffin v. *Breckenridge*, 403 U.S. 88 (1971) **197**
Griffin v. *County Board School Board of Prince Edward County*, 337 U.S. 218 (1964) **566**
Griffin v. *Illinois*, 351 U.S. 12 (1958) **620**
Griffin v. *Maryland*, 378 U.S. 130 (1964) **560–561**
Griffiths, In Re, 413 U.S. 717 (1973) **612, 613**
Griggs v. *Duke Power Co.* (1971) **564**
GRISWOLD v. *CONNECTICUT*, 381 U.S. 479 (1965) **453, 455, 686, 687–688, 689, 695, 698**
Grovey v. *Townsend*, 295 U.S. 45 (1935) **559–560**
Gustafson v. *Florida*, 414 U.S. 260 (1973) **461**
Gwin, White & Prince, Inc. v. *Henneford* (1939) **271n**

Hadley v. *Junior College District of Metropolitan Kansas City*, 397 U.S. 50 (1970) **626n**
Hague v. *Committee for Industrial Organization*, 307 U.S. 496 (1939) **318n, 355–356, 364n**
Hamilton v. *Alabama* **467**
Hamilton v. *Board of Regents of the University of California*, 293 U.S. 245 (1934) **420n**
HAMMER v. *DAGENHART*, 247 U.S. 251 (1918) **191–192, 234–235, 236, 238, 248**
Hampton v. *Wong*, 426 U.S. 88 (1976) **612**
J. W. Hampton, Jr. & Company v. *United States*, 276 U.S. 394 (1928) **237**
HARPER v. *VIRGINIA STATE BOARD OF ELECTIONS*, 383 U.S. 663 (1966) **620, 623, 675**
HARRIS v. *McRAE*, 448 U.S. 297 (1980) **687, 693–694, 714**
Harris v. *New York*, 401 U.S. 222 (1971) **465, 477n**
Harris v. *United States*, 390 U.S. 234 (1968) **459**
HAWAII HOUSING AUTHORITY v. *MIDKIFF*, 467 U.S. 229 (1984) **316, 334**
Hayburn's Case (1792) **59n**
HAZELWOOD SCHOOL DISTRICT v. *KUHLMEIER*, 484 U.S. 260 (1988) **356, 357, 391**

HEART OF ATLANTA MOTEL v. *UNITED STATES*, 379 U.S. 241 (1964) **36, 236, 254**
HECKLER v. *MATHEWS*, 465 U.S. 728 (1984) **617, 661**
Helvering v. *Davis*, 301 U.S. 619 (1937) **239, 241n**
Hepburn v. *Griswold* (1870) **318n**
Herbert v. *Lando*, 441 U.S. 153 (1979) **359**
Herndon v. *Lowry*, 301 U.S. 242 (1937) **347**
Hewitt v. *Helms* (1978) **474**
Hicklin v. *Orbeck* (1978) **271n**
Hines v. *Davidowitz*, 312 U.S. 52 (1940) **265, 271n**
Hipolite Egg Company v. *United States* (1911) **240n**
H.L. v. *Matheson*, 450 U.S. 398 (1981) **696n, 697**
Hodel v. *Indiana*, 452 U.S. 314 (1981) **240n**
Hodel v. *Virginia Surface Mining & Reclamation Association*, 452 U.S. 264 (1981) **240n**
Hodgson v. *Bowerbank* (1809) **59n**
Hoke v. *United States* (1913) **240n**
Holden v. *Hardy*, 169 U.S. 366 (1898) **453**
Holmes v. *City of Atlanta* (1955) **565n**
Holy Spirit Association for the Unification of World Christianity v. *Tax Commission*, 435 N.E. 2d 662 (1982) **421n**
HOME BUILDING AND LOAN ASSOCIATION v. *BLAISDELL*, 290 U.S. 398 (1934) **289–290, 291, 299**
H. P. Hood & Sons v. *DuMond*, 336 U.S. 525 (1949) **265, 269, 272**
Houchins v. *KQED*, 438 U.S. 1 (1978) **357**
Hughes v. *Oklahoma*, 441 U.S. 322 (1979) **272**
Humphrey's Executor v. *United States*, 295 U.S. 602 (1935) **139n**
Hurtado v. *California*, 110 U.S. 516 (1884) **454–455, 457**
Hustler Magazine v. *Falwell*, 485 U.S. 46 (1988) **359, 364**
Hutchinson v. *Proxmire*, 443 U.S. 111 (1979) **93**
Hylton v. *United States*, 3 Dall. 171 (1796) **237**

Idaho v. *Freeman*, 529 F. Supp. 1107 (1981) **103n**
Illinois v. *Gates* (1983) **477n**
IMMIGRATION AND NATURALIZATION SERVICE v. *CHADHA*, 462 U.S. 919 (1983) **100–101, 102, 123**
Ingraham v. *Wright*, 430 U.S. 651 (1977) **471**
In Re Griffiths. See *Griffiths, In Re*
In Re Neagle. See *Neagle, In Re*
In Re Oliver. See *Oliver, In Re*

Jacobson v. *Massachusetts*, 197 U.S. 11 (1905) **417**
James v. *Valtierra*, 402 U.S. 137 (1971) **620–621, 625, 626**
Johnson v. *New Jersey*, 348 U.S. 719 (1966) **475**
Johnson v. *Robinson*, 415 U.S. 361 (1974) **608**
Johnson v. *Virginia* (1963) **565n**
Johnson v. *Zerbst*, 304 U.S. 458 (1938) **466**

Joint Anti-Fascist Refugee Committee v. *McGrath*, 341 U.S. 123 (1951) **476n**
JONES v. *ALFRED H. MAYER COMPANY*, 392 U.S. 409 (1968) **196, 197, 222, 565n**
Jones v. *North Carolina Prisoners' Union* (1977) **473**

Kahn v. *Shevin*, 416 U.S. 351 (1974) **617, 618, 626n**
Karcher v. *Daggett*, 462 U.S. 725 (1983) **621, 626**
Kassel v. *Consolidated Freightways Corporation* (1981) **270, 271n**
Katz v. *Superior Court*, 73 Cal. App. 3d 952 (1977) **421n**
Katz v. *Tyler*, 386 U.S. 942 (1967) **167n**
KATZ v. *UNITED STATES*, 389 U.S. 342 (1967) **462, 502, 688, 689**
Katzenbach v. *McClung*, 379 U.S. 294 (1964) **240n**
Kelley v. *Johnson*, 425 U.S. 238 (1976) **695**
Keyes v. *School District No. 1, Denver, Colorado*, 413 U.S. 189 (1973) **557**
Keyishian v. *Board of Regents*, 385 U.S. 589 (1967) **351**
Kilbourn v. *Thompson*, 103 U.S. 168 (1881) **93, 102n**
Kirkpatrick v. *Preisler* (1969) **626n**
Klopfer v. *North Carolina*, 386 U.S. 213 (1967) **456, 457**
Konigsberg v. *State Bar of California*, 366 U.S. 36 (1961) **351**
KOREMATSU v. *UNITED STATES*, 323 U.S. 214 (1944) **166–167, 179**
Kovacs v. *Cooper*, 336 U.S. 77 (1949) **343, 348**
Kramer v. *Union Free School District No. 15*, 395 U.S. 621 (1969) **623, 627**
Kunz v. *United States*, 340 U.S. 290 (1951) **353, 364n**

Labine v. *Vincent*, 401 U.S. 532 (1971) **613–614**
Laird v. *Tatum*, 408 U.S. 1 (1972) **62**
Lakewood v. *Plain Dealer Publishing Co.* (1988) **355**
Law Students Civil Rights Research Council, Inc. v. *Wadmond*, 401 U.S. 23 (1971) **351**
Lee v. *Washington* (1968) **565n**
LEMON v. *KURTZMAN*, 403 U.S. 602 (1971) **414, 415, 416, 420, 427**
Levitt v. *Committee for Public Education*, 413 U.S. 472 (1973) **416**
Levy v. *Louisiana*, 391 U.S. 68 (1968) **613, 614**
The License Cases, 5 How. 504 (1847) **191, 267**
Lindsey v. *Normet*, 405 U.S. 56 (1972) **624**
Linkletter v. *Walker*, 318 U.S. 618 (1965) **474, 475**
LOCHNER v. *NEW YORK*, 198 U.S. 45 (1905) **313, 315, 327, 605, 690**
Lombard v. *Louisiana*, 373 U.S. 267 (1963) **560**
Los Angeles Department of Water and Power v. *Manhart*, 435 U.S. 702 (1978) **619**
Loving v. *Virginia*, 338 U.S. 1 (1967) **43n**
Lovisi v. *Slayton*, 363 F. Supp. 620 (1973) **697**
Lubin v. *Panish*, 415 U.S. 709 (1974) **623**

LUTHER v. *BORDEN*, 48 U.S. (7 Howard) 1 (1849) **54, 78**
LYNCH v. *DONNELLY*, 465 U.S. 668 (1984) **413, 420, 433**
Lynch v. *Household Finance Corporation*, 405 U.S. 538 (1972) **291n**
LYNG v. *NORTHWEST INDIAN CEMETARY ASSOCIATION*, 485 U.S. 439 (1988) **417, 447**
Lynumn v. *Illinois*, 382 U.S. 528 (1963) **477n**

Mackey v. *United States* (1971) **475**
Madden v. *Kentucky*, 309 U.S. 83 (1940) **310**
Mahan v. *Howell*, 410 U.S. 315 (1973) **622**
Maher v. *Roe*, 432 U.S. 464 (1977) **693–694, 697**
Malloy v. *Hogan*, 378 U.S. 1 (1964) **456, 457, 464**
Manigault v. *Springs*, 199 U.S. 473 (1905) **292n**
MAPP v. *OHIO*, 367 U.S. 643 (1961) **456, 457, 463, 475, 495**
MARBURY v. *MADISON*, 5 U.S. (1 Cranch) 137 (1803) **6, 40, 46–47, 50, 56, 64, 188, 556**
Marchetti v. *United States*, 390 U.S. 39 (1968) **238**
Marsh v. *Chambers* (1985) **413, 420**
Martin v. *Hunter's Lessee*, 1 Wheat. 304 (1816) **47, 198n, 199**
Martin v. *Wilks* (1989) **626n**
Massachusetts v. *Sheppard* (1984) **463, 477n**
MASSACHUSETTS BOARD OF RETIREMENT v. *MURGIA*, 427 U.S. 307 (1976) **609, 614, 624, 655**
Mathews v. *Lucas*, 427 U.S. 495 (1976) **614**
Mayor of Baltimore v. *Dawson* (1955) **565n**
McCARDLE, EX PARTE, 74 U.S. (7 Wallace) 506 (1869) **48–50, 70, 179**
McCleskey v. *Kemp* (1987) **471**
McCollum v. *Board of Education*, 333 U.S. 203 (1948) **412**
McCULLOCH v. *MARYLAND*, 17 U.S. (Wheat.) 316 (1819) **6, 7, 91–92, 102n, 105, 167n, 189–190, 192, 232**
McCrary v. *United States* (1904) **237**
McDaniel v. *Paty*, 435 U.S. 618 (1978) **412**
McGowan v. *Maryland*, 366 U.S. 420 (1961) **412–413**
McGRAIN v. *DAUGHERTY*, 273 U.S. 135 (1927) **94–96, 112**
Meek v. *Pittenger*, 421 U.S. 349 (1975) **415–416**
Mempa v. *Rhay* **467**
Memphis v. *Greene*, 451 U.S. 100 (1981) **199n**
Metro Broadcasting v. *Federal Communications Commission* (1990) **611**
Michael M. v. *Sonoma County Superior Court*, 450 U.S. 464 (1981) **618–619**
MILLER v. *CALIFORNIA*, 413 U.S. 15 (1973) **360–361, 362, 405**
MILLIGAN, EX PARTE, 71 U.S. (4 Wall.) 2 (1866) **166, 176**
MILLIKEN v. *BRADLEY*, 418 U.S. 717 (1974) **558, 583**
Milliken v. *Bradley II*, 433 U.S. 267 (1977) **558**
MIRANDA v. *ARIZONA*, 384 U.S. 436 (1966) **35, 43n, 464–466, 467, 475, 476, 507**

Mississippi v. *Johnson*, 4 Wall 475 (1867) **139**
Mississippi University for Women v. *Hogan*, 458 U.S. 718 (1982) **616, 627**
MISSOURI v. *HOLLAND*, 252 U.S. 346 (1920) **7, 164, 175**
MISSOURI v. *JENKINS*, 110 S. Ct. 1651 (1990) **558, 590**
Missouri Ex Rel Gaines v. *Canada*, 305 U.S. 337 (1938) **553, 554**
Missouri Pacific Company v. *Norwood* (1931) **270**
MISTRETTA v. *UNITED STATES*, 488 U.S. (1989) **100, 119**
Mobile v. *Bolden*, 446 U.S. 55 (1980) **566**
Moody v. *Daggett* (1976) **473**
Moore v. *Ogilvie*, 394 U.S. 814 (1969) **626n**
Moore v. *Sims*, 442 U.S. 415 (1979) **199**
MOOSE LODGE NO. 107 v. *IRVIS*, 407 U.S. 163 (1972) **562, 597**
Morehead v. *New York ex. rel. Tipaldo*, 298 U.S. 587 (1936) **319**
Morrison v. *Olson*, 487 U.S. 654 (1988) **103, 133–134, 135, 148**
Morton v. *Mancari*, 417 U.S. 535 (1974) **627**
Mount Healthy City Board of Education v. *Doyle*, 429 U.S. 274 (1977) **562–563**
MUELLER v. *ALLEN*, 463 U.S. 388 (1983) **415, 430**
Mugler v. *Kansas*, 123 U.S. 623 (1887) **313**
Mulford v. *Smith*, 307 U.S. 38 (1939) **238**
Muller v. *Oregon*, 208 U.S. 412 (1908) **30, 314**
MUNN v. *ILLINOIS*, 94 U.S. 113 (1877) **311, 312, 315, 325**
Murray's Lessee v. *Hoboken Land and Improvement Company*, 59 U.S. 272 (1856) **453**
Muskrat v. *United States*, 219 U.S. 346 (1911) **60n**
MYERS v. *UNITED STATES*, 272 U.S. 52 (1926) **134, 144**

NAACP v. *Alabama*, 357 U.S. 449 (1958) **352, 363n**
NATIONAL LABOR RELATIONS BOARD v. *JONES & LAUGHLIN STEEL CORPORATION*, 301 U.S. 1 (1937) **36, 235, 250**
National League of Cities v. *Usery*, 426 U.S. 833 (1976) **194, 236, 239**
NATIONAL TREASURY EMPLOYEES UNION v. *VON RAAB*, 109 S. Ct. 1384 (1989) **462, 490**
NEAGLE, IN RE, 135 U.S. 1 (1890) **137, 154**
NEAR v. *MINNESOTA*, 283 U.S. 697 (1931) **356–357, 394**
Nebbia v. *New York*, 291 U.S. 502 (1934) **314**
Nebraska Press Association v. *Stuart*, 427 U.S. 539 (1976) **357**
Newberry v. *United States*, 256 U.S. 232 (1921) **559**
NEW JERSEY v. *T.L.O.*, 469 U.S. 325 (1985) **460, 487**
New Orleans v. *Dukes*, 427 U.S. 297 (1976) **319**
New Orleans City Park Improvement Association v. *Detiege* (1958) **565n**
New York v. *Belton*, 101 S. Ct. 2860 (1981) **459–460, 476n**
New York v. *Ferber* (1982) **361**
New York v. *Quarles* (1984) **465**

NEW YORK TIMES v. *SULLIVAN,* 376 U.S. 254 (1964) **349, 358–359, 362, 403**
NEW YORK TIMES COMPANY v. *UNITED STATES,* 403 U.S. 713 (1971) **60n, 357, 396**
NIX v. *WILLIAMS,* 467 U.S. 431 (1984) **465, 514**
Nixon v. *Administrator of General Services,* 433 U.S. 425 (1977) **139**
Nixon v. *Condon,* 286 U.S. 73 (1932) **565n**
Nixon v. *Fitzgerald,* 457 U.S. 731 (1982) **136, 139**
Nixon v. *Herndon,* 273 U.S. 536 (1927) **559**
Nixon v. *Warner Communications,* 435 U.S. 589 (1978) **357**
NLRB v. *Fainblatt* (1939) **240n**
NLRB v. *Friedman-Harry Marks Clothing Company* (1937) **240n**
NOLLAN v. *CALIFORNIA COASTAL COMMISSION,* 483 U.S. 825 (1987) **317, 336**
Noto v. *United States,* 367 U.S. 290 (1961) **350**
Nyquist v. *Mauclet,* 432 U.S. 1 (1977) **612**

Ogden v. *Saunders,* 12 Wheat. 213 (1827) **54, 286–287**
Oliver, In Re, 333 U.S. 257 (1948) **457**
Oliver v. *United States* (1984) **476n**
OLMSTEAD v. *UNITED STATES,* 277 U.S. 438 (1928) **462, 499, 686, 687, 688, 689**
O'Lone v. *Shabazz* (1987) **473**
Oregon v. *Haas,* 420 U.S. 714 (1975) **465**
Oregon v. *Mitchell,* 400 U.S. 112 (1970) **43n**
Organization for a Better Austin v. *Keefe,* 402 U.S. 115 (1971) **357**
Orr v. *Orr,* 440 U.S. 268 (1979) **618**
Oyama v. *California,* 332 U.S. 661 (1948) **318n**

PACIFIC GAS & ELECTRIC COMPANY v. *STATE ENERGY RESOURCES CONSERVATION & DEVELOPMENT COMMISSION,* 461 U.S. 190 (1983) **265, 273**
PALKO v. *CONNECTICUT,* 302 U.S. 319 (1937) **453, 479**
PALMORE v. *SIDOTI,* 446 U.S. 429 (1984) **562, 599**
Panama Refining Company v. *Ryan,* 293 U.S. 388 (1935) **100**
PARIS ADULT THEATER I v. *SLATON,* 413 U.S. 49 (1973) **405**
Parker v. *Gladden,* 385 U.S. 363 (1966) **456, 457**
Pasadena City Board of Education v. *Spangler,* 427 U.S. 424 (1976) **559**
The Passenger Cases, 7 How. 283 (1849) **267**
PATTERSON v. *McLEAN CREDIT UNION,* 109 S. Ct. 2363 (1989) **197, 225, 565n**
PAUL v. *DAVIS,* 424 U.S. 693 (1976) **695, 723**
Pennell v. *City of San Jose* (1988) **317**
Pennsylvania v. *Nelson,* 350 U.S. 497 (1956) **199n**
Pensacola Telegraph Company v. *Western Union Telegraph Company* (1878) **232**

Perez v. *United States*, 402 U.S. 146 (1971) **236, 240n, 241**
Peterson v. *Greenville*, 373 U.S. 244 (1963) **560**
PHILADELPHIA, CITY OF v. *NEW JERSEY*, 437 U.S. 617 (1978) **38–39, 269, 280**
Planned Parenthood of Central Missouri v. *Danforth*, 428 U.S. 52 (1976) **690–691, 697**
PLESSY v. *FERGUSON*, 163 U.S. 537 (1896) **3, 36, 550–551, 552, 554, 573, 610, 611**
Plyler v. *Doe*, 462 U.S. 725 (1983) **609, 626n, 627**
Poe v. *Ullman*, 367 U.S. 497 (1961) **60n, 62**
Pointer v. *Texas*, 380 U.S. 400 (1965) **456, 457**
Police Department of Chicago v. *Mosley*, 408 U.S. 92 (1972) **355, 364n**
Pollock v. *Farmer's Loan & Trust Company*, 157 U.S. 429 (1895) **43n, 237**
POWELL v. *ALABAMA*, 287 U.S. 45 (1932) **466, 467, 504**
Powell v. *McCormack*, 395 U.S. 486 (1969) **62**
Press-Enterprise Co. v. *Superior Court* (1986) **357**
THE PRIZE CASES, Black 635 (1863) **161, 169**
Procunier v. *Martinez* (1974) **472–473**
Prudential Insurance Company v. *Benjamin* (1946) **272n**
Pulley v. *Harris*, 104 S. Ct. 871 (1984) **471, 478**

Rankin v. *McPherson* (1987) **352**
Raymond Motor Transportation, Inc. v. *Rice* (1978) **270**
Red Lion Broadcasting Company v. *FCC*, 395 U.S. 367 (1969) **364**
Reed v. *Reed*, 404 U.S. 71 (1971) **615, 616**
Regan v. *Wald* (1984) **167n**
REGENTS OF THE UNIVERSITY OF CALIFORNIA v. *BAKKE*, 438 U.S. 265 (1978) **30, 33, 551–552, 610, 611, 612, 626n, 632**
Reitman v. *Mulkey*, 387 U.S. 369 (1967) **561–562, 566**
Renton v. *Playtime Theaters* (1986) **361**
REYNOLDS v. *SIMS*, 377 U.S. 533 (1964) **621, 671**
Reynolds v. *United States*, 98 U.S. 145 (1878) **421**
Rhode Island v. *Innis* (1980) **477n**
RICHMOND v. *CROSON*, 109 S. Ct. 706 (1989) **610–611, 639**
Richmond Newspapers, Inc. v. *Virginia*, 448 U.S. 555 (1980) **357, 364**
Robbins v. *California*, 453 U.S. 420 (1981) **459**
ROBERTS v. *LOUISIANA*, 428 U.S. 325 (1976) **536**
Roberts v. *United States Jaycees*, 468 U.S. 609 (1984) **363n**
Robinson v. *California*, 370 U.S. 660 (1962) **456, 457, 470**
Rodgers v. *Richmond*, 365 U.S. 534 (1961) **477n**
ROE v. *WADE*, 410 U.S. 113 (1973) **34, 36, 52–53, 687, 690, 691–693, 694, 695, 702**
ROSTKER v. *GOLDBERG*, 453 U.S. 57 (1981) **167n, 608, 619–620, 663**
Roth v. *United States*, 354 U.S. 476 (1957) **20n, 360**
Rumely v. *United States*, 345 U.S. 41 (1953) **95–96**
Runyon v. *McCrary*, 427 U.S. 160 (1976) **197, 199, 565n**

SAN ANTONIO INDEPENDENT SCHOOL DISTRICT v. *RODRIGUEZ*, 411 U.S. 1 (1973) **608, 609, 620–621, 624, 625, 680**

Santa Cruz v. *NLRB* (1938) **240n**

Santo Bello v. *New York*, 404 U.S. 257 (1971) **469**

Sarnoff v. *Schultz*, 409 U.S. 929 (1972) **167n**

Scales v. *United States*, 367 U.S. 203 (1961) **350, 351**

Schad v. *Mount Ephraim* (1981) **361**

Schall v. *Martin* (1984) **470**

SCHECHTER POULTRY CORPORATION v. *UNITED STATES*, 295 U.S. 495 **100, 117, 240n**

SCHENCK v. *UNITED STATES*, 249 U.S. 47 (1919) **346–347, 350, 363n, 368**

Schilb v. *Kuebel* (1971) **456, 457**

Schiro v. *Bynum* (1964) **565n**

Schlesinger v. *Ballard*, 419 U.S. 498 (1975) **617, 618, 626n**

Schlesinger v. *Reservists' Committee to Stop the War*, 418 U.S. 208 (1974) **52**

Schneckloth v. *Bustamonte* (1973) **477n**

SCHOOL DISTRICT OF ABINGTON TOWNSHIP v. *SCHEMPP*, 374 U.S. 203 (1963) **412, 424**

School District of the City of Grand Rapids v. *Ball*, 105 S. Ct. 3216 (1985) **416**

Scott v. *Illinois*, 440 U.S. 367 (1979) **477n**

Scott v. *Sandford* (1857) **318n**

SELECTIVE SERVICE SYSTEM v. *MINNESOTA PUBLIC INTEREST RESEARCH GROUP*, 468 U.S. 841 (1984) **466**

SHAPIRO v. *THOMPSON*, 394 U.S. 618 (1969) **623–624, 668**

SHELLEY v. *KRAEMER*, 334 U.S. 1 (1948) **561, 566n, 595**

SHERBERT v. *VERNER*, 374 U.S. 398 (1963) **417, 419, 445**

Silkwood v. *Kerr-McGee Corporation* (1984) **265**

Silverman v. *United States*, 365 U.S. 505 (1961) **688, 689**

Skinner v. *Railway Labor Executives Association* (1989) **461, 462**

SKOKIE, VILLAGE OF v. *NATIONAL SOCIALIST PARTY OF AMERICA*, 373 N.E. 2d 21 (1978) **355, 386**

THE SLAUGHTERHOUSE CASES, 83 U.S. (16 Wallace) 36 (1873) **195–196, 309–311, 313, 320, 545, 550**

Smith v. *Allwright*, 321 U.S. 649 (1944) **560**

Smith v. *California* (1959) **363n**

Snepp v. *United States*, 444 U.S. 507 (1980) **357**

Snowden v. *Hughes*, 321 U.S. 1 (1944) **310**

Solem v. *Helm* (1983) **471–472**

Sosna v. *Iowa*, 419 U.S. 393 (1975) **627**

South Carolina Highway Department v. *Barnwell Brothers, Inc.*, 303 U.S. 177 (1938) **270**

SOUTH DAKOTA v. *DOLE*, 483 U.S. 203 (1987) **260**

South Dakota v. *Neville* (1983) **466**

SOUTHERN PACIFIC COMPANY v. *ARIZONA*, 325 U.S. 761 (1945) **270, 271n, 281**
Spano v. *New York*, 360 U.S. 315 (1959) **477n**
Springer v. *United States* (1881) **236**
STANFORD v. *KENTUCKY*, 109 S. Ct. 2969 (1989) **471, 537**
Stanley v. *Georgia*, 394 U.S. 557 (1969) **696n**
State Athletic Cmsm. v. *Dorsey* (1959) **565n**
Steagald v. *United States*, 101 S. Ct. 1662 (1981) **477n**
Steward Machine Company v. *Davis*, 301 U.S. 548 (1937) **239**
Stone v. *Powell*, 428 U.S. 465 (1976) **478**
Stone v. *Mississippi*, 101 U.S. 814 (1880) **288–289**
Sturges v. *Crowninshield*, 4 Wheaton 122 (1819) **286, 292**
Sugarman v. *Dougall*, 413 U.S. 634 (1973) **612**
Superintendent v. *Hill* (1985) **474**
SWANN v. *CHARLOTTE-MECKLENBURG BOARD OF EDUCATION*, 402 U.S. 1 (1971) **556–557, 559, 581**
Sweatt v. *Painter*, 339 U.S. 629 (1950) **553, 554, 566**
Swift & Company v. *United States* (1905) **233–234**

Tate v. *Short*, 401 U.S. 395 (1971) **620**
Teague v. *Lane* (1989) **475**
Terry v. *Ohio*, 392 U.S. 1 (1968) **461**
TEXAS v. *JOHNSON*, 491 U.S. (1989) **354, 383**
Thompson v. *City of Louisville*, 362 U.S. 199 (1960) **23**
Tilton v. *Richardson*, 403 U.S. 672 (1971) **414**
Time v. *Hill*, 385 U.S. 374 (1967) **697**
TINKER v. *DES MOINES*, 393 U.S. 503 (1969) **356,389**
Torasco v. *Watkins*, 367 U.S. 488 (1961) **412**
Townsend v. *Sain* (1963) **477n**
TRIMBLE v. *GORDON*, 430 U.S. 762 (1977) **614, 625, 652**
Trop v. *Dulles*, 356 U.S. 86 (1958) **470**
Turner v. *Memphis* (1962) **565n**
TURNER v. *SAFLEY*, 482 U.S. 78 (1987) **473, 541**
Twining v. *New Jersey*, 211 U.S. 78 (1908) **464, 478**

United Building and Construction Trades Council of Camden County v. *Mayor and Council of the City of Camden* (1984) **198n–199n**
United Jewish Organizations of Williamsburgh v. *Carey*, 430 U.S. 144 (1977) **627**
United Public Workers v. *Mitchell*, 330 U.S. 75 (1947) **60n**
United States v. *Ballard*, 322 U.S. 78 (1948) **418, 421**
United States v. *Brewster*, 408 U.S. 501 (1972) **103n**
UNITED STATES v. *BUTLER*, 297 U.S. 1 (1936) **238, 239, 240n, 255**
UNITED STATES v. *CAROLENE PRODUCTS COMPANY*, 304 U.S. 144 (1938) **60n, 315–316, 334, 345**
United States v. *Classic*, 313 U.S. 299 (1941) **560**

UNITED STATES v. *CURTISS-WRIGHT EXPORT CORPORATION,* 299 U.S. 304 (1936) **163, 164, 172**
United States v. *Darby Lumber Company,* 312 U.S. 100 (1941) **194, 198n, 236, 240n, 241**
United States v. *Guest,* 383 U.S. 745 (1966) **199**
United States v. *Hartwell,* 6 Wall. 385 (1868) **3**
United States v. *Havens* (1980) **477n**
UNITED STATES v. *KAHRIGER,* 345 U.S. 22 (1953) **238, 259**
UNITED STATES v. *E. C. KNIGHT COMPANY,* 156 U.S. 1 (1895) **233, 246**
UNITED STATES v. *LEON,* 468 U.S. 897 (1984) **463, 477n, 518**
UNITED STATES v. *NIXON,* 418 U.S. 683 (1974) **24, 27, 32, 62, 136, 152**
United States v. *O'Brien,* 391 U.S. 367 (1968) **354, 364n**
United States v. *Pink,* 315 U.S. 203 (1942) **168**
United States v. *Richardson,* 418 U.S. 166 (1974) **51–52, 239**
United States v. *Robel,* 389 U.S. 258 (1967) **351**
United States v. *Robinson,* 414 U.S. 218 (1973) **461**
United States v. *Ross,* 102 S. Ct. 2157 (1982) **460, 477n**
United States v. *Salerno* (1987) **470**
United States v. *Seeger,* 380 U.S. 163 (1965) **421n**
United States v. *United States District Court,* 407 U.S. 297 (1972) **478**
United States v. *Wade* (1967) **467**
United States v. *Yale Todd* (1794) **59n**
United States Civil Service Commission v. *National Association of Letter Carriers,* 413 U.S. 548 (1973) **352, 364**
United States Ex Rel. Seals v. *Wiman,* 303 F. 2d 53 (1962) **563**
UNITED STATES TRUST COMPANY v. *NEW JERSEY,* 431 U.S. 1 (1977) **291, 303**

Valley Forge Christian College v. *Americans United for Separation of Church and State,* 454 U.S. 464 (1982) **52, 60n, 62**
Vance v. *Bradley,* 440 U.S. 93 (1979) **614**
Village of Arlington Heights v. *Metropolitan Housing Development Corporation.* See *Arlington Heights, Village of* v. *Metropolitan Housing Development Corporation*
Village of Skokie v. *Nationalist Socialist Party of America.* See *Skokie, Village of* v. *Nationalist Socialist Party of America*
Vlandis v. *Kline,* 412 U.S. 441 (1973) **624**

WALLACE v. *JAFFREE,* 472 U.S. 38 (1985) **412, 413, 420, 436**
Walz v. *Tax Commission* (1970) **412–413**
Warden v. *Hayden,* 387 U.S. 294 (1967) **460**
Wards Cove Packing Co. v. *Antonio,* 109 S. Ct. 2115 (1990) **564, 601**
Washington v. *Chrisman,* 102 S. Ct. 812 (1982) **476n**
WASHINGTON v. *DAVIS,* 426 U.S. 229 (1976) **562–563**

Washington v. *Texas,* 388 U.S. 14 (1967) **456, 457**
WATKINS v. *UNITED STATES,* 354 U.S. 178 (1957) **95–96, 114**
Wayman v. *Southard* (1825) **99**
Weber v. *Aetna Casualty and Surety Company,* 406 U.S. 164 (1972) **614, 627**
WEBSTER v. *REPRODUCTIVE HEALTH SERVICES,* 109 S. Ct. 3040 (1989) **692–693, 707**
Weeks v. *United States,* 232 U.S. 383 (1914) **462, 463**
Weinberger v. *Salfi,* 422 U.S. 749 (1975) **624**
Weinberger v. *Wiesenfeld,* 420 U.S. 636 (1975) **617, 618**
Welsh v. *United States,* 398 U.S. 333 (1970) **421n**
Wengler v. *Druggists Mutual Insurance Company,* 446 U.S. 142 (1980) **627**
Wesberry v. *Sanders,* 376 U.S. 1 (1964) **626n**
WEST COAST HOTEL COMPANY v. *PARRISH,* 300 U.S. 379 (1937) **314–315, 331**
WEST VIRGINIA BOARD OF EDUCATION v. *BARNETTE,* 319 U.S. 624 (1943) **364, 417, 442**
Whalen v. *Roe,* 429 U.S. 589 (1977) **695**
Whitney v. *California,* 274 U.S. 357 (1927) **345, 346, 363n, 364**
WICKARD v. *FILBURN,* 317 U.S. 111 (1942) **235, 236, 252**
Wiener v. *United States,* 357 U.S. 349 (1958) **139n**
Williams v. *Illinois,* 399 U.S. 235 (1970) **620**
Williams v. *Rhodes,* 393 U.S. 23 (1968) **623**
WILLIAMSON v. *LEE OPTICAL COMPANY,* 348 U.S. 483 (1955) **315, 333**
Willson v. *Black Bird Creek Marsh Company,* 2 Pet. 245 (1829) **266, 267–268, 271n**
Wisconsin v. *Yoder,* 406 U.S. 205 (1972) **418**
Wolf v. *Colorado,* 338 U.S. 25 (1949) **457, 462–463**
Wolf v. *McDonald* (1974) **472**
Wolf v. *McDonnell* **474**
Wolman v. *Walter,* 433 U.S. 220 (1977) **416**
WOODSON v. *NORTH CAROLINA,* 428 U.S. 280 (1976) **534**
Wright v. *Emporia City Council,* 407 U.S. 451 (1972) **566**
Wynehamer v. *New York,* 13 N.Y. 378 (1856) **312**

Yates v. *United States,* 354 U.S. 298 (1957) **350, 364n**
Yick Wo v. *Hopkins,* 118 U.S. 356 (1886) **566**
YOUNGER v. *HARRIS,* 401 U.S. 37 (1971) **193, 205**
YOUNGSTOWN SHEET AND TUBE COMPANY v. *SAWYER,* 343 U.S. 579 (1952) **8, 137–138, 140**

Zurcher v. *Stanford Daily,* 436 U.S. 547 (1978) **358**